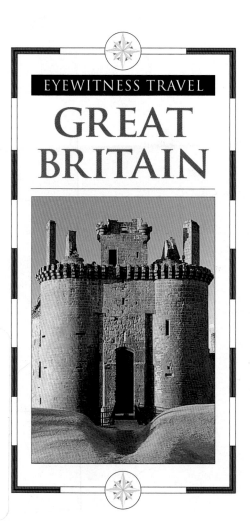

EYEWITNESS TRAVEL

GREAT BRITAIN

EYEWITNESS TRAVEL

GREAT BRITAIN

MAIN CONTRIBUTOR: MICHAEL LEAPMAN

LONDON, NEW YORK,
MELBOURNE, MUNICH AND DELHI
www.dk.com

ART EDITOR Stephen Bere
PROJECT EDITOR Marian Broderick
EDITORS Carey Combe, Sara Harper, Elaine Harries,
Kim Inglis, Ella Milroy, Andrew Szudek, Nia Williams
US EDITOR Mary Sutherland
DESIGNERS Susan Blackburn, Elly King,
Colin Loughrey, Andy Wilkinson

CONTRIBUTORS
Josie Barnard, Christopher Catling,
Juliet Clough, Lindsay Hunt, Polly Phillimore,
Martin Symington, Roger Thomas

MAPS
Jane Hanson, Phil Rose, Jennifer Skelley (Lovell Johns Ltd)
Gary Bowes (Era-Maptec Ltd)

PHOTOGRAPHERS
Joe Cornish, Paul Harris, Rob Reichenfeld, Kim Sayer

ILLUSTRATORS
Richard Draper, Jared Gilby (Kevin Jones Assocs), Paul Guest, Roger Hutchins,
Chris Orr & Assocs, Maltings Partnership,
Ann Winterbotham, John Woodcock

Reproduced by Colourscan (Singapore)
Printed and bound by South China Printing Co. Ltd., China

First American edition 1995
10 11 12 13 10 9 8 7 6 5 4 3 2 1
Published in the United States by DK Publishing,
375 Hudson Street, New York, NY 10014

Reprinted with revisions 1996, 1997, 1999, 2000, 2001,
2002, 2003, 2004, 2005, 2006, 2007, 2008, 2009, 2010

Copyright © 1995, 2010 Dorling Kindersley Limited, London

Published in Great Britain by Dorling Kindersley Limited.

A catalog record for this book is available
from the Library of Congress.

ISSN 1542-1554
ISBN 978-07566-6072-7

THROUGHOUT THIS BOOK, FLOORS ARE REFERRED TO IN ACCORDANCE
WITH EUROPEAN USAGE, I.E., THE "FIRST FLOOR" IS ONE FLIGHT UP FROM GROUND LEVEL.

Front cover main image: Leeds Castle, Maidstone, Kent

We're trying to be cleaner and greener:

- we recycle waste and switch things off
- we use paper from responsibly managed forests whenever possible
- we ask our printers to actively reduce water and energy consumption
- we check out our suppliers' working conditions – they never use child labour

Find out more about our values and best practices at www.dk.com

The information in this
DK Eyewitness Travel Guide is checked annually.
Every effort has been made to ensure that this book is as up-to-date
as possible at the time of going to press. Some details, however,
such as telephone numbers, opening hours, prices, gallery hanging
arrangements and travel information are liable to change. The
publishers cannot accept responsibility for any consequences arising
from the use of this book, nor for any material on third-party
websites, and cannot guarantee that any website address in this
book will be a suitable source of travel information. We value the
views and suggestions of our readers highly. Please write to:
Publisher, DK Eyewitness Travel Guides,
Dorling Kindersley, 80 Strand, London, Great Britain WC2R 0RL.

◁ Cricket, England's national game

CONTENTS

HOW TO USE
THIS GUIDE **6**

A 14th-century illustration
of two knights jousting

INTRODUCING
GREAT BRITAIN

DISCOVERING
GREAT BRITAIN **10**

PUTTING GREAT
BRITAIN ON THE MAP **14**

A PORTRAIT OF
GREAT BRITAIN **20**

THE HISTORY OF
GREAT BRITAIN **38**

GREAT BRITAIN
THROUGH THE YEAR **62**

Beefeater at the Tower of London

LONDON

INTRODUCING LONDON
72

WEST END AND
WESTMINSTER **76**

Eilean Donan Castle on Loch Duich in the Scottish Highlands

Jacobean "Old House" in Hereford

HOW TO USE THIS GUIDE

This guide helps you to get the most from your holidays in Great Britain. It provides both detailed practical information and expert recommendations. *Introducing Great Britain* maps the country and sets it in its historical and cultural context. The six regional chapters, plus *London*, describe important sights, using maps, pictures and illustrations. Features cover topics from houses and famous gardens to sport. Hotel, restaurant, and pub recommendations can be found in *Travellers' Needs*. The *Survival Guide* has practical information on everything from transport to personal safety.

LONDON

The centre of London has been divided into four sightseeing areas. Each has its own chapter, which opens with a list of the sights described. The last section, *Further Afield*, covers the most attractive suburbs. All sights are numbered and plotted on an area map. The information for each sight follows the map's numerical order, making sights easy to locate within the chapter.

Sights at a Glance lists the chapter's sights by category: Historic Streets and Buildings; Museums and Galleries; Churches and Cathedrals; Shops; Parks and Gardens.

2 **Street-by-Street Map**
This gives a bird's-eye view of the key areas in each chapter.

Stars indicate the sights that no visitor should miss.

All pages relating to London have red thumb tabs.

A locator map shows where you are in relation to other areas of the city centre.

1 **Area Map**
For easy reference, the sights are numbered and located on a map. Sights in the city centre are also marked on the Street Finder *on pages 127–47.*

A suggested route for a walk is shown in red.

3 **Detailed information**
The sights in London are described individually. Addresses, telephone numbers, opening hours, admission charges, tours and wheelchair access are also provided, as well as public transport links.

1 Introduction
The landscape, history and character of each region is outlined here, showing how the area has developed over the centuries and what it has to offer the visitor today.

GREAT BRITAIN AREA BY AREA
Apart from London, Great Britain has been divided into 14 regions, each of which has a separate chapter. The most interesting towns and places to visit have been numbered on a *Regional Map*.

Each area of Great Britain can be identified quickly by its colour coding, shown on the inside front cover.

2 Regional Map
This shows the main road network and gives an illustrated overview of the whole region. All entries are numbered and there are also useful tips on getting around the region by car, train and other forms of transport.

3 Detailed information
All the important sights, towns and other places to visit are described individually. They are listed in order, following the numbering on the Regional Map. Within each entry, there is detailed information on important buildings and other sights.

Story boxes explore related topics.

For all the top sights, a Visitors' Checklist provides the practical information you need to plan your visit.

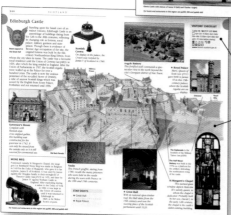

4 The top sights
These are given one or more full pages. Three-dimensional illustrations reveal the interiors of historic buildings. Interesting town and city centres are given street-by-street maps, featuring individual sights.

INTRODUCING GREAT BRITAIN

DISCOVERING GREAT BRITAIN

Each one of Great Britain's counties, that have grown out of kingdoms, principalities, shires, fiefs, boroughs, and parishes, has its own special flavour. This derives from Britain's landscape, its resources and its history, all of which have shaped its peoples, too.

Queen's Life Guardon Parade

There has always been something of a divide between the industrial North and the wealthier South. Regional pride is very strong. Vernacular architecture marks each region, and there is a rich variety of scenery to be found in every corner of this green and bounteous island.

A view of Big Ben and the London Eye

LONDON

- A ride on the London Eye
- Majestic parks
- World-class museums

Britain's capital can be enjoyed in all weathers. So many buildings, from **Big Ben** *(see p77)* to the **Tower of London** *(see pp118–19)*, are emblematic of the city. To get an overview take a bus riverboat or the

London Eye *(see p81)*; visit the West End for the most exciting shops, or stroll through its lovely parks. The **National Gallery** *(see p82–3)* is one of the finest art museums in the world, the **British Museum** *(see pp106–7)* and **Victoria and Albert Museum** *(see pp98–9)* are storehouses of treasures while **Tate Modern** *(see 121)* has set a standard for contemporary art.

THE DOWNS AND CHANNEL COAST

- Great days out from London
- Fairytale castles
- Brighton's brilliant sea front

This is "The Garden of England", green and rural, with rolling Downs. Many places in this corner of the country are accessible on a day trip from London; **Hampton Court** *(see p173)* and **Leeds Castle** *(see p189)* are favourite excursions. Many estates have connections with great

figures from history: Winston Churchill's **Chartwell** *(see p188)*, Queen Victoria's **Osborne** *(see p168)* on the Isle of Wight and J.M.W. Turner's **Petworth** *(see p172)*, an antiques-hunters' paradise. Ancient cathedrals rise from **Chichester** *(see pp171)*, **Winchester** *(see pp170–1)* and **Canterbury** *(see pp186–7)*, which has many tales to tell. Breezy resorts dot the coast. The liveliest is **Brighton** *(see pp174–9)*, known as "London-on-Sea", with its famous Lanes, Palace Pier and seafront promenade.

Punting on the River Cam past King's College Chapel, Cambridge

EAST ANGLIA

- A punt in Cambridge
- Magnificent Ely Cathedral
- A day at the races

This part of the country grew wealthy on the wool trade and its merchants built fabulous half-timbered houses and pretty towns such as **Lavenham** *(see p206)*. In the charming university town of Cambridge *(see p210–15)* try

The promenade and Palace Pier, Brighton, Sussex

◁ *Salisbury Cathedral: from the meadows by John Constable (1776–1837)*

punting on the Backs with the students or, for a less vigourous outing, admire **King's College Chapel** *(see p212–13)*. For another cultural high, visit **Ely Cathedral** *(see pp194–5)*. Spend a day at the races at **Newmarket** *(see p207)*, or visit **Aldeburgh** *(see pp202–203)* during its prestigious annual music festival. The ports on the lovely coast provide seafood for your table.

THAMES VALLEY

- **Attractive riverside pubs**
- **Oxford's dreaming spires**
- **Imposing Blenheim Palace**

The River Thames has long been a pleasure ground. The riverside, from London's outer suburbs to **Windsor** *(see pp235–7)*, **Oxford** *(see pp222–7)* and beyond, has many appealing waterside pubs and restaurants located in attractive towns. Boats can be hired, and the annual rowing regatta at **Henley-on-Thames** *(see p63 and p66)* is the height of the summer season. No wonder that the song of Britain's most exclusive private school, Eton *(see p235)*, which is located by the river, is *The Eton Boating Song*. **Windsor Castle** *(see pp236–7)* is undoubtedly a main draw, easily reached in a day trip from London, as are the beautiful colleges of **Oxford University** *(see pp226–7)*. Not far away are other historic places to visit, including the Churchill family home at **Blenheim Palace** *(see*

Stonehenge, Wiltshire, Great Britain's famous prehistoric monument

pp228–9), the Duke of Bedford's **Woburn Abbey** *(see p230)* and **Stowe** *(see p230)*, which has one of the most magnificent gardens in England.

WESSEX

- **Mysterious Stonehenge**
- **Cheddar cheese and Taunton Cider**
- **Fine architecture in Bath and Salisbury**

The former kingdom of the West Saxons echoes with history and legends. Here are some of the most important Neolithic sites in the country, including the mysterious and magnificent **Stonehenge** *(see pp262–3)*. This is the country of good living, with Cheddar cheese from around the Cheddar Gorge, and Somerset cider. The Georgian spa town of **Bath** *(see pp258–61)* makes an excellent centre to explore the region. There are two coasts – in the north on the Bristol Channel and in the south on the English channel where **Poole** *(see pp270–1)* is a great yachting centre. Bath, **Wells** *(see pp252–3)* and **Salisbury** *(see pp264–5)* all have outstanding cathedrals. There are wild animals at **Longleat** *(see p266)*, wild landscapes on **Exmoor National Park** *(see pp250–1)*, while the **Glastonbury** *(see pp253)* music festival attracts fans in their thousands.

DEVON AND CORNWALL

- **Surfing fit for champions**
- **Seafood and cream teas**
- **Fabulous gardens**

Britain's best beaches are in the West Country, some of which have high cliffs and waves worthy of champion surfers. Its fishing villages have long attracted artists, in particular St Ives, where the **Tate St Ives** gallery *(see p277)* can be visited. Seafood is plentiful, and rich pasturelands brings dairy ice-cream and cream teas. Seafaring is a way of life, as the **National Maritime Museum Cornwall** *(see pp280–1)* in Falmouth attests. **Bodmin Moor** *(see pp284–5)* and **Dartmoor** *(see p81)* present an untamed wilderness but some fine gardens are here, too, including the **Eden Project** *(see pp282–3)*.

A view of Blenheim Palace, Woodstock, Oxfordshire

Eden Project, Cornwall, a garden for the 21st century

THE HEART OF ENGLAND

- **Shakespeare's birthplace**
- **Typically English Cotswold villages**
- **Half-timbered border towns**

There is a great mix of attractions in this region where the Industrial Revolution began *(see pp314–15)*. The most popular sites are **Warwick Castle** *(see pp322–3)* and Shakespeare's birthplace in **Stratford-upon-Avon** *(see pp324–5)*. Cotswold villages built of golden limestone are quintessentially English. Other lovely rural spots include the Malvern Hills and the Wye Vallley. Attractive architecture distinguishes the half-timbered Welsh border towns including the city of **Chester** *(see pp310–11)*.

Anne Hathaway's cottage, Stratford-upon-Avon, Warwickshire

EAST MIDLANDS

- **Chatsworth, a fine country house**
- **Great walking in the Peak District**
- **Buxton spa and opera house**

One of the most impressive country houses, **Chatsworth** *(see pp334–5)*, is a high spot of this region. It sits at the edge of the **Peak District** *(see pp338–9)*, a popular area for walking. There are several attractive towns such as **Buxton** *(see p334)*, a spa town with an opera house while **Lincoln** *(see pp340–1)* has medieval buildings and a fine cathedral.

Mist on Rydal Water, Lake District, Cumbria

LANCASHIRE AND THE LAKES

- **England at its most picturesque**
- **Liverpool, maritime city of Empire**
- **Manchester, capital of the North**

The **Lake District** *(see pp352–68)* is where walking as an activity rather than a chore began, and you will see why when you encounter the stunning scenery of fells and lakes. Serious walkers put on their waterproofs and boots, while Sunday strollers hire row boats, or look in at Dove Cottage, where the poets William and Dorothy Wordsworth lived. To the south is **Liverpool** *(see pp354–5)*, a Unesco World Heritage city, with wonderful architecture and great art galleries. **Blackpool** *(see p371)* is the main resort, known for its illuminations. Inland is **Manchester** *(see pp372–5)* England's second largest city.

YORKSHIRE AND THE HUMBER REGION

- **Haunting abbey ruins**
- **The Brontë sisters' dramatic moors**
- **The ancient city of York**

Yorkshire is known for its striking moors, which the literary Brontë sisters of **Haworth** *(see p412)* knew so well. It is also known for its great abbeys, such as **Fountains** *(see pp390–1)*, **Rievaulx** *(see p393)* and **Whitby** *(see p396)*, which were reduced to haunting ruins after the English church broke from Rome. **York Minster** *(see pp406–407)* remains the most important church in the north and the ancient town is worth exploring. Sculptures by Henry Moore grace **Yorkshire Sculpture Park** *(see p413)*.

Whitby harbour and St Mary's Church, Yorkshire

NORTHUMBRIA

- **The trail of Celtic Christianity**
- **Life as it was lived, in Beamish Open Air Museum**
- **Hadrian's Wall from coast to coast**

A boat trip to the **Farne Islands** *(see p418)* off Lindisfarne is the starting point to unravelling early Celtic Christianity, a journey that can be followed as far as **Durham Cathedral** *(see pp428–9)*. The **Beamish Open Air Museum** *(see pp424–5)*, which re-creates life in the northeast in the 19th century, makes a great family day out. Castles on Northumberland's coast were built to withstand Viking attack, but it is **Hadrian's Wall** *(see pp422–3)*, erected by the Romans to keep out the Scots, that is particularly impressive.

NORTH WALES

- **Wild Snowdonia National Park**
- **Narrow-gauge railways**
- **Stunning medieval castles**

This is the part of Wales, where Welsh is commonly spoken, and the annual Eisteddfod literary festival is held. Its wildness is captured around Snowdon, the highest mountain in England and Wales. The centre for exploring **Snowdonia National Park** *(see pp450–1)* is Llanberis from where a narrow-gauge railway runs to the top. Another former slate-quarry railway takes passengers up from the coast at Porthmadog near **Portmeirion** *(see p454–5)*. Medieval castles keep watch at **Harlech** *(see p454)*, **Caernarfon** *(see p444)* and **Conwy** *(see p438 and p447)*.

SOUTH AND MID WALES

- **Pony trekking in the hills**
- **Scenic coastal walks**
- **Hay-on-Wye literary festival**

This is a region to tour by car, to go walking or pony trekking, across mountains like the **Brecon Beacons** *(see pp468–9)*. The roads are emptier than England's and the valleys are green and lush. The coast has some delightful ports and long-established resorts. The most attractive are around the **Gower Peninsula** *(see p466)*

Cliffs of the Pembrokeshire Coast National Park, South Wales

and in Pembrokeshire in the south west where there is the diminutive **St David's Cathedral** *(see pp464–5)*. Wales is known for its male voice choirs – as well as its men of letters – **Hay-on-Wye** *(see p461)* hosts an annual literary festival.

SCOTTISH LOWLANDS

- **Glasgow, dynamic city of art**
- **Medieval Edinburgh and its Georgian New Town**
- **Magnificent abbeys and castles**

The capital **Edinburgh** *(see pp504–11)* and **Glasgow** *(see pp516–21)* are Scotland's dazzling cities, both full of interest and worth several

days' exploration. Charles Rennie Mackintosh left his Art Nouveau mark on Glasgow, while thousands of hopeful performers attempt to find fame in Edinburgh each August at the famous festival. The capital's high points are **Edinburgh Castle** *(see pp506–7)*, keeper of the Scottish Crown jewels and the **Palace of Holyroodhouse** *(see p510)*, the Queen's official Scottish residence. Castles abound in the Lowlands, notably the Renaissance gem **Stirling** *(see pp497–8)*.

SCOTTISH HIGHLANDS AND ISLANDS

- **Mountain climbing and skiing**
- **The castles of Royal Deeside**
- **Remote, idyllic hills**

This is as wild as Britain gets: mountainous, heather-clad and dramatically remote, drifting into offshore islands. You may well see eagles and stags, while on the west coast seals swoop in on the beautiful shores. **Aberdeen** *(see pp538–40)* is the starting point for a tour of the castles of **Royal Deeside** *(see p540–1)*. Climb mountains, go skiing in Aviemore in the **Cairngorms** *(see pp544–5)*, follow the whisky trails and take a ferry to the Western Isles.

A view of Edinburgh Castle, Scotland

Putting Great Britain on the Map

Lying in northwestern Europe, Great Britain is bounded by the Atlantic Ocean, the North Sea and the English Channel. The island's landscape and climate are varied, and it is this variety that even today affects the pattern of settlement. The remote shores of the West Country peninsula and the inhospitable mountains of Scotland and Wales are less populated than the relatively flat and fertile Midlands and Southeast, where the vast majority of the country's 61 million people live. Due to this population density, the south is today the most built-up part of the country.

KEY

===	Motorway
▬▬	Major road
- - -	Ferry route
···	Channel Tunnel
▬ ▬	National border

0 kilometres 100

0 miles 100

Shetland and Orkney Islands

These islands form the northern-most part of Great Britain, with the Shetlands lying six degrees south of the Arctic Circle. There are transport links to the mainland.

Europe

Great Britain is situated in the northwest corner of Europe. Its nearest neighbours are Ireland to the west, and the Netherlands, Belgium and France across the Channel. Denmark, Norway and Sweden are also easily accessible.

EUROPE

Regional Great Britain: London, the South, the Midlands and Wales

Great Britain has airline connections with most cities in the world. London is the main transport hub with three major international airports, including Heathrow, the world's busiest. Southern England, Britain's most populous area, is divided, within this book, into four regions – Southeast England, the West Country, Wales and the Midlands – with a separate chapter for London. Road and rail links to the North and Scotland (see pp18–19) are plentiful, as are links between all main towns.

KEY TO COLOUR-CODING

- London

Southeast England

- The Downs and Channel Coast
- East Anglia
- Thames Valley

The West Country

- Wessex
- Devon and Cornwall

Wales

- North Wales
- South and Mid-Wales

The Midlands

- The Heart of England
- East Midlands

KEY TO MAP

- Ferry port
- Airport
- Motorway
- Major road
- Railway line
- Channel Tunnel

Dumfries
Carlisle
Keswick
Penr
Windermere
Lancast
Blackpool
Preston
Liverpool
We
Dublin
Dun Laoghaire
Anglesey
Llandudno
Holyhead
Conwy
Caernarfon
Ruthin
Chester
Llanberis
Betws-y-Coed
Blaenau
Ffestiniog
Bala
Llangollen
Dolgellau
Shrewsbury
Tel
Machynlleth
Wolve
Aberdyfi
Aberystwyth
Ludlow
Leomins
Aberaeron
Llandrindod
Wells
Rosslare
Hereford
Fishguard
Llandovery
Hay on
Wye
Carmarthen
Dolgellau
Ross-on-Wye
Monmouth
Pembroke
Tenby
Tintern
Swansea
Newport
CARDIFF
Bri
Weston-
Super-Mare
Wells
Lynton
Glastonb
Appledore
Barnstaple
Bridgwater
Clovelly
Taunton
Bideford
Yeovil
Bude
Sh
Boscastle
Okehampton
Sidmouth
Tintagel
Exeter
Abbotsbury
Bodmin
Weymou
St Austell
Totnes
Torquay
Fowey
Plymouth
Brixham
St Ives
Truro
Falmouth
Dartmouth
Penzance
Helston
Santander
Roscoff
Bilbao

Greater London

Greater London, the area within the M25 motorway ring, is home to 7.5 million people and covers an area of 600 sq miles (1,580 sq km).

Regional Great Britain: The North and Scotland

This part of Great Britain is divided into two sections in this book. Although it is far less populated than the southern sector of the country, there are good road and rail connections, and ferry services link the islands with the mainland.

KEY TO COLOUR-CODING

The North Country

- Lancashire and the Lakes
- Yorkshire and Humber Region
- Northumbria

Scotland

- The Lowlands
- The Highlands and Islands

Isle of Lewis

Stornoway

Tarbert

Ullapool

Lochmaddy

Uig

Isle of Skye

Kyle of Lochalsh

Lochboisdale

Castlebay

Mallaig

Fort William

Arinagour

Tobermory

Scarinish

Craignure

Oban

Crainlarich

Scalasaig

Jura

Greenock

Kennacraig

Islay

Port Ellen

Brodick

Ardrossan

Irvine

Campbeltown

Isle of Arran

Larne

Belfast

Cairnryan

Stranraer

Isle of Man

Douglas

Holyhead

MILEAGE CHART

LONDON

10 = Distance in miles
10 = Distance in kilometres

111 **179**	BIRMINGHAM									
150 **241**	102 **164**	CARDIFF								
74 **119**	185 **298**	228 **367**	DOVER							
372 **599**	290 **466**	373 **600**	442 **711**	EDINBURGH						
389 **626**	292 **470**	374 **602**	466 **750**	45 **72**	GLASGOW					
529 **851**	448 **721**	530 **853**	600 **966**	158 **254**	167 **269**	INVERNESS				
184 **296**	81 **130**	173 **278**	257 **414**	213 **343**	214 **344**	371 **597**	MANCHESTER			
274 **441**	204 **328**	301 **484**	343 **552**	107 **172**	145 **233**	265 **426**	131 **211**	NEWCASTLE		
112 **180**	161 **259**	235 **378**	167 **269**	360 **579**	383 **616**	517 **832**	185 **298**	260 **418**	NORWICH	
212 **341**	206 **332**	152 **261**	287 **462**	427 **784**	426 **785**	545 **1038**	250 **451**	427 **655**	324 **521**	PLYMOUTH

0 kilometres 100

0 miles 100

ORKNEY AND SHETLAND ISLANDS

Shetland Islands

Unst

Yell

Mainland

Foula

Lerwick

Fair Isle

Westray

Sanday

Mainland

Stronsay

Stromness

Kirkwall

Orkney Islands

Hoy

Scrabster

Thurso · WICK

Aberdeen

Stromness

Lerwick

Scrabster

Thurso

Wick

Elgin

Fraserburgh

Peterhead

Aberdeen

Braemar

Forfar

Montrose

Arbroath

Perth · Dundee

St Andrews

Stirling

Kirkcaldy

Dunfermline

EDINBURGH

Berwick-Upon-Tweed

Galashiels

Peebles

Holy Island

Bamburgh

Farne Islands

Hawick

Jedburgh

Alnwick

Warkworth

Dumfries

Morpeth

Hexham

Corbridge

Newcastle Upon Tyne

Carlisle

Durham

Sunderland

Cockermouth

Middleton-in-Teesdale

Hartlepool

Keswick

Penrith

Barnard Castle

Middlesbrough

Grasmere

Appleby-in-Westmorland

Darlington

Goathland · Whitby

Hawkshead

Windermere

Richmond

Helmsley

Scarborough

Barrow-in-Furness

Kendal

Thirsk

Flamborough Head

Heysham

Ripon

Bridlington

Lancaster

Skipton

Harrogate

Stavanger Bergen

Clitheroe

York

Beverley

Blackpool

Burnley

Leeds

Kingston Upon Hull

Southport

Preston

Blackburn

Bradford

Halifax

Wakefield

Bolton

Rochdale

Huddersfield

Scunthorpe

Grimsby

Wigan

Manchester

Barnsley

Doncaster

Liverpool

Stockport

Sheffield

Chester

Lincoln

Zeebrugge Rotterdam

KEY TO MAP

Ferry port

Airport

Motorway

Major road

Railway line

A PORTRAIT OF GREAT BRITAIN

Britain has been assiduous in preserving its traditions, but offers the visitor much more than stately castles and pretty villages. A diversity of landscape, culture, literature, art and architecture, as well as its unique heritage, results in a nation balancing the needs of the present with those of its past.

Britain's character has been shaped by its geographical position as an island. Never successfully invaded since 1066, its people have developed their own distinctive traditions. The Roman invasion of AD 43 lasted 350 years but Roman culture and language were quickly overlain with those of the northern European settlers who followed. Ties with Europe were loosened further in the 16th century when the Catholic church was replaced by a less dogmatic established church.

Although today a member of the European Union, Britain continues to delight in its non-conformity, even in superficial ways such as driving on the left-hand side of the road instead of the right. The opening of the rail tunnel to France is a topographical adjustment that does not necessarily mark a change in national attitude.

Tudor rose

The British heritage is seen in its ancient castles, cathedrals and stately homes with their gardens and Classical parklands. Age-old customs are renewed each year, from royal ceremonies to Morris dancers performing on village greens.

For a small island, Great Britain encompasses a surprising variety in its regions, whose inhabitants maintain distinct identities. Scotland and Wales are separate countries from England with their own legislative assemblies.

Walking along the east bank of the River Avon, Bath

◁ Punting, a popular pastime on the River Cam, Cambridge

Widecombe-in-the-Moor, a Devon village clustered round a church and set in hills

They have different customs, traditions, and, in the case of Scotland, different legal and educational systems. The Welsh and Scots Gaelic languages survive and are sustained by their own radio and television networks. In northern and West Country areas, English itself is spoken in a rich variety of dialects and accents, and these areas maintain their own regional arts, crafts, architecture and food.

The landscape is varied, too, from the craggy mountains of Wales, Scotland and the north, through the flat expanses of the Midlands and eastern England to the soft, rolling hills of the south and west. The long, broad beaches of East Anglia contrast with the picturesque rocky inlets along much of the west coast.

Scottish coat of arms at Edinburgh Castle

Despite the spread of towns and cities over the last two centuries, rural Britain still flourishes. Nearly three-quarters of Britain's land is used for agriculture. The main commercial crops are wheat, barley, sugar beet and potatoes, though what catches the eye in early summer are the fields of bright yellow rape or slate-blue flax.

The countryside is dotted with farms and charming villages, with picturesque cottages and lovingly tended gardens – a British passion. A typical village is built around an ancient church and a small, friendly pub. Here the pace of life slows. To drink a pint of ale in a cosy, village inn and relax before a fire is a time-honoured British custom. Strangers will be welcomed cordially, though perhaps with caution; for even if strict formality is a thing of the past, the British have a tendency to be reserved.

In the 19th and early 20th centuries, trade with the extensive British Empire, fuelled by abundant coal supplies, spurred manufacturing and created wealth. Thousands of people moved from the countryside to towns and cities near mines, mills and factories. By 1850 Britain was the world's strongest industrial nation. Now many

Lake and gardens at Petworth House, Sussex

of these old industrial centres have declined, and today manufacturing employs only 22 per cent of the labour force, while 66 per cent work in the growing service sector. These service industries are located mainly in the southeast, close to London, where modern office buildings bear witness to comparative prosperity.

Crowds at Petticoat Lane market in London's East End

is a multi-cultural society that can boast a wide range of music, art, food and religions. However, prejudice does exist and in some inner-city areas where poorer members of different communities live, racial tensions can occasionally arise. Even though discrimination in housing and employment on the grounds of race is against the law, it does occur in places.

SOCIETY AND POLITICS

British cities are melting-pots for people not just from different parts of the country but also from overseas. Irish immigration has long ensured a flow of labour into the country, and since the 1950s hundreds of thousands have come from former colonies in Africa, Asia and the Caribbean, many of which are now members of the Commonwealth. Nearly six per cent of Britain's 60 million inhabitants are from non-white ethnic groups – and about half of these were born in Britain. The result

Britain's class structure still intrigues and bewilders many visitors, based as it is on a subtle mixture of heredity and wealth. Even though many of the great inherited fortunes no longer exist, some old landed families still live on their

Bosses in Norwich Cathedral cloisters

large estates, and many now open them to the public. Class divisions are further entrenched by the education system. While more than 90 per cent of children are educated free by the state, richer parents often opt for private schooling, and the products of these private schools are disproportionately represented in the higher echelons of government and business.

The monarchy's position highlights the dilemma of a people seeking to preserve its most potent symbol of national unity in an age that is suspicious of inherited privilege. Without real political power, though still head of the Church of England, the Queen and her family are subject to increasing public scrutiny. Following a spate of personal scandals, some citizens advocate the abolition of the monarchy.

Democracy has deep foundations in Britain: there was even a parliament of sorts in London in the 13th century.

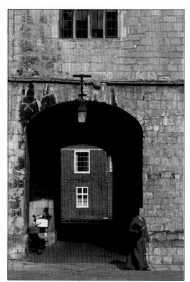

Priest in the Close at Winchester Cathedral

Yet with the exception of the 17th-century Civil War, power has passed gradually from the Crown to the people's elected representatives. A series of Reform Acts between 1832 and 1884 gave the vote to all male citizens, though women were not enfranchised on an equal basis until 1928. Margaret Thatcher – Britain's first woman Prime Minister – held office for 12 years from 1979. During the 20th century, the Labour (left wing) and Conservative (right wing) parties have, during their periods in office, favoured a mix of public and private ownership for industry and ample funding for the state health and welfare systems.

Afternoon tea on the back lawn at the Thornbury Castle Hotel, Avon

The position of Ireland has been an intractable political issue since the 17th century. Part of the United Kingdom for 800 years, but divided in 1921, it has seen conflict between Catholics and Protestants for many years. The Good Friday Peace Agreement of 1998 was a huge step forward and the path to lasting peace now seems possible.

CULTURE AND THE ARTS

Britain has a famous theatrical tradition stretching back to the 16th century and William Shakespeare. His plays

The House of Lords, in Parliament

have been performed on stage almost continuously since he wrote them and the works of 17th- and 18th-century writers are also frequently revived. Contemporary British playwrights such as Tom Stoppard, Alan Ayckbourn and David Hare draw on this long tradition with their vivid language and by using comedy to illustrate serious themes. British actors such as Helen Mirren, Ian McKellen, Ralph Fiennes and Anthony Hopkins have international reputations.

While London is the focal point of British theatre, fine drama is to be seen in many other parts of the country. The Edinburgh Festival and its Fringe are the high point of Great Britain's cultural calendar with theatre and music to suit all tastes. Other music festivals are held across the country, chiefly in summer, while there are annual

Schoolboys at Eton, the famous public school

festivals of literature at Hay-on-Wye and Cheltenham. Poetry has had an enthusiastic following since Chaucer wrote the *Canterbury Tales* in the 14th century: poems from all eras can even be read on the London Underground, where they are interspersed with the advertisements in the carriages and on the station platforms.

In the visual arts, Britain has a strong tradition in portraiture, caricature, landscape and watercolour. In modern times David Hockney and Lucian Freud, and sculptors Henry Moore and Barbara Hepworth, have enjoyed worldwide recognition. Architects including

Christopher Wren, Inigo Jones, John Nash and Robert Adam all created styles that define British cities; and today, Norman Foster and Richard Rogers carry the standard for Post-Modernism. Britain is becoming famous for its innovative fashion designers, many of whom now show their spring and autumn collections in Paris.

Reading the newspaper in Kensington Gardens

The British are avid newspaper readers. There are 11 national newspapers published from London on weekdays: the standard of the serious newspapers is very high; for example, *The Times* is read the world over because of its reputation for strong intentional reporting. Most popular, however, are the tabloids packed with gossip, crime and sport, which account for some 80 per cent of the total.

The indigenous film industry has produced international hits such as *The Queen*; though blockbusters such as the Harry Potter films are often backed by the US. British television is famous for the quality of its news, current affairs and drama programmes. The publicly funded British Broadcasting Corporation (BBC), which controls five national radio networks and two terrestrial television channels, as well as additional radio stations and television channels via digital technology, is widely admired.

The British are great sports fans, and soccer, rugby, cricket and golf are popular. An instantly recognizable English image is that of the cricket match on a village green. Nationwide, fishing is the most popular sporting pastime, and the British make good use of their national parks as keen walkers.

British food used to be derided for a lack of imagination. The cuisine relied on a limited range of quality ingredients, plainly prepared. But recent influences from abroad have introduced a wider range of ingredients and more adventurous techniques. Typical English food – plain home cooking and regional dishes – has also enjoyed a revival in recent years.

In this, as in other respects, the British are doing what they have done for centuries: accommodating their own traditions to influences from other cultures, while leaving the essential elements of their national life and character intact.

Naoमी Campbell, a British supermodel

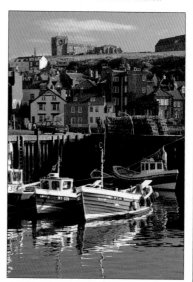
Whitby harbour and St Mary's Church, Yorkshire

Gardens Through the Ages

Styles of gardening in Britain have expanded alongside architecture and other evolving fashions. The Elizabethan knot garden became more elaborate and formal in Jacobean times, when the range of plants greatly increased. The 18th century brought a taste for large-scale "natural" landscapes with lakes, woods and pastures, creating the most distinctively English style to have emerged. In the 19th century, fierce debate raged between supporters of natural and formal gardens, developing into the eclecticism of the 20th century when "garden rooms" in differing styles became popular.

Capability Brown (1715–83)
was Britain's most influential garden designer, favouring the move away from formal gardens to man-made pastoral settings.

Monumental column

A grotto and cascade brought romance and mystery.

Blackthorn

Classical temples were a much appreciated feature in 18th-century gardens and were often exact replicas of buildings that the designers had seen in Greece.

Maple

IDEAL LANDSCAPE GARDEN

Classical Greece and Rome inspired the grand gardens of the early 18th century, such as Stourhead and Stowe. Informal clumps of trees played a critical part in the serene, manicured landscapes.

Winding paths were carefully planned to allow changing vistas to open out as visitors strolled around the garden.

Elaborate parterres *were a feature of aristocratic gardens of the 17th century, when the fashion spread from Europe. This is the Privy Garden at Hampton Court Palace, restored in 1995 to its design under William III.*

DESIGN AND FORMALITY

A flower garden is a work of artifice, an attempt to tame nature rather than to copy it. Growing plants in rows or regular patterns, interspersed with statues and ornaments, imposes a sense of order. Designs change to reflect the fashion of the time and the introduction of new plants.

Medieval gardens usually had a herber (a turfed sitting area) and a vine arbour. A good reconstruction is Queen Eleanor's Garden, Winchester.

Tudor gardens featured edged borders and sometimes mazes. The Tudor House Garden, Southampton also has beehives and heraldic statues.

Herbaceous borders, *full of lush plants, are the glory of the summer garden. Gertrude Jekyll (1843–1932), was high priestess of the mixed border, with her eye for seductive colour combinations.*

Cedar of Lebanon

Yew

Rhododendron

The Palladian bridge was a favourite feature, often decorative rather than practical.

Knot Gardens *were in vogue in the 1500s. Intersecting lines of lavender or box were filled with flowers, herbs or vegetables, as in this restoration at Pitmedden in Scotland.*

VISITORS' CHECKLIST

The "yellow book", Gardens of England and Wales, the annual guide to the National Gardens Scheme, lists gardens open to the public.

DEVELOPMENT OF THE MODERN PANSY

All garden plants derive from wild flowers, bred over the years to produce qualities that appeal to gardeners. The story of the pansy, one of our most popular flowers, is typical.

The wild pansy (Viola tricolor) native to Britain is commonly known as heartsease. It is a small-flowered annual which can vary considerably in colour.

The mountain pansy (Viola lutea) is a perennial. The first cultivated varieties resulted from crossing it with heartsease in the early 19th century.

The Show Pansy was bred by florists after the blotch appeared as a chance seedling in 1840. It was round in form with a small, symmetrical blotch.

The Fancy Pansy, developed in the 1860s, was much larger. The blotch covered all three lower petals save for a thin margin of colour.

Modern hybrids of pansies, violas and violettas, developed by selective breeding, are varied and versatile in a wide range of vibrant new colours.

17th-century gardening was more elaborate. Water gardens like those at Blenheim were often combined with parterres of exotic foreign plants.

Victorian gardens, their formal beds a mass of colour, were a reaction to the landscapes of Capability Brown. Alton Towers has a good example.

20th-century gardens mix historic and modern styles, as at Hidcote Manor, Gloucestershire. Growing wild flowers is becoming a popular choice.

Stately Homes

The grand country house reached its zenith in the 18th and 19th centuries, when the old landed families and the new captains of industry enjoyed their wealth, looked after by a retinue of servants. The earliest stately homes date from the 14th century, when defence was paramount. By the 16th century, when the opulent taste of the European Renaissance spread to England, houses became centres of pleasure and showplaces for fine art *(see pp302–03).* The Georgians favoured chaste Classical architecture with rich interiors, the Victorians flamboyant Gothic. Due to 20th-century social change many stately homes have been opened to the public, some administered by the National Trust.

Adam sketch (c.1760) for ornate panel

The saloon, a domed rotunda based on the Pantheon in Rome, was designed to display the Curzon family's Classical sculpture collection to 18th-century society

The Drawing Room, the main room for entertaining, contains the most important pictures and some exquisite plasterwork.

The Marble Hall *is where balls and other social functions took place among Corinthian columns of pink alabaster.*

The Family Wing is a self-contained "pavilion" of private living quarters; the servants lived in rooms above the kitchen. The Curzon family still live here.

The Music Room is decorated with musical themes. Music was the main entertainment on social occasions.

TIMELINE OF ARCHITECTS

1650				1750

Colen Campbell (1676–1729) designed Burlington House *(see p81)*

William Kent (1685–1748) built Holkham Hall *(see p197)* in the Palladian style

Robert Adam (1728–92), who often worked with his brother James (1730–94) was as famous for decorative details as for buildings

Henry Holland (1745–1806) designed the Neo-Classical south range of Woburn Abbey *(see p230)*

Sir John Vanbrugh *(see p398)* was helped by **Nicholas Hawksmoor** (1661–1736) on Blenheim Palace *(see pp228–29)*

John Carr (1723–1807) designed the Palladian Harewood House *(see p410)*

Castle Howard (1702) by Sir John Vanbrugh

Adam fireplace, Kedleston Hall, adorned with Classical motifs

NATIONAL TRUST

National Trust oak leaf design

At the end of the 19th century, there were real fears that burgeoning factories, mines, roads and houses would obliterate much of Britain's historic landscape and finest buildings. In 1895 a group that included the social reformer Octavia Hill formed the National Trust, to preserve the nation's valuable heritage. The first building acquired by the trust was the medieval Clergy House at Alfriston in Sussex, in 1896 *(see p180)*. Today the National Trust is a charity that runs many historic houses and gardens, and vast stretches of countryside and coastline *(see p671)*. It is supported by more than two million members nationwide.

A corridor links the kitchen to the main house.

The 13th-century church is all that is left of Kedleston village, moved in 1760 to make way for the new house and its grounds.

KEDLESTON HALL

This Derbyshire mansion *(see p336)* is an early work of the influential Georgian architect Robert Adam, who was a pioneer of the Neo-Classical style derived from ancient Greece and Rome. It was built for the Curzon family in the 1760s.

Life Below Stairs by Charles Hunt (c.1890)

LIFE BELOW STAIRS

A large community of resident staff was essential to run a country house smoothly. The butler was in overall charge, ensuring that meals were served on time. The housekeeper supervised uniformed maids who made sure the place was clean. The cook ran the kitchen, using fresh produce from the estate. Ladies' maids and valets acted as personal servants.

1800	1850	

Dining Room, Cragside, Northumberland

Norman Shaw (1831–1912) was an exponent of Victorian Gothic, as in Cragside (above), and a pioneer of the Arts and Crafts movement *(see p328)*

Philip Webb (1831–1915) was a leading architect of the influential Arts and Crafts movement *(see p328)*, whose buildings favoured the simpler forms of an "Old English" style, instead of flamboyant Victorian Gothic

Standen, West Sussex (1891–94) by Philip Webb

Sir Edwin Lutyens (1869–1944) designed the elaborate Castle Drogo in Devon *(see p295)*, one of the last grand country houses

Heraldry and the Aristocracy

Order of the Garter medal

The British aristocracy has evolved over 900 years from the feudal obligations of noblemen to the Norman kings, who conferred privileges of rank and land in return for armed support. Subsequent monarchs bestowed titles and property on their supporters, establishing new aristocratic dynasties. The title of "earl" dates from the 11th century; that of "duke" from the 14th century. Soon the nobility began to choose their own symbols, partly to identify a knight concealed by his armour: these were often painted on the knight's coat (hence the term "coat of arms") and also copied onto his shield.

The College of Arms, London: housing records of all coats of arms and devising new ones

ROYAL COAT OF ARMS

The most familiar British coat of arms is the sovereign's. It appears on the royal standard, or flag, as well as on official documents and on shops that enjoy royal patronage. Over nearly 900 years, various monarchs have made modifications. The quartered shield in the middle displays the arms of England (twice), Scotland and Ireland. Surrounding it are other traditional images including the lion and unicorn, topped by the crown and the royal helm (helmet).

Edward III *(1327–77) was the founder of the chivalric Order of the Garter. The garter, bearing the motto,* Honi soit qui mal y pense *(evil be to him who thinks of evil), goes round the central shield.*

The lion is the most common beast in heraldry.

The red lion is the symbol of Scotland.

The unicorn is a mythical beast, generally regarded as a Scottish royal beast in heraldry.

Henry II *(1154–89) formalized his coat of arms to include three lions. This was developed by his son Richard I to become the "Gules three lions passant guardant or" seen on today's arms.*

The royal helm with gold protective bars was introduced to the arms by Elizabeth I (1558–1603).

Dieu et mon droit (God and my right) has been the royal motto since the reign of Henry V (1413–22).

Henry VII *(1485–1509) devised the Tudor rose, joining the white and red roses of York and Lancaster.*

ADMIRAL LORD NELSON

When people are ennobled they may choose their own coat of arms if they do not already have one. Britain's naval hero (1758–1805) was made Baron Nelson of the Nile in 1798 and a viscount in 1801. His arms relate to his life and career at sea; but some symbols were added after his death.

A seaman supports the shield.

The motto means "Let him wear the palm (or laurel) who deserves it".

A tropical scene shows the Battle of the Nile (1798).

The San Joseph was a Spanish man o'war that Nelson daringly captured.

TRACING YOUR ANCESTRY

For records of births, deaths and marriages in England and Wales since 1837, contact the **General Register Office** (0845 603 7788; www.gro.gov.uk), and in Scotland **New Register House**, 3 West Register St, Edinburgh EH1 3YT (0131 334 0380; www.gro-scotland. gov.uk). For help in tracing family history, consult the **Society of Genealogists**, 14 Charterhouse Bldgs, London EC1 (020 7251 8799).

Inherited titles *usually pass to the eldest son or the closest male relative, but some titles may go to women if there is no male heir.*

The Duke of Edinburgh (born 1921), husband of the Queen, is one of several dukes who are members of the Royal Family.

The Marquess of Salisbury (1830–1903), Prime Minister three times between 1885 and 1902, was descended from the Elizabethan statesman Robert Cecil.

Earl Mountbatten of Burma (1900–79) was ennobled in 1947 for diplomatic and military services.

Viscount Montgomery (1887–1976) was raised to the peerage for his military leadership in World War II.

Lord Byron (1788–1824), the Romantic poet, was the 6th Baron Byron: the 1st Baron was an MP ennobled by Charles I in 1625.

PEERS OF THE REALM

There are nearly 1,200 peers of the realm. In 1999 the process began to abolish the hereditary system in favour of life peerages that expire on the death of the recipient *(see left and below)*. Ninety-two hereditary peers are entitled to sit in the House of Lords, including the Lords Spiritual – archbishops and senior bishops of the Church of England – and the Law Lords. In 1958 the Queen expanded the list of life peerages to honour people who had performed notable public service. From 1999 the system of "peoples peerages" began to replace inherited honours.

KEY TO THE PEERS

☐	25 dukes
☐	35 marquesses
☐	175 earls and countesses
☐	98 viscounts
☐	800+ barons and baronesses

THE QUEEN'S HONOURS LIST

Twice a year several hundred men and women nominated by the Prime Minister and political leaders for outstanding public service receive honours from the Queen. Some are made dames or knights, a few receive the prestigious OM (Order of Merit), but far more receive lesser honours such as OBEs or MBEs (Orders or Members of the British Empire).

Mother Theresa *received the OM in 1983 for her work in India.*

Terence Conran, *founder of Habitat, was knighted for services to industry.*

The Beatles *were given MBEs in 1965. Paul McCartney was knighted in 1997.*

Rural Architecture

For many, the essence of British life is found in villages. Their scale and serenity nurture a way of life envied by those who live in towns and cities. The pattern of British villages dates back some 1,500 years, when the Saxons cleared forests and established settlements, usually centred around a green or pond. Most of today's English villages existed at the time of the *Domesday Book* in 1086, though few actual buildings survive from then. The settlements evolved organically around a church or manor; the cottages and gardens were created from local materials. Today, a typical village will contain structures of various dates, from the Middle Ages onward. The church is usually the oldest, followed perhaps by a tithe barn, manor house and cottages.

Abbotsbury, in Dorset – a typical village built up around a church

A steep-pitched roof covers the whole house.

Timbers are of Wealden oak.

Eaves are supported by curved braces.

Wealden Hall House *in Sussex is a medieval timber-framed house, of a type found in southeast England. It has a tall central open hall flanked by bays of two floors and the upper floor is "jettied", overhanging the ground floor.*

A tiled roof keeps the grain dry.

The entrance is big enough for ox-wagons.

Holes let in air – and birds.

Walls and doors are weatherboarded.

The medieval tithe barn *stored produce for the clergy – each farmer was required to donate one tenth (tithe) of his annual harvest. The enormous roofs may be supported by crucks, large curved timbers extending from the low walls.*

Slender spire from the Georgian era

THE PARISH CHURCH

The church is the focal point of the village and, traditionally, of village life. Its tall spire could be seen – and its bells heard – by travellers from a distance. The church is also a chronicle of local history: a large church in a tiny village indicates a once-prosperous settlement. A typical church contains architectural features from many centuries, occasionally as far back as Saxon times. These may include medieval brasses, wall paintings, misericords *(see p341)*, and Tudor and Stuart carvings. Many sell informative guide books inside.

West elevation

Pinnacled towers dating from the 15th century are situated at the west end.

Bells summon the congregation.

Buttresses support old walls.

Norman arches are rounded.

Stone cottages such as this Pennine longhouse are built from hard, local granite, keeping out the severe winter weather. Farm animals were housed in the barn (on right), and the family home was at the other end (see far right).

Chimneys come in various shapes.

The roof is made from slabs of Lake District stone.

Windows were often small in cold areas.

The roof is surfaced with tiles.

Type of stone used depends on locality. In Cumbria blue-grey Pennine stone was used.

Weatherboard houses were built chiefly in southeast England in the 18th and 19th centuries; the timber boarding acted as cladding to keep out the cold and rain.

Bay windows add light and space.

Thatch is made from reeds or straw.

Thatched cob cottages of the 17th century have a cob covering a timber frame. The cob is made from a mixture of wet earth, lime, dung, chopped reed, straw, gravel, sand and stones.

Walls are 1 m (3 ft) thick.

BUILDING MATERIALS

The choice of materials depended on local availability. A stone cottage in east Scotland or Cornwall would be granite, or in the Cotswolds, limestone. Timber for beams was often oak. Flint and pebble were popular in the chalky south and east. Slate is quarried in Wales and brick was widely used from Tudor times.

Welsh slate, making a durable roof

Tiles made from fired clay

Flint and pebble – common in Norfolk

Wood planks used for weatherboarding

Brick, widely used since Tudor times

Local hard granite from South Wales

South elevation

The nave is often the oldest part of the building, with extensions added in later centuries.

Towers are often later additions, due to their tendency to collapse.

Ropes used by bell-ringers.

The font, where babies are baptized, is often a church's oldest feature.

Pointed arches date from the 13th century.

Many pulpits are Jacobean.

A screen separates nave from chancel.

The chancel houses the choir and altar.

The Countryside

Common Blue butterfly

For its size, Britain contains an unusual variety of geological and climatic conditions that have shaped diverse landscapes, from treeless windswept moorland to boggy marshes and small hedged cattle pastures. Each terrain nurtures its typical wildlife and displays its own charm through the seasons. With the reduction in farming and the creation of footpaths and nature reserves, the countryside is becoming more of a leisure resource.

INDIGENOUS ANIMALS AND BIRDS

There are no large or dangerous wild animals in Britain but a wealth of small mammals, rodents and insects inhabit the countryside, and the rivers and streams are home to many varieties of fish. For bird-watchers there is a great range of songbirds, birds of prey and seabirds.

Livestock graze on low pastures.

Trees provide shelter and protection for wildlife.

Higher land is uncultivated.

Bushes and trees grow between rocks.

Streams flow over a stony bed from mountain springs.

The highest ground is often covered in snow until spring.

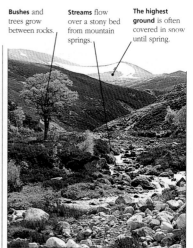

WOODED DOWNLAND

Chalk downland, seen here at Ditchling Beacon on the Downs *(see p181),* has soil of low fertility and is grazed by sheep. However crops are sometimes grown on the lower slopes. Distinctive wild flowers and butterflies thrive here, while beech and yew predominate in the woods.

WILD HILLSIDE

Large tracts of Britain's uplands remain wild terrain, unsuitable for crops or forestry. Purple heather is tough enough to survive in moorland, the haunt of deer and game birds. The highest craggy uplands, such as the Cairngorms *(see p544–45)* in Scotland, pictured here, are the habitat of birds of prey, such as the golden eagle.

Spear thistle *has pink heads in summer that attract several species of butterfly.*

Ling, *a low-growing heather with tiny pink bell-flowers, adds splashes of colour to peaty moors and uplands.*

The dog rose *is one of Britain's best-loved wild flowers; its pink single flower is widely seen in hedgerows.*

Hogweed *has robust stems and leaves with large clusters of white flowers.*

Meadow cranesbill *is a wild geranium with distinctive purple flowers.*

Tormentil *has small yellow flowers. It prefers moist, acid soil and is found near water on heaths and moors in summer.*

Swallows, *swifts and house martins are all summer visitors.*

Kestrels *are small falcons that prey on mammals such as voles.*

Rabbits *are often spotted feeding at the edge of fields or near woods.*

Robins, *common in gardens and hedgerows, have distinctive red breast feathers.*

Foxes, *little bigger than domestic cats, live in hideaways in woods, near farmland.*

Cereal crops ripen in small fields.

Hedgerows provide refuge for wildlife.

Small mixed woods break up the field pattern.

Sheep graze on salty marshes.

Culverts drain water from the field.

Reed beds edge the water.

TRADITIONAL FIELDS

The patchwork fields here in the Cotswolds *(see p304)* reflect generations of small-scale farming. A typical farm would produce silage, hay and cereal crops, and keep a few dairy cows and sheep in enclosed pastures. The tree-dotted hedgerows mark boundaries that may be centuries old.

MARSHLAND

Flat and low-lying wetlands, criss-crossed with dykes and drainage canals, provide the scenery of Romney Marsh *(see also p182)* as well as much of East Anglia. Some areas have rich, peaty soil for crops, or salty marshland for sheep, but there are extensive uncultivated sections, where reed beds shelter wildlife.

The oxeye daisy *is a larger relative of the common white daisy, found in grassland from spring to late summer.*

Orchids *are among the rarer wild flowers. This species is the Common Spotted Orchid.*

Cowslips *belong to the primrose family. In spring they are often found in the grass on open meadowlands.*

Sea lavender *is a saltmarsh plant that is tolerant of saline soils. It flowers in late summer.*

Poppies *glow brilliant red in cornfields.*

Buttercups *are among the most common wild flowers. They brighten meadows in summer.*

Walkers' Britain

Walkers of all levels of ability and enthusiasm are well served in Britain. There is an unrivalled network of long-distance paths through some spectacular scenery, which can be tackled in stages with overnight stays en route, or dipped into for a single day's walking. For shorter walks, Britain is dotted with signposts showing public footpaths across common or private land. You will find books of walk routes in local shops and a large map will keep you on track. Choose river routes for easy walking or take to the hills for a greater challenge.

Walker resting on Scafell Pike, Lake District

The West Highland Way is an arduous 95 mile (153 km) route from Milngavie, near Glasgow, to north of Fort William, across mountainous terrain with fine lochs and moorland scenery (see p494).

Fort William

Glasgow

The Pennine Way *was Britain's first designated long-distance path. The 268 mile (431 km) route from Edale in Derbyshire to Kirk Yetholm on the Scottish border is a challenging upland hike, with long, lonely stretches of moorland. It is only for experienced hill walkers.*

St Bees Head

Offa's Dyke Footpath *follows the boundary between Wales and England. The 168 mile (270 km) path goes through the beautiful Wye Valley (see p461) in the Welsh borders.*

Dales Way runs from Ilkley in West Yorkshire to Bowness-on-Windermere in the Lake District, 81 miles (130 km) of delightful flat riverside walking and valley scenery.

Presta

Pembrokeshire Coastal path *is 186 miles (299 km) of rugged cliff-top walking from Amroth on Carmarthen Bay to the west tip of Wales at Cardigan.*

St Dogmaels

Amroth

Minehea

ORDNANCE SURVEY MAPS

The best maps for walkers are published by the Ordnance Survey, the official mapping agency (08456 050505). Out of a wide range of maps the most useful are the *Explorer* series, which include the more popular regions and cover a large area, on a scale of 1:25,000, and the *Landranger* series, on a scale of 1:50,000.

The Southwest Coastal Path offers varied scenery from Minehead on the north Somerset coast to Poole in Dorset, via Devon and Cornwall – in all a marathon 630 mile (1,014 km) round trip.

SIGNPOSTS

Long-distance paths are well signposted, some of them with an acorn symbol (or with a thistle in Scotland). Many shorter routes are marked with coloured arrows by local authorities or hiking groups. Local councils generally mark public footpaths with yellow arrows. Public bridleways, marked by blue arrows, are paths that can be used by both walkers and horse riders – remember, horses churn up mud. Signs appear on posts, trees and stiles.

TIPS FOR WALKERS

Be prepared: *The weather can change very quickly: dress for the worst. Always take a compass, a proper walking map and get local advice before undertaking any ambitious walking. Pack some food and drink if the map does not show a pub en route.*
On the walk: *Always keep to the footpath and close gates behind you. Never feed or upset farm animals, leave litter, pick flowers or damage plants.*
Where to stay: *The International Youth Hostel Federation (see pp670–71) has a network of hostels which cater particularly for walkers. Bed-and-breakfast accommodation is also available near most routes (see p553).*
Further information: *The Ramblers' Association (020–7339 8500; www.ramblers.org.uk) is a national organization for walkers, with a guide to accommodation.*

The Coast to Coast Walk *crosses the Lake District, Yorkshire Dales and North York Moors, on a 190 mile (306 km) route. This demanding walk covers a spectacular range of North Country landscapes. All cross-country routes are best walked from west to east to take advantage of the prevailing wind.*

< Yetholm

dermere

Robin Hood's Bay

Ilkley

Edale

The Ridgeway *is a fairly easy path that follows an ancient track once used by cattle drovers. Starting near Avebury (see p263) it covers 85 miles (137 km) to Ivinghoe Beacon.*

Peddars Way and the Norfolk Coast Path together make 94 miles (151 km) of easy lowland walking, from Thetford, north to the coast then east to Cromer.

Sheringham

Thetford

Icknield Way, the most ancient prehistoric road in Britain, is 105 miles (168 km) long and links the Ridgeway to Peddars Way.

Ivinghoe

Kemble
epstow

Avebury

Farnham

Winchester

Poole Harbour

The Thames Path follows the river for 213 miles (341 km) from central London to Kemble, its source in Gloucestershire.

London

Dover

Eastbourne

The Isle of Wight Coastal Path circles the entire island on an easy 65 mile (105 km) footpath.

The North Downs Way is an ancient route through 141 miles (227 km) of low-lying hills from Farnham in Surrey to Dover or Folkestone in Kent.

The South Downs Way *is a 101 mile (162 km) walk from Eastbourne on the south coast to Winchester (see p170–71). It can be completed in a week.*

THE HISTORY OF GREAT BRITAIN

Britain began to assume a cohesive character as early as the 7th century, with the Anglo-Saxon tribes absorbing Celtic and Roman influences and finally achieving supremacy. They suffered repeated Viking incursions and were overcome by the Normans at the Battle of Hastings in 1066. Over centuries, the disparate cultures of the Normans and Anglo-Saxons combined to form the English nation, a process nurtured by Britain's position as an island. The next 400 years saw English kings involved in military expeditions to Europe, but their control over these areas was gradually wrested from them. As a result they extended their domain over Scotland and Wales. The Tudor monarchs consolidated this control and laid the foundations for Britain's future commercial success. Henry VIII recognized the vital importance of sea power and under his daughter, Elizabeth I, English sailors ranged far across the world, often coming into conflict with the Spanish. The total defeat of the Spanish Armada in 1588 confirmed Britain's position as a major maritime power. The Stuart period saw a number of internal struggles, most importantly the Civil War in 1641. But by the time of the Act of the Union in 1707 the whole island was united and the foundations for representative government had been laid. The combination of this internal security with continuing maritime strength allowed Britain to seek wealth overseas. By the end of the Napoleonic Wars in 1815, Britain was the leading trading nation in the world. The opportunities offered by industrialization were seized, and by the late 19th century, a colossal empire had been established across the globe. Challenged by Europe and the rise of the US, and drained by its leading role in two world wars, Britain's influence waned after 1945. By the 1970s almost all the colonies had become independent Commonwealth nations.

Medieval knights, masters of the arts of war

Contemporary map showing the defeat of the Armada (1588), making Britain into a world power

◁ **Henry VIII, founder of the British navy, seen here with his son, Edward, and wife Jane Seymour**

Kings and Queens

All English monarchs since the Norman Conquest in 1066 have been descendants of William the Conqueror. Scottish rulers, until James VI and the Union of Crowns in 1603 *(see pp482–3),* have been more diverse. When the Crown passes to someone other than the monarch's eldest son, the name of the ruling family usually changes. The rules of succession have been precisely laid down and strongly favour men over women, but Britain has still had six queens since 1553. In Norman times the monarchy enjoyed absolute power, but today the position is largely symbolic.

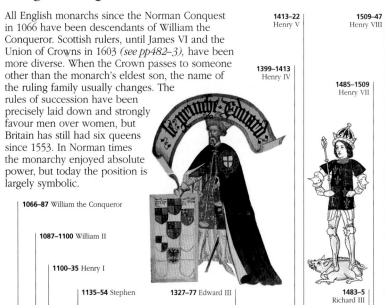

1413–22 Henry V

1399–1413 Henry IV

1509–47 Henry VIII

1485–1509 Henry VII

1066–87 William the Conqueror

1087–1100 William II

1100–35 Henry I

1135–54 Stephen

1327–77 Edward III

1483–5 Richard III

1050	1100	1150	1200	1250	1300	1350	1400	1450	1500
NORMAN		PLANTAGENET					LANCASTER	YORK	TUDO
1050	1100	1150	1200	1250	1300	1350	1400	1450	1500

1154–89 Henry II

1189–99 Richard I

1199–1216 John

1216–72 Henry III

1307–27 Edward II

1272–1307 Edward I

1422–61 and 1470–1 Henry VI

1461–70 and 1471–83 Edward IV

1377–99 Richard II

Matthew Paris's 13th-century chronicle showing clockwise from top left, Richard I, Henry II, John and Henry III

1483 Edward V

1660–85 Charles II

1685–8 James II

1936 Edward VIII

1689–1702
William III and
Mary II

1702–14
Anne

1714–27
George I

53–8 Mary I

1603–25
James I

1837–1901 Victoria

1901–10
Edward VII

1727–60
George II

1952– Elizabeth II

	1600	1650	1700	1750	1800	1850	1900	1950	2000
	STUART			HANOVER			SAXE-COBURG	WINDSOR	
	1600	1650	1700	1750	1800	1850	1900	1950	2000

1830–37
William IV

1936–52 George VI shown
on the George Medal

1649–60 Commonwealth
under Lord Protector
Oliver Cromwell

1820–30
George IV

1910–36
George V

1625–49 Charles I

558–1603 Elizabeth I

–53 Edward VI

1760–1820 George III

Prehistoric Britain

Britain was part of the European landmass until the end of the last Ice Age, around 6000 BC, when the English Channel was formed by melting ice. The earliest inhabitants lived in limestone caves: settlements and farming skills developed gradually through the Stone Age. The magnificent wooden and stone henges and circles are masterworks from around 3000 BC, but their significance is a mystery. Flint mines and ancient pathways are evidence of early trading and many burial mounds (barrows) survive from the Stone and Bronze Ages.

Axe Heads
Stone axes, like this one found at Stonehenge, were used by Neolithic men.

Cup and ring marks were carved on standing stones, such as this one at Ballymeanoch.

MAPPING THE PAST

Monuments from the Neolithic (New Stone), Bronze and Iron Ages, together with artifacts found from these periods, provide a wealth of information about Britain's early settlers, before written history began with the Romans.

Neolithic Tools
Antlers and bones were made into Neolithic leather-working tools. These were found at Avebury (see p263).

Pottery Beaker
The Beaker People, who came from Europe in the early Bronze Age, take their name from these drinking cups often found in their graves.

Gold Breast Plate
Made by Wessex goldsmiths, its spectacular pattern suggests it belonged to an important chieftain.

Pentre Ifan, an impressive Neolithic burial chamber in South Wales, was once covered with a huge earth mound.

Mold Cape
Gold was mined in Wales and Cornwall in the Bronze Age. This intricately worked warrior's cape was buried in a grave at Mold, Clwyd.

This gold cup, found in a Cornish barrow, is evidence of the wealth of Bronze Age tribes.

TIMELINE

6000–5000 As the Ice Age comes to an end, sea levels rise, submerging the landlink between Britain and the Continent

Neolithic flint axes

6000 BC	5500 BC	5000 BC	4500 BC	4000 BC

A gold pendant and button (1700 BC), found in Bronze Age graves

3500 Neolithic Age begins. Long barrows and stone circles built around Britain

Skara Brae is a Neolithic village of about 2500 BC *(see p529).*

Maiden Castle
An impressive Iron Age hill fort in Dorset, its concentric lines of ramparts and ditches follow the contours of the hill top (see p269).

Iron Age Axe
The technique of smelting iron came to Britain around 700 BC, brought from Europe by the Celts.

Iron Age Brochs, round towers with thick stone walls, are found only in Scotland.

Castlerigg Stone Circle is one of Britain's earliest Neolithic monuments *(see p361).*

WHERE TO SEE PREHISTORIC BRITAIN

Wiltshire, with Stonehenge *(p262)* and Avebury *(p263)*, has the best group of Neolithic monuments, and the Uffington White Horse is nearby *(p221)*. The Scottish islands have many early sites and the British Museum *(pp106–7)* houses a huge collection of artefacts.

A circular bank *with over 180 stones encloses the Neolithic site at Avebury (see p263).*

Uffington White Horse
Thought to be 3,000 years old, the shape has to be "scoured" to keep grass at bay (see p221).

A chalk figure, thought to be a fertility goddess, was found at Grimes Graves *(see p194).*

This bronze Celtic helmet (50 BC) was found in the River Thames, London.

Stonehenge was begun around 3,500 years ago *(see pp262–63).*

Snettisham Torc
A torc was a neck ring worn by Celtic men. This one, found in Norfolk, dates from 50 BC and is made from silver and gold.

2500 Temples, or henges, are built of wood or stone	**1650–1200** Wessex is at the hub of trading routes between Europe and the mines of Cornwall, Wales and Ireland		**1000** First farmsteads are settled	**550–350** Migration of Celtic people from southern Europe	**500** Iron Age begins. Hill forts are built	
0 BC	**2500 BC**	**2000 BC**	**1500 BC**	**1000 BC**	**500 BC**	
2100–1650 The Bronze Age reaches Britain. Immigration of the Beaker People, who make bronze implements and build ritual temples		*Chieftain's bronze sceptre (1700 BC)*	**1200** Small, self-sufficient villages start to appear		**150** Tribes from Gaul begin to migrate to Britain	

Roman Britain

Throughout the 350-year Roman occupation, Britain was ruled as a colony. After the defeat of rebellious local tribes, such as Boadicea's Iceni, the Romans remained an unassimilated occupying power. Their legacy is in military and civil

Roman jasper seal

construction: forts, walls, towns and public buildings. Their long, straight roads, built for easy movement of troops, are still a feature of the landscape.

Cavalry Sports Helmet
Found in Lancashire, it was used in tournaments by horsemen. Cavalry races and other sports were held in amphitheatres near towns.

Silver Jug
This 3rd-century jug, the earliest known silver item with Christian symbols, was excavated near Peterborough.

Exercise corridor

Main baths

Entrance hall

Fishbourne Palace was built at the site of a natural harbour and ships could moor here.

Hadrian's Wall
Started in 120 as a defence against the Scots; it marked the northern frontier of the Roman Empire and was guarded by 17 forts housing over 18,500 foot-soldiers and cavalry.

Mithras
This head of the god Mithras was found on the London site of a temple devoted to the cult of Mithraism. The sect demanded of its Roman followers loyalty and discipline.

TIMELINE

54 BC Julius Caesar lands in Britain but withdraws

Julius Caesar (c.102–44 BC)

AD 61 Boadicea rebels against Romans and burns their towns, including St Albans and Colchester, but is defeated *(see p195)*

AD 70 Romans conquer Wales and the North

Boadicea (1st century), Queen of the Iceni

140–143 Romans occupy southern Scotland and build Antonine Wall to mark the frontier

| 55 BC | AD 1 | AD 50 | | 150 |

AD 43 Claudius invades; Britain becomes part of the Roman Empire

AD 78–84 Agricola advances into Scotland, then retreats

120 Emperor Hadrian builds a wall on the border with Scotland

Flavian Mosaic
*Roman floors of the 1st
century used patterns
in black and white stone.
More mosaics survive
at Fishbourne than at
any other British site.*

Courtyard

Guest
apartment

Guest
bathroom

Box
hedges

Aisled
hall

WHERE TO SEE ROMAN BRITAIN

Many of Britain's main towns and cities were established by the Romans and have Roman remains, including York (*see pp404–09*), Chester (*see pp310–11*), St Albans (*see p232*), Colchester (*see p205*), Bath (*see pp258–61*), Lincoln (*see pp340–41*) and London (*see pp70–155*). Several Roman villas were built in southern England, favoured for its mild climate and proximity to Europe.

The Roman baths in Bath
(*see pp258–61*), *known as
Aquae Sulis, were built between
the 1st and 4th centuries
around a natural hot spring.*

FISHBOURNE PALACE

Built during the 1st century for Togidubnus, a pro-Roman governor, the palace (here reconstructed) had sophisticated functions such as under-floor heating and indoor plumbing for baths (*see p171*).

Chi-Rho Symbol
*This early Christian
symbol is from a
3rd-century fresco
at Lullingstone
Roman villa in Kent.*

Battersea Shield
*Found in the Thames
near Battersea, the
shield bears Celtic
symbols and was
probably made at
about the time of the
first Roman invasion.
Archaeologists suspect
it may have been lost
by a warrior while
crossing the river, or
offered as a sacrifice
to one of the many
river gods. It is now
at the British Museum
(see pp106–7).*

206 Tribes from
northern Scotland
attack Hadrian's Wall

254 St Alban is
beheaded, and
becomes Britain's
first Christian
martyr

*Aberlemno Pictish
stone in Scotland*

410 Romans
withdraw
from Britain

| 200 | 250 | 300 | 350 | 400 |

306 Roman troops in
York declare
Constantine emperor

350–69 Border
raids by Picts
and Scots

440–450
Invasions of
Angles, Saxons
and Jutes

209 Septimius Severus
arrives from Rome with
reinforcements

Anglo-Saxon Kingdoms

King Canute (1016–35)

By the mid-5th century, Angles and Saxons from Germany had started to raid the eastern shores of Britain. Increasingly they decided to settle, and within 100 years Saxon kingdoms, including Wessex, Mercia and Northumbria, were established over the entire country. Viking raids throughout the 8th and 9th centuries were largely contained, but in 1066, the last invasion of England saw William the Conqueror from Normandy defeat the Anglo-Saxon King Harold at the Battle of Hastings. William then went on to assume control of the whole country.

Viking Axe
The principal weapons of the Viking warriors were spear, axe and sword. They were skilled metal-workers with an eye for decoration, as seen in this axe-head from a Copenhagen museum.

Vikings on a Raiding Expedition
Scandinavian boat-building skills were in advance of anything known in Britain. People were terrified by these large, fast boats with their intimidating figureheads, which sailed up the Thames and along the coasts.

ANGLO-SAXON CALENDAR

These scenes from a chronicle of seasons, made just before the Norman invasion, show life in late Anglo-Saxon Britain. At first people lived in small farming communities, but by the 7th century towns began to spring up and trade increased. Saxon kings were supported by nobles but most of the population were free peasants.

TIMELINE

c.470–495 Saxons and Angles settle in Essex, Sussex and East Anglia	**c.556** Saxons move across Britain and set up seven kingdoms		*St Augustine (d.604)* **635** St Aidan establishes a monastery on Lindisfarne	**730–821** Supremacy of Mercia, whose king, Offa (d.796), builds a dyke along the Mercia–Wales border
450	500	550	600	650	700	75
450 Saxons first settle in Kent		**563** St Columba lands on Iona	**597** St Augustine sent by Rome to convert English to Christianity	**617–85** Supremacy of Northumbrian kingdom

Mercian coin which bears the name of King Offa

Ox-drawn plough for tilling

Minstrels entertaining at a feast

Hawks, used to kill game

Harold's Death
This 14th-century illustration depicts the victorious William of Normandy after King Harold was killed with an arrow in his eye. The Battle of Hastings (see p181) was the last invasion of Britain.

Alfred Jewel
This 9th-century gold ornament in the Ashmolean Museum (see p224) has the inscription: "Alfred ordered me made". This may refer to the Saxon King Alfred.

Edward the Confessor
In 1042, Edward – known as "the Confessor" because of his piety – became king. He died in 1066 and William of Normandy claimed the throne.

WHERE TO SEE ANGLO-SAXON BRITAIN

The best collection of Saxon artefacts is from a burial ship unearthed at Sutton Hoo in Suffolk in 1938 and now on display at the British Museum *(see pp106–7)*. There are fine Saxon churches at Bradwell in Essex and Bosham in Sussex *(see p171)*. In York the Viking town of Jorvik has been excavated *(see p408)* and actual relics are shown alongside models of people and dwellings.

The Saxon church *of St Laurence (see p255) was built in the late 8th century.*

Legend of King Arthur
Arthur is thought to have been a chieftain who fought the Saxons in the early 6th century. Legends of his knights' exploits appeared in 1155 (see p285).

802–839 After the death of Cenwulf (821), Wessex gains control over most of England

867 Northumbria falls to the Vikings

878 King Alfred defeats Vikings but allows them to settle in eastern England

An invading Norman ship

1016 Danish King Canute *(see p171)* seizes English crown

800	850	900	950	1000	1050	1100

843 Kenneth McAlpin becomes king of all Scotland

c.793 Lindisfarne sacked by Viking invaders; first Viking raid on Scotland about a year later

926 Eastern England, the Danelaw, is reconquered by the Saxons

1042 The Anglo-Saxon Edward the Confessor becomes king (d.1066)

1066 William of Normandy claims the throne, and defeats Harold at the Battle of Hastings. He is crowned at Westminster

The Middle Ages

Noblemen stag hunting

Remains of Norman castles on English hill tops bear testimony to the military might used by the invaders to sustain their conquest – although Wales and Scotland resisted for centuries. The Normans operated a feudal system, creating an aristocracy that treated native Anglo-Saxons as serfs. The ruling class spoke French until the 13th century, when it mixed with the Old English used by the peasants. The medieval church's power is shown in the cathedrals that grace British cities today.

Magna Carta
To protect themselves and the church from arbitrary taxation, the powerful English barons compelled King John to sign a "great charter" in 1215 (see p235). This laid the foundations for an independent legal system.

Becket is received into heaven.

Craft Skills
An illustration from a 14th-century manuscript depicts a weaver and a copper-beater – two of the trades that created a wealthy class of artisans.

Henry II's knights murder Becket in Canterbury Cathedral.

MURDER OF THOMAS BECKET

The struggle between church and king for ultimate control of the country was brought to a head by the murder of Becket, the Archbishop of Canterbury. After Becket's canonization in 1173, Canterbury became a major centre of pilgrimage.

Ecclesiastical Art
Nearly all medieval art had religious themes, such as this window at Canterbury Cathedral (see pp186–7) depicting Jeroboam.

Black Death
A plague swept Britain and Europe several times in the 14th century, killing millions of people. This illustration, in a religious tract, produced around 100 years later, represents death taking its heavy toll.

TIMELINE

1071 Hereward the Wake, leader of the Anglo-Saxon resistance, defeated at Ely

1154 Henry II, the first Plantagenet king, demolishes castles, and exacts money from barons instead of military service

1170 Archbishop of Canterbury, Thomas à Becket, is murdered by four knights after quarrelling with Henry II

1100	1150	1200	1250

1086 The *Domesday Book*, a survey of every manor in England, is compiled for tax purposes

Domesday Book

1215 Barons compel King John to sign the *Magna Carta*

1256 First Parliament to include ordinary citizens

Battle of Agincourt

In 1415, Henry V took an army to France to claim its throne. This 15th-century chronicle depicts Henry beating the French army at Agincourt.

This casket (1190), in a private collection, is said to have contained Becket's remains.

Becket takes his place in Heaven after his canonization.

Two clergymen look on in horror at Becket's murder.

Richard III

Richard, shown in this 16th-century painting, became king during the Wars of the Roses: a bitter struggle for power between two factions of the royal family – the houses of York and Lancaster.

John Wycliffe *(1329–84)*

This painting by Ford Madox Brown (1821–93) shows Wycliffe with the Bible he translated into English to make it accessible to everyone.

WHERE TO SEE MEDIEVAL BRITAIN

The university cities of Oxford *(pp222–27)* and Cambridge *(pp210–15)* contain the largest concentrations of Gothic buildings. Magnificent cathedrals rise high above many historic cities, among them Lincoln *(pp340–41)* and York *(pp404–09)*. Both cities still retain at least part of their ancient street pattern. Military architecture is best seen in Wales *(pp438–9)* with the formidable border castles of Edward I.

All Souls College *in Oxford (see p226), which only takes graduates, is a superb blend of medieval and later architecture.*

Castle Life

Every section of a castle was allotted to a baron whose soldiers helped defend it. This 14th-century illustration shows the coats of arms (see p30) of the barons for each area.

282–3
dward I
onquers
Wales

1296 Edward I invades Scotland but Scots resist stoutly

Edward I (1239–1307)

1314 Scots defeat English at the Battle of Bannockburn *(see p482)*

1348 Europe's population halved by Black Death

| 1300 | 1350 | 1400 | 1450 |

1381 Peasants' revolt after the imposition of a poll tax on everyone in the country over 14

1415 English victory at Agincourt

1387 Chaucer starts writing the *Canterbury Tales (see p186)*

Geoffrey Chaucer (c.1345–1400)

1485 Battle of Bosworth ends Wars of the Roses

1453 End of Hundred Years' War against France

Tudor Renaissance

After years of debilitating civil war, the Tudor monarchs established peace and national self-confidence, reflected in the split from the church of Rome – due to Henry VIII's divorce from Catherine of Aragon – and the consequent closure of the monasteries.

Hawking, a popular pastime

Henry's daughter, Mary I, tried to re-establish Catholicism but under her half-sister, Elizabeth I, the Protestant church secured its position. Overseas exploration began, provoking clashes with other European powers seeking to exploit the New World. The Renaissance in arts and learning spread from Europe to Britain, with playwright William Shakespeare adding his own unique contribution.

Curtains behind the queen are open to reveal scenes of the great English victory over the Spanish Armada in 1588.

Sea Power
Henry VIII laid the foundations of the powerful English navy. In 1545, his flagship, the Mary Rose *(see p169), sank before his eyes in Portsmouth harbour on its way to do battle with the French.*

Theatre
Some of Shakespeare's plays were first seen in purpose-built theatres such as the Globe (see p120) in south London.

The globe signifies that the queen reigns supreme far and wide.

Monasteries
With Henry VIII's split from Rome, England's religious houses, like Fountains Abbey (see pp390–91), were dissolved. Henry stole their riches and used them to finance his foreign policy.

TIMELINE

1497 John Colet denounces the corruption of the clergy, supported by Erasmus and Sir Thomas More

1533–4 Henry VIII divorces Catherine of Aragon and is excommunicated by the Pope. He forms the Church of England

1542–1567 Mary, Queen of Scots rules Scotland

1490

1510

1530

1497 John Cabot (see p256) makes his first voyage to North America

1513 English defeat Scots at Flodden (see p482)

Henry VIII (1491–1547)

1535 Act of Union with Wales

1536–40 Dissolution of the Monasteries

1549 First Book Common Pray introduce

Mary, Queen of Scots
As great-granddaughter of Henry VII, she laid claim to the English throne in 1559. But in 1567, Elizabeth I had her imprisoned for 20 years until her execution for treason in 1587.

Jewels symbolize triumph.

WHERE TO SEE TUDOR BRITAIN
Hampton Court Palace *(p173)* has been altered over the centuries but remains a Tudor showpiece. Part of Elizabeth I's former home at Hatfield *(p231)* still survives. In Kent, Leeds Castle, Knole *(pp188–9)* and Hever Castle *(p189)* all have connections with Tudor royalty. Burghley House *(pp342–3)* and Hardwick Hall *(p302)*, both Midlands mansions, retain their 16th-century character.

This astronomical clock *at Hampton Court (see p173), with its intriguing zodiac symbols, was installed in 1540 by Henry VIII.*

DEFEAT OF THE ARMADA
Spain was England's main rival for supremacy on the seas, and in 1588 Philip II sent 100 powerfully armed galleons towards England, bent on invasion. The English fleet – under Lord Howard, Francis Drake, John Hawkins and Martin Frobisher – sailed from Plymouth and destroyed the Spanish navy in a famous victory. This commemorative portrait of Elizabeth I by George Gower (d.1596) celebrates the triumph.

Protestant Martyrs
Catholic Mary I reigned from 1553 to 1558. Protestants who opposed her rule were burned, such as these six churchmen at Canterbury in 1555.

William Shakespeare (1564–1616)

	1570 Sir Francis Drake's first voyage to the West Indies	**1584** Sir Walter Raleigh tries to colonize Virginia after Drake's first unsuccessful attempt	**1591** First play by Shakespeare performed	**1600** East India Company founded, beginning British involvement on the Indian continent
0	**1570**		**1590**	
1553 Death of Edward VI; throne passes to the Catholic Mary I	**1559** Mary, Queen of Scots lays claim to English throne	**1587** Execution of Mary, Queen of Scots on the orders of Elizabeth I	**1588** Defeat of the Spanish Armada	**1603** Union of Crowns. James VI of Scotland becomes James I of England
	1558 Elizabeth I ascends the throne	*Sir Walter Raleigh (1552–1618)*		

Stuart Britain

The end of Elizabeth I's reign signalled the start of internal turmoil. The throne passed to James I, whose belief that kings ruled by divine right provoked clashes with Parliament. Under his son, Charles I, the conflict escalated into Civil War that ended with his execution. In 1660 Charles II regained the throne, but after his death James II was ousted for Catholic leanings. Protestant-ism was reaffirmed with the reign of William and Mary, who suppressed the Catholic Jacobites (see p483).

A 17th-century barber's bowl

Science

Sir Isaac Newton (1642–1727) invented this reflecting telescope, laying the foundation for a greater under-standing of the universe, including the law of gravity.

Charles I stayed silent at his trial.

Oliver Cromwell

A strict Protestant and a passionate champion of the rights of Parliament, he led the victorious Par-liamentary forces in the Civil War. He became Lord Protector of the Commonwealth from 1653 to 1658.

On the way to his death, the king wore two shirts for warmth, so onlookers should not think he was shivering with fright.

Theatre

After the Restoration in 1660, when Parliament restored the monarchy, theatre thrived. Plays were perform-ed on temporary outdoor stages.

EXECUTION OF CHARLES I

Cromwell was convinced there would be no peace until the king was dead. At his trial for treason, Charles refused to recog-nize the authority of the court and offered no defence. He faced his death with dignity on 30 January 1649, the only English king to be executed. His death was followed by a republic known as the Commonwealth.

TIMELINE

1605 "Gunpowder Plot" to blow up Parliament thwarted	**1614** "Addled Parliament" refuses to vote money for James I	**1620** Pilgrim Fathers sail in the *Mayflower* to New England	**1642** Civil War breaks out	**1653–8** Cromwell rules as Lord Protector

| | 1625 | | 1650 | |

James I (1566–1625)

	1611 New translation of Bible published, known as King James Version	**1638** Scots sign National Covenant, opposing Charles I's Catholic leanings	**1649** Charles I executed outside Banqueting House and Commonwealth declared by Parliament	**1660** Restoration of the monarchy under Charles I.

Restoration of the Monarchy
This silk embroidery celebrates the fact that Charles II escaped his father's fate by hiding in an oak tree. There was joy at his return from exile in France.

WHERE TO SEE STUART BRITAIN

The best work of the two leading architects of the time, Inigo Jones and Christopher Wren, is in London, and includes St Paul's Cathedral (pp114–15). In the southeast two classic Jacobean mansions are Audley End (p208) and Hatfield House (p231). The Palace of Holyrood (p510), in Edinburgh, is another example.

The headless body kneels by the block.

The axeman holds the severed head of Charles I.

Hatfield House (p231) *is a splendid Jacobean mansion.*

Plague
Bills of mortality showed the weekly deaths as bubonic plague swept London in 1665. Up to 100,000 Londoners died.

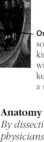

Onlookers soaked up the king's blood with their handkerchiefs to have a memento.

Anatomy
By dissecting corpses, physicians began to gain an understanding of the working of the human body – a crucial step towards modern surgery and medicine.

Pilgrim Fathers
In 1620 a group of Puritans sailed to America. They forged good relations with the native Indians; here they are shown being visited by the chief of the Pokanokets.

665–6 reat Plague

The Great Fire of London

1666 Great Fire of London

1688 The Glorious Revolution: Catholic James II deposed by Parliament

1707 Act of Union with Scotland

1675

1700

1690 Battle of the Boyne: William's English/Dutch army defeats James II's Irish/French army

1692 Glencoe Massacre of Jacobites (Stuart supporters) by William III's forces

William III (1689–1702)

Georgian Britain

Actress Sarah Siddons (1785), Gainsborough

The 18th century saw Britain, now recovered from the trauma of its Civil War, develop as a commercial and industrial powerhouse. London became a centre of banking, and a mercantile and professional class grew up. Continuing supremacy at sea laid the foundations of an empire; steam engines, canals and railways heralded the Industrial Revolution. Growing confidence was reflected in stately architecture and elegant fashions but, as cities became more crowded, conditions for the underclass grew worse.

Slate became the preferred tile for Georgian buildings. Roofs became less steep to achieve an Italian look.

A row of sash windows is one of the most characteristic features of a Georgian house.

Oak was used in the best dwellings for doors and stairs, but pine was standard in most houses.

The saloon was covered in wallpaper, a cheaper alternative to hanging walls with tapestries or fabrics.

The drawing room was richly ornamented and used for entertaining visitors.

The dining room was used for all family meals.

Steps led to the servants' entrance in the basement.

Battle of Bunker Hill

In 1775 American colonists rebelled against British rule. The British won this early battle in Massachusetts, but in 1783 Britain recognized the United States of America.

Watt's Steam Engine

The Scottish engineer James Watt (1736–1819) patented his engine in 1769 and then developed it for locomotion.

Lord Horatio Nelson

Nelson (see p31) became a hero after his death at the Battle of Trafalgar fighting the French.

TIMELINE

1714 George, Elector of Hanover, succeeds Queen Anne, ending the Stuart dynasty and giving Britain a German-speaking monarch

George I (1660–1727)

1720 "South Sea Bubble" bursts: many speculators ruined in securities fraud

1721 Robert Walpole (1646–1745) becomes the first Prime Minister

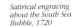
The Dutch Bubblers

Satirical engraving about the South Sea Bubble, 1720

1746 Bonnie Prince Charlie *(see p535)*, Jacobite claimant to throne, defeated at the Battle of Culloden

1757 Britain's first canal completed

1715	1730	1745	1760

The **attics** were where children and servants slept.

The **master bedroom** often had a mahogany four-poster bed.

Furniture was often carved, depicting animal heads and legs.

Canal Barge *(1827)*
Canals were a cheap way to carry the new industrial goods but were gradually superseded by railways during the 19th century.

Chippendale Armchair *(1760)*
Thomas Chippendale (1718–79) designed elegant furniture in a style still popular today.

WHERE TO SEE GEORGIAN BRITAIN

Bath *(see pp258–61)* and Edinburgh *(see pp504–11)* are two of Britain's best-preserved Georgian towns. The Building of Bath Museum in Bath *(see p261)* has a real Georgian flavour and Brighton's Royal Pavilion *(see pp178–9)* is a Regency extravaganza by John Nash.

Charlotte Square (see p504) *in Edinburgh has fine examples of Georgian architecture.*

Hogarth's Gin Lane
Conditions in London's slums shocked William Hogarth (1697–1764), who made prints like this to urge social reform.

GEORGIAN TOWN HOUSE

Tall, terraced dwellings were built to house wealthy families. The main architects of the time were Robert Adam *(see p28)* and John Nash *(see p105).*

The **servants** lived and worked in the basement during the day.

Kitchen

1776 American Declaration of Independence

1788 First convict ships are sent to Australia

1805 The British, led by Lord Nelson, beat Napoleon's French fleet at Battle of Trafalgar

1811–17 Riots against growing unemployment

1815 Duke of Wellington beats Napoleon at Waterloo

Caricature of Wellington (1769–1852)

775   1790   1805   1820

Silver tureen, 1774

1783 Steam-powered cotton mill invented by Sir Richard Arkwright (1732–92)

1807 Abolition of slave trade

1811 Prince of Wales made Regent during George III's madness

1825 Stockton to Darlington railway opens

1829 Catholic Emancipation Act passed

Victorian Britain

When Victoria became Queen in 1837, she was only 18. Britain was in the throes of its transformation from an agricultural country to the world's most powerful industrial nation. The growth of the Empire fuelled the country's confidence and opened up markets for Britain's manufactured goods. The accelerating growth of cities created problems of health and housing and a powerful Labour movement began to emerge. But by the end of Victoria's long and popular reign in 1901, conditions had begun to improve as more people got the vote and universal education was introduced.

Victoria and Disraeli, 1887

Florence Nightingale *(1820–1910) Known as the Lady with the Lamp, she nursed soldiers in the Crimean War and pioneered many improvements in army medical care.*

Newcastle Slum *(1880) Rows of cheap houses were built for an influx of workers to the major industrial cities. The awful conditions spread disease and social discontent.*

Glass walls and ceiling

Prefabricated girders

As well as silk textiles exhibits included carriages, engines, jewels, glass, plants, cutlery and sculptures.

Union Banner *Trade unions were set up to protect industrial workers against unscrupulous employers.*

Ophelia by Sir John Everett Millais *(1829–96) The Pre-Raphaelite painters chose Romantic themes, reflecting a desire to escape industrial Britain.*

TIMELINE

1832 Great Reform Bill extends the vote to all male property owners

1841 London to Brighton railway makes resort accessible

Vase made for the Great Exhibition

1851 Great Exhibition

1867 Second Reform A gives the vote to all ma householders in town

1830	1840	1850	1860

1834 Tolpuddle Martyrs transported to Australia for forming a union

1833 Factory Act forbids employment of children for more than 48 hours per week

1854–6 Britain victorious against Russia in Crimean War

1863 Opening of the London Underground

Triumph of Steam and Electricity

This picture from the Illustrated London News *(1897) sums up the feeling of optimism engendered by industrial advances.*

Elm trees were incorporated into the building along with sparrows, and sparrow hawks to control them.

WHERE TO SEE VICTORIAN BRITAIN

The industrial cities of the Midlands and the North are built around grandiose civic, commercial and industrial buildings. Notable Victorian monuments include the Manchester Museum of Science and Industry *(see p374)* and, in London, the Victoria and Albert Museum *(see pp98–9)* and St Pancras train station.

The Rotunda, Manchester *is a stately Victorian building.*

GREAT EXHIBITION OF 1851

The brainchild of Prince Albert, Victoria's consort, the exhibition celebrated industry, technology and the expanding British Empire. It was the biggest of its kind held up until then. Between May and October, six million people visited Joseph Paxton's lavish crystal palace, in London's Hyde Park. Nearly 14,000 exhibitors brought 100,000 exhibits from all over the world. In 1852 it was moved to south London where it burned down in 1936.

Cycling Craze
The bicycle, invented in 1865, became immensely popular with young people, as illustrated by this photograph of 1898.

1872 The Ballot Act introduces secret voting

1874 Benjamin Disraeli becomes Prime Minister

1884 Telephones introduced

1893 Gladstone's Irish Home Rule Bill defeated

1901 Queen Victoria dies

Cartoon of Gladstone, Vanity Fair *(1869)*

1870   1880   1890   1900

1870 Education Act makes school compulsory for children up to the age of 11

1877 Queen Victoria created Empress of India

Early telephone

1892 First Labour MP elected

1899–1902 Britain defeats South African Dutch settlers in Boer War

Britain from 1900 to 1950

When Queen Victoria's reign ended in 1901, British society threw off many of its 19th-century inhibitions, and an era of gaiety and excitement began. This was interrupted by World War I. The economic troubles that ensued, which culminated in the Depression of the 1930s, brought misery to millions. In 1939 the ambitions of Germany provoked World War II. After emerging victorious from this conflict, Britain embarked on an ambitious programme of social, educational and health reform.

Playwright Noel Coward

Welwyn Garden City was based on the Utopian idea of Sir Ebenezer Howard (1850–1928), founder of the garden city movement.

The Roaring Twenties
Young flappers discarded the rigid social codes of their parents and instead dis- covered jazz, cocktails and the Charleston.

Suffragettes
Women marched and chained themselves to railings in their effort to get the vote; many went to prison. Women over 30 won the vote in 1919.

NEW TOWNS
A string of new towns was created on the outskirts of London, planned to give residents greenery and fresh air. Welwyn Garden City was originally founded in 1919 as a self-contained community, but fast rail links turned it into a base for London commuters.

World War I
British troops in Europe dug into deep trenches protected by barbed wire and machine guns, only metres from the enemy, in a war of attrition that cost the lives of 17 million.

Wireless
Invented by Guglielmo Marconi, radios brought news and entertainment into homes for the first time.

TIMELINE

1903 Suffragette movement founded	**1911** MPs are given a salary for the first time, allowing working men to be elected	**1914–18** World War I		**1924** Fir Labou governme
1905	**1910**	**1915**	**1920**	
Henry Asquith (1852–1928), Prime Minister	**1908** Asquith's Liberal government introduces old age pensions	**1918** Vote given to all women over 30	**1922** First national radio service begins	

Marching for Jobs
These men were among thousands who marched for their jobs after being put out of work in the 1920s. The stock market crash of 1929 and the ensuing Depression caused even more unemployment.

Garden cities
ll had trees,
onds and
pen spaces.

World War II
German night-time air raids targeted transport, military and industrial sites and cities, such as Sheffield, in what was known as the "Blitz".

Modern Homes
Labour-saving devices, such as the vacuum cleaner, invented by William Hoover in 1908, were very popular. This was due to the virtual disappearance of domestic servants, as women took jobs outside the home.

WYN
N CITY

TO LET
PER ANNUM
L PURCHASE TERMS
ESTATE OFFICE
N CITY HERTS.
AVEMENT. E.C.2.

Cheap housing and the promise of a cleaner environment attracted many people to these new cities.

HILLMAN MINX

Family Motoring
By the middle of the century, more families could afford to buy mass-produced automobiles, like the 1950s Hillman Minx pictured in this advertisement.

1926 General Strike		**1936** Abdication of Edward VIII	**1944** Education Act: school leaving age raised to 15; grants provided for university students	**1948** National Health Service introduced
Edward VIII (1894–1972) and Wallis Simpson (1896–1986)				**1947** Independence for India and Pakistan
1930	**1935**		**1940**	**1945**
1929 Stock market crashes	**1936** First scheduled television service begins	**1939–45** Winston Churchill leads Britain to victory in World War II	**1945** Majority Labour government; nationalization of railways, road haulage, civil aviation, Bank of England, gas, electricity and steel
1928 Votes for all men and women over 21		*Food ration book*	

Britain Today

With the deprivations of war receding, Britain entered the Swinging Sixties, an explosion of youth culture characterized by the mini-skirt and the emergence of pop groups. The Age of Empire came to an end as most colonies gained independence by the 1970s – although Britain went to war again in 1982 when Argentina sought to annexe the tiny Falkland Islands.

Designer Vivienne Westwood and Naomi Campbell

People were on the move; immigration from the former colonies enriched British culture – though it also gave rise to social problems – and increasing prosperity allowed millions of people to travel abroad. Britain joined the European Community in 1973, and forged a more tangible link when the Channel Tunnel opened in 1994.

1982 British troops set sail to drive the Argentinians from the British-owned Falkland Islands

1960s The miniskirt takes British fashion to new heights of daring – and Flower Power arrives from California

1970s The outlandish clothes, hair and make-up of Punk Rockers shock the country

1951 Winston Churchill comes back as Prime Minister as Conservatives win general election

1965 Death penalty is abolished

1976 Supersonic Concorde makes first commercial flight

1950	1960	1970	1980

1950	1960	1970	1980

1953 Elizabeth II crowned in first televised Coronation

1963 The Beatles pop group from Liverpool captures the spirit of the age with numerous chart-topping hits

1975 Drilling begins for North Sea oil

1981 Charles Prince of Wales, marries Lady Diana Spencer in "fairytale" wedding at St Paul's Cathedral

1951 Festival of Britain lifts postwar spirits

1959 First motorway, the M1, built from London to the Midlands

1957 First immigrants arrive from the Caribbean by boat

1979 The "Iron Lady" Margaret Thatcher becomes Britain's first woman Prime Minister; her right-wing Conservative Government privatizes several state-owned industries

1973 After years of negotiation, Britain joins the European Community

1984 Year-long miners' strike fails to stop pit closures and heralds decline in trade union power

2005 The Prince of Wales marries Camilla Parker-Bowles at the Guildhall in Windsor

1991 Britain's tallest building, Canada Tower *(see p125)*, erected as part of the huge Docklands development – London's new financial centre

2004 One of London's most distinctive buildings, 30 St Mary Axe, also known as "the Gherkin", opens

2005 London's transport system hit by four bombs in a terrorist attack

2012 Britain is set to host the 2012 Olympic Games

1992 Conservative Government elected for fourth term – a record for this century

1997 New Labour ends 18 years of Conservative government

1990	2000	2010

1990	2000	2010

2007 Gordon Brown takes office as Prime Minister after Tony Blair's resignation

1990 Mrs Thatcher forced to resign by Conservative MPs; replaced by John Major

2005 The Labour party is elected for a record third term under Tony Blair

2003 Britain joins the US-led coalition in the Iraq war and thousands take to the streets to protest against the imminent invasion

1999 Formation of Scottish Parliament and Welsh Assembly

1985 Concern for famine in Africa gives rise to giant Live Aid pop concert to raise money for the starving

1994 Channel Tunnel opens to give direct rail link between Britain and Continental Europe

GREAT BRITAIN THROUGH THE YEAR

Every British season has its particular charms. Most major sights are open all year round, but many secondary attractions may be closed in winter. The weather is changeable in all seasons and the visitor is as likely to experience a crisp, sunny February day as to be caught in a cold, heavy shower in July. Long periods of

Film festival sign

adverse weather and extremes of temperature are rare. Spring is characterized by daffodils and bluebells, summer by roses and autumn by the vivid colours of changing leaves. In wintertime, country vistas are visible through the bare branches of the trees. Annual events and ceremonies, many stemming from age-old traditions, reflect the attributes of the seasons.

Bluebells in spring in Angrove woodland, Wiltshire

SPRING

As the days get longer and warmer, the countryside starts to come alive. At Easter many stately homes and gardens open their gates to visitors for the first time, and during the week before Whit Sunday, or Whitsun (the seventh Sunday after Easter), the Chelsea Flower Show takes place. This is the focal point of the gardening year and spurs on the nation's gardeners to prepare their summer displays. Outside the capital, many music and arts festivals mark the middle months of the year.

MARCH

Ideal Home Exhibition *(second week)*, Earl's Court, London. New products and ideas for the home.
Crufts Dog Show, National Exhibition Centre, Birmingham.
International Book Fair *(third week)*, Olympia, London.
St Patrick's Day *(17 March)*. Musical events in major cities celebrate the feast day of Ireland's patron saint.

APRIL

Maundy Thursday (Thursday before Easter), the Queen gives money to pensioners.
St George's Day *(23 April)*, English patron saint's day.
Antiques for Everyone *(last week)*, National Exhibition Centre, Birmingham.

Water garden exhibited at the Chelsea Flower Show

MAY

Furry Dancing Festival *(8 May)*, Helston, Cornwall. Spring celebration *(see p280)*.
Well-dressing festivals *(Ascension Day)*, Tissington, Derbyshire *(see p337)*.
Chelsea Flower Show *(May)*, Royal Hospital, London.
Brighton Festival *(last three weeks)*. Performing arts.
Glyndebourne Festival Opera Season *(mid-May–end Aug)*, near Lewes, East Sussex. Opera productions.
International Highland Games *(last weekend)*, Blair Atholl, Scotland.

Yeomen of the Guard conducting the Maundy money ceremony

SUMMER

Life moves outdoors in the summer months. Cafés and restaurants place tables on the pavements and pub customers take their drinks outside. The Queen holds garden parties for privileged guests at Buckingham Palace while, more modestly, village fêtes – which include traditional games and local stalls – are organized. Beaches and swimming pools become crowded and office workers picnic in city parks at lunch. The rose, England's national flower, bursts into bloom in millions of gardens. Cultural treats include open-air theatre performances, outdoor concerts, the Proms in London, the National Eisteddfod in Wales, Glyndebourne's opera festival, and Edinburgh's festival of the performing arts.

Glastonbury music festival, a major event attracting thousands of people

Assessment of sheep at the Royal Welsh Show, Builth Wells

Deck chair at Brighton

JUNE

Royal Academy Summer Exhibitions *(Jun–Aug)*. Large and varied London show of new work by many artists.
Bath International Festival *(late May–early Jun)*, various venues. Arts events.
Beaumaris Festival *(27 May–4 Jun)*, various venues. Concerts, craft fairs plus fringe activities.
Trooping the Colour *(Sat closest to 10 Jun)*, Whitehall, London. The Queen's official birthday parade.
Glastonbury Festival *(late June)*, Somerset.
Aldeburgh Festival *(second and third weeks)*, Suffolk. Arts festival with concerts and opera.
Royal Highland Show *(third week)*, Ingliston, near Edinburgh. Scotland's agricultural show.
Leeds Castle *(last week)*. Open-air concerts.
Glasgow International Jazz Festival *(last weekend)*. Various venues.

JULY

Royal Show *(first week)*, near Kenilworth, Warwickshire. National agricultural show.
International Eisteddfod *(first week)*, Llangollen, North Wales. International music and dance competition *(see p450)*.
Hampton Court Flower Show *(early July)*, Hampton Court Palace, Surrey.
Summer Music Festival *(third weekend)*, Stourhead, Wiltshire.
International Henley Royal Regatta *(first week)*, Henley-on-Thames. Rowing regatta on the Thames.
Cambridge Folk Festival *(last weekend)*. Music festival with top international artists.
Royal Welsh Show *(last weekend)*, Builth Wells, Wales. Agricultural show.
International Festival of Folk Arts *(late Jul–early Aug)*, Sidmouth, Devon *(see p289)*.

AUGUST

Royal National Eisteddfod *(early in month)*. Traditional arts competitions, in Welsh *(see p435)*. Various locations.

Reveller in bright costume at the Notting Hill Carnival

Henry Wood Promenade Concerts *(mid-Jul–mid-Sep)*, Royal Albert Hall, London. Famous concert series popularly known as the Proms.
Edinburgh International Festival *(mid-Aug–mid-Sep)*. The largest festival of theatre, dance and music in the world *(see p481)*.
Edinburgh Festival Fringe. Alongside the festival, there are 400 shows a day.
Brecon Jazz *(mid-Aug)*, jazz festival in Brecon, Wales.
Beatles Festival *(last weekend)*, Liverpool. Music and entertainment related to the Fab Four *(see p377)*.
Notting Hill Carnival *(last weekend)*, London. West Indian street carnival with floats, bands and stalls.

Boxes of apples from the autumn harvest

AUTUMN

After the heady escapism of summer, the start of the new season is marked by the various party political conferences held in October and the royal opening of Parliament. All over the country on 5 November, bonfires are lit and fireworks let off to celebrate the foiling of an attempt to blow up the Houses of Parliament by Guy Fawkes and his co-conspirators in 1605. Cornfields become golden, trees turn fiery yellow through to russet and orchards

are heavy with apples and other autumn fruits. In churches throughout the country, thanksgiving festivals mark the harvest. The shops stock up for the run-up to Christmas, their busiest time of the year.

SEPTEMBER

Blackpool Illuminations *(beg Sep–end Oct)*. A 5 mile (8 km) spectacle of lighting along Blackpool's seafront.
Royal Highland Gathering *(first Sat)*, Braemar, Scotland. Kilted clansmen from all over the country toss cabers, shot putt, dance and play the bagpipes. The royal family usually attends.
International Sheepdog Trials *(14–16 Sep)*, all over Britain, with venues changing from year to year.

Shot putting at Braemar

Great Autumn Flower Show *(third weekend)*, Harrogate, N Yorks. Displays by nurserymen and national flower organizations.
Oyster Festival *(Sat at beginning of oyster season)*, Colchester. Lunch hosted by the mayor to celebrate the beginning of the much awaited oyster season.

OCTOBER

Harvest Festivals *(whole month)*, all over Britain especially in farming areas.
Horse of the Year Show *(6–10 Oct)*, NEC, Birmingham.
Nottingham Goose Fair *(second weekend)*. One of Britain's oldest traditional fairs now has a funfair.
Canterbury Festival *(second and third weeks)*. Music, drama and the arts.
Aldeburgh Britten Festival *(third weekend)*. Concerts with music by Britten *(see p201)* and other composers.

Procession leading to the state opening of Parliament

NOVEMBER

Opening of Parliament *(Oct or Nov)*. The Queen goes from Buckingham Palace to Westminster in a state coach, to open the new parliamentary session.
London Film Festival *(end Oct–beg Nov)*. Forum for new films, various venues.
Lord Mayor's Procession and Show *(second Sat)*. Parade in the City, London.
Remembrance Day *(second Sun)*. Services and parades at the Cenotaph in Whitehall, London, and all over Britain.
RAC London to Brighton Veteran Car Rally *(first Sun)*. A 7am start from Hyde Park, London to Brighton, East Sussex.
Guy Fawkes Night *(5 Nov)*, fireworks and bonfires all over the country.
Regent Street Christmas Lights *(mid-Nov)*, London.

Fireworks over Edinburgh on Guy Fawkes Night

Winter landscape in the Scottish Highlands, near Glencoe

WINTER

Brightly coloured fairy lights and Christmas trees decorate Britain's principal shopping streets as shoppers rush to buy their seasonal gifts. Carol services are held in churches across the country, and pantomime, a traditional entertainment for children deriving from the Victorian music hall, fills theatres in major towns.

Brightly lit Christmas tree at the centre of Trafalgar Square

Many offices close between Christmas and the New Year. Shops reopen for the January sales on 27 December – a paradise for bargain-hunters.

DECEMBER

Christmas Tree *(first Thu)*, Trafalgar Square, London. The tree is donated by the

people of Norway and is lit by the Mayor of Oslo; this is followed by carol singing.
Carol concerts *(whole month)*, all over Britain.
Grand Christmas Parade *(beg Dec)*, London. Parade with floats to celebrate myth of Santa Claus.
Midnight Mass *(24 Dec)*, in churches everywhere around Britain.
Allendale Tarbaal Festival *(31 Dec)*, Northumberland. Parade by villagers with burning tar barrels on their heads to celebrate the New Year.

Sprig of holly

JANUARY

Hogmanay and **New Year** *(31 Dec, 1 Jan)*, Scottish celebrations. **Burns Night** *(25 Jan)*. Scots everywhere celebrate poet Robert Burns' birth with poetry, feasting and drinking.

FEBRUARY

Chinese New Year *(late Jan or early Feb)*. Lion dances, firecrackers and processions in Chinatown, London.

PUBLIC HOLIDAYS

New Year's Day (1 Jan).
2 Jan (Scotland only).
Easter weekend (March or April). In England it begins on **Good Friday** and ends on **Easter Monday**; in Scotland there is no Easter Monday holiday.
May Day (usually first Mon in May).
Late Spring Bank Holiday (last Mon in May).
Bank Holiday (first Mon in August, Scotland only).
August Bank Holiday (last Mon in August, except Scotland).
Christmas and Boxing Day (25– 26 December).

Morris dancing on May Day in Midhurst, Sussex

The Sporting Year

Many of the world's major competitive sports, including soccer, cricket and tennis, were invented in Britain. Originally devised as recreation for the wealthy, they have since entered the arena of mass entertainment. Some, however, such as the Royal Ascot race meeting and Wimbledon tennis tournament, are still valued as much for their social prestige as for the sport itself. Other delightful sporting events in Britain take place at a local level: village cricket, point-to-point racing and the Highland Games are all popular amateur events.

Kelly Holmes

Royal Ascot *is the four-day social highlight of the horse racing year. The high class of the thoroughbreds is matched by the high style of the fashions, with royalty attending.*

Oxford and Cambridge Boat Race, *first held in 1829 at Henley, has become a national event, with the two university eights now battling it out between Putney and Mortlake on the Thames.*

The FA Cup Final *is the apex of the football season.*

Derby Day horse races, Epsom

January	February	March	April	May	June

Cheltenham Gold Cup steeplechase *(see p328)*

Grand National steeple-chase, Aintree *(see p376),* **Liverpool**

Rugby League Cup Final, Wembley

Embassy World Snooker Championships, Sheffield

Wimbledon Lawn Tennis Tournment *is the world's most prestigious lawn tennis championship.*

Six Nations Rugby Union *is an annual contest between England, France, Italy, Ireland (left), Scotland (right) and Wales. This league-based competition runs through winter ending in March.*

London Marathon *attracts thousands of long-distance runners, from the world's best to fancy-dressed fund raisers.*

Henley Royal Regatta *(see p234) is an international rowing event on the Thames (first held in 1839). It is also a glamorous social occasion.*

British Grand Prix, *held at Silverstone, is Britain's round of the Formula One World Championship.*

TICKETS AND TOUTS

For many big sporting events, the only official source of tickets is the club concerned. Booking agencies may offer hard-to-get tickets – though often at high prices. Unauthorized touts may lurk at popular events but their expensive tickets are not always valid. Check carefully.

Tickets for the Grand Prix

British Open Golf Championship, *a major golf event, is held at one of several British courses. Here, Nick Faldo putts.*

The Cheltenham and Gloucester Trophy *is the final of a season of competition to find the year's county cricket champions. It takes place at Lord's (see p155).*

Cowes week *(see p168),* a yachting festival, covers all classes of racing.

Horse of the Year Show brings together top show-jumpers to compete on a tough indoor course *(see p64).*

Oxford versus Cambridge rugby union, Twickenham

August	September	October	November	December

European Show jumping Championships at Hickstead

Braemar Highland Games *(see p64)*

British Figure Skating and Ice Dance Champion-ships *are a feast of elegance on ice (various venues).*

Winmau World Masters Darts Champion-ships

Gold Cup Humber powerboat race, Hull

KEY TO SPORT SEASONS

Cricket

River fishing

Football (soccer)

Hunting and shooting

Rugby (union and league)

Flat racing

Jump racing

Athletics – track and field

Road running and cross-country

Polo

Cartier International Polo, *at the Guards Club, Windsor (see p235), is one of the main events for this peculiarly British game, played mainly by royalty and army officers.*

The Climate of Great Britain

Britain has a temperate climate. No region is far from the sea, which exerts a moderating influence on temperatures. Seldom are winter nights colder than -15°C, even in the far north, or summer days warmer than 30°C in the south and west: a much narrower range than in most European countries. Despite Britain's reputation, the average annual rainfall is quite low – 108 cm (42 inches) – and heavy rain is rare. The Atlantic coast is warmed by the Gulf Stream, making the west slightly warmer, though wetter, than the east.

LANCASHIRE AND THE LAKES

°C /°F

	Apr	Jul	Oct	Jan
max	12/54	19/66	14/57	6/43
		13/55	8/46	
min	5/41			2/36
☀	5.5 hrs	6 hrs	3 hrs	1.5 hrs
☂	53 mm	85 mm	104 mm	90 mm
month	Apr	Jul	Oct	Jan

THE HEART OF ENGLAND

°C /°F

	Apr	Jul	Oct	Jan
max	12/54	20/68	13/55	6/43
		13/55	8/46	
min	5/41			2/36
☀	4.5 hrs	5.5 hrs	3 hrs	1.5 hrs
☂	53 mm	69 mm	69 mm	74 mm
month	Apr	Jul	Oct	Jan

Average monthly maximum temperature

Average monthly minimum temperature

Average daily hours of sunshine

Average monthly rainfall

SOUTH AND MID-WALES

°C /°F

	Apr	Jul	Oct	Jan
max	13/55	20/68	14/57	7/45
		13/55	8/46	
min	5/41			2/36
☀	5.5 hrs	6 hrs	3.5 hrs	1.5 hrs
☂	65 mm	89 mm	109 mm	108 mm
month	Apr	Jul	Oct	Jan

NORTH WALES

°C /°F

	Apr	Jul	Oct	Jan
max	11/52	17/63	14/57	6/43
		11/52	8/46	
min	5/41			1/34
☀	3 hrs	3.5 hrs	2.5 hrs	1.5 hrs
☂	144 mm	206 mm	261 mm	252 mm
month	Apr	Jul	Oct	Jan

DEVON AND CORNWALL

°C /°F

	Apr	Jul	Oct	Jan
max	13/55	19/66	15/59	8/46
		13/55	9/48	
min	6/43			4/39
☀	6 hrs	6.5 hrs	3.5 hrs	2 hrs
☂	53 mm	70 mm	91 mm	99 mm
month	Apr	Jul	Oct	Jan

WEST COUNTRY

°C /°F

	Apr	Jul	Oct	Jan
max	14/57	21/70	15/59	7/45
		14/57	9/48	
min	6/43			2/36
☀	5.5 hrs	6.5 hrs	3.5 hrs	2 hrs
☂	49 mm	65 mm	85 mm	74 mm
month	Apr	Jul	Oct	Jan

THAMES VALLEY

°C /°F

	Apr	Jul	Oct	Jan
max	14/57	22/72	15/59	7/45
		13/55	7/45	
min	5/41			1/34
☀	5.5 hrs	6 hrs	3 hrs	1.5 hrs
☂	41 mm	55 mm	64 mm	61 mm
month	Apr	Jul	Oct	Jan

Map labels: Inverness, The Highlands and Islands, EDINBURGH, Glasgow, The Lowlands, Lancashire and the Lakes, Liverpool, North Wales, Caernarfon, South and Mid-Wales, CARDIFF, West Country, Exeter, Devon and Cornwall

THE HIGHLANDS AND ISLANDS

°C /°F			
11/52	17/63	13/55	
	10/50	7/45	7/45
3/37			1/34
4.5 hrs	3.5 hrs	2 hrs	1 hrs
111 mm	137 mm	215 mm	200 mm
month	Apr	Jul	Oct	Jan

THE LOWLANDS

°C /°F			
11/52	19/66	14/57	
	11/52	7/45	6/43
4/39			1/34
5 hrs	5.5 hrs	3 hrs	1.5 hrs
38 mm	69 mm	56 mm	47 mm
month	Apr	Jul	Oct	Jan

NORTHUMBRIA

°C /°F			
11/52	18/64	13/55	
	13/55	8/46	6/43
5/41			2/36
5 hrs	5.5 hrs	3 hrs	1.5 hrs
38 mm	64 mm	61 mm	62 mm
month	Apr	Jul	Oct	Jan

YORKSHIRE

°C /°F			
13/55	21/70	14/57	
	12/54	7/45	6/43
5/41			1/34
5 hrs	5.5 hrs	3 hrs	1.5 hrs
41 mm	62 mm	56 mm	59 mm
month	Apr	Jul	Oct	Jan

EAST MIDLANDS

°C /°F			
13/55	21/70	14/57	
	12/54	6/43	6/43
4/39			0/32
5 hrs	5.5 hrs	3 hrs	1.5 hrs
38 mm	58 mm	56 mm	56 mm
month	Apr	Jul	Oct	Jan

THE DOWNS AND CHANNEL COAST

°C /°F			
14/57	22/72	14/57	
	12/54	6/43	6/43
4/39			0/32
5.8 hrs	7.3 hrs	4 hrs	2 hrs
38 mm	58 mm	56 mm	56 mm
month	Apr	Jul	Oct	Jan

LONDON

°C /°F			
13/55	22/72	16/61	
	15/59	10/50	8/46
7/45			4/39
5 hrs	6 hrs	3.5 hrs	1.5 hrs
39 mm	45 mm	50 mm	44 mm
month	Apr	Jul	Oct	Jan

EAST ANGLIA

°C /°F			
14/57	22/72	15/59	
	12/54	6/43	7/45
4/39			1/34
5 hrs	6 hrs	3.5 hrs	2 hrs
37 mm	58 mm	51 mm	49 mm
month	Apr	Jul	Oct	Jan

rthumbria

wcastle
on Tyne

Yorkshire

York

chester

East Midlands

rmingham

Norwich

Cambridge

art of
land

Thames Valley

East Anglia

Oxford

London

Downs and
Channel Coast

Dover

Portsmouth

LONDON

⚜ London at a Glance

The largest city in Europe, London is home to over seven million people and covers 625 sq miles (1,600 sq km). The capital was founded by the Romans in the first century AD as a convenient administrative and communications centre and a port for trade with Continental Europe. For a thousand years it has been the principal residence of British monarchs as well as the centre of business and government, and it is rich in historic buildings and treasures from all periods. In addition to its diverse range of museums, galleries and churches, London is an exciting contemporary city, packed with a vast array of entertainments and shops. The attractions on offer are virtually endless but this map highlights the most important of those described in detail on the following pages.

Buckingham Palace (pp86–7) *is London home and office to the monarchy. The Changing of the Guard takes place on the palace forecourt.*

REGENT'S PARK AND BLOOMSBURY *(see pp102–107*

WEST END AND WESTMINSTER *(see pp76–*

SOUTH KENSINGTON AND HYDE PARK *(see pp94–101)*

Hyde Park (p75), *the largest central London park, boasts numerous sports facilities, restaurants, an art gallery and Speakers' Corner. The highlight is the Serpentine Lake.*

0 kilometers   1
0 miles   0.5

GREATER LONDON

M25 · A1(M) · A10 · M11 · Enfield · Barnet · Watford · M1 · Edgware · Finchley · A1 · A405 · A12 · A121 · Ruislip · Walthamstow · A127 · M40 · A40 · Hampstead · Bethnal Green · Barking · Dagenham · Uxbridge · Ealing · M4 · London City · Thames · A316 · Greenwich · A2 · Dartford · Heathrow · Richmond · Wandsworth · Bexley · A20 · Staines · A3 · Wimbledon · Dulwich · Beckenham · A21 · Kingston-Upon-Thames · Bromley · Orpington · M20 · M3 · A23 · M26 · Epsom · M25 · A21 · M23

0 kilometers   15
0 miles   15

The Victoria and Albert Museum (pp98–99) *is the world's largest museum of decorative arts. This German cup is 15th century.*

KEY

☐ Main sightseeing area

The British Museum's (pp106–7) *vast collection of antiquities from all over the world includes this Portland Vase from the 1st century BC.*

The National Gallery's (pp82–3) *world-famous collection of paintings includes works such as* Christ Mocked *(c.1495) by Hieronymus Bosch.*

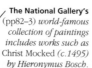

THAMES

THE CITY AND SOUTHWARK *(see pp108–121)*

St Paul's (pp114–15) *huge dome is the cathedral's most distinctive feature. Three galleries around the dome give spectacular views of London.*

Westminster Abbey (pp92–3) *has glorious medieval architecture and is crammed with impressive tombs and monuments to some of Britain's greatest public figures.*

The Tower of London (pp118–19) *is most famous as the prison where enemies of the Crown were executed. The Tower houses the Crown Jewels, including the Imperial State Crown.*

Tate Britain (p91) *displays an outstanding collection of British art ranging from stylized Elizabethan portraiture, such as* The Cholmondeley Ladies, *to cutting edge installation and film.*

London's Parks and Gardens

Camellia japonica

London has one of the world's greenest city centres, full of tree-filled squares and large expanses of grass, some of which have been public land since medieval times. From the elegant terraces of Regent's Park to the Royal Botanic Gardens at Kew, every London park and garden has its own charm and character. Some are ancient crown or public land, while others were created from the grounds of private houses or disused land. Londoners make the most of these open spaces: for exercise, listening to music, or simply escaping the bustle of the city.

Holland Park (see pp122–23) *offers acres of peaceful woodland, an open-air theatre (see p153) and a café.*

Kew Gardens (see p126) *are the world's premiere botanic gardens. An amazing variety of plants from all over the world is complemented by an array of temples, monuments and a landscaped lake.*

Richmond Park (see p126), *London's largest Royal Park, remains unspoiled with roaming deer and magnificent river views.*

```
0 kilometres          1

0 miles         0.5
```

SEASONAL BEST

As winter draws to a close, spectacular drifts of crocuses, daffodils and tulips are to be found peeping above the ground in Green Park and Kew. Easter weekend marks the start of outdoor events with funfairs on many commons and parks. During the summer months the parks are packed with picnickers and sunbathers and you can often catch a free open-air concert in St James's or Regent's parks. The energetic can play tennis in most

Winter in Kensington Gardens, adjoining Hyde Park

parks, swim in Hyde Park's Serpentine or the ponds on Hampstead Heath, or take rowing boats out on the lakes in Regent's and Battersea parks. Autumn brings a different atmosphere, and on 5 November firework displays and bonfires celebrate Guy Fawkes Night *(see p64)*. Winter is a good time to visit the tropical glasshouses and the colourful outdoor winter garden at Kew. If the weather gets really cold, the Round Pond in Kensington Gardens may be fit for ice-skating.

Hampstead Heath *(see p124)* is a breezy open space embracing a variety of landscapes.

Regent's Park (see p103) *has a large boating lake, an open-air theatre (see p153) and London Zoo. Surrounded by Nash's graceful buildings, it is one of London's most civilized retreats.*

St James's Park, *in the heart of the city, is a popular escape for office workers. It is also a reserve for wildfowl.*

Green Park, *with its shady trees and benches, offers a cool, restful spot in the heart of London.*

Battersea Park is a pleasant riverside site with a man-made boating lake.

Greenwich Park (see p125) *is dominated by the National Maritime Museum. There are fine views from the Old Royal Observatory on the hill top.*

Hyde Park and Kensington Gardens (see p101) *are both popular London retreats. There are sporting facilities, a lake and art gallery in Hyde Park. This plaque is from the ornate Italian Garden in Kensington Gardens.*

HISTORIC CEMETERIES

In the late 1830s, a ring of private cemeteries was established around London to ease the pressure on the monstrously overcrowded and unhealthy burial grounds of the inner city. Today the cemeteries, notably **Highgate** *(see p124)* and **Kensal Green**, are well worth visiting for their flamboyant Victorian monuments.

Kensal Green cemetery on the Harrow Road

WEST END AND WESTMINSTER

The West End is the city's social and cultural centre and the London home of the royal family. Stretching from the edge of Hyde Park to Covent Garden, the district bustles all day and late into the night. Whether you're looking for art, history, street- or café-life, it is the most rewarding area in which to begin an exploration of the city.

Horse Guard on Whitehall

Westminster has been at the centre of political and religious power for a thousand years. In the 11th century, King Canute founded Westminster Palace and Edward the Confessor built Westminster Abbey, where all English monarchs have been crowned since 1066. As modern government developed, the great offices of state were established in the area.

SIGHTS AT A GLANCE

Historic Streets and Buildings
Banqueting House **18**
Buckingham Palace pp86–7 **13**
Cabinet War Rooms and Churchill Museum **16**
Downing Street **17**
Houses of Parliament pp90–91 **19**
Piccadilly Circus **8**
Ritz Hotel **10**
Royal Mews **15**
Royal Opera House **3**
The Mall **12**
The Piazza and Central Market **1**

Museums and Galleries
London's Transport Museum **2**
National Gallery pp82–3 **6**
National Portrait Gallery **7**
Royal Academy **9**
Somerset House **4**
Tate Britain **21**
The Queen's Gallery **14**

Churches
Queen's Chapel **11**
Westminster Abbey pp92–3 **20**

Attractions
London Eye **5**

KEY
- ▪ Street-by-Street map pp78–9
- ▪ Street-by-Street map pp84–5
- ▪ Street-by-Street map pp88–9
- ⊖ Underground station
- ⇌ Railway station
- ⛴ River boat pier

GETTING THERE
This area is the hub of the city's public transport system, served by virtually all tube lines and scores of buses (*see pp690–91*). The most convenient tube and railway station is Charing Cross.

0 metres 500
0 yards 500

◁ **Big Ben and the Houses of Parliament**

Street-by-Street: Covent Garden

Until 1973, Covent Garden was an area of decaying streets and warehouses, which only came alive after dark when the fruit and vegetable market traders packed up for the day. Since then the Victorian market and elegant buildings nearby have been converted into stylish shops, restaurants, bars and cafés, creating an animated district which attracts a lively young crowd, night and day.

Seven Dials is a replica of a 17th-century monument marking the crossroads.

Covent Garden

Neal Street and Neal's Yard are lined with many specialist shops converted from former warehouses.

St Martin's Theatre *(see p153)* is home to the world's longest running play, *The Mousetrap.*

Stanfords map shop

The Lamb and Flag, built in 1623, is one of London's oldest pubs.

New Row is lined with little shops and cafés.

St Paul's Church was designed in 1633 by Inigo Jones *(see p53)*, in the style of the Italian Renaissance architect, Andrea Palladio. Jones also designed the original Covent Garden Piazza.

Royal Opera House
*Some of the world's
greatest opera singers
and ballet dancers have
performed at the Royal
Opera House* ❸

LOCATOR MAP
See Street Finder map 11

KEY

– – – Suggested route

| 0 meters | 100 |
| 0 yards | 100 |

**London's
Transport Museum**
*This museum's
intriguing collec-
tion brings to life
the history of the
city's tubes, buses
and trains. It also
displays examples
of 20th-century
commercial art* ❷

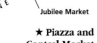
Jubilee Market

★ **Piazza and
Central Market**
*Shops and cafés fill the
piazza and market* ❶

STAR SIGHTS

★ Piazza and Central
Market

The Piazza and
Central Market ❶

Covent Garden WC2. **Map** 11 C2.
⊖ *Covent Garden.* ♿ *cobbled
streets.* **Street performers in Piazza:**
10am–dusk daily.

The 17th-century architect
Inigo Jones *(see p53)* planned
the Piazza in Covent Garden
as an elegant residential
square, modelled on the
piazza in the Tuscan town of
Livorno, which he had seen
under construction during his
travels in Italy. For a brief period, the Piazza became one of
the most fashionable addresses
in London, but it was superseded by the even grander St
James's Square *(see p85)*
which lies to the southwest.
    Decline accelerated when
a fruit and vegetable market
developed. By the mid-18th
century, the Piazza had become a haunt of prostitutes and
most of its houses had turned
into seedy lodgings, gambling
dens, brothels and taverns.

**A mid-18th-century view of
Covent Garden's Piazza**

Meanwhile the wholesale
produce market became the
largest in the country and in
1828 a market hall was erected
to ease congestion. The market, however, soon outgrew
its new home and despite the
construction of new buildings,
such as Floral and Jubilee
halls, the congestion grew
worse. In 1973 the market
moved to a new site in south
London, and over the next
two decades Covent Garden
was redeveloped. Today only
St Paul's Church remains of
Inigo Jones's buildings, and
Covent Garden, with its many
small shops, cafés, restaurants, market stalls and street
entertainers, is one of central
London's liveliest districts.

London's Transport Museum ❷

The Piazza, Covent Garden WC2.
Map 11 C2. **Tel** 020 7379 6344.
🚇 Covent Garden. ⬜ 10am–6pm
Sat–Thu, 11am–9pm Fri. ⬜ ⬜ ⬜
phone in advance. ⬜ ⬜
www.ltmuseum.co.uk

This collection of buses, trams and underground trains ranges from the earliest horse-drawn omnibuses to a present-day Hoppa bus. Housed in the Victorian Flower Market of Covent Garden built in 1872, the museum is particularly good for children, who can sit in the driver's seat of a bus or an underground train, operate signals and chat to an actor playing a 19th-century tube-tunnel miner.

London's bus and train companies have long been prolific patrons of artists, and the museum holds a fine collection of 19th- and 20th-century commercial art. Copies of some of the best posters and works by distinguished artists, such as Paul Nash and Graham Sutherland, are on sale at the museum shop.

Poster by Michael Reilly (1929), London Transport Museum

Royal Opera House ❸

Covent Garden WC2. **Map** 11 C2.
Tel 020 7304 4000. 🚇 Covent
Garden. ⬜ for performances and
guided tours (phone to check). ⬜
www.roh.org.uk

The first theatre on this site was built in 1732, and staged plays as well as concerts. However, the building was destroyed by fire in 1808 and again in 1856. The present

structure was designed in 1858 by E M Barry. John Flaxman's portico frieze, depicting tragedy and comedy, survived from the previous building of 1809.

The Opera House is home to the Royal Opera and Royal Ballet companies. After two years of renovation the building reopened in the new millennium, complete with a second auditorium and new rehearsal rooms. Backstage tours are available, and once a month visitors can watch the Royal Ballet rehearse.

Somerset House ❹

Strand WC2. **Map** 11 C2. **Tel** 020
7845 4600. 🚇 Temple. ⬜ 10am–6pm
daily (last adm: 5.15pm). ⬜ 1 Jan,
24–26 Dec. **Ice rink** ⬜ two months in
winter. ⬜ ⬜ **Courtauld Institute of
Art Gallery.** ⬜ ⬜ ⬜ **Admiralty
Restaurant. Tel** 020 7845 4646.
www.somerset-house.org.uk

Designed in 1770 by William Chambers, Somerset House presents two great collections of art, the **Courtauld Institute of Art Gallery** and the

Somerset House: Strand façade

Embankment Galleries.

The courtyard forms an attractive piazza (which becomes an ice rink in winter), and the riverside terrace has a café. The Admiralty Restaurant is also highly regarded. Located in Somerset House but famous in its own right is the Courtauld Institute of Art Gallery, which includes important Impressionist and Post-Impressionist works by artists such as Manet, Renoir and Cezanne. In spring 2008 the new riverside Embankment Galleries were launched. Occupying 750 square metres of exhibition space on the two

SOHO AND CHINATOWN

Soho has been renowned for pleasures of the table, the flesh and the intellect ever since it was first developed in the late 17th century. At first a fashionable residential area, it declined when high society shifted west to Mayfair and immigrants from Europe moved into its narrow streets. Furniture-makers and tailors set up shop here and were joined in the late 19th century by pubs, nightclubs, restaurants and brothels. In the 1960s, Hong Kong Chinese moved into the area around Gerrard and Lisle streets and they created an aromatic China-town, packed with many restaurants and food shops. Soho's raffish reputation has long attracted artists and writers, ranging from the 18th-century essayist Thomas de Quincey to poet Dylan Thomas and painter Francis Bacon. Although strip joints and peep shows remain, Soho has enjoyed something of a renaissance, and today is full of stylish and lively bars and restaurants.

Lion dancer in February's Chinese New Year celebrations

For hotels and restaurants in this region see pp556–560 and pp608–616

The opulent Palm Court of the Ritz Hotel

lower floors, the changing programme covers a broad range of contemporary arts, including photography, design, fashion and architecture.

London Eye ❺

Jubilee Gardens, South Bank, SE1. **Map** 12 D2. **Tel** 0870 5000 600 (information and 24-hr advance booking – recommended as tickets sell out days in advance). ⬤ Waterloo, Westminster. 🚌 11, 24, 211. 🕐 Oct–May: 10am–8pm daily; Jun–Sept: 10am–9pm daily (Jul & Aug: to 9:30pm). ⬤ 25 Dec & early Jan (for maintenance). 🎫 Pick up tickets at County Hall (adjacent to Eye) at least 30 mins before boarding time. ☐ ☐ ⬤ www.londoneye.com

The London Eye is a 135-m (443-ft) observation wheel that was installed on the South Bank to mark the Millennium. Its enclosed passenger capsules offer a gentle, 30-minute ride as the wheel makes a full turn, with breathtaking views over London and for up to 42 km (26 miles) around. Towering over one of the world's most familiar riverscapes, it has understandably captured the hearts of Londoners and visitors alike, and is one of the city's most popular attractions. "Flights" on the wheel are on the hour and half-hour.

National Gallery ❻

See pp82–3.

National Portrait Gallery ❼

2 St Martin's Place WC2. **Map** 11 B3. **Tel** 020 7312 2463. ⬤ Charing Cross, Leicester Sq. 🕐 10am–6pm Sat–Wed, 10am–9pm Thu & Fri. ⬤ 24–26 Dec. ♿ ☐ ☐ ☐ www.npg.org.uk

This museum celebrates Britain's history through portraits, photographs and sculptures; subjects range from Elizabeth I to David Beckham. The 20th-century section contains paintings and photographs of the royal family, politicians, rock stars, designers, artists and writers.

Piccadilly Circus ❽

W1. **Map** 11 A3. ⬤ Piccadilly Circus.

Dominated by garish neon advertising hoardings, Piccadilly Circus is a hectic traffic junction surrounded by shopping malls. It began as an early 19th-century crossroads between Piccadilly and John Nash's (see p105) Regent Street. It was briefly an elegant space, edged by curving stucco façades, but by 1910 the first electric advertisements had been installed. For years people have congregated at its centre, beneath the delicately poised figure of Eros, erected in 1892.

The Statue of Eros

Royal Academy ❾

Burlington House, Piccadilly W1. **Map** 10 F3. **Tel** 020 7300 8000. ⬤ Piccadilly Circus, Green Park. 🕐 10am–6pm Sat–Thu, 10am–10pm Fri. ⬤ 24–25 Dec, Good Fri. 🎫 ♿ 🎫 by appointment. ☐ ☐ ☐ www.royalacademy.org.uk

Founded in 1768, the Royal Academy is best known for its summer exhibition, which has been an annual event for over 200 years and comprises a rewarding mix of around 1,200 new works by established and unknown painters, sculptors and architects. During the rest of the year, the gallery shows prestigious touring exhibitions from around the world, and the courtyard in front of Burlington House, one of the West End's few surviving mansions from the early 18th century, is often filled with people waiting to get in. Quite apart from its aesthetic delights, the Royal Academy provides the weary traveller with a little lacuna of tranquillity. Its interior decoration inspires calm, and seems to be cut off from the stresses and strains of modern city life.

Ritz Hotel ❿

Piccadilly W1. **Map** 10 F3. **Tel** 020 7493 8181. ⬤ Green Park. ♿ See **Where to Stay** p540. www.theritzlondon.com

Cesar Ritz, the Swiss hotelier who inspired the word "ritzy", had virtually settled down to a quiet retirement by 1906 when this hotel was built and named after him. The colonnaded front of the château-style building was erected in 1906 to suggest just the merest whiff of Paris, where the grandest hotels were to be found at the turn of the century. It still maintains its Edwardian air of *fin de siècle* opulence and sophisticated grandeur, and is a popular venue for afternoon tea (reservations are required). A touch of *soigné* danger may be found in the casino.

National Gallery ❻

The National Gallery is London's leading art museum, with over 2,300 paintings, most on permanent display. It has flourished since 1824, when the House of Commons agreed to purchase 38 major paintings. These became the core of a national collection of European art that now ranges from Cimabue in the 13th century to 19th-century Impressionists. The gallery's particular strengths are in Dutch, Italian Renaissance and 17th-century Spanish painting. To the left of the main gallery lies the Sainsbury Wing, financed by the grocery family and completed in 1991. It houses the Early Renaissance collection.

The Adoration of the Kings (1564)
This realistic work is by Flemish artist Pieter Bruegel the Elder (c.1525–69).

Education Centre entrance ♿

Stairs to lower floor

The Ambassadors
The strange shape in the foreground of this Hans Holbein portrait (1533) is a distorted skull, a symbol of mortality.

KEY TO FLOORPLAN

- ☐ Painting 1250–1500
- ☐ Painting 1500–1600
- ☐ Painting 1600–1700
- ☐ Painting 1700–1900
- ☐ Special exhibitions
- ☐ Non-exhibition space

Link to main building

Stairs to lower floors 🛗

Arnolfini Portrait
Jan van Eyck (c.1385–1441), one of the pioneers of oil painting, shows his mastery of colour, texture, and minute detail in this portrait of 1434.

Entrance to Sainsbury Wing ♿

The Annunciation
This refined work of the early 1450s, by Fra Filippo Lippi, forms part of the gallery's exceptional Italian Renaissance collection.

★ **'The Rokeby Venus'**
*This is Velázquez's only
surviving female nude
(1647–51).*

VISITORS' CHECKLIST

Trafalgar Sq WC2. **Map** 11 B3.
Tel 020 7747 2885.
Charing Cross, Leicester Sq,
Piccadilly Circus. 3, 6, 9, 11,
12, 13, 15, 23, 24, 29, 53, 77A,
88, 91, 139, 159, 176, 453.
Charing Cross.
10am–6pm daily (9pm Fri).
1 Jan, 24–26 Dec. via
Sainsbury Wing and Getty
entrances.
www.nationalgallery.org.uk

★ **The Hay Wain** *(1821)*
*The great age of 19th-century land-
scape painting is represented by
Constable and Turner (see p91).
This picture shows how Constable
caught changing light and shadow.*

Getty
entrance

Trafalgar Square
entrance

The Neo-
Classical façade is
made of Portland stone.

★ **'The Leonardo Cartoon'**
(c.1499–1500)
*The genius of Leonardo da
Vinci glows through this picture
of the Virgin and Child, St
Anne and St John the Baptist.*

GALLERY GUIDE

*Most of the collection
is housed on one floor.
The paintings hang
chronologically, with
the earliest works,
1250–1500, in the
Sainsbury Wing.
Lesser paintings of
all periods are dis-
played on the lower
floor of the main
building. There is
a restaurant on the
first floor in the
Sainsbury Wing.*

STAR PAINTINGS

★ 'The Leonardo Cartoon'
by Leonardo da Vinci

★ 'The Rokeby Venus'
by Diego Velázquez

★ The Hay Wain by
John Constable

At the Theatre *(1876–7)*
*Renoir was one of the greatest
painters of the Impressionist
movement. The theatre was
a popular subject among
artists of the time.*

Street-by-Street: Piccadilly and St James's

As soon as Henry VIII built St James's Palace in the 1530s, the surrounding area became the centre of fashionable court life. Today Piccadilly forms a contrast between the bustling commercial district full of shopping arcades, eateries and cinemas, with St James's, to the south, which is still the domain of the wealthy and the influential.

St James's Church was designed by Sir Christopher Wren in 1684.

★ Royal Academy
The permanent art collection here includes this Michelangelo relief of the Madonna and Child (1505) ⑨

Burlington Arcade, an opulent covered walk, has fine shops and beadles on patrol.

Fortnum & Mason (*see p148*) was founded in 1707.

The Ritz
César Ritz founded one of London's most famous hotels in 1906 ⑩

St James's Palace was built on the site of a leper hospital.

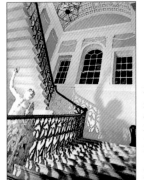

To the Mall and Buckingham Palace (*see pp86–7*)

Spencer House, recently restored to its 18th-century splendour, contains fine period furniture and paintings. This Palladian palace was completed in 1766 for the 1st Earl Spencer, an ancestor of the late Princess of Wales.

STAR SIGHTS

★ Piccadilly Circus

★ Royal Academy

★ Piccadilly Circus
The crowds and dazzling neon lights make this the West End's focal point **❽**

LOCATOR MAP
See Street Finder map 10, 11

KEY

– – – Suggested route

| 0 metres | 100 |
| 0 yards | 100 |

Piccadilly

Jermyn Street has elegant shops selling antiques, unusual gifts and men's clothing.

St James's Square has long been the most fashionable address in London.

Pall Mall is a street of gentlemen's clubs, which admit only members and their guests.

Queen's Chapel
This was the first Classical church in England **⓫**

Royal Opera Arcade is lined with quality shops. Designed by John Nash, it was completed in 1818.

Queen's Chapel ⓫

Marlborough Rd SW1. **Map** 11 A4. *Tel* 020-7930 4832. ⊖ Green Park. ⬜ to the public Sun services (Easter–end Jul) and major Saints' Days only. ♿

The sumptuous Queen's Chapel was designed by Inigo Jones for the Infanta of Spain, the intended bride of Charles I *(see pp52–3)*. Work started in 1623 but ceased when the marriage negotiations were shelved. The chapel was finally completed in 1627 for Charles's eventual queen, Henrietta Maria. It was the first church in England to be built in a Classical style, with a coffered ceiling based on a reconstruction by Palladio of an ancient Roman temple.

Interior of Queen's Chapel

The Mall ⓬

SW1. **Map** 11 A4. ⊖ Charing Cross, Green Park.

This broad triumphal approach from Trafalgar Square to Buckingham Palace was created by Aston Webb when he redesigned the front of the palace and the Victoria Monument in 1911. The spacious tree-lined avenue follows the course of an old path at the edge of St James's Park. The path was laid out in the reign of Charles II, when it became London's most fashionable and cosmopolitan promenade. The Mall is used for royal processions on special occasions. Flagpoles down both sides fly the national flags of foreign heads of state during official visits. The Mall is closed to traffic on Sundays.

Buckingham Palace ⓭

Queen Elizabeth II

Opened to visitors for the first time in 1993 to raise money for repairing fire damage to Windsor Castle *(see pp236–7)*, the Queen's official London home and office is an extremely popular attraction in August and September. John Nash *(see p105)* began converting the 18th-century Buckingham House into a palace for George IV in 1826 but was taken off the job in 1831 for overspending his budget. The first monarch to occupy the palace was Queen Victoria, just after she came to the throne in 1837. The tour takes visitors up the grand staircase and through the splendour of the State Rooms, but not into the royal family's private apartments.

Music Room
State guests are presented and royal babies christened in this room.

White Drawing Room

Green Drawing Room

Grand Staircase

Blue Drawing Room

State Dining Room

The Queen's Gallery
Masterpieces from the Royal Collection, such as Vermeer's The Music Lesson (c.1660), are displayed here in a series of changing exhibitions.

Throne Room
The Queen carries out many formal ceremonial duties here, under the richly gilded ceiling.

View over the Mall
On special occasions the Royal Family wave to crowds from the balcony.

The Royal Standard flies while the Queen is in residence.

The East Wing façade was added by Aston Webb in 1913.

The Changing of the Guard takes place on the palace forecourt.

THE CHANGING OF THE GUARD

Dressed in brilliant scarlet tunics and tall furry hats called bearskins, the palace guards stand in sentry boxes outside the Palace. Crowds gather to watch the colourful and musical military ceremony as the guards march from Wellington Barracks to Buckingham Palace, parading for half an hour while the palace keys are handed by the old guard to the new.

The Queen's Gallery 🟢

Buckingham Palace Rd SW1. **Map** 10 F5. **Tel** 020 7766 7301. 🚇 *St James's Park, Victoria.* ⬭ *10am–5:30pm daily (last admission for exhibitions: 4:30pm).* ● *25, 26 Dec. Call for more details.* 🚻 🖼 www.royalcollection.org.uk

The Queen's art collection is one of the finest and most valuable in the world, rich in the works of old masters such as Rembrandt and Leonardo. The gallery hosts a rotating programme of exhibitions, enabling the year-round display of many masterpieces, drawings and decorative arts from the Queen's collection.

Detail: The Gold State Coach (1762), Royal Mews

Royal Mews 🟢

Buckingham Palace Rd SW1. **Map** 10 E5. **Tel** 020 7766 7302. 🚇 *Victoria.* ⬭ *Apr–Oct: 11am–4pm Sat–Thu (advisable to check opening times on day of visit). Extended opening hrs may operate Aug–Sep.* 🚻 *open 9:30am–5pm daily all year (closed 25, 26 Dec).* 🖼 ♿ www.royalcollection.org.uk

Lovers of horses and royal pomp should not miss this working stable and coach house. Designed by John Nash in 1825, it houses horses and state coaches used on official occasions. Among them is the glass coach used for royal weddings and foreign ambassadors. The star exhibit is the ornate gold state coach, built for George III in 1762, which was used by the Queen during the Golden Jubilee celebrations in 2002. The shop sells interesting merchandise.

Street-by-Street: Whitehall and Westminster

The broad avenues of Whitehall and Westminster are lined with imposing buildings that serve the historic seat of both government and the established church. On weekdays the streets are crowded with civil servants whose work is based here, while at weekends the area takes on a different atmosphere with a steady flow of tourists.

Downing Street
Sir Robert Walpole was the first Prime Minister to live here in 1732 ⓱

Cabinet War Rooms and Churchill Museum
Now open to the public, these were Winston Churchill's World War II headquarters ⓰

St Margaret's Church is a favourite venue for political and society weddings.

★ Westminster Abbey
The abbey is London's oldest and most important church ⓴

Central Hall (1911) is a florid example of the Beaux Arts style.

Richard I's Statue is an 1860 depiction of the king, killed in battle in 1199.

KING CHARLES STREE

STOREY'S GATE

GREAT GEORGE STREET

BROAD   SANCTUARY

PARLIAMENT SQUARE

ST MARGARET STREET

ABINGDON STREET

GREAT COLLEGE STREET

Dean's Yard is a secluded grassy square surrounded by picturesque buildings from different periods, many used by Westminster School.

The Burghers of Calais is a cast of Auguste Rodin's 1886 original in France.

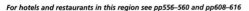
For hotels and restaurants in this region see pp556–560 and pp608–616

To Trafalgar Square

Banqueting House
Inigo Jones designed this elegant building in 1622 **⑱**

LOCATOR MAP
See Street Finder map 11

The Cenotaph (1920) is a war memorial by Sir Edwin Lutyens.

RICHMOND TERRACE

WHITEHALL

VICTORIA EMBANKMENT

Horse Guards is a parade ground protected by a guard, changed twice each day.

Westminster Pier is the main starting point for river trips (pp74–5).

Westminster

★ **Houses of Parliament**
The seat of government is dominated by the clock tower, holding the 14-tonne bell Big Ben, hung in 1858. Its deep chimes are broadcast daily on BBC radio **⑲**

KEY

- - - Suggested route

| 0 metres | 100 |
| 0 yards | 100 |

STAR SIGHTS

★ Westminster Abbey

★ Houses of Parliament

Cabinet War Rooms and Churchill Museum ⑯

Clive Steps, King Charles St SW1.
Map 11 B5. **Tel** *020 7930 6961.*
⊖ *Westminster.* ⏲ *9:30am–6pm daily (last adm: 5pm).* ⬤ *24–26 Dec.*
📷 ♿ 🖥 🏛 www.iwm.org.uk

This warren of cellars below a government office building is where the War Cabinet – first under Neville Chamberlain, then Winston Churchill from 1940 – met during World War II when German bombs were falling on London. The rooms include living quarters for ministers and military leaders and a Cabinet Room, where strategic decisions were taken. They are laid out as they were when the war ended, complete with Churchill's desk, communications equipment, and maps for plotting battles and strategies. The Churchill Museum records and illustrates Churchill's life and career.

Telephones in the Map Room, Cabinet War Rooms

Downing Street ⑰

SW1. **Map** 11 B4. ⊖ *Westminster.*
⬤ *to the public.*

Number 10 Downing Street has been the official residence of the British Prime Minister since 1732. It contains a Cabinet Room in which government policy is decided, an impressive State Dining Room and a private apartment; outside is a well-protected garden.

Next door at No. 11 is the official residence of the Chancellor of the Exchequer, who is in charge of the nation's financial affairs. In 1989, iron gates were erected at the Whitehall end of Downing Street for security purposes.

Banqueting House ⑱

Whitehall SW1. **Map** 11 B4. *Tel 020 3166 6151.* ⊖ *Charing Cross.* ⏱ *10am–5pm Mon–Sat.* ⬤ *pub hols & for functions. Always call before your visit.* 🔲 📷 ♿ www.hrp.org.uk

Completed by Inigo Jones *(see p53)* in 1622, this was the first building in central London to embody the Palladian style of Renaissance Italy. In 1629 Charles I commissioned Rubens to paint the ceiling with scenes exalting the reign of his father, James I. They symbolize the divine right of kings, disputed by the Parliamentarians, who executed Charles I outside the building in 1649 *(see pp52–3).*

Panels from the Rubens ceiling (1629–34), Banqueting House

Houses of Parliament ⑲

SW1. **Map** 11 C5. *Tel 020 7219 3000.* ⊖ *Westminster.* **Visitors' Galleries** ⏱ *2:30–10:30pm Mon & Tue; 11:30am–7:30pm Wed; 11:30am–6:30pm Thu; 9:30am–3pm sitting Fri. Queue or UK residents may apply in advance to local MP.* ⬤ *frequently for parliamentary recesses.* ♿ 📞 *call 0870 906 3773 or go to* www.keithprowse.com *to book tickets for tours.* 🔲 www.parliament.uk

There has been a Palace of Westminster here since the 11th century, though only Westminster Hall remains from that time. The present Neo-Gothic structure by Sir Charles Barry was built after the old palace was destroyed by fire in 1834. Since the 16th century it has housed the two Houses of Parliament, the Lords and the Commons. The House of Commons consists of elected Members of Parliament (MPs).

The party with most MPs forms the Government, and its leader becomes Prime Minister. The House of Lords comprises peers, law lords, bishops and archbishops.

Westminster Abbey ⑳

See pp92–3.

Central Lobby

Victoria Tower

The House of Commons' original chamber was destroyed by fire in 1941.

Royal Gallery

St Stephen's entrance for the public

The House of Lords is a lavishly decorated Gothic Hall designed by Pugin in 1836–7.

Members' entrance

Big Ben has kept exact time for the nation almost continuously since 1859.

Westminster Hall

Portico of Tate Britain

Tate Britain ㉑

Millbank SW1. **Map** 19 B2. **Tel** 020 7887 8888. Pimlico. 77a, 88, C10. Victoria, Vauxhall. to Tate Modern every 40 mins. 10am–5:50pm daily. 24–26 Dec. for major exhibitions. Atterbury St. www.tate.org.uk

Formerly the Tate Gallery, Tate Britain is the national gallery of British art, and includes works from the 16th to the 21st century. Displays draw on the enormous Tate Collection, which also includes the international modern art seen at Tate Modern *(p121)*. A river boat, *Tate to Tate*, takes visitors between the two galleries. Located in the Clore Galleries are works from the Turner Bequest *(see box)*.

The size of the collection necessitates some rotation of displays. Major themes change on a yearly basis, solo artists' rooms and smaller themed rooms more frequently. Loan exhibitions are installed in the ground floor galleries and part of the main floor.

The section on the years 1500–1800 covers a period of dramatic change in British history, from the Tudors and

Recumbent Figure (1938) by Henry Moore

Stuarts through to the age of Thomas Gainsborough. The section concludes with a series of changing displays about the poet and artist William Blake.

The years 1800 to 1900 saw dramatic expansion and change in the arts in Britain. This section shows the new themes that began to emerge. Included are the "Victorian Narrative" painters such as William Powell Frith, and the work of the Pre-Raphaelites, such as John Everett Millais and Dante Gabriel Rossetti. The period 1900–1960 includes the work of Jacob Epstein, that of Wyndham Lewis and his Vorticist group, and the celebrated modernist works of Henry Moore, Barbara Hepworth, Ben Nicholson, Francis Bacon and Lucian Freud.

The Tate collection of British art from 1960 to the present is outstanding, and the displays in this section are changed on a regular basis. From the 1960s, Tate's funding for the purchase of works began to increase substantially, while artistic activity continued to pick up speed, encouraged by public spending. As a result, Tate Britain's collection is particularly rich in this period. Works range from the 1960s Pop artists

The First Marriage (A Marriage of Styles I) (1962) by David Hockney

David Hockney, Richard Hamilton and Peter Blake, through the works of Gilbert and George and the landscape artist Richard Long, to the 1980s paintings of Howard Hodgkin and R B Kitaj. The so-called Young British Artists (YBAs) of the 1990s are well represented by leading figures Damien Hirst, Tracey Emin and Sarah Lucas. A small space called Art Now is dedicated to contemporary artists.

Captain Thomas Lee (1594) by Marcus Gheeraerts II

THE TURNER BEQUEST

The Turner Bequest comprises some 300 oil paintings and 20,000 watercolours and drawings, received by the nation from the great landscape painter J M W Turner some years after his death in 1851. Turner's will had specified that a gallery be built to house his pictures and this was finally done in 1987 with the opening of the Clore Galleries. Most of the oils are on view in the main galleries, and the watercolours are the subject of changing displays.

Shipping at the Mouth of the Thames (c.1806–7)

Westminster Abbey ⑳

Westminster Abbey has been the burial place of
Britain's monarchs since the 11th century and the
setting for many coronations and royal weddings. It
is one of the most beautiful buildings in London, with
an exceptionally diverse array of architectural styles,
ranging from the austere French Gothic of the nave to
the astonishing complexity of Henry VII's chapel. Half
national church, half national museum, the abbey aisles
and transepts are crammed with an extraordinary collection of tombs and monuments honouring some of Britain's
greatest public figures, ranging from politicians to poets.

North Entrance
*The mock-medieval
stonework is
Victorian.*

**Statesmen's
Aisle**

Flying buttresses help
redistribute the great
weight of the roof.

★ Nave
*At a height of 31 m
(102 ft), the nave is
the highest in England.
The ratio of height to
width is 3:1.*

CORONATION
The coronation ceremony
is over 1,000 years old
and since 1066, with the
crowning of William the
Conqueror on Christmas
Day, the abbey has been
its sumptuous setting.
The coronation of Queen
Elizabeth II, in 1953, was
the first to be televised.

Cloisters
*Built mainly in the 13th and
14th centuries, the cloisters
link the Abbey church with
the other buildings.*

STAR FEATURES

★ Nave

★ Henry VII Chapel

★ Chapter House

For hotels and restaurants in this region see pp556–560 and pp608–616

★ Henry VII Chapel

The chapel, built in 1503–19, has superb late Perpendicular vaulting and choir stalls dating from 1512.

The Sanctuary, built by Henry III, has been the scene of 38 coronations.

Poets' Corner

A host of great poets are honoured here, including Shakespeare, Chaucer and T S Eliot.

The Museum has many of the abbey's treasures including wood, plaster and wax effigies of monarchs.

The Pyx Chamber is where the coinage was tested in medieval times.

★ Chapter House

A beautiful octagonal room, remarkable for its 13th-century tile floor. It is lit by six huge stained glass windows showing scenes from the abbey's history.

St Edward's Chapel

The shrine of Edward the Confessor is housed here, along with the tombs of many medieval monarchs.

VISITORS' CHECKLIST

Broad Sanctuary SW1.**Map** 11 B5. **Tel** 020 7222 5152. Westminster. 3, 11, 12, 24, 29, 53, 70, 77, 77a, 88, 109, 159, 170. Victoria. Westminster Pier. **Cloisters** 9am–5:30pm daily. **Abbey (Royal Chapels, Poets' Corner, Choir, Statesmen's Aisle, Nave)** 9:30am–3:45pm Mon–Fri (to 6pm Wed), 9:30am–1:30pm Sat (last adm: 12:45pm). **Chapter House, Pyx Chamber & Museum** 10:30am–4pm daily. **College Garden** Apr–Sep: 10am–6pm Tue–Thu; Oct–Mar: 10am–4pm Tue–Thu. **Evensong** 5pm Mon–Fri (evening prayers Wed), 3pm Sat, Sun. **Concerts.** **www**.westminster-abbey.org

HISTORICAL PLAN OF THE ABBEY

The first abbey church was established as early as the 10th century, but the present French-influenced Gothic structure was begun in 1245 at the behest of Henry III. Because of its unique role as the coronation church, the abbey escaped Henry VIII's onslaught on Britain's monastic buildings (*see pp50–51*).

KEY

- Built between 1055–1350
- Added from 1350–1420
- Built between 1500–1512
- Towers completed 1745
- Restored after 1850

SOUTH KENSINGTON AND HYDE PARK

This exclusive district embraces one of London's largest parks and some of its finest museums, shops, restaurants and hotels. Until the mid-19th century it was a genteel, semi-rural backwater of large houses and private schools lying to the south of Kensington Palace. In 1851, the Great Exhibition, until then the largest arts and science event ever staged *(see pp56–7)*, was held in Hyde Park, transforming the area into a celebration of Victorian learning and self-confidence.

Peter Pan statue in Kensington Gardens

The brainchild of Queen Victoria's husband, Prince Albert, the exhibition was a massive success and the profits were used to buy 35 ha (87 acres) of land in South Kensington. Here, Prince Albert encouraged the construction of a concert hall, museums and colleges devoted to the applied arts and sciences; most of them survive. The neighbourhood soon became modish, full of flamboyant red-brick mansion blocks, garden squares and the elite shops still to be found in Knightsbridge.

SIGHTS AT A GLANCE

Historic Buildings
Kensington Palace ❼

Churches
Brompton Oratory ❷

Shops
Harrods ❶

Parks and Gardens
Hyde Park and Kensington
Gardens ❻

Museums and Galleries
Natural History Museum ❺
Science Museum ❹
*Victoria and Albert Museum
pp98–9* ❸

GETTING THERE

South Kensington station (accessible from an entrance on Exhibition Road) is on the Piccadilly, Circle and District lines; only the Piccadilly line passes through Knightsbridge and Hyde Park Corner. The No. 14 bus runs direct from Piccadilly Circus to South Kensington, via Knightsbridge.

KEY

▨	Street-by-Street map *pp96–7*
⊖	Underground station

◁ **Ennismore Mews in South Kensington, built 1843–6**

Street-by-Street: South Kensington

The numerous museums and colleges created in the wake of the Great Exhibition of 1851 *(see pp56–7)* continue to give this neighbourhood an air of leisured culture. Visited as much by Londoners as tourists, the museum area is liveliest on Sundays and on summer evenings during the Royal Albert Hall's famous season of classical "Prom" concerts *(see p154).*

The Royal Albert Hall opened in 1870 and was modelled on Roman amphitheatres.

The Memorial to the Great Exhibition is surmounted by a bronze statue of its instigator, Prince Albert.

The Royal College of Music, founded in 1882, exhibits historic musical instruments such as this harpsichord dating from 1531.

★ **Science Museum**
Visitors can experiment with over a thousand interactive displays ❹

★ **Natural History Museum**
The Creepy Crawlies exhibition has proved highly popular ❺

STAR SIGHTS

★ Science Museum

★ Natural History Museum

★ Victoria and Albert Museum

Entrance to South Kensington tube

KEY

─ ─ ─ Suggested route

| 0 metres | | 100 |
| 0 yards | | 100 |

The Albert Memorial was built in memory of Queen Victoria's husband who died in 1861.

LOCATOR MAP
See Street Finder maps 8, 16, 17

★ Victoria and Albert Museum
The museum has a fine collection of applied arts and photography from around the world ❸

Brompton Oratory
This ornate Baroque church is famous for its splendid musical tradition
❷

Brompton Square (1821)

To Knightsbridge and Harrods

BROMPTON ROAD
RDENS

Harrods Food Hall

Harrods ❶

Knightsbridge SW1. **Map** 9 B5. **Tel** 020 7730 1234. 🚇 *Knightsbridge.* ⏲ *10am–8pm Mon–Sat, noon–6pm Sun.* ♿ 🍴 🚻 *See* **Shops and Markets** *pp120–21.* www.harrods.com

In 1849 Henry Charles Harrod opened a small grocery shop on Brompton Road, which soon became famous for its impeccable service and quality. The store moved into these extravagant premises in Knightsbridge in 1905.

Brompton Oratory ❷

Brompton Rd SW7. **Map** 17 B1. **Tel** 020 7808 0900. 🚇 *South Kensington.* ⏲ *6:30am–8pm daily.* ♿ 🚻 www.bromptonoratory.com

The Italianate Oratory is a lavish monument to the 19th-century English Catholic revival. It was established as a base for a community of priests by John Henry Newman (later Cardinal Newman), who introduced the Oratorian movement to England in 1848. The church was opened in 1884, and the dome and façade added in the 1890s.

The sumptuous interior holds many fine monuments. The 12 huge 17th-century statues of the apostles are from Siena Cathedral, the elaborate Baroque Lady Altar (1693) is from the Dominican church at Brescia, and the 18th-century altar in St Wilfred's Chapel is from Rochefort in Belgium.

Victoria and Albert Museum ❸

The Glass gallery, room 131

The Victoria and Albert Museum (the V&A) contains one of the world's widest collections of art and design, ranging from early Christian devotional objects and the mystical art of southeast Asia to cutting-edge furniture design. Originally founded in 1852 as the Museum of Manufactures to inspire students of design, it was renamed by Queen Victoria in 1899 in memory of Prince Albert. The museum has undergone a dramatic redisplay of its collection, including work on the Ceramics galleries, Sackler Education Centre and Medieval and Renaissance galleries, which span three levels. The Gilbert Collection also opened here in 2009.

Silver galleries
Radiant pieces such as the Burgess Cup (Britain, 1863) fill these stunning galleries.

★ British Galleries
The Great Bed of Ware has been a tourist attraction since 1601, when Shakespeare sparked interest in it by making reference to it in Twelfth Night.

★ Fashion gallery
In this gallery, European clothing from the mid-1500s to the present day is displayed, such as these famous Vivienne Westwood shoes.

Exhibition Road entrance

KEY TO FLOORPLAN

- Level 0
- Level 1
- Level 2
- Level 3
- Level 4
- Level 6
- Henry Cole Wing
- Non-exhibition space

STAR EXHIBITS

- ★ British Galleries
- ★ Fashion gallery
- ★ Medieval and Renaissance galleries
- ★ Islamic Middle East gallery

GALLERY GUIDE

The V&A has a 7-mile (11-km) layout spread over six levels. Level 1, houses the China, Japan and South Asia galleries, as well as the Fashion gallery and the Cast Courts. The British Galleries are on levels 2 and 4. Level 3 contains the 20th Century galleries and displays of silver, jewellery, ironwork, paintings and works of 20th-century design. The glass display is also on upper level 4. The Ceramics galleries are on level 6. The Henry Cole Wing houses the Sackler Education Centre, RIBA Architecture Study Rooms and the Prints and Drawings Study Rooms.

Architecture gallery
Features highlights from the world class collection of drawings, models, photographs and architectural fragments of the V&A and RIBA collections, such as this 1930s-style doll's house.

VISITORS' CHECKLIST

Cromwell Rd SW7. **Map** 17 A1.
Tel *020 7942 2000.*
🚇 *South Kensington.*
🚌 *14, 74, 414, C1.* ⬜
10am–5:45pm daily (10am– 10pm last Fri of each month).
⬤ *24–26 Dec.* ♿ 📷 🍴
🅿 📱 *www.vam.ac.uk*

★ Medieval and Renaissance galleries
The stunning Burghley Nef (France, 1527) is located in these new galleries in rooms 62–4.

China gallery
This magnificent ancestor portrait is among the many exquisite pieces on show in this gallery.

Aston Webb's façade (1909) is decorated with 32 sculptures of English craftsmen and designers.

★ Islamic Middle East gallery
On display are fantastic objects representing the finest in Islamic art and design, such as this 16th-century Ottoman table.

Main entrance

Science Museum ❹

Exhibition Rd SW7. **Map** 16 F1. *Tel 0870 870 4868.* 🚇 *South Kensington.* ⏰ *10am–6pm daily.* ⬤ *24–26 Dec.* 🎟 *for IMAX, special exhibitions and simulators only.* ♿ 🛍 ✉ 📷
www.sciencemuseum.org.uk

Centuries of continuing scientific and technological development lie at the heart of the Science Museum's massive collections. The hardware displayed is magnificent: from steam engines to aeroengines; spacecraft to the very first mechanical computers. Equally important is the social

Newcomen's Steam Engine (1712), Science Museum

context of science – what discoveries and inventions mean for day-to-day life – and the process of discovery itself. There are many interactive and hands-on displays which are very popular with children.

The museum is spread over seven floors and includes the high-tech Wellcome Wing at the west end of the museum. The basement features the excellent hands-on galleries for children, including The Garden. The Energy Hall dominates the ground floor, and is dedicated to steam power, with the still-operational Harle Syke Mill Engine of 1903. Here too are Space and Making the Modern World, a highlight of which is the display of the scarred Apollo 10 spacecraft, which carried three astronauts to the moon and back in May 1969. In Challenge of Materials, located on the first floor, our

expectations of materials are confounded with exhibits such as a bridge made of glass and a steel wedding dress.

The Flight gallery on the third floor is packed with early flying contraptions, fighter planes, aeroplanes and the Launchpad. The fourth and fifth floors house the medical science galleries, where Science and the Art of Medicine has a 17th-century Italian vase for storing snake bite treatment.

The high-tech Wellcome Wing offers four floors of interactive technology, including 'Who Am I?', a fascinating exhibition exploring the science of you. With an IMAX 3D Cinema and the SimEx simulator ride, it is a breathtaking addition to the museum. The museum cafés and shop are particularly good.

Natural History Museum ❺

Cromwell Rd SW7. **Map** 16 F1. *Tel 020 7942 5000.* 🚇 *South Kensington.* ⏰ *10am–5:50pm daily.* ⬤ *24–26 Dec.* 🍴 ♿ 🛍 🖥
www.nhm.ac.uk

This cathedral-like building's richly sculpted stonework conceals an iron and steel frame; this construction technique was revolutionary when the museum opened in 1881. The imaginative displays tackle fundamental issues such as the ecology and evolution of the planet, the origin of species and the development of human beings – all explained through a dynamic combination of the latest technology, interactive techniques and traditional displays.

The museum is divided

Relief from a decorative panel in the Natural History Museum

into four sections: the Blue Zone, Green Zone, Red Zone and the Orange Zone. In the Blue Zone, the Ecology exhibition explores the complex web of the natural world through a replica of a moonlit rainforest buzzing with the sounds of insects. One of the most popular exhibits is the Dinosaur Gallery, which includes life-like animatronic models of dinosaurs. The Vault, located in the Green Zone, contains a dazzling collection of the finest gems, crystals, metals and meteorites from around the world. The Darwin Centre, which opened in 2009, is the largest curved structure in Europe. The eight-storey-high cocoon houses the museum's vast collection of insects and plants.

The Tuojiangasaurus skeleton (about 150 million years old), Natural History Museum

Statue of the young Queen Victoria outside Kensington Palace, sculpted by her daughter, Princess Louise

Hyde Park and Kensington Gardens ❻

W2. **Map** 9 B3. **Tel** 020 7298 2000.
Hyde Park ⊖ Hyde Park Corner, Knightsbridge, Lancaster Gate, Marble Arch. ⬤ dawn–midnight daily. ♿
Kensington Gardens. Tel 020 7298 2000. ⊖ Queensway, Lancaster Gate. ⬤ dawn–dusk daily. ♿ ⬛ See also pp74–5. **Diana, Princess of Wales Memorial Playground** ⊖ Queensway, Bayswater. ⬤ 10am–dusk daily. ♿ ⬛ www.royalparks.org.uk

The ancient manor of Hyde was part of the lands of Westminster Abbey seized by Henry VIII at the Dissolution of the Monasteries in 1536 (see pp50–51). James I opened the park to the public in the early 17th century, and it was soon one of the city's most fashionable public spaces. Unfortunately it also became popular with duellists and highwaymen, and consequently

William III had 300 lights hung along Rotten Row, the first street in England to be lit up at night. In 1730, the Westbourne River was dammed by Queen Caroline in order to create the Serpentine, an artificial lake that is today used for boating and swimming, and Rotten Row for horse riding. The park is also a rallying point for political demonstrations, while at Speaker's Corner, in the northeast, anyone has had the right to address the public since 1872. Sundays are particularly lively, with many budding orators and a number of eccentrics revealing their plans for the betterment of mankind.

Adjoining Hyde Park is Kensington Gardens, the former grounds of Kensington Palace. Three great attractions for children are the innovative Diana, Princess of Wales Memorial Playground, the bronze statue of J M Barrie's fictional Peter Pan (1912), by George Frampton, and the Round Pond where people sail model boats. Also worthseeing is the dignified Orangery (1704), once used by Queen Anne as a "summer supper house" and now a summer café.

Detail of the Coalbrookdale Gate, Kensington Gardens

Kensington Palace ❼

Kensington Palace Gdns W8. **Map** 8 D4. **Tel** 0844 482 7777. ⊖ High St Ken, Queensway. ⬤ Nov–Feb: 10am–5pm daily; Mar–Oct: 10am–6pm daily (last adm: 1 hr before close). ⬤ 1 Jan, 24–26 Dec. 🎟 📷 ♿ ground floor. 🖥 www.hrp.org.uk

Kensington Palace was the principal residence of the royal family from the 1690s until 1760, when George III moved to Buckingham Palace. Over the years it has seen a number of important royal events. In 1714 Queen Anne died here from a fit of apoplexy brought on by over-eating and, in June 1837, Princess Victoria of Kent was woken to be told that her uncle William IV had died and she was now queen – the beginning of her 64-year reign. Half of the palace still holds royal apartments, but the other half is open to the public. Among the highlights are the 18th-century state rooms with ceilings and murals by William Kent (see p28). After the death of Princess Diana in 1997, the palace became a focal point for mourners who gathered in their thousands at its gates and turned the area into a field of bouquets.

REGENT'S PARK AND BLOOMSBURY

Cream stuccoed terraces built by John Nash *(see p105)* fringe the southern edge of Regent's Park in London's highest concentration of quality Georgian housing. The park, named for the Prince Regent, was also designed by Nash, as the culmination of a triumphal route from the Prince's house in St James's *(see pp84–5)*. Today it is the busiest of the royal parks and boasts a zoo, an open air theatre, boating lake, rose garden, cafés and London's largest mosque. To the northeast is Camden Town *(see p124)* with its popular market, shops and cafés, reached by walking, or taking a boat, along the picturesque Regent's Canal.

Ancient Greek vase, British Museum

Bloomsbury, an enclave of attractive garden squares and Georgian brick terraces, was one of the most fashionable areas of the city until the mid-19th century, when the arrival of large hospitals and railway stations persuaded many of the wealthier residents to move west to Mayfair, Knightsbridge and Kensington. Home to the British Museum since 1753 and the University of London since 1828, Bloomsbury has long been the domain of artists, writers and intellectuals, including the Bloomsbury Group *(see p163)*, George Bernard Shaw, Charles Dickens and Karl Marx. Traditionally a centre for the book trade, it remains a good place for literary browsing.

SIGHTS AT A GLANCE

Historic Streets
Bloomsbury **5**

Museums and Galleries
British Museum pp106–7 **4**

Madame Tussaud's **1**
Sherlock Holmes Museum **2**
Wallace Collection **3**

GETTING THERE
For most of Regent's Park, the nearest tube stations are Regent's Park, Great Portland Street and Baker Street. Buses 13, 139 and 159 run from Trafalgar Square to near Baker Street. The closest station to the zoo is Camden Town. Russell Square tube station is in the heart of Bloomsbury.

KEY
🚇 Underground station

0 metres 500
0 yards 500

◁ St Andrew's Place, Regent's Park

Madame Tussaud's ❶

Marylebone Rd NW1. **Map** 2 D5.
📞 0870 400 3000. 🚇 Baker St.
🕐 9:30am–5:30pm Mon–Fri, 9am–
6pm Sat–Sun. ⬤ 25 Dec. 🎫
📷 ♿ phone first. 🖥
www.madame-tussauds.com

Madame Tussaud began her
wax-modelling career making
death masks of victims of the
French Revolution. She
moved to
England and in 1835
set up an exhib-ition
of her work in
Baker Street, near
the present site.
Traditional tech-
niques are still
used to create
figures of royal-
ty, politicians,
actors, pop stars
and
sporting
heroes. The
main sec-
tions of the
exhi-bition are:

**Wax figure of
Elizabeth II**

Blush, where
visitors get to
feel what it is like to be at a
celebrity A-list party; Première
Night, devoted to the giants of
the entertainment world; and
the World Stage, a collection
of various royalty, statesmen,
world leaders, writers and
artists.

The Chamber of Horrors is
the most renowned part of
Madame Tussaud's for its
recreations of murders and
executions. In the Spirit of
London finale, visitors travel
in stylized taxi-cabs through

**Wax model of Luciano Pavarotti
(1990), Madame Tussaud's**

**Conan Doyle's fictional detective
Sherlock Holmes**

the city's history to "witness"
events, from the Great Fire of
1666 to the Swinging 1960s.
Ticket prices also include
entry to temporary exhibitions
featuring media icons of the
moment. Educational tours
are also available for groups.

Sherlock Holmes Museum ❷

221b Baker St NW1. **Map** 1 C4.
Tel 020-7935 1127. 🚇 Baker St. 🕐
9:30am–6pm daily. ⬤ 25 Dec. 📷 🎫
www.sherlock-holmes.co.uk

Sir Arthur Conan Doyle's
fictional detective was
supposed to live at 221b
Baker Street, which did not
exist. The museum, labelled
221b, actually stands between
Nos. 237 and 239, and is the
only surviving Victorian lodging house in the street. There
is a reconstruction of Holmes's
front room, and memorabilia
from the stories decorate
every room. Visitors can buy
plaques, Holmes hats, Toby
jugs and meerschaum pipes.

Wallace Collection ❸

Hertford House, Manchester Sq W1.
Map 10 D1. 📞 020-7563 9500.
🚇 Bond St, Baker St. 🕐
10am–5pm daily. ⬤ 24–26 Dec, 1
Jan, Good Fri. ♿ phone first. 🍴 🎫
www.wallacecollection.org

One of the world's finest
private collections of European
art, it has remained intact
since 1897. The product of

passionate collecting by four
generations of the Seymour-
Conway family who were
Marquesses of Hertford, it
was bequeathed to the state
on the condition that it would
go on permanent public display with nothing added or
taken away. Hertford House
still retains the atmosphere of
a grand 19th-century house,
and the recent Centenary
Project has created more
gallery space and a stunning
high-level glass roof for the
central courtyard, which now
contains a sculpture garden
and an elegant restaurant.

The 3rd Marquess (1777–
1842), a flamboyant London
figure, used his Italian wife's
fortune to buy works by
Titian and Canaletto, along
with numerous 17th-century
Dutch paintings including
works by Van Dyck. The collection's particular strength is
18th-century French painting,
sculpture and decorative arts,
acquired by the 4th Marquess
(1800–70) and his natural son,
Sir Richard Wallace (1818–90).

**A 16th-century Italian majolica
dish from the Wallace Collection**

The Marquess had a taste for
lush romanticism, and notable
among his acquisitions are
Watteau's *Champs Elysées*
(1716–17), Fragonard's *The
Swing* (1766) and Boucher's
*The Rising and Setting of the
Sun* (1753).

Other highlights at the
Wallace Collection include
Rembrandt's *Titus, the Artist's
Son* (1650s), Titian's *Perseus
and Andromeda* (1554–6)
and Hals's famous *Laughing
Cavalier* (1624). There is also
an important collection of
Renaissance armour, and
superb examples of Sèvres
porcelain and Italian majolica.

John Nash's Regency London

John Nash, the son of a Lambeth millwright, was designing houses from the 1780s. However, it was not until the 1820s that he also became known as an inspired town planner, when his "royal route" was completed. This took George IV from his Pall Mall palace, through Piccadilly Circus and up the elegant sweep of Regent Street to Regent's Park, which Nash bordered with rows of beautiful

Statue of John Nash (1752–1835)

Neo-Classical villas, such as Park Crescent and Cumberland Terrace. Though many of his plans were never completed, this map of 1851, which unusually places the south at the top, shows Nash's overall architectural impact on London. His other work included the revamping of Buckingham Palace *(see pp86–7)*, and the building of several theatres and churches.

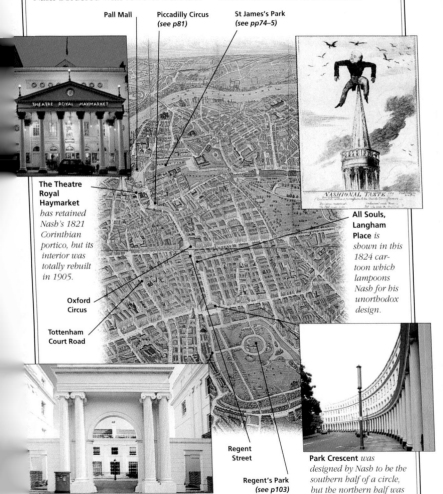

Pall Mall

Piccadilly Circus *(see p81)*

St James's Park *(see pp74–5)*

The Theatre Royal Haymarket *has retained Nash's 1821 Corinthian portico, but its interior was totally rebuilt in 1905.*

Oxford Circus

Tottenham Court Road

All Souls, Langham Place *is shown in this 1824 cartoon which lampoons Nash for his unorthodox design.*

Regent Street

Regent's Park *(see p103)*

Cumberland Terrace, *the longest and most ornate of the stuccoed terraces surrounding Regent's Park, was intended to face a royal palace, which was never built.*

Park Crescent *was designed by Nash to be the southern half of a circle, but the northern half was never built. The interiors were refurbished in the 1960s but the dramatic façade was kept intact.*

British Museum ❹

The oldest public museum in the world, the British Museum was established in 1753 to house the collections of the physician Sir Hans Sloane (1660–1753). Sloane's collection has been added to by gifts and purchases from all over the world, and the museum now contains objects spanning thousands of years. The main part of the building (1823–50) is by architect Robert Smirke, but the architectural highlight is the modern Great Court, with the Reading Room at its centre.

Helmet from Sutton Hoo ship burial

★ Egyptian Mummies
Animals such as this cat (30 BC) were preserved alongside humans by the ancient Egyptians.

Bronze Figure Shiva Nataraja
This statue of the Hindu God Shiva Nataraja (c.1100) from South India forms part of the fine collection of Oriental art.

The Egyptian Gallery on the main floor houses the Rosetta Stone, the inscription that enabled 19th-century scholars to decipher Egyptian hieroglyphs.

Upper floors

90
91
67
95
61
59
60

Montague Place entrance

34
33
24
25
21
20
19
22
9
4
8
17
16
10
15
18
88
89
77
78
79
80
82
85
83
84

Main floor

Lower floor

GALLERY GUIDE
The Greek and Roman, and Middle Eastern collections are found on all three levels of the museum, predominantly on the west side. The African collection is located on the lower floor, while Asian exhibits are found on the main and upper floors on the north side of the museum. The Americas collection is located in the northeast corner off the main floor. Egyptian artifacts are found in the large gallery to the west of the Great Court and on the first floor.

★ Parthenon Sculptures
These reliefs from the Parthenon in Athens were brought to London by Lord Elgin around 1802 and are housed in a special gallery.

STAR EXHIBITS

★ Egyptian Mummies

★ Parthenon Sculptures

★ Lindow Man

KEY TO FLOORPLAN

☐ Asian collection	☐ Middle Eastern collection
☐ Enlightenment	☐ Europe collection
☐ Coins and medals	☐ Temporary exhibitions
☐ Greek and Roman collections	☐ Non-exhibition space
☐ Egyptian collection	☐ World collection

The Great Court is London's largest covered square, with shops, cafés, a restaurant, display areas and educational facilities.

First floor

Mildenhall Treasure
The Great Dish was among the 34 pieces of 4th-century Roman silver tableware ploughed up in Suffolk in 1942.

Paul Hamlyn Library

Reading Room

Main entrance

★ **Lindow Man**
The skin on this 2,000-year-old human body was preserved by the acids of a peat-bog in Cheshire. He was probably killed in an elaborate ritual.

VISITORS' CHECKLIST

Great Russell St WC1. **Map** 3 B5.
Tel 020 7323 8000. ⊖ Holborn,
Russell Sq, Tottenham Court Rd.
🚌 7, 8, 10,14, 19, 24, 25, 29,
30, 38, 55, 134,188. 🚆 Euston,
King's Cross. 🕙 10am–5:30pm
daily (selected galleries until
8:30pm Thu & Fri). 🔴 1 Jan,
Good Fri, 24–26 Dec.
🔲 🔲 🔲 🔲 🔲
www.thebritishmuseum.ac.uk

Private gardens of Bedford Square

Bloomsbury ❺

WC1. **Map** 3 B4. ⊖ Russell Sq,
Tottenham Court Rd. **Charles
Dickens Museum** 48 Doughty St
WC1. **Tel** 020 7405 2127. 🕙
10am–5pm Mon–Sat, 11am–5pm
Sun (last adm: 4:30pm). 🔲 🔲
www.dickensmuseum.com

Home to numerous writers and artists, Bloomsbury is a tradition-al centre of the book trade. It is dominated by the British Museum and the University of London and characterized by several fine Georgian squares. These include **Russell Square**, where the poet T S Eliot (1888–1965) worked for a publisher for 40 years; **Queen Square**, which contains a statue of Queen Charlotte, wife of George III; and **Bloomsbury Square**, laid out in 1661. A plaque here comme-morates members of the Bloomsbury Group (see p163). One of London's best-preserved 18th-century oases is **Bed-ford Square**. Charles Dickens (see p189) lived at 48 Doughty Street during a brief but critical stage in his career, and it was here that he wrote *Oliver Twist* and *Nicholas Nickleby*, both completed in 1839.

Queen Charlotte (1744–1818)

His former home is now the **Charles Dickens Museum**, which has rooms laid out as they were in Dickens's time, with objects taken from his other London homes and first editions of many of his works.

THE CITY AND SOUTHWARK

Dominated today by glossy office blocks, the City is the oldest part of the capital. The Great Fire of 1666 obliterated four-fifths of its buildings. Sir Christopher Wren rebuilt much of it and many of his churches survived World War II (see pp58–9). Commerce has always been the City's lifeblood, and the power of its merchants and bankers secured it a degree of autonomy from state control. Humming with activity in business hours, it empties at night.

In the Middle Ages Southwark, on the south bank of the Thames, was a refuge for pleasure-seekers, prostitutes, gamblers and criminals. Even after 1550, when the area fell under the jurisdiction of the City, its brothels and taverns thrived. There were also several bear-baiting arenas in which plays were staged until the building of theatres such as the Globe (1598), where many of Shakespeare's works were first performed. Relics of old Southwark are mostly on the waterfront, which has been imaginatively redeveloped and provided with a pleasant walkway.

Old bank sign on Lombard Street

SIGHTS AT A GLANCE

Historic Sights and Buildings
HMS Belfast ⓬
Lloyd's Building ➐
Monument ➑
The Old Operating Theatre ⓮
Temple ➌
Tower Bridge ➓
Tower of London pp118–19 ➒

Pubs
George Inn ⓯

Museums and Galleries
Design Museum ⓫
London Dungeon ⓭
Museum of London ➏
Shakespeare's Globe ⓲
Sir John Soane's Museum ➍
Tate Modern ⓳

Markets
Borough Market ⓰

Churches and Cathedrals
St Bartholomew-the-Great ➎
St Paul's Cathedral pp114–15 ➋
St Stephen Walbrook ➊
Southwark Cathedral ⓱

GETTING THERE
The City is served by the Circle, Central, District, Northern and Metropolitan lines and by a number of buses. London Bridge is the main station for Southwark – served by the Northern and Jubilee lines and by trains running from Charing Cross, Cannon Street and Waterloo.

KEY
	Tourist Information
	Street-by-Street map pp110–11
	Underground station
	Railway station
	River boat pier

0 metres 500
0 yards 500

◁ **St Paul's Cathedral in the heart of the City, with the NatWest Tower (1980) to the left**

Street-by-Street: The City

This is the financial heart of London and has been ever since the Romans set up a trading post here 2,000 years ago. For years it was London's main residential area but today very few people live here. The City was severely bombed in World War II and the main clues to its past are streets named after vanished inns and markets. Its numerous churches, many built after the Great Fire of 1666 by the architect Sir Christopher Wren *(see p114)*, are now dwarfed by lavish banks and post-modern developments.

Detail: St Paul's Cathedral

St Mary-le-Bow takes its name from the bow arches in the Norman crypt. Anyone born within earshot of its bells is said to be a true Cockney.

St Paul's station

New Change replaces Old Change, a 13th-century street destroyed in World War II.

Statue of Queen Anne

ST PAUL'S CHURCHYARD

NEW CHANGE

WATLING STREET

BREAD STREET

CANNON STREET

FRIDAY ST

QUEEN VICTORI

QUEEN

St Nicholas Cole Abbey was the first church Wren built in the City (in 1677). It had to be restored after World War II bomb damage.

★ **St Paul's Cathedral**
Built after the Great Fire of 1666, Wren's masterpiece was funded by a tax on coal ❷

Mansion House station

St James Garlickhythe contains unusual sword rests and hat stands, beneath Wren's elegant spire of 1717.

STAR SIGHTS

★ St Paul's Cathedral

★ St Stephen Walbrook

COLLEGE·OF·ARMS

The College of Arms is the official repository of the coats of arms and pedigrees of British families *(see p30)*. It was rebuilt here, on its former site, in the 1670s after the Great Fire.

Mansion House (1753), designed by George Dance the Elder, is the official home of the Lord Mayor. The Palladian façade is a familiar City landmark.

LOCATOR MAP
See Street Finder map 13

Bank of England Museum

The Royal Exchange was founded in 1565 by Sir Thomas Gresham as a centre for commerce. The current building dates from 1844.

Bank station

Lombard Street, named after bankers who came here from Lombardy in the 13th century, retains its traditional banking signs.

KEY

– – – Suggested route

St Mary Abchurch owes its unusually spacious feel to Wren's large dome. The altar carving is by Grinling Gibbons.

★ St Stephen Walbrook
This fine Wren church contains a striking white stone altar by Henry Moore ❶

0 metres   100
0 yards   100

Skinners' Hall
is an 18th-century Italianate building constructed for the ancient guild that controlled trade in fur and leather.

St Stephen Walbrook ❶

39 Walbrook EC4. **Map** 13 B2. **Tel** 020 7626 9000. ⊖ Bank, Cannon St. ◯ 10am–4pm Mon–Thu, 10am–3pm Fri. ● public hols. ✝ 12:45am Thu. **http://ststephenwalbrook.net**

The Lord Mayor's parish church was built by Sir Christopher Wren in the 1670s and is among the finest of all his City churches. The bright, airy interior is flooded with light by a huge dome that appears to float above the eight columns and arches that support it. The dome, deep and coffered with ornate plasterwork, was a forerunner of St Paul's. Original fittings, such as the highly decorative font cover and pulpit canopy, contrast with the stark simplicity of Henry Moore's massive white stone altar (1987). The best time to see the church is during one of its free organ recitals from 12.30 to 1.30pm on Fridays.

St Paul's ❷

See pp116–17.

Effigies in Temple Church

Temple ❸

Inner Temple, King's Bench Walk EC4. **Tel** 020 7797 8250. **Map** 12 E2. ⊖ Temple. ◯ 12:30–3pm Mon–Fri (grounds only). ♿ **Middle Temple Hall,** Middle Temple Ln EC4. **Tel** 020 7427 4800. ◯ 10–11:30am, 3–4pm Mon–Fri. ♿ **Temple Church. Tel** 020 7353 8559. ◯ Wed–Fri; call for times and services. 📷 book ahead.

A cluster of atmospheric squares form the Inner and Middle Temples, two of

London's four Inns of Court, where law students are trained. The name Temple derives from the medieval Knights Templar, a religious order which protected pilgrims to the Holy Land and was based here until 1312. Marble effigies of knights lie on the floor of the circular Temple Church, part of which dates from the 12th century. Middle Temple Hall has a fine Elizabethan interior.

St Bartholomew-the-Great ❺

West Smithfield EC1. **Map** 12 F1. **Tel** 020 7606 5171. ⊖ Barbican, St Paul's. ◯ 8:30am–5pm (4pm in winter) Mon–Fri, 10:30am–4pm Sat, 8:30am–8pm Sun. ● 1 Jan, 25, 26 Dec. 📷 ♿ 📷 by appt. **Concerts. www**.greatstbarts.com

The historic area of Smithfield has witnessed a number of bloody events over the years, among them the execution of rebel peasant leader Wat Tyler in 1381, and, in the reign of Mary I (1553–58), the burning of scores of Protestant martyrs.

Sir John Soane's Museum ❹

13 Lincoln's Inn Fields WC2. **Map** 12 D1. **Tel** 020 7405 2107. ⊖ Holborn. ◯ 10am–5pm Tue–Sat, 6–9pm 1st Tue of month. ● public hols, 24 Dec. ♿ ground floor only. 📷 Sat 2:30pm. **www**.soane.org

One of the most eccentric museums in London, this house was left to the nation by Sir John Soane in 1837, with a stipulation that nothing should be changed. The son of a bricklayer, Soane became one of Britain's leading late Georgian architects developing a restrained Neo-Classical style of his own. After marrying the niece of a wealthy builder, whose fortune he inherited, he bought and reconstructed No. 12 Lincoln's Inn Fields. In 1813 he and his wife moved into No. 13 and in 1824 he rebuilt No. 14, adding a picture gallery and the mock medieval Monk's

Parlour. Today, true to Soane's wishes, the collections are much as he left them – an eclectic gathering of beautiful, instructional and often simply peculiar artifacts. There are casts, bronzes, vases, antique fragments, paintings and a selection of bizarre trivia which ranges from a giant fungus from Sumatra to a scold-bridle, a device designed to silence nagging wives. Highlights include the sarcophagus of Seti I, Soanes's own designs, including those for the Bank of England, models by leading Neo-Classical sculptors and the *Rake's Progress* series of paintings (1734) by William Hogarth, which Mrs Soane bought for £520.

The building itself is full of architectural surprises and illusions. In the main ground floor room, cunningly placed mirrors play tricks with light and space, while an atrium stretching from the basement to the glass-domed roof allows light on to every floor.

A glass dome lets light on to all the floors.

A vast sarcophagus (1300 BC) stands on the floor of the crypt.

Hidden in a quiet corner behind Smithfield meat market (central London's only surviving wholesale food market), this is one of London's oldest churches. It once formed part of a priory founded in 1123 by a monk, Rahere, whose tomb is here. He was Henry I's court jester until he dreamed that St Bartholomew had saved him from a winged monster.

The 13th-century arch, now topped by a Tudor gatehouse, used to be the entrance to the church until the old nave was pulled down during the Dissolution of the Monasteries (*see pp50–51*). The painter William Hogarth was baptized here in 1697. The church featured in the films *Four Weddings and a Funeral* and *Shakespeare in Love*.

St Bartholomew's gatehouse

Delft plate made in London 1600, Museum of London

Museum of London ❻

London Wall EC2. **Map** 13 A1.
Tel 0870 444 3855. 🄴 Barbican, St Paul's. ☐ 10am–6pm daily.
⬤ 24–26 Dec. 🖔🄰🄰
www.museumoflondon.org.uk

This museum traces life in London from prehistoric times to the outbreak of World War I. Displays of archaeological finds and domestic objects alternate with reconstructed street scenes and interiors.

There is also a working model of the Great Fire of 1666 in the London's Burning section. The Roman London gallery has a brightly coloured 2nd-century fresco from a Southwark bath house.

The museum has spent over £20 million redeveloping its lower galleries, retelling London's history from 1666 to the present day with over 4,000 objects and interactive exhibits. The galleries are due to open in the spring of 2010, and visitors will be able to discover the city's many incarnations in the London before London, Roman London and Medieval London galleries.

Every wall is covered and every room filled with artifacts from Soane's voluminous collection.

In the picture gallery, panels covered with paintings unfold to reveal more works of art hidden behind them.

The Monk's Parlour is full of grotesque Gothic casts.

St Paul's Cathedral

The Great Fire of London in 1666 left the medieval cathedral of St Paul's in ruins. Wren was commissioned to rebuild it, but his design for a church on a Greek Cross plan (where all four arms are equal) met with considerable resistance. The authorities insisted on a conventional Latin cross, with a long nave and short transepts, which was believed to focus the congregation's attention on the altar. Despite the compromises, Wren created a magnificent Baroque cathedral, which was built between 1675 and 1710 and has since formed the lavish setting for many state ceremonies.

★ Dome
At 111 m (360 ft), the elaborate dome is one of the highest in the world.

The balustrade along the top was added in 1718 against Wren's wishes.

★ West Front and Towers
Inspired by the Italian Baroque architect, Borromini, the towers were added by Wren in 1707.

The West Portico consists of two storeys of coupled Corinthian columns, topped by a pediment carved with reliefs showing the Conversion of St Paul.

The Nave
An imposing succession of massive arches and saucer domes open out into the vast space below the cathedral's main dome.

West Porch

Main entrance approached from Ludgate Hill

CHRISTOPHER WREN

Trained as a scientist, Sir Christopher Wren (1632–1723) began his impressive architectural career at the age of 31. He became a leading figure in the rebuilding of London after the Great Fire of 1666, building a total of 52 new churches. Although Wren never visited Italy, his work was influenced by Roman, Baroque and Renaissance architecture, as is apparent in his masterpiece, St Paul's Cathedral.

The lantern weighs a massive 850 tonnes.

The Golden Gallery has splendid views over London.

The oculus is an opening through which the cathedral floor can be seen.

Stone Gallery

The High Altar canopy was made in the 1950s, based on designs by Wren.

Entrance to Golden, Whispering and Stone galleries

The South Portico was inspired by the porch of Santa Maria della Pace in Rome. Wren absorbed the detail by studying a friend's collection of architectural engravings.

Entrance to crypt, which has many memorials to the famous.

VISITORS' CHECKLIST

Ludgate Hill EC4. **Map** 13 A2.
Tel 020 7236 4128. ● St
Paul's, Mansion House. ▦ 4,
11, 15, 17, 23, 25, 76, 172.
▦ City Thameslink. **Cathedral**
◯ 8:30am–4pm Mon–Sat.
Galleries, Crypt, Ambulatory
◯ 9:30am–4:15pm. ● for
sightseeing Sun; check website
for closures of all or part of the
cathedral. ▨ ✝ 11am Sun.
♿ ▨ ▯▯ ◻ ◻
www.stpauls.co.uk

★ **Whispering Gallery**
The dome's unusual acoustics mean that words whispered against the wall can be heard clearly on the opposite side.

Choir
Jean Tijou, a Huguenot refugee, created much of the fine wrought iron-work in Wren's time, including these choir screens.

Choir Stalls
The 17th-century choir stalls and organ case were made by Grinling Gibbons (1648–1721), a wood-carver from Rotterdam. He and his team of craftsmen worked on these intricate carvings for two years.

STAR SIGHTS

★ West Front and Towers

★ Dome

★ Whispering Gallery

Richard Rogers's Lloyd's building

Lloyd's Building ⑦

1 Lime St EC3. **Map** 13 C2. **Tel** 020
7327 6586. ⊖ Monument, Bank,
Aldgate. ⬤ to the public.

Lloyd's was founded in the
late 17th century and soon
became the world's main

insurers, issuing policies on
everything from oil tankers
to Betty Grable's legs. The
present building, designed by
Richard Rogers, dates from
1986 and is one of the most
interesting modern buildings
in London. Its exaggerated
stainless-steel external piping
and high-tech ducts echo
Rogers' forceful Pompidou
Centre in Paris. Lloyd's is well
worth seeing floodlit at night.

Monument ⑧

Monument St EC3. **Map** 13 C2. **Tel**
020 7626 2717. ⊖ Monument. ◯
9:30am–5pm daily. ⬤ 1 Jan, 24–26
Dec. ⬚ www.towerbridge.org.uk

This doric column, designed
by Wren to commemorate
the Great Fire of London that
devastated the original walled
city in September 1666, was, in

1681, the tallest isolated stone
column in the world. Topped
with a bronze flame, the
Monument is 62 m (205 ft)
high; the exact distance west to
Pudding Lane, where the fire is
believed to have started. Reliefs
around the column's base
show Charles II restoring the
city after the tragedy.

The now restored column
has 311 tightly spiralled steps
that lead to a tiny viewing
platform. (In 1842, it was
enclosed with an iron cage to
prevent suicides.) The steep
climb is well worth the effort
as the views from the top are
spectacular and visitors are
rewarded with a certificate.

Tower of London ⑨

See pp118–19.

Tower Bridge ⑩

SE1. **Map** 14 D3. **Tel** 020 7403 3761.
⊖ Tower Hill. **The Tower Bridge
Exhibition** ◯ Apr–Sep: 10am–
5:30pm daily; Oct–Mar: 9:30am–5pm
daily (last adm: 4pm). ⬤ 24–26 Dec.
⬚ ♿ access lift. ◻
www.towerbridge.org.uk

This flamboyant piece of
Victorian engineering,
designed by Sir Horace Jones,

was completed in 1894 and
soon became a symbol of
London. Its two Gothic towers
contain the mechanism for
raising the roadway to permit
large ships to pass through.
The towers are made of a
supporting steel framework
clad in stone, and are linked
by two high-level walkways
which were closed between
1909 and 1982 due to
their popularity

with suicides and prostitutes.
The bridge now houses The
Tower Bridge Exhibition, with
interactive displays bringing
the bridge's history to life.
There are fine river views
from the walkways, and a
look at the steam engine
room that powered the lifting
machinery until 1976,
when the system was
electrified.

Walkways, open to the
public, give panoramic views
over the Thames and London.

The roadway, when raised,
creates a space 40 m (135 ft)
high and 60 m (200 ft) wide, big
enough for large cargo ships.

Engine room

South Bank

**Lifts and 300
steps** lead to the
top of the towers.

**The Victorian wind-
ing machinery** was
originally powered
by steam.

Entrance

North Bank

Design Museum ⓫

Butlers Wharf, Shad Thames SE1.
Map 14 E4. **Tel** 0870 909 9009.
Tower Hill, London Bridge.
10am–5:45pm daily (last adm:
5:15pm). 25 & 26 Dec.
Blueprint Café 020 7940 8785
for reservations.
www.designmuseum.org

This museum was the first
in the world to be devoted
solely to modern and contemporary design when it was
founded in 1989. A frequently
changing programme of
exhibitions explores landmarks in modern design
history and the most exciting
innovations in contemporary
design set against the context
of social, cultural, economic
and technological changes.
The Design Museum embraces
every area of design, from
furniture and fashion, to
household products, cars,
graphics, websites and architecture in exhibitions and
new design commissions.
Each spring the museum
hosts Designer of the Year, a
national design prize, with an
exhibition at which the public
can vote for the winner.
    The museum is arranged
over three floors, with major
exhibitions on the first floor.
There is a choice of smaller
displays on the second,
which also houses an
Interaction Space, where
visitors can play vintage video
games and learn about the
designers featured in the
museum in the Design at
the Design Museum online
research archive. The shop
and café are on the ground
floor. On the first floor is the
Blueprint Café restaurant,
which has stunning views of
the Thames (booking ahead
recommended).

Exterior of the Design Museum

**The now familiar sight of the naval
gunship HMS Belfast on the Thames**

HMS Belfast ⓬

Morgan's Lane, Tooley St SE1.
Map 13 C3. 020 7940 6300.
London Bridge, Tower Hill.
Mar–Oct: 10am–6pm daily; Nov–Feb:
10am–5pm daily (last adm: 45 mins
before closing). 24–26 Dec.
limited. **www**.iwm.org.uk

Originally launched in 1938
to serve in World War II,
the 11,500-ton battle ship
HMS *Belfast* was instrumental
in the destruction of the
German battle cruiser
Scharnhorst in the battle of
North Cape, and also played
an important role in the
Normandy Landings.
    After the war, the battle
cruiser, designed for offensive
action and for supporting
amphibious operations, was
sent to work for the United
Nations in Korea. The ship
remained in service with the
British navy until 1965.
    Since 1971, the cruiser has
been used as a floating naval
museum. Part of it has been
atmospherically recreated
to show what the ship was
like in 1943, when it partici-
pated in sinking the German
battle cruiser. Other displays
portray life on board during
World War II, and there are
also special exhibits which
relate to the history of the
Royal Navy.
    As well as being a great
family day out, it is also
possible for children to
take part in the educational
activity weekends that take
place on board the ship.

London Dungeon ⓭

Tooley St SE1. **Map** 13 C3. 0871
360 2049. London Bridge. Jul–
Aug 9:30am–6pm; Easter–Jun, Sep &
Oct 10am–5:30pm; Nov–Easter
10:30am–5pm; daily. 25 Dec.
book in advance to avoid queues.
www.thedungeons.com

In effect a much expanded
version of the chamber of
horrors at Madame Tussaud's
(see p104), this museum is
a great hit with children. It
illustrates the most bloodthirsty events in British history.
It is played strictly for terror,
and screams abound as Druids
perform a human sacrifice at
Stonehenge, Henry VIII's wife
Anne Boleyn is beheaded,
and a room full of people die
in agony during the Great
Plague. Other displays include
torture, murder and witchcraft.

19th-century surgical tools

The Old Operating Theatre ⓮

9a St Thomas St SE1. **Map** 13 B4. **Tel**
020 7188 2679. London Bridge.
10:30am–5pm daily. 15 Dec–
5 Jan. **www**.thegarret.org.uk

St Thomas's Hospital stood
here from its foundation in
the 12th century until it was
moved west in 1862. At this
time most of its buildings
were demolished to make
way for the railway. The
women's operating theatre
(The Old Operating Theatre
Museum and Herb Garret)
survived only because it was
located away from the main
buildings, in a garret over the
hospital church. It lay, bricked
up and forgotten, until the
1950s. Britain's oldest operating theatre, dating back to
1822, it has now been fitted
out as it would have been in
the early 19th century.

Tower of London ❾

Soon after William the Conqueror became king in 1066, he built a fortress here to guard the entrance to London from the Thames Estuary. In 1097 the White Tower was completed in sturdy stone; other fine buildings have been added over the centuries. The tower has served as a royal residence, armoury, treasury and, most famously, as a prison. Some were tortured here and among those who met their death were the "Princes in the Tower", the sons and heirs of Edward IV. Today the tower is a popular attraction, housing the Crown Jewels and other exhibits, such as the displays about the Peasants' Revolt of 1381, the only time the Tower's walls were breached. The most celebrated residents are the ravens; legend has it that the kingdom will fall if they desert the tower. Some guided tours are led by the colourful Beefeaters.

Beauchamp Tower
Many high-ranking prisoners were held here, often with their own retinues of servants. The tower was built by Edward I around 1281.

"Beefeaters"
Thirty-five Yeomen Warders guard the Tower and live here. Their uniforms hark back to Tudor times.

Two 13th-century curtain walls protect the tower.

Tower Green was the execution site for favoured prisoners, away from crowds on Tower Hill, where many had to submit to public execution. Seven people died here, including two of Henry VIII's six wives, Anne Boleyn and Catherine Howard.

Queen's House
This Tudor building is the sovereign's official residence at the Tower.

Main entrance from Tower Hill

THE CROWN JEWELS

The world's best-known collection of precious objects, now displayed in a splendid exhibition room, includes the gorgeous regalia of crowns, sceptres, orbs and swords used at coronations and other state occasions. Most date from 1661, when Charles II commissioned replacements for regalia destroyed by Parliament after the execution of Charles I *(see pp52–3)*. Only a few older pieces survived, hidden by royalist clergymen until the Restoration – notably, Edward the Confessor's sapphire ring, now incorporated into the Imperial State Crown *(see p73)*. The crown was made for Queen Victoria in 1837 and has been used at every coronation since.

The Sovereign's Ring (1831)

The Sovereign's Orb (1661), a hollow gold sphere encrusted with jewels

★ Jewel House
Among the magnificent Crown Jewels is the Sceptre with the Cross (1660), which now contains the world's biggest diamond.

VISITORS' CHECKLIST

Tower Hill EC3. **Map** 14 D3.
Tel 0844 482 7799 for advance booking. ⊖ Tower Hill; Tower Gateway (DLR). 🚌 RV1, 15, X15, 25, 42, 78, 100, D1, D9, D11.
🚆 Fenchurch Street. ◻ Mar–Oct: 9am–6pm (from 10am Sun, Mon); Nov–Feb: 9am–5pm (from 10am Sun, Mon) daily. (Last adm: 1 hr before closing.) ● 1 Jan, 24–26 Dec. 🎦 & limited, except Jewel House. ◻ 🎟 **Ceremony of the Keys:** 9:30pm daily (book in advance). **www**.hrp.org.uk

★ White Tower
When the tower was finished in 1097, it was the tallest building in London at 27 m (90 ft) high.

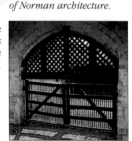

★ Chapel of St John
This austerely beautiful Romanesque chapel is a particularly fine example of Norman architecture.

THAMES

Traitors' Gate
The infamous entrance was used for prisoners brought from trial in Westminster Hall.

Bloody Tower
A new permanent display explores the mysterious disappearance of Edward IV's two sons, who were put here by their uncle, Richard of Gloucester (later Richard III), after their father died in 1483. The princes disappeared and Richard was crowned later that year. In 1674 the skeletons of two children were found nearby.

STAR SIGHTS

★ Jewel House

★ White Tower

★ Chapel of St John

The George Inn, now owned by the National Trust

George Inn ⑮

(NT) 77 Borough High St SE1.
Map 13 B4. *Tel* 020 7407 2056.
⊖ London Bridge, Borough.
◯ 11am–11pm Mon–Sat, noon–
10:30pm Sun. 🍴

Dating from the 17th century,
this building is the only traditional galleried coaching inn
left in London and is mentioned in Dickens's *Little
Dorrit*. It was rebuilt after the
Southwark fire of 1676 in a
style that dates back to the
Middle Ages. There were originally three wings around a
courtyard, where plays were
staged in the 17th century. In
1889 the north and east wings
were demolished, so there is
only one wing remaining.
   The inn is still a popular pub
with a well-worn, comfortable
atmosphere, perfect on a cold,
damp day. In the summer, the
yard fills with picnic tables,
and patrons are occasionally
entertained by actors and
morris dancers. The house bitter is highly recommended.

Borough Market ⑯

8 Southwark St SE1. **Map** 13 B4.
⊖ London Bridge. **Retail market**
◯ 11am–5pm Thu, noon–6pm Fri,
9am–4pm Sat.

Borough Market was until
recently a wholesale fruit and
vegetable market, which had
its origins in medieval times,
and moved to its current
position beneath the railway
tracks in 1756. This hugely

popular fine-food market has
now become well established,
selling gourmet foods from
Britain and abroad, as well as
quality fruit and vegetables,
to locals and tourists alike.

**Shakespeare window (1954),
Southwark Cathedral**

Southwark Cathedral ⑰

Montague Close SE1.
Map 13 B3. *Tel* 020 7367 6700.
⊖ London Bridge. ◯ 8am–6pm
daily. 📷 🌐 www.southwark.
anglican.org/cathedral

Although some parts of this
building date back to the
12th century, it was not until
1905 that it became a cathedral. Many original medieval
features remain, notably the
tomb of the poet John Gower
(c.1325–1408), a contemporary of Chaucer *(see p172)*.
There is a monument to
Shakespeare, carved in 1912,
and a memorial window
(above) installed in 1954.

Shakespeare's Globe ⑱

New Globe Walk SE1. **Map** 13 A3.
Tel 020 7902 1400. Box office: 020
7401 9919. ⊖ Southwark, London
Bridge. **Exhibition** ◯ Late Apr–early
Oct: 9am–12:30pm, 1–5pm Mon–Sat,
9–11:30am & noon–5pm Sun; early
Oct–late Apr: 10am–5pm daily. ●
24, 25 Dec. 📷 ♿ 🎥 every 30 mins.
(Rose Theatre tours for groups of 15
or more by appt only). **Performances**
late Apr–early Oct. ♿ limited. 🍴 📷
🌐 www.shakespeares-globe.org

Opened in 1997, this circular
building is a faithful reproduction of an Elizabethan
theatre, close to the site of the
original Globe where many of
Shakespeare's plays were first
performed. It was built using
handmade bricks and oak
laths, fastened with wooden
pegs rather than metal screws,
and has the first thatched roof
allowed in London since the
Great Fire of 1666. The
theatre was erected thanks
to a heroic campaign by the
American actor and director
Sam Wanamaker. Open to the
elements (although the seats
are protected), it operates
only in the summer, and
seeing a play here can be
a thrilling experience, with
top-quality acting under the
artistic direction of Mark
Rylance among others.
   Beneath the theatre,
Shakespeare's Globe Exhibition is open all year and
covers many aspects of
Shakespeare's work and times.
Groups of 15 or more may
book to see the foundations of
the nearby Rose Theatre.

**Shakespeare's *Henry IV* (performed
at the Globe Theatre around 1600)**

Tate Modern ⑲

Holland St, SE1. **Map** 13 A3. **Tel** 020 7887 8888. 🚇 Blackfriars, Southwark. 🚌 to Tate Britain every 40 mins. 🚇 Blackfriars. ⏰ 10am–6pm Sun–Thu, 10am–10pm Fri & Sat. 🔴 24–26 Dec. 💷 major exhibitions. ♿ 🚻 📷 🎁 www.tate.org.uk/modern

Looming over the southern bank of the Thames, Tate Modern occupies the converted Bankside power station, a dynamic space for one of the world's premier collections of contemporary art. Tate Modern draws its main displays from the expansive Tate Collection, also shown at the other Tate galleries: Tate St Ives (p277), Tate Liverpool (p377) and Tate Britain (p91). A river boat, Tate to Tate, transports visitors between Tate Modern and Tate Britain. Tate Modern completed a major re-hang of its collection in 2006, and displays on level 5 also underwent changes in 2009.

Inverno from Quattro Stagioni (1993–4) by Cy Twombly

The gallery's west entrance leads straight into the massive Turbine Hall. Each year an artist is commissioned to install in this space. Louise Bourgeois was the first to do so, creating three giant towers and a gargantuan spider, *Maman* (2000). In 2008, Dominique Gonzalez-Foerster's *TH 2058* filled the Turbine Hall with 200 yellow and blue bunk beds.

An escalator whisks visitors from the Turbine Hall, up to level 3 where the main galleries are located. In a break with convention, Tate Modern organizes its displays by theme rather than chronology or school – a practice that cuts across movements and mixes up media. Four themes based on traditional genres reveal how traditions have been confronted, extended or rejected by artists throughout the 20th and into the 21st centuries.

Tate Modern's displays are arranged into two thematic wings on level 3 and the displays continue on level 5. The collection focuses on key periods of modern art: Cubism, Futurism and Vorticism; Surrealism and Surrealist tendencies; Abstract Expressionism and European Informal Art; and Minimalism. At the centre of each of the four exhibitions is a focal display, from which all the other displays rotate.

Spatial Concept "Waiting" (1960) by Lucio Fontana

Over 40 per cent of the work on display since the major re-hang in 2006 has never been on display at Tate Modern before. The collection includes works such as the iconic paintings *Whaam!* by Roy Lichtenstein, *Spatial Concept "Waiting"* by Lucio Fontana and *Quattro Stagioni* by Cy Twombly as well as other important pieces by the likes of Francis Picabia and Anish Kapoor. To complement its permanent collection, Tate Modern presents a dynamic programme of temporary exhibitions, including three large-scale shows per year. Major live events are staged each year, taking their inspiration from the Collection.

Soft Drainpipe – Blue (Cool) (1967) by Claes Oldenburg

BANKSIDE POWER STATION

This forbidding fortress was designed in 1947 by Sir Giles Gilbert Scott, the architect of Battersea Power Station, Waterloo Bridge and London's famous red telephone boxes. The power station is of a steel-framed brick skin construction, comprising over 4.2 million bricks. The Turbine Hall was designed to accommodate huge oil-burning generators and three vast oil tanks are still in situ, buried under the ground just south of the building. The tanks are to be employed in a future stage of Tate Modern development. The power station itself was converted by Swiss architects Herzog and de Meuron who designed the two-storey glass box, or lightbeam, which runs the length of the building. This serves to flood the upper galleries with light and also provides wonderful views of London.

The façade, chimney and light beam of Tate Modern

FURTHER AFIELD

Over the centuries London has steadily expanded to embrace the scores of villages that surrounded it, leaving the City as a reminder of London's original boundaries. Although now linked in an almost unbroken urban sprawl, many of these areas have maintained their old village atmosphere and character. Hampstead and Highgate are still distinct enclaves, as are artistic Chelsea and literary Islington. Greenwich, Chiswick and Richmond have retained features that hark back to the days when the Thames was an important artery for transport and commerce, while just to the east of the City the wide expanses of the former docks have, in the last 20 years, been imaginatively rebuilt as new commercial and residential areas.

SIGHTS AT A GLANCE

Camden and Islington **7**
Chelsea **1**
Chiswick **10**
East End and Docklands **8**

Greenwich **9**
Hampstead **4**
Hampstead Heath **5**
Highgate **6**

Holland Park **2**
Notting Hill and
  Portobello Road **3**
Richmond and Kew **11**

KEY

▓	Main sightseeing areas
☐	Greater London
☐	Parks
═	Motorway
▬	Major road
═	Minor road

10 miles = 15 km

Chelsea **1**

SW3. 🚇 *Sloane Square.* **Map** 17 B2.

Riverside Chelsea has been fashionable since Tudor times when Sir Thomas More, Henry VIII's Lord Chancellor

Statue of Sir Thomas More (1478–1535), Cheyne Walk

(*see p50*), lived here. The river views attracted artists and the arrival of the historian Thomas Carlyle and essayist Leigh Hunt in the 1830s began a literary connection. Blue plaques on the houses of **Cheyne Walk** celebrate former residents such as J M W Turner (*see p91*) and writers George Eliot, Henry James and T S Eliot.

Chelsea's artistic tradition is maintained by its galleries and antique shops, many of them scattered among the clothes boutiques on **King's Road**. This begins at **Sloane Square**, named after the physician Sir Hans Sloane, who bought the manor of Chelsea in 1712. Sloane expanded the **Chelsea Physic Garden** (1673) along Swan Walk to cultivate plants and herbs.

Wren's **Royal Hospital**, on Royal Hospital Road was built in 1692 as a retirement home for old soldiers and still houses 400 Chelsea Pensioners.

Arab Hall, Leighton House (1866)

Holland Park **2**

W8, W14. 🚇 *Holland Park.* **Map** 7 B5.

This park is more intimate than the large royal parks such as Hyde Park (*see p101*). It was opened in 1952 on the grounds of **Holland House**, a centre of social and political intrigue in its 19th-century heyday.

Around the park are some magnificent late Victorian houses. **Linley Sambourne**

House was built about 1870 and has received a much-needed facelift, though it remains much as Sambourne furnished it, in the Victorian manner, with china ornaments and heavy velvet drapes. He was a political cartoonist for the satirical magazine *Punch* and drawings cram the walls.

Leighton House, built for the Neo-Classical painter Lord Leighton in 1866, has been preserved as an extraordinary monument to the Victorian Aesthetic movement. The highlight is the Arab Hall, which was added in 1879 to house Leighton's stupendous collection of 13th- to 17th-century Islamic tiles. The best paintings include some by Leighton himself and by his contemporaries Edward Burne-Jones and John Millais.

Georgian house, Hampstead

🏛 Linley Sambourne House
18 Stafford Terrace W8. *Tel 020 7602 3316 (020 7938 1295 Sat, Sun).* 🚇 *High St Ken.* ⏱ *Mar–Dec: tours only, Mon–Fri by appt, Sat & Sun every hr till 3:30pm.* 📷 🎫 ♿

🏛 Leighton House
12 Holland Park Rd W14. *Tel 020 7602 3316.* 🚇 *High St Ken.* ⏱ *11am–5:30pm Wed–Mon.* ⬤ *public hols.* 📷 🎫 *Wed & Thu.* ♿

Notting Hill and Portobello Road ❸

W11. 🚇 *Notting Hill Gate.* **Map** 7 B2.

In the 1950s and 60s, Notting Hill became a centre for the Caribbean community and today it is a vibrant cosmopolitan part of London. It is also home to Europe's largest street carnival *(see p63)* which began in 1965 and takes over the entire area on the August bank holiday weekend, when costumed parades flood through the crowded streets.

Nearby, Portobello Road market *(see pp148–9)* has a bustling atmosphere with hundreds of stalls and shops selling a variety of collectables.

Hampstead ❹

NW3, N6. 🚇 *Hampstead.* 🚈 *Hampstead Heath.*

On a high ridge north of the metropolis, Hampstead is essentially a Georgian village with many perfectly maintained mansions and houses. It is one of London's most desirable residential areas, home to a community of artists and writers since Georgian times.

Situated in a quiet Hampstead street, **Keats House** (1816) is an evocative tribute to the life and work of the poet John Keats (1795–1821). Keats lived here for two years before his tragic death from consumption at the age of 25, and it was under a plum tree in the garden that he wrote his celebrated *Ode to a Nightingale.* Mementoes of Keats and of Fanny Brawne, the neighbour to whom he was engaged, are on show. Renovated in 2009, Keats House now benefits from more extensive displays.

The **Freud Museum**, which opened in 1986, is dedicated to the dramatic life of Sigmund Freud (1856–1939), the founder of psychoanalysis. At the age of 82, Freud fled from Nazi persecution in Vienna to this Hampstead house where he lived and worked for the last year of his life. His daughter Anna, pioneer of child psychoanalysis, continued to live here until her death in 1982. Inside, Freud's rich Viennese-style consulting rooms remain unaltered, and 1930s home movies show moments of Freud's life, including scenes of the Nazi attack on his home in Vienna.

🏛 Keats House
Keats Grove NW3. 📞 020 7435 2062. 🚇 *Hampstead, Belsize Pk.* ⏱ 1–5pm Tue–Sun (am by appt). 📷 **www**.cityoflondon.gov.uk/keats

🏛 Freud Museum
20 Maresfield Gdns NW3. *Tel* 020 7435 2002. 🚇 *Finchley Rd.* ⏱ noon–5pm Wed–Sun. 📷 ♿ *limited.* 📷 **www**.freud.org.uk

Antique shop on Portobello Road

View east across Hampstead Heath to Highgate

Hampstead Heath 5

N6. 🚇 *Hampstead, Highgate.* 🚆 *Hampstead Heath.*

Separating the hill-top villages of Hampstead and Highgate, the open spaces of Hampstead Heath are a precious retreat from the city. There are meadows, lakes and ponds for bathing and fishing, and fine views over the capital from **Parliament Hill**, to the east.

Situated in landscaped grounds high on the edge of the Heath is the magnificent **Kenwood House**, where classical concerts *(see p154)* are held by the lake in summer. The house was remodelled by Robert Adam *(see p28)* in 1764 and most of his interiors have survived, the highlight of which is the library. The mansion is filled with Old Master paintings, such as works by Van Dyck, Vermeer, Turner *(see p91)* and Romney; the star attraction is Rembrandt's self-portrait of 1663.

🏛 Kenwood House
Hampstead Lane NW3. **Tel** 020-8348 1286. ⬜ *daily.* ♿ 🖥 📷
www.english-heritage.org.uk

Handmade crafts and antiques, Camden Lock indoor market

Highgate 6

N6. 🚇 *Highgate, Archway.*

A settlement since the Middle Ages, Highgate, like Hampstead, became a fashionable aristocratic retreat in the 16th century. Today, it still has an exclusive rural feel, aloof from the urban sprawl below, with a Georgian high street and many expensive houses.

Highgate Cemetery *(see p75)*, with its monuments and hidden overgrown corners, has an extraordinary, magical atmosphere. Tour guides (daily in summer, weekends in winter) tell of the many tales of intrigue, mystery and vandalism connected with the cemetery since it opened in 1839. In the eastern section is the tomb of Victorian novelist George Eliot (1819–80) and of the cemetery's most famous incumbent, Karl Marx (1818–83).

🏛 Highgate Cemetery
Swains Lane N6. **Tel** 020-8340 1834. 🚇 *Archway, Highgate.* ⬜ *daily.* ⬤ *during burials, 25–26 Dec.* 🖼 ✶
www.highgate-cemetery.org

Camden and Islington 7

NW1, N1. **Camden** 🚇 *Camden Town, Chalk Farm.* **Islington** 🚇 *Angel, Highbury & Islington.*

Camden is a lively area packed with restaurants, shops and a busy **market** *(see p148–9)*. Thousands of people come here each weekend to browse among the wide variety of stalls or simply to soak up the atmosphere of the lively cobbled area around the canal, which is enhanced by the buskers and street performers.

Neighbouring Islington was once a fashionable spa but the rich moved out in the late 18th century and the area deteriorated rapidly. In the 20th century, writers such as Evelyn Waugh, George Orwell and Joe Orton lived here. In recent decades, Islington has been rediscovered and is again fashionable as one of the first areas in London to become "gentrified", with many professionals buying the old houses.

East End and Docklands ❽

E1, E2, E14. **East End** 🅔 *Aldgate East, Liverpool St, Bethnal Green.* **Docklands** 🅔 *Canary Wharf.*

In the Middle Ages the East End was full of craftsmen practising noxious trades such as brewing, bleaching and vinegar-making, which were banned within the City. The area has also been home to numerous immigrant communities since the 17th century, when French Huguenots, escaping religious persecution moved into Spitalfields, and made it a silk-weaving centre. Even after the decline of the silk industry, textiles and clothing continued to dominate, with Jewish tailors and furriers setting up workshops in the 1880s, and Bengali machinists sewing in cramped premises from the 1950s.

A good way to get a taste of the East End is to explore its Sunday street markets *(see p149)*, and sample freshly baked bagels and spicy Indian food. By way of contrast, anyone interested in contemporary architecture should visit the **Docklands**, an ambitious re-development of disused docks, dominated by the Canada Tower; at 250 m (800 ft) it is London's tallest building. Other attractions include the **V&A Museum of Child-hood**, a delightful toy museum with lots of activities, and **Dennis Severs' House**, in which you are taken on a historic journey from the 17th to the 19th centuries.

Canada Tower, Canary Wharf

Royal Naval College framing the Queen's House, Greenwich

🏛 V&A Museum of Childhood
Cambridge Heath Rd E2. **Tel** 020 8983 5200. ◐ 10am–5.45pm daily. ● 1 Jan, 25–26 Dec. 🅔🖥🖨 **www**.museumofchildhood.org.uk

🏠 Dennis Severs' House
18 Folgate St E1. **Tel** 020 7247 4013. ◐ noon–2pm Mon after 1st & 3rd Sun of month, Mon eve (by candlelight), noon–4pm Sun. 🎟🖨 **www**.dennissevershouse.co.uk

Greenwich ❾

SE10. 🚆 *Greenwich, Maze Hill.* 🅔 *Cutty Sark (DLR).*

The world's time has been measured from the **Royal Observatory Greenwich** (now housing a museum) since 1884. The area is full of maritime and royal history, with Neo-Classical mansions, a park, many antique and book shops and various markets *(see pp148–9)*. The **Queen's House**, designed by Inigo Jones for James I's wife, was completed in 1637 for Henrietta Maria, the queen of Charles I. The Queen's House has now been restored to its original state, and

its highlights include the perfectly cubic main hall and the unusual spiral "tulip staircase".

The adjoining **National Maritime Museum** has exhibits that range from primitive canoes, through Elizabethan galleons, to modern ships. Anyone interested in naval history should visit the **Old Royal Naval College**, which was designed by Christopher Wren *(see p114)* in two halves

An 18th-century compass, National Maritime Museum

so that the Queen's House kept its river view. It began as a royal palace, became a hospital in 1692, and in 1873 the Old Royal Naval College moved here. The Rococo chapel and the 18th-century *trompe l'oeil* Painted Hall are open to the public.

🏛 Royal Observatory Greenwich
Greenwich Park SE10. **Tel** 020 8312 6565. ◐ 10am–5pm daily (last Planetarium show: 4pm). ● 24–26 Dec. 🖨 **www**.rog.nmm.ac.uk

🏛 Queen's House and National Maritime Museum
Romney Rd SE10. **Tel** 020 8312 6565. ◐ daily. ● 24–26 Dec. 🎟🅔 limited. 🖥🖨 **www**.nmm.ac.uk

🏠 Old Royal Naval College
King William Walk, Greenwich SE10. **Tel** 020 8269 4747. ◐ 10am–5pm daily. ● public hols.

Chiswick ❿

W4. ⊖ *Chiswick.*

Chiswick is a pleasant suburb of London, with pubs, cottages and a variety of birdlife, such as herons, along the picturesque riverside. One of the main reasons for a visit is **Chiswick House**, a magnificent country villa inspired by the Renaissance architect Andrea Palladio. It was designed in the early 18th century by the 3rd Earl of Burlington as an annexe to his larger house (demolished in 1758), so that he could display his art collection and entertain friends. The gardens are now fully restored.

Heron

🏛 **Chiswick House**
Burlington Lane W4. **Tel** *020 8995 0508.* ◯ *Apr–Oct: Sun–Wed & bank hols.* 🈲 🔊 *call ahead.* 🎫
www.english-heritage.org.uk

Richmond and Kew ⓫

SW15. ⊖ ⇄ *Richmond.*

The attractive village of Richmond took its name from a palace built by Henry VII (the former Earl of Richmond in Yorkshire) in 1500, the remains of which can be seen off the green. Nearby is the expansive **Richmond Park**, which was once Charles I's royal hunting ground. In summer, boats

Chiswick House

sail down the Thames from Westminster Millennium Pier, making a pleasant day's excursion from central London.

The nobility continued to favour Richmond after royalty had left, and some of their mansions have survived. The Palladian villa, **Marble Hill House**, was built in 1724–9 for the mistress of George II and has been restored to its original appearance. On the opposite side of the Thames, the brooding **Ham House**, built in 1610, had its heyday later that century when it became the home of the Lauderdales. The Countess of Lauderdale inherited the house from her father, who had been Charles I's "whipping boy" – meaning that he was punished whenever the future king misbehaved. He was rewarded as an adult by being given a peerage and the lease of Ham estate.

A little further north along the Thames, **Syon House** has been inhabited by the Dukes and Earls of Northumberland for over 400 years. Numerous attractions here include a butterfly house, a museum of historic cars and a spectacular conservatory built in 1830. The lavish Neo-Classical interiors of the house, created by Robert Adam in the 1760s *(see p28),* remain the highlight.

Brewers Lane, Richmond

On the riverbank to the south, **Kew Gardens**, the world's most complete botanic gardens, feature examples of nearly every plant that can be grown in Britain. There are also conservatories displaying thousands of exotic tropical blooms.

🏛 **Marble Hill House**
(EH) Richmond Rd, Twickenham. **Tel** *020 8892 5115.* ◯ *Apr–Oct: Sat, Sun, pub hols.* 🔊 *limited.* 🍴 🖼 🎫

🏛 **Ham House**
(NT) Ham St, Richmond. **Tel** *020 8940 1950.* ◯ *Apr–Oct: Sat–Wed.*

🏛 **Syon House**
London Rd, Brentford. **Tel** *020 8560 0881.* **House** ◯ *mid-Mar– Oct: Wed, Thu, Sun & pub hols.* **Gardens** ◯ *daily.* ● *Nov–mid-Mar.* 🈲 🔊 *gardens only.* 🖼 🎫 **www**.syonpark.co.uk

🌷 **Kew Gardens**
Royal Botanic Gdns, Kew Green, Richmond. **Tel** *020 8332 5655.* ◯ *daily.* ● *1 Jan, 24–25 Dec.* 🈲 🔊 🖼 🍴 🖼 🎫 **www**.kew.org

LONDON STREET FINDER

The map references given with the sights, hotels, restaurants, shops and entertainment venues based in central London refer to the following four maps. All the main places of interest within the central area are marked on the maps in addition to useful practical information, such as tube, railway and coach stations. The key map below shows the area of London that is covered by the Street Finder. The four main city-centre areas (colour-coded in pink) are shown in more detail on the inside back cover.

KEY

▪ Major sight	ⓘ Tourist information	▭ Motorway
▫ Other sight	✚ Hospital with casualty unit	▭ Pedestrian street
▫ Other building	🚓 Police station	*56 House number (main street)
Ⓔ Underground station	✝ Church	
⬏ British rail	✡ Synagogue	**SCALE OF MAP PAGES**
🚌 Bus stop	⊠ Post office	
⬌ River boat boarding point	═ Railway line	1:11,000

0 metres 200
0 yards 200

SHOPS AND MARKETS

London is one of the great shopping cities of Europe, with bustling, lively street markets, world-famous department stores and a wide variety of eclectic shops selling clothes, antiques, crafts and much more. The best shopping areas range from up-market districts such as Knightsbridge and Bond Street, which sell expensive

Bags from two famous London department stores

designer clothes, to the busy, chaotic stretch of Oxford Street. The vibrant markets of Covent Garden, Berwick Street and Brick Lane are also popular. The city is best known, however, for its huge range of clothes shops selling everything from traditional tweeds to the latest zany designs of the ever-changing high-street fashion trends.

WHEN TO SHOP

In central London, most shops stay open from 10am to about 5.30–6pm Monday to Saturday. Many department stores, however, have longer hours. The "late night" shopping until 7 or 8pm is on Thursday and Friday in Oxford Street and the rest of West End; and on Wednesday in Knightsbridge and Chelsea. Some shops in tourist areas, such as Covent Garden and the Trocadero, are open until 7pm or later every day, including Sunday. Some street markets and a number of other shops are usually open on Sundays as well.

TWICE-YEARLY SALES

The traditional sale season is from January to February and from June to July, when shops slash prices and sell off left-over stock. The department stores have some of the best reductions – queues for the famous Harrods sale start to form long before it opens.

SHOPPING AREAS

London's best shopping areas range from the up-market Knightsbridge, where porcelain, jewellery and couture come at the highest prices, to colourful markets, where getting the cheapest bargains is what it's all about.

The city beckons specialist shoppers with its treasures and collectibles crammed into inviting antiques shops, and streets full of antiquarian booksellers and art galleries.

BEST OF THE DEPARTMENT STORES

Harrods is the king of the city's department stores with over 300 departments and a staff of 5,000. The spectacular food hall with Edwardian tiles displays fish, cheese, fruit and vegetables. Other specialities include fashion, china and glass, kitchenware and electronics. Londoners also often head for the nearby **Harvey Nichols**, which stocks the best of everything. The clothing department is particularly strong, with an emphasis on talented British, European and American names. The food hall, opened in 1992, is one of London's most stylish.

Selfridges, on Oxford Street, has expanded its range in recent years. It has arguably the widest choice of labels, a great lingerie department and a section devoted to emerging designers. It also has a food hall that features delicacies from all over the world.

Originally a drapery, **John Lewis**, to this date, has a good selection of fabrics and haberdashery. Its china, glass and household items make this store and its Sloane Square partner, **Peter Jones**, equally popular with Londoners.

Liberty, near Carnaby Street, has been famous ever since 1875 for its beautiful silks and other Oriental goods. Don't forget to check out the famous scarf department.

Fortnum and Mason's is best known for its ground-floor food department. It has everything from Fortnum's tins of biscuits and tea to cured meats and lovely wicker hampers. In fact, these exquisite delicacies are so engrossing that the upper floors filled with classic fashion and luxury items often remain free of crowds.

Harrods at night, illuminated by 11,500 lights

MARKETS

Whatever you're looking for, it's definitely worth visiting one of London's colourful markets. Many of them mix English traditions with those of more recent immigrants, creating an exotic atmosphere and a truly fascinating array of merchandise. At some, the seasoned hawkers have honed their sales patter to an entertaining art, which reaches fever pitch just before closing, when the plummeting prices at the end of the day are announced. Keep your wits about you, your hand on your purse and join in the fun.

Among the best of the West End markets are **Grays Antiques** and **Jubilee and Apple** markets in Covent Garden. Although it is somewhat touristy, **Piccadilly Crafts** is also very popular. In Soho, the spirited costermongers of **Berwick Street** peddle some of the cheapest and freshest fruit and vegetables in the area.

In the East End, **Petticoat Lane** is probably the most famous of London's street markets. Those in search of the latest street fashions make a beeline for **Old Spitalfields**, while **Brick Lane** is massively popular due

Bustling Petticoat Lane market, officially known as Middlesex Street

to its trendy location. Here you can find everything from shellfish to trainers. Nearby, **Columbia Road** is perfect for greenery and blossoms.

South of the river, **East Street** also has a flower market, but the majority of its traders sell clothes. **Bermondsey Market** is a gathering point for London's antiques traders. Collectors set off early to scrutinize the fine paintings and old jewellery. **Borough** (*see p120*) caters to the restaurant trade with it's fine food and farmer's market. **Brixton Market** stocks a superb

assortment of Afro-Caribbean foods, often to the pounding beat of reggae music.

In north London, **Camden Lock Market** offers a vibrant atmosphere and stalls selling everything from vintage clothes to lovely crafts. In nearby Islington, **Camden Passage** is a quiet cobbled street where charming cafés nestle among quaint antiques shops.

In Notting Hill, **Portobello Road** is actually a bunch of markets rolled into one, and an entire afternoon can be spent browsing there.

DIRECTORY

DEPARTMENT STORES

Fortnum & Mason
181 Piccadilly W1. **Map 11 A3. *Tel* 020 7734 8040.**

Harrods
87–135 Brompton Rd SW1. **Map 9 C5. *Tel* 020 7730 1234.**

Harvey Nichols
109–125 Knightsbridge SW1. **Map 9 C5. *Tel* 020 7235 5000.**

John Lewis
278–306 Oxford St W1. **Map 10 E1. *Tel* 020 7629 7711.**

Liberty
210–20 Regent St W1. **Map 10 F2. *Tel* 020 7734 1234.**

Peter Jones
Sloane Sq, SW1. **Map 18 D2. *Tel* 020 7730 3434.**

Selfridges
400 Oxford St W1. **Map 10 D2. *Tel* 0800 123 400.**

MARKETS

Bermondsey Market
Long Lane & Bermondsey St SE1. **Map 13 C5.**
⏰ *5am–2pm Fri.*

Berwick Street
Berwick St W1.
Map 11 A2.
⏰ *9am–6pm Mon–Sat.*

Borough
8 Southwark St SE1.
Map 13 B4. ⏰ *11am–5pm Thu, noon–6pm Fri, 9am–4pm Sat.*

Brick Lane
Brick Lane E1. **Map 6 E5.**
⏰ *dawn–1pm Sun.*

Brixton Market
Electric Ave SW9.
⏰ *8.30am–5.30pm daily.*

Camden Lock Market
Chalk Farm Rd NW1.
🚇 Camden Town, Chalk Farm.
⏰ *9:30am–5:30pm daily.*

Camden Passage
Camden Passage N1.
Map 4 F1.
⏰ *10am–2pm Wed, 10am–5pm Sat.*

Columbia Road
Columbia Rd E2.
Map 6 D3.
🚇 Shoreditch, Old St.
⏰ *8am–2pm Sun.*

East Street
East St SE17. 🚇 Elephant & Castle. ⏰ *8am–5pm daily (to 2pm Thu & Sun).*

Grays Antiques
58 Davies St, Mayfair.
Map 10 E2.
⏰ *10am–6pm Mon–Fri.*

Greenwich
College Approach SE10.
⏰ *11am–6pm Wed, 10am–5:30pm Thu & Fri, 9am–6pm Sat & Sun.*

Jubilee and Apple
Covent Gdn Piazza WC2.
Map 11 C2. ⏰ *9am–5pm daily.*

Old Spitalfields
Commercial St E1. 🚇 Liverpool St. **Map 6 D1.**
⏰ *9:30am–5:30pm daily.*

Petticoat Lane
Middlesex St E1. **Map 14 E2.** ⏰ *9am–2pm Sun.*

Piccadilly Crafts
St James's Church, Piccadilly W1. **Map 11 A3.**
⏰ *9am–6pm Wed–Sat.*

Portobello Road
Portobello Rd W10.
Map 7 C3. ⏰ *daily (main market Sat).*

Exclusive designer clothes on sale at Harrods, Knightsbridge

CLOTHES

British tailoring and fabrics are world renowned for their high quality. **Henry Poole & Co**, **H Huntsman & Sons** and **Gieves & Hawkes** are among the most highly respected tailors on Savile Row.

The past decade has seen the advent of a new generation of trend conscious tailors who specialize in modern cuts and fabrics. The line-up includes **Richard James** and **Ozwald Boateng**. Several stalwarts of classic British style have also recently reinvented themselves as fashion labels. **Burberry** is the best example, although it still does a brisk trade in its famous trenchcoats, and distinctive accessories. Designers **Margaret Howell** and **Nicole Farhi** create trendsetting versions of British country garments for men as well as women.

London designers are known for their eclectic, irreverent style. *Grande dames* of fashion, **Zandra Rhodes** and **Vivienne Westwood** have been on the scene since the 1970s. Many other British designers of international stature also have their flagship stores in the capital, including the popular **Stella McCartney**, **Alexander McQueen**, **Paul Smith** and **Matthew Williamson**. Designer clothes, however, are not just the preserve of the rich. If you want to flaunt a bit of British design, but can't afford the high prices, it's worth

visiting **Debenhams**, which has harnessed the talents of numerous leading designers. Cheaper versions of all the latest styles appear in the shops almost as soon as they have been sashayed down the catwalk. **Topshop** and **Oasis** have both won celebrity fans for their up-to-the-minute ensembles of hip and youthful fashions for women; young professionals head to **French Connection**. The upmarket chains **Jigsaw** and **Whistles** are more expensive, with their emphasis on beautiful fabrics and shapes. Fashion-conscious young men can turn to **Reiss** and **Ted Baker** for trendy clothing.

SHOES

Some of the most famous names in the footwear industry are based in Britain. If you can spare a few thousand pounds, you can have a pair custom-made by the Royal Family's shoemaker, **John Lobb**. Readymade, traditional brogues and Oxfords are the mainstay of **Church's Shoes**. **Oliver Sweeney** gives classics a contemporary edge. **The British Boot Company** in Camden has the widest range of funky Dr Martens, appropriated by rock'n'rollers and the grunge set. **Jimmy Choo** and **Manolo Blahnik** are two all-time favourites of most fashionable women all over the world. Less expensive, yet good quality designs can be found in **Hobbs** or **Pied à Terre**, while **Faith** and **Office** turn out young, voguish styles.

GIFTS AND SOUVENIRS

Contemporary Applied Arts and the market in Covent Garden Piazza stock uniquely British pottery, knitwear and other crafts. To buy all your gifts under one roof, visit Liberty *(see p148)*, where all kinds of exquisite items can be found in every department.

Leading museums such as the Victoria and Albert *(see pp98–9)*, Natural History and Science Museums *(see p100)* sell unusual mementos as well. Alternatively, try **Hamley's** for gifts and toys.

BOOKS AND MAGAZINES

The bookshops in London rank among its most illustrious specialities. Charing Cross Road is a treasure trove for those hunting for antiquarian, second-hand as well as new volumes. It is the home of **Foyles**, famous for its massive stock. Large branches of chains such as **Waterstone's** and **Borders** co-exist with many specialist stores in this highly learned street.

Hatchards in Piccadilly is the city's oldest bookshop, and also one of its best, offering an extensive choice of titles.

Vintage Magazines in Soho, as its name suggests, stocks publications dating back to the early 1900s – collectors of back issues will be delighted.

Well-stocked bookshop on the legendary Charing Cross Road

ART AND ANTIQUES

Art and antiques shops abound in London, and you are sure to find something of beauty and value within your means.

Cork Street is the centre of Britain's contemporary art world. **Waddington Galleries** is the best known, while **Redfern Art Gallery** and **Flowers** exhibit unusual modern art.

Visit **Roger's Antiques Galleries** and Grays Antiques *(see p148)* for striking vintage jewellery and objets d'art.

The East End is a growing area for contemporary art. The cutting-edge **White Cube Gallery** is there, as is the internationally renowned **Whitechapel Art Gallery**.

For photography, visit the **Photographers' Gallery**, which has the largest collection of originals for sale in Britain. **Hamiltons Gallery** also hosts interesting exhibitions.

DIRECTORY

CLOTHES

Alexander McQueen
4–5 Old Bond St W1.
Map 10 F3.
Tel 020 7355 0088.

Burberry
21–23 New Bond St W1.
Map 10 F2.
Tel 020 7930 3343.
One of several branches.

Debenhams
334–348 Oxford St W1.
Map 10 E2.
Tel 08445 616 161.

French Connection
249–251 Regent St W1.
Map 10 F2.
Tel 020 7493 3124.
One of several branches.

Gieves & Hawkes
1 Savile Row W1. **Map** 10
F3. *Tel 020 7434 2001.*

H Huntsman & Sons
11 Savile Row W1. **Map**
10 F3. *Tel 020 7734 7441.*

Henry Poole & Co
15 Savile Row W1. **Map**
10 F3. *Tel 020 7734 5985.*

Jigsaw
6 Duke of York Sq, Kings
Rd SW3. **Map** 17 C2.
Tel 020 7730 4404.

Margaret Howell
34 Wigmore St W1. **Map**
10 E1. *Tel 020 7009 9009.*

Matthew Williamson
28 Bruton St W1.
Map 10 E3.
Tel 020 7629 6200.

Nicole Farhi
158 New Bond St W1.
Map 10 E2.
Tel 020 7499 8368.

Oasis
12–14 Argyll St W1.
Map 10 F2.
Tel 020 7434 1799.

Ozwald Boateng
30 Savile Row &
9 Vigo St W1. **Map** 10 F3.
Tel 020 7437 0620.

Paul Smith
Westbourne House
120 & 122 Kensington
Park Rd W11. **Map** 7 B2.
Tel 020 7727 3553.

Reiss
Kent House, 14–17
Market Place W1.
Map 10 F1.
Tel 020 7637 9112.
One of several branches.

Richard James
29 Savile Row W1.
Map 10 F2.
Tel 020 7434 0605.

Stella McCartney
30 Bruton St W1.
Map 10 E3.
Tel 020 7518 3100.

Ted Baker
9–10 Floral St WC2.
Map 11 C2.
Tel 020 7836 7808.
One of several branches.

Topshop
Oxford Circus W1.
Map 10 F1.
Tel 08448 487 487.
One of several branches.

Vivienne Westwood
6 Davies St W1.
Map 10 E2.
Tel 020 7629 3757.

Whistles
303 Brompton Rd SW3.
Map 17 B2.
Tel 020 7823 9134.

Zandra Rhodes
79 Bermondsey St, SE1.
Map 11 C5.
Tel 020 7403 5333.

SHOES

The British Boot Company
5 Kentish Town Rd NW1.
Map 2 F1.
Tel 020 7485 8505.

Church's Shoes
201 Regent St W1.
Map 10 F2.
Tel 020 7734 2438.

Faith
192–194 Oxford St W1.
Map 10 F1.
Tel 020 7580 9561.

Hobbs
47–48 South Molton St
W1. **Map** 10 E2.
Tel 020 7629 0750.
One of several branches.

Jimmy Choo
27 New Bond St W1.
Map 10 F2.
Tel 020 7493 5858.

John Lobb
9 St James's St SW1.
Map 10 F4.
Tel 020 7930 3664.

Manolo Blahnik
49–51 Old Church St,
Kings Road SW3. **Map** 17
A4. *Tel 020 7352 8622.*

Office
57 Neal St WC2.
Map 11 B1.
Tel 020 7379 1896.
One of several branches.

Oliver Sweeney
66 New Bond St W1.
Map 10 E2.
Tel 020 7355 0387.

Pied à Terre
179 South Molton St W1.
Map 10 E2.
Tel 020 7629 1362.

GIFTS AND SOUVENIRS

Contemporary Applied Arts
2 Percy St WC1.
Map 11 A1.
Tel 020 7436 2344.

Hamley's
2 Fouberts Place W1.
Map 10 F2.
Tel 0870 333 2450.

BOOKS AND MAGAZINES

Borders
120 Charing Cross Rd
WC2. **Map** 11 B1.
Tel 020 7379 7313.
One of several branches.

Foyles
113–119 Charing Cross Rd
WC2. **Map** 11 B1.
Tel 020 7437 5660.

Hatchards
187 Piccadilly W1.
Map 10 F3.
Tel 020 7439 9921.

Vintage Magazines
39–43 Brewer St W1.
Map 11 A2.
Tel 020 7439 8525.

Waterstone's
203–205 Piccadilly W1.
Map 11 A3.
Tel 020 7851 2400.
One of several branches.

ART AND ANTIQUES

Flowers
21 Cork St W1.
Map 10 F3.
Tel 020 7439 7766.

Hamiltons Gallery
13 Carlos Place W1.
Map 10 E3.
Tel 020 7499 9493.

Photographers' Gallery
16–18 Ramillies St W1.
Map 10 F2.
Tel 0845 262 1618.

Redfern Art Gallery
20 Cork St W1.
Map 10 F3.
Tel 020 7734 1732.

Roger's Antiques Galleries
65 Portobello Road W11.
Map 7 A1.
Tel 020 7467 5787.

Waddington Galleries
11, 12 Cork St W1.
Map 10 F3.
Tel 020 7851 2200.

White Cube Gallery
48 Hoxton Square N1.
Map 5 C3.
Tel 020 7930 5373.

Whitechapel Art Gallery
80–82 Whitechapel
High St E1.
Map 14 E1.
Tel 020 7522 7888.

ENTERTAINMENT IN LONDON

London has the enormous variety of entertainment that only the great cities of the world can provide. The historical backdrop and the lively bustling atmosphere add to the excitement. Whether dancing the night away at a famous disco or making the most of London's varied arts scene, the visitor has a bewildering choice. A trip to London is not complete without a visit to the theatre which ranges from glamorous West End musicals to experimental Fringe plays. There is world-class ballet and opera in fabled venues such as Sadler's Wells and the Royal Opera House. The musical menu covers everything from classical, jazz and rock to rhythm and

Many London cafés have free live music

blues performed in atmospheric basement clubs, old converted cinemas and outdoor venues such as Wembley. Movie buffs can choose from hundreds of films each night. Sports fans can watch cricket at Lord's or participate in a host of activities from water sports to ice skating.

Time Out, published every Tuesday, is the most comprehensive guide to what is on in London, with detailed weekly listings and reviews. *The Evening Standard, The Guardian* (Saturday) and *The Independent* also have reviews and information on events. If you buy tickets from booking agencies rather than direct from box offices, do compare prices – and only buy from ticket touts if you are desperate.

WEST END AND NATIONAL THEATRES

Palace Theatre poster (1898)

The glamorous, glittering world of West End theatreland, emblazoned with the names of world-famous performers, offers an extraordinary range of entertainment.

West End theatres (see Directory for individual theatres) survive on their profits and rely on financial backers, known as "angels". Consequently, they tend to stage commercial productions with mass appeal: musicals, classics, comedies

and plays by bankable contemporary playwrights.

The state-subsidized **National Theatre** is based in the Southbank Centre *(see p154)*. It has three auditoriums – the large, open-staged Olivier, the proscenium-arched Lyttelton, and the small studio space of the Cottesloe.

The **Royal Shakespeare Company** (RSC) regularly stages Shakespeare plays, but its repertoire includes Greek tragedies, Restoration comedies and modern works. Based at Stratford-upon-Avon *(see pp325–27)*, its major productions perform at London West End theatres. The RSC ticket hotline has information. **The Old Vic** has been rejuvenated recently under the artistic directorship of Kevin Spacey, whose exciting programme of drama attracts wide audiences.

Theatre tickets generally cost from £5 to £50 (for a top price West End show) and can be bought direct from box offices, by telephone or post. The "tkts" discount theatre ticket booth in Leicester Square sells tickets for a wide range of shows on the day of performance. It is open Monday to Saturday (10am–7pm) for matinees and evening shows, and Sundays (noon–3pm) for matinees only.

OFF-WEST END AND FRINGE THEATRES

Off-West End theatre is a middle category bridging the gap between West End and Fringe theatre. It includes venues that, regardless of location, have a permanent management team and often provide the opportunity for established directors and actors to turn their hands to more adventurous works in a smaller, more intimate, environment. Fringe theatres, on the other hand, are normally venues hired out to visiting companies. Both offer a vast array of innovative productions, serving as an outlet for new, often experimental writing.

Venues (too numerous to list – see newspaper listings),

The Old Vic, the first home of the National Theatre from 1963

Open-air theatre at Regent's Park

range from tiny theatres or rooms above pubs such as the Gate, which produces neglected European classics, to theatres such as the Donmar Warehouse, which attracts major directors and actors.

OPEN-AIR THEATRE

In summer, a performance of one of Shakespeare's airier creations such as *A Midsummer Night's Dream*, takes on an atmosphere of enchantment among the green vistas of Regent's Park (0870-060 1811). Lavish summer opera productions are staged at Holland Park (020-7602 7856). Shakespeare's Globe *(see p120)* offers open-air theatrical performances in a beautifully recreated Elizabethan theatre.

CINEMAS

The West End abounds with multiplex cinema chains (MGM, Odeon, UCI) which show big budget Hollywood films, usually in advance of the rest of the country, although release dates tend to lag well behind the US and many other European countries.

The Odeon Marble Arch has the largest commercial screen in Europe, while the Odeon Leicester Square boasts London's biggest auditorium with almost 2,000 seats.

Londoners are well-informed cinema-goers and even the larger cinema chains include some low-budget and foreign films in their repertoire. The majority

BFI IMAX Cinema, at Waterloo

of foreign films are subtitled, rather than dubbed. A number of independent cinemas, such as the Renoir and Prince Charles in central London, and the Curzon in Mayfair, show foreign-language and art films.

The largest concentration of cinemas is in and around Leicester Square although there are local cinemas in most areas. Just off Leicester Square, the Prince Charles is the West End's cheapest cinema. Elsewhere in the area you can expect to pay as much as £10 for an evening screening – almost twice the price of the local cinemas. Monday and afternoon performances in the West End are often cheaper.

The BFI Southbank, at the Southbank Centre, is London's flagship repertory cinema. Subsidized by the British Film Institute, it screens a wide range of films, old and new, from all around the world. Nearby at Waterloo is the BFI IMAX, with one of the world's largest screens.

DIRECTORY

Adelphi
Strand. **Map** 11 C3.
Tel 0870 403 0303.

Aldwych
Aldwych. **Map** 11 C2.
Tel 0870 400 0805.

Apollo
Shaftesbury Ave.
Map 11 B2.
Tel 020 7834 6318.

Cambridge
Earlham St. **Map** 11 B2.
Tel 0870 264 3333.

Comedy
Panton St. **Map** 11 A3.
Tel 0870 060 6637.

Criterion
Piccadilly Circus. **Map**
11 A3. *Tel 0870 847 1778.*

Dominion
Tottenham Court Rd. **Map**
11 A1. *Tel 0870 607 7400.*

Duchess
Catherine St. **Map** 11 C2.
Tel 020 7632 9600.

Duke of York's
St Martin's Lane. **Map** 11
B2. *Tel 0870 060 6623.*

Fortune
Russell St. **Map** 11 C2.
Tel 0870 060 6626.

Garrick
Charing Cross Rd. **Map**
11 B2. *Tel 0870 040 0083.*

Gielgud
Shaftesbury Ave. **Map**
11 B2. *Tel 0844 482 5130.*

Her Majesty's
Haymarket. **Map** 11 A3.
Tel 0844 412 2707.

Lyceum
Wellington St. **Map** 11
C2. *Tel 0870 243 9000.*

Lyric
Shaftesbury Ave. **Map** 11
B2. *Tel 0870 890 1107.*

National
South Bank. **Map** 12 D3.
Tel 020 7452 3000.

New London
Drury Lane. **Map** 11 C1.
Tel 0870 890 0141.

Noel Coward
St Martin's Lane. **Map** 11
B2. *Tel 0844 482 5120.*

Novello Theatre
Aldwych. **Map** 12 D2.
Tel 0844 482 5120.

The Old Vic
Waterloo Rd SE1.
Map 12 E4.
Tel 0870 060 6628.

Palace
Cambridge Circus W1. **Map**
11 B2. *Tel 0870 890 0142.*

Phoenix
Charing Cross Rd. **Map** 11
B2. *Tel 0870 060 6629.*

Piccadilly
Denman St. **Map** 11 A2.
Tel 0870 060 0123.

Prince Edward
Old Compton St. **Map** 11
D5. *Tel 0844 482 5151.*

Prince of Wales
Coventry St. **Map** 11 A3.
Tel 0844 482 5115.

Queen's
Shaftesbury Ave. **Map**
11 B2. *Tel 0844 482 5160.*
RSC Tel 01789 403 444.

Shaftesbury
Shaftesbury Ave. **Map**
11 B2. *Tel 0844 482 5160.*

St Martin's
West St. **Map** 11 B2.
Tel 0844 499 1515.

**Theatre Royal:
Drury Lane**
Catherine St. **Map** 11 C2.
Tel 020 7087 7500.

**Theatre Royal:
Haymarket**
Haymarket. **Map** 11 A3.
Tel 0870 844 2353.

Vaudeville
Strand. **Map** 11 C3.
Tel 020 7836 9987.

Wyndham's
Charing Cross Rd. **Map**
11 B2. *Tel 0844 482 5120.*

Royal Festival Hall, South Bank Centre

CLASSICAL MUSIC, OPERA AND DANCE

London is one of the world's great centres for classical music, with five symphony orchestras, internationally renowned chamber groups such as the Academy of St-Martin-in-the-Fields and the English Chamber Orchestra, as well as a number of contemporary groups. There are performances virtually every week by major international orchestras and artists, reaching a peak during the summer Proms season at the **Royal Albert Hall** *(see p63)*. The newly restored **Wigmore Hall** has excellent acoustics and is a fine setting for chamber music, as is the converted Baroque church (1728) of **St John's, Smith Square**.

Although televised and outdoor performances by major stars have greatly increased the popularity of opera, prices at the **Royal Opera House** *(see p80)* are still aimed at corporate entertainment but the policy now is to keep a few cheaper seats. The refurbished building is elaborate and productions are often extremely lavish. English National Opera, based at the **London Coliseum**, has more adventurous productions, appealing to a younger audience (nearly all operas are sung in English). Tickets range from £5 to £200 and it is advisable to book in advance.

The Royal Opera House is also home to the Royal Ballet, and the London Coliseum to the English National Ballet, the two leading classical ballet companies in Britain. Visiting ballets also perform in both. There are numerous young contemporary dance companies, and **The Place** is a dedicated contemporary

dance theatre where many companies perform. Other major dance venues are **Sadler's Wells**, the **ICA**, the **Peacock Theatre** and the **Chisenhale Dance Space**.

The **Barbican Concert Hall** and **Southbank Centre** (comprising the Royal Festival Hall, Queen Elizabeth Hall and Purcell Room) host an impressive variety of events ranging from touring opera and classical music performances to free foyer concerts.

Elsewhere in London many outdoor musical events take place in summer *(see pp62–3)* at venues such as **Kenwood House**. Events to look out for are: the London Opera Festival (June) with singers from all over the world; the City of London Festival (July) which hosts a range of varied musical events; and contemporary dance festivals Spring Loaded (February–April) and Dance Umbrella (October) – see *Time Out* and newspaper listings.

Kenwood House on Hampstead Heath *(see p124)*

DIRECTORY

CLASSICAL MUSIC, OPERA AND DANCE

Barbican Concert Hall
Silk St EC2. **Map** 5 A5. **Tel** 020 7638 4141. www.barbican.org.uk

Chisenhale Dance Space
64–84 Chisenhale Rd E3. Bethnal Green, Mile End. **Tel** 020 8981 6617. www.chisenhaledance space.co.uk

ICA
The Mall SW1. **Map** 11 A4. **Tel** 020 7930 3647. www.ica.org.uk

Kenwood House
(EH) Hampstead Lane NW3. **Tel** 020 8348 1286.

London Coliseum
St Martin's Lane WC2. **Map** 11 B3. **Tel** 0870 145 0200. www.eno.org

Peacock Theatre
Portugal St WC2. **Map** 12 D1. **Tel** 0844 412 4322.

The Place
17 Duke's Rd WC1. **Map** 3 B3. **Tel** 020 7121 1100. www.theplace.org.uk

Royal Albert Hall
Kensington Gore SW7. **Map** 8 F5. **Tel** 020 7589 8212. www.royal alberthall.com

Royal Opera House
Floral St WC2. **Map** 11 C2. **Tel** 020 7304 4000. www.roh.org.uk

Sadler's Wells
Rosebery Ave EC1. **Tel** 0844 412 4300. www.sadlerswells.com

St John's, Smith Sq
Smith Sq SW1. **Map** 19 B1. **Tel** 020 7222 1061. www.sjss.org.uk

Southbank Centre
SE1. **Map** 12 D3. **Tel** 0871 663 2500. www. southbankcentre.co.uk

Wigmore Hall
Wigmore St W1. **Map** 10 D1. **Tel** 020 7935 2141. www.wigmore-hall.org.uk

ROCK, POP, JAZZ AND CLUBS

100 Club
100 Oxford St W1. **Map** 10 F1. **Tel** 020 7636 0933. www.the100club.co.uk

333
333 Old St EC1. **Tel** 020 7739 1800.

Brixton Academy
211 Stockwell Rd SW9. Brixton. **Tel** 0870 771 2000. www.brixton-academy.co.uk

Café de Paris
3 Coventry St W1. **Map** 4 D5. **Tel** 020 7734 7700.

The Hippodrome, Leicester Square

ROCK, POP, JAZZ AND CLUBS

An ordinary week night in London features scores of concerts, ranging from rock and pop, to jazz, Latin, world, folk and reggae. Artists guaranteed to fill thousands of seats play large venues such as **Wembley Arena** or the **Royal Albert Hall**. However, many major bands prefer to play the **Brixton Academy** and the **Forum**, both former cinemas.

There are a number of live jazz venues. Best of the old crop is **Ronnie Scott's**, although the **100 Club, Jazz Café** and **Pizza on the Park** have good reputations.

London's club scene is one of the most innovative in Europe. It is dominated by big-name DJs, who host different nights

in different clubs, and some of the best clubs are one-nighters (see *Time Out* and newspaper listings). The West End discos **Ruby Blue** and the **Café de Paris** are glitzy, expensive and very much on the tourist circuit. The **Hippodrome** was a popular club for more than 20 years. Originally built for circus and variety performances, the building reopened as a performing arts venue in 2008. In contrast, the New York-style **Ministry of Sound**, the camp cabaret of **Madame Jojo's**, the trendy Shoreditch clubs **333** and **Cargo**, and a host of other venues ensure that you will never be short of choice. Alternatives are the excellent laser and light shows at **Heaven**, the glamorous

super-club **Pacha London**, or the live music venue **Koko** in Camden, which also hosts a variety of club nights. **Heaven** and the **Fridge** are among the most popular of London's gay clubs.

Opening times are usually 10pm–3am, but on weekends many clubs open until 6am.

SPORTS

An impressive variety of public sports facilities are to be found in London and they are generally inexpensive to use. Swimming pools, squash courts, gyms and sports centres, with an assortment of keep-fit classes, can be found in most districts, and tennis courts hired in most parks. Water sports, ice skating and golf are among the variety of activities on offer. Spectator sports range from football and rugby at various club grounds to cricket at **Lord's** or the **Oval**, and tennis at the **All England Lawn Tennis Club**, Wimbledon. Tickets for the most popular matches can often be hard to come by (*see p67*). More traditional sports include polo at **Guards**, croquet at **Hurlingham** (private members only) and medieval tennis at **Queen's Club Real Tennis**. See pages 662–665 for more information on sporting activities.

Ticket agency, Shaftesbury Avenue

Cargo
83 Rivington St EC2.
Old St. **Tel** *020 7749 7844.*

Forum
9–17 Highgate Rd NW5.
Kentish Town.
Tel *020 7428 4099.*

Fridge
Town Hall Parade, Brixton Hill SW2. *Brixton.*
Tel *020 7326 5100.*

Heaven
Under the Arches, Villiers St WC2. **Map** 11 C3.
Tel *020 7930 2020.*

Jazz Café
3–5 Parkway NW1.
Camden Town.
Tel *020 7485 6834.*

Koko
1A Camden High St NW1.
Mornington Crescent
Tel *0870 432 5527.*

Madame Jojo's
8–10 Brewer St W1. **Map**
11 A2. **Tel** *020 7734 3040.*

Ministry of Sound
103 Gaunt St SE1.
Elephant & Castle.
Tel *0870 060 0010.*

Pacha London
Terminus Place, SW1. **Map**
18 F1. **Tel** *0845 371 4489.*
www.pachalondon.com

Pizza on the Park
11 Knightsbridge SW1.
Map 10 D5. **Tel** *020 7235 7825.*

Ronnie Scott's
47 Frith St W1.
Map 11 A2.
Tel *020 7439 0747.*
www.ronniescotts.co.uk

Ruby Blue
Leicester Sq WC2. **Map**
4 E5. **Tel** *0871 223 0869.*

SPORTS

All England Lawn Tennis Club
Church Rd, Wimbledon
SW19. *Southfields.*
Tel *020 8946 2244.*

Guards Polo Club
Windsor Great Park,
Englefield Green, Egham.
Egham.
Tel *01784 434212.*

Hurlingham Club
Ranelagh Gdns SW6.
Map 18 D3. **Tel** *020 7736 8411.*

Lord's Cricket Ground
St John's Wood NW8.
St John's Wood.
Tel *020 7289 1611.*

Oval Cricket Ground
The Oval, Kennington
SE11. *Oval.*
Tel *020 7820 5700.*

Queen's Club Real Tennis
Palliser Rd W14.
Barons Court.
Tel *020 7385 3421.*

SOUTHEAST
ENGLAND

Southeast England at a Glance

The old Saxon kingdoms covered the areas surrounding London, and today, while their accessibility to the capital makes them a magnet for commuters, each region retains a character and history of its own. The attractions include England's oldest universities, royal palaces, castles, stately homes and cathedrals, many of which played critical roles in the nation's early history. The landscape is soft, with the green and rounded hills of the south country levelling out to the flat fertile plains and fens of East Anglia, fringed by broad, sandy beaches.

Blenheim Palace (see pp228–9) *is a Baroque masterpiece. The Mermaid Fountain (1892) is part of the spectacular gardens.*

Bedfordshire

Hertfor

Buckinghamshire

THAMES VALLEY
(see pp216–37)

Oxford University's *buildings (see pp222–7) amount to a textbook of English architecture from the Middle Ages to the present. Christ Church College (1525) is the largest in the university.*

Oxfordshire

Surrey

Hampshire

West Susse

Windsor Castle (see pp236–7) *is Britain's oldest royal residence. The Round Tower was built in the 11th century when the palace guarded the western approaches to London.*

Winchester Cathedral (see pp170–1) *was begun in 1097 on the ruins of a Saxon church. The city has been an important centre of Christianity since the 7th century. The cathedral's northwest door is built in a characteristic medieval style.*

◁ **The white cliffs of Dover, Kent**

Ely Cathedral's (see pp194–5) *south transept contains some of the finest stone carving in Britain. The octagonal corona was added in the 14th century when the Norman tower collapsed; the replacement tower dominates the surrounding flat fenland.*

Norfolk

ibridgeshire

EAST ANGLIA
(see pp190–215)

Suffolk

Essex

Cambridge University's (see pp210–15) *buildings are enhanced by the quiet college gardens, the Backs and the public commons. King's College Chapel is the outstanding example of late medieval architecture in the city.*

ONDON
pp70–157)

Kent

THE DOWNS AND CHANNEL COAST
(see pp164–89)

East Sussex

Canterbury Cathedral (see pp186–7) *is the spiritual home of the Church of England. It contains some of the country's most exquisite medieval stained glass such as the nave's west window. It also has some well-preserved 12th-century wall paintings.*

Brighton's Royal Pavilion (see pp178–9) *was built for the Prince Regent and is one of the most lavish buildings in the land. Its design by John Nash (see p107) is based on Oriental themes and it has recently been restored to its original splendour.*

0 kilometres   25

0 miles   25

The Garden of England

With its fertile soil, mild climate and regular rainfall, the Kentish countryside has flourished as a fruit-growing region ever since its first orchards were planted by the Romans. There has been a recent boom in wine-making, as the vine-covered hillsides around Lamberhurst show, and several vineyards may be visited. The orchards are dazzling in the blossom season, and in the autumn the branches sag with ripening fruit – a familiar sight which inspired William Cobbett (1762–1835) to describe the area as "the very finest as to fertility and diminutive beauty in the whole world". Near Faversham, the fruit research station of Brogdale is open to the public, offering orchard walks, tastings and informative displays.

White wine from the southeast

HOPS AND HOPPING

Hop-picking, a family affair

Oast houses, topped with distinc-tive angled cowls, are a common feature of the Kentish landscape and many have now been turned into houses. They were originall

SEASONAL FRUIT

This timeline shows the major crops in each month of the farming year. The first blossoms may appear when the fields are still dusted with snow. As the petals fall, fruit appears among the leaves. After ripening in the summer sun, the fruit is harvested in the autumn.

Peach blossom *is usually to be found on south-facing walls, as its fruit requires warm conditions.*

Orchards *are used to grow plums, pears and apples. The latter (blossoming above) remain Kent's most important orchard crop.*

Raspberries *are a luscious soft fruit Many growers allo you to pick your or from the fields, an then pay by weig*

MARCH	APRIL	MAY	JUNE	JUL

Srawberries *are Britain's favourite and earliest soft fruit New strains allow them to be picked all summer.*

Sour cherry blos-som *is the earliest flower. Its fruit is used for cooking.*

Pear blossom *has creamy white flowers which appear two or three weeks before apple blossom.*

Cherry plum blossom *is one of the most beautiful blossoms; the plum is grown more for its flowers than its fruit.*

Gooseberries *are not always sweet enough to eat raw, though all types are superb in pies and other desserts.*

t to dry hops, an ingredient
rewing beer *(see pp604–5)*.
ny are still used for that, for
ough imports have reduced
nestic hop-growing, more
n four million tonnes are
duced in Britain annually,
stly in Kent.

n summer, the fruiting plants
be seen climbing the rect-
gular wire frames in fields by
roadside. Until the middle of
20th century thousands of
ilies from London's East End
uld move to the Kentish hop
ds every autumn for working
idays harvesting the crop and
nping in barns. That tradition
faded, because now the
ps are picked by machine.

OAST HOUSE

The cowls turn in the wind, providing air which is controlled by trapdoors below.

Hops are dried above a fan which blows hot air from the underlying radiators.

After drying, the hops are cooled and stored.

A press packs the hops into bags, ready for the breweries.

Cherries *are the sweetest of Kent's fruit: two popular varieties are Stella (top) and Duke.*

Plums *are often served stewed, in pies, or dried into prunes. The Victoria plum (left) is the classic English dessert plum and is eaten raw. The Purple plum is also popular.*

Greengages *are green plums. They have a distinctive taste and can be made into jam.*

Bramley Seedling *is one of the best cooking apples, but it is not sweet enough to eat raw.*

Pears, *such as the William (left), should be eaten at the height of ripeness. The Conference keeps better.*

| AUGUST | SEPTEMBER | OCTOBER | NOVEMBER |

The Kentish cob, *a variety of hazelnut, is undergoing a revival, having been eclipsed by European imports. Unlike many nuts, it is best picked fresh from the tree.*

Dessert apples, *such as Cox's Orange Pippin (right), are some of England's best-loved fruits. The newer Discovery is easier to grow.*

urrants *are mong the most assertively avoured fruit and are sed in desserts and jams.*

Peaches, *grown in China 4,000 years ago, came to ngland in the 19th century.*

Vineyards *are now a familiar sight in Kent (as well as Sussex and Hampshire). Most of the wine produced, such as Lamberhurst, is white.*

Houses of Historical Figures

Visiting the homes of artists, writers, politicians and royalty is a rewarding way of gaining an insight into their private lives. Southeast England, near London, boasts many historic houses that have been preserved as they were when their illustrious occupants were alive. All these houses, from large mansions such as Lord Mountbatten's Broadlands to the more modest dwellings, like Jane Austen's House, contain exhibits relating to the life of the famous people who lived there.

Florence Nightingale
(1820–1910), the "Lady with the Lamp", was a nurse during the Crimean War (see p56). She stayed at Claydon with her sister, Lady Verney.

Nancy Astor *(1879–1964) was the first woman to sit in Parliament in 1919. She lived at Cliveden until her death and made it famous for political hospitality.*

Claydon House, Winslow, nr Milton Keynes

The Duke of Wellington *(1769–1852) was given this house by the nation in 1817, in gratitude for leading the British to victory at Waterloo (see p55).*

THAMES VALLEY
(see pp216–17)

Cliveden House, nr Maidenhead

Stratfield Saye, Basingstoke, nr Windsor

Jane Austen *(1775–1817) wrote three of her novels, including* Emma, *and revised the others at this house where she lived for eight years until shortly before her death (see p172).*

Jane Austen's House, Chawton, nr Winchester

Broadlands, nr Southampton

Lord Mountbatten (1900–79), a British naval commander and statesman, was the last Viceroy of India in 1947. He lived here all his married life and remodelled the original house considerably.

Osborne House, Isle of Wight

Queen Victoria (1819–1901) and her husband, Prince Albert, built Osborne House *(see p168)* in 1855 as a seaside retreat for their family because they never truly warmed to the Royal Pavilion in Brighton.

BLOOMSBURY GROUP

A circle of avant-garde artists, designers and writers, many of them friends as students, began to meet at a house in Bloomsbury, London, in 1904 and soon gained a reputation for their Bohemian lifestyle. When Duncan Grant and Vanessa Bell moved to Charleston in 1916 *(see p180)*, it became a Sussex outpost of the celebrated group. Many of the prominent figures associated with the circle, such as Virginia Woolf, EM Forster, Vita Sackville-West and JM Keynes paid visits here. The Bloomsbury Group was also known for the Omega Workshops, which made innovative ceramics, furniture and textiles.

Vanessa Bell at Charleston by Duncan Grant (1885–1978)

Gainsborough's House, Sudbury, nr Ipswich

EAST ANGLIA
(see pp190–215)

Thomas Gainsborough *(1727–88), one of Britain's greatest painters, was born in this house (see p194). He was best known for his portraits, such as this one of Mr and Mrs Andrews.*

Charles Darwin *(1809–82), who developed the theory that man and apes have a common ancestor, wrote his most famous book,* On the Origin of Species, *at the house where he lived.*

Down House, Downe, nr Sevenoaks

THE DOWNS AND CHANNEL COAST
(see pp164–89)

Bleak House, Broadstairs, nr Margate

Charles Dickens (1812–70), the prolific and popular Victorian novelist *(see p189)*, had many connections with Kent. He took holidays at Bleak House, later named after his famous novel.

Chartwell, Westerham, nr Sevenoaks

Batemans, Burwash, nr Hastings

Winston Churchill (1874–1965), Britain's inspirational Prime Minister in World War II *(see p189)*, lived here for 40 years until his death. He relaxed by rebuilding parts of the house.

Rudyard Kipling *(1865–1936), the poet and novelist, was born in India, but lived here for 34 years until his death. His most famous works include* Kim, *the two* Jungle Books *and the* Just So Stories.

Charleston, Lewes

Vanessa Bell (1879–1961), artist and member of the Bloomsbury Group, lived here until her death in 1961. The 18th-century farmhouse reflects her decorative ideas and is filled with murals, paintings and painted furniture *(see p180)*.

THE DOWNS AND CHANNEL COAST

HAMPSHIRE · SURREY · EAST SUSSEX · WEST SUSSEX · KENT

When settlers, invaders and missionaries came from Europe, the southeast coast was their first landfall. The wooded chalk ridges and lower-lying weald beyond them made an ideal base for settlement and proved to be productive farmland.

The Romans were the first to build major fortifications along the Channel Coast to discourage potential attackers from the European mainland. The remains of many of these can be seen today, and some, like Portchester Castle just outside Portsmouth, were incorporated into more substantial defences in later centuries. There also exists substantial evidence of Roman domestic buildings, such as Fishbourne Palace, in coastal areas and further inland.

The magnificence of cathedrals such as Canterbury and Winchester bear witness to their role as important bases of the medieval church, then nearly as powerful as the state. Many Kent and Sussex ports grew prosperous on trade with the Continent – as did the hundreds of smugglers who operated from them. From Tudor times on, monarchs, noblemen and courtiers acquired estates and built manor houses in the countryside between London and the coast, appreciating the area's moderate climate and proximity to the capital. Many of these survive and are popular attractions for visitors. Today the southeast corner of England is its most prosperous and populous region. Parts of Surrey and Kent, up to 20 miles (32 km) from the capital, are known as the Stockbroker Belt: the area has many large, luxurious villas belonging to wealthy people prominent in business and the professions, attracted by the same virtues that appealed to the Tudor gentry.

The fertile area of Kent has long been known as the Garden of England, and despite the incursion of bricks and mortar, it is still a leading area for growing fruit *(see pp160–1)*, being in a prime position for the metropolitan market nearby.

Aerial view of the medieval and moated Leeds Castle

◁ A lush covering of bluebells in the deciduous woodlands of Kent

Exploring the Downs and Channel Coast

The North and South Downs, separated by the lower-lying Weald are ideal walking country as well as being the site of many stately homes. From Tudor times, wealthy, London-based merchants and courtiers built their country residences in Kent, a day's ride from the capital, and many are open to the public. On the coast are the remains of sturdy

View of Brighton Pier from the promenade

castles put up to deter invaders from across the Channel. Today, though, the seashore is largely devoted to pleasure. Some of Britain's earliest beach resorts were developed along this coast, and sea bathing is said to have been invented in Brighton.

Oast houses at Chiddingstone near Royal Tunbridge Wells

0 kilometres   20

0 miles   10

SEE ALSO

- **Where to Stay** pp560–3
- **Where to Eat** pp616–19

GETTING AROUND

The area is well served, with a network of motorways and A roads from London to the major towns. The A259 is a scenic coast road which offers fine views over the English Channel. Bus and rail transport is also good, with a number of coach companies providing regular tours to the major sites. An InterCity train service runs to all the major towns.

SIGHTS AT A GLANCE

KEY

▬	Motorway
▬	Major road
▬	Secondary road
▬	Minor road
▬	Scenic route
▬	Main railway
▬	Minor railway
▲	Summit

Canterbury Cathedral's spire, dominating the skyline

The Victorian Osborne House, Isle of Wight

Isle of Wight ❶

Isle of Wight. 🏛 *138,000.*
🚢 *from Lymington, Southampton,
Portsmouth.* ℹ *Western Esplanade,
Brading Road, Ryde (01983 813813).*
www.islandbreaks.co.uk

A visit to **Osborne House**,
the favoured seaside retreat
of Queen Victoria and Prince
Albert (*see p160*), is alone
worth the ferry ride from the
mainland. Furnished much
as they left it, the house
provides a marvellous insight
into royal life and is dotted
with family mementoes.

The **Swiss Cottage** was
built for the royal children to
play in. It is now a museum
attached to Osborne House.
Adjacent to it you can see the
bathing machine used by the
queen to preserve her modesty
while taking her to the edge
of the sea (*see p369*).

The other main sight on the
island is **Carisbrooke Castle**,
built in the 11th century. A
walk on its outer wall and the
climb to the top of its keep
provides spectacular views. It
was here that Charles I (*see
pp52–3*) was held prisoner in
1647; an attempt to escape
was foiled when he got stuck
between the bars of a window.

The island is a base for
ocean sailing, especially during
Cowes Week (*see p67*). The
scenic highlight is the
Needles – three towers of
rock jutting out of the sea at
the island's western end. This
is only a short walk from

Alum Bay, famous for its
multi-coloured cliffs and sand.

🏛 **Osborne House**
(EH) East Cowes. **Tel** *01983 200022.*
⏲ *daily (Nov–Mar: Wed–Sun for
only, phone for details).* 🎫 &
limited. 🎬 📷 *(also* 📷 *in Swiss
Cottage Apr–Oct only).* 🎁

🏰 **Carisbrooke Castle**
Newport. **Tel** *01983 522107.*
⏲ *daily.* ● *1 Jan, 24–26 Dec.*
& *limited.* 🎬 📷 *in summer.* 🎁

Beaulieu ❷

Brockenhurst, Hampshire. **Tel** *01590
612345.* 🚆 *Brockenhurst then taxi.*
⏲ *daily.* ● *25 Dec.* 🎫 🎬 & 🎁
by appt. 🖥 **www.beaulieu.co.uk**

Palace House, once the gatehouse of Beaulieu Abbey,
has been the home of Lord
Montagu's family since 1538. It
now contains the finest collection of vintage cars in the
country at the **National Motor
Museum**, along with boats
used in the James Bond films.

There is also an exhibition
of monastic life in the ruined
ancient **abbey**, founded in

1204 by King John (*see p48*)
for Cistercian monks. The
original refectory now serves
as the parish church.

Environs: Just south is the
maritime museum at **Buckler's
Hard**, telling the story of shipbuilding in the 18th century.
The yard employed 4,000
men at its peak but declined
when steel began to be used.
Boat trips are available.

🏛 **Buckler's Hard**
Beaulieu. **Tel** *01590 614645.* ◯
daily. ● *25 Dec.* 🎫 & *ltd.* 📷 🎁

New Forest ❸

Hampshire. 🚆 *Brockenhurst.* 🚌
Lymington then bus. ℹ *main car
park, Lyndhurst (023 8028 2269).*
⏲ *10am–5pm daily.* ● *1 Jan, 24–
26 Dec.* **www.thenewforest.co.uk**

This unique expanse of heath
and woodland is, at 145 sq
miles (375 sq km), the largest
area of unenclosed land in
southern Britain.

Despite its name, this is
one of the few primeval oak
woods in England. It was the
popular hunting ground of
Norman kings, and in 1100
William II was fatally wounded here in a hunting accident.

Today it is enjoyed by up to
seven million visitors a year,
who share it with the New Forest ponies, unique to the area,
and over 1,500 fallow deer.

Southampton ❹

Hampshire. 🏛 *220,000.* ✈ 🚆 🚌
🚌 ℹ *9 Civic Centre Road (023 8083
3333).* **www.visit-southampton.co.uk**

For centuries this has been
a flourishing port. The
Mayflower sailed from here
to America in 1620 with the

A 1909 Rolls-Royce Silver Ghost at Beaulieu's National Motor Museum

Pilgrim Fathers, as did the *Titanic* on its maiden and ultimately tragic voyage in 1912.

The **Maritime Museum** has exhibits about both these ships, along with displays on the huge romantic liners that sailed from the port in the first half of the 20th century.

There is a walk around the remains of the medieval city wall. At the head of the High Street stands the old city gate, **Bargate**, the most elaborate gate to survive in England. It still has its 13th-century drum towers and is decorated with intricate, 17th-century armorial carvings. **God's**

The luxurious liner the *Titanic*, which sank in 1912

House Tower Museum of Archaeology consists of a 13th-century gatehouse and 15th-century gallery and tower, and includes displays from the Roman to medieval periods.

🏛 **Maritime Museum**
Town Quay Rd. **Tel** 023 8022 3941. ◯ 10am–4pm Tue–Sat, 1–4pm Sun. ● 1 Jan, 25, 26 Dec, some public hols. ♿ limited. 📷 📱

🏛 **God's House Tower Museum**
Winkle St. **Tel** 023 8063 5904. ◯ 10am–4pm Tue–Sat, 1–4pm Sun. ♿ foyer & shop only. 📱

Portsmouth ❺

Hampshire. 🏘 *190,000.* ✈ 🚉 🛈 The Hard (023 9282 6722). 📅 Thu–Sat. **www**.visitportsmouth.co.uk

Once a vital naval port, Portsmouth is today a quiet town but fascinating for those interested in English naval history.

Under the banner of **Portsmouth Historic Dockyard**, the city's historic dockyard is the hub of Portsmouth's most important sights. Among these is the hull of the *Mary Rose*, the favourite of Henry VIII (*see p50*), which capsized on its maiden voyage as it left to fight the French in 1545. It was recovered from the sea bed in 1982 along with thousands of 16th-century objects now on display nearby, giving an absorbing insight into life at sea in Tudor times.

Alongside it is **HMS Victory**, the English flagship on which Admiral Nelson was killed at Trafalgar (*see p31*) and now restored to its former glory. You can also visit the **Royal Naval Museum** which deals with naval history from the 16th century to the Falklands War, the 19th-century **HMS Warrior,** and galleries telling the story of Nelson.

Portsmouth's other military memorial is the **D-Day Museum**. This is centred on the *Overlord Embroidery*, a masterpiece of needlework commissioned in 1968 from the Royal School of Needlework, depicting the World War II Allied landing in Normandy in 1944.

The figurehead on the bow of HMS *Victory* at Portsmouth

Portchester Castle, on the north edge of the harbour, was fortified in the third century and is the best example of Roman sea defences in northern Europe. The Normans later used the Roman walls to enclose a castle – only the keep survives – and a church. Henry V used the castle as a garrison before the Battle of Agincourt (*see p49*). In the 18th–19th centuries it was a prisoner-of-war camp.

Among less warlike attractions is the **Charles Dickens Museum** (*see p189*), the house where the author was born in 1812.

The striking **Spinnaker Tower** adds an innovative touch to Portsmouth's skyline. Rising to 170 m (558 ft), the views over the harbour and beyond are quite magnificent.

🏛 **Portsmouth Historic Dockyard**
The Hard. **Tel** 023 9272 8060. ◯ daily (last adm: 4pm). ● 24–26 Dec. 📷 ♿ 🍴 📱

🏛 **D-Day Museum**
Museum Rd. **Tel** 023 9282 7261. ◯ daily. ● 24–26 Dec. ♿ ♿

🏰 **Portchester Castle**
Castle St, Porchester. **Tel** 023 9237 8291. ◯ daily. ● 1 Jan, 24–26 Dec. 📷 📱 📱

🏛 **Charles Dickens Museum**
393 Old Commercial Rd. **Tel** 023 9282 7261. ◯ May–Sep: daily; 7 Feb (Dickens's birthday). 📷 📱 🍴

⚓ **Spinnaker Tower**
Gunwharf Quays. **Tel** 023 9285 7520. ◯ daily. 📷 📱 📱

A wild pony and her foal roaming freely in the New Forest

Winchester ❻

Hampshire. 🏠 36,000. 🚌 🚃
ℹ️ Guildhall, High St (01962
840500). 🗓️ Wed–Sat.
www.visitwinchester.co.uk

Capital of the ancient king–
dom of Wessex, the city of
Winchester was also the headquarters of the Anglo-Saxon
kings until the Norman
Conquest (see p47).

William the Conqueror built
one of his first English castles
here. The only surviving part
of the castle is the **Great Hall**,
erected in 1235 to replace the
original. It is now home
to the legendary Round
Table. The story
behind the table is a
mix of history and
myth. King Arthur (see
p285) had it shaped so
no knight could claim
precedence. It was said
to have been built by the
wizard Merlin but was
actually made in the
13th century.

The **Westgate Museum** is
one of the two surviving 12th-
century gatehouses in the city
wall. The room (once a prison)
above the gate has a 16th-
century painted ceiling. It was
moved here from Winchester
College, England's oldest fee-
paying, or "public" school.
Winchester has been an

**The 13th-century Round Table,
Great Hall, Winchester**

ecclesiastical centre for many
centuries. **Wolvesey Castle**
(built around 1110) was the
home of the **cathedral's**
bishops after the Conquest.
The **Hospital of St Cross** is an
almshouse built in 1446.

Author Izaac Walton (1593–1683) is
depicted in the stained glass Anglers'
Window made in 1914.

**These magnificent
choir-stalls** (c.1308)
are England's
oldest.

The Perpendicular nave is the
highlight of the building.

**Jane Austen's
grave**

**Main
entrance**

The Lady Chapel was
rebuilt by Elizabeth of York
(c.1500) after her son was
baptized in the cathedral.

**Visitors'
centre**

WINCHESTER
CATHEDRAL

The Close. **Tel** 01962 857200.
⬜ daily. 📷 ♿ 🍴 🎁
www.winchester-cathedral.org.uk
The first church was built here in
648 but the present building was begun
in 1097. Originally a Benedictine monastery,
much of the Norman architecture remains despite
continual modifications until the early 16th century.

**The
century**
Tournai marble

Weary strangers may claim the "Wayfarer's Dole" a horn (cup) of ale and bread, given out since medieval times.

🏛 Great Hall & Visitor Centre
Castle Ave. **Tel** 01962 846476.
🕐 daily. ● 25, 26 Dec. ♿

🏛 Westgate Museum
High St. **Tel** 01962 869864.
🕐 Feb, Mar: Tue–Sun; Apr–Oct: Mon–Sun. 📷

🏛 Hospital of St Cross
St Cross Rd. **Tel** 01962 851375.
🕐 Mon–Sat. ● Good Fri, 25 Dec.
📷 ♿ www.stcrosshospital.co.uk

The Library has over 4,000 books. This "B" from Psalm 1 is found in the Winchester Bible, an exquisite work of 12th-century illumination.

The Norman chapter house ceased to be used in 1580. Only the Norman arches survive.

Prior's Hall

The Close originally contained the domestic buildings for the monks of the Priory of St Swithun – the name before it became Winchester Cathedral. Most of the buildings, such as the refectory and cloisters, were destroyed during the Dissolution of the Monasteries (see p50).

Chichester ❼

West Sussex. 🏘 26,000. 🚉 🚌 ℹ
29A South St (01243 775888). 🛒
Wed, Sat. www.visitchichester.org

This wonderfully preserved market town, with an elaborate early 16th-century market cross at its centre, is dominated by its **cathedral**, consecrated in 1108. The exterior is a lovely mix of greenish limestone and Caen stone and its graceful spire, said to be the only English cathedral spire visible from the sea, dominates the town. The cathedral still contains much of interest, including a unique detached bell tower dating from 1436.

There are two carved stone panels in the choir, dating from 1140. Modern works include paintings by Graham Sutherland (1903–80), and a stained-glass window by Marc Chagall (1887–1985).

Environs: Just west at Bosham is the Saxon **Holy Trinity Church**, thought to have been used by King Canute (see p46). Myth has it that this was where Canute failed to stop the incoming tide and so proved to his courtiers that his powers had limits. The church appears in the *Bayeux Tapestry*, held in France, because Harold heard mass here in 1064 before he was shipwrecked off Normandy and then rescued by William the Conqueror (see p47).

The refurbished **Fishbourne Roman Palace** (see p45), between Bosham and Chichester, is the largest Roman villa in Britain. It covers 3 ha (7 acres) and was discovered in 1960 by a workman. Constructed from AD 75, it

Chagall's stained-glass window (1978), Chichester Cathedral

was destroyed by fire in 285. The north wing has some of the finest mosaics in Britain, including one of Cupid.

To the north is the 18th-century **Goodwood House**. Its magnificent art collection features works by Canaletto (1697–1768) and Stubbs (1724–1806). This impressive house, home to the Earl of March, has a racecourse on the Downs.

⛪ Chichester Cathedral
West St. **Tel** 01243 782595. 🕐 daily. 🕐 for Mass. ♿ 📷 📚 🛒

🏛 Fishbourne Roman Palace
Fishbourne. **Tel** 01243 785859. 🕐 Feb–mid-Dec: daily; mid-Dec–Jan (café closed): Sat, Sun. 📷 ♿ 📚 🛒 www.sussexpast.co.uk

🏛 Goodwood House
Goodwood. **Tel** 01243 755048. 📠 01243 755040. 🕐 Apr–Sep: Sun–Mon (pm); Aug: Sun–Thu (pm). ● special events, last-minute closures. Always call ahead. 📷 ♿ 📚 🛒

WILLIAM WALKER

At the beginning of the 20th century, the cathedral's east end seemed certain to collapse unless its foundations were underpinned. But because the water table lies only just below the surface, the work had to be done under water. From 1906 to 1911, Walker, a deep-sea diver, worked six hours a day laying sacks of cement beneath the unsteady walls until the building was safe.

William Walker in his diving suit

The dominating position of Arundel Castle, West Sussex

Arundel Castle ❽

Arundel, West Sussex. **Tel** 01903 882173. ◼ Arundel. ◯ Apr–Oct: 10am–4pm Tue–Sun. ◯ public hols. ◻ ◻ by arrangement. ◻ ◻ ◻ www.arundelcastle.org

Dominating the small riverside town below, this vast, grey hill-top castle, surrounded by castellated walls, was first built by the Normans.

During the 16th century it was acquired by the powerful Dukes of Norfolk, the country's senior Roman Catholic family, whose descendants still live here. They rebuilt it after the original was virtually destroyed by Parliamentarians in 1643 *(see p52)*, and restored it again in the 19th century.

In the castle grounds is the parish church of **St Nicholas**. The small Catholic Fitzalan chapel (c.1380) was built into its east end by the castle's first owners, the Fitzalans, and can only be entered from the grounds.

Petworth House ❾

(NT) Petworth, West Sussex. **Tel** 01798 343929. ◼ Pulborough then bus. **House** ◯ Mar–Nov: Sat–Wed. Call for Christmas opening times. **Park** ◯ daily. ◻ ◻ limited. ◻ ◻ www.nationaltrust.org.uk/petworth

This late 17th-century house was immortalized in a series of famous views by the painter J M W Turner *(see p91)*. Some of his best paintings are on display here and are part of Petworth's outstanding art

collection, which also includes works by Titian (1488–1576), Van Dyck (1599–1641) and Gainsborough *(see p163)*. Also extremely well represented is ancient Roman and Greek sculpture, such as the 4th-century BC *Leconfield Aphrodite*, widely thought to be by Praxiteles.

The Carved Room is decorated with intricately carved wood panels of birds, flowers and musical instruments, by Grinling Gibbons (1648–1721).

The large deer park includes some of the earliest work of Capability Brown *(see p26)*.

The Restoration clock on the Tudor Guildhall, Guildford

Guildford ❿

Surrey. 🏠 63,000. ◼ ◼ ◻ ◻ ◻ 14 Tunsgate (01483 444333). ◻ Fri, Sat. www.visitguildford.com

The county town of Surrey, settled since Saxon times, incorporates the remains of a small refurbished Norman

castle. The high street is lined with Tudor buildings, such as the impressive **Guildhall**, and the huge modern red-brick cathedral, completed in 1954, dominates the town's skyline.

Environs: Guildford stands on the end of the North Downs, a range of chalk hills that are popular for walking *(see p37)*. The area also has two famous beauty spots: **Leith Hill** – the highest point in southeast England – and **Box Hill**. The view from the latter is well worth the short, gentle climb from West Humble.

To the north of Guildford is **Wisley** with 97 hectares (240 acres) of beautiful gardens. To the south of the town is **Clandon Park**, an 18th-century house with a sumptuous interior. Its Marble Hall boasts an intricate Baroque ceiling.

Southwest is Chawton, where **Jane Austen's House** *(see p162)* is located. This red-brick house is where Austen wrote most of her witty novels, such as *Emma*. Celebratory events until July 2010 will mark the 200th anniversary of Austen's arrival at the house.

🏛 **Wisley**
(RHS) Off A3. **Tel** 0845 260 9000. ◯ daily. ◻ ◻ ◻ ◻ ◻

🏛 **Clandon Park**
(NT) West Clandon, Surrey. **Tel** 01483 222482. ◯ Mar–Oct: Tue–Thu, Sun; public hols. ◻ ◻ limited. ◻ ◻

🏛 **Jane Austen's House**
Alton, Hants. **Tel** 01420 83262. ◯ Jan–Feb: Sat & Sun; Mar–Dec: daily. ◯ 25 & 26 Dec. ◻ ◻ limited. ◻ ◻

Hampton Court ⓫

East Molesey, Surrey. 📞 0844 482 7777. 🚆 Hampton Court. 🕐 daily. ⭕ 24–26 Dec. 🅿️ ♿ 📷 🏪 🍴 🚻
www.hrp.org.uk

The powerful chief minister and Archbishop of York to Henry VIII *(see pp50–51)*, Cardinal Wolsey, leased a small manor house in 1514 and transformed it into a magnificent country residence. In 1528, to retain royal favour,

Wolsey gave it to the king. After the royal takeover, Hampton Court was extended twice, first by Henry himself and in the 1690s by William and Mary, who used Christopher Wren *(see p114)* as the architect. From the outside the palace is a harmonious blend of Tudor and English Baroque; inside there is a striking contrast between Wren's Classical royal rooms,

Ceiling decoration, Hampton Court

which include the King's Apartments, and Tudor architecture, such as the Great Hall. Many of the state apartments are decorated with paintings and furnishings from the Royal Collection.
The Baroque gardens, with their radiating avenues of majestic limes, collections of rare plants and formal plant beds, have been painstakingly restored.

The Baroque maze *is one of the garden's most famous features; visitors often become lost in it.*

The Queen's Apartments, including the Presence Chamber and Bedchamber, are arranged around the the north and east sides of Fountain Court.

Fountain Court

The Fountain Garden still has a few of the original yews planted by William and Mary *(see p53).* Only one fountain remains out of the original 13 built.

Great Hall

Main entrance

Anne Boleyn's Gateway is at the entrance to Clock Court.

River Thames

The Mantegna Gallery houses Andrea Mantegna's nine canvasses depicting *The Triumphs of Caesar* (1490).

Long Water

Broad Walk

The Pond Garden, *a sunken water garden, was part of Henry VIII's elaborate designs. The small pond in the middle contains a single-jet fountain.*

The Tudor Chapel Royal *was completed by Henry VIII. But the superb woodwork, including the massive reredos by Grinling Gibbons, all date from a major refurbishment by Queen Anne (c.1711).*

Steyning ⑫

West Sussex. 🚉 5,000 🚌 ⓘ *9 The Causeway, Horsham (01403 211661).*

This lovely little town in the lee of the Downs is packed with timber-framed houses from the Tudor period and earlier, with some built of flint and others in sandstone.

In Saxon times, Steyning was an important port and ship-building centre on the River Adur: King Ethelwulf, father of King Alfred (*see p47*), was buried here in 858; his body was later moved to Winchester. The *Domesday Book (see p48)* records that Steyning had 123 houses, making it one of the largest towns in the south. The 12th-century church is spacious and splendid, evidence of the area's ancient prosperity; the tower, of chequered stone and flint, was added around 1600.

In the 14th century the river silted up and changed course away from the town, putting an end to its days as a port. Later it became an important coaching stop on the south coast road: the **Chequer Inn** recalls this prosperous period, with its unusual 18th-century flint and stone façade.

Environs: The remains of a **Norman castle** can be visited at Bramber, east of Steyning. This small, pretty village also contains the timber-framed **St Mary's House** (1470). It has fine panelled rooms, including the Elizabethan Painted Room, and one of the oldest trees in the country, a *Ginkgo biloba.*
Chanctonbury Ring and **Cissbury Ring**, on the hills west of Steyning, were Iron Age forts and the latter has the remains of a Neolithic flint mine. Worthing is the resort where Oscar Wilde (1854–1900) wrote *The Importance of Being Earnest.*

🏛 **St Mary's House**
Bramber. **Tel** *01903 816205.*
◻ May–Sep: Sun, Thu (pm), public hols. 🅿 ⓘ

Street-by-Street: Brighton ⑬

A stick of Brighton rock

As the nearest south coast resort to London, Brighton is perennially popular, but has always been more refined than its boisterous neighbours further east, such as Margate (*see p183*) and Southend. The spirit of the Prince Regent (*see p179*) lives on, not only in the magnificence of his Royal Pavilion, but in the city's reputation as a venue for adulterous weekends in discreet hotels. Brighton has always attracted actors and artists – Laurence Olivier made his final home here.

Old Ship Hotel
Built in 1559, it was later bought by Nicholas Tettersells, with the money given to him by Charles II as a reward for taking him to France during the Civil War (see p52).

★ Brighton Pier
Built in 1899, this typical late-Victorian pier now caters for today's visitors with amusement arcades.

STAR SIGHTS
★ Brighton Pier
★ Royal Pavilion

KEY
– – – Suggested route

★ Royal Pavilion
The Prince Regent's fantastic Oriental palace helped turn Brighton into a fashionable resort, and is today its principal attraction.

e inset

ALBERT STREET

EET

VISITORS' CHECKLIST

East Sussex. 🚶 249,000. 🚂 Brighton Central. 🚌 Pool Valley. ℹ️ Royal Pavilion shop (0906 7112255). 🛍️ Mon–Sat. 🎭 International Arts Festival: May.

Many new plays are first staged in the charming Theatre Royal, established in 1807, before they move to the West End of London.

Brighton Dome, an Indian-style building opposite the Royal Pavilion and once George IV's stables, is now a major arts venue.

NEW ROAD

NORTH STREET

CHURCH STREET

Art Deco
This 1920s Art Deco bronze lamp is on display at the Brighton Museum and Art Gallery.

OLD STEINE

GRAND PARADE

OLD STEINE

| 0 metres | 100 |
| 0 yards | 100 |

THE LANES

PRINCE ALBERT ST
BLACK LION ST
NILE ST
MEETING HOUSE LA
MEETING HOUSE LA
UNION ST
MEETING HOUSE LA
BRIGHTON PL
BARTHOLOMEWS
REGENT ARCADE
MARKET ST
EAST ST
NORTH ST

MARINE PARADE

EIRA DRIVE

Eastbourne

Sea Life Centre
Built in 1872 as a menagerie, it became an aquarium in 1929. Don't miss the sharks and other British marine life.

THE LANES

The Lanes
Today a maze of antique and independent shops, the Lanes were the original streets of the village of Brighthelmstone.

Brighton: Royal Pavilion

As sea bathing became fashionable in the mid-18th century, Brighton was transformed into England's first seaside resort. Its gaiety soon appealed to the rakish Prince of Wales, who became George IV in 1820. When, in 1785, he secretly married Mrs Fitzherbert, it was here that they conducted their liaison. He moved to a farmhouse near the shore and had it enlarged by Henry Holland *(see p28)*. As his parties grew more lavish, George needed a suitably extravagant setting for them, and in 1815 he employed John Nash *(see p105)* to transform the house into a lavish Oriental palace. Completed in 1823, the exterior has remained largely unaltered. Queen Victoria sold the Pavilion to the town of Brighton in 1850.

Central Dome
Nash adopted what he called the Hindu Style, as in this delicate tracery on one of the imposing turban domes.

★ **Banqueting Room**
Fiery dragons feature in many of the interior schemes. This colourful one dominates the centre of the Banqueting Room's extraordinary ceiling, and has a huge crystal chandelier suspended from it.

The exterior is partly built in Bath stone.

Banqueting Room Gallery

South Galleries

The banqueting table, which seats 24 people, is laid as for a splendid feast.

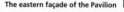

The eastern façade of the Pavilion

Standard Lamps
More dragons, along with dolphins and lotus flowers, figure on the Banqueting Room's eight original standard lamps, made of porcelain, ormolu and gilded wood.

STAR SIGHTS

★ Banqueting Room

★ Great Kitchen

★ **Great Kitchen**
The Prince's epic banquets required a kitchen of huge proportions. The vast ranges and long shelves of gleaming copper pans were used by famous chefs of the day.

◁ **Front façade of George IV's extravagant Royal Pavilion, Brighton**

Saloon
The gilded wall decorations were designed on Indian themes, but the Chinese wallpaper harks back to an earlier decorative scheme. The long couch mimics an Egyptian river boat.

VISITORS' CHECKLIST

Old Steine, Brighton. *Tel* 01273 290900. ☐ Apr–Sep: 9:30am–5:45pm; Oct–Mar: 10am–5:15pm (last adm: 45 mins before closing); daily. ☐ 25, 26 Dec. 🅰 🖊 limited. 🖊 🖊 🖊 🖊
www.royalpavilion.org.uk

Long Gallery
Mandarin figures, which can nod their heads, line the pink and blue walls of this 49 m (162 ft) gallery.

Queen Victoria's Bedroom
This reproduction four-poster is on display in the upper floor apartments that were used by Queen Victoria (see pp56–7).

The Music Room, with its crimson and gold murals, was where a 70-piece orchestra played to the Prince's guests.

The domes are made of cast iron.

Music Room Gallery

Yellow Bow Rooms

PLAN OF THE ROYAL PAVILION

Exit | **Entrance** | **Stairs to upper floor** | **King's Apartments**

Shop

Octagon Hall

eat
tchen

Banqueting Room | **Saloon** | **Long Gallery** | **Music Room** | **Music Room Gallery**

ers
n

Banqueting Room Gallery

Both Holland and Nash made additions and changes to the original farmhouse. The upper floor contains bedrooms, such as the Yellow Bow Rooms, which George's brothers used. The shaded areas represent the artwork above.

PRINCE OF WALES AND MRS FITZHERBERT

The Prince of Wales was only 23 years old when he fell in love with Maria Fitzherbert, a 29-year-old Catholic widow, and secretly married her. They lived in the farmhouse together and were the toast of Brighton society until George's official marriage took place to Caroline of Brunswick in 1795. Mrs Fitzherbert moved into a small house nearby.

Upstairs interior of Anne of Cleves House, Lewes

Lewes ⑭

East Sussex. 🚶 16,000. 🚊
ℹ️ 187 High St (01273 483448).
www.lewes.gov.uk

The ancient county town of
Sussex was a vital strategic site
for the Saxons, because of its
high vantage point looking
out over the coastline. William
the Conqueror built a wooden
castle here in 1067 but this
was soon replaced by a large
stone structure whose remains
can be visited today.

In 1264 it was the site of a
critical battle in which Simon
de Montfort and his barons
defeated Henry III, enabling
them to establish the first
English Parliament.

The Tudor **Anne of Cleves
House** is a museum of local
history, although Anne of
Cleves, Henry VIII's fourth
wife, never actually lived here.

On Guy Fawkes Night (see
p64) lighted tar barrels are
rolled to the river and various
effigies, including of the Pope
and Guy Fawkes, are burned.
This commemorates the town's
17 Protestant martyrs burnt at
the stake by Mary I (see p51).

Environs: Nearby are the 16th-
century **Glynde Place**, a fine
courtyard house, and the charming **Charleston**, home to the
Bloomsbury Group (see p163).

🏛 **Anne of Cleves House**
Lewes. **Tel** 01273 474610. ⏰ Sun–
Thu (Nov–Feb: Sat, Sun; school half
term: daily). 🔵 24–26 Dec. 🈳 🅿️

🏯 **Glynde Place**
Lewes. **Tel** 01273 858224. ⏰ May–
Aug: Wed, Sun, pub hols. 🈳 🖥 🅿️

🏯 **Charleston**
Lewes. **Tel** 01323 811265. ⏰ Apr–
Oct: Wed–Sun, Bank Hol Mon. 🈳
🈳 🖥 🅿️ www.charleston.org.uk

Eastbourne ⑮

East Sussex. 🚶 93,000. 🚊 🚌 ℹ️
Cornfield Rd (0871 663 0031). 🛒
Tue, Sat. www.visiteastbourne.com

This Victorian seaside resort
is a popular place for
retirement, as well as a first-
rate centre for touring the
Downs. The South Downs
Way (see p37) begins at
Beachy Head, the spectacular
163 m (536 ft) chalk cliff just
on the outskirts of the town.
From here it is a bracing walk
to the cliff top at Birling Gap,
with views to the **Seven
Sisters**, the chalk hills that end
abruptly as they meet the sea.

Environs: To the west of Eastbourne is **Seven Sisters Country
Park**, a 285 ha (700 acre) area
of chalk cliffs and Downland
marsh that is open all year.
The **Park Visitor's Centre** contains information on the local
area, history and geology.

Just north is the pretty
village of **Alfriston**, with an
ancient market cross and a
15th-century inn, **The Star**, in
its quaint main street. Near
the church is the 14th-century
Clergy House that, in 1896,
became the first National
Trust property (see p29). To
the east is the huge prehistoric
chalk carving, the **Long Man
of Wilmington** (see p221).

ℹ️ **Park Visitor's Centre**
Exceat, Seaford. **Tel** 01323 870280.
⏰ Apr–Oct: daily; Nov–Mar: Sat,
Sun. 🔵 25 Dec. 🅿️ ♿ 🍴

🏯 **Clergy House**
(NT) Alfriston. **Tel** 01323 870001.
⏰ Sat–Mon, Wed, Thu.
🔵 Jan. 🈳 🅿️

The lighthouse (1902) at the foot of Beachy Head, Eastbourne

The meandering River Cuckmere flowing through the South Downs to the beach at Cuckmere Haven

The Downs ⑯

East Sussex. 🚉 🚌 *Eastbourne.* 🛈 *Cornfield Rd, Eastbourne (0871 663 0031).* **www**.visiteastbourne.com

The North and South Downs are parallel chalk ridges that run from east to west all the way across Kent, Sussex and Surrey, separated by the lower-lying and fertile Kent and Sussex Weald.

The smooth Downland hills are covered with springy turf, kept short by grazing sheep, making an ideal surface for walkers. The hill above the precipitous **Devil's Dyke,** just north of Brighton, offers spectacular views for miles across the Downs. The legend is that the Devil cut the gorge to let in the sea and flood the countryside, but was foiled by divine intervention. The River Cuckmere runs through one of the most picturesque parts of the South Downs.

Located at the highest point of the Downs is **Uppark House**. This neat square building has been meticulously restored to its mid-18th-century appearance after a fire in 1989.

🚪 **Uppark House (NT)** *Petersfield, West Sussex.* **Tel** *01730 825857.* ⬜ *Apr–Oct: Sun–Thu (pm).* 🎫 🚻 🛍 🎁

Hastings ⑰

East Sussex. 🚶 *83,000.* 🚉 🚌 🛈 *Priory Meadow, Queens Square (0845 2741001).* **www**.visithastings.com

This fascinating seaside town was one of the first Cinque Ports *(see p182)* and is still a thriving fishing port. The town is characterized by the unique tall wooden "net shops" on the beach, where for hundreds of years fishermen have stored their nets.

In the 19th century, the area to the west of the Old Town was built up as a seaside resort, which left the narrow, characterful streets of the old

The wooden net shops, on Hastings' shingle beach

fishermen's quarter intact. There are two cliff railways and smugglers' caves displaying where contraband used to be stored *(see p280)*.

Environs: Seven miles (11 km) from Hastings is Battle. The centre square of this small town is dominated by the gatehouse of **Battle Abbey**. William the Conqueror built this on the site of his great victory, reputedly placing the high altar where Harold fell, But the abbey was destroyed in the Dissolution *(see p50)*. There is an evocative walk around the actual battlefield.

⛪ **Battle Abbey (EH)** *High St, Battle.* **Tel** *01424 775705.* ⬜ *daily: Easter–Sep: 10am–6pm; Oct–Easter: 10am–4pm.* ⬛ *1 Jan, 24–26 Dec.* 🎫 🚻 🎁

BATTLE OF HASTINGS

In 1066, William the Conqueror's *(see p47)* invading army from Normandy landed on the south coast, aiming to take Winchester and London. Hearing that King Harold and his army were camped just inland from Hastings, William confronted them. He won the battle after Harold was mortally wounded by an arrow in his eye. This last successful invasion of England is depicted on the *Bayeux Tapestry* in Normandy, France.

King Harold's death, *Bayeux Tapestry*

The fairy-tale 14th-century Bodiam Castle surrounded by its moat

Bodiam Castle ⑱

(NT) Nr Robertsbridge, E Sussex. *Tel 01580 830196.* ⚞ *Robertsbridge then taxi.* ◯ *mid-Feb–Oct: daily; Nov–23 Dec: Wed–Sun; 27 Dec–mid-Feb: Sat, Sun.* ● *24–26 Dec.* ⚑ ♿ ltd. ⬛ ⬛

Surrounded by its wide, glistening moat, this late 14th-century castle is one of the most romantic in England.

It was previously thought to have been built as a defence against French invasion, but is now believed to have been intended as a home for a Sussex knight. The castle saw action during the Civil War *(see p52)*, when it was damaged in an assault by Parliamentary soldiers. They removed the roof to reduce its use as a base for Charles I's troops.

It has been uninhabited since, but its grey stone has proved indestructible. With the exception of the roof, it was restored in 1919 by Lord Curzon who gave it to the nation.

Environs: To the east is **Great Dixter**, a 15th-century manor house restored by Sir Edwin Lutyens in 1910. The late Christopher Lloyd created a magnificent garden with a blend of terraces and borders, and a great nursery, too.

⛩ **Great Dixter**
Northiam, Rye. *Tel 01797 252878.* ◯ *Apr–Oct: 2–5:30pm Tue–Sun & public hols.* ⚑ ⬛
www.greatdixter.co.uk

Rye ⑲

See pp184–5.

Romney Marsh ⑳

Kent. ⚞ *Ashford.* 🚌 *Ashford, Hythe.* ℹ *Dymchurch Rd, New Romney (01797 369487).* ◯ *Feb–Dec.*

Until Roman times Romney Marsh and its southern neighbour Walland Marsh were entirely covered by the sea at high tide. The Romans drained the Romney section, and Walland Marsh was gradually reclaimed during the Middle Ages. Together they formed a large area of fertile land, particularly suitable for the bulky Romney Marsh sheep bred for the quality and quantity of their wool.

Dungeness, a desolate and lonely spot at the southeastern tip of the area, is dominated by a lighthouse and two nuclear power stations that

COASTAL DEFENCE AND THE CINQUE PORTS

Before the Norman Conquest *(see pp46–7),* national government was weak and, with threats from Europe, it was important for Saxon kings to keep on good terms with the Channel ports. So, in return for keeping the royal fleet supplied with ships and men, five ports – Hastings, Romney, Hythe, Sandwich and Dover – were granted the right to levy taxes; others were added later. "Cinque" came from the old French word for five. The privileges were revoked during the 17th century. In 1803, in response to the growing threat from France, 74 fixed defences were built along the coast. Only 24 of these Martello towers still exist.

The cliff-top position of Dover Castle

A Martello tower, built as part of the Channel's defences

break up the skyline. It is also the southern terminus of the popular **Romney, Hythe and Dymchurch Light Railway** which was opened in 1927. During the summer this takes passengers 14 miles (23 km) up the coast to Hythe on trains a third the conventional size.

The northern edge of the marsh is crossed by the Royal Military Canal, built to serve both as a defence and supply line in 1804, when it was feared Napoleon was planning an invasion *(see p55)*.

Dover ㉑

Kent. 🚶 30,000. 🚂 🚌 ⛴
ℹ️ Old Town Gaol, Biggin St
(01304 205108). 📮 Sat.
www.whitecliffscountry.org.uk

Its proximity to the European mainland makes Dover, with its neighbour Folkestone (the terminal for the Channel Tunnel, *see p680*), the leading port for cross-Channel travel. Its famous white cliffs exert a strong pull on returning travellers.

Dover's strategic position and large natural harbour mean the town has always had an important role to play in the nation's defences.

Built on the original site of an ancient Saxon fortification, **Dover Castle**, superbly positioned on top of the high cliffs, has helped defend the town from 1198, when Henry II first built the keep, right up to World War II, when it was used as the command post for the Dunkirk evacuation. Exhibits in the castle and in the labyrinth of tunnels beneath made by prisoners in the Napoleonic Wars *(see p55)* cover all these periods.

Environs: One of the most significant sites in England's early history is the ruin of **Richborough Roman Fort**. Now a large grassy site two miles (3 km) inland, this was where, in AD 43, Claudius's Roman invaders *(see p44)* made their first landing. For hundreds of years afterwards, Rutupiae, as it was known, was one of the most important ports of entry and military bases in the country.

♟ **Dover Castle**
(EH) Castle Hill. *Tel* 01304 211067. 🕐 daily (Nov–Jan: Thu–Mon). 🔴 1 Jan, 24–26 Dec. 💷 🎫 of the tunnels, by appt. 🅿 ♿ 🛍

🏛 **Richborough Roman Fort**
(EH) Richborough. *Tel* 01304 612 013. 🕐 Apr–Sep: daily. 💷 ♿ 🛍

Margate ㉒

Kent. 🚶 40,000. 🚂 🚌
ℹ️ 12–13 The Parade (0870 2646111). **www**.visitthanet.co.uk

A boisterous seaside resort on the Isle of Thanet, Margate has been a popular destination for a long time. Nowdays **The Turner Centre** is the big draw, both architecturally and for its varied contemporary exhibitons.

Environs: Just south is a 19th-century gentleman's residence, **Quex House**, which has two unusual towers in its grounds. The adjoining museum has a fine collection of African and Oriental art, as well as unique dioramas of tropical wildlife. To the west is a Saxon church, built within the remains of the

Visitors relaxing on Margate's popular sandy beach

bleak Roman coastal fort of **Reculver**. Dramatic twin towers, known as the Two Sisters, were added to the church in the 12th century. The church now stands at the centre of a very pleasant, if rather windy, 37 ha (91 acre) camp site.

🏛 **The Turner Centre**
17–18 The Parade. *Tel* 01843 294 208. 🕐 phone for details. 💷 🛍
🌐 **www**.turnercontemporary.org

♜ **Quex House**
Birchington. *Tel* 01843 842168. 🕐 Easter–Oct: Sun–Thu. **House** 🕐 pm only. 💷 ♿ 🎫 for groups. 🍴 🛍

🏛 **Reculver Fort**
(EH) Reculver. *Tel* 01227 361911 (Herne Bay Tourist Information). 🕐 daily (exterior only).

A drainage dyke running through the fertile plains of Romney Marsh

Street-by-Street: Rye ⑲

The Mermaid
Inn sign

This ancient and charming fortified town was added to the original Cinque ports *(see p182)* in the 12th–13th century. A huge storm in 1287 diverted the River Rother so that it met the sea at Rye, and for more than 300 years it was one of the most important Channel ports. However, in the 16th century the harbour began to silt up and the town is now 2 miles (3 km) inland. Rye was frequently attacked by the French, culminating in 1377 when it was burnt to the ground.

★ **Mermaid Street**
This delightful cobbled street, its huddled houses jutting out at unlikely angles, has hardly altered since it was rebuilt in the 14th century.

The Mint
Site of 12th-century Mint in the time of King Stephen.

The Mermaid Inn, rebuilt c.1420, is Rye's largest medieval building. In the 1750s it was the headquarters of notorious and bloodthirsty smugglers called the Hawkhurst gang.

View over the River Tillingham

Strand Quay
The brick and timber warehouses survive from the prosperous days when Rye was a thriving port.

STAR SIGHTS

★ Mermaid Street

★ Ypres Tower

Lamb House
This fine Georgian house was built in 1722. George I stayed here when stranded in a storm, and author Henry James (1843–1916) lived here.

St Mary's Church
The turret clock (1561) is claimed to be the oldest working clock in the country.

↑ Hastings and railway station

Land Gate
Built in the 14th century this is the only survivor of the old fortified town's four gates.

CINQUE PORT STREET

TOWER STREET

HIGH STREET

CONDUIT HILL

HILDERS CLIFF

LION STREET

MARKET STREET

EAST STREET

The 16th-century Flushing Inn

This cistern was built in 1735; horse-drawn machinery was used to raise water to the highest part of the town.

Gun Garden, Ypres Tower

★ Ypres Tower
Built as a castle in 1250, it was turned into a house in 1430. It is now used as the museum.

KEY

- - - Suggested route

| 0 metres | 50 |
| 0 yards | 50 |

Environs: Just 2 miles (3 km) to the south of Rye is the small town of **Winchelsea**. At the behest of Edward I, it was moved to its present position in 1288, when most of the old town on lower land to the southeast, was drowned by the same storm that diverted the River Rother in 1287.

Winchelsea is probably Britain's first coherently planned medieval town. Although not all of it was built as originally planned, its rectangular grid survives today, as does the **Church of St Thomas Becket** (begun c.1300) at its centre. Several raids during the 14th century by the French damaged the church and burned down scores of houses. The church has three tombs, and there are also two well-preserved medieval tombs in the chantry. The three windows (1928–33) in the Lady Chapel were designed by Douglas Strachan as a memorial to those who died in World War I.

Just beyond the edges of present-day Winchelsea are the remains of three of the original gates – showing just how big a town was first envisaged. The beach below is one of the finest on the southeast coast.

Camber Sands, to the east of the mouth of the Rother, is another excellent beach. Once used by fishermen, it is now popular with swimmers and edged with seaside bungalows and a bustling holiday camp. Camber Sands is also a favourite spot in the UK for kite- and windsurfing.

The ruins of **Camber Castle** are west of the sands, near Brede Lock, Rye. This was one of the forts built along this coast by Henry VIII when he feared an attack by the French. When the castle was built it was on the edge of the sea but it was abandoned in 1642 when it became stranded inland as the river silted up.

🏰 **Camber Castle**
(EH) Camber, Rye.
Tel 01797 223862. ☐ Jul–Sep:
Sat, Sun pm for 🚌 only.

Canterbury Cathedral

To match Canterbury's growing ecclesiastical rank as a major centre of Christianity, the first Norman archbishop, Lanfranc, ordered a new cathedral to be built on the ruins of the Anglo-Saxon cathedral in 1070. It was enlarged and rebuilt many times and as a result embraces examples of all styles of medieval architecture. The most poignant moment in its history came in 1170 when Thomas Becket was murdered here *(see p48)*. Four years after his death a fire devastated the cathedral and the Trinity Chapel was built to house Becket's remains. The shrine quickly became an important religious site and until the Dissolution *(see p50)* the cathedral was one of Christendom's chief places of pilgrimage.

Jesus on Christ Church Gate, Canterbury Cathedral

Canterbury ㉓

Kent. 🚉 *50,000.* 🚆 🚌 🛈 *Sun St, Buttermarket (01227 378100).* 🛒 *Wed, Fri.* www.canterbury.co.uk

Its position on the London to Dover route meant Canterbury was an important Roman town even before the arrival of St Augustine in 597, sent by the pope to convert the Anglo-Saxons to Christianity. The town rose in importance, soon becoming the centre of the Christian Church in England.

With the building of the **cathedral** and the martyrdom of Thomas Becket *(see p48)*, Canterbury's future as a religious centre was assured.

Adjacent to the ruins of **St Augustine's Abbey**, destroyed in the Dissolution *(see p50)*, is **St Martin's Church**, the oldest in England. This was where St Augustine first worshipped and it has impressive Norman and Saxon work.

West Gate Museum, with its round towers, is an imposing medieval gatehouse. It was built in 1381 and contains a display of arms and armoury.

The Poor Priests' Hospital, founded in the 12th century, now houses the **Museum of Canterbury**.

🏛 **West Gate Museum**
St Peter's St. **Tel** 01227 789576. ◻ Mon–Sat. ● 1 Jan, Good Fri, 24–28 Dec. 🖼 🔲

🏛 **Museum of Canterbury**
Stour St. **Tel** 01227 475202. ◻ Jun–Sep: daily; Oct–May: Mon–Sat. 🖼 🔲 www.canterbury-museums.co.uk

The nave at 60 m (188 ft) makes Canterbury one of the longest medieval churches.

The South West Porch (1426) may have been built to commemorate the victory at Agincourt *(see p49)*.

Main entrance

★ **Medieval Stained Glass**
This depiction of the 1,000-year-old Methuselah is a detail from the southwest transept window.

GEOFFREY CHAUCER

Considered to be the first great English poet, Geoffrey Chaucer (c.1345–1400), a customs official by profession, wrote a rumbustious and witty account of a group of pilgrims travelling from London to Becket's shrine in 1387 in the *Canterbury Tales*. The pilgrims represent a cross-section of 14th-century English society and the tales remain one of the greatest and most entertaining works of early English literature.

Wife of Bath, *Canterbury Tales*

Bell Harry Tower

The central tower, dominating the skyline, was built in 1498 to house a bell donated by Henry of Eastry 100 years before. The fan vaulting is a superb example of the late Perpendicular style.

VISITORS' CHECKLIST

11 The Precincts, Canterbury. **Tel** 01227 762862. ☐ 9am–4:30pm Mon–Sat (Jun–Sep: to 5pm; also 12:30–2pm Sun). Contact advised. ☐ for services & concerts; Good Friday, 24 & 25 Dec. ☐ ☐ 8am daily; 5:30pm Mon–Fri; 3:15pm Sat, Sun; 11am Sun. ☐ ☐
www.canterbury-cathedral.org

★ Site of the Shrine of St Thomas Becket

This Victorian illustration (anon) portrays Becket's canonization. The Trinity Chapel was built to house his tomb which stood here until it was destroyed in 1538. The spot is now marked by a lighted candle.

Great Cloister

Chapter House

The Great South Window has four stained glass panels (1958) by Erwin Bossanyi.

★ Black Prince's Tomb

This copper effigy is on the tomb of Edward III's son, who died in 1376.

STAR FEATURES

★ Medieval Stained Glass

★ Site of the Shrine of St Thomas Becket

★ Black Prince's Tomb

St Augustine's Chair

The quire (choir), completed in 1184, is one of the longest in England.

Trinity Chapel

The circular Corona Chapel

The keep of Rochester Castle, dominating Rochester and the Medway Valley

Leeds Castle ㉔

Maidstone, Kent. **Tel** 01622 765400.
🚃 Bearsted then bus. ⬜ 10am–5pm
daily. ⬤ for concerts & 25 Dec. 🎫 ♿
🍴 🅿 🛍 www.leeds-castle.com

Surrounded by a lake that reflects the warm buff stone of its crenellated turrets, Leeds is often considered to be the most beautiful castle in England. Begun in the early 12th century, it has been continuously inhabited and its present appearance is a result of centuries of rebuilding and extensions, most recently in the 1930s. Leeds has royal connections going back to 1278, when it was given to Edward I by a courtier seeking favour.

Henry VIII loved the castle and visited it often, escaping from the plague in London. It contains a life-sized bust of Henry from the late 16th century. Leeds passed out of royal ownership when Edward VI gave it to Sir Anthony St Leger in 1552 as a reward for helping to pacify the Irish.

Rochester ㉕

Kent. 🏠 145,000. 🚃 🚉
ℹ 95 High Street (01634 843666).

Clustered at the mouth of the River Medway are the towns of Rochester, Chatham and Gillingham, all rich in naval history, but none more so than Rochester, which

occupied a strategic site on the London to Dover road.

England's tallest Norman keep is at **Rochester Castle**, worth climbing for the views over the Medway. The town's medieval history is still visible, with the original city walls – which followed the lines of the Roman fortifications – on view in the High Street, and some well-preserved wall paintings in the **cathedral**, built in 1088.

Environs: In Chatham, the **Historic Dockyard** is now a museum of shipbuilding and nautical crafts. **Fort Amherst** nearby was built in 1756 to protect the dockyard and river entrance from attack, and has 1,800 m (5,570 ft) of tunnels to explore that were hewn by Napoleonic prisoners of war.

♆ Rochester Castle
Castle Hill. **Tel** 01634 402276. ⬜
10am–4pm (5pm Apr–Sep) daily (last adm: 45 mins before close). ⬤ 1 Jan, 24–26 Dec. 🎫 ♿ grounds only. 🅿

A gladiator, Knole

🏛 Historic Dockyard
Dock Rd, Chatham. **Tel** 01634
823807. ⬜ mid-Feb–Oct: daily;
Nov: Sat, Sun. 🎫 ♿ 🍴 🛍 🅿

♄ Fort Amherst
Dock Rd, Chatham. **Tel** 01634
847747. ⬜ call for details. 🎫 🅿
www.fortamherst.com

Knole ㉖

(NT) Sevenoaks, Kent. **Tel** 01732
450608. 🚃 Sevenoaks then taxi.
House ⬜ Mar–Jul: Wed–Sun (pm);
Aug: Tue–Sun; Sep–Oct: Wed–Sun
(pm), Good Fri & pub hols. **Park** ⬜
daily. 🎫 ♿ ltd. 🅿 by appt. 🛍 🅿

This huge Tudor mansion was built in the late 15th century, and was seized by Henry VIII from the Archbishop of Canterbury at the Dissolution (see p50). In 1566 Queen Elizabeth I gave it to her cousin Thomas Sackville. His descendants have lived here ever since, including the writer Vita Sackville-West, (1892–1962). The house is well known for its 17th-century furniture, such as the elaborate bed made for James II. The 405-ha (1,000-acre) park has deer and lovely walks.

Environs: A small manor house, **Ightham Mote**, east of Knole, is one of the finest examples of English medieval architecture. Its 14th-century timber-and-stone building encloses a central court and is encircled by a moat.

At **Sissinghurst Castle Garden** are gardens created by Vita Sackville-West and her husband Harold Nicolson in the 1930s.

Ightham Mote
(NT) Ivy Hatch, Sevenoaks.
Tel 01732 810378. ☐ mid-Mar–Oct: Wed–Fri, Sun, Mon & public hols. ☐ ☐ ☐ ☐

Sissinghurst Castle Garden
(NT) Cranbrook. **Tel** 01580 710701.
☐ mid-Mar–Oct: 11am–6:30pm Fri–Tue. ☐ ☐ limited. ☐ ☐ ☐

Hever Castle ㉗

Edenbridge, Kent. **Tel** 01732 865224.
☒ Edenbridge Town. ☐ Apr–Oct: daily (Thu–Sun Nov, Dec, Mar). **Gardens** 11am–6pm; **Castle** noon–6pm. ☐ ☐ limited. ☐ ☐ groups by arrangement. ☐ www.hever-castle.co.uk

This small, moated castle is famous as the 16th-century home of Anne Boleyn, the

CHARLES DICKENS

Charles Dickens (1812–70), a popular writer in his own time, is still widely read today. He was born in Portsmouth but moved to Chatham aged five. As an adult, Dickens lived in London but kept up his Kent connections, taking holidays in Broadstairs, just south of Margate – where he wrote *David Copperfield* – and spending his last years at Gad's Hill, near Rochester. The town celebrates the famous connection with an annual Dickens festival.

The façade of Chartwell, Winston Churchill's home

doomed wife of Henry VIII, executed for adultery. She lived here as a young woman and the king often visited her while staying at Leeds Castle. In 1903 Hever was bought by William Waldorf Astor, who undertook a restoration programme, building a Neo-Tudor village alongside it to accommodate guests and servants. The moat and gatehouse date from around 1270.

Environs: To the northwest of Hever is **Chartwell**, the family home of Sir Winston Churchill (*see p59*). It remains furnished as it was when he lived here. Some 140 of his paintings are on display.

Chartwell
(NT) Westerham, Kent. ☐ 01732 868381. ☐ mid-Mar–Jun, Sep–Nov: 11am–5pm Wed–Sun & public hols; Jul–Aug: 11am–5pm Tue–Sun & public hols. ☐ ☐ limited. ☐ ☐

Royal Tunbridge Wells ㉘

Kent. ☒ 55,000. ☒ ☐
☐ Old Fish Market, The Pantiles (01892 515 675). ☒ Sat.
www.visittunbridgewells.com

Helped by royal patronage, the town became a popular spa in the 17th and 18th centuries after mineral springs were discovered in 1606. The Pantiles – the colonnaded and paved promenade – was laid out in the 1700s.

Environs: Nearby is a superb manor house, **Penshurst Place**. Built in the 1340s, it has an 18-m- (60-ft-) high Great Hall.

Penshurst Place
Tonbridge, Kent. **Tel** 01892 870307.
☐ Apr–Oct: daily; Mar: Sat, Sun: **House** noon–4pm; **Gardens** 10:30am–6pm; **Toy Museum** noon–5pm. ☐ ☐ limited. ☐ ☐ ☐

An early 18th-century astrolabe to measure the stars, Hever Castle garden

EAST ANGLIA

NORFOLK · SUFFOLK · ESSEX · CAMBRIDGESHIRE

The bulge of land between the Thames Estuary and the Wash, flat but far from featureless, sits aside from the main north – south axis through Britain, and for that reason it has succeeded in maintaining and preserving its distinctive architecture, traditions and rural character in both cities and countryside.

East Anglia's name derives from the Angles, the people from northern Germany who settled here during the 5th and 6th centuries. East Anglians have long been a breed of plain-spoken and independent people. Two prominent East Anglians – Queen Boadicea in the 1st century and Oliver Cromwell in the 17th century – were famous for their stubbornness and their refusal to bow to constituted authority. During the Civil War, East Anglia was Cromwell's most reliable source of support. The hardy people who made a difficult living hunting and fishing in the swampy fens, which were drained in the 17th century, were called the Fen Tigers. After draining, the peaty soil proved ideal for arable farming, and today East Anglia grows about a third of Britain's vegetables. The rotation of crops, heralding Britain's agricultural revolution, was perfected in Norfolk in the 18th century. Many of the region's towns and cities grew prosperous on the agricultural wealth, including Norwich. The sea also plays a prominent role in East Anglian life. Coastal towns and villages support the many fishermen who use the North Sea, rich in herring in former days but now known mainly for flat fish.

In modern times, the area has become a centre of recreational sailing, both off the coast and on the inland waterway system known as the Norfolk Broads. East Anglia is also home to one of Britain's top universities: Cambridge.

Lavender fields in full bloom in July, Heacham, Norfolk

◁ **Cley windmill overlooking the sea marshes on the north Norfolk coast**

Exploring East Anglia

As you move away from London, you soon reach the countryside immortalized by the painter Constable *(see p204)*, scattered with churches, windmills and medieval agricultural barns. Nature lovers will find it fruitful territory, especially North Norfolk with its bird reserves and seal colonies. Boating enthusiasts, too, are well catered for in this, Britain's driest and sunniest region. The local architecture ranges from a mix of medieval to modern. The distinctive pink-washed cottages in Suffolk, flint cottages in Norfolk and thatched roofs everywhere, are also much in evidence.

Punting on the River Cam in Cambridge

For additional map symbols *see back flap*

KEY

═══	Motorway
═══	Major road
───	Secondary road
⋯⋯	Minor road
▬▬	Scenic route
┄┄	Main railway
∿∿	Minor railway

GETTING AROUND

The region's more isolated sights can be very difficult to reach by public transport and, for a few people, car rental may be a cheaper and more efficient method of travelling around. The M11 motorway runs from London to Cambridge. The coast road from Aldeburgh to King's Lynn takes you through some of the best countryside in the area. There are frequent mainline trains to Norwich, Ipswich and Cambridge although the local trains are more sporadic. There are international and domestic airports at Stansted (*see p682*) and Norwich.

SEE ALSO

Beach huts on Wells-next-the-Sea beach, north Norfolk

SIGHTS AT A GLANCE

0 kilometres 10

0 miles 10

Peterborough ❶

Cambridgeshire. 👥 *156,000.*
🚆 🚌 ℹ️ *3–5 Minster Precinct
(01733 452336).* 🏪 *Tue–Sat.*
www.visitpeterborough.com

Peterborough's coat of arms with a Latin inscription: Upon this Rock

Although one of the oldest settlements in Britain, Peterborough was designated a New Town in 1967, and is now a mixture of ancient and modern.

The city centre is dominated by the 12th-century **St Peter's Cathedral** which gave the city its name. The interior of this classic Norman building, with its vast yet simple nave, was badly damaged by Cromwell's troops (*see p52*), but its unique painted wooden ceiling (1220) has survived intact. Catherine of Aragon, the first wife of

Henry VIII, is buried here, although Cromwell's troops also destroyed her tomb.

Environs: The oldest wheel in Britain (1,300 BC) was found preserved in peat at **Flag Fen Bronze Age Centre**. The site provides a fascinating glimpse into prehistory.

🎵 **Flag Fen Bronze Age Centre**
The Droveway, Northey Rd.
Tel 0844 414 0646. 🕐 *Mar–Oct:
Tue–Sun, public hols.* 🚫 ♿ 📷 🎁
www.flagfen.com

Grimes Graves ❸

(EH) Lynford, Norfolk. **Tel** 01842
810656. 🚆 *Brandon then taxi.*
🕐 *Apr–Sep: daily; Oct, Mar:
Thu–Mon.* 🚫 🎁 ♿

One of the most important Neolithic sites in England, this was once an extensive complex of flint mines – 433 shafts have been located – dating from before 2000 BC.

Using antlers as pickaxes, Stone Age miners hacked through the soft chalk to extract the hard flint below to make weapons and tools. The flint may have been transported long distances around England on the prehistoric network of paths. You can descend 9 m (30 ft) by ladder into one of the shafts and see

Ely ❷

Cambridgeshire. 👥 *14,000.* 🚆
ℹ️ *29 St Mary's St (01353 662062).*
🔵 *Mon.* 🏪 *Thu (general), Sat
(craft & antiques).* **http://**visitely.
eastcambs.gov.uk

Built on a chalk hill, this small city is thought to be named after the eels in the nearby River Ouse. The hill was once an inaccessible island in the then marshy and treacherous Fens (*see p196*). It was also the last stronghold of Anglo-Saxon resistance, under Hereward the Wake (*see p48*), who hid in the cathedral until the Normans crossed the Fens in 1071.

Today this small prosperous city, totally dominated by the huge **cathedral**, is the market centre for the rich agricultural area surrounding it.

The lantern's glass windows admit light into the dome.

This painted wooden angel *is one of hundreds of bosses that were carved all over the south and north transepts in the 13th and 14th centuries.*

Stained glass museum

The tomb is that of Alan de Walsingham, designer of the unique Octagon.

The Octagon, *made of wood, was built in 1322 when the Norman tower collapsed. Its roof, the lantern, took an extra 24 years to build and weighs 200 tonnes.*

Octagon

Area of cutaway

ELY CATHEDRAL
Ely. **Tel** 01353 667735. 🕐 *daily.*
🔵 *special events.* 🚫 ♿ 📷 🍴 🛒 🎁
Begun in 1083, the cathedral took 268 years to complete. It survived the Dissolution (*see p50*) but was closed for 17 years by Cromwell (*see p52*) who lived in Ely for a time.

the galleries where the flint was mined. During excavations, unusual chalk models of a fertility goddess *(see p43)* and a phallus were discovered.

Environs: Nearby, at the centre of the once fertile plain known as the Breckland, is the small market town of **Thetford**.

Once a prosperous trading town, its fortunes dipped in the 16th century, when its priory was destroyed *(see p50)* and the surrounding land deteriorated due to excessive sheep grazing. The area was later planted with pine trees. A mound in the city marks the site of a pre-Norman castle.

The revolutionary writer and philosopher Tom Paine, author of *The Rights of Man,* was born here in 1737.

Oxburgh Hall surrounded by its medieval moat

The huge cathedral *dominates the flat Fens countryside surrounding Ely.*

Painted ceiling, 19th century

The Prior's Door (c.1150)

The south aisle has 12 classic Norman arches at its foot, with pointed Early English windows above.

Swaffham 4

Norfolk. 6,700. Market Place (01760 722255).
Apr–mid-Oct. Sat.
www.aroundswaffham.co.uk

The best-preserved Georgian town in East Anglia and a fashionable resort during the Regency period, Swaffham is at its liveliest on Saturdays when a market is held in the square around the market cross of 1783. In the centre of the town is the 15th-century **Church of St Peter and St Paul**, with a small spire added in the 19th century. It has a magnificent Tudor north aisle, said to have been paid for by John Chapman, the Pedlar of Swaffham. He is depicted on the two-sided town sign near the market place. Myth has it that he went to London and met a stranger who told him of hidden treasure at Swaffham. He returned, dug it up and used it to embellish the church, where he is shown in a window.

Environs: Castle Acre, north of the town, has the remains of a massive Cluniac **priory**. Founded in 1090, its stunning Norman front still stands.

A short drive south is **Oxburgh Hall and Garden**, built by Sir Edmund Bedingfeld in 1482. The hall, entered through a huge 24 m (80 ft) fortified gatehouse, displays the velvet Oxburgh Hangings, embroidered by Mary, Queen of Scots *(see p511).*

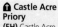

Swaffham town sign

Castle Acre Priory
(EH) Castle Acre.
Tel 01760 755394.
daily (Oct–Mar: Thu–Mon.
1 Jan, 24–26 Dec. ltd.

Oxburgh Hall & Garden
(NT) Oxborough. **Tel** 01366 328258. Mar–Oct: Sat–Wed (Aug: daily). **Garden** Dec: Sat, Sun. ltd.

BOADICEA AND THE ICENI

When the Romans invaded Britain, the Iceni, the main tribe in East Anglia, joined forces with them to defeat the Catuvellauni, a rival tribe. But the Romans then turned on the Iceni, torturing Queen Boadicea (or Boudicca). In AD 61, she led a revolt against Roman rule: her followers burned down London, Colchester and St Albans. The rebellion was put down and the queen took poison rather than submit. At Cockley Cley, near Swaffham, an Iceni camp has been excavated.

Illustration of Queen Boadicea leading her Iceni followers

A windmill on Wicken Fen

The Fens ❺

Cambridgeshire/Norfolk. ⭘ Ely.
🛈 29 St Mary's St, Ely (01353
662062). ⭘ Mon.
www.eastcambs.gov.uk/tourism

This is the open, flat, fertile
expanse that lies between
Lincoln, Cambridge, Bedford
and King's Lynn. Up until
the 17th century it was a
swamp, and settlement was
possible only on "islands",
such as Ely (*see p194*).

Through the 17th century,
speculators, recognizing the
value of the peaty soil for farmland, brought in Dutch experts
to drain the fens. However,
as the peat dried, it
contracted, and the
fens have slowly
been getting lower.
Powerful electric
pumps now keep
it drained.

Nine miles (14 km)
from Ely is Wicken
Fen, 243 ha (600
acres) of undrained
fen providing a
habitat for water
life, wildfowl and
wild flowers.

King's Lynn ❻

Norfolk. 🏠 42,000. ⭘ ⭘
🛈 Custom House, Purfleet Quay
(01553 763044). ⭘ Tue, Fri, Sat.
www.west-norfolk.gov.uk

Formerly Bishop's Lynn, its
name was changed at the
Reformation (*see p50*) to
reflect the changing political
reality. In the Middle Ages
it was one of
England's most
prosperous ports,
shipping grain and
wool from the sur-
rounding countryside
to Europe. There are
still a few warehouses
and merchants'
houses by the River
Ouse surviving
from this period.
At the north end of
the town is **True's**

**Trinity Guildhall,
King's Lynn**

North Norfolk Coastal Tour ❽

This tour takes you through some of the most
beautiful areas of East Anglia; nearly all of the
north Norfolk coast has been designated an Area of
Outstanding Natural Beauty. The sea has dictated the
character of the area. With continuing deposits of silt,
once busy ports are now far inland and the shingle
and sand banks that have been built up are home
to a huge variety of wildlife. Do bear in mind when
planning your journey that this popular route can
get congested during summer.

TIPS FOR DRIVERS

Tour length: 28 miles (45 km)
Stopping-off points: Holkham
Hall makes a pleasant stop for
a picnic lunch. There are some
good pubs in Wells-next-the-Se
(See also pp684–5.)

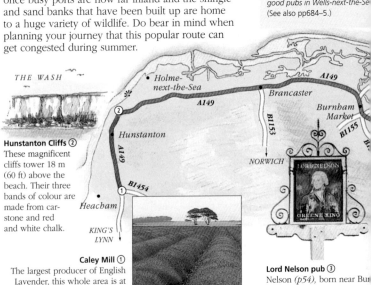

THE WASH

Hunstanton Cliffs ②
These magnificent
cliffs tower 18 m
(60 ft) above the
beach. Their three
bands of colour are
made from car-
stone and red
and white chalk.

Heacham

*KING'S
LYNN*

Hunstanton

Caley Mill ①
The largest producer of English
Lavender, this whole area is at
its best in July and August when
the fields are a blaze of purple.

*Holme-
next-the-Sea*

Brancaster

A149

NORWICH

*Burnham
Market*

Lord Nelson pub ③
Nelson (*p54*), born near Bur
ham Market, dined here befo
he went to sea for the last tim

Yard, a relic of the old fishermen's quarter.

The **Trinity Guildhall**, located in the Saturday Market Place, dates back to the 15th century and was formerly a prison. The handsome **Custom House**, overlooking the river, was built in the 17th century as a merchant exchange. It is now a museum dedicated to the town's colourful maritime history. The Tourist Information Centre is also located here. **St Margaret's Church**, on the Market Place, dates back to 1101, and the interior includes a fine Elizabethan screen. In 1741 the tall spire on the southwest tower collapsed in a storm.

🏛 **Custom House**
Purfleet Quay. **Tel** 01553 763044.
⬜ daily. ♿ ground floor.

Sandringham House, where the Royal Family spend every Christmas

Sandringham ❼

Norfolk. **Tel** 01553 612908. 🚌 from King's Lynn. ⬜ Easter–Oct: daily. ◉ one wk Jul. 📷 ♿ 🍴 all year. 🏠 all year. **www**.sandringhamestate.co.uk

This sizeable Norfolk estate has been in royal hands since 1862 when it was bought by the Prince of Wales, who later became Edward VII. The 18th-century house was elaborately embellished and refurbished by the prince and now retains an appropriately Edwardian atmosphere.

The large stables are now a museum and contain several trophies that relate to hunting, shooting and horse racing – all favourite royal activities. A popular feature is a display of royal motor cars spanning nearly a century. In the park there are scenic nature trails.

Holkham Hall ④
This Palladian home is magnificent. Set in a beautiful landscaped park, it houses an impressive collection of art and Classical sculptures.

KEY

▬▬▬ Tour route

‑ ‑ ‑ Other roads

☀ Viewpoint

The Run

Bob Hall's Sands

…eham …ay

CROMER

Blakeney ⑥

A149

⑤

B1105

Stiffkey

B1388

FAKENHAM

B1156

Glaven

HOLT

Cley Windmill ⑦
This famous landmark overlooks Cley Marshes which became, in 1926, the first nature and bird reserve in Britain.

Blakeney Marshes ⑥
In the 13th century, Blakeney was a substantial trading port. Today, the marsh is inhabited by a seal colony and hundreds of sea birds.

…s-next-the-Sea ⑤
to silting, this port is now a (1.5 km) from the sea. Its sandy beach is popular and with colourful beach huts.

0 kilometres 5

0 miles 3

The symmetrical red-brick façade of the 17th-century Blickling Hall

Blickling Hall ⑨

(NT) Aylsham, Norfolk. *Tel 01263 738 030.* Norwich, then bus. **House** ⬜ *mid-Mar–Oct: Wed–Thu (Aug: daily).* **Garden** ⬜ *dawn–dusk daily.* **Park** ⬜ *daily.* **www**.nationaltrust.org.uk

Approached from the east, its symmetrical Jacobean front framed by trees and flanked by two yew hedges, Blickling Hall offers one of the most impressive vistas of any country house in the area.

Anne Boleyn, Henry VIII's tragic second queen, spent her childhood here, but very little of the original house remains. Most of the present structure dates from 1628, when it was home to James I's Chief Justice Sir Henry Hobart. Later in 1767 the 2nd Earl of Buckinghamshire, John Hobart, celebrated the Boleyn connection with reliefs in the Great Hall depicting Anne and her daughter, Elizabeth I. The Long Gallery is the most

spectacular room to survive from the 1620s. Its ceiling depicts symbolic representations of learning.

The Peter the Great Room marks the 2nd earl's service as ambassador to Russia and was built to display a huge spectacular tapestry (1764) of the tsar on horseback, a gift from, Catherine the Great. It also has portraits (1760) of the ambassador and his wife by Gainsborough *(see p163).*

Norwich ⑩

See pp200–201.

The Broads ⑪

Norfolk. Hoveton, Wroxham. Norwich, then bus. Station Rd, Hoveton (01603 782281) Apr–Oct, or 18 Colegate, Norwich (01603 610 734). **www**.broads-authority.gov.uk

These shallow lakes and waterways south and northeast of Norwich, joined by

six rivers – the Bure, Thurne, Ant, Yare, Waveney and Chet – were once thought to have been naturally formed, but in actual fact they are medieval peat diggings which flooded when the water level rose in the 13th century.

In summer the 125 miles (200 km) of open waterways, uninterrupted by locks, teem with thousands of boating enthusiasts. You can either hire a boat yourself or take one of the many trips on offer to view the plants and wildlife of the area. Look out for Britain's largest butterfly, the swallowtail. Wroxham, the unofficial capital of the Broads, is the starting point for many of these excursions.

The waterways support substantial beds of strong and durable reeds, much in demand for thatching *(see p33).* They are cut in winter and carried to shore in the distinctive Broads punts.

For a more detailed look at the origins of the Broads and their varied wildlife, visit the **Norfolk Wildlife Trust** – a large thatched floating information centre on Ranworth Broad, with displays on all aspects of the area, and a bird-watching gallery.

In the centre of Ranworth is **St Helen's Church** which has a painted medieval screen, a well-preserved 14th-century illuminated manuscript and spectacular views over the entire area from its tower.

🦋 **Norfolk Wildlife Trust**
Ranworth. *Tel 01603 625540.*
⬜ *Apr–Oct: daily.*

Sailing boat, Wroxham Broad, Norfolk

For hotels and restaurants in this region see pp563–566 and pp619–622

Great Yarmouth ⑫

Norfolk. 🏘 90,000. ✈ 🚉
ℹ Marine Parade (01493 846345).
🎪 Wed, Fri (summer), Sat.
www.great-yarmouth.co.uk

Herring fishing was once the major industry of this port, with 1,000 boats engaged in it just before World War I. Over-fishing led to a depletion of stocks and, for the port to survive, it started to earn its living from servicing container ships and North Sea oil rigs.

It is also the most popular seaside resort on the Norfolk coast and has been since the 19th century, when Dickens *(see p189)* gave it useful publicity by setting part of his novel *David Copperfield* here.

The **Elizabethan House Museum** has a large, eclectic display which illustrates the social history of the area.

In the old part of the town, around South Quay, are a number of charming houses including the 17th-century **Old Merchant's House**. It retains its original patterned plaster ceilings as well as examples of old ironwork and architectural fittings from

Fishing trawlers at Lowestoft's quays

nearby houses, which were destroyed during World War II. The guided tour of the house includes a visit to the adjoining cloister of a 13th-century friary.

🏛 Elizabethan House Museum
(NT) 4 South Quay. **Tel** 01493 855746. ☐ Apr–Oct: daily (pm only weekends). 🎟 🛈

🏚 Old Merchant's House
(EH) South Quay. **Tel** 01493 857900. ☐ Apr–Sep: pm daily. 🎟 📷 🛈

WINDMILLS ON THE FENS AND BROADS

The flat, open countryside and the stiff breezes from the North Sea made windmills an obvious power source for East Anglia well into the 20th century, and today they are an evocative and recurring feature of the landscape. On the Broads and Fens, some were used for drainage, while others, such as that at Saxtead Green, ground corn. On the boggy fens they were not built on hard foundations, so few survived, but elsewhere, especially on the Broads, many have been restored to working order. The seven-storey Berney Arms Windmill is the tallest on the Broads. Thurne Dyke Drainage Mill is the site of an exhibition about the occasionally idiosyncratic mills and their more unusual mechanisms.

Corn mill at Saxtead Green, near Framlingham

Herringfleet Smock Mill, near Lowestoft

Lowestoft ⑬

Suffolk. 🏘 55,000. ✈ 🚉
ℹ East Point Pavilion, Royal Plain (01502 533600). 🎪 Tue–Sat.
www.visit-lowestoft.co.uk

The most easterly town in Britain was long a rival to Great Yarmouth, both as a holiday resort and a fishing port. Its fishing industry has only just survived. The coming of the railway in the 1840s gave the town an advantage over other resorts, and the solid Victorian and Edwardian boarding houses are evidence of its popularity.

Lowestoft Museum, in a 17th-century house, has a good display of the fine porcelain made here in the 18th century, as well as exhibits on local archaeology and domestic life.

Environs: Somerleyton Hall is built in Jacobean style on the foundations of a smaller mansion. Its gardens are a real delight, and there is a genuinely baffling yew hedge maze.

🏛 Lowestoft Museum
Oulton Broad. **Tel** 01502 511457. ☐ May–Oct: 10:30am–5pm daily (from 2pm Sun). 🛈 ♿ ltd. 📷 by appt. **www**.lowestoftmuseum.org

🏚 Somerleyton Hall
On B1074. **Tel** 01502 734901. ☐ Easter Sun–Oct: Thu, Sun & pub hols (Jul–Aug: also Tue, Wed). 🛈 🎟 ♿ 📷 by appt. 🅿
www.somerleyton.co.uk

Norwich ⑩

In the heart of the fertile East Anglian countryside, Norwich, one of the best-preserved cities in Britain, is steeped in a relaxed provincial atmosphere. The city was first fortified by the Saxons in the 9th century and still has the irregular street plan of that time. With the arrival of Flemish settlers in the early 12th century and the establishment of a textile industry, the town soon became a prosperous market and was the second city of England until the Industrial Revolution in the 19th century *(see pp56–7)*.

The cobbled street, Elm Hill

Exploring Norwich

The oldest parts of the city are Elm Hill, one of the finest medieval streets in England, and Tombland, the old Saxon market place by the cathedral. Both have well-preserved medieval buildings, which are now incorporated into pleasant areas of small shops.

With a trading history spanning hundreds of years, the colourful market in the city centre is well worth a visit. A good walk meanders around the surviving sections of the 14th-century flint city wall.

🔒 Norwich Cathedral

The Close. *Tel 01603 218300.*
◯ *daily.* **Donations.** ♿ 📷 🍴 🚻
www.cathedral.org.uk
This magnificent building was founded in 1096 by Bishop Losinga and built with stone from Caen in France and Barnack.

The precinct originally included a monastery, and the surviving cloister is the most extensive in England. The thin cathedral spire was added in the 15th century, making it, at 96 m (315 ft), the second tallest in England after Salisbury *(see pp264–5)*. In the majestic

nave, soaring Norman pillars and arches support a 15th-century vaulted roof whose stone bosses, many of which illustrate well-known Bible stories, have recently been beautifully restored.

Easier to appreciate at close hand is the elaborate wood carving in the choir – the canopies over the stalls and the misericords beneath the seats, one showing a small boy being smacked. Not to be missed is the 14th-century Despenser Reredos in St Luke's Chapel. It was hidden for years under a carpenter's table to prevent its destruction by Puritans.

Two gates to the cathedral close survive: **St Ethelbert's**,

One of over a thousand carved bosses in the cathedral cloisters

a 13th-century flint arch, and the **Erpingham Gate** at the west end, built by Sir Thomas Erpingham, who led the triumphant English archers at the Battle of Agincourt in 1415 *(see p49)*.

Beneath the east outer wall is the grave of Edith Cavell, the Norwich-born nurse who was arrested and executed in 1915 by the Germans for helping Allied soldiers escape from occupied Belgium.

🏛 Castle Museum

Castle Meadow. *Tel 01603 493625.*
◯ *daily (Sun pm only).* ● *1 Jan, 25 & 26 Dec.* ♿ 🚪 📷 🚻
www.museums.norfolk.gov.uk
The brooding keep of this 12th-century castle has been a museum since 1894, when it ended 650 years of service as a prison. The most important Norman feature is a carved door that used to be the main entrance.

Exhibits include significant collections of archaeology,

A view of Norwich Cathedral's spire and tower from the southeast

COLMAN'S MUSTARD

It was said of the Colmans that they made their fortune from what diners left on their plate. In 1814 Jeremiah Colman started milling mustard at Norwich because it was at the centre of a fertile plain where mustard was grown. Today at 15 Royal Arcade a shop sells mustard and related items, while a small museum illustrates the history of the company.

A 1950s advertisement for Colman's Mustard

natural history, fine art as well as the world's largest collection of ceramic teapots.

The art gallery is dominated by works from the Norwich School of painters. This group of early 19th century landscape artists painted directly from nature, getting away from the stylized studio landscapes that had been fashionable up to then. Chief among the group were John Crome (1768–1821), whom many compare with Constable (*see p204*), and John Sell Cotman (1782–1842), known for his watercolours. There are also regular exhibitions held here.

🔒 Church of St Peter Mancroft

Market Place. **Tel** 01603 610443.
◻ 10am–4pm Mon–Sat; 10am–4pm Sat (summer), 10am–1pm (winter); Sun (services only). **Donations.** &

This imposing Perpendicular church, built around 1455, so dominates the city centre that many visitors assume it is the cathedral. John Wesley (*see p279*) wrote of it, "I scarcely ever remember to have seen a more beautiful parish church".

The large windows make the church very light, and the dramatic east window still has most of its 15th-century glass. The roof is unusual in having wooden fan tracery – it is normally in stone – covering the hammerbeam construction. The famous peal of 13 bells rang out in 1588 to celebrate the defeat of the Spanish Armada (*see p51*) and is still heard every Sunday.

Its name derives from the Latin *magna crofta* (great meadow) which described the area in pre-Norman times.

🏛 Bridewell Museum

Bridewell Alley. **Tel** 01603 629127.
◻ until 2011. 🏷 ▯

One of the oldest houses in Norwich, this 14th-century flint-faced building was used for years as a jail for women and beggars. It now houses an exhibition of local industries, with displays of old machines and reconstructed shops. A section about the people of Norwich is being developed.

🏛 Guildhall

Gaol Hill. **Tel** 01264 781611. ▯

Above the city's ancient market place is the imposing 15th-century flint and stone Guildhall with its gable of checkered flushwork (now a café).

VISITORS' CHECKLIST

Norfolk. 🏘 125,000. 🚶 ✈ ✚
Thorpe Rd. 🚌 Surrey St.
🛈 The Forum, Millennium Plain (01603 213999). 🏪 Mon–Sat.
www.visitnorwich.co.uk

🏛 Strangers' Hall

Charing Cross. **Tel** 01603 667229.
◻ Wed–Sat; call ahead for times (tickets from Castle Museum).
● 24–31 Dec. 🏷

This 14th-century merchant's house gives a glimpse into English domestic life through the ages. The house was lived in by immigrant weavers – the "strangers". It has a fine 15th-century Great Hall and a costume display featuring a collection of underwear.

🏛 The Sainsbury Centre for Visual Arts

University of E Anglia (on B1108).
Tel 01603 593199. ◻ Tue–Sun.
● 23 Dec–20 Jan. 🏷 & 🏷 by arrangement. ▯ 🏷 **www**.scva.ac.uk

This important art gallery was built in 1978 to house the collection of Robert and Lisa Sainsbury given to the University of East Anglia in 1973.

The collection's strength is in its modern European paintings, including works by Modigliani, Picasso and Bacon, and in its sculptures by Giacometti and Moore. There are also displays of ethnographic art from Africa, the Pacific and the Americas.

The centre, designed by Lord Norman Foster, one of Britain's most innovative architects, was among the first to display its steel structure openly.

Back of the New Mills (1814) by John Crome of the Norwich School

Purple heather in flower on Dunwich Heath

Southwold ⓮

Suffolk. 🏘 3,900. 🚻 🛈 *High Street (01502 724729).* 🏪 *Mon, Thu. Shops closed Wed pm.* **www**.visit-southwold.co.uk

This picture-postcard seaside resort, with its charming white-washed villas clustered around small greens, has, largely by historical accident, remained unspoiled. The railway line which connected it with London was closed in 1929, which effectively isolated this Georgian town from an influx of day-trippers.

This was also once a large port, as testified by the size of the 15th-century **St Edmund King and Martyr Church**, worth a visit for the 16th-century painted screens.

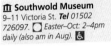

Jack o'the Clock, Southwold

On its tower is a small figure dressed in the uniform of a 15th-century soldier and known as Jack o'the Clock. **Southwold Museum** tells the story of the Battle of Sole Bay, which was fought offshore between the English and Dutch navies in 1672.

Environs: The pretty village of **Walberswick** lies across the creek. By road it is a long detour and the only alternatives are a rowing-boat ferry across the harbour (summer only) or a footbridge across the river half a mile inland. Further inland at Blythburgh, the 15th-century **Holy Trinity Church** dominates the surrounding land. In 1944 a US bomber blew up over the church, killing Joseph Kennedy Jr, brother of the future American president.

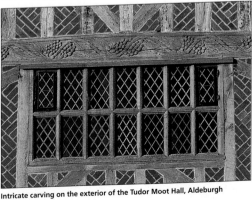

Intricate carving on the exterior of the Tudor Moot Hall, Aldeburgh

🏛 **Southwold Museum**
9–11 Victoria St. **Tel** *01502 726097.* ⏰ *Easter–Oct: 2–4pm daily (also am in Aug).* ♿

Dunwich ⓯

Suffolk. 🏘 *1,400.*

This tiny village is all that remains of a "lost city" consigned to the sea by erosion. In the 7th century Dunwich was the seat of the powerful East Anglian kings. In the 13th century it was still the biggest port in Suffolk and some 12 churches were built. But the land was being eroded at about a metre (3 ft) a year, and the last original church collapsed into the sea in 1919.

Dunwich Heath, to the south, runs down to a sandy beach and is an important nature reserve. **Minsmere Reserve** has observation hides for watching a huge variety of birds.

🦋 **Dunwich Heath**
(NT) Nr Westleton. **Tel** *01728 648501.* ⏰ *dawn–dusk.* 🅿 🚻

🦋 **Minsmere Reserve**
Minsmere, Westleton. **Tel** *01728 648281.* ⏰ *daily.* ⏰ *25, 26 Dec.* 📷 ♿ 🅿 🚻 **www**.rspb.org.uk

Aldeburgh ⓰

Suffolk. 🏘 *3,840.* 🚉
🛈 *High St (01728 453637).*
www.suffolkcoastal.gov.uk/tourism

Best known today for the music festivals at Snape Maltings just up the River Alde, Aldeburgh has been a port since Roman times (the Roman area is now under water).

Erosion has resulted in the fine Tudor **Aldeburgh Museum**, once far inland, now being close to the beach. Its ground floor, originally the market, is now a museum. The large timbered court room above can only be reached by the original outside staircase.

The **church**, also Tudor, contains a large stained-glass window placed in 1979 as a memorial to Benjamin Britten.

🏛 **Aldeburgh Museum**
Moot Hall, Market Cross Pl. **Tel** 01728 454666. ⬤ May–Oct: daily (pm); Easter–Apr: Sat, Sun (pm). 🏚 🛈

Framlingham Castle ⑰

(EH) Framlingham, Suffolk. **Tel** 01728 724189. 🚃 Wickham Market then taxi. ⬤ daily (Nov–Mar: Thu–Mon). ⬤ 1 Jan, 24–26 Dec. 🏚 🛈 🏚

Perched on a hill, the small village of Framlingham has long been an important strategic site, even before the present castle was built in 1190 by the Earl of Norfolk.

Little of the castle from that period survives except the powerful curtain wall and its towers; walk round the top of it for fine views of the town.

Mary Tudor, daughter of Henry VIII, was staying here in 1553 when she heard she was to become queen.

Environs: To the southeast, on the coast, is the 27 m (90 ft) keep of **Orford Castle**, built for Henry II as a coastal defence at around the same time as Framlingham. It is an early example of an English castle with a 16-sided keep; earlier they were square and later round. A short climb to the top of the castle gives fantastic views.

⛪ **Orford Castle**
(EH) Orford. **Tel** 01394 450472. ⬤ daily (Oct–Mar: Thu–Mon). ⬤ 1 Jan, 24–26 Dec. 🏚 🛈

ALDEBURGH MUSIC FESTIVAL
Composer Benjamin Britten (1913–76), born in Lowestoft, Suffolk, moved to Snape in 1937. In 1945 his opera *Peter Grimes* – inspired by the poet George Crabbe (1754–1832), once a curate at Aldeburgh – was performed in Snape. Since then the area has become the centre of musical activity. In 1948, Britten began the Aldeburgh Music Festival, held every June (*see p63*). He acquired the Maltings at Snape and converted it into a music venue opened by the Queen in 1967. It has since become the focus of an annual series of East Anglian musical events in churches and halls throughout the entire region.

Benjamin Britten in Aldeburgh

Ipswich ⑱

Suffolk. 🏙 120,000. 🚃 🛈 🛈 St Stephen's Lane (01473 258070). ⬤ Tue, Thu–Sat. 🎭 IPART (music & arts): last wk Jun–1st wk Jul. **www**.visit-ipswich.com

Suffolk's county town has a largely modern centre but several buildings remain from earlier times. It rose to prominence after the 13th century as a port for the rich Suffolk wool trade (*see p207*). Later, with the Industrial Revolution, it began to export coal.

The **Ancient House** in Buttermarket has a superb example of pargeting – the ancient craft of ornamental façade plastering. The town's museum and art gallery, **Christchurch Mansion**, is a Tudor house from 1548, where Elizabeth I stayed in 1561. It also boasts the best collection of Constable's paintings out of London (*see p204*), including four marvellous Suffolk landscapes, as well as paintings by Gainsborough (*see p163*).

Ipswich Museum contains replicas of the Mildenhall and Sutton Hoo treasures, the originals being in the British Museum (*see pp106–7*).

In the centre of the town is **St Margaret's**, a 15th-century church built in flint and stone with a double hammerbeam roof and 17th-century painted ceiling panels. **Wolsey's Gate**, a Tudor gateway of 1527, provides a link with Ipswich's most famous son, Cardinal Wolsey (*see p173*). He started to build an ecclesiastical college in the town, but fell from royal favour before it was finished.

🏛 **Christchurch Mansion**
Christchurch Pk. **Tel** 01473 433554. ⬤ 10am–5pm daily. ⬤ 1 Jan, Good Fri, 24–27 Dec. 🏚 limited. 🏚 by appt. 🛈 🛈

🏛 **Ipswich Museum**
High St. **Tel** 01473 433550. ⬤ Tue–Sat. 🛈 🏚

Pargeting on the Ancient House in Ipswich

Constable Walk ⑲

This walk in Constable country follows one of the most picturesque sections of the River Stour. The route taken would have been familiar to the landscape painter John Constable (1776–1837). Constable's father, a wealthy merchant, owned Flatford Mill, which was depicted in many of the artist's important paintings. Constable claimed to know and love "every stile and stump, and every lane" around East Bergholt.

The River Stour, used as a backdrop for Constable's *Boatbuilding* (1814)

TIPS FOR WALKERS

Starting point: Park off Flatford Lane, East Bergholt (charge to park). ℹ 01206 299460; **(NT)** Bridge Cottage (01206 298260). *Getting there:* A12 to East Bergholt, then follow signs to Flatford. 🚆 Manningtree is within walking distance of Flatford. 🚌 from Ipswich or Colchester. *Stopping-off point:* Dedham. *Length:* 3 miles (5 km). *Difficulty:* Flat trail along riverside footpath with kissing gates.

Viewpoint ⑤
The view over the valley from the top of the hill shows Constable country at its best.

Car Park ①
Follow the signs to Flatford Mill then cross the footbridge.

↑A12

Dedham Mill

Stour

B1029

P

④ Dedham

B1029

③

Gosnalls Farm

EAST BERGHOLT

P ①

Fen Bridge ③
This modern footbridge replaced one that Constable used as a focus for many of his paintings.

Ram Lock •

Flatford Mill •
②

Dedham Church ④
The tall church tower appears in many of Constable's pictures including the *View on the Stour near Dedham* (1822).

KEY

▪ ▪	Route
═══	B road
───	Minor road
☆	Viewpoint
P	Parking

0 metres	500
0 yards	500

Willy Lott's Cottage ②
This cottage remains much the same as it did when featured in Constable's painting *The Hay-Wain* (see p83).

Colchester 🔟

Essex. 🏃 160,000. ⊕ 🚌 ℹ️ Queen
St (01206 282920). 🚍 Fri, Sat.
www.visitcolchester.com

The oldest recorded town in
Britain, Colchester was the
effective capital of south-east
England when the Romans
invaded in AD 43, and it was
here that the first permanent
Roman colony was established.

After Boadicea *(see p195)*
burnt the town in AD 60, a
2 mile (3 km) wall was built,
3 m (10 ft) thick and 9 m (30 ft)
high, to deter future attackers.
You can still see these walls
and the surviving Roman town
gate, the largest in Britain.

During the Middle Ages
Colchester developed into an
important weaving centre. In
the 16th century, a number of
immigrant Flemish weavers
settled in an area west of the
castle, known as the **Dutch
Quarter**, which still retains
the original tall houses and
steep, narrow streets.

Colchester was besieged for
11 weeks during the Civil War
(see p52) before being captured by Cromwell's troops.

🏛 Tymperleys

Trinity St. **Tel** 01206 282943.
◯ Apr–Oct: Tue–Sat. ♿ limited. ▯
www.colchestermuseums.org.uk
Clock-making was an important craft in Colchester, and it
is celebrated in this restored
half-timbered, 15th-century
mansion, also worth visiting
for its formal Tudor garden.

🏛 Hollytrees Museum

High St. **Tel** 01206 282940. ◯ daily.
🌑 1 Jan, 24–27 Dec. ♿ ▯
www.colchestermuseums.org.uk
This elegant Georgian town-
house was built in 1719. Now
a charming museum of social
history, you can experience
the day-to-day lives of Colchester people and changing
technology over 300 years.

🏛 Castle Museum

High St. **Tel** 01206 282939. ◯
10am–5pm daily (from 11am Sun).
🌑 1 Jan, 24–27 Dec. ▯ 🎦 ♿ ✍
www.colchestermuseums.org.uk
This is the oldest and largest
Norman keep still standing in
England. Twice the size of the
White Tower at the Tower of

**The Norman keep of the Castle
Museum, Colchester**

London *(see pp118–19)*, it was
built in 1076 on the platform
of a Roman temple dedicated
to Claudius *(see p44)*, using
stones and tiles from other
Roman buildings. The museum's displays relate the story
of the town from prehistoric
times to the Civil War. There
is also a medieval prison.

♜ Layer Marney Tower

Off B1022. **Tel** 01206 330784. ◯
Apr–Sep: Wed & Sun (Jul & Aug: Sun–
Thu). 🎦 ♿ limited. 📷 by appt. ▯
📷 www.layermarneytower.co.uk
This remarkable Tudor gatehouse is the tallest in Britain:
its pair of six-sided, eight-
storey turrets reach to 24 m
(80 ft). It was intended to be
part of a larger complex, but
the designer, Sir Henry Marney,
died before it was completed.
The brickwork and terracotta
ornamentation around the
roof and windows are models
of Tudor craftsmanship.

Beth Chatto Garden

Elmstead Market. **Tel** 01206 822007.
◯ Mar–Oct: 9am–5pm daily (pm
only Sun); Nov–Feb: 9am–4pm Mon–
Sat. 🌑 22 Dec–5 Jan. ♿ ▯ 🎦 ▯
www.bethchatto.co.uk
One of Britain's most eminent
gardening writers, Beth Chatto
began this experiment in the
1960s to test her belief that it is
possible to create a garden in
the most adverse conditions.
The dry and windy slopes,
boggy patches, gravel beds
and wooded areas support an
array of plants best suited to
that particular environment.

Coggeshall 🔲

Essex. 🏃 4,000. 🚍 Thu.
www.coggeshall-pc.gov.uk

This town has two of the
most important medieval and
Tudor buildings in the country.
Dating from 1140, **Coggeshall
Grange Barn** is the oldest
surviving timber-framed barn
in Europe. Inside is a display
of historic farm wagons. The
half-timbered merchant's
house, **Paycocke's**, was built
around 1500 and has a beautifully panelled interior. There
is a display of Coggeshall lace.

♜ Coggeshall Grange Barn

(NT) Grange Hill. 📞 01376 562226.
◯ Apr–Oct: Tue, Thu, Sun & public
hols (pm). 🌑 Good Fri. 🎦 ♿

♜ Paycocke's

(NT) West St. **Tel** 01376 561305.
◯ Apr–Oct: Tue, Thu, Sun & public
hols (pm). 🌑 Good Fri. 🎦 ♿

Beth Chatto Garden, Colchester, in full summer bloom

Lavenham ②

Suffolk. 🚶 1,800.
ℹ️ Lady St (01787 248207).

Often considered the most perfect of all English small towns, Lavenham is a treasure trove of beautiful timber-framed houses ranged along streets whose pattern is virtually unchanged from medieval times. For 150 years, between the 14th and 16th centuries, Lavenham was the prosperous centre of the Suffolk wool trade. It still has many outstanding and well-preserved buildings; indeed no less than 300 of the town's buildings are listed, including the magnificent **Little Hall**.

Environs: Gainsborough's House, Sudbury, is a museum on this painter (see p163).

🏛️ **Little Hall** Market Place. **Tel** 01787 247019. ☐ Apr–Oct: Wed, Thu, Sat, Sun; public hols. 🎫

🏛️ **Gainsborough's House** Sudbury. **Tel** 01787 372958. ☐ Mon–Sat. ● 24 Dec–2 Jan, Good Fri. 🚹 ☐ 🖥️ 🎫 www.gainsborough.org

LITTLE HALL

The **solar bedroom** was the best and sunniest room in the house.

Dormitory

The **crown-post roof** is a superb feat of medieval engineering.

Bronze of Egyptian Goddess Cat Bastet

Library

Entrance

Dining room

The **herringbone-style** timber on the exterior was used often in the 14th century.

Bury St Edmunds ②

Suffolk. 🚶 34,000. 🚄 🚌 ℹ️ Angel Hill (01284 764667). ● Wed, Sat. www.stedmundsbury.gov.uk

St Edmund was the last Saxon king of East Anglia, decapitated by Danish raiders in 870. Legend has it that a wolf picked up the severed head – an image that appears in a number of medieval carvings. Edmund was canonized in 900 and buried in Bury, where in 1014 King Canute (see p171) built an **abbey** in his honour, the wealthiest in England until its destruction in the Dissolution of the Monasteries (see p351). The abbey ruins now lie in the town centre.

Nearby are two large 15th-century churches, built when the wool trade made the town wealthy. **St James's** was designated a cathedral in 1914. The best features of **St Mary's** are the north porch and the hammerbeam roof over the nave. A stone slab in the north-east corner marks the tomb of Mary Tudor (see pp50–51).

Just below the **market cross** in Cornhill – remodelled by Robert Adam (see p28) in 1714 – stands the large 12th-century **Moyse's Hall**, a merchant's house that serves as the local history museum, displaying archaeology from the area.

Illustration of St Edmund

Environs: Three miles (5 km) southwest of Bury is the late 18th-century **Ickworth House**. This eccentric Neo-Classical mansion features an unusual rotunda with a

The 18th-century rotunda of Ickworth House, Bury St Edmunds

domed roof flanked by two huge wings. The art collection includes works by Reynolds and Titian. There are also fine displays of silver, porcelain and sculpture, for example, John Flaxman's (1755–1826) moving *The Fury of Athamas*. The house is set in a large park.

The stallion unit at the National Stud, Newmarket

🏛 **Moyse's Hall**
Cornhill. **Tel** 01284 706183.
☐ daily (last adm: 4pm). ⬤
public hols, 24 Dec. 🖼 🚻 🛗

🏯 **Ickworth House (NT)**
Horringer. **Tel** 01284 735270. ☐
Mar–Oct: Fri–Tue. 🖼 🛗 🍴 🛗

Newmarket ㉔

Suffolk. 🏘 *17,000*. 🚉 🖼 🚌 🛈 *Palace House, Palace St (01638 667200)*. ⬤
Tue, Sat. **www**.forest-heath.gov.uk

A walk down the short main street tells you all you need to know about this busy and wealthy little town. The shops sell horse feed and all manner of riding accessories; the clothes on sale are tweeds, jodhpurs and the soft brown hats rarely worn by anyone except racehorse trainers.

Newmarket has been the headquarters of British horse racing since James I decided that its open heaths were ideal for testing the mettle of his fastest steeds against those of his friends. The first ever recorded horse race was held here in 1622. Charles II shared his grandfather's enthusiasm and after the Restoration *(see p53)* would move the whole court to Newmarket, every spring and summer, for the sport – he is the only British king to have ridden a winner.

A horse being exercised on Newmarket Heath

The modern racing industry began to take shape here in the late 18th century. There are now over 2,500 horses in training in and around the town, and two racecourses staging regular race meetings from around April to October *(see pp66–7)*. Training stables are occasionally open to the public but you can view the horses being exercised on the heath in the early morning. Tattersall's, the auction house for thoroughbreds, is in the centre of Newmarket.

The **National Stud** can also be visited. You will see the five or six stallions on stud, mares in foal and if you are lucky a newborn foal – most likely in April or May.

The **National Horseracing Museum** tells the history of the sport and contains many offbeat exhibits such as the skeleton of Eclipse, one of the greatest horses ever, unbeaten in 18 races and the ancestor of most of today's fastest performers. It also has a large display of sporting art.

🛈 **National Stud**
Newmarket. **Tel** 01638 663464. ☐
Feb–Sep: daily; Oct: half term. 🖼 🛗
🅿 ⬤ 🛗 **www**.nationalstud.co.uk

🏛 **National Horseracing Museum**
99 High St, Newmarket. **Tel** 01638
667333. ☐ Apr–Oct: daily. 🖼 🛗
🅿 ⬤ 🛗 **www**.nhrm.co.uk

St Mary's Church, Stoke-by-Nayland, southeast of Bury St Edmunds

THE RISE AND FALL OF THE WOOL TRADE

Wool was a major English product from the 13th century and by 1310 some ten million fleeces were exported every year. The Black Death *(see p48)*, which swept Britain in 1348, perversely provided a boost for the industry: with labour in short supply, land could not be cultivated and was grassed over for sheep. Around 1350 Edward III decided it was time to establish a home-based cloth industry and encouraged Flemish weavers to come to Britain. Many settled in East Anglia, particularly Suffolk, and their skills helped establish a flourishing trade. This time of prosperity saw the construction of the sumptuous churches, such as the one at Stoke-by-Nayland, that we see today – East Anglia has more than 2,000 churches. The cloth trade here began to decline in the late 16th century with the development of water-powered looms. These were not suited to the area, which never regained its former wealth. Today's visitors are the beneficiaries of this decline, because the wool towns such as Lavenham and Bury St Edmunds never became rich enough to destroy their magnificent Tudor halls and houses and construct new buildings.

The façade of Anglesey Abbey

Anglesey Abbey 25

(NT) Lode, Cambridgeshire.
Tel 01223 810080. Cambridge then bus. **House** Mar–Oct: Wed–Sun; **Garden** Wed–Sun. limited.

The original Abbey was built in 1135 for an Augustinian order. But only the crypt – also known as the monks' parlour – with its vaulted ceiling on marble and stone pillars, survived the Dissolution (see p50).

This was later incorporated into a manor house whose treasures include furniture from many periods and a rare seascape by Gainsborough (see p206). The superb garden was created in the 1930s by Lord Fairhaven as an ambitious, Classical landscape of trees, sculptures and borders.

Huntingdon 26

Cambridgeshire. 18,000. Princes St (01480 388588). Wed, Sat.

More than 300 years after his death, Oliver Cromwell (see p52) still dominates this small town. Born here in 1599, a record of his baptism can be seen in the County Records Office in Huntingdon. You can see his name and traces of ancient graffiti scrawled all over it which says "England's plague for five years".
Cromwell Museum, his former school, traces his life with pictures and mementoes, including his death mask.

Cromwell remains one of the most disputed figures in British history. An MP before he was 30, he became embroiled in the disputes between Charles I and Parliament over taxes and religion. In the Civil War (see p52) he proved an inspired general and, after refusing the title of king, was made Lord Protector in 1653, four years after the King was beheaded. Just two years after his death the monarchy was restored by popular demand, and his body was taken out of Westminster Abbey (see pp92–3) to hang on gallows.

There is a 14th-century bridge across the River Ouse which links Huntingdon with Godmanchester, the site of a Roman settlement.

🏛 Cromwell Museum
Grammar School Walk.
Tel 01480 375830. Tue–Sun (Nov–Mar: pm only except Sat). 1 Jan, 24–27 Dec, some public hols.

Cambridge 27

See pp210–15.

Audley End 28

(EH) Saffron Walden, Essex.
Tel 01799 522399. Audley End then taxi. **House** mid-Mar–Oct: Wed–Sun. **Garden** Wed–Sun. 24 Dec–31 Jan. limited.
www.english-heritage.org.uk

This was the largest house in England when built in 1603–14 for Thomas Howard, Lord Treasurer and 1st Earl of Suffolk. James I joked that Audley End was too big for a king but not for a Lord Treasurer. Charles II, his grandson, disagreed and bought it in 1667. He seldom went there, however, and in 1701 it was given back to the Howards, who demolished two thirds of the house.

What remains is a Jacobean mansion, retaining its original hall and many fine plaster ceilings. Robert Adam (see p28) remodelled some of the interior in the 1760s, and these rooms have been restored to his original designs. At the same time, Capability Brown (see p26) landscaped the magnificent 18th-century park.

Stained glass window, installed in 1771, represents the Last Supper.

The Chapel was completed in 1772 to a Gothic design. The furniture was made to complement the wooden pillars and vaulting which are painted to imitate stone.

Main entrance

The Great Hall, hung with family portraits, is the highlight of the house, with the massive oak screen and elaborate hammerbeam roof surviving in their Jacobean form.

Epping Forest ㉙

Essex. ➡ *Chingford.* 🚆 *Loughton,
Theydon Bois.* 🛈 *High Beach, Loughton (020–8508 0028) & Highbridge
St, Waltam Abbey (01992 652295).*

As one of the large open spaces near London, the 2,400 ha (6,000 acre) forest is popular with walkers, just as, centuries ago, it was a favourite hunting ground for kings and courtiers – the word forest

Epping Forest contains oaks and beeches up to 400 years old

denoted an area for hunting. Henry VIII had a lodge built in 1543 on the edge of the forest. His daughter Elizabeth I often used the lodge and it soon became known as **Queen Elizabeth's Hunting Lodge.**

This three-storey timbered building has been fully renovated and now houses an exhibition explaining the lodge's history and other aspects of the forest's life.

The tracts of open land and woods interspersed with a number of lakes, make an ideal habitat for a variety of plant, bird and animal life: deer roam the northern part, many of a special dark strain introduced by James I. The

A depiction of the Battle of Maldon (991) on the *Maldon Embroidery*

Corporation of London bought the forest in the mid-19th century to ensure it remained open to the public.

🏰 **Queen Elizabeth's
Hunting Lodge**
Rangers Rd, Chingford. **Tel** 020–8529
6681. ⬜ Oct–Mar: Fri–Sun; Apr–Sep:
Wed–Sun, pm only. ⬤ 1 Jan, 24–26
Dec. ♿ limited. 📷 by appt. 🅿 ▯

Maldon ㉚

Essex. 👥 21,000. ➡ *Chelmsford
then bus.* 🛈 *Coach Lane (01621
856503).* 🗓 *Thu, Sat.*
www.visitmaldon.co.uk

This delightful old town on the River Blackwater, its High Street lined with shops and inns from the 14th century on, was once an important harbour. One of its best-known industries is the production of Maldon sea salt, panned in the traditional way.

A fierce battle here in 991, when Viking invaders defeated the Saxon defenders, is told in *The Battle of Maldon,* one of the earliest known Saxon poems. The battle is also celebrated in the *Maldon Embroidery* on display in the **Maeldune Centre**. This 13-m-(42-ft-) long embroidery, made by locals, depicts the history of Maldon from 991 to 1991.

Environs: East of Maldon at Bradwell-on-Sea is the sturdy Saxon church of **St Peter's-on-the-Wall**, a simple stone building that stands isolated on the shore. It was built in 654, from the stones of a former Roman fort, by St Cedd, who used it as his cathedral. It was restored in the 1920s.

🏛 **Maeldune Centre**
High St. **Tel** 01621 851628. ⬜ Apr–
Oct: Mon–Sat; Nov–Mar: Thu & Fri;
pm only. ⬤ 1 Jan, 24–26 Dec. 📷

Thomas Howard, *the
1st Earl of Suffolk
(1561–1626), painted
here by Biagio Rebecca,
reputedly spent over
£200,000 on the house.*

**Jacobean
wooden screen
(c.1605)**

Saloon

**The Great Drawing
Room** is an example of
Adam's fine work.

**Little
Drawing
Room**

Street-by-Street: Cambridge 27

Carving, King's
College Chapel

Cambridge has been an important town since Roman times as it was sited at the first navigable point on the River Cam. In the 11th century religious orders began to be established in the town and, in 1209, a group of religious scholars broke away from Oxford University (*see pp222–27*) after academic and religious disputes and came here. Student life dominates the city but it is also a thriving market centre serving a rich agricultural region.

Cyclists in Cambridge

Newmarket → BRIDGE STREET

ST JOHN'S STRE

Magdalene Bridge carries Bridge Street across the Cam from the city centre to Magdalene College.

St John's College has superb Tudor and Jacobean architecture.

Kitchen Bridge

★ **Bridge of Sighs**
Built in 1831 and named after its Venetian counterpart, it is best viewed from the Kitchen Bridge.

Trinity College

Trinity Bridge

The Backs
This is the name given to the grassy strip lying between the backs of the big colleges and the banks of the Cam – a good spot to enjoy this classic view of King's College Chapel.

KEY

– – – Suggested route

STAR SIGHTS

★ Bridge of Sighs

★ King's College Chapel

Clare College

Clare Bridge

Grantchester

0 metres   7

0 yards   75

Round Church
The 12th-century Church of the Holy Sepulchre has one of the few round naves in the country. Its design is based on the Holy Sepulchre in Jerusalem.

Gonville and Caius (pronounced "keys"), founded in 1348, is one of the oldest colleges.

Great St Mary's Church
This clock is over the west door of the university's official church. Its tower offers fine views.

VISITORS' CHECKLIST

Cambridgeshire. 120,000.
Stansted. Cambridge.
Station Rd. Drummer St.
Wheeler St (0871 2268006).
01223 457574. daily.
Folk Festival: July; Strawberry Fair: June. www.visitcambridge.org

★ King's College Chapel
This late medieval masterpiece took 70 years to build (see pp212–13).

Market square
Bus and Coach station

King's College
Henry VIII, king when the chapel was completed in 1515, is commemorated in this statue near the main gate.

Queens' College
Its Tudor courts are among the university's finest. This 18th-century sundial is over the old chapel – now a reading room.

Corpus Christi College

To London and railway station

Mathematical Bridge
It is a myth that this bridge over the Cam at Queens' College was first built without nuts or bolts.

🏛 Fitzwilliam Museum

Trumpington St. **Tel** 01223 332900.
🕐 Tue–Sun; public hols. 🔴 24–27
Dec, 1 Jan, Good Fri. **Donation.** ♿
📷 by arrangement. 🚻 📷
www.fitzmuseum.cam.ac.uk

One of Britain's oldest public museums, this massive Classical building has works of exceptional quality and rarity, especially antiquities, ceramics, paintings and manuscripts.

The core of the collection was bequeathed in 1816 by the 7th Viscount Fitzwilliam. Other gifts have since greatly added to the exhibits.

Works by Titian (1488–1576) and the 17th-century Dutch masters, including Hals, Cuyp and Hobbema's *Wooded Landscape* (1686), stand out among the paintings. French Impressionist gems include Monet's *Le Printemps* (1866) and Renoir's *La Place Clichy* (1880), while Picasso's *Still Life* (1923) is notable among the modern works. Most of the important British artists are represented, from Hogarth in the 18th century through Constable in the 19th to Ben Nicholson in the 20th.

The miniatures include the earliest surviving depiction of Henry VIII. In the same gallery are some dazzling illuminated manuscripts, notably the 15th-century *Metz Pontifical*, a French liturgical work.

The impressive Glaisher collection of European earthenware and stoneware includes a unique display of English delftware from the 16th and 17th centuries.

Handel's bookcase contains folios of his work, and nearby is Keats's original manuscript for *Ode to a Nightingale* (1819).

Portrait of Richard James (c.1740s) by William Hogarth

Cambridge: King's College

King's College Coat of Arms

Henry VI founded this college in 1441. Work on the chapel – one of the most important examples of late medieval English architecture – began five years later, and took 70 years to complete. Henry himself decided that it should dominate the city and gave specific instructions about its dimensions: 88 m (289 ft) long, 12 m (40 ft) wide and 29 m (94 ft) high. The detailed design is thought to have been by master stonemason Reginald Ely, although it was altered in later years.

★ Fan Vaulted Ceiling
This awe-inspiring ceiling, supported by 22 buttresses, was built by master stonemason John Wastell in 1515.

The Fellows' Building was designed in 1724 by James Gibbs, as part of an uncompleted design for a Great Court.

Henry VI's statue
This bronze statue of the college's founder was erected in 1879.

KING'S COLLEGE CHOIR

When he founded the chapel, Henry VI stipulated that a choir of six lay clerks and 16 boy choristers – educated at the College school – should sing daily at services. This still happens in term time but today the choir also gives concerts all over the world. Its broadcast service of carols has become a much-loved Christmas tradition.

Choristers in King's College Chapel

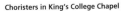
For hotels and restaurants in this region see pp563–566 and pp619–622

Crown and Tudor Rose
This detail of Tudor heraldry on the west door of the Chapel reflects Henry VII's vision of English supremacy.

One of four octagonal turrets

Stained-Glass Windows
The 16th-century windows in the chapel all depict biblical scenes. This one shows Christ baptizing his followers.

Organ
The massive 17th-century organ case above the screen is decorated with two angels playing trumpets.

Side chapels

The screen is a superb example of Tudor woodwork and divides the chapel into antechapel and choir.

Gothic gatehouse, 19th-century

Main entrance

STAR SIGHTS

★ Fan Vaulted Ceiling

★ Altarpiece by Rubens

★Altarpiece by Rubens
Painted in 1634 for the convent of the White Nuns in Belgium, The Adoration of the Magi *was privately donated to King's in 1961.*

Exploring Cambridge University

Cambridge University has 31 colleges (see also pp210–11), the oldest being Peterhouse (1284) and the newest being Robinson (1979). Clustered around the city centre, many of the older colleges have peaceful gardens backing onto the River Cam, which are known as the "Backs". The layout of the older colleges, as at Oxford (see pp226–7), derives from their early connections with religious institutions, although few escaped heavy-handed modification in the Victorian era. The college buildings are generally grouped around squares called courts and offer an unrivalled mix of over 600 years of architecture from the late medieval period through Wren's masterpieces and up to the present day.

The nave of the Wren Chapel at Pembroke College

The imposing façade of Emmanuel College

Emmanuel College
Built in 1677 on St Andrew's Street, Sir Christopher Wren's (see p114) chapel is the highlight of the college. Some of the intricate interior details, particularly the plaster ceiling and Amigoni's altar rails (1734), are superb. Founded in 1584, the college has a Puritan tradition. One notable graduate was the clergyman John Harvard, who emigrated to America in 1636 and left all his money to the Massachusetts college that now bears his name.

Senate House
King's Parade is the site of this Palladian building, which is used primarily for university ceremonies. It was designed by James Gibbs in 1722 as part of a grand square of university buildings – which was never completed.

Corpus Christi College
Just down from Senate House, this was founded in 1352 by the local trade guilds, anxious to ensure that education was not the sole prerogative of

church and nobility. Its Old Court is remarkably well preserved and looks today much as it would have done when built in the 14th century.

The college is connected by a 15th-century gallery of red brick to St Bene't's Church (short for St Benedict's), whose large Saxon tower is the oldest structure in Cambridge.

King's College
See pp212–13.

Pembroke College
The college chapel was the first building completed by Wren (see pp114–15). A formal classical design, it replaced a 14th-century chapel that was turned into a library. The college, just off Trumpington Street, also has fine gardens.

Jesus College
Although founded in 1497, some of its buildings on Jesus Lane are older, as the college took over St Radegond's nunnery, built in the 12th century. There are traces of Norman columns, windows and a well-preserved hammerbeam roof in the college dining hall.

The chapel keeps the core of the original church but the stained glass windows are modern and contain work by William Morris (see pp220–21).

Queens' College
Built in 1446 on Queens' Land, the college was endowed in 1448 by Margaret of Anjou, queen of Henry VI, and again in 1465 by Elizabeth Woodville, queen of Edward IV, which explains the position of the apostrophe. Queens' has a

---

PUNTING ON THE CAM

Punting captures the essence of carefree college days: a student leaning on a long pole, lazily guiding the flat-bottomed river craft along, while others stretch out and relax. Punting is still popular both with students and visitors, who can hire punts from boatyards along the river – with a chauffeur if required. Punts do sometimes capsize, and novices should prepare for a dip.

Punting by the King's College "Backs"

marvellous collection of Tudor buildings, notably the half-timbered President's Gallery, built in the mid-16th century on top of the brick arches in the charming Cloister Court. The Principal Court is 15th century, as is Erasmus's Tower, named after the Dutch scholar.

Pepys Library in Magdalene College

The college has buildings on both sides of the Cam, linked by the bizarre Mathematical Bridge, built in 1749 to hold together without the use of nuts and bolts – although they have had to be used in subsequent repairs.

Magdalene College
Pronounced "maudlin" – as is the Oxford college (see p226) – the college, on Bridge Street, was established in 1482. The diarist Samuel Pepys (1633–1703) was a student here and left his large library to the college on his death. The 12 red-oak bookcases have over 3,000 books. Magdalene was the last all-male Cambridge college and it admitted women students only in 1987.

St John's College
Sited on St John's Street, the imposing turreted brick and stone gatehouse of 1514, with its colourful heraldic symbols, provides a fitting entrance to the second largest Cambridge college and its rich store of 16th- and 17th-century buildings. Its hall, most of it Elizabethan, has portraits of the college's famous alumni, such as the poet William Wordsworth (see p366) and the statesman Lord Palmerston. St John's spans the Cam and boasts two bridges, one built in 1712 and the other, the Bridge of Sighs, in 1831, based on its Venetian namesake.

Peterhouse
The first Cambridge college, on Trumpington Street, is also one of the smallest. The hall still has original features from 1286 but its best details are later – a Tudor fireplace which is backed with 19th-century tiles by William Morris (see pp220–21). A gallery connects the college to the 12th-century church of St Mary the Less, which used to be called St Peter's Church – hence the college's name.

William Morris tiles, Peterhouse

Trinity College
The largest college, situated on Trinity Street, was founded by Henry VIII in 1547 and has a massive court and hall. The entrance gate, with statues of Henry and James I (added later), was built in 1529 for King's Hall, an earlier college incorporated into Trinity. The Great Court features a late Elizabethan fountain – at one time the main water supply. The chapel, built in 1567, has life-size statues of college members, notably Roubiliac's statue of the scientist Isaac Newton (1755).

University Botanic Garden
A delightful place for a leisurely stroll, just off Trumpington Street, as well as an important academic resource, the garden has been on this site since 1846. It has a superb collection of trees and a sensational water garden. The winter garden is one of the finest in the country.

The Bridge of Sighs over the River Cam, linking the buildings of St John's College

THAMES VALLEY

BUCKINGHAMSHIRE · OXFORDSHIRE · BERKSHIRE
BEDFORDSHIRE · HERTFORDSHIRE

The mighty tidal river on which Britain's capital city was founded has modest origins, meandering from its source in the hills of Gloucestershire through the lush countryside towards London. Almost entirely agricultural land in the 19th century, the Thames Valley maintains its pastoral beauty despite the incursion of modern industry.

There are ancient royal connections with the area. Windsor Castle has been a residence of kings and queens for more than 900 years, and played a critical role in history in 1215, when King John set out from here to sign the *Magna Carta* at Runnymede on the River Thames. Further north, Queen Anne had Blenheim Palace built for her military commander, the 1st Duke of Marlborough. Elizabeth I spent part of her childhood at Hatfield House, and part of the Tudor palace still stands.

Several towns in this region, most notably Burford in Oxfordshire, developed as coach staging posts on the important trunk routes between London and the West Country. With the introduction of commuter transportation in the early 20th century, much of the area became an extension of suburbia and saw some imaginative experiments in Utopian town planning such as the garden city of Welwyn and the Quaker settlement at Jordans.

Oxford, the Thames Valley's principal city, owes its importance to the foundation of Britain's first university there in 1167; many of its colleges are gems of medieval architecture. In the 17th century, a number of battles during the Civil War *(see p52)* were fought around Oxford, which for a time was the headquarters of King Charles I, who was supported by the students. When the royalists were forced to flee Oxford, Cromwell made himself chancellor of the university.

Punting on the River Cherwell, Oxford

◁ **Medieval staircase in Christchurch College, Oxford**

Exploring the Thames Valley

The pleasant countryside of the Chiltern Hills and
of the Thames Valley itself appealed to aristocrats
who built stately homes close to London. Many of
these are among the grandest in the country, including
Hatfield House and Blenheim. Around these great
houses grew picturesque villages, with half-timbered
buildings and, as you move towards the Cotswolds,
houses built in attractive buff-coloured stone.
That the area has been inhabited for
thousands of years is shown by the
number of prehistoric remains, including
the most remarkable chalk hillside
figure, the White Horse of Uffington.

SIGHTS AT A GLANCE

Blenheim Palace pp228–9 **6**
Burford **2**
Gardens of the Rose **15**
Great Tew **1**
Hatfield House **13**
Hughendon Manor **16**
Kelmscott **3**
Knebworth House **12**
Oxford pp222–7 **5**
Roald Dahl Museum **10**
St Albans **14**
Stowe **7**
Vale of the White
  Horse **4**
Waddesdon Manor **9**
Windsor pp235–7 **18**
Woburn Abbey **8**
ZSL Whipsnade Zoo **11**

Walks and Tours
Touring the Thames **17**

A thatched cottage, Upper Swarford, Banbury

GETTING AROUND

As an important commuter belt,
the Thames Valley is well served
by public transport, as well as a
good network of motorways and
major roads into London. Mainline
trains travel to all the major towns
and there are many coach services
that run from London to the major
sights and attractions.

0 kilometres 10

0 miles 10

**Marlow Bridge, spanning
the Thames**

Leicester

Rushden

Peterborough

Wollaston

Milton
Ernest

Olney

Bedford

Sandy

Kempston

Cambridge

Newport Pagnell

Biggleswade

Milton Keynes

Clophill   Henlow

Royston

WOBURN
ABBEY **8**

Flitwick

Letchworth   Baldock

Toddington

Barton-le-Clay

Hitchin

Buntingford

Leighton
Buzzard

Dunstable

Luton

Stevenage

Whitchurch

KNEBWORTH
HOUSE **12**

ODESDON
OR

11

Harpenden

Much
Hadham

WHIPSNADE

Welwyn Garden City

Hertford

Tring

Hatfield

HATFIELD
HOUSE **13**

Hoddesdon

Hemel Hempstead

10
AHL
EUM

GARDENS OF
THE ROSE

14 ST ALBANS **15**

Great
Missenden

Chesham

Potter's Bar

Cheshunt

HUGHENDON
MANOR **16**

Watford

Dartford

ligh
mbe

Rickmansworth

London

Beaconsfield

MES
low

Cookham

Maidenhead

Uxbridge

ames

Slough

WINDSOR **18**

Bracknell

okingham

Sandhurst

SEE ALSO

• *Where to Stay* pp566–8

• *Where to Eat* pp622–4

KEY

━━ Motorway

━━ Major road

━━ Secondary road

┈┈ Minor road

━━ Scenic route

┅┅ Main railway

┄┄ Minor railway

Radcliffe Camera, surrounded by Oxford's spires

Great Tew ❶

Oxfordshire. 👥 250. 🚋 Oxford or Banbury then taxi. ℹ️ Castle Quay Shopping Centre, Banbury (01295 259855). **www**.visitnorth oxfordshire.com

This secluded village of ironstone was founded in the 1630s by Lord Falkland for estate workers. It was heavily restored between 1809 and 1811 in the Gothic style. Thatched cottages stand in gardens with clipped box hedges, and in the village centre is the 16th-century pub, the **Falkland Arms**, with its period atmosphere.

Environs: Five miles (8 km) west are the **Rollright Stones**, three Bronze Age monuments. They comprise a stone circle of 77 stones, about 30 m (100 ft) in diameter, known as the King's Men; the remains of a burial chamber called the Whispering Knights; and the solitary King Stone.

Further north is **Banbury**, well known for its spicy flat cakes and its market cross, immortalized in the nursery rhyme, *Ride a Cock-horse to Banbury Cross*. The original medieval cross was destroyed but it was replaced in 1859.

The 19th-century Banbury Cross

🍺 **Falkland Arms Pub**
Great Tew. *Tel* 01608 683653. ◯ daily. ● 25 Dec. 🍴🎵

Burford ❷

Oxfordshire. 👥 1,000. ℹ️ Sheep St (01993 823558).

A charming small town, Burford has hardly changed from Georgian times, when it was an important coach stop between Oxford and the West Country. Cotswold stone houses, inns and shops, many built in the 16th century, line its main street. **Tolsey Hall** is a Tudor house with an open ground floor where stalls are still set up. The house is located on the corner of Sheep Street, itself a reminder of the importance of the medieval wool trade *(see p207)*.

Environs: Just east of Burford is **Swinbrook**, whose church contains the Fettiplace Monuments, six carved figures from the Tudor and Stuart periods.

Two miles (3 km) beyond are the ruins of **Minster Lovell Hall**, a 15th-century manor house whose unusual dovecote survives intact.

A few miles south of Burford is **Cotswold Wildlife Park**, home to a diverse collection of mammals, reptiles and birds. **Witney**, to the west, has a town hall dating from 1730.

🏛 **Minster Lovell Hall**
(EH) Minster Lovell. ◯ daily.

🦌 **Cotswold Wildlife Park**
Burford. *Tel* 01993 823006. ◯ daily. ● 25 Dec. 📷🦽🍴🚻
www.cotswoldwildlifepark.co.uk

Kelmscott ❸

Oxfordshire. 👥 100. ℹ️ 5 Market Place, Faringdon (01367 242191). **www**.faringdon.org

The imaginative designer and writer William Morris lived in this pretty Thameside village from 1871 until his death in 1896. He shared his house, the classic Elizabethan **Kelmscott Manor**, with fellow painter Dante Gabriel Rossetti (1828–82), who left after an affair with Morris's wife Jane – the model for many pre-Raphaelite paintings.

Morris and his followers in the Arts and Crafts movement were attracted by the

Cotswold stone houses, Burford, Oxfordshire

The formal entrance of the Elizabethan Kelmscott Manor

medieval feel of the village and several cottages were later built in Morris's memory.

Today Kelmscott Manor has works of art by members of the movement – including some William de Morgan tiles. Morris is buried in the village churchyard, with a tomb designed by Philip Webb.

Two miles (3 km) to the east is **Radcot Bridge**, thought to be the oldest bridge still standing over the Thames. Built in the 13th century from the local Taynton stone, it was a strategic river crossing, and in 1387 was damaged in a battle between Richard II and his barons.

🚾 **Kelmscott Manor**
Kelmscott. **Tel** 01367 252486. ⏺ Apr–Sep: Wed & some Sat; Gardens & shop: Thu. 🎫 🚻 limited. 🅿️ 🍴
www.kelmscottmanor.co.uk

Vale of the White Horse ❹

Oxfordshire. 🚆 Didcot. 🛈 25 Bridge St, Abingdon (01235 522711); 19 Church St, Wantage (01235 760176). www.abingdon.gov.uk

This lovely valley gets its name from the huge chalk horse, 100 m (350 ft) from nose to tail, carved into the hillside above Uffington. It is believed to be Britain's oldest hillside carving and has sparked many legends: some say it was cut by the Saxon leader Hengist (whose name means stallion in German); while others believe it is to do with Alfred the Great, thought to have been born nearby.

It is, however, a great deal older than either of these stories suggest, having been dated at around 1000 BC.

Nearby is the Celtic earth ramparts of the Iron Age hill fort, **Uffington Castle**. A mile (1.5 km) west along the Ridgeway, an ancient trade route, (see p37), is an even older monument, a large Stone Age burial mound which is known as **Wayland's Smithy**. This is immersed in legends that Sir Walter Scott (see p512) used in his novel *Kenilworth*.

The best view of the horse is to be had from Uffington village, which is also worth visiting for the **Tom Brown's School Museum**. This 17th-century school house contains exhibits devoted to the author Thomas Hughes (1822–96). Hughes set the early chapters of his Victorian novel, *Tom Brown's Schooldays*, here. The museum also contains material about excavations on White Horse Hill.

🏛 **Tom Brown's School**
Broad St, Uffington. 🛈 01367 820259. ⏺ Easter–Oct: Sat, Sun & public hols (pm). 🎫 🚻 limited.
www.museum.uffington.net

HILLSIDE CHALK FIGURES

It was the Celts who first saw the potential for creating large-scale artworks on the chalk hills of southern England. Horses – held in high regard by both the Celts and later the Saxons, and the objects of cult worship – were often a favourite subject, but people were also depicted, notably Cerne Abbas, Dorset (see p269) and the Long Man of Wilmington (see p180). The figures may have served as religious symbols or as landmarks by which tribes identified their territory. Many chalk figures have been obliterated, because without any attention they are quickly overrun by grass. Uffington is "scoured", to prevent encroachment by grass, a tradition once accompanied by a fair and other festivities. There was a second flush of hillside carving in the 18th century, especially in Wiltshire. In some cases – for instance at Bratton Castle near Westbury – an 18th-century carving has been superimposed on an ancient one.

Britain's oldest hillside carving, the White Horse of Uffington

Street-by-Street: Oxford 🔒

Oxford has long been a strategic point on the western routes into London – its name describes its position as a convenient spot for crossing the river (a ford for oxen). The city's first scholars, who founded the university, came from France in 1167. The development of England's first university created the spectacular skyline of tall towers and "dreaming spires".

Old Ashmolean
Now the Museum of the History of Science, this resplendent building was designed in 1683 to show Elias Ashmole's collection of curiosities. The displays were moved in 1845.

The Ashmolean Museum displays one of Britain's foremost collections of fine art and antiquities.

St John's College

Balliol College

Martyrs' Memorial
This commemorates the three Protestant martyrs, Latimer, Ridley and Cranmer, who were burned at the stake for heresy.

Coach station & Oxford Castle

ST GILES

BEAUMONT STREET

MAGDALEN STREET

BROAD STREET

TURL

BRA

| 0 meters | 100 |
| 0 yards | 100 |

KEY

– – – Suggested route

Trinity College

Oxford Story

Jesus College

Lincoln College

CORNMARKET STREET

MARKET STREET

Covered market

Railway station

Lincoln College Library

ST A

Museum of Oxford

PERCY BYSSHE SHELLEY

Shelley (1792–1822), one of the Romantic poets *(see p366)*, attended University College, Oxford, but was expelled after writing the revolutionary pamphlet *The Necessity of Atheism.* Despite that disgrace, the college has put up a memorial to him from his daughter-in-law.

Sheldonian Theatre
The first building designed by Wren (see p114) is the scene of Oxford University's traditional graduation ceremonies.

STAR SIGHTS

★ Radcliffe Camera

★ Christ Church

★ Radcliffe Camera

This Classical rotunda is Oxford's most distinctive building and is now a reading room of the Bodleian. It was one of the library's original buildings (see p227).

VISITORS' CHECKLIST

Oxfordshire. 🖼 134,248. 🚄 Botley Rd. 🚌 Gloucester Green. 🅸 15–16 Broad St (01865 25 2200). 🛒 Wed, 1st & 3rd Thu of mth (farmers' market), Thu (flea market). **www**.visitoxford.org

Bridge of Sighs

Resembling the steeply arched bridge in Venice of the same name, this picturesque landmark was built in 1914 and joins the old and new buildings of Hertford College.

New College

St Mary the Virgin Church

Queen's College

All Souls College

→ London

University College

→ Botanic Garden and Magdalen College

→ Oriel College

Merton College

Corpus Christi College

★ Christ Church

Students still eat at long tables in all the college halls. Senior academics sit at the high table and grace is almost always said in Latin.

Exploring Oxford

A bust on the Sheldonian Theatre

Oxford is more than just a university city; it has one of Britain's most important car factories in the suburb of Cowley. Despite this, Oxford is dominated by institutions related to its huge academic community: like Blackwell's bookshop which has over 20,000 titles in stock. The two rivers, the Cherwell and the Isis (the name given to the Thames as it flows through the city), provide lovely riverside walks, or you can hire a punt and spend an afternoon on the Cherwell.

🏛 Ashmolean Museum

Beaumont St. **Tel** 01865 278000.
◯ Tue–Sun (Sun pm only) & public hols. ● 1 Jan, Good Fri, 25–28 Dec.
🦽 📷 Tue, Fri, Sat. 🔲 🚻
www.ashmolean.org

One of the best museums in Britain outside London, the Ashmolean – the first purpose-built museum in England – opened in 1683, based on a display known as "The Ark" collected by the two John Tradescants, father and son.

On their many voyages to the Orient and the Americas they collected stuffed animals and tribal artifacts. On their death, the collection was acquired by the antiquarian Elias Ashmole, who donated it to the university and had a building made for the exhibits on Broad Street – the Old Ashmolean, now the Museum of the History of Science. In the 1800s, part of the Tradescant collection was moved to the University Galleries, a Neo-Classical building of 1845. This greatly expanded museum is now known as the Ashmolean.

What is left of the original curio collection is overshadowed by the other exhibits in the museum, in particular the paintings. These include Bellini's *St Jerome Reading in a Landscape* (late 15th century); Raphael's *Heads of Two Apostles* (1519); Turner's *Venice: The Grand Canal* (1840); Rembrandt's *Saskia Asleep* (1635); Michelangelo's *Crucifixion* (1557), Picasso's *Blue Roofs* (1901) and a large group of Pre-Raphaelites, including Rossetti and Millais. There are also fine Greek and Roman carvings and a collection of stringed musical instruments. Items of more local interest include a Rowlandson watercolour of Radcliffe Square in about 1790 and the Oxford Crown. This silver coin was minted here during the Civil War in 1644 *(see p52)* and forms part of the second-largest coin collection in Britain. Perhaps the single most important item is the gold enamelled ring known as the Alfred Jewel *(see p47),* which is over 1,000 years old.

A new building designed by Rick Mather, which opened in late 2009 provides the museum with twice as much space as it previously had.

The entrance to the Ashmolean Museum

♣ Botanic Garden

Rose Lane. **Tel** 01865 286690.
◯ daily. ● Good Fri, 25 Dec.
🦽 Mar–Oct. **Donation** Nov–Feb.
🦽 www.botanic-garden.ox.ac.uk

Britain's oldest botanic garden was founded in 1621 – one ancient yew tree survives from that period. The entrance gates were designed by Nicholas Stone in 1633 and paid for, like the garden itself, by the Earl of Danby. His statue adorns the gate, along with those of Charles I and II. This small garden is a delightful spot for a stroll, with an original walled garden, a more recent herbaceous border and rock garden, and a new insectivorous house.

The 17th-century Botanic Gardens

🏰 Carfax Tower

Carfax Sq. **Tel** 01865 790522. ◯ daily. ● 1 Jan, 25 & 26 Dec. 🦽 🚻

The tower is all that remains of the 14th-century Church of St Martin, demolished in 1896 so that the adjoining road could be widened. Be there to watch the clock strike the quarter hours, and climb to the top for a panoramic view of the city. Carfax was the crossing point of the original north-to-south and east-to-west routes through Oxford and the word comes from the French *quatre voies,* or "four ways".

🎵 Holywell Music Room

Holywell St. ◯ concerts only. 🦽 🦽

This was the first building in Europe designed, in 1752, specifically for public musical performances. Previously, concerts had been held in private houses for invited guests only. Its two splendid chandeliers originally adorned Westminster Hall at the coronation of George IV in 1820, and were given by the king to Wadham College, of which the music room technically forms a part. The room is regularly used for contemporary and classical concerts.

🏛 Museum of Oxford
St Aldates. *Tel 01865 252761.* ◯ Tue–Sun. ● 1 Jan, 24–26 Dec, 31 Dec. 🔲 www.moo.org.uk

A well-organized display in the Victorian town hall illustrates the long history of Oxford and its university. Exhibits include a Roman pottery kiln. The main features are a series of well-reconstructed rooms, including one from an Elizabethan inn and an 18th-century student's room.

🎭 Martyrs' Memorial
Magdalen St.

This commemorates the three Protestants burned at the stake on Broad Street – Bishops Latimer and Ridley in 1555, and Archbishop Cranmer in 1556. On the accession of Queen Mary in 1553 *(see p51)*, they were committed to the Tower of London, then sent to Oxford to defend their views before the doctors of divinity who, after the hearing, condemned them as heretics.

The memorial was designed in 1843 by George Gilbert Scott and based on the Eleanor crosses erected in 12 English towns by Edward I (1239–1307) to honour his queen.

🎭 Oxford Castle
44–46 Oxford Castle. *Tel 01865 260666.* ◯ daily. ♿ 🔲 🔲

Following a £40-million development, this 1,000-year-old castle opened in 2005. It forms part of an urban space that includes shops, restaurants and a hotel.

🏛 Oxford Castle Unlocked
44-46 Oxford Castle. *Tel 01865 260666.* ◯ daily. ● 25 Dec. 🔲 🔲 🔲 ♿

The secrets of the castle are revealed in this exhibition that looks at the site's turbulent past. Climb St George's Tower for panoramic views over the city.

🎭 Sheldonian Theatre
Broad St. *Tel 01865 277299.* ◯ call for details. ● Christmas period, Easter & public hols. 🎫 ♿ limited. www.sheldon.ox.ac.uk

Completed in 1669, this was designed by Christopher Wren *(see p114)*, and paid for by Gilbert Sheldon, the Archbishop of Canterbury, as a location for university degree ceremonies. The Classical design of the D-shaped building is based on the Theatre of Marcellus in Rome. The octagonal cupola was built in 1838 and boasts a famous view from its huge Lantern. The theatre's painted ceiling depicts the triumph of religion, art and science over envy, hatred and malice.

⛪ St Mary the Virgin Church
High St. *Tel 01865 279111.* ◯ daily. ● 24, 25, 26 Dec. 🔲 🔲 www.university-church.ox.ac.uk

This, the official university church, is said to be the most visited parish church in England. The oldest parts date from the early 13th century and include the tower, from which there are fine views. Its Convocation House served as the university's first

Thomas Cranmer statue, St Mary the Virgin Church

library until the Bodleian was founded in 1488 *(see p227).* The church is where the three Oxford Martyrs were pronounced heretics in 1555. An architectural highlight is the Baroque south porch.

🏛 University Museum
Parks Rd. *Tel 01865 272950.* ◯ daily. ● Easter, 24–26 Dec. ♿ 🔲 www.oum.ox.ac.uk

🏛 Pitt Rivers Museum
Parks Rd. *Tel 01865 270927.* ◯ daily. ● Easter, 24–26 Dec. ♿ 🔲 www.prm.ox.ac.uk

Two of Oxford's most interesting museums adjoin each other. The first is a museum of natural history containing relics of dinosaurs as well as a stuffed dodo. This flightless bird has been extinct since the 17th century, but was immortalized by Lewis Carroll (an Oxford mathematics lecturer) in his book *Alice in Wonderland*. The Pitt Rivers Museum has an extensive ethnographic collection – masks and totems from Africa and the Far East – and archaeological displays, including exhibits collected by the explorer Captain Cook.

The impressive frontage of the University Museum and Pitt Rivers Museum

Exploring Oxford University

Many of the 36 colleges which go to make up the university were founded between the 13th and 16th centuries and cluster around the city centre. As scholarship was then the exclusive preserve of the church, the colleges were designed along the lines of monastic buildings but were often surrounded by beautiful gardens. Although most colleges have been altered over the years, many still incorporate a lot of their original features.

The spectacular view of All Souls College from St Mary's Church

All Souls College
Founded in 1438 on the High Street by Henry VI, the chapel on the college's north side has a classic hammerbeam roof, unusual misericords *(see p341)* on the choir stalls and 15th-century stained glass.

Christ Church College
The best way to view this, the largest of the Oxford colleges, is to approach through the meadows from St Aldate's. Christ Church dates from 1525 when Cardinal Wolsey founded it as an ecclesiastical college to train cardinals. The upper part of the tower in Tom Quad – a rectangular courtyard – was built by Wren *(see p114)* in 1682 and is the largest in the

city. When its bell, Great Tom, was hung in 1648, the college had 101 students, which is why the bell is rung 101 times at 9:05pm, to mark the curfew for students (which has not been enforced since 1963). The odd timing is because night falls here five minutes later than at Greenwich *(see p125)*. Christ Church has produced 13 British prime ministers in the last 200 years. Beside the main quad is the 12th-century Christ Church Cathedral, one of the smallest in England.

Lincoln College
One of the best-preserved of the medieval colleges, it was founded in 1427 on Turl Street, and the front quad and façade

are 15th century. The hall still has its original roof, including the gap where smoke used to escape. The Jacobean chapel is notable for its stained glass. John Wesley *(see p279)* was at college here and his rooms, now a chapel, can be visited.

Magdalen College
At the end of the High Street is perhaps the most typical and beautiful Oxford college. Its 15th-century quads in contrasting styles are set in a park by the Cherwell, crossed by Magdalen Bridge. Every May Day at 6am, the college choir sings from the top of Magdalen's bell tower (1508) – a 16th-century custom to mark the start of summer.

New College
One of the grandest colleges, it was founded by William of Wykeham in 1379 to educate clergy to replace those killed by the Black Death of 1348 *(see p49)*.

Magdalen Bridge spanning the River Cherwell

Its magnificent chapel on New College Lane, restored in the 19th century, has vigorous 14th-century misericords and El Greco's (1541–1614) famous painting of *St James*.

Queen's College
Most of the college buildings date from the 18th century and represent some of the finest work from that period in Oxford. Its superb library was built in 1695 by Henry Aldrich (1647–1710) The front screen with its bell-topped gatehouse is a feature of the High Street.

STUDENT LIFE

Students belong to individual colleges and usually live in them for the duration of their course. The university gives lectures, sets exams and awards degrees but much of the students' tuition and social life is based around their college. Many university traditions date back hundreds of years, like the graduation ceremonies at the Sheldonian, which are still held in Latin.

Graduation at the Sheldonian *(see p224)*

Merton College seen from Christ Church Meadows

St John's College
The impressive frontage on St Giles dates from 1437, when it was founded for Cistercian scholars. The old library has lovely 17th-century bookcases and stained glass, while the Baylie Chapel has a display of 15th-century vestments.

Trinity College
The oldest part of the college on Broad Street, Durham Quad, is named after the earlier college of 1296, which was incorporated into Trinity in 1555. The late 17th-century chapel has a magnificent reredos and wooden screen.

Corpus Christi College
The whole of the charming front quad on Merton Street dates from 1517, when the college was founded. The quad's sundial, topped by a pelican – the college symbol – bears an early 17th-century calendar. The chapel has a rare 16th-century eagle lectern.

Merton College
Off Merton Street, this is the oldest college (1264) in Oxford. Much of its hall dates from then, including a sturdy decorated door. The chapel choir contains allegorical reliefs representing music, arithmetic, rhetoric and grammar. Merton's Mob Quad served as a model for the later colleges.

BODLEIAN LIBRARY
Founded in 1320, the library was expanded in 1426 by Humphrey, Duke of Gloucester (1391–1447) and brother of Henry V, when his collection of manuscripts would not fit into the old library. It was refounded in 1602 by Thomas Bodley, a wealthy scholar, who insisted on strict rules: the keeper was forbidden to marry. The library is one of the six copyright deposit libraries in the country – it is entitled to receive a copy of every book published in Britain.

The Radcliffe Camera (1748), a domed Baroque rotunda, was built by James Gibbs as a memorial to the physician Dr John Radcliffe (1650–1714).

Main entrance

This extension was built in 1630.

Duke Humphrey's Library *has ceiling panels that carry the university crest and Latin motto* Dominus Illuminatio Mea – *the Lord, my Light.*

The Divinity School (1488) *has a unique vaulted ceiling with 455 carved bosses representing biblical scenes and both mythical and real beasts – one of the country's finest Gothic interiors.*

Blenheim Palace 6

After John Churchill, the 1st Duke of Marlborough, defeated the French at the Battle of Blenheim in 1704, Queen Anne gave him the Manor of Woodstock and had this palatial house built for him in gratitude. Designed by both Nicholas Hawksmoor and Sir John Vanbrugh *(see p398)*, it is a Baroque masterpiece. It was also the birthplace of Britain's World War II leader, Winston Churchill, in 1874.

★ Long Library
This 55 m (183 room was desig by Vanbrugh as picture gallery. portraits include of Queen Anne Sir Godfrey Kne (1646–1723). T stucco on the ceiling is by Isa Mansfield (1725

Winston Churchill and his wife, Clementine

The Grand Bridge was begun in 1708. It has a 31 m (101 ft) main span and contains rooms within its structure.

Chapel
The marble monument to the 1st Duke of Marlborough and his family was sculpted by Michael Rysbrack in 1733.

Water Terraces
These magnificent gardens were laid out in the 1920s by French architect Achille Duchêne in 17th-century style, with detailed patterned beds and fountains.

STAR SIGHTS

★ Long Library

★ Saloon

★ Park and Gardens

Great Hall
This splendid ceiling by Thornhill in 1716, shows the 1st Duke of Marlborough presenting his plan for the Battle of Blenheim to Britannia.

VISITORS' CHECKLIST

Woodstock, Oxfordshire.
Tel 0870 060 2080. from Oxford. Oxford. **Palace & Gardens** Feb–Oct: 10:30am–5:30pm daily; Nov & Dec: Wed–Sun. **Park** 9am–5pm daily. limited.
www.blenheimpalace.com

The Italian Garden contains the Mermaid Fountain (early 1900s) by US sculptor Waldo Story.

East gate

Great Court

Grinling Gibbons lions (1709)

Clock tower

Blenheim Palace: The Untold Story

First State Room

Entrance

The Green Drawing Room has a full-length portrait of the 4th Duke by George Romney (1734–1802).

Red Drawing Room

Green Writing Room

Second State Room

Third State Room

★ **PARK AND GARDENS**

Grand Bridge
Palace
Water Terraces
Temple of Diana
Rose Garden
Arboretum
Column of Victory
Triumphal Arch
Woodstock
Car park
Italian Garden
Narrow-gauge railway
Secret garden
Car park
Butterfly House
Adventure playground
Marlborough Maze

A house fit for a victorious general had to be surrounded by a park with suitably heroic monuments. They were kept when "Capability" Brown (*see p26*) re-landscaped the park (1764–74) and created the lake.

★ **Saloon**
French artist Louis Laguerre (1663–1721) painted the detailed scenes on the walls and ceiling.

Canaletto's Entrance to the Arsenal (1730) hangs at Woburn Abbey

Stowe Gardens ➐

(NT) Buckingham, Buckinghamshire. *Tel* 01494 755568. ⬆ Milton Keynes then bus. ⬤ Mar–Nov: Wed–Sun; Dec–Feb: Sat & Sun, public hols. **Stowe House** ⬤ Access may be restricted due to a 20-year restoration project. 🖼 ♿ limited. 🖥 📷 www. nationaltrust.org.uk/stowegardens

This is the most ambitious and important landscaped garden in Britain, as well as being one of the finest examples of the 18th-century passion for improving on nature to make it conform to fashionable notions of taste.

In the space of nearly 100 years the original garden, first laid out around 1680, was enlarged and transformed by the addition of monuments, Greek and Gothic temples, grottoes, statues, ornamental bridges, artificial lakes and "natural" tree plantings.

Most of the leading designers and architects of the period contributed to the design, including Sir John Vanbrugh, James Gibbs and Capability Brown *(see p26)*.

From 1593 to 1921 the property was owned by the Temple and Grenville families – later the Dukes of Buckingham – until the large Palladian house at its centre was converted into an elite boys' school.

The family were soldiers and politicians in the liberal tradition, and many of the buildings and sculptures in the garden symbolize Utopian ideals of democracy and freedom. Some features deteriorated in the 19th century but a major restoration programme has returned much of the statuary to its former glory.

Woburn Abbey ➑

Woburn, Bedfordshire. *Tel* 01525 290333. ⬆ Flitwick then taxi. ⬤ Mar–Sep: daily. ⬤ Oct–Feb. **Grounds** ⬤ daily. 📷 🖼 ♿ ring first. 📷 by arrangement. 🍴 www.woburnabbey.co.uk

The Dukes of Bedford have lived here for over 350 years and were among the first owners of an English stately home to open their house to the public some 40 years ago.

The abbey was built in the mid-18th century on the foundations of a large 12th-century Cistercian monastery. Its mix of styles range from Henry Flitcroft and Henry Holland *(see p28)*. The abbey's grounds are also popular for their 142-ha (350-acre) safari park and attractive deer park, home to nine species including the Manchurian Sika deer from China.

The home's magnificent state apartments house an important private art collection which includes works by Reynolds (1723–92) and Canaletto (1697–1768).

Waddesdon Manor ➒

Nr Aylesbury, Buckinghamshire. *Tel* 01296 653226. ⬆ Aylesbury then taxi. **House** ⬤ Mar–Dec: Wed–Sun; Jan–Feb: Sat & Sun. **Grounds** ⬤ Mar–23 Dec: 10am–5pm Wed–Sun & bank hol Mon. 🖼 🍴 🖥 📷 www.waddesdon.org.uk

Waddesdon Manor was built between 1874–89 by Baron Ferdinand de Rothschild and designed by French architect Gabriel-Hippolyte Destailleur.

Built in the style of a French 16th-century chateau, the manor houses one of the world's finest collections of French 18th-century decorative art as well as Savonnierie carpets and Sèvres porcelain.

The garden, originally laid out by French landscape gardener Elie Lainé, is renowned for its seasonal displays.

Roald Dahl Museum ➓

81–83 High St, Great Missenden, Buckinghamshire. *Tel* 01494 892192. ⬆ Great Missenden. ⬤ 10am–5pm Tue–Sun & bank hols. 📷 🖼 ♿ www.roalddahlmuseum.org

The magical world of Roald Dahl's stories comes to life in this award-winning museum. A series of biographical galleries explore the life and work of the children's writer, while the Story Centre's interactive exhibits allow children to make their own animation film, record dreams in a "dream bottle" or try their hand at creative writing.

The 17th-century Palladian bridge over the Octagon Lake in Stowe Park

Hatfield House, one of the largest Jacobean mansions in the country

ZSL Whipsnade Zoo ⓫

Nr Dunstable, Bedfordshire. **Tel** 01582 872171. ⯒ Hemel Hempsted or Luton then bus. ◐ daily. ◉ 25 Dec. ⬚ ♿ ▯ www.zsl.org

The rural branch of London Zoo, this was one of the first zoos to minimize the use of cages, confining animals safely but without constriction.

At 240 ha (600 acres), it is Europe's largest conservation park, with more than 2,500 species. You can drive through some areas or go by steam train. Also popular are the adventure playground, the Cheetah Rock exhibit and the sea lions' underwater display.

Knebworth House ⓬

Knebworth, Hertfordshire. **Tel** 01438 812661. ⯒ Stevenage then taxi. ◐ Sat, Sun; two weeks at Easter: daily; Jul–Aug: daily. ▯ ⬚ ♿ limited. ▯ ▯ www.knebworthhouse.com

A notable Tudor mansion, with a beautiful Jacobean banqueting hall, Knebworth was overlain with a 19th-century Victorian Gothic exterior by Lord Lytton, the head of the family. His eldest son, the 1st Earl of Lytton, was Viceroy of India, and exhibits illustrate the Delhi Durbar of 1877, when Queen Victoria became Empress of India.

A visit includes the house, gardens, park, and a dinosaur trail for children.

Hatfield House ⓭

Hatfield, Hertfordshire. **Tel** 01707 287010. ⯒ Hatfield. ◐ Easter Sat–Sep: Wed–Sun & public hols. ▯ ⬚ ♿ ▯ www.hatfield-house.co.uk

One of England's finest Jacobean houses, Hatfield House was built between 1607 and 1611 for the powerful statesman Robert Cecil.

Its chief historical interest, though, lies in the surviving wing of the original Tudor Hatfield Palace, where Queen Elizabeth I (*see pp50–51*) spent much of her childhood. She held her first Council of State here when she was crowned in 1558. The palace was partly demolished in 1607 to make way for the new house, which contains mementoes of her life, including the *Rainbow* portrait painted around 1600 by Isaac Oliver. Visitors can attend medieval banquets in the old palace's Great Hall.

Originally laid out by Robert Cecil with help from John Tradescant, the gardens have been restored to reflect these Jacobean origins.

FAMOUS PURITANS

18th-century engraving of John Bunyan

Three major figures connected with the 17th-century Puritan movement are celebrated in the Thames area. John Bunyan (1628–88), who wrote the allegorical tale *The Pilgrim's Progress,* was born at Elstow, near Bedford. A passionate Puritan orator, he was jailed for his beliefs for 17 years. The Bunyan Museum in Bedford is a former site of Puritan worship. William Penn (1644–1718), founder of Pennsylvania in the USA, lived, worshipped and is buried at Jordans, near Beaconsfield. A bit further north at Chalfont St Giles is the cottage where the poet John Milton (1608–74) stayed to escape London's plague. There he completed his greatest work, *Paradise Lost.* The house is now a museum based on his life and works.

William Penn, founder of Pennsylvania

John Milton painted by Pieter van der Plas

St Albans ⑭

Today a thriving market town and a base for London commuters, St Albans was for centuries at the heart of some of the most stirring events in English history. A regional capital of ancient Britain, it became a major Roman settlement and then a key ecclesiastical centre – so important that during the Wars of the Roses (see p49), two battles were fought for it. In 1455 the Yorkists drove King Henry VI from the town and six years later the Lancastrians retook it.

The martyr St Alban

Exploring St Albans

Part of the appeal of this ancient and fascinating town, little more than an hour's drive from London, is that its 2,000-year history can be traced vividly by visiting a few sites within easy walking distance of one another. There is a large car park within the walls of the Roman city of Verulamium, between the museum and St Michael's Church and across the road from the excavated theatre. From there it is a pleasant lakeside walk across the park, passing more Roman sites, Ye Olde Fighting Cocks inn, the massive cathedral and the historic High Street. Marking the centre of the town, the High Street is lined with several Tudor buildings and a clock tower dating from 1412, from which the curfew bell used to ring at 4am in the morning and 8:30pm at night.

⋔ Verulamium

Just outside the city centre are the walls of Verulamium, one of the first British cities the Romans established after their invasion of Britain in AD 43. Boadicea (see p195) razed it

to the ground during her unsuccessful rebellion against the Romans in AD 62, but its position on Watling Street, an important trading route, meant that it was quickly rebuilt on an even larger scale and the city flourished until 410.

🏛 Verulamium Museum

St Michael's St. **Tel** 01727 751810.
◯ daily (pm only Sun). ● 25 Dec–2 Jan. 🖼 🕭 🖪 www.stalbans museum.org.uk
This excellent museum tells the story of the city, but its main attraction is its splendid collection of well-preserved Roman artefacts, notably some breathtaking mosaic floors, including one depicting the head of a sea god, and another of a scallop shell. Other finds included burial urns and lead coffins.

On the basis of excavated plaster fragments, a Roman room has been painstakingly recreated, its walls painted in startlingly bright colours and geometric patterns.

Between here and St Albans Cathedral are a bath house with a mosaic, remnants of the ancient city wall and one of the original gates.

One of the oldest surviving pubs in England

🍺 Ye Olde Fighting Cocks

Abbey Mill Lane. **Tel** 01727 869152.
◯ daily. 🕭
Believed to be England's oldest surviving pub, Ye Olde Fighting Cocks is certainly, with its octagonal shape, one of the most unusual. It originated as the medieval dovecote of the old abbey and moved here after the Dissolution (see p50).

🏛 Roman Theatre

Bluehouse Hill. **Tel** 01727 835035.
◯ daily. ● 1 Jan, 25, 26 Dec. 🖼 🖪 www.romantheatre.co.uk
Just across the road from the museum are the foundations of the open-air theatre, first built around AD 140 but enlarged several times. It is one of only six known to have been built in Roman Britain. Alongside it are traces of a row of Roman shops and a house, from which many of the museum's treasures – such as a bronze statuette of Venus – were excavated in the 1930s.

🏛 St Michael's Church

St Michael's. **Tel** 01727 835037.
◯ Apr–Sep: phone for details. 🕭
This church was first founded during the Saxon reign and is built partly on bricks taken from Verulamium, which by then was in decline. Numerous additions have been made since then, including a truly splendid Jacobean pulpit.

The church contains an early 17th-century monument to the statesman and writer Sir Francis Bacon; his father owned nearby Gorhambury, a large Tudor house, now in ruins.

A scallop shell, one of the mosaic floors at the Verulamium Museum

🅰 St Albans Cathedral

Sumpter Yard. **Tel** 01727 860780.
⭕ daily. ♿ 📷 11:30am & 2:30pm.
www.stalbanscathedral.org.uk
This outstanding example
of medieval architecture has
some classic features such as
the 13th- and 14th-century wall
paintings on the Norman piers.

It was begun in 793, when
King Offa of Mercia founded
the abbey in honour of St
Alban, Britain's first Christian
martyr, put to death by the
Romans in the third century
for sheltering a priest. The

The splendour of the Gardens of the Rose in June

The imposing west side of
St Albans Cathedral

oldest parts, which still stand,
were first built in 1077 and
are easily recognizable as
Norman by the round-headed
arches and windows. They
form part of the 84 m (276 ft)
nave – the longest in England.

The pointed arches further
east are Early English (13th
century), while the decorated
work of the 14th century was
added when some of the
Norman arches collapsed.

East of the crossing is
what remains of St Alban's
shrine – a marble pedestal
made up of more than 2,000
tiny fragments. Next to it is the
tomb of Humphrey, Duke of
Gloucester (see p227).

It was here at the cathedral
that the English barons drafted
the Magna Carta document
(see p48), which King John
was then forced to sign.

Gardens of the Rose 🕒

Chiswell Green, Hertfordshire. **Tel**
01727 850461. ⭐ St Albans then
bus. ⭕ Jun–Sep: daily, but always
call ahead. 🌐 sometimes Mon, Tue.
📷 ♿ 🛈 📷 www.rnrs.org

As well as being England's
national symbol, the rose
is the most popular flower
with British gardeners.

The 5 ha (12 acre) garden of
the Royal National Rose Society, with over 30,000 plants and
1,700 varieties, is at its peak in
late June. The gardens trace
the history of the flower as far
back as the white rose of
York, the red rose of Lancaster
(see p49) and the Rosa Mundi
– named by Henry II for his
mistress Fair Rosamond after
she was poisoned by Queen
Eleanor in 1177. In 2005–7

the gardens were extensively
redeveloped by leading garden designer Michael Balston.

Hughenden Manor 🕕

(NT) High Wycombe, Bucking-
hamshire. **Tel** 01494 755565. ⭐
High Wycombe then bus. ⭕ Mar–
Oct: Wed–Sun, 2 weeks in Dec.
🌐 Good Fri. 📷 ♿ limited. 🍴

The Victorian statesman and
novelist Benjamin Disraeli,
Prime Minister from 1874 to
1880, lived here for 33 years
until his death. Originally a
Georgian villa, Disraeli
adapted it in 1862 to the
Gothic style. Furnished as
it was in his day, the house
gives an idea of the life of a
wealthy Victorian gentleman
and shows some portraits
of his contemporaries.

GEORGE BERNARD SHAW

Although a controversial playwright and known
as a mischievous character, the Irish-born
George Bernard Shaw (1856–1950) was a man
of settled habits. He lived near St Albans in a
house at Ayot St Lawrence, now called Shaw's
Corner, for the last 44 years of his life,
working until his last weeks in a
summer-house at the bottom
of his large garden. His plays,
combining wit with a powerful
political and social message, still
seem fresh today. One of the most
enduring is Pygmalion (1913),
on which the musical My Fair
Lady is based. The house and
garden are now a museum
of his life and works.

Touring the Thames ⑰

The Thames between Pangbourne and Eton is leafy and romantic and best seen by boat. But if time is short, the road keeps close to its bank for much of the way. Swans glide gracefully below ancient bridges, voles dive into the water for cover, and elegant herons stand impassive at the river's edge. Huge beech trees overhang the banks which are lined with fine houses, their gardens sloping to the water. The tranquil scene has inspired painters and writers through the ages as well as operating, until recently, as an important transport link.

Hambledon Mill ⑥
The white weather-boarded mill, which was operational until 1955, is one of the largest on the Thames as well as one of the oldest in origin. There are traces of the original 16th-century mill.

Beale Park ①
The philanthropist Gilbert Beale (1868–1967) created a 10 ha (25 acre) park to preserve this beautiful stretch of river intact and breed endangered birds like owls, ornamental water fowl, pheasants and peacocks.

Henley ⑤
This lovely old river town boasts houses and churches dating from the 15th and 16th centuries and an important regatta, first held in 1829 (see p66).

Pangbourne ②
Kenneth Grahame (1859–1932), author of *The Wind in the Willows,* lived here. Pangbourne was used as the setting by artists Ernest Shepard in 1908 and Arthur Rackham in 1951 to illustrate the book.

Sonning Bridge ④
The 18th-century bridge is made up of 11 brick arches of varying width.

TIPS FOR DRIVERS

Tour length: 50 miles (75 km).
Stopping-off points: The picturesque town of Henley has a large number of riverside pubs which will make good stops for lunch. If you are boating you can often moor your boat alongside the river bank. (See also pp684–5.)

Whitchurch Mill ③
This charming village, linked to Pangbourne by a Victorian toll bridge, has a picturesque church and one of the many disused watermills that once harnessed the power of this stretch of river.

Cookham ⑦
This is famous as the home of Stanley Spencer (1891–1959), one of Britain's leading 20th-century artists. The former Methodist chapel, where Spencer worshipped as a child, has been converted into a gallery that contains some of his paintings and equipment. This work, entitled *Swan Upping* (1914–19), recalls a Thames custom.

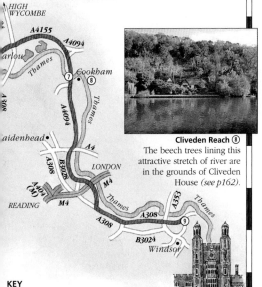

Cliveden Reach ⑧
The beech trees lining this attractive stretch of river are in the grounds of Cliveden House (see p162).

KEY

▬▬ Tour route

═══ Other roads

☆ Viewpoint

| 0 kilometres | 10 |
| 0 miles | 5 |

Eton College ⑨
Founded by Henry VI in 1440, Eton is Britain's most famous public school. It has a superb Perpendicular chapel (1441) with a series of English wall paintings (1479–88).

Salter Bros hire boats, moored at Henley

BOATING TOURS
In summer, scheduled river services run between Henley, Windsor, Runnymede and Marlow. Several companies operate from towns along the route. You can hire boats by the hour or the day or, for a longer tour, you can rent cabin cruisers and sleep on board (see also p689). Ring Salter Bros on 01753 865 832 for more information.

Windsor ⑱

Berkshire. 🏠 *30,000* 🚊
ℹ️ *Windsor Royal Station (01753 743900).* **www**.windsor.gov.uk

The town of Windsor is dwarfed by the enormous **castle** *(see pp236–7)* on the hill above – in fact its original purpose was to serve the castle's needs. The town is full of quaint Georgian shops, houses and inns. The most prominent building on the High Street is the **Guildhall** completed by Wren *(see p114)* in 1689, where Prince Charles and Camilla Parker-Bowles were married in 2005. **Eton College**, the most prestigious school in Britain, lies just a short walk away.

The huge 1,940-ha (4,800-acre) **Windsor Great Park** stretches from the castle three miles (5 km) to Snow Hill, where there is a statue of George III.

Environs: Four miles (7 km) to the southeast is the level grassy meadow, **Runnymede**. This is one of England's most historic sites, where in 1215 King John was forced by his rebellious barons to sign the *Magna Carta (see p48)*, thereby limiting his royal powers. The dainty memorial pavilion at the top of the meadow was erected in 1957.

🏫 **Eton College**
Tel 01753 671177. ⬜ *mid-Mar–Oct: 10:30am–4:30pm. Always call ahead.* **www**.etoncollege.com

King John signing the *Magna Carta*, Runnymede

Windsor Castle

Henry II rebuilt the castle

The oldest continuously inhabited royal residence in Britain, the castle, originally made of wood, was built by William the Conqueror in around 1080 to guard the western approaches to London. He chose the site as it was on high ground and just a day's journey from his base in the Tower of London. Successive monarchs have made alterations that render it a remarkable monument to royalty's changing tastes. King George V's affection for it was shown when he chose Windsor for his family surname in 1917. The castle is an official residence of the Queen and her family who stay here many weekends.

Albert Memorial Chapel
First built in 1240, it was rebuilt in 1485 and finally converted into a memorial for Prince Albert in 1863.

King Henry VIII Gate and main exit

★ St George's Chapel
The architectural highlight of the castle, it was built between 1475 and 1528 and is one of England's outstanding Perpendicular Gothic churches. Ten monarchs are buried here.

The Round Tower was first built in wood by William the Conqueror. In 1170 it was rebuilt in stone by Henry II *(see p48)*. It now houses the Royal Archives and Photographic Collection.

Statue of Charles II

Albert Memorial Chapel (1485)

The Round Tower (1080)

Waterloo Chamber (1820s)

St George's Hall (1357–68)

Middle Ward

Lower Ward

St George's Chapel (1475–1528)

Upper Ward

KEY

▢	11th–13th centuries
▢	14th century
▢	15th–18th centuries
▢	19th–20th centuries

WINDSOR CASTLE'S HISTORY
Founded in 1080 as a motte and bailey (see p486), Henry II and Edward III were responsible for the bulk of the work until the castle was remodelled by George IV in 1823.

Drawings Gallery
This chalk etching of Christ by Michelangelo is part of the Royal Collection. Various pieces in the collection are on display here, including works by Holbein and Leonardo da Vinci among others.

The Audience Chamber is where the Queen greets her guests.

The Queen's Ballroom

Queen Mary's Dolls' House, designed by Sir Edwin Lutyens, was given to Queen Mary in 1924. The wine cellar contains genuine vintage wine.

VISITORS' CHECKLIST

Castle Hill. *Tel* 020 7766 7304.
🕐 9:45am–5:15pm (Nov–Feb: to 4:15pm). (Last adm: 1 hr 15 mins before close.) ⬤ Good Fri, 25 & 26 Dec. ✝ St Georges Chapel (closed for services). ♿ **www**.royalcollection.org.uk

Waterloo Chamber
This banqueting hall was created as part of Charles Long's brief for the remodelling of the castle in 1823.

Brunswick Tower

The East Terrace Garden was created by Sir Jeffry Wyatville for King George IV in the 1820s.

★ **State Apartments**
These rooms contain many treasures, such as this 18th-century bed in the King's State Bedchamber, hung in its present splendour for the visit in 1855 of Napoleon III.

STAR SIGHTS
★ St George's Chapel

★ State Apartments

The Fire of 1992
A devastating blaze began during maintenance work on the State Apartments. St George's Hall was destroyed but has been rebuilt.

THE WEST COUNTRY

The West Country at a Glance

The West Country forms a long peninsula bounded by the Atlantic to the north and the English Channel to the south, tapering down to Land's End, mainland Britain's westernmost point. Whether exploring the great cities and cathedrals, experiencing the awesome solitude of the moors and their prehistoric monuments, or simply enjoying the miles of coastline and mild climate, this region has an enduring appeal for holiday-makers.

Wells (see pp252–3) *is a charming town nestling at the foot of the Mendip Hills. It is famous for its exquisite three-towered cathedral with an ornate west façade, featuring a array of statues. Alongside stan the moated Bishop's Palace an the 15th-century Vicar's Close*

Exmoor's (see pp250–51) *heather-clad moors and wooded valleys, grazed by wild ponies and red deer, lead down to some of Devon and Somerset's most dramatic cliffs and coves.*

St Ives (see p277) *has a branch of the Tate Gallery that shows modern works by artists associated with the area. Patrick Heron's bold coloured glass (1993) is on permanent display.*

Devon

DEVON AND CORNWALL
(see pp272–95)

Cornwall

Dartmoor (see pp294–5) *is a wilderness of great natural beauty covering an area of 365 sq miles (945 sq km). Stone clapper bridges, picturesque villages and weathered granite tors punctuate the landscape.*

◁ **Stunning views of the Lizard Peninsula**

Bath (see pp258–9) is named after the Roman baths that stand at the heart of the old city next to the splendid medieval abbey. It is one of Britain's liveliest and most rewarding cities, full of elegant Georgian terraces, built in local honey-coloured limestone by the two John Woods (Elder and Younger).

Stonehenge (see pp262–3), the world-famous prehistoric monument, was built in several stages from 3000 BC. Moving and erecting its massive stones was an extraordinary feat for its time. It is likely that this magical stone circle was a place of worship to the sun.

WESSEX (see pp246–71)

Wiltshire

Somerset

Dorset

0 kilometres   25

0 miles   25

Salisbury's (see pp264–5) cathedral with its soaring spire was the inspiration for one of John Constable's best-loved paintings. The picturesque Cathedral Close has a number of fine medieval buildings.

Stourhead *garden* (see pp266–7) *was inspired by the paintings of Claude and Poussin. Created in the 18th century, the garden is itself a work of art. Contrived vistas, light and shade and a mixture of landscape and gracious buildings, such as the Neo-Classical Pantheon at its centre, are vital to the overall effect.*

Coastal Wildlife

The long and varied West Country coastline, ranging from the stark, granite cliffs of Land's End to the pebble-strewn stretch of Chesil Bank, is matched with an equally diverse range of wildlife. Beaches are scattered with colourful shells, while rock pools form miniature marine habitats teeming with life. Caves are used by larger creatures, such as grey seals, and cliffs provide nest sites for birds. In the spring and early summer, an astonishing range of plants grow on the foreshore and cliffs which can be seen at their best from the Southwest Coastal Path *(see p36)*. The plants in turn attract numerous moths and butterflies.

Cliff-tops of Land's End with safe ledges for nesting birds

Chesil Bank *is an unusual ridge of pebbles* (see p256) *stretching 18 miles (29 km) along the Dorset coast. The bank was created by storms and the pebbles increase in size from northwest to southeast due to varying strengths of coastal currents. The bank encloses a lagoon called the Fleet, habitat of the Abbotsbury swans, as well as a large number of wildfowl.*

The Painted Lady, *often seen on cliff-top coastal plants, migrates to Britain in the spring.*

High tides wash up driftwood and shell

Cliff-top turf contains many species of wild flowers.

Thrift, *in hummocks of honey-scented flowers, is a familiar sight on cliff ledges in spring.*

Yellowhammers *are to be seen perched on cliff-top bushes.*

Marram grass roots help hold back sand against wind erosion.

Grey seals *come on land to give birth to their young. They can be spotted on remote beaches.*

A BEACHCOMBER'S GUIDE

The best time to observe the natural life of the se shore is when the tide begins to roll back, before the scavenging seagulls pick up the stranded cral fish and sandhoppers, and the seaweed dries up. Much plant and marine life can be found in the secure habitat provided by rock pools.

Durdle Door *was formed by waves continually eroding the weaker chalk layers of this cliff (see p270) in Dorset, leaving the stronger oolite to create a striking arch, known in geology as an eyelet.*

COLLECTING SHELLS

Most of the edible molluscs, such as scallops and cockles, are known as bivalves; others, such as whelks and limpets, are known as gastropods.

Great scallop **Common cockle**

Common whelk **Common limpet**

Seaweed, *such as bladder wrack, can resemble coral or lichen when in water.*

Rocks are colonized by clusters of barnacles, mussels and limpets.

Oystercatchers *have a distinctive orange beak. They hunt along the shore, feeding on all kinds of shellfish.*

Starfish *can be aggressive predators on shellfish. The light-sensitive tips of their tentacles help them to "see" the way.*

Mussels *are widespread and can be harvested for food.*

Rock pools teem with crabs, mussels, shrimps and plant life.

The Velvet Crab, *often found hiding in seaweed, is covered with fine downy hair all over its shell.*

Grey mullet, *when newly hatched, can often be seen in rock pools.*

West Country Gardens

Gardeners have long been attracted to the West Country. Its mild climate is perfect for growing tender and exotic plants, many of which were brought from Asia in the 19th century. As a result, the region has some of England's finest and most varied gardens, covering the whole sweep of garden styles and history *(see pp26–7)*, from the clipped formality of Elizabethan Montacute, to the colourful and crowded cottage-garden style of East Lambrook Manor.

Lanhydrock's (p284) *clipped yews and low box hedges frame a blaze of colourful annuals.*

Trewithen (p281) *is renowned for its rare camellias, rhododendrons and magnolias, grown from seed collected in Asia. The huge garden is at its most impressive in March and June.*

Cotehele *(p293)* has a lovely lush valley garden.

DEVON AN
CORNWAI
(see pp272–

Trelissick *(p281)* has memorable views over the Fal Estuary through shrub-filled woodland.

Glendurgan *(p281)* is a plant-lover's paradise set in a steep, sheltered valley.

Mount Edgcumbe *(p292)* preserves its 18th-century French, Italian and English gardens.

Trengwainton (p276) *has a fine stream garden, whose banks are crowded with moisture-loving plants, beneath a lush canopy of New Zealand tree ferns.*

Overbecks *(near Salcombe) enjoys a spectacular site overlooking the Salcombe Estuary. There are secret gardens, terraces and rocky dells.*

CREATIVE GARDENING

Gardens are not simply collections of plants; they rely for much of their appeal on man-made features. Whimsical topiary, ornate architecture, fanciful statuary and mazes help to create an atmosphere of adventure or pure escapism. The many gardens dotted around the West Country offer engaging examples of the vivid imagination of designers.

Mazes *were created in medieval monasteries to teach patience and persistence. This laurel maze at Glendurgan was planted in 1833.*

Fountains *and flamboyant statuary have adorned gardens since Roman times. Such eye-catching embellishments add poetic and Classical touches to the design of formal gardens, such as Mount Edgcumbe.*

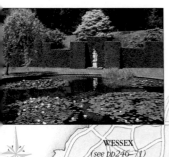

Knightshayes Court (p289) *is designed as a series of formal garden "rooms", planted for scent, colour or seasonal effect.*

WESSEX
(see pp246–71)

East Lambrook Manor *(near South Petherton) is a riot of colours, as old-fashioned cottage plants grow without restraint.*

Stourhead *(see pp266–7)* is a magnificent example of 18th-century landscape gardening.

Athelhampton's *(p269)* gardens make use of fountains, statues, pavilions and columnar yews.

Montacute House *(p268)* has pavilions and a centuries-old yew hedge, and is renowned for its collection of old roses.

0 kilometres   25

0 miles   25

Parnham *(near Beaminster), like many West Country gardens, has several parts devoted to different themes. Here conical yews comple-ment the formality of the stone balustrade; elsewhere there are woodland, kitchen, shade and Mediterranean gardens.*

Many garden buildings *are linked by an element of fantasy; while country houses had to conform to everyday practicalities, the design of many smaller buildings gave more scope for imagination. This fanciful Elizabethan pavilion on the forecourt at Montacute House was first and foremost decora-tive, but sometimes served as a lodging house.*

Topiary *can be traced back to the Greeks. Since that time the sculpting of trees into unusual, often eccentric shapes has been developed over the centuries. The yew topiary of*

1920s Knightshayes features a fox being chased by a pack of hounds. The figures form a delightful conceit and come into their own in winter when little else is in leaf.

WESSEX

WILTSHIRE · SOMERSET · DORSET

The natural and diverse beauty of this predominantly rural region is characterized by rolling hills and charming villages. The area is enriched by a wealth of historical and architectural attractions, ranging from the prehistoric stone circle of Stonehenge to the Roman baths and magnificent Georgian townscape of Bath.

Vast swathes of bare windswept downland give way to lush river valleys, and the contrast between the two may explain the origin in medieval times of the saying, "as different as chalk and cheese". The chalk and limestone hills provided pasture for sheep whose wool was exported to Europe or turned to cloth in mill towns such as Bradford-on-Avon. Meanwhile the rich cow-grazed pastures of the valleys produced the Cheddar cheese for which the region has become famous.

The area's potential for wealth was first exploited by prehistoric chieftains whose large, mysterious monuments, such as Stonehenge and Maiden Castle, are striking features of the landscape. From this same soil sprang King Arthur *(see p285)* and King Alfred the Great, about whom there are numerous fascinating legends. It was King Arthur who is thought to have led British resistance to the Saxon invasion in the 6th century. The Saxons finally emerged the victors and one of them, King Alfred, first united the West Country into one political unit, called the Kingdom of Wessex *(see p47)*.

Wilton House and Lacock Abbey, both former monasteries, were turned into splendid stately homes during the 16th century, due to the Dissolution of the Monasteries *(see pp50–51)*. Today, their previous wealth can be gauged by the size and grandeur of their storage barns.

Matching the many man-made splendours of the region, Wessex is rich in rare wildlife and plants.

Two visitors enjoying the Elizabethan gardens of Montacute House, Somerset

◁ Eighteenth-century cottages lining Gold Hill, Shaftesbury

Exploring Wessex

From the rolling chalk plains around Stonehenge
to the rocky cliffs of Cheddar Gorge and the
heather-covered uplands of Exmoor, Wessex
is a scenically varied microcosm of England.
Reflecting the underlying geology, each part
of Wessex contributes its own distinctive
architecture, with the Neo-Classically inspired
buildings of Bath giving way to the mellow brick
and timber of Salisbury and the thatched flint-
and-chalk cottages of the Dorset landscape.

Bath's abbey and Georgian townscape

KEY

▭▭	Motorway
▭▭	Major road
▬▬	Secondary road
▭▭	Minor road
▬▬	Scenic route
▭▭	Main railway
—	Minor railway
△	Summit

Exmoor National Park

SEE ALSO

- **Where to Stay** pp568–71
- **Where to Eat** pp624–6

SIGHTS AT A GLANCE

Huge sarsen stones of Stonehenge, dating from around 3000 BC

GETTING AROUND

Bath and Bristol are served by fast mainline trains, other major towns and seaside resorts by regional railways and long-distance bus services. Popular sights such as Stonehenge feature on many tour operators' bus excursions. The rural heart of Wessex, however, has little in the way of public transport and unless you have the time to walk the region's footpaths, you will need a car.

Exmoor National Park ❶

Curlew

The majestic cliffs plunging into the Bristol Channel along Exmoor's northern coast are interrupted by lush, wooded valleys carrying rivers from the high moorland down to sheltered fishing coves. Inland, wild rolling hills are grazed by sturdy Exmoor ponies, horned sheep and the local wild red deer. Buzzards are also a common sight wheeling over the bracken-clad terrain looking for prey. For walkers, Exmoor offers 1,000 km (620 miles) of wonderful public paths and varied, dramatic scenery, while the tamer perimeters of the National Park offer less energetic attractions – everything from traditional seaside entertainments to picturesque villages and ancient churches.

View east along the South West Coast Path

Combe Martin is a pretty setting for the Pack of Cards Inn *(see p288).*

Parracombe Old Church has a Georgian interior with a complete set of wooden furnishings

Heddon's Mouth
The River Heddon passes through woodland and meadows down to this attractive point on the coast.

The Valley of Rocks
Sandstone outcrops, eroded into fantastical shapes, characterize this natural gorge.

KEY

ℹ️	Tourist information
▬▬	A road
▭▭	B road
═══	Minor road
– –	Coast path
☀	Viewpoint

Lynmouth
Above the charming fishing village of Lynmouth stands hill-top Lynton. The two villages are connected by a cliff railway (see p288).

Watersmeet
The East Lyn and Hoar Oak Water join together in a tumbling cascade at this spot in the middle of a beautifully wooded valley. There is also a tearoom with a pretty garden.

Culbone church, a mere 10.6 m (35 ft) in length, claims to be Britain's smallest parish church.

Oare's church commemorates the writer R D Blackmore, whose romantic novel *Lorna Doone* (1869) is set in the area.

VISITORS' CHECKLIST

Somerset/Devon.
🚆 🚌 Tiverton then bus.
🛈 Lee Rd, Lynton (01598
752225).
Dunster Castle (NT), Dunster.
Tel 01643 821314. ☐ Apr–Oct:
Sat–Wed. 🎫 ♿ 🏠
www.nationaltrust.org.uk
National Park Centre
Dulveton ☐ all year
Tel 01398 323841. **www**.
exmoor-nationalpark.gov.uk

Porlock
The flower-filled village of Porlock has retained its charm, with winding streets, thatched houses and a fascinating old church.

Selworthy is a picturesque village of thatched cottages.

Minehead is a major resort built around a pretty quay. A steam railway runs all the way from here to Bishop's Lydeard.

Dunster has an ancient castle and an unusual octagonal Yarn Market (c.1609) where local cloth was once sold.

Simonsbath is a good starting point for walkers. The Exmoor ponies found locally are thought to descend from prehistoric ancestors.

Dunkery Beacon
Rising to a height of 520 m (1,700 ft), this is the highest point on Exmoor.

Tarr Steps is an ancient "clapper" bridge built of stone slabs.

0 kilometres   5

0 miles   3

Malmsmead · Culbone · Oare · Porlock · A39 · Selworthy · Minehead · Water · Exe · DUNKERY BEACON · 520 m · 1,704 ft · Dunster · A396 · A39 · B3223 · BRENDON HILLS · ath · Exford · B3224 · Barle · Exe · A396 · B3223 · B3190 · TAUNTON · Dane's Brook · B3224 · TIVERTON · WIMBLEBALL LAKE · Barle · Dulverton · B3222 · TIVERTON

Taunton ❷

Somerset. 🏘 77,000. 🚉 🔌 🅸
Paul St (01823 336 344). 🏠 *Thu
(farmers'), Tue & Sat (livestock).*
www.heartofsomerset.com

Taunton lies at the heart of a
fertile region famous for its
apples and cider, but it was
the prosperous wool industry
that financed the massive
church of **St Mary Magdalene**
(1488–1514) with its glorious
tower. Taunton's **castle** was
the setting for the notorious
Bloody Assizes of 1685 when
"Hanging" Judge Jeffreys dispensed harsh retribution on
the Duke of Monmouth and
his followers for an uprising
against King James II. The
12th-century building now
houses the **Museum of Somerset**.
A star exhibit is the Roman
mosaic from a villa at Low
Ham, Somerset, showing the
story of Dido and Aeneas.

**Environs: Hestercombe
Garden** is one of Sir Edwin
Lutyens and Gertrude
Jekyll's great masterpieces.

🏛 **Museum of Somerset**
Castle Green. **Tel** 01823
320201. 🔲 call for details. 🔲
for refurbishment until summer
2010. 🅰 ground floor. 🔌
🌺 **Hestercombe Garden**
Cheddon Fitzpaine. **Tel** 01823
413923. 🔲 daily. 🔌 🔲 🔌
🅰 **www**.hestercombe
gardens.com

SOMERSET CIDER

Somerset is one of the few
English counties where
real farmhouse cider,
known as "scrumpy",
is still made using
the traditional
methods. Cider
once formed
part of the farm
labourer's wages
and local folk-
lore has it that
various unsav-
oury additives,
such as iron
nails, were added to give
strength. Cider-making can
be seen at **Sheppy's** farm,
on the A38 near Taunton.

**Scrumpy
cider**

Wells ❸

Somerset. 🏘 10,000. 🔌 🅸 *Market
Place (01749 672552).* 🏠 *Wed
(farmers'), Sat.* **www**.wellstourism.com

Wells is named after St
Andrew's Well, the sacred
spring that bubbles up from
the ground near the 13th-
century **Bishop's
Palace**, residence
of the Bishop of
Bath and Wells. A
tranquil city, Wells
is famous for its
magnificent cathe-
dral which was
begun in the late
1100s. Penniless
Porch, where
beggars once
received alms,
leads from the
bustling market
place to the calm
of the cathedral
close. **Wells & Mendip Museum**
has prehistoric finds from nearby
Wookey Hole and other caves.

**Cathedral
clock
(1386–92)**

Environs: To the northeast of
Wells lies the impressive cave
complex of **Wookey Hole**,
which has an extensive range
of popular amusements.

🏛 **Wells & Mendip Museum**
8 Cathedral Green. **Tel** 01749 673477.
🔲 daily 🔌 🅰 limited. 🔌
🔌 **www**.wellsmuseum.org.uk
🛢 **Wookey Hole**
Off A371. **Tel** 01749 672243. 🔲 daily.
🔌 🔌 🔌 🔌 **www**.wookey.co.uk

The West Front
*features 300 fine
medieval statues of
kings, knights and
saints – many of
them life-size.*

**The Vicars'
Close**, built in
the 14th century
for the Vicars'
Choir, is one
of the oldest
complete streets
in Europe.

The Chain Gate (1460)

Cloisters

**Path leading
round the moat**

This graceful flight of steps
*curves up to the octagonal
Chapter House which has delicate vaulting dating from 1306.
The 32 ribs springing from the
central column create a
beautiful palm-tree effect.*

Glastonbury Abbey, left in ruins in 1539 after the Dissolution

Bishops' tombs *circle the chancel. This sumptuous marble tomb, in the south aisle, is that of Bishop Lord Arthur Hervey, who was Bishop of Bath and Wells (1869–94).*

The palace moat *is home to swans which ring a bell by the gatehouse when they want to be fed. Feeding times are at 11am and 4pm.*

The Bishop's Palace (1230–40)

13th-century ruins of the Great Hall

WELLS CATHEDRAL AND THE BISHOP'S PALACE

The Close. **Tel** *01749 674483.*
☐ *daily.* ☐ *limited.*
Bishop's Palace Tel *01749 678691.*
☐ *Apr–Oct: Tue–Fri, Sun & public hols (Aug: daily).* ☐ ☐

Wells has maintained much of its medieval character with its cathedral, Bishop's Palace and other buildings around the close forming a harmonious group. The most striking features of the cathedral are the west front and the "scissor arches" installed in 1338 to support the tower.

Glastonbury ❹

Somerset. ☐ *9,000.* ☐ ☐ *Tribunal, High St (01458 832954).* ☐ *Tue.*
www.glastonburytic.co.uk

Shrouded in Arthurian myth and rich in mystical association, the town of Glastonbury was once one of the most important destinations for pilgrims in England. Now thousands flock here for the annual rock festival *(see p63)* and for the summer solstice on Midsummer's Day (21 June).

Over the years history and legend have become intertwined, and the monks who founded **Glastonbury Abbey**, around 700, found it profitable to encourage the association between Glastonbury and the mythical "Blessed Isle" known as Avalon – alleged to be the last resting place of King Arthur and the Holy Grail *(see p285)*.

The great abbey was left in ruins after the Dissolution of the Monasteries *(see p50)*. Even so, some magnificent relics survive, including parts of the vast Norman abbey church, the unusual Abbot's Kitchen, with its octagonal roof, and the Victorian farmhouse, now the **Somerset Rural Life Museum**.

Growing in the abbey grounds is a cutting from the famous Glastonbury thorn which is said to have miraculously grown from the staff of St Joseph of Arimathea. According to myth, he was sent around AD 60 to convert England to Christianity. The English hawthorn flowers at Christmas as well as in May.

The **Lake Village Museum** has some interesting finds from the Iron Age settlements that once fringed the marshlands around **Glastonbury Tor**. Seen for miles around, the Tor is a hill crowned by the remains of a 14th-century church.

血 Somerset Rural Life Museum
Chilkwell St. **Tel** *01458 831197.*
☐ *Tue–Sun (Nov–Apr: Tue–Sat & pub hols).* ☐ *1 Jan, Good Fri, 24–26 Dec.* ☐ *limited.* ☐ *closed winter.* ☐

血 Lake Village Museum
Tribunal, High St. **Tel** *01458 832954.*
☐ *daily.* ☐ *25, 26 Dec.* ☐ ☐

Cheddar Gorge ❺

Described as a "deep frightful chasm" by novelist Daniel Defoe in 1724, Cheddar Gorge is a spectacular ravine cut through the Mendip plateau by fast-flowing streams during the interglacial phases of the last Ice Age. Cheddar has given its name to a rich cheese that originates from here and is now produced worldwide. The caves in the gorge provide the perfect environment of constant temperature and high humidity for storing and maturing the cheese.

VISITORS' CHECKLIST

On B3135, Somerset. 🛈 01934 744071. 🚌 from Wells and Weston-super-Mare. 🅿 🍴 🖾
Cheddar Caves & Gorge
Tel 01934 742343. ◯ daily. ◯ 24, 25 Dec. 🎫 ♿ limited. 🖾
📷 www.cheddarcaves.co.uk
Cheddar Gorge Cheese Co.
Tel 01934 742810. ◯ daily.
♿ 🖾 📷 www.cheddargorge cheeseco.co.uk

The Cheddar Gorge Cheese Company *is the only working Cheddar dairy in Cheddar. Visitors can see Cheddar being made, and taste and buy cheese in the new store.*

The B3135 road winds round the base of the 3 mile (5 km) gorge.

"Cheddar Man", *a 9,000-year-old skeleton, is on display at Cheddar Caves and Gorge. The museum here looks at the pre-historic world of our cannibal ancestors.*

A footpath follows the top of the gorge on its southern edge.

Gough's Cave is noted for its cathedral-like proportions.

Tourist information

Cox's Cave contains unusually shaped stalactites and stalagmites.

The gorge *is a narrow, winding ravine with limestone rocks rising almost vertically on either side to a height of 140 m (460 ft).*

A flight of 274 steps leads to the top of the gorge.

The rare Cheddar Pink *is among the astonishing range of plant and animal life harboured in the rocks.*

Lookout Tower has far-reaching views over the area to the south and west.

Bristol ❻

See pp256–7.

Bath ❼

See pp258–61.

Bradford-on-Avon ❽

Wiltshire. 🏠 *9,500.* 🚇 🚌 *St Margaret St (01225 865797).* 🛒 *Thu.*
www.bradfordonavon.co.uk

This lovely Cotswold-stone town with its steep flagged lanes is full of flamboyant houses built by wealthy wool and cloth merchants in the 17th and 18th centuries. One fine Georgian example is **Abbey House**, on Church Street. A little further along, **St Laurence Church** is a remarkably complete Saxon building founded in 705 *(see p47).* The

Typical Cotswold-stone architecture in Bradford-on-Avon

church was converted to a school and cottage in the 12th century and was rediscovered in the 19th century when a vicar recognized the characteristic cross-shaped roof.

At one end of the medieval **Town Bridge** is a small stone cell, built as a chapel in the 13th century but later used as a lock-up for 17th-century vagrants. A short walk away, near converted mill buildings and a stretch of the Kennet and Avon Canal, is the massive 14th-century **Tithe Barn** *(see p32).*

🏛 Tithe Barn
(EH) Pound Lane. 🕐 *daily.* 🔒 *25, 26 Dec.* ♿

Corsham ❾

Wiltshire. 🏠 *12,000.*
ℹ️ *31 High St (01249 714660).*
www.visitwiltshire.co.uk

The streets of Corsham are lined with stately Georgian houses in Cotswold stone. **St Bartholomew's Church** has an elegant spire and a lovely carved alabaster tomb (1960) to the late Lady Methuen, whose family founded Methuen publishers. The family acquired **Corsham Court** in 1745 with its picture gallery and a remarkable collection of Flemish, Italian and English

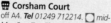

Peacock in grounds, Corsham Court

paintings, including works by Van Dyck, Lippi and Reynolds. Peacocks wander through the grounds, adding their colour and elegance to the façade of the Elizabethan mansion.

🏛 Corsham Court
off A4. **Tel** *01249 712214.* 🕐 *mid-Mar–Sep: Tue–Thu, Sat, Sun; Oct–mid-Mar: Sat, Sun (pm).* 🔒 *Dec.* 📷 ♿

Lacock ❿

Wiltshire. 🏠 *1,000.*

Maintained in its pristine state by the National Trust, with very few modern intrusions, Lacock is a picturesque and delightful village to explore. The meandering River Avon forms the boundary to the north side of the churchyard, while humorous stone figures look down from **St Cyriac Church**. Inside the 15th-century church is the splendid Renaissance-style tomb of Sir William Sharington (1495–1553). He acquired **Lacock Abbey** after the Dissolution of the Monasteries *(see p50),* but it was a later owner, John Ivory Talbot, who had the buildings remodelled in the Gothic

revival style, in vogue in the early 18th century. The abbey is famous for the window (in the south gallery) from which his descendant William Henry Fox Talbot, an early pioneer of photography, took his first picture in 1835, and for the sheets of snowdrops which cover the abbey grounds in early spring. A 16th-century barn at the abbey gates has been converted to the **Fox Talbot Museum**, which has displays on his experiments.

Environs:
Designed by Robert Adam *(see pp32–3)* in 1769, **Bowood House** includes the laboratory where Joseph Priestley discovered oxygen in 1774, and a rich collection of sculpture, costumes and paintings. Italianate gardens surround the house while the lake-filled grounds, landscaped by Capability Brown *(see p30),* contain a Doric temple, grotto, cascade and an adventure playground.

🏛 Lacock Abbey
(NT) Lacock. **Tel** *01249 730459.* 🕐 *Mar–Oct: Wed–Mon (pm).* 🔒 *Good Fri.* 📷 ♿ *limited in house.* **www**.nationaltrust.org.uk

🏛 Fox Talbot Museum
(NT) Lacock. **Tel** *01249 730459.* 🕐 *daily (Nov–Feb: Sat & Sun only).* 🔒 *Good Fri.* 📷 ♿

🏛 Bowood House
Derry Hill, nr Calne. **Tel** *01249 812102.* 🕐 *Apr–Oct: daily.* 📷 ♿ 🍴 📷 📷

William Henry Fox Talbot (1800–77)

Bristol 6

It was in 1497 that John Cabot sailed from Bristol on his historic voyage to North America. The city, at the mouth of the Avon, became the main British port for transatlantic trade, pioneering the era of the ocean-going steam liner with the construction of Brunel's ss *Great Britain*. The city flourished as a major trading centre, growing rich on the distribution of wine, tobacco and, in the 17th century, slaves.

King Brennus, St John's Gate

Because of its docks and aero-engine factories, Bristol was heavily bombed during World War II and the city centre bears witness to the ideas of post-war planners. The docks have been shifted to deeper waters at Avonmouth and the old dock area has been transformed, taking on new life characterized by waterside cafés, shops and art galleries.

Exploring Bristol

The oldest part of the city lies around Broad, King and Corn streets, known as the Old Quarter. The lively St Nicholas covered market, part of which occupies the **Corn Exchange**, was built by John Wood the Elder (*see p258*) in 1743. Outside are the famous Bristol Nails, four bronze 16th–17th-century pedestals which Bristol merchants used as tables when paying for goods – hence the expression "to pay on the nail". **St John's Gate**, at the head of Broad Street, has medieval statues of Bristol's two mythical founders, King Brennus and King Benilus. Between Lewins Mead and Colston Street, **Christmas Steps** is a steep lane lined with specialist shops and cafés. The **Chapel of the Three Kings** at the top was founded in 1504.

A group of buildings around the cobbled King Street include the 17th-century timber-framed **Llandoger Trow** inn. It is here that Daniel Defoe is said to have met Alexander

The Two Sisters (c.1889) by Renoir, City Museum and Art Gallery

Selkirk, whose true-life island exile served as the inspiration for Defoe's novel *Robinson Crusoe* (1719). Just up from here is the **Theatre Royal**, built in 1766, and home to the famous Bristol Old Vic.

Not far away, the renowned gallery the **Arnolfini**, on Narrow Quay, is a showcase for contemporary art, drama, dance and cinema.

On the Harbourside, **Explore-At-Bristol** (www.at-bristol.org.uk) combines an exciting, interactive science centre with an aquarium.

Not far from the Harbourside, elegant **Clifton** revels in ornate Regency crescents. The impressive **Clifton Suspension Bridge** by Brunel, completed in 1864, perfectly complements the drama of the steep Avon gorge. **Bristol Zoo Gardens** houses over 400 exotic and endangered species set in stunning gardens.

Bow of Brunel's ss Great Britain

Memorial to William Canynge the Younger (1400–74)

🔒 St Mary Redcliffe

Redcliffe Way. **Tel** *0117 9291487.* ☐ *daily.* ♿ 📷 *by arrangement.* 🌐 *www.stmaryredcliffe.co.uk*

This magnificent 14th-century church was claimed by Queen Elizabeth I to be "the fairest in England". The church owes much to the generosity of William Canynge the Elder and Younger, both famous mayors of Bristol. Inscriptions on the tombs of merchants and sailors tell of lives devoted to trade in Asia and the West Indies. Look out for the Bristol maze in the north aisle.

🏛 Brunel's ss *Great Britain*

Gas Ferry Rd. 📞 *0117 9260680.* ☐ *daily.* ● 24, 25 Dec. 🎟 *ticket valid for one year.* ♿ 📷 *by appt.* 📧 🌐 *www.ssgreatbritain.com*

Designed by Isambard Kingdom Brunel, this is the world's first large iron passenger ship. Launched in 1843, she travelled 32 times round the world before being abandoned in the Falkland Islands in 1886. The ship has recently been fully restored.

🏠 Georgian House

7 Great George St. **Tel** *0117 9211362.* ☐ *Sat–Wed.* www.bristol-city.gov.uk/museums

Life in a wealthy Bristol merchant's house of the 1790s is illustrated by furnishings in the elegant drawing room and the servants' area.

🏛 Museum of Bristol

Princes Wharf, Harbourside. ☐ *consult the website for more information.* www.bristol-city.gov.uk/museums

After a massive rebuild, the old Industrial Museum will reopen in 2011 as the Museum of Bristol. The focus will be on the individual lives, stories and memories of the city's residents while retaining the best of the original building's industrial heritage. This project is part of the regeneration of Bristol's Harbourside.

Warehouses overlooking the Floating Harbour

🏛 Bristol Blue Glass Factory and Shop

Brislington. **Tel** 0117 972 0818.
🖥 daily. www.bristol-glass.co.uk
The Bristol Blue Glass name
is over 350 years old and
represents the best tools,
techniques and traditions from
the past. Every piece of glass
is free blown and hand-made,
making each one unique and
collectable. Glass blowing
demonstrations take place
at the visitor centre, where
there is also a gallery shop.

🏛 City Museum and Art Gallery

Queen's Rd. **Tel** 0117 922 3571. 🖥
daily. 🔴 24, 25 Dec. 🚹 limited. 🅿
🖥 www.bristol-city.gov.uk/museums
Varied collections include
Egyptology, dinosaur fossils,
Roman tableware, the largest
collection of Chinese glass
outside China and a fine
collection of European paintings including works by Renoir
and Bellini. Bristol artists include Sir Thomas Lawrence
and Francis Danby.

🕀 Bristol Cathedral

College Green. **Tel** 0117 9264879.
🖥 daily. **Donation.** 🚹 limited.
www.bristol-cathedral.co.uk
Bristol's cathedral, begun in
1140, took an unusually long
time to build. Rapid progress
was made between 1298 and
1330, when the inventive choir
was rebuilt; the transepts and
tower were finished in 1515,
and another 350 years passed
before the Victorian architect,
G E Street, built the nave.
Humorous medieval carving
abounds – a snail crawling
across the stone foliage in the
Berkeley Chapel, musical mon-
keys in the Elder Lady Chapel,
and a fine set of wooden
misericords in the choir.

BRISTOL CITY CENTRE

Bristol Cathedral ③
Brunel's ss
  Great Britain ④
City Museum and
  Art Gallery ①
Georgian House
  ②
Museum of
  Bristol ⑤
St Mary
  Redcliffe ⑥

0 metres   250
0 yards   250

Key to Symbols *see back flap*

Street-by-Street: Bath ❼

Bath owes its magnificent Georgian town-scape to the bubbling pool of water at the heart of the Roman Baths. The Romans transformed Bath into England's first spa resort and it regained fame as a spa town in the 18th century. At this time the two John Woods (Elder and Younger), both architects, designed the city's Palladian-style buildings. Many houses bear plaques recording the numerous famous people who have resided here.

The Circus
This is a daring departure from typical Georgian square, by John the Elder (1705–

No. 1 Royal Crescent

No. 17 is where the 18th-century painter Thomas Gainsborough lived *(see p163).*

Assembly Rooms and Museum of Costume

★ Royal Crescent
Hailed the most majestic street in Britain, this graceful arc of 30 houses (1767–74) is the masterpiece of John Wood the Younger. West of the Royal Crescent, Royal Victoria Park (1830) is the city's largest open space.

Jane Austen *(see p162),* the writer, stayed at No. 13 Queen Square on one of many visits to Bath in her youth.

Milsom Street and New Bond Street contain some of Bath's most elegant shops.

Theatre Royal (1805)

KEY

— — — Suggested route

0 metres   100
0 yards   100

THE KING'S SPRING

STAR SIGHTS

★ Royal Crescent

★ Roman Baths

★ Bath Abbey

Pump Rooms
These tearooms once formed the social hub of the 18th-century spa community. They contain this decorative drinking fountain.

Pulteney Bridge
This charming bridge (1769–74), designed by Robert Adam, is lined with shops and links the centre with the magnificent Great Pulteney Street. Look out for a rare Victorian pillar box on the east bank.

VISITORS' CHECKLIST

Bath. 85,000. Bristol International Airport, 20 miles (32 km) W Bath. Dorchester St. Abbey Chambers, Abbey Church Yard (0906 7112000) 50p per min. daily. International Festival: May–Jun.

The Building of Bath Museum

★ Roman Baths
Built in the 1st century, this bathing complex is one of Britain's greatest memorials to the Roman era.

Holburne Museum

★ Bath Abbey
The splendid abbey stands at the heart of the old city in the Abbey Church Yard, a paved courtyard enlivened by buskers. Its unique façade features stone angels climbing Jacob's Ladder to heaven.

Parade Gardens
Courting couples came to this pretty riverside park for secret liaisons in the 18th century.

Rail & coach stations

Sally Lunn's House (1482) is one of Bath's oldest houses.

PARAGON

BROAD STREET

WALCOT STREET

NEW BOND STREET

BOROUGH WALLS

UNION STREET

HIGH STREET

GATE STREET

CHEAP STREET

GRAND PARADE

ORANGE GROVE

PIERREPOINT STREET

YORK STREET

Exploring Bath

Piazza cellist

The beautiful and compact city of Bath is set among the rolling green hills of the Avon valley, and wherever you walk you will enjoy spendid views of the surrounding countryside. The traffic-free heart of this lively city is full of street musicians, museums, cafés and enticing shops, while the elegant honey-coloured Georgian houses, so characteristic of Bath, form an elegant backdrop to city life.

Bath Abbey, at the heart of the old city, begun in 1499

🔒 Bath Abbey

13 Kingston Bldgs, Abbey Churchyard. *Tel* 01225 422462. ☐ daily. ◉ during services. **Donation.** ♿ ☐ **www**.bathabbey.org

This splendid abbey was supposedly designed by divine agency. According to legend, God dictated the form of the church to Bishop Oliver King in a dream; this story has been immortalized in the wonderfully eccentric carvings on the west front. The bishop began work in 1499, rebuilding a church that had been founded in the 8th century. Memorials cover the walls and the varied Georgian inscriptions make fascinating reading. The spacious interior is remarkable for the fan vaulting of the nave, an addition made by Sir George Gilbert Scott in 1874.

🏛 National Trust Assembly Rooms and Museum of Costume

Bennett St. *Tel* 01225 477789. ☐ daily. ◉ 25, 26 Dec. ◉ for Museum of Costume. ♿ ☐ ◉ **www**.museumofcostume.co.uk

The Assembly Rooms were built by Wood the Younger in 1769, as a meeting place for the fashionable elite and as an elegant backdrop for many glittering balls. Jane Austen's novel *Northanger Abbey* (1818) describes the atmosphere of gossip and flirtation here. In the basement is a collection of costumes in period settings. The display illustrates fashions from the 16th century to the present day.

🏛 No. 1 Royal Crescent

Royal Crescent. *Tel* 01225 428 126. ☐ Tue–Sun & public hols. ◉ Dec, Jan, Good Fri. ◉ **www**.bath-preservation-trust.org.uk

This museum lets you inside the first house of this beautiful Georgian crescent, giving a glimpse of what life was like for 18th-century aristocrats, such as the Duke of York, who probably lived here. It is furnished down to such details as the dog-powered spit used to roast meat in front of the fire.

🏛 Holburne Museum of Art

Great Pulteney St. *Tel* 01225 466669. ☐ call for details. ◉ for refurbishment. ◉ ♿ limited. ☐ ☐ **www**.bath.ac.uk/holburne

This historic building is named after William Holburne of Menstrie (1793–1874), whose collections form the nucleus of the display of fine and decorative arts. Paintings can be seen by British artists such as Gainsborough and Stubbs.

ROMAN BATHS MUSEUM

Entrance in Abbey Churchyard. 🖪 01225 477785. ☐ daily. ◉ 25, 26 Dec. ◉ ♿ limited. **www**.romanbaths.co.uk

According to legend, Bath owes its origin to the Celtic King Bladud who discovered the curative properties of its natural hot springs in 860 BC. Cast out from his kingdom as a leper, Bladud cured himself by imitating his swine and rolling in the hot mud at Bath.

In the first century, the Romans built baths around the spring, and a temple dedicated to the goddess Sulis Minerva, who combined the attributes of the Celt water goddess Sulis and the Roman goddess Minerva. Among the Roman relics is a bronze head of the goddess.

Gilded bronze head of Sulis Minerva

Medieval monks of Bath Abbey also exploited the springs' properties, but it was when Queen Anne visited in 1702–3 that Bath reached its zenith as a fashionable watering place.

🏛 Building of Bath Museum

The Vineyards. *Tel 01225 333895.*
◯ *Tue–Sun & public hols.* ● *end-Nov–mid-Feb.* 🎫 ♿ *limited.* 📷
www.bath-preservation-trust.org.uk
This museum, housed in an old Methodist chapel, is an excellent starting point for exploring the city. It shows how, in the 18th century, Bath was transformed from a medieval wool town into one of Europe's most elegant spas. John Wood and his son designed the Classically inspired stone fronts of the Royal Crescent and the Circus, leaving individual property speculators to develop the houses behind. While the façades speak of harmony and order, the houses behind show the result of rampant individualism, with no two houses alike. The museum looks at every aspect of the buildings, from their construction to a new gallery of Georgian interiors.

🏛 American Museum

Claverton Manor, Claverton Down.
Tel 01225 460503. ◯ *Aug, mid-Nov–mid-Dec: daily (pm); Mar–Oct: Tue–Sun (pm) & pub hols.* 🎫 ♿ *limited.* 📷 📷 **www**.american museum.org
Founded in 1961, this was the first American museum to be established in this country. Rooms in the 1820 manor house are decorated in many styles, from the rudimentary dwellings of the first settlers to opulent 19th-century homes. There are special sections on Shaker furniture, quilts and Native American art, and a replica of George Washington's Mount Vernon garden of 1785.

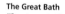

A 19th-century American Indian weathervane

The Great Bath

The open-air Great Bath, which stands at the heart of the Roman spa complex, was not discovered until the 1870s. Leading off this magnificent pool were various bathing chambers which became increasingly sophisticated over the four centuries the Romans were here. The baths fell into ruin, but extensive excavations have revealed the remarkable skill of Roman engineering.

he dome (1897) is based on St Stephen Walbrook church in London (see p112).

Around the edges of the bath are the bases of piers that once supported a barrel-vaulted roof.

York Street

A late 19th-century terrace bears statues of famous Romans such as Julius Caesar.

The sacred spring is enclosed by a reservoir now named the King's Bath.

The water flows from the spring into the corner of the bath at a constant temperature of 46° C (115° F).

The lead-lined bath, steps, column bases and paving stones around the edge all date from Roman times.

Stonehenge ⓫

Built in several stages from about 3000 BC, Stonehenge is Europe's most famous prehistoric monument. We can only guess at the rituals that took place here, but the alignment of the stones leaves little doubt that the circle is connected with the sun and the passing of the seasons, and that its builders possessed a sophisticated understanding of both arithmetic and astronomy. Despite popular belief, the circle was not built by the Druids, an Iron Age priestly cult that flourished in Britain from around 250 BC – more than 1,000 years after Stonehenge was abandoned.

Stonehenge as it is today

Finds from a burial mound near Stonehenge (Devizes Museum)

The Heel Stone casts a long shadow straight to the heart of the circle on Midsummer's day.

The Avenue forms a ceremonial approach to the site.

The Slaughter Stone, named by 17th-century antiquarians who believed Stonehenge to be a place of human sacrifice, was in fact one of a pair forming a doorway.

The Outer Bank, dug around 3000 BC, is the oldest part of Stonehenge.

BUILDING OF STONEHENGE

Stonehenge's monumental scale is more impressive given that the only tools available were made of stone, wood and bone. The labour involved in quarrying, transporting and erecting the huge stones was such that its builders must have been able to command immense resources and vast numbers of people. One method is explained below.

RECONSTRUCTION OF STONEHENGE

This illustration shows what Stonehenge probably looked like about 4,000 years ago.

A sarsen stone *was moved on rollers and levered into a pit.*

With levers *supported by timber packing, it was gradually raised.*

The stone *was then pulled upright by about 200 men hauling on ropes.*

The pit *round the ba was packed tightly u stones and chalk.*

WILTSHIRE'S OTHER PREHISTORIC SITES

The open countryside of the Salisbury Plain made this area an important centre of prehistoric settlement, and today it is covered in many ancient remains. Ringing the horizon around Stonehenge are scores of circular barrows, or burial mounds, where members of the ruling class were honoured with burial close to the temple site. Ceremonial bronze weapons and other finds excavated around Stonehenge and the other local prehistoric sites can be seen in the museum at Salisbury (*see pp264–5*) and the main museum at Devizes.

Silbury Hill (NT) is Europe's largest prehistoric earthwork, but despite extensive excavations its purpose remains a mystery. Built out of chalk blocks around 2750 BC, the hill covers 2 ha (5 acres) and rises to a height of 40 m (131 ft). Nearby **West Kennet Long Barrow** (NT) is the biggest

Silbury Hill

The Sarsen Circle was erected around 2500 BC and is capped by lintel stones held in place by mortice and tenon joints.

The Bluestone Circle was built around 2500 BC out of some 80 slabs quarried in south Wales. It was never completed.

Horseshoe of Bluestones

Horseshoe of Sarsen Trilothons

Sarsen stone forming part of the Avebury Stone Circle

Avebury ⑫

(EH/NT) Wiltshire. 600. ➔ Swindon then bus. *Green St (01672 539250).* ◯ daily. **www**.nationaltrust.org.uk

Built around 2500 BC, the **Avebury Stone Circle** surrounds the village of Avebury and was probably once some form of religious centre. Although the stones used are smaller than those at Stonehenge, the circle itself is wider. Superstitious villagers smashed many of the stones in the 18th century, believing the circle to have been a place of pagan sacrifice.

The original form of the circle is best appreciated by a visit to the excellent **Alexander Keiller Museum** to the west of the site, which illustrates in detail the construction of the circle. There is also a fascinating exhibition called "6,000 Years of Mystery", which explains the changing landscape of Avebury.

St James's Church has a Norman font carved with sea monsters, and a rare 15th-century choir screen.

Environs: A few minutes' drive east, **Marlborough** is an attractive town with a long and broad High Street lined with colonnaded Georgian shops.

ернate ends of the lintel were fired up.

The weight of the lintel was supported by a timber platform.

The lintel *was then levered sideways on to the uprights.*

chambered tomb in England, with numerous stone-lined "rooms" and a monumental entrance. Built as a communal cemetery around 3250 BC, it was in use for several centuries – old bodies were taken away to make room for newcomers.

Old Sarum is set within the massive ramparts of a 1st-century Romano-British hill fort. The Norman founders of Old Sarum built their own motte and bailey castle inside this ready-made fortification, and the remains of this survive along with the foundations of the huge cathedral of 1075. Above ground nothing remains of the town that once sat within the ramparts. The town's occupants moved to the fertile river valley site that became Salisbury during the early 12th century *(see pp264–5)*.

Old Sarum

(EH) Castle Rd. **Tel** 01722 335398. ◯ daily. ● 1 Jan, 24–26 Dec.

The chambered tomb of West Kennet Long Barrow (c.3250 BC)

Alexander Keiller Museum

(NT) Off High St. **Tel** 01672 538015. ◯ daily. ● 24–26 Dec. **www**.nationaltrust.org.uk

Salisbury ⑬

The "new" city of Salisbury was founded in 1220, when the old hill-top settlement of Old Sarum *(see p263)* was abandoned, being too arid and windswept, in favour of a new site among the lush water meadows where the rivers Avon, Nadder and Bourne meet. Locally sourced Purbeck marble and Chilmark stone were used for the construction of a new cathedral which was built mostly in the early 13th-century, over the remarkably short space of 38 years. Its magnificent landmark spire – the tallest in England – was an inspired afterthought added in 1280–1310.

The early 14th-century house of John A'Port, Queen's Street

Bishop's Walk and a sculpture by Elisabeth Frink (1930–93), Cathedral Close

Exploring Salisbury

The spacious and tranquil **Close**, with its schools, alms-houses and clergy housing, makes a fine setting for Salisbury's cathedral. Among the numerous elegant buildings here are the **Matrons' College**, built in 1682 as a home for widows and unmarried daughters of the clergy, and 13th-century **Malmesbury House** with its splendid early Georgian façade (1719), fronted by lovely wrought-iron gates. Other buildings of interest include the 13th-century **Medieval Hall**, the 13th-century **Wardrobe**, now a regimental museum, and the **Cathedral School**, housed in the 13th-century Bishop's Palace and famous for the quality of its choristers.

Beyond the walls of the Cathedral Close, Salisbury

developed its chessboard layout, with areas devoted to different trades, perpetuated in street names such as Fish Row and Butcher Row. Leaving the Close through **High Street Gate**, you reach the busy High Street leading to the 13th-century **Church of St Thomas**, which has a lovely carved timber roof (1450), and a late 15th-century Doom painting, showing Christ seated in judgement and demons seizing the damned. Nearby in Silver Street, **Poultry Cross** was built in the 14th century as a covered poultry market. An intricate network of alleys

fans out from this point with a number of fine timber-framed houses. In the large bustling **Market Place** the **Guildhall** is an unusual cream stone building from 1787–95, used for civic functions. More attractive are the brick and tile-hung houses on the north side of the square, many with Georgian façades concealing medieval houses.

The Cloisters are the largest in England. They were added between 1263 and 1284 in the Decorated style.

The Chapter House has an original of the *Magna Carta*. Its walls have stone friezes of the Old Testament.

Choir stalls

The Trinity Chapel contains the grave of St Osmund who was bishop of Old Sarum from 1078–1099.

Bishop Audley's Chantry, a magnificent 16th-century monument to the bishop, is one of several small chapels clustered round the altar.

FISH ROW

Street signs reflecting trades of 13th-century Salisbury

✠ Mompesson House

(NT) The Close. **Tel** 01722 420980.
◯ Apr–Oct: Sat–Wed. 🖼 ⚙ limited.
🖥 www.nationaltrust.org.uk

Built by a wealthy Wiltshire family in 1701, the handsomely furnished rooms of this house give an indication of life for the Close's inhabitants in the 18th century. The delightful garden, bounded by the north wall of the Close, has fine herbaceous borders.

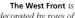

The graceful spire soars to a height of 123 m (404 ft).

The West Front is decorated by rows of lavish symbolic figures and saints in niches.

A roof tour takes you up to an external gallery at the base of the spire with views of the town and Old Sarum.

🏛 Salisbury and South Wiltshire Museum

The Close. **Tel** 01722 332151. ◯
Mon–Sat (Jul–Aug: Sun pm). 🖼 🖥
🖥 www.salisburymuseum.org.uk

In the medieval King's House, this museum has displays on early man, Stonehenge and nearby Old Sarum (see p263).

The clock dating from 1386 is the oldest working clock in Europe.

The nave is divided into ten bays by columns of polished Purbeck marble.

North transept

Numerous windows add to the airy and spacious atmosphere of the interior.

SALISBURY CATHEDRAL

The Close. **Tel** 01722 555120. ◯ daily. **Donation.** ⚙ 🖥
🖥 www.salisburycathedral.org.uk

The cathedral was mostly built between 1220 and 1258. It is a fine example of Early English Gothic architecture, typified by tall, sharply pointed lancet windows.

VISITORS' CHECKLIST

Wiltshire. 🚶 40,000. 🚆 South Western Rd. 🚌 Endless St.
ℹ Fish Row (01722 334956). 🏛 Tue, Sat. 🎭 Salisbury International Arts Festival: end May–early Jun
www.visitsalisbury.com

Environs: The town of Wilton is renowned for its carpet industry, founded by the 8th Earl of Pembroke using French Huguenot refugee weavers. The town's ornate **church** (1844) is a brilliant example of Neo-Romanesque architecture, incorporating genuine Roman columns, Flemish Renaissance woodwork, German and Dutch stained glass and Italian mosaics.

Wilton House has been home to the Earls of Pembroke since it was converted from a nunnery after the Dissolution (see p50). The house, largely rebuilt by Inigo Jones in the 17th century, includes one of the original Tudor towers, a fine collection of art and a landscaped park with a Palladian bridge (1737). The Single and Double Cube State Rooms have magnificently frescoed ceilings and gilded stucco work, and were designed to hang a series of family portraits by Van Dyck.

✠ Wilton House

Wilton. **Tel** 01722 746729. ◯
Easter weekend, May–Aug: Sun–Thu, bank hol Sat. 🖼 ⚙ 🍴 🖥

Double Cube room, designed by Inigo Jones in 1653

The Longleat Tree tapestry (1980) depicting a 400-year history

Longleat House ⑭

Warminster, Wiltshire. **Tel** 01985 844400. ⬛ Warminster then taxi. **House** ◯ daily. ◉ 25 Dec. **Safari Park** ◯ Feb–Nov: daily. 📷 ♿ 🍴 🛍 🎁 www.longleat.co.uk

The architectural historian John Summerson coined the term "prodigy house" to describe the exuberance and grandeur of Elizabethan architecture that is so well represented at Longleat. The house was started in 1540, when John Thynne bought the ruins of a priory on the site for £53. Over the centuries subsequent owners have added their own touches. These include the Breakfast Room and Lower Dining Room (dating from the 1870s), modelled on the Venetian Ducal Palace, and erotic murals painted by the present owner, the 7th Marquess of Bath. Today, the Great Hall is the only remaining room which belongs to Thynne's time.

In 1949, the 6th Marquess was the first landowner in Britain to open his stately home to the public, in order to fund the maintenance and preservation of the house and its estate. Parts of the grounds, landscaped by Capability Brown *(see p26)*, were turned into an expansive safari park in 1966, where lions, tigers and other wild animals roam freely. This, along with other additions such as England's longest hedge maze, the Adventure Castle and Blue Peter Maze, and special events, now draw even more visitors than the house.

Stourhead ⑮

Stourhead is among the finest examples of 18th-century landscape gardening in Britain *(see pp26–7)*. The garden was begun in the 1740s by Henry Hoare (1705–85), who inherited the estate and transformed it into a breathtaking work of art. Hoare created the lake, surrounding it with rare trees and plants, and Neo-Classical Italianate temples, grottoes and bridges. The Palladian-style house, built by Colen Campbell *(see p28)*, dates from 1724.

Pantheon
Hercules is among the statues of Roman gods housed in the elegant Pantheon (1753).

Gothic Cottage (1806)

Iron Bridge

A walk of 2 miles (3 km) round the lake provides artistically contrived vistas.

The lake was created from a group of medieval fishponds. Hoare dammed the valley to form a single expanse of water.

Turf Bridge

Temple of Flora (1744)

★ Temple of Apollo
The Classical temples that dot the garden were all designed by influential architect Henry Flitcroft (1679–1769).

Grotto

Tunnels lead to an artificial cave with a pool and a life-size statue of the guardian of the River Stour, sculpted by John Cheere in 1748.

VISITORS' CHECKLIST

(NT) Stourton, Wiltshire. **Tel** 01747 841152. 🚆 Gillingham (Dorset) then taxi. **House** ⬤ Mar–Oct: 11am–5pm Fri–Tue. **Gardens** ⬤ 9am–7pm (or dusk if earlier) daily. 🅿 🚻 limited. 🛒 🍴 🖥 🛍 **www**.national-trust.org.uk/stourhead

★ Stourhead House

Reconstructed after a fire in 1902, the house contains fine Chippendale furniture. The art collection reflects Henry Hoare's Classical tastes and includes The Choice of Hercules (1637) by Nicolas Poussin.

Colourful shrubs around the house include fragrant rhododendrons in spring.

Stourton village was incorporated into Hoare's overall design. 🍴 🛍

Pelargonium House is a historical collection of over 100 species and cultivars.

The reception offers information to help you enjoy your visit.

Entrance and car park

St Peter's Church

The parish church contains monuments to the Hoare family. The medieval Bristol Cross, nearby, was brought from Bristol in 1765.

STAR SIGHTS

★ Temple of Apollo

★ Stourhead House

Shaftesbury ⓰

Dorset. ⌂ *8,000.* 🚌 🚻 ℹ *8 Bell St
(01747 853514).* 🛍 *Thu.*
www.ruraldorset.com

Hilltop Shaftesbury, with its
cobbled streets and 18th-
century cottages is often used
as a setting for films to give a
flavour of Old England.
Picturesque **Gold Hill** is lined
on one side by a wall of the
demolished **abbey**, founded
by King Alfred in 888. Only
the excavated remains of the
abbey church survive, and
many masonry fragments are
found in the local museum.

**The Almshouse (1437) adjoining
the Abbey Church, Sherborne**

Sherborne ⓱

Dorset. ⌂ *9,500.* 🚊 🚌 ℹ *Digby
Rd (01935 815341).* 🛍 *Thu, Sat.*
www.westdorset.com

Few other towns in Britain
have such a wealth of
unspoilt medieval buildings.
Edward VI *(see p41)* founded
the famous Sherborne School
in 1550, saving intact the
splendid **Abbey Church** and
other monastic buildings that
might otherwise have been
demolished in the Dissolution
(see p50). Remains of the Saxon
church can be seen in the
abbey's façade, but the most
striking feature is the 15th-
century fan-vaulted ceiling.

Sherborne Castle, built by
Sir Walter Raleigh *(see p51)* in
1594, is a wonderfully varied
building that anticipates the
flamboyant Jacobean style.
Raleigh also lived briefly in
the early 12th-century **Old
Castle**, which now stands
in ruins, demolished during
the Civil War *(see p52)*.

Environs: West of Sherborne,
past Yeovil, is the magnificent
Elizabethan **Montacute House**
(see p245), set in 120 ha (300
acres) of grounds. It is noted
for tapestries, and for the
Tudor and Jacobean portraits
in the vast Long Gallery.

⛪ Sherborne Castle
Off A30. **Tel** *01935 813182.*
Castle ◻ *Apr–Oct: Tue–Thu, Sat,
Sun & bank hols (pm).* **Grounds**
◻ *Apr–Oct: Thu–Tue.* 🎫 ▢ 🎁
www.sherbornecastle.com

⛪ Old Castle
(EH) Off A30. **Tel** *01935 812730.*
◻ *Easter–Oct: daily.* 🎫 ♿ 🎁

🏛 Montacute House
(NT) Montacute. **Tel** *01935 823289.*
House ◻ *Mar–Oct: Wed–Mon.*
Grounds ◻ *Apr–Nov: Wed–Mon.*
🎫 🍴 🎁

Abbotsbury ⓲

Dorset. ⌂ *400.* ℹ *Bakehouse
Market St (01305 871130).*
www.abbotsbury-tourism.co.uk

The name Abbotsbury recalls
the town's 11th-century
Benedictine abbey of which
little but the huge tithe barn,
built around 1400, remains.
Nobody knows when the
Swannery here was founded,
but the earliest record dates
to 1393. Mute swans come to
nest in the breeding season,
attracted by the reed beds
along the Fleet, a brackish
lagoon protected from

The Swannery at Abbotsbury

the sea by a high ridge of
pebbles called **Chesil Bank**
(see p242). Its wild atmosphere
makes an appealing contrast
to the south coast resorts,
although strong currents make
swimming too dangerous.
**Abbotsbury Sub-Tropical
Gardens** are the frost-free
home to many new plants, discovered by botanists travelling
in South America and Asia.

🦢 Swannery
New Barn Rd. **Tel** *01305 871858.* ◻
mid-Mar–Oct: daily. 🎫 ♿ 🎁

**🌺 Abbotsbury Sub-Tropical
Gardens**
Off B3157. **Tel** *01305 871387.* ◻
daily. ● *24 Dec–1 Jan.* 🎫 ♿ ▢ 🎁

Weymouth ⓳

Dorset. ⌂ *62,000.* 🚊 🚌 ⛴
ℹ *King's Statue, The Esplanade
(01305 785747).* 🛍 *Thu.*

Weymouth's popularity as a
seaside resort began in 1789,
when George III paid the first
of many summer visits here.
The king's bathing machine
can be seen in the old brewery
complex, **Brewers' Quay**; his

Weymouth Quay, Dorset's south coast

For hotels and restaurants in this region see pp568–571 and pp624–626

statue is a prominent feature on the seafront. Here gracious Georgian terraces and hotels look across to the beautiful expanse of Weymouth Bay. Different in character is the old town around Custom House Quay with its fishing boats and old seamen's inns. Weymouth will host the sailing events at the 2012 London Olympics.

🏛 Brewers' Quay

Hope Sq. *Tel* 01305 777622. ☐ *daily.* ● *25 & 26 Dec, 2 wks in Jan.* 📷

Dorchester ⑳

Dorset. 🏘 *16,000.* 🚌 ❚ *Antelope Walk (01305 267992).* 🛒 *Wed.* **www**.visit-dorchester.co.uk

Dorchester, the county town of Dorset, is still recognizably the town in which Thomas Hardy based his novel *The Mayor of Casterbridge* (1886). Here, among the many 17th- and 18th-century houses lining the High Street, is the **Dorset County Museum**, where the original manuscript of the novel is displayed. Dorchester has the only example of a **Roman town house** in Britain. The remains reveal architectural details including a fine mosaic. There are also finds from Iron Age and Roman sites on the outskirts of the

A 55 m (180 ft) giant carved on the chalk hillside, Cerne Abbas (NT)

town. **Maumbury Rings** (Weymouth Avenue), is a Roman amphitheatre, originally a Neolithic henge. To the west, many Roman graves have been found below the Iron Age hill fort, **Poundbury Camp**.

Environs: Just southwest of Dorchester, **Maiden Castle** *(see p43)* is a massive monument dating from around 100 BC. In AD 43 it was the scene of a battle when the Romans fought the Iron Age people of southern England.

To the north lies the charming village of **Cerne Abbas** with its magnificent medieval tithe barn and monastic buildings. The huge chalk figure of a giant on the hillside here is a fertility figure thought to represent either the Roman god Hercules or an Iron Age warrior.

East of Dorchester are the churches, thatched villages and rolling hills immortalized in Hardy's novels. Picturesque **Bere Regis** is the Kingsbere of *Tess of the D'Urbervilles*, where the tombs of the family whose name inspired the novel may be seen in the Saxon **church**. **Hardy's Cottage** is where the writer was born and **Max Gate** is the house he designed and lived in from 1885 until his death. His heart is buried with his family at **Stinsford** church – his body was given a public funeral at Westminster Abbey *(pp92–3).*

There are beautiful gardens *(see p245)* and a magnificent medieval hall at 15th-century **Athelhampton House**.

Hardy's statue, Dorchester

🏛 Dorset County Museum

High West St. *Tel* 01305 262735. ☐ *Mon–Sat (Jul–Sep: daily).* ● *25, 26 Dec.* 📷 *valid for one year.* ♿ *ltd.* 🌐 www.dorsetcountymuseum.org

🏠 Hardy's Cottage

(NT) Higher Bockhampton. *Tel* 01305 262366. ☐ *Apr–Oct: Sun–Thu.* 📷 ♿ *garden only.*

🏠 Max Gate

(NT) Alington Ave, Dorchester. *Tel* 01305 262538. ☐ *Apr–Sep: Sun, Mon & Wed (pm).* 📷 ♿

🏛 Athelhampton House

Athelhampton. *Tel* 01305 848363. ☐ *Sun–Thu (Nov–Feb: Sun).* 📷 ♿ *gardens only.* 📷 📷 **www**.athelhamptonhouse.co.uk

---

THOMAS HARDY (1840–1928)

The vibrant, descriptive novels and poems of Thomas Hardy, one of England's best-loved writers, are set against the background of his native Dorset. The Wessex countryside provides a constant and familiar stage against which his characters enact their fate. Vivid accounts of rural life record a key moment in history, when mechanization was about to destroy ancient farming methods, just as the Industrial Revolution had done in the towns a century before *(see pp54–5).* Hardy's powerfully visual style has made novels such as *Tess of the D'Urbervilles* (1891) popular with modern film-makers, and drawn literary pilgrims to the villages and landscapes that inspired his fiction.

Nastassja Kinski in Roman Polanski's film *Tess* (1979)

Corfe Castle **㉑**

(NT) Dorset. **Tel** *01929 481294.* ⇌
Wareham then bus. ⬜ *daily.* ⬤ *25
& 26 Dec.* 🅿 ♿ *limited.* 🎫
Mar–Oct; Nov–Feb by arrangement.
📷 🏠 www.nationaltrust.org.uk

The spectacular ruins of
Corfe Castle romantically
crown a jagged pinnacle of
rock above the charming unspoilt village that shares its
name. The castle has dominated the landscape since the
11th century, first as a royal
fortification, then as the dramatic ruins seen today. In
1635 the castle was purchased
by Sir John Bankes, whose
wife and her retainers – mostly
women – courageously held
out against 600 Parliamentary
troops, in a six-week siege
during the Civil War *(see
pp52–3)*. The castle was
eventually taken through trea-
chery and in 1646 Parliament
voted to have it "slighted" –
deliberately blown up to
prevent it being used again.
From the ruins there are far-
reaching views over the Isle of
Purbeck and its coastline.

The ruins of Corfe Castle, dating mainly from Norman times

Isle of Purbeck **㉒**

Dorset. ⇌ *Wareham.* 🚢 *Shell Bay,
Studland.* ℹ *Swanage (01929
422885).* **www**.swanage.gov.uk

The Isle of Purbeck, which
is in fact a peninsula, is the
source of the grey shelly
limestone, known as Purbeck
marble, from which the castle
and surrounding houses were
built. The geology changes to
the southwest at **Kimmeridge**,
where the muddy shale is rich
in fossils and recently

discovered oil reserves. The
Isle, a World Heritage site, is
fringed with unspoilt beaches.
Studland Bay (NT) – with its
white sand and its sand-dune
nature reserve, rich in birdlife
– has been rated one of
Britain's best beaches.
Sheltered **Lulworth Cove** is
almost encircled by white
cliffs, and there is a fine cliff-
top walk to Durdle Door *(see
p243)*, a natural chalk arch.

The main resort in the area
is **Swanage**, the port where
Purbeck stone was trans-
ported by ship to London, to
be used for everything from
street paving to church building. Unwanted masonry from
demolished buildings was
shipped back and this is how
Swanage got its wonderfully
ornate **Town Hall** façade, designed by Wren around 1668.

Poole **㉓**

Dorset. 👥 *142,000.* ⇌ 🚌 🚢
ℹ *The High St (01202 253253).*
www.pooletourism.com

Situated on one of the largest
natural harbours in the world,
Poole is an ancient, still thriving, seaport. The quay is lined
with old warehouses, modern
apartments and a marina,
overlooking a safe sheltered
bay. The **Waterfront
Museum**, partly housed in
15th-century cellars on the
quay, has undergone a major
refurbishment, and re-opened
during 2007.

Nearby **Brownsea Island**
(reached by boat from the
quay) is given over to a
woodland nature reserve with

Beach adjoining Lulworth Cove, Isle of Purbeck

For hotels and restaurants in this region see pp568–571 and pp624–626

a waterfowl and heron sanctuary. The fine views of the Dorset coast add to the appeal of the island.

🏛 **Waterfront Museum**
High St. **Tel** 01202 262600.
☐ daily. ● 1 Jan, 25, 26 Dec. &
www.poole.gov.uk

🦋 **Brownsea Island**
(NT) Poole. **Tel** 01202 707744.
☐ Apr–Nov: daily (boat trips leave the quayside every 30 mins during the season). &

Boats in Poole harbour

Wimborne Minster ㉔

Dorset. 🏘 6,500. 🚌 ℹ 29 High St (01202 886116). 🛍 Fri–Sun. www.ruraldorset.com

The fine collegiate church of Wimborne's **Minster** was founded in 705 by Cuthburga, sister of King Ina of Wessex. It fell prey to marauding Danish raiders in the 10th century, and the imposing grey church we see today dates from the refounding by Edward the Confessor (see p47) in 1043. Stonemasons made use of the local Purbeck marble, carving beasts, biblical scenes, and a mass of zig-zag decoration.

The 16th-century **Priest's House Museum** has rooms furnished in the style of different periods and an enchanting hidden garden.

Environs: Designed for the Bankes family after the destruction of Corfe Castle, **Kingston Lacy** was acquired by the National Trust in 1981. The estate has always been farmed by traditional methods

and is astonishingly rich in wildlife, rare flowers and butterflies. This quiet, forgotten corner of Dorset is grazed by rare Red Devon cattle and can be explored using paths and "green lanes" that date back to Roman and Saxon times. The fine 17th-century house on the estate contains an outstanding collection of paintings, including works by Rubens, Velázquez and Titian.

🏛 **Priest's House Museum**
High St. **Tel** 01202 882533. ☐ Apr–Oct: Mon–Sat. & limited. 🅿 🅿

🏛 **Kingston Lacy**
(NT) on B3082. **Tel** 0845 0511700. **House** ☐ Apr–Oct: Wed–Sun; 2 wks at Christmas. **Gardens** ☐ Apr–Oct: daily; Nov–Mar: Sat & Sun. & gardens only. 🍴 🅿

Bournemouth ㉕

Dorset. 🏘 165,000. ✈ 🚌 🚆. ℹ westover road (01202 451700). www.bournemouth.co.uk

Bournemouth's popularity as a seaside resort is due to an almost unbroken sweep of sandy beach, extending from the mouth of Poole Harbour to Hengistbury Head. Most of the seafront is built up, with large seaside villas and exclusive hotels. To the west there are numerous clifftop parks and gardens, interrupted by beautiful wooded river ravines, known as "chines". The varied and colourful garden of **Compton Acres** was conceived as a museum of many different garden styles.

In central Bournemouth the amusement arcades, casinos, nightclubs and shops cater for the city's many visitors. In the summer, pop groups, TV comedians and the highly

Marchesa Maria Grimaldi by Sir Peter Paul Rubens (1577–1640), Kingston Lacy

regarded Bournemouth Symphony Orchestra perform at various venues in the city. The **Russell-Cotes Art Gallery and Museum**, housed in a late Victorian villa, has an extensive collection, with many fine Oriental and Victorian artefacts.

Environs: The magnificent **Christchurch Priory**, east of Bournemouth, is 95 m (310 ft) in length – the longest church in England. It was rebuilt between the 13th and 16th centuries and presents a sequence of different styles. The original nave, built around 1093, is an impressive example of Norman architecture, but the highlight is the intricate stone reredos, which features a Tree of Jesse, tracing the lineage of Christ. Next to the Priory are the ruins of a Norman **castle**.

Between Bournemouth and Christchurch, **Hengistbury Head** is well worth climbing for grassland flowers, butterflies and sea views, while **Stanpit Marsh**, to the west of Bournemouth, is an excellent spot for viewing herons and other wading birds.

🌷 **Compton Acres**
Canford Cliffs Rd. **Tel** 01202 700778. ☐ daily. 🅿 & 🍴 www.comptonacres.co.uk

🏛 **Russell-Cotes Art Gallery and Museum**
Eastcliff. **Tel** 01202 451800. ☐ Tue–Sun. & 🍴 🅿 www.russell-cotes.bournemouth.gov.uk

A toy train on the popular seafront at Bournemouth

DEVON AND CORNWALL

DEVON · CORNWALL

Miles of magnificently varied coastline dominate this magical corner of Britain. Popular seaside resorts alternate with secluded coves and unspoilt fishing villages rich in maritime history. In contrast there are lush, exotic gardens and the wild terrain of the moorland interior, dotted with tors and historic remains.

Geographical neighbours, the counties of Devon and Cornwall are very different in character. Celtic Cornwall, with its numerous villages named after early Christian missionaries, is mostly stark and treeless at its centre. In many places it is still scarred by the remains of tin and copper mining that has played an important part in the economy for some 4,000 years. Yet this does not detract from the beauty and variety of the coastline dotted with lighthouses and tiny coves, and penetrated by deep tidal rivers.

Devon, by contrast, is a land of lush pasture divided into a patchwork of tiny fields and threaded with narrow lanes, whose banks support a mass of flowers from the first spring primroses to summer's colourful mixture of campion, foxglove, oxeye daisies and blue cornflowers. The leisurely pace of rural life here, and in Cornwall, contrasts with life in the bustling cities. Exeter with its magnificent cathedral, historic Plymouth, elegant Truro and Elizabethan Totnes are urban centres brimming with life and character.

The spectacular coastline and the mild climate of the region attract families, boating enthusiasts and surfers. For those in search of solitude, the Southwest Coastal Path provides access to the more tranquil areas. There are fishing villages and harbours whose heyday was in the buccaneering age of Drake and Raleigh *(see p51),* and inland the wild moorland of Bodmin and Dartmoor, which provided inspiration for many romantic tales. Many of these are associated with King Arthur *(see p285)* who, according to legend, was born at Tintagel on Cornwall's dramatically contorted north coast.

Beach huts on the seafront at Paignton, near Torquay

◁ Fishing boats in Port Isaac, on Cornwall's north coast

Exploring Devon and Cornwall

Romantic Moorland dominates the inland parts of
Devon and Cornwall, ideal walking country with
few roads and magnificent views stretching for miles.
By contrast the extensive coastline is indented by
hundreds of sheltered river valleys, each one seem-
ingly isolated from the rest of the world – one reason
why Devon and Cornwall can absorb so many visitors
and yet still seem uncrowded. Wise tourists get to
know one small part of Devon or Cornwall intimately,
soaking up the atmosphere of the region, rather than
rushing to see everything in the space of a week.

KEY

▬	Motorway
▬	Major road
▬	Secondary road
▭	Minor road
▬	Scenic route
▬	Main railway
▬	Minor railway
△	Summit

SIGHTS AT A GLANCE

Appledore ⑯
Barnstaple ⑰
Bideford ⑮
Bodmin ⑪
Buckfastleigh ㉓
Buckland Abbey ㉖
Bude ⑬
Burgh Island ㉔
Clovelly ⑭
Cotehele ㉗
Dartmoor pp294–5 ㉙
Dartmouth ㉑
Eden Project pp282–3 ⑨
Exeter ⑲
Falmouth ⑥
Fowey ⑩
Helston and the
   Lizard Peninsula ⑤
Lynton and Lynmouth ⑱
Morwellham Quay ㉘
Penzance ③
Plymouth ㉕
St Austell ⑧
St Ives ②
St Michael's Mount
   pp278–9 ④
Tintagel ⑫
Torbay ⑳
Totnes ㉒
Truro ⑦

Walks and Tours

Penwith Tour ①

The dramatic cliffs of Land's End,
England's most westerly point

SEE ALSO

• *Where to Stay* pp571–5

• *Where to Eat* pp626–9

Lundy

Barr
Bide

Hartland Point   CLOVE
Hartland
Morewenstow
Holsw
BUDE ⑬
Bude Bay   Marha
Week St Mary   As
Boscastle   Boyt
🎵⑫ TINTAGEL
Brown Willy   Launce
Camelford   *420m*   Altar
Polzeath   *Bodmin Moor*
Bolventor
Padstow   *Colliford*
    Reservoir Ce
Wadebridge   St Neot
St Mawgan   BODMIN ⑪   Lis
St Columb   *Lanhydrock*
Newquay   Major   Lostwithiel   St C
Bugle
Newlyn East   EDEN PROJECT ⑨   East Looe
ST AUSTELL ⑧
St. Agnes   ⑩   Polperr
Trewithen   FOWEY
Portreath   ⑦ TRURO   *Heligan*   Mevagissey
Camborne   Redruth   *Trelissick*   Gorran Haven
Dodman Point
ST IVES ②   Penryn   Gerrans
Chysauster   Hayle
St Just   PENZANCE   *Poldark*   ⑥ FALMOUTH
PENWITH   ③ ④   *Mine*   Mawnan Smith
TOUR ①   ST MICHAEL'S   ⑤ HELSTON
Sennen   Mousehole   MOUNT
Mount's   *Goonhilly*
Bay   Mullion   *Earth Station*
    Coverack
⑤ LIZARD PENINSULA
Lizard   *Lizard Point*

Sub-tropical gardens at Torquay, the popular seaside resort

GETTING AROUND

Large numbers of drivers, many towing caravans (trailers), travel along the M5 motorway and A30 trunk road from mid-July to early September and travel can be slow, especially on Saturdays. Once in Devon and Cornwall, allow ample time if you are travelling by car along the region's narrow and high-banked lanes.

The regular train services, running from Paddington to Penzance, along Brunel's historic Great Western Railway, stop at most major towns. Aside from this, you are dependent on taxis or infrequent local buses.

Typical thatched, stone cottages, Buckland-in-the-Moor, Dartmoor

0 kilometres 15

0 miles 10

Penwith Tour ❶

This tour passes through a spectacular, remote Cornish landscape, dotted with relics of the tin mining industry, picturesque fishing villages and many prehistoric remains. The magnificent coastline varies between the gentle rolling moorland in the north and the rugged, windswept cliffs that characterize the dramatic south coast. The beauty of the area, combined with the clarity of light, has attracted artists since the late 19th century. Their work can be seen in Newlyn, St Ives and Penzance.

TIPS FOR DRIVERS

Tour length: 31 miles (50 km)
Stopping-off points: There are pubs and cafés in most villages. Sennen Cove makes a pleasant mid-way stop. (See also pp684–5.)

Zennor ①
The carved mermaid in the church recalls the legend of the mermaid who lured the local squire's son to her ocean lair.

Lanyon Quoit ②
One of many prehistoric monuments, this chambered tomb is visible on the left from the road to Madron.

Botallack Mine ⑧
Derelict engine-houses clinging to the cliffside are a vivid reminder of the region's former industry of tin-mining.

Trengwainton ③
These gardens are noted for their luxuriance (p244).

Land's End ⑦
England's most westerly point is noted for its dramatic and wild landscape. A local exhibition reveals its history, geology and wildlife.

Minack Theatre ⑥
This Ancient Greek-style theatre (1923) overlooks a magical bay of Porthcurno. It forms a magnificent backdrop for productions in summer.

Merry Maidens ⑤
This Bronze Age stone circle is said to be 19 girls turned to stone for dancing on Sunday.

Newlyn ④
Cornwall's largest fishing port gave its name to a school of artists founded in the 1880s (p278). Examples of their work can be seen in the art gallery here.

0 kilometres   3

0 miles   2

KEY

▬▬▬	Tour route
═══	Other roads
☀	Viewpoint

St Ives ❷

Cornwall. 🏘 *11,000.* � 🚉
ℹ *Street-an-Pol (01736 796297).*
www.visit-westcornwall.com

St Ives's **Barbara Hepworth Museum and Sculpture Garden** and **Tate St Ives** celebrate the work of a group of artists who set up a seaside art colony here from the 1920s. The former presents the sculptor's work in the house and garden where she lived and worked for many years. Tate St Ives, designed to frame a panoramic view of Porthmeor Beach, reminds visitors of the natural surroundings that inspired the art on display within. A new museum at the Leach Pottery (Tel: 01736 799703) celebrates the life and work of potter Bernard Leach, another luminary of the St Ives Society of Artists.

The Lower Terrace, Tate St Ives

The town of St Ives remains a typical English seaside resort, surrounded by a crescent of golden sands. Popular taste rules in the many other art galleries tucked down winding alleys with names such as Teetotal Street, a legacy of the town's Methodist heritage. Many galleries are converted cellars and lofts where fish were once salted and packed. In between are whitewashed cottages with tiny gardens brimming with flowers, their vibrant colours made intense by the unusually clear light that first attracted artists to St Ives.

🏛 **Barbara Hepworth Museum and Sculpture Garden**
Barnoon Hill. **Tel** *01736 796226.*
⏰ *daily (Nov–Feb: Tue–Sun).* ●
24–26 Dec. 🎫 ♿ *by appt.* 📷

🏛 **Tate St Ives**
Porthmeor Beach. **Tel** *01736 796226.* ⏰ *daily (Nov–Feb: Tue–Sun).* ● *24–26 Dec; occasionally for rehanging – phone to check.* 🎫 ♿ 🍴 📷 **www.**tate.org.uk/stives

---

TWENTIETH-CENTURY ARTISTS OF ST IVES

Ben Nicholson and Barbara Hepworth formed the nucleus of a group of artists that made a major contribution to the development of abstract art in Europe. In the 1920s, St Ives together with Newlyn *(see p276)* became a place for aspiring artists. Among the prolific artists associated with the town are the potter Bernard Leach (1887–1979) and the painter Patrick Heron (1920–99), whose *Coloured Glass Window (see p240)* dominates the Tate St Ives entrance. Much of the art on display at Tate St Ives is abstract and illustrates new responses to the rugged Cornish landscape, the human figure and the ever-changing patterns of sunlight on sea.

John Wells' *(1907–2000) key interests are in light, curved forms and birds in flight, as revealed in* Aspiring Forms *(1950).*

Barbara Hepworth *(1903–75) was one of the foremost abstract sculptors of her time.* Madonna and Child *(1953) can be seen in the church of St Ia.*

Ben Nicholson's *(1894–1982) work shows a change in style from simple scenes, such as the view from his window, to a preoccupation with shapes – as seen in this painting* St Ives, Cornwall *(1943–5). Later, his interest moved towards pure geometric blocks of colour.*

Penzance ❸

Cornwall. 🚶 *15,000.* 🚆 🚌 ⛴ ℹ️
Station Approach (01736 362207).
www.visit-westcornwall.com

Penzance is a bustling resort
with a climate so mild that
palm trees and sub-tropical
plants grow happily in the lush
Morrab Gardens. The town
commands fine views of St
Michael's Mount and a great
sweep of clean sandy beach.

The main road through the
town is Market Jew Street, at
the top of which stands the
magnificent domed Market
House (1837), fronted by a
statue of Sir Humphrey Davy
(1778–1829). Davy, who came
from Penzance, invented the
miner's safety lamp which
detected lethal gases.

Chapel Street is lined with
curious buildings, none more
striking than the flamboyant
Egyptian House (1835), with
its richly painted façade and
lotus bud decoration. Just as
curious is **Admiral Benbow
Inn** (1696) on the same street,
which has a pirate perched on
the roof looking out to sea.
The town's **Museum and Art
Gallery** has pictures by the
Newlyn School of artists.

Environs: A short distance
south of Penzance, **Newlyn**
(see p276) is Cornwall's largest
fishing port, which has given
its name to the local school of
artists founded by Stanhope
Forbes (1857–1947). They
painted outdoors, aiming to
capture the fleeting impres-
sions of wind, sun and sea.
Continuing south, the coastal
road ends at **Mousehole**
(pronounced Mowzall), a
pretty, popular village with a

The Egyptian House (1835)

tiny harbour, tiers of cottages
and a maze of narrow alleys.

North of Penzance, over-
looking the magical Cornish
coast, **Chysauster** is a fine
example of a Romano-British
village. The site has remained
almost undisturbed since it

St Michael's Mount ❹

(NT) Marazion, Cornwall. *Tel 01736
710507; tide and ferry information
01736 710265.* 🚢 *from Marazion
(Mar–Oct) or on foot at low tide.* ⭕
*Mar–Oct: Sun–Fri; Nov–Mar guided
tours only (book ahead).* 🎫 🚻 🅿️
📷 www.stmichaelsmount.co.uk

St Michael's Mount emerges
dramatically from the waters
of Mounts Bay. According to
ancient Roman historians, the
mount was the island of Ictis,
an important centre for the
Cornish tin trade during the
Iron Age. It is dedicated to
the archangel St Michael
who, according to legend,
appeared here in 495.

When the Normans con-
quered England in 1066 *(see
pp46–7)*, they were struck by
the island's resemblance to
their own Mont-St-Michel,
whose Benedictine monks
were invited to build a small
abbey here. The abbey was
absorbed into a fortress at the
Dissolution *(see p351)*, when
Henry VIII set up a chain of
coastal defences to counter an
expected attack from France.
In 1659 St Michael's Mount
was purchased by Colonel John St
Aubyn, whose descendants
subsequently turned the fortress into a magnificent house.

View of St Michael's Mount
from Marazion

**Harbourside
village**

Access to the island is by boat from
Marazion or on foot
by a cobbled cause-
way at low tide.

The rocky slopes were
planted with sub-tropical
trees and shrubs by the
St Aubyn family.

**PLAN OF
MAIN FLOOR**

Priory
Church

Choir

Blue Drawing
Room

Exit

North
Terrace

Hall

Entrance

Map
Room

Sir John's
Room

Ante Room

South
Terrace

Long
Passage

Library

Staircase
to Armoury
and Exit

Chevy
Chase Room

Smoking
Room

was abandoned during the 3rd century.

From Penzance, regular boat and helicopter services depart for the **Isles of Scilly**, a beautiful archipelago forming part of the same granite mass as Land's End, Bodmin Moor and Dartmoor. Along with tourism, flower-growing forms the main source of income here.

🏛 Penlee House Gallery and Museum
Morrab Rd.
Tel 01736 363625. ☐ May–Sep: 10am–5pm Mon–Sat; Oct–Apr: 10:30am–4:30pm Mon–Sat.
⬤ 25–26 Dec, 1 Jan. 🎫 🖼 but free admission on Sat. ♿ 🛍
www.penleehouse.org.uk

⛪ Chysauster
(EH) Off B3311.
Tel 07831 757934.
☐ Apr–Oct: daily. 🖼 🛍

THE GROWTH OF METHODISM

The hard-working and independent mining and fishing communities of the West Country had little time for the established church, but they were won over by the new Methodist religion, with its emphasis on hymn singing, open-air preaching and regular or "methodical" Bible reading. When John Wesley, the founder of Methodism, made the first of many visits to the area in 1743, sceptical Cornishmen pelted him with stones. His persistence, however, led to many conversions and by 1762 he was preaching to congregations of up to 30,000 people. Simple places of worship were built throughout the county; one favoured spot was the amphitheatre **Gwennap Pit**, at Busveal, south of Redruth. Methodist memorabilia can be seen in the Royal Cornwall Museum in Truro (see p281).

John Wesley (1703–91)

Castle entrance

The South Terrace forms the roof of the large Victorian wing. Beneath it there are five floors of private quarters.

The Blue Drawing Room *was formed from the Lady Chapel in the mid-18th century and is decorated in charming Rococo Gothic style. It contains fine plaster work, furniture and paintings by Gainsborough and Thomas Hudson.*

The Armoury displays sporting weapons and military trophies brought back by the St Aubyn family from various wars.

The Priory Church, *rebuilt in the late 14th century, forms the summit of the island. Beautiful rose windows are found at both ends.*

The Chevy Chase Room *takes its name from a plaster frieze (1641) representing hunting scenes.*

Pinnacles of serpentine rock at Kynance Cove (NT), Lizard Peninsula

Helston and the Lizard Peninsula ❺

Cornwall. 🚌 *from Penzance.*
ℹ️ *Station Approach, Penzance*
(01736 362207).
www.visit-westcornwall.com

The attractive town of Helston makes a good base for exploring the windswept coastline of the Lizard Peninsula. The town is famous for its Furry Dance, which welcomes spring with dancing through the streets *(see p62);* the **Folk Museum** explains the history of this ancient custom. The Georgian houses and inns of Coinagehall Street are a reminder that Helston was once a thriving stannary town where tin ingots were brought for weighing and stamping before being sold. Locally mined tin was brought down river to a harbour at the bottom of this street until access to the sea was blocked in the 13th century by a shingle bar that formed across the estuary. The bar created the freshwater lake, Loe Pool, and an attractive walk skirts its wooded shores. In 1880, Helston's trade was taken over by a new harbour created to the east on the River Helford, at Gweek. Today, Gweek is the home of the **National Seal Sanctuary**, where sick seals are nursed before being returned to the sea.

Cornwall's tin mining industry, from Roman to recent times, is covered at the **Poldark Mine** where underground tours show the working conditions of 18th-century miners. Another major attraction is **Flambards Experience**, with its recreation of a Victorian village and of Britain during the Blitz.

Further south, huge satellite dishes rise from the heathland. The **Goonhilly Earth Station** visitors' centre here explores the world of satellite communications.

Local shops sell souvenirs carved from serpentine, a soft greenish stone which forms the unusual-shaped rocks that rise from the sandy beach at picturesque **Kynance Cove**.

🏛 **Folk Museum**
Market Place, Helston. **Tel** 01326
564027. ⏱ *Mon–Sat (am only).*
● *Christmas week.* 🅿️ ♿ *limited.*
🌐 **www**.kerrierleisure.org.uk

🦭 **National Seal Sanctuary**
Gweek. **Tel** 01326 221361.
⏱ *daily.* ● *25 Dec.* 🅿️ ♿ 🛒 🌐
www.sealsanctuary.co.uk

🏛 **Poldark Mine**
Wendron. **Tel** 01326 573173.
⏱ *2 wks at Easter, Jul & Aug: daily;*
Apr–Jun, Sep & Oct: Sun–Fri; Nov–
Mar: tours only, by appt. 🅿️ ♿ 🌐
www.poldark-mine.co.uk

🏛 **Flambards Experience**
Culdrose Manor, Helston. **Tel** 0845
6018684. ⏱ *Easter–Aug: daily;*
Oct–Mar: Tue–Thu. 🅿️ ♿ 🍴 🌐
www.flambards.co.uk

🏛 **Goonhilly Earth Station**
Nr Helston, off B3293. **Tel** 0800
679 593. ⏱ *daily.* 🅿️ ♿ 🛒 🌐
www.goonhilly.bt.com

CORNISH SMUGGLERS

In the days before income tax was invented, the main form of government income came from tax on imported luxury goods, such as brandy and perfume. Huge profits were to be made by evading these taxes, which were at their height during the Napoleonic Wars (1780–1815). Remote Cornwall, with its coves and rivers penetrating deep into the mainland, was prime smuggling territory; estimates put the number of people involved, including women and children, at 100,000. Some notorious families resorted to deliberate wrecking, setting up deceptive lights to lure vessels onto the sharp rocks, in the hope of plundering the wreckage.

Falmouth ❻

Cornwall. 🏘 22,000. 🚌 🚆 ⛴
ℹ️ *11 Market Strand (01326
312300).* **www**.acornishriver.co.uk

Falmouth stands at the point where seven rivers flow into a long stretch of water called the **Carrick Roads**. The drowned river valley is so deep that huge ocean-going ships can sail up almost as far as Truro. Numerous creeks are ideal for boating excursions to view the varied scenery and birdlife.

Falmouth has the third largest naturally deep harbour after Sydney and Rio de Janeiro, and it forms the most interesting part of this seaside resort. On the harbour waterfront stands the recently constructed **National Maritime Museum Cornwall**, part of a projected large new waterside complex, to include cafés, shops and restaurants. With an exterior that is oak-clad to reflect the history of wooden boat sheds in the area, the museum is dedicated to the great maritime tradition of Cornwall, and contains Britain's finest public collection of historic and contemporary small craft. The building is designed to bring to life the stories of boats, maritime themes and Cornwall's heritage, as well as the story of the people whose lives depended on the sea. It aims to be accessible to the whole family.

The many old houses on the harbour include the striking **Customs House** and the chimney alongside, known as the "King's Pipe" because it was used for burning contraband tobacco seized from smugglers in the 19th century. **Pendennis Castle** and St Mawes Castle opposite, were built by King Henry VIII.

Environs: To the south, **Glendurgan** *(see p244)* and **Trebah** gardens are both set in sheltered valleys leading down to delightful sandy coves on the Helford River.

Truro Cathedral, designed by J L Pearson and completed in 1910

🏛 **National Maritime Museum Cornwall**
Discovery Quay, Falmouth. **Tel** 01326 313388. ☐ daily. ● 25, 26 Dec. ☐
www.nmmc.co.uk

⚓ **Pendennis Castle (EH)** The Headland. **Tel** 01326 316594. ☐ daily. ● 1 Jan, 24–26 Dec. 🅿 limited. 🔲 🔲 🔲

🌿 **Glendurgan (NT)** Mawnan Smith. **Tel** 01326 250906. ☐ mid-Feb–mid-Nov: Tue–Sat & pub hols (Aug: Mon–Sat). ● Good Fri. 🅿 🔲 🔲

🌿 **Trebah**
Mawnan Smith. **Tel** 01326 252200. ☐ daily. 🔲 🅿 🔲 🔲
www.trebah-garden.co.uk

Ship's figure-head, Falmouth

Truro ➐

Cornwall. 🏘 19,000. 🚉 🔲
🛈 Boscawen St (01872 274555). 🛒 Wed (cattle), Wed & Sat (farmers' market). **www**.acornishriver.co.uk

Once a market town and port, Truro is now the administrative capital of Cornwall. Truro's many gracious Georgian buildings reflect its prosperity during the tin mining boom of the 1800s. In 1876 the 16th-century parish church was rebuilt to create the first new **cathedral** to be built in England since Wren built St Paul's *(see pp114–15)* in the 17th century. With its central tower, lancet windows and spires, the cathedral is an exuberant building that looks more French than English.

Truro's cobbled streets and alleys lined with craft shops are also a delight to explore. The **Royal Cornwall Museum** provides an excellent intro-duction to the history of the county with displays on tin mining, Methodism *(see p279)* and smuggling.

Environs: On the outskirts of the city lie **Trewithen** and **Trelissick** gardens *(see p244).* The former has a rich collection of Asiatic plants.

🏛 **Royal Cornwall Museum**
River St. **Tel** 01872 272205. ☐ Mon–Sat. ● public hols. 🅿 🔲 🔲
www.royalcornwallmuseum.org.uk

🌿 **Trewithen**
Grampound Rd. **Tel** 01726 883647. ☐ Mar–May: daily; Jun–Sep: Mon–Sat. 🅿 🔲 by arrangement. 🔲
🔲 **www**.trewithengardens.co.uk

🌿 **Trelissick (NT)** Feock. **Tel** 01872 862090. ☐ Mar–May: daily; Jun–Sep: Mon–Sat. 🅿 🔲 🔲 🔲

The "Cornish Alps": china-clay spoil tips north of St Austell

St Austell ➑

Cornwall. 🏘 20,000. 🚉 🔲
🛈 Jet Service Station, Southbourne Rd (0845 094 0428). 🛒 Fri–Sun.
www.cornish-riviera.co.uk

The busy industrial town of St Austell is the capital of the local china-clay industry which rose to importance in the 18th century. Clay is still a vital factor here; until recently, China was the only other place where such quality and quantity of clay could be found. Spoil tips are a prominent feature; on a sunny day they look like snow-covered peaks, meriting the local name the "Cornish Alps".

Environs: The famous **Lost Gardens of Heligan** are an amazing restoration project to recreate the extraordinary gardens created by the Tremayne family from the 16th century to World War I. At the **Wheal Martyn China Clay Museum**, nature trails weave through clay works that oper-ated from 1878 until the 1920s.

🌿 **Lost Gardens of Heligan**
Pentewan. **Tel** 01726 845100. ☐ daily. ● 24 & 25 Dec. 🅿 🔲
🔲 🔲 **www**.heligan.com

🏛 **Wheal Martyn China Clay Museum**
Carthew. **Tel** 01726 850362. ☐ Feb–Sep: daily. 🅿 🔲 limited. 🔲 🔲 **www**.wheal-martyn.com

Eden Project ❾

Built in a china clay pit that had reached the end of its useful life, the Eden Project is a global garden for the 21st century, and a dramatic setting in which to tell the fascinating story of mankind's dependence on plants. Two futuristic conservatories called Biomes have been designed to mimic the environments of warmer climes: one hot and humid, the other warm and dry. The outer Biome is planted with species that thrive in the Cornish climate. The Eden Project seeks to educate by telling the story of plants, people and places. The relationship between humans and nature is interpreted by artists throughout the site. An impressive education centre, the Core, was opened in 2006 and is used for exhibitions, films and workshops.

④ **Tropical South America**
Some plants in this area reach enormous proportions. The leaves of the giant waterlily can be up to 2 m (6 ft) across.

③ **West Africa**
Iboga is central to the African religion Bwiti. Highly hallucinogenic, it is an integral part of initiation ceremonies.

② **Malaysia**
The Titan arum grows within this rainforest display. The flower will grow to 1.5 m (4 ft) and smell of rotting flesh.

① **Tropical Islands**
Set apart from the rest of the world, these islands have many fascinating plants. The rare Madagascar Periwinkle (Catharanthus roseus) is thought to help cure leukemia.

THE SITE

Access to the outdoor and the covered Biomes is via the Visitor Centre.

Rainforest Biome
① Tropical Islands
② Malaysia
③ West Africa
④ Tropical South America
⑤ Crops & cultivation

Mediterranean Biome
⑥ The Mediterranean
⑦ South Africa
⑧ California
⑨ Crops & cultivation

VISITORS' CHECKLIST

Bodelva, St Austell, Cornwall.
Tel 01726 811911. St Austell.
dedicated bus service from St
Austell. Apr–Oct: 10am–
6pm daily (last adm 5pm); Nov–
Mar: 10am–4:30pm daily (last
adm 3pm). 24, 25 Dec.
For events details
see **www**.edenproject.com

Building Eden

*Cornwall's declining china clay industry has left behind
many disused pits. The Eden Project makes ingenious use
of this industrial landscape. After partly infilling a pit,
the massive Biomes were nestled into its base and walls.*

Transparent hexagons
made of ultra-light hi-
tech plastic

⑤ **Crops and cultivation**
The coffee plant (Coffea
arabica) *is one of the many
plants on display that are
used in our everyday lives.*

The entrance to both
the Rainforest and
Mediterranean Biomes is
via the Link, where two
restaurants are located.

RAINFOREST BIOME

vast conservatory houses a lush jungle of 8,000
and plants. The dome is high enough to allow
rainforest trees to grow to their full height.

oor Biome
llination
rnish crops
nts for taste
obal gardeners
er & brewing
pe & fibre
mp
eppe & Prairie
o-engineering
a
vender
echanical theatre
el
yth & folkore
odiversity & Cornwall

㉕ Play
㉖ Flowers in the making
㉗ Health
㉘ Flowerless garden

KEY

Land Train

The
Stage

Eden
Arena

The
Core

Visitor Centre

0 metres 150

0 yards 150

View of Polruan across the estuary from Fowey

Fowey ❿

Cornwall. 🏘 2,000. 🚢
🅸 5 South St (01726 833616).
www.fowey.co.uk

Fowey (pronounced Foy),
has been immortalized
under the name of Troy Town
in the humorous novels of Sir
Arthur Quiller-Couch (1863–
1944), who lived here in a
house called **The Haven**.
A resort favoured by many
wealthy Londoners with a taste

DAPHNE DU MAURIER

The period romances of
Daphne du Maurier (1907–
89) are inextricably linked
with the wild Cornish landscape where she grew up.
Jamaica Inn established
her reputation in 1936, and
with the publication of
Rebecca two years later
she found herself one of
the most popular authors
of her day. *Rebecca* was
made into a film directed
by Alfred Hitchcock, star-
ring Joan Fontaine and
Lord Laurence Olivier.

for yachting and expensive
seafood restaurants, Fowey is
the most gentrified of the
Cornish seaside towns. The
picturesque charm of the
flower-filled village is undeniable, with its tangle of tiny
steep streets and its views
across the estuary to Polruan.
The church of **St Fimbarrus**
marks the end of the ancient
Saint's Way footpath from
Padstow – a
reminder of the
Celtic missionaries
who arrived on the
shores of Cornwall
to convert people to
Christianity. Its
flower-lined path
leads to a majestic
porch and carved
tower. Inside there
are some fine 17th-
century memorials to
the Rashleigh family
whose seat, Menabilly,
became Daphne du Maurier's
home and featured as Mander-
ley in *Rebecca* (1938).

Jamaica Inn,
Bodmin Moor

Environs: For a closer look at
the town of **Polruan** and the
ceaseless activity of the harbour there is a number of
river trips up the little creeks.
At the estuary mouth are the
twin towers from which
chains were once hung to de-
mast invading ships – an
effective form of defence.
  A fine stretch of coast leads
further east to the picturesque
fishing villages of **Polperro**,
nestling in a narrow green ravine, and neighbouring **Looe**.
  Upriver from Fowey is the
tranquil town of **Lostwithiel**.
Perched on a hill just to the
north are the remains of the
Norman **Restormel Castle**.

⚓ **Restormel Castle**
(EH) Lostwithiel. **Tel** 01208 872687.
◻ Apr–Oct: daily. 🎫 🅿 ♿

Bodmin ⓫

Cornwall. 🚂 Bodmin Parkway. 🚌
Bodmin. 🅸 Mount Folly Sq, Bodmin
(01208 76616). www.bodminlive.com

Bodmin, Cornwall's ancient
county town, lies on the
sheltered western edge of the
great expanse of moorland
that shares its name. The
history and archaeology of
the town and moor are covered by **Bodmin Town Museum**,
while **Bodmin Jail**, where
public executions took place
until 1909, is a gruesome tourist attraction. The churchyard
is watered by the ever-gushing
waters of a holy spring, and it
was here that St Guron established a Christian cell in the 6th
century. The **church** is dedicated to St Petroc, a Welsh
missionary who founded a
monastery here. The
monastery has dis-
appeared, but the
bones of St Petroc
remain, housed in
a splendid 12th-
century ivory casket
in the church.
  For a pleasant day
out, ride the **Bodmin
& Wenford Railway**,
a steam train which
departs from Bodmin
Station, or take part in
a Victorian murder
trial at **The Courtroom Experience**, run by the tourist office.
  South of Bodmin is the
Lanhydrock estate. Amid its
extensive wooded acres and
formal gardens *(see p244)* lies
the massive Victorian manor
house, rebuilt after a fire in
1881, but retaining some
Jacobean features. The fine
17th-century plaster ceiling in
the Long Gallery depicts
scenes from the Bible.
  The desolate wilderness of
Bodmin Moor is noted for its
network of prehistoric field
boundaries. The main attraction, however, is the 18th-
century **Jamaica Inn**, made
famous by Daphne du
Maurier's tale of smuggling
and romance. Today there
is a restaurant and bar based
on du Maurier's novel, and a
small museum. A 30-minute
walk from the Inn is **Dozmary
Pool**, reputed to be bottom-
less until it dried up in 1976.

The ruins of Tintagel Castle on the north coast of Cornwall

According to legend, the dying King Arthur's sword Excalibur was thrown into the pool.

To the east is **Altarnun**. Its spacious 15th-century church of **St Nonna** is known as the "Cathedral of the Moor".

🏛 Bodmin Town Museum
Mt Folly Sq, Bodmin. **Tel** 01208 77067. ☐ Easter–Oct: Mon–Sat, Good Fri. ● pub hols. & ltd.

🏚 Bodmin Jail
Berrycombe Rd, Bodmin. **Tel** 01208 76292. ☐ daily. ● 25 Dec. 🍴 ▯ www.bodminjail.org

🏚 Lanhydrock
(NT) Bodmin. **Tel** 01208 265950. House ☐ Apr–Oct: Tue–Sun & public hols. **Gardens** ☐ daily.

Tintagel ⑫

Cornwall. 🏘 1,700. 🚉 Bossiney Rd (01840 779084). 🚌 Thu (summer). www.visitboscastleandtintagel.com

The romantic and mysterious ruins of **Tintagel Castle**, built around 1240 by Earl Richard of Cornwall, sit high on a hill-top surrounded by slate cliffs. Access to the castle is via two steep staircases clinging to the cliffside where pink thrift and purple sea lavender abound.

The earl was persuaded to build in this isolated, windswept spot by the popular belief, derived from Geoffrey of Monmouth's fictitious

History of the Kings of Britain, that this was the birthplace of the legendary King Arthur.

Large quantities of fine eastern Mediterranean pottery dating from around the 5th century have been discovered, indicating that the site was an important trading centre, long before the medieval castle was built. Whoever lived here, perhaps the ancient Kings of Cornwall, could evidently afford a luxurious lifestyle.

A clifftop path leads from the castle to Tintagel's **church**, which has Norman and Saxon masonry. In Tintagel village the **Old Post Office** is a rare example of a 14th-century restored and furnished Cornish manor house.

Environs: A short distance to the east, **Boscastle** is a pretty National Trust village. The River Valency runs down the middle of the main street to the fishing harbour, which is sheltered from the sea by high slate cliffs. Access from the harbour to the sea is via a channel cut through the rocks.

🏰 Tintagel Castle
(EH) Off High St. **Tel** 01840 770328. ☐ daily. ● 1 Jan, 24–26 Dec. 🍴 www.english-heritage.org.uk/tintagel

🏚 Old Post Office
(NT) Fore St. **Tel** 01840 770024. ☐ Mar–Oct: daily. ▯ 🍴

Bude ⑬

Cornwall. 🏘 9,000. 🚉 Crescent car park (01288 354240). 🚌 Fri (summer). www.visitbude.info

Wonderful beaches around this area make Bude a popular resort for families. The expanse of clean golden sand that attracts visitors today once made Bude a bustling port. Shelly, lime-rich sand was transported along a canal to inland farms where it was used to neutralize the acidic soil. The canal was abandoned in 1880 but a short stretch survives, providing a haven for birds such as kingfishers and herons.

Kingfisher

KING ARTHUR

Historians think the legendary figure of King Arthur has some basis in historical fact. He was probably a Romano-British chieftain or warrior who led British resistance to the Saxon invasion of the 6th century *(see pp46–7)*. Geoffrey of Monmouth's *History of the Kings of Britain* (1139) introduced Arthur to literature with an account of the many legends connected with him – how he became king by removing the sword Excalibur from a stone, his final battle with the treacherous Mordred, and the story of the Knights of the Round Table *(see p170)*. Other writers, such as Alfred, Lord Tennyson, took up these stories and elaborated on them.

King Arthur, from a 14th-century chronicle by Peter of Langtoft

Clovelly ⑭

Devon. 📷 350. **Tel** 01237 431781.
Town & Visitors' Centre ⬜ daily.
⬤ 25 & 26 Dec. 📷 ♿ Visitors'
Centre. **www**.clovelly.co.uk

Clovelly has been a noted beauty spot since the novelist Charles Kingsley (1819–75) wrote about it in his stirring story of the Spanish Armada, *Westward Ho!* (1855). The whole village is privately owned and has been turned into a tourist attraction, with little sign of the flourishing fishing industry to which it owed its birth. It is a charming, picturesque village with steep, traffic-free cobbled streets rising up the cliff from the harbourside, white-washed houses and gardens brimming with brightly coloured flowers. There are superb views from the lookout points and fine coastal paths to explore from the tiny quay.

Hobby Drive is a scenic 3-mile (5-km) approach on foot to the village which runs through woodland along the coast. The road was constructed in 1811–29 to give

Bideford's medieval bridge, 203 m (666 ft) long with 24 arches

employment to local men who had been made redundant at the end of the Napoleonic Wars *(see pp54–5)*.

Bideford ⑮

Devon. 📷 14,000. 🚌 ℹ️ Kingsley
Rd (01237 477676). 🏪 Tue, Sat.

Strung out along the estuary of the River Torridge, Bideford grew and thrived on importing tobacco from the New World. Some 17th-century merchants' houses survive in Bridgeland Street, including the splendid bay-windowed house at No. 28 (1693). Beyond is Mill Street, leading to the parish church

and the fine medieval bridge. The quay stretches from here to a pleasant park and a statue that commemorates Charles Kingsley, whose novels helped bring visitors to the area in the 19th century.

Environs: To the west of Bideford, the village **Westward Ho!** was built in the late 19th century and named after Kingsley's popular novel. The development failed, and the Victorian villas and hotels are now part of a holiday resort. Rudyard Kipling *(see p163)* was at school here and the hill to the south, known as **Kipling Tors**, was the background for *Stalky & Co* (1899).

Also to the west is **Hartland Abbey**, built as a monastery c.1157, now a family home. The BBC filmed parts of *Sense and Sensibility* here. Visitors can enjoy a museum, art and antiques, as well as gardens.

Henry Williamson's *Tarka the Otter* (1927) describes the otters of the **Torridge Valley** and naturalists are hoping to reintroduce otters here. Part of a Tarka Trail has been laid out along the Torridge and bicycles can be hired from the old railway station. The trail passes close to the magnificent **Rosemoor Garden**.

Day trips run from either Bideford or Ilfracombe (depending on the tide) to **Lundy** island, which is abundant in birds and wildlife.

🌺 **RHS Rosemoor Garden**
Great Torrington. **Tel** 01805
624067. ⬜ daily. ⬤ 25 Dec. 📷
♿ 🚻 📷 **www**.rhs.org.uk

🏛️ **Hartland Abbey**
nr. Bideford. **Tel** 01237 441264.
⬜ Apr–May: Wed, Thu, Sun;
Jun–Sep: Sun–Thu. 📷 🖥️ ⬜ 📷
limited. **www**.hartlandabbey.com

Fishing boats in Clovelly's harbour

videos on local trades such as fishing and shipbuilding.

🏛 **North Devon Maritime Museum**
Odun Rd. **Tel** 01237 474852. ◯ May–Sep: daily; Apr, Oct: pm. 🖼 ♿ ltd. 🖥 www.devonmuseums.net

Barnstaple ⑰

Devon. 🏠 33,000. 🚋 🚌 🚹 The Square (01271 375000). 🏪 Mon–Sat. www.staynorthdevon.co.uk

Although Barnstaple is an important distribution centre for the whole region, its town centre remains calm due to the exclusion of traffic. The massive glass-roofed **Pannier Market** (1855) has stalls of organic fruit and vegetables, honey and eggs, much of it produced by farmers' wives to supplement their income. Nearby is **St Peter's Church** with its twisted broach spire, said to have been caused by a lightning strike which warped the timbers in 1810.

On the Strand is a wonderful arcade topped with a statue of Queen Anne, now the **Heritage Centre**. This was built as an exchange where merchants traded the contents of their cargo boats moored on the River Taw alongside. Nearby is the 15th-century bridge and the **Museum of Barnstaple and North Devon**, where displays cover local history and the 700-year-old pottery industry, as well as local wildlife, such as the otters. The 180-mile (290 km) Tarka Trail circuits around Barnstaple; 35 miles (56 km) of it can be cycled.

Environs: Just west of Barnstaple, **Braunton "Great Field"** covers over 120 ha (300 acres) and is a well-preserved relic of medieval open-field

Fishermen's cottages, Appledore

Appledore ⑯

Devon. 🏠 3,000. 🚹 Bideford (01237 477676).

Appledore's remote position at the tip of the Torridge Estuary has helped to preserve its charms intact. Busy boatyards line the long riverside quay, which is also the departure point for fishing trips and ferries to the sandy beaches of Braunton Burrows on the opposite shore. Timeworn Regency houses line the main street which runs parallel to the quay, and behind is a network of narrow cobbled lanes with 18th-century fishermen's cottages. Several shops retain their original bow-windows and sell an assortment of crafts, antiques and souvenirs.

Uphill from the quay is the **North Devon Maritime Museum**, with an exhibition on the experiences of Devon emigrants in Australia and displays explaining the work of local shipyards. The tiny **Victorian Schoolroom** which is affiliated to the museum, shows various documentary

Barnstaple's Pannier Market

Statue of Queen Anne (1708)

cultivation. Beyond lies **Braunton Burrows**, one of the most extensive wild-dune reserves in Britain. It is a must for plant enthusiasts who would like to spot sea kale, sea holly, sea lavender and horned poppies growing in their natural habitat. The sandy beaches and pounding waves at nearby Croyde and Woolacombe, are favourites among surfing enthusiasts, but there are also calmer areas of warm shallow water and rock pools.

Arlington Court, north of Barnstaple, has a collection of model ships, magnificent perennial borders and a lake. The stables house a collection of horse-drawn vehicles. Carriage rides are available.

🏛 **Museum of Barnstaple and North Devon**
The Square. **Tel** 01271 346747. ◯ Mon–Sat. ◯ 24 Dec–1 Jan. ♿ ltd. 🖥 www.devonmuseums.net

🏰 **Arlington Court**
(NT) Arlington. **Tel** 01271 850296. ◯ Easter–Oct: Sun–Fri. 🖼 ♿ limited. 🖥 🖥

The village of Lynmouth

Lynton and Lynmouth ⑱

Devon. 🏛 2,000. 🚌 ℹ️ *Town Hall, Lee Rd, Lynton (0845 660 3232).* www.lynton-lynmouth-tourism.co.uk

Situated at the point where the East and West Lyn rivers meet the sea, Lynmouth is a picturesque, though rather commercialized, fishing village. The pedestrianized main street, lined with shops selling clotted cream and seaside souvenirs, runs parallel to the Lyn, now made into a canal with high embankments as a precaution against flash floods. One flood devastated the town at the height of the holiday season in 1952. The scars caused by the flood, which was fuelled by heavy rain on Exmoor, are now overgrown by trees in the pretty **Glen Lyn Gorge**, which leads north out of the village. Lynmouth's sister town, Lynton, is a mainly Victorian village perched on the clifftop 130 m (427 ft) above, giving lovely views across the Bristol Channel to the Welsh coast. It can be reached from the harbour front by a cliff railway, by road or by a steep path.

Environs: Lynmouth makes an excellent starting point for walks on Exmoor. There is a 2 mile (3 km) trail that leads southeast to tranquil **Water-smeet** *(see p251)*. On the western edge of Exmoor, **Combe Martin** *(see p250)* lies in a sheltered valley. On the main street, lined with Victorian villas, is the 18th-century Pack of Cards Inn, built by a gambler with 52 windows, for each card in the pack.

Exeter ⑲

Exeter is Devon's capital, a bustling and lively city with a great deal of character, despite the World War II bombing that destroyed much of its city centre. Built high on a plateau above the River Exe, the city is encircled by substantial sections of Roman and medieval wall, and the street plan has not changed much since the Romans first laid out what is now the High Street. Elsewhere the Cathedral Close forms a pleasant green, and there are cobbled streets and narrow alleys which invite leisurely exploration. For shoppers there is a wide selection of big stores and smaller speciality shops.

Exploring Exeter
The intimate green and the close surrounding Exeter's distinctive cathedral were the setting for Anthony Trollope's novel *He Knew He Was Right* (1869). Full of festive crowds listening to buskers in the summer, the close presents an array of architectural styles. One of the finest buildings here is the Elizabethan **Mol's Coffee House**. Among the other historic buildings that survived World War II are the magnificent **Guildhall** (1330) on the High Street (one of Britain's oldest civic buildings), the opulent **Custom House** (1681) by the quay, and the elegant 18th-century **Rougement House** which stands near the remains of a Norman **castle** built by William the Conqueror *(see pp46–7)*.

The port area has been transformed into a tourist attraction with its early 19th-century warehouses converted into craft shops, antique galleries and cafés. Boats can be hired for cruising down the short stretch of canal. The **Quay House Interpretation Centre**

The timber-framed Mol's Coffee House (1596), Cathedral Close

West front and south tower, Cathedral Church of St Peter

(open daily April–October; weekends November–March) has audio-visual and other displays on the history of Exeter.

🏛 Cathedral Church of St Peter
Cathedral Close. *Tel 01392 255573.* ⏰ daily. 📷 ♿ 🍴
Exeter's cathedral is one of the most gloriously ornamented in Britain. Except for the two Norman towers, the cathedral is mainly 14th century and built in the style aptly known as Decorated because of the swirling geometric patterns of the stone work. The West Front, the largest single collection (66) of medieval figure sculptures in England, includes kings, apostles and prophets. Started in the 14th century, it was completed by 1450. Inside, the splendid Gothic vaulting sweeps from one end of the church to the other, impressive in its uniformity and punctuated by gaily painted ceiling bosses.

Among the tombs around the choir is that of Edward II's treasurer, Walter de Stapledon (1261–1326), who was murdered by a mob in London. Stapledon raised much of the money needed to fund the building of this cathedral.

Collection of shells and other objects in the library of A La Ronde

North of Sidmouth lies the magnificent church at **Ottery St Mary**. Built in 1338–42 by Bishop Grandisson, the church is clearly a scaled-down version of Exeter Cathedral, which he also helped build. In the churchyard wall is a memorial to the poet Coleridge who was born in the town in 1772.

Nearby **Honiton** is famous for its extraordinarily intricate and delicate lace, made here since Elizabethan times.

To the north of Exeter, **Killerton** is home to the National Trust's costume collection. Here, displays of bustles and corsets and vivid tableaux illustrate aristocratic fashions from the 18th century to the present day.

Further north near Tiverton, is **Knightshayes Court**, a Victorian Gothic mansion with fine gardens (see p245).

Underground Passages

Paris St. *Tel 01392 665 887*. ☐ Jun–Sep: daily; Oct–May: Tue–Sun.
Under the city centre lie the remains of Exeter's medieval water-supply system. An excellent video and guided tour explain how the stone-lined tunnels were built in the 14th and 15th centuries on a slight gradient in order to bring in fresh water for townspeople from springs outside the town. The site was refurbished in 2007 and includes the new Heritage Centre.

St Nicholas Priory

The Mint. *Tel 01392 665858*. ☐ for conservation work – phone for details
Built in the 12th century, this building has retained many of its original features and rooms. These help visitors to trace its fascinating history from austere monastic beginnings, through its secular use as a Tudor residence for wealthy merchants, to its 20th-century incarnation as five separate business premises occupied by various tradesmen including a bootmaker and an upholsterer.

Royal Albert Memorial Museum and Art Gallery

Queen St. *Tel 01392 665858*. ☐ call for details. ● for refurbishment until 2011.
This museum has a wonderfully varied collection, including Roman remains, a zoo of stuffed animals, West Country art and a particularly good ethnographic display. Highlights include displays on silverware, watches and clocks.

19th-century head of an Oba, Royal Albert Museum

Environs: South of Exeter on the A376, the eccentric **A La Ronde** is a 16-sided house built in 1796 by two spinster cousins, who decorated the interior with shells, feathers and souvenirs gathered while on tour in Europe.

Further east, the unspoilt Regency town of **Sidmouth** lies in a sheltered bay. There is an eclectic array of architecture, the earliest buildings dating from the 1820s when Sidmouth became a popular summer resort. Thatched cottages stand opposite huge Edwardian villas, and elegant terraces line the seafront. In summer the town hosts the famous International Festival of Folk Arts (see p63).

A La Ronde

(NT) Summer Lane, Exmouth. *Tel 01395 265514*. ☐ Mar–Oct: Sat–Wed.

Killerton

(NT) Broadclyst. *Tel 01392 881345*. **House** ☐ Mar–Sep: Wed–Mon; Aug & Christmas: daily; Oct: Wed–Sun. **Garden** ☐ daily.

Knightshayes Court

(NT) Bolham. *Tel 01884 254665*. ☐ mid-Feb–Oct: Sat–Thu, Good Fri. **Gardens** ☐ Apr–Nov: daily. limited.

Mexican dancer at Sidmouth's International Festival of Folk Arts

Torbay ⑳

Torbay. ≊ ⊞ Torquay, Paignton. ⓘ Vaughan Parade, Torquay (01803 211211). www.englishriviera.co.uk

The seaside towns of Torquay, Paignton and Brixham form an almost continuous resort around the great sweep of sandy beach and blue waters of Torbay. Because of its mild climate, semi-tropical gardens and exuberant Victorian hotel architecture, this popular coastline has been dubbed the English Riviera. In the Victorian era Torbay was patronized by the wealthy. Today, the theme is mass entertainment, and there are plenty of attractions, mostly in and around Torquay.

Torre Abbey includes the remains of a monastery founded in 1196. It is currently undergoing a massive restoration programme, the first phase of which focused on the abbey's oldest part. Future phases will redevelop the abbey's galleries and restore the historic gardens. **Torquay**

Museum nearby covers natural history and archaeology, including finds from **Kents Cavern**, on the outskirts of the town. This is one of England's most important prehistoric sites, and the spectacular caves include displays on people and animals who lived here up to 350,000 years ago.

The charming miniature town of **Babbacombe Model Village** is north of Torquay, while a mile (1.5 km) inland is the lovely village of **Cockington**. Visitors travel by horse-drawn carriage to the preserved Tudor manor house, church and thatched cottages.

In Paignton, the celebrated **Paignton Zoo** teaches children about the planet's wildlife, and from here you can take the steam railway – an ideal way to visit Dartmouth.

Continuing south from Paignton, the pretty town of Brixham was once England's most prosperous fishing port.

🏠 **Torre Abbey**
King's Drive, Torquay. **Tel** 01803 293593. ◯ daily. 🏷 🗓 🔌 🛒 🖼

Bayards Cove, Dartmouth

🏛 **Torquay Museum**
Babbacombe Rd, Torquay. **Tel** 01803 293975. ◯ daily (Nov–Easter: Mon–Sat). ● Christmas wk. 🏷 🔌 🖳
📷 www.torquaymuseum.org

🕳 **Kents Cavern**
Ilsham Rd, Torquay. 📷 01803 215 136. ◯ daily. ● 25 & 26 Dec. 🏷
🗓 🍴 🖳 www.kents-cavern.co.uk

🏛 **Babbacombe Model Village**
Hampton Ave, Torquay. **Tel** 01803 315315. ◯ daily. 🏷 🔌 🖳

🦒 **Paignton Zoo**
Totnes Rd, Paignton. 📷 01803 697 500. ◯ daily. ● 25 Dec. 🏷 🔌
🍴 🖳 www.paigntonzoo.org.uk

Dartmouth ㉑

Devon. 🏠 5,500. ≊ ⓘ Mayors Ave (01803 834224). 🛒 Tue–Fri am. www.discoverdartmouth.com

Sitting high on the hill above the River Dart is the **Royal Naval College**, where British naval officers have trained since 1905. Dartmouth has always been an important port and it was from here that English fleets set sail to join the Second and Third Crusades. Some 18th-century houses adorn the cobbled quay of Bayards Cove, while carved timber buildings line the 17th-century Butterwalk, home to **Dartmouth Museum**. To the south is **Dartmouth Castle** (1388).

🏛 **Dartmouth Museum**
Butterwalk. **Tel** 01803 832923. ◯ Mon–Sat. ● 1 Jan, 25 & 26 Dec. 🏷 📷 www.devonmuseums.net

🏰 **Dartmouth Castle**
(EH) Castle Rd. **Tel** 01803 833588. ◯ daily (Nov–Easter: Sat & Sun). ● 1 Jan, 24–26 Dec. 🏷 📷

Torquay, on the "English Riviera"

Stained-glass window in Blessed Sacrament Chapel, Buckfast Abbey

Totnes ❷

Devon. 🏔 7,500. 🚊 🚉 🚌
ℹ Town Mill (01803 863168).
🚌 Tue am (May–Sep), Fri, Sat.
www.totnesinformation.co.uk

Totnes sits at the highest navigable point on the River Dart with a Norman **castle** perched high on the hill above. Linking the two is the steep High Street, lined with bow-windowed Elizabethan houses. Bridging the street is the **Eastgate**, part of the medieval town wall. Life in the town's heyday is explored in the **Totnes Elizabethan Museum**, which also has a room devoted to the mathematician Charles Babbage (1791–1871), who is regarded as the pioneer of modern computers. There is a **Guildhall**, and a **church** with a delicately carved and gilded rood screen. On Tuesdays in the summer, market stallholders dress in Elizabethan costume.

Environs: A few miles north of Totnes, **Dartington Hall** has 10 ha (25 acres) of lovely gardens and a famous music school where concerts are held in the timbered 14th-century Great Hall.

Stallholders in Totnes market

⛰ **Totnes Castle**
(EH) Castle St. **Tel** 01803 864406.
◯ Apr–Oct: daily. 🎟

🏛 **Totnes Elizabethan Museum**
Fore St. **Tel** 01803 863821. ◯
Easter–Oct: Mon–Fri. 🎟 🚹 limited.

🏛 **Guildhall**
Rampart Walk. **Tel** 01803 862147.
◯ Apr–Oct: Mon–Fri. 🎟

🌷 **Dartington Hall Gardens**
Tel 01803 862367. ◯ daily.
www.dartingtonhalltrust.com

Buckfastleigh ❷

Devon. 🏔 3,300. 🚊 ℹ Fore St
(01364 644522).

This market town, situated on the edge of Dartmoor (see pp294–5), is dominated by **Buckfast Abbey**. The original abbey, founded in Norman times, fell into ruin after the Dissolution of the Monasteries and it was not until 1882 that a small group of French Benedictine monks set up a new abbey here. Work on the present building was financed by donations and carried out by the monks. The abbey was completed in 1938 and lies at the heart of a thriving community. The fine mosaics and modern stained-glass window are also the work of the monks.

Nearby is the **Buckfast Butterfly Farm and Otter Sanctuary**, and the **South Devon Steam Railway** terminus where steam trains leave for Totnes.

🏛 **Buckfast Abbey**
Buckfastleigh. **Tel** 01364 645500.
◯ daily. 🔴 Good Fri, 25–27 Dec.
🚹 🚻 🏠 **www**.buckfast.org.uk

🦋 **Buckfast Butterfly Farm and Otter Sanctuary**
Buckfastleigh. **Tel** 01364 642916.
◯ Easter–Nov: daily. 🎟 🚹
www.ottersandbutterflies.co.uk

Burgh Island ❷

Devon. 🚊 Plymouth, then taxi. ℹ
The Quay, Kingsbridge (01548 853 195). **www**.kingsbridgeinfo.co.uk

The short walk across the sands at low tide from Bigbury-on-Sea to Burgh Island takes you back to the era of the 1920s and 1930s. It was here that the millionaire Archibald Nettlefold built the luxury **Burgh Island Hotel** (see p567) in 1929. Created in Art Deco style with a natural rock sea-bathing pool, this was the exclusive retreat of figures such as the Duke of Windsor and Noel Coward. The restored hotel is worth a visit for the photographs of its heyday and the Art Deco fittings. You can also explore the island and **Pilchard Inn** (1336), reputed to be haunted by the ghost of a smuggler.

The Art Deco style bar in Burgh Island Hotel

Plymouth 25

Plymouth. 250,000. The Mayflower, The Barbican (01752 306330). daily.
www.plymouth.gov.uk

The tiny port from which Drake, Raleigh, the Pilgrim Fathers, Cook and Darwin all set sail on pioneering voyages has now grown to a substantial city, much of it boldly rebuilt after wartime bombing. Old Plymouth clusters around the **Hoe**, the famous patch of turf on which Sir Francis Drake is said to have calmly finished his game of bowls as the Spanish Armada approached the port in 1588 *(see pp50–51)*. Today the Hoe is a pleasant park and parade ground surrounded by memorials to naval men, including Drake himself. Alongside is Charles II's **Royal Citadel**, built to guard the harbour in

Drake's coat of arms

the 1660s. On the harbour is the **National Marine Aquarium**. Nearby is the **Mayflower Stone and Steps**, the spot where the Pilgrim Fathers set sail for the New World in England's third and successful attempt at colonization in 1620. The popular **Plymouth Mayflower Exhibition** explores the story of the Mayflower and the creation of the harbour. Interactive graphics are used to tell the tales of merchant families and emigration to the New World.

Environs: A boat tour of the harbour is the best way to see the dockyards where warships have been built since the Napoleonic Wars. There are also splendid views of various fine gardens, such as **Mount Edgcumbe Park** *(see p244)*, scattered around the coastline. East of the city, the 18th-century **Saltram House** has two rooms

Mid-18th-century carved wood chimneypiece, Saltram House

by Adam *(see pp28–9)* and portraits by Reynolds, who was born in nearby Plympton.

🏰 Royal Citadel
(EH) The Hoe. **Tel** 0117 9750700.
May–Sep: Tue & Thu. only.

🐠 National Marine Aquarium
Rope Walk, Coxside. **Tel** 01752 600
301. daily. 25 Dec.
www.national-aquarium.co.uk

🏛 Plymouth Mayflower Exhibition
3–5 The Barbican. **Tel** 01752 306
330. daily (Nov–Apr: Mon–Sat).

🌿 Mount Edgcumbe Park
Cremyll, Torpoint. from Torpoint
car park. **Tel** 01752 822236. **House**
Apr–Sep: Sun–Thu. **Grounds**
all year.
www.mountedgcumbe.gov.uk

🏛 Saltram House
(NT) Plympton. **Tel** 01752 333500.
Gallery Mar–Nov: Sat–Thu; Jan
& Feb: Sat. **Gardens** all year.
open all year.

Buckland Abbey 26

(NT) Yelverton, Devon. **Tel** 01822
853607. from Yelverton. Fri–
Wed (Nov–Mar: Sat & Sun pm).
Christmas–mid-Feb.
www.nationaltrust.org.uk

Founded by the Cistercian monks in 1278, Buckland Abbey was converted to a house after the Dissolution of the Monasteries and became the home of Drake from 1581–96. Many of the monastic buildings survive in a garden setting, notably the 14th-century tithe barn *(see p28)*. Drake's life is explained through paintings and memorabilia in the house.

View of Plymouth Harbour from the Hoe

Cotehele 27

(NT) St Dominick, Cornwall.
Tel 01579 351346. ⌷ Calstock.
House ☐ Apr–Oct: Sat–Thu &
Good Fri. **Grounds** ☐ daily. ☐ ☐
☐ limited. ☐ ☐

Magnificent woodland and
lush river scenery make Cotehele (pronounced Coteal) one
of the most delightful spots
on the River Tamar and a
rewarding day can be spent
exploring the estate. Far from
civilization, tucked into its
wooded fold in the Cornish
countryside, Cotehele has
slumbered for 500 years. The
main attraction is the house
and valley garden at its centre.
Built mainly between 1489
and 1520, it is a rare example
of a medieval house, set
around three courtyards with a
magnificent open hall, kitchen,
chapel and a warren of private
parlours and chambers. The
romance of the house is enhanced by colourful terraced
gardens to the east, leading via
a tunnel into a richly planted
valley garden. The path
through this garden passes a
large domed medieval dovecote and descends to a quay,
to which lime and coal were
once shipped. There are fine
views up and down the winding reed-fringed Tamar from
Prospect Tower, and a gallery
on the quayside specializes in
local arts and crafts. The estate
includes a village, a quay with
a small maritime museum,
working mill buildings, ancient
lime kilns and workshops
with 19th-century equipment.

Spanish Armada and British fleets in the English Channel, 1588

SIR FRANCIS DRAKE

Sir Francis Drake (c.1540–1596) was the first Englishman to
circumnavigate the globe and he was knighted by Elizabeth I
in 1580. Four years later he introduced tobacco and potatoes
to England, after bringing home 190 colonists who had tried
to establish a settlement in Virginia. To many, however,
Drake was no more than an opportunistic rogue, renowned
for his exploits as a "privateer", the polite name for a pirate.
Catholic Spain was the bitter enemy and Drake further
endeared himself to queen and people by his part in the
victory over Philip II's Armada *(see pp50–51)*, defeated by
bad weather and the buccaneering spirit of the English.

Morwellham Quay 28

Near Tavistock, Devon.
Tel 01822 832766. ⌷ Gunnislake.
☐ daily. ☐ 1 Jan, 24–26 Dec.
☐ ☐ ☐ limited. ☐ ☐
www.morwellham-quay.co.uk

Morwellham Quay was a
neglected and overgrown
industrial site until 1970, when
members of a local trust began
restoring the abandoned cottages, schoolhouse, farmyards,
quay and copper mines to
their original condition.
    Today, Morwellham Quay
is a thriving and rewarding
industrial museum, where
you can easily spend a whole
day partaking in the typical
activities of a Victorian
village, from preparing the
shire horses for a day's work,
to riding a tramway deep into
a copper mine in the hillside
behind the village. The
museum is brought to life by
characters in costumes, some
of whom give demonstrations
throughout the day. You can
watch, or lend a hand to the

Industrial relics at Morwellham
Quay in the Tamar Valley

cooper while he builds a
barrel, attend a lesson in the
schoolroom, take part in
Victorian playground games
or dress up in 19th-century
hooped skirts, bonnets, top
hats or jackets. The staff, who
convincingly play the part of
villagers, lead you through
their lives and impart a huge
amount of information about
the history of this small
copper-mining community.

Medieval dovecote in the gardens
of Cotehele estate

Dartmoor National Park ㉘

Buzzard

The high, open moorland of central Dartmoor provides the eerie background for Conan Doyle's thriller, *The Hound of the Baskervilles* (1902). Here at Princetown, surrounded by weathered outcrops of granite tors is one of Britain's most famous prisons. Also dotting the landscape are scores of prehistoric remains which have survived because of the durability of granite. Elsewhere the mood is very different. Streams tumble through wooded and boulder-strewn ravines forming cascades and waterfalls, and thatched cottages nestle in the sheltered valleys around the margins of the moor. Many establishments offer cream teas and warming fires to weary walkers.

Characteristic moorland, eastern Dartmoor

Okehampton has the Museum of Dartmoor Life and a ruined 14th-century castle.

Lydford Gorge (NT) (open Apr–Oct) is a dramatic ravine, leading to a waterfall.

The Ministry of Defence uses much of this area for training but access is available on non-firing days (0800 458 4868 to check).

High Moorland Visitor Centre

Brentor
This volcanic hill crowned by a tiny church (first built in 1130) is visible for miles.

KEY

🚩	Information centre
▬▬	A road
▬▬	B road
═══	Minor road
�ූ	Viewpoint

0 kilometres   5

0 miles   5

High Willhays
621 m
2,038 ft

MELDON RESERVOIR

MINISTRY OF DEFENCE FIRING RANGES

Two Bridges

Merrivale   Blackbroo

Princetown

BURRATOR RESERVOIR

Postbrid

PLYMOU

Ivy

Postbridge
Dartmoor's northern moor can be explored from the village of Postbridge. The gently rolling moorland is crossed by many dry-stone walls.

Dartmoor Ponies
These small, tough ponies have lived on the moor since at least the 10th century.

Grimspound is the impressive remains of a Bronze Age settlement.

Castle Drogo (NT) is a magnificent mock-castle built by the architect Sir Edwin Lutyens (*see p29*) in 1910–30.

VISITORS' CHECKLIST

Devon. 🚆 🚌 *Exeter, Plymouth, Totnes then bus.* ℹ️ *Dartmoor National Park Authority's Centre (01822890414),* www.dartmoor-npa.gov.uk. **Okehampton Castle**, Castle Lane, Okehampton. **Tel** *01837 52844.* ☐ *Apr–Sept: daily.* 🎟️ **Museum of Dartmoor Life**, West St, Okehampton. **Tel** *01837 52295.* ☐ *10:15am–4:15pm Tue & Fri (closed for lunch).* ● *24 Dec–1 Jan.* 🎟️ ♿ *limited.* **Castle Drogo (NT)**, Drewsteignton. **Tel** *01647 433 306.* ☐ *Apr–Nov: Wed–Mon.* **Gardens** ☐ *daily.* 🎟️ ♿ *gardens only.* 🍴 🛒 🔲

Becky Falls is a 22-m (72-ft) waterfall set in delightful woodlands.

EXETER
Drewsteignton
Teign

EXETER
Moretonhampstead

RTHY JIR
Bovey

Manaton

EXETER
Bovey Tracey

Buckland-in-the-Moor

NFORD SERVOIR
Buckfastleigh

Ashburton

ON DAM SERVOIR

Hound Tor
Nearby lie the remains of a Medieval settlement abandoned in the 14th century.

Bovey Tracey has an extensive woodland reserve.

Haytor Rocks is one of the most popular of the many tors.

South Devon Steam Railway

Buckfast Abbey was founded by King Canute (*see p159*) in 1018.

Dartmoor Butterfly and Otter Sanctuary

artmeet
arks the lovely onfluence point f the East and Vest Dart rivers.

Buckland-in-the-Moor
One of the many picturesque villages on Dartmoor.

THE
MIDLANDS

The Midlands at a Glance

The Midlands is an area that embraces
wonderful landscapes and massive industrial
cities. Visitors come to discover the wild beauty
of the rugged Peaks, cruise slowly along the
Midlands canals on gaily painted narrowboats
and explore varied and enchanting gardens.
The area encompasses the full range of
English architecture from mighty cathedrals and humble churches to charming
spa towns, stately homes and country
cottages. There are fascinating industrial
museums, many in picturesque settings.

Cheshire

Staffordshire

Shropshire

Tissington Trail (see
p337) *combines a walk
through scenic Peak
District countryside with
an entertaining insight
into the ancient custom
of well-dressing.*

THE HEART OF ENGLAND
(see pp304–329)

Ironbridge Gorge (see pp314–15) *was the
birthplace of the Industrial Revolution (see
pp348–9). Now a World Heritage Centre, the
site is a reminder of the lovely countryside in
which the original factories were located.*

Worcestershire

Herefordshire

Gloucestershire

The Cotswolds (see
pp304–5) *are full of
delightful houses built
from local limestone, on
the profits of the medieval
wool trade. Snowshill
Manor (left) is situated
near the unspoilt village
of Broadway.*

| 0 kilometres | 25 |
| 0 miles | 25 |

◁ **The front of the half-timbered Lord Leycester Hospital, Warwick**

Chatsworth House (see pp334–5), *a magnificent Baroque edifice, is famous for its gorgeous gardens. The "Conservative" Wall, a greenhouse for exotic plants, is pictured above.*

Lincoln Cathedral (see p341), *a vast, imposing building, dominates the ancient town. Inside are splendid misericords and the superb 13th-century Angel Choir, which has 30 carved angels.*

Nottinghamshire

Lincolnshire

Derbyshire

EAST MIDLANDS
(see pp330–343)

Leicestershire

Burghley House (see pp342–3) *is a dazzling landmark for miles around in the flat East Midlands landscape, with architectural motifs from the European Renaissance.*

Warwickshire

Warwick Castle (see pp322–3) *is an intriguing mixture of medieval power base and country house, complete with massive towers, battlements, a dungeon and state apartments, such as the Queen Anne Bedroom.*

Northamptonshire

Stratford-upon-Avon (see pp324–7) *has many picturesque houses connected with William Shakespeare's life, some of which are open to visitors. These black and white timber-framed buildings, which abound in the Midlands, are a typical example of Tudor architecture (see pp302–3).*

Canals of the Midlands

One of England's first canals was built by the 3rd Duke of Bridgewater in 1761 to link the coal mine on his Worsley estate with Manchester's textile factories. This heralded the start of a canal-building boom and by 1805, a 3,000 mile (4,800 km) network of waterways had been dug across the country, linking into the natural river system. Canals provided the cheapest, fastest way of transporting goods, until competition began to arrive from the railways in the 1840s. Cargo transport ended in 1963 but today nearly 2,000 miles (3,200 km) of canals are still navigable, for travellers who wish to take a leisurely cruise on a narrowboat.

The Grand Union Canal *(pictured in 1931) is 300 miles (485 km) long and was dug in the 1790s to link London with the Midlands.*

Lockside inns cater for narrowboats.

Lock-keepers were provided with canalside houses.

The Farmer's Bridge *is a flight of 13 locks in Birmingham. Locks are used to raise or lower boats from one level of the canal to another. The steeper the gradient, the more locks are needed.*

Heavy V-shaped timber gates close off the lock.

Water pressing against the gate keeps it shut.

The towpath is where horses pulled the canal boats before engines were invented. They were changed periodically for fresh animals.

Narrowboats *have straight sides and flat bottoms and are pointed at both ends. Cargo space took up most of the boat, with a small cabin for the crew. Exteriors were brightly painted.*

NO 7   BILL O TOMS   NEW MARTON LOCK

MIDLANDS CANAL NETWORK

The industrial Midlands was the birthplace of the English canal system and still has the biggest concentration of navigable waterways.

VISITORS' CHECKLIST

Companies specializing in canal boat holidays: Blake's Holidays **Tel** *01603 739400*; Hoseasons **Tel** *01502 501010*; Canal Cruising Co **Tel** *01785 813982*; Black Prince Holidays **Tel** *01527 575115*; Alvechurch Boat Centres Ltd **Tel** *0121 445 2909*;
Canal museums: Phone to check opening times: National Waterways Museum (*see p329*); Canal Museum, Stoke Bruerne, Towcester **Tel** *01604 862229*; Boat Museum, Ellesmere Port. **Tel** *0151 3555017*.
www.thewaterwaystrust.co.uk

Canal

Footbridge

A **windlass** fills or lowers water levels.

A **balance beam** swings the gates open.

CANAL LOCKS

Canals used tunnels, embankments and locks for the speedy transportation of goods across country. Locks were used to convey boats up or down hills.

The Edstone Aqueduct, *just north of Stratford-upon-Avon, carries the canal in a cast iron trough. This is supported on brick piers for 180 m (495 ft), over roads and a busy railway line.*

CANAL ART

Canal boat cabins are very small and every inch of space is utilized to make a comfortable home for the occupants. Interiors were enlivened with colourful paintings and attractive decorations.

Furniture was designed to be functional and to brighten up the cramped cabin.

Narrowboats are often decorated with ornamental brass.

Water cans were also painted. The most common designs were roses and castles, with local variations in style.

Tudor Manor Houses

Many striking manor houses were built in central England during the Tudor Age *(see pp50–51)*, a time of relative peace and prosperity. The abolition of the monasteries meant that vast estates were broken up and sold to secular landowners, who built houses to reflect their new status *(see p28)*. In the Midlands, wood was the main building material, and the gentry flaunted their wealth by using timber panelling for flamboyant decorative effect.

The Lucy family arms

The decorative moulding *on the south wing dates from the late 16th century. Ancient motifs, such as vines and trefoils, are combined with the latest imported Italian Renaissance styles.*

The rectangular moat *was for decoration rather than defence. It surrounds a recreated knot garden (see p26) that was laid out in 1972 using plants known to have been available in Tudor times.*

The Long Gallery *was the last part of the Hall to be built (c.1560–1562). It has original plasterwork portraying Destiny (left) and Fortune.*

Brickwork chimney

Jetties (overhanging upper stories)

TUDOR MANSIONS AND TUDOR REVIVAL

There are many sumptuously decorated Tudor mansions in the Midlands. In the 19th century Tudor Revival architecture became a very popular "Old English" style, intended to invoke family pride and values rooted in the past.

Hardwick Hall *in Derbyshire, whose huge kitchen is pictured, is one of the finest Tudor mansions in the country. These buildings are known as "prodigy" houses (see p342) due to their gigantic size.*

Charlecote Park, *Warwickshire, is a brick mansion built by Sir Thomas Lucy in 1551– 59. It was heavily restored in Tudor style in the 19th century, but has a fine original gatehouse. According to legend, the young William Shakespeare (see pp324–7) was caught poaching deer in the park.*

The Parlour *was an informal reception room. Biblical scenes such as* Susannah and the Elders *(right) expressed religious faith and learning.*

Entrance

Wood panelling

Courtyard

The Great Hall *(c.1504–1508) is the oldest part of the house, and in Tudor times was the most important. The open-plan hall was the main communal area for dining and entertainment.*

LITTLE MORETON HALL
The Moreton family home *(see p311)* was built between 1504 and 1610, from a number of box-shapes, fitted together. Wood panelling and jetties displayed the family's wealth.

The patterned glazing *in the great bay window is typically 16th century: small pieces of locally made glass were cut into diamond shapes and held in place by lead glazing bars.*

Packwood House *in Warwickshire is a timber-framed mid-Tudor house with extensive 17th–century additions. The unusual garden of clipped yew trees dates from the 17th century and is supposed to represent the Sermon on the Mount.*

Moseley Old Hall, *Staffordshire, has a red brick exterior concealing its early 17th-century timber frame. The King's Room is where Charles II hid after the Battle of Worcester (see pp52–3).*

Wightwick Manor, *West Midlands, was built in 1887–93. It is a fine example of Tudor Revival architecture and has superb late 19th-century furniture and decorations.*

Building with Cotswold Stone

The Cotswolds are a range of limestone hills running over 50 miles (80 km) in a north-easterly direction from Bath *(see pp258–61)*. The thin soils are difficult to plough but ideal for grazing sheep, and the wealth engendered by the medieval wool trade was poured into building majestic churches and opulent town houses. Stone quarried from these hills was used to build London's St Paul's Cathedral *(see pp114–15)*, as well as the villages, barns and manor houses that make the landscape so picturesque.

Dragon, Deerhurst Church

Arlington Row Cottages *in Bibury, a typical Cotswold village, were built in the 17th century for weavers whose looms were set up in the attics.*

Windows were taxed and glass expensive. Workers' cottages had only a few, not very large windows made of small panes of glass.

A drip mould keeps rain off the chimney.

The roof is steeply pitched to carry the weight of the tiles. These were made by master craftsmen who could split blocks of stone into sheets by using natural fault lines.

COTSWOLD STONE COTTAGE

The two-storey Arlington Row Cottages are asymmetrical and built of odd-shaped stones. Small windows and doorways make them quite dark inside.

Timber lintels and doors

Timber framing was cheaper than stone, and was used for the upper rooms in the roof.

VARIATIONS IN STONE

Cotswold stone is warmer-toned in the north, pearly in central areas and light grey in the south. The stone seems to glow with absorbed sunlight. It is a soft stone that is easily carved and can be used for many purposes, from buildings to bridges, headstones and gargoyles.

"Tiddles" *is a cat's gravestone in Fairford churchyard.*

Lower Slaughter *gets its name from the Anglo-Saxon word slough, or muddy place. It has a low stone bridge, over the River Eye.*

COTSWOLD STONE TOWNS AND VILLAGES

The villages and towns on this map are prime examples of places built almost entirely from stone. By the 12th century almost all of the villages in the area were established. Huge deposits of limestone resulted in a wealth of stone buildings. Masons worked from distinctive local designs that were handed down from generation to generation.

① Winchcombe
② Broadway
③ Stow-on-the-Wold
④ Upper and Lower Slaughter
⑤ Bourton-on-the-Water
⑥ Sherborne
⑦ Northleach
⑧ Painswick
⑨ Bibury
⑩ Fairford

Wool merchants' houses were built of fine ashlar (dressed stone) with ornamental cornerstones, doorframes and windows.

The eaves here have a dentil frieze, so-called because it resembles a row of teeth.

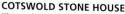

COTSWOLD STONE HOUSE

This early Georgian merchant's house in Painswick shows the fully developed Cotswold style, which borrows decorative elements from Classical architecture.

The door frame has a rounded pediment on simple pilasters.

STONE GARGOYLES

In Winchcombe's church, 15th-century gargoyles reflect a combination of pagan and Christian beliefs.

Pagan gods warded off pre-Christian evil spirits.

Fertility figures, always important in rural areas, were incorporated into Christian festivals.

Human faces often caricatured local church dignitaries.

Animal gods represented qualities such as strength in pagan times.

Dry-stone walling *is an ancient technique used in the Cotswolds. The stones are held in place without mortar.*

A stone cross *(16th century) in Stanton village, near Broadway, is one of many found in the Cotswolds.*

Table-top and "tea caddy", *fine 18th-century tombs, can be found in Painswick churchyard.*

THE HEART OF ENGLAND

CHESHIRE · GLOUCESTERSHIRE · HEREFORDSHIRE
SHROPSHIRE · STAFFORDSHIRE · WARWICKSHIRE · WORCESTERSHIRE

*B*ritain's great attraction is its variety, and nowhere is this more true than at the heart of the country, where the Cotswold hills, enfolding stone cottages and churches, give way to the flat, fertile plains of Warwickshire. Shakespeare country borders on the industrial heart of England, once known as the workshop of the world.

Coventry, Birmingham, the Potteries and their hinterlands have been manufacturing iron, textiles and ceramics since the 18th century. In the 20th century these industries have declined, and a new type of museum has developed to commemorate the towns' industrial heyday and explain the manufacturing processes which were once taken for granted. Ironbridge Gorge and Quarry Bank Mill, Styal, where the factories are now living museums, are fascinating industrial sites and enjoy beautiful surroundings.

These landscapes may be appreciated from the deck of a narrowboat, making gentle progress along the Midlands canals, to the region on the border with Wales known as the Marches. Here the massive walls of Chester and the castles at Shrewsbury and Ludlow recall the Welsh locked in fierce battle with Norman barons and the Marcher Lords. The Marches are now full of rural communities served by the peaceful market towns of Leominster, Malvern, Ross-on-Wye and Hereford. The cities of Worcester and Gloucester both have modern shopping centres, yet their majestic cathedrals retain the tranquillity of an earlier age.

Cheltenham has Regency terraces, Cirencester a rich legacy of Roman art and Tewkesbury a solid Norman abbey. Finally, there is Stratford-upon-Avon, where William Shakespeare, the Elizabethan dramatist, lived and died.

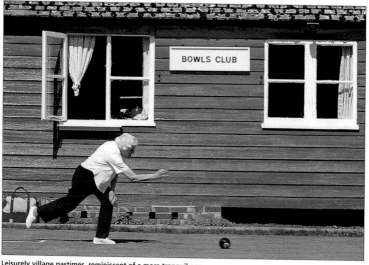

Leisurely village pastimes, reminiscent of a more tranquil age

◁ Cotswold stone: an extremely popular building material in the Heart of England

Exploring the Heart of England

The heart of England, more than any other region, takes its character from the landscape. Picturesque houses, pubs and churches, made from timber and Cotswold stone, create a harmonic appearance that delights visitors and adds greatly to the pleasures of exploration. The area around Birmingham and Stoke-on-Trent, however – once the industrial hub of England – contrasts sharply. The bleak concrete skyline may not appeal, but the area has a fascinating history that is reflected in the self-confident Victorian art and architecture, and a series of award-winning industrial heritage museums.

Arlington Row: stone cottages in the Cotswold village of Bibury

SIGHTS AT A GLANCE

Birmingham ⑬
Cheltenham ⑳
Chester ❷
Chipping Campden ⑱
Cirencester ㉒
Coventry ⑭
Gloucester ㉑
Great Malvern ⑪
Hereford ❽
Ironbridge pp314–15 ❺
Ledbury ⑩
Leominster ❼
Ludlow ❻
Quarry Bank Mill, Styal ❶
Ross-on-Wye ❾
Shrewsbury ❹
Stoke-on-Trent ❸
*Stratford-upon-Avon
    pp324–7* ⑰
Tewkesbury ⑲
Warwick pp321–3 ⑯
Worcester ⑫

Walks and Tours
Midlands Garden Tour ⑮

GETTING AROUND

The Heart of England is easily reached by train, with mainline rail services to Cheltenham, Worcester, Birmingham, and Coventry. The M5 and M6 motorways are the major road routes but are frequently congested. Long-distance buses provide regular shuttle services to Cheltenham and Birmingham. Travelling within the region is best done by car. Rural roads are delightfully empty, although major attractions, such as Stratford-upon-Avon, may be very crowded during the summer.

SEE ALSO

Warrin
Runcorn
Mersey
Ellesmere
  Port
CHESTER ❷
Tarvin
Aldford   Bunt
A41
Wrexham
Chirk   Whitchur
Oswestry   A495   Pree:
West Felton
A483
Nesscliffe
Severn
Middletown
A458   SHREWSBURY ❹
Minsterley
A483
Chirbury
Church
Stretto
A489
Lydham
Newcastle
Teme   Craven A
Stokesay Castle   A489
LUDLOW ❻
Knighton   Wooff
Wigmore
Presteigne
LEOMINSTER ❼
Pembridge
Eardisley   Hope under
    Dinmore
Clifford
HEREFORD ❽
Kingstone   A465
A49
Kilpeck
Abbey Dore
ROSS
Abergavenny
Goodrich Cas
Monmouth
Chepstow

0 kilometres   10
0 miles   10

View of the Wye Valley, near Ross-on-Wye

KEY

▬▬	Motorway
▬▬	Major road
▬▬	Secondary road
▭▭▭	Minor road
▬▬	Scenic route
▬▬▬	Main railway
▬▬	Minor railway

Reader's House, Ludlow, opposite
St Laurence's Church

Quarry Bank Mill, a working reminder of the Industrial Revolution

Quarry Bank Mill, Styal ❶

(NT) Cheshire. **Tel** 01625 445896.
✈ Manchester Airport, then bus.
◯ Mar–Oct: daily; Nov–Jan: Wed–Sun
(& Mon in school hols). 🔒 24 & 25
Dec. 📷 🚻 limited. 🍴 🛍
www.nationaltrust.org.uk

The history of the Industrial
Revolution (see pp54–5) is
brought vividly to life at Quarry
Bank Mill, an early factory now
transformed into a museum
and private garden. Here, mill
master Samuel Greg first used
the waters of the Bollin Valley
in 1784 to power the water
frame, a machine for spinning
raw cotton fibres into thread.
By the 1840s, the Greg cotton
empire was one of the biggest
in Britain, and the mill produced bolts of material to be
exported all over the world.

Today the massive old mill
buildings have been restored
to house a living museum of
the cotton industry. This dominated the Manchester area for
nearly 200 years, but was
finally destroyed by foreign
competition. The entire process, from the spinning and
weaving to the bleaching,
printing and dyeing, is shown
through a series of reconstructions, demonstrations and

hands-on displays. The weaving shed is full of clattering
looms producing textiles.
There are fascinating contraptions that demonstrate how
water can be used to drive
machinery, including an enormous wheel, 50 tons in weight
and 7 m (24 ft) high, that is
still used to power the looms.

The Greg family
realized the importance
of having a healthy,
loyal and stable work-
force. A social history
exhibition explains
how the mill workers
were housed in the
purpose-built village
of Styal, in spacious
cottages which had
vegetable gardens and
toilets. Details of their
wages, working con-
ditions and medical
facilities are displayed
on information boards.

There are guided
tours of the nearby
Apprentice House.
Local orphans lived
here, and were sent to work
up to 12 hours a day at the
mill when they were just six
or seven years old. Visitors can
try the beds in the house and
even sample the medicine they
were given. Quarry Bank Mill
is surrounded by over 115 ha
(284 acres) of woodland.

Chester ❷

Cheshire. 🏛 125,000. ✈ 🚉
ℹ Town Hall, Northgate St
(01244 402111). 🛒 Mon–Sat.
www.chestertourist.com

First settled by the Romans
(see pp44–5), who established
a camp in AD 79 to defend
fertile land near the River
Dee, the main streets of
Chester are now lined with
timber buildings. These are
the **Chester Rows**, which,
with their two tiers of shops
and continuous upper gallery,
anticipate today's multi-storey
shops by several centuries.

Although their oriel windows
and decorative timber-work
are mostly 19th century, the
Rows were first built in the
13th and 14th centuries, and
the original structures can be
seen in many places. The
façade of the 16th-
century **Bishop Lloyd's
House** in Watergate
Street is the most richly
carved in Chester. The
Rows are at their most
varied and attractive
where Eastgate Street
meets Bridge Street.
Here, views of the
cathedral and the town
walls give the impres-
sion of a perfectly
preserved medieval
city. This illusion is
helped by the Town
Crier, who calls the
hour and announces
news in summer
from the Cross, a
reconstruction of
the 15th-century stone
crucifix that was destroyed
in the Civil War (see pp52–3).

The **Grosvenor Museum**,
south of the Cross, explains
the town's history. To the
north is the **cathedral**. The
choir stalls have splendid
misericords (see p341), with

Chester's 1897
clocktower

Examples of the intricate carving on Bishop Lloyd's House, a Tudor building in Watergate Street, Chester

The Chester Rows, where shops line the first-floor galleries

scenes including a quarrelling couple. In sharp contrast are the delicate spire-lets on the stall canopies. The cathedral is surrounded on two sides by the **city walls**, originally Roman but rebuilt at intervals. The best stretch is from the cathedral to Eastgate, where a wrought-iron **clock** was erected in 1897. The route to Newgate leads to a **Roman amphitheatre** built in AD 100.

🏛 **Grosvenor Museum**
Grosvenor St. *Tel* 01244 402008.
◯ Mon–Sat, Sun pm. ● 1 Jan,
Good Fri, 25 & 26 Dec. 🅿 &
limited. **www**.chester.gov.uk

🎭 **Roman Amphitheatre**
Little St John St. *Tel* 01244 402009.
◯ daily.

Stoke-on-Trent ❸

Stoke-on-Trent. 🚶 252,000.
🚆 🚍 🛈 Victoria Hall Cultural
Quarter (01782 236000). ▲ Mon–
Sat. **www**.visitstoke.co.uk

From the mid-18th century, Staffordshire became a leading centre for mass-produced ceramics. Its fame arose from the fine bone china and porcelain products of Wedgwood,

Minton, Doulton and Spode, but the Staffordshire potteries also make a wide range of utilitarian products such as baths, toilets and wall tiles.

In 1910 a group of six towns – Longton, Fenton, Hanley, Burslem, Tunstall and Stoke – merged to form the conurbation of Stoke-on-Trent, also known as the Potteries. Fans of the writer Arnold Bennett (1867–1931) may recognise this area as the "Five Towns",

a term he used in a series of novels about the region (Fenton was excluded).

The **Gladstone Pottery Museum** is a Victorian complex of workshops, kilns, galleries and an engine house. There are demonstrations of traditional pottery techniques. The **Potteries Museum and Art Gallery** in Hanley has historic and modern ceramics.

Josiah Wedgwood began his earthenware firm in 1769 and built a workers' village, Etruria. The last surviving steam-powered pottery mill is on display at the **Etruria Industrial Museum**.

Environs: About 10 miles (16 km) north of Stoke-on-Trent is **Little Moreton Hall** *(see p303)*, a Tudor manor house.

🏛 **Gladstone Pottery Museum**
Uttoxeter Rd, Longton.
Tel 01782 319 232. ◯ daily.
● 24 Dec–2 Jan. 🅿 & 🗖 🗖
www.stoke.gov.uk/gladstone

🏛 **Potteries Museum and
Art Gallery**
Bethesda St, Hanley. *Tel* 01782
232323. ◯ daily. ● 25 Dec–1
Jan. 🗖 🗖 🗖 **www**.stoke.gov.
uk/museums

🏛 **Etruria Industrial Museum**
Lower Bedford St, Etruria. *Tel* 01782
233144. ◯ Jan–Mar: Mon–Wed;
Apr–Dec: Sat–Wed. ● 25 Dec–1
Jan. 🗖 🗖 by arrangement. 🗖 🗖

🏰 **Little Moreton Hall**
(NT) Congleton, off A34. *Tel* 01260
272018. ◯ Mar–Oct: Wed–Sun &
public hols; Nov–Feb: Sat & Sun. 🗖

STAFFORDSHIRE POTTERY

An abundance of water, marl, clay and easily mined coal to fire the kilns enabled Staffordshire to develop as a ceramics centre; and local supplies of iron, copper and lead were used for glazing. In the 18th century, pottery became widely accessible and affordable. English bone china, which used powdered animals' bones for strength and translucence, was shipped all over the world, and Josiah Wedgwood (1730–95) introduced simple, durable crockery – though his best known design is the blue jasperware decorated with white Classical themes. Coal-powered bottle kilns fired the clay until the 1950s Clean Air Acts put them out of business. They have been replaced by electric or gas-fired kilns.

Wedgwood candlesticks, 1785

Timber-framed, gabled mansions in Fish Street, Shrewsbury

Shrewsbury ❹

Shropshire. 🏘 96,000. 🚆 🚌
ℹ️ The Square (01743 281200).
🛒 Tue, Wed, Fri, Sat. 🌸 Shrewsbury Flower Show (mid Aug).

Shrewsbury is almost an island, enclosed by a great loop of the River Severn. A gaunt **castle** of red sandstone, first built in 1083, guards the entrance to the town, standing on the only section of land not surrounded by the river. Such defences were necessary on the frontier between England and the wilder Marches of Wales, whose inhabitants fiercely defied Saxon and Norman invaders *(see pp46–7)*. The castle, rebuilt over the centuries, now houses the Shropshire Regimental Museum.

In AD 60 the Romans *(see pp44–5)* built the garrison town of Viroconium, modern Wroxeter, 5 miles (8 km) east of Shrewsbury. Finds from the excavations are displayed at **Shrewsbury Museum and Art Gallery**, including a decorated silver mirror from the 2nd century and other luxury goods imported by the Roman army.

The town's medieval wealth as a centre of the wool trade is evident in the many timber-framed buildings found along the High Street, Butcher Row,

Roman silver mirror in Rowley's House Museum

and Wyle Cop. Two of the grandest High Street houses, **Ireland's Mansions** and **Owen's Mansions**, are named after Robert Ireland and Richard Owen, the wealthy wool merchants who built them in 1575 and 1570 respectively. Similarly attractive buildings in Fish Street frame a view of the **Prince Rupert Hotel**, which was briefly the headquarters of Charles I's nephew, Rupert, in the English Civil War *(see pp52–3)*.

Outside the loop of the river, the **Abbey Church** survives from the medieval monastery. It has a number of interesting memorials, including one to Lieutenant WES Owen MC, better known as the war poet Wilfred Owen (1893–1918), who taught at the local Wyle Cop school and was killed in the last days of World War I.

Environs: To the south of Shrewsbury, the road to Ludlow passes through the landscapes celebrated in the 1896 poem by AE Housman (1859–1936), *A Shropshire Lad*. Highlights include the bleak moors of **Long Mynd**, with 15 prehistoric barrows, and **Wenlock Edge**, wonderful walking country with glorious, far-reaching views.

♜ **Shrewsbury Castle**
Castle St. **Tel** 01743 361196.
🕐 Tue–Sat. 🔴 late Dec–mid-Feb.
♿ ♿ 🛍

🏛 **Shrewsbury Museum and Art Gallery**
Barker St. **Tel** 01743 361196.
🔴 for refurbishment until 2011.
♿ limited. 🖥 www.shrewsbury museums.com

Ironbridge Gorge ❺

See pp314–15.

Ludlow ❻

Shropshire. 🏘 10,000. 🚆 ℹ️ Castle St (01584 875053). 🛒 Mon, Wed, Fri, Sat. 🎵 music & drama (end Jun). www.ludlow.org.uk

Ludlow attracts large numbers of visitors to its splendid castle, but there is much else to see in this town, with its small shops and its lovely Georgian and half-timbered Tudor buildings. Ludlow is an important area of geological research and the **museum**, just off the town centre, has fossils of the oldest known animals and plants.

The ruined **castle** is sited on cliffs high above the River Teme. Built in 1086, it was damaged in the Civil War *(see pp52–3)* and abandoned in 1689. *Comus*, a court masque using music and drama, by John Milton (1608–74) was first performed here in 1634 in the Great Hall.

The 13th-century south tower and hall of Stokesay Castle, near Ludlow

Prince Arthur (1486–1502), elder brother of Henry VIII *(see pp50–51)*, died at Ludlow Castle. His heart is buried in **St Laurence Church** at the other end of Castle Square, as are the ashes of the poet A E Housman. The east end of the church backs onto the **Bull Ring**, with its ornate timber buildings. Two inns vie for attention across the street: **The Bull**, with its Tudor back yard, and **The Feathers**, with its flamboyant façade, whose name recalls the feathers used in arrow-making, once a local industry.

Environs: About 5 miles (8 km) north of Ludlow, in a lovely setting, is **Stokesay Castle**, a fortified manor house with a colourful moated garden.

♣ **Ludlow Castle**
The Square. **Tel** 01584 873355.
☐ daily (Dec & Jan: Sat & Sun only).
⟐ ♿ ▢ ⟐ ▢

🏛 **Ludlow Museum**
Castle St. **Tel** 01584 873857. ☐ Apr–Oct: Mon–Sat (Jun–Aug: daily). ♿

♣ **Stokesay Castle**
(EH) Craven Arms, A49. **Tel** 01588 672544. ☐ Mar–Oct: Wed–Sun; (Apr–Sep: daily); Nov–Feb: Thu–Sun.
⟐ ▢ ▢

Leominster ⑦

Herefordshire. 🏠 11,000. ≋
ℹ Corn Sq (01568 616460).
📅 Fri. www.herefordshire.gov.uk

Farmers come to Leominster (pronounced "Lemster") from all over this rural region to buy supplies. There are two buildings of note in the town, which has been a wool-manufacturing centre for 700 years. In the town centre stands the magnificent **Grange Court**, carved with bold and bizarre figures in 1633. Nearby is the **priory**, whose imposing Norman portal is carved with an equally strange mixture of mythical birds and beasts. The lions, at least, can be explained: medieval monks believed that the name of Leominster was derived from *monasterium leonis*, "the monastery of the lions". In fact, *leonis* probably comes from medieval, rather than Classical Latin, and it means

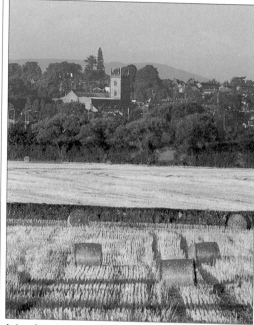

A view of Leominster, set on the River Lugg in rolling border country

"of the marshes". The aptness of this description can readily be seen in the green lanes around the town, following the lush river valleys.

Environs: South of the town, the magnificent gardens and parkland at **Hampton Court** have recently been restored and include island pavilions and a maze. To the west of the town, along the River Arrow, are the villages of **Eardisland** and **Pembridge**, with their well-kept gardens and timber-framed houses. **Berrington Hall**, 3 miles (5 km) north of Leominster,

Gatehouse of Stokesay Castle, near Ludlow

is a Neo-Classical house set in grounds by Capability Brown. Inside are beautifully preserved ceiling decorations and period furniture.

To the northeast of Leominster is **Tenbury Wells**, which enjoyed brief popularity as a spa in the 19th century. The River Teme flows through it, full of minnows, trout and other fish and beloved of the composer Sir Edward Elgar *(see p317)*, who came to seek inspiration on its banks. The river also feeds **Burford House Gardens**, on the western outskirts of Tenbury Wells, where the water is used to create streams, fountains and pools that are rich in unusual moisture-loving plants.

♣ **Hampton Court Gardens**
nr Hope Under Dinmore. **Tel** 01568 797 777. ☐ Apr–21 Dec: 11am–5pm (to 4pm Nov–Dec) Tue–Sun. ⟐ ♿
▢ ▢ www.hamptoncourt.org.uk

♔ **Berrington Hall**
(NT) Berrington. **Tel** 01568 615721. ☐ mid-Mar–Oct: Sat–Wed; Nov–mid-Mar: Sat & Sun. ⟐ ▢ ▢

♣ **Burford House Gardens**
Tenbury Wells. **Tel** 01584 810777. ☐ daily. ● 1 Jan, 25 & 26 Dec. ⟐
♿ ▢ ▢ www.burford.co.uk

Ironbridge Gorge ⑤

Ironbridge Gorge was one of the most important centres of the Industrial Revolution (see pp54–5). It was here, in 1709, Abraham Darby I (1678–1717) pioneered the use of inexpensive coke, rather than charcoal, to smelt iron ore. The use of iron in bridges, ships and buildings transformed Ironbridge Gorge into one of the world's great iron-making centres. Industrial decline in the 20th century led to the Gorge's decay, although today it has been restored as an exciting complex of industrial archaeology, with several museums strung along the wooded banks of the River Severn.

VISITORS' CHECKLIST

Shropshire. 2,900. Telford then bus (Telford Travelink 01952 200005). Ironbridge town (01952 884391). daily. 1 Jan, 24, 25 Dec. Some sites closed Nov–Apr, call for details. most sites. by arrangement.
www.ironbridge.org.uk

The Museum of Iron, topped by a cast- and wrought-iron clock

COALBROOKDALE MUSEUM OF IRON

The history of iron and the men who made it is traced in this remarkable museum. Abraham Darby I's discovery of how to smelt iron ore with coke allowed the mass production of iron, paving the way for the rise of large-scale industry. His original blast furnace forms the museum's centrepiece.

One of the museum's themes is the history of the Darby dynasty, a Quaker family who had a great impact on the Coalbrookdale community.

Ironbridge led the world in industrial innovation, producing the first iron wheels and cylinders for the first steam engine. Cast-iron statues, many of them commissioned for the 1851 Great Exhibition (see pp56–7), are among the many Coalbrookdale Company

products on display. They include a bronze figure of Andromeda and many sculptures of stags and hounds.

One of the Darby family's homes in the nearby village of Coalbrookdale, **Rosehill House** (open during the summer), has been furnished in mid-Victorian style.

MUSEUM OF THE GORGE

This partly castellated, Victorian building was a warehouse for storing products from the ironworks before they were shipped down the River Severn. The warehouse is now home to the Museum of the Gorge, and has displays illustrating the history of the Severn and the development of the water industry. Until the arrival of the railways in the mid-19th century, the Severn was the main form of transport and communication to and from the Gorge. Sometimes too shallow, at other times in flood, the river was not a particularly reliable means of transportation; by the 1890s river trading had stopped completely.

The highlight of the museum is a wonderful 12 m (40 ft) model of the Gorge as it would have appeared in 1796, complete with foundries, cargo boats and growing villages.

Europe (1860), statue in the Museum of Iron

JACKFIELD TILE MUSEUM

There have been potteries in this area since the 17th century, but it was not until the Victorian passion for decorative tiles that Jackfield became famous. There were two tile-making factories here – Maw and Craven Dunnill – that produced a tremendous variety of tiles from clay mined nearby.

Peacock Panel (1928), one of the tile museum's star attractions

Talented designers created an astonishing range of images. The Jackfield Tile Museum, in the old Craven Dunnill works, has a collection of the decorative floor and wall tiles that were produced here from the 1850s to the 1960s. On certain days, visitors can watch small-scale demonstrations of traditional methods of tile-making in the old factory buildings, including the kilns and the decoration workshops.

IRONBRIDGE GORGE SIGHTS

Blists Hill Victorian Town ⑥
Coalbrookdale
　Museum of Iron ①
Coalport China
　Museum ⑤
Iron Bridge ③
Jackfield Tile
　Museum ④
Museum of the Gorge ②

0 kilometres　　2

0 miles　　　1

COALPORT CHINA MUSEUM

In the mid-19th century the Coalport Works was one of the largest porcelain manufacturers in Britain, and its name was synonymous with fine china. The Coalport Company still makes porcelain but has long since moved its operations to Stoke-on-Trent *(see p311)*. Today the china workshops have been converted into a museum, where visitors can watch demonstrations of the various stages of making porcelain, including the skills of pot-throwing, painting and gilding. There is a superb collection of 19th-century china housed in one of the museum's distinctive bottle-shaped kilns.

Coalport China Museum with its bottle-shaped kiln

Nearby is the **Tar Tunnel**, an important source of natural bitumen discovered 110 m (360 ft) underground in the 1700s. It once yielded 20,500 litres (4,500 gal) of tar every week. Visitors can still explore part of the tunnel (Apr–Oct).

THE IRON BRIDGE

Abraham Darby III (grandson of the first man to smelt iron with coke) cast the world's first iron bridge in 1779, revolutionizing building methods in the process. Spanning the Severn, the bridge is a monument to the ironmasters' skills. The toll-house on the south bank charts its construction.

BLISTS HILL VICTORIAN TOWN

This enormous open-air museum recreates Victorian life in an Ironbridge Gorge town. A group of 19th-century buildings has been reconstructed on the 20 ha (50 acre) site of Blists Hill, an old coal mine that used to supply the ironworks in the Gorge. Here, people in period costume enact roles and perform tasks such as iron forging.

The site has period housing, a church and even a Victorian school. Visitors can change money into old coinage to buy items from the baker or even pay for a drink in the local pub.

The centrepiece of Blists Hill is a complete foundry that still produces wrought iron. One of the most spectacular sights is the Hay Inclined Plane, which was used to transport canal boats up and down a steep slope. Other attractions include steam engines, a saddlers, a doctors, a chemist, a candlemakers and a sweetshop.

Hereford ⓼

Herefordshire. 🏘 50,000. ✈ 🚌
🛈 *King St (01432 268430).*
🛒 *Wed (cattle, general), Sat (general).*
www.visitherefordshire.co.uk

Once the capital of the Saxon kingdom of West Mercia, Hereford is today an attractive town which serves the needs of a primarily rural community. A cattle market is held here every Wednesday, and local produce is sold at the covered market in the town centre. Almost opposite, the Jacobean timber-framed **Old House** of 1621 is now a museum of local history.

In the **cathedral**, only a short stroll away, interesting features include the Lady Chapel, in richly ornamented Early English style, the *Mappa Mundi* (see below) and the Chained Library, whose 1,500 books are tethered by iron chains to bookcases as a precaution against theft. The story of these national treasures is told through models, original artifacts and interactive computer technology. The best place for an overall view of the cathedral is at the Bishop's Meadow, south of the centre, leading down to the banks of the Wye.

Hereford's many rewarding museums include the **City Museum and Art Gallery**, noted for its Roman mosaic and for watercolours by local artists, and the **Cider**

Hereford's 17th-century Old House, furnished in period style

Detail of figures on Kilpeck Church

Museum and King Offa Distillery. In the museum, visitors can discover the history of traditional cider making. The King Offa Distillery, which is open for visits and tastings, is the first distillery licensed to produce cider brandy for 200 years.

Environs: During the 12th century, Oliver de Merlemond made a pilgrimage from Hereford to Spain. Impressed by several churches he saw on the way, he brought French masons over to England and introduced their techniques to this area. One result was **Kilpeck Church**, 6 miles (10 km) southwest, covered in

lustful figures showing their genitals, and tail-biting dragons. At **Abbey Dore**, 4 miles (6 km) west, the Cistercian abbey church is complemented by the serene riverside gardens of **Abbey Dore Court**.

🏛 **Old House**
High Town. **Tel** *01432 260694.*
⏰ *Apr–Sep: Tue–Sun; Oct–Mar: Tue–Sat; public hols.* ● *25 & 26 Dec, 1 Jan, Good Fri.* ♿ *limited.* 📷
www.herefordshire.gov.uk/museums

🏛 **City Museum and Art Gallery**
Broad St. **Tel** *01432 260692.* ⏰
Apr–Sep: Tue–Sun; Oct–Mar: Tue–Sat, public hols. ● *25 & 26 Dec, 1 Jan, Good Fri.* ♿ 📷
www.herefordshire.gov.uk

🏛 **Cider Museum and King Offa Distillery**
Ryelands St. **Tel** *01432 354207.*
⏰ *Tue–Sat & public hols.*
● *25 & 26 Dec, 1 Jan.* 🎫 ♿
limited. 🎫 *by arrangement.* 📷
🛈 **www**.cidermuseum.co.uk

Ross-on-Wye ⓽

Herefordshire. 🏘 10,000. 🚌 🛈
Edde Cross St (01989 562768). 🛒 *Thu, Sat; farmers' market 1st Fri of month.*
www.visitherefordshire.co.uk

The fine town of Ross sits on a cliff of red sandstone above the water meadows of the River Wye. There are wonderful views over the river from the cliff-top gardens,

---

MEDIEVAL VIEW

Hereford Cathedral's most celebrated treasure is the *Mappa Mundi*, the Map of the World, drawn in 1290 by a clergyman, Richard of Haldingham. The world is depicted here on Biblical principles: Jerusalem is at the centre, the Garden of Eden figures prominently and monsters inhabit the margins of the world.

Central detail, Mappa Mundi

The wooded Wye Valley near Ross

given to the town by a local benefactor, John Kyrle (1637–1724). Kyrle was lauded by the poet Alexander Pope (1688–1744) in his *Moral Essays on the Uses of Riches* (1732) for using his wealth in a practical way, and he came to be known as "The Man of Ross". There is a memorial to Kyrle in **St Mary's Church**.

Environs: From Hereford to Ross, the **Wye Valley Walk** follows 16 miles (26 km) of gentle countryside. From Ross it continues south for 33 miles (54 km), over rocky ground in deep, wooded ravines.

Goodrich Castle, 5 miles (8 km) south of Ross, is a 12th-century red sandstone fort on a rock above the river.

♣ **Goodrich Castle**
(EH) Goodrich. **Tel** 01600 890538.
☐ daily (Nov–Feb: Wed–Sun). 🎫 ☐
(Apr–Sep). **www**.english-heritage.org.uk

Ledbury ⑩

Herefordshire. 🏠 8,000. ☎ ☐
ℹ The Masters House (01531 636147). **www**.visitledbury.co.uk

Ledbury's main street is lined with timbered houses, including the **Market Hall** which dates from 1655. Church Lane, a cobbled lane running up from the High Street, has lovely 16th-century buildings: the **Heritage Centre** and **Butcher Row House** are both now museums. **St Michael and All Angels Church** has a massive detached bell tower, ornate Early English decoration and interesting monuments.

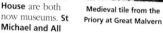

Medieval tile from the Priory at Great Malvern

🏛 **Heritage Centre**
Church Lane. ☐ Easter–Oct: daily. ♿
🏛 **Butcher Row House**
Church Lane. ☐ Easter–Oct: daily.

Great Malvern and the Malverns ⑪

Worcestershire. 🏠 35,000. ☎ ☐
ℹ 21 Church St (01684 892289).
☐ Fri; farmers' market 3rd Sat of month. **www**.malvernhills.gov.uk

The ancient granite rock of the Malvern Hills rises from the plain of the River Severn, its 9 miles (15 km) of glorious scenery visible from afar. Composer Sir Edward Elgar (1857–1934) wrote many of his greatest works here, including the oratorio *The Dream of Gerontius* (1900), inspired by what the diarist John Evelyn (1620–1706) described as "one of the goodliest views in England". Elgar's home was in **Little Malvern**, whose truncated Church of St Giles, set on a steep, wooded hill, lost its nave when the stone was stolen during the Dissolution *(see p339).* **Great Malvern**, capital of the hills, is graced with 19th-century buildings which look like Swiss sanitoria: patients would stay at institutions such as Doctor Gulley's Water Cure Establishment. The water gushing from the hillside at St Ann's Well, above the town, is bottled and sold throughout Britain. The town is home to the famous Morgan cars (contact 01684 573104 to arrange a factory visit).

Malvern's highlight is the **Priory**, with its 15th-century stained-glass windows and medieval misericords. The old monastic fishponds below the church form the lake of the **Priory Park**. Here the theatre hosts performances of Elgar's music and plays by George Bernard Shaw.

A view of the Malverns range, formed of hard Pre-Cambrian rock

Worcester ⑫

Worcestershire. ⏵ 95,000.
⏵ ⏵ ⓘ High St (01905 726311).
⏵ Mon–Sat.
www.visitworcester.com

Worcester is one of many
English cities whose character
has been transformed by
modern development. The
architectural highlight remains
the **cathedral**, off College
Yard, which suffered a collapsed tower in 1175 and a
disastrous fire in 1203, before
the present structure was
started in the 13th century.

The nave and central tower
were completed in the 1370s,
after building was severely
interrupted by the Black Death,
which decimated the labour
force (see p48). The most
recent and ornate addition
was made in 1874, when Sir
George Gilbert Scott (see p465)
designed the High Gothic
choir, incorporating 14th-
century carved misericords.

There are many interesting
tombs, including King John's,

Charles I holding a symbol of the
Church on Worcester's Guildhall

a masterpiece of medieval
carving, in front of the altar.
Prince Arthur, Henry VIII's
brother (see p313), who died
at the age of 15, is buried in
the chantry chapel south of
the altar. Underneath, the
huge Norman crypt survives
from the first cathedral (1084).

From the cathedral cloister,
a gate leads to College Green
and out into Edgar Street and

its Georgian houses. Here the
Worcester Porcelain Museum
displays Royal Worcester porcelain dating back to 1751.
On the High Street, north of
the cathedral, the **Guildhall**
of 1723 is adorned with
statues of Stuart monarchs,
reflecting the city's Royalist
allegiances. In Cornmarket
is **Ye Olde King Charles
House**, in which Prince
Charles, later Charles II, hid
after the Battle of Worcester
in 1651 (see pp52–3).

Some of Worcester's finest
timber buildings are found
in Friar Street: **The Greyfriars**,
built around 1480, has been
restored in period style. The
Commandery was originally
an 11th-century hospital. It
was rebuilt in the 15th century
and used by Prince Charles
as a base during the Civil
War. Now a museum, it has
a fine hammerbeam roof.

Elgar's Birthplace was the
home of composer Sir Edward
Elgar (see p318) and contains
memorabilia of his life.

🏛 **Worcester Porcelain
Museum**
Severn St. **Tel** 01905 746000. ⬜
daily. ⬤ 25 Dec. 🈵 ♿ 🚻 🍴 🛍

🏚 **The Greyfriars**
(NT) Friar St. **Tel** 01905 23571.
⬜ Mar–Dec: Wed–Sat; Jul & Aug:
Wed–Sun & public hols. 🈵

🏛 **Commandery**
Sidbury. **Tel** 01905 361821.
⬜ daily (Nov–Mar: Mon–Thu &
Sat). ⬤ 1 Jan, 25–26 Dec. 🅿 🈵

🏛 **Elgar's Birthplace**
Lower Broadheath. **Tel** 01905
333224. ⬜ daily. ⬤ 24 Dec–
mid-Jan. 🈵 ♿ limited. 🅿
www.elgarfoundation.org

Birmingham ⑬

Birmingham. ⏵ 1,000,000.
⏵ ⏵ ⓘ The Rotunda
(0844 888 3883). ⏵ Mon–Sat.
www.visitbirmingham.com

Brum, as it is affectionately
known to its inhabitants, grew
up as a major centre of the
Industrial Revolution in the
19th century. A vast range
of manufacturing trades was
based in Birmingham and
was responsible for the rapid
development of grim factories
and cramped housing. Since

Worcester Cathedral, overlooking the River Severn

The Last of England, Ford Madox Brown, Birmingham Art Gallery

The clearance of several of these areas after World War II, Birmingham has raised its cultural profile. The city succeeded in enticing Sir Simon Rattle to conduct the City of Birmingham Symphony Orchestra, and persuaded the former Royal Sadler's Wells Ballet (now the Birmingham Royal Ballet) to leave London for the more up-to-date facilities of Birmingham. The **National Exhibition Centre**, 8 miles (13 km) east of the centre, draws thousands of people to its conference, lecture and exhibition halls.

Set away from the massive Bullring shopping centre, Birmingham's 19th-century civic buildings are excellent examples of Neo-Classical architecture. Among them are the **City Museum and Art Gallery**, where the collection includes outstanding works by pre-Raphaelite artists such as Sir Edward Burne-Jones (1833–98), who was born in Birmingham, and Ford Madox Brown (1821–93). The museum also organizes some interesting

temporary exhibitions of art, such as works by J M W Turner (1775–1851).

Birmingham's extensive canal system is now used mainly for leisure boating *(see pp300–01)*, and several former warehouses have been converted into museums and galleries. **Thinktank – The Birmingham Museum of Science and Discovery** celebrates the city's contributions to the world of railway engines, aircraft, and the motor trade. The old jewellery quarter has practised its traditional crafts here since the 16th century.

Suburban Birmingham has many attractions, including the **Botanical Gardens** at Edgbaston, and **Cadbury World** at Bournville, where there is a visitor centre dedicated to chocolate (booking ahead is advisable). Bournville village was built in 1890 by the Cadbury brothers for their workers and is a pioneering example of a garden suburb.

🏛 City Museum and Art Gallery
Chamberlain Sq. **Tel** 0121 303 2834. ☐ call for details. ● 25 & 26 Dec. ⬤ ☐ ⬤

🏛 Thinktank
Millennium Point. **Tel** 0121 202 2222. ☐ daily. ● 24–26 Dec.

🌺 Botanical Gardens
Westbourne Rd, Edgbaston. **Tel** 0121 454 1860. ☐ daily. ● 25 Dec. ⬤ ⬤ ⬤ ⬤ by appt. ⬤

🏛 Cadbury World
Linden Rd, Bournville. **Tel** 0845 450 3599. ☐ daily (Nov–Jan: call for details). ● first two weeks Jan. ⬤ ⬤

Coventry ⑭

Coventry. 🏙 300,000. ⬛ ☐ ⬤
Cathedral Tower (024 7622 7264). ⬤
Mon–Sat. **www**.visitcoventry.co.uk

As an armaments centre, Coventry was a prime target for German bombing raids in World War II, and in 1940 the **cathedral** in the city centre was hit. After the war the first totally modern cathedral by Sir Basil Spence (1907–76) was built alongside the ruins. It includes sculptures by

Epstein's *St Michael Subduing the Devil*, on Coventry Cathedral

Sir Jacob Epstein and a tapestry by Graham Sutherland.

The **Herbert Gallery and Museum** has displays on the 11th-century legend of Lady Godiva, who rode naked through the streets. The recently renovated **Coventry Transport Museum** has the largest collection of Britain's road transport in the world, including cars, cycles and models, and features the fastest car in the world as well as interactive displays.

🏛 Herbert Gallery and Museum
Jordan Well. **Tel** 024 7683 2386. ☐ daily (Sun: pm) 1 Jan. ⬤ ⬤

🏛 Coventry Transport Museum
Hales St. **Tel** 024 7623 4270. ☐ daily. ● 24–26 Dec. ⬤ ⬤ ⬤ **www**.transport-museum.com

Stately civic office buildings in Victoria Square, Birmingham

Midlands Garden Tour ⑮

The charming Cotswold stone buildings perfectly complement the lush gardens for which the region is famous. This picturesque route from Warwick to Cheltenham is designed to show every type of garden, from tiny cottage plots, brimming with bell-shaped flowers and hollyhocks, to the deer-filled, landscaped parks of stately homes. The route follows the escarpment of the Cotswold Hills, taking in spectacular scenery and some of the prettiest Midlands villages on the way.

Plum tree in blossom

TIPS FOR DRIVERS

Tour length: 35 miles (50 km).
Stopping-off points: Hidcote Manor has excellent lunches and teas; there are refreshments at Kiftsgate Court and Sudeley Castle. Travellers will find a good choice in Broadway, from traditional pubs and tea shops to the de luxe Lygon Arms. (See also pp684–5.)

Cheltenham Imperial Gardens ⑨
These colourful public gardens on the Promenade were laid out in 1817–18 to encourage people to walk from the town to the spa *(see p328).*

Sudeley Castle ⑧
The restored castle is complemented by box hedges, topiary and an Elizabethan knot garden *(see p26).* Catherine Parr, Henry VIII's widow, died here in 1548.

EVESHAM

M5

GLOUCESTER
M5

STROUD

CIRENCESTER

CHELTENHAM

OXFORD

Broadway ⑤
Wisteria and cordoned fruit trees cover 17th-century cottages, fronted by immaculate gardens.

Winchcombe

Stanway House ⑦
This Jacobean manor has many lovely trees in its grounds and a pyramid above a cascade of water.

Snowshill Manor ⑥
This Cotswold stone manor contains an extraordinary collection, from bicycles to Japanese armour. There are walled gardens and terraces full of *objets d'art* such as the clock (left). The colour blue is a recurrent theme.

Warwick Castle ①
The castle's gardens
(see pp322–3) include
Mound, planted in
medieval style, with
ss, oaks, yew trees
and box hedges.

COVENTRY

BIRMINGHAM

e Hathaway's Cottage ②
s has a pretty, informal 19th-
ury- style garden (see p327).

WARWICK

LONDON

Avon

ford-upon-Avon

BANBURY

CIRENCESTER

BANBURY

OXFORD

Hidcote Manor Gardens ③
Started in the early
years of the last century,
these beautiful gardens
pioneered the idea of
a garden as a series
of outdoor "rooms",
enclosed by high yew
hedges and planted
according to themes.

Kiftsgate Court Garden ④
This charmingly naturalistic garden
lies opposite Hidcote Manor. It has
many rare and unusual plants on a
series of hillside terraces, including
the enormous "Kiftsgate" Rose,
nearly 30 m (100 ft) high.

KEY

▬▬▬	Motorway
▬▬▬	Tour route
═══	Other roads
☆	Viewpoint

0 kilometres   5

0 miles   5

Warwick ⑯

Warwickshire. 🏠 28,000.
🚌 🚉 ℹ The Courthouse,
Jury St (01926 492212). 🛍 Sat.
www.warwickshire.gov.uk

Warwick suffered a major fire
in 1694, but some medieval
buildings survived. **St John's
House Museum** in St John's is
a charming Jacobean mansion
housing reconstructions of a
Victorian parlour, kitchen and
classroom. At the west end
of the High Street, a row of
medieval guild buildings were
transformed in 1571 by the Earl
of Leicester, who founded the
Lord Leycester Hospital as a
refuge for his old soldiers.

The arcaded **Market Hall**
(1670) is part of the Warwickshire Museum, renowned for
its unusual tapestry map of
the county, woven in 1558.

In Church Street, to the
south of St Mary's Church, is
the **Beauchamp Chapel** (1443–
64). It is a superb example of
Perpendicular architecture
and has tombs of the Earls of
Warwick. There is a view of
Warwick Castle (see pp322–3)
from St Mary's tower.

🏛 **St John's House Museum**
St John's. **Tel** 01926 412132.
⬜ May–Sep: Tue–Sun; Oct–Apr:
Tue–Sat; bank hol Mon. ⬆ limited.

🏥 **Lord Leycester Hospital**
High St. **Tel** 01926 491422. ⬜ Tue–
Sun & public hols. ⬤ Good Fri, 25
Dec. **Gardens** ⬜ same as house but
Easter–Sep only. 🎫 🚻 ⬆ ltd. 📷

🏛 **Market Hall**
Market Place. **Tel** 01926 412500.
⬜ Tue–Sat (May–Sep: Tue–Sun).
⬆ limited. 📷

The Lord Leycester Hospital,
now a home for ex-servicemen

Warwick Castle

Neville family at prayer (c.1460)

Warwick's magnificent castle is the finest medieval fortress in the country. The original Norman castle was rebuilt in the 13th and 14th centuries, when huge outer walls and towers were added, mainly to display the power of the great feudal magnates, the Beauchamps and, in the 1400s, the Nevilles, the Earls of Warwick. The castle passed in 1604 to the Greville family who, in the 17th and 18th centuries, transformed it into a great country house. In 1978 the owners of Madame Tussaud's *(see p104)* bought the castle and set up tableaux of wax portraits to illustrate its history.

The Ghost Tower is where the ghost of Sir Fulke Greville, murdered in London by a servant in 1628, is said to walk.

The Mound has remains of the motte and bailey ca *(see p486)* and the 1 century keep

Royal Weekend Party
The portrait of the valet is part of the award-winning exhibition of the Prince of Wales's visit in 1898.

★ **Great Hall and State Rooms**
Medieval apartments were transformed into the Great Hall and State Rooms. A mark of conspicuous wealth, they display a collection of family treasures from around the world.

The Mill and Engine House

Kingmaker Attraction
Dramatic displays recreate medieval life as "Warwick the Kingmaker", Richard Neville, prepared for battle in the Wars of the Roses.

View of Warwick Castle, south front, by Antonio Canaletto (1697–1768)

Ramparts and towers, of local
grey sandstone, were added
in the 14th and 15th
centuries.

★ **Guy's Tower**
*Completed around 1393,
the tower had lodgings for
guests and members of the
Earl of Warwick's retinue.*

Dream of Battle Show
creates the drama, noise
and adrenaline-charged
terror of medieval battle
through the dreams of 14-
year-old Squire William.

Entrance

STAR SIGHTS

★ Great Hall and
State Rooms

★ Guy's Tower

**The underground
dungeon**

The Gatehouse is
defended by portcullises
and "murder holes"
through which boiling
pitch was dropped onto
attackers beneath.

**Caesar's
Tower**

TIMELINE

1068
Norman
motte and
bailey
castle built

1264 Simon de
Montfort, champion
of Parliament
against Henry III,
attacks Warwick
Castle

Shield (1745)

1478 Castle reverts to
Crown after murder of
Richard Neville's son-in-law

1890s–1910
Visits from future
Edward VII

1000	1200	1400	1600	1800

Richard Neville

1604 James I
gives castle to Sir
Fulke Greville

1642 Siege
of the Castle
of Royalist
Troops

1871 Fire
damages the
Great Hall

1268–1445 Much of the present castle built
by the Beauchamp family, Earls of Warwick

1449–1471 Richard Neville, Earl of Warwick,
plays leading role in Wars of the Roses

1600–1800 Interiors remodelled and gardens landscaped

Street-by-Street: Stratford-upon-Avon **⑰**

Situated on the west bank of the River Avon, in the heart of the Midlands, is one of the most famous towns in England. Stratford-upon-Avon dates back to at least Roman times but its appearance today is that of a small Tudor market town, with mellow, half-timbered architecture and tranquil walks beside the tree-fringed Avon. This image belies its popularity as the most visited tourist attraction outside London, with eager hordes flocking to see buildings connected to William Shakespeare or his descendants.

A 1930s jester

Bancroft Gardens
There is an attractive boat-filled canal basin here and a 15th-century causeway.

Tourist information

WATE

UNION STREET

BRIDGE STREET

HIGH STREET

★ Shakespeare's Birthplace
This building was almost entirely reconstructed in the 19th century, but in the style of the Tudor original.

0 metres   100

0 yards   100

Shakespeare Centre

HENLEY STREET

MEER STREET

WOOD STREET

ELY STREET

To train station

P

Harvard House
The novelist Marie Corelli (1855–1924) had this house restored. Next door is the 16th-century Garrick Inn.

STAR SIGHTS

- ★ Shakespeare's Birthplace
- ★ Hall's Croft
- ★ Holy Trinity Church

Town Hall
Built in 1767, there are traces of 18th-century graffiti on the front of the building saying God Save the King.

Royal Shakespeare Theatre and Swan Theatre
Closed for redevelopment from April 2007 to 2010, the RSC will instead perform at the Courtyard Theatre.

VISITORS' CHECKLIST

Warwickshire. 🏙 22,000.
✈ 20 miles (32 km) NW of
Stratford-upon-Avon. 🚆
Alcester Rd. 🚌 Bridge St.
ℹ️ Bridge Foot **Tel** 0870 160
7930. 🚕 Fri. 🎭 Shakespeare's
Birthday: Apr; Stratford Festival:
Jul. **www**.shakespeare.org.uk

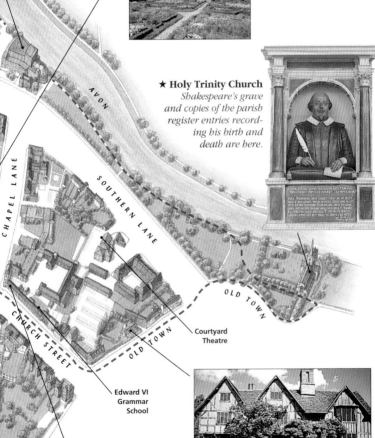

Nash's House
The foundations of New Place, where Shakespeare died, form the garden beside this house.

★ Holy Trinity Church
Shakespeare's grave and copies of the parish register entries recording his birth and death are here.

Courtyard
Theatre

Edward VI
Grammar
School

Guild
Chapel

KEY

– – – Suggested route

away's
ge

★ Hall's Croft
John Hall, Shakespeare's son-in-law, was a doctor. This delightful house includes an exhibition of medicine in Shakespeare's time.

Exploring Stratford-upon-Avon

Mosaic of Shakespeare on the
beautiful Old Bank (1810)

William Shakespeare was born in Stratford-upon-Avon on St George's Day, 23 April 1564. Admirers of his work have been coming to the town since his death in 1616. In 1847 a public appeal successfully raised the money to buy the house in which he was born. As a result Stratford has become a literary shrine to Britain's greatest dramatist. It also has a thriving cultural reputation as the provincial home of the prestigious Royal Shakespeare Company, whose dramas are usually performed in Stratford before playing a second season in London (see pp152–3).

Around Stratford

The centre of Stratford-upon-Avon has many buildings that are connected with William Shakespeare and his descendants. On the High Street corner is the **Cage**, a 15th-century prison. It was converted into a house where Shakespeare's daughter Judith lived, and is now a shop. At the end of the High Street, the **Town Hall** has a statue of Shakespeare on the façade given by David Garrick (1717–79), the actor who in 1769 organized the first Shakespeare festival.

The High Street leads into Chapel Street where the half-timbered **Nash's House** is a

Anne Hathaway's Cottage, home of Shakespeare's wife

museum of local history. It is also the site of **New Place**, where Shakespeare died in 1616, and which is now a herb and knot garden (see p26). In Church Street opposite, the **Guild Chapel** (1496) has a *Last Judgement* painting (c.1500) on the chancel wall. Shakespeare is thought to have attended the **Edward VI Grammar School** (above the former Guildhall) next door.

A left turn into Old Town leads to **Hall's Croft**, home of Shakespeare's daughter Susanna, which displays 16th- and 17th-century medical artefacts. An avenue of lime trees leads to **Holy Trinity Church**, where Shakespeare is buried. A walk along the river follows the Avon to **Bancroft Gardens**, which lies at the junction of the River Avon and the Stratford Canal.

🏛 Shakespeare's Birthplace

Henley St. **Tel** 01789 204016. ◯ daily. ◉ 23–26 Dec. 🖼 ♿ limited. 🖥 www.shakespeare.org.uk

Bought for the nation in 1847, when it was a public house, Shakespeare's Birthplace was converted back to Elizabethan style. Objects associated with Shakespeare's father, John, a glovemaker and wool merchant, are on display. There is a birth room, in which Shakespeare was supposedly born, and another room has a window etched with visitors' autographs, including that of Sir Walter Scott (see p512).

Holy Trinity Church, seen across the River Avon

🏠 Harvard House

High St. **Tel** *01789 204507.* ☐ *May, Jun & Sep: Fri–Sun; Jul & Aug: Wed–Sun.* 🔲 **www**.shakespeare.org.uk

Built in 1596, this ornate house was the home of Katherine Rogers, whose son, John Harvard, emigrated to America and in 1638 left his estate to a new college, later renamed Harvard University. The house contains a Museum of British Pewter and displays relating to John Harvard.

Environs: No tour of Stratford would be complete without a visit to **Anne Hathaway's Cottage**. Before her marriage to William Shakespeare she lived at Shottery, 1 mile (1.5 km) west of Stratford. Despite fire damage in 1969, the cottage is still impressive, with some original 16th-century furniture. The Hathaway descendants lived here until the early 20th century *(see p321).*

🏠 Anne Hathaway's Cottage

Cottage Lane. **Tel** *01789 292100.* ☐ *daily.* ⬤ *23–26 Dec.* 🔲 🔲 **www**.shakespeare.org.uk

Kenneth Branagh in *Hamlet*

THE ROYAL SHAKESPEARE COMPANY

The Royal Shakespeare Company is renowned for its new interpretations of Shakespeare's work. The company performs at the 1932 Royal Shakespeare Theatre, a windowless brick building adjacent to the Swan Theatre, built in 1986 to a design based on an Elizabethan playhouse. Next to it is a building displaying sets, props and costumes. The RSC also performs at the 150-seat theatre, known as the Other Place, and in London *(see pp152–3).*

Grevel House, the oldest house in Chipping Campden

Chipping Campden ⓲

Gloucestershire. 🏘 *2,500.* 🅸 *High St (01386 841206).* **www**.visitchippingcampden.com

This perfect Cotswold town is kept in pristine condition by the Campden Trust. Set up in 1929, the Trust has kept alive the traditional skills of stonecarving and repair that make Chipping Campden such a unified picture of golden-coloured and lichen-patched stone. Visitors travelling from the northwest along the B4035 first see a group of ruins: the remains of **Campden Manor**, begun around 1613 by Sir Baptist Hicks, 1st Viscount Campden. The manor was burned by Royalist troops to stop it being sequestered by Parliament at the end of the Civil War *(see pp52–3),* but the almshouses opposite the gateway were spared. They were designed in the form of the letter "I" (which is Latin for "J"), a symbol of the owner's loyalty to King James I.

The town's **Church of St James**, one of the finest in the Cotswolds, was built in the 15th century, financed by merchants who bought wool from Cotswold farmers and exported it at a high profit. Inside the church there are many elaborate tombs, and a magnificent brass dedicated to William Grevel, describing him as "the flower of the wool merchants of England". He built **Grevel House** (c.1380) in the High Street, the oldest in a fine row of buildings, which is distinguished by a double-storey bay window.

Viscount Campden donated the **Market Hall** in 1627. His contemporary, Robert Dover, founded in 1612 the "Cotswold Olimpicks", long before the modern Olympic Games had been established. The 1612 version included such painful events as the shin-kicking contest. It still takes place on the first Friday after each Spring Bank Holiday, followed by a torchlit procession into town ready for the Scuttlebrook Wake Fair on the next day. The setting for the games is a spectacular natural hollow on **Dover's Hill** above the town, worth climbing on a clear day for the marvellous views over the Vale of Evesham.

The 17th-century Market Hall in Chipping Campden

Tewkesbury's abbey church overlooks the town, crowded onto the bank of the River Severn

Tewkesbury ⑲

Gloucestershire. 🏠 11,000.
ℹ️ Church St (01684 855040).
🛒 Wed, Sat. www.visitcotswolds
andsevernvale.gov.uk

This lovely town sits on the
confluence of the rivers
Severn and Avon. It has one of
England's finest Norman abbey
churches, **St Mary the Virgin**,
which locals saved during the
Dissolution of the Monasteries
(see p50) by paying Henry VIII
£453. Around the church, with
its bulky tower and Norman
façade, timbered
buildings are
crammed within
the bend of the
river. Warehouses
are a reminder of
past wealth, and
Borough Mill
on Quay Street,
the only mill
left harnessed
to the river's energy,
still grinds corn.

Pump Room detail,
Cheltenham

Environs: Boat trips run from
the river to **Twyning**'s riverside
pub, 6 miles (10 km) north.

Cheltenham ⑳

Gloucestershire. 🏠 107,000. 🚄 🚌
ℹ️ 77 Promenade (01242 522878).
🛒 Sun; farmers' market 2nd & last Fri
of month. www.visitcheltenham.com

Cheltenham's reputation for
elegance was first gained in
the late 18th century, when
high society flocked to the spa

town to "take the waters",
following the example set by
George III (see pp54–5). Many
gracious terraced houses were
built, in a Neo-Classical style,
along broad avenues. These
survive around the Queen's
Hotel, near **Montpellier**, a
lovely Regency arcade lined
with craft and antique shops,
and in the **Promenade**, with
its smart department stores and
couturiers. A more modern
atmosphere prevails in the
newly built Regency Arcade,
where the star attraction is the
1987 **clock** by Kit Williams:
visit on the hour to
see fish blowing
bubbles over the
onlookers' heads.
The **Museum and
Art Gallery** is
worth a visit to
see its unusual
collection of
furniture and
other crafts
made by members of
the influential Arts
and Crafts Movement (see p29),
whose strict principles of utilitarian design were laid down
by William Morris (see p220).
The **Pittville Pump Room**
(1825–30), modelled on the
Greek Temple of Ilissos in
Athens, is frequently used for
performances during the
town's renowned annual
festivals of music (July) and
literature (October).
The event that really attracts
the crowds is the Cheltenham
Gold Cup – the premier event
of the National Hunt season –
held in March (see p66).

🏛️ **Museum and
Art Gallery**
Clarence St. **Tel** 01242 237431.
◻️ Mon–Sat. ⬤ 1 Jan, 25 Dec &
public hols. ♿ 📷 by arrangement.
📷 ℹ️ www.cheltenham
museum.org.uk

🏺 **Pittville Pump Room**
Pittville Park. **Tel** 01242 523852.
◻️ Wed–Mon. ⬤ 1 Jan, 25 &
26 Dec, public hols & frequently
for functions: call to check. ♿
www.pittvillepumproom.org.uk

Fantasy clock, by Kit Williams,
in Cheltenham's Regency Arcade

Gloucester Cathedral's nave

Gloucester ㉑

Gloucestershire. 🏠 110,000. 🚉🚌🛈 28 Southgate St (01452 396572). 🛒 Wed, Sat. www.visitgloucester.info

Gloucester has played a prominent role in the history of England. It was here that William the Conqueror ordered a vast survey of all the land in his kingdom, that was to be recorded in the *Domesday Book* of 1086 *(see p48)*.

The city was popular with the Norman monarchs and in 1216 Henry III was crowned in its magnificent **cathedral**. The solid, dignified nave was begun in 1089. Edward II *(see p439)*, who was murdered in 1327 at Berkeley Castle, 14 miles (22 km) to the southwest, is buried in a tomb near the high altar. Many pilgrims came to honour Edward's tomb, leaving behind generous donations, and Abbot Thoky was able to begin rebuilding in 1331. The result was the wonderful east window and the cloisters, where the fan vault was developed and then copied in other churches all over the country.

The impressive buildings around the cathedral include College Court, with its **House of the Tailor of Gloucester** museum, in the house that the children's author Beatrix Potter used as the setting *(see p367)* for her illustrations of that story. A museum complex has been created in the **Gloucester Docks**, part of which is still a port, linked to the Bristol Channel by the Gloucester and Sharpness Canal (opened in 1827). In the old port, and housed in a Victorian warehouse, the **National Waterways Museum** relates the history of canals. A new gallery, Move It, looks at how canals were built.

🏛 **House of the Tailor of Gloucester**
College Court. **Tel** 01452 422856. ◯ Mon–Sat (Sun: pm only). ● public hols. 🚻 ♿

🏛 **National Waterways Museum**
Llanthony Warehouse, Gloucester Docks. **Tel** 01452 318200. ◯ daily. ● 25 Dec. 🚻 ♿ 🅿 📷
www.nwm.org.uk

Cirencester ㉒

Gloucestershire. 🏠 20,000. 🚌 🛈 Market Place (01285 654180). 🛒 Mon, Tue (cattle) & Fri. www.cotswold.gov.uk

Known as the capital of the Cotswolds, Cirencester has as its focus a market place, where there is a market every Monday and Friday. Overlooking the market is the **Church of St John Baptist**, whose "wineglass" pulpit (1515) is one of the few pre-Reformation pulpits to survive in England. To the west, **Cirencester Park** was laid out by the 1st Earl of Bathurst from 1714, with help from the poet Alexander Pope *(see p317)*. The mansion is surrounded by a massive yew hedge. Clustering round the park entrance are the 17th- and 18th-century wool merchants' houses of Cecily Hill, built in grand Italianate style. Much humbler Cotswold houses are to be found in Coxwell Street, and underlying this is a Roman town, evidence of which emerges whenever the ground is dug.

The **Corinium Museum**, since its renovation in 2004, is a must-see site. It features excavated objects in a series of tableaux illustrating life in a Roman household.

🌳 **Cirencester Park**
Cirencester Park. **Tel** 01285 653135. ◯ daily. ♿
www.cirencesterpark.co.uk

🏛 **Corinium Museum**
Park St. **Tel** 01285 655611. ◯ daily (Sun pm only). ● 1 Jan, 25 & 26 Dec. 📷 ♿ 🅿 🚻
www.cotswold.gov.uk

Cirencester's fine parish church, one of the largest in England

---

ART AND NATURE IN THE ROMAN WORLD

Cirencester was an important centre of mosaic production in Roman days. Fine examples of the local style are shown in the Corinium Museum and mosaics range from Classical subjects, such as Orpheus taming lions and tigers with the music of his lyre, to the naturalistic depiction of a hare. At

Chedworth Roman Villa, 8 miles (13 km) north, mosaics are inspired by real life. In the *Four Seasons* mosaic, *Winter* shows a peasant, dressed in a woollen hood and a wind-blown cloak, clutching a recently caught hare in one hand and a branch for fuel in the other.

Hare mosaic, Corinium Museum

EAST MIDLANDS

DERBYSHIRE · LEICESTERSHIRE · LINCOLNSHIRE
NORTHAMPTONSHIRE · NOTTINGHAMSHIRE

Three very different kinds of landscape greet visitors to the East Midlands. In the west, wild moors rise to the craggy heights of the Peak District. These give way to the low-lying plain and the massive industrial towns at the region's heart. In the east, hills and limestone villages stretch to a long, flat seaboard.

The East Midlands owes much of its character to a conjunction of the pastoral with the urban. The spa resorts, historical villages and stately homes coexist within a landscape shaped by industrialization. Throughout the region there are swathes of scenic countryside – and grimy industrial cities.

The area has been settled since prehistoric times. The Romans mined lead and salt, and they built a large network of roads and fortresses. Anglo-Saxon and Viking influence is found in many of the place names. During the Middle Ages profits from the wool industry enabled the development of towns such as Lincoln, which still has many fine old buildings. The East Midlands was the scene of ferocious battles during the Wars of the Roses and the Civil War, and insurgents in the Jacobite Rebellion reached as far as Derby.

In the west of the region is the Peak District, Britain's first national park. Created in 1951, it draws crowds in search of the wild beauty of the heather-covered moors, or the wooded dales of the River Dove. The peaks are very popular with rock climbers and hikers.

The eastern edge of the Peaks descends through stone-walled meadows to sheltered valleys. The Roman spa of Buxton adds a final note of elegance before the flatlands of Derbyshire, Leicestershire and Nottinghamshire are reached. An area of coal mines and factories since the late 18th century, the landscape is being transformed, as part of a ten-year-long project, into The National Forest.

Well-dressing dance, an ancient custom at Stoney Middleton in the Peak District

◁ **West front of Chatsworth House, a superb Baroque stately home in the Peak District**

Exploring the East Midlands

The East Midlands is a popular tourist destination, easily accessible by road, but best explored on foot. Numerous well-marked trails pass through the Peak District National Park. There are superb country houses at Chatsworth and Burghley and the impressive historic towns of Lincoln and Stamford to discover.

SIGHTS AT A GLANCE

Burghley pp342–3 ❽
Buxton ❶
Chatsworth pp334–5 ❷
Lincoln pp340–41 ❼
Matlock Bath ❸
Northampton ❿
Nottingham ❻
Stamford ❾

Walks and Tours

Peak District Tour ❺
Tissington Trail ❹

GETTING AROUND

The M6, M1 and A1 are the principal road routes to the East Midlands, but they are subject to frequent delays because of the volume of traffic they carry. It can be faster and more interesting to find cross-country routes to the region, for example through the attractive countryside and villages around Stamford and Northampton. Roads in the Peak District become very congested during the summer and an early start to the day is advisable. Lincoln and Stamford are well served by fast mainline trains from London. Rail services in the Peak District are far more limited, but local lines run as far as Matlock and Buxton.

View of Burghley House from the north courtyard

SEE ALSO

- **Where to Stay** pp578–80
- **Where to Eat** pp632–4

KEY

▬▬	Motorway
▬▬	Major road
▬▬	Secondary road
⋯⋯	Minor road
───	Scenic route
▬▬	Main railway
───	Minor railway
△	Summit

Peak District countryside seen from the Tissington Trail

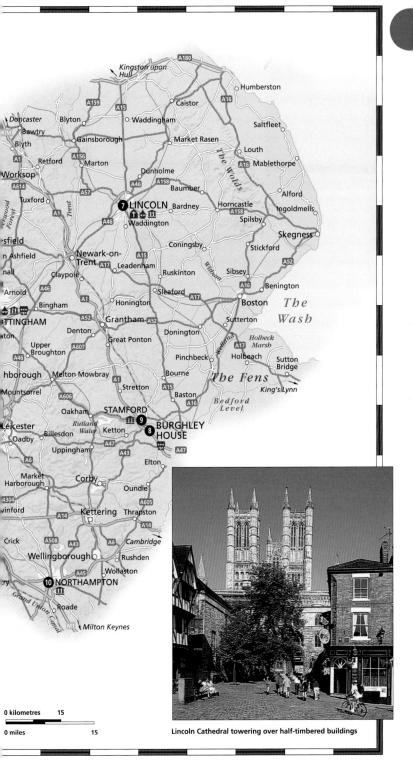

A180
Kingston upon Hull
Humberston
A159
A15
Caistor   A16
Saltfleet
Doncaster   Blyton   Waddingham
Bawtry
Blyth   Market Rasen   Louth
A1(M)   Gainsborough   A16 Mablethorpe
A1   Retford   A156   Marton   The Wolds
Worksop   Dunholme   Horncastle   Alford
A614   A57   A46   A158   Ingoldmells
Tuxford   Trent   Baumber   A158 Spilsby
Sherwood   Skegness
Forest   7 LINCOLN Bardney   A52
sfield   A46   Waddington   Coningsby   Stickford
n Ashfield   Newark-on-   Sibsey   Benington
nall   Trent A17 Leadenham   A15 Ruskinton   A16 Boston
Claypole   Sleaford A17
Arnold   A46   Honington   Sutterton   The
Bingham   A52 Grantham A52   Wash
TTINGHAM   A1   Donington
ton   Denton   Great Ponton   Holbeck
Upper   Pinchbeck   A17 Marsh
Broughton   A607   Bourne Holbeach Sutton
A46   Bridge
hborough Melton Mowbray A1 Stretton   The Fens King's Lynn
Mountsorrel A606   Baston A15
Oakham STAMFORD A16   Bedford
Leicester Rutland 9   Level
Oadby   Billesdon Water Ketton 8 BURGHLEY
Uppingham A47 A43   HOUSE
A6   Elton   A47
Market   A605
Harborough   Corby   Oundle
4304   A14
vinford   Kettering Thrapston
A14
Crick   A508 A43 A6 Cambridge
Wellingborough Rushden
A45
ry   10 NORTHAMPTON Wollaston
Grand Union Canal Roade
Milton Keynes

0 kilometres   15

0 miles   15

Lincoln Cathedral towering over half-timbered buildings

Buxton Opera House, a late 19th-century building restored in 1979

Buxton ❶

Derbyshire. 🏛 20,000. 🚆 🚌
🛈 Pavilion Gardens (01298 25106).
🛒 Tue, Sat. www.highpeak.gov.uk

Buxton was developed as a spa town by the 5th Duke of Devonshire during the late 18th century. It has many fine Neo-Classical buildings, including the **Devonshire Royal Hospital** (1790), originally stables, at the entrance to the town. The **Crescent** was built (1780–90) to rival Bath's Royal Crescent *(see p258)*.

At its southwest end, the tourist information office is housed in the former town baths. Here, a spring where water surges from the ground at a rate of 7,000 litres (1,540 gallons) an hour can be seen. Buxton water is bottled and sold but there is a public fountain at **St Ann's Well**, opposite.

Steep gardens known as the Slopes lead from the Crescent to the small, award-winning **Museum and Art Gallery**, with geological and archaeological displays. Behind the Crescent, overlooking the Pavilion Gardens, is the striking 19th-century iron and glass **Pavilion**, and the splendidly restored **Opera House**, where a Music and Arts Festival is held in summer.

🏛 Buxton Museum and Art Gallery
Terrace Rd. *Tel 01298 24658.* 🕐 Easter–Sep: Tue–Sun; Oct–Easter: Tue–Sat. 🕐 25 Dec–2 Jan. 🚻 🅿 🛒
www.derbyshire.gov.uk

🚻 Pavilion Gardens
St John's Rd. *Tel 01298 23114.*
🕐 daily. 🕐 25 Dec. 🚻 🍴 🛒 🅿

Chatsworth House and Gardens ❷

Chatsworth is one of Britain's most impressive stately homes. Between 1687 and 1707, the 4th Earl of Devonshire replaced the old Tudor mansion with this Baroque palace. The house has beautiful gardens, landscaped in the 1760s by Capability Brown *(see p26)* and developed by the head gardener, Joseph Paxton *(see pp56–7)*, in the mid-19th century.

First house built in 1552 by Bess of Hardwick

Summerhouse

Round ponds, known as the Spectacles

★ **Cascade**
Water tumbles down the steps of the Cascade, built in 1696 to a French design.

STAR SIGHTS

★ Cascade

★ Chapel

Paxton's "Conservative" Wall
This wood-and-glass conservatory wall was designed in 1848 by Joseph Paxton, the creator of Chatsworth's Great Conservatory (now demolished).

Garden entrance

House entrance

South front and canal pond with Emperor fountain

VISITORS' CHECKLIST

Derbyshire. 🚆 Chesterfield,
then bus. **Tel** 01246 565300.
🕐 mid-Mar–Dec: 11am–4:30pm
(gardens: 11am–5pm) daily. 🅿️
♿ gardens & some of house. 🍴
🌐 📷 www.chatsworth.org

Maze: site of
Paxton's Great
Conservatory

Rhododendron Walk

Grotto

★ **Chapel**
*The chapel (1693) is
resplendent with
art and marble.*

War Horse
*This sculpture
(1991) is by
Elisabeth Frink.*

Canal pond

Sea-horse
fountain

★ **State Rooms**
*The rooms have
fine interiors and
superb art, such as
this* trompe l'oeil *by Jan
van der Vaart (1651–1727).*

Matlock ❸

Derbyshire. 🚶 23,000. 🚉
ℹ Crown Square (01629 583388).
www.visitderbyshire.co.uk

Matlock was developed as a spa from the 1780s. Interesting buildings include the massive structure (1853) on the hill above the town, built as a hydrotherapy centre but now council offices. On the hill opposite is the mock-Gothic **Riber Castle**.

From Matlock, the A6 winds through the outstandingly beautiful **Derwent Gorge** to **Matlock Bath**. Here, cable cars ascend to the **Heights of Abraham** pleasure park, with caves, nature trail and extensive views. Lead-mining is the subject of the **Peak District Mining Museum**, and visitors can inspect the old **Temple Mine** nearby. **Sir Richard Arkwright's Cromford Mill** (1771), a world heritage site and the first ever water-powered cotton spinning mill, lies at the southern end of the gorge (see p339).

🎿 **Heights of Abraham**
On A6. **Tel** 01629 582365. ⬜ Feb–Nov: daily. 🦽 ♿ limited. 🎫 📷 🛒
www.heightsofabraham.com

🏛 **Peak District Mining Museum**
The Pavilion, off A6. **Tel** 01629 583834. ⬜ daily. 🎫 ♿ 📷 🛒
www.peakmines.co.uk

⛏ **Temple Mine**
Temple Rd, off A6. **Tel** 01629 583834. ⬜ call for details. 🎫

⛏ **Cromford Mill**
Mill Lane, Cromford. **Tel** 01629 824297. ⬜ daily. ⬤ 25 Dec. 🎫
♿ 🍴 📷 www.cromfordmill.co.uk

Cable cars taking visitors to the Heights of Abraham

Tissington Trail ❹

See p337.

Peak District Tour ❺

See pp338–9.

Nottingham ❻

Nottinghamshire. 🚶 269,000. 🚉
🚌 ℹ Smithy Row (0844 477 5678).
🛏 daily. www.nottinghamcity.gov.uk

The name of Nottingham often conjures up the image of the evil Sheriff, adversary of Robin Hood. **Nottingham Castle** stands on a rock riddled with underground passages. The castle houses a museum, with displays on the city's history, and what was Britain's first municipal art gallery, featuring works by Sir Stanley Spencer (1891–1959) and Dante Gabriel Rossetti (1828–82). At the foot of the castle, Britain's oldest tavern, the **Trip to Jerusalem** (1189), is still in business. Its name may refer to the 12th- and 13th-century crusades, but much of it is 17th-century.

There are several museums near the castle, including **Tales of Robin Hood**, which tells the story of the outlaw, and the **Museum of Nottingham Life**, which looks at life in Nottingham over the last 300 years.

Nottingham's redeveloped city centre includes an award-winning Old Market Square.

Environs: Stately homes within a few miles of Nottingham include the Neo-Classical **Kedleston Hall** (see pp28–9). "Bess of Hardwick", Countess of Shrewsbury (see p334), built the spectacular **Hardwick Hall** (see p302).

♣ **Nottingham Castle and Museum**
Friar Lane. **Tel** 0115 9153700.
⬜ daily. ⬤ 1 Jan, 24–27 Dec.
🎫 ♿ 📷 of the caves. 📷 🛒

🏛 **Tales of Robin Hood**
30–38 Maid Marion Way.
Tel 0115 9483284. ⬜ daily.
⬤ 25 & 26 Dec. 🎫 ♿ 📷 🛒

🏛 **Museum of Nottingham Life**
Castle Boulevard. **Tel** 0115 915 3600. ♿ ⬜ daily. ⬤ 1 Jan, 24–26 Dec. 🎫 📷 www.nottinghamcity.gov.uk

🏰 **Kedleston Hall**
(NT) off A38. **Tel** 01332 842191.
⬜ Mar–Oct: Sat–Wed (pm). 🎫
♿ 🍴 📷

🏰 **Hardwick Hall**
(NT) off A617. **Tel** 01246 850430.
⬜ Apr–Oct: Wed, Thu, Sat, Sun & public hols. 🎫 ♿ limited. 🍴 📷

ROBIN HOOD OF SHERWOOD FOREST

England's most colourful folk hero was a legendary swordsman, whose adventures are depicted in numerous films and stories. He lived in Sherwood Forest, near Nottingham, with a band of "merry men", robbing the rich to give to the poor. As part of an ancient oral tradition, Robin Hood figured mainly in ballads; the first written records of his exploits date from the 15th century. Today historians think that he was not one person, but a composite of many outlaws who refused to conform to medieval feudal constraints.

Victorian depiction of Friar Tuck and Robin Hood

Tissington Trail ❹

The full-length Tissington Trail runs for 13 miles (22 km), from the village of Ashbourne to Parsley Hay, where it meets the High Peak Trail. This is a short version, taking an easy route along a dismantled railway line around Tissington village and providing good views of the beautiful White Peak countryside. The Derbyshire custom of well-dressing is thought to have originated in pre-Christian times. It was revived in the early 17th century, when the Tissington village wells were decorated in thanksgiving for deliverance from the plague, in the belief that the fresh water had had a medicinal effect. Well-dressing is still an important event in the Peakland calendar, and can be seen in other villages where the water supplies were prone to dry up.

Crakelow Cutting ③
The view to the north is of open farmland, dotted with small stands of trees.

Crakelow Farm

④

③

Railway Cutting ②
The old railway's limestone cuttings are now home to wild flowers, lizards and butterflies.

②

Downhill Track ④
The track runs along an 18th-century dry-stone wall, built as a result of land enclosure.

KEY

– –	Route
═══	Minor road
P	Parking
ℹ	Information
⛪	Church
🚻	Toilets

A515

Town Head Farm

⑤

Tissington ⛪

Old Station ①
Tissington's old railway station has a refreshment hatch.

①

A515

B5056

TIPS FOR WALKERS

Starting point: Old Station. ℹ Ashbourne Tourist Information (01335 343666). **Getting there:** Car from Buxton, Matlock or Ashbourne. **Length:** 3 miles (5 km). **Difficulty:** Mostly flat trail along unused railway track and path. www.derbyshiredales.gov.uk

Tissington Hall Well ⑤
This and the other four wells in Tissington are decorated on Ascension Day (the 40th day after Easter). Framed boards have a layer of clay into which rice, seeds and flower petals are pressed.

0 metres	500
0 yards	500

Peak District Tour ❺

Detail, Buxton Opera House

The Peak District's natural beauty and sheep-grazed crags contrast with the factories of nearby valley towns. Designated Britain's first National Park in 1951, the area has two distinct types of landscape. In the south are the gently rolling hills of the limestone White Peak. To the north, west and east are the wild, heather-clad moorlands of the Dark Peak peat bogs, superimposed on millstone grit.

Edale ⑤
The high plateau of scenic Edale mark the starting point of the 256 mile (412 km) Pennine Way footpath *(see p36)*.

Buxton ⑥
This lovely spa town's opera house *(see p334)* is known as the "theatre in the hills" because of its magnificent setting.

Arbor Low ⑦
This stone circle, known as the "Stonehenge of the North", dates from around 2000 BC and consists of 46 recumbent stones enclosed by a ditch.

TIPS FOR DRIVERS

Tour length: 40 miles (60 km).
Stopping-off points: There are refreshments at Crich Tramway Village and Arkwright's Mill in Cromford. Eyam has good old-fashioned tea shops. The Nag's Head in Edale is a charming Tudor inn. Buxton has many pubs and cafés. (See also pp684–5.)

KEY

▬▬	Tour route
═══	Other roads
❊	Viewpoint

Dovedale ⑧
Popular Dovedale is one of the prettiest of the Peak District's river valleys, with its stepping stones, thickly wooded slopes and wind-sculpted rocks. Izaac Walton (1593–1683), author of *The Compleat Angler,* used to fish here.

STOCKPORT, MANCHESTER

HOLLIN

A625

A6

Wye

Hathersage ④

There are spectacular panoramic views over the moors above Hathersage, which is thought to be "Morton" in Charlotte Brontë's *(see p412) Jane Eyre*.

Eyam ③

This is famous for the villagers' self-imposed quarantine to contain the plague of 1665–6. There is a fine Saxon cross in the churchyard.

Crich Tramway Village ②

This unique museum is in a disused quarry. Visitors can take rides on old trams from all over the world, along reconstructed Victorian streets.

Cromford ①

Arkwright's Mill *(see p336)* was the world's first water-powered cotton mill. It stands next to the Cromford Canal, part of which can be toured by horse-drawn narrowboats in the summer.

HIGH RAKE
391 m
1,283 ft

HARBORO ROCKS
379 m
1,243 ft

0 kilometres 3

0 miles 2

Street-by-Street: Lincoln ❼

Carving in Angel Choir

Surrounded by the flat landscape of the Fens, Lincoln rises dramatically on a cliff above the River Witham, the three towers of its massive cathedral visible from afar. The Romans *(see pp44–5)* founded the first fortress here in AD 50. By the time of the Norman Conquest *(see p47)*, Lincoln was one of the most important cities in England (after London, Winchester and York). The city's wealth was due to its strategic importance for the export of wool from the Lincolnshire Wolds to Europe. Lincoln has managed to retain much of its historic character. Many remarkable medieval buildings have survived, most of which are along the aptly named Steep Hill, leading to the cathedral.

3rd-century Newport Arch

Museum of Lincolnshire Life

WESTGATE

CASTLE HILL

DRURY LANE

Norman House (1180)

MICHAELGATE

★ Lincoln Castle
The early Norman castle, rebuilt at intervals, acted as the city prison from 1787 to 1878. The chapel's coffin-like pews served to remind felons of their fate.

KEY

– – – Suggested route

Jew's House
Lincoln had a large medieval Jewish community. This mid-12th-century stone house, one of the oldest of its kind, was owned by a Jewish merchant.

15th-century Stonebow Gate and bus and railway stations

| 0 meters | | 100 |
| 0 yards | | 100 |

STAR SIGHTS

★ Lincoln Castle

★ Lincoln Cathedral

VISITORS' CHECKLIST

Lincoln. 90,000. Humberside, 30 miles (48 km); E Midlands, 51 miles (82 km). St Mary St. Melville St. Castle Hill (01522 873800). www.lincoln.gov.uk

★ Lincoln Cathedral
The west front is a harmonious mix of Norman and Gothic styles. Inside, the best features include the Angel Choir, with the figure of the Lincoln Imp.

Alfred, Lord Tennyson
A statue of the Lincolnshire-born poet (1809–92) stands in the grounds.

EASTGATE

Exchequergate Arch

POTTERGATE

MINISTER YARD

The 14th-century Pottergate Arch

Victorian Arboretum

GREENSTONE PLACE

Ruins of Medieval Bishop's Palace

Greenstone Stairs

DANESGATE

LINDUM ROAD

TERRACE

Usher Art Gallery
This is packed with clocks, ceramics, and silver. There are paintings by Peter de Wint (1784–1849) and J M W Turner (see p91).

MISERICORDS

Misericords are ledges that project from the underside of the hinged seat of a choir stall, which provide support while standing.

St Francis of Assisi

Lincoln Cathedral's misericords in the early Perpendicular-style canopied choir stalls are some of the best in England. The wide variety of subjects includes parables, fables, myths, biblical scenes and irreverent images from daily life.

One of a pair of lions

Burghley House ⓭

Portrait of Sir Isaac Newton, Billiard Room

William Cecil, 1st Lord Burghley (1520–98) was Queen Elizabeth I's adviser and confidant for 40 years and built the wonderfully dramatic Burghley House in 1555–87. The roof line bristles with stone pyramids, chimneys disguised as Classical columns and towers shaped like pepper pots. The busy skyline resolves itself into a symmetrical pattern when viewed from the west, where a lime tree stands, one of many planted by Capability Brown *(see p26)* when the surrounding deer park was landscaped in 1760. The interior walls are lavishly decorated with Italian paintings of Greek gods enacting their dramas. An Elizabethan "Garden of Surprises" and an education and visitor centre opened in 2007.

★ Old Kitchen
Gleaming copper pans hang from the walls of the fan-vaulted kitchen, little altered since the Tudor period.

North Gate
Intricate examples of 19th-century wrought-iron work adorn the principal entrances.

The Billiard Room
has many fine portraits inset in oak panelling.

Cupolas were very fashionable details, inspired by European Renaissance architecture.

A chimney has been disguised as a Classical column.

Mullioned windows were added in 1683 when glass became less expensive.

The Gatehouse, with its side turrets, is a typical feature of the "prodigy" houses of the Tudor era *(see p302).*

West Front
Featuring the Burghley crest, the West Front was finished in 1577 and formed the original main entrance.

STAR SIGHTS

★ Old Kitchen

★ Heaven Room

★ Hell Staircase

★ Heaven Room
Gods tumble from the sky, and satyrs and nymphs play on the walls and ceiling in this masterpiece by Antonio Verrio (1639–1707).

Obelisk and clock (1585)

The Great Hall has a double hammer-beam roof and was a banqueting hall in Elizabethan days.

The wine cooler (1710) is thought to be the largest in existence.

The Fourth George Room, one of a suite, is panelled in oak stained with ale.

★ Hell Staircase
Verrio painted the ceiling to show Hell as the mouth of a cat crammed with tormented sinners. The staircase, of local stone, was installed in 1786.

VISITORS' CHECKLIST

Off A1 SE of Stamford, Lincs. **Tel** 01780 752451. ⬚ Stamford. ⬚ Apr–Oct: 11am–5pm daily. ⬚ 4 days Sep (horse trials). ⬚ ⬚ ⬚ ⬚ **www**.burghley.co.uk

Stamford ⑨

Lincolnshire. 🏠 18,000. ⬚ ⬚ ⬚ 27 St Mary's St (01780 755611). ⬚ Fri. **www**.southkesteven.gov.uk

Stamford is a showpiece town, famous for its churches and Georgian townhouses. The town retains a medieval street plan, with a warren of winding streets and cobbled alleys.

The spires of the medieval churches (five survive of the original eleven) give Stamford the air of a miniature Oxford.

Barn Hill, leading up from All Saints Church, is the best place for a view of Stamford's Georgian architecture in all its variety. Below it is Broad Street, where the **Stamford Museum** covers the history of the town. Exhibits include a model of Britain's fattest man, Daniel Lambert, who was 336 kg (53 stone) and died while attending Stamford Races in 1809, and the 6-m- (20-ft)-long Stamford Tapestry.

🏛 **Stamford Museum**
Broad St. **Tel** 01780 766317. ⬚ Apr–Sep: daily (Sun: pm); Oct–Mar: Mon–Sat. ⬚ ⬚ **www**.lincoln shire.gov.uk/stamfordmuseum

Northampton ⑩

Northamptonshire. 🏠 187,000. ⬚ ⬚ ⬚ Sessions House, George Row (01604 838800). ⬚ Mon–Sat (Thu: antiques). **www**.northampton.gov.uk

This market town was once a centre for shoe-making, and the **Central Museum and Art Gallery** holds the world's largest collection of footwear. One of many fine old build-ings is the Victorian Gothic **Guildhall**. Six miles west of the town is **Althorp House**, family home of Diana Princess of Wales. Visitors can tour the house, grounds, see an exhibition on Diana and her island resting place.

🏛 **Central Museum and Art Gallery**
Guildhall Rd. **Tel** 01604 838111. ⬚ daily (Sun: pm). ⬚ 25, 26 Dec. ⬚ ⬚

🏛 **Althorp House**
Great Brington (off A428). **Tel** 01604 770107. ⬚ Jul & Aug. ⬚ 31 Aug. ⬚ ⬚ ⬚ ⬚ **www**.althorp.com

THE NORTH COUNTRY

The North Country at a Glance

Rugged coastlines, spectacular walks and climbs, magnificent stately homes and breathtaking cathedrals all have their place in the north of England, with its dramatic history of Roman rule, Saxon invasion, Viking attacks and border skirmishes. Reminders of the industrial revolution are found in towns such as Halifax, Liverpool and Manchester, and peace and inspiration in the dramatic scenery of the Lake District, with its awe-inspiring mountains and waters.

Hadrian's Wall (see pp422–3), *built around 120 to protect Roman Britain from the Picts to the north, cuts through rugged Northumberland National Park scenery.*

NORTHUMB**
(see pp414–4

Northumber

Dur**

The Lake District (see pp354–69) *is a combination of superb peaks, tumbling rivers and falls and shimmering lakes such as Wast Water.*

Cumbria

Yorkshire Dales National Park (see pp384–86) *creates a delightful environment for walking and touring the farming landscape, scattered with attractive villages such as Thwaite, in Swaledale.*

Lancashire

LANCASHIRE AND THE LAKES (see pp354–379)

The Walker Art Gallery (see pp378–9) *in Liverpool is one of the jewels in the artistic crown of the north, with an internationally renowned collection ranging from Old Masters to modern art. Sculpture includes John Gibson's* Tinted Venus *(c.1851–6).*

Manchester

Liverpool

◁ **The 11th-century Alnwick Castle, Alnwick, Northumberland, from across the River Aln**

Fountains Abbey (see pp390–91), *one of the finest religious buildings in the north, was founded in the 12th century by monks who desired simplicity and austerity. Later the abbey became extremely wealthy.*

Durham Cathedral (see pp428–9), *a striking Norman structure with an innovative southern choir aisle and fine stained glass, has towered over the city of Durham since 995.*

Castle Howard (see pp398–9), *a triumph of Baroque architecture, offers many magnificent settings, including this Museum Room (1805–10), designed by CH Tatham.*

Cleveland

North Yorkshire

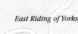

YORKSHIRE AND THE HUMBER REGION *pp380–413)*

Leeds

East Riding of Yorkshire

York (see pp404–409) *is a city of historical treasures, ranging from the medieval to Georgian. Its magnificent minster has a large collection of stained glass and the medieval city walls are well preserved. Other sights include churches, narrow alleyways and notable museums.*

0 kilometres   25

0 miles   25

The Industrial Revolution in the North

The face of Northern England in the 19th century was dramatically altered by the development of the coal mining, textile and shipbuilding industries. Lancashire, Northumberland and the West Riding (*see p381*) of Yorkshire all experienced population growth and migration to cities. The hardships of urban life were partly relieved by the actions of several wealthy industrial philanthropists, but many people lived in extremely deprived conditions. Although most traditional industries have now declined sharply or disappeared as demand has moved elsewhere, a growing tourist industry has developed in many of the former industrial centres.

Back-to-backs *or colliers' rows, such as these houses at Easington, were provided by colliery owners from the 1800s onwards. They comprised two small rooms for cooking and sleeping, and an outside toilet.*

1815 Sir Humphrey Davy invented a safety oil lamp for miners. Light shone through a cylindrical gauze sheet which prevented the heat of the flame igniting methane gas in the mine. Thousands of miners benefited from this device.

Coal mining *was a family industry in the North of England with women and children working alongside the men.*

1750		1800	
PRE-STEAM		STEAM AGE	
1750		1800	

1781 Leeds-Liverpool Canal opened. The building of canals facilitated the movement of raw materials and finished products, and aided the process of mechanization immeasurably.

1830 Live and Manchester ra opened, connecting t the biggest cities o London. Within a mon railway carried passe

Halifax's Piece Hall (see p413), *restored in 1976, is the most impressive surviving example of industrial architecture in northern England. It is the only complete 18th-century cloth market building in Yorkshire. Merchants sold measures of cloth known as "pieces" from rooms lining the cloisters inside.*

Hebden Bridge (see p412), *a typical West Riding textile mill town jammed into the narrow Calder Valley, typifies a pattern of workers' houses surrounding a central mill. The town benefited from its position when the Rochdale Canal (1804) and then the railway (1841) took advantage of this relatively low-level route over the Pennines.*

Saltaire (see p411) *was a model village built by the wealthy cloth merchant and mill-owner Sir Titus Salt (1803–76), for the benefit of his workers. Seen here in the 1870s, it included houses and facilities such as shops, gardens and sportsfields, with almshouses, a hospital, school and chapel. A disciplinarian, Salt banned alcohol and pubs from Saltaire.*

George Hudson *(1800–71) built the first railway station in York (see p408) in 1840–42. In the 1840s he owned more than a quarter of the railways in Britain and was known as the "railway king".*

1842 Coal Mines Act prevented women and children from working in harsh conditions in the mines.

Port Sunlight (see p379) *was founded by William Hesketh Lever (1851–1925) to provide housing for workers at his Sunlight soap factory. Between 1889 and 1914 he built 800 cottages. Amenities included a pool.*

Strikes to improve working conditions were common. Violence flared in July 1893 when colliery owners locked miners out of their pits and stopped their pay after the Miners' Federation resisted a 25 per cent wage cut. Over 300,000 men struggled without pay until November, when work resumed at the old rate.

1850		1900
FULL MECHANIZATION		
1850		1900

Power loom weaving *transformed the textile industry while creating unemployment among skilled hand loom weavers. By the 1850s, the West Riding had 30,000 power looms, used in cotton and woollen mills. Of 79,000 workers, over half were to be found in Bradford alone.*

Furness dry dock *was built in the 1890s when the shipbuilding industry moved north, in search of cheap labour and materials. Barrow-in-Furness, Glasgow (see pp516–19) and Tyne and Wear (see p424) were the new centres.*

Joseph Rowntree *(1836–1925) founded his chocolate factory in York in 1892, having formerly worked with George Cadbury. As Quakers, the Rowntrees believed in the social welfare of their workers (establishing a model village in 1904), and, with Terry's confectionary (1767), they made a vast contribution to York's prosperity. Today, Nestlé Rowntree is the world's largest chocolate factory and York is Britain's chocolate capital.*

North Country Abbeys

Northern England has some of the finest and best preserved religious houses in Europe. Centres of prayer, learning and power in the Middle Ages, the larger of these were designated abbeys and were governed by an abbot. Most were located in rural areas, considered appropriate for a spiritual and contemplative life. Viking raiders had destroyed many Anglo-Saxon religious houses in the 8th and 9th centuries *(see pp46–7)* and it was not until William the Conqueror founded the Benedictine Selby Abbey in 1069 that monastic life revived in the north. New orders, Augustinians in particular, arrived from the Continent and by 1500 Yorkshire had 83 monasteries.

Cistercian monk

Ruins of St Mary's Abbey today

The Liberty of St Mary was the name given to the land around the abbey, almost a city within a city. Here, the abbot had his own market, fair, prison and gallows – all exempt from the city authorities.

ST MARY'S ABBEY

Founded in York in 1086, this Benedictine abbey was one of the wealthiest in Britain. Its involvement in the wool trade in York and the granting of royal and papal privileges and land led to a relaxing of standards by the early 12th century. The abbot was even allowed to dress in the same style as a bishop, and was raised by the pope to the status of a "mitred abbot". As a result, 13 monks left in 1132, to found Fountains Abbey *(see pp390–91).*

Gatehouse and St Olave's church

Interval tower

Water tower

Hospitium or guest house

MONASTERIES AND LOCAL LIFE

As one of the wealthiest landowning sections of society, the monasteries played a vital role in the local economy. They provided employment, particularly in agriculture, and dominated the wool trade, England's largest export during the Middle Ages. By 1387 two thirds of all wool exported from England passed through St Mary's Abbey, the largest wool trader in York.

Cistercian monks tilling their land

WHERE TO SEE ABBEYS TODAY

Fountains Abbey *(see pp390–91),* founded by Benedictine monks and later taken over by Cistercians, is the most famous of the numerous abbeys in the region. Rievaulx *(see p393),* Byland *(see p392)* and Furness *(see p368)* were all founded by the Cistercians, and Furness became the second wealthiest Cistercian house in England after Fountains. Whitby Abbey *(see p396),* sacked by the Vikings, was later rebuilt by the Benedictine order. Northumberland is famous for its early Anglo-Saxon monasteries, such as Ripon, Lastingham and Lindisfarne *(see pp418–19).*

Mount Grace Priory (see p394) *founded in 1398, is the best-preserved Carthusian house in England. The former individual gardens and cells of each monk are still clearly visible.*

THE DISSOLUTION OF THE MONASTERIES (1536–40)

By the early 16th century, the monasteries owned one-sixth of all English land and their annual income was four times that of the Crown. Henry VIII ordered the closure of all religious houses in 1536, acquiring their wealth in the process. His attempt at dissolution provoked a large uprising of Catholic northerners led by Robert Aske later that year. The rebellion failed and Aske and others were executed for conspiracy. The dissolution continued under Thomas Cromwell, who became known as "the hammer of the monks".

Thomas Cromwell (c.1485–1549)

The large Abbot's House testified to the grand lifestyle that late medieval abbots adopted.

The Chapter House, an assembly room, was the most important building after the church.

Lavatory

Kitchen

The Warming House was the only room in the monastery, apart from the kitchen, which had a fire.

Refectory

The Abbey Wall had battlements added in 1318 to protect it against raids by Scottish armies.

Common parlour

Cloister

Kirkham Priory, *an Augustinian foundation of the 1120s, enjoys a tranquil setting on the banks of the River Derwent, near Malton. The finest feature of the ruined site is the 13th-century gatehouse which leads into the priory complex.*

Kirkstall Abbey *was founded in 1152 by monks from Fountains Abbey. The well-preserved ruins of this Cistercian house near Leeds include the church, the late Norman chapter house and the abbot's lodging. This evening view was painted by Thomas Girtin (1775–1802).*

Easby Abbey *lies beside the River Swale, outside the pretty market town of Richmond. Among the remains of this Premonstratensian house, founded in 1155, are the 13th-century refectory and sleeping quarters and 14th-century gatehouse.*

The Geology of the Lake District

The Lake District contains some of England's most spectacular scenery. Concentrated in just 900 sq miles (231 sq km) are the highest peaks, deepest valleys and longest lakes in the country. Today's landscape has changed little since the end of the Ice Age 10,000 years ago, the last major event in Britain's geological history. But the glaciated hills which were revealed by the retreating ice were once part of a vast mountain-chain whose remains can also be found in North America. The mountains were first raised by the gradual fusion of two ancient landmasses which, for millions of years, formed a single continent. Eventually the continent broke into two, forming Europe and America, separated by the widening Atlantic Ocean.

Piece of Lake District slate

Honister Pass, *with its distinctive U-shape, is an example of a glaciated valley, once completely filled with ice.*

GEOLOGICAL HISTORY

The oldest rock formed as sediment under an ocean called Iapetus. Some 450 million years ago, Earth's internal movements made two continents collide, and the ocean disappear.

1 **The collision** *buckled the former sea bed into a mountain range. Magma rose from Earth's mantle, altered the sediments and cooled into volcanic rock.*

2 **In the Ice Age,** *glaciers slowly excavated huge rock basins in the mountainsides, dragging debris to the valley floor. Frost sculpted the summits.*

3 **The glaciers retreated** *10,000 years ago, their meltwaters forming lakes in valleys dammed by debris. As the climate improved, plants colonized the fells.*

RADIATING LAKES

The diversity of lakeland scenery owes much to its geology: hard volcanic rocks in the central lakes give rise to rugged hills, while soft slates to the north produce a more rounded topography. The lakes form a radial pattern, spreading out from a central volcanic rock zone.

Scafell Pike is the highest peak in England. One of the three Scafell Pikes, its two neighbours are Broad Crag and Ill Crag.

▲ **Great Gable**

▲ **Old Man of Coniston**

Coniston Water

Wast Water *is the deepest of the lakes. Its southeastern cliffs are streaked with granite scree – the debris formed each year as rock shattered by the winter frost tumbles down during the spring thaw.*

MAN ON THE MOUNTAIN

The sheltered valley floors with their benign climate and fertile soils are ideal for settlement. Farmhouses, dry-stone walls, pasture and sheep pens are an integral part of the landscape. Higher up, the absence of trees and bracken are the result of wind and a cooler climate. Old mine workings and tracks are the relics of once-flourishing industries.

Plantations *of coniferous trees are a recent feature of the landscape. Some see them as harming traditional views and disturbing the ecology.*

Summer grazing

Copper and graphite mines

Tracks

Dry-stone walls *(see p305)*

400–500m (130–170ft)

300–400m (100–130 ft)

Slate *and other local stone has long been incorporated into buildings: slate roofs, stone walls, lintels and bridges.*

Hedges

Sheep pens for winter grazing

vaite

Blencathra

t Water

Helvellyn

Ullswater

Place Fell

High Street

Windermere

Skiddaw *is composed of slate, formed when the muddy sediment of the ancient ocean floor was altered by extreme pressure.*

Striding Edge *is a long, twisting ridge which leads to the summit of Helvellyn. It was sharpened by the widening of the valleys on either side caused by the build up of glaciers.*

The Langdale Pikes *are remnants of the volcanic activity which once erupted in the area. They are made of hard igneous rocks, known as Borrowdale Volcanics. Unlike the Skiddaw Slates, they have not eroded smoothly, so they leave a craggy skyline.*

LANCASHIRE AND THE LAKES

CUMBRIA · LANCASHIRE

The landscape painter John Constable (1776–1837) declared that the Lake District, now visited by 18 million people annually, had "the finest scenery that ever was". The Normans built many religious houses here, and William II created estates for English barons. Today, the National Trust is its most important landowner.

Within the 30 mile (45 km) radius of the Lake District lies an astonishing number of fells and lakes. Today, all looks peaceful, but from the Roman occupation to the Middle Ages, the northwest was a turbulent area, as successive kings and rulers fought over the territory. Historians can revel in the various Celtic monuments, Roman remains, stately homes and monastic ruins. Although the scenery is paramount, there are many outdoor activities as well as spectator sports, such as Cumbrian wrestling, and wildlife to observe.

Lancashire's portfolio of tourist attractions includes the fine county town of Lancaster, bright Blackpool with its autumn illuminations and fairground attractions, and the peaceful seaside beaches to the south. Inland, the most appealing regions are the Forest of Bowland, a sparse expanse of heathery grouse moor, and the picturesque Ribble Valley.

Further south still are the industrial conurbations of Manchester and Merseyside, where the attractions are more urban.

There are many fine Victorian buildings in Manchester, where the industrial quarter of Castlefield has been revitalized. Liverpool, with its restored Albert Dock, is best known as the seaport city of the Beatles. It has a lively club scene and is increasingly used as a film location. Both cities have good art galleries and museums.

Jetty at Grasmere, one of the most popular regions of the Lake District

◁ Restored Albert Dock, lining the River Mersey in Liverpool

Exploring Lancashire and the Lakes

The Lake District's natural scenery outweighs any of its man-made attractions. Its natural features are the result of geological upheavals over millennia *(see pp352–3)*, and four of its peaks are more than 1,000 m (3,300 ft). Human influences have left their mark too: the main activities are quarrying, mining, farming and tourism.

The Lakes are most crowded in summer when activities include lake trips and hillwalking. The best bases are Keswick and Ambleside, while there are also good hotels on the shores of Windermere and Ullswater and in the Cartmel area.

Lancashire's Bowland Forest is an attractive place to explore on foot, with picturesque villages. Further south, Manchester and Liverpool have excellent museums and galleries.

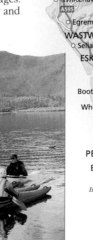

Watersports on Derwentwater in the Northern Fells and Lakes area

GETTING AROUND

For many, the first glimpse of the Lake District is from the M6 near Shap Fell, but the A6 is a more dramatic route. You can reach Windermere by train, but you need to change at Oxenholme, on the mainline route from Euston to Carlisle. Penrith also has rail services and bus links into the Lakes. L'al Ratty, the miniature railway up Eskdale, and the Lakeside & Haverthwaite railway, which connects the steamers on Windermere, make for enjoyable outings. Regular buses link all the main centres where excursions are organized. One of the most enterprising is the Mountain Goat minibus, in Windermere and Keswick.

Lancaster, Liverpool and Manchester are on the main rail and bus routes and also have airports. For Blackpool, you need to change trains in Preston. Wherever you go in the area, one of the best means of getting around is on foot.

View over Crummock Water, north of Buttermere,
one of the quieter Western Lakes

SIGHTS AT A GLANCE

KEY

═══	Motorway
═══	Major road
───	Secondary road
┈┈┈	Minor road
───	Scenic route
╌╌╌	Main railway
───	Minor railway
△	Summit

0 kilometres   20

0 miles   10

SEE ALSO

Preserved docks and Liver Building, Liverpool

-in-
land

Darlington

Skipton

Barnoldswick

Colne

Burnley

Darwen

Ramsbottom   Littleborough

Rochdale   Leeds

Oldham   Sheffield

28 SALFORD QUAYS
29 MANCHESTER

Stockport

Birmingham

Carlisle ❶

Cumbria. 🏛 102,000. ✈ mainly private. 🚉 🚌 ℹ The Old Town Hall, Green Market (01228 625600). www.historic-carlisle.org.uk

Due to its proximity to the Scottish border, this city has long been a defensive site. Known as Luguvalium by the Romans, it was an outpost of Hadrian's Wall (see pp422–3). Carlisle was sacked and pillaged repeatedly by the Danes, the Normans and border raiders, and suffered damage as a Royalist stronghold under Cromwell (see p52).

Today, Carlisle is the capital of Cumbria. In its centre are the timber-framed Guildhall and market cross, and fortifications still exist around its West Walls, drum-towered gates and its Norman **castle**. The castle tower has a small museum devoted to the King's Own Border Regiment. The cathedral dates from 1122 and features a decorative east window. Carlisle's **Tullie House Museum** recreates the city's past with sections on Roman history and Cumbrian wildlife. Nearby lie the evocative ruins of

Saxon iron sword in the Tullie House Museum

Façade of Hutton-in-the-Forest with medieval tower on the right

Lanercost Priory (c.1166) and the remains of the unique **Birdoswald Roman Fort**.

⛫ **Carlisle Castle**
(EH) Castle Way. **Tel** 01228 591922. ⬤ daily. ⬤ 24–26 Dec, 1 Jan. 🎫 🅿 limited. 🎥 📷

🏛 **Tullie House Museum**
Castle St. **Tel** 01228 618718. ⬤ daily (Sun: pm). 🎫 🅿 📷 🍴

⛪ **Lanercost Priory**
(EH) Nr Brampton. **Tel** 016977 3030. ⬤ Mar–Sep: daily, Oct: Thu–Mon; Nov & Dec: Sat & Sun. 📷 🎫 🅿 limited.

⛫ **Birdoswald Roman Fort**
(EH) Gilsland, Brampton. **Tel** 016977 47602. ⬤ Mar–Oct: daily. 🎫 🅿 limited. 🖥 📷

Penrith ❷

Cumbria. 🏛 15,000. ℹ Robinson's School, Middlegate (017688 67466). ⬤ Tue, Sat, Sun. www.visiteden.co.uk

Timewarp shopfronts on the market square and a 14th-century **castle** of sandstone are Penrith's main attractions.

There are some strange hog-back stones in St Andrew's churchyard, allegedly a giant's grave, and the 285 m (937 ft) Beacon provides stunning views of distant fells.

Environs: Just northeast of Penrith at Little Salkeld is a famous Bronze Age circle (with 66 tall stones) known as **Long Meg and her Daughters**. Six miles (9 km) northwest of Penrith lies **Hutton-in-the-Forest**. The oldest part of this house is the 13th-century tower. Inside is a magnificent Italianate staircase, a sumptuously panelled 17th-century Long Gallery, a delicately stuccoed Cupid Room dating from the 1740s, and several Victorian rooms. Outside, you can walk around the walled garden and topiary terraces, or explore the woods.

⛫ **Penrith Castle**
(EH) Ullswater Rd. ⬤ daily. ♿ in grounds.

🏰 **Hutton-in-the-Forest**
Off B5305. **Tel** 017684 84449. **House** ⬤ Easter–Sep: Wed, Thu, Sun & pub hols (pm). **Grounds** ⬤ Apr–Oct: Sun–Fri. 🎫 ♿ ltd. 🖥 📷

Dalemain ❸

Penrith, Cumbria. **Tel** 017684 86450. 🚉 🚌 Penrith then taxi. ⬤ Apr–Oct: Sun–Thu. 🎫 ♿ limited. 🎥 🖥 📷 www.dalemain.com

A seemly Georgian façade gives this fine house near Ullswater the impression of architectural unity, but hides a much-altered medieval and Elizabethan structure with a maze of rambling passages. Public rooms include a superb Chinese drawing room with

---

TRADITIONAL CUMBRIAN SPORTS

Cumberland wrestling is one of the most interesting sports to watch in the summer months. The combatants, often clad in longjohns and embroidered velvet pants, clasp one another in an armlock and attempt to topple each other over. Technique and good balance outweigh physical force. Other traditional Lakeland sports include fell-racing, a gruelling test of speed and stamina up and down local peaks at ankle-breaking speed. Hound-trailing is also a popular sport in which specially bred hounds follow an aniseed trail over the hills. Sheep-dog trials, steam fairs, flower shows and gym-khanas take place in summer. The Egremont Crab Fair in September holds events such as greasy-pole climbing.

Cumberland wrestlers

Sheep resting at Glenridding, on the southwest shore of Ullswater

hand-painted wallpaper, and a panelled 18th-century drawing room. Several small museums occupy various outbuildings, and the gardens contain a fine collection of fragrant shrub roses and a huge silver fir.

Sumptuous Chinese drawing room at Dalemain

Ullswater ➍

Cumbria. ➡ *Penrith.* ℹ *Main car park, Glenridding, Penrith (017684 82414).* **www.lake-district.gov.uk**

Often considered the most beautiful of all Cumbria's lakes, Ullswater stretches from gentle farmland near Penrith to dramatic hills and crags at its southern end. The main western shore road can be very busy. In summer, two restored Victorian steamers ply

regularly from Pooley Bridge to Glenridding. One of the best walks crosses the eastern shore from Glenridding to Hallin Fell and the moorland of Martindale. The western side passes Gowbarrow, where Wordsworth's immortalized "host of golden daffodils" bloom in spring *(see p366)*.

Keswick ➎

Cumbria. ⬛ *5,000.* ℹ *Moot Hall, Market Sq (017687 72645).* **www.keswick.org**

Popular as a tourist venue since the advent of the railway in Victorian times, Keswick now has guest houses, a summer repertory theatre, outdoor equipment shops and a serious parking problem in high season. Its most striking central building is the **Moot Hall**, dating from 1813, now used as the tourist office. The town prospered on wool and leather until, in Tudor times, deposits of graphite were discovered. Mining then took over as the main industry and Keswick became an important centre for pencil manufacture. In World War II, hollow pencils were made to hide espionage maps on thin paper. The factory includes the **Pencil Museum** with interesting

audiovisual shows. Among the many fine exhibits at the **Keswick Museum and Art Gallery** are the original manuscripts of Lakeland writers, musical stones and many other curiosities.

To the east of the town lies the ancient stone circle of Castlerigg, thought to be older than Stonehenge.

🏛 **Pencil Museum**
Carding Mill Lane. **Tel** 017687 73626.
◯ *daily.* ⬤ *1 Jan, 25, 26 Dec.* 🎫
♿ 🔲 **www.pencilmuseum.co.uk**

🏛 **Keswick Museum and Art Gallery**
Fitz Park, Station Rd. **Tel** 017687 73263. ◯ *Easter–Oct: Tue–Sat & public hols.* ♿ 🔲

Outdoor equipment shop in Keswick

Northern Fells and Lakes ❻

The rare red squirrel, native to the area

Many visitors praise this northern area of the Lake District National Park for its scenery and geological interest (*see pp352–3*). It is ideal walking country, and nearby Derwentwater, Thirlmere and Bassenthwaite provide endless scenic views, rambles and opportunities for watersports. Large areas surrounding the regional centre of Keswick (*see p359*) are accessible only on foot, particularly the huge mass of hills known as Back of Skiddaw – located between Skiddaw and Caldbeck – or the Helvellyn range, east of Thirlmere.

The Whinlatter Pass is an easy route from Keswick to the farmland of Lorton Vale. It gives good view of Bassenthwaite Lak and a glimpse of Grisedale Pike.

Bassenthwaite is best view from the east shore; howe accessibility is limited. Par is easier from the west si

Lorton Vale
The lush, green farmland south of Cockermouth creates a marked contrast with the more rugged mountain landscapes of the central Lake District. In the village of Low Lorton is the private manor house of Lorton Hall, dating from the 15th century.

Derwentwater
Surrounded by woodland slopes and fells, this attractive oval lake is dotted with tiny islands. One of these was inhabited by St Herbert, a disciple of St Cuthbert (see p419), who lived there as a hermit until 687. A boat from Keswick provides a lake excursion.

THE MAJOR PEAKS

The Lake District hills are the highest in England. Although they seem small by Alpine or world standards, the scale of the surrounding terrain makes them look extremely grand. Some of the most important peaks are shown on the following pages. Each peak is regarded as having its own personality. This section shows the Skiddaw fells, which are north of Keswick.

KEY

▬ From ① Blencathra to ② Cockermouth (*see opposite*)

▬ From ③ Grisedale Pike to ④ the Old Man of Coniston (*see pp362–3*)

▬ From ⑤ the Old Man of Coniston to ⑥ Windermere and Tarn Crag (*see pp364–5*)

— National Park boundary

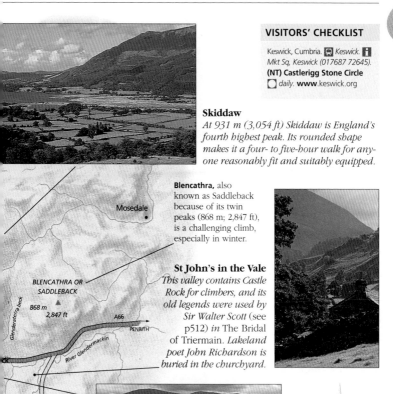

Skiddaw

At 931 m (3,054 ft) Skiddaw is England's fourth highest peak. Its rounded shape makes it a four- to five-hour walk for anyone reasonably fit and suitably equipped.

Blencathra, also known as Saddleback because of its twin peaks (868 m; 2,847 ft), is a challenging climb, especially in winter.

St John's in the Vale

This valley contains Castle Rock for climbers, and its old legends were used by Sir Walter Scott (see p512) in The Bridal of Triermain. *Lakeland poet John Richardson is buried in the churchyard.*

Mosedale

BLENCATHRA OR SADDLEBACK

868 m
2,847 ft

A66
PENRITH

River Glendermackin

Legburthwaite

Thirlmere was created as a reservoir to serve Manchester in 1879.

Castlerigg Stone Circle

Described by Keats (see p123) as "a dismal cirque of Druid stones upon a forlorn moor", *these ancient stones overlook Skiddaw, Helvellyn and Crag Hill.*

KEY

ℹ️	Information
▬	Major road
▭	Minor road
☀	Viewpoint

0 kilometres	5
0 miles	3

②

Blencathra
868 m (2,847 ft)
Hart Side

Great Dodd

Ullock Pike

Helvellyn
950 m (3,116 ft)

Dodd Wood

Keswick
Derwentwater
Sale Fell

Lord's Seat

Ullscarf

Lorton Fell
Ullscarf

Grisedale Pike 790 m
(2,591 ft)

Great Cockup
Great Calva

Skiddaw
931 m
(3,054 ft)

A591

B5291

Bassenthwaite Lake

A66 to
Cockermouth

Bassenthwaite Village

Crummock Water, one of the quieter "western lakes"

Cockermouth ⓿

Cumbria. 🏯 *8,000.* 🚉
Workington. 🚌 ℹ️ *Town Hall,
Market St (01900 822634).*
www.western-lakedistrict.co.uk

Colourwashed terraces and
restored workers' cottages
beside the river are especially
attractive in the busy market
town of Cockermouth, which
dates from the 12th century.
The place not to miss is the
handsome **Wordsworth
House**, in the Main Street,
where the poet was born *(see
p366)*. This fine Georgian

building still contains a few of
the family's possessions, and
is furnished in the style of the
late 18th century. Wordsworth
mentions the attractive
terraced garden, which overlooks the River Derwent, in
his *Prelude*. The local parish
church contains a Wordsworth
memorial window.

Cockermouth **castle** is partly
ruined but still inhabited and
closed to the public. The town
has small museums of printing,
toys and a mineral collection,
and an art gallery. The
Jennings Brewery invites
visitors for tours and tastings.

🏛 **Wordsworth House**
(NT) Main St. **Tel** 01900 820884. ◯
Mar–Oct: Mon–Sat. 🔲 *non-members.*
🔲 **www**.wordsworthhouse.org.uk

🍺 **Jennings Brewery**
Castle Brewery. **Tel** 0845 1297185.
◯ *Mon–Sat (Jul, Aug: daily).* 🔲
🔲 **www**.jenningsbrewery.co.uk

Newlands Valley ⓿

Cumbria. 🚉 *Workington then bus.* 🚌
Cockermouth. ℹ️ *Town Hall, Market
St, Cockermouth (01900 822634);
Market Sq, Keswick (017687 72645).*
www.lake-district.gov.uk

From the gently wooded
shores of Derwentwater, the
Newlands Valley runs through
a scattering of farms towards
rugged heights of 335 m
(1,100 ft) at the top of the
pass, where steps lead
to the waterfall, Moss Force.
Grisedale Pike, Grasmoor
and Knott Rigg all provide
excellent fell walks. Local
mineral deposits of copper,
graphite, lead and even small
amounts of gold and silver
were extensively mined here
from Elizabethan times
onwards. **Little Town** was
used as a setting by Beatrix
Potter *(see p367)* in *The Tale
of Mrs Tiggywinkle.*

Kitchen, with an old range and tiled floor, at Wordsworth House

③

Blencathra
*868 m
(2,847 ft)*

**Grisedale
Pike**
*790 m
(2,591 ft)*

Grasmoor
850 m (2788 ft)
Wandope

White
Pike

Robinson
Great Dodd

Fleetwith Pike

Dalehead

Raise

Looking
Stead

Helvellyn
*950 m
(3,118 ft)*

③

④

Knott Rigg

Crummock Water

Ennerdale

Buttermere

Buttermere village

Innominate Tarn
and Haystacks

Pillar

Mosedale

Black Sail
Pass

Kirk Fell

Great
*899 m
(2,949*

Buttermere **9**

Cumbria. 🚃 Penrith. 🚌 Cocker-mouth. 🚌 Penrith to Keswick; Keswick to Buttermere. **ℹ️** Town Hall, Market St, Cockermouth (01900 822634).

Interlinking with Crummock Water and Loweswater, Buttermere and its surround-ings contain some of the most appealing countryside in the region. Often known as the "western lakes", the three are remote enough not to become too crowded. Buttermere is a jewel amid grand fells: High Stile, Red Pike and Haystacks. Here the ashes of the cele-brated hill-walker and author of fell-walking books, A W Wainwright, are scattered.

The village of Buttermere, with its handful of houses and inns, is a popular starting point for walks round all three lakes. Loweswater is hardest to reach and therefore the quietest, surrounded by woods and hills. Nearby Scale Force is the highest waterfall in the Lake District, plunging 36 m (120 ft).

Verdant valley of Borrowdale, a favourite with artists

Borrowdale **10**

Cumbria. 🚃 Workington. 🚌 Cockermouth. **ℹ️** Town Hall, Market St, Cockermouth (01900 822634).

This romantic valley, subject of a myriad sketches and watercolours before photo-graphy stole the scene, lies beside the densely wooded shores of Derwentwater under towering crags. It is a popular trip from Keswick and a great variety of walks are possible along the valley.

The tiny hamlet of **Grange** is one of the prettiest spots, where the valley narrows dramatically to form the "Jaws of Borrowdale". Nearby Castle Crag has superb views.

From Grange you can com-plete the circuit of Derwent-water along the western shore, or move southwards to the more open farmland around Seatoller. As you head south by road, look out for a National Trust sign *(see p29)* to the **Bowder Stone**, a delicately poised block weighing nearly 2,000 tonnes, which may have fallen from the crags above or been deposited by a glacier millions of years ago.

Two attractive hamlets in Borrowdale are **Rosthwaite** and **Stonethwaite**. Also worth a detour, preferably on foot, is Watendlath village, off a side road near the famous beauty spot of **Ashness Bridge**.

WALKING IN THE LAKE DISTRICT

Two long-distance footpaths pass through the Lake District's most spectacular scenery. The 70 mile (110 km) Cumbrian Way runs from Carlisle to Ulverston via Keswick and Coniston. The western section of the Coast-to-Coast Walk *(see pp36–7)* passes through this area. There are hundreds of shorter walks along lake shores, nature trails or following more challenging uphill routes. Walkers should stick to paths to avoid erosion, and check weather conditions at National Park information centres.

Typical Lake District stile over dry-stone wall

Scafell Pike 978 m (3,210 ft) · Langdale Pikes · Hard Knott 550 m (1,803 ft) · Hardknott Pass · Carrs · Grey Friar · Swirl How · Dow Crag · Old Man of Coniston 803 m (2,633 ft) · Caw

East-water · Crinkle Crags 924 m (2,816 ft) · Blea Tarn · Wastwater Screes · Harter Fell · Eskdale · Ravenglass and Eskdale Railway · Seathwaite Tarn · Seathwaite · River Duddon

④

Convivial Wasdale Head Inn at Wasdale Head

Wastwater ⓫

Cumbria. ⌗ *Whitehaven.* 🛈 *12 Main St, Egremont (01946 820693).*

A silent reflection of truly awesome surroundings, black, brooding **Wastwater** is a mysterious, evocative lake. The road from Nether Wasdale continues along its northwest side. Along its eastern flank loom walls of sheer scree over 600 m (2,000 ft) high. Beneath them the water looks inky black, whatever the weather, plunging an icy 80 m (260 ft) from the waterline to the bottom to form England's deepest lake. You can walk along the screes, but it is an uncomfortable and dangerous scramble. Boating on the lake is banned for conservation reasons, but fishing permits are available from the nearby National Trust camp site.

At **Wasdale Head** lies one of Britain's grandest views: the austere pyramid of **Great Gable**, centrepiece of a fine mountain composition, with the huge forms of Scafell and **Scafell Pike**. The scenery is utterly unspoilt, and the only buildings lie at the far end of the lake: an inn and a tiny church commemorating fallen climbers. Here the road ends, and you must turn back or take to your feet, following signs for Black Sail Pass and Ennerdale, or walk up the grand fells ahead. Wasdale's irresistible backdrop was the inspiration of the first serious British mountaineers, who flocked here during the 19th century, insouciantly clad in tweed jackets, carrying little more than a length of rope slung over their shoulders.

Eskdale ⓬

Cumbria. ⌗ *Ravenglass then narrow-gauge railway to Eskdale (Easter–Oct: daily; Dec–Feb: phone to check).* 🛈 *12 Main St, Egremont (01946 820693).* **www**.eskdale.info

The pastoral delights of Eskdale are best encountered over the gruelling **Hardknott Pass**, which is the most taxing drive in the Lake District, with steep gradients. You can pause at the 393-m (1,291-ft) summit to explore the Roman **Hardknott Fort** or enjoy the lovely view. As you descend into Eskdale, rhododendrons and pines flourish in a landscape of small hamlets, narrow lanes and gentle farmland. The main settlements below are the attractive village of Boot and coastal Ravenglass, both with old corn mills.

Just south of Ravenglass is the impressive **Muncaster Castle**, the richly furnished home of the Pennington family. Another way to enjoy the scenery is to take the miniature railway (La'l Ratty) from Ravenglass to Dalegarth.

⌂ **Muncaster Castle**
Ravenglass. **Tel** *01229 717614.* **Castle** ◯ *mid-Feb–mid-Nov: Sun–Fri (pm) & public hols.* **Garden** ◯ *Feb–Dec: daily.* 🅿 🚻 🅶 *ground floor and garden.* **www**.muncaster.co.uk

Remains of the Roman Hardknott Fort, Eskdale

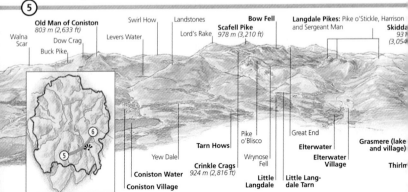

⑤

Old Man of Coniston
803 m (2,633 ft)

Walna Scar

Dow Crag

Buck Pike

Swirl How

Levers Water

Landstones

Lord's Rake

Scafell Pike
978 m (3,210 ft)

Bow Fell

Langdale Pikes: Pike o'Stickle, Harrison and Sergeant Man

Skidda
93 (3,054

⑥

⑤

Yew Dale

Coniston Water

Coniston Village

Tarn Hows

Crinkle Crags
924 m (2,816 ft)

Little Langdale

Pike o'Blisco

Wrynose Fell

Little Langdale Tarn

Great End

Little Lang-dale Tarn

Elterwater

Elterwater Village

Grasmere (lake and village)

Thirlm

Autumnal view of Seathwaite, in the Duddon Valley, a popular centre for walkers and climbers

Duddon Valley ⓭

Cumbria. ☒ Foxfield, Ulverston.
🚹 The Square, Broughton-in-Furness
(01229 716115; Easter–Oct only).
www.southlakeland.gov.uk

Also known as Dunnerdale,
this picturesque tract of
countryside inspired 35 of
Wordsworth's sonnets (see
p366). The prettiest stretch lies
between Ulpha and Cockley
Beck. In autumn the colours
of heather moors and a light
sprinkling of birch trees are
particularly beautiful. Stepping
stones and bridges span the
river at intervals, the most
charming being Birk's Bridge,
near Seathwaite. At the southern end of the valley, where
the River Duddon meets the
sea at Duddon Sands, is the
pretty village of Broughton-
in-Furness. Note the stone
slabs used for fish on market
day in the square.

Langdale ⓮

Cumbria. ☒ Windermere. 🚹 Market
Cross, Ambleside (015394 32582).
www.southlakeland.gov.uk

Stretching from Skelwith
Bridge, where the Brathay
surges powerfully over waterfalls, to the summits of Great
Langdale is the two-pronged
Langdale Valley. Walkers and
climbers throng here to take
on **Pavey Ark**, **Pike o'Stickle**,
Crinkle Crags and **Bow Fell**.
The local mountain rescue
teams are the busiest in Britain.

Great Langdale is the more
spectacular valley and it is
often crowded, but quieter
Little Langdale has many
attractions too. It is worth
completing the circuit back to
Ambleside via the southern
route, stopping at Blea Tarn.
Reedy **Elterwater** is a picturesque spot, once a site of the
gunpowder industry. Wrynose
Pass, west of Little Langdale,
climbs to 390 m (1,281 ft), a
warm-up for Hardknott Pass
further on. At its top is Three
Shires Stone, marking the
former boundary of the old
counties of Cumberland,
Westmorland and Lancashire.

Rydal Water, one of the major attractions of the Lake District

Grasmere and Rydal ⑮

Cumbria. **Grasmere** 🏛 *700.*
Rydal 🏛 *100.* 🚍 *Grasmere.*
ℹ *Central Buildings, Market Cross,
Ambleside (015394 32582).*
www.lake-district.gov.uk

The poet William Wordsworth lived in both these villages on the shores of two lakes. Fairfield, Nab Scar and Loughrigg Fell rise steeply above their reedy shores and offer good opportunities for walking. Grasmere is now a sizable settlement, and the famous Grasmere sports *(see p358)* attract large crowds every August.

The Wordsworth family is buried in St Oswald's Church, and crowds flock to the annual ceremony of strewing the church's earth floor with fresh rushes. Most visitors head for **Dove Cottage**, where the poet spent his most creative years. The museum in the barn behind includes such artefacts as the great man's socks. The Wordsworths moved to a larger house, **Rydal Mount**, in

Rydal in 1813 and lived here until 1850. The grounds have waterfalls and a summerhouse. Dora's Field nearby is a blaze of daffodils in spring and Fairfield Horseshoe offers an energetic, challenging walk.

🏛 Dove Cottage and the Wordsworth Museum
Off A591 nr Grasmere. **Tel** 015394 35544. ☐ *daily.* ● *24–26 Dec, mid-Jan–mid-Feb.* 🖼️ 🗓️ 🚻 ◻
www.wordsworth.org.uk

🏛 Rydal Mount
Rydal. **Tel** 015394 33002. ☐ *Mar–Oct: daily; Nov–Feb: Wed–Mon.* ● *Dec & Jan.* 🖼️ 🚻 *limited.* ◻

Ambleside ⑯

Cumbria. 🏛 *3,400.* 🚍
ℹ *Central Buildings, Market Cross (015394 32582).* 🛒 *Wed.*
www.lake-district.gov.uk

Ambleside has good road connections to all parts of the Lakes and is an attractive base, especially for walkers and climbers. Mainly Victorian in character, it has a good range of outdoor clothing, crafts and specialist food shops. An enterprising little cinema and a summer classical music festival add life in the evenings. Sights in town are small-scale: the remnants of the Roman fort of Galava, AD 79, Stock Ghyll Force waterfall and **Bridge House**, now a National Trust information centre.

Environs: Within easy reach are the wooded Rothay valley and **Touchstone Interiors** at Skelwith Bridge, with their contemporary design products. At nearby Troutbeck is the restored farmhouse of **Townend**, dating from 1626,

The tiny Bridge House over Stock Beck in Ambleside

WILLIAM WORDSWORTH (1770–1850)
Best known of the Romantic poets, Wordsworth was born in the Lake District and spent most of his life there. After school in Hawkshead and a period at Cambridge, a legacy enabled him to pursue his literary career. He settled at Dove Cottage with his sister Dorothy and in 1802 married an old school friend, Mary Hutchinson. They lived simply, walking, bringing up their children and receiving visits from poets such as Coleridge and de Quincey. Wordsworth's prose works include one of the earliest guidebooks to the Lake District.

BEATRIX POTTER AND THE LAKE DISTRICT

Although best known for her children's stories with characters such as Peter Rabbit and Jemima Puddleduck, which she also illustrated, Beatrix Potter (1866–1943) became a champion of conservation in the Lake District after moving there in 1906. She married William Heelis, devoted herself to farming, and was an expert on Herdwick sheep. To conserve her beloved countryside, she donated land to the National Trust.

Cover illustration of *Jemima Puddleduck* (1908)

whose interior gives an insight into Lakeland domestic life.

🏛 **Touchstone Interiors**
Skelwith Bridge. *Tel* 015394 34002. ◻ daily. ● 24–26 Dec. 🔲 🔲 🔲

🏛 **Townend**
(NT) Troutbeck, Windermere. *Tel* 015394 32628. ◻ Apr–Oct: Wed–Sun; Sun & bank hol Mon: pm. 🔲

Windermere ⑰

Cumbria. 🚉 *Windermere.* 🚌
Victoria St. 🛈 Victoria St (015394 46499) or Glebe Rd, Bowness-on-Windermere (015394 42895). **www**.southlakeland.gov.uk

At over 10 miles (16 km) long, this dramatic watery expanse is England's largest mere. Industrial magnates built mansions around its shores long before the railway arrived. Stately **Brockhole**, now a national park visitor centre, was one such grand

estate. When the railway reached Windermere in 1847, it enabled crowds of workers to visit the area on day trips.

Today, a year-round car ferry service connects the lake's east and west shores (it runs between Ferry Nab and Ferry House), and summer steamers link Lakeside, Bowness and Ambleside on the north-south axis. Belle Isle, a wooded island on which a unique round house stands, is one of the lake's most attractive features, but landing is not permitted. **Fell Foot Park** is at the south end of the lake, and there are good walks on the northwest shore. A quite stunning viewpoint is Orrest Head 238 m (784 ft) northeast of Windermere town.

Environs: Bowness-on-Windermere, on the east shore, is a hugely popular centre. Many of its buildings display Victorian details, and

St Martin's Church dates back to the 15th century. The **Windermere Steamboat Museum** has a collection of superbly restored craft, and one of these, *Swallow*, makes regular lake trips. The **World of Beatrix Potter** recreates her characters in an exhibition, and a film tells her life story.

Beatrix Potter wrote many of her books at **Hill Top**, the 17th-century farmhouse at Near Sawrey, northwest of Windermere. Hill Top is furnished with many of Potter's possessions, and left as it was in her lifetime. The **Beatrix Potter Gallery** in Hawkshead holds annual exhibitions of her manuscripts and illustrations.

🛈 **Brockhole Visitor Centre**
On A591. *Tel* 015394 46601. ◻ Feb–Nov: daily. 🔲 🔲 🔲

🍃 **Fell Foot Park**
(NT) Newby Bridge. *Tel* 015395 31273. ◻ daily. 🔲 🔲

🏛 **Windermere Steamboat Museum**
Rayrigg Rd, Windermere. *Tel* 015394 45565. ◻ late Mar–Nov: daily. 🔲 🔲 🔲 🔲 🔲

🏛 **World of Beatrix Potter**
The Old Laundry, Crag Brow. *Tel* 015394 88444. ◻ daily. ● 25 Dec, last three wks in Jan. 🔲 🔲 🔲 🔲 limited. **www**.hop-skip-jump.com

🏚 **Hill Top**
(NT) Near Sawrey, Ambleside. *Tel* 015394 36269. ◻ Apr–Oct: Sat–Thu. 🔲 🔲

🏛 **Beatrix Potter Gallery**
(NT) The Square, Hawkshead. *Tel* 015394 36355. ◻ Apr–Oct: Sat–Wed. 🔲 🔲

Boats moored along the shore at Ambleside, the north end of Windermere

Peaceful Coniston Water, the setting of Arthur Ransome's novel, *Swallows and Amazons* (1930)

Coniston Water ⑱

Cumbria. ⚡ *Windermere then bus.* 🚌 *Ambleside then bus.* ⓘ *Coniston car park, Ruskin Ave (015394 41533).* **www**.conistontic.org

For the finest view of this stretch of water just outside the Lake District, you need to climb. The 19th-century art critic, writer and philosopher John Ruskin, had a fine view from his house, **Brantwood**, where his paintings and memorabilia can be seen today. Contemporary art exhibitions and events take place throughout the year.

An enjoyable excursion is the summer lake trip from Coniston Pier on the National Trust steam yacht, *Gondola*, calling at Brantwood. Coniston was also the scene of Donald Campbell's fatal attempt on the world water speed record in 1967. The green slate village of Coniston, once a centre for copper-mining, now caters for local walkers.

Also interesting is the traffic-free village of **Hawkshead** to the northwest, with its quaint alleyways and timber-framed houses. To the south is the vast Grizedale Forest, dotted with woodland sculptures.

Just north of Coniston Water is the man-made **Tarn Hows**, a landscaped tarn surrounded by woods. There is a pleasant climb up the 803 m (2,635 ft) Old Man of Coniston.

🏛 **Brantwood**
Off B5285, nr Coniston. **Tel** *015394 41396.* ⓘ *mid-Mar–mid-Nov: daily; mid-Nov–mid-Mar: Wed–Sun.* 🎫 🍴 🅿 ⓘ **www**.brantwood.org.uk

Kendal ⑲

Cumbria. 🏠 *26,000.* ⚡ ⓘ *Town Hall, Highgate (01539 725758).* 🛒 *Wed, Sat.* **www**.southlakeland.gov.uk

A busy market town, Kendal is the administrative centre of the region and the southern gateway to the Lake District. Built in grey limestone, it has an arts centre, the **Brewery**, and a central area which is best enjoyed on foot. **Abbot Hall,**

Kendal mint cake, the famous lakeland energy-booster for walkers

built in 1759, has paintings by Turner and Romney as well as Gillows furniture. In addition, the hall's stable block contains the **Museum of Lakeland Life**, with occasional lively workshops demonstrating local crafts and trades. There are dioramas of geology and wild-life in the **Museum of Natural History and Archaeology**. About 3 miles (5 km) south of the town is 14th-century

---

Sizergh Castle, with a fortified tower, carved fireplaces and a lovely garden.

🏛 **Abbot Hall Art Gallery & Museum of Lakeland Life**
Kendal. **Tel** *01539 722464.* ⓘ *mid-Jan–20 Dec: Mon–Sat.* 🎫 ⓖ *gallery.* 📷 *by arrangement.* 🅿 ⓘ **www**.abbothall.org.uk

🏛 **Kendal Museum of Natural History and Archaeology**
Station Rd. **Tel** *01539 721374.* ⓘ *Thu–Sat.* 🅿 ⓘ **www**. kendalmuseum.org.uk

⚓ **Sizergh Castle**
(NT) off A591 & A590. **Tel** *015395 60951.* ⓘ *Apr–Oct: Sun–Thu.* 🎫 ⓖ *ground floor & grounds.* 🅿 ⓘ

Furness Peninsula ⑳

Cumbria. ⚡ 🚌 *Barrow-in-Furness.* ⓘ *Forum 28, Duke St, Barrow-in-Furness (01229 876505).* **www**.barrowtourism.co.uk

Barrow-in-Furness *(see p349)* is the peninsula's main town. Its **Dock Museum**, built over a Victorian dock where ships were repaired, traces the history of Barrow using interactive computer displays.

Ruins of the red sandstone walls of **Furness Abbey** remain in the wooded Vale of Deadly Nightshade, with a small exhibition of monastic life. The historic town of Ulverston received its charter in 1280. Stan Laurel, of Laurel and Hardy fame, was born here in 1890. His memorabilia **museum** has a cinema. In the nearby village of Gleaston is the **Gleaston Water Mill**, a 400-year-old, working corn mill.

🏛 **Dock Museum**
North Rd, Barrow-in-Furness. *Tel* 01229 876400. ◯ *Easter–Oct: Tue–Sun; Nov–Easter: Wed–Sun (Sat, Sun: pm); public hols.* 🔲 ◻ ◻
www.dockmuseum.org.uk

⛪ **Furness Abbey**
Vale of Deadly Nightshade. *Tel* 01229 823420. ◯ *Easter–Sep: daily; Oct–Easter: Thu–Mon.* ◉ *1 Jan, 24–26 Dec.* ◻ ◻ ◻ *limited.*

♒ **Gleaston Water Mill**
Gleaston. *Tel* 01229 869244. ◯ *Tue–Sun.*

🏛 **Laurel and Hardy Museum**
Upper Brook St, Ulverston. *Tel* 01229 582292. ◯ *daily.* ◉ *Jan, 25 Dec.* ◻ ◻

Staircase at Holker Hall

Cartmel ㉑

Cumbria. 🚶 *700.* 🛈 *Main St, Grange-over-Sands (015395 34026).* www.grangeoversands.net

The highlight of this pretty village is its 12th-century **priory**, one of the finest Cumbrian churches. Little remains of the original priory except the gatehouse in the village centre. The restored church has an attractive east window, a stone-carved 14th-century tomb, and beautiful misericords.

Cartmel also boasts a small racecourse. The village has given its name to its surroundings, a hilly district of green farmland with mixed woodland and limestone scars.

A major local attraction is **Holker Hall**, former residence of the Dukes of Devonshire. Inside are lavishly furnished rooms, with fine marble fireplaces, and a superb oak staircase. Outside are stunning gardens and a deer park.

♒ **Holker Hall**
Cark-in-Cartmel. *Tel* 015395 58328. ◯ *Mar–Oct: Sun–Fri.* ◻ ◻ *limited.* ◻ *by arrangement.* ◻ ◻
www.holker-hall.co.uk

Levens Hall ㉒

Nr Kendal, Cumbria. *Tel* 015395 60321. 🚌 *from Kendal or Lancaster.* ◯ *Apr–mid-Oct: Sun–Thu.* ◻ ◻ ◻ *gardens only.* ◻
www.levenshall.co.uk

The outstanding attraction of this Elizabethan mansion is its topiary, but the house itself has much to offer. Built around a 13th-century tower, it contains a fine collection of Jacobean furniture and water-colours by Peter de Wint (1784–1849). Also of note are the ornate ceilings, Charles II dining chairs, the earliest example of English patchwork and the gilded hearts on the drainpipes.

The 18th-century Turret Clock has a single hand, a common design of the period.

Main entrance

The yew and box topiary was designed in 1694 by French horticulturist Guillaume Beaumont.

Box hedges were a common component of geometrically designed gardens of this period.

Over 300 years old, the garden's box-edged beds are filled with colourful herbaceous displays.

The complex topiary, shaped into cones, spirals and pyramids, is kept in shape by gardeners. Some specimens are 6 m (20 ft) high.

Morecambe Bay, looking northwest towards Barrow-in-Furness

Morecambe Bay ㉓

Lancs. 🚉 *Morecambe.* ⛴ *Heysham (to Isle of Man).* 🛈 *Marine Rd. (01524 582808).* **www**.lancaster.gov.uk

The best way to explore Morecambe Bay is by train from Ulverston to Arnside. The track follows a series of low viaducts across a huge expanse of glistening tidal flats where thousands of wading birds feed and breed. The bay is one of the most important bird reservations in the country. On the Cumbrian side of the bay, retirement homes have expanded the sedate Victorian resort of Grange-over-Sands, which grew up after the arrival of the railway in 1857. Nearby, **Hampsfield Fell** and **Humphrey Head Point** give fine views along the bay.

Leighton Hall ㉔

Carnforth, Lancashire. **Tel** 01524 734 474. 🚌 *to Yealand Conyers (from Lancaster).* ◯ *May–Sep: 2–5pm Tue–Fri & bank hols (also Sun in Aug).* 💷 & *ground floor only.* 📷 ▢ ▢
www.leightonhall.co.uk

Leighton Hall's estate dates back to the 13th century, but most of the building is 19th-century, including its Neo-Gothic façade. It is owned by the Gillow family, of the Lancastrian furniture business, whose products are now prized antiques. Excellent pieces can be seen here, including a ladies' work-box inlaid with biblical scenes. In

the afternoon, weather permitting, the hall's large collection of birds of prey display their aerial prowess.

Lancaster ㉕

Lancashire. 🏘 *50,000.* 🚉 🚌 🛈 *Castle Hill (01524 32878).* 🛒 *Mon–Sat.* **www**.lancaster.gov.uk

This county town of Lancashire is tiny compared to Liverpool or Manchester (now counties in their own right), but it has a long history. The Romans named it after their camp over the River Lune. Originally a defensive site, it developed into a prosperous port largely on the proceeds of the slave trade. Today, its university and cultural life still thrive. The Norman **Lancaster Castle** was expanded in the 14th and 16th centuries. It has been a crown court and a prison since the 13th century. The Shire Hall is decorated with 600 heraldic shields. Some fragments from Hadrian's Tower (which has a collection of torture instruments) are 2,000 years old.

The nearby priory church of **St Mary** is on Castle Hill. Its main features include a Saxon doorway and carved 14th-century choir stalls. There is an outstanding museum of furniture in the 17th-century **Judge's Lodgings**, while the **Maritime Museum**, in the Georgian custom house on St George's Quay, contains displays on the port's history. The **City Museum**, based in the old town hall, concentrates on the history of Lancaster.

The splendid **Lune Aqueduct** carries the canal over the River Lune on five wide arches. Other attractions are found in **Williamson Park**, site of

Tawny eagle at Leighton Hall

the 1907 Ashton Memorial. This folly was built by the local linoleum magnate and politician, Lord Ashton.

CROSSING THE SANDS

Morecambe Bay sands are very dangerous. Travellers used to cut across the bay at low tide to shorten the long trail around the Kent estuary. Many perished as they were caught by rising tides or quicksand, and sea fogs hid the paths. Locals who knew the bay became guides, and today you can travel with a guide from Kents Bank to Hest Bank near Arnside.

The High Sheriff of Lancaster Crossing Morecambe Sands (anon)

There are fine views from the top of this 67 m (220 ft) domed structure. Opposite is the tropical butterfly house and the pavilion café.

♠ Lancaster Castle
Castle Parade. **Tel** 01524 64998. ○ daily. ● mid-Dec–early Jan. only (limited when court is in session). www.lancastercastle.com

� Judge's Lodgings
Church St. **Tel** 01524 32808. ○ Apr–Jun, Oct: daily (Sat & Sun: pm only); Jul–Sep: daily. ● Nov–Good Fri. limited.

⑪ Maritime Museum
Custom House, St George's Quay. **Tel** 01524 382264. ○ daily (Nov–Easter: pm). ● 24–26, 31 Dec, 1 Jan. www.lancashire.gov.uk

⑪ City Museum
Market Sq. **Tel** 01524 64637. ○ Mon–Sat. ● 24 Dec–2 Jan.

♣ Williamson Park
Wyresdale Rd. **Tel** 01524 33318. ○ daily. limited. www.williamsonpark.com

Ribble Valley ㉖

Lancashire. 🚋 Clitheroe. 🚌 Market Place, Clitheroe (01200 425566). 🚌 Tue, Thu, Sat. www.ribblevalley.gov.uk

Clitheroe, a small market town with a hilltop castle, is a good centre for exploring the Ribble Valley's rivers and old villages, such as Slaidburn. Ribchester has a **Roman Museum**, and there is a ruined **Cistercian abbey** at Whalley. To the east is 560 m (1,830 ft) Pendle Hill, with a Bronze Age burial mound at its peak.

⑪ Roman Museum
Ribchester. **Tel** 01254 878261. ○ daily. by arrangement.

♠ Whalley Abbey
Whalley. **Tel** 01254 828400. ○ daily. ● 24 Dec–2 Jan. www.whalleyabbey.co.uk

Blackpool ㉗

Lancashire. 🏠 150,000. ✈ 🚋 🚌 Clifton St (01253 478222). www.visitblackpool.com

British holiday patterns have changed in the past few decades, and Blackpool is no longer the apogee of seaside entertainment, but it remains a unique experience. A wall of amusement arcades, piers, bingo halls and fast-food stalls stretch behind the sands. At night, entertainers strut their stuff under the bright lights. The town attracts thousands of visitors in September and October when the Illuminations trace the skeleton of the 158 m (518 ft) Blackpool Tower. Blackpool's resort life dates back to the 18th century, but it burst into prominence when the railway first arrived in 1840, bringing Lancastrian workers to their holiday resort.

Coming from the Mill (1930) by L S Lowry (See p375)

Blackpool Tower, painted gold for its centenary in 1994

Salford Quays ㉘

Salford. 🚋 Harbour City (from Manchester). 🚌 The Lowry, Pier 8 (0161 848 8601). www.visitsalford.info

The Quays, to the west of Manchester city centre (15 minutes by tram), were once the terminal docks for the **Manchester Ship Canal**. After the docks closed in 1982, the area became sadly run down but since the 1990s a massive redevelopment plan has changed the area dramatically. A world-class business, cultural and residential area of great architectural and regional significance has been created and more people are now employed at the Quays than in its heyday as a major seaport.

There is a wealth of entertainment, leisure and cultural facilities on offer, including **The Lowry** (see p375), the **Manchester United Museum** (see p375), the **Imperial War Museum North** (see p375), the **Salford Museum and Art Gallery** and The Lowry Outlet Mall, as well as numerous bars, restaurants and shops.

There are various water-based activities and ship-canal cruises. The Quays was also a venue for the Commonwealth Games in 2002, and now hosts the Triathlon World Cup.

⑪ Salford Museum and Art Gallery
Peel Park, The Crescent. **Tel** 0161 778 0800. ○ Mon–Fri, Sat–Sun pm. ● 25, 26 Dec.

Manchester 29

Sign for the John Rylands Library

Manchester dates back to Roman times, when in AD 79, Agricola set up a base called Mancunium. It rose to prominence in the late 18th century, when Richard Arkwright introduced cotton processing. By 1830, the first railway linked Manchester and Liverpool, and in 1894 the Manchester Ship Canal (see p371) opened, allowing cargovessels inland. Civic buildings sprang up from the proceeds of cotton wealth, but these were in stark contrast to the slums of the millworkers. Social discontent led writers, politicians and reformers to espouse liberal or radical causes.

The achievements of football team Manchester United and the international success of bands such as The Smiths and The Stone Roses, gave Manchester a cachet of cool during the 1980s and 1990s. Devastation caused by an IRA carbombing of the city centre in 1996 was seized as an opportunity to redevelop the main shopping areas. This regeneration has since spread to other areas of the city, notably the old dockside area of Salford Quays.

Exploring Manchester

Manchester is a fine, compact city with much to see in its central areas. The Victorian era of cotton wealth has gifted the city an imposing heritage of industrial architecture, much of which is providing sites for development. The former central railway station, for example, is now **Manchester Central**, a huge exhibition and conference complex. Among other fine 19th-century buildings are the dramatic **John Rylands Library** on Deansgate, founded over 100 years ago by the widow of a local cotton millionaire, and the 1856 Renaissance-style **Free Trade Hall**, now the Radisson Edwardian hotel, which stands on the site of the Peterloo Massacre.

Urbis, an interactive attraction on life in cities

MANCHESTER CITY CENTRE

Free Trade Hall ①
John Rylands Library ③
Manchester Art Gallery ⑦
Manchester Central ②
Manchester Town Hall ④
Museum of Science and Industry in Manchester ⑧
Royal Exchange ⑤
Urbis ⑥

*Map labels:*
Victoria Station
M62
MILLER ST
Chetham's School of Music
Urbis ⑥
SHUDE HILL
Cathedral
Corn Exchange
Printworks
WITHY GROVE
Victoria Bridge
BOLTON
VICTORIA ST
EXCHANGE SQUARE
CORPORATION ST
Arndale Centre
OLDHAM LEEDS
HIGH ST
CHURCH ST
Irwell
ST MARY'S PARSONAGE
Royal Exchange ⑤
MARKET STREET
ST ANN'S ST
SPRING GARDENS
PICCADILLY
People's History Museum
BRIDGE STREET
GARTSIDE STREET
DEANSGATE
CROSS STREET
KING STREET
YORK ST
Piccadilly Gardens
PARKER ST
IRWELL STREET
John Rylands Library ③
BRAZENOSE ST
ST ALBERT SQUARE
PRINCESS ST
MOSLEY STREET
CHINA TOWN
Piccadilly Gardens Bus Station
AYTOUN STREET
LONDON ROAD
Opera House
QUAY STREET
Manchester Town Hall ④
Manchester Art Gallery ⑦
CHORLTON ST
WATER STREET
LOWER BYROM STREET
Museum of Science and Industry in Manchester ⑧
PETER STREET
Central Library
ST PETER'S SQUARE
GEORGE ST
FALKNER ST
Chorlton St Coach Station
GAY VILLAGE
Picca Sta
LIVERPOOL Salford Quays
LIVERPOOL ROAD
Upper Campfield Market
PETERS FIELDS
Free Trade Hall ①
OXFORD STREET
PORTLAND ST
PRINCESS ST
CANAL
FAIRFIELD ST
POTATO WHARF
DEANSGATE
Manchester Central Great Northern ②
Bridgewater Hall
LOWER MOSLEY STREET
WEST WHITWORTH STREET
CASTLEFIELD
Roman Fort
WHITWORTH STREET
GREAT BRIDGEWATER ST
Rochdale Canal
The Green Room
The Cornerhouse
Deansgate Station
Oxford Road Station
University
Whitworth Art Gallery
Manchester Museum
Manchester Airport 18 km (11 miles)
ALTRINCHAM

0 metres   250
0 yards   250

Key to Symbols *see back flap*

The Neo-Gothic Town Hall by Alfred Waterhouse

🏛 Manchester Town Hall

Albert Square. **Tel** 0161 234 5000.
⭘ Mon–Fri. ♿

Manchester's majestic town hall was designed by Liverpool-born Alfred Waterhouse (1830–1905), an architect who would later find fame with his Natural History Museum in London. Waterhouse won the commission for the building in an architectural competition, his design finding favour for making best use of the awkward triangular site.

The building was completed in 1877 in an English Gothic style with its roots in the 13th century. Tours take place at 2pm every other Saturday but visitors can also explore the building on their own. Sign in inside the main entrance, where a statue of General Agricola, the Roman who founded Manchester in AD 79, looks down on passers-by. The highlight is the Great Hall adorned by 12 murals painted by Ford Maddox Brown, the celebrated Pre-Raphaelite painter.

Throughout the building the decoration includes numerous examples of cotton flowers and bees, the latter a symbol of Manchester's industriousness. In the square in front of the town hall is Manchester's **Albert Memorial**, dedicated to the consort of Queen Victoria, which is similar in style but predates the one in London's Hyde Park.

🏛 Royal Exchange

St Ann's Square.
Tel 0161 833 9833.
⭘ Mon–Sat. ♿
📧 🌐 www.royal
exchange.co.uk

Built in 1729, the Manchester Royal Exchange, as it was then known, was once claimed to be the "biggest room in the world". It was built as the main trading hall of the cotton industry and at the end of the 19th century it was reckoned that over 80 percent of world trade in cloth was controlled from these premises. During the Second World War the building was severely damaged by bombs. This coincided with the decline of the cotton trade in the United Kingdom and when the Exchange was rebuilt it was reduced to half its original size. The doors were finally closed to trading in 1968. A daring scheme saw the main hall converted into a theatre in the mid-1970s with the auditorium enclosed in a high-tech structure supported by the old building's pillars; it nestles like a lunar module beneath the great dome. The rest of the Exchange building contains an arcade, shops and cafés.

🏛 Urbis

Cathedral Gdns. **Tel** 0161 605 8200.
⭘ 10am–6pm daily. 📷 for temporary exhibitions only.
♿ 🍴 📧 🌐 www.urbis.org.uk

The Urbis, opened in 2002, explores life around the world in different cities. It's housed in a striking ski slope-shaped glass building. The visit begins with a glass-elevator ride up the incline, then proceeds via an introductory film show down through three staggered floors of interactive exhibits.

The lower level houses temporary exhibitions on an urban theme, for which there is usually an admission fee. The interactive galleries, on levels two to four, explore the people, place and pulse of the modern city.

Across the plaza from Urbis is **Manchester Cathedral**, which largely dates from the 19th century but stands on a site that has been occupied by a church for over a millennium.

THE PETERLOO MASSACRE

In 1819, the working conditions of Manchester's factory workers were so bad that social tensions reached breaking point. On 16 August, 50,000 people assembled in St Peter's Field to protest at the oppressive Corn Laws. Initially peaceful, the mood darkened and the poorly trained mounted troops panicked, charging the crowd with their sabres. Eleven were killed and many wounded. The incident was called Peterloo (the Battle of Waterloo had taken place in 1815). Reforms such as the Factory Act came in that year.

G Cruikshank's Peterloo Massacre cartoon

Museum of Science and Industry, set in old passenger railway buildings

🏛 Manchester Art Gallery

Mosley St & Princess St. *Tel 0161 235 8888.* ☐ *Tue–Sun.* ⬤ *Mon (except Bank Holidays), 24–26, 31 Dec, 1 Jan, Good Fri.* 📷 ♿ 🍽 💻 🛍
www.manchestergalleries.org

The gallery reopened in summer 2002, doubling its display space after a £35 million makeover and a brand new extension by architect Sir Michael Hopkins. The original building was designed by Sir Charles Barry (1795–1860) in 1824, and contains an excellent collection of British art, notably Pre-Raphaelites such as Holman Hunt and Dante Gabriel Rossetti. Early Italian, Flemish and French Schools are also represented.

The gallery has a fine collection of decorative arts, from the Greeks to Picasso to contemporary craftworkers, in the Gallery of Craft & Design. There is also a changing programme of special exhibitions in two fantastic new galleries on the top floor. Most exhibitions are free and there is a programme of accompanying events for adults and families.

A new and lively space called the Clore Interactive Gallery offers a combination of real artworks and hands-on activities for children.

🏛 Museum of Science and Industry

Liverpool Rd. *Tel 0161 832 2244.* ☐ *daily.* ⬤ *24–26 Dec.* ♿ 💻 🍽
🖥 www.msim.org.uk

One of the largest science museums in the world, the spirit of scientific enterprise and industrial might of Manchester's heyday is conveyed here. Among the best sections are the Power Hall, a collection of working steam engines, the Electricity Gallery, tracing the history of domestic power, and an exhibition on the Liverpool and Manchester Railway. A collection of planes that made flying history are displayed in the Air and Space Gallery.

🏛 Manchester Museum

Oxford Road. *Tel 0161 275 2634,* ☐ *daily.* ♿ 🍽 💻 🛍
www.museum.man.ac.uk.

Part of Manchester University, this venerable museum (opened 1885) houses around six million items from all ages and all over the world, but it specializes in Egyptology and zoology. The collection of ancient Egyptian artefacts is one of the largest in the United Kingdom and numbers about 20,000 objects including monumental stone sculpture and a number of mummies, displayed together with their coffins and funerary

goods. There are also various sections that deal with funerary masks, tomb models and mummified animals. The zoological collections number over 600,000 objects, ranging from stuffed animals to a cast of one of the most complete skeletons of a T Rex dinosaur, which was added to the museum in November 2004.

The original museum building was designed by Alfred Water-house, the same architect responsible for the city's magnificent Town Hall (*see p373*).

🏛 Whitworth Art Gallery

University of Manchester, Oxford Rd. *Tel 0161 275 7450.* ☐ *daily (Sun: pm).* ⬤ *24 Dec–2 Jan, Good Fri.* ♿ 💻 🛍
www.whitworth.man.ac.uk

Jacob Epstein's Genesis, Whitworth Art Gallery

The Stockport-born machine tool manufacturer and engineer Sir Joseph Whitworth bequeathed money for this gallery, originally intended to be a museum of industrial art and design that would inspire the city's textile trade. Founded in 1889, it has been a part of the University of Manchester since 1958. The fine red-brick building is from the Edwardian period, while the modern interior dates from the 1960s.

The gallery houses a superb collection of drawings, sculpture, contemporary art, textiles and prints. Jacob Epstein's *Genesis* nude occupies the entrance, and there is an important collection of British watercolours by Turner (*see p91*), Girtin and others. Look out for the Japanese woodcuts and the Collection of historic and modern wallpapers, built up from donations from wallpaper manufacturers, as well as through the gallery's active Collecting Policy.

There is a well-developed Education Department that organizes a full programme of activities for groups and individuals of all ages and abilities, for both formal and informal learning.

Lawrence Alma-Tadema, *Etruscan Vase Painters*, Manchester Art Gallery

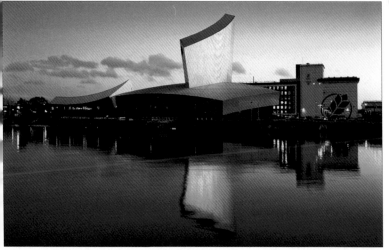

Exterior of the Imperial War Museum North, designed by Daniel Libeskind to represent a globe shattered by conflict

🏛 Lowry Centre

Pier 8, Salford Quays. **Tel** *0870 787 5788.* ◯ *daily. Admission free, but donations requested.* 🚻 🍴 📷 🏪 **www**.thelowry.com.

On a prominent site beside the Manchester Ship Canal, the Lowry is a shimmering, silvery arts and entertainment complex that combines two theatres, a restaurant, terrace bars and cafes, art galleries and a shop.

The centre is named after celebrated reclusive artist Laurence Stephen Lowry (1887–1976), who was born locally and lived all his life in the Manchester area. A rent collector by day, in his leisure hours he painted cityscapes dominated by the smoking chimneys of industry beneath heavy soot filled skies.

However, he is most famous as a painter of "matchstick men", the term frequently applied to the crowds of slight and ghostly figures peopling his canvases. Some of Lowry's work is displayed in one of the galleries here; another hosts regularly changing temporary exhibitions. There is also a room where a 20-minute documentary "Meet Mr Lowry" is screened throughout the day.

The centre provides many facilities and activities for children, and is perfect for a family day out.

🏛 Imperial War Museum North

Trafford Wharf Road, Salford Quays. **Tel** *0161 836 4000.* ◯ *daily.* ● *24–26 Dec.* 🎫 🚻 🍴 📷 🏪 **www**.iwm.org.uk.

This most striking piece of modern architecture comes courtesy of Daniel Libeskind, the architect nominated to design a replacement for New York's World Trade Centre. His Manchester building is a waterfront collision of three great aluminium shards, representing a globe shattered by conflict. Inside, a vast, irregular space is used to display a small but well presented collection of military hardware and ephemera, with nine "silos" devoted to exhibits on people's experiences of war.

On the hour the lights are extinguished for an audio-visual display using the angled walls of the main hall.

As visitors leave they are invited to take the elevator up the 55-metre (180-ft) "Air Shard" for views over the city.

🏛 Manchester United Museum

Salford Quays. **Tel** *0161 868 8000.* ◯ *daily. Tours must be booked in advance.* 🎫 📷 🏪 **www**.manutd.com

Premier League football (soccer) team Manchester United's ground Old Trafford also includes a purpose-built museum. In addition to the historic displays there is much interactive fun such as a chance to test your own penalty-taking skills.

The museum tour takes in the dressing rooms, the trophy room and the players' lounge and culminates in a walk down the tunnel tracing the route taken by players at every home game.

Manchester United Museum on the grounds of Old Trafffford football stadium

Liverpool ⑳

Traces of settlement on Merseyside date back to the 1st century. In 1207 "Livpul", a fishing village, was granted a charter by King John. The population was only 1,000 in Stuart times, but during the 17th and 18th centuries Liverpool's westerly seaboard gave it a leading edge in the lucrative Caribbean slave trade. The first docks opened in 1715 and eventually stretched 7 miles (11 km) along the Mersey. Liverpool's first ocean steamer set out from here in 1840, and would-be emigrants to the New World poured into the city from Europe, including a flood of Irish refugees from the potato famine. Many settled permanently in Liverpool and a large, mixed community developed. Today, the port handles even greater volumes of cargoes than in the 1950s and 1960s, but container ships use Bootle docks. Despite economic and social problems, the irrepressible "Scouse" or Liverpudlian spirit re-emerged in the Swinging Sixties, when four local lads stormed the pop scene. Many people still visit Liverpool to pay homage to the Beatles, but the city is also known for its orchestra, the Liverpool Philharmonic, its sport (football and the Grand National steeplechase) and its universities.

Liver Bird on the Royal Liver Building

Victorian ironwork, restored and polished, at Albert Dock

Exploring Liverpool

Liverpool's waterfront by the Pier Head, guarded by the mythical Liver Birds (a pair of cormorants with seaweed in their beaks) on the **Royal Liver Building**, is one of the most easily recognized in Britain. Nearby are the famous ferry terminal across the River Mersey and the revitalized

LIVERPOOL CITY CENTRE

Beatles Story ⑥
Cavern Quarter ①
Merseyside Maritime
  Museum ⑧
Metropolitan Cathedral ⑤
Museum of Liverpool Life ⑨
Royal Liver Building ⑩

St George's Hall ④
Tate Liverpool ⑦
Town Hall ⑪
The Walker pp378–9 ③
World Museum Liverpool ②

docklands. Other attractions include top-class museums and fine galleries, such as the **Walker** (*see pp378–9*). Its wealth of interesting architecture includes some fine Neo-Classical buildings in the city centre, such as the gargantuan **St George's Hall**, and two cathedrals.

Albert Dock

ⓘ *0151 708 7334.* ◯ *daily.* ● *1 Jan, 25 Dec.* ◩ *some attractions.* ♿
www.albertdock.com

There are five warehouses surrounding Albert Dock, all designed by Jesse Hartley in 1846. The docks were closed by 1972. After a decade of dereliction, these Grade I listed buildings were restored in a development that includes museums, galleries, shops, restaurants, bars and businesses.

Albert Dock quay beside the River Mersey

🏛 Merseyside Maritime Museum

Albert Dock. **Tel** *0151 478 4499.* ◯ *daily.* ♿ *limited.* ▣ ▮
www.liverpoolmuseums.org.uk

Devoted to the history of the Port of Liverpool, this large complex has good sections on shipbuilding and the Cunard and White Star liners. The area on the Battle of the Atlantic in World War II includes models and charts. Another gallery deals with emigration to the New World. The **HM Customs and Excise National Museum** is also located here, and examines the history of the subject, including smuggling, as well as customs and excise today. Next door is the new **International Slavery Museum**. Across the quayside is the rebuilt Piermaster's House and the Cooperage.

Ship's bell in the Maritime Museum

🏛 Museum of Liverpool Life

Pier Head, Albert Dock. **Tel** *0151 478 4080.* ● *for refurbishment until 2010.* ♿ ▮

Many aspects of Liverpool culture converge here. Exhibits cover the history of Liverpool, its people and their contribution to international life. The *City Soldier's* gallery explores life in the King's Regiment in times of war and peace. Other interactive exhibits and accounts of daily life tell stories of sporting and political events since the 1800s.

VISITORS' CHECKLIST

Liverpool. ⚐ *450,000.* ✈ *7 miles (11 km) SE Liverpool.* ⛟ *Lime St.* ⛟ *Norton St.* ⛴ *from Pier Head to the Wirral, also sightseeing trips; to Isle of Man & N Ireland.* ⓘ *Whitechapel (0151 233 2008).* ⚑ *Sun (heritage market).* ☎ *0906 680 6886; Liverpool Show: May; Clipper Round the World Yacht Race: Jun; Beatles Week: Aug.* **www**.visitliverpool.com

🏛 Beatles Story

Britannia Vaults. **Tel** *0151 709 1963.* ◯ *daily.* ● *25, 26 Dec.* ◩ ♿ ▮
www.beatlesstory.com

In a walk-through exhibition, this museum records the history of The Beatles' meteoric rise to fame, from their first record, *Love Me Do,* through Beatlemania to their last live appearance together in 1969, and their eventual break-up. The hits that mesmerized a generation can be heard.

🏛 Tate Liverpool

Albert Dock. **Tel** *0151 702 7400.* ◯ *Tue–Sun (Jun–Aug: daily).* ● *1 Jan, Good Fri, 24–26 Dec.* ◩ *some exhibitions.* ♿ ☞ *by arrangement.* ▣ ▮ **www**.tate.org.uk/liverpool

Tate Liverpool has one of the best contemporary art collections outside London. Marked by bright blue and orange panels and arranged over three floors, the gallery was converted from an old warehouse by architect James Stirling. It opened in 1988 as Tate Britain's *(see p91)* first outstation.

THE BEATLES

Liverpool has produced many good bands and a host of singers, comedians and entertainers before and since the 1960s. But the Beatles – John Lennon, Paul McCartney, George Harrison and Ringo Starr – were the most sensational, and locations associated with the band, however tenuous, are revered as shrines in Liverpool. Bus and walking tours trace the hallowed ground of the Salvation Army home at *Strawberry Fields* and *Penny Lane* (both outside the city centre), as well as the boys' old homes. The most visited site is Mathew Street, near Moorfields Station, where the Cavern Club first throbbed to the Mersey Beat. The original site is now a shopping arcade, but the bricks have been used to create a replica. Nearby are statues of the Beatles and *Eleanor Rigby*.

Liverpool: The Walker

Italian dish (c. 1500)

Founded in 1877 by Sir Andrew Barclay Walker, a local brewer and Mayor of Liverpool, this gallery houses one of the finest art collections in Britain. Paintings range from early Italian and Flemish works to Rubens, Rembrandt, Poussin, and French Impressionists such as Degas's *Woman Ironing* (c.1892–5). Among the strong collection of British artists from the 18th century onward are works by Millais and Turner and Gainsborough's *Countess of Sefton* (1769). There is 20th-century art by Hockney and Sickert, and the sculpture collection includes works by Henry Moore.

Seashells *(1874) Albert Moore painted female figures based on antique statues. Influenced by Whistler (see p519), he adopted subtle shading.*

Interior at Paddington
(1951) Lucian Freud's friend Harry Diamond posed for six months for this picture, intended by the artist to "make the human being uncomfortable".

Big Art for Little Artists Gallery

Ground floor

15

14

13

12

5

8

9

10

11

First floor

Façade was designed by H H Vale and Cornelius Sherlock.

Main entrance

The Sleeping Shepherd Boy
(c.1835) The great Neo-Classical sculptor of the mid-19th century, John Gibson (1790–1866), used traditional colours to give his statuary a smooth appearance.

GALLERY GUIDE
All the picture galleries are on the first floor.
Rooms 1–2 house medieval and Renaissance paintings; Rooms 3 and 4 have 17th-century Dutch, French, Italian and Spanish art. British 18th- and 19th-century works are in Rooms 5–9. Rooms 11–15 have 20th-century and contemporary British art, and Room 10 has Impressionists and Post-Impressionists.

The 7th-century Kingston Brooch in World Museum Liverpool

🏛 **World Museum Liverpool**
William Brown St. **Tel** 0151 478
4393. ◻ 10am–5pm daily.
● 1 Jan, 24–26 Dec. ⚹ ◻ ◻
www.liverpoolmuseums.org.uk
Six floors of exhibits in this
excellent museum include
collections of Egyptian, Greek
and Roman pieces, natural
history, archaeology, space and
time. Highlights include the
hands-on Weston Discovery
Centre, a planetarium, the
Close Natural History Centre,
an aquarium, a world cultures
gallery and a Bug House.

🔒 **Anglican Cathedral**
St James' Mount. **Tel** 0151 709
6271. ◻ daily. ⚹ ◻ ◻
www.liverpoolcathedral.org.uk
Although Gothic in style, this
building was only completed
in 1978. The largest Anglican
cathedral in the world is a fine
red sandstone edifice designed
by Sir Giles Gilbert Scott. The
foundation stone was laid
in 1904 by Edward VII but,
dogged by two world wars,
building work dragged on to
modified designs.

🔒 **Metropolitan Cathedral
of Christ the King**
Mount Pleasant. **Tel** 0151 709 9222.
◻ daily. **Donation.** ⚹ ◻ www.
liverpoolmetrocathedral.org.uk
Liverpool's Roman Catholic
cathedral rejected traditional
forms in favour of a striking
modern design. Early plans,
drawn up by Pugin and later
by Lutyens *(see p29)* in the
1930s, proved too expensive.
The final version, brainchild
of Sir Frederick Gibberd and
built from 1962–7, is a circular
building surmounted by a
stylized crown of thorns 88 m
(290 ft) high. It is irreverently
known as "Paddy's Wigwam"
by non-Catholics (a reference
to Liverpool's large Irish

population). Inside, the stained-
glass lantern, designed by John
Piper and Patrick Reyntiens,
floods the circular nave with
diffused blueish light. There
is a fine bronze of Christ by
Elisabeth Frink (1930–94).

Environs: A spectacular richly
timbered building dating from
1490, **Speke Hall** lies 6 miles
(10 km) east of Liverpool's
centre, surrounded by lovely
grounds. The oldest parts of
the hall enclose a cobbled
courtyard dominated by two
yew trees, Adam and Eve.
  Birkenhead on the Wirral
peninsula has been linked to
Liverpool by ferry for over
800 years. Now, road and rail
tunnels supplement access.
The Norman Priory is still in
use on Sundays, and stately
Hamilton Square was designed
from 1825–44 by J Gillespie
Graham, one of the architects
of Edinburgh's New Town.
  On the Wirral side is **Port
Sunlight Village** *(see p349)*, a
Victorian garden village built
by enlightened soap manufacturer William Hesketh Lever
for his factory workers. He also
founded the **Lady Lever Art
Gallery** here for his collection
of works of art, including Pre-
Raphaelite paintings.

🏚 **Speke Hall**
(NT) The Walk, Speke. **Tel** 0151 427
7231. ◻ Apr–Oct: Wed–Sun (pm);
Nov–mid-Dec: Sat, Sun (pm); public
hols. 🏚 ⚹ limited. ◻ ◻
www.nationaltrust.org.uk

🏚 **Port Sunlight Village &
Heritage Centre**
95 Greendale Rd, Port Sunlight, Wirral.
Tel 0151 644 6466. ◻ Apr–Oct:
10am–4pm; Nov–Mar: 11am–4pm
daily. ● Christmas wk. 🏚 🏚 ⚹
◻ ◻ www.portsunlightvillage.com

**Entrance to the half-timbered
manor house of Speke Hall**

**Christ Discovered in the
Temple** *(1342)*
*Simone Martini's Holy
Family conveys emotional
tension through highly
expressive body language.*

KEY TO FLOOR PLAN

◻ 13th–17th-century European

◻ 18th–19th-century British,
  Pre-Raphaelites and Victorian

◻ Impressionist/Post-Impressionist

◻ 20th-century and
  contemporary British

◻ Sculpture gallery

◻ Craft and design gallery

◻ Special exhibitions

◻ Non-exhibition space

YORKSHIRE AND THE HUMBER REGION

NORTH YORKSHIRE · EAST RIDING OF YORKSHIRE

With the historic city of York at its heart, this is an area of picturesque moorland and valleys. To the north lie the Yorkshire Dales and the North York Moors; eastwards, a coastline of beaches; and southwards, a landscape of lush meadows.

Yorkshire was originally made up of three separate counties, formerly known as "Ridings". Today it covers over 5,000 sq miles (12,950 sq km). The northeast section has dramatic limestone scenery that was carved by glaciers in the Ice Age. Farming was the original livelihood, and the dry-stone walls weaving up precipitous scars and fells were used to divide the land. Imposed on this were the industries of the 19th century; blackened mill chimneys and crumbling viaducts are as much a part of the scenery as the grand houses of those who profited from them.

Close to the Humber, the landscape is very different, dominated historically by the now flagging fishing industry, and geographically by lush, sprawling meadows. Its coastline is exceptional, and further north are the attractions of wide, sandy beaches and bustling harbour towns. Yet it is the contrasting landscapes that make the area so appealing, ranging from the bleak moorland of the Brontë novels to the ragged cliff coast around Whitby, and the flat expanse of Sunk Island.

The city of York, where Roman and Viking relics exist side by side, is second only to London in the number of visitors that tread its streets. Indeed the historical centre of York is the region's foremost attraction. Those in search of a real taste of Yorkshire, however, should head for the countryside. In addition to excellent touring routes, a network of rewarding walking paths range from mellow ambles along the Cleveland Way to rocky scrambles over the Pennine Way at Pen-y-Ghent.

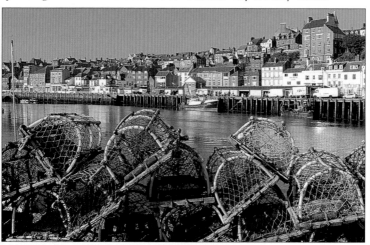

Lobster pots on the quayside at the picturesque fishing port of Whitby

◁ The peaceful valley of Rosedale, North York Moors

Exploring Yorkshire and the Humber Region

Yorkshire covers a wide area, once made up of three counties or "Ridings". Until the arrival of railways, mining and the wool industry in the 19th century, the county was a farming area. Dry-stone walls dividing fields still pepper the northern part of the county, alongside 19th-century mill chimneys and country houses. Among the many abbeys are Rievaulx and the magnificent Fountains. The medieval city of York is a major attraction, as are Yorkshire's beaches. The Humber region is characterized by the softer, rolling countryside of the Wolds, and its nature reserves attract enormous quantities of birds.

Rosedale village in the North York Moors

SIGHTS AT A GLANCE

Bempton and Flamborough Head 26
Beverley 27
Bradford 35
Burton Agnes 25
Burton Constable 28
Byland Abbey 10
Castle Howard pp398–9 22
Coxwold 11
Eden Camp 23
Fountains Abbey pp390–91 7
Grimsby 31
Halifax 38
Harewood House 33
Harrogate 3
Haworth 36
Hebden Bridge 37
Helmsley 13
Holderness and Spurn Head 30
Hutton-le-Hole 16
Kingston upon Hull 29
Knaresborough 4

Leeds 34
Magna 41
Mount Grace Priory 15
National Coal Mining Museum 39
Newby Hall 6
North York Moors 17
North York Moors Railway 18
Nunnington Hall 12
Rievaulx Abbey 14
Ripley 5
Ripon 8
Robin Hood's Bay 20
Scarborough 21
Sutton Bank 9
Whitby 19
Wharram Percy 24
York pp404–9 32
Yorkshire Dales 1
Yorkshire Sculpture Park 40

Walks
Malham Walk 2

Map labels:
Penrith
Durh
A66
A66
Scotch Corner
Richmond
Thwaite   *Swaledale*   Catter
Reeth
Hardraw   Castle Bolton   Leyburn
Hawes   *Wensleydale*   Middleha
Aysgarth
YORKSHIRE
DALES
NATIONAL
Kendal   Kettlewell
Horton in   PARK
Ribblesdale   *Wharfedale*   FOUNTAINS ABBE
A65   Grassington   Patele
MALHAM   Burnsall
Settle   WALK 2   RIP
Malham
Long Preston   Bolton Abbey   A59   HARRO
Skipton   *Wharfe*
A629   Ilkley   HAREW
Keighley
Bingley
HAWORTH 36
Burnley   BRADFORD 35   LE
HEBDEN
BRIDGE 37   A646   38 HALIFAX
Sowerby Bridge
NATIONAL COAL
MINING MUSEUM
Huddersfield
Manchester   YORKSHIR
SCULPTURE PAR
Holmfirth
A628   Peniston
Stocksbri
Pea
Distr

SEE ALSO

• *Where to Stay* pp583–6

• *Where to Eat* pp637–40

Section of Lendal Bridge (1863)
crossing the Ouse in York

KEY

▬	Motorway
▬	Major road
▬	Secondary road
▭	Minor road
▬	Scenic route
▬	Main railway
▬	Minor railway

GETTING AROUND

The area is served by the A1, the M1,
the M62 and the A59. Trains run to
major cities such as York and Leeds,
and there are train or coach (bus) links
between many towns and hamlets. The
Yorkshire Dales and North York Moors
national parks are good for walkers,
and cyclists can enjoy rides around
York and the River Humber.

0 kilometres   15

0 miles   10

Yorkshire Dales ❶

The Yorkshire Dales is a farming landscape, formed from three principle dales, Swaledale, Wharfedale and Wensleydale, and a number of small ones, such as Deepdale. Glaciation in the Ice Age helped carve out these steep-sided valleys, and this scenery contrasts with the high moorlands. However, 12 centuries of settlement have altered the landscape in the form of cottages, castles and villages which create a delightful environment for walking. A national park since 1954, the area provides recreation while serving local community needs.

Malham Walk
(see p387)

KEY

▬▬▬	Major road
▭▭▭	Minor road
═══	Other roads
▬▬▬	National Park boundary

0 kilometres   20

0 miles   15

The green, rolling landscape of Deepdale, near Dent

Monk's Wynd – one of Richmond's narrow, winding streets

Exploring Swaledale

Swaledale's prosperity was founded largely on wool, and it is famous for its herd of sheep that graze on the wild higher slopes in the harshest weather. The fast-moving river Swale that gives the northernmost dale its name travels from bleak moorland down magnificent waterfalls into the richly wooded lower slopes, passing through the village of Reeth and the town of Richmond.

♠ Richmond Castle

(EH) Tower Street. **Tel** 01748 822493. ⬜ Oct–Apr: Thu–Mon; May–Sep: daily. 🎫 ♿ limited. ⬜
Swaledale's main point of entry is the medieval market town of Richmond, which has the largest cobbled marketplace in England. Alan Rufus, the Norman 1st Earl of Richmond, began building the castle in 1071, and some of the masonry on the curtain walls probably dates from that time. It has a fine Norman keep, 30 m (100 ft) high with walls 3.3 m (11 ft) thick. An 11th-century arch leads into a courtyard containing Scolland's Hall (1080), one of England's oldest buildings.

Richmond's marketplace was once the castle's outer bailey. Its quaint, narrow streets gave rise to the song, *The Lass of Richmond Hill* (1787), written by Leonard McNally for his wife, Frances I'Anson, who was brought up in Hill House, on Richmond Hill. Turner *(see p91)* depicted the town many times. The Georgian Theatre (1788) is the only one of its age still surviving.

🏛 Swaledale Folk Museum
Reeth Green. *Tel* 01748 884118.
◯ Easter–Oct: Wed–Fri, Sun & public hols; Nov–Easter: Sun. 🏷🅿🚻
Reeth, a town that became known as the centre of the lead-mining industry, houses this museum in a former Methodist Sunday school (1830). Included in it are mining and wool-making artifacts (wool from the hardy Swaledale sheep was another mainstay of the economy) and brass band memorabilia.

🦅 Buttertubs
Near Thwaite, on the B6270 Hawes road, are a series of potholes that streams fall into. These became known as the Buttertubs when farmers going to market lowered their butter into the holes to keep it cool.

Buttertubs, near Thwaite

Exploring Wensleydale
The largest of the Yorkshire dales, Wensleydale is famous for its cheese and more recently for James Herriot's books and the television series, *All Creatures Great and Small.* It is easy walking country for anyone seeking an alternative to major moorland hikes.

🏛 Dales Countryside Museum
Station Yard, Hawes. *Tel* 01969 666210. ◯ daily. ● 24–26 Dec, 1 Jan. 🏷🅿🚻
In a former railway goods warehouse in Hawes, capital of Upper Wensleydale, is a

Barrels at the Theakston Brewery

fascinating museum, filled with items from life and industry in the 18th- and 19th-century Upper Dales. This includes cheese- and butter-making equipment. Wensleydale cheese was created by monks at nearby Jervaulx Abbey. There is also a rope-making works a short walk away.

Hawes itself is the highest market town in England, at 259 m (850 ft) above sea level. It is a thriving centre where thousands of sheep and cattle are auctioned each summer.

🦅 Hardraw Force
🏷 at Green Dragon Inn, Hardraw.
At the tiny village of Hardraw, nearby, is England's tallest single-drop waterfall, with no outcrops to interrupt its 29 m (96 ft) fall. It became famous in Victorian times when the daredevil Blondin walked across it on a tightrope. Today, you can walk right under this fine waterfall, against the rock face, and look through the stream without getting wet.

🦅 Aysgarth Waterfalls
ℹ National Pk Centre (01969 662910). ◯ Fri–Sun.
An old packhorse bridge gives a clear view of the point at which the previously placid River Ure suddenly begins to plunge in foaming torrents over wide limestone shelves. Turner painted the impressive lower falls in 1817.

🏛 Theakston Brewery
Masham. *Tel* 01765 680000. ◯ daily. ● 23 Dec–early Jan. 🏷📷 🚻 www.theakstons.co.uk
The pretty town of Masham is the home of Theakston brewery, creator of the potent ale Old Peculier. The history

VISITORS' CHECKLIST
N Yorkshire. 🚉 *Skipton.* 🚌 ℹ 01756 792809. www.yorkshiredales.org.uk

of this local family brewery from its origin in 1827 is on display in the visitors' centre. Masham village itself has an attractive square once used for sheep fairs, surrounded by 17th- and 18th-century houses. There is a medieval church.

♟ Bolton Castle
Castle Bolton, nr Leyburn. *Tel* 01969 623981. ◯ daily. ● 23–25 Dec. 🏷🅿🚻 www.boltoncastle.co.uk
Situated in the village of Castle Bolton, this castle was built in 1379 by the 1st Lord Scrope, Chancellor of England. It was used as a fortress from 1568 to 1569 when Mary, Queen of Scots *(see p511)* was held prisoner here by Elizabeth I *(see pp50–51).*

♟ Middleham Castle
(EH) Middleham, nr Leyburn. *Tel* 01969 623899. ◯ Apr–Sep: 10am–6pm daily; Oct–Mar: 10am–4pm Mon–Wed, Sat & Sun. ● 1 Jan, 24–26 Dec. 🏷📷 ♿ limited.
Owned by Richard Neville, Earl of Warwick, it was built in 1170. The castle is better known as home to Richard III *(see p49)* when he was made Lord of the North. It was once one of the strongest fortresses in the north but became un-inhabited during the 15th century, when many of its stones were used for nearby buildings. The keep provides a fine view of the landscape.

Remains of Middleham Castle, once residence of Richard III

Extensive ruins of Bolton Priory, dating from 1154

Exploring Wharfedale

This dale is characterized by gritstone moorland, contrasting with quiet market towns along meandering sections of river. Many consider Grassington a central point for exploring Wharfedale, but the showpiece villages of Burnsall, overlooked by a 506 m (1,661 ft) fell, and Buckden, 701 m (2,302 ft), near Buckden Pike, also make excellent bases.

Nearby are the Three Peaks of Whernside, 736 m (2,416 ft), Ingleborough, 724 m (2,376 ft) and Pen-y-Ghent 694 m (2,278 ft). They are known for their potholes and tough terrain, but this does not deter keen walkers from attempting to climb them all in one day. If you sign in at the Pen-y-Ghent café at Horton-in-Ribblesdale, at the centre of the Three Peaks, and complete the 20 mile (32 km) course, reaching the summit of all three peaks in less than 12 hours, you can qualify for membership of the Three Peaks of Yorkshire Club.

Burnsall

St Wilfrid's, Burnsall. *Tel 01756 720331.* ○ *Apr–Oct: daily to dusk.* &
Preserved in St Wilfrid's church graveyard are the original village stocks, gravestones from Viking times and a head-stone carved in memory of the Dawson family by sculptor Eric Gill (1882–1940). The village has a five-arched bridge and hosts Britain's oldest fell race every August.

🏛 Grassington Museum

The Square, Grassington.
○ *Mar–Oct: daily (pm).* 🎫
& *limited.*
This folk museum is set in two 18th-century lead miners' cottages. Its exhibits illustrate the domestic and working history of the area, including farming and lead mining.

🏰 Bolton Priory

Bolton Abbey, Skipton. *Tel 01756 718009.* ○ *daily.* &
One of the most beautiful areas of Wharfedale is around the village of Bolton Abbey, set in an estate owned by the Dukes of Devonshire. While preserving its astounding beauty, its managers have incorporated over 30 miles (46 km) of foot-paths, many suitable for the disabled and young families.

The ruins of Bolton Priory, established by Augustinian canons in 1154 on the site of a Saxon manor, are extensive.

They include a church, chapter house, cloister and prior's lodging. These all demonstrate the wealth accumulated by the canons from the sale of wool from their flocks of sheep. The priory nave is still used as a parish church. Another attraction of the estate is the "Strid", a point where the River Wharfe surges spectacularly through a gorge, foaming yellow and gouging holes out of the rocks.

🦇 Stump Cross Caverns

Greenhow Hill, Pateley Bridge. *Tel 01756 752780.* ○ *Mar–Nov: daily; Dec–Feb: Sat, Sun & pub hols.* 🎫 ▯
🖥 www.stumpcrosscaverns.co.uk
These caves were formed over a period of half a million years: trickles of underground water formed intertwining passages and carved them into fantastic shapes and sizes. Sealed off in the last Ice Age, the caves were only discovered in the 1850s, when lead miners sank a mine shaft into the caverns.

♟ Skipton Castle

High St. *Tel 01756 792442.* ○ *daily (Sun: pm).* ● *25 Dec.* 🎫 ▯ 🛈
www.skiptoncastle.co.uk
The market town of Skipton is still one of the largest auctioning and stockraising centres in the north. Its 11th-century castle was almost entirely rebuilt by Robert de Clifford in the 14th century. Beautiful Conduit Court was added by Henry, Lord Clifford, in Henry VIII's reign. The central yew tree was planted by Lady Anne Clifford in 1659 to mark restoration work to the castle after Civil War damage.

Conduit Court (1495) and yew tree at Skipton Castle

For hotels and restaurants in this region see pp583–586 and pp637–640

Malham Walk ❷

The Malham area, shaped by glacial erosion 10,000 years ago, has one of Great Britain's most dramatic limestone landscapes. The walk from Malham village can take over four hours if you pause to enjoy the viewpoints and take a detour to Gordale Scar. Those who are short of time tend to go only as far as Malham Cove. This vast natural amphitheatre, formed by a huge geological tear, is like a giant boot-heel mark in the landscape. Above lie the deep crevices of Malham Lings, where rare flora such as hart's-tongue flourishes. Unusual plants grow in the lime-rich Malham Tarn, said to have provided inspiration for Charles Kingsley's *The Water Babies* (1863). Coot and mallard visit the tarn in summer and tufted duck in winter.

Sandpiper at Malham Tarn

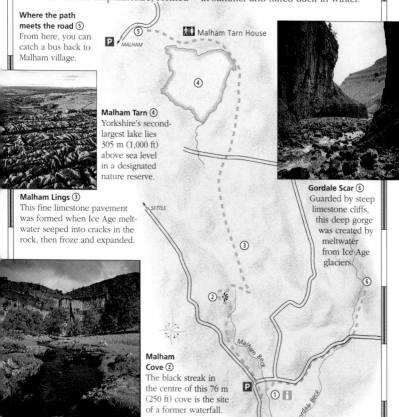

Where the path meets the road ⑤
From here, you can catch a bus back to Malham village.

Malham Tarn House

Malham Tarn ④
Yorkshire's second-largest lake lies 305 m (1,000 ft) above sea level in a designated nature reserve.

Malham Lings ③
This fine limestone pavement was formed when Ice Age meltwater seeped into cracks in the rock, then froze and expanded.

SETTLE

Gordale Scar ⑥
Guarded by steep limestone cliffs, this deep gorge was created by meltwater from Ice Age glaciers.

Malham Cove ②
The black streak in the centre of this 76 m (250 ft) cove is the site of a former waterfall.

Malham Beck

Gordale Beck

SKIPTON

KEY

▬▬	Walk route
═══	Minor road
☆	Viewpoint
P	Parking
i	Tourist information
🚻	Toilets

Malham ①
An attractive riverside village, it has an information centre with details of drives and walks.

0 kilometres   1
0 miles   ½

TIPS FOR WALKERS

*Starting point: Malham. **Getting there:** Leave M65 at Junction 14 and take A56 to Skipton, then follow signs to Malham which is off A65. **Length:** 7 miles (11 km). **Difficulty:** Malham Cove is steep but the Tarn area is flatter.*
i 01729 830363.

A 1920s poster advertising the spa town of Harrogate

Harrogate ❸

North Yorkshire. 🏛 *69,000.*
🚆 🚌 🚏 *The Royal Baths,*
Crescent Rd (0845 389 3223).
www.harrogate.gov.uk

Between 1880 and World War I, Harrogate was the north's leading spa town, with nearly 90 medicinal springs. It was ideal for aristocrats who, after a tiring London season, were able to stop for a health cure before journeying on to grouse-shooting in Scotland.

Today, Harrogate's main attractions are its spa town atmosphere, fine architecture, public gardens and its convenience as a centre for visiting North Yorkshire and the Dales.

The naturally welling spa waters may not currently be in use, but you can still go for a Turkish bath in one of the country's most attractive steam rooms. The entrance at

the side of the Royal Bath Assembly Rooms (1897) is unassuming, but once inside, the century-old **Harrogate Turkish Baths** are a visual feast of tiled Victoriana.

The town's spa history is recorded in the **Royal Pump Room Museum**. At the turn of the century, the waters were thought to be rich in iron early in the day. So, between 7am and 9am the 1842 octagonal building would have been filled with rich and fashionable people drinking glasses of water. Poorer people could take water from the pump outside. Today you can sample the waters and enjoy the museum's exhibits, including a Penny Farthing bicycle.

Harrogate is also known for the rainbow-coloured flower-beds in **The Stray**, a common space to the south of the town centre, and for the ornamental **RHS Harlow Carr Gardens**,

owned by the Royal Horticultural Society. Visitors can enjoy the delicious cakes at **Betty's Café Tea Rooms** *(see p628).*

🛁 Harrogate Turkish Baths
The Royal Baths, Crescent Rd.
Tel *01423 556746.* ⬜ **Men:** *Mon, Wed & Fri: (pm); Sat.* **Women:** *Mon (am); Tue & Thu: (pm); Fri (am); Sun.* **Mixed** *(in bathing suits): Tue (am); (couples only in bathing suits): Wed & Fri (both eve); Sun (eve).* 🖼

🏛 Royal Pump Room Museum
Crown Pl. ***Tel*** *01423 556188.*
⬜ *daily (Sun: pm only).*
● *1 Jan, 24–26 Dec.* 🖼 👟 🚻

🛁 Betty's Café Tea Rooms
1 Parliament St. ***Tel*** *01423 814070.*
⬜ *daily.* ● *1 Jan, 25–26 Dec.*
www.bettysandtaylors.co.uk

🌸 RHS Harlow Carr Gardens
Crag Lane. ***Tel*** *01423 702746.* ⬜
daily. 🖼 👟 🍴 🖥 **www**.rhs.org.uk

Knaresborough ❹

North Yorkshire. 🏛 *14,000.* 🚆 🚌
from Harrogate. 🚏 *9 Castle Courtyard, Market Place (01423 866886).* 🛍 *Wed.*

Perched precipitously above the River Nidd is one of England's oldest towns, mentioned in the Domesday Book of 1086 *(see p48).* Its historic streets – which link the church, John of Gaunt's ruined castle, and the market place with the river – are now lined with fine 18th-century houses.

Nearby is **Mother Shipton's Cave**, reputedly England's oldest tourist attraction. It first went on show in 1630 as the birthplace of Ursula Sontheil,

Mother Shipton's cave, with objects encased in limestone

The south front of Newby Hall

a famous local prophetess. Today, people can view the effect the well near her cave has on objects hung below the dripping surface. Almost any item, from umbrellas to soft toys, will become encased in limestone within a few weeks.

🎋 Mother Shipton's Cave
Prophesy House, High Bridge.
Tel 01423 864600. ☐ *Easter–Oct: daily; Feb–Easter: Sat, Sun.*
● *Nov–Jan.* 🈲 📷 🚻 📷 📷

Ripley ❺

North Yorkshire. 🏃 150. 🚌 *from Harrogate or Ripon.* ❗ *Town Hall (01773 841488).*
www.harrogate.gov.uk

Since the 1320s, when the first generation of the Ingilby family lived in an early incarnation of **Ripley Castle**, the village has been made up almost exclusively of castle employees. The influence of one 19th-century Ingilby had the most visual impact. In the 1820s, Sir William Amcotts Ingilby was so entranced by a village in Alsace Lorraine that he created a similar one in French Gothic style, complete with an *Hotel de Ville*. Present-day Ripley has a cobbled market square, and quaint cottages line the streets.

Ripley Castle, with its 15th-century gatehouse, was where Oliver Cromwell *(see p52)* stayed following the Battle of Marston Moor. The 28th generation of Ingilbys live here, and it is open for tours. The attractive grounds contain two lakes and a deer park, as well as more formal gardens.

♠ Ripley Castle
Ripley. **Tel** 01423 770152.
☐ *Apr–Oct: daily; Nov–Mar: Tue, Thu, Sat–Sun; Dec–Feb: Sat–Sun.*
● *25 Dec.* 🈲 🚻 📷 📷 📷

Newby Hall ❻

Nr Ripon, North Yorkshire. **Tel** 01423 322583. ☐ *Apr–Jun & Sep: Tue–Sun; Jul & Aug: daily.* 🈲 🚻 🍴 📷
www.newbyhall.com

Newby Hall stands on land once occupied by the de Nubie family in the 13th century, and has been in the hands of the current family since 1748. The central part of the present house was built in the late 17th century in the style of Sir Christopher Wren.

Visitors will find 25 acres of gardens to explore. Laid out in a series of compartmented areas off a main axis, each garden is planted to come into flower during a different season. There is also a Woodland Discovery Walk, where contemporary sculpture is displayed.

For children, there is an adventure garden with activities and a miniature railway that runs through the gardens alongside the river Ure. River boat rides are also available. Each year a number of special events are staged, including Plant Fairs, a Historic Vehicle Rally and two Craft Fairs.

Fountains Abbey ❼

See pp390–91.

Ripon ❽

North Yorkshire. 🏃 14,000.
🚌 *from Harrogate.* ❗ *Minster Rd (0845 389 0178).* 🛒 *Thu.*
www.visitripon.org

Ripon, a charming small city, is best known for the cathedral and "the watch", which has been announced since the Middle Ages by the Wakeman. In return for protecting Ripon citizens, he would charge an annual toll of two pence per household. Today, a man still blows a horn in the Market Square each evening at 9pm, and every Thursday a handbell is rung to open the market.

The **Cathedral of St Peter and St Wilfrid** is built above a 7th-century Saxon crypt. At less than 3 m (10 ft) high and just over 2 m (7 ft) wide, it is held to be the oldest complete crypt in England. The cathedral is known for its collection of misericords *(see p341)*, which include both pagan and Old Testament examples. The architectural historian Sir Nikolaus Pevsner (1902–83) considered the cathedral's West Front the finest in England.

Ripon's **Prison and Police Museum**, housed in the 1686 "House of Correction", looks at police history and the conditions in Victorian prisons.

🏛 Prison and Police Museum
St Marygate. **Tel** 01765 690799.
☐ *Apr–Oct: daily (pm only).*
● *Nov–Mar.* 🈲 🚻 📷
www.riponmuseums.co.uk

Ripon's Wakeman, blowing his horn in the Market Square

Fountains Abbey ❼

Nestling in the wooded valley of the River Skell are the extensive sandstone ruins of Fountains Abbey and the outstanding water garden of Studley Royal. Fountains Abbey was founded by Benedictine monks in 1132 and taken over by Cistercians three years later. By the mid-12th century it had become the wealthiest abbey in Britain, though it fell into ruin during the Dissolution (see p50). In 1720, John Aislabie, the MP for Ripon and Chancellor of the Exchequer, developed the land and forest of the abbey ruins. He began work, continued by his son William, on the famous water garden, the statuary and Classical temples in the grounds. This makes a dramatic contrast to the simplicity of the abbey.

THE ABBEY

The abbey buildings were designed to reflect the Cistercians' desire for simplicity and austerity. The abbey frequently dispensed charity to the poor and the sick, as well as travellers.

The Chapel of Nine Altars *at the east end of the church was built from 1203 to 1247. It is ornate, compared to the rest of the abbey, with an 18-m (60-ft) high window complemented by another at the western end of the nave.*

Chapter house

Cloister

Abbot's house

Kitchen

Monks' infirmary hall

Refectory

Lay brothers' infirmary   Lay brothers' refectory

Cellarium and dormitory undercroft, *with vaulting 90 m (300 ft) long, was used for storing fleeces which the abbey monks sold to Venetian and Florentine merchants.*

Fountains Hall
Built by Sir Stephen Proctor around 1611, with stones from the abbey ruins, its design is attributed to architect Robert Smythson. It included a great hall with a minstrels' gallery and an entrance flanked by Classical columns.

Fountains Mill is one of the finest monastic watermills in Britain.

To visitor centre and car park

River Skell

Paths leading to the estate park

★ **Abbey**
This was built by using stones taken from the Skell valley.

STAR SIGHTS

★ Abbey

★ Temple of Piety

St Mary's Church
This sumptuous Victorian Gothic church was built by architect William Burges in 1871–8. Inside, the choir stalls are decorated with multi-coloured carved parrots.

Octagon Tower

Footpath to St Mary's Church

Lake

Banqueting House

Moon Pond

Cascade

Canal

VISITORS' CHECKLIST

(NT) Studley Royal Estate, Ripon. **Tel** 01765 608888. from Ripon (May–Sep) or Harrogate. Mar–Oct: 10am–5pm daily; Nov–Feb: 10am–4pm (or dusk if earlier) daily (Nov–Jan: Sat–Thu only). 24 & 25 Dec.
www.fountainsabbey.org.uk

Anne Boleyn's Seat
This Gothic alcove, with a fine view of the abbey, was built in the late 18th century to replace her statue.

Temple of Fame
The columns of this domed building are made of hollow timber but look like sandstone.

★ Temple of Piety
This garden house was originally dedicated to Hercules. It was renamed as a symbol of filial piety by William Aislabie after his father's death in 1742.

The 19th-century white horse, seen on one of the walks around Sutton Bank

Sutton Bank ❾

North Yorkshire. 🚲 Thirsk. ℹ️
Sutton Bank (01845 597426).

Notorious among motorists for its 1 in 4 gradient, which climbs for about 107 m (350 ft), Sutton Bank itself is well known for its panoramic views. On a clear day you can see from the Vale of York to the Peak District *(see pp338–9)*. William and his sister Dorothy Wordsworth stopped here to admire the vista in 1802, on their way to visit his future wife, Mary Hutchinson, at Brompton. Apart from Sutton Bank, where you can walk round the white horse, the area is less wild than the coastal side, and suitable for children.

Byland Abbey ❿

(EH) Coxwold, York. **Tel** 01347 868 614. 🚌 from York or Helmsley. 🚲 Thirsk. ⬜ Apr–Jul & Sep: Thu–Mon; Aug: daily. 🏷️ ♿ limited. **www.** english-heritage.org.uk/yorkshire

This Cistercian monastery was founded in 1177 by monks from Furness Abbey in Cumbria. It featured what was then the largest Cistercian church in Britain, 100 m (328 ft) long and 41 m (135 ft) wide across the transepts. The layout of the monastery, including cloisters and the west front of the church, is still visible, as is the green and yellow glazed tile floor. Fine workmanship is shown in carved stone details and in the capitals, kept in the small museum.

In 1322 the Battle of Byland was fought nearby, and King Edward II *(see p40)* narrowly escaped capture when the invading Scottish army learned that he was dining with the Abbot. In his hurry to escape, the king had to leave many treasures behind, which were looted by the invading soldiers.

Coxwold ⓫

North Yorkshire. 🏠 160. ℹ️ 49 Market Place, Thirsk (01845 522755). **www.**herriotcountry.com

Situated just inside the bounds of the North York Moors National Park *(see p395)*, this charming village nestles at the foot of the Howardian Hills. Its pretty houses are built from local stone, and the 15th-century church has some fine Georgian

Shandy Hall, home of author Laurence Sterne, now a museum

box pews and an impressive octagonal tower. But Coxwold is best known as the home of the author Laurence Sterne (1713–68), whose writings include *Tristram Shandy* and *A Sentimental Journey.*

Sterne moved here in 1760 as the church curate. He rented a rambling house that he named **Shandy Hall** after a Yorkshire expression meaning eccentric. Originally built as a timber-framed, open-halled house in the 15th century, it was modernized in the 17th century and Sterne later added a façade. His grave lies beside the porch at Coxwold's church.

The miniature Queen Anne drawing room at Nunnington Hall

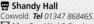
Shandy Hall
Coxwold. *Tel* 01347 868465.
May–Sep: Wed & Sun (pm).
limited. **Gardens** Sun–Fri.
www.hambleton.gov.uk

Nunnington Hall ⑫

(NT) Nunnington, York. *Tel* 01439 748283. Malton, then bus or taxi. Tue–Sun. ground floor.

Set in alluring surroundings, this 17th-century manor house is a combination of architectural styles, including features from the Elizabethan and Stuart periods. Both inside and outside, a notable architectural feature is the use of the broken pediment (the upper arch is left unjoined).

Nunnington Hall was a family home until 1952, when Mrs Ronald Fife donated it to the National Trust. A striking feature is the panelling in the Oak Hall. Formerly painted, it extends over the three-arched screen to the Great Staircase. Nunnington's collection of 22 miniature furnished period rooms is popular with visitors.

A mid-16th-century tenant Dr Robert Huickes, physician to Henry VIII *(see p50–51)*, is best known for advising Elizabeth I that she should not, at the age of 32, consider having any children.

Helmsley ⑬

North Yorkshire. 2,000. from Malton or Scarborough. Helmsley Castle (01439 770173). Fri. www.ryedale.gov.uk/tourism

This pretty market town is noted for its **castle**, now an imposing ruin. Built from 1186 to 1227, its main function and strength as a fortress is illustrated by the remaining keep, tower and curtain walls. The original D-shaped keep had one part blasted away in the Civil War *(see p52)*, but remains the dominant feature. The castle was so impregnable that there were few attempts to force entry. However, in 1644, after holding out for a three-month seige against Sir Thomas Fairfax, the Parliamentary general, the castle was finally taken.

Helmsley church tower

Rievaulx Abbey ⑭

(EH) Nr Helmsley, North Yorkshire. *Tel* 01439 798228. Thirsk or Scarborough, then bus or taxi. Apr–Sep: daily; Oct–Mar: Thu–Mon. 24–26 Dec, 1 Jan. limited.

Rievaulx is perhaps the finest abbey in the area, due to both its dramatic setting in the steep wooded valley of the River Rye and its extensive remains. It is surrounded by steep banks that form natural barriers from the outside world. Monks of the French Cistercian order from Clairvaux founded this, their first major monastery in Britain, in 1132. The main buildings were finished before 1200. The layout of the chapel, kitchens and infirmary give an idea of monastic life.

Rievaulx Abbey, painted by Thomas Girtin (1775–1802)

Mount Grace Priory ruins, with farm and mansion in foreground

Mount Grace Priory ⑮

(EH/NT) On A19, NE of Northallerton, North Yorks. *Tel* 01609 883494. ⊠ *Northallerton then bus.* ◯ *Apr–Sep: Thu–Mon; Oct–Mar: Thu–Sun.* 🖼 ♿ *ground floor, shop & grounds.* ◻ www.english-heritage.org.uk/yorkshire

Founded by Thomas Holland, Duke of Surrey, and in use from 1398 until 1539, this is the best-preserved Carthusian or charterhouse monastery *(see pp350–51)* in England. The monks took a vow of silence and lived in solitary cells, each with his own garden and an angled hatch so that he would not even see the person serving his food. They only met at matins, vespers and feast-day services. Attempts at escape by those who could not endure the rigour of the rules were punished by imprisonment.

The ruins of the priory include the former prison, gatehouse and outer court, barns, guesthouses, cells and the church. The 14th-century church, the best-preserved section of the site, is particularly small, as it was only rarely used by the community. A cell has been reconstructed to give an impression of monastic life.

Hutton-le-Hole ⑯

North Yorkshire. 👥 *400.* ⊠ *Malton then bus.* ℹ *The Ropery, Pickering (01751 473791).* www.ryedale.gov.uk/tourism

This picturesque village is characterized by a spacious green, grazed by roaming sheep, and surrounded by houses, an inn and shops. Lengths of white wood, replacing stone bridges, span the moorland stream. Its cottages, some with date panels over the doors, are made from limestone, with red pantiled roofs. In the village centre is the excellent

Wheelwright's workshop at Ryedale Folk Museum

Ryedale Folk Museum, which records the lifestyle of an agricultural community using Romano-British artifacts and reconstructed buildings.

🏛 **Ryedale Folk Museum**
Hutton-le-Hole. *Tel* 01751 417367. ◯ *late Jan–mid-Dec: daily.* 🖼 ♿ ◻

North York Moors ⑰

See p395.

North Yorkshire Moors Railway ⑱

Pickering & Grosmont, North Yorkshire. *Tel* 01751 472508. ◯ *Apr–Oct: daily; Nov–Mar: some weekends (call for details).* 🖼 ♿ 🚽 ◻ www.nymr.co.uk

Designed in 1831 by George Stephenson as a route along the North York Moors and links with the Esk Valley, Pickering and Whitby *(see p382)*, this railway was considered an engineering miracle. Due to budget constraints, Stephenson was not able to build a tunnel, so had to lay the route down the mile-long (1.5 km) incline between Beck Hole and Goathland. The area around Fen Bog was stabilized using timber, heather, brushwood and fleeces so that a causeway could be built over it. A horse was used to pull a coach along the track at 10 miles (16 km) per hour. After horsepower came steam, and for almost 130 years the railway linked Whitby to the rest of the country. In the early 1960s the line was closed but in 1967, a group of locals began a campaign to relaunch it, and in 1973 it was officially reopened. Today, the 18 mile (29 km) line runs from Pickering via Levisham, Newtondale Halt and Goathland before stopping at Grosmont, through the scenic heart of the North York Moors.

North York Moors ⑰

The area between Cleveland, the Vale of York and the Vale of Pickering is known as the North York Moors National Park. The landscape consists of bleak yet beautiful moors interspersed with lush green valleys. Agriculture is still the main source of income here as it has been for centuries, and until the advent of coal, the communities' local source of fuel was turf. In the 19th century, the geology of the area created extractive industries which included ironstone, lime, coal and building stone.

Mallyan Spout
A footpath leads to this waterfall from Goathland.

Farndale
During springtime, this area is famous for the beauty and profusion of its daffodils.

"Fat Betty" White Cross Crosses and standing stones are a feature of the Moors.

Goathland
A centre for forest and moorland walks, it has 19th-century houses and good accommodation.

THE MOORS CENTRE, DANBY

EGTON BRIDGE

LEAHOLM

WHITBY

West Beck

Wheeldale Gill

THORGILL

Seven

Hartoft Beck

Rutmoor Beck

Blawarth Beck

Dove

Rosedale Abbey
Named after the priory that has long since gone, this beautiful village still has some remains of the kilns from its 19th-century ironstone mining industry.

Hutton-le-Hole
This lovely village has the excellent Ryedale Folk Museum.

Spaunton

Wade's Causeway
Often called the Roman Road, its origins and destination are unknown. Long considered Roman in date, this is now less certain, although it may date from towards the end of the Roman occupation.

VISITORS' CHECKLIST

North Yorkshire. 🚆 *Pickering*. 🚌 *Pickering (Easter–Oct)*. **Moorsbus Tel** 01845 597000. 🛈 Pickering (01751 473791); Moors Centre (01439 772737). **www**.visit northyorkshiremoors.co.uk

Lastingham
Lastingham's church, dating from 1078, has a Norman crypt with stone carving.

0 kilometres   2

0 miles   2

Whitby ⑲

Whitby's known history dates back to the 7th century, when a Saxon monastery was founded on the site of today's famous 13th-century abbey ruins. In the 18th and early 19th centuries it became an industrial port and shipbuilding town, as well as a whaling centre.

Jet comb (c.1870)

In the Victorian era, the red-roofed cottages at the foot of the east cliff were filled with workshops crafting jet into jewellery and ornaments. Today, the tourist shops that have replaced them sell antique-crafted examples of the distinctive black gem.

VISITORS' CHECKLIST

North Yorkshire. ⛵ 13,500. ⬆ Teeside, 50 miles (80 km) NW Whitby. 🚉 Station Sq. ⓘ Langborne Rd (01723 383637). 🛒 Tue, Sat. 🎭 Whitby Festival: Jun; Angling Festival: Apr; Lifeboat Day: Jul or Aug; Folk Week: 17–23 Aug; Whitby Regatta: Aug. **www.** discoveryorkshirecoast.com

Exploring Whitby

Whitby is divided into two by the estuary of the River Esk. The Old Town, with its pretty cobbled streets and pastel-hued houses, huddles round the harbour. High above it is St Mary's Church with a wood interior reputedly fitted by ships' carpenters. The ruins of the 13th-century Whitby Abbey, nearby, are still used as a landmark by mariners. From them you get a fine view over the still-busy harbour, strewn with colourful nets. A pleasant place for a stroll, the harbour is overlooked by an imposing bronze clifftop statue of the explorer Captain James Cook (1728–79), who was apprenticed as a teenager to a Whitby shipping firm.

Lobster pots lining the quayside of Whitby's quaint harbour

Medieval arches above the nave of Whitby Abbey

⛪ Whitby Abbey

(EH) Abbey Lane. **Tel** 01947 603568. ⭕ Mar–Oct: daily; Nov–Feb: Thu–Mon. 🅿️ ♿ 🛍️

The monastery founded in 657 was sacked by Vikings in 870. In the 11th century it was rebuilt as a Benedictine Abbey. The ruins date mainly from the 13th century. A visitor centre has recently been added.

⛪ St Mary's Parish Church

East Cliff. **Tel** 01947 603421. ⭕ daily. Stuart and Georgian alterations to this Norman church have left a mixture of twisted wood columns and maze-like 18th-century box pews. The 1778 triple-decker pulpit has rather avant-garde decor – ear-trumpets used by a Victorian rector's deaf wife.

🏛 Captain Cook Memorial Museum

Grape Lane. **Tel** 01947 601900. ⭕ Mar–Oct & Feb half-term: daily. 🅿️ 🛍️ **www.**cookmuseumwhitby.co.uk

The young James Cook slept in the attic of this 17th-century harbourside house when he was apprenticed nearby. The museum has displays of period furniture in the style described in the inventories of the house, and watercolours by artists who travelled on his voyages.

🏛 Whitby Museum and Pannett Art Gallery

Pannett Park. **Tel** 01947 602908 (museum), 01947 602051 (gallery). ⭕ Tue–Sun & public hols. ☀ Sun: am; 24 Dec–2 Jan. 🅿️ museum only. ♿ limited. 🛍️

The Pannett Park grounds, museum and gallery were a gift of Whitby solicitor, Robert Pannett (1834–1920), to house his art collection. Among the museum's treasures are objects illustrating local history, such as jet jewellery, and Captain Cook artifacts.

The three-storey extension at the museum, completed in 2005, houses a costume gallery and photography and map collections.

⛪ Caedmon's Cross

East Cliff.

On the path side of the abbey's clifftop graveyard is the cross of Caedmon, an illiterate labourer who worked at the abbey in the 7th century. He experienced a vision that inspired him to compose cantos of Anglo-Saxon religious verse, which are still sung today.

Cross of Caedmon (1898)

Robin Hood's Bay ⑳

North Yorkshire. 🏘 1,400.
🚆 🚌 *Whitby.* ℹ *Langbourne Rd, Whitby (01723 383637).*
www.discoveryorkshirecoast.com

Legend has it that Robin Hood *(see p336)* kept his boats here in case he needed to make a quick getaway. The village has a history as a smugglers' haven, and many houses have ingenious hiding places for contraband. The cobbled main street is so steep that visitors need to leave their vehicles in the car park. In the village centre, attractive, narrow streets full of colour-washed stone cottages huddle around a quaint quay. There is a rocky beach with rock pools for children to play in. At low tide, the pleasant walk south to Boggle Hole takes 15 minutes, but you need to keep an eye on the tides.

Cobbled alley in the Bay Town area of Robin Hood's Bay

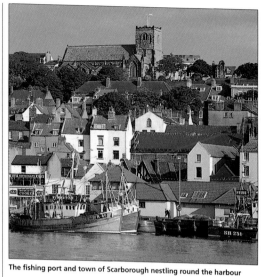

The fishing port and town of Scarborough nestling round the harbour

Scarborough ㉑

North Yorkshire. 🏘 54,000. 🚆
🚌 ℹ *Valley Bridge Rd (01723 383636).* 🛒 *Mon–Sat.* **www**.
discoveryorkshirecoast.com

The history of Scarborough as a resort can be traced back to 1626, when it became known as a spa. In the Industrial Revolution *(see pp348–9)* it was nicknamed "the Queen of the Watering Places", but the post-World War II trend for holidays abroad has meant fewer visitors. The town has two beaches; the South Bay amusement arcades contrast with the quieter North Bay. Playwright Alan Ayckbourn premiers his work at the Stephen Joseph theatre, and Anne Brontë *(see p412)* is buried in St Mary's Church.

Bronze and Iron Age relics have been found on the site of **Scarborough Castle**. The **Rotunda** (1828–9), which underwent a major refurbishment during 2007, was one of Britain's first purpose-built museums. Works by the local artist Atkinson Grimshaw (1836–93) hang in **Scarborough Art Gallery**. The **Sea-Life and Marine Sanctuary**'s baby seals are its main attraction.

⚓ **Scarborough Castle**
(EH) Castle Rd. **Tel** 01723 372451.
🕐 *Apr–Sep: daily; Oct–mid-Mar: Thu–Mon.* ● 1 Jan, 24–26 Dec.
🚫 👶 🚻 🅿

🏛 **Rotunda Museum**
Vernon Rd. **Tel** 01723 374839.
🕐 *Jun–Sep: Tue–Sun; Oct–May: Tue, Sat, Sun & public hols.*
● 1 Jan, 25 & 26 Dec. 🚫 🅿

🏛 **Scarborough Art Gallery**
The Crescent. **Tel** 01723 374753.
🕐 *Tue–Sun.* ● 1 Jan, 25 & 26 Dec. 🚫 👶 ♿ **www**.scarborough museums.org.uk

🐠 **Sea-Life and Marine Sanctuary**
Scalby Mills Rd. **Tel** 01723 376125.
🕐 *daily.* ● 25 Dec. 🚫 👶 🚻 🅿
www.sealifeeurope.com

THE GROWING POPULARITY OF SWIMMING

During the 18th century, sea-bathing came to be regarded as a healthy pastime, and from 1735 onwards men and women, on separate stretches of the coast, could be taken out into the sea in bathing huts, or "machines". In the 18th century, bathing was segregated although nudity was permitted. The Victorians brought in fully clothed bathing, and 19th-century workers from Britain's industrial heartlands used the new steam trains to visit the coast for their holidays. At this time, British seaside resorts such as Blackpool *(see p371)* and Scarborough expanded to meet the new demand.

A Victorian bathing hut on wheels

Castle Howard ❷

Pillar detail in the Great Hall, carved by Samuel Carpenter

Still owned and lived in by the Howard family, Castle Howard was created by Charles, 3rd Earl of Carlisle. In 1699, he commissioned Sir John Vanbrugh, a man of dramatic ideas but with no previous architectural experience, to design a palace for him. Vanbrugh's grand designs of 1699 were put into practice by architect Nicholas Hawksmoor *(see p28)*, and the main body of the house was completed by 1712. The West Wing was built in 1753–9, using a design by Thomas Robinson, son-in-law of the 3rd Earl. In the 1980s, Castle Howard was used as the location for the television version of Evelyn Waugh's novel *Brideshead Revisited* (1945) and again for the film version in 2008.

Temple of the Four Winds
Vanbrugh's last work, designed in 1724, has a dome and four Ionic porticoes. Situated in the grounds at the end of the terrace, it is typical of an 18th-century "landscape building".

The front façade boldly faces north, which is unusual for the 17th century, while all the state rooms have a southerly aspect, with superb views over the gardens.

East Wing

North Front

★ Great Hall
Rising 20 m (66 ft), from its 515 sq m (5,500 sq ft) floor to the dome, the Great Hall has columns by Samuel Carpenter (1660–1713), wall paintings by Pellegrini and a circular gallery.

SIR JOHN VANBRUGH

Vanbrugh (1664–1726) trained as a soldier, but became better known as a playwright, architect and member of the Whig nobility. He collaborated with Hawksmoor over the design of Blenheim Palace, but his bold architectural vision, later greatly admired, was mocked by the establishment. He died while working on the garden buildings and grounds of Castle Howard.

Chapel Stained Glass

Admiral Edward Howard ~~ered~~ the chapel in 1870–75. The windows were designed by Edward Burne-Jones and ~~ade~~ by William Morris & Co.

Bust of the 7th Earl

J H Foley sculpted this portrait bust, which stands at the top of the Grand Staircase in the West Wing, in 1870.

VISITORS' CHECKLIST

A64 from York. *Tel* 01653 648 444. ◼ York then bus, or Malton then taxi. **House** ◻ Mar–Oct: 11am–4pm daily. **Grounds** ◻ 10am–4:30pm daily. ◪ ◻ ◻
◻ www.castlehoward.co.uk

★ Long Gallery

Displayed here are paintings and sculptures commissioned by the Howard family, including works by Reynolds and Pannini.

West Wing

Tourist entrance

Antique Passage

Antiquities collected in the 18th and 19th centuries by the various Earls of Carlisle are on display here. The plethora of mythical figures and gods reflects contemporary interest in Classical civilizations.

STAR SIGHTS

★ Great Hall
_____
★ Long Gallery

Museum Room

Furniture here includes Regency chairs, a bronze collection and this 17th-century cabinet.

Eden Camp ㉓

Malton, North Yorkshire. **Tel** 01653 697777. ⊞ Malton then taxi. ◯ mid-Jan–late Dec: daily. ▢ ▥ ▧ ▢
www.edencamp.co.uk

This is an unusual, award-winning theme museum which pays tribute to the British people during World War II. Italian and German prisoners of war were kept at Eden Camp between 1939 and 1948. Today, some original huts built by Italian prisoners in 1942 are used as a museum, with period tableaux and a soundtrack. Each hut adopts a theme to take the visitor through civilian life in war-time, from Chamberlain's radio announcement of the outbreak of hostilities to the coming of peace. Visitors, including schoolchildren and nostalgic veterans, can see the Doodle-bug V-1 bomb which crashed outside the Officers' Mess, take tea in the canteen or experience a night in the Blitz. A tour can last for several hours.

British and American flags by the sign for Eden Camp

Wharram Percy ㉔

(EH) North Yorkshire. **Tel** 01904 601 901. ⊞ Malton, then taxi. ◯ daily.
www.english-heritage.org.uk

This is one of England's most important medieval village sites. Recent excavations have unearthed evidence of a 30-household community, with two manors, and the remains of a medieval church. There is also a millpond which has beautiful wild flowers in late spring. Wharram Percy is set in a pretty valley, sign-posted off the B1248 from Burdale, in the heart of the green, rolling Wolds. It is about 20 minutes' walk from the car park, and makes an ideal picnic stop.

Alabaster carving on the chimney-piece at Burton Agnes

Burton Agnes ㉕

On A614, nr Driffield, East Yorks. **Tel** 01262 490324. ⊞ Driffield, then bus. ◯ Apr–Oct: daily. ▥ ▧ limited. ▢
▢ **www**.burton-agnes.com

Of all the grand houses in this area, Burton Agnes Hall is a firm favourite. This is partly because the attractive, red-brick Elizabethan mansion has such a homely atmosphere. One of the first portraits you see in the Small Hall is of Anne Griffith, whose father, Sir Henry, built the house. There is a monument to him in the local church.

Burton Agnes has remained in the hands of the original family and has changed little since it was built, between 1598 and 1610. You enter it by the turreted gatehouse, and the entrance hall has a fine Elizabethan alabaster chimney piece. The massive oak stair-case is an impressive example of Elizabethan woodcarving.

In the library is a collection of Impressionist and Post-Impressionist art, pleasantly out of character with the rest of the house, including works by André Derain, Renoir and Augustus John. The extensive grounds include a purpose-built play area for children.

Bempton and Flamborough Head ㉖

East Yorkshire. ▦ 4,300. ⊞ Bempton. ▢ Bridlington. ▮ 25 Prince St, Bridlington (01262 673474).
www.eastriding.gov.uk

Bempton, which consists of 5 miles (8 km) of steep chalk cliffs between Speeton and Flamborough Head, is the largest seabird-breeding colony in England, and is famous for its puffins. The ledges and fissures provide ideal nest-sites for more

Nesting gannet on the chalk cliffs at Bempton

than 100,000 pairs of birds. Today, eight different species, including skinny black shags and kittiwakes, thrive on the Grade 1 listed *(see p671)* Bempton cliffs. Bempton is the only mainland site for goose-sized gannets, well known for their dramatic fishing techniques. May, June and July are the best bird-watching months.

The spectacular cliffs are best seen from the north side of the Flamborough Head peninsula.

Beverley ㉗

East Riding of Yorkshire. 🚉 30,000.
🛈 34 Butcher Row (01482 391672).
🖂 Sat. **www**.eastriding.gov.uk

The history of Beverley dates back to the 8th century, when Old Beverley served as a retreat for John, later Bishop of York, who was canonized for his healing powers. Over the centuries Beverley grew as a medieval sanctuary town. Like York, it is an attractive combination of both medieval and Georgian buildings.

The best way to enter Beverley is through the last of five medieval town gates, the castellated North Bar (rebuilt

Minstrel Pillar in St Mary's Church

1409–10). The bars were constructed so that market goods had to pass through them and a toll (levy) paid.

The skyline is dominated by the twin towers of the magnificent **minster**. This was co-founded in 937 by Athelstan, King of Wessex, in place of the church that John of Beverley had chosen as his final resting place in 721. The decorated nave is the earliest surviving building work which dates back to the early 1300s. It is particularly famous for its 16th-century choir stalls and 68 misericords *(see p341)*.

The minster contains many early detailed stone carvings, including a set of four from about 1308 that illustrate figures with ailments such as toothache and lumbago. On the north side of the altar is the richly carved 14th-century Gothic Percy tomb, thought to be that of Lady Idoine Percy. Also on the north side is the Fridstol, or Peace Chair, said to date from 924-39, the time of Athelstan. Anyone who sat on it would be granted 30 days' sanctuary.

Within the North Bar, **St Mary's Church** has a 13th-century chancel and houses Britain's largest number of medieval

The inspiration for Lewis Carroll's White Rabbit, St Mary's Church

stone carvings of musical instruments. The brightly painted 16th-century Minstrel Pillar is particularly notable. Painted on the panelled chancel ceiling are portraits of monarchs after 1445. On the richly sculpted doorway of St Michael's Chapel is the grinning pilgrim rabbit said to have inspired Lewis Carroll's White Rabbit in *Alice in Wonderland*.

There is a great day out to be had at **Beverley Races**, with various theme days throughout the season and excellent food and drink.

⏻ **Beverley Races**
York Rd. **Tel** 01482 867488.
◯ 20 meetings Apr–Sep.
🅿️ ♿ 🍴 @ info@
beverleyracecourse.co.uk

Beverley Minster, one of Europe's finest examples of Gothic architecture

Burton Constable ㉘

Nr Hull, East Yorkshire. **Tel** 01964 562400. 🚃 Hull then taxi. ◌ Easter–Oct: Sat–Thu. 🎟️ ♿ 🅿️ 🚻 🖼️ www.burtonconstable.com

The Constable family have been leading landowners since the 13th century, and have lived at Burton Constable Hall since work began on it in 1570. It is an Elizabethan house, altered in the 18th century by Thomas Lightholer, Thomas Atkinson and James Wyatt. Today, its 30 rooms include Georgian and Victorian interiors. It has a fine collection of Chippendale furniture and family portraits dating from the 16th century. Most of the collections of prints, textiles and drawings belong to Leeds City Art Galleries. The family still lives in the south wing.

Painting of Burton Constable (c.1690) by an anonymous artist

In Victoria Square is the **Maritime Museum**. Built in 1871 as the offices of the Hull Dock Company, it traces the city's maritime history. Among its exhibits are an ornate whalebone and vertebrae bench and a display of complicated rope knots such as the Eye Splice and the Midshipman's Hitch.

An imposing Elizabethan building, **Hands on History**, explores Hull's story through a collection of some of its families' artifacts.

In the heart of the Old Town, the **William Wilberforce House** is one of the surviving examples of the High Street's brick merchants' dwellings. Its first-floor oak-panelled rooms date from the 17th century, but most of the house is dedicated to the Wilberforce family. The house has

recently undergone a huge refurbishment costing around £1.6 million.

Nearby is the **Streetlife Transport Museum**, Hull's most popular and noisiest museum, loved by children. It features Britain's oldest tramcar. New to Hull, at the mouth of the River Hull, **The Deep** is the world's only submarium, in a stunning building and dramatic setting. With lots of exciting sea life and state-of-the-art technology, it is ideal for families.

🏛 **Maritime Museum**
Queen Victoria Sq **Tel** 01482 613903. ◌ daily (Sun: pm). ♿ 🅿️ www.hullcc.gov.uk/museums

🏛 **Hands on History**
South Churchside. **Tel** 01482 613902. ◌ daily (Sun: pm). ● 23-27 Dec, 1 Jan, Good Fri. 🚻 ♿

The Princes' Dock in Kingston upon Hull's restored docks area

Kingston upon Hull ㉙

Kingston upon Hull. 🚶 270,000. 🚃 🚉 🚌 🛈 Paragon St. (01482 223559). 🛒 Mon–Sat. www.hullcc.gov.uk

There is a lot more to Hull than the heritage of a thriving fishing industry. The restored town centre docks are attractive, and Hull's Old Town, laid out in medieval times, is all cobbled, winding streets and quaintly askew red-brick houses. You can follow the "Seven Seas" Fish Trail, a path of inlaid metal fishes on the city's pavements that illustrates the many different varieties that have been landed in Hull, from anchovy to shark.

WILLIAM WILBERFORCE (1758–1833)

William Wilberforce, born in Hull to a merchant family, was a natural orator. After studying Classics at Cambridge, he entered politics and in 1784 gave one of his first public addresses in York. The audience was captivated, and Wilberforce realized the potential of his powers of persuasion. From 1785 onwards, adopted by the Pitt government as spokesman for the abolition of slavery, he conducted a determined and conscientious campaign. But his speeches won him enemies, and in 1792, threats from a slave-importer meant that he needed a constant armed guard. In 1807 his bill to abolish the lucrative slave trade became law.

A 19th-century engraving of Wilberforce by J Jenkins

🏛 **William Wilberforce Hse**
High St, Hull. **Tel** 01482 613921.
⬜ daily (Sun: pm). 🔲 🔲 🚻 limited.

🏛 **Streetlife Transport Museum**
High St, Hull. **Tel** 01482 613956.
⬜ Mon–Sat, Sun pm. 🚻 🔲

🐟 **The Deep**
Hull (via Citadel Way). **Tel** 01482 381 000. ⬜ daily. ⬤ 24, 25 Dec. 🚻 📷
🔲 🔲 🅿 **www**.thedeep.co.uk

Holderness and Spurn Head 30

East Riding of Yorkshire. 🚂 Hull
(Paragon St) then bus. 🚌 120
Newbegin, Hornsea (01964 536404).

This curious flat area east of Hull, with straight roads and delicately waving fields of oats and barley, in many ways resembles Holland, except that its mills are derelict. Beaches stretch for 30 miles (46 km) along the coastline. The main resort towns are **Withernsea** and **Hornsea**.

The Holderness landscape only exists because of erosion higher up the coast. The sea continues to wash down tiny bits of rock which accumulate. Around 1560, this began to form a sandbank, and by 1669 it had became large enough to be colonized as Sonke Sand. The last bits of silting mud and debris joined the island to the mainland as recently as the 1830s. Today, you can drive through the eerie, lush wilderness of Sunk Island on the way east to Spurn Head. This is located at the tip of the Spurn Peninsula,

a 3.5 mile (6 km) spit of land that has also built up as the result of coastal erosion elsewhere. Flora, fauna and birdlife have been protected here by the Yorkshire Wildlife Trust since 1960. Walking here gives the eerie feeling that the land could be eroded from under your feet at any time. A surprise discovery at the end of Spurn Head is a tiny community of pilots and lifeboat crew, constantly on call to guide ships into Hull harbour, or help cope with disasters.

Fishing boat at Grimsby's National Fishing Heritage Centre

Grimsby 31

NE Lincs. 🏙 92,000. 🚲 🔲 🚹
Alexandra Dock, Cleethorpes (01472
323222). **www**.nelincs.gov.uk

Perched at the mouth of the River Humber, Grimsby was founded in the Middle Ages by a Danish fisherman by the name of Grim, and rose to prominence in the 19th century as one of the world's largest fishing ports. Its first dock was opened in 1800 and, with the arrival of the railways, the town secured the means of transporting its catch all over the country. Even though the traditional fishing industry had declined by the 1970s, dock area redevelopment has ensured that Grimsby's unique heritage is retained.

This is best demonstrated by the award-winning **National Fishing Heritage Centre**, a museum that recreates the industry in its 1950s heyday, capturing the atmosphere of the period. Visitors sign on as crew members on a trawler and, by means of a variety of vivid interactive displays, travel from the back streets of Grimsby to the Arctic fishing grounds. On the way, they can experience the roll of the ship, the smell of the fish and the heat of the engine. The tour can be finished off with a guided viewing of the restored 1950s trawler, the *Ross Tiger*.

Other attractions in Grimsby include an International Jazz Festival every September, a restored Victorian shopping street called Abbeygate, a market, a wide selection of restaurants, and the nearby seaside resorts of Cleethorpes, Mablethorpe and Skegness.

🏛 **National Fishing Heritage Centre**
Heritage Sq, Alexandra Dock. **Tel**
01472 323345. ⬜ Easter–Oct: daily.
⬤ 25 & 26 Dec. 📷 🚻 📷 🔲 🔲

Isolated lighthouse at Spurn Head, at the tip of Spurn Peninsula

Street-by-Street: York ⏱

The city of York has retained so much of its medieval structure that walking into its centre is like entering a living museum. Many of the ancient timbered houses, perched on narrow, winding streets, such as the Shambles, are protected by a conservation order. Much of the centre is pedestrianised and there are always student bikes bouncing over cobbled streets.
Its strategic position led to its development as a railway centre in the 19th century.

Monk Bar coat of arms

★ York Minster
England's largest medieval church was built in 1220 (see pp40...)

Stonegate
The medieval red devil is a feature of this street, built over a Roman road.

York Art Gallery

St Mary's Abbey

Yorkshire Museum is home to some of the most fascinating archeology in the country.

Lendal Bridge

Railway station, coach station, National Railway Museum, and Leeds

Ye Old Starre Inne is one of the oldest pubs in York.

St Olave's Church
The 11th-century church, next to the gatehouse of St Mary's Abbey (see p350), was founded by the Earl of Northumbria in memory of St Olaf, King of Norway. To the left is the Chapel of St Mary on the Walls.

Guildhall
This two-headed medieval roof boss is on the 15th-century Guildhall, situated beside the River Ouse and restored after bomb damage during World War II

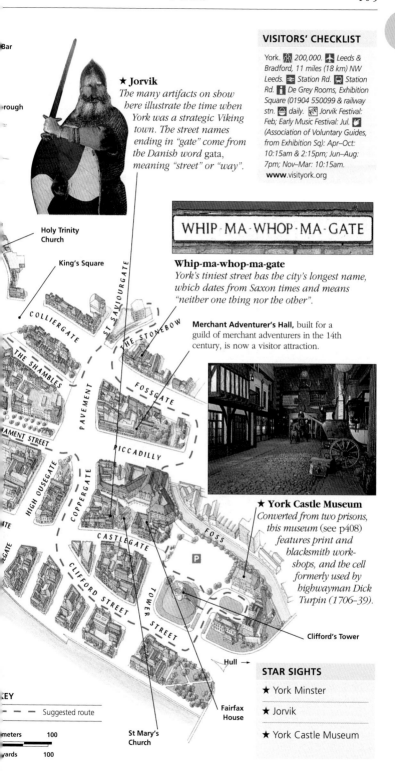

Bar

rough

★ Jorvik
The many artifacts on show here illustrate the time when York was a strategic Viking town. The street names ending in "gate" come from the Danish word gata, *meaning "street" or "way".*

VISITORS' CHECKLIST

York. 🏠 200,000. ✈ Leeds & Bradford, 11 miles (18 km) NW Leeds. 🚆 Station Rd. 🚍 Station Rd. ℹ De Grey Rooms, Exhibition Square (01904 550099 & railway stn. 🏛 daily. 🎭 Jorvik Festival: Feb; Early Music Festival: Jul. 🎫 (Association of Voluntary Guides, from Exhibition Sq): Apr–Oct: 10:15am & 2:15pm; Jun–Aug: 7pm; Nov–Mar: 10:15am.
www.visityork.org

Holy Trinity Church

King's Square

COLLIERGATE

ST SAVIOURGATE

THE STONEBOW

WHIP·MA·WHOP·MA·GATE

Whip-ma-whop-ma-gate
York's tiniest street has the city's longest name, which dates from Saxon times and means "neither one thing nor the other".

Merchant Adventurer's Hall, built for a guild of merchant adventurers in the 14th century, is now a visitor attraction.

THE SHAMBLES

PAVEMENT

FOSSGATE

LIAMENT STREET

PICCADILLY

HIGH OUSEGATE

COPPERGATE

FOSS

★ York Castle Museum
Converted from two prisons, this museum (see p408) features print and blacksmith workshops, and the cell formerly used by highwayman Dick Turpin (1706–39).

CASTLEGATE

ATE

GATE

CLIFFORD STREET

TOWER STREET

Clifford's Tower

🅿

Hull →

KEY

- - - Suggested route

meters   100

yards   100

Fairfax House

St Mary's Church

STAR SIGHTS

★ York Minster

★ Jorvik

★ York Castle Museum

York Minster

Central sunflower in rose window

The largest Gothic cathedral north of the Alps, York Minster is 158 m (519 ft) long and 76 m (249 ft) wide across the transepts, and houses the largest collection of medieval stained glass in Britain (see p409). The word "minster" usually means a church served by monks, but priests always served at York. The first minster began as a wooden chapel used to baptize King Edwin of Northumbria in 627. There have been several cathedrals on or near the site, including an 11th-century Norman structure. The present minster was begun in 1220 and completed 250 years later. In July 1984, the south transept roof was destroyed by fire. Restoration cost £2.25 million.

Central Tower
This lantern tower was reconstructed in 1420–65 (after partial collapse in 1407) from a design by the master stonemason William Colchester.

Great East Window (p409)

The Choir has a vaulted entrance with a 15th-century boss of the Assumption of the Virgin.

South transept entrance

The 16th-century rose window

★ **Choir Screen**
Sited between the choir and the nave, this 15th-century stone screen depicts kings of England from William I to Henry VI, and has a canopy of angels.

The Nave, begun 1291, was severely damaged by fire in 1840. Rebuilding costs were heavy, but it was re-opened with a new peal of bells in 1

★ **Chapter House**
A Latin inscription near the entrance of the wooden-vaulted Chapter House (1260–85) reads: "As the rose is the flower of flowers, so this is the house of houses".

VISITORS' CHECKLIST

Deangate, York. *Tel 01904 557216.* ☐ *Mon–Sat: 9am–5pm (from 9:30am Nov–Mar); Sun: noon–3:45pm. Opening times may change subject to major services.* ● *Good Fri, Easter Sun, 24 & 25 Dec.* ☒ *to Minster, Undercroft & the Tower.* ✝ *Mon–Sat: 7:30am, 7:45am, 12:30pm (also at noon Sat), 5:15pm (evensong); Sun: 8am, 10am, 11:30am, 4pm.* ☒ *main floors.* ☒ ⛪ ☐
www.yorkminster.org

Timbered interior of the Merchant Adventurers' Hall

The western towers, with their 15th-century decorative panelling and elaborate pinnacles, contrast with the simpler design of the north transept. The southwest tower is the minster belfry.

Great West Door

West Window

STAR SIGHTS

★ Chapter House

★ Choir Screen

⛩ Monk Bar

This is one of York's finest original medieval gates, situated at the end of Goodramgate. It is vaulted on three floors, and the portcullis still works. In the Middle Ages, the rooms above it were rented out, and it was a prison in the 16th century. Its decorative details include men holding stones ready to drop on intruders.

🏛 York Art Gallery

Exhibition Sq. *Tel 01904 687687.* ☐ *daily.* ● *1 Jan, 24–26 Dec.* ☒☒☒☐☐
www.yorkartgallery.org.uk
This Italianate building of 1879 holds a wide-ranging collection of paintings from western Europe dating from the early 14th century. There is also a collection of British and foreign studio pottery, including work by Bernard Leach, William Staite Murray and Shoji Hamada.

A 15th-century French portrait of St Anthony in York Art Gallery

⛩ Clifford's Tower

(EH) Clifford's St. *Tel 01904 646940.* ☐ *daily.* ● *1 Jan, 24–26 Dec.* ☐ ☒ www.english-heritage.org.uk
Sited on top of a mound that William the Conqueror built for his original wooden castle, destroyed by fire during anti-Jewish riots in 1190, Clifford's Tower dates from the 13th century. Built by Henry III, it was named after the de Clifford family, who were constables of the castle.

🏛 DIG – An Archaeological Adventure

St Saviourgate. *Tel 01904 543403.* ☐ *daily (best to book in advance).* ● *24–25 Dec.* ☒☒☐☐
Housed in a restored medieval church, this centre invites visitors to become archaeological detectives and discover how archaeologists have pieced together clues from the past to unravel the history of the Viking age in York.

⛩ Merchant Adventurers' Hall

(EH) Fossgate. *Tel 01904 654818.* ☐ *Easter–Sep: daily; Oct–Easter: Mon–Sat.* ● *24 Dec–3 Jan.* ☒☒
www.theyorkcompany.co.uk
Built by the York Merchants' Guild, which controlled the northern cloth trade in the 15th–17th centuries, this building has fine timberwork. The Great Hall is probably the best example of its kind in Europe. Among its paintings is an unattributed 17th-century copy of Van Dyck's portrait of Charles I's queen, Henrietta Maria. Below the Great Hall is the hospital, which was used by the guild until 1900, and a private chapel.

Exploring York

The appeal of York is its many layers of history. A medieval city constructed on top of a Roman one, it was first built in AD 71, when it became capital of the northern province and was known as Eboracum. It was here that Constantine the Great was made emperor in 306, and reorganized Britain into four provinces. A hundred years later, the Roman army had withdrawn. Eboracum was renamed Eoforwic, under the Saxons, and then became a Christian stronghold. The Danish street names are the reminder that it was a Viking centre from 867, and one of Europe's chief trading bases. Between 1100 and 1500 it was England's second city. The glory of York is the minster *(see pp406–7)*. The city also boasts 18 medieval churches, 3 mile long (4.8 km) medieval city walls, elegant Jacobean and Georgian architecture and fine museums.

Grand staircase and fine plaster ceiling at Fairfax House

The Middleham Jewel, Yorkshire Museum

🏛 York Castle Museum

The Eye of York. **Tel** 01904 687687. ⬤ daily. ⬤ 1 Jan, 25 & 26 Dec. ♿ ground floor only. 📷 🅿 📱 www.york.castle.museum.org.uk

Housed in two 18th-century prisons, the museum has a fine folk collection, started by Dr John Kirk of the market town of Pickering. Opened in 1938, its period displays include a Jacobean dining room, a moorland cottage, and a 1950s front room. It also contains an exhibition on the traditions of birth, marriages and death in Britain from 1700 to 2000.

The most famous exhibits include the reconstructed Victorian street of Kirkgate, complete with shopfronts, and the Anglo Saxon York Helmet, discovered in 1982.

🏠 York Minster

See pp406–7.

🏛 Jorvik

Coppergate. **Tel** 01904 543400. ⬤ daily. ⬤ 25 Dec. ♿ ring first. 📱 www.jorvik-viking-centre.co.uk

This centre is built on the site of the original Viking settlement which archaeologists uncovered at Coppergate. Using new technology, a dynamic vision of 10th-century York is recreated, with smells bringing the Viking world to life. At the centre's sister attraction, DIG, visitors can take part in an archaeological excavation.

🏛 Yorkshire Museum and St Mary's Abbey

Museum Gardens. **Tel** 01904 687687. ⬤ daily. ♿ 🅿 📱

Yorkshire Museum was in the news when it purchased the 15th-century Middleham Jewel for £2.5 million, one of the finest pieces of English Gothic jewellery found this century. Other exhibits include 2nd-century Roman mosaics and an Anglo-Saxon silver gilt bowl.

St Mary's Abbey *(see p350)* in the riverside grounds is where the medieval York Mystery Plays are set every few years.

🛏 Fairfax House

Castlegate. **Tel** 01904 655543. ⬤ mid-Feb–Dec: daily (Sun: pm only). ⬤ 24, 26 & 31 Dec, Jan, early Feb. 📷 📱 ♿ limited. 📱 www.fairfaxhouse.co.uk

From 1755 to 1762 Viscount Fairfax built this fine Georgian town house for his daughter, Anne. The house was designed by John Carr *(see p28)*, and restored in the 1980s. Between 1920 and 1965 it was a cinema and dancehall. Today, visitors can see the bedroom of Anne Fairfax (1725–93), and a fine collection of 18th-century furniture, porcelain and clocks.

🏛 National Railway Museum

Leeman Rd. **Tel** 01904 621261. ⬤ daily. ⬤ 24–26 Dec. ♿ 🅿 📱 www.nrm.org.uk

In what is the world's largest railway museum, nearly 200 years of history are explored using a variety of visual aids. Visitors can try wheel-tapping and shunting in the interactive gallery, or find out what made Stephenson's *Rocket* so successful. Exhibits include uniforms, rolling stock from 1797 onward and Queen Victoria's Royal Train carriage, as well as the very latest rail innovations.

Reproduction of Stephenson's Rocket (right) and 1830s first-class carriage in York's National Railway Museum

The Stained Glass of York Minster

York Minster houses the largest collection of medieval stained glass in Britain, some of it dating from the late 12th century. The glass was generally coloured during production, using metal oxides to produce the desired colour, then worked on by craftsmen on site. When a design had been produced, the glass was first cut, then trimmed to shape. Details

Window detail

were painted on, using iron oxide-based paint which was fused to the glass by firing in a kiln. Individual pieces were then leaded together to form the finished window.

Part of the fascination of the minster glass is its variety of subject matter. Some windows were paid for by lay donors who specified a particular subject, others reflect ecclesiastical patronage.

Miracle of St Nicholas *(late 12th century) was put in the nave over 100 years after it was made. It shows a Jew's conversion.*

The Five Sisters *in the north transept are the largest examples of grisaille glass in Britain. This popular 13th-century technique involved creating fine patterning on clear glass and decorating it with black enamel.*

St John the Evangelist, *in part of the Great West Window (c.1338), is holding an eagle, itself an example of stickwork, where paint is scraped off to reveal clear glass.*

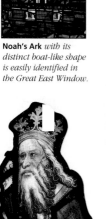

Noah's Ark *with its distinct boat-like shape is easily identified in the Great East Window.*

The Great East Window *(1405–8), the size of a tennis court, is the largest area of medieval painted glass in the world. The Dean and Chapter paid master glazier John Thornton four shillings a week for this celebration of the Creation.*

Edward III *is a fine example of the 14th-century "soft" style of painting, achieved by stippling the paint.*

Walter Skirlaw, *whose bishopric was revoked in favour of Richard Scrope, donated this window on its completion in 1408.*

Harewood House ❸❸

Leeds. **Tel** 0113 2181010. �æ *Leeds then bus.* ⬜ *mid-Mar–Nov: daily.* 📷
♿ 🎫 *by arrangement.* 🖥 📷
www.harewood.org

Designed by John Carr in 1759, Harewood House is the Yorkshire home of the Earl and Countess of Harewood.

The grand Palladian exterior is impressive, with interiors created by Robert Adam and an unrivalled collection of 18th-century furniture made specifically for Harewood by Yorkshire-born Thomas Chippendale (1711–79). There is a collection of paintings by Italian and English artists, including Reynolds and Gainsborough, and two watercolour rooms. The grounds by Capability Brown *(see p26)* include the **Harewood Bird Garden**, which has exotic species and a breeding programme of certain endangered varieties.

Bali starling, one of Harewood's rare birds

Leeds ❸❹

Leeds. 🏙 750,000. 🚶 🚆 🚌
🈐 *Leeds City Station (0113 2425242).* 🈐 *Mon–Sat.*
www.leedsliveitloveit.com

The third-largest of Britain's provincial cities, Leeds was at its most prosperous during the Victorian period. The most impressive legacy from this era is a series of ornate, covered shopping arcades. Also of note is the **Town Hall**, designed by Cuthbert Brodrick and opened by Queen Victoria in 1858.

Today, although Leeds is primarily an industrial city, it also offers a thriving cultural scene. Productions at **The Grand** by Opera North, one of Britain's top operatic companies, are of a high quality.

The **City Art Gallery** has impressive collections of British 20th-century art and of Victorian paintings, including works by local artist Atkinson Grimshaw (1836–93). Among the late 19th-century French art are works by Signac, Courbet and Sisley. The Henry Moore Institute, added in 1993, is devoted to the research and display of sculpture of all periods. It comprises a study centre, library, galleries and an archive of material on Moore and other sculptural pioneers.

The **Armley Mills Museum**, in a 19th-century woollen mill, explores the industrial heritage of Leeds. Filled with original equipment, recorded sounds and models in 19th-century workers' clothes, it traces the history of the ready-to-wear industry. The **Leeds City Museum** charts the history of Leeds with ethnographical and archaeological exhibits.

A striking waterfront development by the River Aire has attracted two museums. The **Royal Armouries Museum**, from the Tower of London, tells the story of arms and armour around the world in battle, sport and fashion. The **Thackray Medical Museum** is an interactive display of medical advances, from a re-created Victorian slum to modern-day medical challenges.

For children, **Tropical World** features crystal pools, a rainforest house, butterflies and tropical fish. There is also a farm and a Rare Breeds

The County Arcade, one of Leeds' restored shopping arcades

centre in the grounds of the Tudor-Jacobean **Temple Newsam House**, which has major art and furniture collections including Chippendale pieces.

🏛 **City Art Gallery**
The Headrow. **Tel** 0113 2478248.
⬜ *daily (Sun: pm).* 🈐 ♿ 📷

🏛 **Armley Mills Museum**
Canal Rd, Armley. **Tel** 0113 2637 861. ⬜ *Tue–Sun (Sun: pm), pub hols.*
⬤ *1 Jan, 25, 26 Dec.* 📷 ♿ 📷

🏛 **Leeds City Museum**
Millennium Sq. **Tel** 0113 2243732.
⬜ *daily.* ⬤ *pub hols.* ♿ 🈐 📷

🏛 **Royal Armouries**
Armouries Drive. **Tel** 0113 2201999.
⬜ *daily.* ⬤ *24, 25 Dec.* ♿ 🈐 📷

🏛 **Thackray Medical Museum**
Beckett St. 🈐 *0113 2457084.* ⬜ *daily.* ⬤ *1 Jan, 24–26, 31 Dec.* 📷
♿ 🈐 📷 **www**.thackraymuseum.org

🍀 **Tropical World**
Canal Gdns, Princes Ave. **Tel** 0113 2661850. ⬜ *daily.* ⬤ *25, 26 Dec.*
📷 ♿ 🈐 📷

🏛 **Temple Newsam House**
Off A63. **Tel** 0113 2645535. ⬜ *Tue–Sun.* ⬤ *25 & 26 Dec, Jan.* 📷 🈐 📷

Working loom at the Armley Mills Museum in Leeds

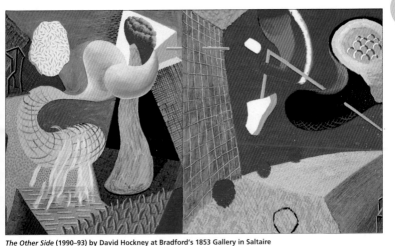

The Other Side (1990–93) by David Hockney at Bradford's 1853 Gallery in Saltaire

Bradford 35

Bradford. 492,000. ✈ ≋ ⌷
City Hall, Centenary Square
(01274 433678). Mon–Sat.
www.visitbradford.com

In the 16th century, Bradford was a thriving market town, and the opening of its canal in 1774 boosted trade. By 1850, it was the world's capital for worsted (fabric made from closely twisted wool). Many of the city's well-preserved civic and industrial buildings date from this period, such as the Wool Exchange on Market Street. In the 1800s a number of German textile manufacturers settled in what is now called Little Germany. Their houses are characterized by decorative stone carvings that illustrated the wealth and standing of the occupants.

The **National Media Museum**, founded in 1983, explores the technology and art of these media. There is a television section called TV Heaven, where visitors can ask to watch their favourite programme. They are also encouraged to see themselves read the news on TV. The giant IMAX screen uses the world's largest film format. Film subjects include journeys

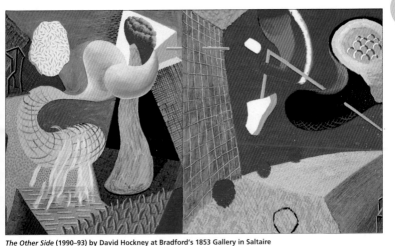

Daguerreotype camera by Giroux (1839)

into space, the ocean and the natural world.

The **Colour Museum** traces dyeing and textile printing from ancient Egypt to the present day with an emphasis on hands-on elements.

Bradford Industrial Museum is housed in an original spinning mill. As well as seeing and hearing all the mill machinery, you can ride on a horse-drawn tram. Saltaire, a Victorian industrial village (*see p349*), is on the outskirts of the city. Built by Sir Titus Salt for his Salts Mill workers, it was completed in 1873. The **1853 Gallery** has the world's largest collection of works by David Hockney, born in Bradford.

🏛 **National Media Museum**
Pictureville. *Tel* 01274 202030.
☐ daily (school hols); Tue–Sun (school terms); public holidays. ● 24–26 Dec.
🅿 & 🍴 www.nmpft.org.uk

🏛 **Colour Museum**
1 Providence St. *Tel* 01274 390955.
☐ Tue–Sat. ● 24 Dec–2 Jan.
🅿 🍴 &
www.colour-experience.org

🏛 **Bradford Industrial Museum**
Moorside Mills, Moorside Rd. *Tel* 01274 435900. ☐ Tue–Sat, Sun (pm), public hols. ● 25 & 26 Dec. & 🅿
www.bradfordmuseums.org

🏛 **1853 Gallery**
Salts Mill, Victoria Rd. *Tel* 01274 531 163. ☐ daily. ● 25 & 26 Dec. &
🍴 🅿 🅿 www.saltsmill.org.uk

BRADFORD'S INDIAN COMMUNITY

Immigrants from the Indian subcontinent originally came to Bradford in the 1950s to work in the mills, but with the decline of the textile industry many began small businesses. By the mid-1970s there were 1,400 such enterprises in the area. Almost one fifth were in the food sector, born out of simple cafés catering for mill-workers whose families were far away. As Indian food became more popular, these restaurants thrived, and today there are over 200 serving the highly spiced dishes of the Indian subcontinent.

Balti in a Bradford restaurant

Haworth Parsonage, home to the Brontë family, now a museum

Haworth ❸

Bradford. 🕍 5,000. 🚊 Keighley.
🚉 2–4 West Lane (01535 642329).
www.visithaworth.com

The setting of Haworth, in bleak Pennine moorland dotted with farmsteads, has changed little since it was home to the Brontë family. The village boomed in the 1840s, when there were more than 1,200 hand-looms in operation, but it is more famous today for the Brontë connection.

You can visit the **Brontë Parsonage Museum**, home from 1820–61 to novelists Charlotte, Emily and Anne, their brother Branwell and their father, the Revd Patrick Brontë. Built in 1778–9, the house remains decorated as it was during the 1850s. Eleven rooms, including the children's study and Charlotte's room, display letters, manuscripts,

furniture and personal objects. The nostalgic Victorian **Keighley and Worth Valley Railway** runs through Haworth. It stops at Oakworth station, where parts of *The Railway Children* were filmed. At the end of the line is the Railway Museum at Oxenhope.

🏛 **Brontë Parsonage Museum**
Church St. **Tel** 01535 642323.
⭘ daily. ⬤ 24–27 Dec; Jan. 🅿 🎧
♿ limited. **www**.bronte.org.uk

Charlotte Brontë's childhood story book, for her sister, Anne

THE BRONTË SISTERS

During a harsh, motherless childhood, Charlotte, Emily and Anne retreated into fictional worlds of their own, writing poems and stories. As adults, they had to work as governesses, but still published a poetry collection in 1846. Only two copies were sold, but in the following year Charlotte's *Jane Eyre*, became a bestseller, arousing interest in Emily's *Wuthering Heights* and Anne's *Agnes Grey*. After her

Charlotte Brontë (1816–55)

siblings' deaths in 1848–9, Charlotte published her last novel, *Villette*, in 1852. She married the Revd Nicholls, her father's curate, in 1854, but died shortly afterwards.

Hebden Bridge ❸

Calderdale. 🕍 12,500. 🚊 🚉
New Rd (01422 843831). ⬤ Thu.
www.hebdenbridge.co.uk

Hebden Bridge is a delightful South Pennines former mill town, surrounded by steep hills and former 19th-century mills. The houses seem to defy gravity as they cling to the valley sides. Due to the gradient, one house is made from two bottom floors, and the top two floors form another unit. To separate ownership of these "flying freeholds", an Act of Parliament was devised.

There is a superb view of Hebden Bridge from nearby **Heptonstall**, where the poet Sylvia Plath (1932–63) is buried. The village contains a Wesleyan chapel (1764).

Halifax ❸

Calderdale. 🕍 88,000. 🚊 🚉
🚉 Piece Hall (01422 368725). ⬤
Thu–Sat. **www**.visitcalderdale.com

Halifax's history has been influenced by textiles since the Middle Ages, but today's visual reminders date mainly from the 19th century. The town inspired William Blake's vision of "dark Satanic mills" in his poem *Jerusalem* (1820). The wool trade helped to make the Pennines into Britain's industrial backbone.

Until the mid-15th century cloth production was modest, but vital enough to contribute towards the creation of the 13th-century Gibbet Law, which stated that anyone caught stealing cloth could be executed. There is a replica of the gibbet used for decapitation at the bottom of Gibbet Street. Many of Halifax's 18th- and 19th-century buildings owe their existence to wealthy cloth traders. Sir Charles Barry (1795–1860), architect of the Houses of Parliament, was commissioned by the Crossley family to design the Town Hall. They also paid for the landscaping of the People's Park by the creator of the Crystal Palace, Sir Joseph Paxton (1801–65). Thomas Bradley's

Large Two Forms (1966–9) by Henry Moore in Bretton Country Park

18th-century **Piece Hall** was where wool merchants once sold their cloth, trading in one of the 315 "Merchants' Rooms". It has a massive Italianate courtyard, now beautifully restored. Today, Halifax's market takes place here.

Eureka! is a hands-on children's museum, with exhibits such as the Giant Mouth Machine. **Shibden Hall Museum** is a fine period house, parts of which date to the 15th century.

Environs: The nearby village of **Sowerby Bridge** was an important textile centre from the Middle Ages to the 1960s. Today visitors come to enjoy the scenic canals.

🏛 **Eureka!**
Discovery Rd. 📞 01422 330069.
⭕ daily. ⚫ 24–26 Dec. ♿ 🚻 🖥
www.eureka.org.uk

🏛 **Shibden Hall Museum**
Listers Rd. *Tel* 01422 352246.
⭕ daily (Sun: pm). ⚫ 24 Dec–
2 Jan. 🏛 📷 🖥

National Coal Mining Museum ㊴

Wakefield. *Tel* 01924 848806. 🚃
Wakefield then bus. ⭕ daily (last tour
3:15pm – booking advised). Children
under 5 not allowed underground.
⚫ 24–26 Dec, 1 Jan. ♿ 📷 🖥 📷
www.ncm.org.uk

Housed in the old Caphouse Colliery, this museum offers the chance to go into a real mine shaft: warm clothing is advised. An underground tour takes you 137 m (450 ft) down,

equipped with a hat and a miner's lamp. Enter narrow seams and see exhibits such as life-size working models. Other displays depict mining from 1820 to the present day.

Yorkshire Sculpture Park ㊵

Wakefield. *Tel* 01924 832631.
🚃 Wakefield then bus. ⭕ daily.
⚫ 24, 25, 29–31 Dec. ♿ 🖥 📷
www.ysp.co.uk

This is one of Europe's leading open-air galleries, situated in 200 ha (500 acres) of 18th-century parkland dotted with changing exhibitions of the work of Henry Moore, Anthony Caro, Eduardo Chillida, Barbara Hepworth, Antony Gormley and others. The indoor display spaces include the ambitious visitor centre, which leads on to the stunning new Underground Gallery exhibition space.

Magna ㊶

Rotherham. *Tel* 01709 720002.
🚃 Rotherham Central or Sheffield
then bus (No. 69). ⭕ Mar–Sep:
daily; Oct–Feb: Tue–Sun.
⚫ 24 & 25 Dec. 📷 ♿ 🚻 🖥 📷
www.visitmagna.co.uk

A former steel works has been imaginatively converted into a huge science adventure centre, with an emphasis on interactive exhibits, noise and spectacle designed to appeal to 4–15-year-olds. In the Air, Fire, Water and Earth Pavilions visitors can get close to a tornado, operate real diggers or discover what it's like to detonate a rock face. There are also multimedia displays on the lives of steelworkers and on how a giant furnace operated, as well as a show that features robots with artificial intelligence that evolve and learn as they hunt each other down.

The Face of Steel display at Magna

NORTHUMBRIA

NORTHUMBERLAND · COUNTY DURHAM

England's northeast extremity is a tapestry of moorland, ruins, castles, cathedrals and huddled villages. With Northumberland National Park and Kielder Water reservoir to the north, a rugged eastern coastline, and the cities of Newcastle and Durham to the south, the area combines a dramatic history with abundant natural beauty.

The empty peaceful hills, elusive wildlife and panoramic vistas of Northumberland National Park belie the area's turbulent past. Warring Scots and English, skirmishing tribes, cattle drovers and whisky smugglers have all left traces on ancient routes through the Cheviot Hills. Slicing through the southern edge of the park is the famous reminder of the Romans' 400-year occupation of Britain, Hadrian's Wall, the northern boundary of their empire.

Conflict between Scots and English continued for 1,000 years after the Romans departed, and even after the 1603 union between the two crowns. A chain of massive crenellated medieval castles punctuates the coastline, while other forts that once defended the northern flank of England along the River Tweed lie mostly in ruins. Seventh-century Northumbria was the cradle of Christianity under St Aidan, but this was sharply countered by Viking violence from 793 onward, as the Scandinavian invaders raided the monasteries. But a reverence for Northumbrian saints is in the local psyche, and St Cuthbert and the Venerable Bede are both buried in Durham Cathedral. The influence of the Industrial Revolution, concentrated around the mouths of the rivers Tyne, Wear and Tees, made Newcastle upon Tyne the north's main centre for coal mining and ship-building. Today, the city is famous for its "industrial heritage" attractions and urban regeneration schemes.

Section of Hadrian's Wall, built by the Romans in about 120, looking east from Cawfields

◁ The towers of Durham Cathedral, rising above the River Wear

Exploring Northumbria

Historic sites are plentiful along Northumbria's coast.
South of Berwick-upon-Tweed, a causeway leads to the
ruined priory and castle on Lindisfarne, and there are
major castles at Bamburgh, Alnwick and Warkworth. The
hinterland is a region of wide open spaces, with wilderness
in the Northumberland National Park, and fascinating Roman
remains of Hadrian's Wall at Housesteads and elsewhere.
The glorious city of Durham is dominated by its castle and
cathedral, and Newcastle upon Tyne has a lively nightlife.

SIGHTS AT A GLANCE

Alnwick Castle **5**
Bamburgh **4**
Barnard Castle **17**
Beamish Open Air Museum **13**
Berwick-upon-Tweed **1**
Cheviot Hills **8**
Corbridge **10**
Durham pp428–9 **14**
Farne Islands **3**
Hadrian's Wall pp422–3 **11**
Hexham **9**
Kielder Water **7**
Lindisfarne **2**
Middleton-in-Teesdale **16**
Newcastle upon Tyne **12**
Warkworth Castle **6**

Walks and Tours
North Pennines Tour **15**

SEE ALSO

The wilderness of Upper Coquetdale in the sparsely
populated Cheviot Hills

Eyemouth
**BERW
UPON-TW**
Tweedn

Tweed

Coldstream

Crookham

A69

W

*The Cheviot
816m*

*Kidland
Forest*

Jedburgh

CHEVIOT
HILLS **8**
Al

Kielder Forest

A68

Northumberland Nationa

Rede

Rochester

Be

Kielder

**KIELDER
WATER** **7**

Otterburn

A6

B6320

Ridsc

Bellingham

A68

Wark

Colwell

HADRIAN'S WALL

Hu

Housesteads **11** Chesters
Great   Fort
Chesters Fort   Vindolanda

Chesters
Fort

COR

A69

Haydon
Bridge

9
HEXHA

Carlisle

Haltwhistle

P

NORTH PENNINES TOUR

Allendale
Town

D
Re

15

B6295

Bla

e

Allenheads

n

Cowshill

A689

Stan

n

i

n

e

s

*Cow Green
Reservoir*

**MIDDLETON IN
TEESDALE** **16**

Penrith

B

A66

0 kilometres   10

0 miles   10

The rugged coastline of Northumberland, with Bamburgh Castle in the distance

GETTING AROUND

North of Newcastle, the A1068 meets the A1 linking the sights of the Northumbrian coast, and continuing on to Scotland. Two spectacular inland routes, the A696 and the A68, merge near Otterburn to skirt the Northumberland National Park. A mainline railway links Durham, Newcastle and Berwick, but a car is necessary to explore Northumbria comprehensively.

KEY

▬▬	Motorway
▭▭	Major road
▬	Secondary road
▭▭▭	Minor road
▬	Scenic route
▭▭	Main railway
───	Minor railway
△	Summit

ARNE ▲ 2

E ISLANDS 3

4 BAMBURGH ▲ 🏛 Seahouses

B1340

A1

Embleton

rton

n

Aln

CASTLE 5 ▲ 🏛 Alnmouth

Shilbottle

WARKWORTH 6
CASTLE ▲ Amble

y

ington Broomhill

Felton

rsley Widdrington

A697 A1068

Ashington

Morpeth

343

ton Bedlington Blyth

Belsay A189

A1 Cramlington

nteland ✈

Whitley Bay

ewburn Gosforth A19

Tynemouth

South Shields

12 NEWCASTLE UPON TYNE

dhoe Gateshead Boldon

A692

Washington

MISH OPEN
IR MUSEUM 13 🏛 A1(M)
Sunderland

Stanley Chester le-Street

Consett

Houghton-le-Spring

chester A691 A690 Hetton-le-Hole

14 DURHAM Peterlee

Brandon Wheatley Hill

v Coxhoe A19

Willington

m Hartlepool

Spennymoor Ferryhill

p Auckland Sedgefield

Shildon A689 Seaton Carew

A688 Newton Aycliffe Redcar

A68 Billingham

Staindrop Saltburn-by-the-Sea

Stockton-on-Tees Loftus

NARD A1(M) Middlesbrough
LE Tees A66 Whitby

York Darlington A171

Northallerton

Guildhall, Newcastle upon Tyne

View over Berwick-upon-Tweed's three bridges

Berwick-upon-Tweed ❶

Northumberland. 👥 *13,000*. 🚢
🛈 *106 Mary Gate (01289 330733)*.
🛒 *Wed, Sat.*
www.berwick-upon-tweed.gov.uk

Between the 12th and 15th centuries Berwick-upon-Tweed changed hands 14 times in the wars between the Scots and English. Its position, at the mouth of the river which divides the two nations, made the town strategically vital.

The English finally gained permanent control in 1482 and maintained Berwick as a fortified garrison. Ramparts dating from 1555, 1.5 miles (2.5 km) long and 7 m (23 ft) thick, offer superb views over the Tweed. Within the 18th-century barracks are the **King's Own Scottish Borderers Regimental Museum**, an **art** gallery, and **By Beat of Drum**, charting the history of British infantrymen.

🏛 King's Own Scottish Borderers Regimental Museum
The Barracks. **Tel** *01289 307427.*
◻ *Easter–Oct: Mon–Sat;*
Nov–Easter: Wed–Sun. ● *22 Dec–3 Jan, public hols.* 📷 🛈

Lindisfarne ❷

Northumberland. 🚢 *Berwick-upon-Tweed then bus.* 🛈 *106 Mary Gate, Berwick-upon-Tweed (01289 330733).* **www**.lindisfarne.org.uk

Twice daily a long, narrow neck of land sinks under the North Sea tide for five hours, separating Lindisfarne, or Holy Island, from the coast. At low tide, visitors stream over the causeway to the island made famous by St Aidan, St Cuthbert and the Lindisfarne gospels. Nothing remains of the Celtic monks' monastery, finally abandoned in 875 after successive Viking attacks, but the magnificent arches of the 11th-century **Lindisfarne Priory** are still visible.

After 1540, stones from the priory were used to build **Lindisfarne Castle**, which was restored and made into a private home by Sir Edwin Lutyens *(see p29)* in 1903. It includes a walled garden by Gertrude Jekyll *(see p27)*.

⚓ Lindisfarne Castle
(NT) Holy Island. **Tel** *01289 389244.*
◻ *Mar–Oct & Feb half-term: Tue–Sun. Opening times depend on tide – phone to check.* 📷

Farne Islands ❸

(NT) Northumberland. 🚢 *from Sea-houses (Apr–Oct).* 🛈 *106 Mary Gate, Berwick-upon-Tweed (01289 330733)*

There are between 15 and 28 Farne Islands off the coast from Bamburgh, some of them periodically covered by sea. Nature wardens and lighthouse keepers share them with seals, puffins and other seabirds. Boat tours depart from **Seahouses** harbour and can land on Staple and Inner Farne, site of St Cuthbert's 14th-century chapel, or Longstone, where Grace Darling's lighthouse is located.

Lindisfarne Castle (1540), the main landmark on the island of Lindisfarne

Celtic Christianity

St Cuthbert on a sea voyage

The Irish monk St Aidan arrived in Northumbria in 635 from the island of Iona, off western Scotland, to evangelize the north of England. He founded the monastery on the island of Lindisfarne, and it became one of the most important centres for Christianity in England. This and other monastic communities thrived in Northumbria, becoming rich in scholarship, although the monks lived simply. It also emerged as a place of pilgrimage after miracles were reported at the shrine of St Cuthbert, Lindisfarne's most famous bishop. But the monks' pacifism made them defenceless against 9th-century Viking raids.

St Aidan's Monastery *was added to over the centuries to become Lindisfarne Priory. This 8th-century relic with interlaced animal decorations is from a cross at the site.*

The Venerable Bede *(673–735), the most brilliant early medieval scholar, was a monk at the monastery of St Paul in Jarrow. He wrote* The Ecclesiastical History of the English People *in 731.*

St Aidan *(600–651), an Irish missionary, founded a monastery at Lindisfarne and became Bishop of Northumbria in 635. This 1960 sculpture of him, by Kathleen Parbury, is in Lindisfarne Priory grounds.*

St Cuthbert *(635–87) was the monk and miracle worker most revered of all. He lived as a hermit on Inner Farne (a chapel was built there in his memory) and later became Bishop of Lindisfarne.*

Lindisfarne Priory *was built by Benedictines in the 11th century, on the site of St Aidan's earlier monastery.*

THE LINDISFARNE GOSPELS

Held in the British Library, this book of richly illustrated portrayals of Gospel stories is one of the masterpieces of the "Northumbrian Renaissance" which left a permanent mark on Christian art and history-writing. The work was carried out by monks at Lindisfarne under the direction of Bishop Eadfrith, around 700. Monks managed to save the book and took it with them when they fled from Lindisfarne in 875 after suffering Viking raids. Other treasures were plundered.

Elaborately decorated initial to the *Gospel of St Matthew* **(c.725)**

Illustration of Grace Darling from the 1881 edition of *Sunday at Home*

Bamburgh ❹

Northumberland. 🏰 *1,100.* ⬛
Berwick. ℹ️ *Seahouses (01665 720884; Apr–Oct); 106 Mary Gate, Berwick-upon-Tweed (01289 330733).*

Due to Northumbria's history of hostility against the Scots, there are more strongholds and castles here than in any other part of England. Most were built from the 11th to the 15th centuries by local warlords, as was Bamburgh's red sandstone **castle**. Its coastal position had been fortified since prehistoric times, but the first major stronghold was built in 550 by a Saxon chieftain, Ida the Flamebearer.

In its heyday between 1095 and 1464, Bamburgh was the royal castle that was used by the Northumbrian kings for coronations. By the end of the Middle Ages it had fallen into obscurity, then in 1894 it was bought by Newcastle arms tycoon Lord Armstrong, who restored it. Works of art are exhibited in the cavernous Great Hall, and there are suits of armour and medieval artifacts in the basement.

Bamburgh's other main attraction is the tiny **Grace Darling Museum** which celebrates the bravery of the 23-year-old, who, in 1838, rowed through tempestuous seas with her father, the keeper of the Longstone lighthouse, to rescue nine people from the wrecked *Forfarshire* steamboat.

Carrara marble fireplace (1840) at Alnwick Castle

🏰 **Bamburgh Castle**
Bamburgh. **Tel** *01668 214515.*
⬜ *Mar–Oct: daily.* ⬛ 🍴 📷 ♿ 🏪
www.bamburghcastle.com

🏛️ **Grace Darling Museum**
Radcliffe Rd. ⬜ *Easter–Oct: daily.* ♿

Alnwick Castle ❺

Alnwick, Northumberland. **Tel** *01665 510777.* ⬛ 🚌 *Almouth.* ⬜
April–Oct: daily. 📷 ♿ *limited.* 📷
🎦 www.alnwickcastle.com

Dominating the market town on the River Aln is another great fortress, Alnwick Castle. Described by the Victorians as the "Windsor of the north", it is the main seat of the Duke of Northumberland, whose family, the Percys, have lived here since 1309.

This border stronghold has survived many battles, but now peacefully dominates the pretty market town of Alnwick, overlooking landscape designed by Capability Brown. The stern medieval exterior belies the treasure house within, furnished in palatial Renaissance style with a collection of Meissen china and paintings by Titian, Van Dyck and Canaletto. The Postern Tower contains early British and Roman relics. The **Regimental Museum of Royal Northumberland Fusiliers** is in the Abbot's Tower. Other attractions are the Percy State coach, the dungeon and superb countryside views.

Warkworth Castle ❻

(EH) Warkworth, nr Amble. **Tel** *01665 711423.* ⬜ *Nov–Mar: Sat–Mon; Apr–Oct: daily.* ● *1 Jan, 24–26 Dec.* 📷 📷 ♿ *limited.*

Warkworth Castle sits on a green hill overlooking the River Coquet. It was one of the Percy family homes. Shakespeare's *Henry IV* features the castle in the scenes between the Earl of Northumberland and his son, Harry Hotspur. Much of the present-day castle remains date from the 14th century. The unusual turreted, cross shaped keep, also added in the 14th century, is a central feature of the castle tour.

Warkworth Castle reflected in the River Coquet

Kielder Water ❼

Yarrow Moor, Falstone, Hexham.
Tel *0870 2403549.* ⬜ *daily.* ♿
www.visitkielder.com

One of the top attractions of Northumberland, Kielder Water lies close to the Scottish border, surrounded by spectacular scenery. With a perimeter of 27 miles (44 km), it is Europe's largest man-made lake, and offers facilities for sailing, windsurfing, canoeing, water-skiing and fishing. In summer, the cruiser *Osprey* departs from Leaplish on trips around the lake. The Kielder Water Exhibition, next to the Tower Knowe Visitor Centre, depicts the history of the valley from the Ice Age to the present day

Cheviot Hills ⑧

These bare, lonely moors, smoothed into rounded humps by Ice Age glaciers, form a natural border with Scotland. Walkers and outdoor enthusiasts find a near-wilderness unmatched anywhere else in England. This remotest extremity of the Northumberland National Park nevertheless has a long and vivid history. Roman legions, warring Scots and English border raiders, cattle drovers and whisky smugglers have all left traces along the ancient routes and tracks they carved out here.

VISITORS' CHECKLIST

Northumberland. ≈ *Hexham.* ℹ *Wooler (01668 282123), Eastburn, South Park.* **Tel** *01434 605555.*

The Cheviots' *isolated burns and streams are among the last habitats in England for the shy, elusive otter.*

Chew Green Camp, *which to the Romans was ad fines, or, "towards the last place", has fine views from the remaining fortified earthworks.*

The Pennine Way *starts in Derbyshire and ends at Kirk Yetholm in Scotland. The final stage (shown here) goes past Byrness, crosses the Cheviots and traces the Scottish border.*

Uswayford Farm track

Uswayford Farm, *is perhaps the most remote farm in England, and one of the hardest to reach. It is set in deserted moorland.*

KEY

⬛ A roads

▬ B roads

═ Minor roads

- - - Pennine Way

✳ Viewpoint

Map labels: BERWICK-UPON-TWEED, B6351, Kirk Yetholm, Wooler, A697, College Burn, Harthope Burn, KIDLAND FOREST, Beamish, CHEVIOT HILLS, Clennel/Street track, Oswey Burn, Uswayford, Alwin, Alwinton, Harbottle, Byrness, Holystone, Rede, A68, B6341, Grasslees Burn, Otterburn, Elsdon, A696, NEWCASTLE-UPON-TYNE

0 kilometres 5

0 miles 5

Alwinton, *a tiny village built mainly from grey stone, is situated beside the River Coquet. It is an access point for many fine walks in the area, and the wild landscape is deserted except for sheep.*

Hexham ⑨

Northumberland. 👥 *14,000.* 🚆
🅿 🚻 *Wentworth Car Park
(01434 652220).* 🚌 *Tue.*
www.hadrianswallcountry.org

The busy market town of Hexham was established in the 7th century, growing up around the church and monastery built by St Wilfrid, but the Vikings sacked and looted it in 876. In 1114, Augustinians began work on a priory and abbey on the original church ruins to create **Hexham Abbey**, which still towers over the market square. The Saxon crypt, built partly with stones from the former Roman fort at Corbridge, is all

**Ancient stone carvings at
Hexham Abbey**

that remains of St Wilfrid's Church. The south transept has a 12th-century night stair: stone steps leading from the dormitory. In the chancel is the Frith Stool, a Saxon throne in the centre of a circle which protected fugitives.

Medieval streets, many with Georgian and Victorian shopfronts, spread out from the market square, The 15th-century Moot Hall was once a council chamber and the old gaol (jail) contains a **museum** of border history.

Hadrian's Wall ⑪

On the orders of Emperor Hadrian, work began in AD 120 on a 73 mile (117 km) wall to be erected across northern England, to mark and defend the northern limits of the British province and the northwest border of the Roman Empire. Troops were stationed at milecastles along the wall, and large turrets, later forts, were built at 5 mile (8 km) intervals. The wall, now the responsibility of English Heritage, was abandoned in 383 as the Empire crumbled, but much of it remains.

**Location of
Hadrian's Wall**

Vindolanda *is the site of several forts. The first timber fort dated from AD 90 and a stone fort was not built until the 2nd century. The museum has a collection of Roman writing tablets providing details of food, clothes and work.*

Great Chesters Fort was built facing east to guard Caw Gap, but there are few remains today. To the south and east of the fort are traces of a civil settlement and a bathhouse.

Carvoran Fort is probably pre-Hadrianic. Little of the fort survives, but the Roman Army museum nearby covers the wall's history.

Emperor Hadrian *(76–138) came to Britain in 120 to order a stronger defence system. Coins were often cast to record emperors' visits, such as this bronze sestertius. Until 1971, the penny was abbreviated to d, short for* denarius, *a Roman coin.*

Housesteads Settlement includes the remains of terraced shops or taverns.

Cawfields, *2 mile (3 km) north of Haltwhistle, is the access point to one of the highest and most rugged sections of the wall. To the east, the remains of a milecastle sit on Whin Sill crag.*

🏛 **Hexham Abbey**
Market Place. **Tel** 01434 602031.
⬭ daily. ⬤ ⬤ ⬤

🏛 **Border History Museum**
Old Gaol, nr Hallgate. **Tel** 01434
652349. ⬭ Feb–Oct: daily; Nov:
Mon, Tue, Sat. 🖼 ⬤ ⬤

Corbridge ⑩

Northumberland. 🏘 4,000. ➤
🛈 Hill St (01434 632815).

This quiet town conceals
a few historic buildings
constructed with stones from
the Roman garrison town of

**The parson's 14th-century fortified
tower house at Corbridge**

nearby Corstopitum. Among
these are the thickset Saxon
tower of St Andrew's Church
and the 14th-century fortified
tower house built to protect
the local clergyman. Excavations of Corstopitum, now
known as **Corbridge Roman
Site and Museum**, have
exposed earlier forts, a well-
preserved granary, temples,
fountains and an aqueduct.

🏛 **Corbridge Roman Site
and Museum**
(EH) **Tel** 01434 632349. ⬭ Apr–Oct:
daily; Nov–Mar: Sat & Sun. ⬤ 24–26
Dec, 1 Jan. 🖼 ⬤ limited. 🔲 ⬤

THE WALL COAST-TO-COAST

The wall runs eastward from Bowness on the
Solway Firth to the mouth of the Tyne at Wallsend.
The B6318 and A69 provide access to major sites.

KEY

ᴜᴜᴜ   Route of the wall

```
0 kilometres        20
0 miles             20
```

Carrawburgh Fort, a 500-man
garrison, guarded the Newbrough
Burn and North Tyndale approaches.

Limestone Corner Milecastle is
sited at the northernmost part of
the wall and has magnificent views
of the Cheviot Hills (see p421).

Sewingshields Milecastle, with
magnificent views west to Housesteads,
is one of the best places for walking.
This reconstruction shows the layout
of a Roman milecastle on the wall.

Chesters Fort was a
bridgehead over the
North Tyne. In the
museum are altars, sculp-
tures and inscriptions.

Chesters Bridge crossed the
Tyne. The original Hadrianic
bridge was rebuilt in 207. The
remains of this second bridge
abutment can still be seen.

Housesteads Fort is the best-
preserved site on the wall, with
fine views over the countryside.
The excavated remains include
the commanding officer's house
and a Roman hospital.

```
0 metres        500
0 yards         500
```

Newcastle upon Tyne ⑫

🏙 273,000. ✈ 🚂 🚌 🚢 ℹ
Quayside (0191 2778000). 🛍 Sun.
www.visitnewcastlegateshead.com

Newcastle owes its name to its Norman **castle** which was founded in 1080 by Robert Curthose, the eldest son of William the Conqueror (see p47). The Romans had bridged the Tyne and built a fort on the site 1,000 years earlier. During the Middle Ages it was used as a base for English campaigns against the Scots. From the Middle Ages, the city flourished as a coal mining and exporting centre. It was known in the 19th century for engineering, steel production and later as the world's foremost

shipyard. The city's industrial base has recently declined, but "Geordies", as inhabitants of the city are known, have refocused their civic pride on the ultra-modern Metro Centre shopping mall at Gateshead, southwest of the city, and Newcastle United soccer team.

Bridges crossing the Tyne at Newcastle

The city's lively night scene includes clubs, pubs and ethnic restaurants. The visible trappings of its past are reflected in the magnificent **Tyne Bridge** and in **Earl Grey's Monument**, as well as the grand façades in the city centre thoroughfares, such as Grey Street. On the quayside there are some dramatic new features, notably **Baltic**, the contemporary art centre, **The Sage Gateshead**, the international centre for music, and the tilting **Gateshead Millennium Bridge**.

⚓ **The Castle**
St Nicholas St. **Tel** 0191 232 7938. ⬜ daily. ⬛ 1 Jan, Good Fri, 24–26 Dec. 🎫 📷
Curthose's original wooden "new castle" was rebuilt in stone in the 12th century. Only

Beamish, The North of England Open Air Museum ⑬

This giant open air museum, spread over 120 ha (300 acres) of County Durham, re-creates an authentic picture of family, working and community life in the northeast in the 19th and early 20th centuries.

It has a 1913 Town Street, colliery village with drift mine, working farm and railway station. A tramway serves the different parts of the museum, which carefully avoids romanticizing the past.

Tram symbol

The station, which dates back to 1913, has a platform, a signal box, a wrought-iron footbridge and a goods yard.

Home Farm recreates the atmosphere of an old-fashioned farm. Rare breeds of cattle and sheep, more common before the advent of mass breeding, can be seen.

🏚 🚃
School

Miners' houses were tiny, oil-lit dwellings, backing onto vegetable gardens and owned by the colliery.

Chapel

the thickset, crenellated keep remains intact with two suites of royal apartments. A series of staircases spiral up to the renovated battlements, from which there are fine views over the city and the Tyne.

St Nicholas Cathedral

St Nicholas Sq. **Tel** 0191 2321939. ☐ daily. &

This is one of Britain's tiniest cathedrals. There are remnants inside of the original 11th-century Norman church on which the present 14th- and 15th-century structure was founded. Its most striking feature is its ornate "lantern tower" – half tower, half spire – of which there are only three others in Britain.

Bessie Surtees' House

(EH) 41–44 Sandhill. **Tel** 0191 2611585. ☐ Mon–Fri. ● 25 Dec–2 Jan, public hols. & limited.

The story of beautiful, wealthy Bessie, who lived here before

Reredos of the Northumbrian saints in St Nicholas Cathedral

eloping with penniless John Scott, later Lord Chancellor of England, is the romantic tale behind these half-timbered 16th- and 17th-century houses. The window through which Bessie escaped now has a blue glass pane.

Tyne Bridge

Newcastle–Gateshead. ☐ daily. &

Opened in 1928, this steel arch was the longest of its type in Britain with a span of 162 m (531 ft). Designed by Mott, Hay and Anderson, it soon became the city's most potent symbol.

Earl Grey's Monument

Grey St.

Benjamin Green created this memorial to the 2nd Earl Grey, Liberal Prime Minister from 1830 to 1834.

Baltic

The Centre for Contemporary Art Gateshead. **Tel** 0191 478 1810. ☐ daily. 🅿 ⏹ 🖥 www.balticmill.com

This former grain warehouse has been converted by architect Dominic Williams into a major new international centre for contemporary art, one of the biggest in Europe, with amazing views of Tyneside from its rooftop restaurant.

The Town has a sweet factory, newspaper office, solicitor, dentist and music teacher. There is also a pub.

VISITORS' CHECKLIST

Beamish, Co. Durham. **Tel** 0191 3704000. 🚆 🚌 Newcastle, then bus. ☐ Apr–Oct: 10am–5pm daily (last adm: 3pm); Nov–Mar: Town and Colliery Village only 10am–4pm Tue–Thu, Sat & Sun. 🖥 🛈 www.beamish.org.uk

The Co-op stocked everything a family needed at the turn of the century. A full range of foods available in 1913 is displayed.

Pockerley Manor

The 1825 Railway

Steam Winding Engine

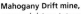

Mahogany Drift mine, *a tunnel driven into coal seams near the surface, was here long before the museum and was worked from the 1850s to 1958. Visitors are given guided tours underground.*

Entrance

Houses built by the London Lead Company in Middleton-in-Teesdale

Durham ⑭

See pp428–9.

North Pennines Tour ⑮

See p427.

Cotherstone cheese, a speciality of the Middleton-in-Teesdale area

Middleton-in-Teesdale ⑯

Co. Durham. 🏠 1,100. 🚂 Darlington. 🛈 10 Market Place (01833 690909). www.visitteesdale.co.uk

Clinging to a hillside amid wild Pennine scenery on the River Tees is this old lead mining town. Many of its rows of grey stone cottages were built by the London Lead Company, a paternalistic, Quaker-run organization who influenced every corner of its employees' daily lives.

The company began mining in 1753, and soon it virtually owned the town. Workers were expected to observe strict temperance, send their children to Sunday school and conform to the many

company maxims. Today, mining has all but ceased in Teesdale, with Middleton standing as a monument to the 18th-century idea of the "company town". The offices of the London Lead Company can still be seen, as well as Nonconformist chapels from the era and a memorial fountain made of iron.

The crumbly Cotherstone cow's milk cheese, a speciality of the surrounding dales, is available in the shops.

Barnard Castle ⑰

County Durham. 🏠 5,000. 🚂 Darlington. 🛈 Woodleigh, Flatts Rd (01833 690909). 🛒 Wed. www.teesdalediscovery.com

Barnard Castle, known in the area as "Barney", is a little town full of character,

with old shopfronts and a cobbled market overlooked by the ruins of the Norman castle from which it takes its name. The original Barnard Castle was built around 1125–40 by Bernard Balliol, ancestor of the founder of Balliol College, Oxford (see p222). Later, the market town grew up around the fortification.

Today, Barnard Castle is known for the extraordinary French-style château to the east of the town, surrounded by acres of formal gardens. Started in 1860 by the local aristocrat John Bowes and his French wife Josephine, an artist and actress, it was never a private residence, but always intended as a museum and public monument. The château finally opened in 1892, by which time the couple were both dead. Nevertheless, the **Bowes Museum** stands as a monument to his wealth and her extravagance.

The museum houses a strong collection of Spanish art which includes El Greco's *The Tears of St Peter,* dating from the 1580s, and Goya's *Don Juan Meléndez Váldez,* painted in 1797. Clocks, porcelain, furniture, musical instruments, toys and tapestries are among its treasures.

🏛 **Bowes Museum**
Barnard Castle. **Tel** 01833 690606.
🕐 daily. ⬤ 1 Jan, 25 & 26 Dec. 🎫
♿ 📷 (summer). 🍴 🛈
www.bowesmuseum.org.uk

The Bowes Museum, a French-style château near Barnard Castle

North Pennines Tour ⑮

Starting just to the south of Hadrian's Wall, this tour explores the South Tyne Valley, and Upper Weardale. It crosses one of England's wildest and most remote tracts of moorland, then heads north again. The high ground is mainly blanketed with heather, dotted with sheep or criss-crossed with dry-stone

Sheep grazing on the moors

walls, a feature of this region. Harriers and other birds hover above, and streams tumble into valleys of tightly huddled villages.

Celts, Romans and other settlers have left imprints on the North Pennines. The wealth of the area was based on lead mining and stone quarrying which has long co-existed with farming.

Haltwhistle ①

In the Church of the Holy Cross is the tombstone of John Ridley, brother of Protestant martyr, Nicholas Ridley, burnt at the stake in 1555 *(see p222).*

Haydon Bridge ③

There are some delightful walks near this spa town where the painter John Martin was born in 1789. Nearby Langley Castle is worth a visit.

Hexham ④

A pretty old town *(see p422),* Hexham has a fine abbey.

Blanchland ⑤

Some houses in this lead-mining village are built on the site of a 12th-century abbey, using the original stone.

Bardon Mill ②

To the north is the Roman fort and civilian settlement of Vindolanda *(see p422).*

NEWCASTLE UPON TYNE

← *CARLISLE* A69

River Tyne

South Tyne　North Tyne

A69　B6305　B6531　B6307

West Dipton Burn　Ham Burn　Devil's Water

A686　B6305　B6295　River East Allen

Allendale Town　Beldon Burn

A69　A686

Derwent reservoir

B6278　*Edmund-byers*

B6278

Allenheads

Rookhope Burn

A689　*Cowshill*　*Wearhead*　*Eastgate*　A689

Killhope Burn　*Burnhope Burn*　*Westgate*　*River Wear*　A689

DURHAM →

Allendale ⑦

With its capital at Allendale Town, this is an area of spectacular scenery, with many walking and trout fishing opportunities.

KEY

━━ Tour route

═══ Other roads

☀ Viewpoint

TIPS FOR DRIVERS

Length: 50 miles (80 km)
Stopping-off points: Several pubs in Stanhope serve bar meals, and the Durham Dales Centre provides teas all year round. Horsley Hall Hotel at Eastgate serves meals all day. (See also pp684–5.)

Stanhope ⑥

An 18th-century castle overlooks the market square. The giant stump of a fossilized tree, said to be 250 million years old, guards the graveyard.

0 kilometres　5

0 miles　　　5

Durham ⑭

Cathedral Sanctuary knocker

The city of Durham was built on Island Hill or "Dunholm" in 995. This rocky peninsula, which defies the course of the River Wear's route to the sea, was chosen as the last resting place for the remains of St Cuthbert. The relics of the Venerable Bede were brought to the site 27 years later, adding to its attraction for pilgrims. Durham Cathedral was treated by architects as an experiment for geometric patterning, while the Castle served as the Episcopal Palace until 1832, when Bishop William van Mildert gave it up and surrendered part of his income to found Britain's third university. The 23 ha (57 acre) peninsula has many footpaths, views and fine buildings.

★ **Cathedral**
Built from 1093 to 1274, it is a striking Norman structure.

Old Fulling Mill, a largely 18th-century building, houses a museum of archaeology.

Prebend's footbridge was built in 1777. A sculpture by Colin Wilbourn is situated at the "island" end.

College Green

Monastic kitchen

Church of St Mary the Less

College gatehouse

South Bailey

St Cuthbert's Tomb

"Our Daily Bread" Window
This modern stained-glass window in the north nave aisle was donated in 1984 by a local department store.

Galilee Chapel
Architects began work on the exotic Galilee Chapel in 1170, drawing inspiration from the Great Mosque of Cordoba in Andalusia. It was altered by Bishop Langley (d.1437) whose tomb is by the west door.

STAR SIGHTS
★ Cathedral

★ Castle

★ Castle

Begun in 1072, the castle is a fine Norman fortress. The keep, sited on a mound, is now part of the university.

Town Hall (1851)

St Nicholas' Church (1857)

Tunstal's Chapel

Situated at the end of the Tunstal's Gallery, the castle chapel was built c.1542. Its fine woodwork includes this unicorn misericord (see p341).

University buildings were built by Bishop John Cosin in the 17th century.

Castle Gatehouse

Traces of Norman stonework can be seen in the outer arch, while the sturdy walls and upper floors are 18th century, rebuilt in a style dubbed "gothick" by detractors.

CATHEDRAL ARCHITECTURE

The vast dimensions of the 900-year-old columns, piers and vaults, and the inventive giant lozenge and chevron, trellis and dogtooth patterns carved into the stone columns, are the main innovative features of Durham Cathedral. It is believed that 11th- and 12th-century architects such as Bishop Ranulph Flambard tried to unify all parts of the structure. This can be seen in the south aisle of the nave below.

Ribbed vaults, *criss-crossing above the nave, are now common in church ceilings. One of the major achievements of Gothic architecture, they were first built at Durham.*

Church of St Mary le Bow

Kingsgate Footbridge, built from 1962–3, leads to North Bailey.

The lozenge *shape is a pattern from prehistoric carving, but never before seen in a cathedral.*

Chevron patterns *on some of the piers in the nave are evidence of Moorish influence.*

WALES

Wales at a Glance

Wales is a country of outstanding natural beauty with varied landscapes. Visitors come to climb dramatic mountain peaks, go walking in the forests, fish in the broad rivers and enjoy the miles of unspoilt coastline. The country's many seaside resorts have long been popular with English holidaymakers. As well as outdoor pursuits there is the vibrancy of Welsh culture, with its strong Celtic roots, to be experienced. Finally there are many fine castles, ruined abbeys, mansions and cities full of magnificent architecture.

Anglesey

Caernarfonshire & Merionethshire

Card

Carmarthensh

Pembrokeshire

Beaumaris Castle *was intended to be a key part of Edward I's "iron ring" to contain the rebellious Welsh (see p436). Begun in 1295 but never completed, the castle (see p438) has a sophisticated defence structure that is unparalleled in Wales.*

Portmeirion (see pp454–5) *is a private village whose astonishing buildings seem rather incongruous in the Welsh landscape. The village was created by the architect Sir Clough Williams-Ellis to fulfill a personal ambition. Some of the buildings are assembled from pieces of architecture taken from sites around the country.*

St David *is the smallest city in Britain. The cathedral (see pp464–5) is the largest in Wales, and its nave is noted for its carved oak roof and beautiful rood screen. Next to the cathedral is the medieval Bishop's Palace, now a ruin.*

◁ **Caernarfon's colourful quayside marina**

Llanberis and Snowdon
(see p451) *is an area
famous for dangerous, high
peaks, long popular with
climbers. Mount Snowdon's
summit is most easily
reached from Llanberis. Its
Welsh name,* Yr Wyddfa
Fawr, *means "great tomb"
and it is the legendary
burial place of a giant slain
by King Arthur (see p285).*

*conwy
olwyn*   *Flintshire*

    Denbighshire

NORTH WALES
(see pp440–55)

    Wrexham

Conwy Castle *guards one of the
best-preserved medieval fortified
towns in Britain (see pp446–7).
Built by Edward I, the castle
was besieged and came close
to surrender in 1294. It was
taken by Owain Glyndŵr's
supporters in 1401.*

The Brecon Beacons *(see pp468–9) is a national park,
a lovely area of mountains, forest and moorland in South
Wales, which is a favourite with walkers and naturalists.
Pen-y-Fan is one of the principal summits.*

Powys

OUTH AND MID-WALES
(see pp456–75)

Cardiff Castle's
*(see pp472–3) Clock
Tower is just one of
many 19th-century
additions by the
eccentric but gifted
architect William
Burges. His flamboy-
ant style still delights
and amazes visitors.*

Monmouthshire

iff, Swansea & Environs

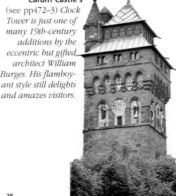

| 0 kilometres | 25 |
| 0 miles | 25 |

A PORTRAIT OF WALES

*L*ong popular with British holidaymakers, the many charms of Wales are now becoming better known internationally. They include spectacular scenery and a vibrant culture specializing in male-voice choirs, poetry and a passionate love of team sports. Governed from Westminster since 1536, Wales has its own distinct Celtic identity and in 1999 finally gained partial devolution.

Much of the Welsh landmass is covered by the Cambrian Mountain range, which effectively acts as a barrier from England. Wales is warmed by the Gulf Stream and has a mild climate, with more rain than most of Britain. The land is unsuitable for arable farming, but sheep and cattle thrive; the drove roads, along which sheep used to be driven across the hills to England, are now popular walking trails. It is partly because of the rugged terrain that the Welsh have managed to maintain their separate identity and their ancient language.

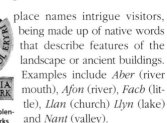
One of Wales's splendid National Parks

Welsh is an expansive, musical language, spoken by only one-fifth of the 2.7 million inhabitants, but in parts of North Wales it is still the main language of conversation. There is an official bilingual policy: road signs are in Welsh and English, even in areas where Welsh is little spoken. Welsh place names intrigue visitors, being made up of native words that describe features of the landscape or ancient buildings. Examples include *Aber* (river mouth), *Afon* (river), *Fach* (little), *Llan* (church) *Llyn* (lake) and *Nant* (valley).

Wales was conquered by the Romans, but not by the Saxons. The land and the people therefore retained Celtic patterns of settlement and husbandry for six centuries before the Norman Conquest in 1066. This allowed time for the development of a distinctive Welsh nation whose homogeneity continues to this day.

The early Norman kings subjugated the Welsh by appointing "Marcher Lords" to control areas bordering England. A string

Rugby: the popular Welsh sport

of massive castles provides evidence of the turbulent years when Welsh insurrection was a constant threat. It was not until 1535 that Wales formally became part of Britain, and it would take nearly 500 years before the people of Wales regained partial autonomy.

Religious non-conformism and radical politics are deeply rooted in Welsh consciousness. Saint David converted the country to Christianity in the 6th century. Methodism, chapel and teetotalism became firmly entrenched in

Mountain sheep: a familiar sight in rural Wales

gorsedd (assembly) of bards at the eisteddfod

ancient bards: minstrels and poets, who may have been associated with the Druids. Bardic tales of quasi-historical figures and magic were part of the oral tradition of the Dark Ages. They were first written down in the 14th century as the *Mabinogion,* which has inspired Welsh poets up to the 20th century's Dylan Thomas. The male-voice choirs found in many towns, villages and factories, particularly in the industrial south, express the Welsh musical heritage. Choirs compete in eisteddfods: festivals that celebrate Welsh culture.

he Welsh psyche during the 19th entury. Even today some pubs stay losed on Sundays. A long-standing oral tradition in Wales has produced many outstanding public peakers, politicians and actors. Velsh labour leaders have played mportant roles in the British rade union movement and the levelopment of socialism.

Welsh heritage is steeped in song, music, poetry and legend ather than handicrafts, lthough one notable exception is the arved Welsh lovespoon – a craft ecently revived. The well-known Velsh love of music derives from the

Welsh lovespoon

In the 19th century, the opening of the South Wales coalfield in Mid-Glamorgan – for a time the biggest in the world – led to an industrial boom, with mass migration from the countryside to the iron and steelworks. This prosperity was not to last: apart from a brief respite in World War II, the coal industry has been in terminal decline for decades, causing severe economic hardship. Today tourism is being promoted in the hope that the wealth generated, by outdoor activities in particular, will be able to take "King Coal's" place.

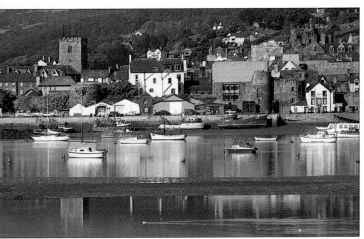

onwy's picturesque, medieval walled town, fronted by a colourful harbour

The History of Wales

St David, patron saint of Wales

Wales has been settled since prehistoric times, its history shaped by many factors, from invasion to industrialization. The Romans set up bases in the mountainous terrain, but it was effectively a separate Celtic nation when Offa's Dyke was built as the border with England in 770. Centuries of cross-border raids and military campaigns followed before England and Wales were formally united by the Act of Union in 1535. The rugged northwest, the former stronghold of the Welsh princes, remains the heartland of Welsh language and culture.

Owain Glyndwr, heroic leader of Welsh opposition to English rule

THE CELTIC NATION

Ornamental Iron Age bronze plaque from Anglesey

Wales was settled by waves of migrants in prehistoric times. By the Iron Age *(see pp42–3)*, Celtic farmers had established hillforts and their religion, Druidism. From the 1st century AD until the legions withdrew around 400, the Romans built fortresses and roads, and mined lead, silver and gold. During the next 200 years, Wales was converted to Christianity by missionaries from Europe. St David *(see pp464–5)*, the Welsh patron saint, is said to have turned the leek into a national symbol. He persuaded soldiers to wear leeks in their hats to distinguish themselves from Saxons during a 6th-century skirmish.

The Saxons *(see pp46–7)* failed to conquer Wales, and in 770 the Saxon King Offa built a defensive earthwork along the unconquered territory *(see p461)*. Beyond Offa's Dyke the people called

themselves *Y Cymry* (fellow countrymen) and the land *Cymru*. The Saxons called the land "Wales" from the Old English *wealas*, meaning foreigners. It was divided into kingdoms of which the main ones were Gwynedd in the north, Powys in the centre and Dyfed in the south. There were strong trade, cultural and linguistic links between each.

MARCHER LORDS

The Norman invasion of 1066 *(see p47)* did not reach Wales, but the border territory ("the Marches") was given by William the Conqueror to three powerful barons based at Shrewsbury, Hereford and Chester. These Marcher Lords made many incursions into Wales and controlled most of the lowlands. But the Welsh

Edward I designating his son Prince of Wales in 1301

princes held the mountainous northwest and exploited English weaknesses. Under Llywelyn the Great (d.1240), North Wales was almost completely independent; in 1267 his grandson, Llywelyn the Last, was acknowledged as Prince of Wales by Henry III.

In 1272 Edward I came to the English throne. He built fortresses and embarked on a military campaign to conquer Wales. In 1283 Llywelyn was killed in a skirmish, a shattering blow for the Welsh. Edward introduced English law and proclaimed his son Prince of Wales *(see p444)*.

OWAIN GLYNDWR'S REBELLION

Welsh resentment against the Marcher Lords led to rebellion. In 1400 Owain Glyndŵr (c.1350–1416), a descendant of the Welsh princes, laid waste to English-dominated towns and castles. Declaring himself Prince of Wales, he found Celtic allies in Scotland, Ireland, France and Northumbria. In 1404 Glyndŵr captured Harlech and Cardiff, and formed a parliament in Machynlleth *(see p462)*. In 1408 the French made a truce with the English king, Henry IV. The rebellion then failed and Glyndŵr went into hiding until his death.

UNION WITH ENGLAND

Wales suffered greatly during the Wars of the Roses (*see p49*) as Yorkists and Lancastrians tried to gain control of the strategically important Welsh castles. The wars ended in 1485, and the Welshman Henry Tudor, born in Pembroke, became Henry VII. The Act of Union in 1535 and other laws abolished the Marcher Lordships, giving Wales parliamentary representation in London instead. English practices replaced inheritance customs and English became the language of the courts and administration. The Welsh language survived, partly helped by the church and by Dr William Morgan's translation of the Bible in 1588.

Miners from South Wales pictured in 1910

Vernacular Bible, which helped to keep the Welsh language alive

INDUSTRY AND RADICAL POLITICS

The industrialization of south and east Wales began with the development of open-cast coal mining near Wrexham and Merthyr Tydfil in the 1760s. Convenient ports and the arrival of the railways helped the process. By the second half of the 19th century open-cast mines had been superseded by deep pits in the Rhondda Valley.

Living and working conditions were poor for industrial and agricultural workers. A series of "Rebecca Riots" in South Wales between 1839 and 1843, involving tenant farmers (dressed as women) protesting about tithes and rents, was forcibly suppressed. The Chartists, trade unions and the Liberal Party had much Welsh support.

The rise of Methodism (*see p279*) roughly paralleled the growth of industry: 80 per cent of the population was Methodist by 1851. The Welsh language persisted, despite attempts by the British government to discourage its use, which included punishing children caught speaking it.

WALES TODAY

In the 20th century the Welsh became a power in British politics. David Lloyd George, although not born in Wales, grew up there and was the first British Prime Minister to come from a Welsh family. Aneurin Bevan, a miner's son who became a Labour Cabinet Minister, helped create the National Health Service (*see p59*).

Welsh nationalism continued to grow: in 1926 Plaid Cymru, the Welsh Nationalist Party, was formed. In 1955 Cardiff was recognized as the capital of Wales (*see p470*) and four years later the red dragon became the emblem on Wales' new flag. Plaid Cymru won two parliamentary seats at Westminster in 1974, and in a 1998 referendum the Welsh espoused limited home rule. The National Assembly for Wales is housed in the stunning Y Senedd, on the waterfront in Cardiff Bay.

The 1967 Welsh Language Act made Welsh compulsory in schools, and the television channel S4C (Sianel 4 Cymru), formed in 1982, broadcasts many programmes in Welsh.

From the 1960s the steel and coal industries declined, creating mass unemployment. This has been partly alleviated by the emergence of high-tech industries, and by growth in tourism: Cardiff is home to many major tourist attractions including the Millennium Stadium and Cardiff Bay, Europe's largest waterfront development (*see pp470–71*).

Girl in traditional Welsh costume

Castles of Wales

A French 15th-century painting of Conwy Castle

Wales is rich in romantic medieval castles. Soon after the Battle of Hastings, in 1066 *(see p47)*, the Normans turned their attentions to Wales. They built earth and timber fortifications, later replaced by stone castles, initiating a building programme that was pursued by the Welsh princes and invading forces. Construction reached its peak during the reign of Edward I *(see p436)*. As the need for security lessened in the later Middle Ages, some castles became stately homes.

The north gatehouse was planned to be 18 m (60 ft) high, providing lavish royal accommodation, but its top storey was never built.

The inner ward was lined with a hall, granary, kitchens and stables

Rounded towers, with fewer blind spots than square ones, gave better protection.

Arrow slit

BEAUMARIS CASTLE

The last of Edward I's Welsh castles *(see p444)*, this perfectly symmetrical, concentric design was intended to combine impregnable defence with comfort. Invaders would face many obstacles before reaching the inner ward.

Moat

Curtain wall

WHERE TO SEE WELSH CASTLES

In addition to Beaumaris, in North Wales there are medieval forts at Caernarfon *(see p444)*, Conwy *(see p446)* and Harlech *(see p454)*. Edward I also built Denbigh, Flint (near Chester) and Rhuddlan (near Rhyll). In South and mid-Wales, Caerphilly (near Cardiff), Kidwelly (near Carmarthen) and Pembroke were built between the 11th and 13th centuries. Spectacular sites are occupied by Cilgerran (near Cardigan), Criccieth (near Porthmadog) and Carreg Cennen *(see p468)*. Chirk Castle, near Llangollen, is a good example of a fortress that has since become a stately home.

Caerphilly, *6 miles (10 km) north of Cardiff, is a huge castle with concentric stone and water defences that cover 12 ha (30 acres).*

Harlech Castle (see p454) *is noted for its massive gatehouse, twin towers and the fortified stairway to the sea. It was the headquarters of the Welsh resistance leader Owain Glyndŵr (see p436) from 1404–8.*

CASTELL-Y-BERE

This native Welsh castle at the foot of Cader Idris (see p440) was founded by Llywelyn the Great in 1221 (see p422), to secure internal borders rather than to resist the English.

Entrance

The D-shaped, elongated tower is a typical feature of Welsh castles.

The castle's construction follows the shape of the rock. The curtain walls are too low and insubstantial to be of much practical use.

Drawbridge

Chapel Tower has a beautiful medieval chapel.

The protected dock, on a channel that originally led to the sea, received supplies during sieges.

...er wall, with an ...assage, was higher ...e curtain wall to ...simultaneous firing.

Twin-towered gatehouse

Edward I (see p436) was the warrior king whose castles played a key role in the subjugation of the Welsh people.

EDWARD I AND MASTER JAMES OF ST GEORGE

In 1278 Edward I brought over from Savoy a master stonemason who became a great military architect, James of St George. Responsible for planning and building at least 12 of Edward's fine Welsh castles, James was paid well and liberally pensioned off, indicating the esteem in which he was held by the king.

A plan of Caernarfon Castle illustrates how its position, on a promontory surrounded by water, has determined the building's shape and defence.

Caernarfon Castle (see p444), birthplace of the ill-fated Edward II (see p327), was intended to be the official royal residence in North Wales, and has palatial private apartments.

Castell Coch was restored in Neo-Gothic style by Lord Bute and William Burges (see p472). Mock-castles were built by many Victorian industrialists.

Conwy Castle (see p447), like many other castles, required forced labour on a massive scale for its construction.

NORTH WALES

ABERCONWY & COLWYN · ANGLESEY · CAERNARFONSHIRE &
MERIONETHSHIRE · DENBIGHSHIRE · FLINTSHIRE · WREXHAM

The North Wales landscape has a dramatic quality reflected in its history. In prehistoric times, Anglesey was a stronghold of the religious elite known as the Druids. Roman and Norman invasions concentrated on the coast, leaving the mountains to the Welsh. These wild areas are the centre of Welsh language and culture.

Defence and conquest have been constant themes in Welsh history. North Wales was the scene of ferocious battles between the Welsh princes and Anglo-Norman monarchs determined to establish English rule. The string of formidable castles which still stand in North Wales are as much a testament to Welsh resistance as to the wealth and strength of the invaders. Several massive fortresses, including Beaumaris, Caernarfon and Harlech, almost surround the rugged high country of Snowdonia, an area that even today maintains an untamed quality.

Sheep and cattle farming are the basis of the rural economy here, though there are also large areas of forestry. Along the coast, tourism is a major activity. Llandudno, a purpose-built Victorian resort, popularized the sandy northern coastline in the 19th century. The area continues to attract large numbers of visitors, though major development is confined to the narrow coastal strip that lies between Prestatyn and Llandudno, leaving the island of Anglesey and the remote Llyn Peninsula largely untouched.

The Llyn Peninsula remains one of the strongholds of the Welsh language, along with rather isolated inland communities, such as Dolgellau and Bala.

No part of North Wales can truly be called industrial, though there are still remnants of the once-prosperous slate industry in Snowdonia, where the stark, grey quarries provide a striking contrast to the natural beauty of the surrounding mountains. At the foot of Snowdon (the highest mountain in Wales), the villages of Beddgelert, Betws-y-Coed and Llanberis are popular bases for walkers who come to enjoy the spectacular views and striking beauty of this remote region.

Caernarfon Castle, one of the forbidding fortresses built by Edward I

◁ The River Dee at Llangollen, still an area of unspoilt natural beauty

Exploring North Wales

The dominant feature of North Wales is Snowdon, the highest mountain in Wales. Snowdonia National Park extends dramatically from the Snowdon massif south beyond Dolgellau, with thickly wooded valleys, mountain lakes, moors and estuaries. To the east are the softer Clwydian Hills, and unspoilt coastlines can be enjoyed on Anglesey and the beautiful Llyn Peninsula.

A lighthouse perched on the sea cliffs of Anglesey

KEY

▬▬▬	Major road
▬▬▬	Minor road
▭▭▭	Secondary road
▬▬▬	Scenic route
▭▭▭	Main railway
▬▬▬	Minor railway
△	Summit

Carmel Head

Cemaes A5025 Amlwch

Holyhead Bay

Llyn Alaw A5111

Moelfre

Benllech

Great Ormes Head

LLANDUDNO

Holy Island

Holyhead

Anglesey

Gwalchmai

Pentraeth

BEAUMARIS

CONWY

Penmae

Rhosneigr

Llangefni A5025

Llanfairfechan

Bangor

Aberffraw A4080

Port Dinorwic

Bethesda

Dolgarrog

Newborough

Carnedd Llyw 1064m

Llan

CAERNARFON

Llanberis

Capel Curig

Caernarfon Bay

LLANBERIS AND SNOWDON

BETWS CO

Penygroes

Snowdon 1085m

Dolwydde

Llanllyfni

BEDDGELERT

A498

A470

BLAEN FFESTI

Ffestinic

Llanaelhaearn

A487

A498

Tan-y-Bwlch

Maentwrog

Nefyn

A4417

Porthmadog

PORTMEIRION

LLYN PENINSULA

Tudweiliog

Pwllheli

Criccieth

Tremadog Bay

Traws

HARLECH

Llanbedrog

A499

B4413

Abersoch

Llanbedr

Rhinog Fawr 720m

Plas-yn-Rhiw

Aberdaron

Braich y Pwll

Porth Neigwl

Cardigan Bay

Y Llethr 754m

Snowdonia National

Bardsey Island

Llanaber

DOLGELLAU

Barmouth

Cader Idris 892m

Barmouth Bay

Fairbourne

A493

Llwyngwril

Abergynolwyn

A487

Tywyn

A493

Aberystwyth

ABERDYFI

The peaks and moorland of Snowdonia

For additional map symbols see back flap

GETTING AROUND

The main route into North Wales from the northwest of
England is the A55, a good dual carriageway which bypasses
several places that used to be traffic bottlenecks, including
Conwy. The other main route through the region is the A5
Shrewsbury to Holyhead road, which follows a trail through
the mountains pioneered by the 19th-century engineer Thomas
Telford (see p447). Rail services run along the coast to Holyhead,
connecting with ferries across the Irish Sea to Dublin and
Dun Laoghaire. Scenic branch lines travel from Llandudno
Junction to Blaenau Ffestiniog (via Betws-y-Coed) and along
the southern Llyn Peninsula.

SIGHTS AT A GLANCE

Aberdyfi **16**
Bala **7**
Beaumaris **2**
Beddgelert **11**
Betws-y-Coed **8**
Blaenau Ffestiniog **9**
Caernarfon **1**
Conwy pp446–7 **3**
Dolgellau **15**
Harlech **14**
Llanberis and Snowdon **10**
LLandudno **4**
LLangollen **6**
Llyn Peninsula **12**
Portmeirion pp454–5 **13**
Ruthin **5**

The imposing castle built at Conwy by Edward I in the 13th century

Caernarfon Castle, built by Edward I as a symbol of his power over the conquered Welsh

Caernarfon ❶

Caernarfonshire & Merionethshire (Gwynedd). 🚶 10,000. 🚌
🛈 Castle St (01286 672232).
🚌 Sat. **www**.gwynedd.gov.uk

One of the most famous castles in Wales, Caernarfon Castle, looms over this busy town. Both town and castle were created after Edward I's defeat of the last native Welsh prince, Llywelyn ap Gruffydd (Llywelyn the Last) in 1283 (see p436). The town walls merge with modern streets that spread beyond the medieval centre to a market square.

THE INVESTITURE

In 1301 the future Edward II became the first English Prince of Wales (see p436), a title since held by the British monarch's eldest son. In 1969 the investiture in Caernarfon Castle of Prince Charles (above) as Prince of Wales drew 500 million TV viewers.

Overlooking the town and its harbour, **Caernarfon Castle** (see p439), with its polygonal towers, was built as a seat of government for North Wales. Caernarfon was a thriving port in the 19th century, and during this period the castle ruins were restored by the architect Anthony Salvin. Displays in the castle include the Royal Welch Fusiliers Museum, and exhibitions tracing the history of the Princes of Wales and exploring the theme "Chieftains and Princes".

Situated on the hill above the town are the ruins of **Segontium**, a Roman fort built in about AD 78. Local legend claims that the first Christian Emperor of Rome, Constantine the Great, was born here in 280.

♣ **Caernarfon Castle**
Y Maes. **Tel** 01286 677617.
⬜ daily. 🔲 📷 call for details. 🔲
📷 **www**.caernarfon.com

🏰 **Segontium**
(NT) Beddgelert Rd. **Tel** 01286
675625. ⬜ Tue–Sun (Sun: pm).
● 1 Jan, 24, 26 Dec. 🔲 limited.
📷 **www**.segontium.org.uk

Beaumaris ❷

Anglesey (Gwynedd). 🚶 2,000. 🚌
🛈 Llanfair PG, Station Site, Holyhead Rd, Anglesey (01248 713177).
www.visitanglesey.co.uk

Handsome Georgian and Victorian architecture gives Beaumaris the air of a resort on England's southern coast. The buildings reflect this

sailing centre's past role as Anglesey's chief port, before the island was linked to the mainland by the road and railway bridges built across the Menai Strait in the 19th century. This was the site of Edward I's last, and possibly greatest, **castle** (see p438), which was built to command this important ferrying point to the mainland of Wales.

Ye Olde Bull's Head inn, on Castle Street, was built in 1617. Its celebrated literary patrons have included Dr Samuel Johnson (1709–84) and Victorian novelist Charles Dickens (see p189).

The town's **Courthouse**, was built in 1614 and the recently restored 1829 **Gaol** preserves its soundproofed punishment room and a huge treadmill for prisoners. Two public hangings took place here. Richard Rowlands, the last victim, protested his innocence and cursed the church clock as he was led to the gallows, declaring that its four faces would never show the same times again. It failed to show consistent times until it had an overhaul in 1980.

♣ **Beaumaris Castle**
Castle St. **Tel** 01248 810361.
⬜ daily. 🔲 🔲
www.beaumaris.com

🏛 **Courthouse**
Castle St. **Tel** 01248 811691.
⬜ Apr–Sep: daily. 🔲 🔲 🔲

🏛 **Gaol**
Bunkers Hill. **Tel** 01248 810921.
⬜ Apr–Sep: daily. 🔲 🔲 limited.
📷 **www**.angleseyheritage.org

ALICE IN WONDERLAND

The Gogarth Abbey Hotel, Llandudno, was the summer home of the Liddells. Their friend, Charles Dodgson (1832–98), would entertain young Alice Liddell with stories of characters such as the White Rabbit and the Mad Hatter. As Lewis Carroll, Dodgson wrote his magical tales in *Alice's Adventures in Wonderland* (1865) and *Through the Looking-Glass* (1871).

Arthur Rackham's illustration (1907) of *Alice in Wonderland*

🏛 **Llandudno Museum**
Gloddaeth St. *Tel* 01492 876517.
⏰ *Easter–Oct: 10:30am–1pm, 2–5pm Tue–Sun.* ♿ limited.

⛏ **Great Orme Copper Mines**
Off A55. *Tel* 01492 870447.
⏰ *mid-Mar–Oct: daily.*
📷 ♿ limited. 🅿 🚻
www.greatormemines.info

Ruthin ❺

Denbighshire (Clwyd). 👥 *5,000.*
🚌 ℹ *Craft Centre, Park Rd (01824 703992).* 🛒 *1st Tue of every month; Thu (indoor).*
www.borderlands.co.uk

Ruthin's long-standing prosperity as a market town is reflected in its fine half-timbered medieval buildings. These include the National Westminster and Barclays banks in St Peter's Square. The former was a 15th-century courthouse and prison, the latter the home of Thomas Exmewe, Lord Mayor of London in 1517–18. **Maen Huail** ("Huail's stone"), a boulder outside Barclays, is said to be where King Arthur *(see p285)* beheaded Huail, his rival in a love affair.

St Peter's Church, on the edge of St Peter's Square, was founded in 1310 and has a Tudor oak roof in the north aisle. Next to the Castle Hotel is the 17th-century pub **The Seven Eyes** (formerly the Myddleton Arms), whose seven unusual, Dutch-style, dormer windows are known locally as the "eyes of Ruthin".

Conwy ❸

See pp446–7.

Llandudno ❹

Gwynedd. 👥 *19,000.* 🚉 🚌 ℹ *Library Building, Mostyn St (01492 577577).* www.visitllandudno.org.uk

Llandudno's crescent-shaped bay

Llandudno retains much of the holiday spirit of the 19th century, when the new railways brought crowds to the coast. Its **pier**, more than 700 m (2,295 ft) long, and its canopied walkways recall the heyday of seaside holidays. The town is also proud of its association with the author Lewis Carroll *(see above)*. The exhibits at the **Llandudno Museum** explore Llandudno's history from Roman times onwards.

Llandudno's cheerful seaside atmosphere owes much to a strong sense of its Victorian roots – unlike many British seaside towns, which embraced the flashing lights and funfairs of the 20th century. To take full advantage of its sweeping beach, Llandudno was laid out between its two headlands, Great Orme's Head and Little Orme's Head.

Great Orme's Head, now a Country Park and Nature Reserve, rises to 207 m (670 ft) and has a long history. In the Bronze Age copper was mined here; the **copper mines** and their excavations are open to the public. The **church** on the headland was built from timber in the 6th century by St Tudno, rebuilt in stone in the 13th century, restored in 1855 and is still in use. Local history and wildlife can be traced in an information centre on the summit.

There are two effortless ways to reach the summit: on the **Great Orme Tramway**, one of only three cable-hauled street tramways in the world (the others are in San Francisco and Lisbon), or by the **Llandudno Cable Car**. Both operate only in summer.

The "eyes of Ruthin", an unusual feature in Welsh architecture

Street-by-Street: Conwy ❸

Conwy is one of Britain's most underrated historic towns. Until the early 1990s it was famous as a traffic bottleneck, but thanks to a town bypass, its concentration of architectural riches – unparalleled in Wales – can now be appreciated. The castle dominates: a brooding, intimidating monument built by Edward I *(see p438)*. But Conwy is set apart from other medieval towns by its amazingly well-preserved town walls. Fortified with 21 towers and three gateways, the walls form an almost unbroken shield around the old town.

Smallest House
This fisherman's cottage on the quayside, just over 3 m (10 ft) high, is said to be the smallest house in Britain.

Plas Mawr, the "Great Mansion", was built by a nobleman, Robert Wynne, in 1576.

St Mary's Church
This medieval church, on the site of a 12th-century Cistercian abbey, is set in peaceful grounds.

Bangor

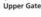

Upper Gate

Llywelyn's Statue
Llywelyn the Great (see p436) was arguably Wales's most successful medieval leader.

Aberconwy House
This restored 14th-century house was once the home of a wealthy merchant.

THOMAS TELFORD

Thomas Telford (1757–1834) was the gifted Scottish engineer responsible for many of Britain's roads, bridges and canals. The Menai Bridge (see p444), the Pontcysyllte Aqueduct (see p450) and Conwy Bridge are his outstanding works in Wales. Telford's graceful bridge at Conwy has aesthetic as well as practical qualities. Completed in 1826 across the mouth of the Conwy estuary, it was designed in a castellated style to blend with the castle. Before the bridge's construction the estuary could only be crossed by ferry.

VISITORS' CHECKLIST

Conwy. 8,000. Conwy.
01492 592248. **Aberconwy House (NT).** Tel 01492 592246.
Wed–Mon. Nov–Mar. **Conwy Castle** Tel 01492 592358. daily. **Smallest House** Tel 01492 593484. Apr–Oct: daily.
www.gonorthwales.co.uk

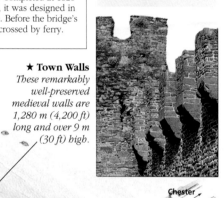

★ **Town Walls**
These remarkably well-preserved medieval walls are 1,280 m (4,200 ft) long and over 9 m (30 ft) high.

Chester

NEW BRIDGE

CASTLE STREET

CASTLE STREET

Telford's bridge

Railway bridge

0 metres 50

0 yards 50

Entrance to castle

KEY

— — Suggested route

STAR SIGHTS

★ Town Walls

★ Conwy Castle

★ **Conwy Castle**
This atmospheric watercolour, Conwy Castle (c.1770), is by the Nottingham artist Paul Sandby.

Pontcysyllte Aqueduct, built in 1795–1805, carrying the Llangollen Canal

Choristers at the Eisteddfod, a popular Welsh festival

Llangollen ❻

Denbighshire. 🚶 *5,000.* 🚇 ℹ️
y Capel, Castle St (01978 860828).
🚌 *Tue.* **www**.llangollen.org.uk

Best known for its annual Eisteddfod (festival), this pretty town sits on the River Dee, which is spanned by a 14th-century bridge. The town became notorious in the 1700s, when two Irishwomen, Sarah Ponsonby and Lady Eleanor Butler, the "Ladies of Llangollen", set up house together in the half-timbered **Plas Newydd**. Their unconventional dress and literary enthusiasms attracted such celebrities as the Duke of Wellington *(see p162)* and William Wordsworth *(see p366)*. The ruins of a 13th-century castle, **Castell Dinas Brân**, occupy the summit of a hill overlooking the house.

Environs: Boats on the **Llangollen Canal** sail from Wharf Hill in summer and cross the spectacular 300 m (1,000 ft) long Pontcysyllte Aqueduct, built by Thomas Telford *(see p447)*.

🏛 **Plas Newydd**
(NT) Hill St. ***Tel*** *01248 715272.*
⏰ *Easter–Oct: Sat–Wed.* 📷 ♿
limited. 🖥 🅿️

Bala ❼

Gwynedd. 🚶 *2,000.* 🚌 *from Llangollen.* ℹ️ *Penllyn, Pensarn Rd (01678 521021).* **www**.visitsnowdonia.info

Bala Lake, Wales's largest natural lake, lies between the Aran and Arenig mountains at the fringes of Snowdonia National Park. It is popular for water-sports and boasts a unique fish called a *gwyniad*, which is related to the salmon.

The little grey-stone town of Bala is a Welsh-speaking community, its houses strung out along a single street at the eastern end of the lake. Thomas Charles (1755–1814), a Methodist church leader, once lived here. A plaque on his former home recalls Mary Jones who walked 28 miles (42 km) barefoot from Abergynolwyn to buy a Bible. This led to Charles establishing the Bible Society, providing cheap bibles to the working classes.

The narrow-gauge **Bala Lake Railway** follows the lake shore from Llanuwchllyn, 4 miles (6 km) southwest.

Betws-y-Coed ❽

Conwy. 🚶 *600.* 🚆 ℹ️ *Royal Oak Stables (01690 710426).*
www.betws.org.uk

This village near the peaks of Snowdonia has been a hill-walking centre since the 19th century. To the west are the **Swallow Falls**, where the River Llugwy flows through a wooded glen. The bizarre **Ty Hyll** ("Ugly House"), is a *tŷ unnos* ("one-night house"); traditionally, houses erected between dusk and dawn on common land were entitled to freehold rights, and the owner could enclose land as far as he could throw an axe from the door. To the east is **Waterloo Bridge**, built by Thomas Telford to celebrate the victory against Napoleon.

🏛 **Ty Hyll**
Capel Curig. ***Tel*** *01690 720287.*
House ⏰ *Easter–Sep: daily.*
Grounds ⏰ *Easter–Sep: daily; Oct–Easter: Mon–Fri.* 📷 ♿ *limited.*

The ornate Waterloo Bridge, built in 1815 after the famous battle

◁ **The picturesque village of Beddgelert in Snowdonia National Park**

A view of the Snowdonia countryside from Llanberis Pass, the most popular route to Snowdon's peak

Blaenau Ffestiniog ⑨

Gwynedd. 5,500. Betws-y-Coed (01690 710426); Jun–Sep: 01766 830360. Tue (Jun–Sep).

Blaenau Ffestiniog, once the slate capital of North Wales, sits among mountains riddled with quarries. The **Llechwedd Slate Caverns**, overlooking Blaenau, opened to visitors in the early 1970s, marking a new role for the declining industrial town. The electric Miners' Tramway takes passengers on a tour into the original caverns.

On the Deep Mine tour, visitors descend on Britain's steepest passenger incline railway to the underground chambers, while sound effects recreate the atmosphere of a working quarry. The dangers included landfalls and floods, as well as the more gradual threat of slate dust breathed into the lungs.

There are slate-splitting demonstrations on the surface, a quarryman's cottage and a re-creation of a Victorian village to illustrate the cramped and basic living conditions endured by workers between the 1880s and 1945.

The popular narrow-gauge **Ffestiniog Railway** *(see pp452–3)* runs from Blaenau to Porthmadog.

Llechwedd Slate Caverns
Off A470. **Tel** 01766 830306.
daily. except the Deep Mine. www.llechwedd-slate-caverns.co.uk

Llanberis and Snowdon ⑩

Gwynedd. 2,100. High St, Llanberis (01286 870765).
www.gwynedd.gov.uk

Snowdon, which at 1,085 m (3,560 ft) is the highest peak in Wales, is the main focus of the vast Snowdonia National Park, whose scenery ranges from this rugged mountain country to moors and sandy beaches.

The easiest route to Snowdon's summit begins in Llanberis: the 5 mile (8 km) **Llanberis Track**. From Llanberis Pass, the Miners' Track (once used by copper miners) and the Pyg Track are alternative paths. Walkers should beware of sudden weather changes and dress accordingly. The narrow-gauge **Snowdon Mountain Railway**, which opened in 1896, is an easier option.

Llanberis was a major 19th-century slate town, with grey terraces hewn into the hills. Other attractions are the 13th-century shell of **Dolbadarn Castle**, and, above Lake Peris, the **Electric Mountain**, which has tours of Europe's biggest hydro-electric pumped storage station.

Dolbadarn Castle
Off A4086 nr Llanberis.
Tel 01286 870765. daily.

Electric Mountain
Llanberis. **Tel** 01286 870636.
daily. Jan. www.fhc.co.uk

BRITAIN'S CENTRE OF SLATE

Welsh slates provided roofing material for Britain's new towns in the 19th century. In 1898, the slate industry employed nearly 17,000 men, a quarter of whom worked at Blaenau Ffestiniog. Foreign competition and new materials later took their toll. Quarries such as Dinorwig in Llanberis and Llechwedd in Blaenau Ffestiniog now survive on the tourist trade.

The dying art of slate-splitting

The village of Beddgelert, set among the mountains of Snowdonia

Beddgelert ⓫

Gwynedd. 🏠 500.
ℹ️ Canolfan-Hebog (01766 890615).
www.eryri-npa.gov.uk

Beddgelert enjoys a spectacular location in Snowdonia. The village sits on the confluence of the Glaslyn and Colwyn rivers at the approach to two mountain passes: the beautiful Nant Gwynant Pass, which leads to Snowdonia's highest reaches, and the Aberglaslyn Pass, a narrow wooded gorge which acts as a gateway to the sea.

Business was given a boost by Dafydd Pritchard, the landlord of the Royal Goat Hotel, who in the early 19th century adapted an old Welsh legend to associate it with Beddgelert. Llywelyn the Great *(see p436)* is said to have left his faithful hound Gelert to guard his infant son while he went hunting. He returned to find the cradle overturned and Gelert covered in blood. Thinking the dog had savaged his son, Llywellyn slaughtered Gelert, but then discovered the boy, unharmed, under the cradle. Nearby was the corpse of a wolf, which Gelert had killed to protect the child. To support the tale, Pritchard created **Gelert's Grave** (*bedd Gelert* in Welsh) by the River Glaslyn, a mound of stones a short walk south of the village.

Environs: There are many fine walks in the area: one leads south to the Aberglaslyn Pass and along a disused part of the Welsh Highland Railway. The **Sygun Copper Mine**, 1 mile (1.5 km) northeast of Beddgelert, offers self-guided tours of caverns recreating the life of Victorian miners.

🏔 **Sygun Copper Mine**
On A498. *Tel* 01766 890595.
⏰ Mar–Oct: daily; Feb half term.
💷 ♿ limited. 🅿 🎁
www.syguncoppermine.co.uk

Ffestiniog Railway

Railway crest

The Ffestiniog narrow-gauge railway takes a scenic 14 mile (22 km) route from Porthmadog Harbour to the mountains and the slate town of Blaenau Ffestiniog *(see p451)*. Designed to carry slate from the quarries to the quay, the railway replaced a horse-drawn tramway constructed in 1836, operating on a 60 cm (2 ft) gauge. After closure in 1946, it was reconstructed by volunteers and re-opened in sections from 1955–82.

Steam traction *trains were first used on the Ffestiniog Railway in 1863. There are some diesel engines but most trains on the route are still steam-hauled.*

Llyn Peninsula ⑫

Gwynedd. 🚊 🚌 *Pwllheli.* ⛴
Aberdaron to Bardsey Island. 🛈
Min-y-don, Station Sq, Pwllheli (01758 613000). **www.**nwt.co.uk

This 24-mile (38-km) finger of land points southwest from Snowdonia into the Irish Sea. Although it has popular beaches, notably at Pwllheli, Criccieth, Abersoch and Nefyn, the coast's overriding feature is its untamed beauty. Views are at their most dramatic in the far west and along the mountain-backed northern shores.

The windy headland of **Braich-y-Pwll**, to the west of Aberdaron, looks out towards Bardsey Island, the "Isle of 20,000 Saints". This became a place of pilgrimage in the 6th century, when a monastery was founded here. Some of the saints are said to be buried in the churchyard of the ruined

13th-century **St Mary's Abbey**. Close by is **Porth Oer**, a small bay also known as "Whistling Sands" (the sand is meant to squeak, or whistle, underfoot).

East of Aberdaron is the 4 mile (6.5 km) bay of **Porth Neigwl**, known in English as Hell's Mouth, the scene of many shipwrecks due to the bay's treacherous currents. Hidden in sheltered grounds above Porth Neigwl bay, 1 mile (1.5 km) northeast of Aberdaron, is **Plas-yn-Rhiw**,

a small, medieval manor house with Tudor and Georgian additions and lovely gardens.

The former quarrying village and "ghost town" of **Llithfaen**, tucked away below the sheer cliffs of the mountainous north coast, is now a centre for Welsh language studies.

🏠 **Plas-yn-Rhiw**
(NT) *off B4413.* **Tel** *01758 780219.*
🕐 *Apr–Oct: Thu–Sun; May, Jun & Sep: Thu–Mon; Jul & Aug: Wed–Mon.*
🅿 ♿ *limited.*

Llithfaen village, now a language centre, on the Llyn Peninsula

Tan-y-Bwlch station is part of a National Park by the same name set in the heart of Snowdonia. Nature trails lead from this stop to the park's lakes and forests.

Moelwyn Tunnel

Campbell's Platform

Tan-y-Bwlch 🅿

Dduallt

Plas Halt

A487

A496

DOLGELLAU, BALA

Tan-y-Grisiau is request stop for a ˳ver station visitor ˳tre, and is near a ˳erfall and a lake.

BETWYS-Y-COED

A470

Blaenau Ffestiniog 🛈

🚶 Tan-y-Grisiau

A496

VISITORS' CHECKLIST

🛈 *01766 516000.*
Tel *bookings 01766 516024.*
🚊 *Porthmadog.* 🕐 *daily.*
🔴 *25 Dec.* 💳 ♿ 🚻 📷
www.festrail.co.uk

KEY

▭▬	Ffestiniog Railway
○	Station
—	British Rail
▭▭	Major roads

Portmeirion ⑬

Gwynedd. **Tel** 01766 770000.
🚋 Minffordd. ◯ daily ● 25 Dec.
🅿 & limited. ⚑ 🛏 🛍 ☕
www.portmeirion-village.com

This bizarre Italianate village on a private peninsula at the top of Cardigan Bay was created by Welsh architect Sir Clough Williams-Ellis (1883–1978). He fulfilled a childhood dream by building a village "to my own fancy on my own chosen site". About 50 buildings surround a central piazza, in styles from Oriental to Gothic. Visitors can stay at the luxurious hotel or in one of the charming village cottages. Portmeirion has been an atmospheric location for many films and television programmes, including the popular 1960s television series *The Prisoner*.

Sir Clough Williams-Ellis at Portmeirion

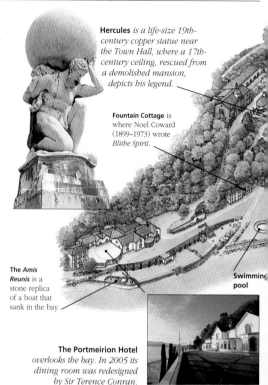

Hercules *is a life-size 19th-century copper statue near the Town Hall, where a 17th-century ceiling, rescued from a demolished mansion, depicts his legend.*

Fountain Cottage is where Noel Coward (1899–1973) wrote *Blithe Spirit*.

The *Amis Reunis* is a stone replica of a boat that sank in the bay.

Swimming pool

The Portmeirion Hotel *overlooks the bay. In 2005 its dining room was redesigned by Sir Terence Conran.*

Harlech ⑭

Gwynedd. 🏘 1,300. 🚋 ⓘ High St
(01766 780658). 🏛 Sun (summer).
www.gwynedd.gov.uk

This small town with fine beaches is dominated by **Harlech Castle**, a medieval fortress *(see p438)* built by Edward I between 1283 and 1289. The castle sits on a precipitous crag, with superb views of Tremadog Bay and the Llyn Peninsula to the west, and Snowdonia to the north. When the castle was built, the sea reached a fortified stairway cut into the cliff, so that supplies could arrive by ship, but now the sea has receded. A towering gatehouse protects the inner ward, enclosed by walls and four round towers.

Despite its defences, Harlech Castle fell to Owain Glyndŵr *(see p436)* in 1404, and served as his court until its recapture four years later. The song *Men of Harlech* is thought to have been inspired by the castle's heroic resistance during an eight-year siege in the Wars of the Roses *(see p49)*.

🏰 **Harlech Castle**
Castle Sq. **Tel** 01766 780552.
◯ daily. ● 1 Jan, 24–26 Dec.
🅿 🛍 **www**.harlech.com

Dolgellau ⑮

Gwynedd. 🏘 2,650. ⓘ Eldon Sq
(01341 422888). 🏛 Fri (livestock).

The dark local stone gives a stern, solid look to this market town, where the Welsh language and customs are still very strong. It lies in the long shadow of the 892 m (2,927 ft) mountain of Cader Idris where, according to legend, anyone who spends a night on its summit will awake a poet or a madman – or not at all.

Dolgellau was gripped by gold fever in the 19th century, when high-quality gold was

Harlech Castle's strategic site overlooking mountains and sea

For hotels and restaurants in this region see pp588–590 and pp642–644

Triumphal Arch

Central Piazza

Lodge

mpanile

yal
lphin
ttage

Bristol
Colonnade

Viewing
platform

The Ship Shop *sells Portmeirion's famous flowered pottery.*

The Pantheon *was built in 1960–61, but lack of funds meant that the dome was originally made from plywood instead of copper and painted green. The Pantheon's unusual façade is formed by the upper half of a music room fireplace by Norman Shaw (see p29).*

Dolgellau's grey-stone buildings, dwarfed by the mountain scenery

discovered in the Mawddach Valley nearby. The deposits were not large enough to sustain an intensive mining industry for long. Nevertheless, up until 1999, small amounts were mined and crafted locally into fine jewellery.

Dolgellau is a good centre for walking, whether you wish to take gentle strolls through beautiful leafy countryside or strenuous hikes across extreme terrain with dramatic mountain views. The lovely **Cregennen Lakes** are set high in the hills

above the thickly wooded **Mawddach Estuary** to the northwest; north are the harsh, bleak **Rhinog moors**, one of Wales's last true wildernesses.

Aberdyfi ⑯

Gwynedd. 🏘 *900.* 🚊 🚻 *Wharf Gardens (01654 767321).*
www.gwynedd.gov.uk

Perched on the mouth of the Dyfi Estuary, this little harbour resort and sailing centre makes the most of its splendid but rather confined location, its houses occupying every yard of a narrow strip of land between mountain and sea. In the 19th century, local slate was exported from here, and between the 1830s and the 1860s about 100 ships were built in the port. *The Bells of Aberdovey*, a song by Charles Dibdin for his opera *Liberty Hall* (1785), tells the legend of Cantref-y-Gwaelod, thought to have been located here, which was protected from the sea by dykes. One stormy night, the sluice gates were left open by Prince Seithenyn, when he was drunk, and the land was lost beneath the waves. The submerged church bells are said to peal under the water to this day.

Neat Georgian houses by the sea, Aberdyfi

SOUTH AND MID-WALES

CARDIFF, SWANSEA & ENVIRONS · CARDIGANSHIRE
CARMARTHENSHIRE · MONMOUTHSHIRE · POWYS · PEMBROKESHIRE

South and mid-Wales are less homogeneous regions than North Wales. Most of the population lives in the southeast corner. To the west is Pembrokeshire, the loveliest stretch of Welsh coastline. To the north the industrial valleys give way to the wide hills of the Brecon Beacons and the rural heartlands of central Wales.

South Wales's coastal strip has been settled for many centuries. There are prehistoric sites in the Vale of Glamorgan and Pembrokeshire. The Romans established a major base at Caerleon, and the Normans built castles all the way from Chepstow to Pembroke. In the 18th and 19th centuries, coal mines and ironworks opened in the valleys of South Wales, attracting immigrants from all over Europe. Close communities developed here, focused on the coal trade, which turned Cardiff from a sleepy coastal town into the world's busiest coal-exporting port.

The declining coal industry has again changed the face of this area: slag heaps have become green hills, and the valley towns struggle to find alternative forms of employment. Coal mines such as Blaenafon's Big Pit are now tourist attractions; today, many of the tour guides taking visitors underground are ex-miners, who can offer a first-hand glimpse of the hard life found in mining communities before the pits closed.

The southern boundary of the Brecon Beacons National Park marks the beginning of rural Wales. With a population sparser than anywhere in England, this is an area of small country towns, hill-sheep farms, forestry plantations and spectacular man-made lakes.

The number of Welsh-speakers increases and the sense of Welsh culture becomes stronger as you travel further from the border with England, with the exception of an English enclave in south Pembrokeshire.

The changing face of the coal industry: former miners take visitors down the Big Pit in Blaenafon

◁ Magnificent coastal scenery near St David's, Pembrokeshire

Exploring South and Mid-Wales

Magnificent coastal scenery marks the Pembrokeshire
Coast National Park and cliff-backed Gower Peninsula,
while Cardigan Bay and Carmarthen Bay offer quieter
beaches. Walkers can enjoy grassy uplands in the Brecon
Beacons and gentler country in the leafy Wye Valley. Urban
life is concentrated in the southeast of Wales, where old
mining towns line the valleys north of Cardiff, the capital.

**Cliffs of the Pembrokeshire
Coast National Park**

GETTING AROUND

The M4 motorway is the major route
into Wales from the south of England,
and there are good road links west of
Swansea running to the coast. The
A483 and A488 give access to mid-
Wales from the Midlands. Frequent
rail services connect London with
Swansea, Cardiff and the ferry
port of Fishguard.

MACHYNLL

Aberdyfi

Borth

ABERYSTWYTH 🟤 **7**

Cardigan   Devil'

Bay

Llanon   Pontrhydfer

Strata Flori

ABERAERON **8**

New Quay   Tregar

Llanarth   Ystrad Aeron

Aberporth   Lampe

Cemaes Head   Llanybydder   Pumsaint

Cardigan   *Teifi*   Llandysul

Goodwick   Newport   Newcastle   Rhos
Emlyn

Fishguard   Crymych

Pembrokeshire Coast National Park   Llar

Letterston   Cynwyl Elfed   Llandeilo

9 **ST. DAVIDS**   Treffgarne   Carmarthen   Carreg Cenn
Gas.

St. Brides   Whitland   *Tywi*
Bay   Haverfordwest   St. Clears

Skomer   Narberth   Cross Hands
Island

Dale   Milford   Kilgetty   Kidwelly   Pontarddulais
Haven   Neyland   Saundersfoot

Broad Sound   Pembrey   Llanelli

Pembroke   **10** **TENBY**   *Carmarthen*   Gorseinon

Manorbier   *Caldey*   *Bay*   **SWANSEA**
Island   Llanrhidian

St Govan's Head   Rhossili   *Gower*   Mumbles
Peninsula

Port-Eynon   S

SIGHTS AT A GLANCE

Aberaeron **8**
Aberystwyth **7**
Blaenafon **16**
*Brecon Beacons
pp468–9* **13**
Caerleon **15**
Cardiff pp470–71 **14**
Elan Valley **5**
Hay-on-Wye **3**
Knighton **2**
Llandrindod Wells **4**

Machynlleth **6**
Monmouth **17**
Powis Castle **1**
St Davids pp464–5 **9**
Swansea and the
Gower Peninsula **11**
Tenby **10**
Tintern Abbey **18**

Walks and Tours
Wild Wales Tour **12**

SEE ALSO

• *Where to Stay* pp590–93

• *Where to Eat* pp644–46

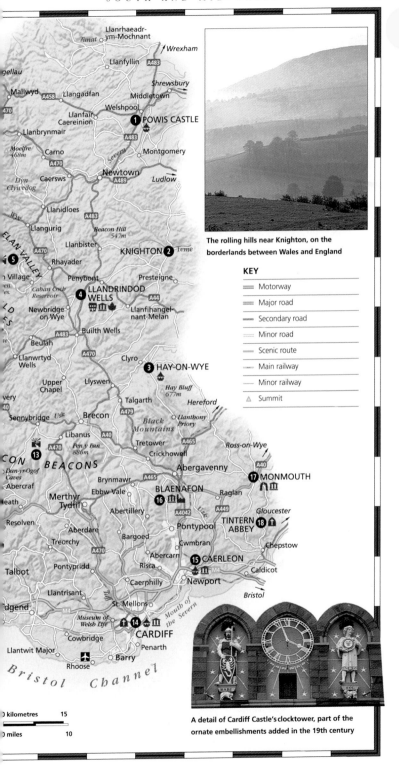

The rolling hills near Knighton, on the borderlands between Wales and England

KEY

▬▬	Motorway
▬▬	Major road
▬▬	Secondary road
⋯⋯	Minor road
───	Scenic route
┈┈	Main railway
──	Minor railway
△	Summit

A detail of Cardiff Castle's clocktower, part of the ornate embellishments added in the 19th century

**Map labels:**

Llanrhaeadr-ym-Mochnant
Tanat
Wrexham
Llanfyllin A483
Shrewsbury
Mallwyd A458 Langadfan
Middletown
Welshpool
1 POWIS CASTLE
Llanfair Caereinion
A483
Llanbrynmair
Moelfre 468m
Carno
Montgomery
A470
Caersws
Newtown A489
Ludlow
Llyn Clywedog
Llanidloes A483
Llangurig
Beacon Hill 547m
Llanbister
KNIGHTON 2
Teme
ELAN VALLEY
5
A470
Rhayader
n Village
es.
Caban Coch Reservoir
Penybont
Presteigne
4 LLANDRINDOD WELLS
A44
Newbridge-on-Wye
Llanfihangel-nant-Melan
Beulah
A483 Builth Wells
Llanwrtyd Wells
A470
Clyro
3 HAY-ON-WYE
Upper Chapel
Llyswen
Hay Bluff 677m
very
Talgarth
Hereford
40
Sennybridge Usk
Brecon A479
Black Mountains
Llanthony Priory
Libanus
Pen y Fan 886m
Tretower
A40
Crickhowell
A465
Ross-on-Wye
13
A470
BEACONS
Abergavenny
A40
CON
Dan-yr-Ogof Caves
Brynmawr
A465
17 MONMOUTH
Abercraf
Ebbw Vale
BLAENAFON
Raglan
eath
Merthyr Tydfil
16
A4042
A449
Resolven
Abertillery
Pontypool
Gloucester
Aberdare
Bargoed
A470
Cwmbran
TINTERN ABBEY 18
Treorchy
Abercarn
Chepstow
Pontypridd
Risca
15 CAERLEON
Talbot
Caerphilly
Newport
Llantrisant
St Mellons
Caldicot
Bristol
dgend
M4
Mouth of the Severn
Museum of Welsh Life
14 CARDIFF
Cowbridge
Penarth
Llantwit Major
Barry
Rhoose
Bristol Channel

0 kilometres 15
0 miles 10

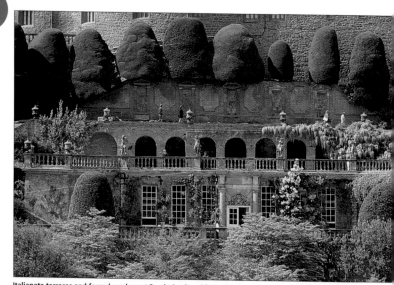

Italianate terraces and formal gardens at Powis Castle, adding a Mediterranean air to the Welsh borderlands

Powis Castle ❶

(NT) Welshpool, Powys. 📞 *01938 551944.* 🚌 *Welshpool then bus.* ⏰ *Apr–Jun & Sep–Oct: Thu–Mon; Jul–Aug: Wed–Mon & public hols; Nov & Mar: Sat & Sun.* ♿ ⬆ *limited.* 🖥 📷 *www.castlewales.com/powis*

Powis Castle – the spelling is an archaic version of "Powys" – has outgrown its military roots. Despite its sham battlements and dominant site, 1 mile (1.6 km) to the southwest of the town of Welshpool, this red-stone building has served as a country mansion for centuries. It began life in the 13th century as a fortress, built by the princes of Powys to control the border with England.

The castle is entered through one of few surviving medieval features: a gateway, built in 1283 by Owain de la Pole. The gate is flanked by two towers.

The castle's lavish interiors soon banish all thoughts of war. A **Dining Room**, decorated with fine 17th-century panelling and family portraits, was originally designed as the castle's Great

Hall. The **Great Staircase**, added in the late 17th century and elaborately decorated with carved fruit and flowers, leads to the main apartments: an early 19th-century library, the panelled **Oak Drawing Room** and the Elizabethan **Long Gallery**, where ornate plasterwork on the fireplace and ceiling date from the 1590s. In the **Blue Drawing Room** there are three 18th-century Brussels tapestries.

The Herbert family bought the property in 1587 and were proud of their Royalist connections; the panelling in

The richly carved 17th-century Great Staircase

the **State Bedroom** bears the royal monogram. Powis Castle was defended for Charles I in the Civil War *(see pp52–3),* but fell to Parliament in 1644. The 3rd Baron Powis, a supporter of James II, had to flee the country when William and Mary took the throne in 1688 *(see pp52–3).*

The castle's **Clive Museum** has an exhibition concerning "Clive of India" (1725–74), the general and statesman who helped strengthen British control in India in the mid-18th century. The family's link with Powis Castle was established by the 2nd Lord Clive, who married into the Herbert family and became the Earl of Powis in 1804.

The gardens at Powis are among the best-known in Britain, with their series of elegant Italianate terraces, adorned with statues, niches, balustrades and hanging gardens, all stepped into the steep hillside beneath the castle walls. Created between 1688 and 1722, these are the only formal gardens of this period in Britain that are still kept in their original form *(see pp26–7).*

Knighton ❷

Powys. 🏘 *3,500.* 🚄 ℹ️ *Offa's Dyke Centre, West St (01547 528753).* 🛍 *Thu.* **www.**offasdyke.demon.co.uk

Knighton's Welsh name, Tref y Clawdd ("The Town on the Dyke"), reflects its status as the only original settlement on **Offa's Dyke**. In the 8th century, King Offa of Mercia (central and southern England) constructed a ditch and bank to mark out his territory, and to enable the enforcement of a Saxon law: "Neither shall a Welshman cross into English land without the appointed man from the other side, who should meet him at the bank and bring him back again without any offence being committed." Some of the best-preserved sections of the 6-m-(20-ft-) high earthwork lie in the hills around Knighton. The Offa's Dyke Footpath runs for 177 miles (285 km) along the border between England and Wales.

Knighton is set on a steep hill, sloping upwards from **St Edward's Church** (1877) with its medieval tower, to the summit, where a castle once stood. The main street leads via the market square, marked by a 19th-century clock tower, along **The Narrows**, a Tudor street with little shops. **The Old House** on Broad Street is a medieval "cruck" house (curved timbers form a frame to support the roof), with a hole in the ceiling instead of a chimney.

Knighton's clock

Hay-on-Wye ❸

Powys. 🏘 *1,300.* ℹ️ *Oxford Rd (01497 820144).* 🛍 *Thu.* **www.**hay-on-wye.co.uk

Book-lovers from all over the world come to this quiet border town in the Black Mountains. Hay-on-Wye has over 30 second-hand book-shops stocking millions of titles, and in early summer hosts a prestigious Festival of Literature. The town's love affair with books began when a bookshop was opened in the 1960s by Richard Booth, who claims the (fictitious) title of King of Independent Hay and lives in **Hay Castle**, a 17th-century mansion in the grounds of the original 13th-century castle. Hay's oldest inn the 16th–century **Three Tuns** on Bridge Street, is still functioning and has an attractive half-timbered façade.

Environs: Hay sits on the approach to the Black Mountains and is surrounded by rolling hills. To the south are the heights of Hay Bluff and the Vale of Ewyas, where the 12th-century ruins of **Llanthony Priory** (*see p469*) retain fine pointed arches.

⚓ **Hay Castle**
Tel 01497 820503. ⭘ *daily.* ⬤ *25 Dec.* 🎟 *grounds only.* ♿

Llandrindod Wells ❹

Powys. 🏘 *5,000.* 🚄 ℹ️ *Memorial Gardens (01597 822600).* 🛍 *farmers' market last Thu of month; Fri.*

Llandrindod is a perfect example of a Victorian town, with canopied streets, delicate wrought ironwork,

One of Hay-on-Wye's bookshops

gabled villas and ornamental parklands. This purpose-built spa town became Wales's premier inland resort of the 19th century. Its sulphur and magnesium spring waters were taken to treat skin complaints and a range of other ailments.

The town now makes every effort to preserve its Victorian character, with a lake and the well-tended **Rock Park Gardens**. The restored 19th-century **Pump Room** in Temple Gardens is where, during the last full week of August, residents don period costume and cars are banned from the town centre.

The **Radnorshire Museum** traces the town's past as one of a string of 19th-century Welsh spas which included Builth, Llangammarch and **Llanwrtyd** (now a pony trekking centre).

🏛 **Radnorshire Museum**
Temple Street. ***Tel*** *01597 824513.* ⭘ *Phone for opening times.* ⬤ *1 Jan, 25 & 26 Dec.* 🎟 ♿

Victorian architecture on Spa Road, Llandrindod Wells

Craig Goch, one of the original chain of Elan Valley reservoirs

Elan Valley ❺

Powys. �／Llandrindod.
ℹ️ Rhayader (01597 810898).
www.elanvalley.org.uk

A string of spectacular reservoirs, the first of the country's man-made lakes, has made this one of Wales's most famous valleys. **Caban Coch, Garreg Ddu, Pen-y-Garreg** and **Craig Goch**, were created between 1892 and 1903 to supply water to Birmingham, 73 miles (117 km) away. They form a chain of lakes about 9 miles (14 km) long, holding 50 billion litres (13 billion gallons) of water. Victorian engineers selected these high moorlands on the Cambrian Mountains, for their high annual rainfall of 1,780 mm (70 inches). The choice created bitter controversy and resentment: more than 100 people had to move from the valley that was flooded in order to create Caban Coch.

Unlike their more utilitarian modern counterparts, these dams were built during an era when decoration was seen as an integral part of any design. Finished in dressed stone, they have an air of grandeur which is lacking in the huge **Claerwen** reservoir, a stark addition built during the early 1950s to double the lakes' capacity. Contained by a 355 m (1,165 ft) dam, it lies 4 miles (6 km) along the B4518 that runs through Elan Valley and offers magnificent views.

The remote moorlands and woodlands surrounding the lakes are an important habitat for wildlife; the red kite can often be seen here. The **Elan Valley Visitors' Centre**, beside the Caban Coch dam, describes the construction of the lakes, as well as the valley's own natural history. **Elan Village**, set beside the centre, is an unusual ex-ample of a model workers' village, built during the 1900s to house the water-works staff. Outside the centre is a statue of the poet Percy Bysshe Shelley (see p222), who stayed in the valley at the mansion of Nantgwyllt in 1810 with his wife, Harriet. The house now lies underneath the waters of Caban Coch, along with the rest of the old village. Among the buildings submerged were the village school and a church.

The trail from Machynlleth to Devil's Bridge, near Aberystwyth

Machynlleth ❻

Powys. 🚍 2,200. 🚂 ℹ️ Penrallt S. (01654 702401). 🛒 Wed.
www.exploremidwales.com

Half-timbered buildings and Georgian façades appear among the grey-stone houses in Machynlleth. It was here that Owain Glyndŵr, Wales's last native leader (see p436), held a parliament in 1404. The restored **Parliament House** has displays on his life and a brass-rubbing centre.

The ornate **Clock Tower**, in the middle of Maengwyn Street, was erected in 1874 by the Marquess of Londonderry to mark the coming of age of his heir, Lord Castlereagh. The Marquess lived in **Plas Machynlleth**, a 17th-century house in parkland off the main street, which is now a centre of Celtic heritage and culture.

Environs: In an old slate quarry 2.5 mile (4 km) to the north, a "village of the future" is run by the **Centre for Alternative Technology**. A water-balanced cliff railway takes summer visitors to view low-energy houses and organic gardens, to see how to make the best of Earth's resources.

Parliament House sign, Machynlleth

🏛 **Parliament House**
Maengwyn St. **Tel** 01654 702827.
🕐 Easter–Sep: Mon–Sat. ♿ ℹ️
🏛 **Centre for Alternative Technology** On A487. **Tel** 01654 705950. 🕐 daily. ● early Jan. 🅿️ ♿ 🍴 ℹ️ **www**.cat.org.uk

Aberystwyth ❼

Ceredigion. 🚍 11,000. 🚂 🚍 ℹ️ Terrace Rd (01970 612125).
www.ceredigion.gov.uk

This seaside and university town claims to be the cultural capital of mid-Wales. By the standards of this rural area, "Aber" is a big place, its population increased for much of the year by students.

To Victorian travellers, Aberystwyth was the "Biarritz

f Wales". There have been o great changes along the promenade, with its gabled otels, since the 19th century. Constitution Hill, a steep outcrop at the northern end, an be scaled in summer on the electric **Cliff Railway**, built n 1896. At the top, in a *camera obscura*, a lens

uskers on Aberystwyth's seafront

projects views of the town. The ruined **Aberystwyth Castle** (1277) is located south of the promenade. In the town centre, the **Ceredigion Museum**, set in a former music hall, traces the history of the town.

To the northeast of the town centre, **The National Library of Wales**, next to Aberystwyth University, has a valuable collection of ancient Welsh manuscripts.

SAVIN'S HOTEL

When the Cambrian Railway opened in 1864, businessman Thomas Savin put £80,000 into building a new hotel in Aberystwyth for package tourists. The scheme made him bankrupt, but the seafront building, complete with mock-Gothic tower, was bought by campaigners attempting to establish a Welsh university. The "college by the sea" opened in 1872, and is now the Theological College.

Mosaics on the college tower

Environs: During the summer the narrow-gauge Vale of Rheidol Railway runs 12 miles (19 km) to **Devil's Bridge**, where a dramatic series of waterfalls plunges through a wooded ravine and a steep trail leads to the valley floor.

🏛 **Ceredigion Museum**
Terrace Rd. *Tel 01970 633088.* ⚪
Mon–Sat. ⚫ *Good Fri, 25 Dec–2 Jan.* 📷 ♿ www.ceredigion.gov.uk

Aberaeron ❽

Ceredigion. 🏚 *1,500.*
🚆 *Aberystwyth, then bus.*
ℹ *The Quay (01545 570602).*
www.tourism.ceredigion.gov.uk

Aberaeron's harbour, lined with Georgian houses, became a trading port and shipbuilding centre in the early 19th century. Its orderly streets were laid out in pre-railway days, when the ports along Cardigan Bay enjoyed considerable wealth. The last boat was built here in 1994 and its harbour is now full of holiday sailors. The harbour can be crossed via a wooden footbridge.

On the quayside, the popular Honey Bee Ice Cream Parlour serves world-renowned ice creams to a loyal clientele. There is also a centre of local crafts in the town, Clos Pengarreg.

Rows of brightly painted Georgian houses lining the purpose-built harbour at Aberaeron

St Davids ❾

St David, the patron saint of Wales, founded a monastic settlement in this remote corner of southwest Wales in about 550, which became one of the most important Christian shrines. The present cathedral, built in the 12th century, and the Bishop's Palace, added a century later, are set in a grassy hollow below St Davids town, officially Britain's smallest city. The date of St David's death, 1 March, is commemorated throughout Wales.

Icon of Elijah, south transept

St Davids' Cathedral, the largest in Wales

The Private Chapel was a late 14th-century addition, built, like the rest of the palace, over a series of vaults.

Entrance

★ Great Hall
The open arcade and decorated parapet were added by Bishop Gower (1328–47) to unify different sections of the palace.

BISHOP'S PALACE
The bishop's residence, built between 1280 and 1350 and now in ruins, had lavish private apartments.

Palace latrines

Typical medieval window

Rose window

The Bishop's Hall, smaller than the Great Hall, may have been reserved for private use.

GREAT HALL
This reconstruction shows the hall before the lead was stripped from the roof. Bishop Barlow, St Davids' first Protestant bishop (1536–48), is thought to have been responsible for the lead's removal.

Wooden screen

Vault

STAR SIGHTS

- ★ Great Hall
- ★ Nave Ceiling
- ★ St David's Shrine

★ Nave Ceiling
The roof of the nave is lowered and hidden by an early 16th-century oak ceiling. A beautiful 14th-century rood screen divides the nave from the choir.

VISITORS' CHECKLIST

Cathedral Close, St Davids.
Tel 01437 720199.
Haverfordwest then bus.
9am–5:30pm daily (Sun: pm).
www. stdavidscathedral.org.uk

CATHEDRAL
St David was one of the founders of the 6th-century monastic movement, so this was an important site of pilgrimage. Three visits here equalled one to Jerusalem.

Stained-Glass Window
In the nave's west end, eight panels, produced in the 1950s, radiate from a central window showing the dove of peace.

St Mary's College Chapel

Bishop Vaughan's Chapel has a fine fan-vaulted early Tudor roof.

Entrance

Tower Lantern Ceiling
The medieval roof was decorated with episcopal insignia when restored in the 1870s by Sir George Gilbert Scott.

★ St David's Shrine
A statue of the saint is placed near the shrine. Thought to symbolize the Holy Spirit, a dove is said to have landed on David's shoulder as he spoke to a gathering of bishops.

Sixteenth-Century Choir Stalls
The royal coat of arms on one of the carved choir stalls shows that the sovereign is a member of St Davids' Chapter. There are some interesting misericords (see p341) in these stalls.

Tenby ⓾

Pembrokeshire. 👥 5,000. 🚋 🚌 🚻
ℹ️ Upper Park Road (01834 842
402). www.pembrokeshire.gov.uk

Tenby has successfully trodden the fine line between over-commercialization and popularity, refusing to submit its historic character to the garish excesses of some seaside towns. Georgian houses overlook its handsome harbour, which is backed by a well-preserved medieval clifftop town of narrow streets and passages. The old town was defended by a headland fortress, now ruined, flanked by two wide beaches and a ring of 13th-century walls. These survive to their full height in places, along with a fortified gateway, the **Five Arches**.

The three-storeyed **Tudor Merchant's House** is a 15th-century relic of Tenby's highly prosperous seafaring days, with original fireplaces and chimneys. There are regular boat trips from the harbour to **Caldey Island**, 3 miles (5 km) offshore, home of a perfume-making monastic community.

🏛 **Tudor Merchant's House**
(NT) Quay Hill.
Tel 01834 842279.
⭕ Mar–Oct: Sun–Fri. 🎟
🎫 for pre-booked parties.

A partly medieval restaurant next to the Tudor Merchant's House

Swansea and the Gower Peninsula ⓫

Swansea. 👥 230,000. 🚋 🚌 🚻
ℹ️ Plymouth St (01792 468321).
🗓 Mon–Sat. www.swansea.gov.uk

Swansea, Wales's second city, is set along a wide, curving bay. The city centre was rebuilt after heavy bombing in World War II but, despite the modern buildings, a traditional Welsh atmosphere prevails. This is particularly noticeable in the excellent food market, full of Welsh delicacies such as laverbread *(see p606)* and locally caught cockles.

The award-winning **Maritime Quarter** redevelopment has transformed the old docklands, and is worth a visit.

A statue of copper magnate John Henry Vivian (1779–1855) overlooks the marina. The Vivians, a leading Swansea family, founded the **Glynn Vivian Art Gallery**, which has exquisite Swansea pottery and porcelain. Archaeology and Welsh history feature at the **Swansea Museum**, the oldest museum in Wales.

The life and work of local poet Dylan Thomas (1914–53) is celebrated in the recently opened **Dylan Thomas Centre**. A permanent exhibition, Man and Myth, includes the original drafts of his poems, letters and memorabilia. His statue overlooks the Maritime Quarter. Thomas spent his childhood in the city's suburbs. **Cwmdonkin Park** was the scene of an early poem, *The Hunchback in the Park*, and its water garden has a memorial stone quoting from his *Fern Hill*.

Swansea's austere **Guildhall** (1934) has a surprisingly rich interior. The huge panels, by Sir Frank Brangwyn (1867–1956), on the theme of the British Empire, were originally painted for the House of Lords.

Swansea's most celebrated son, the poet Dylan Thomas

Picturesque fishermen's cottages at the Mumbles seaside resort

Swansea Bay leads to the **Mumbles**, a popular watersports centre at the gateway to the 19-mile-long (30 km) Gower Peninsula, which in 1956 was the first part of Britain to be declared an Area of Outstanding Natural Beauty. A string of sheltered, south-facing bays leads to Oxwich and Port-Eynon beaches.

Rhossili's enormous beach leads to north Gower and a coastline of low-lying burrows, salt marshlands and cockle beds. The peninsula is littered with ancient sites such as **Parc Le Breose**, a prehistoric burial chamber.

Near Carmarthen is the **National Botanic Garden of Wales**, with formal gardens centred on The Great Glasshouse which contains a Mediterranean ecosystem.

🏛 **Glynn Vivian Art Gallery**
Alexandra Rd. *Tel* 01792 516900.
⭕ Tue–Sun & public hols.
♿ limited. 🎫 by arrangement.
🖥 www.glynnviviangallery.org

🏛 **Swansea Museum**
Victoria Rd. *Tel* 01792 653763. ⭕
Tue–Sun & public hols. ♿ limited.
🖥 www.swanseaheritage.net

🏛 **Dylan Thomas Centre**
Somerset Pl. *Tel* 01792 463980.
⭕ daily. ♿ 🎫 by arrangement.
🍴 🖥 📷 www.swansea.gov.uk

🏛 **Guildhall**
St Helen's Rd. *Tel* 01792 635489.
⭕ Mon–Fri. 🔴 public hols. ♿

🌿 **National Botanic Garden of Wales**
Middleton Hall, Llanarthne.
Tel 01558 668768. ⭕ daily.
🔴 25 Dec. 🎟 ♿ 🍴 📷 📷
www.gardenofwales.org.uk

Wild Wales Tour ⑫

This tour weaves across the Cambrian Mountains' windswept moors, green hills and high, deserted plateaux. New roads have been laid to the massive Llyn Brianne Reservoir, north of Llandovery, and the old drover's road across to Tregaron has a tarmac surface. But the area is still essentially a "wild Wales" of hidden hamlets, isolated farmsteads, brooding high-lands and traditional, quiet market towns.

Llanidloes ⑥
The town was a centre of religious and social unrest in the 17th and 18th centuries (*see p437*). There is a rare example of a free-standing Tudor market hall. The medi-eval church was restored in the late 19th century.

Devil's Bridge ④
This is a popular, romantic beauty spot with waterfalls, rocks, wooded glades and an ancient stone bridge – built by the Devil, according to legend.

Elan Valley ⑤
This is an area of lakes and important wildlife habitats (*see p462*).

Strata Florida ③
This famous ruined abbey was an important poli-tical, religious and educa-tional centre during the Middle Ages.

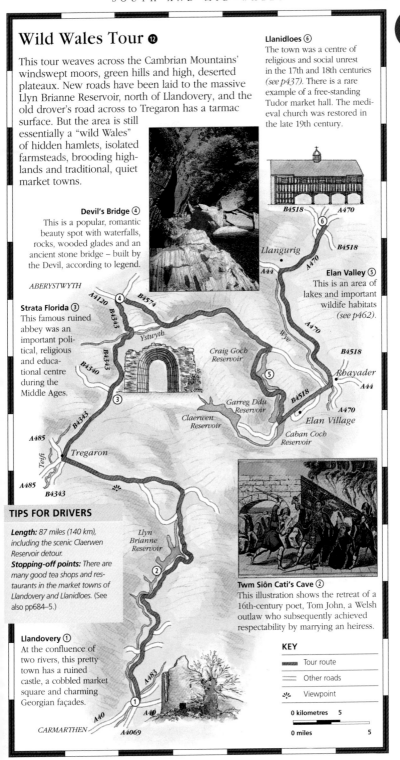

TIPS FOR DRIVERS

Length: 87 miles (140 km), including the scenic Claerwen Reservoir detour.
Stopping-off points: There are many good tea shops and res-taurants in the market towns of Llandovery and Llanidloes. (See also pp684–5.)

Llandovery ①
At the confluence of two rivers, this pretty town has a ruined castle, a cobbled market square and charming Georgian façades.

Twm Siôn Cati's Cave ②
This illustration shows the retreat of a 16th-century poet, Tom John, a Welsh outlaw who subsequently achieved respectability by marrying an heiress.

KEY

▄▄▄▄	Tour route
══	Other roads
☀	Viewpoint

0 kilometres 5

0 miles 5

Brecon Beacons ⑬

Trekking in the Beacons

The Brecon Beacons National Park covers 520 sq miles (1,345 sq km) from the Wales–England border almost all the way to Swansea. There are four mountain ranges within the park: the Black Mountain (to the west), Fforest Fawr, the Brecon Beacons and the Black Mountains (to the east). Much of the area consists of high, open country with smooth, grassy slopes on a bedrock of red sandstone. The park's southern rim has limestone crags, wooded gorges, waterfalls and caves. Visitors can enjoy many outdoor pursuits, from fishing in the numerous reservoirs to pony trekking, caving and walking.

Llyn y Fan Fach
This remote, myth-laden glacial lake is a 4 mile (6.5 km) walk from Llanddeusant.

The Black Mountain, a largely unexplored wilderness of knife-edged ridges and high, empty moorland, fills the western corner of the National Park.

BUILTH WELLS
LAMPETER
Llandovery A40
Sennybridge Usk
USK RESERVOIR
Clai A40
A4069
A4067
A421
Li
A40
CARMARTHEN Tywi
Llandeilo
Llanddeusant
Trapp
B L A C K   M O U N T A I N
YSTRADFELLT RESERVOIR
A4067
FFOREST FAWR
A4069
A483
Twrch
Gied
Mellte
Hepste
Llandybie
A471
Tawe
A4059
LLANELLI
Ammanford
A4068
SWANSEA
A4221
Ystradgynlais
A4109
A465
NEATH
Hirwaun

0 kilometres 10
0 miles 5

Fforest Fawr ("Great Forest") is named after an area that was a medieval royal hunting ground.

Carreg Cennen Castle
Spectacularly sited, the ruined medieval fortress of Carreg Cennen (see p438) stands on a sheer limestone cliff near the village of Trapp.

Dan-yr-Ogof Caves
A labyrinth of caves runs through the Brecon Beacons. Guided tours of two large caves are offered here.

KEY

▬▬	A road
▭▭	B road
═	Minor road
= =	Footpath
⚹	Viewpoint

For hotels and restaurants in this region see pp590–593 and pp644–646

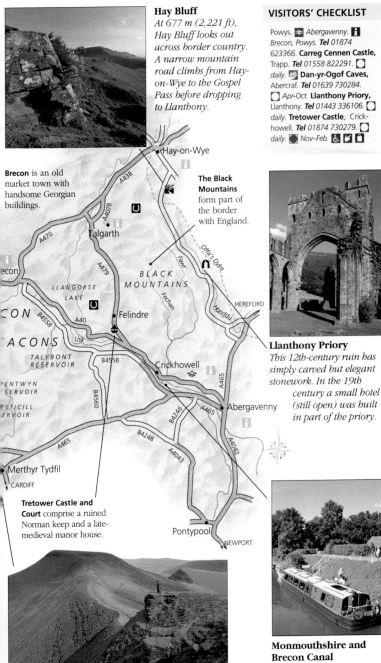

Hay Bluff

At 677 m (2,221 ft), Hay Bluff looks out across border country. A narrow mountain road climbs from Hay-on-Wye to the Gospel Pass before dropping to Llanthony.

Brecon is an old market town with handsome Georgian buildings.

The Black Mountains form part of the border with England.

Llanthony Priory

This 12th-century ruin has simply carved but elegant stonework. In the 19th century a small hotel (still open) was built in part of the priory.

Tretower Castle and Court comprise a ruined Norman keep and a late-medieval manor house.

Monmouthshire and Brecon Canal

This peaceful waterway, completed in 1812, was once used to transport raw materials between Brecon and Newport. It is now popular with leisure boats.

Pen y Fan

At 886 m (2,907 ft), Pen y Fan is the highest point in South Wales. Its distinctive, flat-topped summit, once a Bronze Age burial ground (see pp42–3), can be reached by footpaths from Storey Arms on the A470.

Cardiff ⑭

Cardiff was first occupied by the Romans, who built a fort here in AD 75 *(see pp44–5)*. Little is known of its subsequent history until Robert FitzHamon *(see p472)*, a knight in the service of William the Conqueror, was given land here in 1093. By the 13th century, the settlement was substantial enough to be granted a royal charter, but it remained a quiet country town until the 1830s when the Bute family, who inherited land in the area, began to develop it as a port. By 1913 this was the world's busiest coal-exporting port, profiting from rail links with the South Wales mines. Its wealth paid for grandiose architecture, while the docklands became a raucous boom-town. Cardiff was confirmed as the first Welsh capital in 1955, by which time demand for coal was falling and the docks were in decline. The city is now being transformed by urban renewal programmes.

Fireplace detail in the Banqueting Hall, Cardiff Castle

City Hall's dome, adorned with a dragon, the emblem of Wales

Exploring Cardiff

Cardiff is a city with two focal points. The centre, laid out with Victorian and Edwardian streets and gardens, is the first of these. There is a Neo-Gothic castle and Neo-Classical civic buildings, as well as indoor shopping malls and a 19th-century **covered market**. Canopied arcades, lined with shops, lead off the main streets, the oldest being the **Royal Arcade** of 1858. The **Millennium Stadium** (on the site of Cardiff Arms Park, the first home of Welsh rugby) opened in 1999 with the Rugby World Cup, and is open for tours most days.

To the south of the centre, the docklands are now being transformed into the second focal point by the creation of a freshwater lake and waterfront. **Y Senedd**, which opened in 2006, houses the National Assembly for Wales. Free guided tours are available but

booking is essential. Other attractions in the area are **Techniquest**, a hands-on science museum, and the impressive **Wales Millennium Centre**. A leading cultural venue, it stages a range of arts performances including musicals, ballet and stand-up comedy. It is also home to the Welsh National Opera.

The wooden **Norwegian Church** was first erected in 1868 for Norwegian sailors bringing wooden props for use in the coal pits of the South Wales valleys. Once surrounded by warehouses, it was taken apart and rebuilt during the dockland development.

Also in Cardiff Bay, the Red Dragon Centre houses the **Doctor Who Up Close Exhibition**, featuring many of the props and costumes seen in the TV series, which is shot in Cardiff (open daily; www. doctorwhoexhibitions.com). The **Cardiff Bay Visitor Centre** (www.cardiffharbour.com), on the waterfront, offers great views of the bay and displays about the history and development of the area.

♣ Cardiff Castle
See pp472–3.

⊞ City Hall and Civic Centre
Cathays Park. **Tel** *029 2087 1727.*
◻ *Mon–Fri.* ● *public hols.* & ⓑ
www.cardiffcityhall.com

Cardiff's civic centre of Neo-Classical buildings in white Portland stone is set among parks and avenues around Alexandra Gardens. The City Hall (1905), one of its first buildings, is dominated by its 60 m (200 ft) dome and clock

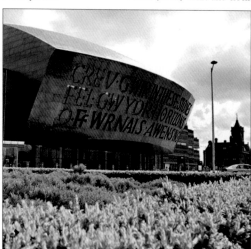
The entrance to the Wales Millennium Centre

tower. Members of the public can visit the first-floor Marble Hall, which is furnished with Siena marble columns and statues of Welsh heroes, among them St David, Wales's patron saint (see pp464–5). Cardiff University is based in the Civic Centre.

⛫ National Museum Cardiff

Cathays Park. **Tel** 029 2039 7951. ◷ Tue–Sun, public hols. ● 1, 2 Jan & 24, 25 Dec. ᵹ ◧ by appt. ◨ ◧ www.museum wales.ac.uk

Opened in 1927, the museum occupies an impressive civic building with a colonnaded portico, guarded by a statue of David Lloyd George (see p437). The art collection is among the finest in Europe, with works on display by Renoir, Monet and Van Gogh.

Statue of Welsh politician David Lloyd George

⛫ Craft in the Bay

The Flourish, Lloyd George Ave, Cardiff Bay. **Tel** 029 2048 4611. ◷ 10:30am–5:30pm daily. ᵹ ◧

An extensive craft gallery, organized by the Makers' Guild in Wales, opened here in June 2002. The building now houses a wide variety of craft displays and demonstrations, including textile weaving and ceramic making.

Environs: Established during the 1940s at St Fagans, on the western edge of the city, the open-air **St Fagans' National History Museum** was one of the first of its kind. Buildings from all over Wales, including workers' terraced cottages, farmhouses, a tollhouse, row of shops, chapel and old schoolhouse have been carefully reconstructed within the 40-ha (100-acre) parklands, along with a recreated Celtic village. There is also a Tudor mansion which can be visited, boasting

VISITORS' CHECKLIST

Cardiff. 🏟 321,000. ✈ Rhoose. 🚂 Central Sq. 🚌 Wood St. ◨ The Hayes (0870 121 1258). 🎭 Cardiff Festival: Jul, Aug. www.visitcardiff.com

its own beautiful gardens in the grounds.

Llandaff Cathedral lies in a deep, grassy hollow beside the River Taf at Llandaff, 2 miles (3 km) northwest of the city centre. The cathedral was first a medieval building, occupying the site of a 6th-century monastic community.

Restored after suffering severe bomb damage during World War II, it was eventually reopened in 1957 with the addition of Sir Jacob Epstein's huge, stark statue, Christus, which is mounted on a concrete arch.

⛫ St Fagans' National History Museum

St Fagans. **Tel** 029 2057 3500. ◷ daily. ᵹ ◧ www.museumwales.ac.uk

CARDIFF CITY CENTRE

Cardiff Castle pp472–3 ③
Cardiff Market ⑤
City Hall & Civic Centre ②
Craft in the Bay ⑥
Millennium Stadium ④
National Museum Cardiff ①
Norwegian Church ⑨
Techniquest ⑦
Y Senedd ⑧

0 metres 500
0 yards 500

Key to Symbols see back flap

Cardiff Castle

Cardiff Castle began life as a Roman fort, whose remains are separated from later work by a band of red stone. A keep was built within the Roman ruins in the 12th century. Over the following 700 years, the castle passed to several powerful families and eventually to John Stuart, son of the Earl of Bute, in 1776. His great-grandson, the 3rd Marquess of Bute, employed the "eccentric genius", architect William Burges, who created an ornate mansion between 1869 and 1881, rich in medieval images and romantic detail.

Arab Room
The gilded ceiling, with Islamic marble and lapis lazuli decorations, was built in 1881.

Animal Wall
A lion and other creatures guard the wall to the west of the castle. They were added between 1885 and 1930.

Herbert Tower

★ Summer Smoking Room
This was part of a complete bachelor suite in the Clock Tower, that also included a Winter Smoking Room.

Clock Tower

Main entrance to apartments

TIMELINE

AD 75 Roman fort constructed	**1107** Castle inherited by Mabel FitzHamon, whose husband is made Lord of Glamorgan	**1423–49** Beauchamp family adds the Octagon Tower and Great Hall ceiling	**1869** 3rd Marquess of Bute begins reconstruction
	1183 Castle damaged during Welsh uprising	**1445–1776** Castle passes in turn to Nevilles, Tudors and Herberts	

1000	**1200**	**1400**	**1600**	**1800**

1093 First Norman fort built by Robert FitzHamon of Gloucester	**1308–1414** Despenser family holds castle		**1776** Bute family acquires the castle
		Chaucer Room wall detail	**1947** The castle is given in trust to the city of Cardiff

VISITORS' CHECKLIST

Castle St, Cardiff. *Tel* 029-2087
8100. ☐ Mar–Oct: 9am–6pm
daily; Nov–Feb: 9:30am–5pm
daily. 🖼 🚻 🚻 🚻
www.cardiffcastle.com

★ Banqueting Hall
The design and decoration of this room depicts the castle's history, making impressively ingenious use of the murals and castellated fireplace.

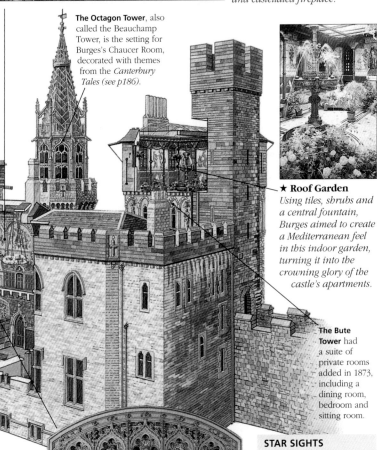

The Octagon Tower, also called the Beauchamp Tower, is the setting for Burges's Chaucer Room, decorated with themes from the *Canterbury Tales* (see p186).

★ Roof Garden
Using tiles, shrubs and a central fountain, Burges aimed to create a Mediterranean feel in this indoor garden, turning it into the crowning glory of the castle's apartments.

The Bute Tower had a suite of private rooms added in 1873, including a dining room, bedroom and sitting room.

STAR SIGHTS

- ★ Banqueting Hall
- ★ Library
- ★ Summer Smoking Room
- ★ Roof Garden

★ Library
Carved figures representing ancient characters of Greek, Assyrian, Hebrew and Egyptian alphabets decorate the library's chimneypiece.

Remains of Caerleon's amphitheatre, built in the 2nd century

Caerleon ⑮

Newport (Gwent). 🏠 11,000.
🚌 5 High St (01633 422656).
www.caerleon-tourism.org

Together with York (see pp404–5) and Chester (see pp310–11), Caerleon was one of only three fortress settlements in Britain built for the Romans' elite legionary troops. From AD 74 Caerleon (*Isca* to the Romans, after the River Usk, which flows beside the town) was home to the 2nd Augustan Legion, which had been sent to Wales to crush the native Silures tribe. The remains of their base now lie between the modern town and the river.

An altar at Caerleon's Legion Museum

The excavations at Caerleon are of great social and military significance. The Romans built not just a fortress for their crack 5,500-strong infantry division but a complete town to service their needs, including a stone amphitheatre. Judging by the results of the excavation work carried out since the archaeologist Sir Mortimer Wheeler unearthed the amphitheatre in 1926, Caerleon is one of the largest and most important Roman military sites in Europe. The defences enclosed an area of 20 ha (50 acres), with 64 rows of barracks, arranged in pairs, a hospital, and a bath-house complex.

Outside the settlement, the amphitheatre's large stone foundations have survived in an excellent state of preservation.

Six thousand spectators could enjoy the blood sports and gladiators' combat.

More impressive still is the fortress baths complex, which opened to the public in the mid-1980s. The baths were designed to bring all the home comforts to an army posted to barbaric Britain. The Roman troops could take a dip in the open-air swimming pool, play sports in the exercise yard or covered hall, or enjoy a series of hot and cold baths.

Nearby are the foundations of the only Roman legionary barracks on view in Europe. The many excavated artifacts, including a collection of engraved gemstones, are displayed at the **National Roman Legion Museum**.

🏛 **National Roman Legion Museum**
High St. **Tel** 01633 423134. ⭕ Mon–Sat, Sun (pm). ● 1 Jan, 24–26 Dec. 🔲 🔲 **www**.nmgw.ac.uk

Big Pit Mining Museum, reminder of a vanished industrial society

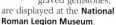

Blaenafon ⑯

Torfaen. 🏠 6,000. 🚌 Monmouth Rd, Abergavenny (01873 853254). **www**.blaenafontic.com

Commercial coal-mining has now all but ceased in the South Wales valleys – an area which only 100 years ago was gripped by the search for its "black gold". Though coal is no longer produced at **Big Pit** in Blaenafon, the **Mining Museum** provides a vivid reminder of this tough industry. The Big Pit closed as a working mine in 1980, and opened three years later as a museum. Visitors follow a marked-out route around the mine's surface workings to the miners' baths, the blacksmith's forge, the workshops and the engine house. There is also a replica of an underground gallery, where mining methods are explained. But the climax of any visit to Big Pit is beneath the ground. Kitted out with helmets, lamps and safety batteries, visitors descend by cage 90 m (300 ft) down the mineshaft and then are guided by ex-miners on a tour of the underground workings and pit ponies' stables.

Blaenafon also has remains of the iron-smelting industry. Across the valley from Big Pit stand the 18th-century smelting furnaces and workers' cottages that were once part of the **Blaenavon Ironworks**, and which are now a museum.

🏛 **Big Pit Mining Museum**
Blaenafon. **Tel** 01495 790311. ⭕ mid-Feb–Nov: daily; Dec & Jan: phone for details. 🔲 phone first. 🔲 🔲 🔲

🏛 **Blaenavon Ironworks**
North St. **Tel** 01495 792615. ⭕ mid-Mar–Oct: daily. 🔲 🔲 🔲

Monmouth ⑰

Monmouthshire (Gwent). 🏠 12,000.
🚌 🚌 Priory St (01600 713899). 🅿 Fri, Sat. **www**.visitwyevalley.com

This market town, which sits at the confluence of the Wye and Monnow rivers, has many historical associations. The 11th-century castle, behind Agincourt Square, is in ruins but the **Regimental Museum**,

Monnow Bridge in Monmouth, once a watchtower and jail

beside it, remains open to the public. The castle was the birthplace of Henry V (see p49) in 1387. Statues of Henry V (on the façade of Shire Hall) and Charles Stewart Rolls stand in the Square. Rolls, born at nearby Hendre, co-founded Rolls-Royce cars, and died in a flying accident in 1910.

Lord Horatio Nelson (see p54), the famous admiral, visited Monmouth in 1802. An excellent collection of Nelson memorabilia, gathered by Lady Llangattock, mother of Charles Rolls, is displayed at the **Nelson Museum**.

Monmouth was the county town of the old Monmouthshire. The wealth of elegant Georgian buildings, including the elaborate **Shire Hall**, which dominates Agincourt Square, reflect its former status. The most famous architectural feature in Monmouth is **Monnow Bridge**, a narrow 13th-century gateway on its western approach, thought to be the only surviving fortified bridge gate in Britain.

For a lovely view over the town, climb the Kymin, a 256 m (840 ft) hill crowned by a **Naval Temple** built in 1801.

Monmouth Castle and Regimental Museum

The Castle. *Tel 01600 772175.* ◻ *Apr–Oct: daily (pm); Nov–Mar: Sat & Sun (pm).* ● *25 Dec.* ♿ www. monmouthcastlemuseum.org.uk

Nelson Museum

Priory St. *Tel 01600 710630.* ◻ *daily (Sun: pm).* ♿ ▣

Tintern Abbey ⑱

Monmouthshire (Gwent). *Tel 01291 689251.* ◼ *Chepstow then bus.* ◻ *daily* ● *24–26 Dec, 1 Jan.* ▣ ▨ ♿ www.cadw.wales.gov.uk

Ever since the 18th century, travellers have been enchanted by Tintern's setting in the steep and wooded Wye Valley and by the majestic ruins of its abbey. Poets were often inspired by the scene. Wordsworth's sonnet, *Lines composed a few miles above Tintern Abbey*, embodied his romantic view of landscape:

> *once again*
> *Do I behold these steep and*
> *lofty cliffs,*
> *That on a wild, secluded*
> *scene impress*
> *Thoughts of more deep*
> *seclusion*

The abbey was founded in 1131 by Cistercian monks, who cultivated the surrounding lands (now forest), and developed it as an influential religious centre. By the 14th century this was the richest abbey in Wales, but along with other monasteries it was dissolved in 1536. Its skeletal ruins are now roofless and exposed, the soaring arches and windows giving them a poignant grace and beauty.

Tintern Abbey in the Wye Valley, in the past a thriving centre of religion and learning, now a romantic ruin

SCOTLAND

Scotland at a Glance

Stretching from the rich farmlands of the Borders to a chain of isles only a few degrees south of the Arctic Circle, the Scottish landscape has a diversity without parallel in Britain. As you travel northwest from Edinburgh, the land becomes more mountainous and its archaeological treasures more numerous. In the far northwest, Scotland's earliest relics stand upon the oldest rock on Earth.

Western Isles

THE HIGHLAND AND ISLANDS *(see pp520–49)*

Skye (see pp534–5) *renowned for its dramatic scenery, has one of Scotland's most striking coast-lines. On the east coast, a stream plunges over Kilt Rock, a cliff of hexagonal basalt columns named after its likeness to an item of Scottish national dress.*

Argyll and Bute

Clyde Valley

Ayrsh

The Trossachs (see pp494–5) *are a beautiful range of hills straddling the border between the Highlands and the Lowlands. At their heart, the forested slopes of Ben Venue rise above the still waters of Loch Achray.*

Culzean Castle (see pp522–3) *stands on a cliff's edge on the Firth of Clyde, amid an extensive country park. One of the jewels of the Lowlands, Culzean is a magnificent showcase of work by the Scottish-born architect, Robert Adam (see p28).*

◁ Loch Lomond, the Lowlands

Shetland

Orkney

ghland

The Cairngorms (see pp544–45) *cover an area prized for its beauty and diversity of wildlife, though there are also many historical relics to be found, such as this early 18th-century arch at Carrbridge.*

Moray

Aberdeenshire

Royal Deeside (see pp540–41) *in the Grampians has been associated with British royalty since Queen Victoria bought Balmoral Castle in 1852.*

Perthshire & Tayside

al

Fife

The Lothians

THE LOWLANDS
(see pp490–523)

The Borders

mfries
&
lloway

Edinburgh (see pp504–11) *is the capital of Scotland. Between its medieval castle and the Palace of Holyroodhouse stretches the Royal Mile – a concentration of historic sights, ranging from the old Scottish Parliament buildings to the house of John Knox. Georgian terraces predominate in the New Town.*

The Burrell Collection (see pp520–21), *on the southern outskirts of Glasgow, is a museum of some of the city's greatest art treasures. It is housed in a spacious, glass building opened in 1983.*

0 kilometres	50
0 miles	50

A PORTRAIT OF SCOTLAND

From the grassy hills of the Borders to the desolate Cuillin Ridge of Skye, the landscape of Scotland is breathtaking in its variety. Lonely glens, sparkling lochs and ever-changing skies give the land a challenging character, which is reflected in the qualities of the Scottish people. Tough and self-reliant, they have made some of Britain's finest soldiers, its boldest explorers and most astute industrialists.

The Scots are proud of their separate identity and their own systems of law and education and, in 1998, voted overwhelmingly for their own parliament. Many Scots welcomed this as a long-awaited reversal of the Act of Union that united the English and Scottish parliaments in 1707. But despite their national pride, they are not a homogeneous people, the main division is between traditionally Gaelic-speaking Highlanders, and the Lowlanders who spoke Scots, a form of Middle English which is now extinct. Today, though Gaelic survives (chiefly in the Western Isles), most people speak regional dialects or richly accented English. Many Scottish surnames derive from Gaelic: the prefix "mac" means "son of". A Norse heritage can be found in the far north, where Shetlanders welcome the annual return of the sun during the Viking fire festival, Up Helly Aa.

A hammer-thrower at the Braemar Games

In the 16th century, a suspicion of authority and dislike of excessive flamboyance attracted many Scots to the Presbyterian church with its absence of bishops and its stress on simple worship. The Presbyterian Church of Scotland was established in 1689, though a substantial Catholic minority remained which today predominates in the crofting (small-scale farming) communities of the Western Isles. Now sparsely populated, the Isles preserve a rural culture that once dominated the Highlands, a region that is the source of much that is distinctively Scottish. The clan system originated there, along with the tartans, the bagpipes and such unique sports as tossing the caber – a large tree trunk. Highland sports, along with traditional dances, are still performed at annual games *(see p64)*.

Edinburgh bagpiper

Resourcefulness has always been a prominent Scottish virtue, and Scotland has produced a disproportionately high number of Britain's geniuses. James Watt designed the first effective steam engine to power the Industrial Revolution, while Adam Smith became the 18th century's most influential economist. In the 19th century, James Simpson discovered the anaesthetic qualities of

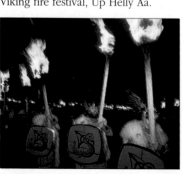
The Viking festival, Up Helly Aa, in Lerwick, Shetland

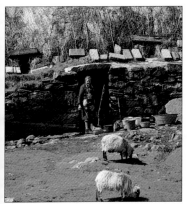

A traditional stone croft on the Isle of Lewis

With some of the harshest weather conditions in Europe it is perhaps less surprising that Scotland has bred numerous explorers, including polar explorer William Speirs Bruce and African missionary David Livingstone. There is also a strong intellectual and literary tradition, from the 18th-century philosopher David Hume, through novelists Sir Walter Scott and Robert Louis Stevenson, to the poetry of Robert Burns. Today Scotland hosts a variety of arts festivals, such as Edinburgh's.

chloroform, James Young developed the world's first oil refinery and Alexander Bell revolutionized communications by inventing the telephone. The 20th century saw one of the greatest advances in medicine with the discovery of penicillin by Alexander Fleming.

The Scots are also known for being shrewd businessmen, and have always been prominent in finance: both the Bank of England and the Royal Bank of France were founded by Scots, while Andrew Carnegie created one of 19th century-America's biggest business empires.

Detail of Edinburgh's Festival Fringe office

With a population density only one-fifth of England and Wales, Scotland has vast tracts of untenanted land which offer numerous outdoor pleasures. It is richly stocked with game, and the opening of the grouse season on 12 August is a highlight on the social calendar. Fishing and hill-walking are popular and in winter thousands flock to the Cairngorms and Glencoe for skiing. Though the weather may be harsher than elsewhere, the Scots will claim that the air is purer – and that enjoying rugged conditions is what distinguishes them from their soft southern neighbours.

The blue waters of Loch Achray in the heart of the Trossachs, north of Glasgow

The History of Scotland

Since the Roman invasion of Britain, Scotland's history has been characterized by its resistance to foreign domination. The Romans never conquered the area, and when the Scots extended their kingdom to its present boundary in 1018, a long era of conflict began with England. After many wars, the Scots finally accepted union with the "auld enemy": first with the union of crowns, and then with the Union of Parliament in 1707. In 1999 the inauguration of the Scottish Parliament was a dramatic change.

Bonnie Prince Charlie, by G Dupré

An elaborately carved Pictish stone at Aberlemno, Angus

EARLY HISTORY

There is much evidence in Scotland of important prehistoric population centres, particularly in the Western Isles, which were peopled mostly by Picts who originally came from the Continent. By the time Roman Governor Julius Agricola invaded in AD 81, there were at least 17 independent tribes, including the Britons in the southwest, for him to contend with.

The Romans reached north to the Forth and Clyde valleys, but the Highlands deterred them from going further. By 120, they had retreated to the line where the Emperor Hadrian had built his wall to keep the Picts at bay (not far from today's border). By 163 the Romans had retreated south for the last time. The Celtic influence began when

"Scots" arrived from Ireland in the 6th century, bringing the Gaelic language with them.

The Picts and Scots united under Kenneth McAlpin in 843, but the Britons remained separate until 1018, when they became part of the Scottish kingdom.

THE ENGLISH CLAIM

The Norman Kings regarded Scotland as part of their territory but seldom pursued the claim. William the Lion of Scotland recognized English sovereignty by the Treaty of Falaise (1174), though English control never spread to the northwest. In 1296 William Wallace, supported by the French (the start of the Auld Alliance, which lasted two centuries), began the long war of independence. During this bitter conflict, Edward I seized the sacred Stone of Destiny from Scone *(see p498)*, and took it to Westminster Abbey. The war lasted for more than 100 years. Its great hero was Robert the Bruce, who defeated the English in 1314 at Bannockburn. The English held the upper hand after that, even though the Scots would not accept their rule.

John K statue Edinbu

THE ROAD TO UNION

The seeds of union between the crowns were sown in 1503 when James IV of Scotland married Margaret Tudor, daughter of Henry VII. When her brother, Henry VIII, came to the throne, James sought to assert independence but was defeated and killed at Flodden Field in 1513. His granddaughter, Mary, Queen of Scots *(see p511)*, married the French Dauphin in order to cement the Auld Alliance and gain assistance in her claim to

Bruce in Single Combat at Bannockburn (1906) by John Hassall

the throne of her English cousin, Elizabeth I. She had support from the Catholics wanting to see an end to Protestantism in England and Scotland. However, fiery preacher John Knox won support for the Protestants and established the Presbyterian Church in 1560. Mary's Catholicism led to the loss of her Scottish throne in 1568, and her subsequent flight to England, following defeat at Langside. Finally, after nearly 20 years of imprisonment she was executed for treason by Elizabeth in 1587.

The factories on Clydeside, once creators of the world's greatest ships

UNION AND REBELLION

On Elizabeth I's death in 1603, Mary's son, James VI of Scotland, succeeded to the English throne and became James I, king of both countries. Thus the crowns were united, though it was 100 years before the formal Union of Parliaments in 1707. During that time, religious differences within the country

Articles of Union between England and Scotland, 1707

reached boiling point. There were riots when the Catholic-influenced Charles I restored bishops to the Church of Scotland and authorized the printing of a new prayer book. This culminated in the signing, in Edinburgh in 1638, of the National Covenant, a document that condemned all Catholic doctrines. Though the Covenanters were suppressed, the Protestant William of Orange took over the English throne in 1688 and the crown passed out of Scottish hands.

In 1745, Bonnie Prince Charlie (see p535), descended from the Stuart kings, tried to seize the throne from the Hanoverian George II. He

marched far into England, but was driven back and defeated at Culloden field (see p537) in 1746.

INDUSTRIALIZATION AND SOCIAL CHANGE

In the late 18th and 19th centuries, technological progress transformed Scotland from a nation of crofters to an industrial powerhouse. In the notorious Highland Clearances (see p531), from the 1780s on, landowners ejected tenants from their smallholdings and gave the land over to sheep and other livestock. The first ironworks was established in 1760 and was soon followed by coal mining, steel production and shipbuilding on the Clyde. Canals were cut, railways and bridges built.

A strong socialist movement developed as workers sought to improve their conditions. Keir Hardie, an Ayrshire coal miner, in 1892 became the first socialist elected to parliament, and in 1893 founded the Independent Labour Party. The most enduring symbol of this time is the spectacular Forth rail bridge (see p502).

SCOTLAND TODAY

Although the status of the country appeared to have been settled in 1707, a strong nationalist sentiment remained

and was heightened by the Depression of the 1920s and '30s which had severe effects on the heavily industrialized Clydeside. This was when the Scottish National Party formed, advocating self-rule. The Nationalists asserted themselves in 1950 by stealing the Stone of Scone from Westminister Abbey.

The discovery of North Sea oil in 1970 encouraged a nationalist revival and, in 1979, the Government promised to establish a separate assembly if 40 per cent of the Scottish electorate endorsed the plan in a referendum. This figure was finally surpassed in 1998, and the Scottish Parliament was duly inaugurated in 1999.

A North Sea oil rig, helping to provide prosperity in the 1970s

Clans and Tartans

The clan system, by which Highland society was divided into tribal groups led by autocratic chiefs, can be traced to the 12th century, when clans were already known to wear the chequered wool cloth later called tartan. All members of the clan bore the name of their chief, but not all were related by blood. Though they had noble codes of hospitality, the clansmen had to be warriors to protect their herds, as can be seen from their mottoes. After the Battle of Culloden *(see p537)*, all the clan lands were forfeited to the Crown, and the wearing of tartan was banned for nearly 100 years.

The Mackays, *also known as the Clan Morgan, won lasting renown during the Thirty Years War.*

The MacLeods *are of Norse heritage. The clan chief still lives in Dunvegan Castle, Skye (see p534).*

The Mackenzies *received much of the lands of Kintail (see p530) from David II in 1362.*

The MacDonalds *were the most powerful of all the clans, holding the title of Lords of the Isles.*

CLAN CHIEF

The chief was the clan's patriarch, judge and leader in war, commanding absolute loyalty from his clansmen who gave military service in return for his protection. The chief summoned his clan to do battle by sending a runner across his land bearing a burning cross.

Bonnet with eagle feathers, clan crest and plant badge.

Dirk

Sporran, or pouch, made of badger's skin.

Feileadh-mor, or "great plaid" (the early kilt), wrapped around waist and shoulder.

Basket-hilted sword

The Campbells *were a widely feared clan who fought the Jacobites in 1746 (see p537).*

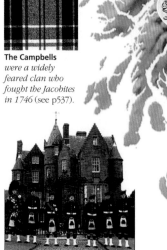

The Black Watch, *raised in 1729 to keep peace in the Highlands, was one of the Highland regiments in which the wearing of tartan survived. After 1746, civilians were punished by exile for up to seven years for wearing tartan.*

The Sinclairs *came from France in the 11th century and became Earls of Caithness in 1455.*

The Frasers *came to Britain from France with William the Conqueror (see p47) in 1066.*

George IV, *dressed as a Highlander, visited Edinburgh in 1822, the year of the tartan revival. Many tartan "setts" (patterns) date from this time, as the original ones were lost.*

The Gordons *were famously good soldiers; the clan motto is "by courage, not by craft".*

The Stuarts *were Scotland's royal dynasty. Their motto was "no one harms me with impunity".*

CLAN TERRITORIES

The territories of 10 prominent clans are marked here with their clan crests. Dress tartans tend to be colourful, while hunting tartans are darker.

The Douglas *clan were prominent in Scottish history, though their origin is unknown.*

PLANT BADGES

Each clan had a plant associated with its territory. It was worn on the bonnet, especially on the day of battle.

Scots pine was worn by the MacGregors of Argyll.

Rowan berries were worn by the Clan Malcolm.

Ivy was worn by the Clan Gordon of Aberdeenshire.

Spear thistle, now a national symbol, was a Stuart badge.

Cotton grass was worn by the Clan Henderson.

HIGHLAND CLANS TODAY

Once the daily dress of the clansmen, the kilt is now largely reserved for formal occasions. The one-piece *feileadh-mor* has been replaced by the *feileadh-beag*, or "small plaid", made from approximately 7 m (23 ft) of material with a double apron fastened at the front with a silver pin. Though they exist now only in name, the clans are still a strong source of pride for Scots, and many still live in areas traditionally belonging to their clans. Many visitors to Britain can trace their Scots ancestry *(see p31)* to the Highlands.

Modern Highland formal dress

Evolution of the Scottish Castle

There are few more romantic sights in the British Isles than a Scottish castle on an island or at a lochside. These formidable retreats, often in remote settings, were essential all over the Highlands, where incursions and strife between the clans were common. From the earliest Pictish *brochs (see p43)* and Norman-influenced motte and bailey castles, the distinctively Scottish stone tower-house evolved, first appearing in the 14th century. By the mid-17th century fashion had become more important than defence, and there followed a period in which numerous huge Scottish palaces were built.

Detail of the Baroque façade, Drumlanrig

MOTTE AND BAILEY

These castles first appeared in the 12th century. They stood atop two adjacent mounds enclosed by a wall, or palisade, and defensive ditches. The higher mound, or motte, was the most strongly defended as it held the keep and chief's house. The lower bailey was where the people lived. Of these castles little more than earthworks remain today.

Keep, with chief's house, lookout and main defence

All that remains today of Duffus Castle, Morayshire

Duffus Castle, *(c.1150), was atypically made of stone rather than wood. Its fine defensive position dominates the surrounding flatlands north of Elgin.*

Motte of earth or rock, sometimes partially man-made

Bailey enclosing dwellings and storehouses

EARLY TOWER-HOUSE

Designed to deter local attacks rather than a major assault, the first tower-houses appeared in the 13th century, though their design lived on for 400 years. They were built initially on a rectangular plan, with a single tower divided into three or four floors. The walls were unadorned, with few windows. Defensive structures were on top, and extra space was made by building adjoining towers. Extensions were made as vertically as possible, to minimize the area open to attack.

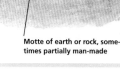

Crenellated parapet for sentries

Featureless, straight walls with arrow slits for windows

Claypotts Castle (c.1570) with uniquely projecting garrets above its towers

Braemar Castle (c.1630), a conglomeration of extended towers

Neidpath Castle, *standing upon a steep rocky crag above the River Tweed, is an L-shaped tower-house dating from the late 14th century. Once a stronghold for Charles II, its walls still bear damage from a siege conducted by Oliver Cromwell (see p52).*

Small, inconspicuous doorway

LATER TOWER-HOUSE

Though the requirements of defence were being replaced by those of comfort, the style of the early tower-house remained popular. By the 17th century, wings for accommodation were being added around the original tower (often creating a courtyard). The battlements and turrets were kept more for decorative than defensive reasons.

Drum Castle (see p541), a 13th-century keep with a mansion house extension from 1619

Priest's room with secret access

The original 15th-century tower-house

Round angle tower, containing stairway

A 16th-century horizontal extension

Traquair House (see p513), *by the Tweed, is reputedly the oldest continuously inhabited house in Scotland. The largely unadorned, roughcast exterior dates to the 16th century, when a series of extensions were built around the original 15th-century tower-house.*

Decorative, corbelled turret

Blair Castle (see p543), incorporating a medieval tower

CLASSICAL PALACE

By the 18th century, the defensive imperative had passed and castles were built in the manner of country houses, rejecting the vertical tower-house in favour of a horizontal plan (though the building of imitation fortified buildings continued into the 19th century with the mock-Baronial trend). Outside influences came from all over Europe, including Renaissance and Gothic revivals, and echoes of French châteaux.

Dunrobin Castle (c.1840), Sutherland

Larger windows due to a lesser need for defence

Balustrades instead of battlements

Decorative cupola

Drumlanrig Castle (see p514) *was built in the 17th century. There are many traditional Scots aspects as well as such Renaissance features as the decorated stairway and façade.*

Renaissance-style colonnade

Baroque horseshoe stairway

The Flavours of Scotland

At its best, Scottish food is full of the natural flavour of the countryside. Served with few sauces or spices, its meat is lean and tasty. Beef doesn't get better than Aberdeen Angus, the lamb is full flavoured, and the venison superb. Scottish salmon and trout are renowned, but there are also excellent mussels, lobster and crabs. Wheat does not grow here, so oatcakes and bannocks (flat, round loaves) replace bread. The Scots have a sweet tooth, not just for cakes and shortbread but also for toffee and butterscotch.

Smoked Salmon

Pedigree Aberdeen Angus cattle grazing the Scottish moors

THE LOWLANDS

The pasturelands of southern Scotland nourish dairy cattle and sheep, producing cheeses such as Bonnet, Bonchester and Galloway Cheddar. To accompany them are summer fruits such as loganberries, tayberries and strawberries that ripen in the Carse of Gowrie beside the River Tay. Oats, the principal cereal,

appears in much Scottish cookery, from porridge to oatcakes. Pearl barley is also a staple, used in Scotch Broth (made with mutton and vegetables) or in a milk pudding. Oats are also used in the making of haggis, a round sausage of sheep or venison offal – the "chieftain o' the puddin' race", as the poet Robert Burns described it. It is often served with "neeps and tatties" (mashed swede and potato).

THE HIGHLANDS

From the Highlands comes wonderful game, including grouse, partridge, caper-caillie (a large type of grouse) and deer. Fish are smoked around the coast, the west coast producing kippers, the east coast Finnan haddock, notably Arbroath Smokies. Smoked white fish is the main ingredient of Cullen Skink, a soup served on Burns' Night.

Lobster　Trout　　　　Oysters　Salmon
Mussels

Selection of fresh Scottish fish and seafood

TRADITIONAL SCOTTISH FOOD

Kippers (oak-smoked herrings) are one way to start the day in Scotland, and porridge – traditionally served with salt rather than sugar – is another, although oatcakes or some other kind of griddled scone are usually present. A bowl of porridge would once last all week, just as one-pot Scotch broths bubbled in iron cauldrons over peat fires for days. Sometimes broths were made with kale or lentils, or they might contain an old boiling fowl and leeks, in which case they were known as cock-a-leekie. Any leftover meat went into making stovies, a potato and onion hash. The evening meal in Scotland is traditionally "high tea" taken in the early evening which might start with smoked fish, cold meats and pies, followed by shortbread, fruit cake or drop scones, all washed down with cups of tea.

Oats

Haggis with neeps and tatties
This is the definitive Scottish dish, traditionally served on Burns' Night (25 January).

HOW WHISKY IS MADE

Traditionally made from just barley, yeast and stream water, Scottish whisky (from the Gaelic *usquebaugh*, or the "water of life") takes a little over three weeks to produce, though it must be given at least three years to mature. Maturation usually takes place in oak casks, often in barrels previously used for sherry. The art of blending was pioneered in Edinburgh in the 1860s.

Barley grass

1 *Malting is the first stage. Barley grain is soaked in water and spread on the malting floor. With regular turning the grain germinates, producing a "green malt". Germination stimulates the production of enzymes which turn the starches into fermentable sugars.*

2 *Drying of the barley halts germination after 12 days of malting. This is done over a peat fire in a pagoda-shaped malt-kiln. The peat-smoke gives flavour to the malt and eventually to the mature whisky. The malt is gleaned of germinated roots and then milled.*

3 *Mashing of the ground malt, or "grist", occurs in a large vat, or "mash tun", which holds a vast quantity of hot water. The malt is soaked and begins to dissolve, producing a sugary solution called "wort", which is then extracted for fermentation.*

4 *Fermentation occurs when yeast is added to the cooled wort in wooden vats, or "washbacks". The mixture is stirred for hours as the yeast turns the sugar into alcohol, producing a clear liquid called "wash".*

5 *Distillation involves boiling the wash twice so that the alcohol vaporizes and condenses. In copper "pot stills", the wash is distilled – first in the "wash still", then in the "spirit still". Now purified, with an alcohol content of 57 per cent, the result is young whisky.*

6 *Maturation is the final process. The whisky mellows in oak casks for a legal minimum of three years. Premium brands give the whisky a 10- to 15-year maturation, though some are given up to 50 years.*

Traditional drinking vessels, or *quaichs*, made of silver

Blended whiskies *are made from a mixture of up to 50 different single malts.*

Single malts *vary according to regional differences in the peat and stream water used.*

THE LOWLANDS

CLYDE VALLEY · CENTRAL SCOTLAND · FIFE · THE LOTHIANS
AYRSHIRE · DUMFRIES AND GALLOWAY · THE BORDERS

S *outheast of the Highland boundary fault line lies a part of*
Scotland very different in character from its northern neighbour.
If the Highlands embody the romance of Scotland, the Lowlands
have traditionally been her powerhouse. Lowlanders have always pros-
pered in agriculture and, more recently, in industry and commerce.

Being the region of Scotland clos-est to the English border, the Lowlands inevitably became the crucible of Scottish his-tory. For centuries after the Romans built the Antonine Wall (*see p44*) across the Forth–Clyde isthmus, the area was engulfed in conflict. The Borders are scattered with the castles of a territory in uneasy proximity to rapacious neighbours, and the ramparts of Stirling Castle overlook no fewer than seven differ-ent battlefields fought over in the cause of independence.

The ruins of medieval abbeys, such as Melrose, also bear witness to the dangers of living on the invasion route from England, though the woollen trade founded by their monks still flourishes in Peebles and Hawick.

North of the Borders lies Edinburgh, the cultural and administrative capi-tal of Scotland. With its Georgian squares dominated by a medieval cas-tle, it is one of Europe's most elegant cities. While the 18th and 19th cen-turies saw a great flowering of the arts in Edinburgh, the city of Glasgow became a merchant city second only to London. Fuelled by James Watt's devel-opment of the steam engine in the 1840s, Glasgow became the cradle of Scotland's Industrial Revolution, which created a prosperous cotton industry and launched the world's greatest ships.

Both cities retain this dynamism today: Edinburgh annually hosts the world's largest arts festival, and Glasgow is acclaimed as a model of industrial renaissance.

A juggler performing at the annual arts extravaganza, the Edinburgh Festival

◁ **Glamis Castle, 12 miles (19 km) north of Dundee, with its typically Scottish turreted exterior**

Exploring the Lowlands

The Lowlands are traditionally all the land south of the fault line stretching northeast from Loch Lomond to Stonehaven. Confusingly, they include plenty of wild upland country. The region illustrates the diversity of Scotland's scenery. The wooded valleys and winding rivers of the borders give way to the stern hills of the Cheviots and Lammermuirs. Fishing villages cling to the rocky east coast, while the Clyde coast and its islands are dotted with holiday towns. Inland lies the Trossachs, a romantic area of mountain, loch and woodland east of Loch Lomond that is a magnet for walkers (see pp36–7) and well within reach of Glasgow.

Loch Katrine seen from the Trossachs

SEE ALSO

- *Where to Stay* pp593–6
- *Where to Eat* pp646–9

SIGHTS AT A GLANCE

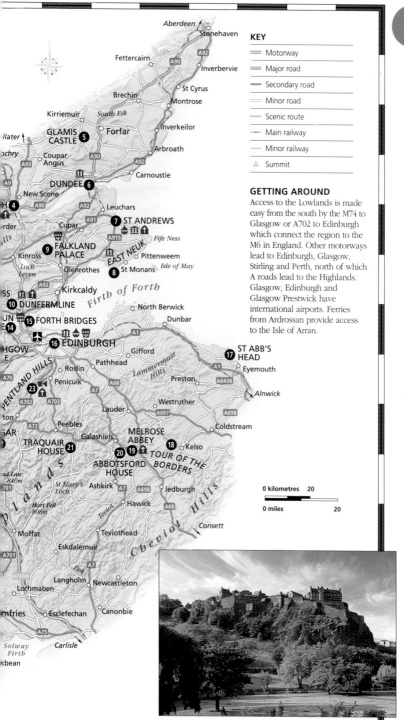

Aberdeen
Stonehaven
Fettercairn
A90
A92
Inverbervie
St Cyrus
Brechin
Montrose
Kirriemuir
South Esk
Inverkeilor
llater
GLAMIS
CASTLE **5**
Forfar
ochry
Coupar
Angus
A93
A90
A92
Arbroath
A9
DUNDEE **6**
New Scone
Carnoustie
4
A90
A92
Leuchars
rder
Cupar
A91
7 ST ANDREWS
lls
A915
Fife Ness
9 FALKLAND
PALACE
EAST NEUK
Kinross
Pittenweem
Loch
Leven
Glenrothes
8 St Monans
Isle of May
SS
A92
Kirkcaldy
Firth of Forth
10 DUNFERMLINE
North Berwick
UN
15 FORTH BRIDGES
Dunbar
14
HGOW
16 EDINBURGH
Gifford
17 ST ABB'S
HEAD
E
Roslin
Pathhead
Lammermuir
Hills
A1
Eyemouth
A70
PENTLAND HILLS
Penicuik
Preston
A6438
A7
A68
Alnwick
A702
A703
Lauder
Westruther
Alnwick
ton
A697
A698
Coldstream
AR
A72
Peebles
MELROSE
ABBEY
23
Galashiels
20 **19**
18 Kelso
21 TRAQUAIR
HOUSE
ABBOTSFORD
HOUSE
TOUR OF THE
BORDERS
ad Law
840m
St Mary's
Loch
Ashkirk
A7
A698
Jedburgh
701
Hart Fell
808m
Hawick
A68
Moffat
Teviot
Consett
A701
Teviothead
Eskdalemuir
Esk
Cheviot Hills
A74M
Langholm
Newcastleton
Lochmaben
mfries
Ecclefechan
Canonbie
A75
Solway
Firth
Carlisle
kbean

KEY

═══ Motorway

▭▭▭ Major road

━━━ Secondary road

┄┄┄ Minor road

─── Scenic route

╌╌╌ Main railway

─── Minor railway

△ Summit

GETTING AROUND

Access to the Lowlands is made
easy from the south by the M74 to
Glasgow or A702 to Edinburgh
which connect the region to the
M6 in England. Other motorways
lead to Edinburgh, Glasgow,
Stirling and Perth, north of which
A roads lead to the Highlands.
Glasgow, Edinburgh and
Glasgow Prestwick have
international airports. Ferries
from Ardrossan provide access
to the Isle of Arran.

0 kilometres   20

0 miles   20

Edinburgh Castle viewed from Princes Street

The Trossachs ①

Combining the ruggedness of the Grampians with the pastoral tranquillity of the Borders, this beautiful region of craggy hills and sparkling lochs is the colourful meeting place of the Lowlands and Highlands. Home to a wide variety of wildlife, including the golden eagle, peregrine falcon, red deer and the wildcat, the Trossachs have inspired numerous writers, including Sir Walter Scott

Golden eagle

(see p512) who made the area the setting for several of his novels. It was the home of Scotland's folk hero, Rob Roy, who was so well known that, in his own lifetime, he was fictionalized in *The Highland Rogue* (1723), a novel attributed to Daniel Defoe.

Loch Katrine
The setting of S. Walter Scott's Li of the Lake (18 this freshwater loch can be explored on the Victorian steam SS Sir Walter Sc which cruises fr the Trossachs Pi

Loch Lomond
Britain's largest freshwater lake was immortalized in a ballad composed by a local Jacobite soldier, dying far from home. He laments that though he will return home before his companions who travel on the high road, he will be doing so on the low road (of death).

The West Highland Way provides a good footpath through the area.

KEY

🛈	Tourist information
▬▬	A road
▭▭	B road
═══	Minor road
– –	Footpath
☼	Viewpoint

0 kilometres   5

0 miles   5

Luss
With its exceptionally picturesque cottages, Luss is one of the prettiest villages in the Lowlands. Surrounded by grassy hills, it occupies one of the most scenic parts of Loch Lomond's western shore.

Map labels: FORT WILLIAM, Inveruglas, LOCH ARKLET, Tarbet, BEN LOMOND ▲ 974 m 3,196 ft, Kinloc, BEN UIRD ▲ 596 m 1,955 ft, Luss, Baln, LOCH LOMOND, Balloch, GLASGOW, A82, A811, B829, B831

Inchmahome Priory

Mary, Queen of Scots (see p511) was hidden in this island priory to escape the armies of Henry VIII (see p512).

VISITORS' CHECKLIST

Stirling. 🚆 Stirling. 🚌 Callander.
🛈 Visit Scotland, Ancaster Sq,
Callander (0870 7200628).
www.visitscotland.com
Loch Lomond Aquarium Visitor
Centre (01389 721500). 🕐 daily.
www.sealifeeurope.com
Inchmahome Priory off A81,
nr Aberfoyle; by ferry to Lake of
Monteith. **Tel** 0870 7200628.
🕐 Apr–Sep: daily. 🎦 🚻 limited.
SS **Sir Walter Scott**: ring Visitor
Centre (01877 376316).

Balquhidder ⛪
PERTH

Rob Roy's grave

LOCH VOIL

A84

TROSSACHS

LOCH LUBNAIG

BEN LEDI
▲
878 m
2,881 ft

A84

NUE

Callander

LOCH ACHRAY

Brig O'Turk

A821

LOCH VENNACHAR

A81

MENTEITH HILLS

Aberfoyle

A81

B8304

Goodie Water

A873

B822

STIRLING

LAKE OF MENTEITH

A81

A811

STIRLING

A811

Arnprior

A875

Balfron

Killearn

Callander

This is the most popular town from which to explore the Trossachs and films of the area are shown at the information centre.

ROB ROY (1671–1734)

Robert MacGregor, known as Rob Roy (Red Robert) from the colour of his hair, grew up as a herdsman near Loch Arklet. After a series of harsh winters, he took to raiding richer Lowland properties to feed his clan, and was declared an outlaw by the Duke of Montrose who then burned his house to the ground. After this, Rob's Jacobite *(see p537)* sympathies became inflamed by his desire to avenge the crime. Plundering the duke's lands and repeatedly escaping from prison earned him a reputation similar to England's Robin Hood *(see p336)*. He was pardoned in 1725 and spent his last years freely in Balquhidder, where he is buried.

The Duke's Pass, between Callander and Aberfoyle, affords some of the finest views in the area.

Queen Elizabeth Forest Park

There are woodland walks through this vast tract of countryside, home to black grouse and red deer, between Loch Lomond and Aberfoyle.

The 17th-century town house of the Dukes of Argyll, Stirling

Stirling ❷

Stirling. 41,000. 🚂 🚌 🅹 41 Dunbarton Rd (08707 200614). www.visitscottishheartlands.com

Situated between the Ochil Hills and the Campsie Fells, Stirling grew up around its castle, historically one of Scotland's most important fortresses. Below the castle the Old Town is still protected by the original 16th-century walls, built to keep Mary Queen of Scots safe from Henry VIII. The medieval **Church of the Holy Rude**, on Castle Wynd, where the infant James VI was crowned in 1567, has one of Scotland's few surviving hammerbeam oak roofs. The ornate façade of **Mar's Wark** is all that remains of a grand palace which, though never completed, was commissioned in 1570 by the 1st Earl of Mar. It was destroyed by the Jacobites (see p537) in 1746. Opposite stands the beautiful 17th-century town house of the Dukes of Argyll.

Environs: Two miles (3 km) south, the **Bannockburn Heritage Centre** stands by the field where Robert the Bruce defeated the English (see p482). After the battle, he dismantled the castle so it would not fall back into English hands. A bronze equestrian statue commemorates the man who is an icon of Scottish independence.

🅸 **Bannockburn Heritage Centre**
(NTS) Glasgow Rd. **Tel** 01786 812664. ◯ Mar–Oct: 10am–5:30pm daily; other times by appointment. ● 24 Dec–Feb. 🈺 🅰

Stirling Castle

Rising high on a rocky crag, this magnificent castle, which dominated Scottish history for centuries, now remains one of the finest examples of Renaissance architecture in Scotland. Legend says that King Arthur (see p285) wrested the original castle from the Saxons, but there is no evidence of a castle before 1124. The present building dates from the 15th and 16th centuries and was last defended, against the Jacobites (see p537), in 1746. From 1881 to 1964 the castle was a depot for recruits into the Argyll and Sutherland Highlanders, though now it serves no military function.

Gargoyle on castle wall

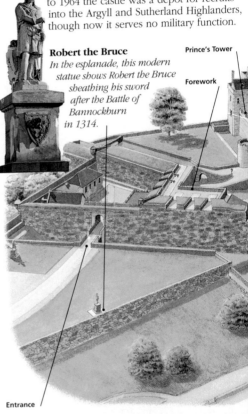

Robert the Bruce
In the esplanade, this modern statue shows Robert the Bruce sheathing his sword after the Battle of Bannockburn in 1314.

Prince's Tower

Forework

Entrance

Stirling Castle in the Time of the Stuarts, painted by Johannes Vorsterman (1643–99)

★ Palace
The otherwise sparse interiors of the royal apartments contain the Stirling Heads. These Renaissance roundels depict 38 figures, thought to be contemporary members of the royal court.

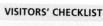

VISITORS' CHECKLIST

Castle Wynd, Stirling. **Tel** 01786 450000. ☐ 9:30am–6pm (Oct–Mar: to 5pm) daily. (Palace closed for restoration until 2011.) ☐ 25–26 Dec. 🅿️ 📷 except museum. ♿ limited. 🎫 🚻 🍴 🛍️ **www. historic-scotland.gov.uk**

The King's Old Building houses the Regimental Museum of the Argyll and Sutherland Highlanders.

★ Chapel Royal
Seventeenth-century frescoes by Valentine Jenkins adorn the chapel, reconstructed in 1594.

Nether Bailey

STAR SIGHTS

★ Palace

★ Chapel Royal

The Great Hall, built in 1500, has been restored to its former splendour.

The Elphinstone Tower was made into a gun platform in 1714.

Grand Battery
Seven guns stand on this parapet, built in 1708 during a strengthening of defences following the revolution of 1688 (see p53).

STIRLING BATTLES

At the highest navigable point of the Forth and holding the pass to the Highlands, Stirling occupied a key position in Scotland's struggles for independence. Seven battlefields can be seen from the castle; the 67-m (220-ft) Wallace Monument at Abbey Craig recalls William Wallace's defeat of the English at Stirling Bridge in 1297, foreshadowing Bruce's victory in 1314 (see p482).

The Victorian Wallace Monument

Perth seen from the east across the Tay

Doune Castle ❸

Doune, Stirling. *Tel 01786 841742.*
🚉 📍 *Stirling then bus.* 🕐 *Apr–Sep:*
9:30am–5:30pm daily; Oct–Mar:
9:30am–4:30pm Sat–Wed; last entry
30 mins before close. 🌑 *21 Dec–*
8 Jan. 📷 *limited.*
www.historic-scotland.gov.uk

Built as the residence of
Robert, Duke of Albany, in the
14th century, **Doune Castle** was
a Stuart stronghold until it fell
into ruin in the 18th century.
Now fully restored, it is one of
the most complete castles of its
time and offers a unique insight
into the royal household.

The Gatehouse, once a
self-sufficient residence, leads
through to the central courtyard from which the Great
Hall can be entered. Complete
with its reconstructed open-
timber roof, minstrels' gallery
and central fireplace, the Hall
adjoins the Lord's Hall and
Private Room. A number of
private stairs and narrow
passages reveal the ingenious
ways the royal family tried to
hide during times of danger.
The castle was the setting for
the 1975 film, *Monty Python
and the Holy Grail*.

Perth ❹

Perthshire. 🏘 *45,000.* 🚉 📍
ℹ️ *West Mill St (01738 450600).*
www.perthshire.co.uk

Once the capital of medieval
Scotland, Perth's rich heritage
is reflected in many of its buildings. It was in the **Church of
Saint John**, founded in 1126,
that John Knox *(see p483)*
delivered many of his fiery
sermons. The Victorianized **Fair
Maid's House**, on North Port,
is one of the oldest houses in
town (c.1600) and was the
fictional home of the heroine
of Sir Walter Scott's *(see p512)
The Fair Maid of Perth* (1828).

In **Balhousie Castle**, the
Museum of the Black Watch
commemorates the first
Highland regiment, while the
Perth Museum & Art Gallery
has displays on local industry
and exhibitions of Scottish art.

Environs: Two miles (3 km)
north of Perth, the Gothic
mansion of **Scone Palace**
stands on the site of an abbey
destroyed in 1559. Between
the 9th and 13th centuries,
Scone guarded the sacred
Stone of Destiny *(see pp482–3)*,
now kept in Edinburgh Castle
(see pp506–7). Some of Mary,
Queen of Scots' *(see p511)*
embroideries are on display.

⚓ **Balhousie Castle**
RHQ Black Watch, Hay St. *Tel 0131
310 8530.* 🕐 *10am–4:30pm Mon–
Sat (Oct–Apr: to 3:30pm Mon–Fri).*

🏛 **Perth Museum & Art
Gallery**
78 George St. *Tel 01738 632488.*
🕐 *10am–5pm daily (from 1pm Sun;
Sep–Apr: Mon–Sat only).* ♿

⚓ **Scone Palace**
A93 to Braemar. *Tel 01738 552300.*
🕐 *Apr–Oct: 9:30am–5pm daily (to
4pm Sun). Grounds close at 6pm.*
📷 ♿ www.scone-palace.co.uk

Glamis Castle ❺

Forfar, Angus. *Tel 01307 840393.*
🚉 📍 *Dundee then bus.* 🕐 *Mar–
Oct: 10:30am–4:30pm daily; Nov &
Dec: 10am–6pm daily (last tour 4pm).*
📷 📹 www.glamis-castle.co.uk

With the pinnacled fairytale
outline of a Loire chateau,
the imposing medieval tower-
house of **Glamis Castle** began

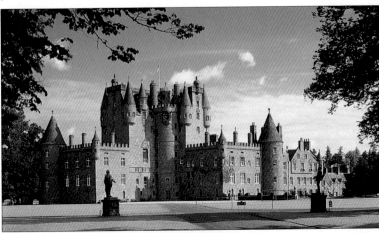

Glamis Castle with statues of James VI (left) and Charles I (right)

as a royal hunting lodge in the 11th century but underwent extensive reconstruction in the 17th century. It was the childhood home of Queen Elizabeth the Queen Mother, and her former bedroom can be seen with a youthful portrait by Henri de Laszlo (1878–956).

Many rooms are open to the public, including Duncan's Hall, the oldest in the castle and Shakespeare's setting for the king's murder in *Macbeth*. Together, the rooms present an array of china, paintings, tapestries and furniture spanning five centuries. In the grounds stand a pair of wrought-iron gates made for the Queen Mother on her 80th birthday in 1980.

View of St Andrews over the ruins of the cathedral

Dundee 6

Dundee City. 🏠 144,000. ✈ ≈ 🚌
🚶 Discovery Point, Discovery Quay (01382 527527). 🚢 Tue, Fri–Sun; farmers' market 3rd Sat of month.
www.angusanddundee.co.uk

Famous for its cake, marmalade and the DC Thomson publishing empire (creators of children's magazines *Beano* and *Dandy*), **Dundee** was also a major ship-building centre in the 18th and 19th centuries, a period which can be atmospherically recreated by a trip to the Victoria Docks.
HMS *Unicorn*, built in 1824, is the oldest British-built warship still afloat and is still fitted as it was on its last voyage. Berthed at Riverside is the royal research ship *Discovery*, built here in 1901 for Captain

Scott's first voyage to the Antarctic. Housed in a Victorian Gothic building, the **McManus Galleries** provide a glimpse of Dundee's industrial heritage, as well as exhibitions on archaeology and Victorian art. The **Howff Burial Ground**, near City Square, has intriguing Victorian tombstones.

🏛 **HMS** *Unicorn*
Victoria Docks, City Quay. **Tel** 01382 200900. ◯ Apr–Oct: daily; Nov–Mar: Wed–Sun. 🎫 ♿ limited.

🏛 **Discovery**
Discovery Point. **Tel** 01382 309060. ◯ daily (Sun pm). 🎫 ♿ **www**.rrsdiscovery.com

🏛 **McManus Galleries**
Albert Sq. **Tel** 01382 432350. ◯ call for opening times. ♿ **www**.dundeecity.gov.uk

St Andrews 7

Fife. 🏠 16,000. ≈ Leuchars. 🚌 Dundee. 🚶 70 Market St (01334 472021). **www**.visit-standrews.co.uk

Scotland's oldest university town and one-time ecclesiastical capital, **St Andrews** is now a shrine to golfers from all over the world *(see below)*. Its three main streets and numerous cobbled alleys, full of crooked housefronts, dignified university buildings and medieval churches, converge on the venerable ruins of the 12th-century cathedral. Once the largest in Scotland, the cathedral was later pillaged for stones to build the town. **St Andrew's Castle** was built for the bishops of the town in 1200. The dungeon can still be seen. The city's golf courses to the west are each open for a modest fee. The **British Golf Museum** tells how the city's Royal and Ancient Golf Club became the ruling arbiter of the game.

St Mary's College insignia, St Andrews University

♦ **St Andrew's Castle**
The Scores. **Tel** 01334 477196. ◯ Apr–Sep: 9:30–6:30pm daily; Oct–Mar: 9:30–4:30pm daily. ● 1 & 2 Jan, 25 & 26 Dec. 🎫 ♿

🏛 **British Golf Museum**
Bruce Embankment. **Tel** 01334 460 046. ◯ Mar–Oct: 9:30am–5:30pm Mon–Sat, 10am–5pm Sun; Nov–Mar: 10am–4pm daily. 🎫 ♿

THE ANCIENT GAME OF GOLF

Scotland's national game was pioneered on the sandy links around St Andrews. The earliest record dates from 1457, when golf was banned by James II on the grounds that it was interfering with his subjects' archery practice.

Mary, Queen of Scots *(see p511)* enjoyed the game and was berated in 1568 for playing straight after the murder of her husband Darnley.

Mary, Queen of Scots at St Andrews in 1563

The central courtyard of Falkland Palace, bordered by rose bushes

East Neuk ❽

Fife. 🚆 *Leuchars.* 🚌 *Glenrothes & Leuchars.* ℹ️ *70 Market Street, St Andrews (01334 472021).*

A string of pretty fishing villages scatters the shoreline of the **East Neuk** (the eastern "corner") of Fife, stretching from Earlsferry to Fife Ness. Much of Scotland's medieval trade with Europe passed through these ports, a connection reflected in the Flemish-inspired crow-stepped gables of many of the cottages. Although the herring industry has declined and the area is now a peaceful holiday centre, the sea still dominates village life. Until the 1980s, fishing boats were built at St Monans, a charming town of narrow twisting streets, while Pittenweem is the base for the East Neuk fishing fleet.

The town is also known for **St Fillan's Cave**, the retreat of a 9th-century hermit whose relic was used to bless the army of Robert the Bruce *(see p482)* before the Battle of Bannockburn. A church stands among the cobbled lanes and colourful cottages of Crail; the stone by the church gate is said to have been hurled to the mainland from the Isle of May by the Devil.

Several 16th- to 19th-century buildings in the village of Anstruther contain the **Scottish Fisheries Museum** which tells the area's history with the aid of interiors, boats and displays on whaling. From the village you can embark for the nature reserve on the **Isle of May** which teems with seabirds and grey seals. The statue of Alexander Selkirk in Lower Largo recalls the local boy whose adventures inspired Daniel Defoe's *Robinson Crusoe* (1719). Disagreeing with his captain, he was dumped on a desert island for four years.

🏛 **Scottish Fisheries Museum**
St Ayles, Harbourhead, Anstruther. *Tel 01333 310628.* ⭕ *Apr–Sep: 10am–5:30pm Mon–Sat (to 4:30pm Oct–Mar), 11am–5pm Sun (from noon Oct–Mar).* ● *25 & 26 Dec, 1 & 2 Jan.* 📷 ♿ **www.scotfishmuseum.org**

THE PALACE KEEPER

Due to the size of the royal household and the necessity for the king to be itinerant, the office of Keeper was created by the medieval kings who required custodians to maintain and replenish the resources of their many palaces while they were away. Now redundant, it was a hereditary title and gave the custodian permanent and often luxurious lodgings.

James VI's bed in the Keeper's Bedroom, Falkland Palace

Falkland Palace ❾

(NTS) Falkland, Fife. *Tel 01337 857397.* 🚆 🚌 *Ladybank, Kirkcaldy, then bus.* ⭕ *Mar–Oct: 10am–5pm daily (Sun: pm).* 📷 🍴 ♿ **www.nts.org.uk**

This stunning Renaissance palace was designed as a hunting lodge of the Stuart kings. Although its construction was begun by James IV in 1500, most of the work was carried out by his son, James V *(see p510)*, in the 1530s. Under the influence of his two French wives he employed French workmen to redecorate the façade of the East Range with dormers, buttresses and medallions, and to build the beautifully proportioned South Range. The palace fell into ruin during the years of the Commonwealth *(see p52)* and was occupied briefly by Rob Roy *(see p495)* in 1715.

After buying the estates in 1887, the 3rd Marquess of Bute became the Palace Keeper and restored it. The richly panelled interiors are filled with superb furniture and portraits of the Stuart monarchs. The royal tennis court is the oldest in Britain.

Dunfermline ❿

Fife. 🏙 *55,000.* 🚆 🚌 ℹ️ *1 High St (01383 720999).* **www.standrews.com/fife**

Scotland's capital until 1603, Dunfermline is dominated by the ruins of the 12th-century abbey and palace which recall its royal past. In the 11th century, the town was the seat of King Malcolm III, who founded a priory on the present site of the **Abbey Church**. With its Norman nave and 19th-century choir, the church contains the tombs of 22 Scottish kings and queens, including Robert the Bruce *(see p482)*.

The ruins of King Malcolm's **palace** soar over the beautiful gardens of Pittencrieff Park. Dunfermline's most famous son, philanthropist Andrew Carnegie (1835–1919), had been forbidden entrance to the park as a boy. After making his fortune, he bought the entire Pittencrieff estate and gave it to the people of Dunfermline. He was born in the town, though moved to Pennsylvania in his teens. There he made a vast fortune in the iron and steel industry. The **Carnegie Birthplace Museum** is still furnished as it was when he lived there, and tells the story of his meteoric career.

🏛 **Carnegie Birthplace Museum**
Moodie St. **Tel** 01383 724302.
◯ Apr–Oct: 11am–5pm Mon–Sat; 2–5pm Sun. 🗎 ♿

The 12th-century Norman nave of Dunfermline Abbey Church

Culross ⓫

(NTS) Fife. 🚶 450. 🚇 Dunfermline. 🚌 Dunfermline. ℹ NTS, The Palace (01383 880359). ◯ Easter–Sep: noon–5pm daily. **Garden** ◯ 10am–dusk all year. 📷 ♿ limited. 🎫 🗎 🎺 Music & Arts Festival: early Aug.

An important religious centre in the 6th century, the town of Culross is said to have been the birthplace of St

Mungo in 514. Now a beautifully preserved 16th- and 17th-century village, Culross prospered in the 16th century with the growth of its coal and salt industries, most notably under Sir George Bruce. He took charge of the Culross colliery in 1575 and created a drainage system called the "Egyptian Wheel" which cleared a mile-long (1.5 km) mine beneath the River Forth.

During its subsequent decline Culross stood unchanged for over 150 years. The National Trust for Scotland began restoring the town in 1932 and now provides a guided tour, which starts at the **Visitors' Centre**.

Built in 1577, Bruce's **palace** has the crow-stepped gables, decorated windows and red pantiles typical of the period. The interior retains its original early 17th-century painted ceilings. Crossing the Square, past the **Oldest House**, dating from 1577, head for the **Town House** to the west. Behind it, a cobbled street known as the Back Causeway (with its raised section for nobility) leads to the turreted **Study**, built in 1610 as a house for the Bishop of Dunblane. The main room is open to visitors and should be seen for its original Norwegian ceiling. Continuing northwards to the ruined abbey, fine church and Abbey House, don't miss the Dutch-gabled **House with the Evil Eyes**.

The 16th-century palace of industrialist George Bruce, Culross

Linlithgow Palace ⓬

Linlithgow, West Lothian. **Tel** 01506 842896. 🚇 🚌 ◯ Apr–Sep: 9:30am–5:30pm daily; Oct–Mar: 9:30am–4:30pm daily. ◯ 25, 26 Dec, 1, 2 Jan. ♿ limited. **www**.historic-scotland.gov.uk

On the edge of Linlithgow Loch stands the former royal palace of **Linlithgow**. Today's remains are mostly of the palace of James I in 1425. The scale of the building is demonstrated by the 28 m (94 ft) long Great Hall, with its huge fireplace and windows. Mary, Queen of Scots (see p511), was born here in 1542.

Falkirk Wheel ⓭

Lime Rd, Falkirk. **Tel** 08700 500208 (booking line). 🚇 Falkirk. ◯ Feb–Nov: **Boat trips** range from 5 trips daily in winter to 3 trips per hour in summer. **Visitor Centre** daily. Nov–Feb: phone for times. 📷 boat trip. 🖥 🗎 **www**.thefalkirkwheel.co.uk

This impressive boat lift is the first ever to revolve, and the centrepiece of Scotland's canal regeneration scheme. Once important for commercial transport, the Union and the Forth and Clyde canals were blocked by several roads in the 1960s. Now the Falkirk Wheel gently swings boats between the two waterways creating an uninterrupted link between Glasgow and Edinburgh. Visitors can ride the wheel on boats that leave from the Visitor Centre.

The rotating Falkirk Wheel boat lift

Hopetoun House ⓮

West Lothian. **Tel** *0131 331 2451.*
🚃 *Dalmeny then taxi.* ⏰ *mid-Mar–late Sep: 10:30am–5pm (last entry 4pm).* 📷 ♿ limited.
📹 *for groups – book ahead.* 💻
www.hopetounhouse.com

An extensive parkland by the Firth of Forth, designed in the style of Versailles, is the setting for one of Scotland's finest stately homes. The original house was built by 1707; it was later absorbed into William Adam's grand extension. The dignified, horse-shoe-shaped plan and lavish interior plasterwork represent Neo-Classical 18th-century architecture at its finest. The drawing rooms, with their Rococo plasterwork and highly ornate mantelpieces, are particularly impressive. The Marquess of Linlithgow, whose family still occupies part of the house, is a descendant of the 1st Earl of Hopetoun, for whom the house was built.

A wooden panel above the main stair, depicting Hopetoun House

Forth Bridges ⓯

Edinburgh. 🚃 🚌 *Dalmeny, Inverkeithing.* ℹ️ *1 High Street, Dunfermline (01383 720999).*

The small town of South Queensferry is dominated by the two great bridges that span the mile (1.6 km) across the River Forth to North Queensferry. The spectacular rail bridge, the first major steel-built bridge in the world, was opened in 1890 and

The shattered crags and cliffs of St Abb's Head

remains one of the greatest engineering achievements of the late Victorian era. Its massive cantilevered sections are held together by more than 6.5 million rivets, and the painted area adds up to some 55 ha (135 acres). The saying "like painting the Forth Bridge" has become a byword for non-stop, repetitive endeavour. The bridge also inspired *The Bridge* (1986) by writer Iain Banks.

The neighbouring road bridge was the largest suspension bridge outside the USA when it opened in 1964, a distinction now held by the Humber Bridge in England. A new bridge is due to open across the Forth in 2016.

South Queensferry got its name from the 11th-century Queen Margaret *(see p507)*, who used the ferry here on her journeys between Edinburgh and the royal palace at Dunfermline *(see p501)*.

Edinburgh ⓰

See pp504–11.

St Abb's Head ⓱

(NTS) Scottish Borders. 🚃 *Berwick-upon-Tweed.* 🚌 *from Edinburgh.*

The jagged cliffs of St Abb's Head, rising 91 m (300 ft) from the North Sea near the southeastern tip of Scotland, offer a spectacular view of thousands of seabirds wheeling and diving below. This 80 ha (200 acre) nature reserve is an important site for cliff-nesting sea birds and becomes, during the May to June breeding season, the home of more than 50,000 birds, including fulmars, guillemots, kittiwakes and puffins that throng the headland near the fishing village of St Abbs. The village has one of the few unspoiled working harbours on Britain's east coast. A clifftop trail begins at the **Visitors' Centre**, where displays include identification boards and a touch table where young visitors can get to grips with wings and feathers.

ℹ️ **Visitors' Centre**
St Abb's Head. **Tel** *018907 71443.*
⏰ *Apr–Oct: 10am–5pm daily.* 📹

The huge, cantilevered Forth Rail Bridge, seen from South Queensferry

A Tour of the Borders ⑱

Because of their proximity to England, the Scottish Borders are scattered with the ruins of many ancient buildings destroyed in the conflicts between the two nations. Most poignant of all are the Border abbeys, whose magnificent architecture bears witness to their former spiritual and political power. Founded during the 12th-century reign of David I, the abbeys were destroyed by Henry VIII *(see p512)*.

Kelso Abbey ②
The largest of the Border Abbeys, Kelso was once the most powerful ecclesiastical establishment in Scotland.

Melrose Abbey ⑥
Once one of the richest abbeys in Scotland, it is here that Robert the Bruce's heart is buried *(see p512)*.

Floors Castle ①
The largest inhabited castle in Scotland, it is the Duke of Roxburghe's ancestral home and was built in the 18th century by William Adam.

Scott's View ⑤
This was Sir Walter Scott's favourite view of the Borders. Out of habit his horse stopped here during Scott's funeral procession.

KEY

▬▬	Tour route
══	Other roads
☀	Viewpoint

Dryburgh Abbey ④
Set on the banks of the Tweed, Dryburgh is considered the most evocative monastic ruin in Scotland. Sir Walter Scott is buried here.

TIPS FOR DRIVERS

Length: 32 miles (50 km).
Stopping-off points: There is a delightful walk northwards from Dryburgh Abbey to the footbridge over the River Tweed.

0 kilometres	5
0 miles	3

Jedburgh Abbey ③
Though established in 1138, fragments of 9th-century Celtic stonework survive from an earlier structure. A Visitors' Centre illustrates the lives of the Augustinian monks who once lived here.

Edinburgh ⑯

With its striking medieval and Georgian districts, overlooked by the extinct volcano of Arthur's Seat and, to the northeast, Calton Hill, Edinburgh is widely regarded as one of Europe's most handsome capitals. The city is famous for the arts (it was once known as "the Athens of the North"), a pre-eminence reflected in its hosting every year of Britain's largest arts extravaganza, the Edinburgh Festival *(see p509)*. Its museums and galleries display the riches of many cultures.

Royal Scots soldiers from the castle

Exploring Edinburgh

Edinburgh falls into two main sightseeing areas, divided by Princes Street, the city's most famous thoroughfare and commercial centre. The Old Town straddles the ridge between the castle and the Palace of Holyroodhouse, with most of the city's medieval history clustered in the alleys of the Grassmarket and Royal Mile areas. The New Town, to the north, evolved after 1767 when wealthy merchants expanded the city beyond its medieval walls. This district contains Britain's finest concentration of Georgian architecture.

🏛 National Gallery of Scotland

The Mound. **Tel** *0131 624 6200.* ◯ *10am–5pm Fri–Wed, 10am–7pm Thu (extended during the festival).* 🎫 *for special exhibitions.* ♿ 🎫 *by appt.* **www**.nationalgalleries.org

One of Scotland's finest art galleries, the National Gallery of Scotland is worth visiting for its 15th- to 19th-century British and European paintings alone,

though plenty more can be found to delight the art-lover. Highlights among the Scottish works include portraits by Allan Ramsay and Henry Raeburn, such as his *Reverend Robert Walker Skating on Duddingston Loch* (c.1800). The Early German collection includes Gerard David's almost comic-strip treatment of the *Three Legends of Saint Nicholas* (c.1500). Works by Raphael, Titian and Tintoretto accompany southern European paintings such as Velázquez's *An Old Woman Cooking Eggs* (1620) and the entire room devoted to *The Seven Sacraments* (c.1640) by Nicholas Poussin.

The new £30-million Weston Link is an underground complex that connects the gallery with the Royal Scottish Academy. It contains a lecture theatre/cinema, shop, restaurant, café, and an IT and education room.

Raeburn's *Rev. Robert Walker Skating on Duddingston Loch*

The doorway of the Georgian House, 7 Charlotte Square

🏠 Georgian House

(NTS) 7 Charlotte Sq. **Tel** *0844 493 2118.* ◯ *Mar & Nov: 11am–3pm daily; Apr–Jun & Sep–Oct: 10am–5pm daily; Jul–Aug: 10am–7pm daily. (Last adm: half an hour before closing.)* 🎫 *mid-Dec–mid-Jan.* 🎫 ♿ *limited.* **www**.nts.org.uk

In the heart of the New Town, Charlotte Square is a superb example of Georgian architecture, its north side, built in the 1790s, being a masterwork by the architect Robert Adam *(see pp28–9)*. The Georgian House at No. 7 has been furnished and repainted in its original 18th-century colours which provide a memorable introduction to the elegance of wealthy New Town life. In stark contrast, "below stairs" is the household staff's living quarters, demonstrating how Edinburgh's working class lived and worked.

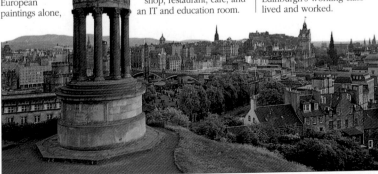

The view from Duncan's Monument on Calton Hill, looking west towards the castle

🏛 Scottish National Gallery of Modern Art & Dean Gallery

Belford Rd. **Tel** 0131 624 6200. ◯ 10am–5pm daily (7pm Thu). 🛇 www.nationalgalleries.org

Housed in a 19th-century school to the northwest of the city centre, this gallery features most European and American 20th-century greats, from Vuillard and Picasso, to Magritte and Lichtenstein. Work by John Bellany can be found among the Scottish painters. Sculpture by Henry Moore is on display in the garden. The Dean Gallery shows a Dada and Surrealist collection.

Medieval chessmen, National Museum of Scotland

Lichtenstein's *In the Car*, National Gallery of Modern Art

🏛 National Museum of Scotland

Chambers St. **Tel** 0131 225 7534. ◯ 10am–5pm Mon–Sat (Tue to 8pm), noon–5pm Sun. ● 25 Dec. 🔲 🛇 📷 free. 🍴 www.nms.ac.uk

This purpose-built museum houses the Scottish Collections of the National Museums of Scotland. Exhibitions tell the story of Scotland, the land and its people, dating from its geological beginnings right up to the constitutionally exciting events of today.

Key exhibits include the famous medieval *Lewis Chessmen*; *Pictish Chains*, known as Scotland's earliest crown jewels, and the *Ellesmere* railway locomotive. There is also a new special exhibition gallery which houses fascinating temporary displays.

🏛 Scottish National Portrait Gallery

1 Queen St. **Tel** 0131 624 6200. ◯ 10am–5pm daily (Thu to 7pm). 🛇 📷 by appointment. www.nationalgalleries.org

The National Portrait Gallery provides a unique visual history of Scotland told through the portraits of those who shared it, from Robert the Bruce *(see p482)* to Queen Anne. Memorabilia from many reigns include Mary, Queen of Scots' *(see p511)* jewellery and a silver travelling canteen abandoned by Bonnie Prince Charlie *(see p535)* at Culloden *(see p537)*. The upper gallery has portraits of famous Scots, including Robert Burns *(see p515)* by Alexander Nasmyth.

EDINBURGH CITY CENTRE

Key to Symbols see back flap

Edinburgh Castle

Beam support in the Great Hall

Standing upon the basalt core of an extinct volcano, Edinburgh Castle is an assemblage of buildings dating from the 12th to the 20th centuries, reflecting its changing role as fortress, royal palace, military garrison and state prison. Though there is evidence of Bronze Age occupation of the site, the original fortress was built by the 6th-century Northumbrian King Edwin, from whom the city takes its name. The castle was a favourite royal residence until the Union of Crowns (see p483) in 1603, after which the king resided in England. After the Union of Parliaments in 1707, the Scottish regalia were walled up in the Palace for over a hundred years. The castle is now the zealous possessor of the so-called Stone of Destiny, a relic of ancient Scottish kings which was seized by the English from Scone Palace, Perthshire and not returned until 1996.

Scottish Crown
On display in the palace, the Crown was restyled by James V of Scotland in 1540.

Military Prison

Governor's House
Complete with Flemish-style crow-stepped gables, this building was constructed for the governor in 1742. It can only be viewed from the outside only as it is still reserved for ceremonial use.

Old Back Parade

Vaults
This French graffiti, dating from 1780, recalls the many prisoners who were held in the vaults during the wars with France in the 18th and 19th centuries.

MONS MEG

Positioned outside St Margaret's Chapel, the siege gun (or *bombard*) Mons Meg was made in Belgium in 1449 for the Duke of Burgundy, who gave it to his nephew, James II of Scotland. It was used by James against the Douglas family in their stronghold of Threave Castle (see p515) in 1455, and later by James IV against Norham Castle in England. After exploding during a salute to the Duke of York in 1682, it was kept in the Tower of London until it was returned to Edinburgh in 1829, at Sir Walter Scott's request.

STAR SIGHTS

★ Great Hall

★ Royal Palace

Argyle Battery
This fortified wall commands a spectacular view to the north beyond the city's Georgian district of New Town.

VISITORS' CHECKLIST

Castle Hill. **Tel** *0131 225 9846.*
9:30am–6pm daily (Oct–Mar: to 5pm). (Last adm: 45 mins before closing.) 25, 26 Dec. *book tickets online to avoid queuing.* **www**.edinburghcastle.gov.uk

★ **Royal Palace**
Mary, Queen of Scots (see p511) gave birth to James VI in this 15th-century palace, where the Scottish regalia are on display.

Entrance

Royal Mile

The Esplanade is the location of the Military Tattoo *(see p509).*

The Half Moon Battery was built in the 1570s as a platform for the artillery defending the northeastern wing of the castle.

St Margaret's Chapel
This stained-glass window depicts Malcolm III's saintly queen, to whom the chapel is dedicated. Probably built by her son, David I, in the early 12th century, the chapel is the castle's oldest existing building.

★ **Great Hall**
With its restored open-timber roof, the Hall dates from the 15th century and was the meeting place of the Scottish parliament until 1639.

Exploring the Royal Mile: Castlehill to High Street

The Royal Mile is a stretch of four ancient streets (from Castlehill to Canongate) which formed the main thoroughfare of medieval Edinburgh, linking the castle to the Palace of Holyroodhouse. Confined by the city wall, the "Old Town" grew upwards, with some tenements climbing to 20 storeys. It is still possible, among the 66 alleys and closes off the main street, to sense the city's medieval past.

Eagle sign outside Gladstone's Land

THE PALACE OF HOLYROODHOUSE

EDINBURGH CASTLE

Locator map

Gladstone's Land is a preserved 17th-century merchant's house.

Scotch Whisky Heritage Centre introduces visitors to Scotland's national drink.

The Camera Obscura contains an observatory from which to view the city, plus optical illusions and giant kaleidoscopes.

← Edinburgh Castle

CASTLE HILL

LAWNMARKET

Lady Stair's House
This 17th-century house is now a museum of the lives and works of Burns, Scott (see p512) and Stevenson.

The "Hub" (c.1840) has the city's highest spire.

🏛 Gladstone's Land

(NTS) 477B Lawnmarket. *Tel 0844 493 2120.* ◯ *Easter–Oct: 10am–5pm daily (Jul & Aug: to 7pm). (Last adm: 30 mins before closing.)* 🎫 ♿
This 17th-century merchant's house provides a window on

life in a typical Old Town house before overcrowding drove the rich to the Georgian New Town. "Lands", as they were known, were tall, narrow buildings erected on small plots of land. The six-storey Gladstone's Land was named after Thomas Gledstanes, the merchant who built it in 1617. The house still has the original arcade booths on the street front and a painted ceiling with fine Scandinavian floral designs. Though extravagantly furnished, it also contains items which are a reminder of the less salubrious side of the old city, such as wooden overshoes which had to be worn in the dirty streets. A chest in the

beautiful Painted Chamber is said to have been given by a Dutch sea captain to a Scottish merchant who saved him from a shipwreck. A similar house, Morocco Land, can be found on Canongate *(see p511)*.

🏛 Parliament House

Parliament Sq, High St. *Tel 0131 225 2595.* ◯ *9am–5pm Mon–Fri.* ⬤ *public hols.* ♿ *limited.*
This majestic, Italianate building was constructed in the 1630s for the Scottish parliament. Parliament House has been home to the Court of Session and the Supreme Court since the Union of Parliaments *(see p483)* in 1707. It is worth seeing, as much for the spectacle of its gowned and wigged advocates as for the stained-glass window in its Great Hall, commemorating the inauguration of the Court of Session by James V, in 1532.

The bedroom of Gladstone's Land

For hotels and restaurants in this region see pp593–596 and pp646–649

The Signet Library has a lavish interior; it was described by King George IV as the "finest drawing room in Europe".

St Giles Cathedral
A bagpiping angel can be found on the arched entrance to the Chapel of the Thistle.

The City Chambers were designed by John Adam in the 1750s.

BANK STREET

HIGH STREET

GEORGE IV BRIDGE

Charles II Statue

The Heart of Midlothian is an arrangement of granite cobblestones on the former site of the city jail.

Parliament House was built in 1639. The Scottish parliament convened here from 1640 until 1707.

Rib-vaulting in the Thistle Chapel, St Giles Cathedral

⌂ St Giles Cathedral

Royal Mile. **Tel** *0131 225 9442.* ◯ *May–Sep: 9am–7pm Mon–Fri, 9am–5pm Sat, 1–5pm Sun; Oct–Apr: 9am–5pm Mon–Sat, 1–5pm Sun.* ⬤ *1 Jan, 25 & 26 Dec.* 🖾 *donation appreciated.* 🖳 www.stgilescathedral.org.uk
Properly known as the High Kirk (church) of Edinburgh, it is ironic that St Giles is popularly known as a cathedral. Though it was twice the seat of a bishop in the 17th century, it was from here that John Knox *(see p483)* directed the Scottish Reformation with its emphasis on individual worship freed from the authority of bishops. A tablet marks the place where Jenny Geddes, a stallholder from a local market, scored a victory for the Covenanters *(see p483)* by hurling her stool at a preacher reading from an English prayer book in 1637.

The Gothic exterior is dominated by a 15th-century tower.

Inside, the impressive Thistle Chapel can be seen, with its elaborate rib-vaulted roof and carved heraldic canopies. The chapel honours the knights, past and present, of the Order of the Thistle. The carved royal pew in the Preston Aisle is used by the Queen when she stays in Edinburgh.

EDINBURGH FESTIVAL

Every year, for three weeks in late summer *(see p63)*, Edinburgh hosts one of the world's most important arts festivals, with every available space (from theatres to street corners) overflowing with performers. It has been held in Edinburgh since 1947 and brings together the best in international contemporary theatre, music, dance and opera. The alternative Festival Fringe balances the classic productions with a host of innovative performances. The most popular event is the Edinburgh Military Tattoo, held on the Castle Esplanade – a spectacle of Scottish infantry battalions marching to pipe bands. Also popular is the Edinburgh Book Festival and Edinburgh Film Festival (held in June).

Street performer from the Edinburgh Festival Fringe

Exploring the Royal Mile: High Street to Canongate

The second section of the Royal Mile passes two monuments to the Reformation: John Knox House and the Tron Kirk. The latter is named after a medieval *tron* (weighing beam) that stood nearby. The Canongate was once an independent district, owned by the canons of the Abbey of Holyrood, and sections of its south side have been restored. Beyond Morocco's Land, the road stretches for the final half-mile (800 m) to the Palace of Holyroodhouse.

THE PALACE OF HOLYROODHOUSE

EDINBURGH CASTLE

LOCATOR MAP

HIGH STREET

SOUTH BRIDGE STREET

The Mercat Cross marks the city centre. It was here that Bonnie Prince Charlie *(see p535)* was proclaimed king in 1745.

The Tron Kirk was built in 1630 for the Presbyterians who left St Giles Cathedral when it came under the Bishop of Edinburgh's control.

🏛 Museum of Childhood

42 High St. **Tel** 0131 529 4142.
⬜ 10am–5pm Mon–Sat (& Sun pm during Festival). ⬛ 25–27 Dec.
♿ limited. **www**.cac.org.uk

This lovely museum is not merely a toy collection but a magical insight into childhood. Founded in 1955 by a city councillor, Patrick Murray (who claimed to enjoy eating children for breakfast), it was the first museum in the world to be devoted to the history and theme of childhood. The collection includes medicines, school books and prams as well as galleries full of old-fashioned toys. With its nickel-odeon, antique slot machines

An 1880 automaton of the Man on the Moon, Museum of Childhood

The entrance to the Palace of Holyroodhouse, seen from the west

and the general enthusiasm of visitors, this has been called the world's noisiest museum.

🏰 Palace of Holyroodhouse

East end of Royal Mile. **Tel** 0131 556 5100. ⬜ Apr–Oct: 9:30am–6pm; Nov–Mar: 9:30am–4:30pm daily. ⬛ ♿ limited. **www**.royalcollection.org.uk

Now the Queen's official Scottish residence, the Palace of Holyroodhouse is named after the "rood", or cross, which King David I is said to have seen between the antlers of a stag he was hunting here in 1128. The present palace was built in 1529 to accommodate James V *(see p501)* and his French wife, Mary of Guise, though it was remodelled in

the 1670s for Charles II. The Royal Apartments (including the Throne Room and Royal Dining Room) are used for investitures and banquets whenever the Queen visits the palace, though they are otherwise open to the public. A chamber in the James V tower is associated with the unhappy reign of Mary, Queen of Scots. It was here, in 1566, that she saw the murder of her trusted Italian secretary, David Rizzio, by her jealous husband, Lord Darnley. She had married Darnley a year earlier in Holyroodhouse chapel.

Bonnie Prince Charlie held court here in 1745 in the Jacobite *(see p537)* rising.

John Knox House

Dating from 1490, the oldest house in the city was the home of John Knox (see p483) in the 1560s. It has recently undergone an extensive refurbishment.

Morocco Land is a reproduction of a 17th-century tenement house. It takes its name from the statue of a Moor which adorns the entrance.

→ **The Palace of Holyroodhouse**

CANONGATE

Museum of Childhood

Though created as a museum for adults by a city councillor who was known to dislike children, this lively musem now attracts flocks of young visitors.

MUSEUM OF CHILDHOOD

Moubray House was to be the signing place of the Treaty of Union in 1707 *(see p469)*, until a mob forced the authorities to retreat to another venue.

🏛 National Museum of Scotland

Chambers St. **Tel** *0131 247 4219.*
◯ *10am–5pm daily.* ● *25 Dec.*
📷 ♿ ✆ 🍴 www.nms.ac.uk

The National Museum first opened its doors in 1866. The Main Hall features a fine collection of Asian sculptures, including one of the Hindu Goddess Parvati, while European Art from 1200 to 1800 is on the first floor. On the second floor are rare scientific instruments, and geological specimens, and Eastern decorative arts are on the top floor. On the ground floor, the new science and technology gallery, Connect, is where Dolly the Sheep can be found.

Parvati, at the National Museum of Scotland

The museum will be partially closed until late summer 2011, while renovations take place.

🐕 Greyfriars Bobby

On an old drinking fountain near the gateway to Greyfriars Church stands the statue of a little Skye terrier. This commemorates the dog who, for 14 years, guarded the grave of his master, John Gray, who died in 1858. The people of Edinburgh fed him until his death in 1872. He was also granted citizenship to prevent him being destroyed as a stray.

MARY, QUEEN OF SCOTS (1542–87)

Born only days before the death of her father, James V, the young Queen Mary spent her childhood in France, after escaping Henry VIII's invasion of Scotland *(see p512)*. A devout Catholic, she married the French Dauphin, and made claims on the English throne. This alarmed Protestants throughout England and Scotland, and when she returned as a widow to Holyroodhouse, aged 18, she was harangued for her faith by John Knox *(see p483)*. In 1567 she was accused of murdering her second husband, Lord Darnley. Two months later, when she married the Earl of Bothwell (also implicated in the murder), rebellion ensued. She lost her crown and fled to England where she was held prisoner for 20 years, before being charged with treason and beheaded at Fotheringhay.

The ruins of Melrose Abbey, viewed from the southwest

Melrose Abbey ⑲

Abbey Street, Melrose, Scottish
Borders. **Tel** 01896 822562. ◯
9:30am–4:30pm daily (Apr–Sep: to
5:30pm). (Last adm: 30 mins before
closing.) ◯ 1, 2 Jan, 25, 26 Dec. ◯
❧ ltd. **www**.historic-scotland.gov.uk

The rose-pink ruins of this
beautiful Border abbey (see
p503) bear testimony to the
hazards of standing in the path
of successive English invasions.
Built by David I in 1136 for
Cistercian monks from Yorkshire, and also to replace a
7th-century monastery, Melrose
was repeatedly ransacked by
English armies, notably in
1322 and 1385. The final blow,
from which none of the
abbeys recovered, came in

1545 during Henry VIII's
destructive Scottish policy
known as the "Rough Woo-
ing". This resulted from the
failure of the Scots to ratify
a marriage treaty between
Henry VIII's son and the
infant Mary, Queen of Scots
(see p511). What remains of
the abbey are the outlines
of cloisters, the kitchen and
other monastic buildings and
the shell of the abbey church
with its soaring east window
and profusion of medieval
carvings. The rich decorations
of the south exterior wall
include a gargoyle shaped like
a pig playing the bagpipes.

An embalmed heart, found
here in 1920, is probably that
of Robert the Bruce (see
p482), who had decreed that

his heart be taken on a crusade to the Holy Land. It was
returned to Melrose after its
bearer, Sir James Douglas (see
p515), was killed in Spain.

Abbotsford House ⑳

Galashiels, Scottish Borders. **Tel**
01896 752043. 🚍 from Galashiels.
◯ late Mar–late Oct: 9:30am–5pm
Mon–Sat, 11am–4pm Sun (except
Jun–Sep). 🞵 ❧ limited. 📷
www.scottsabbotsford.co.uk

Few houses bear the stamp
of their creator so intimately as
Abbotsford House, the home
of Sir Walter Scott for the last
20 years of his life. He bought
a farm here in 1811, known
as Clarteyhole ("dirty hole"
in Scots), though he soon
renamed it Abbotsford, after
the monks of Melrose Abbey
who used to cross the River
Tweed nearby. He later
demolished the house to
make way for the turreted
building we see today, funded
by the sales of his novels.

Scott's library contains more
than 9,000 rare books and his
collections of historic relics
reflect his passion for the
heroic past. An extensive
collection of arms and armour
includes Rob Roy's broad-
sword (see p495). Stuart
mementoes include a crucifix
that belonged to Mary, Queen
of Scots and a lock of Bonnie
Prince Charlie's (see p535)
hair. The small study in which
he wrote his *Waverley* novels
can be visited as can the
room, overlooking the river,
in which he died in 1832.

SIR WALTER SCOTT

Sir Walter Scott (1771–1832)
was born in Edinburgh and
trained as a lawyer. He is best
remembered as a major champion and literary figure of
Scotland, whose poems and
novels (most famously his
Waverley series) created
enduring images of a heroic
wilderness filled with the
romance of the clans. His
orchestration, in 1822, of the
state visit of George IV to
Edinburgh (see p485) was an
extravaganza of Highland culture that helped re-establish
tartan as the national dress of Scotland. He served as Clerk of
the Court in Edinburgh's Parliament House (see p508) and for
30 years was Sheriff of Selkirk in the Scottish Borders, which
he loved. He put the Trossachs (see pp494–5) firmly on the
map with the publication of the *Lady of the Lake* (1810). His
final years were spent writing to pay off a £114,000 debt following the failure of his publisher in 1827. He died with his
debts paid, and was buried at Dryburgh Abbey (see p503).

The Great Hall at Abbotsford,
adorned with arms and armour

Traquair House ㉑

Peebles, Scottish Borders. **Tel** 01896 830 323. from Peebles. Easter–May & Sep: noon–5:30pm; Jun–Aug: 10:30am–5pm; Oct: 11am–4pm; daily; Nov: noon–4pm Sat & Sun. limited. **www**.traquair.co.uk

As Scotland's oldest continuously inhabited house, Traquair has deep roots in Scottish religious and political history, stretching back over 900 years. Evolving from a fortified tower to a stout-walled 17th-century mansion *(see p487)*, the house was a Catholic Stuart stronghold for 500 years. Mary, Queen of Scots *(see p511)* was among the many monarchs to have stayed here and her bed is covered by a counterpane which she made. Family letters and engraved Jacobite *(see p537)* drinking glasses are among relics recalling the period of the Highland rebellions.

Mary, Queen of Scots' crucifix, Traquair House

After a vow made by the 5th Earl, Traquair's Bear Gates (the "Steekit Yetts"), which closed after Bonnie Prince Charlie's *(see p535)* visit in 1745, will not reopen until a Stuart reascends the throne. A secret stairway leads to the Priest's Room which attests to the problems faced by Catholic families until Catholicism was legalized in 1829. Traquair House Ale is still produced in the 18th-century brewhouse.

Biggar ㉒

Clyde Valley. 2,000. High St (01899 221066).

This typical Lowland market town has a number of museums worth visiting. The **Gladstone Court Museum** boasts a reconstructed Victorian street complete with a milliner's, printer's and a village library, while the grimy days of the town's industrial past are recalled at the **Gasworks Museum**, with its collection of engines, gaslights and appliances. Established in 1839 and preserved in the 1970s, the Biggar Gasworks is the only remaining rural gasworks in Scotland.

🏛 **Gladstone Court Museum**
Northback Rd. **Tel** 01899 221050. Apr–Oct: 11am–4:30pm Mon–Sat, 2–4:30pm Sun.
🏛 **Gasworks Museum**
Gasworks Rd. **Tel** 01899 221070. Jun–Sep: 2–4:30pm daily.

Pentland Hills ㉓

The Lothians. Edinburgh, then bus. Regional Park Headquarters, Biggar Rd, Edinburgh (0131 4453383).

The Pentland Hills, stretching for 16 miles (26 km) southwest of Edinburgh, offer some of the best hill-walking country in the Lowlands. Leisurely walkers can saunter along the many signposted footpaths, while the more adventurous can take the chairlift at the Hillend dry ski slope to reach the higher ground leading to the 493 m (1,617 ft) hill of Allermuir. Even more ambitious is the classic scenic route along the ridge from Caerketton to West Kip.

To the east of the A703, in the lee of the Pentlands, stands the exquisite and ornate 15th-century **Rosslyn Chapel**. It was originally intended as a church, but after the death of its founder, William Sinclair, it was also used as a burial ground for his descendants. The delicately wreathed Apprentice Pillar recalls the legend of the apprentice carver who was killed by the master stonemason in a fit of jealousy at his pupil's superior skill.

🔒 **Rosslyn Chapel**
Roslin. **Tel** 0131 4402159. daily (Sun: pm only).

Details of the decorated vaulting in Rosslyn Chapel

The Classical 18th-century tenements of New Lanark on the banks of the Clyde

New Lanark ㉔

Clyde Valley. 🚶 185. 🚆 🚌 Lanark.
ℹ Horsemarket, Ladyacre Rd
(01555 661661). 🚌 Mon (Apr only).
www.newlanark.org

Situated by the falls of the
River Clyde, the village of
New Lanark was founded in
1785 by the industrial entrepreneur David Dale. Ideally

DAVID LIVINGSTONE

Scotland's great missionary
doctor and explorer was
born in Blantyre where he
began working life as a
mill boy at the age of ten.
Livingstone (1813–73)
made three epic journeys
across Africa, from 1840,
promoting "commerce and
Christianity". He became
the first European to see
Victoria Falls and died in
1873 while searching for
the source of the Nile. He
is buried in Westminster
Abbey (see pp92–3).

located for the working of its
water-driven mills, the village
had become Britain's largest
cotton producer by 1800.
Dale and his successor, Robert
Owen, were philanthropists
whose reforms proved that
commercial success need not
undermine the wellbeing of
the workforce. Now a museum,
New Lanark is a window on to
working life in the early 19th
century. The **New Millennium
Experience** provides a special-
effects ride through time, from
the life of a mill girl in 1820 to
the 23rd century.

Environs: 15 miles (24 km)
north, Blantyre has a memorial to the famous Scottish
explorer David Livingstone.

🏛 **New Millennium
Experience**
New Lanark Visitor Centre. **Tel** 01555
661345. 🕐 11am–5pm daily. 🎫 ♿
📷 groups only, by appt – book ahead.

Glasgow ㉕

See pp516–21.

Sanquhar ㉖

Dumfries & Galloway. 🚶 2,500. 🚆
🚌 ℹ 64 Whitesands, Dumfries
(01387 253862).

Now of chiefly historic
interest, the town of
Sanquhar was famous in the
history of the Covenanters

(see p483). In the 1680s, two
declarations opposing the rule
of bishops were pinned to the
Mercat Cross, the site of which
is now marked by a granite
obelisk. The first protest was
led by a local teacher, Richard
Cameron, whose followers
became the Cameronian regiment. The Georgian **Tolbooth**
was designed by William
Adam (see p548) in 1735 and
houses a local interest museum
and tourist centre. The Post
Office, opened in 1763, is the
oldest in Britain, predating
the mail coach service.

Drumlanrig
Castle ㉗

Thornhill, Dumfries & Galloway.
Tel 01848 331555. 🚆 🚌 Dumfries,
then bus. 🔲 Grounds Apr–Oct:
11am–5pm daily. **Castle** Easter–
Aug: 11am–5pm daily. 🎫 ♿ 📷
www.buccleuch.com

Rising squarely from a
grassy platform, the
massive fortress-palace of
Drumlanrig (see p487) was
built from pink sandstone

The Baroque front steps and
doorway of Drumlanrig Castle

between 1679 and 1691 on the site of a 15th-century Douglas stronghold. A formidable multi-turreted exterior contains a priceless collection of art treasures such as paintings by Holbein and Rembrandt, as well as such Jacobite relics as Bonnie Prince Charlie's camp kettle and sash. The emblem of a crowned and winged heart, shown throughout the castle, recalls Sir James, the "Black Douglas", who bore Robert the Bruce's *(see p482)* heart while on crusade. After being mortally wounded he threw the heart at his enemies with the words "forward brave heart!"

The sturdy island fortress of Threave Castle on the Dee

Threave Castle ㉘

Castle Douglas, Dumfries & Galloway. *Tel* 07711 223101. 🚆 Dumfries. ◯ mid-Mar–Sep: 9:30am–5:30pm daily; Oct: 9:30am–4:30pm. (Last boat leaves island 6pm.) 🅿️ www.historic-scotland.gov.uk

This menacing giant of a tower, a 14th-century Black Douglas *(see above)* stronghold standing on an island in the Dee, commands the most complete medieval riverside harbour in Scotland. Douglas's struggles against the early Stewart kings culminated in his surrender here after a two-month siege in 1455 – but only after James II had brought the cannon Mons Meg *(see p506)* to batter the castle. Threave was dismantled after Protestant Covenanters *(see p483)* defeated its Catholic defenders in

1640. Inside the tower, only the shell of the kitchen, great hall and domestic levels remains. Over the 15th-century doorway is the "gallows knob", a reminder of when the owners are said to have boasted that it never lacked its noose. Access to the castle is by small boat.

Whithorn ㉙

Dumfries & Galloway. 🔼 1,000. 🚆 Stranraer. 🅿️ 🛈 Dashwood Sq, Newton Stewart (01671 402431). www.visitdumfriesandgalloway.co.uk

The earliest site of continuous Christian worship in Scotland, Whithorn (meaning white house) takes its name from the white chapel built here by St Ninian in 397. Though nothing remains of his chapel, a guided tour of the archaeological dig reveals evidence of Northumbrian, Viking and Scottish settlements ranging from the 5th to the 19th centuries. A visitors' centre, **The Whithorn Story**, provides information on the excavations and contains a collection of carved stones. One, dedicated to Latinus, dates to 450, making it Scotland's earliest Christian monument.

🏛 **The Whithorn Story**
The Whithorn Trust, 45–47 George St. *Tel* 01988 500508. ◯ Apr–Oct: 10:30am–5pm daily. 🅿️ 🛈 www.whithorn.com

Culzean Castle ㉚

See pp522–3.

Robert Burns surrounded by his creations, by an unknown artist

Burns Cottage ㉛

Burns National Heritage Park, Alloway, South Ayrshire. *Tel* 01292 443700. 🚆 Ayr, then bus. ◯ Oct–Mar: 10am–5pm; Apr–Sep: 10am–5:30pm; daily. ⬤ 25 & 26 Dec, 1 & 2 Jan. 🅿️ 🛈 www.burnsheritagepark.com

Robert Burns (1759–96), Scotland's favourite poet, was born and spent his first seven years in this small thatched cottage in Alloway. Built by his father, the restored cottage still contains much of its original furniture. There is also a small museum next door displaying many of Burns's manuscripts along with early editions of his works. Much of his poem *Tam o' Shanter* (1790) is set in Alloway, which commemorates him with a huge monument on the outskirts of the village.

Burns became a celebrity following the publication in 1786 of the Kilmarnock Edition of his poems. Scots everywhere gather to celebrate Burns Night *(see p65)* on his birthday, 25 January.

SCOTTISH TEXTILES

Weaving in the Scottish Borders goes back to the Middle Ages, when monks from Flanders established a thriving woollen trade with the Continent. Cotton became an important source of wealth in the Clyde Valley during the 19th century, when handloom weaving was overtaken by power-driven mills. The popular Paisley patterns were based on Indian designs.

A colourful pattern from Paisley

Glasgow

Though its Celtic name, *Glas cu*, means "dear green place", Glasgow is more often associated with its industrial past, and once enjoyed the title of Second City of the Empire (after London). Glasgow's architectural standing, as Scotland's finest Victorian city, reflects its era of prosperity, when ironworks, cotton mills and shipbuilding were fuelled by Lanarkshire coal. The Science Centre sits on the Clyde's revitalized south bank, and Glasgow rivals Edinburgh *(see pp504–11)* in the arts, with galleries such as the Kelvingrove and the Burrell Collection *(see pp520–21)*.

St Mungo with the Glasgow symbols

Glasgow's medieval cathedral viewed from the southwest

Exploring Glasgow

With some relics of its grimy industrial past and glossy new image, modern Glasgow is a city of contrasts. The deprived East End, with its busy weekend market, "the Barras", stands by the restored 18th-century Merchant City and Victorian George Square. The more affluent West End prospered in the 19th century as a retreat for wealthy merchants escaping the industrialized Clydeside, and it is here that restaurants, bars, parks and Glasgow University can be found. South Side, next to affluent Pollokshields, is Pollok Country Park, site of the Burrell Collection. An underground network and good bus and rail links provide easy travel around the city.

🏠 Glasgow Cathedral

2 Castle St. **Tel** *0141 5528198.* ⬤
Apr–Sep: 9:30am–5:30pm Mon–Sat, 1–5:30pm Sun; Oct–Mar: 9:30am–4pm Mon–Sat, 1–4pm Sun. ♿
As one of the only cathedrals to escape destruction during the Scottish Reformation *(see pp482–3)* – by adapting itself

to Protestant worship – this is a rare example of an almost complete 13th-century church. It was built on the site of a chapel founded by the city's patron saint, St Mungo, a 6th-century bishop of Strathclyde. According to legend, Mungo placed the body of a holy man named Fergus on a cart yoked to two wild bulls, telling them to take it to the place ordained by God. In the "dear green place" at which the bulls stopped he built his church. The cathedral is on two levels.

GLASGOW CITY CENTRE

Art Gallery and Museum ③
Glasgow Cathedral ⑧
Glasgow School of Art ⑤
Hunterian Art Gallery ①
Museum of Transport ②
Provand's Lordship ⑦
People's Palace ⑩
St Mungo Museum of Religious Art ⑨
Tenement House ④
Willow Tea Room ⑥

0 kilometres 1
0 miles 0.5

Dali's *Christ of St John of the Cross* at the Kelvingrove Art Gallery *(see p519)*

Situated in the cathedral precinct, this museum is a world first. The main exhibition illustrates religious themes with superb artifacts, including a 19th-century dancing Shiva and an Islamic painting entitled the *Attributes of Divine Perfection* (1986) by Ahmed Moustafa. Other religious paintings on display include *Crucifixion VII* (1988) by Scottish artist Craigie Aitchison. An exhibition on religion in Glasgow throws light on the life of the missionary David Livingstone *(see p514)*. Outside you can visit Britain's only permanent Zen Buddhist garden.

The crypt contains the tomb of St Mungo, surrounded by an intricate forest of columns springing up to end in delicately carved rib-vaulting. The Blackadder Aisle, reputed to have been built over a cemetery blessed by St Ninian *(see p515)*, has a ceiling thick with decorative bosses.

⛪ St Mungo Museum of Religious Life and Art

2 Castle St. **Tel** 0141 2761625. ◯ 10am–5pm daily (from 11am Fri & Sun). ♿ 🅿 by appointment. 🖳 🛈

⛪ Tenement House

(NTS) 145 Buccleuch St. **Tel** 0141 3330183. ◯ Mar–Oct: 1–5pm daily. 🚫 🅿 by appt. **www.nts.org.uk**
Less a museum than a time capsule, the Tenement House is an almost undisturbed record of life in a modest Glasgow flat in a tenement estate during the early 20th century. Glasgow owed much of its vitality and neighbourliness to tenement life, though many of these Victorian and Edwardian apartments were to earn a bad name for poverty and overcrowding,

The preserved Edwardian kitchen of the Tenement House

and many have now been pulled down. The Tenement House was first owned by Miss Agnes Toward who lived here from 1911 until 1965. It remained largely unaltered and, since Agnes threw very little away, it is now a treasure trove of social history. The parlour, previously used only on formal occasions, has afternoon tea laid out on a white lace cloth. The kitchen, with its coal-fired range and box bed, is filled with the tools of a vanished era such as a goffering iron for crisping waffles, a washboard and a stone hot-water bottle.

Agnes's lavender water and medicines are still in the bathroom, as though she had stepped out for a minute 70 years ago, and forgotten to return home.

The Kelvingrove Art Gallery and the Glasgow University buildings, viewed from the south

Glasgow's medieval house, Provand's Lordship

🏠 Provand's Lordship
3 Castle St. *Tel 0141 5528819.* ◯
*10am–5pm daily (from 11am Fri &
Sun).* **www**.glasgowmuseums.com
Now a museum, Provand's
Lordship was built as a canon's
house in 1471, and is the city's
oldest surviving house. Its low
ceilings and austere wooden
furnishings create a vivid
impression of life in a wealthy
15th-century household. It is
thought that Mary, Queen of

Mackintosh's interior of the
Willow Tea Room

Scots *(see p511)* may have
stayed here in 1566 when she
made a visit to see her cousin
and husband, Lord Darnley.

🏠 Willow Tea Room
217 Sauchiehall St (also 97 Buchanan
St). *Tel 0141 332 0521.* ◯ *9am–
5pm Mon–Sat, 11am–4:15pm Sun.*
📷 **www**.willow
tearooms.co.uk
This is the sole
survivor of a
series of delight-
ful tea rooms
created by
Charles Rennie
Mackintosh in
1904 for the
celebrated
restaurateur Miss
Kate Cranston. Everything
from the high-backed chairs
to the tables and cutlery was
his design. In particular, the
1904 Room de Luxe sparkles
with silver furniture and
flamboyant leaded glass
work. The No. 97 Buchanan
Street branch opened in 1997,
and recreates Cranston's original Ingram Street Tea Rooms.

🏛 Museum of Transport
1 Bunhouse Rd. *Tel 0141 2872720.*
◯ *10am–5pm Mon–Thu, Sat;
11am–5pm Fri, Sun.* 🚻 🎫 🛈
www.glasgowmuseums.com
Model ships and ranks of
gleaming Scottish-built steam
engines, cars and motorcycles
recall the 19th and early 20th
centuries, when Glasgow's
supremacy in shipbuilding,
trade and manufacturing made
her the "second city" of the
British Empire. Old Glasgow
can be seen through fascinating footage of the town in the
cinema and through a reconstruction of a 1938 street, with
Art Deco shop fronts, a cinema
and an Underground station.
The museum will close in 2010
and reopen at a new location,
on the banks of the Clyde, at
Pointhouse Quay in Yorkhill,
in spring 2011.

The Museum of Transport's
reconstructed 1938 street, with Underground station

🏛 Glasgow Necropolis
Cathedral Sq. *Tel 0141 2873961.*
◯ *daily.* 🛈 🚻 *limited.*
Behind the cathedral, the
reformer John Knox *(see
p483)* surveys the city from
his Doric pillar overlooking a
Victorian cemetery. It is filled
with crumbling monuments
to the dead of Glasgow's
wealthy merchant families.

CHARLES RENNIE MACKINTOSH
Glasgow's most celebrated designer, Charles Rennie Mackintosh
(1868–1928), entered Glasgow School of Art at 16. After his
first big break with the Willow Tea Room, he became a leading
figure in the Art Nouveau movement, developing a unique
style that borrowed from Gothic and Scottish Baronial
designs. He believed a building should be a fully
integrated work of art, creating furniture and fittings
that complemented the overall construction. Nowhere is this total design better seen than in the

A Mackintosh
floral design
Glasgow School of Art, which he designed in 1896.
Unrecognized in his lifetime, Mackintosh's work is
now widely imitated. Its characteristic straight lines and flowing
detail are the hallmark of early 20th-century Glasgow style, in
all fields of design from textiles to architecture.

🏛 People's Palace

Glasgow Green. **Tel** *0141 2760788.*
◯ *10am–5pm Mon–Thu & Sat,*
11am–5pm Fri & Sun. ● *1 & 2 Jan,*
25 & 26 Dec. 🔲 🖵 🖸
www.glasgowmuseums.com

This Victorian sandstone structure was built in 1898 as a
cultural museum for the people
of Glasgow's East End. It
houses everything from temperance tracts to trade-union
banners, suffragette posters
to comedian Billy Connolly's
banana-shaped boots, providing a social history of the
city from the 12th century. A
conservatory at the back contains an exotic winter garden.

🏛 Glasgow School of Art

167 Renfrew St. **Tel** *0141 3534500.*
◯ *by appointment only.* 🖾
🖾 🔲 *limited.* **www**.gsa.ac.uk

Widely considered to be
Charles Rennie Mackintosh's
greatest architectural work,
the Glasgow School of Art
was built between 1897 and
1909 to a design he submitted
in a competition. It was built
in two periods due to financial
constraints. The later, western
wing displays a softer design
than the more severe eastern
half, built only a few years
earlier and compared by a
contemporary critic to a prison.

A student guide takes you
through the building to the
Furniture Gallery, Board
Room and the Library, the
latter a masterpiece of spatial
composition. Each room is an
exercise in contrasts between
height, light and shade with
innovative details echoing the
architectural themes of the
structure. How much of the
school can be viewed depends
on curricular requirements at
the time of visiting.

🏛 Hunterian Art Gallery

82 Hillhead St. **Tel** *0141 3305431.*
◯ *9:30am–5pm Mon–Sat.* ● *24*
Dec–5 Jan & public hols. 🔲 🔲
limited. **www**.hunterian.gla.ac.uk

Built to house a number of
paintings bequeathed to
Glasgow University by ex-
student and physician Dr
William Hunter (1718–83), the
Hunterian Art Gallery contains
Scotland's largest print collec-
tion and works by major
European artists stretching
back to the 16th century. A

George Henry's *Japanese Lady with a Fan* **(1894)**, Art Gallery and Museum

collection of work by Charles
Mackintosh is supplemented
by a complete reconstruction
of No. 6 Florentine Terrace,
where he lived from 1906 to
1914. A major collection of
19th- and 20th-century Scottish
art includes work by William
McTaggart (1835–1910), but the
gallery's most famous collection
is of work by the painter James
McNeill Whistler (1834–1903).

Whistler's *Sketch for Annabel Lee*
(c.1869), Hunterian Art Gallery

🏛 Kelvingrove Art Gallery and Museum

Argyle St, Kelvingrove. **Tel** *0141 276
9599.* ◯ *10am–5pm Mon–Thu & Sat
(to 8pm Thu), 11am–5pm Fri & Sun.*
● *1 & 2 Jan, 25 & 26 Dec.*
www.glasgowmuseums.com

The imposing red sandstone
building that is Kelvingrove is
a striking Glasgow landmark –
even though it was supposedly
built the wrong way round –
and the gallery and museum
is the most visited in Scotland.
Having undergone a major
(£27.9 million) refurbishment,
the gallery and museum house
an impressive array of art and
artifacts. The outstanding
collection has paintings of
inestimable value, including
works by Botticelli, Giorgione
(*The Adulteress Brought Before
Christ*), Rembrandt and Dalí
(*Christ of St John of the Cross,
see p517*). Its impressive representation of 17th-century Dutch
and 19th-century French art is
augmented by the home-grown
talent of the Glasgow Boys and
the Scottish Colourists.

The Georgian Pollok House, viewed from the south

🏛 Pollok House

(NTS) 2060 Pollokshaws Rd. *Tel* (0141) 616 6410. ☐ 10am–5pm daily. ● 1 & 2 Jan, 25 & 26 Dec. 🎫 Apr–Oct only. **www**.nts.org.uk

Pollok House is Glasgow's finest 18th-century domestic building and contains one of Britain's best collections of Spanish paintings. The Neo-Classical central block was finished in 1750, the sobriety of its exterior contrasting with the exuberant plasterwork within. The Maxwells have lived at Pollok since the mid-13th century, but the male line ended with Sir John Maxwell, who added the grand entrance hall in the 1890s and designed most of the terraced gardens and parkland beyond.

Hanging above the family silver, porcelain, hand-painted Chinese wallpaper and Jacobean glass, the Stirling Maxwell collection is strong on British and Dutch schools, including William Blake's *Sir Geoffrey Chaucer and the Nine and Twenty Pilgrims* (1745) and William Hogarth's portrait of James Thomson, who wrote the words to *Rule Britannia*.

Spanish 16th- to 19th-century art predominates: El Greco's *Lady in a Fur Wrap* (1541) hangs in the library, while the drawing room contains works by Francisco de Goya and Esteban Murillo. In 1966 Anne Maxwell Macdonald gave the house and 146 ha (361 acres) of parkland to the City of Glasgow. The park provides the site for the city's fascinating Burrell Collection.

Glasgow: The Burrell Collection

Given to the city in 1944 by Sir William Burrell (1861–1958), a wealthy shipping owner, this internationally acclaimed collection is the jewel in Glasgow's crown, with objects of major importance in numerous fields of interest. The building was purpose-built in 1983. In the sun, the stained glass blazes with colour, while the shaded tapestries seem a part of the surrounding woodland.

Hutton Castle Drawing Room
This is a reconstruction of the Drawing Room at Burrell's own home – the 16th-century Hutton Castle, near Berwick-upon-Tweed. The Hall and Dining Room can also be seen nearby.

Bull's Head
Dating from the 7th century BC, this bronze head from Turkey was once part of a cauldron handle.

Figure of a Lohan
This sculpture of Buddha's disciple dates from the Ming Dynasty (1484).

Hornby Portal
This detail shows the arch's heraldic display. The 14th-century portal comes from Hornby Castle in Yorkshire.

Main entrance

STAR EXHIBITS

★ Stained Glass

★ Tapestries

Rembrandt van Rijn

This self-portrait, signed and dated 1632, has pride of place among the paintings hanging in the 16th- and 17th-century room.

Mezzanine floor

Matthijs Maris

This popular Dutch painter's ethereal style appealed to late 19th-century tastes. The Sisters (1875) is one of over 50 Maris works acquired by Burrell.

Ground floor

Lecture theatre

VISITORS' CHECKLIST

2060 Pollokshaws Rd, Glasgow.
Tel (0141) 287 2550. Pollokshaws West. 45, 47, 48, 57
from Glasgow. 10am–5pm
Mon–Thu, Sat; 11am–5pm Fri,
Sun.
www.glasgowmuseums.com

GALLERY GUIDE

Except for a mezzanine-floor display of paintings, the exhibitions are on the ground floor. Right of the entrance hall, rooms are devoted to tapestries, stained glass and sculpture, while ancient civilizations, Oriental art and the period galleries are ahead.

KEY TO FLOORPLAN

- ☐ Ancient civilizations
- ☐ Oriental art
- ☐ Medieval and post-medieval European art, stained glass and tapestries
- ☐ Period galleries
- ☐ Hutton Castle Rooms
- ☐ Paintings and drawings
- ☐ Temporary exhibition area

★ Stained Glass

This 15th-century Norwich School panel, depicting a youth snaring birds, is one of many secular themes illustrated in the stained-glass display.

★ Tapestries

Scenes from the Life of the Virgin (c.1450), a Swiss work in wool and linen, is one of many tapestries on show.

Culzean Castle ㉚

Robert Adam by
George Willison

Standing on a cliff's edge in
an extensive parkland estate,
the 16th-century keep of
Culzean (pronounced Cullayn),
home of the Earls of Cassillis,
was remodelled between 1777
and 1792 by the Neo-Classical
architect Robert Adam *(see p28)*.
Restored in the 1970s, it is now
a major showcase of his later
work. The grounds became Scotland's first
public country park in 1969 and, with farming
flourishing alongside ornamental gardens, they
reflect both the leisure and everyday activities
of a great country estate.

View of Culzean Castle (c.1815), by Nasmyth

Lord Cassillis' Rooms contain
typical mid-18th-century furnishings, including a gentleman's
wardrobe of the 1740s.

A PLAN OF CULZEAN CASTLE

FIRST FLOOR

- Lord Cassillis' Rooms
- Saloon Ante Room
- Saloon
- Front Hall
- Entrance
- Blue Drawing Room
- Long Drawing Room
- State Bedroom
- Dressing Room
- Eisenhower Presentation

- Kitchen
- Scullery
- Ailsa Exhibition
- Library
- Dining Room
- Armoury
- Oval Staircase

GROUND FLOOR

The clock tower, fronted by the circular carriageway, was originally the
coach house and stables. The clock was
added in the 19th century, and today
the buildings are used for residential
and educational purposes and a shop.

STAR SIGHTS

★ Saloon

★ Oval Staircase

Armoury
Displayed on the walls is the world's most important collection of flintlock pistols, used by the British Army and Militia between the 1730s and 1830s.

VISITORS' CHECKLIST

(NTS) 4 miles (6 km) West of Maybole. *Tel* 0844 493 2149.
🚆 *Ayr, then bus.* **Castle** ☐ *Apr–Oct: 10:30am–5pm daily (last adm: 4pm).* **Grounds** ☐ *dawn until dusk daily.* 🚻 ♿ 🅿️
ℹ️ www.culzeanexperience.org

The Eisenhower Presentation honours the general who was given the top floor of Culzean in gratitude for his role in World War II.

Fountain Court
This sunken garden is a good place to begin a tour of the grounds to the east.

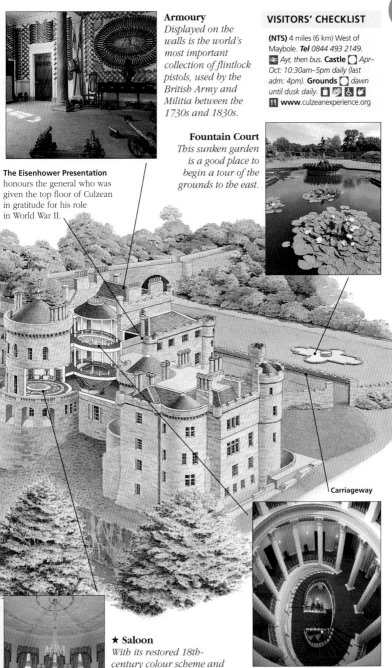

Carriageway

★ Saloon
With its restored 18th-century colour scheme and Louis XVI chairs, this elegant saloon perches on the cliff's edge 46 m (150 ft) above the Firth of Clyde. The carpet is a copy of the one designed by Adam.

★ Oval Staircase
Illuminated by an overarching skylight, the staircase, with its Ionic and Corinthian pillars, is considered one of Adam's finest achievements.

THE HIGHLANDS AND ISLANDS

ABERDEENSHIRE · MORAY · ARGYLL & BUTE · PERTH & KINROSS
SHETLAND · ORKNEY · WESTERN ISLES · HIGHLANDS · ANGUS

Most of the stock images of Scottishness – clans and tartans, whisky and porridge, bagpipes and heather – originate in the Highlands and enrich the popular picture of Scotland as a whole. But for many centuries the Gaelic-speaking, cattle-raising Highlanders had little in common with their southern neighbours.

Clues to the non-Celtic ancestors of the Highlanders lie scattered across the Highlands and Islands in the form of stone circles, brochs and cairns some over 5,000 years old. By the end of the 6th century, the Gaelic-speaking Celts had arrived from Ireland, along with St Columba who taught Christianity. Its fusion with Viking culture in the 8th and 9th centuries produced St Magnus Cathedral in the Orkney Isles.

For over 1,000 years, Celtic Highland society was founded on a clan system, built on family ties to create loyal groups dependent on a feudal chief.

However, the clans were systematically broken up by England after 1746, following the defeat of the Jacobite attempt on the British crown, led by Bonnie Prince Charlie *(see p521)*. A more romantic vision of the Highlands started in the early 19th century. Its creation was largely due to Sir Walter Scott, whose novels and poetry depicted the majesty and grandeur of a country previously considered merely poverty-stricken and barbaric. Another great popularizer was Queen Victoria, whose passion for Balmoral helped to establish the trend for acquiring Highland sporting estates. But behind the sentimentality lay harsh economic realities that drove generations of Highlanders to seek a new life overseas.

Today, over half the inhabitants of the Highlands and Islands still live in communities of less than 1,000. Oil and tourism have supplemented fishing and whisky as the main businesses and population figures are rising.

A wintry dawn over the Cairngorms, the home of Britain's only herd of reindeer

◁ **The stunningly sited castle of Eilean Donan, Loch Duich in Glen Shiel**

Exploring the Highlands and Islands

To the north and west of Stirling (the historic gateway to the Highlands) lie the magnificent mountains and glens, fretted coastlines and lonely isles that are the epitome of Scottish scenery. Inverness, the Highland capital, makes a good starting point for exploring Loch Ness and the Cairngorms, while Fort William holds the key to Ben Nevis. Inland from Aberdeen lie Royal Deeside and the Spey Valley whisky heartland. The romantic Hebrides can be reached by ferry from Oban or Ullapool.

0 kilometres 25

0 miles 25

Cape W

Butt of Lewis   Port of Ness

Kinlochberv

Barvas   North Tolsta

Standing Stones
of Callanish   Portnaguran

Stornoway   Quine
808

Isle   Lechinver

of Lewis   Ledr

Hushinish   Lemreway   Summer
Isles

Tarbert

Harris   Inverewe
Garden   A832

4   Leverburgh   Poolewe

Newtonferry

North   Lochmaddy   Uig   Staffin

Uist   7

Gramsdale   Torridon   A890

Benbecula   Dunvegan   Portree   Lochcarro

Carbost   Kyle of
Lochalsh

South   Broadford   A87   Morvi

Uist   Cuillins   The Saddle   6 FIV

Lochboisdale   Sea   1020m   SIS

of the   Elgol

Barra   Hebrides   Ardvasar

Castlebay   Rhum   Mallaig   ROAD TO TH

Eigg   A830   ISLES TOUR

Mingulay   Muck   Glenfinnan

Fort Willian

Inner   Coll

Hebrides   Aringaur   Tobermory   GLENCOE

Tiree   A828

Scarinish   Lochaline

27   Torosay   OBAN

Staffa   Craignure   Castle   26

ISLAND OF   LOCH AWE

Iona   MULL

Fionnphort   INVERARAY CASTL

AUCHINDRAIN MUSEUM 30

Colonsay   A816   31 C

32   G

JURA   Lochgil

Loch Fy

Paps of   Tarber
Jura
Port Askaig   Craighouse

Port Charlotte   ISLAY   Loc

33   Gigha   34

Port Ellen   Tayinloan

Carradale

Isle
Arra

KINTYRE   Campbeltow

Mull of
Kintyre

Highland cattle grazing on the Isle of Skye

SEE ALSO

• **Where to Stay** pp596–9

• **Where to Eat** pp649–51

GETTING AROUND

There are no motorways in the region, though travel by car is made easy by a good system of A roads. Single-track roads predominate on the isles, which are served by a ferry network and a toll-free bridge to Skye. The rail link ends to the west at Kyle of Lochalsh and to the north at Wick and Thurso. There are regular flights from London to Inverness, Aberdeen and Wick.

Colour-washed houses at the
harbour of Tobermory, Mull

KEY

▬▬	Motorway
▬▬	Major road
▬▬	Secondary road
▭▭	Minor road
▬	Scenic route
▬▬	Main railway
▬	Minor railway
△	Summit

SIGHTS AT A GLANCE

Shetland ❶

Shetland. 🚶 *22,000.* ✈ ⛴ *from Aberdeen and Stromness on mainland Orkney.* 🛈 *Lerwick (08701 999440).* **www**.visitshetland.com

Lying six degrees south of the Arctic Circle, the rugged Shetland islands are Britain's most northerly region and were, with Orkney, part of the kingdom of Norway until 1469. In the main town of Lerwick, this Norse heritage is remembered during the ancient midwinter festival Up Helly Aa *(see p480),* in which costumed revellers set fire to a replica Viking longship. Also in the town, the **Shetland Museum** tells the story of a people dependent on the sea, right up to modern times with the discovery of North Sea oil and gas in the 1970s.

The Iron Age tower, **Mousa Broch**, can be visited on its isle by boat from Sandwick. There is more ancient history at Jarlshof where a museum explains the sprawling sea-front ruins which span 3,000 years.

A boat from Lerwick sails to the isle of Noss where grey seals bask beneath sandstone cliffs crowded with Shetland's seabirds – a spectacle best seen between May and June. Other wildlife includes otters and killer whales.

🏛 **Shetland Museum**
Hay's Dock, Lerwick. *Tel 01595 694688.* ⭘ *daily (pm only Sun).* **www**.shetland-museum.org.uk

Orkney ❷

Orkney. 🚶 *19,800.* ✈ ⛴ *from Gills Bay, Caithness; John o'Groats (May–Sep); Scrabster, Aberdeen.* 🛈 *Broad St, Kirkwall (01856 872856).* **www**.visitorkney.com

The fertile isles of Orkney are remarkable for the wealth of prehistoric monuments which place them among Europe's most treasured archaeological sites. In the town of Kirkwall, the sandstone **St Magnus Cathedral** stands amid a charming core of narrow streets. Its many interesting tombs include that of its 12th-century patron saint.

For hotels and restaurants in this region see pp596–599 and pp649–651

THE SHETLAND SEABIRD ISLES

As seabirds spend most of their time away from land, nesting is a vulnerable period in their lives. The security provided by the inaccessible cliffs at such sites as Noss and Hermaness on Unst finds favour with thousands of migrant and local birds.

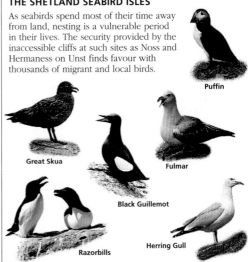

Puffin

Great Skua

Fulmar

Black Guillemot

Razorbills

Herring Gull

Nearby, the early 17th-century **Earl's Palace** is widely held to be one of Scotland's finest Renaissance buildings. To the west of Kirkwall lies Britain's most impressive chambered tomb, the cairn of **Maes Howe**. Dating from 2000 BC, the tomb has runic graffiti on its walls believed to have been left by Norsemen returning from the crusades in 1150.

Nearby, the great **Standing Stones of Stenness** may have been associated with Maes Howe rituals, though these still remain a mystery. Further west, on a bleak heath, stands the Bronze Age **Ring of Brodgar**.

Another archaeological treasure can be found in the Bay of Skail – the complete Stone Age village of **Skara Brae**. It was unearthed by a storm in 1850, after lying buried for 4,500 years. Further south, the

The Norman façade of the St Magnus Cathedral, Orkney

town of Stromness was a vital centre of Scotland's herring industry in the 18th century. Its story is told in the newly renovated local museum, while the **Pier Arts Centre** displays British and international art.

🏰 **Earl's Palace**
Palace Rd, Kirkwall. *Tel 01856 871918.* ⭘ *Apr–Sep: daily.* 🄯 ♿ *ltd.* **www**.historic-scotland.gov.uk

🏛 **Pier Arts Centre**
Victoria St, Stromness. *Tel 01856 850209.* ⭘ *Mon–Sat.* **www**.pierartscentre.com

John o'Groats ❸

Highland. 🚶 *500.* ✈ ⛴ 🚌 *Wick* ⛴ *John o'Groats to Burwick, Orkney (May–Sep).* 🛈 *John o'Groats (01955 611373).*

Some 876 miles (1,409 km) north from Land's End, Britain's most northeasterly mainland village faces Orkney, 8 miles (13 km) across the turbulent Pentland Firth. The village takes its name from a 15th-century Dutchman John de Groot, who, to avoid accusations of favouritism, is said to have built an octagonal house here with one door for each of his eight heirs. The spectacular cliffs and rock stacks of Duncansby Head lie a few miles further east.

Western Isles ❹

Western Scotland ends with this remote chain of islands, made of some of the oldest rock on Earth. Almost treeless landscapes are divided by countless waterways, the western, windward coasts edged by miles of white sandy beaches. For centuries, the eastern shores, composed largely of peat bogs, have provided the islanders with fuel. Man has been here for 6,000 years, living off the sea and the thin turf, though such monuments as an abandoned Norwegian whaling station on Harris attest to the difficulties in commercializing the islanders' traditional skills. Gaelic, part of an enduring culture, is widely spoken.

The Black House Museum, a traditional croft on Lewis

The Uists, Benbecula and Barra

Western Isles. 🚶 7,200. ✈ Barra, Benbecula. 🚢 Uig (Skye), Ullapool, Oban. 🚌 🚆 Oban, Mallaig, Kyle of Lochalsh. 🛈 Lochmaddy, North Uist (01876 500321); Lochboisdale, South Uist (01878 700286); Castlebay, Barra (01871 810336). www.visitthebrides.com

After the dramatic scenery of Harris, the lower-lying, largely waterlogged southern isles may seem an anticlimax, though they nurture secrets well worth discovering. Long, white, sandy beaches fringe the Atlantic coast, edged with one of Scotland's natural treasures: the lime-rich soil known as *machair*. During the summer months, the soil is covered with wild flowers.

From **Lochmaddy**, North Uist's main village, the A867 crosses 3 miles (5 km) of causeway to Benbecula, the isle from which Flora MacDonald smuggled Bonnie Prince Charlie (*see p535*) to Skye. Another causeway leads to South Uist, with its golden beaches renowned as a National Scenic Area. From Lochboisdale, a ferry sails to the tiny isle of Barra. The ferry docks in Castlebay, affording an unforgettable view of **Kisimul Castle**, the ancestral stronghold of the MacNeils of Barra.

The monumental Standing Stones of Callanish in northern Lewis

Lewis and Harris

Western Isles. 🚶 22,000. ✈ Stornoway. 🚢 Uig (Skye), Ullapool, Kyle of Lochalsh. 🛈 Stornoway, Lewis (01851 703088). www.visitthebrides.com **Black House Museum**. *Tel* 01851 710395. 🕘 9:30am–4pm daily (to 5:30pm in summer). 🚫 🕭 ♿ 📷 🛈

Forming the largest landmass of the Western Isles, Lewis and Harris is a single island, though Gaelic dialects differ between the two areas. From **Stornoway**, with its bustling harbour and colourful house fronts, the ancient **Standing Stones of Callanish** are only 16 miles (26 km) to the west. Just off the road on the way to Callanish are the ruins of **Carloway Broch**, a Pictish (*see p482*) tower over 2,000 years old. The more recent past can be explored at Arnol's **Black House Museum** – a showcase of crofting life as it was until only 50 years ago.

South of the rolling peat moors of Lewis, a range of mountains marks the border with Harris, which one enters as one passes Aline Lodge at the head of Loch Seaforth. Only a little less spectacular than the "Munros" (peaks over 914 m; 3,000 ft) of the

mainland and the Isle of Skye (*see pp534–5*), the mountains of Harris are a paradise for the hillwalker and, from their summits on a clear day, the distant Isle of St Kilda can be seen 50 miles (80 km) to the west.

The ferry port of Tarbert stands on a slim isthmus separating North and South Harris. Some local weavers of the famous Harris Tweed still follow the old tradition of using plants to make their dyes.

From the port of Leverburgh, close to the southern tip of Harris, a ferry can be taken to the isle of North Uist, where a causeway has been built to Berneray.

The remote and sandy shores of South Uist

The western side of the Five Sisters of Kintail, seen from above Loch Duich

Skye ❺

See pp534–5.

The Five Sisters ❻

Skye & Lochalsh. 🚆 *Kyle of Loch-alsh.* 🚌 *Glenshiel.* ⓘ *Bayfield Road, Portree, Isle of Skye (01478 612137).* **www**.visithighlands.com

Dominating one of Scotland's most haunting regions, the awesome summits of the Five Sisters of Kintail rear into view at the northern end of Loch Cluanie as the A87 enters Glen Shiel. The **Visitor Centre** at Morvich offers ranger-led excursions in the summer. Further west, the road passes **Eilean Donan Castle**, connected by a bridge. A Jacobite *(see p537)* stronghold, it was destroyed in 1719 by English warships. In the 19th century it was restored and now contains Jacobite relics.

♠ **Eilean Donan Castle**
Off A87, nr Dornie. **Tel** 01599 555202. ⬤ *Apr–Oct: 10am–5:30pm daily.* 📷

Wester Ross ❼

Ross & Cromarty. 🚆 *Achnasheen, Strathcarron.* ⓘ *Visit Scotland (01445 712130).* **www**.visithighlands.com

Leaving Loch Carron to the south, the A890 suddenly enters the northern Highlands and the great wilderness of Wester Ross. The Torridon

Estate includes some of the oldest mountains on Earth (Torridonian rock is over 600 million years old), and is home to red deer, wild cats and wild goats. Peregrine falcons and golden eagles nest in the towering sandstone mass of Liathach, above the village of Torridon with its breathtaking views over Applecross to Skye. The **Torridon Countryside Centre** provides guided walks in season and essential information on the natural history of the region.

To the north, the A832 cuts through the Beinn Eighe National Nature Reserve in which remnants of the ancient Caledonian pine forest still stand on the banks and isles of Loch Maree.

Along the coast, exotic gardens thrive in the warming currents of the Gulf Stream, most impressive being **Inver-ewe Garden** created in 1862 by Osgood Mackenzie (1842–1922). May and June are the months to see the display of

Typical Torridonian mountian scenery in the Wester Ross

rhododendrons and azaleas; July and August for the herbaceous borders.

🏛 **Torridon Countryside Centre**
(NTS) Torridon. **Tel** 0844 493 2229. ⬤ *Easter–Sep: 10am–6pm daily.* 📷 ♿ **www**.nts.org.uk;

♣ **Inverewe Garden**
(NTS) off A832, nr Poolewe. **Tel** 0844 493 2225. ⬤ *daily.* 📷 ♿

Dornoch ❽

Sutherland. 🏠 *2,200.* 🚆 *Golspie, Tain.* ⓘ *The Square, Dornoch (01862 810916).* **www**.visithighlands.com

With its first-class golf course and extensive sandy beaches, **Dornoch** is a popular holiday resort, though it has retained a peaceful atmosphere. Now the parish church, the medieval cathedral was all but destroyed in a clan dispute in 1570; it was finally restored in the 1920s for its 700th anniversary. A stone at the beach end of River Street marks the place where Janet Horne, the last woman to be tried in Scotland for witchcraft, was executed in 1722.

Environs: Twelve miles (19 km) northeast of Dornoch is the stately Victorianized pile of **Dunrobin Castle**, magnificently situated in a great park with formal gardens overlooking the sea. Since the 13th century, this has been the seat of the Earls of Sutherland.

Many of its rooms are open to visitors. A steam-powered fire engine is among the miscellany of objects on display.

South of Dornoch stands the town of **Tain**. Though patronized by medieval kings as a place of pilgrimage, it became an administrative centre of the Highland Clearances. All is explained in the heritage centre, **Tain Through Time**.

♣ **Dunrobin Castle**
Nr Golspie. **Tel** 01408 633177.
⬜ Mar–May, Sep & Oct: 10:30am–4:30pm daily (from noon Sun); Jun–Aug: 10:30am–5:30pm daily. 🏷

🏛 **Tain Through Time**

Tower St. **Tel** 01862 894089. ⬜
Apr–Oct: 10am–5pm Mon–Sat. 🏷
♿ 🅿 www.tainmuseum.org.uk

The serene cathedral precinct in the town of Dornoch

Strathpeffer ⑨

Ross & Cromarty. 🏘 1,400. 🚂
Dingwall, Inverness. 🚌 Inverness. 🛈
Visit Scotland (01463 731505; Easter–Oct). www.undiscoveredscotland.co.uk

Standing 5 miles (8 km) from the Falls of Rogie and to the east of the Northwest Highlands, the popular town of Strathpeffer still has the refined charm for which it was well known in Victorian times, when it flourished as a spa and health resort. The grand hotels, individually designed buildings and gracious layout of Strathpeffer recall the days when royalty from all over Europe used to flock to the chalybeate- and sulphur-laden springs, which were believed to help in the cure of tuberculosis, and in the treatment of rheumatism.

The shores of the Black Isle in the Moray Firth

The Black Isle ⑩

Ross & Cromarty. 🚂 🚌 Inverness.
🛈 Visit Scotland (01463 731505; Easter–Oct).

Though the drilling platforms in the Cromarty Firth are reminders of how oil has changed the local economy, the peninsula of the Black Isle is still largely composed of farmland and fishing villages. The town of **Cromarty** was an important port in the 18th century, with thriving rope and lace industries. Many of its merchant houses still stand; the museum in the **Cromarty Courthouse** provides heritage tours of the town. The **Hugh Miller Museum** is a museum to the theologian and geologist Hugh Miller (1802–56), who was born in the cottage; adjacent is the superb, new

Miller House, which has exhibitions on three floors. **Fortrose** boasts a ruined 14th-century cathedral, while a stone on Chanonry Point commemorates the Brahan Seer, a 17th-century prophet burnt alive in a tar barrel by the Countess of Seaforth after he foresaw her husband's infidelity. For local archaeology, visit **Groam House Museum** in Rosemarkie.

🏛 **Cromarty Courthouse**
Church St, Cromarty. **Tel** 01381 600 418. ⬜ Mar–Oct: daily. 🏷

🏚 **Hugh Miller Museum**
(NTS) Church St, Cromarty. **Tel** 0844 493 2158. ⬜ Easter–Sep: daily; Oct: Sun–Wed pm. 🏷 ♿ limited.

🏛 **Groam House Museum**
High St, Rosemarkie. **Tel** 01381 620 961. ⬜ May–Sep: 10am–5pm daily (Sun pm); Oct–Apr: Sat & Sun (pm).

THE HIGHLAND CLEARANCES

During the heyday of the clan system (see p484), tenants paid their clan chiefs rent for their land in the form of military service. However, with the decline of the clan system after the Battle of Culloden (see p537) and the coming of sheep from the borders, landowners were able to command a financial rent their tenants were unable to afford and the land was bought up by Lowland and English farmers. In what became known as "the year of the sheep" (1792), thousands of tenants were evicted to make way for sheep. Many emigrated to Australia, America and Canada. Ruins of their crofts can still be seen in Sutherland and Wester Ross.

The Last of the Clan (1865) by Thomas Faed

Isle of Skye 36

Otter by the coast at Kylerhea

The largest of the Inner Hebrides, Skye can be reached by the bridge linking Kyle of Lochalsh and Kyleakin. A turbulent geological history has given the island some of Britain's most varied and dramatic scenery. From the rugged volcanic plateau of northern Skye to the ice-sculpted peaks of the Cuillins, the island is divided by numerous sea lochs, leaving the traveller never more than 8 km (5 miles) from the sea. North of the Dunvegan are small caves and white beaches, while Limestone grasslands predominate in the south, where the hillsides, home of sheep and cattle, are scattered with the ruins of crofts abandoned during the Clearances (*see p531*). Historically, Skye is best known for its association with Bonnie Prince Charlie.

Skeabost has the ruins of a chapel which is associated with St Columba. Medieval tombstones can be found in the graveyard.

Grave of Flora MacDonald

WESTERN ISLES

LOCH SNIZORT

• Lusta

B886

• Milovaig

B884

Dunvegan

Ske

A850

A863

Dunvegan Castle
For over seven centuries, Dunvegan Castle has been the seat of the chiefs of the Clan MacLeod. It contains the Fairy Flag, a fabled piece of magic silk treasured for its protection in battle.

| 0 kilometres | 10 |
| 0 miles | 5 |

Portnalong

B8009

Talisker   Carbost

The Talisker Distillery
produces one of the best Highland malts, often described as "the lava of the Cuillins".

Cuillins
Britain's finest mountain range is within walking distance of Sligachan, and in summer a boat sails from Elgol to the desolate inner sanctuary of Loch Coruisk. As he fled across the surrounding moorland, Bonnie Prince Charlie is said to have claimed: "Even the Devil shall not follow me here!"

KEY

🛈	Tourist information
▰▰	Major road
▱▱	Minor road
—	Narrow lane
🗻	Viewpoint

◁ Dawn over the desolate tablelands of northern Skye, viewed from the Quiraing

Quiraing

A series of landslides has exposed the roots of this volcanic plateau, revealing a fantastic terrain of spikes and towers. They are easily explored off the Uig to Staffin road.

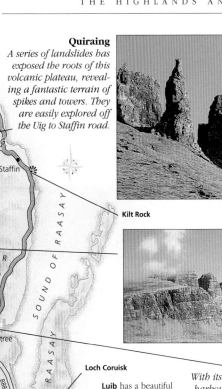

Kilt Rock

The Storr

The erosion of this basalt plateau has created the Old Man of Storr, a monolith rising to 49 m (160 ft) by the Portree road.

Loch Coruisk

Luib has a beautiful thatched cottage, preserved as it was 100 years ago.

Portree

With its colourful harbour, Portree (meaning "port of the king") is Skye's metropolis. It received its name after a visit by James V in 1540.

Bridge to mainland

KYLE OF LOCHALSH

Otters can be seen from the haven in Kylerhea.

Armadale Castle Gardens and Museum of the Isles houses the Clan Donald visitor centre.

BONNIE PRINCE CHARLIE

The last of the Stuart claimants to the Crown, Charles Edward Stuart (1720–88), came to Scotland from France in 1745 to win the throne. After marching as far as Derby, his army was driven back to Culloden where it was defeated. Hounded for five months through the Highlands, he escaped to Skye, disguised as the maidservant of a woman called Flora MacDonald, from Uist. From the mainland, he sailed to France in September 1746, and died in Rome. Flora was buried in 1790 at Kilmuir, on Skye, wrapped in a sheet taken from the bed of the "bonnie" (handsome) prince.

The prince, disguised as a maidservant

Kilchrist Church

This ruined pre-Reformation church's last service was held in 1843. It once served Skye's most populated areas, though the surrounding moors are now deserted.

The ruins of Urquhart Castle on the western shore of Loch Ness

Loch Ness ⓫

Inverness. 🚆 🚌 Inverness. 🛈 Castle Wynd, Inverness (01463 234353). www.loch-ness-scotland.com

At 24 miles (39 km) long, one mile (1.5 km) at its widest and up to 305 m (1,000 ft) deep, **Loch Ness** fills the northern half of the Great Glen fault from Fort William to Inverness. It is joined to lochs Oich and Lochy by the 22-mile (35-km) Caledonian Canal,

THE LOCH NESS MONSTER

First sighted by St Columba in the 6th century, "Nessie" has attracted increasing attention since ambiguous photographs were taken in the 1930s. Though serious investigation is often undermined by hoaxers, sonar techniques continue to yield enigmatic results: plesiosaurs, giant eels and too much whisky are the most popular explanations. Nessie appears to have a close relative in the waters of Loch Morar (see p546).

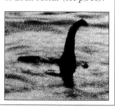

designed by Thomas Telford (see p447). On the western shore, the A82 passes the ruins of the 16th-century **Urquhart Castle**, which was blown up by government supporters in 1692 to prevent it falling into Jacobite hands. A short distance west, **Loch Ness 2000 Exhibition Centre** offers a wealth of audio-visual information.

⚓ **Urquhart Castle**
Nr Drumnadrochit. **Tel** 01456 450551.
🕙 9:30am–6pm daily (Oct–Easter: to 4:30pm). (Last adm: 45 mins before closing.) 🎫 🚻 📷

🏛 **Loch Ness 2000 Exhibition Centre**
Drumnadrochit. **Tel** 01456 450573.
🕙 daily, with longer opening hours in peak season and shorter opening hours in winter. 🎫 🚻 🖥 📷

Inverness ⓬

Highland. 🚶 60,000. 🚆 🚌
🛈 Castle Wynd (0845 2255121).
www.visithighlands.com

As the Highland capital, Inverness makes an ideal base from which to explore the surrounding countryside. The Victorian castle dominates the town centre, the oldest buildings of which are found in nearby Church Street. Today

the castle is used as law courts. The **Inverness Museum and Art Gallery** provides a good introduction to the history of the Highlands with exhibits including a lock of Bonnie Prince Charlie's (see p535) hair and a fine collection of Inverness silver. The **Scottish Kiltmaker Visitor Centre** explores the history and tradition of Scottish kilts as well as workshops, while those in search of tartans and knitwear should visit the **James Pringle Weavers of Inverness**.

Jacobite Cruises run a variety of year-round cruises along the Caledonian Canal and on to Loch Ness. The unfolding scenery makes this a most pleasant and tranquil way to spend a sunny afternoon.

Kilt maker with royal Stuart tartan

🏛 **Museum and Art Gallery**
Castle Wynd. **Tel** 01463 237114.
🕙 10am–5pm Mon–Sat. ♿
www.invernessmuseum.com

🧵 **James Pringle Weavers of Inverness**
Holm Woollen Mill, Dores Rd.
Tel 01463 223311. 🕙 daily. ♿

🏛 **Scottish Kiltmaker Visitor Centre**
Huntly St. **Tel** 01463 222781.
🕙 May–Sep: daily; Oct–Apr: Mon–Sat. ● 1 Jan, 25 Dec. 🎫

Jacobite Cruises
Glenurquhart Road.
Tel 01463 233999. 🕙 daily.
🎫 ♿ www.jacobite.co.uk

Culloden ⑬

(NTS) Inverness. 🚃 🚌 *Inverness.*
www.nts.org.uk

A desolate stretch of moorland, Culloden looks much as it did on 16 April 1746, the date of the last battle to be fought on British soil *(see p483)*. Here the Jacobite cause, with Bonnie Prince Charlie's *(see p535)* leadership, finally perished under the onslaught of Hanoverian troops led by the Duke of Cumberland. All is explained in the excellent **NTS Visitor Centre**.

Environs: Signposted for a mile (1.5 km) or so east are the outstanding Neolithic burial sites, the **Clava Cairns**.

🚩 **NTS Visitor Centre**
On the B9006 east of Inverness.
Tel 01463 790607. 🗓 *Apr–Sep:*
daily. ⚫ *24–26 Dec, Jan.* 🅿️ ♿

Fort George ⑭

Inverness. *Tel* 01667 460232.
🚃 🚌 *Inverness, Nairn.* 🗓 *Apr–*
Sep: 9:30am–6pm daily (to 4:30pm
Oct–Mar). ⚫ *25 & 26 Dec.* 🅿️ ♿
🖥️ **www**.historic-scotland.gov.uk

One of the finest works of European military architecture, Fort George stands on a windswept promontory jutting into the Moray Firth, ideally located to suppress the Highlanders. Completed in 1769, the fort was built after the Jacobite risings to discourage further rebellion in the Highlands and has remained a military garrison

THE JACOBITE MOVEMENT

The first Jacobites (mainly Catholic Highlanders) were the supporters of James II of England (James VII of Scotland) who was deposed by the "Glorious Revolution" of 1688 *(see p53)*. With the Protestant William of Orange on the throne, the Jacobites' desire to restore the Stuart monarchy led to the uprisings of 1715 and 1745. The first, in support of James VIII, the "Old Pretender", ended at the Battle of Sheriffmuir (1715). The failure of the second uprising, with the defeat at Culloden, saw the end of Jacobite hopes and led to the end of the clan system and the suppression of Highland culture for over a century *(see p485)*.

James II, by Samuel Cooper (1609–72)

The drawbridge on the eastern side of Cawdor Castle

ever since. The Fort houses the **Regimental Museum** of the Highlanders Regiment, and some of its barrack rooms reconstruct the conditions of the common soldiers stationed here more than 200 years ago. The **Grand Magazine** contains an outstanding collection of arms and military equipment. The battlements also make an excellent place from which to watch dolphins in the Moray Firth.

Cawdor Castle ⑮

On B9090 (off A96). *Tel* 01667
404401. 🚃 *Nairn, then bus.*
🚌 *from Inverness.* 🗓 *May–mid-Oct:*
10am–5:30pm daily. 🅿️ ♿ *gardens*
& ground floor only. 🚩
www.cawdorcastle.com

With its turreted central tower, moat and drawbridge, Cawdor Castle is one of the most romantic stately homes in the Highlands. Though the castle is famed for being the 11th-century home of Shakespeare's *(see p322)* Macbeth and the scene of his murder of King Duncan, it is not historically proven that either came here.

An ancient holly tree preserved in the vaults is said to be the one under which, in 1372, Thane William's donkey, laden with gold, stopped for a rest during its master's search for a place to build a fortress. According to legend, this was how the site for the castle was chosen. Now, after 600 years of continuous occupation (it is still the home of the Thanes of Cawdor) the house is a treasury of family history, containing a number of rare tapestries and portraits by the 18th-century painters Joshua Reynolds (1723–92) and George Romney (1734–1802). Furniture in the Pink Bedroom and Woodcock Room includes work by Chippendale and Sheraton. In the Old Kitchen, the huge Victorian cooking range stands as a shrine to below-stairs drudgery. The grounds provide nature trails and a nine-hole golf course.

A contemporary picture, *The Battle of Culloden* (1746), by D Campbell

Elgin ⑯

Moray. 🚶 *21,000*. 🚃 🖼
ℹ️ *17 High St, Moray (01343 542666).*

With its cobbled marketplace and crooked lanes, the popular holiday centre of Elgin still retains much of its medieval layout. The 13th-century **cathedral** ruins next to King Street are all that remain of one of Scotland's architectural triumphs, the design of its tiered windows reminiscent of the cathedral at St Andrews *(see p499)*. Once known as the Lantern of the North, the cathedral was severely damaged in 1390 by the Wolf of Badenoch (the son of Robert II) in revenge for his excommunication by the Bishop of Moray. Worse damage came in 1576 when the Regent Moray ordered the stripping of its lead roofing. Among its remains is a Pictish cross-slab in the nave, and a basin in a corner where one of Elgin's benefactors,

Details of the central tower of Elgin Cathedral

Andrew Anderson, was kept as a baby by his homeless mother. Next to the cathedral are the **Biblical Gardens** with all 110 plants mentioned in the Bible, while the **Elgin Museum** has anthropological displays and the **Moray Motor Museum** has over 40 vehicles.

🏛 **Elgin Museum**
1 High St. *Tel 01343 543675*. ◯
Apr–Oct: Mon–Sat. 🖼 ♿ *limited.*
🖥 *www.elginmuseum.org.uk*

🏛 **Moray Motor Museum**
Bridge St, Bishopmill. *Tel 01343 541120*. ◯ *Easter–Oct: 11am–5pm daily.* 🖼 ♿

Aberdeen ⑰

Scotland's third largest city and Europe's offshore oil capital, Aberdeen has prospered since the discovery of petroleum in the North Sea in 1970. The sea bed has now yielded over 100 oilfields. Widely known as the Granite City, its rugged outlines are softened by sumptuous year-round floral displays in its public parks and gardens, the Duthie Park Winter Gardens being one of the largest indoor gardens in Europe. The picturesque village of Footdee, which sits at the end of the city's 2-mile (3-km) beach, has good views back to the busy harbour.

The spires of Aberdeen, rising behind the city harbour

Exploring Aberdeen
The city centre flanks the mile-long (1.5 km) Union Street ending to the east at the Mercat Cross. The cross stands in Castlegate, the one-time site of the city castle. From here the cobbled Shiprow winds southwest and passes Provost Ross's House *(see p540)* on its way to the harbour with its fish market. A bus can be taken a mile (1.5 km) north of the centre to Old Aberdeen which, with its medieval streets and wynds, has the peaceful character of a separate village. Driving is restricted in some streets.

🏫 King's College
College Bounds, Old Aberdeen. *Tel 01224 272092*. **Chapel** ◯ *Opening times vary – phone to check.* ♿
King's College was founded in 1495 as the city's first university. The inter-denominational chapel (the only part of the college open to the public), in the past consecutively Catholic and Protestant, has a lantern tower rebuilt after a storm in 1633. Stained-glass windows by Douglas Strachan add a contemporary touch to the interior which contains a 1540 pulpit, later carved with heads of Stuart monarchs.

⛪ St Andrew's Cathedral
King St. *Tel 01224 640290*.
◯ *May–Sep: 11am–4pm Tue–Fri.*
♿ 🅿 *by appointment.*
The Mother Church of the Episcopal Communion in America, St Andrew's has a memorial to Samuel Seabury, the first Episcopalian bishop in the United States, who was consecrated in Aberdeen in 1784. Coats of arms adorn the ceiling above the north and south aisles, contrasting colourfully with the white walls and pillars. They represent the American States and local Jacobite *(see p537)* families.

The elegant lantern tower of the chapel at King's College

PROVOST SKENE'S HOUSE

Guestrow. *Tel 01224 641086*. ☐ *10am–5pm Mon–Sat, 1–4pm Sun (limited access to upper floors)*. ● *25 & 26, 31 Dec–2 Jan*. **www**.aagm.co.uk

Once the home of Sir George Skene, a 17th-century provost (mayor) of Aberdeen, the house was built in 1545. Inside, period rooms span 200 years of design. The Duke of Cumberland stayed here before the Battle of Culloden *(see p537)*.

The 18th-century Parlour, with its walnut harpsichord and covered chairs by the fire, was the informal room in which the family would have tea.

The Regency Room typifies early 19th-century elegance. A harp dating from 1820 stands by a Grecian-style sofa and a French writing table.

The Painted Gallery has one of Scotland's most important cycles of religious art. The panels are early 17th century, though the artist is unknown.

The 17th-century Great Hall contains heavy oak dining furniture. Provost Skene's wood-carved coat of arms hangs above the fireplace.

The Georgian Dining Room, with its Classical design, was the main formal room in the 16th century and still has its original flagstone floor.

Entrance

ABERDEEN CITY CENTRE

Aberdeen Art Gallery ①
St Andrew's Cathedral ⑤
Marischal College ④
Maritime Museum ⑦
Mercat Cross ⑥
Provost Skene's House ③
St Nicholas Kirk ②

0 metres   200
0 yards   200

🏛 Art Gallery

Schoolhill. **Tel** 01224 523700. ☐
10am–5pm Tue–Sat, 2–5pm Sun. ●
25 Dec–2 Jan. &. www.aagm.co.uk
Housed in a Neo-Classical
building, purpose-built in
1884, the Art Gallery has a
wide range of exhibitions,
with an emphasis on contemporary work. A fine collection
of Aberdonian silver can be
found among the decorative
arts on the ground floor,
and is the subject of
a video
presentation.
A permanent
collection of
18th–20th-century
fine art features
such names as
Toulouse-Lautrec,
Reynolds and Zoffany.
Several of the works
were bequeathed in
1900 by a local granite
merchant, Alex
Macdonald. He
commissioned many of the
paintings in the Macdonald

**Aberdonian
silver in the
Art Gallery**

Room, which displays 92 self-
portraits by British artists. Occasional poetry-readings, music
recitals and films are on offer.

⛪ St Nicholas Kirk

Union St. **Tel** 01224 643494.
☐ May–Sep: noon–4pm Mon–Fri &
Sun, 1–3pm Sat. &.
Founded in the 12th century,
St Nicholas is Scotland's
largest parish church. Though
the present structure dates
from 1752, many
relics of earlier
times can be
seen inside.
After being dam-
aged during the
Reformation, the
interior was divided
into two. A chapel in
the East Church con-
tains iron rings used to
secure witches in the
17th century, while in
the West Church there
are some embroidered
panels attributed to one Mary
Jameson (1597–1644).

🏛 Maritime Museum

Shiprow. **Tel** 01224 337100. ☐
10am–5pm Tue–Sat, noon–3pm Sun.
&. ☐ ☐ www.aagm.co.uk
Overlooking the harbour is
Provost Ross's House, which
dates back to 1593 and is one
of the oldest residential buildings in the town. This museum
traces the history of Aberdeen's
seafaring tradition. Exhibitions
include ship-wrecks, rescues,
shipbuilding and the oil instal-
lations off Scotland's east coast.

⛪ St Machar's Cathedral

The Chanonry. **Tel** 01224 485988. ☐
9am–5pm daily (10am–4pm winter). &.
Dominating Old Aberdeen,
the 15th-century edifice of St
Machar's is the oldest granite
building in the city. The stonework of one arch even dates
as far back as the 14th century.
The impressive nave now
serves as a parish church and
its magnificent oak ceiling is
adorned with the coats of
arms of 48 popes, emperors
and princes of Christendom.

Royal Deeside Tour ⑱

Since Queen Victoria's purchase of the
Balmoral estate in 1852, Deeside has
been best known as the summer
home of the British Royal Family,
though it has been associated with
royalty since the time of Robert the
Bruce (see p482). The route follows
the Dee, formerly a prolific salmon
river, through some magnificent
Grampian scenery.

**Muir of Dinnet
Nature Reserve ④**
An information centre
on the A97 provides an
excellent place from
which to explore this
beautiful mixed wood-
land area, formed by
the retreating glaciers
of the last Ice Age.

Balmoral ⑥
Bought by Queen Victoria for
30,000 guineas in 1852, after its
owner choked to death on a
fishbone, the castle was rebuilt
in the Scottish Baronial style at
Prince Albert's request.

Ballater ⑤
The old railway town of
Ballater has royal warrants
on many of its shop fronts.
It grew as a 19th-century
spa town, its waters
reputedly providing a
cure for tuberculosis.

Dunkeld ⓳

Perth & Kinross. 🏠 *2,500.* 🚊 *Birnam.*
🚌 ℹ️ *The Cross (01350 727688).*
www.visitdunkeld.com

Situated by the River Tay, this ancient and charming village was all but destroyed in the Battle of Dunkeld, a Jacobite *(see p537)* defeat, in 1689. The **Little Houses** lining Cathedral Street were the first to be rebuilt, and are fine examples of imaginative restoration. The ruins of the 14th-century **cathedral** enjoy an idyllic setting on shady lawns beside the Tay, against a backdrop of steep and wooded hills. The choir is used as the parish church and its north wall contains a Leper's Squint: a hole through which lepers could see the altar during mass. It was while on holiday in the Dunkeld country-side that Beatrix Potter *(see p367)* found the location for her Peter Rabbit stories.

The ruins of Dunkeld Cathedral

Pitlochry ⓴

Perth & Kinross. 🏠 *2,900.* 🚊 🚌
ℹ️ *22 Atholl Rd (01796 472215).*
www.perthshire.co.uk

Surrounded by pine-forested hills, Pitlochry became famous after Queen Victoria *(see p56)* described it as one of the finest resorts in Europe. In early summer, salmon swim up the ladder built into the Power Station Dam, on their way to spawning grounds upriver. There is a viewing chamber here to see them. The **Power Station Visitor Centre** outlines the hydro-electric scheme that harnesses the waters of the River Tummel. The home of Bell's whisky, the **Blair Atholl Distillery**, gives an insight into whisky making *(see p489)* and is open for tours. Scotland's famous **Festival Theatre** puts on a summer season when the programme changes daily.

ℹ️ **Power Station Visitor**
Centre Pitlochry. **Tel** *01796 473152.* ⭕ *Apr–Oct: 10am–5:30pm Mon–Fri (Jul & Aug: daily).* 📷 📷

🎭 **Festival Theatre**
Port-na-Craig. **Tel** *01796 484626.* ⭕ *daily.* 📷 ♿ 📷

🏭 **Blair Atholl Distillery**
Perth Rd. **Tel** *01796 482003.* ⭕ *Easter–Sep: Mon–Sat (& Sun pm Jun–Sep); Oct–Mar: Mon–Fri.* ⭕ *22 Dec–3 Jan.* 📷 ♿ *limited.* 📷 🏪
www.discovering-distilleries.com

TIPS FOR DRIVERS

Length: 69 miles (111 km).
Stopping-off points: Crathes Castle café (May–Sep: daily); Station Restaurant, Ballater (food served all day). (See also pp684–5.)

Drum Castle ①
This impressive 13th-century keep was granted by Robert the Bruce to his standard bearer in 1323, in gratitude for his services.

PETERHEAD

A96

ABERDEEN

A956

A93

Banchory ③
Local lavender is a popular attraction here. From the 18th-century Brig o' Feugh, salmon can be seen.

A980

A93

B974

① ● *Peterculter*

Dee

② *Crathes*

③

B9077

A90

A956

STONEHAVEN

Crathes Castle and Gardens ②
This is the family home of the Burnetts, who were made Royal Foresters of Drum by Robert the Bruce. Along with the title, he gave Alexander Burnett the ivory Horn of Leys which is still on display.

0 kilometres		5

0 miles		4

KEY

▬▬▬ Tour route

═══ Other roads

✳️ Viewpoint

Killiecrankie Walk ㉑

In an area famous for its scenery and historical connections, this circular walk offers typical Highland views. The route is fairly flat, though ringed by mountains, and follows the River Garry south to Loch Faskally, meandering through a wooded gorge, passing the Soldier's Leap and a Victorian viaduct. There are several ideal picnic spots along the way. Returning along the River Tummel, the walk crosses one of Queen Victoria's favourite Highland areas, before doubling back along the rivers to complete the circuit.

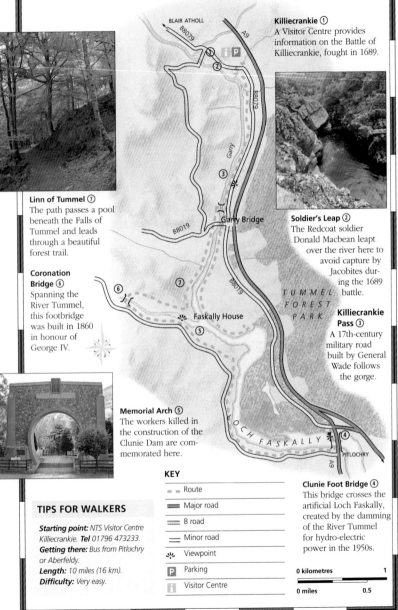

Killiecrankie ①
A Visitor Centre provides information on the Battle of Killiecrankie, fought in 1689.

Linn of Tummel ⑦
The path passes a pool beneath the Falls of Tummel and leads through a beautiful forest trail.

Coronation Bridge ⑥
Spanning the River Tummel, this footbridge was built in 1860 in honour of George IV.

Soldier's Leap ②
The Redcoat soldier Donald Macbean leapt over the river here to avoid capture by Jacobites during the 1689 battle.

Killiecrankie Pass ③
A 17th-century military road built by General Wade follows the gorge.

Memorial Arch ⑤
The workers killed in the construction of the Clunie Dam are commemorated here.

Clunie Foot Bridge ④
This bridge crosses the artificial Loch Faskally, created by the damming of the River Tummel for hydro-electric power in the 1950s.

BLAIR ATHOLL

Garry Bridge

Faskally House

TUMMEL FOREST PARK

LOCH FASKALLY

PITLOCHRY

KEY

▰ ▰	Route
▰▰▰	Major road
▱	B road
	Minor road
�☆	Viewpoint
P	Parking
i	Visitor Centre

0 kilometres   1
0 miles   0.5

TIPS FOR WALKERS

Starting point: *NTS Visitor Centre Killiecrankie.* **Tel** *01796 473233.*
Getting there: *Bus from Pitlochry or Aberfeldy.*
Length: *10 miles (16 km).*
Difficulty: *Very easy.*

The Three Sisters, Glencoe, in late autumn

Blair Castle ㉒

Blair Atholl, Perthshire. *Tel* 01796
481207. ☎ Blair Atholl. ◯ Apr–Oct:
9:30am–4:30pm daily: Nov–Mar: Tue
& Sat. ◯ two weeks end Dec. ♿
limited. www.blair-castle.co.uk

This rambling, turreted castle
has been altered so often in
its 700-year history that it provides a unique insight into the
history of Highland aristocratic
life. The 18th-century wing,
with its Victorian passages
hung with antlers, has a display
containing the gloves and pipe

of Bonnie Prince Charlie *(see
p535)* who spent two days
here gathering Jacobite *(see
p537)* support. Family portraits
cover 300 years and include
paintings by such masters as
Johann Zoffany and Sir Peter
Lely. Sir Edwin Landseer's
Death of a Stag in Glen Tilt
(1850) was painted nearby.
    In 1844 Queen Victoria vis-
ited the castle and conferred
on its owners, the Dukes of
Atholl, the distinction of being
allowed to maintain a private
army. The Atholl Highlanders
still flourish.

The Cairngorms ㉓

See pp544–5.

Glencoe ㉔

Highland. ☎ Fort William. ◻
Glencoe. ℹ Visit Scotland (01855
811866). www.glencoe-scotland.net

Renowned for its awesome
scenery and savage history,
Glencoe was compared by
Dickens to "a burial ground of
a race of giants". The precipitous cliffs of Buachaille Etive
Mor and the knife-edged
ridge of Aonach Eagach (both
over 900 m; 3,000 ft) present
a formidable challenge even to
experienced mountaineers.
    Against a dark backdrop
of craggy peaks and the tumbling River Coe, the Glen
offers superb hill-walking in
the summer. Stout footwear,
waterproofs and attention to
safety warnings are essential.
Details of routes, ranging from
the easy half-hour between
the **NTS Visitor Centre** and
Signal Rock (from which the
signal was given to commence
the massacre) to a stiff 6 mile
(10 km) haul up the Devil's
Staircase can be had from the
Visitor Centre. Guided walks
are offered in summer by the
NTS Ranger service.

ℹ **NTS Visitor Centre**
Glencoe. *Tel* 01855 811307. ◯
daily. ♿ ltd. www.nts.org.uk

THE MASSACRE OF GLENCOE

In 1692, the chief of the Glencoe MacDonalds was five
days late in registering an oath of submission to William
III, giving the government an excuse to root out a nest of
Jacobite *(p537)* supporters. For ten days 130 soldiers, cap-
tained by Robert Campbell, were hospitably entertained by
the unsuspecting MacDonalds. At dawn on 13 February, in
a terrible breach of trust, the soldiers fell on their hosts,
killing some 38 MacDonalds. Many more died in their wintry
mountain hideouts. The mas-
sacre, unsurprisingly, became
a political scandal, though
there were to be no
official reprimands
for three years.

**Detail of *The
Massacre of Glencoe*
by James Hamilton**

The Cairngorms ㉒

Wild Goat

Rising to a height of 1,309 m (4,296 ft), the Cairngorm mountains form the highest landmass in Britain. Cairn Gorm itself is the site of one of Britain's first ski centres. A weather station at the mountain's summit provides regular reports, essential in an area known for sudden changes of weather. Walkers should be sure to follow the mountain code without fail. The funicular railway that climbs Cairn Gorm affords superb views over the Spey Valley. Many estates in the valley have centres which introduce the visitor to Highland land use.

Strathspey Steam Railway
This track between Aviemore and Broomhill dates from 1863.

Aviemore, the commercial centre of the Cairngorms, provides buses to the ski area 13 km (9 miles) away.

Kincraig Highland Wildlife Park
Driving through this park, the visitor can see bison alongside wolves and wild boar. All of these animals were once common in the Highlands.

Rothiemurchus Estate
Highland cattle can be seen among many other creatures at Rothiemurchus. A visitor centre provides guided walks and illustrates life on a Highland estate.

The Cairngorms by Aviemore

Loch Garten Nature Reserve

Ospreys now thrive in this reserve in Abernethy Forest, which was established in 1959 to protect the first pair seen in Britain for 50 years.

GRANTOWN-ON-SPEY

roomhill

A 95

Nethy Bridge

B970

The **Cairngorm Reindeer Centre** provides walks in the hills among Britain's only herd of reindeer.

Skiing

From the Coire Cas car park, a funicular railway can be taken to the restaurant at the summit. There are 28 ski runs in all.

P

CAIRN GORM
▲
1,245 m
(4,084 ft)

EN MACDHUI
▲
1,309 m
(4,296 ft)

CAIRNGORM

MOUNTAINS

Ben MacDhui is Britain's second highest peak, after Ben Nevis.

FLORA OF THE CAIRNGORMS

With mixed woodland at their base and the summits forming a sub-polar plateau, the Cairngorms present a huge variety of flora. Ancient Caledonian pines (once common in the area) survive in Abernethy Forest, while arctic flowers flourish in the heights.

1,200 m (4000 ft)

The Cairngorm plateau holds little life except lichen (Britain's oldest plant), wood rush and cushions of moss campion, which is often completely covered with pink flowers.

1,000 m (3,300 ft)

Shady corries are important areas for alpine plants such as arctic mouse-ear, hare's foot sedge, mountain rock-cress and alpine speedwell.

800 m (2,600 ft)

Pinewoods occupy the higher slopes, revealing purple heather as they become sparser.

600 m (2,000 ft)

Mixed woodland covers the lower ground which is carpeted with heather and deergrass.

400 m (1,300 ft)

200 m (650 ft)

0 m (0 ft)

An idealized section of the Cairngorm plateau

KEY

ℹ	Tourist information
▰▰▰	Major road
▱▱▱	Minor road
▱▱▱	Narrow lane
- -	Footpath
⚜	Viewpoint

Road to the Isles Tour ㉕

This scenic route goes past vast mountain-corridors, breathtaking beaches of white sand and tiny villages, to the town of Mallaig, one of the ferry ports for the isles of Skye, Rum and Eigg. As well as the stunning scenery, the area is steeped in Jacobite history *(see p537)*.

SKYE ⑦

A830

Mallaig ⑦
The Road to the Isles ends at Mallaig, an active little fishing port with a very good harbour and one of the ferry links to Skye *(see pp534–5)*.

Arisaig

⑥

⑤

TIPS FOR DRIVERS

Tour length: 45 miles (72 km).
Stopping-off points: Glenfinnan NTS Visitors' Centre (01397 722 250) explains the Jacobite risings and serves refreshments; the Old Library Lodge, Arisaig, has good Scottish food. (See also pp684–5.)

LOCH MORAR

LOCH EIL

LOCH NAN UAMH

ARDNISH

LOCH AILORT

Morar ⑥
The road continues through Morar, an area renowned for its white sands, and Loch Morar, rumoured to be the home of a 12-m (40-ft) monster known as Morag.

Prince's Cairn ⑤
Crossing the Ardnish Peninsu to Loch Nan Uamh, a cairn marks the spot from which Bonnie Prince Charlie finally left Scotland for France in 174

Oban ㉖

Argyll & Bute. 🚶 8,500. 🚢 🚌 ⛴
ℹ *Argyll Sq (01631 563122).*
www.oban.org.uk

Located on the Firth of Lorne and commanding a magnificent view of the Argyll coast, the bustling port of Oban is a popular destination for travellers on their way to Mull and the Western Isles *(see p529).*

Dominating the skyline is McCaig's Tower, an unfinished Victorian imitation of the Colosseum in Rome. It is worth making the 10-minute climb from the town centre for the sea views alone. Attractions in the town include working centres for glass, pottery and whisky; the Oban distillery produces one of the country's finest malt whiskies *(see p489).* The **Scottish Sealife Sanctuary** rescues injured and orphaned seals and has displays of underwater life. A busy harbour shelters car ferries going to Barra and South Uist, Mull, Tiree and Colonsay islands.

🏛 **Scottish Sealife Sanctuary**
Barcaldine. **Tel** 01631 720386.
⭕ daily. ⬤ 1 Jan, 25 Dec. 🈲 ♿
🍴 🏠 **www**.sealsanctuary.co.uk

Mull ㉗

Argyll & Bute. 🚶 2,800. ⛴ from Oban, Kilchoan, Lochaline. ℹ Main Street, Tobermory (01688 302182).

Most roads on this easily accessible Hebridean island follow the sharply indented rocky coastline, affording wonderful sea views. From Craignure, the Mull and West Highland Railway serves the baronial **Torosay Castle**. A pathway through its gardens is lined with statues, while inside, 19th-century furniture and paintings can be found. On a promontory to the east lies **Duart Castle**, home of the chief of Clan Maclean. Visitors can see the Banqueting Hall and State Rooms in the 13th-century keep. Its dungeons once held prisoners from a Spanish Armada galleon sunk by a Donald Maclean in 1588.

Looking out to sea across Tobermory Bay, Mull

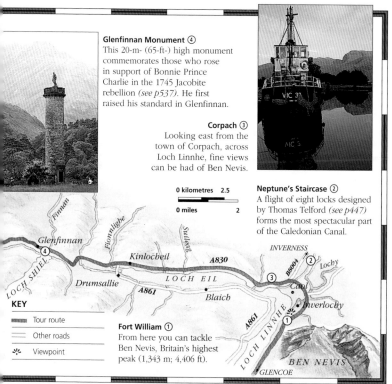

Glenfinnan Monument ④
This 20-m- (65-ft-) high monument
commemorates those who rose
in support of Bonnie Prince
Charlie in the 1745 Jacobite
rebellion *(see p537)*. He first
raised his standard in Glenfinnan.

Corpach ③
Looking east from the
town of Corpach, across
Loch Linnhe, fine views
can be had of Ben Nevis.

Neptune's Staircase ②
A flight of eight locks designed
by Thomas Telford *(see p447)*
forms the most spectacular part
of the Caledonian Canal.

0 kilometres 2.5
0 miles 2

KEY

▬▬▬ Tour route

═══ Other roads

🌿 Viewpoint

Fort William ①
From here you can tackle
Ben Nevis, Britain's highest
peak (1,343 m; 4,406 ft).

Environs: From Fionnphort,
a ferry goes to **Iona**, where St
Columba *(see p525)* began his
mission in Scotland in 563.
North of Iona, the Isle of
Staffa should be visited for
its magnificent **Fingal's Cave**.

⛪ **Torosay Castle**
Off A849, Nr Craignure. *Tel 01680
812421.* **Castle** ◯ *Easter–Oct:
10:30am–5pm daily.* **Gardens**
◯ *10am–5pm daily (dawn–dusk in
winter).* 🏞 ♿ 🖥 🎁 *for groups.*

⛪ **Duart Castle**
Off A849, nr Craignure.
Tel 01680 812309. ◯ *Apr–Oct:
10:30am–5:30pm daily.* 🏞

The ruins of Kilchurn Castle on the shore of Loch Awe

Loch Awe ㉘

Argyll & Bute. 🚆 🚌 *Dalmally.*
ℹ *Inveraray (01499 302063).*
www.loch-awe.com

One of the longest of
Scotland's freshwater lochs,
Loch Awe fills a 25-mile (40-
km) glen in the southwestern
Highlands. A short drive east
of the village of Lochawe

leads to the lochside remains
of **Kilchurn Castle**, abandoned
after being struck by lightning
in the 18th century. Dwarfing
the castle is the huge bulk of
Ben Cruachan, whose summit
can be reached by the narrow
Pass of Brander, in which
Robert the Bruce *(see p482)*
fought the Clan MacDougal in
1308. From the A85, a tunnel
leads to the cavernous
Cruachan Power Station.

Near the village of Taynuilt
the preserved Lorn Furnace at
Bonawe is a reminder of the
iron-smelting industry that
caused the destruction of
much of the area's woodland
in the 18th and 19th centuries.
Marked prehistoric cairns are
found off the A816 between
Kilmartin and Dunadd. The
latter boasts a 6th-century hill
fort from which the Stone of
Destiny *(see p482)* originated.

Inveraray Castle ㉙

Inveraray, Argyll & Bute.
🚆 Arrochar, then bus. **Tel** 01499
302203. ◯ Apr–Oct: 10am–
5:45pm Mon–Sat (Sun: pm only).
🈂 ♿ limited. ▢ ▣ ▯
www.inveraray-castle.com

This multi-turreted mock
Gothic palace is the
family home of the powerful
Clan Campbell who have
been the Dukes of Argyll
since 1701. The castle was
built in 1745 by architects
Roger Morris and William
Adam on the ruins
of a 15th-century castle,
and the conical towers
added later, after a fire in
1877. Magnificent interiors,
designed by Robert Mylne
in the 1770s, form a backdrop to a huge collection
of Oriental and European
porcelain and Regency
furniture and portraits
by Ramsay, Gainsborough
and Raeburn. The Armoury
Hall features a display
of weaponry collected by
the Campbells to fight the
Jacobites *(see p537)*.

Auchindrain Museum ㉚

Inveraray, Argyll & Bute.
Tel 01499 500235. 🚌 Inveraray,
then bus. ◯ Apr–Oct: 10am–
5pm daily. ▯ 🈂 ♿ limited.
www.auchindrain-museum.org.uk

The first open-air museum
in Scotland, Auchindrain
illuminates the working lives
of the kind of farming community that was typical of the
Highlands until the late 19th
century. Originally a township
of some 20 thatched buildings,
the site was communally
farmed by its tenants until
the last one retired in 1962.
Visitors can
wander through
the buildings,

The pinnacled, Gothic exterior of Inveraray Castle

many of which combine living
space, kitchen and cattle shed
under one roof. Some are
furnished with box beds and
old rush lamps. The homes of
Auchindrain are a fascinating
memorial to the time before
the transition from of subsis-
tence to commercial farming.

An old hay turner at the
Auchindrain Museum

Crarae Gardens ㉛

Crarae, Argyll & Bute. **Tel** 01546
886614 or NTS (01852 200366).
🚌 Inveraray, then bus. ◯ 9.30am–
sunset daily. **Visitor Centre** ◯ Easter–
Sep 10am–5pm daily. 🈂 ♿ limited.

Considered the most
beguiling of the gardens of
the West Highlands. the
Crarae Gardens were created
in the 1920s by Lady Grace
Campbell. She was the aunt
of explorer Reginald Farrer,
whose specimens from Tibet
were the beginnings of a
collection of exotic plants.
The gardens are nourished by
the warmth of the Gulf

Stream and the high rainfall.
Although there are many
unusual Himalayan rhodo-
dendrons flourishing here,
the gardens are also home
to exotic plants from various
countries including Tasmania,
New Zealand and the USA.
Plant collectors still contribute
to the gardens, which are
best seen in spring and early
summer against the blue
waters of Loch Fyne.

Jura ㉜

Argyll & Bute. 🚶 200. 🚢 from
Kennacraig to Islay, then Islay to Jura.
🛈 Bowmore (01496 810254).

Barren, mountainous and
overrun by red deer, the isle
of Jura has only one road
which connects the single
village of Craighouse to the
Islay ferry. Though walking is
restricted during the stalking
(deer hunting) season between August and October,
the island offers superb hill-
walking, especially on the
slopes of the three main peaks,
known as the Paps of Jura.
The tallest of these is Beinn
An Oir at 784 m (2571 ft). Beyond the northern tip of the isle
are the notorious whirlpools
of Corryvreckan. The novelist
George Orwell (who came to
the island to write his final
novel, *1984*) nearly lost his
life here in 1946 when he fell
into the water. A legend tells

Lagavulin distillery, producer of one Scotland's finest malts, on Islay

For hotels and restaurants in this region see pp596–599 and pp649–651

Mist crowning the Paps of Jura, seen at sunset across the Sound of Islay

of Prince Breackan who, to win the hand of a princess, tried to keep his boat anchored in the whirlpool for three days, held by ropes made of hemp, wool and maidens' hair. The Prince drowned when a single rope, containing the hair of a girl who had been untrue, finally broke.

Islay ❸❸

Argyll & Bute. 🚶 3,500. ⛴ from Kennacraig. 🛈 The Square, Bowmore (0870 7200617). www.isle-of-islay.com

The most southerly of the Western Isles, Islay (pronounced 'Eyeluh') is the home of respected Highland single malt whiskies Lagavulin and Laphroaig. Most of the island's distilleries produce heavily peated malts with a distinctive tang of the sea. The Georgian village of Bowmore has the island's oldest distillery and a circular church designed to minimize the Devil's possible lurking-places. The **Museum of Islay Life** in Port Charlotte contains fascinating information on social and natural history. Seven miles (11 km) east of Port Ellen stands the Kildalton Cross. A block of local green stone adorned with Old Testament scenes, it is one of the most impressive 8th-

century Celtic crosses in Britain. Worth a visit for its archaeological and historical interest is the medieval stronghold of the Lords of the Isles, **Finlaggan**. Islay's beaches support a variety of bird life, some of which can be observed at the RSPB reserve at Gruinart.

🏛 **Museum of Islay Life**
Port Charlotte. **Tel** 01496 850358. 🕐 Easter–Oct: 10am–5pm Mon–Sat, 2–5pm Sun. 🚫 ♿

Kintyre ❸❹

Argyll & Bute. 🚶 6,000. ⛴ Oban. 🚍 Campbeltown. 🛈 MacKinnon House, The Pier, Campbeltown (01586 552056). www.kintyre.org

A long, narrow peninsula stretching far south of Glasgow, Kintyre has superb views across to the islands of Gigha, Islay and Jura. The 9 mile (14 km) Crinan Canal,

opened in 1801, is a delightful inland waterway, its 15 locks bustling with pleasure craft in the summer. The town of Tarbert (meaning "isthmus" in Gaelic) takes its name from the neck on which it stands, which is narrow enough to drag a boat across between Loch Fyne and West Loch Tarbert. This feat was first achieved by the Viking King Magnus Barfud who, in 1198, was granted by treaty as much land as he could sail around. Travelling south past Campbeltown, the B842 ends at the headland known as the Mull of Kintyre, which was made famous when former Beatle Paul McCartney commercialized a traditional pipe tune of the same name. Westward lies the isle of Rathlin, where Robert the Bruce *(see p482)* learned patience in his struggles against the English by watching a spider weaving a web in a cave.

Fishing boats and yachts moored at Tarbert harbour, Kintyre

TRAVELLERS' NEEDS

WHERE TO STAY

Whatever your budget or accommodation preferences, you should be able to find somewhere to suit you from the large choice given in the hotel listings section that follows *(see pp556–99)*. The listings include over 500 suggestions, ranging from palatial five-star establishments to humble guest-houses. The common factor in this selection is that they are all good of their kind, offering distinctive character or exceptional qualities of hospi-

Hotel doorman, London

tality, facilities or value for money. Location is another prime consideration for inclusion. All the hotels and guesthouses listed make convenient touring bases for one or more of the destinations featured in this book, or have attractive or interesting settings enjoyable in their own right. On the next few pages we outline some of the types of accommodation available in Britain, along with various aspects of choosing, booking and paying for somewhere to stay.

COUNTRY-HOUSE HOTELS

The quintessentially British country-house hotel has proliferated in the last few decades. Many indifferent hotels try to claim the title with a cursory decorative makeover, but the genuine article stands head and shoulders above them. Individual examples vary widely, but the best country-house hotels are usually set in buildings of architectural or historic interest filled with antiques or high-quality traditional furnishings. They generally have extensive grounds, but are not always in deeply rural locations. Comfort, even luxury, is assured, along with good food and service – frequently with a high price tag. Many such hotels are still owned and personally managed by resident proprietors; others belong to groups or chains.

BOUTIQUE AND DESIGNER HOTELS

There is a new breed of sophisticated, contemporary hotel that has been making waves in Britain for some years now. These ultra-cool temples of style revel in innovative architecture, funky décor and hip high-tech gadgetry. Most exude an air of uncluttered minimalism, and some have outstanding restaurants. The best-known examples are perhaps in London (the Metropolitan, *p557,* for instance, or the Sanderson, *p558),* but they can be found elsewhere too, usually in city centres. Trend-setting, upmarket micro-chains like **Malmaison** or **Hotel du Vin** could perhaps be included in this category. Most of these hotels are expensive, but facilities, furnishings, service and privacy justify the cost.

Atholl Palace Hotel *(see p599)*

HOTEL GROUPS

New hotel groups have taken the place of many of the long-established names, providing reliably standardized accommodation at all price levels in most parts of Britain. The majority of chain hotels (operated by the same company under identical corporate branding) lie in accessible, convenient locations. Though lacking in much individuality, they are practical and efficiently run, and usually represent good value for money.

Budget chains offering no-frills, motel-lodge-style accommodation include **Ibis**, **Travelodge** and **Premier Travel Inn**; further up the scale are mid-market chains like **Holiday Inn** or **Novotel**. Chain-hotel rates generally don't include breakfast, but look out for inclusive leisure-

Buckland Manor *(see p576),* **Worcestershire**

◁ **The 11th-century ruins of Corfe Castle, Dorset**

The Swan at Lavenham, Suffolk *(see p565)*, a converted coaching inn

break rates at pricier chains like **Moat House**.

Hotel consortiums – groups of similar but individually owned hotels which market themselves under the same umbrella – include **Best Western** and **Pride of Britain**. There's also **Wolsey Lodges**, a group of private houses, many beautifully furnished and often sited in buildings of notable architectural or historic interest.

INNS AND PUBS WITH ROOMS

The coaching inn is a familiar concept in Britain. Many of these fine old hostelries date from the 18th century, though some are even older, such as The George of Stamford *(see p580)*, and often provide reliable restaurants, traditional décor and a warm and friendly atmosphere.

Other types of pub or inn now offer accommodation and reputable food, and many have become much more welcoming to families. Britain's best inns are very comfortable and stylish and bear comparison with any good hotel. Some budget hotel chains, such as the already mentioned Premier Travel Inn, specialize in adding purpose-built accommodation blocks to existing branded dining pubs like Beefeater or Vintage Inns.

BED-AND-BREAKFASTS AND GUEST HOUSES

The B&B is probably the best-known and certainly the most widely used type of budget accommodation in Britain. These establishments are generally family-owned private homes or farmhouses. Accommodation and facilities tend to be simple (bedrooms may not have TV, telephones, or en-suite bathrooms, for instance), but the best can be quite sophisticated. Prices include breakfast (generally a traditional British fry-up, but other options are usually available as well).

Many B&Bs are reluctant to accept credit cards or travellers' cheques, or may charge a premium for doing so. It's advisable to have some alternative method of payment, preferably cash or, for British residents, a personal cheque backed by a cheque guarantee card. Any regional tourist office should be able to supply a list of local registered B&Bs on request, though they cannot make specific recommendations, and may charge a fee or a commission for making bookings on your behalf.

HOTEL GRADINGS

Recent but only partially successful attempts have been made to harmonize the confusing and often conflicting systems of accommodation classification used by the various tourist boards and motoring organizations, such as the AA and RAC. In England, hotel gradings are now based on a system of one to five stars awarded for facilities and service (the more stars, the more luxurious you can expect your hotel to be). Guesthouses and B&Bs are graded with one to five diamonds, a quality score which is based on various aspects of the accommodation, including cleanliness and hospitality. Special awards (gold and silver, ribbons, rosettes, eggcups, etc) are given for excellence in certain categories, such as an exceptional breakfast or a warm welcome. Scotland and Wales have their own quality-based gradings.

Hintlesham Hall, Suffolk *(see p564)*

PRICES AND BOOKINGS

Make sure you understand clearly what terms you are being offered when you book. Some hotels just quote room rates, others quote a B&B or half board (dinner, bed and breakfast) rate per person. Rates are generally inclusive of VAT and service but some top-range hotels make additional charges; most charge hefty single-person supplements.

Prices in London start at around £80 per night for a standard en-suite double room, including breakfast, but could be well over £200 (without breakfast) at the top end of the scale. Outside London, prices tend to be cheaper, starting from around £60 for an en-suite double

The folly of Doyden Castle, Cornwall, now a National Trust holiday cottage

The elegant hallway of the Gore Hotel in London *(see p560)*

with breakfast. Bed-and-breakfast accommodation outside London starts from around £35 per person per night (though prices vary seasonally and regionally). Farm guesthouses (which often include dinner) can be very good value, at around £30 for half board per person.

Most hotels request confirmation in writing and a deposit in advance (a credit card number will generally do). E-mail bookings are now commonplace, and some hotels have an on-line booking facility. Websites are usually updated more often than hotel brochures and tariffs. Business or chain hotels often give big discounts; contact central reservations as well as the hotel

itself to see which one will give you the best deal. Sometimes it is also possible to negotiate a discount during the low season.

Any hotel booking is a legally binding contract. If you don't show up, the full cost of your stay may be charged. Most hotels will refund your deposit if they are able to relet the room, but some will charge a penalty, depending how close to your stay you cancel. Most travel insurance policies cover cancellation charges for pre-booked UK hotel stays of more than two days, if you have a satisfactory reason.

Watch out for those hidden extras. Telephone charges from hotel rooms have a high mark-up, and rates quoted per unit do not always indicate too clearly how much time you get for your money. Consider using a lobby payphone instead.

Certain chains have a regrettable policy of charging meals or other extras to your credit card weeks after you have left the hotel; check your card statement carefully.

There is no need to tip staff unless they go out of their way to perform some very exceptional duty, such as booking theatre tickets or restaurants for you.

Roadside signboard for bed-and-breakfast

SELF CATERING

Self catering has many attractions, especially for families on a budget and with young children. Tourist boards give accommodation a one to five star rating for quality and facilities, much the same as for hotels. The range of places to let for holiday rentals is huge, from luxury apartments to log cabins or converted farm buildings. Character properties are available from conservation organizations such as the **Landmark Trust**, which restores buildings of historic or architectural interest and makes them available for short-term lets, or the **National Trust** *(see p29)*, which has a number of holiday cottages on its estates. They tend to be very popular, so book well ahead.

Annually updated self-catering guides are a useful source of listings. Also try specialist agencies, tour operators and the small ads in newspapers. Tourist offices can supply up-to-date regional lists and can also offer a booking service.

Confirm what is included in the price (cleaning, electricity, etc.) and check whether any extra fees, deposits or insurance charges will be added to the bill.

CARAVANNING, CAMPING AND MOTOR HOMES

Most of Britain's campsites and caravan (trailer) parks open only for about six months of the year (typically from Easter to October), but you will need to make reservations in advance. Helpful organizations in Britain include the **Camping and Caravanning Club** and the Caravan Club, which publish lists of their member parks and operate their own grading systems.

Camping or caravanning pitches typically cost between £15 and £20 per night. The **Forestry Commission** operates a number of sites in scenic woodland locations throughout the UK.

Motor homes give greater freedom to explore at your own pace and a wider choice of places to stay – including most campsites and caravan parks. Some operators will let you pick up your vehicle directly from an airport or ferry terminal. The **Motor Caravanners' Club** produces a useful monthly magazine.

Campsite, Ogwen Valley, Snowdonia

DISABLED TRAVELLERS

All the UK's tourist boards now provide detailed information about disabled access in their accommodation and sight-seeing guides, and can send further information on request. National Accessible Scheme gradings are awarded to properties inspected and approved under the Tourism for All initiative for various categories of disability.

For more information on these gradings, or other advice on accommodation and travel for disabled visitors, contact **Tourism for All**. Another useful organization is **RADAR** (the Royal Association for Disability and Rehabilitation), which publishes a yearly *Holidays in the British Isles: A Guide for Disabled People*. The listings on pp556–99 indicate which hotels have wheelchair access, but you are strongly advised to check when booking that it matches your needs. The same is true of camping and caravan sites.

DIRECTORY

For more tips on different types of accommodation, see www.visitbritain.com

HOTELS

Accor Hotels
(Ibis, Novotel)
Tel 0870 600 961.
www.accorhotels.com

Best Western
Tel 08454 567050.
www.bestwestern.co.uk

Book Direct Rooms
www.bookdirectrooms.
com

Hilton International
Tel 0870 590 9090.
www.hilton.co.uk

Holiday Inn
Tel 0871 423 4876.
www.holidayinn.co.uk

Hotel du Vin
Tel 01962 841414
or 0845 365 4247.
www.hotelduvin.com

Malmaison
Tel 08453 654247.
www.malmaison.com

Premier Travel Inn
Tel 0870 242 8000.
www.premiertravel
inn.com

Pride of Britain
Tel 0870 609 3012.
www.prideofbritain
hotels.com

QMH Hotels
Tel 01708 730522.
www.qmh-hotels.com

Travelodge
www.travelodge.co.uk

Wolsey Lodges
Tel 01473 822058.
www.wolsey-lodges.
co.uk

CARAVANNING, CAMPING AND MOTOR HOMES

Camping and Caravanning Club
Tel 0845 130 7633.
www.campingand
caravanningclub.co.uk

Forestry Commission
Tel 0845 130 8223.
www.forestholidays.co.uk

Motor Caravanners' Club
Tel 020 8893 3883.
www.motorcaravanners.eu

SELF-CATERING

Landmark Trust
Tel 01628 825925.
www.landmarktrust.
org.uk

National Trust
Tel 0844 800 2070.
www.nationaltrust
cottages.co.uk

National Trust for Scotland
Wemyss Hse, 28 Charlotte Square, Edinburgh EH2 4ET. *Tel* 0844 493 2100.
www.nts.org.uk

Snowdonia Tourist Services
High Street, Porthmadog, Gwynedd LL49 9PG. *Tel* 01766 513829. www.
snowdoniatourist.com

DISABLED TRAVELLERS

RADAR
Unit 12, City Forum, 250 City Road, London, EC1V 8AF. *Tel* 020 7250 3222.
www.radar.org.uk

Tourism for All
c/o Vitalise, Shap Road Industrial Estate, Kendal, Cumbria LA9 6NZ.
Tel 0845 124 9971.
www.tourismforall.
org.uk

Choosing a Hotel

The hotels in this guide have been selected across a wide price range for their excellent, facilities, good value and location. Many also have a recommended restaurant. The chart lists the hotels by region, starting with London. For more details on restaurants see pages 608–651.

PRICE CATEGORIES
For a standard double room per night, inclusive of service charge and any additional taxes such as VAT:

£ under £65
££ £65–£100
£££ £100–£150
££££ £150–£200
£££££ £200 plus

LONDON

WEST END AND WESTMINSTER Dover Hotel   ££

42–44 Belgrave Rd, SW1 **Tel** 020 7821 9085 **Fax** 020 7834 6425 **Rooms** 34   **Map** 18 F2

This well-maintained hotel is terrific value for money. It may not be luxurious once past the grand stucco façade, but the decor is refreshingly modern and every room has satellite TV and pristine en suite shower and WC. It's handy for Victoria Station and Pimlico's many pubs and cafés. **www.dover-hotel.co.uk**

WEST END AND WESTMINSTER B&B Belgravia   £££

64–66 Ebury St, SW1 **Tel** 020 7259 8570 **Fax** 020 7259 8591 **Rooms** 17   **Map** 18 E2

Recently renovated to provide a contemporary interior, this Victorian building caters for the discerning traveller's every need. Facilities include flat screen TVs in all rooms and free internet access, and with cooked breakfasts made to order you will really feel at home. **www.bb-belgravia.com**

WEST END AND WESTMINSTER Citadines Covent Garden/Holborn   £££

94–99 High Holborn, WC1 **Tel** 020 7395 8800 **Fax** 020 7395 8799 **Rooms** 192   **Map** 11 C1

This central branch of the French apart'hotel chain underwent a refurbishment in 2009. It offers pleasant, good-value accommodation for up to four people. Studios or one-bedroom apartments have kitchenettes, dining tables, satellite TVs and hi-fis. There are also handy business facilities and an on-site breakfast room. **www.citadines.com**

WEST END AND WESTMINSTER Elizabeth Hotel and Apartments   £££

37 Eccleston Square, SW1 **Tel** 020 7828 6812 **Fax** 020 7828 6814 **Rooms** 37 & 5 apartments   **Map** 18 E2

The rates are surprisingly reasonable in this elegant town house hotel on a grand garden square, Winston Churchill used to live a couple of doors down. Rooms are simple yet tastefully furnished and guests have access to the private gardens and stately drawing room with newspapers, tea, coffee and biscuits. **www.elizabethhotel.com**

WEST END AND WESTMINSTER City Inn Westminster   £££££

30 John Islip St, SW1 **Tel** 020 7630 1000 **Fax** 020 7233 7575 **Rooms** 460   **Map** 19 B2

Around the corner from Tate Britain, City Inn is unpretentiously modern. Rooms have floor-to-ceiling windows, some of which command Thames views, and luxuries such as robes, flatscreen TVs and DVD players. There's a red cocktail lounge and café with outside tables. Enquire about cheap weekend deals. **www.cityinn.com**

WEST END AND WESTMINSTER Claridges   £££££

Brook St, W1 **Tel** 020 7629 8860 **Fax** 020 7499 2210 **Rooms** 203   **Map** 10 E2

Favoured by the European aristocracy in the 19th century, Empress Eugènie wintered here. Nowadays it attracts show business *glitterati* and business clients alike. Rooms range from Victorian to contemporary by way of fabulous Art Deco suites. Gordon Ramsay's fêted restaurant and a smart bar are further draws. **www.claridges.co.uk**

WEST END AND WESTMINSTER Covent Garden Hotel   £££££

10 Monmouth St, WC2 **Tel** 020 7806 1000 **Fax** 020 7806 1100 **Rooms** 58   **Map** 11 B2

This exquisite hotel's Covent Garden location is one reason why it's popular with thespians. Part of the Firmdale chain, it is decorated in contemporary-English style with antiques and fresh fabrics. Brasserie Max is a popular meeting spot and films are shown in the luxurious screening room at weekends. **www.firmdalehotels.com**

WEST END AND WESTMINSTER Metropolitan   £££££

Old Park Lane, W1 **Tel** 020 7447 1047 **Fax** 020 7447 1147 **Rooms** 150   **Map** 10 D3

The Metropolitan redefined the London luxury hotel when it opened in 1997 and its blond wood, pale fabrics and large plate-glass windows still epitomise modern chic. With holistic spa treatments, a top Japanese restaurant upstairs and entry to the exclusive Met Bar, you won't have to stray far. **www.metropolitan.co.uk**

WEST END AND WESTMINSTER One Aldwych   £££££

1 Aldwych, WC2 **Tel** 020 7300 1000 **Fax** 020 7300 1001 **Rooms** 105   **Map** 11 C2

A grand contemporary hotel in former Edwardian newspaper offices. Impressive details include original art and tarazzo-stone bathrooms with heated floors and mini TVs. There's a spacious health club with a swimming pool, two fabulous restaurants and the buzzing, high-ceilinged Lobby Bar. **www.onealdwych.com**

Key to Symbols *see back cover flap*

WEST END AND WESTMINSTER Radisson Edwardian Hampshire ££££££

31–36 Leicester Square, WC2 **Tel** *020 7839 9399* **Fax** *020 7930 8122* **Rooms** *124* **Map** *11 B2*

Colourful Leicester Square is a good base if you want to make the most of London's nightlife, as it's well placed for the theatre district, bars, clubs and restaurants. This luxurious Radisson has designer bedrooms with Philippe Starck bathrooms and Bose sound systems in the suites. Conference rooms also available. **www.radissonedwardian.com**

WEST END AND WESTMINSTER Ritz ££££££

150 Piccadilly, W1 **Tel** *020 7493 8181* **Fax** *020 7493 2687* **Rooms** *136* **Map** *10 F3*

There are two staff for every room in this famous grand hotel on the edge of Green Park. You can even have your luggage unpacked for you. Rooms are in lavish Louis XVI style with antique furnishings and gold leaf, plus all mod cons. The Rivoli Bar has been restored to its Art Deco splendour. **www.theritzlondon.com**

WEST END AND WESTMINSTER Savoy ££££££

Strand, WC2 **Tel** *020 7836 4343* **Fax** *020 7240 6040* **Rooms** *263* **Map** *11 C2*

This legendary hotel was an afterthought, Richard D'Oyly Carte capitalized on the success of his Savoy Theatre by providing a place to stay. The rest is history. Monet painted the Thames view from his window, Elton John flooded a bathroom and the dry martini was made popular in the bar. There's a rooftop pool as well. **www.fairmont.com/savoy**

WEST END AND WESTMINSTER The Connaught ££££££

Carlos Place, W1 **Tel** *020 7499 7070* **Fax** *020 7495 3262* **Rooms** *92* **Map** *10 E3*

The Connaught maintains its traditional charm while moving with the times. Facilities include butler service and a state-of-the-art gym. The interior feels less stuffy since many of the public rooms, including the Grill and the Connaught Bar, were restyled by renowned designer Nina Campbell. **www.theconnaught.com**

WEST END AND WESTMINSTER The Dorchester ££££££

Park Lane, W1 **Tel** *020 7629 8888* **Fax** *020 7629 8080* **Rooms** *250* **Map** *10 D3*

The epitome of the glamorous luxury hotel, with an outrageously lavish lobby and a star-studded history, the Dorchester has recently been revamped but maintains its tasteful floral bedrooms. The Art Deco-style marble baths are probably the deepest in London. For even more pampering, pop down to the fabulous Art Deco spa. **www.thedorchester.com**

SOUTH KENSINGTON AND HYDE PARK Edward Lear ££

28–30 Seymour St, W1 **Tel** *020 7402 5401* **Fax** *020 7706 3766* **Rooms** *31* **Map** *9 C2*

This characterful small hotel is in the former home of Victorian poet and artist Edward Lear. Rooms are tidy and spacious with satellite TVs. Opt for en suite or shared facilities to keep the cost down. There's a computer with free Internet access and leather seating in the pleasant guests' lounge. **www.edlear.co.uk**

SOUTH KENSINGTON AND HYDE PARK Knightsbridge Green Hotel ££££

159 Knightsbridge, SW1 **Tel** *020 7584 6274* **Fax** *020 7225 1635* **Rooms** *29* **Map** *9 C5*

A shopaholic's dream, this well-kept hotel is right on Knightsbridge, and rates are reasonable. The tidy, modern rooms are regularly upgraded and feature air conditioning, satellite TVs and wireless internet access. Some have views over Hyde Park. There's also a small business centre on-site. **www.thekghotel.com**

SOUTH KENSINGTON AND HYDE PARK The Rockwell ££££

181–183 Cromwell Rd, SW5 **Tel** *020 7244 2000* **Fax** *020 7244 2001* **Rooms** *40* **Map** *16 D2*

Sumptuous and classy, the rooms at The Rockwell are a haven from the bustle of the capital. Egyptian cotton sheets and plush feather pillows, combined with bathroom fittings by Philippe Starck and Hans Grohe, provide guests with a thoroughly rejuvenating experience. **www.therockwell.com**

SOUTH KENSINGTON AND HYDE PARK The Capital Hotel ££££££

22–24 Basil St, SW3 **Tel** *020 7589 5171* **Fax** *020 7225 0011* **Rooms** *49* **Map** *9 C5*

Situated between Harrods and Harvey Nichols, this service-oriented hotel even offers personal shoppers and jogging partners. Its Michelin two-starred restaurant has been refurbished in 1940s-influenced style. Bedrooms feature king-size beds, designer fabrics and the latest technology. **www.capitalhotel.co.uk**

SOUTH KENSINGTON AND HYDE PARK The Franklin Hotel ££££££

22–28 Egerton Gardens, SW3 **Tel** *020 7584 5533* **Fax** *020 7584 5449* **Rooms** *47* **Map** *17 B1*

Occupying four 19th-century town houses in a quiet street, the Franklin creates the pleasant illusion of chic London living. Rooms (all en suite) are designed to combine their Victorian heritage with modern European comforts. Best of all are the large, secluded gardens at the back, shared with well-heeled residents. **www.franklinhotel.co.uk**

SOUTH KENSINGTON AND HYDE PARK The Halkin ££££££

5 Halkin St, SW1 **Tel** *020 7333 1000* **Fax** *020 7333 1100* **Rooms** *41* **Map** *10 D5*

Modern comforts meet Eastern serenity at this gracious luxury hotel. Warm wood, curving lines and creamy bed linen are accented by Southeast Asian art handpicked by the Singaporean owner. Be sure to have a meal at Nahm, it's the only Michelin-starred Thai restaurant outside Thailand. **www.halkin.como.bz**

REGENT'S PARK AND BLOOMSBURY Crescent Hotel ££

49–50 Cartwright Gardens, WC1 **Tel** *020 7387 1515* **Fax** *020 7383 2054* **Rooms** *27* **Map** *3 B4*

One of several hotels in this striking Regency Street, the Crescent has been run by the same family since the 1950s. Most of the well-kept bedrooms have en suite facilities. Soft drinks and snacks are served in the lounge, and guests can use the tennis courts in the private gardens. **www.crescenthoteloflondon.com**

REGENT'S PARK AND BLOOMSBURY Hotel Cavendish ⓔⓔ

75 Gower St, WC1 **Tel** *020 7636 9079* **Fax** *020 7580 3609* **Rooms** *31* **Map** *3 A5*

This characterful B&B near London University has a fascinating history, DH Lawrence and the Beatles stayed here once. Rooms are simple yet comfortably furnished, and some have original fireplaces. Original artworks brighten up the breakfast room and there's a pretty garden as well. Shared facilities available. **www.hotelcavendish.com**

REGENT'S PARK AND BLOOMSBURY 22 York Street 🚹 ⓔⓔⓔ

22 York St, W1 **Tel** *020 7224 2990* **Fax** *020 7224 1990* **Rooms** *10* **Map** *1 C5*

This beautiful property is a cut above most B&Bs. Liz and Michael Callis ensure that rooms in these two immaculately preserved Georgian houses are spotless and stylishly furnished with antiques and French quilts. A gourmet continental breakfast is served in the rustic kitchen. **www.22yorkstreet.co.uk**

REGENT'S PARK AND BLOOMSBURY Euston Square Hotel 🔲🍴🚹 ⓔⓔⓔ

152–156 North Gower St, NW1 **Tel** *020 7388 0099* **Fax** *020 7383 7165* **Rooms** *75* **Map** *3 A4*

A chic stopover close to Euston Station. Rooms may be on the small side, but they are stylishly kitted out in dark wood and cream leather, with flatscreen TVs, a music library and tasteful tiled bathrooms. Complimentary papers and squashy sofas are on offer in the airy lounge and there's also a restaurant. **www.euston-square-hotel.com**

REGENT'S PARK AND BLOOMSBURY Durrants Hotel 🔲🍴🚹🗐🚹 ⓔⓔⓔⓔ

26–32 George St, W1 **Tel** *020 7935 8131* **Fax** *020 7487 3510* **Rooms** *92* **Map** *10 D1*

Established in 1790, Durrants occupies a row of terraced houses and its warren of creaky rooms is delightfully old fashioned. Decor is traditional, old prints and antiques, but TVs are hidden in cabinets and bathrooms are modern. The restaurant and bar are period pieces. Only a few rooms are air conditioned. **www.durrantshotel.co.uk**

REGENT'S PARK AND BLOOMSBURY Charlotte Street Hotel 🔲🅿🍴🚹🗐🚹 ⓔⓔⓔⓔⓔ

15 Charlotte St, W1 **Tel** *020 7806 2000* **Fax** *020 7806 2002* **Rooms** *52* **Map** *11 A1*

The ground floor bar is always buzzing with local workers as well as guests in this exquisitely designed hotel in a street full of restaurants. Reflecting the area's history, its decor nods to the Bloomsbury Set period with original artworks by Vanessa Bell and others. Weekend films in the screening room. **www.charlottestreethotel.com**

REGENT'S PARK AND BLOOMSBURY Sanderson 🔲🅿🍴🚹🗐🚹 ⓔⓔⓔⓔⓔ

50 Berners St, W1 **Tel** *020 7300 1400* **Fax** *020 7300 1401* **Rooms** *150* **Map** *10 F1*

The Sanderson's witty decor, red lips sofa and a framed portrait that seems to hang in mid-air, is like a surreal stage set. Rooms have every comfort, and the Malaysian restaurant, Suki, and two sophisticated cocktail bars are destinations in their own right. The Agua spa offers holistic pampering. **www.sandersonlondon.com**

REGENT'S PARK AND BLOOMSBURY Sherlock Holmes Hotel 🔲🍴🚹🗐🚹 ⓔⓔⓔⓔⓔ

108 Baker St, W1 **Tel** *020 7486 6161* **Fax** *020 7958 5211* **Rooms** *119* **Map** *1 C5*

The name may suggest a tacky theme hotel, yet this is anything but that. You enter this Baker Street boutique hotel via its stylish bar. Contemporary rooms, many with wooden floors, are softened with tactile throws and cushions; there are thoughtful details such as European and US sockets. The gym has spa facilities. **www.parkplaza.com**

REGENT'S PARK AND BLOOMSBURY The Langham, London 🔲🍴🏊🚹🗐🚹 ⓔⓔⓔⓔⓔ

1C Portland Place, W1 **Tel** *020 7636 1000* **Fax** *020 7323 2340* **Rooms** *382* **Map** *10 E1*

The Langham was Europe's first grand hotel when it opened in 1865 and still offers an ultra-luxurious experience behind its sprawling Victorian façade. Rooms achieve a tasteful middle ground between modern and traditional and there are extensive spa facilities including a swimming pool. Near Regent's Park. **www.langhamhotels.com**

THE CITY AND SOUTHWARK Travel Inn London County Hall 🔲🍴🚹 ⓔⓔⓔ

Belvedere Rd, SE1 **Tel** *0870 238 3300* **Fax** *020 7902 1619* **Rooms** *313* **Map** *12 D5*

This branch of the budget Premier Inn chain is housed in the massive former County Hall on the Thames. The more expensive Marriott, which shares the building, has all the river views, but it's a good-value option next to the London Eye, near Waterloo and the Southbank arts complex. Wireless Internet on-site. **www.premierinn.com**

THE CITY AND SOUTHWARK The Zetter 🔲🍴🚹🗐🚹 ⓔⓔⓔⓔ

86–88 Clerkenwell Rd, EC1 **Tel** *020 7324 4444* **Fax** *020 7324 4445* **Rooms** *59* **Map** *4 F4*

In an area known for its loft apartments, this is a loft hotel in a 19th-century warehouse. Rooms have exposed brick, quirky 1970s furniture, old Penguin books, hot-water bottles and high-tech extras, while vending machines on each floor dispense necessities. Hip Italian restaurant at street level. **www.thezetter.com**

THE CITY AND SOUTHWARK Andaz Liverpool Street 🔲🅿🍴🚹🗐🚹 ⓔⓔⓔⓔⓔ

40 Liverpool St, EC2 **Tel** *020 7961 1234* **Fax** *020 7961 1235* **Rooms** *267* **Map** *13 C1*

This magnificent 19th-century railway hotel has been given a 21st-century makeover. The bedrooms have all been designed to create the ultimate modern hotel experience, and there are four fabulous eateries and three bars. Special weekend deals are available. **www.london.liverpoolstreet.andaz.com**

THE CITY AND SOUTHWARK Novotel London City South 🔲🅿🍴🚹🗐🚹 ⓔⓔⓔⓔ

53–61 Southwark Bridge Rd, SE1 **Tel** *020 7089 0400* **Fax** *020 7089 0410* **Rooms** *182* **Map** *13 A3*

Billed as a "New Generation" Novotel, the interior has an airy, minimalist feel. Rooms are equipped with extras such as wireless Internet, minibar and even a radio in the bathroom. The fitness centre has a sauna and steam room, and the location is convenient for the venues and galleries of the South Bank. **www.novotel.com**

Key to Price Guide *see p556* **Key to Symbols** *see back cover flap*

THE CITY AND SOUTHWARK Rookery

₤₤₤₤₤

12 Peter's Lane, Cowcross St, EC1 **Tel** *020 7336 0931* **Fax** *020 7336 0932* **Rooms** *33* **Map** *4 F5*

Occupying six Georgian houses and shops (with faded butcher's and baker's signs still visible on some), this Dickensian hideaway retains many original features, such as flagstone floors in the hall and ceiling beams in some of the rooms. Decorated with antiques throughout, it also offers all the latest technology. **www.rookeryhotel.com**

FURTHER AFIELD Garden Court Hotel

₤₤

30–31 Kensington Gardens Square, W2 **Tel** *020 7229 2553* **Fax** *020 7727 2749* **Rooms** *32* **Map** *8 D2*

An antique Beefeater guards the airy lobby of this well-maintained family hotel on a lovely garden square. The rooms of this Victorian townhouse are tastefully furnished and to keep the cost down, you can opt for shared facilities. Breakfast is included. Good value and close to Portobello Market. **www.gardencourthotel.co.uk**

FURTHER AFIELD Hampstead Village Guesthouse

P ⚡   **₤₤**

2 Kemplay Rd, NW3 **Tel** *020 7435 8679* **Rooms** *9*

This Victorian home, in the picturesque village of Hampstead, is intriguingly cluttered with antiques and curios. Breakfast is served in the garden in summer, English weather permitting. Rooms are equipped with hot-water bottles and fridge. The rates are cheaper if you forego en suite facilities. Non-smoking. **www.hampsteadguesthouse.com**

FURTHER AFIELD Rushmore

⚡   **₤₤**

11 Trebovir Rd, SW5 **Tel** *020 7370 3839* **Fax** *020 7370 0274* **Rooms** *22* **Map** *15 C2*

Like the nearby Mayflower, the Rushmore is proof that accommodation doesn't have to be expensive to be stylish. Each room in this Victorian townhouse has been designed in a different style; even the bathrooms have been customized to fit in with the mood. Breakfast is served in a chic conservatory. **www.rushmore-hotel.co.uk**

FURTHER AFIELD Stylotel

⚡ P   **₤₤**

160–162 Sussex Gardens, W2 **Tel** *020 7723 1026* **Fax** *020 7262 2983* **Rooms** *40* **Map** *9 A2*

Offering some of the cheapest rates in central London, Stylotel is true to its name, although the high-tech style may not suit all tastes. Rooms have wooden floors, aluminium walls, light-box bedside tables and futuristic bathrooms. There's a groovy lounge with curved stainless steel bar and blue leather seats. **www.stylotel.com**

FURTHER AFIELD The London B&B Agency

₤₤

71 Fellows Rd, NW3 **Tel** *020 7586 2768* **Fax** *020 7586 6567*

This accommodation agency offers a vast selection of bed-and-breakfast lodgings throughout London at affordable prices. Among their offers is a gated house near Highgate Village in north London, with luxury bathroom and access to a communal swimming pool. All bookings must go through the agency. **www.londonbb.com**

FURTHER AFIELD Guesthouse West

☰ ♿   **₤₤₤**

163–165 Westbourne Grove, W11 **Tel** *020 7792 9800* **Fax** *020 7792 9797* **Rooms** *20* **Map** *7 C2*

Formerly the Westbourne, Guesthouse West is a budget-conscious design hotel in an Edwardian house. Minimalist dark wood and beige rooms boast high-tech entertainment systems and Molton Brown toiletries. The hip Parlour Bar has terrace tables and Westbourne Grove's bars and boutiques are on the doorstep. **www.guesthousewest.com**

FURTHER AFIELD Mayflower Hotel

⚡ P ⚡   **₤₤₤**

26–28 Trebovir Rd, SW5 **Tel** *020 7370 0991* **Fax** *020 7370 0994* **Rooms** *48* **Map** *16 D2*

This beautifully furnished, budget-boutique hotel is a cut above the rest. The spacious, contemporary rooms have wooden floors and Eastern elements such as elaborately carved beds and rich silks. Marble bathrooms, ceiling fans and CD players are luxurious perks. There are also 35 tasteful apartments nearby. **www.mayflower-group.co.uk**

FURTHER AFIELD Mornington

⚡ ⚡   **₤₤₤**

12 Lancaster Gate, W2 **Tel** *020 7262 7361* **Fax** *020 7706 1028* **Rooms** *66* **Map** *8 F2*

This formerly Swedish-owned hotel is now part of the quality Best Western chain. Bedrooms in the grand Victorian building near Hyde Park maintain a light, airy Scandinavian feel and a buffet smorgasbord-style breakfast caters to the many Swedish clientele. Inquire about special rates. **www.bw-morningtonhotel.co.uk**

FURTHER AFIELD Pavilion Hotel

⚡ P   **₤₤₤**

34–36 Sussex Gardens, W2 **Tel** *020 7262 0905* **Fax** *020 7262 1324* **Rooms** *30* **Map** *9 A1*

The Pavilion's understated brick exterior may not stand out in this hotel-lined strip, but inside it's a world away from boring B&Bs. The fabulously themed rooms, from the rich panelling and tartan of "Highland Fling" to the antique Chinese chests and silks of "Enter the Dragon" are favoured by rock stars. **www.pavilionhoteluk.com**

FURTHER AFIELD Aster House

⚡ ☰   **₤₤₤₤**

3 Sumner Place, SW7 **Tel** *020 7581 5888* **Fax** *020 7584 4925* **Rooms** *13* **Map** *17 A2*

Three-time winner of the Tourist Board's best B&B award, this friendly hotel in a white stucco house has immaculate bedrooms in a typical English-country style. A superior breakfast served in the palm-filled conservatory and a pretty garden complete with pond and resident ducks attract guests. Check the website for special deals. **www.asterhouse.com**

FURTHER AFIELD Colonnade

⚡ P ⛔ ⚡ ☰   **₤₤₤₤**

2 Warrington Crescent, W9 **Tel** *020 7286 1052* **Fax** *020 7286 1057* **Rooms** *43*

Near the picturesque canals of Little Venice, this hotel in two Victorian mansions has been operating since the 1930s. Freud stayed here while his house was being redecorated, and JFK paid a visit in the 1960s. The interior is grand yet unintimidating and every luxurious room has a different feel. **www.theetoncollection.com**

FURTHER AFIELD The Petersham

££££

Nightingale Lane, Richmond, Surrey, TW10 **Tel** *020 8940 7471* **Fax** *020 8939 1098* **Rooms** *60*

This sprawling Victorian hotel perches on Richmond Hill overlooking the Thames. The elegant rooms are in keeping with the building's period grandeur, while integrating modern elements; some have spectacular views of the Thames. Unsurprisingly given its romantic location, it is popular for weddings. **www.petershamhotel.co.uk**

FURTHER AFIELD The Portobello Hotel

££££

22 Stanley Gardens, W11 **Tel** *020 7727 2777* **Fax** *020 7792 9641* **Rooms** *21*   **Map** *7 B2*

This divinely decadent Notting Hill mansion has lured rock royalty for over 30 years with its hip location and extravagantly decorated rooms. Choose from such exotic retreats as the serene Japanese room with private grotto garden and the notorious "Round Bed Room", with its freestanding Victorian bath. **www.portobellohotel.com**

FURTHER AFIELD The Royal Park

££££

3 Westbourne Terrace, W2 **Tel** *020 7479 6600* **Fax** *020 7479 6601* **Rooms** *48*   **Map** *8 F2*

This new town house hotel near Hyde Park has a discreet luxury, which has attracted celebrity guests. Classic, unfussy rooms are furnished with exquisite fabrics, original prints and stone-tiled bathrooms. All the usual gadgetry, plus complimentary welcome drink and evening champagne in the gracious drawing room. **www.theroyalpark.com**

FURTHER AFIELD Blakes Hotel

£££££

33 Roland Gardens, SW7 **Tel** *020 7370 6701* **Fax** *020 7373 0442* **Rooms** *45*   **Map** *16 F2*

Blakes is the original "boutique hotel", created by designer Anouska Hempel over two decades ago. Rooms range in style from baronial manor to opulent Oriental and contain pieces collected on her travels. The discreet residential location has made it a favourite celebrity hideaway. Only some suites are air conditioned. **www.blakeshotels.com**

FURTHER AFIELD Sydney House

£££££

9–11 Sydney St, SW3 **Tel** *020 7376 7711* **Fax** *020 7376 4233* **Rooms** *21*   **Map** *17 A2*

This small hotel is located just steps away from the chic shops of Brompton Cross. Airy rooms are furnished with blond wood furniture, Frette linen, contemporary art and thoughtful features such as American sockets in the ultra-modern bathrooms. Check the website for special rates. **www.sydneyhousechelsea.com**

FURTHER AFIELD The Gore

£££££

190 Queen's Gate, SW7 **Tel** *020 7584 6601* **Fax** *020 7589 8127* **Rooms** *50*   **Map** *8 F5*

The Gore has been in operation for more than 110 years and, although all the modern amenities are available, it still preserves the atmosphere of a bygone age. Rooms feature four-poster beds, framed pictures, luxurious draperies and opulent fabrics. There's a panelled bar and casual bistro as well. **www.gorehotel.com**

FURTHER AFIELD The Milestone Hotel

£££££

1 Kensington Court, W8 **Tel** *020 7917 1000* **Fax** *020 7917 1010* **Rooms** *57 & 6 apartments*   **Map** *8 E5*

This plush hotel opposite Kensington Palace features originally designed rooms, from the smart "Savile Row" to the Colonial-style "Safari Suite". Extras include gym and resistance pool, broadband Internet and Penhaligon's toiletries, 24-hour butler and use of the hotel Bentley. **www.milestonehotel.com**

THE DOWNS AND CHANNEL COAST

BATTLE Fox Hole Farm

£

Kane Hythe Rd, Battle, Sussex, TN33 9QU **Tel** *01424 772053* **Rooms** *3*

A delightful retreat with just three rooms to let. Originally an 18th-century woodcutter's cottage, this gem has heavily beamed ceilings, an inglenook fireplace and everything else that makes an English country dream home. There's a large shrub- and flower-filled garden. Non-smoking.

BEAULIEU Master Builders House Hotel

££££

Bucklers Hard, Beaulieu, Hampshire, SO42 7XB **Tel** *01590 616253* **Fax** *01590 616297* **Rooms** *25*

Marketed by Distinguished Hotels, the Master Builders House stands on the creek where the famed "Hearts of Oak" ships of the Royal Navy were once built. It is on Lord Montagu's estate, which puts the National Motor Museum within minutes while the glorious New Forest is also at the doorstep. Breakfast included. **www.themasterbuilders.co.uk**

BRIGHTON Premier Travel Inn

££

144 North St, Brighton, East Sussex, BN1 1RE **Tel** *0870 990 6340* **Fax** *0870 990 6341* **Rooms** *160*

Finding clean, comfortable and, above all, affordable accommodation in the centre of bustling Brighton is no easy task, or wasn't until the Premier Travel Inn value hotel chain came to the rescue with this perfectly sited location. The Lanes *(see p175)* and the Royal Pavilion are just steps away. **www.premiertravelinn.com**

BRIGHTON De Vere Grand Brighton

£££

97–99 Kings Rd, Brighton, East Sussex, BN1 2FW **Tel** *01273 224300* **Fax** *01273 720613* **Rooms** *201*

Brighton's only five-star hotel, this is arguably the nation's finest big seaside hotel, located right on the seafront. There is a gymnasium and a magnificent Victorian dining room and bar that serves a classic British menu, as well as delicious cream teas. Includes breakfast. **www.devere-hotels.com**

Key to Price Guide *see p556* **Key to Symbols** *see back cover flap*

BRIGHTON Hotel Du Vin Brighton

2–6 Ship St, Brighton, East Sussex, BN1 1AD **Tel** *01273 718588* **Fax** *01273 718599* **Rooms** *49*

Set in the Lanes conservation area, a stone's throw away from the seafront, this cutting-edge hotel and bistro is housed in a collection of eccentric, Gothic Revival and mock-Tudor buildings. All the bedrooms are decorated with Egyptian linen and handsprung mattresses. In 2009 a new Pub du Vin was added next door. **www.hotelduvin.com**

BROCKENHURST Balmer Lawn

Lyndhurst Rd, Brockenhurst, Hampshire, SO42 7ZB **Tel** *01590 623116* **Fax** *01590 623864* **Rooms** *55*

Built in the 1880s as a hunting lodge in the New Forest, Balmer Lawn is now an oasis of comfort and good service. The in-house Beresford's Restaurant has two AA Rosettes for fine dining. Indoor and outdoor heated pools, health spa and tennis courts are among the leisure amenities. Breakfast is included. **www.balmerlawnhotel.com**

BROCKENHURST Rhinefield House

Rhinefield Rd, Brockenhurst, Hampshire, SO42 7QB **Tel** *01590 622922* **Fax** *01592 622800* **Rooms** *50*

Set in a New Forest clearing and surrounded by rhododendrons, Rhinefield is a magnificent 19th-century Jacobean Revival mansion, with Grindling Gibbons wood carvings and other priceless features. Star of the show is the Moorish-style Alhambra Room, now a gracious bar. Breakfast included. **www.handpicked.co.uk/rhinefieldhouse**

CANTERBURY The Falstaff

8–10 St Dunstans St, Canterbury, Kent, CT2 8AF **Tel** *01227 462138* **Fax** *01227 463525* **Rooms** *46*

The Falstaff, at the heart of one of England's most historic cities, celebrated its 600th year in 2005. The one-time coaching inn has been extended into a recently restored wood mill. All rooms are en suite, and have TV and hot drink facilities. It stands next to the imposing Westgate Tower. **www.foliohotels.com/falstaff**

CANTERBURY The Abode

30–33 High St, Canterbury, Kent, CT1 2RX **Tel** *01227 766266* **Fax** *01227 451512* **Rooms** *72*

Located on the pedestrianized High Street, The Abode dates from the 16th century and has many original features. All the bedrooms, some furnished in Tudor or Georgian style, have satellite TV. There is a champagne bar, a fine dining restaurant and The Old Brewery for pub food. Breakfast included. **www.abodehotels.co.uk**

DORKING Burford Bridge

Box Hill, Dorking, Surrey, RH5 6BX **Tel** *0870 400 8283* **Fax** *01306 880386* **Rooms** *57*

Just outside the M25 circle and at the foot of the wooded South Downs, this hotel gives easy access to both London and the South Coast. Try a walk to the summit of Box Hill or visit Denbies winery, across the road, or the many antique shops in nearby Dorking. Then return to a true gourmet experience. **www.mercure-uk.com**

DOVER Wallett's Court Country Hotel & Spa

Westcliffe, Dover, Kent, CT15 6EW **Tel** *01304 852424* **Fax** *01304 853430* **Rooms** *17*

Relax in a Tudor-style room in the manor house, with fine sea views and an oak-beamed ceiling, or enjoy a room in one of the converted ancient barns. The Spa, set in the grounds of Wallett's Court, has a Romanesque exercise pool, sauna and a mineral steam room. Breakfast included. Check the website for special deals. **www.wallettscourt.com**

EAST GRINSTEAD Gravetye Manor

Vowels Lane, East Grinstead, West Sussex, RH1 94LJ **Tel** *01342 810567* **Fax** *01342 810080* **Rooms** *18*

Regarded by many as the establishment that started the country-house hotel movement. A Relais et Châteaux affiliate, it has an oak-panelled Michelin-star restaurant. In 1884, William Robinson, one of England's great gardeners, laid out the wonderful shrubs and flowerbeds. Activities include croquet and shooting. **www.gravetyemanor.co.uk**

EASTBOURNE The Grand Hotel

King Edwards Parade, Eastbourne, East Sussex, BN21 4EQ **Tel** *01323 412345* **Fax** *01323 412233* **Rooms** *152*

Appropriately named, the imposing Grand is one of Britain's classic seaside hotels. Owners Elite Hotels have lavishly refurbished the property to meet 21st-century five-star requirements. Ideal for touring Sussex or just taking the sea air with strolls down the prom. Prices include breakfast. **www.grandeastbourne.com**

FOLKESTONE Clifton Hotel

Leas, Folkestone, Kent, CT20 2EB **Tel** *01303 851231* **Fax** *01303 223949* **Rooms** *80*

The Clifton is set amid the manicured lawns and well-tended gardens of the cliff-top Leas area in the heart of Folkestone. Built in 1864, this imposing Victorian edifice offers sweeping Channel views and is very close to the Le Shuttle Eurotunnel terminal and the ferry port of Dover. Breakfast included. **www.thecliftonhotel.com**

FOLKESTONE Quality Hotel Burlington

Earls Avenue, Folkestone, Kent, CT20 2HR **Tel** *01303 255301* **Fax** *01303 251301* **Rooms** *60*

This Victorian boutique hotel, situated close to the beach, has extensive public rooms, including a choice of lounges, the Bay Tree restaurant and a large cocktail bar. Bedrooms are pleasantly decorated and equipped with modern facilities. Some rooms have sea views. **www.theburlingtonhotel.com**

FOREST ROW Ashdown Park

Wych Cross, Forest Row, East Sussex, RH18 5JR **Tel** *01342 824988* **Fax** *01342 826206* **Rooms** *105*

Set in 186 acres, in the heartland of Ashdown Forest and boasting its own golf course and country club, with a pool and spa. This Victorian Gothic stately home has been carefully restored and modernized. Splendid rooms and suites plus the award-winning Anderida restaurant make it a winner. Breakfast included. **www.elitehotels.co.uk**

GUILDFORD Angel Posting House & Livery   ££££

91 High St, Guildford, Surrey, GU1 3DP **Tel** *01483 564555* **Fax** *01483 533770* **Rooms** *21*

Jane Austen and Admiral Nelson have been guests at this town centre coaching inn that welcomed its first guests in 1500. Old-world charm and high standards of hospitality ensure popularity. The atmospheric salon has a minstrel gallery, a fireplace and a 1685 coaching clock. **www.angelpostinghouse.com**

LENHAM Chilston Park   ££££

Sandway, Lenham, Kent, ME17 2BE **Tel** *01622 859803* **Fax** *01622 858588* **Rooms** *53*

The M20 motorway is just minutes away but thankfully the traffic noises are out of earshot as you stroll in what was once Lord Chilston's estate. This is country-house style at its finest – overflowing with antiques and reeking of log fires. Offers conference rooms as well. The cuisine is of true gourmet standard. **www.handpicked.co.uk/chilstonpark**

LEWES Millers   ££

134 High St, Lewes, East Sussex, BN7 1XS **Tel** *01273 475631* **Rooms** *3*

Behind a neat Georgian frontage in Lewes's charming conservation area stands a 16th-century timber-framed building, which once belonged to the first Duke of Newcastle. Two of the double letting rooms have magnificent four-poster beds. Book in advance. The town is renowned for its antiques shops. Non-smoking. **www.millersbedandbreakfast.com**

MIDHURST Spread Eagle Hotel & Health Spa   ££££

South St, Midhurst, West Sussex, GU29 9NH **Tel** *01730 816911* **Fax** *01730 815668* **Rooms** *39*

Built in 1430, it once hosted Queen Elizabeth I and still features vast fireplaces and impressive bread ovens. The restaurant spotlights head chef Gary Moreton-Jones's modern classic menu, while bedrooms are elegant and spacious. The Aquila Health Spa has a beauty centre and a fully equipped gym. Includes full breakfast. **www.hshotels.co.uk**

NEW MILTON Chewton Glen   £££££

Christchurch Rd, New Milton, Hampshire, BH25 6QS **Tel** *01425 275341* **Fax** *01425 272310* **Rooms** *70*

The epitome of Edwardian elegance, Chewton Glen is located close to the sea. It is renowned for its food and the hotel also boasts a magnificent indoor pool and spa in addition to a range of outdoor sports and leisure activities. The rooms are constantly being updated to offer a high standard of comfort. **www.chewtonglen.com**

RINGWOOD Moortown Lodge   ££

244 Christchurch Rd, Ringwood, Hampshire, BH24 3AS **Tel** *01425 471404* **Fax** *01425 476527* **Rooms** *7*

This unpretentious country inn at the gateway to the New Forest, offers all modern in-room amenities, including high-speed Internet via broadband. Guests have access to the adjacent David Lloyd club, with its gym and pool. A full English breakfast is included. **www.moortownlodge.co.uk**

ROYAL TUNBRIDGE WELLS Hotel Du Vin & Bistro   ££££

Crescent Rd, Tunbridge Wells, Kent, TN1 2LY **Tel** *01892 526455* **Fax** *01892 512044* **Rooms** *34*

Superb quality without unnecessary frills. Sensible prices and trendy service are the key to success for the small but steadily growing Vin & Bistro chain. This branch opened in 1997 and immediately became a favourite for its modern styles of accommodation and cuisine catered in a spacious historic building. **www.hotelduvin.com**

RYE Jeake's House   ££

Mermaid St, Rye, East Sussex, TN31 7ET **Tel** *01797 222828* **Fax** *01797 222263* **Rooms** *11*

Creeper-clad Jeake's House is tucked away in Rye's atmospheric jumble of little cobbled streets. Guests are welcomed by the two resident cats and proprietors Jenny Hadfield and Richard Martin. There's an oak-beamed parlour and a book-lined bar, plus roaring fires on colder days. Breakfast included. **www.jeakeshouse.com**

SEAVIEW Seaview   £££

High St, Seaview, Isle of Wight, PO34 5EX **Tel** *01983 612711* **Fax** *01983 613729* **Rooms** *28*

Once described as "the perfect seaside hotel", this is just the spot for an idyllic weekend. It's good for family holidays too. The kitchen has just been refurbished and the food is as deliciously inventive as ever. Crisp linen, maritime bric-à-brac and a warren of corridors and stairways all add to the romance. **www.seaviewhotel.co.uk**

SOUTHAMPTON Elizabeth House   ££

42–44 The Avenue, Southampton, Hampshire, SO17 1XP **Tel** *023 8022 4327* **Fax** *023 8022 4327* **Rooms** *27*

Set in a quiet residential area, less than a mile from Southampton city centre, the Elizabeth House gives easy access to the new West Quay Shopping Centre and the cruise and ferry terminals. Southampton's attractions include ancient city walls while the New Forest and the Isle of Wight are nearby. Breakfast included. **www.elizabethhousehotel.com**

SOUTHSEA Seacrest   ££

11/12 South Parade, Southsea, Hampshire, PO5 2JB **Tel** *023 9273 3192* **Fax** *023 9283 2523* **Rooms** *28*

This hotel has been constantly improved and upgraded to give guests the best in comfort. A premier position on Southsea's seafront commands fine views across the Solent towards the Isle of Wight. All the rooms are individually designed. Includes breakfast. Call ahead for the best rates. **www.seacresthotel.co.uk**

VENTNOR The Royal Hotel   ££££

Belgrave Rd, Ventnor, Isle of Wight, PO38 1JJ **Tel** *01983 852186* **Fax** *01983 855395* **Rooms** *55*

The Isle of Wight's largest premier hotel can be found in the elegant Victorian town of Ventnor. Gourmets can indulge in inspired cuisine in a palatial dining room replete with rich drapes, high ceilings and massive chandeliers. Explore the island or the staff can arrange a yacht charter. Breakfast included. **www.royalhoteliow.co.uk**

Key to Price Guide *see p556* **Key to Symbols** *see back cover flap*

WICKHAM Old House Hotel & Restaurant ⬛⬛ ©©©
The Square, Wickham, Hampshire, PO17 5JG **Tel** *01329 833049* **Fax** *01329 833672* **Rooms** *12*

Located just off the M27 motorway, this is a good option for those wishing to explore the Portsmouth, Southampton, Winchester triangle. Built in 1715 as a gentleman's town house, the building was converted into a hotel in 1970. You can also stay in a three-bedroom cottage a short walk away. Breakfast included. **www.oldhousehotel.co.uk**

WINCHESTER Lainston House ⬛⬛⬛⬛ ©©©©
Sparsholt, Winchester, Hampshire, SO21 2LT **Tel** *01962 776088* **Fax** *01962 776672* **Rooms** *50*

One of England's most handsome hotels, Lainston House has country style yet is just minutes from the centre of Winchester. Behind that imposing Queen Anne red-brick frontage is a friendly welcome. There are 63 acres to wander in, a gourmet restaurant and you can always order a DVD from room service. **www.exclusivehotels.co.uk**

WORTHING The Beach Hotel ⬛⬛⬛⬛ ©©©
Marine Parade, Worthing, Sussex, BN11 3QJ **Tel** *01903 234001* **Fax** *01903 234567* **Rooms** *79*

Lovingly restored by the Farnes family, The Beach is an Art Deco time warp, located right on Worthing's seafront promenade. Every period detail has been painstakingly renovated, but the amenities are now fully modern. Lifts serve all four floors and the hotel has its own car park. Inclusive of breakfast. **www.thebeachhotel.co.uk**

EAST ANGLIA

ALDEBURGH Wentworth ⬛⬛⬛ ©©©
Wentworth Rd, Aldeburgh, Suffolk, IP15 5BD **Tel** *01728 452312* **Fax** *01728 454343* **Rooms** *35*

Replete with antiques and log fires, the Wentworth Hotel has been run by succeeding generations of the Pritt family since 1920. All the bedrooms are well equipped with latest facilities, including satellite TV, and offer fine sea views. There are also three local golf courses. Includes breakfast. **www.wentworth-aldeburgh.com**

BUCKDEN Lion ⬛⬛ ©©
High St, Buckden, Cambridgeshire, PE19 5XA **Tel** *01480 810313* **Fax** *01480 811070* **Rooms** *15*

Rescued from corporate ownership in 1982, this 15th-century, Grade II listed hotel is a classic country inn. It also has a resident ghost. Well-furnished bedrooms. The oak-panelled restaurant offers excellent wholesome food using the best of local produce. There is also a bar and lounge. Breakfast is included. **www.lionhotel.co.uk**

BURNHAM MARKET The Hoste Arms ⬛⬛⬛ ©©©
The Green, Burnham Market, King's Lynn, Norfolk, PE31 8HD **Tel** *01328 738777* **Fax** *01328 730103* **Rooms** *36*

You can choose to stay in the pretty main part of the inn; in the Zulu wing with its modern African-flavoured styling and leather couches; in an old railway station, a five minutes' walk away; or in the luxury Georgian boutique hotel known as the Vine House. There is a great wine list. Rate includes breakfast. **www.hostearms.co.uk**

BURY ST EDMUNDS Angel Hotel ⬛⬛⬛⬛ ©©©
Angel Hill, Bury St Edmunds, Suffolk, IP33 1LT **Tel** *01284 714000* **Fax** *01284 714001* **Rooms** *75*

The virginia creeper-clad Angel dominates Bury St Edmunds' largest square. Rooms are individually decorated with modern flair or classical grace. Its public areas have always been the place for the local elite to meet. These days they are joined by a global clientele drawn by the hotel's reputation for contemporary British fine dining. **www.theangel.co.uk**

BURY ST EDMUNDS Ounce House ⬛ ©©©
Northgate St, Bury St Edmunds, Suffolk, IP33 1HP **Tel** *01284 761779* **Fax** *01284 768315* **Rooms** *5*

A merchant's house dating from 1870, this spacious family home stands at the top of one of the finest residential streets in Bury St Edmunds. Bedrooms have a chintzy, Victorian style and are equipped with all the modern facilities. A bar operates in the drawing room. Includes breakfast. **www.ouncehouse.co.uk**

CAMBRIDGE Cambridge Fourwentways ⬛⬛ ©
A11/A1307 Fourwentways, Cambridgeshire, CB8 6AP **Tel** *0871 984 6019* **Fax** *01223 839479* **Rooms** *71*

Convenient for both the M11 and the A14, this branch of the nationwide budget hotel chain is ideally located close to the Imperial War Museum's aviation displays at Duxford as well as the equestrian museums and training gallops of Newmarket. A Little Chef eatery is on the same site. Offers good online deals. **www.travellodge.co.uk**

CAMBRIDGE Arundel House Hotel ⬛⬛ ©©©
Chesterton Rd, Cambridge, Cambridgeshire, CB4 3AN **Tel** *01223 367701* **Fax** *01223 367721* **Rooms** *103*

This hotel, created from a terrace of late 19th-century Victorian houses, overlooks the River Cam and is a short walk across the park from the city centre. The historic façade and gracefully decorated rooms have been retained while providing all the latest amenities. Parking is available. Includes continental breakfast. **www.arundelhousehotels.co.uk**

CAMPSEA ASHE The Old Rectory ⬛⬛ ©©
Campsea Ashe, Woodbridge, Suffolk, IP13 0PU **Tel** *01728 746524* **Rooms** *8*

All the delights of the Suffolk coastline are in easy reach – the music and culture of Snape Maltings, the Sutton Hoo Saxon burial ground and the towns of Woodbridge and Aldeburgh. An elegant Georgian house encircled by gardens, it's furnished in chic contemporary style. Includes breakfast. **www.theoldrectorysuffolk.com**

CLACTON-ON-SEA Chudleigh Hotel ££

13 Agate Rd, Marine Parade West, Essex, CO15 1RA **Tel** *01255 425407* **Fax** *01255 470280* **Rooms** *10*

Near the pier, the promenade and Clacton's shopping area, the Chudleigh overlooks the resort's central gardens. It has been run by the same caring family for 41 years. This is classic English seaside hospitality at its best. Comfortable bedrooms providing all modern facilities including DVDs. **www.chudleighhotel.com**

COGGESHALL The White Hart ££

Market End, Coggeshall, Essex, CO6 1NH **Tel** *01376 561654* **Fax** *01376 561789* **Rooms** *18*

Sleepy Coggeshall once boasted of having more inns and pubs per capita than any other town in the country. The atmospheric White Hart is one of the survivors, offering outstanding value for money in one of East Anglia's secret gems. All the rooms have en suite facilities. Full breakfast is included. **www.whitehart-coggeshall.com**

DEDHAM Maison Talbooth ££££

Stratford Rd, Dedham, Colchester, Essex, CO7 6HN **Tel** *01206 322367* **Fax** *01206 322752* **Rooms** *10*

The Milsom family are a legend in Constable country, taking hospitality to new levels of excellence. The essence of Victorian country-house grace and style, the hotel is just a few minutes from the riverside half-timbered Le Talbooth restaurant and the sister Milsom's hotel. There is a pool in the summer and a tennis court. **www.milsomhotels.com**

DUNWICH Ship Inn ££

St James St, Dunwich, Suffolk, IP17 3DT **Tel** *01728 648219* **Fax** *01728 648675* **Rooms** *10*

Before it sank into the sea, medieval Dunwich was East Anglia's busiest port and had a population of 3,000. The 500-year old ship survived and offers simple rooms in an out-of-the-way location. The restaurant is renowned for simply prepared home food, including fish and chips. Some rooms are dog-friendly. **www.shipatdunwich.co.uk**

ELY Lamb Hotel ££

2 Lynn Rd, Ely, Cambridgeshire, CB7 4EJ **Tel** *01353 663574* **Fax** *01353 662023* **Rooms** *31*

The Lamb makes no secret of its 15th-century coaching inn origins at the heart of the Fens *(see p196)*, close to the glorious cathedral. Oak panelling, arched picture-end windows, antique furnishings and candle-lit suppers – it's a haven of traditional values. Includes breakfast. Check the website for special rates. **www.oldenglishinns.co.uk**

GREAT DUNMOW The Starr £££

Market Place, Gt Dunmow, Essex, CM6 1AX **Tel** *01371 874321* **Fax** *01371 876642* **Rooms** *8*

The Starr's elegant conservatory is just the place to enjoy the owners', Terry and Louise George, good food and fine wines before retiring to one of the eight comfortable bedrooms located in a cleverly converted stable block. One room has a four-poster and an impressive Victorian bathtub. Breakfast included. **www.the-starr.co.uk**

HARWICH The Pier Hotel & Restaurant £££

The Quay, Harwich, Essex, CO12 3HH **Tel** *01255 241212* **Fax** *01255 551922* **Rooms** *14*

Set close to where the Pilgrim Fathers set off on their epic voyage, The Pier overlooks neighbouring Felixstowe, the UK's busiest commercial port. Not surprisingly, there's an emphasis on fresh fish in the restaurant. The lovingly and individually furnished rooms are the latest in modern chic style. Includes continental breakfast. **www.milsomhotels.com**

HERTFORD The Ponsbourne Park Hotel £££

New Gate St Village, Hertford, Hertfordshire, SG13 8QT **Tel** *01707 876191* **Fax** *01707 875190* **Rooms** *52*

Originally developed as a training centre and hotel, this stylish conversion of a one-time convent school offers modern minimalism within a gracious Victorian shell. Features include a nine-hole golf course, a heated outdoor pool and five all-weather tennis courts. Includes breakfast. **www.ponsbournepark.co.uk**

HINTLESHAM Hintlesham Hall ££££

George St, Hintlesham, Ipswich, Suffolk, IP8 3NS **Tel** *01473 652334* **Fax** *01473 652463* **Rooms** *33*

Hintlesham Hall has a long-standing reputation as one of England's most exquisite country-house hotels. There is a charming health club with an outdoor heated pool and a year-round programme of special culinary events. You can even learn to cook here. Includes breakfast. **www.hintleshamhall.co.uk**

HUNTINGDON Old Bridge £££

1 High St, Huntingdon, Cambridgeshire, PE29 3TQ **Tel** *01480 424300* **Fax** *01480 411017* **Rooms** *24*

While the rooms are comfortable in this ivy-clad hostelry, the focus is very much on food and wine. A light pasta lunch or a full dinner – they cater for it all with aplomb and gusto and will send a menu on request. There is also a wine shop, and they do wine tastings, too. Breakfast is included. Business centre is a plus. **www.huntsbridge.com**

IPSWICH Salt House Harbour £££

1 Neptune Quay, Ipswich, Suffolk, IP4 1AX **Tel** *01473 226789* **Fax** *01473 226927* **Rooms** *43*

Set right on the River Orwell, from which the writer George Orwell took his name. A substantial old seven-storey warehouse by Neptune Marina has been converted into a trendy loft-style hotel. Bedrooms are en suite with TVs, DVDs and Internet access. The food is equally good and they have an interesting wine list. **www.salthouseharbour.co.uk**

IPSWICH Swallow Belstead Brook Hotel £££

Belstead Rd, Ipswich, Suffolk, IP2 9HB **Tel** *01473 684241* **Fax** *01473 681249* **Rooms** *88*

Hidden away in secluded gardens on the outskirts of Ipswich, this hotel has an indoor pool, air-conditioned gym and sauna. Enjoy delicious cuisine in the elegant oak-panelled Manor restaurant. Originally a 16th-century hunting lodge, this is now a modern hotel, catering to business and leisure travellers. Includes breakfast. **www.swallow-hotels.com**

Key to Price Guide *see p556* **Key to Symbols** *see back cover flap*

KINGS LYNN Hotel Elizabeth Dukes Head
Tuesday Market Place, Kings Lynn, Norfolk, P30 1JS **Tel** *01553 774996* **Fax** *01553 763556* **Rooms** *71*

The Duke's Head has pride of place on King Lynn's Market Square, where public executions took place until 1801. Modern-day guests can anticipate an altogether more attentive, friendly welcome, with such facilities as TV, conference suites and a private car park. **www.elizabethhotels.co.uk**

KINGS LYNN Knights Hill Hotel
South Wootton, Norfolk, PE30 3HQ **Tel** *01553 675566* **Fax** *01553 675568* **Rooms** *79*

Close to King's Lynn, the royal estate at Sandringham and the North Norfolk coast, Knights Hill is a restored farm complex in 11 acres of gardens. Style ranges from the relaxed elegance of Rising Lodge to the rustic charms of the Farmers Arms. The health and leisure centre provides a pool and exercise areas. **www.bw-knightshillhotel.co.uk**

LAVENHAM Lavenham Priory
Water St, Lavenham, Sudbury, Suffolk, C010 9RW **Tel** *01787 247404* **Fax** *01787 248472* **Rooms** *6*

At this 13th-century hotel you can have an-out-of-the-world experience at affordable prices, with exposed beams, polished floors and beds carved by a local craftsman. All the rooms are comfortably furnished with all the latest facilities. Breakfast included in the price. **www.lavenhampriory.co.uk**

LAVENHAM Swan
High St, Lavenham, Sudbury, Suffolk, C010 9QA **Tel** *01787 247477* **Fax** *01787 248286* **Rooms** *46*

Luxuriate below a wealth of exposed beams in a wonderful bedroom named after a local village. Other comforts include rich fabrics, cotton sheets and feather pillows. Some rooms have four-poster beds. The heavily-beamed restaurant has fine food and an extensive wine list. The Garden Bar is much simpler. **www.theswanatlavenham.co.uk**

LOWESTOFT Premier Travel Inn
249 Yarmouth Rd, Lowestoft, Suffolk, NR32 4AA **Tel** *08701 977165* **Fax** *01502 581223* **Rooms** *60*

This coastal Suffolk budget hotel provides a low-cost base for visiting a rich kaleidoscope of castles, stately homes, formal gardens and historic fishing ports such as Lowestoft and Yarmouth. A nationwide brand, Premier Travel Inn provides quality and convenient location. Close to reasonably priced restaurants. **www.premiertravelinn.com**

LOWESTOFT Ivy House Country Hotel
Ivy Lane, Beccles Rd, Lowestoft, Suffolk, NR33 8HY **Tel** *01502 501353* **Fax** *01502 501539* **Rooms** *20*

Surrounded by countryside, Ivy House has huge gardens, with herbaceous borders and lily ponds. Rooms come with colour TV, tea and coffee making machines and en suite bathrooms. Also has conference rooms and the Crooked Barn restaurant is famous for its cuisine. Includes breakfast. **www.ivyhousecountryhotel.co.uk**

MALDON Five Lakes Resort
Colchester Rd, Tolleshunt Knights, Maldon, Essex, CM9 8HX **Tel** *01621 868888* **Fax** *01621 869696* **Rooms** *194*

Set in the country seclusion of Essex, the stylish Four Lakes Resort is close to the charming little town of Maldon *(see p209)*, where Danes and Saxons once fought. Besides the huge indoor pool and extensive spa and leisure facilities, the big attraction comes from two superbly landscaped 18-hole golf courses. **www.fivelakes.co.uk**

NEWMARKET The Rutland Arms
33 High St, Newmarket, Suffolk, CB8 8MB **Tel** *01638 664251* **Fax** *01638 666298* **Rooms** *46*

Newmarket is England's horse-racing capital, and owners, trainers and jockeys are among the regulars at a hotel that is jam-packed with period features. It's one of Newmarket High Street's prime buildings and has a pleasant courtyard for alfresco summer meals. The restaurant serves modern European food. **www.oxfordhotelsandinns.com**

NORTH WALSHAM Beechwood
20 Cromer Rd, North Walsham, Norfolk, NR28 0HD **Tel** *01692 403231* **Fax** *01692 407284* **Rooms** *17*

In 2003 this establishment became the first two-star hotel ever to win the VisitBritain "Hotel of the Year". Rooms are styled with antique furniture, some with four-poster beds. The highlight of the hotel is chef Steven Norgate's speciality, the "Ten-Mile Dinner", with all ingredients sourced from within 10 miles. **www.beechwood-hotel.co.uk**

NORWICH Beeches Hotel & Victorian Gardens
2–6 Earlham Rd, Norwich, Norfolk, NR2 3DB **Tel** *01603 621167* **Fax** *01603 620151* **Rooms** *43*

Just a short stroll from the city centre, the Beeches offers peace and quiet, with spacious traditionally furnished rooms and the hidden delights of an amazing sunken garden. A crunchy gravel drive and sheltering trees give a country-house ambience. The included breakfast is substantial. **www.mjbhotels.com**

NORWICH The Old Rectory
103 Yarmouth Rd, Norwich, Norfolk, NR7 0HF **Tel** *01603 700772* **Fax** *01603 300772* **Rooms** *8*

The Old Rectory overlooks the River Yare in a pleasant suburb that is now a conservation area. Rooms are beautifully furnished, and chef James Perry has earned a good reputation for his daily changing menus. The outdoor heated pool is a real treat. A self-catering cottage for two is also available. Includes breakfast. **www.oldrectorynorwich.com**

PETERBOROUGH Purple Hotel
Gt North Rd, Haddon, Cambridgeshire, PE7 3UQ **Tel** *01733 396850* **Fax** *01733 396869* **Rooms** *82*

Budget priced, yes, but Purple Hotel properties have consistently high standards of modern accommodation. A good night's sleep and you are ready to hit the famous A1 for the Midlands, Yorkshire and all points north into Scotland. It's just as good if you use it as a base for exploring the Fens. **www.purplehotels.com**

PETERBOROUGH Marriott

The Lynchwood Business Park, Cambridgeshire, PE2 6GB **Tel** *01733 371111* **Fax** *01733 236725* **Rooms** *163*

Though it features one of England's oldest cathedrals, Peterborough is a modern business city, a fact that keeps this thoroughly modern hotel busy. Don't be put off by the business park location, the hotel is pleasantly landscaped and has all the amenities you would expect from a Marriott. Includes breakfast. **www.peterboroughmarriott.co.uk**

SOUTHWOLD The Crown Hotel

90 High St, Southwold, Suffolk, IP18 6DP **Tel** *01502 722275* **Fax** *01502 727263* **Rooms** *14*

Next to its sister Adnams hotel, the Swan, this traditional hotel with modern facilities stands at the heart of East Anglia's most gracious little seaside resort. The beach is just five minutes walk away. A venue for all four seasons, it's a wonderful retreat from big city pressures and has a delightful bistro-bar. Includes breakfast. **www.adnams.co.uk**

SOUTHWOLD The Swan Hotel

Market Place, Southwold, Suffolk, IP18 6EG **Tel** *01502 722186* **Fax** *01502 724800* **Rooms** *42*

Paintings and photographs of local scenes make the Swan an evocative showcase for what is East Anglia's most delightful resort town. Being owned by Adnams, the town's brewers and wine importers, ensures the quality of beverages offered. Individualized rooms are part of the experience. Includes breakfast. **www.adnams.co.uk**

WOODBRIDGE Seckford Hall

Woodbridge, Suffolk, IP13 6NU **Tel** *01394 385678* **Fax** *01394 380610* **Rooms** *32*

One of East Anglia's most successful country-house hotels, the Tudor façade features mullion windows and giant chimneys above a huge carved oak entrance door. The bedrooms have en suite facilities, and leisure activities include a pool, gym, beauty salon; and a golf club for a small fee. Includes breakfast. **www.seckford.co.uk**

THAMES VALLEY

AYLESBURY Hartwell House

Oxford Rd, Aylesbury, Oxfordshire, HP17 8NR **Tel** *01296 747444* **Fax** *01296 747450* **Rooms** *52*

A member of the Pride of Britain consortium, this hotel was once the home of the exiled King of France. Relax in palatial reception rooms with decorative ceilings, antique furniture and fine paintings. Enjoy the gourmet restaurant, the luxurious spa or walk in the Lancelot "Capability" Brown designed grounds. **www.hartwell-house.com**

BEDFORD Woodland Manor

Green Lane, Clapham, Bedfordshire, MK41 6EP **Tel** *01234 363281* **Fax** *01234 272390* **Rooms** *35*

Gracious country living awaits at this secluded Grade II listed manor house, with comfortable, well-appointed bedrooms offering sweeping views across the lawns and gardens. Facilities include conference rooms, ample parking space and special offers on particular days. Includes breakfast. **www.woodlandmanorhotel.co.uk**

BICESTER Bignell Park Hotel

Chesterton, Bicester, Oxfordshire, OX26 1UE **Tel** *01869 326550* **Fax** *01869 322729* **Rooms** *22*

Built in 1740 and set in two and a half well-tended acres, the picturesque Bignell Park Hotel offers outstanding views from its luxurious individually styled rooms. Modern cuisine tempts the taste buds and romantic suppers may be taken on the minstrel's gallery. Includes breakfast. **www.bignellparkhotel.co.uk**

BRACKNELL Coppid Beech Hotel

John Nike Way, Bracknell, Berkshire, RG12 8TF **Tel** *01344 303333* **Fax** *01344 301200* **Rooms** *205*

This popular family and business venue has its own dry ski slope and ice rink. There's a conference room, an evening entertainment programme and a health and fitness suite, which includes a children's pool. The restaurant has a good reputation, and there are also a bistro-pub and a nightclub. Includes breakfast. **www.coppidbeech.com**

BURFORD The Lamb Inn

Sheep St, Burford, Oxfordshire, OX18 4LR **Tel** *01993 823155* **Fax** *01993 822228* **Rooms** *17*

Among the best in Burford, The Lamb Inn is a classic golden stone building with beamed ceilings. All the bedrooms are comfortably designed with en suite facilities. You can enjoy lunch or a traditional tea here, and dinner is served at the bar or in the main dining room (6:30–9:30pm). Close to many local attractions. **www.cotswold-inns.co.uk/lamb**

CHARLBURY The Bell at Charlbury

Church St, Charlbury, Oxfordshire, OX7 3PP **Tel** *01608 810278* **Fax** *01608 811447* **Rooms** *12*

Mellow golden Cotswold stone gives a handsome air to this convenient town-centre inn. Comfortable accommodation, fine food and drink and proximity to all the Cotswold attractions keep it eternally popular. Charlbury was once a centre for glove makers and Quakers. **www.bellhotel-charlbury.co.uk**

CHIPPERFIELD Two Brewers

The Common, Chipperfield, Hertfordshire, WD4 9BS **Tel** *01923 265266* **Fax** *01923 261884* **Rooms** *20*

Set on the edge of a common in the peaceful village of Chipperfield, the Two Brewers was once the training quarters for great boxers such as Jem Mace and Bob Fitzsimmons. There's a stone-floored taproom and the food is of gastro-pub quality. Bedrooms are furnished in keeping with the country-inn feel. Includes breakfast. **www.twobrewers.com**

Key to Price Guide *see p556* **Key to Symbols** *see back cover flap*

GLOUCESTERSHIRE Lower Slaughter Manor 🔲🔲 ££££££

Lower Slaughter, nr Cheltenham, Gloucestershire, GL54 2HP **Tel** *01451 820456* **Fax** *01451 822150* **Rooms** *19*

Hidden in a deep fold of the Cotswold Hills, this is one of England's most charming secrets. The manor stands in its own private walled grounds, and splendid plaster ceilings, stone fireplaces and antiques add to the ambience. Superb cuisine and an impressive wine list. Includes breakfast. **www.lowerslaughter.co.uk**

GREAT TEW Falkland Arms 🔲 ££

Great Tew, Chipping Norton, Oxfordshire, OX7 4DB **Tel** *01608 683653* **Fax** *01608 683656* **Rooms** *5*

Oak beams, a flagstone floor and an inglenook fireplace set the mood in a Cotswold premises that is part thatch-roofed. This local pub is famous for its drinks and also provides comfortable B&B accommodation. All the rooms have en suite facilities and a colour TV. **www.falklandarms.org.uk**

HARPENDEN Harpenden House 🔲🔲 £££

18 Southdown Rd, Harpenden, Hertfordshire, AL5 1PE **Tel** *01582 449955* **Fax** *01582 769858* **Rooms** *76*

Conveniently located close to the M1, Luton Airport and for travelling to London, Harpenden House is a well-integrated mix of modern and traditional, with a loyal following among the business community. The main four-storey building is a handsome Georgian edifice. Also has a cocktail bar. **www.foliohotels.com**

HENLEY-ON-THAMES Red Lion 🔲🔲 £££

Hart St, Henley-on-Thames, Oxfordshire, RG9 2AR **Tel** *01491 572161* **Fax** *01491 410039* **Rooms** *34*

Overlooking the Royal Regatta course on the Thames and next to the church where the singer Dusty Springfield is buried, the Red Lion is a charming redbrick riverside inn. The pleasant, individually decorated rooms, many of them with river views, offer en suite facilities, and also has a restaurant and a bar. **www.redlionhenley.co.uk**

LONG CRENDON Angel 🔲 ££

47 Bicester Rd, Long Crendon, Buckinghamshire, HP18 9EE **Tel** *01844 208268* **Fax** *01844 202497* **Rooms** *4*

In a village 32 km (20 miles) from Oxford, the age-old Angel is renowned for its good food. A Pacific Rim influence pervades the kitchen's mouthwatering output. There are just four elegantly decorated rooms, so personal attention is assured. The Cotswolds are in easy reach, as is Milton Keynes. Includes breakfast. **www.angelrestaurant.co.uk**

MAIDENHEAD Elva Lodge Hotel 🔲🔲🔲 ££

Castle Hill, Maidenhead, Berkshire, SL6 4AD **Tel** *01628 622948* **Fax** *01628 778954* **Rooms** *26*

A standard-style modern hotel close to the centre of Maidenhead, the Elva Lodge is convenient for touring Windsor Castle, Henley and the other attractions of the Thames Valley. Service is efficient and while the hotel is orientated to business travellers, families will also feel welcome. Includes breakfast. **www.elvalodgehotel.co.uk**

MARLOW Cliveden 🔲🔲🔲🔲🔲🔲 £££££

Taplow, Berkshire, SL6 OJF **Tel** *01628 668561* **Fax** *01628 661837* **Rooms** *38*

Built by the second Duke of Buckingham in 1666 and once the home of Lord and Lady Astor, this palace above the Thames has welcomed royalty, film stars and writers. All the rooms are handsomely decorated, and they have indoor and outdoor pools and extensive leisure facilities, including tennis, squash and boating. **www.clivedenhouse.co.uk**

MARLOW Danesfield House Hotel & Spa 🔲🔲🔲🔲🔲 ££££££

Henley Rd, Marlow, Buckinghamshire, SL7 2EY **Tel** *01628 891010* **Fax** *01628 890408* **Rooms** *87*

Tucked away in the Chilterns, overlooking the Thames as it winds between Henley and Marlow, this gracious and much extended mansion sits in 65 acres of glorious gardens. The extensive state-of-the-art spa has a pool, gym and treatment rooms. Bedrooms are luxurious, and the restaurant classy. **www.danesfieldhouse.co.uk**

MARLOW MacDonald Compleat Angler 🔲🔲🔲 ££££££

Marlow Bridge, Marlow, Buckinghamshire, SL7 1RG **Tel** *0870 400 8100* **Fax** *01628 486388* **Rooms** *64*

This is one of England's most renowned historic hostelries. All the rooms are comfortably furnished with en suite facilities and have satellite TV, CD players, playstations and a minibar. Service standards are legendary. Its location overlooking Marlow Weir attracts guests. **www.macdonaldhotels.co.uk/compleatangler**

MILTON Le Manoir Aux Quat' Saisons 🔲🔲🔲 ££££££

Church Rd, Great Milton, Oxfordshire, OX44 7PD **Tel** *01844 278881* **Fax** *01844 278847* **Rooms** *32*

This is where French expat Raymond Blanc literally carved his reputation as one of Britain's most acclaimed gourmet chefs. As if the food was not enough, the building is a handsome manor, surrounded by herb gardens, while the bedrooms are a mix of contemporary and traditional styles. **www.manoir.com**

MILTON KEYNES Innkeeper's Lodge 🔲🔲 £

Burchard Cres., Milton Keynes, Buckinghamshire, MK5 6HQ **Tel** *0870 243 0500* **Fax** *01738 44359* **Rooms** *50*

The new Inkeeper's Lodge chain already has 75 locations across the country, lifting the "pub with rooms" concept to a new level of consistency. The Milton Keynes location gives an easy-on-the-pocket base for trips to Woburn Abbey, the Cotswolds and the South Midlands. Includes breakfast. **www.innkeeperslodge.com**

MOULSFORD Beetle & Wedge 🔲🔲 ££

Ferry Lane, Moulsford on Thames, Oxfordshire, OX10 9JF **Tel** *01491 651381* **Fax** *01491 651376* **Rooms** *3*

A gorgeous Thames-side setting is the highlight of this ever-popular upscale hotel and its renowned restaurant, where it always pays to pre-book a table. The style is Anglo-French. The room decor is classic and there are river views and an opulent bathroom. **www.beetleandwedge.co.uk**

NEWBURY The Vineyard At Stockcross

Stockcross, Newbury, Berkshire, RG20 8JU **Tel** *01635 528770* **Fax** *01635 528398* **Rooms** *49*

The Vineyard raises the bar when it comes to country-house style. Best rooms are in the original house, but those in the modern wing are also outstanding for their contemporary look. Also available are a spa and treatment rooms. The Michelin-starred restaurant serves highly inventive British cuisine. Includes breakfast. **www.the-vineyard.co.uk**

OXFORD Travel Lodge Oxford Peartree

Woodstock Rd, Oxford, Oxfordshire, OX2 8JZ **Tel** *08719 848484* **Fax** *01865 513474* **Rooms** *150*

Travel Lodge has a number of their budget properties within easy striking distance of Oxford's fabled dreaming spires. This one sits on the northern section of the Ring Road, making it especially convenient for visitors travelling from the Midlands and North. All rooms are en suite and have TV and tea-making facilities. **www.travellodge.co.uk**

OXFORD Macdonald Randolph Hotel

Beaumont St, Oxford, Oxfordshire, OX1 2LN **Tel** *0870 400 8200* **Fax** *01865 791678* **Rooms** *151*

The refined Randolph has starred in the TV series *Inspector Morse* and numerous movies, including *Shadowlands*. It's the veritable heart of Oxford, and a favourite for students' parents, American tourists and the business community. Rooms are tastefully decorated. Dining is in classical silver-service mode. **www.macdonaldhotels.co.uk**

OXFORD Old Bank

92–94 High St, Oxford, Oxfordshire, OX1 4BN **Tel** *01865 799599* **Fax** *01865 799598* **Rooms** *42*

This handsome stone building in the heart of this university city used to serve as a bank. Money still flows here as it is often fully booked – tribute to the sharp Armani styling of the rooms and the tempting new British cuisine. Conference room and beauty treatments are a plus; an off-site gym can also be used. **www.oldbank-hotel.co.uk**

OXFORD The Old Parsonage Hotel

1 Banbury Rd, Oxford, Oxfordshire, OX2 6NN **Tel** *01865 310210* **Fax** *01865 311262* **Rooms** *30*

Walls of Cotswold stone screen the Old Parsonage from Oxford's passing hubbub, creating the pleasing illusion of a country retreat. The luxurious bedrooms are air conditioned and now have broadband Internet. Fresh Jersey lobsters are served in the restaurant from May through September. **www.oldparsonage-hotel.co.uk**

READING Premier Travel Inn

Goring Lane, Grazeley Green, Reading, Berkshire, RG7 1LS **Tel** *0870 990 6454* **Fax** *0870 990 6455* **Rooms** *32*

Premier Travel Inn is a brand name worth remembering if you are seeking quality budget accommodation in convenient locations. This one is set just south of Reading, with convenient access to the M4 corridor. Comfortably furnished rooms, with a few especially adapted for disabled guests. **www.premiertravelinn.com**

READING Millennium Madejski Hotel Reading

Madejski Stadium (Jct 11 on M4), Reading, Berkshire, RG2 0FL **Tel** *0118 925 3500* **Fax** *0118 925 3501* **Rooms** *201*

John Madejski made his fortune from *Auto Trader* magazines, then saved Reading Football Club from extinction and built them a new stadium of which this hotel is a part. His love of fine food explains the high quality of the fare on offer; the rooms are of an equally high standard. Check the website for special rates. **www.millenniumhotels.com**

ST ALBANS Comfort

Ryder House, Holywell Hill, St Albans, Hertfordshire, AL1 1HG **Tel** *01727 848849* **Fax** *01727 812210* **Rooms** *60*

One of America's biggest groups, Choice and their Comfort brand are now making their mark in the UK thanks to consistent quality and value prices. All the rooms are spacious, with big and firm beds. This hotel occupies a historic building in the centre of this hilltop town that was once a Roman stronghold. **www.choicehotels.com**

WINDSOR Sir Christopher Wren's House Hotel & Spa

Thames St, Windsor, Berkshire, SL4 1PX **Tel** *01753 861354* **Fax** *01753 860172* **Rooms** *96*

Stroll through the pedestrianized Thames Bridge from Eton College and on the right side is this handsome Georgian mansion. The riverside setting makes for a romantic dining experience while the spacious, individualized rooms brim with antiques. They also have a gym and a spa offering beauty treatments. **www.sirchristopherwren.co.uk**

YATTENDON Royal Oak

The Square, Yattendon, Thatcham, Berkshire, RG18 0UG **Tel** *01635 201325* **Fax** *01635 201926* **Rooms** *5*

A classic country pub in Berkshire, serving a pretty little village and tourists alike. The mood is smart and informal, and the contemporary take on traditional food is deservedly award-winning. All rooms are individually decorated and en suite. Includes breakfast. **www.royaloakyattendon.com**

WESSEX

ABBOTSBURY The Abbey House

Church St, Abbotsbury, Dorset, DT3 4JJ **Tel** *01305 871330* **Rooms** *5*

Set in a large, stone country house, this charming guesthouse is well situated for exploring the beautiful Jurassic coast. The rooms offer a high level of comfort, with flat-screen TVs and king-size beds; most are en suite and one has a private sitting room. The restaurant and tea room is open Apr–Oct. **www.theabbeyhouse.co.uk**

Key to Price Guide *see p556* **Key to Symbols** *see back cover flap*

BATH The Windsor Guest Hotel

69 Gt Pulteney St, Bath, Somerset, BA2 4DL **Tel** *01225 422100* **Fax** *01225 422550* **Rooms** *13*

Set in an elegant Grade I protected Georgian terrace, just a short walk from Poultney Bridge and the heart of Bath, the rooms in this hotel are individually decorated. Rooms are elegantly furnished and facilities include 24-hour room service and broadband access. Includes breakfast. **www.bathwindsorguesthouse.co.uk**

BATH Villa Magdala

Henrietta Rd, Bath, Somerset, BA2 6LX **Tel** *01225 466329* **Fax** *01225 483207* **Rooms** *18*

Roy and Lois Thwaites create a homey ambience at this Victorian mansion basking in a peaceful location overlooking lovely Henrietta Park. It's a five-minute flat walk to the Roman baths and city centre shops. This is one of the few local hotels to have on-site guest parking. **www.villamagdala.co.uk**

BATH Royal Crescent

16 Royal Crescent, Bath, Somerset, BA1 2LS **Tel** *01225 823333* **Fax** *01225 339401* **Rooms** *45*

Located at the centre of Bath's glorious semi-circle of Georgian grandiosity. The simple but imposing Bath stone façade is the first glimpse of one of Britain's great hotels. Rooms brim with antiques, beds are luxuriant, there's a spa and the restaurant is elegance personified. **www.royalcrescent.co.uk**

BLANDFORD FORUM Best Western Crown Hotel

West St, Blandford Forum, Dorset, DT11 7AJ **Tel** *01258 456626* **Fax** *01258 451084* **Rooms** *32*

A former coaching inn at the heart of a pretty market town, on the edge of Salisbury Plain, with strong military connections, including a fascinating tank museum nearby. Rooms are spacious and well equipped. Popular wood-panelled bar and restaurant and a small private bar for residents. Includes breakfast. **www.bestwestern.co.uk**

BOURNEMOUTH Miramar

East Overcliff Dr, Bournemouth, Dorset, BH1 3AL **Tel** *01202 556581* **Fax** *01202 291242* **Rooms** *43*

The Miramar occupies a stunning vantage point, with views to the Isle of Wight and the Purbeck Hills. This attractive Edwardian mansion offers a wide range of rooms and suites. There are two restaurants as well as terraces with lawns sweeping down towards the sea. Guests can use a local gym. **www.miramar-bournemouth.com**

BOURNEMOUTH Arlington Hotel

Exeter Park Rd, Bournemouth, Dorset, BH2 5BD **Tel** *01202 552879* **Fax** *01202 298317* **Rooms** *28*

Situated in the town centre, the Arlington stands in its own grounds among scented pine trees. The well-equipped rooms are comfortable, and the hotel prides itself on friendly hospitality. The hotel's private gateways lead directly into the Bournemouth flower gardens, which are just a short walk from the beach. **www.arlingtonbournemouth.co.uk**

BOURNEMOUTH Bay View Court

35 East Overcliff Drive, Bournemouth, Dorset, BH1 3AH **Tel** *01202 294449* **Fax** *01202 292883* **Rooms** *70*

An East Cliff location gives lovely panoramic views across Bournemouth Bay. This comfortable family-run hotel serves international cuisine. A large heated indoor pool, spa bath, steam room, snooker, pool, darts and games machines are located in the popular Purbeck suite. There are relaxing lounges and sun terraces. **www.bayviewcourt.co.uk**

BRADFORD-ON-AVON Bradford Old Windmill

4 Masons Lane, Bradford-on-Avon, Wiltshire, BA15 1QN **Tel** *01225 866842* **Fax** *01225 866648* **Rooms** *3*

And now for something completely different. Yes, it really is an old and extremely atmospheric stone windmill – and the round room has a circular bed. Evening meals are vegetarian but breakfast offers hearty fare for meat-eaters, vegetarians and vegans alike. Price includes breakfast. **www.bradfordoldwindmill.co.uk**

BRISTOL The Town & Country Lodge

Bridgewater Rd, Bristol, Somerset, BS13 8AG **Tel** *01275 392441* **Fax** *01275 393362* **Rooms** *36*

This modern hotel has easy access to the M4 and M5 motorways and to Temple Meads station, with its high-speed links to London and other cities. Providing friendly and efficient hospitality in a comfortable atmosphere, Town and Country Lodge is popular with the business community as well as leisure travellers. **www.tclodge.co.uk**

BRISTOL Westbourne

40–44 St Pauls Rd, Clifton, Bristol, Somerset, BS8 1LR **Tel** *0117 973 4214* **Fax** *0117 974 3552* **Rooms** *29*

The well-located Westbourne Hotel provides superb accommodation for business travellers and families alike, within easy reach of the city centre and all its attractions. The cuisine and levels of service are exemplary, though there are plenty of good restaurants within walking distance. Includes breakfast. **www.westbournehotel-bristol.co.uk**

BRISTOL Mercure Brigstow

5–7 Welsh Back, Bristol, Somerset, BS1 4SP **Tel** *0117 929 1030* **Fax** *0117 9292030* **Rooms** *116*

Occupying a prime city centre position on the banks of the River Avon, the Mercure Brigstow is at the heart of an historic but vigorously modern city. Facilities are first rate, including air conditioning and even a plasma screen in the bathroom. The business centre is well equipped, and guests can use a local health club. **www.mercure.com**

CALNE Lansdowne Strand Hotel

The Strand, Calne, Wiltshire, SN11 0EH **Tel** *01249 812488* **Fax** *01249 815323* **Rooms** *26*

In the centre of the market town, this 16th-century former coaching inn still retains many period features. Individually decorated rooms vary in size. There are two bars; one offers a wide selection of ales and a cosy fire to sit by. An interesting menu and choice of wines is available in the brasserie-style restaurant. **www.lansdownestrand.co.uk**

CASTLE COMBE The Manor House Hotel & Golf Club
Castle Combe, Chippenham, Wiltshire, SN14 7HR **Tel** *01249 782206* **Fax** *01249 782159* **Rooms** *48*

A secluded valley position on its own golf course makes this a truly idyllic retreat within easy reach of both Bath and the Cotswolds. Accommodation is in a row of individual cottages and dining in the main Jacobean-styled house. They also have meeting and private dining rooms. Excellent cuisine. **www.exclusivehotels.co.uk**

CHIPPENHAM Angel Hotel
Market Place, Chippenham, Wiltshire, SN15 3HD **Tel** *01249 652615* **Fax** *01249 443210* **Rooms** *50*

Originally an 18th-century coaching inn, this is now a modern hotel offering 15 rooms of individual character and 35 executive suites. Popular with business guests due to its conference facilities and location, this is also a great place to come for a relaxing break, with its own leisure club, bar and restaurant. **www.angelhotelchippenham.co.uk**

CHIPPENHAM Stanton Manor Hotel
Stanton Saint Quinton, nr Chippenham, Wiltshire, SN14 6DQ **Tel** *01666 837552* **Fax** *01666 837022* **Rooms** *22*

Set in seven acres within a mile of the M4, the original classic Wiltshire stone house has been extended to create a traditional country hotel that offers spacious rooms and the acclaimed Gallery Restaurant. It is also well suited for business travellers. Special rates are available if bookings are done online. **www.stantonmanor.co.uk**

DORCHESTER Casterbridge
49 High East St, Dorset, DT1 1HU **Tel** *01305 264043* **Fax** *01305 260884* **Rooms** *14*

Here's a peaceful haven in a busy county town. Dorchester was the Casterbridge in Thomas Hardy's novel, *The Mayor of Casterbridge,* hence the name of this hotel. Ground floor rooms enjoy a patio and wheelchair access. Four-poster room available. Enjoy a generous breakfast in the dining room or the conservatory. **www.casterbridgehotel.co.uk**

DULVERTON Ashwick House
Dulverton, Somerset, TA22 9QD **Tel** *01398 323868* **Rooms** *8*

Ashwick House is a delightful little Edwardian country estate. Manicured lawns sweep down through the six-acre grounds to water gardens and the River Barle. The suites are baronial. Dinner can be taken on the terrace. Breakfast is included. **www.ashwickhouse.com**

EVERSHOT Summer Lodge
Evershot, Dorset, DT2 0JR **Tel** *01935 482000* **Fax** *01935 482040* **Rooms** *24*

Set in the picturesque village of Evershot, this Relais et Châteaux property has a spa as well as a large heated indoor swimming pool. Enjoy croquet, tennis or an alfresco afternoon tea. In the 2005 Tatler Awards, Summer Lodge was rated as having the best out-of-town restaurant. Includes breakfast. **www.summerlodgehotel.co.uk**

EYPE'S Eype's Mouth Country Hotel
Eype, Bridport, Dorset, DT6 6AL **Tel** *01308 423300* **Fax** *01308 420033* **Rooms** *18*

With dramatic sea views and located just a few minutes walk to the beach, this hotel occupies a coveted position on the heritage coast, with immediate access to the much-lauded coastal path. Family-run, it exudes a welcoming and relaxed atmosphere, ensuring a pleasant and comfortable stay. Includes breakfast. **www.eypesmouthhotel.co.uk**

GILLINGHAM Stock Hill House Hotel & Restaurant
Stockhill, Dorset, SP8 5NR **Tel** *01747 823626* **Fax** *01747 825628* **Rooms** *9*

A beech-lined drive leads to the very definition of peace and seclusion. Stock Hill is one of the country's finest country-house hotels. Chef and patron Peter Hauser and his wife Nita have spent two decades refurbishing to exacting standards. Provides business facilities, and price includes dinner. **www.stockhillhouse.co.uk**

LACOCK The Sign of the Angel
6 Church St, Lacock, Wiltshire, SN15 2LB **Tel** *01249 730230* **Fax** *01249 730527* **Rooms** *10*

If you are looking for character, you've found it. Run by the Levis family since 1953, the hotel has low beams, log fires and squeaky floorboards. Luxuriously furnished bedrooms with TVs, tea and coffee making facilities and phone lines. Includes breakfast. Lacock is now owned by the National Trust. **www.lacock.co.uk**

LYME REGIS Hotel Alexandra
Pound St, Lyme Regis, Dorset, DT7 3HZ **Tel** *01297 442010* **Fax** *01297 443229* **Rooms** *25*

Lauded for its hospitality, comfort and good food, the Alexandra has sloping lawns and magnificent views of the Cobb. All the bedrooms are finely decorated with private bathrooms, TVs, hairdryers and all the standard facilities. Elegant dining room with first-class menu and wine list. **www.hotelalexandra.co.uk**

MALMESBURY The Old Bell
Abbey Row, Wiltshire, SN16 0BW **Tel** *01666 822344* **Fax** *01666 825145* **Rooms** *33*

Established in 1220 adjacent to historic Malmesbury Abbey, this is reputed to be Britain's oldest purpose-built hotel. Welcoming rooms and outstanding levels of service amid the ambience of a bygone age. Pretty terrace for outdoor dining in summer. Outstanding wine list. Includes breakfast. **www.oldbellhotel.co.uk**

PORLOCK WEIR Andrews on the Weir
Porlock Weir, Minehead, Somerset, TA24 8PB **Tel** *01643 863300* **Fax** *01643 863311* **Rooms** *5*

Andrews on the Weir stands on one of Europe's most beautiful stretches of coast, where thick woods sweep down to the sea. Bedrooms are comfortably furnished and the inventively presented food is quite exquisite. It also has a beautiful garden and is close to nearby attractions. Breakfast included. **www.andrewsontheweir.co.uk**

Key to Price Guide *see p556* **Key to Symbols** *see back cover flap*

SHEPTON MALLET Charlton House

Charlton Rd, Somerset, BA4 4PR **Tel** *01749 342008* **Fax** *01749 346362* **Rooms** *25*

Decorated with imagination, flair and a sense of theatre, this country-house hotel is set amid rolling hills just 18 miles (30 km) south of Bath. Relaxation comes easy in an ambience of informal splendour. The outstanding restaurant uses local produce and the spa is special. Includes breakfast. **www.charltonhouse.com**

STON EASTON Ston Easton Park

Ston Easton, nr Bath, Somerset, BA3 4DF **Tel** *01761 241631* **Fax** *01761 241377* **Rooms** *22*

An elegant Palladian mansion sited on a romantic estate offering upscale country life at its best. Wonderfully ornate ceilings, masses of antique furniture and priceless paintings make for a comfortable stay while the cuisine is truly sublime. Facilities include conference and business meeting rooms. Inclusive of breakfast. **www.stoneaston.co.uk**

SWINDON, WILTS Marsh Farm Hotel

Wooton Bassett, Swindon, Wiltshire, SN4 8ER **Tel** *01793 848044* **Fax** *01793 851528* **Rooms** *50*

In three acres, surrounded by open countryside, this large Victorian farmhouse has been restored, converted and extended into a 50-bedroom luxury hotel located to the west of Swindon close to Junction 16 of the M4. Various kinds of meeting rooms are available with all sorts of mod cons. **www.marshfarmhotel.co.uk**

TAUNTON The Mount Somerset

Lower Henlade, Somerset, TA3 5NB **Tel** *01823 442500* **Fax** *01823 442900* **Rooms** *11*

Cradled by the Quantock and Blackdown Hills, the Regency-styled Mount is noted for the elegance and warmth of its greeting. Log fires, abundant scatter cushions and a superb sweeping staircase reek of the good life. Just the place for a calm, unhurried stay. Includes breakfast. **www.mountsomersethotel.co.uk**

WAREHAM The Priory

Church Green, Wareham, Dorset, BH20 4ND **Tel** *01929 551666* **Fax** *01929 554519* **Rooms** *18*

Landscaped gardens fronting the River Frome, it offers fine views of the Purbeck Hills. Sumptuous yet relaxed in style, this 16th-century masterpiece has moorings for those arriving by boat. Furnished with antiques, all rooms are en suite, and you may stay in the main house or the hotel's houseboats. Includes breakfast. **www.theprioryhotel.co.uk**

WELLINGTON Bindon Country House

Langford, Budville, Somerset, TA21 0RU **Tel** *01823 400070* **Fax** *01823 400071* **Rooms** *12*

Extravagantly decorated bedrooms and great food draw people back to this unusually styled and historic Somerset mansion with its extensive gardens, swimming pool, croquet lawn and bicycles. Opt for a four-poster bedroom. Exmoor is within striking distance. Includes breakfast. **www.bindon.com**

WELLS The Crown At Wells

Market Place, Wells, Somerset, BA5 2RP **Tel** *01749 673457* **Fax** *01749 679792* **Rooms** *15*

Set in the bustling market place at the centre of one of England's smallest cities, this attractive Grade II listed building is overlooked by the cathedral and the Bishops Palace, with its moat. All the bedrooms are comfortably furnished with en suite facilities, and Anton's Bistrot is well known for its excellent food. **www.crownatwells.co.uk**

WEYMOUTH Seaham

3 Waterloo Place, Dorset, DT4 7NU **Tel** *01305 782010* **Rooms** *5*

The highest graded guesthouse in town, the Seaham is conveniently located close to the vibrant town centre and picturesque harbour. Recently refurbished, the bedrooms are warmly decorated and have en suite facilities. Breakfast included. Children are not welcome. **www.theseahamweymouth.co.uk**

WOOKEY HOLE Glencot House

Glencot Lane, Wookey Hole, Somerset, BA5 1BH **Tel** *01749 677160* **Fax** *01749 670210* **Rooms** *15*

Glencot House is a Jacobean inspired late-Victorian mansion perfectly set in 18 acres of amazing gardens and parkland, facing the river. It also has its own cricket pitch. All the rooms are beautifully furnished and have four-poster beds. Also has an indoor plunge pool, sauna and a library. Includes breakfast. **www.relaxatglencot.co.uk**

WOOLTON School House Hotel and Restaurant

Hook St, Hook, Wiltshire, SN4 8EF **Tel** *01793 851198* **Fax** *01793 851025* **Rooms** *11*

Close to Swindon and at the gateway to the Cotswolds, this transformed Victorian school building is just minutes from Junction 16 on the M4. Car hire, station and airport transfers can be arranged. The restaurant has a Victorian beamed ceiling. Suitable for business travellers as well. Includes breakfast. **www.schoolhotel.com**

DEVON AND CORNWALL

BIGBURY-ON-SEA Burgh Island

Burgh Island, Bigbury-On-Sea, South Devon, TQ7 4BG **Tel** *01548 810514* **Fax** *01548 810243* **Rooms** *25*

This Art Deco treasure set 200 m (656 ft) off the South Devon coast is where Agatha Christie did her famous disappearing act. Rooms are individually decorated with all the modern facilities. Call for the elevated four-wheel drive or stroll by the sea. Guests can swim in a natural rock pool. Inclusive of breakfast and dinner. **www.burghisland.com**

BOSCASTLE The Bottreaux Hotel & Restaurant

Boscastle, Cornwall, PL35 OBG **Tel** *01840 250231* **Fax** *01840 250170* **Rooms** *8*

Just five minutes stroll from Boscastle's Elizabethan harbour, this town house is at the heart of the busy one-time fishing village. Bedrooms and public areas have been refurbished to very high standards and guest amenities include a car park. Quality restaurant with breakfast inclusive. **www.boscastlecornwall.co.uk**

BOSCASTLE The Old Rectory

St Juliot, Boscastle, Cornwall, PL35 OBT **Tel & Fax** *01840 250225* **Rooms** *4*

Beautiful gardens surround the house where Thomas Hardy fell in love with Emma Lavinia Gifford, leading to some of his best poetry. A family home that has been renovated and decorated beautifully in period style. The breakfast is all-inclusive in this B&B close to the coast and the Eden Project. **www.stjuliot.com**

BUDE The Falcon Hotel

Breakwater Rd, Cornwall, EX23 8SD **Tel** *01288 352005* **Fax** *01288 356359* **Rooms** *29*

There's 200 years of tradition behind this much-expanded one-time coaching inn overlooking the Bude Canal. All the rooms are tastefully decorated and one is a four-poster bedroom with its own luxury spa bath. It also has a stylish restaurant. The Falcon Inn is reputed for its food. **www.falconhotel.com**

CHAGFORD Three Crowns Hotel

High St, Chagford, Devon, TQ13 8AJ **Tel** *01647 433444* **Fax** *01647 433117* **Rooms** *18*

This 13th-century stone-built inn evokes a long history with its mullion windows, massive oak beams, great open fireplace and four-poster rooms. It is at the heart of Dartmoor National Park and conveniently located close to the Eden Project and the Lost Gardens of Heligan. Breakfast is included. **www.chagford-accom.co.uk**

CHAGFORD Gidleigh Park

Gidleigh, Chagford, Devon, TQ13 8HH **Tel** *01647 432367* **Fax** *01647 432574* **Rooms** *24*

Gidleigh Park has long been established as one of the UK's finest country-house hotels. It carries the prestigious Relais et Châteaux branding with pride. The rooms are comfortably furnished with all the modern facilities. Enjoy walks on its gardens, then savour the cuisine that has won two Michelin stars for chef Michael Caines. **www.gidleigh.com**

EXETER Innkeeper's Lodge Exeter East

Clyst St George, Exeter, Devon, EX3 OQJ **Tel** *01392 876121* **Fax** *01392 876904* **Rooms** *21*

A fast-growing nationwide chain of modern budget hotels, Innkeeper's Lodge choose their sites well. This one is located just off the M5, making it a suitable jumping off point for forays into the deepest West Country. Deals include two nights for the price of one, while Continental breakfast is complimentary. **www.innkeeperslodge.com**

EXETER Barcelona

Magdalen St, Exeter, Devon, EX2 4HY **Tel** *01392 281000* **Fax** *01392 281001* **Rooms** *46*

This brilliantly converted former eye hospital gives the wink to inspired 1950s style with all the convenience of a modern hotel. The rooms are stylishly furnished with comforts such as satellite TV, video players and Internet. Business facilities are available, and Café Paradiso prepares Mediterranean cuisine. **www.aliashotels.com**

FALMOUTH Budock Vean Hotel On The River

Helford Passage, Mawnan Smith, Falmouth, Cornwall, TR11 5LG **Tel** *01326 250288* **Fax** *01326 250892* **Rooms** *57*

This hotel is set in 65 acres of grounds that lead down to the Helford River. The bedrooms have all the latest facilities, and some have fine views of the gardens and the golf course. They also have a swimming pool, health spa, two tennis courts and a fine restaurant, and they offer boat trips. Includes breakfast and dinner. **www.budockvean.co.uk**

FOWEY Marina Villa

17 The Esplanade, Fowey, Cornwall, PL23 1HY **Tel** *01726 833315* **Fax** *01726 832779* **Rooms** *17*

The Marina Villa is set on a wooded inlet on Cornwall's beautiful south coast. The hotel boasts stunning sea and river views but the real delights wait inside. The rooms are stylish and the acclaimed Waterside Restaurant, headed by chef Nathan Outlaw, is a destination in its own right. **www.marinavillahotel.co.uk**

FOWEY The Old Quay House

28 Fore St, Fowey, Cornwall, PL23 1AQ **Tel** *01726 833302* **Fax** *01726 833668* **Rooms** *11*

The individually styled rooms at this waterside hotel offer an experience of luxurious indulgence, with natural fabrics, warm colours and splendid views of the surrounding area. The Old Quay House was voted Best Small Hotel of the Year in 2008 and boasts an award-winning restaurant run by chef Ben Bass. **www.theoldquayhouse.com**

ISLES OF SCILLY Hell Bay

Bryher, Isles of Scilly, TR23 OPR **Tel** *01720 422947* **Fax** *01720 423004* **Rooms** *25*

New England and the Caribbean meet Cornwall's offshore islands. Lloyd Loom furnishing and Malabar fabrics are set against cool ocean blues and greens. Robert and Lucy Dorrien-Smith have filled this secluded haven of tranquility with the works of renowned artists. Breakfast and dinner inclusive. **www.hellbay.co.uk**

LANDEWEDNACK Landewednack House

Church Cove, Landewednack, The Lizard, Cornwall, TR12 7PQ **Tel** *01326 290909* **Fax** *01326 290192* **Rooms** *5*

This former rectory is today a quintessential country-house B&B. There is a secluded two-acre walled garden with sea views and a heated swimming pool to keep you on-site, though the surrounding countryside is delightful. There is also a self-contained two-bedroom annexe. Full breakfast is included in the price. **www.landewednackhouse.com**

Key to Price Guide *see p556* **Key to Symbols** *see back cover flap*

LYNMOUTH The Rising Sun

Harbourside, Lynmouth, Devon, EX35 6EG **Tel** *01598 753223* **Fax** *01598 753480* **Rooms** *14*

Percy Bysshe Shelley honeymooned in this 14th-century thatched smugglers inn. It overlooks Lynmouth's picturesque harbour and the highest hogback cliffs in England. Oak panelling, wonky ceilings, beachstone walls and uneven floorboards – it's atmosphere all the way, with well-appointed rooms. **www.risingsunlynmouth.co.uk**

MEMBURY Lea Hill

Membury, Axminster, Devon, EX13 7AQ **Tel** *01404 881881* **Rooms** *2*

Superb walks along the South West Coastal Path, now a World Heritage Site, await at the doorstep of this former hotel, now offering a mix of B&B and self-catering accommodation. Lea Hill also offers six fully furnished cottages and apartments. Rates include breakfast. **www.leahill.co.uk**

MORTEHOE Lundy House Hotel

Chapel Hill, Mortehoe, North Devon, EX34 7DZ **Tel** *01271 870372* **Fax** *01271 871001* **Rooms** *9*

Wet suits and surfboards can be rented at nearby Woolacombe Beach or you can ramble over Exmoor. You might, though, prefer to simply relax while admiring the view over to the romantic offshore Lundy Island and watch the sunset before retiring to contemporary four-poster luxury. Closed Oct–Mar. **www.lundyhousehotel.co.uk**

MOUSEHOLE Old Coast Guard Hotel

The Parade, Mousehole, Penzance, Cornwall, TR19 6PR **Tel** *01736 731222* **Fax** *01736 731720* **Rooms** *14*

Razed in 1595 by raiders from the Spanish Armada, tiny Mousehole has survived as a classic Cornish fishing village. As the name implies, this friendly hotel, with all the mod-con facilities, overlooks the local maritime scene. Most rooms have sea views and several have balconies. Breakfast included. **www.oldcoastguardhotel.co.uk**

MULLION The Polurrian Hotel

Polurrian Hotel, Mullion, South Cornwall, TR12 7EN **Tel** *01326 240421* **Fax** *01326 240083* **Rooms** *39*

Excellent service is still a hallmark here, but what guests always talk about most is the stunning cliff-top location, set in beautiful landscaped gardens and with glorious views across to St Michael's Mount. All rooms are en suite and most have sea views. The hotel also offers beauty treatment rooms. **www.polurrianhotel.com**

NEWQUAY Barrowfield Hotel

Hill Grove Rd, Newquay, Cornwall, TR7 2QY **Tel** *01637 878878* **Fax** *01637 879490* **Rooms** *81*

This family hotel offers honeymoon suites, four posters and suites with separate sleeping areas for children. Golf breaks are another speciality. The location overlooks Tolcarne and Lusty Glaze beaches and is a short and flat walk to Newquay's prime shopping area. **www.daishstravel.com**

NEWQUAY Sands Resort

Watergate Rd, Porth, Newquay, Cornwall, TR7 3LX **Tel** *01637 872864* **Fax** *01637 876365* **Rooms** *88*

Spacious rooms with separate sleeping space for children await at this North Cornwall family favourite. Close to the golden sand beaches and surf, this full-on holiday resort features the Ocean Breeze Spa's relaxing therapies plus four age-banded children's clubs. Rates include full breakfast. **www.sandsresort.co.uk**

NEWQUAY The Headland Hotel

Fistral Beach, Newquay, Cornwall, TR7 1EW **Tel** *01637 872211* **Fax** *01637 872212* **Rooms** *104*

High Victorian Gothic architecture dominating the cliff above one of Newquay's finest beaches gives this four-star hotel an imposing setting. Inside it is a friendly, family-orientated place and they also run a nearby holiday park. The rooms are comfortably furnished, and many have sea view. Full breakfast is standard. **www.headlandhotel.co.uk**

OAK HAMPTON Lewtrenchard Manor

Lewdown, nr Oak Hampton, Devon, EX20 4PN **Tel** *01566 783222* **Fax** *01566 783332* **Rooms** *14*

Barely touched by time, this Jacobean delight is built on the site of an even earlier manor. It is famed for its heavenly 17th-century gardens, and is also ideal for business travellers. All the rooms are individually styled and have modern facilities. Full breakfast is inclusive. **info@lewtrenchard.co.uk**

OTTERY ST MARY Tumbling Weir

Canaan Way, Ottery St Mary, nr Exeter, Devon, EX11 1AQ **Tel** *01404 812752* **Fax** *01404 812752* **Rooms** *10*

A thatched hotel set in half-an-acre of beautiful gardens beside a millstream. Conveniently located close to the M5 and Exeter, this gem is a short drive from historic Exeter and the coast. Comfortable beds and new bathrooms, while the restaurant creates wonderful dishes from local produce. **www.tumblingweir-hotel.co.uk**

PADSTOW The Seafood Restaurant

Riverside, Padstow, Cornwall, PL28 8BY **Tel** *01841 532700* **Fax** *01841 532942* **Rooms** *14*

Described as "a restaurant-with-rooms" rather than a hotel, this harbour-side gem is the perfect showcase for Rick Stein's renowned fish cookery. Rooms are simple and tasteful while romantics will enjoy watching the coming and going of the fishing fleet. Breakfast is included. **www.rickstein.com**

PENZANCE Queens Hotel

Promenade, Penzance, TR18 4HG **Tel** *01736 362371* **Fax** *01736 350033* **Rooms** *70*

This family run hotel has a Victorian elegance and is situated right on the town's promenade, with sweeping views across Mount Bay to St Michael's Mount. Fresh local fish is a speciality in the dining room. Ideal for the Tate St Ives gallery. Offers yoga classes, a hair salon and is suited for business travellers as well. **www.queens-hotel.com**

PENZANCE Summer House · 🍴 · ££££

Cornwall Terrace, Penzance, Cornwall, TR18 4HL **Tel** *01736 363744* **Fax** *01736 360959* **Rooms** *5*

This charming Garde II listed Regency house has been converted into a delightfully intimate hotel and lies very close to the sea. Tropical walled garden, fresh-cut flowers, polished wooden floors and inventive Mediterranean inspired cuisine await. All the bedrooms are individually styled. Breakfast is inclusive. **www.summerhouse-cornwall.com**

PLYMOUTH Athenaeum Lodge · 🚶♿ · ££

4 Athenaeum St, The Hoe, Plymouth, Devon, PL1 2RQ **Tel** *01752 665005* **Rooms** *8*

Conveniently set near Plymouth Hoe, with the Theatre Royal and the historic Barbican nearby, this Grade II listed Georgian building is also close to the Brittany Ferries terminal. If you have difficulty with stairs, a downstairs guest room is available. Wi-Fi internet and laptop available for use. Breakfast is inclusive. **www.athenaeumlodge.com**

PLYMOUTH Novotel · 🏊🍴♿🚶♿ · ££££

Plymouth Road, Marsh Mills, Plymouth, Devon, PL6 8NH **Tel** *01752 221422* **Fax** *01752 223922* **Rooms** *100*

Marsh Mills is the gateway into Plymouth, with all the delights of Devon and Cornwall within easy reach. Each of the modern rooms features a large double and a single bed and up to two under 16s stay free on a B&B basis when sharing their parents' room. Also has a swimming pool and private parking space. **www.novotel.com**

ROCK St Enodoc · 🍴♿🚶 · ££££

Rock, nr Wadebridge, Cornwall, PL27 6LA **Tel** *01208 863394* **Fax** *01208 863970* **Rooms** *20*

Overlooking the beautiful Camel Estuary, and a short drive from the foodie mecca of Padstow, the St Enodoc hotel offers a bright, comfortable feel, with original paintings adding wit and colour. Rooms have microwaves and fridges. They also have a children's playroom, games room and outdoor pool. Breakfast included. **www.enodoc-hotel.co.uk**

ST BLAZEY Nanscawen Manor · 🏊 · ££

Prideaux Rd, Luxulyan Valley, St Blazey, Cornwall, PL24 2SR **Tel** *01726 814488* **Rooms** *3*

Don't be misled by the valley address – this is a hilltop-sited gem with lawns sweeping down to breathtaking views – and you can enjoy these from the sizeable outdoor pool or the hot tubs. The owner adds flair and a gracious welcome to a charming building with 14th-century roots. Breakfast is inclusive. **www.nanscawen.com**

ST HILARY Ennys · 🏊♿ · ££

Trewhella Lane, St Hilary, Penzance, Cornwall, TR20 9BZ **Tel** *01736 740262* **Fax** *01736 740055* **Rooms** *5*

An idyllic country hideaway whose private fields stretch down to the delightful River Hayle. Sheltered formal gardens frame a large heated swimming pool and tennis courts. The rooms are comfortably furnished. Ideal for Lands End, St Michael's Mount, the Eden Project and the Lizard peninsula. Rates include an outstanding breakfast. **www.ennys.co.uk**

ST IVES The Garrack Hotel · 🍴🏊♿📺♿ · ££££

Burthallam Lane, St Ives, Cornwall, TR26 3AA **Tel** *01736 796199* **Fax** *01736 798955* **Rooms** *18*

Unusually for the busy little artists' haunt of St Ives, the Garrack has its own on-site car parking, as well as delightfully themed subtropical gardens. All rooms have private bathrooms and TV while some have jacuzzi or spa baths. Dine on seafood, meat and vegetarian specialities. Includes breakfast. **www.garrack.com**

ST IVES The Gunard's Head · 🅿️🍴♿ · ££££

Near Zennor, St Ives, Cornwall, TR26 3DE **Tel** *01736 796928* **Rooms** *7*

A handsome inn set between the coast road and stonewall-crossed countryside. This restaurant with rooms provides the perfect base from which to explore St Ives. The restaurant uses fresh ingredients and serves local beer and the accommodation is comfortable. **www.gunardshead.co.uk**

ST MAWES Rising Sun · 🍴♿ · ££££

The Square, St Mawes, Truro, Cornwall, TR2 5DJ **Tel** *01326 270233* **Fax** *01326 270198* **Rooms** *8*

Rooms are bright and cheery in this hotel with all the modern comforts. The property fronts directly on to St Mawes' picturesque little harbour, with views of the Roseland Peninsula. Award-winning chef, Ian Rogers, presides over the Rising Sun's much-acclaimed AA Rosette-awarded restaurant. **www.risingsunstmawes.com**

ST MAWES Hotel Tresanton · 🍴♿ · £££££

St Mawes, Truro, Cornwall, TR2 5DR **Tel** *01326 270055* **Fax** *01326 270053* **Rooms** *29*

St Anthony's Lighthouse is a beacon for one of Cornwall's best-loved hotels, formerly a club for yachtsmen. Two years' of re-design and restoration saw Olga Polizzi create a casually elegant venue ideal for weddings and holidays alike. Facilities include a conference room and a variety of treatments. Breakfast is inclusive. **www.tresanton.com**

STOKE CANON Barton Cross Hotel & Restaurant · 🍴♿♿ · ££££

Huxham, Stoke Canon, Exeter, Devon, EX5 4EJ **Tel** *01392 841245* **Fax** *01392 841942* **Rooms** *9*

Set in lush Devon countryside, close to Exeter city and an hour from bustling Torbay, this traditional hotel also accesses a number of magnificent National Trust properties. Fishing and three excellent golf courses are nearby, and you can relax in the timber-beamed lounge afterwards. Includes full breakfast. **www.bartoncrosshotel.co.uk**

TAVISTOCK The Bedford · 🍴♿ · ££

1 Plymouth Road, Tavistock, Devon, PL19 8BB **Tel** *01822 892347* **Fax** *01822 892347* **Rooms** *30*

Formerly a Benedictine Abbey, this elegant hotel was once the residence of the Dukes of Bedford. The rooms are charming and tastefully furnished to a high standard. Situated in the historic market town of Tavistock, the Bedford makes an excellent base from which to explore the wild beauty of Dartmoor. **www.bedford-hotel.co.uk**

Key to Price Guide *see p556* **Key to Symbols** *see back cover flap*

TAVISTOCK The Horn of Plenty
P 🍴   ££££

Gulworthy, Tavistock, Devon, PL19 8JD **Tel** *01822 832528* **Rooms** *10*

Set in two hectares (five acres) of spectacular gardens and with breathtaking views, this elegant country house hotel has a unique character and charm. Rooms offer a combination of elegance and classic sophistication and the hotel boasts an award-winning restaurant under head chef Peter Gorton. **www.thehornofplenty.co.uk**

TEIGNMOUTH Thomas Luny House
££

Teign St, Teignmouth, Devon, TQ14 8EG **Tel** *01626 772976* **Rooms** *4*

Once frequented by the captains of Nelson's navy, this Georgian house is furnished with antiques and collectibles. Tea and home-made cake are offered to afternoon arrivals, which may be enjoyed in the secluded garden. All rooms are individually designed, and expect faultless hospitality. Includes breakfast. **www.thomas-luny-house.co.uk**

TORQUAY Palace Hotel
££££

Babbacombe Rd, Torquay, Devon, TQ1 3TG **Tel** *01803 200200* **Fax** *01803 299899* **Rooms** *141*

Overlooking St Anstey's Cove and featuring a nine-hole golf course, tennis courts and indoor and outdoor swimming pools, this uncrowned queen of the English Riviera stands in 26 acres of glorious gardens. Well placed for visiting Dartmoor. Additionals include conference facilities and tennis tutorials. **www.palacetorquay.co.uk**

WIDEGATE Coombe Farm
££

Widegates, Looe, Cornwall, PL13 1QN **Tel** *01503 240223* **Rooms** *3*

Spacious rooms offer fine views of the wooded valley and the sea, and horse riding and sea and lake fishing are among other attractions. The rooms are warmly decorated and in self-contained cottages. Dartmoor, Bodmin Moor and the Cornish Coastal Path are all at hand. Breakfast included. **www.coombefarmhotel.co.uk**

THE HEART OF ENGLAND

BIBURY The Swan
££££

Bibury, Gloucestershire, GL7 5NW **Tel** *01285 740695* **Fax** *01285 740473* **Rooms** *22*

A picturesque hotel set in a converted 17th-century coaching inn in the Cotswolds. The rooms are luxurious with views over the peaceful River Coln and expansive hotel gardens. Some rooms have en suite jacuzzis. The Swan also boasts an award-winning restaurant. **www.swanhotel.co.uk**

BIRMINGHAM Plough & Harrow
££

135 Hagley Rd, Edgbaston, Birmingham, B16 8LS **Tel** *0121 454 4111* **Fax** *0121 454 1868* **Rooms** *44*

Part of the Crerar hotel chain, this red brick, Victorian hotel is full of character. It is located near the Birmingham city centre and Edgbaston cricket ground, and is a reasonably priced choice for both business travellers and families. The amenities are mostly basic, but the rooms are spacious. Also has conference facilities. **www.swallow-hotels.com**

BIRMINGHAM Hotel du Vin & Bistro
££££

Church St, Birmingham, B3 2NR **Tel** *0121 200 0600* **Fax** *0121 236 0889* **Rooms** *66*

Large, elegant hotel in a converted Victorian building in the city's trendy Jewellery Quarter. Many of the building's original features, including the sweeping staircase and granite pillars, have been retained. Features a well-reputed bistro restaurant and the popular Cellar Bar. Also has a beauty spa. **www.hotelduvin.com**

BIRMINGHAM Malmaison
££££

1 Wharfside St, Birmingham, B1 1RD **Tel** *0121 246 5000* **Fax** *0121 246 5002* **Rooms** *189*

A stylish, award-winning hotel in a former 1960s Royal Mail sorting office, Malmaison sits amid designer stores and within walking distance of the city centre. The rooms are furnished in chic chocolate and cream, with moody lighting and CD libraries. Also has a spa with sauna, Jacuzzi and choice of treatments. **www.malmaison-birmingham.com**

BLACKWELL Blackwell Grange
££

Blackwell, Shipston-on-Stour, Warwickshire, CV36 4PF **Tel** *01608 682357* **Fax** *01608 682856* **Rooms** *3*

Small B&B in a 17th-century farmhouse, complete with low-beamed ceilings and stone-flagged floors, to the north of the Cotswolds. Offers two self-catering cottages; one for up to six persons and the other for two. A great spot for walking. Picnics are provided on request. Also functions as a working farm. **www.blackwellgrange.co.uk**

BLOCKLEY The Crown Inn
££

High St, Blockley, Moreton-In-Marsh, Gloucestershire, GL56 9EX **Tel** *01386 700245* **Fax** *01386 700247* **Rooms** *24*

A converted 14th-century coaching inn with wood-beamed ceilings, whitewashed walls and log fires. Has individually furnished rooms with fireplaces and four-poster beds. The restaurant boasts an impressive cellar and an extensive choice of Real Ales. The nearby countryside is great for walking and horse riding. **www.crowninnblockley.com**

BROAD CAMPDEN Malt House
£££

Broad Campden, Chipping Campden, Gloucestershire, GL55 6UU **Tel** *01386 840295* **Fax** *01386 841334* **Rooms** *7*

Elegant and well-located B&B, which prides itself on its personal touch. Each of the six bedrooms (and one garden suite) is individually decorated with antique furnishings, four-poster beds, fine china and freshly cut flowers from its carefully-tended gardens. Offers a large breakfast with home-made bread and jams. **www.malt-house.co.uk**

BUCKLAND Buckland Manor

Buckland, Gloucestershire, WR12 7LY **Tel** *01386 852626* **Fax** *01386 853557* **Rooms** *13*

This 13th-century country-house hotel, near Broadway, features antiques-filled rooms and fine views over the grounds. Hosts croquet lawns, tennis courts and a private putting green. The award-winning restaurant serves seasonal fruit, vegetables and herbs from the nearby Vale of Evesham. **www.bucklandmanor.com**

CHELTENHAM Georgian House

77 Montpellier Terrace, Cheltenham, Gloucestershire, GL50 1XA **Tel** *01242 515577* **Fax** *01242 545929* **Rooms** *3*

Small, reasonably-priced B&B in a terraced Georgian house built in 1807. The rooms are large and have period fireplaces, wall hangings and furnishings; one of the rooms has a balcony overlooking the garden. Serves hearty breakfasts. Garage parking is available, but it is best to reserve in advance. **www.georgianhouse.net**

CHELTENHAM Hotel Kandinsky

Bayshill Rd, Montpellier, Cheltenham, Gloucestershire, GL50 3AS **Tel** *01242 527788* **Rooms** *48*

An eclectic hotel with contrasting Regency exterior, located in the heart of Cheltenham. The rooms are large and luxurious. Features a sunlit conservatory and a large lounge for guests, and has a contract with a local gym, just ten minutes away. Also has a Mediterranean restaurant. **www.hotelkandinsky.com**

CHELTENHAM Hotel on the Park

38 Evesham Rd, Cheltenham, Gloucestershire, GL52 2AH **Tel** *01242 511526* **Rooms** *12*

In the heart of the Cotswolds and close to Cheltenham's town centre, the luxurious Hotel on the Park combines exceptional standards of hotel keeping with friendly hospitality. Peace, elegance and refinement with full business facilities and an award-winning restaurant. **www.hotelonthepark.com**

CHIPPING CAMPDEN Nineveh Farm

Campden Rd, Mickleton, Chipping Campden, Gloucestershire, GL55 6PS **Tel** *01386 438923* **Rooms** *29*

Cosy and welcoming B&B in a 200-year-old Cotswold farmhouse, within easy reach of Chipping Campden and Stratford-upon-Avon. Rooms are furnished with oak beams, flagstone floors and log fires, with views over the vast grounds. Provides ample parking space, and offers discounts for longer stays. **www.ninevehfarm.co.uk**

CHIPPING CAMPDEN Badgers Hall

High St, Chipping Campden, Gloucestershire, GL55 6HB **Tel** *01386 840839* **Rooms** *3*

This B&B and traditional English tearoom offers a friendly and comfortable stay in the beautiful old Cotswolds market town of Chipping Campden. The bedrooms are large, with antique pine furnishings and wood-beamed ceilings. Serves plentiful breakfasts and authentic cream teas – everything is home-made on the premises. **www.badgershall.com**

CHIPPING CAMPDEN Cotswold House

Chipping Campden, Gloucestershire, GL55 6AN **Tel** *01386 840330* **Fax** *01386 840310* **Rooms** *29*

Located in a Regency town house, this elegant property offers a luxurious, relaxing break in some of England's most beautiful countryside. The deluxe rooms have fireplaces, hot tubs, king-sized beds and state-of-the-art facilities. **www.cotswoldhouse.com**

COLWALL Colwall Park Hotel

Colwall, Malvern, Worcestershire, WR13 6QG **Tel** *01684 540000* **Fax** *01684 540847* **Rooms** *22*

The Colwall Park Hotel offers comfortable, individually decorated rooms, some with views over the beautiful Malvern Hills. Guests can relax in the cosy lounge with a roaring fire in winter and deep armchairs, or head to the library or the games room. Modern British dishes are served in the restaurant. WiFi access. **www.colwall.co.uk**

EVESHAM Evesham Hotel

Coopers Lane, off Waterside, Evesham, Worcestershire, WR11 1DA **Tel** *01386 765443* **Rooms** *40*

Family-friendly and well-priced hotel, often ranked among the top ten places to stay in Britain. The rooms provide all modern amenities, but are decorated to befit the building's Georgian heritage; some rooms offer great views of the grounds. Has an indoor swimming pool. **www.eveshamhotel.com**

GLEWSTONE Glewstone Court

Near Ross-on-Wye, Herefordshire, HR9 6AW **Tel** *01989 770367* **Fax** *01989 770282* **Rooms** *8*

Ideally located in the Wye Valley Area of Outstanding Natural Beauty. This family-run hotel is well placed for walking, horse riding, canoeing and other outdoor activities. Rooms are comfortably furnished to a high standard. The restaurant has open log fires and serves fresh seasonal fare. **www.glewstonecourt.com**

HEREFORD The Priory

Stretton Sugwas, Hereford, Herefordshire, HR4 7AR **Tel** *01432 760264* **Fax** *01432 761809* **Rooms** *8*

Small, but grand, family-run hotel in an 18th-century building, on the outskirts of Hereford. Rooms are large with antique furnishings, including luxurious four-poster beds. The surrounding countryside is stunning and well worth a visit. The restaurant serves local produce (reservations should be made in advance). **www.hotelpriory.co.uk**

HEREFORD Pilgrim Hotel

Much Birch, Hereford, Herefordshire, HR2 8HJ **Tel** *01981 540742* **Fax** *01981 540620* **Rooms** *20*

Delightful three-star, country-house hotel, set amid a vast parkland in the Wye Valley just outside Hereford. The rooms are cosy, with views over the rolling mountains into Wales. Guests can enjoy scenic walks through the Dore Valley. The Pilgrim also boasts a restaurant that uses local produce. **www.pilgrimhotel.co.uk**

Key to Price Guide *see p556* **Key to Symbols** *see back cover flap*

HEREFORD Castle House Hotel 🍴 ⛵ ♿ ££££

Castle St, Hereford **Tel** *01432 356321* **Fax** *01432 365909* **Rooms** *15*

Set in the heart of historic Hereford, Castle House occupies a gracious Georgian town house. Its award-winning restaurant and quiet gardens with views over the old castle moat really make this a special place to stay. The rooms are elegantly furnished with fine antiques and all have modern amenities. **www.castlehse.co.uk**

ILMINGTON Howard Arms 🍴 £££

Lower Green, Ilmington, nr Shipston-on-Stour, Warwickshire, CV36 4LT **Tel** *01608 682226* **Rooms** *8*

Traditional Cotswolds pub offering B&B accommodation on the village green. The rooms at this hotel have a beamed ceiling and antique, country-style furnishings. Voted "UK Dining Pub of the Year 2005" by the Good Pub Guide for its fresh seasonal produce and an extensive selection of wine and cask ale. **www.howardarms.com**

IRONBRIDGE Library House ££

11 Severn Bank, Ironbridge, Telford, Shropshire, TF8 7AN **Tel** *01952 432299* **Fax** *01952 433967* **Rooms** *3*

A distinguished guesthouse, housed in a restored Grade II listed building in the World Heritage Site of Ironbridge Gorge. This hotel sits in a peaceful location among immaculately-tended gardens, and is a short distance from the Telford town centre. Each of the rooms has en suite facilities. **www.libraryhouse.com**

LEYSTERS Hills Farm ££

Leysters, Leominster, Herefordshire, HR 6OHP **Tel** *01568 750205* **Rooms** *3*

A family-run farmhouse B&B, set amid working farmland in the heart of rural Herefordshire. The bedrooms have en suite facilities, and are located in converted barn houses. Offers a sitting room, as well as maps and touring guides of the area. **www.thehillsfarm.co.uk**

LITTLE MALVERN Holdfast Cottage 🍴 ££

Little Malvern, nr Malvern, Worcestershire, WR13 6NA **Tel** *01684 310288* **Fax** *01684 311117* **Rooms** *8*

This country-house hotel is a delightful place to unwind. Boasts attractive woodland gardens and magnificent views of the Malvern Hills. The cosy, oak-beamed rooms have en suite facilities, and the intimate dining room serves home baked cuisine using herbs and vegetables grown in the grounds. **www.holdfast-cottage.co.uk**

MALVERN WELLS Cottage in the Wood 🍴 ⛵ £££

Holywell Rd, Malvern Wells, Worcestershire, WR14 4LG **Tel** *01684 575859* **Fax** *01684 560662* **Rooms** *31*

An award-winning hotel, renowned for its unique location high on the Malvern Hills, and for one of the best views in England – panoramas extend as far as the Cotswolds and the spires of Cheltenham. This family-run hotel comprises three buildings shielded within vast woodlands. **www.cottageinthewood.co.uk**

MORETON IN MARSH Redesdale Arms 🅿 🍴 ⛵ ♿ ££

High St, Moreton in Marsh, Gloucestershire, GL56 0AW **Tel** *01608 650308* **Fax** *01608 651843* **Rooms** *24*

Originally an old stable inn, this hotel offers all traditional comforts in impressive surroundings. The executive rooms have four-poster beds and two of the guestrooms are fitted with whirlpool baths. The hotel is set in the heart of the north Cotswolds and is an ideal base for walkers. **www.redesdalearms.com**

NORTON Hundred House 🍴 ⛵ £££

Bridgnorth Rd (A442), Norton, nr Shifnal, Shropshire, TF11 9EE **Tel** *01952 730353* **Fax** *01952 730355* **Rooms** *10*

Each room in this friendly, acclaimed hotel offers something a little bit different: one has a four-poster bed and period furniture; another has a velvet covered swing; and another has patchwork drapes and fragrant bed sheets. The pub serves a weekly changing menu using locally sourced ingredients. **www.hundredhouse.co.uk**

PAINSWICK The Painswick Hotel & Old Rectory Restaurant 🍴 ⛵ ££££

Kemps Lane, Painswick, Gloucestershire, GL6 6YB **Tel** *01452 812160* **Fax** *01452 814059* **Rooms** *19*

Oft-considered Britain's best country-house hotel, this former rectory sits in the heart of the Cotswold Hills. The rooms are decorated with stylish period furniture and some contemporary designs, luxury fabrics and open fires. The award-winning restaurant offers classic British dishes and an extensive wine list. **www.painswickhotel.com**

PRESTBURY White House Manor ♿ £££

Prestbury, Cheshire, SK10 4HP **Tel** *01625 829376* **Fax** *01625 828627* **Rooms** *12*

Popular manor house, located within easy reach of Manchester. The rooms are luxurious and individually furnished with antiques, collectibles and rich fabrics. All the rooms offer basic amenities such as central heating and TV, as well as a range of tea, coffee and alcoholic beverages. **www.thewhitehouse.uk.com**

SHREWSBURY Albright Hussey Manor Hotel & Restaurant 🍴 ⛵ £££

Shrewsbury, Shropshire, SY4 3AF **Tel** *01939 290523/290571* **Fax** *01939 291143* **Rooms** *26*

Converted moated manor house with splendid views over the Shropshire countryside. All the rooms offer en suite facilties, and boast an atmospheric blend of historic oak panelling, open fireplaces, Tudor beams and modern ameni-ties. Six of the rooms feature original four-poster beds, spa baths and antique furnishings. **www.albrighthussey.co.uk**

STAFFORD The Swan 🍴 ⛵ ♿ £££

46 Greengate St, Stafford, ST16 2JA **Tel** *01785 258142* **Fax** *01785 223372* **Rooms** *31*

The Swan, a former 16th-century coaching inn, benefits from a central town location. Lovingly restored, many of the rooms have original features including stone fireplaces and exposed beams. There are amenities for business and leisure travellers as well as a brasserie and coffee shop. **www.theswanstafford.co.uk**

STRATFORD-UPON-AVON The Old Manor House
££

Halford, Stratford-upon-Avon, Warwickshire, CV36 5BT **Tel** *01789 740264* **Fax** *01789 740609* **Rooms** *3*

Friendly B&B in a Grade II listed, part-Tudor manor house, overlooking vast parklands. The rooms have oak-beamed ceilings, modern furnishings and fine views over the surrounding Warwickshire countryside. Also has a tennis court. The price includes a hearty breakfast, but dinner is only by arrangement. **www.oldmanor-halford.co.uk**

STRATFORD-UPON-AVON Victoria Spa Lodge
££

Bishopton Lane, Bishopton, Stratford-upon-Avon, Warwickshire, CV37 9QY **Tel** *01789 267985* **Rooms** *7*

Built in 1837, this Victorian spa hotel was visited by Queen Victoria, hence its name and the appearance of her coat of arms in the hotel gables. The bedrooms face forward onto the hotel grounds; some overlook Stratford-upon-Avon's canal. Family rooms are also available. Serves a generous breakfast. **www.victoriaspalodge.co.uk**

STRATFORD-UPON-AVON Willow Corner
££

Armscote, Stratford-upon-Avon, Warwickshire, CV37 8DE **Tel** *01608 682391* **Rooms** *3*

Small, luxury B&B in a beautiful, 300-year-old thatched cottage, a short drive from Stratford-upon-Avon. The rates include a full English breakfast with home-made bread and jams, served beside the magnificent inglenook fireplace in the main lounge. **www.willowcorner.co.uk**

SUTTON COLDFIELD New Hall
£££

Walmley Rd, Sutton Coldfield, West Midlands, B76 1QX **Tel** *0121 378 2442* **Fax** *0121 311 1745* **Rooms** *60*

The oldest, inhabited moated house in England, this Grade 1 listed building is set in 26 acres (10.5 ha) of peaceful grounds. The rooms have oak-panelling, four-poster beds and stained-glass windows. Also features a croquet lawn, putting green, tennis court, nine-hole golf course and beauty spa. **www.newhalluk.com**

TEWKESBURY Corse Lawn House Hotel
££££

Tewkesbury, Gloucestershire, GL19 4LZ **Tel** *0870 4188123* **Fax** *01452 780840* **Rooms** *19*

On the edge of a quiet village green, this elegant, Grade II listed Queen Anne building has been extended to create a stunning country house hotel. The Corse Lawn is set in 12 acres of beautiful grounds and the atmosphere here is relaxed and the service attentive and unobtrusive. **www.corselawn.com**

TRUMPET The Verzon
£££

Hereford Rd, Trumpet, Nr Ledbury, HR8 2PZ **Tel** *01531 670381* **Fax** *01531 670830* **Rooms** *8*

The Verzon is a stylish boutique hotel situated 2 miles (3 km) from the historic market town of Ledbury. All rooms have been recently refurbished. The Mulbery bar and brasserie offer informal dining. Stunning views of the Malvern Hills can be appreciated from the deck terrace. **www.theverzon.co.uk**

WINCHCOMBE Wesley House
££

High St, Winchcombe, Gloucestershire, GL54 5LJ **Tel** *01242 602366* **Fax** *01242 609046* **Rooms** *5*

Historic, half-timbered restaurant-with-rooms. The rooms overlook the North Cotswolds, and are small, but cosy. The Almsbury room has a private terrace and the best view, and the Preacher's room once gave shelter to the founder of the Methodist Church, John Wesley. **www.wesleyhouse.co.uk**

EAST MIDLANDS

BABWORTH The Barns Country Guesthouse
£

Morton Farm, Babworth, Retford, Nottinghamshire, DN22 8HA **Tel** *01777 706336* **Rooms** *6*

Non-smoking B&B in the heart of Robin Hood Country. Offers peaceful rooms in a converted, 18th-century farmhouse, near the busy market town of Retford. Vine-covered exterior walls, original oak beams and country furniture all add to the rural charm. Serves a hearty breakfast. **www.thebarns.co.uk**

BARNBY MOOR Ye Olde Bell Hotel
££££

Barnby Moor, Retford, Nottinghamshire, DN22 8QS **Tel** *01777 705121* **Fax** *01777 860424* **Rooms** *48*

Set in expansive, tranquil grounds on the edge of Sherwood Forest, this privately owned converted coaching inn is one of Nottinghamshire's most characterful hotels. The rooms are decorated with oak panelling, log fires and leaded windows, and the restaurant serves award-winning cuisine. **www.yeoldebell.net**

BASLOW Hotel Cavendish
££££

Baslow, Derbyshire, DE45 1SP **Tel** *01246 582311* **Fax** *01246 582312* **Rooms** *24*

This beautiful property is located on the Chatsworth Estate, at the heart of the Peak District National Park. Most of the furnishings – an elegant blend of antiques and modern art – come from Chatsworth House itself. The hotel is within reach of the spa town of Buxton. **www.cavendish-hotel.net**

BIGGIN-BY-HARTINGDON Biggin Hall
££

Biggin-by-Hartington, Buxton, Derbyshire, SK17 0DH **Tel** *01298 84451* **Fax** *01298 84681* **Rooms** *20*

A peaceful, 17th-century country-house hotel, in the Peak District National Park. This Grade II listed building is set amid typical Derbyshire landscape, with heather-clad moorlands and deep wooded valleys. Offers spacious rooms, furnished with four-poster beds and open fires, as well as self-contained apartments. **www.bigginhall.co.uk**

Key to Price Guide *see p556* **Key to Symbols** *see back cover flap*

EAST BARKWITH Bodkin Lodge

£

Torrington Lane, E Barkwith, Market Rasen, Lincolnshire, LN8 5RY **Tel & Fax** *01673 858249* **Rooms** *2*

This welcoming B&B, located on a working farm, is a popular stopping-off point for walkers – a nature trail departs from the door – and racing fans, who can visit the Cadwell Park Racing Circuit nearby. Hosts spacious rooms, and serves a generous breakfast, with Lincolnshire sausages.

GLOSSOP Wind in the Willows

£££

Glossop, Derbyshire, SK13 7PT **Tel** *01457 868001* **Fax** *01457 853354* **Rooms** *12*

Early Victorian country house with great views of the Peak District National Park. Boasts delightful oak-panelled rooms with antique furnishings and modern facilities. The popular restaurant serves traditional English fare in its period dining room. A nine-hole golf course adjoins the hotel. **www.windinthewillows.co.uk**

HOPE Underleigh House

££

Off Edale Rd, Hope, Derbyshire, S33 6RF **Tel** *01433 621372* **Fax** *01433 621324* **Rooms** *5*

This small B&B is located in prime walking area, and offers panoramic views over the surrounding Peak District. Set in a converted cottage and barn, it provides comfortable, spacious rooms, and a generous breakfast in its stone-flagged dining room. The staff is friendly and helpful. **www.underleighhouse.co.uk**

HOUGH ON THE HILL The Brownlow Arms

££

Grantham Rd, Hough on the Hill, Lincolnshire, NG32 2A2 **Tel** *01400 250234* **Fax** *01400 251993* **Rooms** *4*

Truely exceptional accommodation; the four bedrooms are individually and tastefully furnished to a high standard to provide every comfort for guests. Enjoy exploring diverse local attractions and unspoilt countryside before returning to dine at the hotel's excellent restaurant. **www.thebrownlowarms.com**

LANGAR Langar Hall

£££

Langar, Nottinghamshire, NG13 9HG **Tel** *01949 860559* **Fax** *01949 861045* **Rooms** *12*

This stately country-house hotel is popular for weddings and other celebrations. The elegant rooms are split between the main house and the chalet next to the croquet lawn. The restaurant serves simple English cuisine, including Stilton from Colston Bassett and fruits from the Belvoir fruit farm. **www.langarhall.com**

LINCOLN Bail House

££

34 Bailgate, Lincoln, Lincolnshire, LN1 3AP **Tel** *01522 520883* **Fax** *01522 521829* **Rooms** *10*

A 14th-century B&B, just a short walk from the town's castle and cathedral. The rooms have oak-beamed ceilings and a mix of period and modern furnishings. There is a patio for sunbathing in the summer, an outdoor pool and a large gravel car park. Also offers self-catering accommodation. **www.bailhouse.co.uk**

LINCOLN Branston Hall

£££

Branston, Lincoln, Lincolnshire, LN4 1PD **Tel** *01522 793305* **Fax** *01522 790734* **Rooms** *50*

Elegant country-house hotel, set amid an expansive stretch of wooded parkland and lakes. The award-winning, lakeside restaurant has oak-panelled walls and fantastic views over the hotel grounds. Also has an indoor heated pool, jacuzzi, sauna and gym. **www.branstonhall.com**

LOUTH The Priory

££

149 Eastgate, Louth, Lincolnshire, LN11 9AJ **Tel** *01507 602930* **Fax** *01507 609767* **Rooms** *10*

This newly refurbished, Grade II listed building boasts beautiful gardens, a stunning wood-panelled bar, a Gothic function room (generally used for weddings) and a communal lounge for playing cards. The rooms are modern, but in line with the building's original architecture. **www.theprioryhotel.com**

MATLOCK BATH Hodgkinson's Hotel & Restaurant

££

150 S Parade, Matlock Bath, Derbyshire, DE4 3NR **Tel** *01629 582170* **Fax** *01629 584891* **Rooms** *7*

This stylish hotel dates back to the Georgian spa era, and is housed in a Grade II listed building. Offers carefully-renovated, luxurious rooms, furnished with original antiques and four-poster beds. The elegant restaurant serves delicious Mediterranean cuisine. **www.hodgkinsons-hotel.co.uk**

MATLOCK BATH Whitworth Park Hotel

££

Dale Rd N, Matlock, Derbyshire, DE4 2FT **Tel** *01629 733111* **Fax** *01629 735222* **Rooms** *5*

An intimate hotel in a recently-renovated, Victorian building. The rooms in this Grade II listed property have oak-panelled walls and period furnishings. Advance reservations are recommended for the restaurant, which opens daily for lunch and dinner. **www.whitworthparkhotel.co.uk**

NOTTINGHAM Greenwood Lodge

££

Third Ave, Sherwood Rise, Nottingham, NG7 6JH **Tel** *0115 962 1206* **Fax** *0115 962 1206* **Rooms** *6*

A small guesthouse, just a short distance from the city centre. The hotel is set in a charming courtyard garden, and offers rooms with four-poster beds and exquisite antique furnishings. Children below the age of 12 are not allowed. **www.greenwoodlodgecityguesthouse.co.uk**

NOTTINGHAM Lace Market

£££

29–31 High Pavement, The Lace Market, Nottingham, NG1 1HE **Tel** *0115 852 3232* **Tel** *0115 852 3223* **Rooms** *42*

This trendy hotel is home to a brasserie, gastropub and a cocktail bar. The luxurious rooms are equipped with modern facilities, and offer great views over St Mary's Church and the Galleries of Justice. Serves a variety of good food and drink, and provides free access to the nearby Holme's Place health club. **www.lacemarkethotel.co.uk**

NOTTINGHAM Restaurant Sat Bains 🍴🏃 ££££

Restaurant Sat Bains, Old Lenton Lane, Nottingham, NG7 2SA **Tel** *0115 986 6566* **Fax** *0115 986 0343* **Rooms** *7*

Highly regarded and popular restaurant-with-rooms. The rooms feature Molton Brown toiletries, freshly brewed coffee and Egyptian cotton linen. Also boasts a kitchen workshop, and offers a selection of holiday-package deals. This is Nottingham's only Michelin-starred restaurant. **www.restaurantsatbains.net**

OAKHAM The Old Wisteria Hotel & Restaurant 🍴♿ ££

4 Catmose St, Oakham, Rutland, Leicestershire, LE15 6HW **Tel** *01572 722844* **Fax** *01572 724473* **Rooms** *25*

Some sections of this welcoming country-house hotel date back to 1604. This former Georgian hunting lodge offers small, but elegant rooms, all equipped with en suite facilities. Also presents splendid views over Rutland Water. The restaurant serves traditional local cuisine. **www.wisteriahotel.co.uk**

OAKHAM Hambleton Hall 🍴🖥 £££££

Oakham, Rutland, Leicestershire, LE15 8TH **Tel** *01572 756991* **Fax** *01572 724721* **Rooms** *17*

Part of the Relais & Chateaux network of hotels, this sophisticated country-house hotel has a stunning lakeside setting. The spacious rooms are decorated with comfortable furnishings and rich fabrics, and the gourmet restaurant offers a fine wine list. Also has a heated outdoor pool and tennis courts. **www.hambletonhall.com**

SARACENS HEAD Pipwell Manor £

Washway Rd, Saracens Head, Holbeach, Spalding, Lincolnshire, PE12 8AL **Tel & Fax** *01406 423119* **Rooms** *3*

This stylish B&B, set in the heart of Lincolnshire, is the perfect destination for nature lovers and bird-watchers hoping to explore the Fens. A former outpost of Pipwell Abbey, the manor retains much of its original 1700s character, but for a few modern additions, such as the miniature railway around the large gardens. **www.smoothhound.co.uk/hotels**

STAMFORD George of Stamford 🍴🏃♿ ££££

71 St Martins, Stamford, Lincolnshire, PE9 2LB, **Tel** *01780 750750* **Fax** *01780 750701* **Rooms** *47*

Historic coaching inn with magnificent oak-panelled walls. The rooms are comfortable and spacious, equipped with en suite facilities and modern amenities. The well-reputed restaurant serves mouthwatering cuisine, which includes traditional English fare. Also has a business centre. **www.georgehotelofstamford.com**

WORKSOP Charnwood Hotel 🍴🏃♿ ££

Sheffield Rd, Blyth, Worksop, Nottinghamshire, S81 8HF **Tel** *01909 591610* **Fax** *01909 591429* **Rooms** *44*

A modern hotel, set in vast gardens, and well placed for exploring the countryside. Has large bedrooms and a reasonably-priced lounge bar. Popular with business travellers for its meeting facilities and conference equipment. The restaurant serves typical English specialities. **www.thecharnwoodhotel.com**

LANCASHIRE AND THE LAKES

AMBLESIDE Wateredge Inn 🍴 ££

Waterhead Bay, Ambleside, Cumbria, LA22 OEP **Tel** *01539 432332* **Fax** *01539 431878* **Rooms** *22*

Delightful inn set in two adjoining 17th-century fishermen's cottages, near Lake Windermere. The colourfully decorated rooms have en suite facilities; many offer great views of the lake. Well-placed for exploring the scenic countryside and other local attractions. Includes breakfast. **www.wateredgeinn.co.uk**

AMBLESIDE Drunken Duck 🍴 £££

Barngates, Ambleside, Cumbria, LA22 ONG **Tel** *01539 436347* **Fax** *01539 436781* **Rooms** *16*

This lively dining-pub-with-rooms has been welcoming travellers for more than 400 years. Wood fires, oak floors and ales brewed on site add to the appeal. Offers breathtaking views of Lake Windermere. The rooms are stylish; ask for the Garden Room with its open-beamed ceiling. Room rate includes breakfast. **www.drunkenduckinn.co.uk**

BASSENTHWAITE Pheasant 🍴 £££

Bassenthwaite Lake, Cockermouth, Cumbria, CA13 9YE **Tel** *01768 776234* **Fax** *01768 76002* **Rooms** *15*

This well-loved hostelry retains its traditional and tranquil ambience. Built 500 years ago as a farmhouse, it became an alehouse in 1778. Has bright and cheery bedrooms; all have en suite facilities. The snug bar is highly popular. Also has a spacious lounge. Includes breakfast. **www.the-pheasant.co.uk**

BLACKBURN Northcote Manor 🍴♿ £££££

Northcote Rd, Blackburn, Lancashire, BB6 8BE **Tel** *01254 240555* **Fax** *01254 246568* **Rooms** *14*

A luxurious manor-with-rooms, housed in an elegant manor amid lovely gardens. This comfortable house is renowned for its warmth and friendly welcome, as well as superb cuisine. Offers individually decorated rooms, with modern amenities, a traditional English breakfast and complimentary newspaper. **www.northcote.com**

BLACKPOOL Raffles 🍴🏃 £

73–77 Hornby Rd, Blackpool, Lancashire, FY1 4QJ **Tel** *01253 294713* **Fax** *01253 294240* **Rooms** *19*

Flower-decked, white-and-blue painted B&B close to the famous Blackpool Tower. A decided notch above the usual seaside offering, it offers a warm welcome along with bright and stylish rooms. A great place for afternoon tea; the evening meals are generous. Includes breakfast. **www.raffleshotelblackpool.co.uk**

Key to Price Guide *see p556* **Key to Symbols** *see back cover flap*

BLACKPOOL Hotel Sheraton
54–62 Queens Promenade, Blackpool, Lancashire, FY2 9RP **Tel** *01253 352723* **Fax** *01253 595499* **Rooms** *104*

Features an entertainment programme every night of the week, as well as several attractions for kids. The public areas and well-appointed bedrooms are exceptionally spacious, and the service standards high. Also has a large indoor pool. Includes breakfast. **www.hotelsheraton.co.uk**

BLACKPOOL The Imperial
N Promenade, Blackpool, Lancashire, FY1 2HB **Tel** *01253 623971* **Fax** *01253 751784* **Rooms** *180*

Part of the Barcelo Hotel Group, this opulent hotel is ideally located – it presents spectacular views over the beach and the sea, and is only minutes from the local attractions. Rooms and suites are elegantly furnished. Also has a sauna, steam room and spa. Includes breakfast. **www.barcelo-hotels.co.uk**

BOLTON The Last Drop Village Hotel and Spa
Bromley Cross, Bolton, Lancashire, BL7 9PZ **Tel** *01204 591131* **Fax** *01204 304122* **Rooms** *128*

One of a kind, this charming retreat is a re-creation of a typical North Country moorland village. Features arts and crafts shops and a range of eating options. Rooms are modern and well equipped. The glorious Pennine Hills are close by, and it's a short drive into bustling Manchester. Includes breakfast. **www.mercure-uk.com**

BOWNESS-ON-WINDERMERE Lindeth Fell Country House Hotel
Lyth Valley Rd, Bowness-On-Windermere, Cumbria, LA23 3JP **Tel** *01539 443286* **Fax** *01539 447455* **Rooms** *14*

Relaxing country-house hotel, located in the beautiful hills above Lake Windermere. The decor is fresh and stylish, with original works of art adorning the walls. Has spacious, attractively furnished rooms, equipped with modern amenities. Includes breakfast. **www.lindethfell.co.uk**

BOWNESS-ON-WINDERMERE Linthwaite House
Crook Rd, Bowness-On-Windermere, Cumbria, LA23 3JA **Tel** *01539 488600* **Fax** *01539 488601* **Rooms** *30*

A fine country house, located on a sublime hilltop setting, overlooking the beautiful waters of Lake Windermere. The rooms are elegantly decorated, with modern conveniences and great views. This romantic retreat is an ideal venue for a wedding or honeymoon. Complimentary use of nearby fitness centre. Includes breakfast. **www.linthwaite.com**

BUTTERMERE Wood House
Buttermere, Cockermouth, Cumbria, CA13 9XA **Tel** *01768 770208* **Fax** *01768 770241* **Rooms** *3*

Magnificent views across the Lake District fells. The rooms personify simple elegance, furnished with lovely antiques. However, the greatest appeal of this tiny hideaway is the owner's home-baked bread. Also has a delightful stone cottage that can be rented on a weekly basis. Includes breakfast. **www.wdhse.co.uk**

CARLISLE Number Thirty-One
31 Howard Place, Carlisle, Cumbria, CA1 1HR **Tel** *01228 597080* **Fax** *01228 597080* **Rooms** *3*

A stylish Victorian town house in a quiet residential area, yet just a short distance from the city centre. The decor is bold and full of panache. Offers evening meals, provided they are pre-ordered as only fresh ingredients are used. Charming rooms, equipped with modern conveniences. Includes breakfast. **www.number31.co.uk**

CHIPPING The Gibbon Hotel
Chipping, Forest of Bowland, Preston, Lancashire, PR3 2TQ **Tel** *01995 61456* **Fax** *01995 61277* **Rooms** *29*

Stone-built, luxury hotel located in the Forest of Bowland – designated as an Area of Outstanding Natural Beauty. Offers fine dining, expansive gardens and tastefully decorated rooms. A profusion of country pursuits such as walks, cycling and bird-watching are available. Includes breakfast. **www.gibbon-bridge.co.uk**

CHORLEY Park Hallhotel
Charnock Richard, Chorley, Preston, Lancashire, PR7 5LP **Tel** *01257 455000* **Fax** *01257 451838* **Rooms** *140*

Contemporary hotel set beside a peaceful lake, and owned by the operators of the Camelot theme park next door. The spacious rooms have amenities such as modem points and a Sony PlayStation keypad. Entertainment includes a cabaret and a medieval banquet hall. Wireless broadband available. Includes breakfast. **www.parkhall-hotel.co.uk**

COCKERMOUTH The Trout
Crown St, Cockermouth, Cumbria, CA13 0EJ **Tel** *01900 823591* **Fax** *01900 827514* **Rooms** *47*

An appropriate name for a comfortable, if a little impersonal hotel that stands by the fast-moving River Derwent in the northern reaches of Lake District. Just a short walk into delightful Cockermouth – if you can tear yourself away from the hotel's lovely gardens. Room rates include breakfast. **www.trouthotel.co.uk**

GRANGE-INN-BORROWDALE Borrowdale Gates
Grange-Inn-Borrowdale, Keswick, Cumbria, CA12 5UQ **Tel** *01768 777204* **Fax** *01768 777254* **Rooms** *27*

In a wooded valley close to the shores of Derwentwater, "The Queen of the English Lakes". This relaxing hotel is a sensible base for walking, climbing and touring this scenic region. The ever-changing colours of the seasons add to the charm of this smart and well-managed hotel. Includes breakfast. **www.borrowdale-gates.com**

GRASSMERE Howfoot Lodge
Town End, Grassmere, Cumbria, LA22 9SQ **Tel** *01539 435366* **Fax** *01539 435268* **Rooms** *7*

This Victorian guesthouse is owned by the Wordsworth Trust. It stands in landscaped gardens and is furnished with period antiques in keeping with the house. Has pleasant and cheerful rooms, two of which are deluxe standard. An excellent place for outdoor activities such as walks and bicycling. Includes breakfast. **www.howfoot.co.uk**

HAWKSHEAD Queens Head Hotel
££££

Main St, Hawkshead, Cumbria, LA22 ONS **Tel** *01539 436271* **Fax** *01539 436722* **Rooms** *14*

At the heart of one of the prettiest Lakeland villages. Low, exposed oak-beamed ceilings, flagstone floors and a profusion of memorabilia create a relaxed and informal ambience. Some rooms have four-poster beds. Also has family rooms. Food is prepared using fresh local produce. Includes breakfast. **www.queensheadhotel.co.uk**

KENDAL Riverside Hotel Kendal
£££

Stramongate Gate, Beezon Rd, Kendal, Cumbria, LA9 6EL **Tel** *01539 734861* **Fax** *01539 734863* **Rooms** *47*

This charming hotel is housed in an imposing and highly photogenic building, built in 1625. The rooms are tastefully decorated, with en suite facilities and other modern amenities; most offer striking views of the river. Well placed for exploring the various attractions the Lake District has to offer. Includes breakfast. **www.riversidekendal.co.uk**

KESWICK The Grange
££

Manor Brow, Keswick, Cumbria, CA12 4BA **Tel** *01768 772500* **Fax** *01768 772500* **Rooms** *10*

The only five-star establishment in the Keswick area, this small guesthouse was once a hotel and it has retained the hotel-style facilities, which have brought guests back time and again. The scenic views of England's highest mountains are breathtaking, the hospitality faultless. Includes breakfast. **www.grangekeswick.com**

LANCASTER Lancaster House
££££

Green Lane, Ellel, Lancaster, LA1 4GJ **Tel** *01524 844822* **Fax** *01524 844766* **Rooms** *99*

Savour the good things in life in this modern and elegant hotel, with its gourmet restaurant, intimate bar and balconied lounge. A recent £3.2 million development scheme has added new, well-appointed suites, with modern conveniences, as well as a spa and hot tubs in its leisure club. Includes breakfast. **www.elh.co.uk**

LIVERPOOL Hard Days Night Hotel
£££

Central Buildings, North John St, Liverpool, L2 6RR **Tel** *0151 236 1964* **Rooms** *110*

This stylish boutique hotel in the heart of the city attracts Beatles fans from around the world. Specially commissioned art work and memorabilia adorns the walls of this converted Grade II listed building that pays homage to the Fab Four. Business facilities are available. Check the website for special deals. **www.harddaysnighthotel.com**

LIVERPOOL Hope Street Hotel
££££

40 Hope St, Liverpool, L1 9DA **Tel** *0151 709 3000* **Fax** *0151 709 2454* **Rooms** *48*

Built in 1860 in the style of a Venetian palazzo, Liverpool's first boutique hotel is set in the city's beautiful Georgian quarter. The contemporary rooms are individually designed and feature solid wood floors, large beds and Egyptian cotton sheets. A good base from which to explore the city. Includes breakfast. **www.hopestreethotel.co.uk**

LYTHAM ST ANNES Lindum Hotel
££

63–67 S Promenade, Lytham St Annes, Lancashire, FY8 1LZ **Tel** *01253 721534* **Fax** *01253 721364* **Rooms** *78*

A delightful, family-run hotel, located within easy walking distance of the city centre. This seaside retreat has attractively decorated rooms, equipped with modern facilities; most rooms have great views and a sauna and jacuzzi. Serves fresh local produce. Sunday lunch is a much-anticipated affair. Room rates include breakfast. **www.lindumhotel.co.uk**

MANCHESTER Campanile
£

55 Ordsall Lane, Salford, Lancashire, M5 4RS **Tel** *0161 833 1845* **Fax** *0161 833 1847* **Rooms** *104*

Part of the Campanile chain of hotels. Although pitched at the budget end of the market, this hotel offers pleasant rooms with nice little touches such as tea and coffee makers, big beds and well-equipped bathrooms. The in-house restaurant offers good value French country-style food. **www.campanile.com**

MANCHESTER Malmaison
£££

Piccadilly, Manchester, Lancashire, M1 3AQ **Tel** *0161 278 1000* **Fax** *0161 278 1002* **Rooms** *167*

Stylish hotel housed in a converted, 19th-century building, located in the centre of town. Close to the Piccadilly train station, several shops and other downtown attractions. Offers contemporary rooms, decorated in bright, bold colours. Also has a bistro-style restaurant and a spa. **www.malmaison.com**

MANCHESTER The Midland Hotel
££££

Peter St, Manchester, Lancashire, M60 2DS **Tel** *0161 236 3333* **Fax** *0161 932 4100* **Rooms** *312*

This imposing, red sandstone hotel has been one of Manchester's most familiar landmarks since it opened in 1903. Elegance, luxury and high standards of service, accommodation and cuisine are on offer. Also has an indoor pool and a spa. Breakfast is included in the room rates. **www.qhotels.co.uk**

MANCHESTER The Lowry
£££££

50 Dearmans Place, Chapel Wharf, Salford, Greater Manchester, M3 5LH **Tel** *0161 827 4000* **Rooms** *165*

This ultra-modern, ultra-chic riverside hotel is a member of the prestigious Leading Hotels of the World consortium. Frequented by celebrities, fashion icons, pop stars and sports personalities. Rooms are modern and elegant, while the restaurant purveys modernistic British cuisine. **www.roccofortecollection.com**

MELLOR Millstone
££

3 Church Lane, Mellor, Blackburn, Lancashire, BB2 7JR **Tel** *01254 813333* **Fax** *01254 812628* **Rooms** *21*

A former coaching inn that retains its original charm, while adding modern amenities. One of the highest-rated, two-star hotels in the country, it offers neat, practical bedrooms. A good base for those interested in exploring the countryside. Room rates include breakfast. **www.millstonehotel.co.uk**

Key to Price Guide *see p556* **Key to Symbols** *see back cover flap*

OLD TRAFFORD Old Trafford Lodge   ££

Lancashire County Cricket Club, Old Trafford, Manchester, Lancashire, M16 OPX **Tel** *0161 874 3333* **Rooms** *68*

Built next to the cricket ground and just minutes from Manchester United's ground and the huge Old Trafford shopping centre. This modern hotel offers comfortable rooms, with en suite facilities and modern conveniences. A short drive from the city centre. Includes breakfast. **www.lccc.co.uk**

PENRITH North Lakes Hotel & Spa   £££

Ullswater Rd, Penrith, Cumbria, CA11 8QT **Tel** *01768 868111* **Fax** *01768 868291* **Rooms** *84*

The use of local stone, natural wood and open log fires create a genuine "away from it all" mood at this delightful family resort. Features a children's activity programme, massive indoor pool and a spa. This contemporary hotel is a Shire Hotels property. Breakfast included in the room rate. **www.northlakeshotel.com**

PRESTON Hotel Ibis   ££

Garstang Rd, Broughton, Preston, Lancashire, PR3 5JE **Tel** *01772 861800* **Fax** *01772 861900* **Rooms** *82*

Part of the French Accor group's mid-market brand, this smart hotel guarantees consistent quality. The rooms are bright and family-friendly, furnished with modern amenities. The culinary offer here is French, bistro style. Well placed for exploring the Pennines and the Lakes. Includes breakfast. **www.ibishotel.com**

PRESTON Barton Grange Hotel   £££

Garstang Road, Barton, Preston, Lancashire PR3 5AA **Tel** *01772 862551* **Fax** *01772 671967* **Rooms** *51*

This hotel was originally designed as a fine gentlemen's residence. Its most recent refurbishment, inspired by the hotel's history, successfully recreated the Edwardian ambiance of the oak panelled lounge, and restored many of the original features. Staff are friendly and non-intrusive. Includes breakfast. **www.bartongrangehotel.co.uk**

SAWREY Sawrey Hotel   ££

Far Sawrey, Ambleside, Cumbria, LA22 OLQ **Tel** *01539 443425* **Fax** *01539 443425* **Rooms** *19*

Set in the conservation area for Beatrix Potter's Hilltop Farm, this charming property has a homely atmosphere. The bedrooms are spacious and tastefully furnished; most of them offer stunning views of the surroundings. Attractions such as Estwaite Water and Grizedale Forest are located nearby. Includes breakfast. **www.sawreyhotel.co.uk**

ULLSWATER Sharrow Bay   £££££

Ullswater, Penrith, Cumbria, CA10 2LZ **Tel** *01768 486301* **Fax** *01768 486349* **Rooms** *24*

An exquisite country-house hotel, located in a magnificent lakeside setting. Renowned for its excellent cuisine, stylish decor and perfect service. The rooms are appropriately luxurious, and the view from the dining room is claimed as one of England's most beautiful. Dinner and breakfast are included in the room rate. **www.sharrowbay.co.uk**

ULVERSTON Bay Horse   £££

Canal Foot, Ulverston, Cumbria, LA12 9EL **Tel** *01229 583972* **Fax** *01229 580502* **Rooms** *9*

This 18th-century, half-timbered hostelry is situated at the edge of the Leven Estuary. Offers individually decorated, en suite rooms; some with French windows that present striking views of the sea. Ideal for bird-watchers. Warm and welcoming ambience. Includes breakfast. **www.thebayhorsehotel.co.uk**

WHITEWELL Inn At Whitewell   £££

Whitewell, Forest of Bowland, Lancashire, BB7 3AT **Tel** *01200 448222* **Fax** *01200 448298* **Rooms** *23*

Old-fashioned, yet sophisticated riverside inn. This welcoming and friendly retreat shares its premises with an art gallery and a wine merchant. Parts of the building date to the early 1300s. The rooms are stylishly spectacular. Serves delicious food and wines. A memorable experience. Includes breakfast. **www.innatwhitewell.com**

WINDERMERE Gilpin Lodge   £££££

Crook Rd, Windermere, Cumbria, LA23 3NE **Tel** *01539 488818* **Fax** *01539 488058* **Rooms** *20*

Several acres of gardens, woods and moorland provide a glorious setting for this long-established country-house hotel. The roaring log fires, fine wines and superb food in the AA Rosette-awarded restaurant add to the feeling of utter contentment. Rooms are spacious and beautifully furnished. Includes breakfast. **www.gilpinlodge.co.uk**

WINDERMERE Holbeck Ghyll   £££££

Holbeck Lane, Windermere, Cumbria, LA23 1LU **Tel** *015394 323 75* **Fax** *015394 347 43* **Rooms** *23*

An oasis of calm, perfect for relaxing on the terrace and soaking up fantastic views across Lake Windermere to the rugged fells beyond. Food is mouthwateringly good, and the plush armchairs and open fire of the lounge encourage an indulgent way of life. Also has a spa and sauna. Includes breakfast. **www.holbeckghyll.com**

YORKSHIRE AND THE HUMBER REGION

AMPLEFORTH Shallowdale House   ££

Ampleforth, nr York, North Yorkshire, YO62 4DY **Tel** *01439 788325* **Fax** *01439 788885* **Rooms** *3*

Refined guesthouse, just 32 km (20 miles) from York and on the southern edge of the North York Moors National Park. This small retreat was built in the 1960s, and overlooks an exquisite landscape of unspoilt Yorkshire countryside. The rooms are simple, yet stylish. Includes breakfast. **www.shallowdalehouse.co.uk**

BARNSLEY Brooklands Hotel   £££

Barnsley Rd, Dodsworth, Barnsley, South Yorkshire, S75 3JT **Tel** *01226 299571* **Fax** *01226 249465* **Rooms** *77*

This four-star hotel features well-appointed rooms, blending traditional elegance with modern conveniences. Includes executive suites and some rooms with four-poster beds. Holds a license for conducting civil wedding ceremonies. Also has nine conference rooms. Includes breakfast. **www.brooklandshotel.com**

BEVERLEY Tickton Grange Hotel   £££

Main St, Tickton, Beverley, East Yorkshire, HU17 9SH **Tel** *01964 543666* **Fax** *01964 542556* **Rooms** *20*

A charming Georgian country-house hotel, set amid lovely, landscaped grounds. Offers tastfully decorated, en suite bedrooms, with thoughtful touches adding to the charm. The tranquil setting is ideal for both weddings and conferences. Serves mouthwatering desserts. Includes breakfast. **www.ticktongrange.co.uk**

BRADFORD Dubrovnik Hotel   ££

3 Oak Avenue, Bradford, West Yorkshire, BD8 7AQ **Tel** *01274 543511* **Rooms** *45*

Bradford's oldest privately owned hotel has spacious, comfortable rooms and a relaxed atmosphere. Situated in the leafy suburbs, this former mill owner's residence also has a well-renowned restaurant that is popular with locals and guests alike. Special deals are available at weekends, and there is live jazz on Mondays. **www.dubrovnik.co.uk**

EAST WITTON Blue Lion   £££

E Witton, Leyburn, North Yorkshire, DL8 4SN **Tel** *01969 624273* **Fax** *01969 624189* **Rooms** *15*

A classy, 18th-century coaching inn, set amid beautiful surroundings. Offers simple, but comfortable rooms, with modern conveniences. Also caters for weddings, conferences and other events. The hotel is located just a short distance from many attractions, including Jervaulx Abbey. Includes breakfast. **www.thebluelion.co.uk**

FLAMBOROUGH Manor House   ££

Flamborough, Bridlington, East Yorkshire, YO15 1PD **Tel** *01262 850943* **Fax** *01262 850943* **Rooms** *2*

An elegant Georgian country house in a Grade II listed building. Offers just two rooms, both traditionally decorated, yet with modern amenities. Ideal for those looking for an intimate and quiet retreat. The surrounding countryside is a favourite among walkers and bird-watchers. Includes breakfast. **www.flamboroughmanor.co.uk**

GRASSINGTON Ashfield   ££

Summersfold, Grassington, North Yorkshire, BD23 5AE **Tel** *01756 752584* **Fax** *07092 376562* **Rooms** *8*

This peaceful 17th-century hotel near Summersfold's cobbled square has elegantly furnished rooms with modern conveniences; the restaurant serves set meals only. Well placed to explore the beauty of the surrounding Yorkshire Dales. Activities such as fishing, sailing and horse riding are available. Includes breakfast. **www.ashfieldhouse.co.uk**

HALIFAX Holdsworth House   £££

Holdsworth Rd, Holmfield, Halifax, West Yorkshire, HX2 9TG **Tel** *01422 240024* **Fax** *01422 245174* **Rooms** *40*

Grand, 17th-century Jacobean manor, just a short distance from Halifax. Has individually decorated rooms and suites, with modern amenities; some with four-poster beds. The expansive gardens are ideal for hosting weddings. Also offers conference facilities. Includes breakfast. **www.holdsworthhouse.co.uk**

HARROGATE Balmoral   £££

Franklin Mount, Harrogate, North Yorkshire, HG1 5EJ **Tel** *01423 508208* **Fax** *01423 530652* **Rooms** *23*

A mock-Tudor frontage makes this luxurious hotel easy to spot. Offers tastefully furnished rooms, as well as well-equipped business facilities. The decor here is a perfect mix of traditional and contemporary. Boasts an award-winning restaurant. Room rate includes breakfast. **www.balmoralhotel.co.uk**

HAWORTH Old White Lion Hotel   ££

Main St, Haworth, Keighley, West Yorkshire, BD22 8DU **Tel** *01535 642313* **Fax** *01535 646222* **Rooms** *14*

A 300-year-old family-run coaching inn, set at the top of the cobbled main street in Haworth, a Yorkshire town redolent with memories of the Brontë sisters. The parsonage and the museum are a few steps away, and the Keighley & Wortley steam railway stops nearby. Offers comfortable rooms. Includes breakfast. **www.oldwhitelionhotel.com**

HELMSLEY Feversham Arms   ££££

1–8 High St, Helmsley, North Yorkshire, YO62 5AG **Tel** *01439 770766* **Fax** *01439 770346* **Rooms** *24*

This comfortable, refurbished coaching inn has been around for more than 150 years. Located next to the parish church, the hotel offers pleasant rooms. The cuisine here is impeccable, yet unpretentious. Also has a heated swimming pool. Includes breakfast. **www.fevershamarmshotel.com**

HOVINGHAM Worsley Arms   £££

Main St, Hovingham, Yorkshire, YO62 4LA **Tel** *01653 628234* **Fax** *01653 628130* **Rooms** *19*

Built in the 1840s as a spa hotel, this exquisite and timeless country house features open log fires and stylish furnishings. The informal and relaxing environment, in the depths of the Yorkshire countryside, is perfect for a stress-relieving break. Room rate includes breakfast. **www.worsleyarms.com**

HUDDERSFIELD Huddersfield Hotel   £

33–47 Kirkgate, Huddersfield, West Yorkshire, HD1 1QT **Tel** *01484 512111* **Fax** *01484 421552* **Rooms** *39*

A member of the nationwide GE Link Hotels group, this town-centre hotel offers comfortable accommodation with en suite facilities, tea and coffee makers and a free car park. Within the complex they also have the Rosemary Lane Bistro, a traditional pub and Johnny's nightclub. Includes breakfast. **www.thehuddersfieldhotel.com**

Key to Price Guide *see p556* **Key to Symbols** *see back cover flap*

KIRKBYMOORSIDE George & Dragon Hotel

17 Market Place, Kirkbymoorside, North Yorkshire, YO62 6AA **Tel** *01751 433334* **Fax** *01751 432933* **Rooms** *20*

A charming hotel housed in a building composed of three adjoining establishments – a 17th-century inn, a rectory and a cornmill. Offers spacious, elegantly furnished rooms; some with four-poster beds. All have modern amenities. Close to several sightseeing attractions. Serves real ale. Includes breakfast. **www.georgeanddragon.net**

LEEDS Bewley's Hotel Leeds

City Walk, Sweet St, Leeds, West Yorkshire, LS1 9AT **Tel** *0113 234 2340* **Fax** *0113 234 2349* **Rooms** *334*

Opened in 2003, this is Leeds' largest hotel. Conveniently situated in the heart of the city's commercial and shopping district, it offers great value for money. The rooms are large and stylishly furnished, with Internet access, TVs, en suite facilities and more. The city station is just a ten-minute walk away. Includes breakfast. **www.bewleyshotels.com**

LEEDS Haley's Hotel & Restaurant

Shire Oak Rd, Headingley, Leeds, West Yorkshire, LS6 2DE **Tel** *0113 278 4446* **Fax** *0113 275 3342* **Rooms** *27*

Located in a leafy suburb, just a short distance from the city centre. The bedrooms are individually furnished with style and flair, and equipped with many modern conveniences. The cuisine is inventive and well presented by people who really care. Room rate includes breakfast. **www.haleys.co.uk**

LEEDS Malmaison Leeds

1 Swine Gate, Leeds, West Yorkshire, LS1 4AG **Tel** *0113 398 1000* **Fax** *0113 398 1002* **Rooms** *100*

Conceived ten years ago as a chic brasserie and bar with themed rooms, this stylish hotel has grown into a chain with its finger on the pulse of contemporary-style hospitality. Situated in the centre of town, it is an easy walk from all local attractions. Offers striking views of the town's skyline. Includes breakfast. **www.malmaison.com**

LEEDS 42 The Calls

42 The Call, Leeds, West Yorkshire, LS2 7EW **Tel** *0113 244 0099* **Fax** *0113 234 4100* **Rooms** *41*

A refreshingly different town-house hotel that manages to be trendy without becoming a cliché. This converted cornmill, set beside River Nidd, features beamed ceilings, original mill mechanisms, modern handmade beds and a collection of original works of art. Offers luxurious rooms. Includes breakfast. **www.theetoncollection.co.uk**

PICKERING White Swan

Market Place, Pickering, North Yorkshire, Y018 7AA **Tel** *01751 472288* **Fax** *01751 475554* **Rooms** *21*

Set in the picturesque Vale of Pickering, at the foot of the North Yorks Moors, this delightful country-house inn is priced affordably. Offers pleasant rooms that are plain, yet practical. Also has conference facilities. The restaurant serves highly appreciated food. Includes breakfast. **www.white-swan.co.uk**

RICHMOND King's Head

Market Place, Richmond, North Yorkshire, DL10 4HS **Tel** *01748 850220* **Fax** *01748 850635* **Rooms** *30*

Close to King Henry VIII's favourite castle and overlooking the fast-flowing River Swale. The rooms at this hotel are individually styled and tastefully furnished. Local attractions such as the Georgian Theatre Royal are also nearby. Boasts an acclaimed bar, and serves afternoon tea in the lounge. Includes breakfast. **www.kingsheadrichmond.com**

ROYDHOUSE Three Acres Inn

Roydhouse, Shelley, West Yorkshire, HD8 8LR **Tel** *01484 602606* **Fax** *01484 608411* **Rooms** *20*

A rambling old millstone building with lots of character. The rooms are simple, yet comfortably furnished; many offer views of the open moorland. Has independent cottages as well, each with its own garden. Also hosts a traditional shop with pickles, spices and preserves. Ample car parking space. Room rate includes breakfast. **www.3acres.com**

SCARBOROUGH Interludes

32 Princess St, Scarbourough, North Yorkshire, YO11 1QR **Tel** *01723 360513* **Rooms** *5*

A refined guesthouse in a lively seaside town. Housed in a Grade II listed building, this hotel offers pleasant rooms; most with en suite facilities and sea views. Guests can avail of special theatre packages organized by the owners. Parking space is scarce during peak season. Gay-friendly. Includes breakfast. **www.interludeshotel.co.uk**

SETTLE The Plough Inn At Wigglesworth

Wigglesworth, nr Settle, Skipton, North Yorkshire, BD23 4RJ **Tel** *01729 840243* **Fax** *01729 840401* **Rooms** *9*

This charming, 17th-century inn has spectacular views of Pen-y-Ghent and Ingleborough, two of the renowned Three Peaks. The en suite rooms are simply decorated in bright, cheerful colours. Famous for good food and real ale. Ideally placed for exploring the surrounding countryside. Includes breakfast. **www.ploughinn.info**

THORNTON WATLASS The Buck Inn

Thornton Watlass, Ripon, North Yorkshire, HG4 4AH **Tel** *01677 422461* **Fax** *01677 422447* **Rooms** *7*

An archetypal village hostelry with real ale, quality home-cooked food and comfortable bedrooms. The pub wall marks the boundary of the village cricket green. At the rear is a large and secluded garden with a children's play area. Located a short distance from the bustling A1 trunk road. Includes breakfast. **www.thebuckinn.net**

WHITBY White Horse & Griffin

Church St, Whitby, North Yorkshire, YO22 4BH **Tel** *01947 604857* **Fax** *01947 604857* **Rooms** *10*

Quaint old inn set at the core of Whitby, home to the famous explorer Captain Cook. Offers tastefully refurbished rooms, and serves delicious fresh fish and other seafood. Also has two, self-catering cottages. Close to the ruins of Whitby Abbey and its 119 steps. Includes breakfast. **www.whitehorseandgriffin.co.uk**

YARM Judges Country House Hotel
🛏 ♿ 🍴   ££££

Kirklevington Hall, Yarm, Cleveland, North Yorkshire, TS15 9LW **Tel** *01642 789000* **Fax** *01642 782878* **Rooms** *21*

A luxury hotel housed in Kirklevington Hall, a glorious country mansion. The bedrooms and suites are stylishly decorated, with modern amenities such as jacuzzis, CD players, hairdryers, complimentary newspapers and more. Showcases several antiques and works of art as well. Includes breakfast. **www.judgeshotel.co.uk**

YORK Beechwood Close
🛏 ♿   ££

19 Shipton Rd, Cliffton, York, Yorkshire, YO30 5RE **Tel** *01904 658378* **Fax** *01904 647124* **Rooms** *14*

A relaxing and welcoming hotel set amid scenic surroundings. Traditionally decorated bedrooms are comfortable and well equipped. Hosts a restaurant, with splendid views of the secluded garden, and a friendly and well-stocked bar. Includes breakfast. **www.beechwood-close.co.uk**

YORK The Royal York
📶 🛏 ♨ ♿ 🍴   £££

Station Rd, York, Yorkshire, YO24 1AA **Tel** *01904 653681* **Fax** *01904 623503* **Rooms** *167*

Part of the Principal Hotels chain, this magnificent Victorian retreat is set in vast, landscaped gardens. Offers en suite, luxury rooms, with all modern amenities; has two, specially designed rooms for the disabled as well. Also has a conference centre. Just a few steps from the centre of town. Includes breakfast. **www.royalhotelyork.co.uk**

YORK Middlethorpe Hall
📶 🛏 ♨ ♿ 🍴 ⬆   ££££

Bishopthorpe Rd, York, Yorkshire, YO23 2GB **Tel** *01904 641241* **Fax** *01904 620176* **Rooms** *29*

One of the selective Historic House Hotels chain and, arguably, its finest. Set on 20 acres of outstanding gardens and parkland, this country-house hotel is filled with antiques and works of art. Built in 1699, it offers elegant accommodation in the main house and the adjacent mews cottages. Includes breakfast. **www.middlethorpe.com**

NORTHUMBRIA

ALNMOUTH The Schooner Hotel
🛏 ♿   £££

Northumberland St, Alnmouth, Alnwick, Northumberland, NE66 2RS **Tel** *01665 830216* **Fax** *01665 30287* **Rooms** *32*

Comfort with character is the theme at this historic, 17th-century inn. Famous guests include Charles Dickens, John Wesley, Douglas Bader and King George III, but it is a certain Parson Smyth who is said to haunt the place. Offers comfortable, pleasant rooms and a welcoming ambience. Includes breakfast. **www.theschoonerhotel.co.uk**

BAMBURGH Victoria Hotel
🛏 ♿   £££

Front St, Bamburgh, Northumberland, NE69 7BP **Tel** *01668 214431* **Fax** *01688 214404* **Rooms** *30*

In the heart of Bamburgh, this 19th-century hotel has cheery rooms, decorated with period furniture and antiques. Candle-lit suppers can be enjoyed in the glass-domed restaurant. Close at hand is Bamburgh's magnificent castle. Also offers facilities for weddings and conferences. Includes breakfast. **www.thevictoriahotelbamburgh.co.uk**

BELFORD Blue Bell Hotel
🛏 ♿   £££

Market Place, Belford, Northumberland, NE70 7NE **Tel** *01668 213543* **Fax** *01668 213787* **Rooms** *28*

Virginia creeper covers the entire frontage of this 17th-century coaching inn, a popular, family-run hotel with expansive gardens and a traditional restaurant. The rooms are comfortably furnished, and are equipped with modern amenities. Includes breakfast. **www.bluebellhotel.com**

BELFORD Waren House Hotel
🛏   ££££

Waren Mill, Belford, Northumberland, NE70 7EE **Tel** *01668 214581* **Fax** *01668 214484* **Rooms** *13*

This small hotel enjoys outstanding views of the Cheviot Hills from its six acres of mature woodlands and formal gardens. Features individually decorated rooms and suites. Its location next to Budle Bay, a bird life sanctuary, makes it a favourite with bird-watchers. Includes breakfast. **www.warenhousehotel.co.uk**

BERWICK-UPON-TWEED Number One Sallyport
🛏   £££

Off Bridge St, Berwick-Upon-Tweed, Northumberland, TD15 1EZ **Tel** *01289 308827* **Fax** *01289 308827* **Rooms** *7*

This delightful 17th-century inn, set in a Grade II listed building, was voted the "Top B&B in England" for 2005 by *The Sunday Times*. The rooms are spacious and comfortable, furnished with white cotton linen and en suite facilities. This contemporary, yet traditional retreat serves an excellent breakfast. **www.sallyport.co.uk**

CHESTER-LE-STREET Lumley Castle
🛏 ♿   ££££

Chester-le-St, Durham, DH3 4NX **Tel** *0191 389 1111* **Fax** *0191 387 1437* **Rooms** *73*

A genuine medieval castle, complete with battlements and arrow slits, that has been converted into a luxurious hotel. The en suite rooms are elegantly decorated; some with antiques and four-poster beds. A perfect choice for a romantic break. Located a short distance from Durham and Newcastle. Includes breakfast. **www.lumleycastle.com**

CROOKHAM Coach House
🛏 ♿ ⬆   ££

Crookham, Cornhill-on-Tweed, Northumberland, TD12 4TD **Tel** *01890 820293* **Fax** *01890 820284* **Rooms** *10*

Welcoming guesthouse set in a complex of renovated farm buildings that include a 1680s cottage and an old-smithy, all surrounding a sun-trap courtyard. The Coach House offers excellent home cooking and comfortable rooms, and has a reputation for maintaining high, award-winning standards. Includes breakfast. **www.coachhousecrookham.com**

Key to Price Guide *see p556* **Key to Symbols** *see back cover flap*

DURHAM Durham Marriott Hotel Royal County
Old Elvet, Durham, County Durham, DH1 3JN **Tel** *0191 386 6821* **Fax** *0191 386 0704* **Rooms** *150*

Well placed in a historic city, dominated by a massive cathedral and castle. This large hotel offers spacious, tastefully furnished rooms, equipped with modern conveniences. Local attractions such as Beamish North Country Museum are within easy walking distance. Includes breakfast. **www.marriott.com**

DURHAM Whitworth Hall Country Park Hotel
Near Spennymoor, Durham, County Durham, DL16 7OX **Tel** *01388 811772* **Fax** *01388 818669* **Rooms** *29*

A Grade II listed building set amid several acres of lovely gardens. Offers stately en suite rooms; some with views. The deer grazing in the surrounding grounds enhance the hotel's tranquil and relaxing ambience. An idyllic location for weddings. Also provides conference facilities. Includes dinner and breakfast. **www.whitworthhall.co.uk**

HALTWHISTLE Centre Of Britain
Main St, Haltwhistle, Northumberland, NE49 0BH **Tel** *01434 322422* **Fax** *01434 322655* **Rooms** *12*

Part of the 15th-century Pele Tower, this building served as a manor house, post office, coaching inn and more before it was converted into a hotel. The original architectural features have been retained and tastefully combined with modern touches. Has simple rooms. Includes breakfast. **www.centre-of-britain.org.uk**

HEXHAM The County Hotel & Restaurant
Priestpopple, Hexham, Northumberland, NE46 1PS **Tel & Fax** *01434 603601* **Rooms** *7*

Housed in a listed building that originally was a terrace of three houses, the County offers lovely soft furnishings, warm hearths and relaxed Northumbrian surroundings. Expect genuine hospitality and breathtaking scenery; Hadrian's Wall is close by. The restaurant uses all local produce. Includes breakfast. **www.thecountyhexham.co.uk**

HEXHAM De Vere Slaley Hall
Slaley, Hexham, Northumberland, NE47 0BX **Tel** *01434 673350* **Fax** *01474 673962* **Rooms** *139*

The northern flagship of the De Vere chain of hotels. This award-winning, Edwardian resort features two championship golf courses and other outdoor activities such as fishing, archery and hot-air ballooning. Offers large, luxurious en suite rooms; some with jacuzzis. Conference facilities also available. Includes breakfast. **www.devere-hotels.com**

MIDDLETON-IN-TEESDALE The Teesdale Hotel
Market Place, Middleton-in-Teesdale, County Durham, DL12 0QG **Tel** *01833 640264* **Fax** *01883 640651* **Rooms** *14*

This 17th-century, former coaching inn is located in the centre of the village. The rooms have recently been refurbished but are sympathetic to the original style of the inn; all offer en suite facilities. The vast moorland and scenic surroundings provide a relaxing break. Enjoy good home cooking and fine wines. Includes breakfast. **www.teesdalehotel.com**

MORPETH Linden Hall
Longhorsley, Morpeth, Northumberland, NE65 8XF **Tel** *0844 879 9084* **Fax** *01670 500001* **Rooms** *50*

Several hundred acres of woods and parkland, including an award-winning 18-hole golf course, frame this magnificent Georgian mansion. Boasts a health, leisure and fitness spa, a traditional pub and a much-acclaimed restaurant. Has well-appointed and stylish rooms. Includes breakfast. **www.macdonaldhotels.co.uk**

NEWCASTLE UPON TYNE Caledonian
Osborne Rd, Jesmond, Newcastle, Newcastle, NE2 2AT **Tel** *0191 281 7881* **Fax** *0191 281 6241* **Rooms** *91*

Situated in the popular town of Jesmond, this unassuming hotel is just a five-minute drive from Newcastle's city centre. All the key local attractions are within easy reach. The rooms are pleasant, tastefully decorated and equipped with modern amenities. A good base for exploring the countryside. Includes breakfast. **www.peelhotel.com**

NEWCASTLE UPON TYNE Malmasion Newcastle
104 Quayside, Newcastle Upon Tyne, NE1 3DX **Tel** *0191 245 5000* **Fax** *0191 245 4545* **Rooms** *122*

Sophisticated warehouse conversion on the quayside, adjacent to the Millennium Bridge and opposite the outstanding Baltic arts centre. Part of the Malmaison chain of boutique hotels, which is renowned for its finger-on-the-pulse modern style, with much use of primary colours. Includes breakfast. **www.malmaison.com**

ROMALDKIRK Rose & Crown
Romaldkirk, Barnard Castle, County Durham, DL12 9EB **Tel** *01833 650213* **Fax** *01833 650828* **Rooms** *12*

Picture postcard England at its best. The village green makes a charming backdrop for this delightful little inn. Inside, it is smart, yet reassuringly traditional. Serves home-made soup and delicious food. The rooms are small, but cosy. Ideal for an intimate getaway. Includes breakfast. **www.rose-and-crown.co.uk**

SEAHOUSES Olde Ship
7–9 Main St, Seahouses, Northumberland, NE68 7RD **Tel** *01665 720200* **Fax** *01665 721383* **Rooms** *18*

Defiantly traditional, this charming inn sits above the tiny Northumbrian fishing village of Seahouses. It's a veritable museum of the sea, with maritime artefacts from fishing vessels and lifeboats. The rooms are attractive, and the menu features fresh fish and seafood. Includes breakfast. **www.seahouses.co.uk**

STANNERSBURN Pheasant
Stannersburn, Kielder Water, Northumberland, NE48 1DD **Tel** *01434 240382* **Fax** *01434 240382* **Rooms** *8*

An ivy-covered inn near Kielder Water, the largest man-made lake in Europe. A friendly and warm place, full of character, offering spacious en suite rooms, many with countryside views. Food is freshly prepared, using local produce. Located close to Newcastle and Edinburgh. Includes breakfast. **www.thepheasantinn.com**

TILLMOUTH PARK Tillmouth Park Country House Hotel ▯▯ ▯ £££
Cornhill-On-Tweed, Northumberland, TD12 4UU **Tel** *01890 882255* **Fax** *01890 882540* **Rooms** *14*

Hunting, shooting, fishing and golf are all on the menu at this elegant venue. Serves contemporary British cuisine in an award-winning dining room. Organizes chauffeured limousine pick ups from Edinburgh and Newcastle airports, as well as from Berwick station. Includes breakfast. **www.tillmouthpark.co.uk**

WALLSEND Hadrian Lodge Hotel ▯▯ ▯ £
Hadrian Rd, Wallsend, Newcastle, NE28 6HH **Tel** *0191 262 7733* **Fax** *0191 263 0714* **Rooms** *24*

Located at the eastern limit of Hadrian's Wall, hence this hotel's name. Offers simple, yet comfortable rooms, and the room rates include breakfast. A sensible and economical base for a visit to the Newcastle city centre, which is placed just a ten-minute drive away, or for a cross-country walk along the Roman wall. **www.hadrianlodgehotel.co.uk**

NORTH WALES

ABERDYFI Penhelig Arms ▯▯ ▯ £
Aberdyfi, Gwynedd, LL35 0LT **Tel** *01654 767215* **Fax** *01654 767690* **Rooms** *16*

This whitewashed, seafront hotel is spread over three buildings – Penhelig House, Bodhelig and The Cottage. Offers lavish, contemporary rooms and suites, well-equipped with modern amenities. Most rooms boast splendid views of the sea. Serves tasty cuisine, and features an extensive wine list. **www.penheligarms.com**

ABERDYFI Trefiddian Hotel ▯▯▯▯▯ ££
Gwynedd, LL35 0SB **Tel** *01654 767213* **Fax** *01654 767777* **Rooms** *59*

A four-star, family-run hotel, located to the south of Snowdonia National Park, and overlooking Cardigan Bay. Has an indoor heated pool, a tennis court, a play area for children and a nine-hole putting green; an 18-hole golf course lies next door. Offers comfortable rooms with en suite facilities. Price includes dinner. **www.trefwales.com**

ABERSOCH Porth Tocyn Country Hotel ▯▯▯▯ £££
Abersoch, Pwllheli, Gwynedd, LL53 7BU **Tel** *01758 713303* **Fax** *01758 713538* **Rooms** *17*

Country-house hotel renowned for its fine cuisine. Boasts fine views across Cardigan Bay. The rooms are furnished with antiques; those on the ground floor are suitable for disabled travellers (call in advance). Also hosts a children's play area, equipped with a TV, Nintendo, video and board games. Open Apr–Oct. **www.porth-tocyn-hotel.co.uk**

BEAUMARIS Ye Olde Bull's Head Inn ▯▯▯▯ £££
Castle St, Beaumaris, Isle of Anglesey, LL58 8AP **Tel** *01248 810329* **Fax** *01248 811294* **Rooms** *26*

This charming inn on the Isle of Anglesey occupies a Grade II listed building dating back to the 15th century. The rooms combine modern facilities with ancient oak-beamed ceilings and antique furniture and fittings. Hosts an award-winning restaurant and a traditional freehouse bar that serves real ale. **www.bullsheadinn.co.uk**

BEDDGELERT Sygun Fawr Country House ▯▯▯ ££
Beddgelert, Gwynedd, LL55 4NE **Tel** *01766 890258* **Rooms** *11*

Set in a truly rural setting, this four-star, country-house hotel sits amid a vast expanse of mountains and gardens. The rooms at this former, 17th-century manor feature exposed stone work, oak beams and inglenook fireplaces. The dining room, located in the oldest part of the building, has antique furniture. **www.sygunfawr.co.uk**

BETWS-Y-COED Craig-y-Dderwen Riverside Hotel ▯▯▯▯ ££
Betws-y-Coed, Snowdonia National Park, North Wales, LL24 0AS **Tel** *01690 710293* **Fax** *01690 710362* **Rooms** *16*

Country-house hotel, set amid 16 acres of gardens in the heart of Snowdonia National Park. Boasts tastefully furnished rooms, with four-poster beds and log fires and modern amenities; a specially equipped room is available for disabled guests. This tranquil retreat also has a play area for children and free parking. **www.snowdoniahotel.com**

BODELWYDDAN Bodelwyddan Castle Hotel ▯▯▯▯▯ ££
Bodelwyddan, Rhyl, Denbighshire, N Wales, LL18 5YA **Tel** *01745 585088* **Fax** *01705 585089* **Rooms** *186*

Large luxury hotel, housed in a Grade II listed castle. Features many modern facilities, including a heated indoor swimming pool and a sauna and steam room. Activities such as tennis, croquet and archery are also on offer in the magnificent grounds. Has stylish rooms with four-poster beds and patios. Specialises in short break stays. **www.warnerbreaks.co.uk**

CAPEL GARMON Tan-y-Foel Country House ▯▯ £££
Near Betws-y-Coed, Llanrwst, Conwy, LL26 0RE **Tel** *01690 710507* **Fax** *01690 710681* **Rooms** *5*

This quiet and luxurious, family-run hotel is located within striking distance of Conwy Valley and Snowdonia. The rooms in this 17th-century, Welsh stone building are beautifully crafted to fuse traditional and modern styles. Activities such as hiking, horse riding and bird-watching are available nearby. **www.tyfhotel.co.uk**

COLWYN BAY Bryn Holcombe Hotel ▯ £
9 Grosvenor Rd, Colwyn Bay, Conwy, LL29 7YF **Tel** *01492 530423* **Rooms** *5*

A peaceful, two-star hotel, well-placed for exploring Snowdonia National Park. Also a short drive from the World Heritage Site of Conwy Castle, the medieval walled town of Conwy, the Great Orme nature reserve and miles of sandy beaches. The price of the rooms includes a traditional Welsh breakfast.

Key to Price Guide *see p556* **Key to Symbols** *see back cover flap*

COLWYN BAY Rathlin Country House

48 Kings Rd, Colwyn Bay, Conwy, LL29 7YH **Tel** *01492 532173* **Fax** *0871 6619887* **Rooms** *3*

Small, luxury B&B in a beautiful conservation area, just minutes from Colwyn Bay. The rooms at this non-smoking retreat have en suite facilities; one even has a jacuzzi. The cosy dining room features an inglenook fireplace, oak panelling and oak parquet flooring. Also has a sauna. Serves a traditional Welsh breakfast. **www.rathlincountryhouse.co.uk**

CRICCIETH Mynydd Ednyfed Country House Hotel

Caernarfon Rd, Criccieth, Gwynedd, LL52 0PH **Tel** *01766 523269* **Fax** *01766 522929* **Rooms** *9*

Secluded, 400-year-old, country-house hotel. Small, intimate rooms overlook expansive gardens, woods, an orchard and a paddock. Offers striking views of Tremadog Bay and Criccieth Castle as well. This family-run, Welsh retreat is licensed to conduct civil marriage ceremonies too. Tennis courts and a holistic therapy room are available. **www.criccieth.net**

GANLLWYD Plas Dolmelynllyn Country Hotel

Ganllwyd, Dolgellau, Gwynedd, LL40 2HP **Tel** *01341 440273* **Fax** *01341 440640* **Rooms** *9*

Spacious National Trust country-house hotel, ideally placed for sports enthusiasts. Outdoor pursuits such as walking, mountain biking, horse riding, fishing, golf and water sports are all available nearby. Those looking for a peaceful and relaxing break will enjoy the vast, undisturbed gardens, as well as the waterfalls and woods. **www.dolly-hotel.co.uk**

HARLECH Gwrach Ynys

Harlech, Talsarnau, Gwynedd, LL47 6TS **Tel** *01766 780742* **Fax** *01766 781199* **Rooms** *7*

A secluded B&B overlooking Snowdonia National Park. The rooms are cosy and modern, and the ground floor has two lounges. This Edwardian country house is located within reach of Harlech Castle, Royal St David's Golf Club, the Morfa Harlech Nature Reserve and the beach. **www.gwrachynys.co.uk**

LLANABER Llwyndu Farmhouse

Llanaber, Barmouth, Gwynedd, LL42 1RR **Tel** *01341 280144* **Rooms** *7*

Historic farmhouse set in a Grade II listed building, overlooking Cardigan Bay. This early 17th-century hotel has been renovated to provide en suite accommodation, and features oak-beamed ceilings, inglenook fireplaces and a stone spiral staircase, as well as many antiques and curios. **www.llwyndu-farmhouse.co.uk**

LLANBERIS Plas Coch

High St, Llanberis, Gwynned, LL55 4HB **Tel** *01286 872122* **Fax** *01286 872648* **Rooms** *8*

Welcoming guesthouse at the foot of Snowdon. Offers modern B&B accommodation in a spacious Victorian house, built around 1865. All rooms are en suite. This family-friendly hotel is located a short distance from Snowdon Mountain Railway, Llanberis Lake Railway and Padarn Country Park. **www.plas-coch.co.uk**

LLANDRILLO Tyddyn Llan

Near Corwen, Denbighshire, LL21 0ST **Tel** *01490 440264* **Fax** *01490 440414* **Rooms** *12*

Award-winning restaurant-with-rooms occupying an elegant Georgian house, and located in the Vale of Edeyrnion. Rooms are spacious and tastefully furnished, with en suite facilties; most rooms have great views. Sports activities such as fishing, golf, sailing, horse riding and walking are all within easy reach. **www.tyddynllan.co.uk**

LLANDUDNO St Tudno Hotel & Restaurant

The Promenade, Llandudno, Conwy, LL30 2LP **Tel** *01492 874411* **Fax** *01492 860407* **Rooms** *18*

Luxurious hotel with a highly acclaimed restaurant. Occupies a Victorian seafront terrace with great views over the town's promenade, gardens and beach, and the nearby Great Orme headland. The lavish rooms and suites are individually decorated, with modern facilities. Also has spacious lounges. **www.st-tudno.co.uk**

LLANDUDNO The Imperial

The Promenade, Llandudno, Conwy, LL30 1AP **Tel** *01492 877466* **Fax** *01492 878043* **Rooms** *98*

This stylish, contemporary hotel is located on Llandudno's main promenade, and offers splendid views of the bay. The rooms are elegantly decorated, with several modern conveniences. The restaurant boasts fine views over the sea and some great local cuisine. Also provides conference facilities. **www.theimperial.co.uk**

LLANDUDNO Bodysgallen Hall

Llandudno, Conwy, LL30 1RS **Tel** *01492 584466* **Fax** *01492 582519* **Rooms** *32*

Impressive, historic country-house hotel, set amid an expansive wooded parkland. Features a fabulous 17th-century rockery and walled garden. The luxurious rooms offer stunning views over Conwy Castle and the mountains of Snowdonia. Hosts an award-winning restaurant. **www.bodysgallen.com**

LLANGOLLEN The Wild Pheasant Hotel

Berwyn Road, Llangollen, Clwyd, LL20 8AD **Tel** *01978 860629* **Fax** *01978 861837* **Rooms** *46*

Charming hotel in a renovated 19th-century inn, the Wild Pheasant sits picturesquely in the beautiful surroundings of the Vale of Llangollen. Everything can be catered for here, from health and beauty spa retreats to gourmet breaks and even whitewater rafting, laser clay pigeon shooting and off-road driving. **www.wildpheasanthotel.co.uk**

PENMAENPOOL Penmaenuchaf Hall

Dogellau, Gwynedd, LL40 1YB **Tel** *01341 422129* **Fax** *01341 422787* **Rooms** *14*

Relaxing country-house retreat situated in Snowdonia National Park. The tastefully decorated rooms have wonderful views over the surrounding mountains. Outdoor pursuits such as mountain biking, fishing, walking, golf and horse riding are available nearby. The up-market restaurant serves modern British food. **www.penhall.co.uk**

PORTMEIRION Portmeirion

Portmeirion, Gwynedd, LL48 6ET **Tel** *01766 770000* **Fax** *01766 771331* **Rooms** *68*

This village-like complex, built initially by Clough Williams-Ellis as a private peninsula, is now a holiday retreat with a popular hotel, self-catering cottage, shops and restaurants. The lavish rooms and suites are furnished in a contemporary style, and are well-equipped with modern facilities. **www.portmeirion-village.com**

RUTHIN Ruthin Castle Hotel

Ruthin, Denbighshire, LL15 2NU **Tel** *01824 702664* **Fax** *01824 705978* **Rooms** *62*

This luxurious, converted, 13th-century castle occupies a part of the former Crown Estate. The castle sits amid an ancient walled dry moat, with acres of landscaped gardens and parkland alongside the pretty River Clywd. Offers fine dining, a beauty spa and private fishing. Golf course located nearby. **www.ruthincastle.co.uk**

TALSARNAU Maes-y-Neuadd

Talsarnau, Harlech, Gwynedd, LL47 6YA **Tel** *01766 780200* **Fax** *01766 780211* **Rooms** *15*

Charming, 14th-century manor house, beautifully placed at the base of Snowdonia National Park. Houses lavish, well-equipped rooms. The award-winning restaurant is noted for Wales's lamb, fish and farmhouse cheese, while the intimate bar features an ancient inglenook fireplace and period curios. **www.neuadd.com**

SOUTH AND MID-WALES

ABERGAVENNY Clytha Arms

Clytha, nr Abergavenny, Monmouthshire, NP7 9BW **Tel** *01873 840206* **Rooms** *4*

Small, welcoming hotel-restaurant just outside the market town of Abergavenny with an award-winning pub for its real ale. Well placed for exploring the Brecon Beacons and the Sugar Loaf Mountain. The rooms are homely and cheerful, with views over the large grounds. Fishing trips can be arranged on request. **www.clytha-arms.com**

ABERYSTWYTH Conrah Country House

Chancery, Aberystwyth, Ceredigion, SY23 4DF **Tel** *01970 617941* **Fax** *01970 624546* **Rooms** *17*

Stunning country-house with vast woodland grounds and gardens. Located on the outskirts of town, this traditional hotel features a croquet lawn and many footpaths leading down to the coast. The rooms are relaxing, but luxurious, with oak-beamed ceilings and panoramic views. Serves British cuisine with a French twist. **www.conrah.co.uk**

AMMANFORD Glynhir Estate

Glynhir Rd, Llandybie, Carmarthenshire, SA18 2TD **Tel** *01269 850438* **Rooms** *4*

This secluded B&B is housed in a stylish mansion, on an 18th-century Huguenot estate, located at the foothills of the Black Mountains. It features a cascading waterfall and lovely gardens. Has comfortable rooms and self-catering cottages. Offers courses in painting, photography, quilting and sculpture. **www.theglynhirestate.com**

BRECON Cantre Selyf

5 Lion St, Brecon, Powys, LD3 7AU **Tel** *01874 622904* **Fax** *01874 622315* **Rooms** *3*

Small, historic B&B in a 17th-century town house. This non-smoking hotel is situated in Brecon's town centre. The rooms are cosy with beamed ceilings, Georgian fireplaces and cast-iron beds. Ask for a room overlooking the large walled garden and the Norman Town Wall that encloses it. **www.cantreselyf.co.uk**

BRECON Castle of Brecon

The Castle Square, Brecon, Powys, LD3 9DB **Tel** *01874 624611* **Fax** *01874 623737* **Rooms** *30*

The oldest hotel in Wales and located in the town centre, this outstanding family-run establishment occupies the remains of Brecon castle. The rooms are spacious, with en suite facilities; the south-facing rooms have breathtaking views over Brecon Beacons National Park. Ideally located for walking and horse riding. **www.breconcastle.co.uk**

BROAD HAVEN Druidstone

Broad Haven, Haverfordwest, Pembrokeshire, SA62 3NE **Tel** *01437 781221* **Rooms** *11*

Perched high above the sandy beach of Druidstone Haven, this seaside hotel offers splendid views. Accommodation here is split between en suite rooms in the main house and five, individually decorated cottages. Dining room, sitting room and cellar bar overlook the sea. Children and pets are welcome. **www.druidstone.co.uk**

CARDIFF The Big Sleep Hotel

Bute Terrace, Cardiff, CF10 2FE **Tel** *02920 636363* **Fax** *02920 636364* **Rooms** *81*

A stylish hotel at affordable prices, housed in a converted 1960s office block. The interior is self-consciously retro, but the rooms are contemporary and comfortable, with en suite amenities. Offers stunning views as far as the Severn Bridge. Highly popular with both business and leisure travellers. **www.thebigsleephotel.com**

CARDIFF St David's Hotel & Spa

Havannah St, Cardiff, CF10 5SD **Tel** *02920 454045* **Fax** *02920 313075* **Rooms** *132*

Overlooking Cardiff's trendy waterfront bay, this five-star hotel and spa is one of Wales's most luxurious hotels. Offers plush rooms and state-of-the-art leisure amenities. Each room has a private, deck-style balcony with views across the bay. Tailormade spa packages are available, as are conference facilities. **www.thestdavidshotel.com**

CARDIFF The Park Inn

Circle Way E, Llanedeyrn, Cardiff, CF23 9XF **Tel** *02920 589988* **Fax** *02920 549092* **Rooms** *132*

Friendly hotel located just a ten-minute drive from the city centre. A popular choice for business travellers thanks to its conference facilities, but also ideal for exploring the nearby attractions, including Cardiff Bay, Cardiff Castle and Millennium Stadium. Also has a heated indoor swimming pool, spa and sauna. **www.parkinn.com**

CHEPSTOW Marriott St Pierre Hotel and Country Club

St Pierre Park, Chepstow, Monmouthshire, NP16 6YA **Tel** *0870 400 7224* **Fax** *0870 629 975* **Rooms** *148*

Luxury hotel in a converted, 14th-century manor, set amid 400 acres of parkland. The lavish rooms retain the building's original features, while offering all modern facilities. Ask for a room overlooking the ornamental lake. Hosts business centres, two golf courses and a beauty salon. **www.marriothotels.co.uk**

CRICKHOWELL The Bear Hotel

Crickhowell, Powys, NP8 1BW **Tel** *01873 810408* **Fax** *01873 811696* **Rooms** *36*

Charismatic, timbered hotel in the centre of the old market town of Crickhowell, A popular stopping off point for tourists and locals alike. This former coaching inn dates back to 1432, and has retained its cobbled forecourt and inner courtyard. Offers colourful, cheerful rooms and a much-liked low-beamed bar. **www.bearhotel.co.uk**

CRICKHOWELL Gliffaes Country House

Crickhowell, Powys, NP8 1RH **Tel** *01874 730371* **Fax** *01874 730463* **Rooms** *23*

Welcoming, Victorian country-house, set on expansive gardens and grouse-filled woodland. This scenic retreat is located just outside Crickhowell, on the road to Brecon Beacons National Park. It's proximity to River Usk makes it a popular destination for fly fishing enthusiasts. **www.gliffaeshotel.com**

EGLWYSFACH Ynyshir Hall

Eglwysfach, Machynlleth, Powys, SY20 8TA **Tel** *01654 781209* **Fax** *01654 781366* **Rooms** *9*

Nestled in secluded, picturesque countryside above the Dovey estuary, this 16th-century house was once owned by Queen Victoria. Its nearness to one of Britain's finest wildfowl reserves makes it a favourite with bird-watchers. The non-smoking rooms are tastefully decorated with antique furnishings. **www.ynyshirshall.co.uk**

HAVERFORDWEST The Wolfe Inn

Wolfscastle, Haverfordwest, Pembrokeshire, SA62 5LS **Tel** *01437 741662* **Fax** *01437 741676* **Rooms** *4*

Historic, stone-built coaching inn in the small village of Wolfscastle, just a ten-minute drive from Haverfordwest. Offers comfortable rooms, carefully furnished to match the original oak-beamed ceilings. Also has an award-winning brasserie. Children and pets are welcome. Cosy log fires in winter.

HAVERFORDWEST The Druidstone Hotel

Broad Haven, Haverfordwest, Pembrokeshire, SA62 3NE **Tel** *01437 781221* **Fax** *01437 781133* **Rooms** *11*

Standing in eight hectares (20 acres) of wild land overlooking the sandy beach of Druidstone Haven, this hotel has a warm atmosphere and helpful, hospitable owners. It is ideally located for young families and pet lovers. There are also cottages available for rent. **www.druidstone.co.uk**

LAKE VYRNWY Lake Vyrnwy

Llanwyddyn, nr Welshpool, Powys, SY10 0LY **Tel** *01691 870692* **Fax** *01691 870259* **Rooms** *52*

Converted Victorian fishing lodge on the massive Vyrnwy Estate. Boasts fabulous views over mountains, untamed moorland, forests and, of course, Lake Vyrnwy itself. Has elegant rooms; some with luxuries such as jacuzzis, four-poster beds and balconies. Leisure facilities include a sauna and lakeside gym. **www.lakevyrnwy.com**

LAMPETER Falcondale Mansion Hotel

Falcondale Drive, Lampeter, Ceredigion, SA48 7RX **Tel** *01570 422910* **Fax** *01570 423559* **Rooms** *19*

Part of the Best Western chain of hotels, this Victorian mansion is set within a vast parkland, a short drive from the market town of Lampeter. The en suite rooms have four-poster beds and small balconies overlooking the well-tended gardens. The award-winning restaurant serves Welsh cuisine. **www.falcondalehotel.com**

LAMPHEY Lamphey Court Hotel & Spa

Lamphey, Pembrokeshire, SA71 5NT **Tel** *01646 672273* **Fax** *01646 672480* **Rooms** *38*

Magnificent Georgian mansion on the edge of Pembrokeshire National Park. This Best Western hotel boasts luxurious rooms, some fine views and modern amenities. Hosts a leisure spa with an indoor heated pool and jacuzzi, as well as floodlit tennis courts. Offers conference facilities. **www.lampheycourt.co.uk**

LLANIGON Old Post Office

Llanigon, Hay-on-Wye, Powys, HR3 5QA **Tel** *01497 820008* **Rooms** *3*

Small, but charming, 17th-century B&B on the edge of Brecon Beacons, just outside Hay-on-Wye. The non-smoking rooms are located beneath wood-beamed ceilings at the top of a winding oak staircase. Serves a vegetarian breakfast. **www.oldpost-office.co.uk**

LLANTHONY Llanthony Priory

Llanthony, Abergavenny, Monmouthshire, NP7 7NN **Tel** *01873 890487* **Fax** *01873 890844* **Rooms** *4*

Stunning, retreat-style B&B in a 12th-century Augustinian priory on the edge of the Black Mountains. The rooms, housed in former abbey cells, are simple, with minimal furnishings. The low ceilings add to their character and charm. Perfectly located for exploring the scenic countryside. **www.llanthonyprioryhotel.co.uk**

LLYSWEN Llangoed Hall

Llyswen, Brecon, Powys, LD3 0YP **Tel** *01874 754 525* **Fax** *01874 754545* **Rooms** *23*

Luxury hotel housed in a stunning Edwardian country house in the middle of Wye Valley. Features a carved timber staircase, oak doors and antique furnishings in the rooms; works of art by renowned artists such as Whistler and Augustus John adorn the walls. Organizes fishing, rock climbing and other outdoor pursuits on request. **www.llangoedhall.com**

MILEBROOK Milebrook House

Knighton, Powys, LD7 1LT **Tel** *01547 528632* **Fax** *01547 520509* **Rooms** *10*

A converted, stone-built Georgian house, located on the border of England and Wales. This small hotel is perfectly placed for exploring Offa's Dyke, the man-made earthwork that marks the border. The comfortable rooms and restaurant overlook some fabulous countryside. Also has a croquet lawn. **www.milebrookhouse.co.uk**

MONMOUTH The Crown at Whitebrook

Near Monmouth, Monmouthshire, NP25 4TX **Tel** *01600 860254* **Fax** *01600 860607* **Rooms** *8*

This acclaimed restaurant-with-rooms sits in large gardens, in a tiny village on the edge of the Wye Valley Area of Outstanding Natural Beauty. The rooms at this 17th-century eatery are luxurious and beautifully decorated, but it is the gourmet cuisine that draws most visitors. **www.crownatwhitebrook.co.uk**

NEWPORT Cnapan Country House Hotel

East St, Newport, SA42 0SY **Tel** *01239 820575* **Fax** *01239 820878* **Rooms** *5*

A charming and intimate country house with a cheerful and welcoming ambience. Offers spacious rooms, carefully decorated with traditional oak Welsh furnishings. Serves excellent Welsh cuisine. The service is efficient and the hotel is ideally located to explore the countryside. **www.cnapan.co.uk**

PENALLY Penally Abbey Country House Hotel

Penally, Pembrokeshire, SA70 7PY **Tel** *01834 843033* **Fax** *01834 844714* **Rooms** *17*

Neo-Gothic architectural flourishes give this country house considerable character. Set amid expansive gardens and woodlands, this vine-covered hotel has peaceful rooms, with views over Tenby golf course and Carmarthen Bay. The elegant dining room features seasonal produce and an extensive wine list. **www.penally-abbey.com**

PEN-Y-CAE Craig-y-Nos Castle

Brecon Rd, Pen-y-cae, Powys, SA9 1GL **Tel** *01639 731167* **Fax** *01639 731077* **Rooms** *26*

Located in the Brecon Beacons, this impressive castle offers a not-to-be-missed glimpse into Wales's feudal history. Houses en suite rooms; some with great views of the gardens. This popular wedding venue once belonged to the renowned opera singer, Adelina Patti. Ideal for walkers and bird-watchers. **www.craigynoscastle.co.uk**

PORTHKERRY Egerton Grey

Porthkerry, Barry, South Glamorgan, CF62 3BZ **Tel** *01446 711666* **Fax** *01446 711690* **Rooms** *9*

Refined Victorian country-house hotel boasting a vast collection of antiques. The rooms are furnished with a wealth of period furnishings, original brasswork, open fireplaces, ornate mouldings and oak panelling – even the food in the restaurant is served on antique china. The huge grounds include a croquet lawn. **www.egertongrey.co.uk**

REYNOLDSTON Fairyhill

Reynoldston, Gower, Swansea, SA3 1BS **Tel** *01792 390139* **Fax** *01792 391358* **Rooms** *8*

Secluded country house set amid vast, mature woodlands on the Gower Peninsula Area of Outstanding Natural Beauty. Hosts luxurious rooms and an award-winning restaurant that serves a fusion of Welsh and European cuisine. Therapy treatments such as massages, reflexology and reiki are available on request. **www.fairyhill.net**

SPITTAL Lower Haythog Farm

Spittal, Haverfordwest, Pembrokeshire, SA62 5QL **Tel** *01437 731279* **Fax** *01437 731279* **Rooms** *6*

Converted, 14th-century farmhouse, set on several acres of working farmland. This reasonably priced hotel offers a luxurious experience. The en suite rooms are comfortably furnished and retain their cottage-like feel. Also has two, self-catering cottages. Serves home-cooked food, using local produce. **www.lowerhaythogfarm.co.uk**

ST DAVID'S Lochmeyler Farm Guest House

Pen-y-Cwm, near Solva, St David's, Pembrokeshire, SA62 6LL **Tel** *01348 837724* **Rooms** *11*

This quiet guesthouse, on a huge working dairy farm, is a popular stopping off point on the Pembrokeshire Long Distance Coast Path. The accommodation is split between the main 16th-century farmhouse, the cottages and the barn. The rooms are tastefully furnished and equipped with modern amenities. **www.lochmeyler.co.uk**

ST DAVID'S The Old Cross Hotel

Cross Sq, St David's, Pembrokeshire, SA62 6SP **Tel** *01437 720387* **Fax** *01437 720394* **Rooms** *11*

This friendly and comfortable hotel is situated in the centre of the town, just a short walk from the famous cathedral. Bedrooms are spacious and have a good range of facilities. Public areas include comfortable lounges, a popular bar and an airy restaurant where good wholesome food is offered. **www.oldcrosshotel.co.uk**

SWANSEA Windsor Lodge

Mount Pleasant, Swansea, SA1 6EG **Tel** *01792 642158* **Fax** *01792 648996* **Rooms** *20*

Small hotel and restaurant in a 200-year-old, Grade II listed building. This two-star lodge, near the city centre, provides a reasonably priced break. The rooms are modern and comfortable, and the acclaimed restaurant draws both locals and travellers by serving British food with a French twist. **www.windsor-lodge.co.uk**

Key to Price Guide *see p556* **Key to Symbols** *see back cover flap*

TENBY Fourcroft Hotel

🖥 🍴 ♨ 🐕 ♿ ⓔⓔⓔ

North Beach, Tenby, Pembrokeshire, SA70 8AP **Tel** *01834 842886* **Fax** *01834 842888* **Rooms** *40*

This charming hotel offers striking views of Tenby's sheltered North Beach and the fishing harbour. Boasts secluded trails leading down to the beach. The rooms are simple, yet comfortably furnished, with most modern amenities. The restaurant serves local produce with an emphasis on fresh seafood. **www.fourcroft-hotel.co.uk**

TENBY Heywood Lodge Country House Hotel

🍴 ⓔⓔⓔ

Heywood Lane, Tenby, Pembrokeshire, SA70 8BN **Tel** *01834 842684* **Fax** *01834 843976* **Rooms** *12*

Beautiful Victorian house that's a luxury four-star hotel. Offers elegant, en suite rooms with traditional furniture; some have four-poster beds. This country house hotel features a conservatory and king size, hydra spa baths. Welcomes pets. **www.heywoodlodge.com**

THE MUMBLES Carlton Mumbles

🍴 🐕 ⓔⓔ

654–656 Mumbles Rd, Mumbles, Swansea, SA3 4EA **Tel** *01792 360450* **Fax** *01792 360450* **Rooms** *32*

Friendly and affordable B&B located in the hometown of the famous poet, Dylan Thomas. The rooms are plain, but comfortably furnished; some with great views over Swansea Bay. Water-skiing, sailing and powerboating facilities are available nearby, as are a number of golf courses. **www.carltonmumbles.co.uk**

THE MUMBLES The Shoreline Hotel

🍴 🐕 ⓔⓔ

648 Mumbles Rd, Mumbles, Swansea, SA3 4EA **Tel** *01792 366322* **Rooms** *11*

Located on the seafront and close to local amenities, The Shoreline Hotel has been recently renovated to offer high levels of comfort. All rooms have TVs and there is a communal bar area and beautiful views across Swansea Bay. Ideally located to explore the area or play a round of golf at the course nearby. **www.shorelinehotel.co.uk**

TINTERN Parva Farmhouse

🍴 ⓔⓔ

Tintern, Chepstow, Gwent, NP16 6SQ **Tel** *01291 689411/689511* **Fax** *01291 689941* **Rooms** *8*

Farmhouse and restaurant on the banks of River Wye. This welcoming stone house is well placed for exploring Tintern Abbey and its surrounding countryside. The rooms offer great views over the river; some have four-poster beds. There is a guest lounge area and a restaurant with a 4 m (14 ft) high beamed fireplace. **www.hoteltintern.co.uk**

THE LOWLANDS

ARGYLL Bealach Country House

🅿 🍴 ⓔⓔⓔ

Salachan Glen, Duror, Argyll **Tel** *01631 740298* **Rooms** *3*

Originally a shepherd's croft, this country house has been extended to provide large, comfortable accommodation in the West Highlands of Scotland. The rural setting makes it ideal for walkers and the guesthouse is within easy reach of Fort William, Glencoe and other sights. **www.bealach-house.co.uk**

AUCHTERARDER The Gleneagles Hotel

🖥 🍴 ♨ 🐕 📺 ⓔⓔⓔⓔ

A9, Auchterarder, Perthshire, PH3 1NF **Tel** *0800 3893737* **Fax** *01764 662134* **Rooms** *266*

World-renowned château-style resort hotel with high standards of service, cuisine, and amenities. Boasts championship golf courses and state-of-the-art spa and leisure facilities. Well equipped to accommodate the most demanding of guests. Popular with both business travellers and families. **www.gleneagles.com**

AYR The Ivy House

🍴 🐕 ⓔⓔ

2 Allloway, Ayr, Ayrshire, KA7 4NL **Tel** *01292 442336* **Fax** *01292 445572* **Rooms** *5*

Located near the famous Robbie Burns Cottage, this attractive hotel offers individually furnished, comfortable rooms, with modern amenities. Serves delicious food. This is an ideal place to explore the surrounding Ayrshire countryside. Within easy distance of Culzean Castle.

BALQUHIDDER Monachyle Mhor

🍴 🐕 ⓔⓔⓔ

Balquhidder, Lochearnhead, Perthshire, FK19 8PQ **Tel** *01877 384622* **Fax** *01877 384305* **Rooms** *14*

A beautiful, family-run hotel situated in the heart of Highland Perthshire, near the picturesque shores of Loch Voil. Offers luxury rooms and suites, some with log fires, as well as self-catering cottages. Service is outstanding. Also has an award-winning restaurant. **www.monachylemhor.com**

BLAIRGOWRIE Kinloch House

🍴 ♨ 📺 ⓔⓔⓔ

By Blairgowrie, Perthshire, PH10 6SG **Tel** *01250 884237* **Fax** *01250 884333* **Rooms** *18*

This family-run, country-house hotel is set in a particularly scenic locale at the end of a remote lochside glen road. Has an especially warm and welcoming atmosphere. The rooms and suites are comfortable and well equipped with modern facilities. Hosts a sauna and spa, and serves good food. **www.kinlochhouse.com**

CLINTMAINS Clint Lodge

ⓔⓔⓔ

Clinthill, St Boswells, Melrose, Roxburghshire, TD6 0DZ **Tel** *01835 822027* **Fax** *01835 822656* **Rooms** *5*

A traditional country-guesthouse and B&B, run by hospitable hosts. The hotel has great views of the Tweed, and its location close to Melrose Abbey makes it ideal for exploring the surrounding countryside. The rooms are tastefully decorated, with en suite facilities and modern amenities. Serves an excellent breakfast. **www.clintlodge.co.uk**

CUPAR Peat Inn   🍴 🏃 ♿   ££££

Peat Inn, by Cupar, Fife, KY15 5H **Tel** *01334 840206* **Fax** *01334 840530* **Rooms** *8*

Relaxed and informal award-winning restaurant-with-rooms. Boasts luxury suites, elegantly decorated with plush furnishings. The renowned restaurant serves mouthwatering dishes and an extensive selection of wines. Located just a short distance from St Andrews and other sightseeing attractions. **www.thepeatinn.co.uk**

DOLLAR Castle Campbell   🍴 🏃   £££

11 Bridge St, Dollar, Clackmannanshire, FK14 7DE **Tel** *01259 742519* **Fax** *01259 743742* **Rooms** *9*

A simple, but dignified Georgian building, set in the town centre. Has non-smoking, spacious rooms, with en suite facilities and modern conveniences such as colour TVs, tea and coffee makers and telephones. A good base for enjoying the excellent walks in the surrounding countryside. **www.castle-campbell.co.uk**

EDINBURGH 7 Danube Street   £££

7 Danube St, Edinburgh, EH4 1NN **Tel** *0131 332 2755* **Fax** *0131 343 3648* **Rooms** *3*

A delightful B&B, housed in a Georgian town house, in a quiet, but central part of Edinburgh. The comfortable, non-smoking rooms have attached bathrooms, and provide modern amenities such as computer points and a personal key and entrance. Within easy reach of many attractions and eateries. **www.aboutedinburgh.com/danube.html**

EDINBURGH The Glenora Guest House   P 🍴   £££

14 Rosebery Crescent, Edinburgh, EH12 5JY **Tel** *0131 3371186* **Fax** *0131 3371119* **Rooms** *11*

Set in a beautiful Georgian townhouse in the city centre, the Glenora offers luxurious accommodation and an excellent restaurant. The interior is modern and stylish and the award-winning restaurant serves superb organic Scottish breakfasts. Well located close to all amenities. **www.glenorahotel.co.uk**

EDINBURGH Walton Guest House   P 🏃   £££

79 Dundas St, Edinburgh, EH3 6SD **Tel** *0131 556 1137* **Fax** *0131 557 8367* **Rooms** *10*

Located in Edinburgh's New Town, the Walton Guest House occupies a fine Georgian townhouse. The accommodation comprises compact doubles, larger triples and family rooms, all decorated to a high standard. Close to the city centre and ideal both for tourists and those on business. **www.waltonhotel.com**

EDINBURGH The Bonham   📺 🍴 🏃 ♿   ££££

35 Drumsheugh Gardens, Edinburgh, EH3 7RN **Tel** *0131 274 7400* **Fax** *0131 226 6080* **Rooms** *48*

Ultra-smart town house, boasting a rich interior with a perfect blend of many original features and some contemporary touches, including modern works of art and furniture. The oak-panelled restaurant is popular and the cooking is skilled. Offers opulent and well-equipped rooms. **www.thebonham.com**

EDINBURGH The Balmoral   📺 🍴 ♨ 🍽   £££££

1 Princes St, Edinburgh, EH2 2EQ **Tel** *0131 556 2414* **Fax** *0131 557 3747* **Rooms** *188*

Boasting the best known address in Edinburgh, The Balmoral is favoured by those who are accustomed to the very best in life. This elegant hotel has luxurious, tastefully furnished suites and rooms, with Internet access, Fax machines, TVs, and more. Also offers conference facilities, a spa and excellent eateries. **www.thebalmoralhotel.com**

EDINBURGH The Scotsman   📺 🍴 ♨ 🏃 🍽 ♿   £££££

20 N Bridge, Edinburgh, EH1 1YT **Tel** *0131 556 5565* **Fax** *0131 652 3652* **Rooms** *69*

This stylish hotel is housed in the converted former offices of *The Scotsman* newspaper, and offers great views of the city. The luxurious rooms and suites are decorated with authentic Scottish estate tweeds, and feature amenities such as DVD and CD players, TVS, Internet access, coffee makers and more. **www.thescotsmanhotel.co.uk**

EDNAM Edenwater House   🍴   £££

Ednam, Kelso, Roxburghshire, TD5 7QL **Tel** *01573 224070* **Fax** *01573 226615* **Rooms** *4*

A quiet, family-run traditional guesthouse located on the edge of the village. This stone building is comfortably furnished, and offers lovely views of the surrounding Cheviot Hills. The delicious home-cooked meals, made with local produce, are accompanied by a particularly interesting wine list. **www.edenwaterhouse.co.uk**

GLASGOW Premier Inn   📺 🍴 🏃   ££

80 Ballater St, Glasgow, G5 0TW **Tel** *0141 429 4233* **Fax** *0141 429 4244* **Rooms** *114*

This city-centre budget hotel offers modern, spacious and well-equipped rooms with facilities such as satellite TV, walk-in shower rooms and trouser presses. Families are well catered for here, and children under 16 stay for free. Full-Scottish breakfast is served in the trendy hotel bistro. **www.premierinn.com**

GLASGOW Radisson SAS   📺 🍴 🍽   £££

301 Argyle St, Glasgow, G2 8DL **Tel** *0141 204 3333* **Fax** *0141 204 3344* **Rooms** *250*

This contemporary, award-winning hotel is mainly recognized for its innovative design. Hosts lavishly furnished rooms, suites and an apartment, well-equipped with many innovative features. Also has conference rooms, a popular bar and a good restaurant. A definite choice for those who appreciate modern surroundings. **www.radisson.com**

GLASGOW Hotel du Vin at One Devonshire Gardens   🍴 🍽 🏃 ♿   ££££

One Devonshire Gardens, Glasgow, G12 0UX **Tel** *0141 339 2001* **Fax** *0131 337 1663* **Rooms** *49*

A beautiful town house, located in the city's trendy and leafy West End. The rooms have been glamorously furnished and opulently decorated, and the food in the three AA Rosettes restaurant is extremely refined. Well equipped with a high standard of service to match – a place for a serious treat. **www.hotelduvin.com**

Key to Price Guide *see p556* **Key to Symbols** *see back cover flap*

GLASGOW Park Inn

2 Port Dundas Place, Glasgow, G2 3LD **Tel** *0141 333 1500* **Fax** *0141 333 5700* **Rooms** *100*

A glamorous, style-conscious boutique hotel with two trendy restaurants, beauty salon, spa and leisure amenities. The bedrooms are comfortably minimalist. An excellent location for those who enjoy shopping. Also offers meeting and conference facilties. **www.glasgow.parkinn.co.uk**

GLENROTHES Balbirnie

Balbirnie Park, Markinch, Glenrothes, Fife, KY7 6NE **Tel** *01592 610066* **Fax** *01592 610529* **Rooms** *30*

This elegant Georgian mansion evokes an air of tastefully restrained hedonism. The hotel is family run and has been frequently recognised for its quality of service and dining. The ambience is luxurious and proves popular with corporate and leisure customers. Has opulent and comfortable rooms. **www.balbirnie.co.uk**

GULLANE Golf Inn

Main St, Gullane, East Lothian, EH31 2AB **Tel** *01620 843259* **Fax** *01620 842066* **Rooms** *14*

An intimate inn, set in a lovely village in East Lothian – a short drive from Edinburgh – which makes it popular for day trips. Decorated with pine furnishings and crisp colour schemes. The accommodation here is comfortable, but not too expensive, and the appetizing meals are of excellent value. **www.golfinngullane.com**

HEITON Roxburghe

Heiton, Kelso, Roxburghshire, TD5 8JZ **Tel** *01573 450331* **Fax** *01573 450611* **Rooms** *22*

Grand, Jacobean-style house, set in acres of beautiful estate grounds. The house is luxuriously appointed in traditional style, with comfortable rooms. This hotel is a perfect base to enjoy the scenic Borders. Offers a range of outdoor activities such as golf, fishing, mountain biking, walks and more. **www.roxburghe.net**

INVERSNAID Inversnaid Lodge

Inversnaid, Aberfoyle, Stirlingshire, FK8 3TU **Tel** *01877 386254* **Rooms** *9*

This photogenic, lodge-style accommodation on the eastern shores of Loch Lomond is mainly geared towards photographers. Has simple, cottage-style bedrooms, and offers straightforward cooking. Good value for money. Makes an ideal setting for exploring the surrounding countryside. **www.inversnaidphoto.com**

JEDBURGH Hundalee House

Hundalee, Jedburgh, Roxburghshire, TD8 6PA **Tel** *01835 863011* **Fax** *01835 863011* **Rooms** *5*

Stylish B&B in a refined, Georgian-style property, which has been tastefully maintained. The classic interior, a welcoming ambience and good home cooking offers excellent value to its guests. This part of the Borders is perfectly placed for experiencing the scenic environs. **www.accommodation-scotland.org**

LINLITHGOW Champany Inn

Champany, Linlithgow, West Lothian, EH49 7LU **Tel** *01506 834532* **Fax** *01506 834302* **Rooms** *16*

Stylish restaurant-with-rooms. Has spacious bedrooms, with en suite facilities, tasteful and elegant furnishings, bow windows with tartan curtains, and modern amenities. Serves an excellent Scottish breakfast. Located close to several sightseeing attractions and golf courses. **www.champany.com**

MELROSE Burts Hotel

Market Square, Melrose, Roxburghshire, TD6 9PL **Tel** *01896 822285* **Fax** *01896 822870* **Rooms** *20*

Family-run, traditional hotel, carefully maintained over the years. Has a well-earned reputation, both locally and abroad. The restaurant and bar serve superb local produce in convivial surroundings. Offers a warm welcome and good service. Situated close to several golf courses. **www.burtshotel.co.uk**

MELROSE The Townhouse Hotel

Market Square, Melrose, Roxburghshire, TD6 9PQ **Tel** *01896 822645* **Fax** *01896 823474* **Rooms** *11*

A smart hotel, decorated in a sensitive, yet modern style. The owners have a long-standing reputation as welcoming hosts. The chic brasserie serves tasty contemporary cooking. A good place from which to explore this delightful corner of the Borders. **www.thetownhousemelrose.co.uk**

ST ANDREWS Old Course Hotel

Old Station Rd, St Andrews, Fife, KY16 9SP **Tel** *01334 474371* **Fax** *01334 475234* **Rooms** *144*

Situated just on the edge of the town, this hotel boasts splendid views of Old Course – the legendary sea-side links. Features glamorous interiors and exemplary amenities. The luxurious rooms and suites are decorated in a contemporary style. Also has specially designed rooms for disabled guests and wonderful spa facilities. **www.oldcoursehotel.co.uk**

ST ANDREWS St Andrews Bay Hotel

St Andrews Bay, St Andrews, Fife, KY16 8PN **Tel** *01334 837000* **Fax** *01334 471555* **Rooms** *209*

Just a short distance from St Andrews, this resort hotel is self contained and has just about everything one could look for – wonderful views, excellent facilities, a high standard of accommodation and good service. Also boasts a conference centre, two world-class golf courses and a relaxing spa. **www.standrewsopen.com**

ST BOSWELLS Buccleuch Arms

The Green, St Boswells, Dumfriesshire, TD6 0EW **Tel** *01835 822243* **Fax** *01835 823965* **Rooms** *19*

A 16th-century coaching inn, which remains a popular meeting place for visitors to the area and an ideal spot to explore the countryside. The accommodation is comfortable and unpretentious, and the service is friendly and relaxed. The restaurant and bar serve good food. **www.buccleucharms.com**

ST BOSWELLS Dryburgh Abbey Hotel 🛋️🍴🎽🎿 ££££

St Boswells, Melrose, Dumfriesshire, TD6 ORQ **Tel** 01835 822261 **Fax** 01835 823945 **Rooms** 38

An imposing, red sandstone baronial mansion, located in a picturesque setting on the edge of River Tweed. The ruined abbey adjacent to the building adds to the character of the setting. Offers large rooms, and is a popular destination for weddings, conferences and other celebrations. **www.dryburgh.co.uk**

ST FILLANS Four Seasons 🍴 £££

St Fillans, Perthshire, PH6 2NF **Tel** 01764 685333 **Fax** 01764 685444 **Rooms** 12

Set in particularly stunning countryside, with a waterfront location, this small hotel has comfortable rooms, with en suite facilities and striking views of Loch Earn. Also hosts six self-catering log cabin chalets for those who want to enjoy a more intimate stay. This cosy retreat is ideal for a romantic getaway. **www.thefourseasonshotel.co.uk**

TIGHABRUAICH An Lochan Hotel 🍴 £££

Shore Rd, Tighnabruaich, Argyll, PA21 2BE **Tel** 01700 811239 **Fax** 01700 811300 **Rooms** 11

Fine, family-run hotel, set on the picturesque shore. Offers comfortable and spacious accommodation. Dining here can be on a formal or informal basis, and the quality of food and ingredients is extremely high. The service is efficient and friendly. **www.anlochan.co.uk**

TROON Highgrove House Hotel 🍴🎽 £££

Old Loans Rd, Troon, Ayrshire, KA7 7HL **Tel** 01292 312511 **Rooms** 9

An intimate and stylish hotel, designed by a sea captain in the 1920s, with fantastic views over the Firth of Clyde to the Isle of Arran and beyond. A popular place with golfers and for weddings, it's a haven to relax, enjoy good food and convenient for many Ayrshire attractions. **www.costleyhotels.co.uk**

TROON Lochgreen House 🛋️🍴🎽👤 £££££

Monktonhill Rd, Troon, Ayrshire, KA10 7EN **Tel** 01292 313343 **Fax** 01292 318661 **Rooms** 42

Elegant, antiques-filled Edwardian hotel. The bedrooms are large and luxurious, as are the public rooms. The restaurant is modern, but baronial in style, and the cooking is superb. Also has well-maintained grounds. A delightful place to stay. **www.costleyhotels.co.uk**

TURNBERRY The Westin Turnberry Resort 🛋️🍴🎽🎿👤 ££££

Turnberry, Ayrshire, KA26 9LT **Tel** 01655 331000 **Fax** 01655 331706 **Rooms** 219

One of the trendiest places to stay in Scotland. Boasts championship golf courses, a spa, and conference facilities. The well-appointed, en suite rooms are elegantly furnished, with modern amenities. Also has rooms with facilities for disabled guests. Allows pets. The restaurant serves excellent food. **http://turnberry.co.uk/**

YARROW Tibbie Shiels Inn 🍴🎽 £

St Mary's Loch, Selkirk, Selkirkshire, TD7 5LH **Tel** 01750 42231 **Fax** 01750 42302 **Rooms** 5

Once a hostelry favoured by Sir Walter Scott, this 18th-century inn remains a popular place to eat and stay while in the area. Many original features of this B&B have been retained. Has simply furnished, clean rooms, as well as camping facilities. Offers good food, warm service and a genuine welcome. **www.tibbieshielsinn.com**

THE HIGHLANDS AND ISLANDS

ABERDEEN Udny Arms 🍴🎽 ££

Main St, Newburgh, Aberdeenshire, AB41 6BL **Tel** 01358 789444 **Fax** 01358 789012 **Rooms** 28

A comfortable, traditional hotel. The bright, cheerful bedrooms have attached bathrooms, and are decorated with antique furnishings and several modern conveniences. The public rooms are relaxing and welcoming. Located close to three championship golf courses. Also offers facilities for biking and archery. **www.oxfordhotelsandinns.com**

ABERDEEN Ardoe House Hotel 🛋️🍴🎽🎿👤 £££

S Deeside Rd, Aberdeen, Aberdeenshire, AB12 5YP **Tel** 0870 1942104 **Fax** 01224 861283 **Rooms** 109

Located 5 km (3 miles) from the city centre, this is one of Aberdeen's best hotels. The rooms at this luxurious retreat are lavish and tastefully decorated. The suites have four-poster beds. All rooms offer striking views of the countryside. Also has amenities such as a jacuzzi, tennis courts and beauty salons. **www.mercure-uk.com**

ABERDEEN Marcliffe at Pitfodels 🛋️🍴👤 £££££

N Deeside Rd, Pitfodels, Aberdeenshire, AB15 9YA **Tel** 01224 861000 **Fax** 01224 868860 **Rooms** 42

Situated on the outskirts of the city, this up-market hotel has beautiful interiors and a warm and welcoming ambience. The stylish bedrooms offer en suite facilities and many other modern amenities. The conservatory restaurant is bright and airy, and the menus feature Aberdonian quality produce. **www.marcliffe.com**

ACHILTIBUIE Summer Isles 🍴 £££

Achiltibuie, Ross-shire, IV26 2YG **Tel** 01854 622282 **Rooms** 13

A remote and picturesque setting overlooking the Summer Isles makes this charmingly low-key place an idyllic retreat. The hotel interior is sophisticated, and houses lovely, well-appointed bedrooms. The restaurant serves food made with locally grown ingredients. Check opening timings. **www.summerisleshotel.co.uk**

Key to Price Guide *see p556* **Key to Symbols** *see back cover flap*

APPLECROSS Applecross Inn

P 🍴 🏃 ♿ | £££

Applecross, Wester Ross, IV54 8LR **Tel** *01520 744262* **Fax** *01520 744400* **Rooms** *7*

Boasting a stunning rural location with views across the bay to Skye, this newly refurbished inn retains all its character and charm while offering high-quality accommodation and dining. An award-winning hotel with a warm, family atmosphere and one of the best seafood restaurants in Scotland. **www.applecross.uk.com**

ARISAIG Old Library Lodge

🍴 | £££

Road to the Isles, Arisaig, Perthshire, PH39 4NH **Tel** *01687 450651* **Fax** *01687 450219* **Rooms** *6*

Modest and well-run restaurant-with-rooms, set on the Road to the Isles. Housed in a 200-year-old former stable, the hotel offers great views and comfortably furnished rooms. Dining here is a rich culinary experience, with five choices at each course – all beautifully prepared. Sometimes closed Nov, Dec. **www.oldlibrary.co.uk**

AULDEARN Boath House

🍴 🏃 ♿ | £££££

Auldearn, by Nairn, Inverness-shire, IV12 5TE **Tel** *01667 454896* **Fax** *01667 455469* **Rooms** *8*

Known as a "jewel in the Highland crown", this gorgeous mansion is a must-see attraction. The rooms are elegantly furnished with antiques, works of art and modern amenities; all offer excellent views of the estate and the gardens. Also hosts a beauty salon and spa, and serves award-winning cuisine. **www.boath-house.com**

BALLATER Darroch Learg

🍴 🏃 ♿ | ££££

Braemar Rd, Ballater, Royal Deeside, Aberdeenshire, AB35 5UX **Tel** *013397 55443* **Fax** *013397 55252* **Rooms** *17*

Set on a hill in Ballater, amid attractive gardens, this charming Victorian hotel offers splendid views of Lochnagar. The accommodation is comfortable, and the cooking is highly skilled, using the best local produce. A superb wine list completes the experience. **www.darrochlearg.co.uk**

BEAULY Lovat Arms Hotel

🍴 🏃 ♿ | ££

Beauly, Inverness-shire, IV4 7BS **Tel** *01463 782313* **Fax** *01463 782862* **Rooms** *28*

This family-run, traditional hotel is more than 200 years old. Has two popular restaurants and a bar. The rooms are en suite, equipped with modern amenities such as TVs, modem outlets, coffee makers and more. Plenty of golfing and fishing opportunities nearby. Good Scottish fare served by friendly staff. **www.lovatarms.com**

CLACHAN SEIL Willowburn

🍴 | ££££

Clachan Seil, by Oban, Argyll, PA34 4TJ **Tel** *01852 300276* **Fax** *01852 300597* **Rooms** *7*

Located just over Clachan Bridge, this delightful, family-run hotel is housed in a whitewashed cottage. Offers magnificent views of the surrounding countryside. The decor here is simple, and rooms are well equipped. Serves good food, made with locally sourced produce and freshly grown vegetables. B&B and dinner only. **www.willowburn.co.uk**

CRINAN Crinan Hotel

📺 🍴 🏃 ♿ | £££££

Crinan, by Lochgilphead, Argyll, PA31 8SR **Tel** *01546 830261* **Fax** *01546 830292* **Rooms** *20*

A popular base from where to enjoy the panoramic views over Loch Fyne and Jura Sound. The distinctive whitewashed building accommodates a bar and restaurant, where seafood is a speciality. The bedrooms are simply, but tastefully decorated. A friendly and bustling place. **www.crinanhotel.com**

DUNKELD The Pend

🍴 🏃 | ££

5 Brae St, Dunkeld, Perthshire, PH8 0BA **Tel** *01350 727586* **Fax** *01350 727173* **Rooms** *3*

High-quality accommodation in a quiet, Georgian town house, located just off High Street. The interiors are furnished with many antiques and period pieces. Welcoming hosts offer the best of Scottish hospitality, and serve imaginative and superbly-prepared dishes. **www.thepend.com**

DUNKELD Kinnaird

🏊 🍴 | £££££

Kinnaird Estate, by Dunkeld, Perthshire, PH8 0LB **Tel** *01796 482440* **Fax** *01796 482289* **Rooms** *9*

Charming country-house accommodation on an enormous Tayside sporting estate. The setting is tranquil and the amenities are extensive. Features elegantly furnished rooms, with en suite facilities. Provides self-catering cottages as well. Also has tennis courts and a croquet lawn. **www.kinnairdestate.com**

ERISKA Isle of Eriska Hotel

🍴 🏊 🏃 📺 ♿ | £££££

Ledaig, by Oban, Argyll, PA37 1SD **Tel** *01631 720371* **Fax** *01631 720531* **Rooms** *17*

Family-run country estate, located on an island. Houses individually decorated rooms, as well as private cottages; all equipped with modern amenities. This luxurious, romantic hideaway offers several leisure facilities and elaborate dinners. Tranquil and peaceful surroundings. **www.eriska-hotel.co.uk**

FORRES Cluny Bank Hotel

🍴 🏃 | £££

69 St Leonard's Rd, Forres, Moray, Inverness-shire, IV36 1DW **Tel** *01309 674304* **Fax** *01309 671400* **Rooms** *8*

This historic, family-run hotel is located in the quiet residential part of Forres, and retains many of its original features. The bedrooms are comfortable and tastefully decorated, while the public rooms are welcoming and airy. The friendly staff can help arrange outdoor pursuits such as golfing, fishing, cycling and more. **www.clunybankhotel.co.uk**

FORT WILLIAM Ashburn House

££

4 Achintore Rd, Fort William, Perthshire, PH33 6RQ **Tel** *01397 706000* **Fax** *01397 702024* **Rooms** *7*

This traditional, Highland B&B overlooking Loch Linnhe, extends a typical Scottish welcome. The bedrooms of this Victorian house are attractively decorated and well equipped to ensure a comfortable stay. Located a short walking distance from the town centre. Offers hearty breakfasts. **www.highland5star.co.uk**

FORT WILLIAM The Grange   £££

Grange Rd, Fort William, Perthshire, PH33 6JF **Tel** *01397 705516* **Fax** *01397 701595* **Rooms** *4*

This historic B&B has been skilfully and lovingly restored. Enjoys lovely views across Loch Linnhe, and is run by welcoming hosts. The interior is beautifully decorated with great attention to detail, and the rooms are individually furnished with antique beds and lavish bathrooms. Serves a generous breakfast. **www.thegrange-scotland.co.uk**

GLENLIVET Minmore House   ⑪   £££

Glenlivet, Banffshire, Aberdeenshire, AB37 9DB **Tel** *01807 590378* **Fax** *01807 590472* **Rooms** *9*

An elegant country house, set in the grand surroundings of the Glenlivet Estate – formerly the home of the distillery's founder. Offers elegant rooms, furnished with modern conveniences. Serves appetizing meals, made with fresh produce and presented with care. **www.minmorehousehotel.com**

INVERNESS Glenmoriston Town House   ⑪   £££

20 Ness Bank, Inverness, Inverness-shire, IV2 4SF **Tel** *01463 223777* **Fax** *01463 712378* **Rooms** *30*

A traditional town-house hotel that has been tastefully and luxuriously upgraded. The hotel overlooks the River Ness and is only minutes from the town centre. The rooms are furnished in a contemporary style, with modern amenities. Boasts an award-winning French restaurant. **www.glenmoriston.com**

ISLE OF HARRIS Leachin House   ⑪   £££

Tarbert, Isle of Harris, Outer Hebrides, HS3 3AH **Tel** *01859 502157* **Fax** *01859 502157* **Rooms** *3*

A Victorian stone building, originally the home of the father of Harris Tweed – Norman McLeod. The rooms have en suite facilities, as well as amenities such as TVs and central heating. A delightful place to stay and experience this particular corner of the Hebrides.

ISLE OF HARRIS Scarista House   🅿 ⑪ ⚹   ££££

Sgarasta Bheag, Isle of Harris, HS3 3HX **Tel** *01859 550238* **Fax** *01859 550277* **Rooms** *5*

Set in a Georgian-style house, this hotel offers traditional comfort in well furnished, comfortable rooms, all with stunning views of the surrounding remote scenery. There is a library with an open fire and no television to disturb the peace and tranquility of the area. The hotel restaurant is excellent. **www.scaristahouse.com**

ISLE OF IONA Argyll Hotel   ⑪ ⚹   ££

Isle of Iona, Agryll and Bute, PA76 6SJ **Tel** *01681 700334* **Fax** *01681 700510* **Rooms** *16*

A relaxing retreat with views over the Sound of Iona. This traditional hotel has a comfortable and welcoming ambience, enhanced by log fires. The bright, cheerful rooms are simply decorated and furnished with modern facilities. Also boasts a sunny conservatory, and serves good food. **www.argyllhoteliona.co.uk**

ISLE OF LEWIS Galson Farm   ££

S Galson, Isle of Lewis, Outer Hebrides, HS2 0SH **Tel** *01851 850492* **Fax** *01851 850492* **Rooms** *4*

Charming, 18th-century farmhouse on the west coast of Lewis. Offers simple, homely accommodation. This working farm is set in a beautiful location, with striking views of the surroundings. Serves good home cooking with interesting vegetarian options. Bunkhouse accommodation also available. **www.galsonfarm.freeserve.co.uk**

ISLE OF MULL Druimard Country House   ⑪   ££

Dervaig, Isle of Mull, Argyll, PA75 6QW **Tel** *01688 400345* **Fax** *01688 400345* **Rooms** *7*

Welcoming and cosy Victorian hotel, set in a quiet Glenside setting. This stone building hosts Mull's Little Theatre in its grounds. The rooms are tastefully decorated and furnished with modern amenities. Offers simple, but tasty home cooking. **www.druimard.co.uk**

ISLE OF SKYE Duisdale   ⑪   £££

Sleat, Isle Ornsay, Isle of Skye, Inverness-shire, IV43 8QW **Tel** *01471 833202* **Fax** *01471 833404* **Rooms** *17*

Friendly Victorian house set on a hill, with magnificent views of the Sound of Sleat. This small hotel has been flamboyantly decorated and has lots of character. The rooms are spacious and comfortably furnished. Also offers delicious food and lovely gardens. **www.duisdale.com**

ISLE OF SKYE Flodigarry Hotel   🅿 ⑪ ⚹   £££

Flodigarry, Isle of Skye, Inverness-shire, IV51 9HZ **Tel** *01470 552203* **Rooms** *18*

This award-winning country house hotel is located in ancient woodland overlooking the sea towards mainland Scotland. The hotel occupies the former home of Scottish heroine Flora MacDonald and offers comfortably furnished rooms, all with stunning views. This is an excellent base from which to embark on outdoor activities. **www.flodigarry.co.uk**

ISLE OF SKYE Three Chimneys   ⑪ ⚹ ⚹   £££££

Colbost, Dunvegan, Isle of Skye, Inverness-shire, IV55 8ZT **Tel** *01470 511258* **Fax** *01470 511358* **Rooms** *6*

Arguably the finest restaurant-with-rooms in Scotland, this intimate hotel is recognized for the excellence of its cooking and hospitality of the owners. Features modern and luxurious accommodation. The retreat's spectacular location makes for a memorable visit. **www.threechimneys.co.uk**

KILLIECRANKIE Killiecrankie Hotel   ⑪ ⚹ ⚹   ££££

Killiecrankie, by Pitlochry, Perthshire, PH16 5LE **Tel** *01796 473220* **Fax** *01796 472451* **Rooms** *10*

A relaxing and informal hotel, set by the scenic wooded cliffs of the Killiecrankie Pass – a Royal Society for the Protection of Birds reserve. The decor is stylish and bright, and the accommodation is comfortable and spacious. Known for serving good food; light meals are also available. **www.killiecrankiehotel.co.uk**

Key to Price Guide *see p556* **Key to Symbols** *see back cover flap*

KINGUSSIE The Cross

🍴 £££££   ££££

Tweed Mill Brae, Ardbroilach Rd, Kingussie, Perthshire, PH21 1LB **Tel** *01540 661166* **Fax** *01540 661080* **Rooms** *8*

Highly acclaimed restaurant-with-rooms, located in a converted tweed mill near the Cairngorms. The smartly refurbished and attractively decorated interior is light and bright. An ideal base for those interested in exploring this area. Three AA Rosettes restaurant, excellent wine list and caring hosts. **www.thecross.co.uk**

KIRRIEMUIR Lochside Lodge and Roundhouse Restaurant

🍴 🏃 ♿   £££

Bridgend of Lintrathen, by Kirriemuir, Forfarshire, DD8 5JJ **Tel** *01575 560340* **Fax** *01575 560251* **Rooms** *6*

A beautifully converted farm steading, set in a scenic location. This family-run hotel is known for the superb skills of the chef. The bedrooms are well appointed and comfortable, and feature hayloft windows and original coomed ceilings. Dogs are welcome. Many golf courses nearby. **www.lochsidelodge.com**

LOCHINVER The Albannach

🍴 £££££

Lochinver, Sutherland, Inverness-shire, IV27 4LP **Tel** *01571 844407* **Fax** *01571 844285* **Rooms** *5*

Set on a hill on the outskirts of Lochinver, this small hotel is a Mecca for those who enjoy the finer things in life. Offers great views of the countryside. The cooking is quite superb, making innovative use of fresh local produce. Welcoming and hospitable owners. Three suites also available. Closed Jan, Feb. **www.thealbannach.co.uk**

LOCHRANZA Apple Lodge

📺   ££

Lochranza, Isle of Arran, Bute, KA27 8HJ **Tel** *01770 830229* **Fax** *01770 830229* **Rooms** *4*

This charming guesthouse is an excellent base for exploring the sights of Arran. Close to the Kintyre ferry with fine views over the nearby castle. Bedrooms are prettily floral; there is also a self-contained cottage annexe. Serves good home cooking. **www.a1tourism.com/uk/applelodge2**

MUIR OF ORD The Dower House

🍴 🏃   £££

Highfield, Muir of Ord, Inverness-shire, IV6 7XN **Tel** *01463 870090* **Fax** *01463 870090* **Rooms** *4*

This attractive, 18th-century hotel is one of the best-kept secrets in the Highlands. Offers tastefully decorated, pleasant rooms, equipped with modern amenities. The restaurant is renowned for its appetizing home-cooked meals, which emphasize the versatility of good local produce. **www.thedowerhouse.co.uk**

OBAN Lerags House

££££

Lerags, by Oban, Argyll, PA34 4SE **Tel** *01631 563381* **Rooms** *6*

Located on the outskirts of Oban, this lovely country house is run by caring and welcoming hosts. Has clean, simply furnished bedrooms, with modern facilities. A great place to relax and and enjoy the scenic surroundings. Price includes dinner, bed and breakfast. **www.leragshouse.com**

ORKNEY ISLANDS Foveran

🍴   £££

St Ola, Kirkwall, Orkney, KW15 1SF **Tel** *01856 872389* **Fax** *01856 876430* **Rooms** *8*

A fine, family-run hotel, with splendid views over Scapa Flow. The hotel has been tastefully refurbished to a high standard, and the staff give a true taste of Orcadian hospitality. A wonderful base for exploring these magical islands. Offers superb cooking and pleasant accommodation. **www.foveranhotel.co.uk**

PITLOCHRY Atholl Palace

🏊 🍴 🏃 🏃   ££££

Pitlochry, Perthshire, PH16 5LY **Tel** *01796 472400* **Fax** *01796 473036* **Rooms** *108*

This grandiose hotel is an excellent example of Scottish baronial architecture. The accommodation is on a large scale with spacious bedrooms and public areas. Features a wide range of leisure and spa facilities, as well as varying dining options to suit all tastes. **www.athollpalace.com**

PLOCKTON Plockton Hotel

📺 🍴   ££

Harbour St, Plockton, Ross-shire, IV52 8TN **Tel** *01599 544274* **Fax** *01599 544475* **Rooms** *14*

A comfortable and tastefully furnished hotel, set across the waterfront, with breathtaking views of the countryside. The bedrooms are stylishly simple, with en suite facilities; many overlooking the loch and the mountains. Serves good food, using fresh local produce. **www.plocktonhotel.co.uk**

STRONTIAN Kilcamb Lodge

🍴   £££

Strontian, Argyll, PH36 4HY **Tel** *01967 402257* **Fax** *01967 402041* **Rooms** *10*

This elegant country house is located on the quiet Ardnamurchan peninsula. A lovely place to relax and enjoy the striking views over a winding sea loch. Welcoming hosts, excellent food and intimate ambience complete the experience. **www.kilcamblodge.co.uk**

TORLUNDY Inverlochy Castle

🍴 £££££

Torlundy, Fort William, Perthshire, PH33 6SN **Tel** *01397 702177* **Fax** *01397 702953* **Rooms** *17*

A grand, luxurious castle, set amid beautiful grounds, on the outskirts of Fort William. The interior is decorated in a traditional, classic style. Offers high standards of food, accommodation and service. Dining here is a memorable experience. Fishing, tennis and croquet facilities are also available. **www.inverlochycastlehotel.com**

ULLAPOOL Tanglewood House

📺 🏃   ££

Ullapool, Ross-shire, IV26 2TB **Tel** *01854 612059* **Rooms** *3*

This modern, highly individual house commands panoramic vistas of Loch Broom from its huge picture windows. The hotel is tastefully furnished and extremely comfortable. The hostess is a highly accomplished cook, who serves imaginative and innovative cuisine. Bring your own alcohol. **www.tanglewoodhouse.co.uk**

WHERE TO EAT

British food need strike no terrors to the visiting gourmet's heart; the UK's restaurant scene has moved far from its once dismal reputation. This is partly due to an

Hakkasan in central London
(see p610)

influx of foreign chefs and cooking styles; you can now sample a wide range of cuisine throughout Britain, with the greatest choice in London and the other major cities. British chefs are now celebrated among the most innovative in the world and the indigenous cooking (once thought to consist only of fish and chips, overcooked vegetables, meat pies and lumpy custard)

has improved out of all recognition in the last 20 years. You can now also eat very well in Britain whatever your budget – and at most times of day in the towns. Much less elaborate, but well-prepared, affordable food is making a mark in all types of restaurants and cafés throughout the country; more modern approaches combine fresh produce and dietary common sense with influences from around the world. The restaurant listings *(see pp608–651)* feature some of the very best places as well as those with a steady track record.

WHAT'S ON THE MENU?

The choice seems endless in large cities, particularly London. Cuisines from all over the world are represented, as well as their infinite variations – Thai and Tex-Mex, Turkish and Tuscan, Tandoori, Bhel Poori and Balti. There are many more unusual styles of cooking such as Hungarian, Polish, Caribbean and Pacific Rim. French and Italian restaurants are still highly regarded, offering everything from pastries and espresso coffee to the highest standards of *haute cuisine*. Outside the major cities the food scene is more limited, but things are improving and more and more Rosette-

awarded pubs and restaurants are popping up. The vague term "modern-international cuisine" adopted by many restaurants disguises a diverse rag-bag of styles. The spectrum ranges from French to Asian recipes, loosely characterized by the imaginative use of fresh, high-quality ingredients, which are cooked simply with imaginative seasonings.

Nostalgic yearnings for British food have produced a revival of hearty traditional dishes such as steak and kidney pie and treacle pudding *(see p607)*, though "Modern British" cooking adopts a lighter, more innovative approach to old-fashioned stodge. The distinctions between this and Modern

International food are starting to blur, which is mostly a change for the better as young chefs apply Oriental and Mediterranean flavours to home-grown ingredients.

BREAKFAST

It used to be said that the best way to enjoy British food was to eat breakfast three times a day. Traditional British breakfast starts with cereal and milk followed by bacon, eggs and tomato, perhaps with fried black pudding *(see p606)* in the North and Scotland. It is finished off with toast and marmalade washed down with tea. Or you can just have black coffee and fruit juice, with a croissant or two (known as Continental breakfast in hotels). The price of breakfast is often included in hotel tariffs in Britain.

LUNCH

Many restaurants offer light lunches at fixed prices, sometimes of only two courses. The most popular lunchtime foods are sandwiches, salads, baked potatoes with fillings and ploughman's lunches *(see p606)*, the latter found mainly in pubs. A traditional Sunday lunch of roast chicken, lamb or beef is served in some pubs and restaurants.

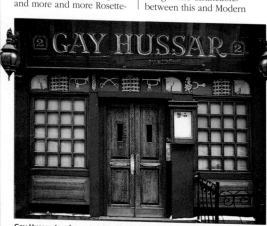

Gay Hussar, London, a top Hungarian restaurant *(see p608)*

AFTERNOON TEA

No visitor should miss the experience of a proper English afternoon tea, which rivals breakfast as the most enjoyable meal of the day *(see p606)*. Some of the most palatial teas are offered by country-house and top London hotels such as the Ritz or Browns. The area that is best known for its classic "cream teas" is the West Country; these always include scones, spread with clotted cream, butter and jam. Wales, Scotland, Yorkshire and the Lake District also offer tasty teas with regional variations; in the North Country a slice of apple pie or fruit cake is served hot with a piece of North Yorkshire Wensleydale cheese on top.

Leith Docks in Edinburgh, a centre of good pubs, bars and restaurants

An afternoon tea including sandwiches, cakes and scones

DINNER

At dinner time, the grander restaurants and hotels offer elaborately staged meals, sometimes billed as five or six courses (though one may be simply a sorbet, or coffee with *petits fours*). Dessert is often followed by cheese and biscuits (crackers). Confusingly, in the North of England and Scotland "lunch" can be called "dinner" and "dinner" may be called "tea".

Generally, you can choose to take your dinner before 6pm or after 9pm only in larger towns, where there is a broad choice of ethnic restaurants, bars and all-day brasseries, which often have long opening hours.

PLACES TO EAT

Eating venues are extremely varied, with brasseries, bistros, wine bars, tearooms, *tapas* bars and theatre cafés now competing with the more conventional cafés and restaurants. Many pubs also now serve excellent bar food at often reasonable prices *(see p652–5)*.

BRASSERIES, BISTROS AND CAFES

French-style café-brasseries are now popular in Britain. Sometimes they stay open all day, serving coffee, snacks and fairly simple dishes along with a selection of beers and wines. Alcoholic drinks, however, may only be available at certain times of day. The atmosphere is usually young and urbane, with decor to match. Drinks such as imported bottled beers, exotic spirits or cocktails may be fairly expensive.

The café at Tate St Ives, Cornwall
(see p628)

Wine bars are similar to brasseries, but with a better selection of wines, which may include English varieties *(see p160)*. Some bars have a good range of ciders and real ales as well *(see p604)*. Bistros are another French import, serving full meals at lunch and dinner time with less formality and more moderate prices than you would expect at a restaurant. You should expect to pay anything from £12 to £30 for a standard three-course meal in a bistro.

RESTAURANTS-WITH-ROOMS AND HOTELS

Restaurants-with-rooms are a new breed of small establishments with only a handful of bedrooms and usually excellent food. They tend to be expensive and are usually in a rural location.

Many hotel restaurants happily serve non-residents. They tend to be expensive, but the best can be unparalleled. Hotels serving a high standard of food are also included on pages 556–99.

RESTAURANT ETIQUETTE

As a rule of thumb, the more expensive the restaurant, the more formal the dress code – though few restaurants nowadays will expect men to wear a shirt and tie. If you are not sure, ring first.

A total smoking ban in public places was implemented throughout the UK in 2007.

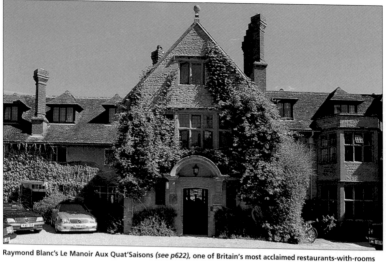

Raymond Blanc's Le Manoir Aux Quat'Saisons *(see p622)*, one of Britain's most acclaimed restaurants-with-rooms

ALCOHOL

Britain's laws concerning the sale of alcohol, the "licensing laws", were once among the most restrictive in Europe. Now they are much more relaxed, with some restaurants operating extended opening hours, especially at weekends. Some establishments, however, may only serve alcohol at set times with food. Some unlicensed restaurants operate a "Bring Your Own" policy; a corkage fee is often charged. It is illegal to sell alcohol to under 18s.

VEGETARIAN FOOD

Britain is ahead of many of its European counterparts in providing vegetarian alternatives to meat dishes. A few places in this section serve only vegetarian meals, but most also cater for carnivores. Vegetarians who want a wider choice should seek out South Indian, Chinese and other ethnic restaurants which have a tradition of vegetarian cuisine.

FAST FOOD

Fast food usually costs well under £10. Apart from the numerous individually owned fish and chip shops, there are many of the usual fast food chains in Britain, as well as some more up market options such as Pizza Express and Yo

Sushi. Sandwich bars are very popular, and are often good value; some also have seating. Budget cafés, nicknamed "greasy spoons", serve simple, inexpensive food, often in the form of endless variations of the breakfast fry-up *(see p606)*.

Blackfriars restaurant *(see p641)*

BOOKING AHEAD

It is always safer to book a table first before making a special journey to a restaurant; city restaurants can be very busy and some of the more renowned establishments can be fully booked a month in advance. If you cannot keep a reservation, you should ring up and cancel. A lot of restaurants operate on knife-edge profit margins, and customers not turning up can threaten their livelihood.

CHECKING THE BILL

All restaurants are required by law to display their current prices outside the door. These amounts include Value Added Tax (VAT), currently at 17.5 per cent. Service and cover charges (if any) are also specified. So you should have a rough idea of what a meal may cost beforehand.

Wine is always pricey in Britain, and extras like coffee or bottled water can be disproportionately expensive.

Service charges (usually between 10 per cent and 15 per cent) are sometimes automatically added to your bill. If you feel that the service has been poor, you are entitled to subtract this service charge. If no service charge has been added, you are expected to add 10 to 15 per cent to the bill, but it is your decision.

Some restaurants may leave the "total" box of credit card slips blank, hoping customers will add something extra to the service charge. Another growing trend is for smart restaurants to boost their sagging profit margins with a "cover charge" for flowers, bread and butter, etc. Live entertainment may also be costed. The majority of restaurants accept credit cards, or UK cheques with a guarantee card, but traditional pubs and cafés will often expect cash.

MEALTIMES

Breakfast is a moveable feast. It may be as early as 6:30am in a city business hotel (most hoteliers will make special arrangements if you have a plane to catch or some other reason for checking out early) or as late as 10:30am in relaxed country house establishments. Few hoteliers relish cooking bacon and eggs that late, however, and some insist you are up and about by 9:00 sharp if you want anything to eat. But you can find breakfast all day long in some urban restaurants. The American concept of Sunday "brunch" (a leisurely halfway house between breakfast and lunch) is becoming increasingly popular in some hotels, restaurants and cafés.

Lunch in pubs and restaurants is usually served between noon and 2:30pm. Try to arrive in time to order the main course before 1:30pm, or you may find choice restricted and service peremptory. Most tourist areas have plenty of cafés, fast-food diners and coffee bars where you can have a snack at any time of day. During peak hours there may be a minimum charge.

If you are lucky enough to be in one of the places where you can get a traditional afternoon tea, it is usually served between 3pm and 5pm.

Dinner is usually served from 6pm until 10pm; some places, especially ethnic restaurants, stay open later. In guest houses or small hotels, dinner may be served at a specific time (sometimes uncomfortably early).

CHILDREN

The continental norm of dining out *en famille* is steadily becoming more acceptable in Britain, and visiting a restaurant may no longer entail endless searches for a babysitter. Many places welcome junior diners, and some actively encourage

Langan's Brassserie, a popular choice for Anglo-French cuisine *(see p609)*

Ice-cream parlour sign

families, at least during the day or early evening. Formal restaurants sometimes cultivate a more adult ambience at dinner time, and some impose age limits. If you want to take young children to a restaurant, check when you book. Italian, Spanish, Indian, fast-food restaurants and ice-cream parlours nearly always welcome children, and sometimes provide special menus or high chairs for them. Even traditional English pubs, which were once a strictly adult preserve, are now relaxing their rules to accommodate families and may even provide special rooms or play areas.

The places that welcome and cater for children are indicated in both the pubs guide *(see pp652–55)* and the restaurant listings.

DISABLED ACCESS

As in most walks of life, restaurant facilities in Britain could be better for disabled visitors, but things are gradually improving. Modern premises usually take account of mobility problems, but it's always best to check first if you have special needs.

PICNICS

Eating outside is becoming more popular in Britain, though it is more likely that you will find tables outside pubs in the form of a beer garden, than outside restaurants. One inexpensive option is to make up your own picnic; most towns have good delicatessens and bakeries where you can collect provisions, and in Britain you do not usually have to worry about shops closing at mid-day as they often do on the Continent.

Look out for street markets to pick up fresh fruit and local cheeses at bargain prices. Department stores like Marks & Spencer and supermarkets such as Sainsbury's and Tesco often sell an excellent range of pre-packed sandwiches and snacks; large towns usually have several sandwich bars to choose from. Your hotel or guest house may also be able to provide a packed lunch. Ask for it the night before.

An option for a chillier day is a hot takeaway meal; fish and chips with salt and vinegar all wrapped in paper is not only a British cliché but a national institution.

Eating alfresco at Grasmere in the Lake District

The Traditional British Pub

Beer label c.1900

Every country has its bars, but Britain is famous for its pubs or "public houses". Ale was brewed in England in Roman times – mostly at home – and by the Middle Ages there were inns and taverns which brewed their own. The 18th century was the heyday of the coaching inn as stage coaches brought more custom. In the 19th century came railway taverns for travellers and "gin palaces" for the new industrial workers. Today, pubs come in all styles and sizes and many cater to families, serving food as well as drink *(see pp652–55)*.

Early 19th-century coaching inn – also a social centre and post office

THE VICTORIAN PUB

A century ago, many pubs in towns and cities had smart interiors, to contrast with the poor housing of their clients.

Pint glasses (containing just over half a litre) are used for beer.

The Red Lion pub name is derived from Scottish heraldry *(see p26)*.

Elaborately etched glass is a feature of many Victorian interiors.

Pub games, *such as cribbage, bar billiards, pool and dominoes are part of British pub culture. Here some regular customers are competing against a rival pub's darts team.*

Beer gardens *outside pubs are a favourite venue for family summer treats.*

Old-fashioned cash register contributes to the period atmosphere of the bar.

Pewter tankards, seldom used by drinkers today, add a traditional touch.

WHAT TO DRINK

Draught bitter is the most traditional British beer. Brewed from malted barley, hops, yeast and water, and usually matured in a wooden cask, it varies from region to region. In the north of England the sweeter mild ale is popular, and lagers served in bottles or on tap are also widely drunk. Stout, made from black malt, is another variation.

Beer pump

Draught bitter is drunk at cellar temperature.

Draught lager is a light-coloured, carbonated beer.

Guinness is a thick, creamy Irish stout.

Pavement tables, crowded with city drinkers during the summer months

A village pub, offering a waterside view and serving drinks in the garden

PUB SIGNS

Early medieval inns used vines or evergreens as signs – the symbol of Bacchus, the Roman god of wine. Soon pubs acquired names that signalled support for monarchs or noblemen, or celebrated victories in battle. As many customers could not read, pub signs had vivid images.

The George *may derive from one of the six English kings of that name, or, as here, from England's patron saint.*

Bottles of spirits, as well as the popular port and sherry, are ranged behind the bar.

Glass lamps imitate the Victorian style.

The Bat and Ball *celebrates cricket, and may be sited near a village green where the game can be played.*

Wine, once rarely found in pubs, is now increasingly popular.

The Green Man *is a woodland spirit from pagan mythology, possibly the basis for the legend of Robin Hood (see p336).*

A deep-toned mahogany bar forms part of the traditional setting.

The Magna Carta *sign commemorates and illustrates the "great charter" signed by King John in 1215 (see p48).*

Draught beer, served from pumps or taps, comes from national and local brewers.

Optics dispense spirits in precise measures.

The Bird in Hand *refers to the ancient country sport of falconry, traditionally practised by noblemen.*

Mild may be served by the pint or in a half-pint tankard (as above).

Top cocktails are gin-and-tonic (right) and Pimm's.

The Flavours of Britain

A rich agriculture that provides meat and dairy products such as well as fruit, vegetables and cereals, gives the British table a broad scope. Traditional dishes – cooked breakfasts, roast beef, fish and chips – are famous, but there is much more on offer, varying from region to region. Many towns give their names to produce and dishes. Seasonal choices include game and seafood, while other produce can be seen at the increasingly popular farmers' markets. Britons still have a penchant for pies and puddings, and most regions have cakes and buns they can call their own. Scotland has its own distinctive cuisine *(see p488).*

Asparagus

Local fresh beetroot on sale at a greengrocer's shop

CENTRAL AND SOUTHERN ENGLAND

All tastes are catered for in the metropolis, and the surrounding countryside has long been given over to its demands. The flat lands of East Anglia provide vegetables and root crops; the South Downs have been shorn by sheep; geese have

made Nottingham famous; and the county of Kent is known as "the Garden of England" for its glorious orchards and its fields of soft fruits. From around the coast come Dover sole, Whitstable oysters (popular since Roman times) and the Cockney favourites, cockles and whelks. The game season runs from November to February, and pheasant is often on the menu.

WEST OF ENGLAND

The warmest part of England is renowned for its classic cream teas, the key ingredient provided by its dairy herds. In Cornwall, pasties have long been a staple. Once eaten by tin miners and filled with meat at one end and jam the other, to give two courses in one, they are now generally made with meat and veg-

Cornish Yarg   Cider-washed   Dorstone goats'-   Cropwell
        Celtic Promise   milk cheese   Bishop Stilton

Montgomery
Cheddar

Ewes'-milk
Wigmore

Selection of fine, farm-produced British cheeses

TRADITIONAL BRITISH FOOD

Though many traditional dishes, such as Lancashire hotpot, beef Wellington and even fish and chips, can be harder to hunt down than tapas, pizza or chicken tikka masala, other reliable regulars remain. Among them are shepherd's pie (minced lamb with mashed potatoes), steak and kidney pie (beef and kidney in gravy baked in a pastry crust), or game pie and "bangers and mash" (sausages with mash potatoes and onion gravy). For pudding there is a variety of trifles, pies, tarts and crumbles, often eaten with custard, as well as a lighter summer pudding of seasonal fruit. A "full English breakfast" is a fry-up of sausages, eggs, bacon, tomatoes, mushrooms and bread, perhaps with black pudding or laverbread. Lunchtime snacks include a "Ploughman's lunch" of cheese and pickles with a "doorstep" of bread.

Dover sole *This is the most tasty flatfish, best served simply grilled with lemon, spinach and new potatoes.*

Display of British breads at a local farmers' market

etables. The clear waters around the peninsula offer up such seafood as sardines, mackerel and crab in abundance, and many of the region's best restaurants specialize in fish. Bath gives its name to special biscuits and buns.

NORTH OF ENGLAND

Cumberland sausage, Lancashire hotpot, Goosnargh duck and Yorkshire pudding – the names tell you exactly where the food on your plate originated. These are the staples, but restaurants these days are creating new dishes from old, such as trout with black (blood) pudding, and even being adventurous with "mushy" peas. Bradford, with its large Asian community, is the best place to eat Indian food.

WALES

The green grass of Wales is appreciated by sheep, who turn into fabulous lamb that is simply roasted and eaten with mint sauce – a favourite all over Britain. The grass is

A Cornish fishmonger displays a locally caught red mullet

good for dairy products, too, including white, crumbly Caerphilly. Cheese is the principal ingredient of Welsh rarebit (pronounced rabbit), made with cheese grilled on toast and occasionally augmented with beer. Look out for prize-winning Welsh Black beef – prime fillets are often accompanied by horseradish sauce. The Irish Sea provides plenty of fish, but there is also freshwater trout and salmon. A curiosity of the South Wales seashore is laver, a kind of sea spinach, which is mixed with oatmeal and fried in small cakes called *bara lawr*, or laverbread, to be served with sausage and bacon for breakfast.

BRITISH CHEESES

Caerphilly Fresh, white, mild cheese from Wales.

Cheshire Crumbly, silky and full-bodied cheese.

Cheddar Often imitated, never bettered; the best comes from the West Country.

Double Gloucester Mellow flavoured, smooth and creamy.

Sage Derby Flavoured with green veins of sage.

Stilton The king of British cheeses, a strong, blue-veined cheese with a creamy texture. Popular at Christmas.

Wensleydale Young, moist and flaky-textured, with a mild, slightly sweet flavour.

Cornish mackerel *The ideal partner for this rich fish is a piquant sauce make of English gooseberries.*

Roast beef *Horseradish sauce is a traditional accompaniment, as are crisp Yorkshire puddings made of batter.*

Welsh lamb with leeks *The leek is the national vegetable of Wales, and perfectly complements roast lamb.*

Choosing a Restaurant

The restaurants in this guide have been selected across a wide range of price categories for their good value, exceptional food and interesting location. This chart lists the restaurants by region, starting with London. It also highlights some of the factors that may influence your choice. For pub listings, see pages 652–657.

PRICE CATEGORIES
Include a three-course meal for one, half a bottle of house wine, and all unavoidable extra charges such as cover, service, VAT:

£ under £20
££ £20–£35
£££ £35–£45
££££ £45–£55
£££££ over £55

LONDON

WEST END AND WESTMINSTER Bigun's Ribs
£
2 Warwick Way, SW1V 1RU **Tel** *020 7834 7350*
Map 18 F2

A typical American restaurant, Bigun's Ribs is known to serve generous proportions of food at rock-bottom prices. A little too noisy for romantic dining, it's ideal for a hearty meal. Though ribs are the main attraction, dishes such as rack of lamb are also really good value for money. The service is brisk and ambience bustling.

WEST END AND WESTMINSTER Busaba Eathai
£
106–110 Wardour St, W1F 0TR **Tel** *020 7255 8686*
Map 11 A2

The immense popularity of Busaba Eathai rests on its reasonably priced Thai food and efficient service. Get there early, as the queue here can be of legendary proportions after 7pm. However, be prepared to share a table whatever time you arrive. Food is good – try Thai calamari and the rose apple wok dish. One of three branches.

WEST END AND WESTMINSTER Bam-Bou
££
1 Percy St, W1T 1DB **Tel** *020 7323 9130*
Map 11 A1

A nice bar upstairs lures you in for a few drinks before you descend to the restaurant proper. Seated at a low table with just candlelight playing off dark wood, you feel a million miles from London. This is not your average Pan-Asian restaurant. The food is excellent and the atmosphere relaxed and warm. Private rooms are also available.

WEST END AND WESTMINSTER Café Mode
££
57 Endell St, WC2H 9AJ **Tel** *020 7240 8085*
Map 11 C2

Great salads, pizzas and vegetarian dishes, and warm, friendly staff all contribute to a winning formula at Café Mode. Always great value and very popular, this restaurant is also preferred by lone diners. The little Med-inspired gem is a cool retreat from the hustle and bustle of Covent Garden.

WEST END AND WESTMINSTER Gay Hussar
££
2 Greek St, W1D 4NB **Tel** *020 7437 0973*
Map 11 A1

Once the place of choice for old journalists to meet and gossip and enjoy second-rate food that reminded them of their private schools. Now, however, it provides a proper insight into authentic Hungarian cuisine, wines and spirits. Good value for money.

WEST END AND WESTMINSTER The Ebury
££
11 Pimlico Rd, SW1W 8NA **Tel** *020 7730 6784*
Map 18 D2

Diners come to this sleek restaurant housed in a converted pub to enjoy a varied modern European menu with British and Mediterranean accents. First-rate ingredients are used in dishes such as ricotta and herb gnocchi, and slow-cooked pork belly with Parmesan polenta. The dining room is bright and airy, exuding understated elegance.

WEST END AND WESTMINSTER Vasco & Piero's Pavilion
££
15 Poland St, W1F 8QE **Tel** *020 7437 8774*
Map 11 A2

Of Umbrian heritage, the owner of this restaurant ensures that chickpeas and lentils feature frequently on the largely Italian menu which changes twice daily. The pasta is made in-house, with the finest quality ingredients. The truffles, particularly, make the place worth a visit. In season, black or white truffles are imported from Umbria.

WEST END AND WESTMINSTER Atrium
£££
4 Millbank, SW1P 3JA **Tel** *020 7233 0032*
Map 19 B1

Bright and modern Atrium has a vast glass-covered space. The well-priced menu changes with the seasons, but always mixes and matches ingredients to wonderful effect, as witnessed in dishes such as seared scallops with Provençal tomatoes; roast monkfish, tomato, olive and fennel stew; or pan-fried guinea fowl with chickpea hot pot.

WEST END AND WESTMINSTER Belgo Centraal
£££
50 Earlham St, WC2H 9LJ **Tel** *020 7813 2233*
Map 11 B2

Nice and handy for Neal Street, Belgo Centraal remains popular every night. The cool young staff whip up a great variety of Belgian cuisine, from *moules marinières* to more exotic creations featuring Belgium's famous beers. Meat-eaters are also catered for. Eat at the long refectory tables and enjoy the fun.

Key to Symbols *see back cover flap*

WEST END AND WESTMINSTER Beotys

79 Saint Martins Lane, WC2N 4AA **Tel** *020 7836 8768*   **Map** *11 B2*

Reputedly the best Greek restaurant in London, Beotys is a perfect place to sample all that Greek cuisine has to offer. Authentic Greek favourites are available, including a bewildering yet tasty variety of meze (small portioned dishes). Ever pulsating with a lively crowd, the atmosphere is very friendly. Closed on Sundays.

WEST END AND WESTMINSTER Bertorelli

44A Floral St, WC2E 9DA **Tel** *020 7836 3969*   **Map** *11 C2*

An Italian institution in Covent Garden, Bertorelli's Roman empire now extends further afield. This is the flagship, though, not the one you may have seen in the film *Sliding Doors*. Freshly prepared and flavourful home cooking is served in a friendly ambience. Sensible prices are an extra bonus. Closed Sundays.

WEST END AND WESTMINSTER Café Pacifico

5–6 Langley St, WC2H 9JA **Tel** *020 7379 7728*   **Map** *11 B2*

Café Pacifico is frequented by the young and young-at-heart. Occasional Mexican live music and a buzzy atmosphere promise a lively night, though those looking for a romantic dinner might want to stay away. A few cocktails followed by some filling and reasonably priced food will send you singing out into the street.

WEST END AND WESTMINSTER Elena's L'Etoile

30 Charlotte St, W1T 2NA **Tel** *020 7636 7189*   **Map** *11 A1*

This long-standing local eatery is extremely busy at lunchtime, with advertizing media people from surrounding ad agencies and TV companies. The time-tested menu delivers classic French bistro food under the gaze of celebrity pictures that cover the walls. It's not cheap but guarantees quality and that indefinable extra – real atmosphere.

WEST END AND WESTMINSTER Indigo

1 Aldwych, WC2B 4B2 **Tel** *020 7300 0400*   **Map** *12 D2*

This stylish restaurant offers an eclectic mix of modern European and International dishes, all beautifully presented. Enjoy a drink in the Grand Bar upstairs before descending in the lift to the plush dining room. Plenty of choice for all tastes and a useful "mix and match" salad and pasta course. On Sundays, they have a brunch-and-movie deal.

WEST END AND WESTMINSTER Langan's Brasserie

Stratton St, W1J 8LB **Tel** *020 7491 8822*   **Map** *10 F3*

The original and perhaps still the best in this chain of restaurants, Langan's faithfully adheres to the style of its late eponymous owner. Service is discreetly attentive and the staff are friendly. Try and get a table downstairs where they serve soufflé with anchovy sauce. Try the house speciality, Langan's bangers and mash with white onion sauce.

WEST END AND WESTMINSTER L'Escargot Marco Pierre White

48 Greek St, W1D 4EF **Tel** *020 7437 6828*   **Map** *11 A1*

Another Soho institution, this restaurant is now run by Marco Pierre White, a legendary chef. Expect high standards but be surprised by the very reasonable prices. In the Picasso Room you can look at some of the master's works while eating artistically crafted fine food. Try the parfait of foi gras *en gelée* with toasted Poilane. Closed on Sundays.

WEST END AND WESTMINSTER Little Italy

21 Frith St, W1D 4RN **Tel** *020 7734 4737*   **Map** *11 A2*

As the name suggests, this tiny restaurant re-creates Italy in its delicious home cooking. It's a busy and vibrant place with a late licence until 4am. The large variety of pasta dishes is a safe bet. The main courses are good too. You might miss the unassuming doorway so back up and look again, it's there. Some music and dancing most nights.

WEST END AND WESTMINSTER Loch Fyne

2–4 Catherine St, WC2B 5JS **Tel** *020 7240 4999*   **Map** *11 C2*

At Loch Fyne, a seafood restaurant, the fish and shellfish are brought in fresh from Scotland. The wine list is suitably chosen to match the crustaceans and other edible sea creatures on offer. Portions are generous whether you choose a platter of oysters or a large plate of poached smoked haddock.

WEST END AND WESTMINSTER Mango Tree

46 Grosvenor Place, SW1X 7EQ **Tel** *020 7823 1888*   **Map** *10 E5*

Just opposite the back gate of Buckingham Palace, Mango Tree was created from the remains of the Enron building. Taking Thai cuisine to a new level, the menu performs fresh twists, as the chefs here create remarkable tastes and effects. The service and decor are impeccable. The three-course lunch menu is great value at £20.

WEST END AND WESTMINSTER Palm Court Brasserie

39 King St, WC2E 8JS **Tel** *020 7240 2939*   **Map** *11 C2*

A good location and a sophisticated interior make Palm Court Brasserie a firm favourite with the locals. Mediterranean flavours are well infused with the southern sunshine. Sharing platters are good fun and great value, while a roast rump of lamb is quite filling. There are special pre-theatre deals, too. Reservations strongly recommended.

WEST END AND WESTMINSTER Porter's English Restaurant

17 Henrietta St, WC2E 8QH **Tel** *020 7836 6466*   **Map** *11 C2*

A great place for proper fish and chips, Porter's is known for serving hearty British "grub" with tasty pie dishes such as steak and Guinness, cod, salmon and prawn. Desserts are equally large and not for those on a diet. Prices are good for the location. A special lunch deal (£29.50) includes a ticket for the London Eye. Cheerful staff.

WEST END AND WESTMINSTER Rock Garden
6–7 The Piazza, WC2E 8HB **Tel** *020 7836 4052*

Map 11 C2

Contrary to its name, this is not a tacky themed restaurant. The Rock Garden serves Modern European cuisine with a wide variety of meat, fish and vegetarian dishes. Weekly specials are made with seasonal produce. It is ideal for children. The location is one of the best in Covent Garden, especially in summer.

WEST END AND WESTMINSTER Signor Zilli
41 Dean St, W1D 4PY **Tel** *020 7734 3924*

Map 11 A2

The owner of this eponymous restaurant is often in attendance, adding a special touch to the place. The Italian food is first rate, if sometimes unadventurous, and the atmosphere is always inviting. The prices are a little steep, but worth it for the large, hearty portions. Closed on Sundays.

WEST END AND WESTMINSTER Sofra
36 Tavistock St, WC2E 7PB **Tel** *020 7240 3773*

Map 11 C2

A reputed London institution, Sofra has been serving superior Turkish food for many years. The speciality is the healthy option involving a variety of little dishes to share. Bread and olives come free throughout the meal, while dips such as hummous and *tzatziki* always taste fresh and clean.

WEST END AND WESTMINSTER Thai Metro
38 Charlotte St, W1F 2NN **Tel** *020 7436 4201*

Map 3 A5

Thai Metro offers top-notch Thai cuisine at affordable prices. The green curry is a must-try, but be warned about the chillies. The zingy flavours that characterize Thai food are all here in abundance. If the weather is warm, you can enjoy your food in the fresh air. Service is brisk, which may not be ideal for a relaxed meal. Good lunch deals.

WEST END AND WESTMINSTER The Gaucho Grill
125–126 Chancery Lane, WC2A 1PU **Tel** *020 7242 7727*

Map 12 E1

There are a few of branches of the Gaucho around London and they remain of consistent value. The star attraction is still its delicious steak. A large wine list helps wash down an enormous meal and the cocktails are good too. Ideal for a pleasant, no-frills dining, it's a well-priced place in a reasonably expensive area. Closed Sundays.

WEST END AND WESTMINSTER Tiger Green Brasserie
Half Moon St, W1J 7BN **Tel** *020 7629 7522*

Map 10 E4

Located in the recently refurbished Hilton London Green Park hotel, this restaurant welcomes all with an arresting menu. The classic combination of contemporary and modern design with an eclectic mix of traditional and international cuisine is well worth the experience. They also have a wide range of cocktails to choose from.

WEST END AND WESTMINSTER Christopher's American Grill
18 Wellington St, WC2E 7DD **Tel** *020 7240 4222*

Map 11 C2

Rather more formal than you might expect from an American restaurant, but then this is a superior establishment. There are plenty of American favourites to choose from, including delicious ham hocks, large steaks and excellent lobsters. There is a Martini bar on the ground floor, and views over Waterloo Bridge from the upstairs restaurant.

WEST END AND WESTMINSTER ECapital
8 Gerrard St, W1D 5PJ **Tel** *020 7434 3838*

Map 11 A2

ECapital's pink interior could be a little garish for some, but the food more than makes up for it. Shanghai-style cooking is a speciality and the menu offers a distinct Shanghai meal that's unique to the locality. The "cubed belly of pork in the poet's style" is particularly good. Service is unusually unhurried and the set menus can be a bargain.

WEST END AND WESTMINSTER Green's Restaurant & Oyster Bar
36 Duke St, SW1Y 6DF **Tel** *020 7930 4566*

Map 10 F3

With wonderful old-world ambience and an extensive (and expensive) champagne list, this is a great establishment. Excellent lobster salads, first-class chips and, of course, a nice choice of oysters, most of them down from Scotland that very day. Those who don't fancy fish can try Green's steak tartare. Closed on Sundays from May to September.

WEST END AND WESTMINSTER Hakkasan
8 Hanway Place, W1T 14B **Tel** *020 7927 7000*

Map 11 A1

A very expensive Chinese restaurant, Hakkasan has maintained a consistently high turnover. The decor is superbly stylish and the food even more so. No windows mean you can't peer in to check it out before entering. Though busy, it's a great choice for gourmets who can afford it. Don't miss the dim sums.

WEST END AND WESTMINSTER Just St James
12 St James St, SW1A 1ER **Tel** *020 7976 2222*

Map 10 F4

With plush surroundings, as befits a restaurant in St James, this impressive place was built from a former Edwardian banking hall. The high-class cooking constantly surprises with its far-reaching, but not overambitious, choices. Strong modern British favourites sit alongside dishes of more global provenance on the frequently-changing menu.

WEST END AND WESTMINSTER L'Oranger
5 St James St, SW1A 1EF **Tel** *020 7839 3774*

Map 10 F4

A very formal French restaurant in the heart of London, L'Oranger exudes classic opulence. The decor is heavy with timeless quality and the traditionally cooked dishes are classy in their presentation. Tables are beautifully laid with expensive linen, high-quality glasses and plates. The regularly changing menu features Provençal dishes.

WEST END AND WESTMINSTER Umu

14–16 Bruton Place, W1J 6L **Tel** *020 7499 8881*

Map *10 E3*

Seriously expensive but extremely stylish, the Michelin-starred Umu offers a beautiful interior, traditional Kyoto cuisine and friendly service by great staff. With a remarkable sake list, this is one of the few places in London where you can find genuine Japanese *kaiseki*. There's also a good, though expensive, tasting menu. Closed 24 Dec–7 Jan.

WEST END AND WESTMINSTER Wilton's

55 Jermyn St, SW1Y 6LX **Tel** *020 7629 9955*

Map *11 A3*

A landmark institution, there has been a Wilton's in London since 1742. A quintessential expensive club-dining experience. Morecambe Bay potted shrimps, grilled Dover sole, Scottish lobster thermidor and West Mersey Oysters are the main attractions here, but you will also want to bask in the atmosphere and in the attentive and well-mannered service.

SOUTH KENSINGTON AND HYDE PARK Dione

1 Kensington High St, W8 5NP **Tel** *020 7937 0393*

Map *8 E5*

Persian/Greek food par excellence with perfect kebabs grilled to smoky brilliance. Tasty, moist pieces of marinated lamb and/or chicken over saffron-scented, buttery rice. Friendly staff are happy to advise on choice of dishes and to stop you from over-ordering, as you may be tempted to do so. Good value, too.

SOUTH KENSINGTON AND HYDE PARK La Maja

43–45 Porchester Road, W2 5DP **Tel** *020 7792 5885*

Map *8 D1*

Loads of lovely tapas, as well as generous main courses, keep the locals coming back for more. La Maja really feels authentic in an unforced way, and the variety of dishes is mouthwatering. A great range of robust Riojas complements the food, which is hearty and garlicky and just perfect for accompanying lively conversation.

SOUTH KENSINGTON AND HYDE PARK Aphrodite Taverna

15 Hereford Rd, W2 4AB **Tel** *020 7229 2206*

Map *8 D2*

Small and unpretentious, this little tavern tries hard and succeeds. Halloumi, *kleftiko*, moussaka, baklava and all the Greek delicacies are well cooked, and their stuffed vine leaves aren't bathed in brine. Though not home-made, they are carefully prepared. Aphrodite excels at starters and is popular with guests from nearby hotels.

SOUTH KENSINGTON AND HYDE PARK Bugis Street Brasserie

The Millennium Gloucester Hotel, Ashburn Place, SW7 4LH **Tel** *020 7331 6211*

Map *16 E2*

Though called a brasserie, this place doesn't offer French cuisine. Expat Singapore natives regard it as the best in London for their kind of food. Dishes are robust, extremely tasty and come in gigantic portions. Plus, for the area, it's not very expensive. For starters, the salt and pepper squid is exceptional.

SOUTH KENSINGTON AND HYDE PARK Racine

239 Brompton Rd, SW3 2EP **Tel** *020 7584 4477*

Map *17 B1*

Racine sets out to showcase French cuisine and succeeds very well. Genuine French food, French waiters and great atmosphere all combine to keep locals coming back for more. The venison, when in season, is excellent and the menu changes regularly. The service is good.

SOUTH KENSINGTON AND HYDE PARK Whits

21 Abingdon Road, W8 6AH **Tel** *020 7938 1122*

Map *15 C1*

A neighbourhood restaurant on a side lane off busy High Street Kensington. Because of its position it does not attract the masses. Try the house special, King & Queen Scallop Risotto, or the roast duck confit. Other mains include pork with crackling or Elwy lamb. Food is consistently good and very seasonal, but always very affordable.

SOUTH KENSINGTON AND HYDE PARK Amaya

15 Halkin Arcade, off Motcomb Street, SW1 8JT **Tel** *020 7823 1166*

Map *10 D5*

A very distinguished Indian restaurant, Amaya is spacious, stylish and with the kitchen on honest display. Specializing in grills, it has three stations – tandoori, sigra and tawa – in action all evening. The range of meats and vegetables is brilliant and the presentation and service faultless. Though it is expensive, it's worth dining here.

SOUTH KENSINGTON AND HYDE PARK Cambio de Tercio

163 Old Brompton Rd, SW5 0LJ **Tel** *020 7244 8970*

Map *16 F2*

This unmistakably Spanish restaurant offers traditional Spanish cuisine such as plump king prawns cooked with chilli and garlic. Most of the ingredients used here are brought over from Spain. Cambio de Tercio was voted "best Spanish restaurant outside of Spain" by the Spanish Ministry of Agriculture, Fishing and Food in 2004.

SOUTH KENSINGTON AND HYDE PARK L'Étranger

36 Gloucester Rd, SW7 4QT **Tel** *020 7584 1118*

Map *16 E1*

L'Étranger is a gem of a place serving extremely good French-Asian fusion food in very stylish surroundings. People rave about the caramelized black cod with miso and with good reason. Every dish on the menu is delectable and there's a massive wine list that has been created with passion and love. You can dance in the club downstairs.

SOUTH KENSINGTON AND HYDE PARK Nahm

The Halkin, 5 Halkin St, SW1X 7DJ **Tel** *020 7333 1234*

Map *10 D5*

This remarkable Thai restaurant has a Michelin star so you can arrive with high expectations. The set menu doesn't disappoint. A recommended appetizer is *ma hor* (minced prawns and chicken simmered in palm sugar with deep fried shallots, garlic and peanuts, served on pineapple and mandarin orange). Not cheap but worth the price.

SOUTH KENSINGTON AND HYDE PARK Pasha 🎵 £££££
1 Gloucester Rd, SW7 4PP **Tel** *020 7589 7969*

Map 16 E1

North Africans love lamb, and here it comes at its best in a spicy tagine with loads of couscous to mop the lovely juices. The tables are rather tiny and it can be tricky keeping all your dishes from tumbling to the floor. Breads and *mezza* are delicious. Live music and belly dancers every night.

SOUTH KENSINGTON AND HYDE PARK Zafferano 🏃♿📖 £££££
5 Lowndes St, SW1X 9EY **Tel** *020 7235 5800*

Map 18 D1

Zafferano has long been recognized as one of the capital's premier Italian restaurants. It's a discreet place, where the emphasis is firmly on the food. Dishes such as risotto with white wine truffle and char-grilled lamb with aubergine (eggplant) allow the quality of the ingredients to shine through.

SOUTH KENSINGTON AND HYDE PARK 1880 at The Bentley ♿📖📖 £££££
27–33 Harrington Gardens, SW7 4JX **Tel** *020 7244 5555*

Map 16 F2

This restaurant is very expensive, but you won't get much better in London with seven-, eight- and nine-course "grazing menus". There is an opulent interior and attentive staff. They enjoy your gastronomic journey with you and the sommelier is a joy. Specialities include seared foie gras, coulis of green apple and confit duck neck.

SOUTH KENSINGTON AND HYDE PARK Foliage ♿📖 £££££
Mandarin Oriental Hyde Park, 66 Knightsbridge, SW1X 7LA **Tel** *020 7201 3723*

Map 9 C5

Foliage is a fantastic restaurant, which seems able to serve the most remarkable food at very reasonable prices. Even the spectacular views of Hyde Park will not distract you from the menu. The three-course set meal includes little tasters in between and the service is faultless. A real jewel.

SOUTH KENSINGTON AND HYDE PARK Mju 🏃♿ £££££
Millennium Knightsbridge, 17 Sloane Street, SW1X 9NU **Tel** *020 7201 6330*

Map 17 C1

The food is a bit hard to categorize at Mju but the restaurant isn't. In this location you expect style and you get it. The best way to appreciate the food is to go for the multicourse tasting menu. Each small dish is assembled with a smart precision. Try oysters with ginger and mirin as well as sea urchin and *foie gras* custard served in a shot glass!

SOUTH KENSINGTON AND HYDE PARK Tom Aikens ♿📖📖 £££££
43 Elystan St, SW3 3NT **Tel** *020 7584 2003*

Map 17 B2

Chef Aikens is the twinkliest star in the cooking firmament with other chefs praising his cooking no end. That said, some people find the cuisine a touch rich but everyone loves the experience. Dishes are lovingly constructed and beautifully plated with flavours finely balanced with a watchmaker's care. Very popular so book ahead.

SOUTH KENSINGTON AND HYDE PARK Zuma 🏃♿ £££££
5 Raphael St, SW7 1DL **Tel** *020 7584 1010*

Map 9 C5

Zuma is a very fashionable restaurant, right opposite Harrods. Celebrities can be spotted here but they come for the great food just like everyone else. Great sashimi, *nigiri*, sushi and tempura with fancy service and fancy prices. It's definitely an experience, but be prepared to dig deep into your pocket.

REGENT'S PARK AND BLOOMSBURY Ishtar 🏃🎵 ££
10–12 Crawford St, W1U 6AZ **Tel** *020 7224 2446*

Map 1 C5

Modern Turkish, so no exotic dancers and no photos of the Istanbul landmarks, either. You can dine on two levels, including under some romantic cellar arches and the dishes are familiar but updated. Go for pan-fried sea bass with potatoes and saffron sauce or some well-marinated kebabs. Leave room for some pastries too.

REGENT'S PARK AND BLOOMSBURY Nippon Tuk 📖 ££
23rd Floor, Hilton London Metropole, 225 Edgware Rd, W2 1DS **Tel** *020 7616 6496*

Map 1 A5

Located on the 23rd floor of the Hilton London Metropole, this Oriental restaurant offers an exquisite dining experience coupled with some of the best views in London. Try sushi, sashimi or even Japanese fish and chips. Before dining, sip a cocktail at the bar and enjoy the view.

REGENT'S PARK AND BLOOMSBURY Caffe Caldesi 🏃📖 £££
118 Marylebone Lane, W1U 2QF **Tel** *020 7935 1144*

Map 10 D1

This airy Italian restaurant offers classic dishes and a very reasonable wine list, with a slightly more formal dining space upstairs. Sit down to a traditional home-cooked dinner. Try the fresh ravioli stuffed with beetroot and ricotta with sage and butter sauce. There is also a patisserie, a delicatessen and a bar.

REGENT'S PARK AND BLOOMSBURY Michael Moore 🏃📖 £££££
19 Blandford St, W1U 3DH **Tel** *020 7224 1898*

Map 10 D1

This popular restaurant mixes excellent food with a genuinely friendly ambience. Michael Moore (no relation to the American film-maker) is there virtually every night and tours the tables for a chat. A very accomplished chef, he changes his menu regularly and keeps his regulars flocking back for more. Special lunch deals are available.

REGENTS PARK AND BLOOMSBURY Defune 🏃♿ £££££
34 George St, W1U 7DP **Tel** *020 7935 8311*

Map 10 D1

Top-class sushi at a high price, but well worth it. A charming minimalist decor is matched by an atmosphere that some find austere but is really just a cool appreciation of the food. This is a decent place and the service is superb. When you're eating raw fish you expect the highest standards and you pay for them.

Key to Price Guide *see p608* **Key to Symbols** *see back cover flap*

REGENT'S PARK AND BLOOMSBURY Orrery

55 Marylebone High Street, W1U 5RB **Tel** *020 7616 8000*

Map *2 D5*

Housed in an old stable block, the dining room is a calm oasis offering stylish dining and contemporary French cuisine. Head for the summer roof terrace for alfresco dining and choose from the menu du jour or the à la carte. The intimate bar area is a good place to sample fine Cuban cigars.

THE CITY AND SOUTHWARK Bengal Cuisine

12 Brick Lane, E1 6RF **Tel** *020 7377 8405*

Map *6 E5*

Just about every building in Brick Lane is an Indian restaurant, but the quality varies. Bengal Cuisine is certainly a lot more modern than most of them. The food is very good value and the cook goes easy on the chilli to suit the Western palate. Staff are happy to advise on dishes if asked. There's a good Sunday buffet as well.

THE CITY AND SOUTHWARK East is East

230 Commercial Rd, E1 2NB **Tel** *020 7702 7222*

Map *16 E1*

A very decent Indian restaurant that doesn't serve all the Bangladeshi dishes like some do. Of course, you are spoiled for choice in this part of London for "Indian" food, but this restaurant gets top marks every time for its authentic cuisine and friendly service. It's also reasonably priced, which is always a bonus.

THE CITY AND SOUTHWARK Fusebox

12 Stoney St, SE1 9AD **Tel** *020 7407 9888*

Map *13 B4*

Fusebox is not so much a restaurant as a good place to eat lunch when exploring Borough Market. Pan-Asian is the main food style with dishes such as tea-smoked salmon and aubergine (eggplant) with oyster mushrooms. There's a great selection of hot and cold things to try and the price is right too.

THE CITY AND SOUTHWARK Baltic

74 Blackfriars Rd, SE1 8HA **Tel** *020 7928 1111*

Map *12 F4*

Located inside a former coach house with exciting high ceilings, Baltic exudes charm. The eastern European influence is noticeable in Baltic's beetroot and vodka cured salmon. There's a massive range of vodkas and the food constantly surprises with dishes such as roast saddle of wild boar. The kitchen is on show and there's often live jazz.

THE CITY AND SOUTHWARK El Vergel

8 Lant St, SE1 1QR **Tel** *020 7357 0057*

Map *13 A5*

Perhaps the only restaurant in town for Chilean food and it does it well. Home-cooked *empanadas*, and *pastel de choclo* are very popular. A small place and not really styled for fine dining, it has a very friendly atmosphere and portions can be huge. Rather charming and very Chilean.

THE CITY AND SOUTHWARK Georgetown Restaurant

10 London Bridge St, SE1 9SG **Tel** *020 7357 7359*

Map *13 B4*

The colonial setting and ambience at Georgetown Restaurant is enhanced by the Singapore Sling cocktails. The menu features a variety of Asian dishes including dim sums, curries with chicken and prawn dumplings as well as the outstanding lamb curry with beans. Look out for special deals.

THE CITY AND SOUTHWARK Haz

9 Cutler St, E1 7DJ **Tel** *020 7929 7923*

Map *14 D1*

Lively, fun and a little posh too, this is a true touch of Turkey in the city. Go for a mixed *meze* starter. They just keep coming and they're all delicious. Go for the well-marinated meat dishes and kebabs and mop up the juice with the lovely flat bread. The office workers throng into Haz at lunchtime so get here before noon.

THE CITY AND SOUTHWARK Kennington Tandoori

313 Kennington Rd, SE11 4QE **Tel** *020 7735 9247*

Map *20 E3*

One of the best Indian curry houses in London, Kennington Tandoori offers reliable food in calm oasis. Its proximity to Westminster means that many curry-loving MPs can be found debating policy over a chicken jalfrezi. Besides classic dishes, there are some unique innovations such as their own Nilgiri *murgh*.

THE CITY AND SOUTHWARK Mar I Terra

14 Gambia St, Waterloo, SE1 0XH **Tel** *020 7928 7628*

Map *12 F4*

Described as a little gem by its fans, this local Spanish restaurant has also been steadily building custom. The quality of the ingredients is one of its secrets as is its location off the main drag. This means the diners are discerning gourmets who have come for the food and the cheerful atmosphere.

THE CITY AND SOUTHWARK Ming Court

54–56 Ludgate Hill, EC4M 7HX **Tel** *020 7248 4303*

Map *12 F2*

Just into the city, Ming Court is close to China in quality and style. Though slightly more expensive than comparable places in China Town, it is ahead of them in decor and ambience. Peking duck scores highly here. The staff are welcoming and the service good.

THE CITY AND SOUTHWARK Rajasthan

49 Monument St, Monument, EC3R 8BU **Tel** *020 7626 1920*

Map *13 C3*

A newly built Indian restaurant, Rajasthan is bright and airy, with fresh flowers on show and not a Bengal tiger or Taj Mahal in sight. The staff are happy to help you avoid the usual curry cliché dishes, but are equally happy to give you chicken tikka masala if that's what you require. Or try something extra special such as a whole poussin. Closed Sundays.

THE CITY AND SOUTHWARK Silka

6–8 Southwark St, London Bridge, SE1 1RQ **Tel** *020 7378 6161*
Map 13 B4

Ayurvedic food is a speciality here, which is essentially food balanced for body and soul, and is particularly good for vegetarians. Of course, there are also all the usual Indian dishes too. There is some reluctance on the staff's part to write down your order so do check that what arrives is actually what you asked for. Closed Sundays.

THE CITY AND SOUTHWARK Story Deli

3 Dray Walk, The Old Truman Brewery, 91 Brick Lane, E1 6QL **Tel** *020 7247 3137*

The menu at this refreshing, organic pizzeria and café uses innovative ingredients, ranging from prawns to pumpkin, to top its tasty, thin-crust pizzas. A great alternative lunch option, with fresh juices and soups as well as tea, coffee and wine. Very popular so bag a seat early. Open daily until 10:30pm.

THE CITY AND SOUTHWARK The Don

The Courtyard, 20 St Swithin's Lane, EC4N 8AD **Tel** *020 7626 2606*
Map 13 B2

This used to be a wine warehouse so it's no surprise that it has an excellent winelist. It also has very attentive staff, who go out of their way to be helpful. A good sommelier and a range of interesting and unique dishes make this a very popular restaurant indeed and reservations are pretty much obligatory. Closed Sundays.

THE CITY AND SOUTHWARK Tito's

4–6 London Bridge **Tel** *020 7407 7787*
Map 8 D4

Tito's is a Peruvian restaurant that serves up plentiful portions at great prices. Typical Peruvian staples such as seafood, fish soups, fried yucca and rice are on the menu. The ceviche and king prawn chupe are recommended as are the Pisco-based cocktails.

THE CITY AND SOUTHWARK Wagamama (Barbican)

1 Ropemaker Street, London EC2 **Tel** *020 7588 2688*
Map 5 B5

A favourite amongst busy city workers who come here for good food and fast service. This branch of the ever popular Japanese chain does not disappoint. Choose from a huge variety of noodle dishes, fresh juices, raw salads and dumplings. An ideal spot for lunch if you are visiting the Barbican arts centre.

THE CITY AND SOUTHWARK Abacus

24 Cornhill, EC3V 3ND **Tel** *020 7337 6767*
Map 13 B2

Hidden away in a basement near Bank Station, Abacus is a true jewel and expects you to pay accordingly. Meals are punctuated by small *amuse-bouches*, tiny, tasty creations from the chef many of which are so delicious they could be courses on their own. There's a seasonal menu and superior levels of service and presentation. A real treat. Closed Sundays.

THE CITY AND SOUTHWARK County Hall

London Marriott County Hall, Queens Walk, SE1 7PB **Tel** *020 7902 8000*
Map 11 C5

A great view of the Thames is just one reason to dine here, close to the Houses of Parliament. Prices are reasonable for the location (the evening set menu comes in at £27.50), and the food never fails to do a good job with dishes such as slow-cooked pork with a chorizo and pea risotto and enjoyable smoked duck.

THE CITY AND SOUTHWARK Moro

34–36 Exmouth Market, EC1R 4QE **Tel** *020 7833 8336*
Map 4 E4

Moro is well known for its Spanish-Moroccan cuisine and serves up consistently good food to regulars. Courgette (zucchini) and mint tortilla is an example of light, flavoursome food and there are some very good breads. Buy ingredients next door and take their famous cookbook home with you.

THE CITY AND SOUTHWARK Ozu

County Hall, Riverside Building, Westminster Bridge Rd, SE1 7PB **Tel** *020 7928 7766*
Map 11 C5

At Ozu, the French owner's classic taste in Japanese food has been inspired by Japanese director Yasujiru Ozu. There is exquisite attention to detail here. Relaxed ambience, a big flat screen used for projecting movies and the 1940s-and '50s-style decor are worth it. A perfect place to enjoy the French-Japanese dishes with a glass of wine.

THE CITY AND SOUTHWARK Tentazioni

2 Mill St, SE1 2BD **Tel** *020 7237 1100*
Map 14 E5

Although a bit more expensive than the average Italian eatery, Tentazioni matches the price with its very high standards. Excellent food is on offer and the five-course tasting menu is a delight, especially at the very reasonable price. A busy and friendly restaurant that's well worth making the walk from Tower Bridge. Closed Sundays.

THE CITY AND SOUTHWARK The Chancery

9 Cursitor St, EC4A 1LL **Tel** *020 7831 4000*
Map 12 E1

This little gem is a stylish new-wave restaurant tucked away down a side street. The well-cooked food is adventurous, modern and very reasonably priced. Try the parfait of foie gras and chicken livers, quince chutney and toasted brioche, or peppered monkfish tail, sweetcorn and pancetta chowder.

THE CITY AND SOUTHWARK The Lobster Pot

3 Kennington Lane, SE11 4RG **Tel** *020 7582 5556*
Map 20 F2

The French owners set out to recreate Brittany (even down to seagull soundtracks) and succeed brilliantly. The eight-course "surprise" menu is fantastic, and the fish is always superbly fresh. Do book in advance, as it's not very big. Downstairs is a brasserie serving classic French fare at slightly lower prices, and there is a wine bar upstairs.

Key to Price Guide *see p608* **Key to Symbols** *see back cover flap*

FURTHER AFIELD Base ⚑ ♟ £
71 Hampstead High St, NW3 1QP **Tel** *020 7431 2224*

During the day, Base is a gourmet bar serving Mediterranean cuisine. In the evening it becomes a bistro serving sumptuous Mediterranean fusion food with an emphasis on fresh ingredients. The menu changes regularly and is complemented by an extensive wine list. Another branch is located at 195 Baker Street.

FURTHER AFIELD Fujiyama ⚑ £
5–7 Vining St, Brixton, SW9 8QA **Tel** *020 7737 6583*

Serving freshly cooked Japanese dishes, Fujiyama has been a Brixton favourite for many years. Noodle soups, pan-fried noodles, bento boxes and sushi are all on offer. There is also a wide variety of vegetarian options, in particular try the *don buri*, an all-in-one meal accompanied by pickles and miso soup.

FURTHER AFIELD Haché Burger ⚑ ♿ £
329–331 Fulham Rd, SW10 9QL **Tel** *020 7823 3515*   **Map** *16 F4*

This chic, modern "bespoke" hamburger place is popular with cinema-goers and posh teenagers. Gourmet burgers are served on a fresh ciabatta bun with rocket, tomato, sweet red onion and the special Haché mayonnaise. Choose from a range of beef, lamb, venison, chicken, fish, duck or veggie burgers.

FURTHER AFIELD Borscht n Tears ♫ ££
46 Beauchamp Place, SW3 1NX **Tel** *020 7584 9911*   **Map** *17 B1*

This place has been here since before the Berlin Wall came down, doing its very best bit for Anglo-Russian relations. The vodka flows pretty freely and the tables can become dance floors. The food is traditional and delicious, if occasionally a bit heavy. You'll have a fun night, even if you cannot remember anything afterwards!

FURTHER AFIELD Brown's West India Quay ⚑ ♿ ♟ ££
Hertsmere Road, E14 8JJ **Tel** *020 7987 9777*

The Brown's empire began in Brighton and is now established throughout the country. The main draw is its solid British cooking while the decor – dark wooden café chairs, palms and ceiling fans – create a colonial feel. Alfresco dining is possible in this former sugar warehouse near Canary Wharf.

FURTHER AFIELD Cumin ⚑ ♿ ££
O2 Centre, 255 Finchley Rd, NW3 6LU **Tel** *020 7794 5616*

One of *Time Out* magazine's top 50 Indian restaurants in London, Cumin is perfect for a pre- or post-movie meal, being located opposite the Vue cinema in West Hampstead. Mouthwatering dishes from northern India are prepared without using any colourings or additives. Try the chicken kahdai, cooked in a fiery tomato and onion sauce.

FURTHER AFIELD Karma ££
44 Blythe Rd, W14 0HA **Tel** *020 7602 9333*

A modern Indian restaurant, Karma takes you on a culinary journey of the Indian sub-continent, exploring the many regional styles of cooking that India has to offer. The chef Dilwar Khan's signature dishes are classic Goan recipes, Chicken Vindaloo and Lamb Xacuti. The wine list has been specially created to complement the cuisine. Closed Mon.

FURTHER AFIELD Mezedepolio ⚑ ♿ ♟ ££
14–15 Hoxton Market, N1 6HG **Tel** *020 7739 8212*   **Map** *5 C3*

Join the crowd at Mezedepolio and choose from a massive selection of Greek dishes. The home-style cooking is unique, and many of the dishes on the menu have never been seen in the country before. They're all very tempting but be warned to keep an eye on the prices. The Real Greek wine bar serves Greek wines as well.

FURTHER AFIELD Mosob ⚑ ££
339 Harrow Rd, W9 3RB **Tel** *020 2766 2012*

Located a short walk from Westbourne Park tube, this family-run restaurant serves Eritrean food in a colourful dining room decorated with African-flavoured furnishings. All dishes on the menu are served with *injera*, a typically Eritrean bread that also doubles as an eating utensil. The vegetarian menu is 100 per cent vegan.

FURTHER AFIELD North Pole ⚑ ♫ 🍴 ££
131 Greenwich High Rd, SE10 8JA **Tel** *020 8853 3020*

A little Greenwich gem, North Pole is comfortably warm with a nice bar downstairs and a fire in the grate upstairs. A small piano tinkles away in the background. Food is of a very high standard. It has a Michelin rating but the prices don't reflect this too badly. Traditional Sunday roasts of beef or chicken are available with all the trimmings.

FURTHER AFIELD The Belvedere ⚑ ♫ 🍴 ♟ ££
Holland House, Abbotsbury Road, W8 6LU **Tel** *020 7602 1238*   **Map** *7 B5*

Tucked away in leafy Holland Park, the Belvedere has a perfect location. The opulence of the main room doesn't get reflected in the bill. Instead, a brilliant variety of dishes is effortlessly combined with a very fair price. "Gastro-pub" type food means hearty and heartening meals that comfort the senses while tickling the palate.

FURTHER AFIELD The Lane Restaurant ⚑ ♫ ♿ ££
12–20 Osborn St, E1 6TE **Tel** *020 7456 1067*   **Map** *14 E1*

Located at the south end of famous Brick Lane, but not an Indian restaurant. It's actually a rather cool and trendy place doing a variety of dishes at very reasonable prices. The cocktail bar area is nice too. It's in an up-and-coming area, so you may find yourself surrounded by young people with cool clothes and a disposable income.

FURTHER AFIELD The Spread Eagle
1–2 Stockwell St, SE10 9JN **Tel** *020 8853 2333*

Fiercely championed by locals, this place radiates confidence with its innovative French cuisine. Small, intimate booths to dine in and a real, roaring fire in winter all conspire to make you want to stay long after the coffee has been cleared away. The food is rich and satisfying and the whole experience is equal to the West End and at half the price.

FURTHER AFIELD Cibo
3 Russell Gardens, W14 8EZ **Tel** *020 7371 6271*

Map 7 A5

Cibo has been around long enough to become a dependable local institution. Its clever mix of tried and trusted northern Italian favourites, combined with more adventurous dishes, never fails to satisfy its young crowd. There's plenty of bread and olives to savour while waiting at the table. The wine list matches the restaurant's high quality.

FURTHER AFIELD Rivington Grill
178 Greenwich High Rd, Greenwich, SE10 8NN **Tel** *020 8293 9270*

Located next to the cinema, Rivington is a great spot for lunch, dinner or drinks before or after a movie or tour around historic Greenwich. Hearty British cuisine is served in a modern dining room with exposed brickwork, crisp white linen tablecloths and low lighting. The Market Breakfast is good. Closed Mon and Tue dinner.

FURTHER AFIELD Yas
7 Hammersmith Rd, Kensington Olympia, W14 8XJ **Tel** *020 7603 9148*

Map 15 A1

Persian food means plenty of meat on the main course, although vegetarians can fill up on a great variety of dips. At Yas, the bread is baked on the premises. Open well past midnight, this remarkable place begins to get busy at a rather late hour. On a warm night, sit outside and watch the world go by.

FURTHER AFIELD Le Vacherin
76–77 South Parade, W4 5LF **Tel** *020 8742 2121*

Le Vacherin is a chef-patron restaurant in deepest Chiswick, a lovely area of London. Here they have re-created a charming Parisian bistro, serving top-notch food in a nice unpretentious way to a loyal local clientele. Sunday brunch is particularly popular. October to March they serve the speciality cheese, le Vacherin, baked with black truffles, almonds and white wine.

FURTHER AFIELD Gordon Ramsay At 68 Royal Hospital Road
68 Royal Hospital Rd, SW3 4HP **Tel** *020 7352 4441*

Map 17 C4

Awarded with three Michelin stars, this restaurant strives for perfection and the effort reflects in everything from place settings to service. For an astonishing average of £110 per person, it is reputedly the best restaurant in London as well as all of England. As a souvenir of London, meal memories here will last a lifetime.

FURTHER AFIELD The River Café
Thames Wharf, Rainville Rd, Hammersmith, W6 9HA **Tel** *020 7386 4200*

The michelin-starred River Café is a well-established favourite among Londoners and tourists alike. With outstanding service, beautifully prepared rustic Italian dishes such as buffalo ricotta and turbot, and an excellent wine list, it's well worth the price. Floor-to-ceiling windows offer lovely views of the gardens and river beyond.

THE DOWNS AND CHANNEL COAST

ARUNDEL Amberley Castle
Amberley, nr Arundel, West Sussex, BN18 9LT **Tel** *01798 831992*

Nestled in some wonderfully imposing 18-m (60-ft) walls with a 12th-century portcullis, this fine restaurant offers a seasonally adjusted menu of local treats. Afternoon tea is served Mon–Thu. Its popularity as a wedding venue makes it necessary to book ahead.

ASHFORD The Manor Restaurant
Eastwell Park, Boughton Lees, Ashford, Kent, TN25 4HR **Tel** *01233 213000*

Set against a backdrop of the North Downs, Eastwell Manor has a formal, wood-panelled dining room called the Manor Restaurant. Modern English cuisine, with the odd Gallic flourish, is served here. The Brasserie, also on the premises, is ideal for afternoon tea and savouries out on the terrace.

BRIGHTON Momma Cherri's Soul Food
2–3 Little East St, Brighton, East Sussex, BN2 1HA **Tel** *01273 325305*

There is a fantastic atmosphere at this welcoming restaurant where the food just keeps on coming. The menu, with its roots in the American deep south, is based on corn and salt pork back as well as seasonal fruit and vegetables. Try the *Jambalya* (a mixture of meats, rice and seasonings), hot wings or BBQ ribs. Follow up with superb chocolate brownies.

BRIGHTON La Fourchette
105 Western Rd, Brighton, East Sussex, BN1 2AA **Tel** *01273 722556*

Lauded as one of Brighton's best restaurants, this handsome bistro is a relaxed showcase for confident regional Gallic comfort classics. The odd Moroccan twist spices up proceedings. An excellent wine list to match, while the choice of desserts will test the strongest resolve.

Key to Price Guide *see p608* **Key to Symbols** *see back cover flap*

BRIGHTON Seven Dials
1 Buckingham Place, Seven Dials, Brighton, East Sussex, BN1 3TD **Tel** *01273 885555*

A bustling eatery much beloved by Brighton's Sunday supplement set, Seven Dials is housed in a converted bank. The menu makes good use of Sussex farmland and local organic produce. Private dining is provided in the downstairs Vault, while a summer terrace offers the perfect spot for al fresco people-watching.

BRIGHTON China Garden
88–91 Preston St, Brighton, East Sussex, BN1 2HG **Tel** *01273 325124*

A well-regarded and well-established Brightonian Chinese institution, China Garden benefits from a recent face-lift: the swish new decor has the feel of a 1930s ocean liner. The balanced menu waves the flag for Cantonese seafood and other more meatier options. Veggies get a good deal too.

BRIGHTON Hotel du Vin
Ship St, Brighton, East Sussex, BN1 1AD **Tel** *01273 718588*

Part of the reliable, cheerful Hotel du Vin mini-chain, this natty bistro is tucked away in the Lanes. The menu opts for modern European with French influence. Vegetarians are also catered for. Some choice selections from the extensive wine list are on offer. The new Pub du Vin next door serves traditional pub fare with ales and wine.

BRIGHTON Seattle Restaurant
Hotel Seattle, Brighton Marina, Brighton, East Sussex, BN2 5WA **Tel** *01273 679799*

A sleek Brighton favourite overlooking the Marina, this restaurant lays stress on mod-European flavours and seafood delicacies. It also serves up a decent selection of pastas. Try the salmon and dill fishcakes or the pan-seared skate served with capers and lemon. The well-stocked and busy cocktail bar adds to the chic buzz.

BROCKENHURST Simply Poussin
The Courtyard, Brookley Road, Brockenhurst, Hampshire, SO42 7RB **Tel** *01590 623063*

This brasserie is hidden away in a village mews that enjoys a more informal air than its hugely popular sister restaurant nearby. The quality of food is equally good. The two-course daily set menu is great value and the predominantly New World wine list is extensive. Closed Sundays and Mondays.

CANTERBURY The Goods Shed
Station Road West, Canterbury, Kent, CT2 8AN **Tel** *01227 459153*

At this farmers' market diner-cum-café, there's a simple blackboard menu offering well-constructed treats. The simple home cooking uses the best of the day's produce from the myriad stalls. As it is increasingly popular with local foodies, seating is at quite a premium during peak times. Closed Mondays; lunch only Sundays.

CHICHESTER The George and Dragon Inn
North St, Chichester, West Sussex, PO19 1NQ **Tel** *01243 785660*

This smartly refurbished pub now features a comfortable and relaxed restaurant in the conservatory, with tables spilling over on to the courtyard in the summer months. The menu offers quality home-made food as well as bar snacks. Located on the North Walls walk, near the famous Chichester Festival Theatre.

CHICHESTER Comme Ça
67 Broyle Rd, Chichester, West Sussex, PO19 6BD **Tel** *01243 788724*

Just around the corner from Chichester's historic centre, Comme Ça is a busy centrepiece for full-blooded Normandy cooking genially served in a comfortably rustic ambience. Outside dining is available on the terrace during the summer months, while the Garden Room is a popular spot for private functions. Closed Mon.

EAST CHILTINGTON The Jolly Sportsman
Chapel Lane, East Chiltington, East Sussex, BN7 3BA **Tel** *01273 890400*

This acclaimed gastropub is a relaxed rural retreat, famed for its free-range chicken and duck, with enjoyable Euro stylings elsewhere on a surprisingly refined menu. Contemporary art adorns the walls, while the shaded terrace has a distinctly Moroccan feel. Microbrewery on the premises. Closed Sunday evening, Mondays.

EAST GRINSTEAD Gravetye Manor
Nr East Grinstead, West Sussex, RH19 4LJ **Tel** *01342 810567*

Michelin-starred Gravetye Manor is an oak-panelled country house with a sophisticated air. Its refined ambience complements the stately Anglo-French menu enriched with vegetables freshly picked from its gardens. The long and winding wine list includes over 600 bins. Children aged over seven are welcome. Smart casual dress code.

EAST LAVANT Royal Oak
Pook Lane, East Lavant, West Sussex, PO18 0AX **Tel** *01243 527434*

Once the local watering hole in an off-the-beaten-track Downland village close to Goodwood, the Royal Oak is now a highly reputed gastro pub and still maintains its original 200-year-old charm. On the menu you'll find high-class renditions of pub classics plus specials with a more modern accent.

EMSWORTH 36 on the Quay
47 South St, Emsworth, Hampshire, PO10 7EG **Tel** *01243 375592*

Located in a fishing village overlooking the bay, this bright and affable dining room focuses largely on fish. In addition, plenty of landlubber local produce feature on the menu. The "Little Big" tasting menu allows diners to enjoy a little bit of everything. Overnight accommodation available.

EVERSLEY New Mill Restaurant

New Mill Rd, Eversley, Hampshire, RG27 0RA **Tel** *01189 732277*

Rural honey pot perched on the banks of River Blackwater and the Millpond. The main restaurant is home to à la carte lighter fare, while the grill room, basing itself on the rural gastropub template, is the place for belt-loosening, comfort classics. There's an award-winning wine list.

FAVERSHAM Read's Restaurant with Rooms

Macknade Manor, Canterbury Rd, Faversham, Kent, ME13 8XE **Tel** *01795 535344*

Traditional Georgian manor house with self-styled "restaurant-with-rooms", Read's is set in its own wooded grounds. The kitchen produces a delicious range of seasonal, modern British fare. Plenty of vegetables, fresh from its own walled garden, are accompanied by locally caught game and fish.

HASLEMERE Auberge de France

Lythe Hill Hotel and Spa, Petworth Rd, Haslemere, Surrey, GU27 3BQ **Tel** *01428 651251*

Auberge de France, the oak-panelled dining room at Lythe Hill Hotel, dates from the 14th century. The extensive menu covers a range of Gallic gastro points. Antiques and candlelight add to the cosy Tudor feel, while the windows overlook a nearby lake and parkland. Private dining rooms available.

HAYWARDS HEATH Jeremy's at Borde Hill

Borde Hill Gardens, Balcombe Rd, Haywards Heath, West Sussex, RH16 1XP **Tel** *01444 441102*

Overlooking a walled Victorian garden, this family-run restaurant cooks up modern European dishes, with a strong Mediterranean influence. Local artwork on the walls and friendly service add to the pleasingly relaxed air. The outdoor dining on the terrace is a perfect spot for Sunday lunch.

HYTHE BAY Hythe Bay Fish Restaurant

Marine Parade, Hythe Bay, Kent, CT21 6AW **Tel** *01303 267024*

This beachfront charmer conjures up a whole range of innovative recipes with the local catch. The oysters are a house speciality. Vegetarian dishes are on offer too. The well-established Sunday buffets draw a buzzy, family crowd, as does the sunny terrace, weather permitting.

JEVINGTON The Hungry Monk

Jevington, nr Polegate, East Sussex, BN26 5QF **Tel** *01323 482178*

Local game and fish jostle for position and are given a Gallic twist on the enjoyable menu on offer at this 14th-century flint cottage. A one-time monastic retreat, complete with log fireplaces, candlelight and assorted antiques, the Hungry Monk is at its finest when the nights are drawing in. Half of the extensive wine list is under £20 a bottle.

LENHAM Culpeper's Restaurant

Sandway, Lenham, nr Maidstone, Kent, ME17 2BE **Tel** *01622 859803*

Housed in a country pile, this restaurant sits pretty in what used to be the entrance hall, complete with chandeliers and formal family portraits. The menu features modern British food, and the signature dish is smoked venison. The cellar straddles old and new worlds, while a post-meal brandy in the Drawing Room is a fine way to round off the evening.

LEWES Bill's Produce Store

56 Cliffe High St, Lewes, East Sussex, BN7 2AN **Tel** *01273 476918*

People come from miles around and from as far as London to eat at this deli/café/restaurant. The amazing variety of dishes is served in generous portions and beautifully presented. There is always a queue, but it moves fast, and the service is friendly and efficient. Another branch is in Brighton. Closes at 5pm Mon–Sat, 4pm Sun.

NEWBURY Dew Pond

Old Burghclere, Newbury, Berkshire, RG20 9LH **Tel** *01635 278408*

A cosy country-house restaurant on the edge of Watership Down, Dew Pond specializes in Scottish beef. Closer to home, Hampshire cheeses and local game also feature on the menu. Oak beams and outside decking add to the allure. Watch out for a series of monthly gastro evenings featuring five-course dinners.

PORTSMOUTH A Bar Bistro

58 White Hart Rd, Portsmouth, Hampshire, PO1 2JA **Tel** *02392 811585*

There's much to enjoy in this affable seafood restaurant overlooking the fish market. The A Bar Bistro has an airy feel, with French windows and a terrace. For mains, try the salmon wellington, mussels or local catch of the day. Certainly not ideal if you are just having drinks, though you can get yourself a passable martini here.

RIPLEY Drakes

The Clock House, High Street, Ripley, Surrey, GU23 6AQ **Tel** *01483 224777*

A fine Queen Anne town house with variegated brickwork and a very attractive garden, Drakes is becoming an increasingly popular destination for London foodies. Well-crafted modern French favourites are created by a confident young chef, whose impressive CV includes stints with über-chefs Marco Pierre White and Nico Landenis.

RYE Landgate Bistro

5–6 Landgate, Rye, Sussex, TN31 7LH **Tel** *01797 222829*

The Landgate Bistro is famed for its agreeably uncomplicated modern British fare that has a growing army of fans. Its fishcakes and other clever tricks with seafood are much celebrated. Also on offer are local meats and game. Among the menu highlights are the delicious leek and Roquefort tarts. Closed Mondays and Tuesdays.

Key to Price Guide *see p608* **Key to Symbols** *see back cover flap*

SEAVIEW Priory Bay Hotel 🏃 £££

Priory Drive, Seaview, Isle of Wight, PO34 5BU **Tel** *01983 613146*

Dating back to the medieval times, this hotel has a pair of hotel dining rooms set on the bay itself, with their own private beach. The Priory Oyster specializes in seafood and light mod-Med flavours that come with a good and healthy zing. It also welcomes children, unlike the Island Room, which is preferred by the less calorie-conscious.

STOCKBRIDGE The Greyhound 🏃♿🍴 £££

31 High St, Stockbridge, Hampshire, SO20 6EY **Tel** *01264 810833*

Superior gastropub serving modern English cuisine, the Greyhound makes plentiful use of produce from the nearby New Forest and the River Test, which runs through the grounds. On the menu, meat options outweigh the fish-based dishes. Though the place can get loud, there's much to recommend here. Closed Sun dinner, Mon.

TUNBRIDGE WELLS Thackeray's 🍴 £££££

85 London Rd, Tunbridge Wells, Kent, TN1 1EA **Tel** *01892 511921*

Thackeray's offers agreeable modern French flavours in a Grade II-listed building, once home to the eponymous novelist. The warm, chatty atmosphere draws a contended clientele, both local and from further afield. Cocktails are served beforehand in the Gold Room, and a post-meal Scotch in the gold leaf-lined Throne Room.

WHITSTABLE Wheelers Oyster Bar 📖🏃♿ ££

8 High St, Whitstable, Kent, CT5 1BQ **Tel** *01227 273311*

Justly celebrated shellfish emporium that closes at 9pm, Wheelers Oyster Bar is the oldest fish and shellfish establishment in Britain. It doesn't have a licence so bring your own wine to the Oyster Parlour, tucked behind the main seafood bar, or nip over to the pebble beach for an impromptu picnic. Closed Wednesdays.

WHITSTABLE Whitstable Oyster Fish Company 🏃♿🍴 £££

Horsebridge, Whitstable, Kent, CT5 1BU **Tel** *01227 276856*

This is a popular seafood restaurant based in an old Naval warehouse overlooking the North Sea. There's a busy open kitchen with skilled staff getting to grips with fish freshly caught by the company's own band of fishermen. The nautically themed decor is enthusiastic but stops short of going overboard. Closed Mon (except bank hols).

WICKHAM The Old House Hotel Restaurant 🏃♿ £££

The Square, Wickham, Hampshire, PO17 5JG **Tel** *01329 833049*

Converted from an old Georgian house, this hotel dining room is an atmospheric spot to enjoy some interesting European dishes made with locally sourced produce. Fish is a house speciality. The room is a cosy affair, with exposed old oak beams and some wonderful original 17th-century fittings. Extensive wine list.

WILMINGTON Crossways Hotel 🍴 ££££

Wilmington, nr Polegate, East Sussex, BN26 5SG **Tel** *01323 482455*

A short stroll from the famed Long Man of Wilmington, the Crossways is a great spot for those visiting Glyndebourne. Its modern British cuisine uses fresh local ingredients. Though the classic dining room may not impress the style-conscious, it's well worth the experience.

EAST ANGLIA

ALDEBURGH 152 Aldeburgh 🏃♿ ££

152 High St, Aldeburgh, Suffolk, IP15 5AX **Tel** *01728 454594*

A leisurely pebble's throw from the beach, chic little 152 Aldeburgh serves up modern European cooking with a bias towards flavours from south of the Alps. Open for breakfast, lunch and dinner, the restaurant benefits from a well-travelled kitchen and the bountiful fresh produce on its doorstep. Closed first two weeks of January.

ALDEBURGH Regatta Restaurant and Wine Bar 🏃🍴 ££

171–173 High St, Aldeburgh, Suffolk, IP15 5AN **Tel** *01728 452011*

Favoured spot for seasonal asparagus, this cheery, family-run restaurant waves the flag for Suffolk's acclaimed regional produce. Specialities include good fish from the beach and game from the surrounding estates in winter. A worthy addition to Aldeburgh's burgeoning foodie scene.

ALDEBURGH The Lighthouse 🏃♿🍴 £££

77 High St, Aldeburgh, Suffolk, IP15 5AU **Tel** *01728 453377*

The Lighthouse is a breezy, busy bistro that specializes in fishy flavours, courtesy of deck-fresh produce from the Suffolk coast. The lunch and dinner menus change daily, while there are also good fixed-price options. The summer terrace is a local favourite, weather permitting.

BURY ST EDMUNDS Maison Bleue 🏃♿🍴 ££

31 Churchgate St, Bury St Edmunds, Suffolk, IP33 1RG **Tel** *01284 760623*

Maison Bleue specializes in Gallic fish, though the daily-changing menu does include a special "butcher's corner" for the meat-lovers. The smart dining room is well served by a kitchen that conjures up interesting, yet simple, fare using the best of the local catch. The nautical-themed bar is decorated with paintings of the sea.

CAMBRIDGE Riverside Brasserie

The Cambridge Garden House Hotel, Granta Place, Mill Lane, Cambridge, Cambridgeshire, CB2 1RT **Tel** *01223 259988*

Perched on the side of the River Cam, this brasserie is beautifully set in its own secluded gardens. Lighter, French-influenced fare makes it a popular drop-in for the city's ladies-who-lunch, though evening visits are delightful too. A brisk stroll away from Cambridge's historic centre.

CAMBRIDGE The Arts Roof Garden

4th Floor, Cambridge Arts Theatre, 6 St Edwards Passage, Cambridge, Cambridgeshire, CB2 3PJ **Tel** *01223 367333*

Artful modern European creations attract local culture vultures to The Arts Roof Garden, one of the city centre's best restaurants. The dining room is airy and light, and the ideal place for pre-theatre meals. It's an increasingly popular venue for wedding receptions, so booking is advised. Closed Sun, Mon (unless there is a show on).

CAMBRIDGE Graffiti at Hotel Felix

Whitehouse Lane, Huntingdon Rd, Cambridge, Cambridgeshire, CL3 0LX **Tel** *01223 277977*

Overlooking landscaped gardens, this handsome hotel dining room is set in a converted Victorian mansion. The menu features a selection of mod-Med dishes as well as a choice of game. Despite being just a short distance away from the bustle of Cambridge city centre, the place is quite peaceful. There is a good-value three-course lunch deal.

CAMBRIDGE Restaurant 22

22 Chesterton Rd, Cambridge, Cambridgeshire, CB4 3AX **Tel** *01223 351880*

Small but perfectly formed, Restaurant 22 is set in a smart Victorian town house that serves British and French favourites, with the odd Asian twist added for extra interest. The decent wine list is predominantly French, but does travel further afield to good effect.

CAMBRIDGE Midsummer House

Midsummer Common, Cambridge, Cambridgeshire, CB4 1HA **Tel** *01223 369299*

On the banks of the River Cam, Midsummer House is a plush restaurant that boasts an array of awards. The elegant ambience is well served by a kitchen with a heavy French accent. A recent face-lift adds to the charm, with a slate floor and warm shades giving a distinctly Mediterranean feel to proceedings. Closed Sun, Mon; Tue lunch.

CLAVERING The Cricketers

Whyken Rd, Clavering, nr Saffron Walden, Cambridgeshire, CB11 4QT **Tel** *01799 550442*

This award-winning rural retreat has become a popular destination for London foodies. The extra allure is provided by the fact that this is actually TV chef Jamie Oliver's family home. Menus change seasonally, with the robust cooking treading that well-worn path between the UK and Italy. Good selection of wine and real ales.

COLCHESTER The Warehouse Brasserie

The Old Chapel, Chapel St North, Colchester, Essex, CO2 7AT **Tel** *01206 765656*

One of the better dining options in the area, the Warehouse Brasserie is set in the heart of Colchester. A decent collection of British comfort food classics is served to an appreciative mix of diners in a relaxed, friendly atmosphere. The attentive service here makes for a pleasant dining experience. Closed Sun, Mon.

CROMER Bolton's Bistro

The Cliftonville Hotel, Seafront, Cromer, Norfolk, NR27 9AS **Tel** *01263 512543*

There's a really traditional look to this seafront bistro affair with its daily-changing blackboard menu displaying prepared-to-order fresh fish specialities, including some fine seasonal Cromer crab and lobster. Red meat-eaters and vegetarians get their share of goodies too, while the ice cream has a local fan club.

FRESSINGFIELD EYE The Fox and Goose Inn

Church Rd, Fressingfield Eye, Suffolk, IP21 5PB **Tel** *01379 586247*

Once a poorhouse, the Fox and Goose Inn has been a local favourite since the mid-1800s. Over the years, the restaurant has maintained its good standards, and perfected its interpretation of regional specialities, with a pro-European touch added occasionally. Closed Mondays; first two weeks in Jan.

HARWICH The Harbourside Restaurant

The Pier Hotel and Restaurant, The Quay, Harwich, Essex, CO12 3HH **Tel** *01255 241212*

Living up to its name, the Pier has a nautical setting, complete with fishing boats moored at the front door and the Stour and Orwell estuaries stretching out to the horizon. Seafood understandably tends to get most of the attention here but there's also a range of meat dishes featured on the menu.

HOLKHAM The Victoria at Holkham

Holkham Estate, nr Wells-Next-The-Sea, Norfolk, NR23 1RG **Tel** *01328 713230*

A stroll from the windswept sands of Holkham Beach, this neat hotel diner serves local shellfish, organic delicacies and wild game. Crab and mussels are the house specialities. On-site microbrewery produces plenty of quaffable delights to wash it all down with. Barbeques in the summer months.

HOLT Morston Hall

Holt, nr Blakeney, Norfolk, NR25 7AA **Tel** *01263 741041*

Increasingly popular honeypot for happy-go-lucky locals and yachting types from nearby Morston Quay, Morston Hall is an inviting, relaxed place. The five-course daily-changing menu features superior cooking with French foundations. Afternoon tea is served daily by the open fire. Closed first week in Jan.

Key to Price Guide *see p608* **Key to Symbols** *see back cover flap*

HORRINGER Fredericks at The Ickworth

Horringer, nr Bury St Edmunds, Suffolk, IP29 5QE **Tel** *01284 735350*

Set in one of the wings of a very stately country house, Frederick's is the centrepiece of a sleek hotel. A range of ambitious modern European cooking is on offer for a well-heeled clientele. The smooth service comes with a cheery geniality. The ambience is warm and relaxing, the dress code smart casual. Open for dinner only.

HUNTINGDON The Terrace

The Old Bridge, 1 High St, Huntingdon, Cambridgeshire, PE29 3TQ **Tel** *01480 424300*

With light, airy decor, the Terrace is known for its well-regarded food with a global reach but local starting points. All the food, including bread, is made on the premises and served in a cheery, informal ambience. There's a good-value set lunch menu on offer, while the excellent wine list is worth exploring.

HUNTINGDON The Pheasant

Keyston, Huntingdon, Cambridgeshire, PE18 0RE **Tel** *01832 710241*

This thatched inn, with oaked-beam dining room, is home to some heartening Anglo-French fare. The secret of its outstanding cooking lies in the successful blending of classical French techniques with the pick of local game. The well-considered wine list includes a wide by-the-glass choice.

IPSWICH Il Punto

Neptune Quay, Ipswich, Suffolk, IP4 1AX **Tel** *01473 289748*

A former Belgian gunboat dating from the 1800s, Il Punto now serves as a floating brasserie with a distinctly Gallic outlook. The interior makes good use of its original fittings, while there's plenty of outside deck dining to be enjoyed when waters are calmer. No lunch served on Saturdays.

MELBOURN Sheene Mill

Station Rd, Melbourn, Cambridgeshire, SG8 6DX **Tel** *01763 261393*

The cosy interior and chatty, informal air belie the meticulous kitchen at this restored rural mill. Proudly waving the flag for British cuisine, albeit with plenty of influences from sunnier climes, the cooking here is of a very high quality. The vegetables and herbs are all from the garden on the premises.

NORWICH Tatlers

21 Tombland, Norwich, Norfolk, NR3 1RF **Tel** *01603 766670*

A long-standing brasserie, Tatler's is situated in the heart of town, just around the corner from the cathedral. The staff dispense modern British fare for an appreciative mix of diners in an informal atmosphere. The seasonal menu uses local ingredients and includes decent vegetarian options. Closed Sunday evenings.

NORWICH St Giles House Restaurant

41–45 St Giles St, Norwich, Norfolk, NR2 1AB **Tel** *01603 275180*

The philosophy of this restaurant specializing in modern European cuisine is simple: offering top-quality food made with the finest local and seasonal ingredients. There is an extensive wine list covering both the old and new worlds, and a wide range of wines by the glass. Located in a Grade II listed building in the centre of town.

OULTON BROAD The Crooked Barn Restaurant

Ivy House Country Hotel, Ivy Lane, Oulton Broad, Suffolk, NR33 8HY **Tel** *01502 501353*

An 18th-century thatched barn, Crooked Barn Restaurant is ideal for candlelit dining in a light and spacious room. The excellent cooking, which uses local free-range and organic produce, is predominantly British. The odd garnish from further afield is also added to good effect, with touches from southern Europe, as well as Down Under.

STANTON The Leaping Hare Restaurant

Wyken Hall, Stanton, Bury St Edmunds, Suffolk, IP31 2DW **Tel** *01359 250287*

This well-known restaurant stands in a converted 18th-century barn. The attractive dining room is set on the edge of a country estate, nestled among woods, vineyards and perfect gardens. An appealing rustic menu featuring Suffolk fare matches the ambience. The excellent wine list includes wines produced from the Wyken vineyard.

WELLS-NEXT-THE-SEA The Crown Hotel

The Buttlands, Wells-Next-The-Sea, NR23 1EX **Tel** *01328 710209*

Restored from a 16th-century coaching inn, the Crown serves decent British fare with a few interesting Pacific Rim touches. The kitchen enjoys the best of fresh produce caught in the picturesque harbour town on the Norfolk coast. Lighter bites, served on a black slate, are available in the bar, with an open fire and old oak beams.

WERRINGTON The Cherry House Restaurant

125 Church St, Werrington, Cambridgeshire, PE4 6QF **Tel** *01733 571721*

In a relaxed, rural setting, this smart Francophile eatery has earned a good reputation for quality. The chef's elaborate, confident cooking uses the best of local ingredients and a wealth of experience gained from stints in some of London's more celebrated hotel kitchens. There's an excellent, if slightly short, wine list. Closed Mondays.

WOODBRIDGE Crown & Castle

Orford, Woodbridge, Suffolk, IP12 2LJ **Tel** *01394 450205*

Sitting in the shadows of a Norman castle, this relaxed, elegant hotel dining room plays to its strengths: a quintessentially English menu for such a perfect English setting. The recently refurbished private dining room is home to a large round table, and suitable for small dinner parties.

WYMONDHAM Number 24 Restaurant ✖ & ▮ ££££
24 Middleton St, Wymondham, Norfolk, NR18 0AD **Tel** *01953 607750*

Located in a charming Grade II listed building, this restaurant has a seasonal menu featuring contemporary English cuisine. The Sunday lunch, however, tends to follow a more traditional route. Closed Sunday dinner, Tuesday lunch and all day Monday.

THAMES VALLEY

BRAY-ON-THAMES The Fat Duck ✖ ▮ £££££
High St, Bray, Berkshire, SL6 2AQ **Tel** *01628 580333*

One of the most exquisite restaurants in the region, Fat Duck is located in a 15th-century listed building. The exterior gives way to clean, modernist decor, where diners undergo a once-in-a-lifetime experience. Multiple, double-figure courses include such culinary inventions as snail porridge and egg and bacon ice cream.

BUCKINGHAM Prego Restaurant and Wine Bar ✖ & ▮ ££
4 High St, Buckingham, Buckinghamshire, MK18 1NT **Tel** *01280 821205*

This friendly family restaurant exudes sunny Mediterranean ambience. Well located on Buckingham high street, it specializes in authentic Italian home cooking including fine pizza and pasta dishes. Free parking is available directly opposite the restaurant.

DINTON La Chouette ✖ ££££
Westlington Green, Dinton, Buckinghamshire, HP17 8UW **Tel** *01296 747422*

Forget calories and fat content as you enter this Belgian restaurant situated on the village green. The fabulously rich menu caters to the indulgent food-lover. Dishes are modern European blended with a little Belgian stodge. Perfect place for jazz-loving beer connoisseurs, but watch out for low beams as you walk away from the bar.

EASINGTON The Mole and Chicken ✖ & ▮ ££
Easington, nr Long Crendon, Buckinghamshire, HP189EY **Tel** *01844 208387*

Well-heeled diners come from afar to this former 19th-century village store for views of the Buckinghamshire and Oxfordshire countryside. The adventurous cooking features modern European cuisine using local produce. There's also a good wine list. While it's open-plan and snug inside, visitors flock to the garden in summer. Book in advance.

GODSTOW The Trout Inn ✖ & ▮ ££
195 Godstow Rd, Lower Wolvercote, Oxford, Oxfordshire, OX2 8PN **Tel** *01865 510930*

Built in 1133 and steeped in history, the Trout Inn was where Lewis Carroll dreamt up *Alice in Wonderland*, and Colin Dextor, the creator of Inspector Morse, regularly sunk a pint. On the banks of Oxford Canal, punters enjoy passing boats and feed the fish, ducks swans and peacocks as they tuck into traditional pub grub.

GREAT MILTON Le Manoir aux Quat' Saisons ✖ ⅋ & ▮ £££££
Church Rd, Great Milton, Oxford, Oxfordshire, OX44 7PD **Tel** *01844 278881*

Acclaimed as an art gallery for the taste buds, this restaurant has a two-acre kitchen garden producing the vegetables and herbs used in their imaginatively crafted dishes. The new season milk-fed lamb is one of the specialities. Lovingly prepared picnic hampers sustain explorations around the surrounding countryside.

GREAT MISSENDEN La Petite Auberge ✖ ▮ £££
107 High St, Great Missenden, Buckinghamshire, HP16 0BB **Tel** *01494 865370*

Set in the idyllically quiet Chiltern village, La Petite Auberge is a quaint French restaurant run by a self-effacing French couple. Though the decor is modest and traditional, the impeccable authentic French cuisine more than makes up for it. The restaurant has a loyal following of locals and travellers.

KINTBURY The Dundas Arms ✖ ▮ ▮ ££
53 Station Rd, Kintbury, Berkshire, RG17 9UT **Tel** *01488 658263*

Nestled on the banks of the River Kennet and Kennet and Avon Canal, the Dundas Arms is a late 18th-century restaurant-pub. Local produce is imaginatively whipped up into creative dishes and served amid simple but effective decor. The beer and wine selections are handsome, beefed up by local Butts and West Berkshire brews.

MAIDENHEAD The Waterside Inn ✖ & ▮ ▮ £££££
The Waterside Inn, Ferry Rd, Bray, Berkshire, SL6 2AT **Tel** *01628 620691*

Boasting three Michelin stars, the crown in chef entrepreneur Michel Roux's restaurant empire is a formal establishment offering French dining at its very finest. Enjoy roasted Challandais duck with lemon, while the Thames refracts throughout this riverside gem. Finish up with indulgent digestifs in one of the summerhouses or by the fire. Open Wed–Sun.

MOULSFORD Beetle and Wedge ✖ ▮ ££
Moulsford-on-Thames, Oxfordshire, OX10 9JF **Tel** *01491 651381*

Beetle and Wedge is encircled by beautiful gardens running alongside the river immortalized in Kenneth Grahame's *The Wind in the Willows*. The relaxed Boathouse Restaurant is not to be missed during long evenings when dishes are grilled to perfection. Inside, the dining room is used exclusively for private parties. Booking ahead is a must.

OXFORD Al-Shami

25 Walton Crescent, Oxford, Oxfordshire, OX1 2JG **Tel** *01865 310066*

For those who have never explored Lebanese cuisine, Al-Shami is worth a try. Going beyond the typical vine leaves, the menu is spectacular, with prices to suit everyone's budget. Highlights are the *mohammara bil-jawz* (mixed crushed nuts, red capsicum, olive oil and spices) and charcoal grill selection. Don't miss the Lebanese wines.

OXFORD Browns

5–11 Woodstock Rd, Oxford, Oxfordshire, OX2 6HA **Tel** *01865 511995*

A branch of the booming brasserie chain, Browns is a firm favourite with business folk and weekend lunchers. The menu has recently been polished with more contemporary dishes, such as asparagus and wild mushroom risotto, to complement snacks and salads, sandwiches and steaks. Pretty seating spills out onto the pavement in summer.

OXFORD Cherwell Boathouse

Bardwell Rd, Oxford, Oxfordshire, OX2 6SR **Tel** *01865 552746*

With a riverfront location at a punting station, Cherwell Boathouse is a favourite with wine buffs and romancers. Simple, but flawless, modern European cooking is enhanced by a well-priced and famously good wine selection. Try the honed-to-perfection goat's cheese or adventurous dishes such as pan-fried pollock.

OXON Sir Charles Napier

Sprigg's Alley, nr Chinnor, Oxon, Oxfordshire, OX39 4BX **Tel** *01494 483011*

A favourite with showbiz types seeking retreat, this isolated pub-restaurant in the Chiltern hills is not easily accessed, but the stunning views make it more than worth it. The British menu is slightly pricey, but features some rare dishes. Check the restaurant website as the menu is constantly changing. Remarkable garden sculptures and paintings.

PENN STREET VILLAGE Hit or Miss Inn

Penn St Village, Penn St, Amersham, Buckinghamshire, HP7 0PX **Tel** *01494 713109*

Hit or Miss is a gastro-pub in the most traditional sense. Its location, opposite a cricket club, makes it a favourite destination for locals or walkers strolling from Penn Wood. The menu is vast, covering everything from crayfish to a reasonable set Sunday roast. Watch out for special Morris dancing, jazz events and a beer fest in July.

POTTERS BAR Paparazzi

1 Barnet Rd, Potters Bar, Hertfordshire, EN6 2QX **Tel** *01707 662623*

Paparazzi lives up to its name: national football teams, minor celebrities and anyone who wants to be seen comes to dine here. The menu is simple and Italian, with plenty of well-priced options. Although there is no formal entertainment, watch out if it's your birthday, as you're likely to be serenaded by the whole restaurant.

READING Pepe Sale

3 Queens Walk, Reading, Berkshire, RG1 7QF **Tel** *01189 597700*

A Sardinian-Italian restaurant, Pepe Sale is a stone's throw from busy Broad Street and local Hexagon Theatre. The menu offers Mediterranean specialities such as wild boar for the adventurous diner, plus dishes both traditional and unorthodox. Rustic yet minimalist decor, warm ambience and a decent wine list add to the appeal.

READING London Street Brasserie

2–4 London St, Reading, Berkshire, RG1 4SE **Tel** *01189 505036*

Reading prides itself on being an antidote to generic, conveyor-belt eateries. Waiting staff wear black, but are allowed to express individuality in no set uniform. The menu mixes British, French and Mediterranean cuisine, yet manages to avoid becoming confusing, while the contemporary decor makes this brasserie a romantic dining destination.

READING L'Ortolan

Church Lane, Shinfield, Reading, Berkshire, RG2 9BY **Tel** *01189 888500*

One of the best restaurants in the country, this British and French eatery is an absolute pleasure. Its lovely setting in luxurious gardens is complemented by the terrace and conservatory. Wine-tasting evenings emphasize their focus on fine drinking as well as dining. Set lunches and menus are tasty and affordable.

REED The Cabinet at Reed

The Cabinet, High St, Reed, nr Royston, Hertfordshire, SG8 8AH **Tel** *01763 848366*

Boasting a unique blend of English, French and transatlantic fare, the Cabinet is a rising star in the quiet Hertfordshire countryside. It is housed in a 16th-century building, with a pleasant decor comprising beamed ceilings and leather chairs. Outside, it is stunning with a large al fresco dining area and a wood-burning rotisserie.

SPEEN The Old Plow Bistro & Restaurant

Flowers Bottom Lane, Speen, Buckinghamshire, HP27 0PZ **Tel** *01494 488300*

A 17th-century building set in the heart of the Chiltern countryside, Old Plow is famed for a very high quality of modern eclectic cuisine. Specialities are French dishes with wonderful sauces, and seafood which arrives direct from the Devon coast. Friendly service to match the excellent standards of this bistro-restaurant. Closed Sun, Mon.

STREATLEY The Swan at Streatley

Streatley-on-Thames, Berkshire, RG8 9HR **Tel** *01491 878800*

The restaurant at this efficient business and leisure hotel serves carefully prepared dishes with the best local produce. The star attraction on the menu is the roast breast of Gressingham duck with citrus fruits. Adjourn from the Riverside Terrace to the Drawing Room Bar for a coffee or liqueur for the full dining experience.

THAME The Thatch
29–30 Lower High St, Thame, Oxfordshire, OX9 2AA **Tel** *01844 214340*

Set in a 16th-century half-timbered building, the Thatch offers a well-considered menu, which makes excellent use of seasonal and ethically produced ingredients. The restaurant also boasts an airy dining room, open fires and a secluded patio garden. The attentive staff ensure eating and drinking here is a relaxed affair.

THURLEIGH The Jackal
3 High St, Thurleigh, Bedfordshire, MK44 2DB **Tel** *01234 771293*

Recently taken over and revitalized, this pub-restaurant offers outstanding and award-winning bistro-style food. With a huge outdoor garden and an inviting interior filled with sofas and easy chairs, it's the perfect place to spend an evening or lunch time. The home-made sticky toffee pudding is fast becoming famous across the district.

WINDSOR Al Fassia
27 St Leonards Rd, Windsor, Berkshire, SL4 3BP **Tel** *01753 855370*

Shining out among the traditional Windsor restaurants, Al Fassia serves a host of North African delights. The caring concern of a family-run business is matched with a strictly professional attention to detail. The fluffy, melt-in-the-mouth couscous is well worth a try. Some specialities must be ordered a couple of days ahead.

WINDSOR Mango Lounge
9 Datchet Rd, Windsor, Berkshire, SL4 1QB **Tel** *01753 855576*

With views across to Windsor Castle, this is a stylish and contemporary Indian restaurant. The innovative menu reflects the entire Indian sub-continent, including Goan, Bengali, Gujarati and Rajasthani influences. Try the king prawn moilee, cooked in a coconut and curry leaf sauce, or the Karai chicken, flavoured with chilli flakes and cumin.

WOBURN Paris House
Woburn Park, Woburn, Bedfordshire, MK17 9QP **Tel** *01525 290692*

A mock-Tudor building set in the grounds of Woburn Abbey, Paris House is a fancy, but friendly, restaurant serving contemporary French cuisine. Varied menus range from gastronomic to special occasions (such as *Phantom of the Opera* evenings) to fine à la carte choices. Don't miss the wonderfully dripping hot raspberry soufflé.

WOODSTOCK The Feathers Hotel
Market St, Woodstock, Oxfordshire, OX20 1SX **Tel** *01993 812291*

Situated next to historic landmarks such as Blenheim Palace and the Oxford University's "dreaming spires", the Feathers successfully combines modern cuisine with traditional dishes. Originally seven separate 17th-century houses, the building has a cosy and charismatic interior, with roasting log fires and interesting antique furniture.

WESSEX

AVEBURY The Circle Restaurant
High St, Avebury, Marlborough, Wiltshire, SN8 1RF **Tel** *01672 539514*

Vegetarians and wholefood fans rave about this counter-service restaurant beside the ancient stone circle. Using local products, they serve up wonderful home-made soups and organic teas – all at an extremely reasonable price. It's a perfect place to allow the wonder of Avebury stone circle to properly sink in, along with their nutritious flapjacks.

BATH Hole in the Wall
16 George St, Bath, Somerset, BA1 2EN **Tel** *01225 425242*

With probably the best menu in Bath, this vaulted restaurant has been refurbished to bring sleek minimalism to dazzling period features. The old-fashioned service and subdued atmosphere merely adds to its glamour. The contemporary British cuisine, with a French flair, is superb. Don't miss the buttered cabbage.

BATH Moon and Sixpence
6A Broad St, Bath, Somerset, BA1 5LJ **Tel** *01225 460962*

A well-kept secret, Moon and Sixpence is a favourite with locals and discerning visitors. Slightly hidden up a cobbled path, it offers quiet dining right in the bustling city centre. The reasonably priced food is loosely termed modern-international. Particularly pleasant in summer when table service is provided in the downstairs conservatory.

BATH The Bath Priory
Weston Road, Bath, Somerset, BA1 2XT **Tel** *01225 331922*

Not the original Priory, this top-notch establishment stands in a vast 19th-century Bath property, surrounded by four acres of award-winning gardens. Chef Michael Caines has two Michelin stars and is renowned for his innovative modern-European cuisine. Tasting and seasonal menus are available.

BEAMINSTER Bridge House Hotel
Prout Bridge, Beaminster, Dorset, DT8 3AY **Tel** *01308 862200*

A few minutes from the Dorset coast, among beautiful countryside, this ancient clergy makes a great refreshment break. Local produce is transformed into dishes that change daily, but are likely to include fresh scallops or their speciality – organic pork, chicken and lamb. An additional brasserie serves French-inspired fare at slightly lower prices.

Key to Price Guide *see p608* **Key to Symbols** *see back cover flap*

BISHOPSTON The Barn Restaurant

The Annexe Courtyard, Seymour Rd, Bishopston, Bristol, BS7 9EQ **Tel** *01179 049996*

Steeped in history, this inviting family-run establishment is housed in a 17th-century converted barn. While the interior exudes period charm, traditional English dishes are presented in a stylish contemporary way. The ingredients, too, are served with a culinary twist, such as special apple cider sauce.

BOURNEMOUTH Chez Fred

10 Seamoor Rd, Westbourne, Bournemouth, Dorset, BH4 9AN **Tel** *01202 761023*

The only place to eat fish and chips by the seaside, Chez Fred is famous for its interpretation of the national delicacy as well as mouthwatering puddings. Quintessentially British, the setting of this family-run eatery is welcoming and the atmosphere children-friendly and lively, with competitions to win extra portions of chips.

BRADFORD-ON-AVON Woolley Grange

Woolley Green, Bradford-on-Avon, Wiltshire, BA15 1TX **Tel** *01225 864705*

This intriguing 17th-century Jacobean manor house, built of Bath stone, is beautifully surrounded by 14 acres of leafy grounds. The extensive menu features everything from children's food to fine international cuisine using locally sourced produce. A casual, cosy atmosphere prevails in the dining room decorated with Oriental rugs and antiques.

BRISTOL Howards Restaurant

1a Avon Crescent, Hotwells, Bristol, BS1 6XQ **Tel** *01179 262921*

Beautifully set in a Georgian waterside building, Howards offers an extensive, modern French menu with a well-considered accompanying wine list, all at very reasonable prices. The main dining room has delightful views over the harbour below. Staff are famously polite and attentive.

BRISTOL Riverstation

The Grove, Bristol, BS1 4RB **Tel** *01179 144434*

Formerly a harbourside police station left in decline, Riverstation has fully exploited its potential to become one of the city's top restaurants offering modern European cuisine. Of its two floors, the dock floor has a bar and kitchen which is busy and buzzing all day long. The other floor is a light and airy restaurant.

COLERNE Lucknam Park

Colerne, Chippenham, Wiltshire, SN14 8AZ **Tel** *01225 742777*

Situated in a splendid country manor with hotel, spa and equestrian facilities, the restaurant is a suitably posh addition. The menu includes specialities such as pot-roast pork with pan-fried foie gras and caramelised apple. The hotel is steeped heavily in tradition and the dress code is casual but smart. No children under five.

LACOCK Sign of the Angel

Church St, Lacock, Wiltshire, SN15 2LB **Tel** *01249 730230*

The only sheep that this converted 15th-century wool merchant's house comes across now, is in the form of delicious roast lamb. The ambience is that of a quaint village restaurant, with log fires, oak panelling, low beams and squeaky floorboards, all teeming with history and character. The friendly, informal staff serve stellar steak and kidney pie.

MAIDEN NEWTON Le Petit Canard

Dorchester Road, Maiden Newton, Dorchester, DT2 0BE **Tel** *01300 320536*

Enjoy fine dining at this Michelin-listed, AA Rosette restaurant. Their success is reflected in the deliciously unique dishes such as the loin fillet of local venison with redcurrant sauce. The service is impeccable and the cottage environment endearing.

POOLE Museum Inn

Farnham, nr Blandford Forum, Dorset, DT11 8DE **Tel** *01725 516261*

With a timber-panelled dining room, a huge inglenook fireplace, flagstoned floors and wooden tables, this is a classic English pub-restaurant. The clientele may include the hunting jet set. The weekly menu is reasonable and perfectly executed.

POOLE Storm Fish Restaurant

16 High Street, Poole, Dorset, BH15 1BP **Tel** *01202 674970*

With a rustic interior and a cosy, intimate atmosphere, Storm is perfect for a romantic dinner. Owner Pete Miles is a fisherman by day and chef by night, serving up the freshest produce in what is reputedly Poole's finest seafood restaurant. Desserts are home-made and the "Piggies' Platter" allows those with a sweet tooth to mix and match.

SALISBURY Da Vinci

68 Castle St, Salisbury, Wiltshire, SP1 3TS **Tel** *01722 328402*

This Italian restaurant is very popular with the locals. The service is friendly and efficient, and the menu includes a number of tried-and-tested classics. Opt for one of the many delectable pasta dishes or the fillet steak with *paesana* sauce. The locally sourced veal is equally tempting.

SANDBANKS La Roche

The Haven, Banks Rd, Sandbanks, Dorset, BH13 7QL **Tel** *01202 707333*

Perched at the very tip of the exclusive Sandbanks peninsula with breathtaking views across the bay, this glass-fronted dining room provides a stylish backdrop for a showcase of local fish and seafood. Luxurious ingredients and modern flavours are expertly coordinated without over-indulgence. Popular, so book early.

STON EASTON Cedar Tree
Ston Easton Park Hotel, Ston Easton, nr Bath, Somerset, BA3 4DF **Tel** *01761 241631*

Overlooking the River Nor and Ston Easton Park's beautiful gardens, this Georgian restaurant harks back to a bygone era. The food, however, is modern British, with European influences, made with fresh local produce. Open to both residential and non-residential hotel guests.

STURMINSTER NEWTON Plumber Manor
Sturminster Newton, Dorset, DT10 2AF **Tel** *01258 472507*

In the middle of Thomas Hardy's "Vale of Little Dairies" and in the centre of a triangle of charming country towns, this family-run country house and restaurant is an idyllic stopping point. Portraits adorn the walls and friendly Labradors greet guests as they come to enjoy fine food, particularly fish as well as delightful desserts.

SWANAGE Cauldron Bistro
5 High St, Swanage, Dorset, BH19 2LN **Tel** *01929 422671*

Quality ingredients fresh from the sea have long been the secret to the success of this town-centre restaurant close to the quay, with French posters adding to the classic bistro atmosphere. Firm, juicy scallops are heavenly, whether served with lemon, garlic and balsamic or as a classic *coquilles* St Jacques. Invigorate the palate with the ginger ice cream.

TAUNTON Castle Hotel
Castle Green, Taunton, Somerset, TA1 1NF **Tel** *01823 272671*

Once a Norman fortress, this hotel has been welcoming travellers since the 12th century, and has been run by the same family for the last half-century. While the antiquated interior is preserved, the food is the main focus in the restaurant. The steamed oxtail pudding is superb, or you can try the reasonably priced Great British classics menu.

WARMINSTER The Mulberry Restaurant
Bishopstrow House, Warminster, Wiltshire, BA12 9HH **Tel** *01985 212312*

Named after a tree in Bishopstrow House's beautiful grounds, golden-yellow Mulberry Restaurant is gracious with a Georgian feel. It may look old and rambling but its clientele is young. Enjoy light lunches and dinners overlooking acres of land and opt for the set meals. Outstanding value and good-quality food.

WEST BAY Riverside
West Bay, Bridport, Dorset, DT6 4EZ **Tel** *01308 422011*

This restaurant boasts wonderful service, superb food and a festive atmosphere indoors. Its position as one of the best fish restaurants in the Southwest is quite an achievement, since most coastal places serve seafood. The langoustines with mayonnaise or char-grilled mackerel with chips are heavenly.

WEST BEXINGTON Manor Hotel
Beach Rd, West Bexington, Dorchester, Dorset, DT2 9DF **Tel** *01308 897785*

Just when you think you've taken one coastal path too far, you'll hit upon this gorgeous old stone inn. The restaurant serves a range of delicious dishes, while the daily-changing menu features local produce and seafood. The Cellar Bar offers a selection of wines from around the world. Walk off the burn later with a jaunt to Chesil beach.

WILTSHIRE The Compasses Inn
Lower Chicksgrove, Tisbury SP3 6NB **Tel** *01722 714318*

The Compasses Inn is situated in a designated area of outstanding natural beauty. This superbly run restaurant is housed in a traditional thatched cottage and has a pleasant, relaxed atmosphere. The award-winning imaginative English and modern European menu is complimented by a good choice of wines and friendly service.

YEOVIL Little Barwick House
Little Barwick House, Barwick, Yeovil, Somerset, BA22 9TD **Tel** *01935 423902*

Located right on the Devon and Somerset border, this idyllic family-run hotel is a great place to stop for food while touring each county's gorgeous scenery. The decor is elegantly minimalistic, to let you focus on the fine British food, such as the celebrated roast guinea fowl with wild mushroom risotto. Children over five years welcome.

DEVON AND CORNWALL

AVONWICK Avon Inn
Avonwick South Brent, Devon, TQ10 9NB **Tel** *01364 73475*

On the banks of the Avon, this dining pub owned by Dennis and Debbie is a perfect respite during a river walk. English food is prepared with a Continental twist. Specialities include the steak and ale pie and the whole roast pork hock. Enjoy fine wines or real ales. Friendly pub quiz on Mondays.

BARNSTAPLE The Restaurant at Broomhill
Broomhill Art Hotel, Muddiford Rd, Barnstaple, Devon, EX31 4EX **Tel** *01271 850262*

Part of an intriguing sculpture garden art gallery and hotel, this restaurant provides a three-course gourmet lunch that can last the entire afternoon, and even push on late into the evening. Food is cheap and top quality, and they make a strong effort to use local and organic produce. Impromptu jazz concerts create a convivial ambience.

Key to Price Guide *see p608* **Key to Symbols** *see back cover flap*

BIGBURY Oyster Shack

Milburn Orchard Farm, Stakes Hill, Bigbury, Devon, TQ7 4BE Tel 01548 810876

The name suggests that Oyster Shack is little more than a shack with a tarpaulin, but the front remains secondary to the unmissable food served here. The main draw is the ultra-fresh seafood: local mussels and oysters, pan-fried sardines, potted shrimp, shell-on prawns or whatever the catch of the day might be. Booking is essential.

CHAGFORD 22 Mill Street

22 Mill St, Chagford, Devon, TQ13 8AW Tel 01647 432244

Nestled behind a cream-and-green shop front, this modern European restaurant lies on a street of attractive old town houses. The atmosphere is relaxing, welcoming and unintimidating. Attention to detail, clear flavours and attractive presentation make the place worth its slightly high prices. Savour the wide-ranging wine list too.

CHAGFORD Gidleigh Park

Gidleigh Park, Chagford Devon, TQ13 8HH Tel 01647 432367

Officially one of the best restaurants this country has to offer, Gidleigh Park has won several awards and accolades. The attention to detail is what sets it apart. Menus change according to the season, but expect fine quality whatever the month. The wine choice is also among the nation's best. Perfect for special occasions.

DARTINGTON Cott Inn

Dartington, Totnes, Devon, TQ9 6HE Tel 01803 863777

Charming Cott Inn is a 14th-century restaurant-with-rooms with all the antiquated extras: exposed beams, open fireplace, horse brasses, soft lights. The restaurant has cosy cushioned pews, wall lanterns and a very reasonable menu, while the bar is ideal for the occasional a sing-along and to watch Friday night morris dancers.

DARTMOUTH The New Angel

2 South Embankment, Dartmouth, Devon, TQ6 9BH Tel 01803 839425

Formerly called Carved Angel, this restaurant takes its new name from its present Michelin-starred owner. Unlike formal, old-fashioned dining rooms, it welcomes the entire family, except dogs, in an unpretentious environment. No fixed-price menus, just individually priced dishes. Get there early for 8.30am coffee, croissants and cooked breakfast.

DODDISCOMBSLEIGH The Nobody Inn

Doddiscombsleigh, nr Exeter, Devon, EX6 7PS Tel 01647 252394

A 16th-century country inn set in the rolling Devon countryside, Nobody Inn was renamed after an unfortunate incident with a deceased landlord. Enjoy the traditional interior and fresh local produce as well as its imaginative wine and whisky list, comprehensive selection of local cheeses and creative cooking. Unspoilt old-world charm.

EXETER Thai Orchid

5 Cathedral Yard, Exeter, Devon, EX1 1HJ Tel 01392 214215

Very friendly and welcoming service greets you as soon as you step inside this pleasing Oriental establishment. Authentic Thai cuisine is on offer in the 16th-century building, where the stone-masons who built Exeter's glorious cathedral originally boarded. Fresh orchids on each table are a thoughtful finishing touch.

HONITON Combe House Hotel and Restaurant

Gittisham, Devon, EX14 3AD Tel 01404 540400

This restaurant has a deserved reputation for fine food and friendly, dedicated service. Choose from select cuts of meat and game in season or locally caught fish, all prepared by a Master Chef of Britain award winner. All vegetables are sourced from the restaurant's kitchen garden. Good wine selection.

KINGSBRIDGE Buckland-Tout-Saints Hotel

Goveton, Kingsbridge, Devon, TQ7 2DS Tel 01548 853055

Set in a wonderful 1690 Grade II listed residence in the middle of lush woodland countryside, Buckland-Tout-Saints is a magnificent manor house from Queen Anne's time, with plenty of character. Winner of a double AA Rosette Award, the restaurant serves British cuisine with a Scottish influence. Don't miss the luxury wines.

LEWDOWN Lewtrenchard Manor

Lewdown, Okehampton, Devon, EX20 4PN Tel 01566 783222

Mentioned in the *Domesday Book* of 1086, this impressive manor was once a popular hangout of knights. Even today, diners are treated to generous helpings of well-cooked, wholesome modern English food. An excellently stocked cellar features modestly-priced bottles from every region in the world.

LIFTON The Arundell Arms Hotel

Fore St, Lifton, Devon, PL16 0AA Tel 01566 784666

The Arundell Arms serves as an escape from the hustle and bustle. The lovely surrounding countryside provides activities such as fishing, riding, walking and golf. The restaurant serves fixed-price menus featuring local game and fish, created by two of Britain's official master chefs. Bar snacks are also available for lunch or dinner.

LYNMOUTH The Rising Sun

Harbourside, Lynmouth, Devon, EX35 6EG Tel 01598 753223

Percy Bysshe Shelley stayed at this 14th-century thatched smugglers' inn that overlooks a picturesque harbour and Lynmouth Bay. Lobster literally lands at their door, as well as local Exmoor game and salmon fished from the River Lyn. There are also plenty of other offerings served in the romantic candlelit, oak-panelled dining room.

MARLDON Church House Inn

Village Rd, Marldon, Devon, TQ3 1SL **Tel** *01803 558279*

Located in the centre of the village, delightful Church House Inn is as old as the 14th-century church beside it. The restaurant, renowned for its traditional menu with a Mediterranean twist, serves as the centre of the local community. A perfect slice of quintessential countryside life comes with a full-bodied pint.

MOUSEHOLE Old Coastguard Hotel

Mousehole, Penzance, Cornwall, TR19 6PR **Tel** *01736 731222*

As the name suggests, this restaurant-hotel is right on the tip of the coast, with some absolutely beautiful views from the rooms and restaurant. The menu is modern and dishes are made to perfection. Don't miss the kippers and poached egg for breakfast. The "Real Fishy Feast", with sea bass and roasted tomatoes, is outstanding.

PADSTOW The Seafood Restaurant

Riverside, Padstow, Cornwall, PL28 8BY **Tel** *01841 532700*

Much more special than its matter-of-fact name, this fish and shellfish restaurant has been around since 1975. Just across the quay from the lobster boats and trawlers, it procures much of the fish literally straight off the boats. Expertly cooked by the chef, Rick Stein, seafood is fresh and succulent.

PENZANCE Bay Restaurant

Britons Hill, Penzance, Cornwall, TR18 3AE **Tel** *01736 366890*

This stylish two AA Rosette restaurant has an outdoor deck that opens out in summer for magnificent views across Mount's Bay and over the rooftops to Penzance Harbour. Generous and creative European cuisine is served by knowledgeable staff. Local fish, vegetables and herbs are complemented by excellent Cornish wine.

PENZANCE Harris's

46 New St, Penzance, Cornwall, TR18 2LZ **Tel** *01736 364408*

Run by the Harris family for over 30 years, this small restaurant wins acclaim for freshly made dishes served with local produce and fish from nearby Newlyn market. The menu highlights modern British cuisine with an excellent range of seafood dishes. The crab Florentine comes highly recommended.

POLPERRO Kitchen

The Coombes, Polperro, Cornwall, PL13 2RQ **Tel** *01503 272780*

This delightful little restaurant serves mainly home-made food. Bread is baked daily and ice cream is made nearby. Delicious fish is garnered from Cornish day boats, with the exception of the odd exotic dish. The atmosphere is cosy, and while service is unobtrusive during the meal, diners can often go into the kitchen for a chat and tour afterwards. Lunch only.

PORT ISAAC Slipway Hotel and Seafood Restaurant

The Habour Front, Port Isaac, Cornwall, PL29 3RH **Tel** *01208 880264*

Recently taken over by new owners, this quaint fish restaurant offers a perfect sample of Cornish fishy fare in season. Though there's no live music inside, diners can hear the tuneful noise of fisherman singing in the forecourt, or else a local live band. Reasonably-priced and consistently good, with a 40-plus wine list to boot.

SALCOMBE Winking Prawn

Waterfront Brasserie and Garden, North Sands, Salcombe, Devon, **Tel** *01548 842326*

In a thickly wooded valley, this little place appears beside an empty beach. There's an evening barbecue of steak and king prawns that can be taken outside on fine days. When it rains, the restaurant offers bowls of soup and *fruits de mer*. This beach-side restaurant is a real holiday treat.

ST IVES Tate Café and Restaurant

Porthmeor Beach, St Ives, Cornwall, TR26 1TG **Tel** *01736 796226*

Enjoy the views over the old town of St Ives and Porthmeor Beach from this art-gallery brasserie while tucking into wholefood dishes made from produce created by Cornish growers and suppliers where possible. They stock and sell premium Cornish goods, ranging from cheese to fish, potatoes to ice cream and cider to wine.

ST IVES Alba

Old Lifeboat House, Wharf Rd, St Ives, Cornwall, TR26 1LF **Tel** *01736 797222*

With spectacular views of the bay, mesmerizing Alba is housed in the old lifeboat building. Equally breathtaking is the double AA Rosette cuisine, predominantly seafood, all sourced locally. The accompanying wine list is as impressive. The restaurant is split between two floors.

ST MAWES Hotel Tresanton

27 Lower Castle Rd, St Mawes, Cornwall, TR2 5DR **Tel** *01326 270055*

Situated at the edge of the unspoiled village of St Mawes, the Tresanton was created in the 1940s as a yachtsmen's club. Its unique interior comprises old houses on different levels. The lovely restaurant has pretty views of the sea, looking towards St Anthony's Lighthouse. The food is exquisite and benefits from the local seafood easily available.

SUMMERCOURT Viners

Carvynick, Summercourt, Cornwall, TR8 5AF **Tel** *01872 510544*

A former pub, this bar and restaurant is run by Kevin Viner, the first-ever chef in Cornwall to win a Michelin star. The interior has been tranformed with flair. Moving from his former fine dining, the owner-chef strives to keep the dishes simple. The emphasis is on the stand-alone strength of first-rate local fish and shellfish, Cornish lamb and beef.

TAVISTOCK The Horn of Plenty 🕭🖳 £££££
Gulworthy, Tavistock, Devon, PL19 8JD Tel 01822 832528

With stunning views over the tranquil Tamar Valley near Tavistock in Devon, this inviting country-house hotel is set in five acres of immaculate gardens and wild orchards. The award-winning restaurant excels itself under the baton of its executive head chef, TV chef Peter Gorton. Children welcome at lunchtimes.

TOTNES Willow 🕭🎵🖳 ££
87 High St, Totnes, Devon, TQ9 5PB Tel 01803 862605

Willow holds the crown in the area for vegetarian cuisine, offering low-priced wholesome dishes and an organic wine list amid cheerful decor with a pretty courtyard at the back. The staff are helpful, and welcoming towards children. Wednesdays are Curry Nights and music sessions on Fridays are regularly jammed, so it's worth booking ahead of time.

TORQUAY Mulberry House 🍽🕭🖳🕭 £££
1 Scarborough Rd, Torquay, Devon, TQ2 5UJ Tel 01803 213639

A calm and soothing atmosphere exudes at this restaurant-with-rooms. The menu changes frequently and all dishes are home-made to complement local seasonal produce. The bread and cakes are remarkable. It also serves traditional Victorian meals using locally sourced, fresh produce.

TREBURLEY Springer Spaniel 🕭🖳🕭 ££
Treburley, nr Launceston, Cornwall, PL15 9NS Tel 01579 370424

Picturesque, award-winning Springer Spaniel is a country-food pub, set in an attractive 18th-century beamed building. The staff are friendly and laid-back, and an easy-going ambience prevails throughout. The menu changes frequently, reflecting the owner's desire to use local produce including home-grown vegetables and salads.

VIRGINSTOW Percy's 🕭🖳 £££££
Coombeshead Estate, Virginstow, Devon, EX21 5EA Tel 01409 211236

Award-winning dishes burst with colour and flavour at this restaurant and hotel. The kitchen, supervised by one of Devon's top female chefs, Tina Bricknell-Webb, creates consistently good contemporary country cuisine, with a wine selection to match. The comfortable lounges are available for private hire.

THE HEART OF ENGLAND

ANSLOW The Burnt Gate 🕭🕭 ££
59 Hopley Rd, Anslow, Burton upon Trent, Staffordshire, DE13 9PY Tel 01283 563664

Friendly pub and restaurant with a homely decor featuring dark wood beams and an open coal fire. This award-winning eatery serves traditional dishes made with fresh, local produce, and is well known for steak, gammon, poultry, seasonal game and a variety of seafood. Also has dedicated menus for vegetarians and coeliacs.

BIRMINGHAM Chez Jules 🕭 £
5a Ethel St, Birmingham, B2 4BG Tel 0121 633 4664

Located in the heart of Birmingham, this busy French bistro offers simple, tasty food at surprisingly low prices. The menu includes old favourites such as *coq au vin*, moules marinières (mussels in white wine and garlic), crème brûlée and chocolate mousse, all using produce from local markets. Relaxed and friendly atmosphere.

BIRMINGHAM Titash Balti Restaurant 🕭🕭 ££
2278 Coventry Rd, Birmingham, B26 3JR Tel 0121 722 2080

A must-try speciality here is Balti, a spicy, aromatic dish that was originally introduced by the city's large Kashmiri Pakistani community, and is cooked in a wok-like pot. This winner of "Curry Chef of the Year" has recently been refurbished. An à la carte menu offers delicious food and dishes are accompanied by naan bread.

BIRMINGHAM Berlioz Restaurant 🕭 £££
6 Burlington Arcade, 126 New St, Birmingham, B2 4JQ Tel 0121 633 1737

Bright and airy, and with an undeniable historical grandeur, Berlioz is comfortably relaxed and offers impressive views over the New Street shopping area. The international cuisine is innovative and represents excellent value for money, especially the reasonable fixed-price dinner menu.

BIRMINGHAM The Brasserie Malmaison 🕭 £££
One Wharfside St, Birmingham, B1 1RD Tel 0121 246 5000

The Malmaison is beautifully designed and offers a traditional French brasserie dining experience with a modern British twist and plenty of charisma. The food is beautifully presented and divinely tasty, prepared with fine-quality locally sourced ingredients. Try the loin of Shropshire venison or the baked cod fillet with garlic mash.

CHELTENHAM Le Champignon Sauvage 🕭🕭🖳 £££
24–26 Suffolk Rd, Cheltenham, Gloucestershire, GL50 2AQ Tel 01242 573449

Renowned French restaurant and winner of several awards. The interior is lovingly decorated in cream, with modern art on the walls and large, comfortable chairs for an informal dining experience. The seasonal menu has a strong emphasis on local ingredients. Eel tortellini, Wiltshire pork and pigeon breast are some of the favourites here.

CHELTENHAM Le Petit Blanc
The Queen's Hotel, The Promenade, Cheltenham, Gloucestershire, GL50 1NN **Tel** *01242 266800*

Fine dining under the helm of award-winning chef Raymond Blanc. Set in an elegant Georgian building, this modern, vibrant brasserie is as well known for its cocktail bar as it is for its rich, French food. The kids menu offers a mix of haute cuisine and popular favourites such as gratinèed macaroni cheese and home-made French fries.

CHELTENHAM Off the Square
8 The Courtyard, Montpellier St, Cheltenham, Gloucestershire, GL50 1SR **Tel** *01242 227757*

A neat restaurant with a cream-and-blue decor and an alfresco terrace. The friendly waiters serve large, tasty dishes from a menu that features new, imaginative combinations every two months. The popular dessert menu offers a hot liquid chocolate pudding with home-made banana ice cream. A good choice for vegetarians.

CHIPPENHAM Bybrook Restaurant
Manor House Hotel and Golf Club, Castle Combe, nr Bath, Wiltshire, SN14 7HR **Tel** *01249 782206*

Outstanding food in a breathtaking setting in the Manor House hotel on the southern edge of the Cotswolds. Named after the Bybrook River that runs beside the hotel, this restaurant uses fresh produce from the house's kitchen garden and orchards. Stained-glass windows offer views over the Italian garden and the adjacent golf course.

COVENTRY Ryton Organic Gardens
Ryton Organic Gardens, nr Wolston, Coventry, Warwickshire, CV8 3LG **Tel** *02476 308213*

Organic restaurant run by a registered organic association. The menu features home-made dishes cooked to order, using organically grown produce from the gardens. Vegan and vegetarian meals also feature on the menu, which changes periodically.

GLOUCESTER The Fountain Inn
Westgate Street, Gloucester, Gloucestershire, GL1 2NW **Tel** *01452 522562*

With a pretty patio and delightful flower garden, this place is great for alfresco dining in the summer. Everyone is catered for, with a good mixture of mediterrannean dishes, seafood and traditional pub fare. The Sunday menu is particularly tempting.

HEREFORD Castle House
Castle St, Hereford, Herefordshire, HR1 2NW **Tel** *01432 356321*

Award-winning restaurant in the Castle House hotel. The seasonal menu here draws on fresh meat and produce delivered daily from the hotel's farm nearby. Try the Hereford prime beef and finish with a vanilla crème brûlée with cinnamon roast pear. Also hosts a cocktail bar for a pre-meal apéritif.

INGLESHAM Inglesham Forge Restaurant
Inglesham, Highworth, Swindon, Wiltshire, SN6 7QY **Tel** *01367 252298*

Welcoming restaurant set in a 15th-century forge. The decor is old fashioned, with wood-beamed ceilings. Serves a tasty range of modern English cuisine with a French influence. The specials vary from season to season, but can include anything from escargot Bourguignonne to breast of duck with morello cherries.

LEAMINGTON SPA Newbold Bar & Brasserie
18 Newbold St, Leamington Spa, Warwickshire, CV32 4HN **Tel** *01926 424667*

Atmospheric setting and friendly service make this restaurant a favourite with the pre-theatre crowd. Occupies two floors of an airy, old Georgian building near the centre of town. The à la carte menu on the upper floor serves a wide variety of mouthwatering international cuisine, while the long bar downstairs serves bar snacks.

LITTLE BEDWYN The Harrow at Little Bedwyn
Little Bedwyn, Marlborough, Wiltshire, SN8 3JP **Tel** *01672 870871*

Rated by the *Wine Spectator* as having one of the finest restaurant wine lists in the world. This Michelin-star eatery is primarily known for its extensive collection of Australian premium wines, and diners can opt for the "tasting menu with Aussie wines" meal. Also serves an à la carte menu.

LUDLOW Ego Café Bar
Quality Square, Ludlow, Shropshire, SY8 1AR **Tel** *01584 878000*

Stylish bistro in a renovated bakery, with bright furnishings and art-covered walls. Features a small, but delicious British menu and a bustling outdoor patio. The cuisine draws on local produce, and ranges from guinea fowl and venison steak to roasted organic red pepper and *Dolcelatte pithivier* (a French pastry).

LUDLOW The Clive Restaurant with Rooms
Bromfield, Ludlow, Shropshire, SY8 2JR **Tel** *01584 856565*

This converted farmhouse, with 15 bedrooms, has been decorated to emphasize many of the building's original features, including whitewashed walls and wood-beamed ceilings. The seasonal menu serves high-quality British fare, using produce from the surrounding countryside. The atmosphere is warm and informal.

PAXFORD The Churchill Arms
Paxford, Chipping Campden, Gloucestershire, GL55 6XH **Tel** *01386 594000*

Restaurant with four rooms on a B&B basis, set in a small, working Cotswolds village. Offers an appetizing menu of local produce to accompany the popular real ales from local breweries. The menu is constantly updated, but dishes such as grilled fish, braised local lamb shank and poached chicken are regular favourites.

Key to Price Guide *see p608* **Key to Symbols** *see back cover flap*

ROSS-ON-WYE The Bridge Restaurant   🚩   £££

*The Bridge at Wilton, Herefordshire, HR9 6AA **Tel** 01989 562655*

Housed in a Georgian country house on the banks of the River Wye, this AA Rosette-rated restaurant attracts gourmet food enthusiasts from around the country. Head chef James Arbaune creates unique, exciting and truly imaginative modern European dishes. Rooms also available.

SALT Holly Bush Inn   🚹 🖼   ££

*Salt, nr Stafford, Staffordshire, ST18 0BX **Tel** 01889 508234*

This picturesque country inn with a large beer garden is one of England's oldest pubs. Serves award-winning food. Dishes range from green shelled mussels to home-made steak and kidney pudding, as well as pan-fried Cornish brie. Ideal for a family stop-off point.

STOW-ON-THE-WOLD The King's Arms   🚹   ££

*Market Square, Stow-on-the-Wold, Gloucestershire, GL54 1AF **Tel** 01451 830364*

A charming, 500-year-old coaching inn, which can trace its history back to 1645, when King Charles I was reported to have stayed here. The menu focuses on fresh local ingredients, including trout, Gloucester Old Spot pork and British cheeses. Has two dining areas, with log fires. Also offers accommodation on a B&B basis.

STRATFORD-UPON-AVON Marlowe's Restaurant   🚹   £££

*18 High St, Stratford-upon-Avon, Warwickshire, CV37 6AU **Tel** 01789 204999*

Two restaurants housed in an Elizabethan town house, in the heart of Stratford. Opt for the silver-service formal restaurant – perfect for business clients and posh events – or book a private party in the more informal bistro. Autographed pictures of visiting glitterati such as Vanessa Redgrave and Sir Alec Guinness line the bar.

SWINDON Pear Tree Restaurant   🚹 ♿   ££££

*Church End, Purton, Swindon, Wiltshire, SN5 4ED **Tel** 01793 772100*

AA Rosette-winning restaurant in an elegant Cotswold stone hotel on the outskirts of Purton. Has 17 luxury bedrooms and a small conservatory dining room with great views over the Marlborough Downs. Menu offers modern English cooking, including seasonal asparagus, roasted guinea fowl and delicious chocolate desserts.

TETBURY The Trouble House Inn   🚹 ♿   ££

*Cirencester Rd, Tetbury, Gloucestershire, GL8 8SG **Tel** 01666 502206*

Excellent local food in a stunning historical setting. Offers everything from the local ale to a fabulous three-course meal. Specials such as Gloucester Old Spot sausages with creamy mashed potato and onion gravy are a clear favourite. Features an atmospheric dining room with polished wooden floors, black beams and ancient fireplaces.

TITLEY The Stagg Inn & Restaurant   🚹 ♿ 🚩   £££

*Titley, Kington, Herefordshire, HR5 3RL **Tel** 01544 230221*

Small hotel and restaurant overlooking the beautiful Welsh Marshes. A well-reputed wine list accompanies its classic menu of regional English fare. Diners have a choice of eating in the bar, the non-smoking dining room or the garden. The produce, which includes organic rare breed pork and home-cured bacon, is sourced from local shops.

ULLINGSWICK Three Crowns Inn   🚹 ♿   ££

*Ullingswick, nr Hereford, Herefordshire, HR1 3JQ **Tel** 01432 820279*

An unassuming gastro-pub, with one of the best-priced menus in the area, the Three Crowns Inn serves simple British favourites. Fish and other seafood make a good showing, as does traditional Welsh fare, especially the borderland cheeses. Menu highlights include the peppered sirloin of Herefordshire beef and grilled line-caught bass.

WINCHCOMBE 5 North Street   🚹 🚩   £££

*5 North St, Winchcombe, Gloucestershire, GL54 5LH **Tel** 01242 604566*

Small, Michelin-starred restaurant, set in a picturesque village. The cosy interior features heavy wood beams, and has a cottage-like feel. Presents a tasty menu of traditional English fare with a French twist. Serves pork, crackling, stuffed cabbage and cider *jus*, as well as brill braised in red wine with bubble and squeak.

WINCHCOMBE Wesley House   🚹 🚩   £££

*Wesley House, High St, Winchcombe, Gloucestershire, GL54 5LJ **Tel** 01242 602366*

Hotel and restaurant in the old Cotswolds town of Winchcombe. The food here is simple, with an emphasis on seasonal local ingredients. Specialities to look out for include braised lamb shank and roasted duck breast. Keep some space for the delicious home-made desserts, such as the outstanding amaretti crème brûlée.

WISTANSTOW The Plough Inn   🚹 ♿   £

*Wistanstow, Craven Arms, Shropshire, SY7 8DG **Tel** 01588 673251*

Timeless village pub with a warm and welcoming ambience. The inn may look unexceptional from outside, but the menu makes it well worth the visit. A great choice for family Sunday lunches. Home-made chutneys and sauces all add to the charm. Fabulous real ale is provided by the brewery located next door.

WORCESTER King Charles II Restaurant   🚹   ££

*29 New St, Worcester, Worcestershire, WR1 2DP **Tel** 01905 22449*

Historic restaurant serving international cuisine. The decor is stylish, and features fine lace tablecloths, crystal glasses and an elegant ambience. It was from here that King Charles II escaped Cromwell's forces after his defeat in the Battle of Worcester in 1651. There is a dungeon situated in the restaurant.

EAST MIDLANDS

BAKEWELL Renaissance

Bath St, Bakewell, Derbyshire, DE45 1BX **Tel** *01629 812687*

An atractively converted barn houses this relaxed restaurant serving traditional French cuisine made from fresh local produce. Light starters such as blue cheese soufflé with leek casserole prepare the appetite for the rich and hearty main courses to follow. If there's room, try one of the original and beautifully presented desserts.

BASLOW Fischer's

Baslow Hall, Calver Rd, Baslow, Derbyshire, DE45 1RR **Tel** *01246 583259*

An award-winning restaurant, located in a popular country-house hotel on the edge of the Chatsworth estate. The Michelin-starred menu serves dishes made using the local produce; some from Chatsworth's farm shop. Venison, wild hare and spring lamb provide the seasonal highlights. Dress code is smart casual.

BECKINGHAM Black Swan

Hillside, Beckingham, Lincolnshire, LN5 0RQ **Tel** *01636 626474*

Fabulous country inn serving French and modern English cuisine. This friendly and welcoming restaurant has been winning awards for the past 20 years. Dishes are made from locally sourced produce. Favourites such as Colston Bassett Stilton make its mark on the three-course table d'hote menu. Patio dining available in summer.

BIRCH VALE The Waltzing Weasel Inn

New Mills Rd, Birch Vale, High Peak, Derbyshire, SK22 1BT **Tel** *01663 743402*

This highly acclaimed restaurant is located at the bottom of Kinder Scout, and is very popular with Ramblers, a UK-based walking association. Special gastronomic evenings are arranged through the week, and there is also a good gluten-free menu and a varied vegetarian menu. Also hosts eight panoramic en suite bedrooms.

BUCKMINSTER The Tollemache Arms

Main St, Buckminster, Lincolnshire, NG33 5SA **Tel** *01476 860007*

Country pub with restaurant and accommodation, the Tollemache Arms sits in a prime location near the market towns of Oakham, Melton Mowbray and Grantham. The smart restaurant serves a beautifully presented blend of modern and classic cuisine, such as "Grilled sea bass with basil mash and baby chorizo sausages".

CAUNTON Caunton Beck

Main St, Caunton, Newark, Nottinghamshire, NG23 6AB **Tel** *01636 636793*

Lovingly run gastro-pub in a delightfully restored 16th-century ale house. The family friendly restaurant has a welcoming ambience, and a modern European menu that is served at any time of the day. Also features a large and popular outdoor terrace in the summer.

CHESTERFIELD Buckinghams

85–87 Newbold Rd, Newbold, Chesterfield, Derbyshire, S41 7PU **Tel** *01246 201041*

Hotel and unusual restaurant, with just one table that seats up to eight diners. The chef consults with the guests before the meal, and provides a unique, "surprise" seasonal menu depending on their requirements and wishes. The setting is cosy, and the decor elegant. The hotel also offers cooking courses.

CLIPSHAM Olive Branch

Main St, Clipsham, Oakham, Rutland, LE15 7SH **Tel** *01780 410355*

A country pub, housed in three adjacent cottages that were joined in 1890 and later renovated. This delightful eatery has a reputation for fine dining and holds a Michelin star. In addition to a wide range of delicious regional dishes, the gastro-pub also offers sloe gin and damson vodka. The decor is traditional, with antique furnishings.

COLSTON BASSETT Martins Arms Inn

School Lane, Colston Bassett, Nottingham, Nottinghamshire, NG12 3FD **Tel** *01949 81361*

Well-reputed for its game and fish, not to mention the Stilton produced in the village of Colston Bassett itself. Provides a great stopping-off point in the agricultural haven of the Vale of Belvoir. The food is modern European making the most of local ingredients. A welcoming fire and comfortable sofas add to the informal ambience.

DAVENTRY Fawsley Hall

Fawsley, Daventry, Northamptonshire, NN11 3BA **Tel** *01327 892000*

Magnificent Tudor country-house hotel with a panoramic restaurant. Offers some of the best desserts in the country. The dark chocolate tart and banana ice cream warrants a visit in itself. The main courses, which include dishes such as rabbit with langoustine and bass stuffed with crab, all add to the richness. The menu changes regularly.

FOTHERINGHAY The Falcon

Fotheringhay, Northamptonshire, PE8 5HZ **Tel** *01832 226254*

Welcoming inn known as much for its selective wine list as it is for its real ales. International menu featuring pub fare as it should be served. Whole roast sea bass, char-grilled pave of lamb and sirloin steak with thyme *salmoriglio* (an Italian sauce) are some of the notable options. Log fires and eclectic decoration add to the effect.

Key to Price Guide *see p608* **Key to Symbols** *see back cover flap*

LEICESTER Sayonara Thali   🚹   ⓔ

49 Belgrave Rd, Leicester, Leicestershire, LE4 6AR **Tel** *0116 2665 888*

Popular South Indian restaurant on Leicester's Golden Mile, so-called for its gold jewellery shops. Serves thali food – curry dishes served on a large metal plate along with chapatis and deep fried bread made with plain flour. Delicious milk drinks flavoured with pistachio and cardamom are also available.

LEICESTER Alloro   🚹 ♿ 🍴   ⓔⓔ

29 Millstone Lane, Leicester, Leicestershire, LE1 5JN **Tel** *0116 291 0004*

Elegant restaurant in a converted factory; the menus here present a wide range of traditional Italian dishes including seafood risotto and fillet steak. The two-course lunch and dinner specials are good value and there is a bar area where you can enjoy a coffee after dinner.

LEICESTER Entropy   🚹 🎵 ♿   ⓔⓔ

3 Dover St, Leicester, Leicestershire, LE1 6PW **Tel** *0116 254 8530*

Modern cuisine in a contemporary setting. Serves an updated version of classical French fare. Terrine of chicken and leek is offered along with Puy lentils; pigeon *pot au feu* with tarragon ravioli; and *foie gras* sauce fillet of local beef with sautéed ratte potatoes. Closed on Sunday.

LEICESTER The Case   🚹 🍴   ⓔⓔ

4–6 Hotel St, St Martins, Leicester, Leicestershire, LE1 5AW **Tel** *0116 251 7675*

A modern European menu with an English twist. This trendy restaurant has built a reputation for innovative and imaginative cuisine. Specials include grilled lemon sole with prawn, lemon and caper brown butter, and Cajun-spiced monkfish on bubble and squeak. Features wine-tasting evenings.

LINCOLN Jews House   🚹 🍴   ⓔⓔ

15 The Strait, Lincoln, Lincolnshire, LN2 1JD **Tel** *01522 524851*

Reputedly Lincoln's oldest building, this l2th-century, Jewish merchant's house is also the town's most famous restaurant. Located beside the town's cathedral, the venue is small, cosy and exclusive; advance booking is recommended. A well-stocked wine cellar accompanies a menu featuring a mix of British and French cuisines.

LINCOLN Lea Gate Inn   🚹 ♿   ⓔⓔ

Leagate Rd, Conningsby, Lincolnshire, LN4 4RS **Tel** *01526 342370*

Built in the mid-16th century, this former fen guide house is now a friendly pub with rooms. Many of its period features, including beam ceilings and inglenook fireplaces, have been retained. Offers traditional specialities such as steak and kidney pie and Lincolnshire sausages with mash. Also has a children's playground.

MATLOCK Red House   🍴   ⓔⓔⓔ

Old Rd, Darley Dale, Matlock, Derbyshire, DE4 2ER **Tel** *01629 734854*

Country-house hotel with just ten bedrooms. This small, AA Rosette-awarded restaurant is well reputed in Derbyshire for its panoramic dining room and home-made cuisine. Locally sourced ingredients create such dishes as baked duck with red cabbage and fillet of venison with red wine *jus*. The dress code is smart casual.

MELTON MOWBRAY The Gringling Gibbons   🚹   ⓔⓔⓔ

Stapleford Park, nr Melton Mowbray, Leicestershire, LE14 2EF **Tel** *01572 787015*

A highly-renowned restaurant, set in a tranquil country hotel and spa. The menu is traditionally English with an emphasis on fish, including seared turbot with braised baby fennel and roast John Dory with smoked eel. Also offers a children's menu. Smart casual attire is requested in the restaurant.

MELTON MOWBRAY The Tollemache Arms   🚹 🍴   ⓔⓔⓔ

48 Main St, Buckminster, nr Melton Mowbray, NG33 5SA **Tel** *01476 860007*

Country gastro-pub with rooms. This non-smoking inn is a modern, friendly dining venue, located on the outskirts of town. The menu is traditional, made with fresh local produce. Features specialities such as pan-fried pigeon breast with onion marmalade and calves' liver with sauté potatoes and tomato fondue. The desserts are also worth trying.

NEWHAVEN Carriages Italian Restaurant   🚹 ♿   ⓔⓔⓔ

Newhaven, nr Hartingdon, Buxton, Derbyshire, SK17 0DU **Tel** *01298 84528*

Heartwarming Italian welcome followed by an appetizing variety of traditional Sicilian cuisine and fresh seafood. The decor features two railway carriages bedecked with velvet armchairs and period style table lamps. Favourites include *saltimbocca alla Romana* (veal medallions) and *filetto al Dolcelatte* (fillet steaks with blue cheeses and port).

NEWTON-LINFORD Gibson's Grey Lady   🚹   ⓔⓔⓔ

Sharpley Hill, Newtown Linford, Leicestershire, LE6 0AH **Tel** *01530 243558*

Scenic restaurant set in a quaint thatched cottage. This charming eatery prides itself on using the freshest ingredients for preparing its dishes. House specialities include steak, braised shank of lamb and grilled Dover sole. Also features a delightful selection of home-made chocolate desserts. An idyllic, relaxing spot.

NORTH KILWORTH Wordsworth Restaurant   🚹 ♿   ⓔⓔⓔⓔ

Lutterworth Rd, N Kilworth, Leicestershire, LE17 6JE **Tel** *01858 880058*

This elegant restaurant is located in the Kilworth House Hotel, and provides an attractive setting for an evening meal. The classy interior features glittering chandeliers, a domed ceiling and stained-glass windows. Treats such as sweetbread salad with grape compote and white gazpacho with pepper jelly are on offer.

NORTHAMPTON The New French Partridge

Horton, Northampton, Northamptonshire, NN7 2AP **Tel** *01604 870033*

Stylish country dining in an acclaimed restaurant-with-rooms. Offers an innovative array of classic dishes. Braised belly of pork comes with sautéed artichoke hearts and ginger liqueur, while red mullet is accompanied by scallop and salmon roulade, mussel and saffron broth, and poached crayfish.

NOTTINGHAM French Living

27 King St, Nottingham, Nottinghamshire, NG1 2AY **Tel** *0115 958 5885*

Presenting an authentic taste of France in Nottingham, this delightful restaurant draws its set, seasonal menus from the best classic French cuisine. Look out for crisp, fruity desserts in summer and hot vegetable soups in winter. The red-brick cellar and scent of freshly-brewed coffee all add to the effect.

NOTTINGHAM Hart's

1 Standard Court, Park Row, Nottingham, Nottinghamshire, NG1 6GN **Tel** *0115 911 0666*

Impressive hotel and restaurant, well known for its fantastic British cooking. Food is sourced locally, but given an international twist, which produces such dishes as honey-glazed Gressingham duck breast with pak choi. Fabulous desserts include white chocolate parfait with mixed berries and espresso parfait with amaretto sabayon.

NOTTINGHAM Ye Olde Trip to Jerusalem

Brewhouse Yard, Nottingham, Nottinghamshire, NG1 6AD **Tel** *0115 947 3171*

With ancient cellar rooms and engravings on the walls, the atmosphere of Britain's oldest pub doesn't disappoint. The food is typical pub fare with a strong local influence. Ploughman's salad and chicken tikka masala make an appearance, as does Stilton and vegetable crumble and rump steak.

NOTTINGHAM World Service

Newdigate House, Castlegate, Nottingham, Nottinghamshire, NG1 6AF **Tel** *01158 475587*

An award-winning restaurant, this eatery has fast gained a reputation for serving outstanding local produce with an Eastern twist. Organic salmon comes with beetroot and orange salsa, while fried monkfish tail is accompanied with a curry sauce. The bar provides the perfect setting for a pre-meal drink.

PLUMTREE Perkins

Old Railway Station, Plumtree, Nottingham, Nottinghamshire, NG12 5NA **Tel** *0115 937 3695*

Friendly restaurant and bar, occupying a converted, late 19th-century village station. The main restaurant extends into a conservatory and garden patio. The seasonal menu changes every four weeks, and features everything from leek and rosemary soup to local Clipston fillet steak.

STAMFORD Berritos

1–2 Castle St, Stamford, Lincolnshire, PE9 2RA **Tel** *01780 762739*

Stylish restaurant occupying an elegant 17th-century, stone building in Stamford's medieval town centre. The terrace seating overlooks Wellend River, home to weeping willows, oak trees and varied wildfowl and bird life. The menu features traditional American fare. Ideal for nature lovers.

STONY STRATFORD Calcutta Brasserie

7 St Paul's Court, High St, Stony Stratford, Buckinghamshire, MK11 1LJ **Tel** *01908 566577*

Outlandish Indian restaurant in a converted chapel. The building's original 200-year-old panelling and a copy of the Michelangelo fresco, *The Creation* from the Sistine Chapel, have been retained as part of the decor. Dining here has a slightly surreal feel as a result, but the modern food and friendly service add to the fun. Good vegetarian choice.

WINTERINGHAM Winteringham Fields

Winteringham, Lincolnshire, DN15 9PF **Tel** *01724 733096*

Gastronomic hotspot in a rambling old 16th-century manor house hotel, beautifully set in a peaceful country village. With five AA Rosettes, the award-winning menu doesn't disappoint. Try the six-course surprise menu for the region's and season's best cuisine. A wide variety of seafood, poultry, game and delicious desserts.

LANCASHIRE AND THE LAKES

AMBLESIDE Rothay Manor Hotel and Restaurant

Rothay Bridge, Ambleside, Cumbria, LA22 0EH **Tel** *01539 433605*

Renowned for its afternoon teas, this comfortable, family-run hotel and restaurant offers outstanding service. The smoked salmon and breast of guinea fowl served with wild mushrooms, asparagus and champagne and cream sauce are among the tempting dishes offered.

AMBLESIDE Drunken Duck Inn

Barngates, Ambleside, Cumbria, LA22 0NG **Tel** *0153 9436347*

Oak beams and open log fires create a traditional setting in this 400-year-old inn. Serves imaginative dishes in a relaxed and informal atmosphere. The varied menu features specialities such as smoked haddock and pan-fried monkfish with sautéed baby leeks. Guests can also sample the delicious home-brewed beers.

Key to Price Guide *see p608* **Key to Symbols** *see back cover flap*

AMBLESIDE The Samling

Ambleside Rd, Ambleside, Cumbria, LA23 1LR **Tel** *015394 31922*

This delightful, award-winning restaurant offers dining in unashamed comfort. Line-caught sea bass, hand-dived scallops and succulent Herdwick lamb are some of the dishes on the gourmet menu. The well-stocked cellar holds choice wines from across the world, plus some fine old whiskies.

APPLETHWAITE Underscar Manor

Underscar Manor, Applethwaite, Cumbria, CA12 4PH **Tel** *01768 775000*

A Victorian country house built in the Italianate style, set amid several acres of woodland and formal gardens. Serves a variety of inspirational dishes, which, in season, include venison, pheasant and fish from Scottish waters. Patrons can dine à la carte or opt for the six course "menu surprise". Children below the age of 12 are not allowed.

BLACKPOOL September Brasserie

15 Queen St, Blackpool, Lancashire, FY1 1NL **Tel** *01253 623282*

Enjoy food, simply cooked, but with a twist, from an eclectic menu that reflects the changing seasons and uses organic produce wherever possible. The same care extends to the collection of wines, which highlights a different country or region each month. The venue is popular with theatre-goers, and advance booking is recommended.

CARLISLE Number 10

10 Eden Mount, Stanwix, Carlisle, Cumbria, CA3 9LY **Tel** *01228 524183*

Friendly service and excellent cooking are the hallmarks of this delightful little restaurant. Locally sourced fish, beef, lamb, vegetables and cheese are the main features on the menu. Specialities such as roast smoked salmon and watercress tart are available. Many interesting vegetarian options are on offer as well.

CARTMEL Uplands

Haggs Lane, Cartmel, Cumbria, LA11 6HD **Tel** *01539 536248*

A family-run hotel and restaurant, which enjoys several repeat customers. Serves modern British cooking in the relaxed and comfortable setting of an Edwardian gentleman's residence. The four-course set dinner provides options at each course, and includes a tureen of home-made soup served with delicious bread, hot from the oven.

CARTMEL L'Enclume Restaurant with Rooms

Cavendish St, Cartmel, Cumbria, LA11 6PZ **Tel** *01539 536362*

Dining at this former village smithy is nothing short of a culinary adventure; a definite stop for discerning foodies. Award-winning chef Simon Rogan's bold and creative style explores unusual ingredients such as myrrh and ancient herbs. Choose from the à la carte menu or try one of the taste-and-texture menus offering 20 mini-taster courses.

COCKERMOUTH Quince and Medlar

11–13 Castlegate, Cockermouth, Cumbria, CA13 9EU **Tel** *01900 823579*

A historic, Georgian building near Cockermouth Castle is home to this family-run, vegetarian restaurant. The stylish surroundings enhance the intimate candlelit dinners. For 18 years, this eatery has been serving imaginative dishes, exploiting modern vegetarian cuisine to the full and drawing inspiration from around the world.

KENDAL Bridge Street

Bridge St, Kendal, Cumbria, LA9 7DD **Tel** *01539 738855*

Photographs of old Kendal decorate the walls of this fine historic house, where the small dining rooms create an intimate setting. Chef Julian Ankers exploits the flavours of traditional English fare and local produce to create exciting and tasty dishes.

LANGHO Northcote Manor

Northcote Rd, Langho, Blackburn, Lancashire, BB6 8BE **Tel** *01254 240555*

Set within the refined luxury of a 19th-century country house, the emphasis in this award-winning restaurant is on superlative cooking. Chef Nigel Haworth's inventiveness focuses on seasonal regional produce, creating some unique twists to local dishes. Black pudding and pink trout served with mustard and nettle sauce is a signature dish.

LIVERPOOL Everyman Bistro

5–9 Hope St, Liverpool, Merseyside, L1 9BH **Tel** *0151 708 9545*

Award-winning head chef, Tom Gill, offers fresh food made with prime ingredients sourced from local producers. The extensive menu includes a variety of cuisines from around the world and offers a good choice of vegetarian and gluten-free dishes. Modern interior and fast, friendly service.

LIVERPOOL Simply Heathcotes

25 The Strand, Beetham Plaza, Liverpool, Merseyside, L2 0XL **Tel** *0151 236 3536*

Overlooking the waterfront in the heart of the city, this lively, modern restaurant turns everyday food into a feast. There is something for everyone, from a light snack to a full evening dinner. Traditional dishes such as home-made black puddings and bread-and-butter pudding are popular, or visit on a gourmet evening for something special.

LIVERPOOL The Side Door

29A Hope St, Liverpool, Merseyside, L1 9BQ **Tel** *0151 707 7888*

Located midway between the city's two cathedrals, this friendly restaurant offers imaginative modern British and European cooking, often with a Thai influence, but biased towards local cuisine. Expect to be guided through the carefully selected wine list, which features many unusual varieties from both the old and new world.

LIVERPOOL 60 Hope Street
60 Hope St, Liverpool, Merseyside, L1 9BZ **Tel** *0151 707 6060*

Ideal for a casual meal, the Café Bar in the basement serves a range of light meals, from sandwiches and salads to more substantial dishes. For a formal setting, choose the restaurant, which offers modern European cuisine within relaxed and unpretentious surroundings. The wine selection complements the food.

LONGRIDGE The Longridge Restaurant
104–106 Higher Rd, Longridge, Preston, Lancashire, PR3 3SY **Tel** *01772 784969*

Opened in 1990, this is acclaimed chef Paul Heathcote's flagship restaurant. Traditional local dishes such as black pudding and bread-and-butter pudding appear beside more flamboyant creations based on Goosnargh chicken and duck. The reasonably priced, two-course lunch is of great value.

LONGRIDGE Thyme
1–3 Inglewhite Rd, Longridge, Preston, Lancashire, PR3 3JR **Tel** *01772 786888*

Chef Alex Coward has built a fine reputation for this lively town-centre restaurant with his easy-going, yet ambitious cooking. From snack lunches to special occasion dinners, his award-winning cuisine draws on local ingredients to produce favourites such as Barry Pugh's suckling pig served with black pudding, mashed potato and red wine jus.

MANCHESTER Yang Sing
34 Princess St, Manchester, Lancashire, M1 4JY **Tel** *0161 236 2200*

A highly acclaimed Chinese restaurant, and a culinary experience not to be missed. Expert waiters guide you through the extensive, 400 dish menu to create an individual banquet that perfectly suits your taste. Features a good range of Chinese beers.

MANCHESTER Restaurant Bar & Grill
14 John Dalton St, Manchester, Lancashire, M2 6JR **Tel** *0161 839 1999*

This vibrant, modern restaurant, close to many of Manchester's major venues, is a popular city-centre meeting place, both at lunch time and in the evening. Asian influences colour the à la carte menu with dishes such as Malay spiced chicken or crispy duck on Chinese greens.

MANCHESTER The Modern
The Modern at Urbis, Levels 5 & 6, Cathedral Gardens, Manchester, Lancashire, M3 4BG **Tel** *0161 605 8282*

From its lofty location above Urbis, this stylish restaurant treats diners to a spectacular panorama of the Manchester skyline. Serves excellent modern French cuisine, which has an unexpected Manchester flavour. Features fresh regional produce that includes seafood, poultry and game.

MANCHESTER The Moss Nook Restaurant
Ringway Rd, Manchester, Lancashire, M22 5WA **Tel** *0161 437 4778*

Everything on the menu is a speciality at this fine restaurant, located close to Manchester Airport. On offer is French-style cuisine including lobster and foie gras. The pan-fried scallops and crispy roast duckling are particularly recommended. In good weather, the garden terrace offers a delightfully relaxed setting for a meal.

MELMERBY Village Bakery
Melmerby, Penrith, Cumbria, CA10 1HE **Tel** *01768 881811*

The smell of fresh bread and home baking greet guests as they enter one of the country's first totally organic restaurants. Even the wines, beers and ciders are organic. Noted for its warm and unfussy service, the eatery offers hearty breakfasts, wholesome lunches (with hot and cold selections) and teas, as well as tasty treats through the day.

SALFORD The River Restaurant
Lowry Hotel, 50 Dearman's Place, Salford, Lancashire, M3 5LH **Tel** *0161 827 4003*

Overlooking River Irwell, this stylish restaurant features a contemporary, yet classical decor. Offers modern European food with an English influence. Steaks are a speciality here, and guests might like to try fillet of beef with potato rosti and Madeira *jus*. A popular dessert is the *assiette*, a large plate of different chocolate desserts. Pianist most evenings.

SAWLEY The Spread Eagle
The Spread Eagle, Sawley, nr Clitheroe, Lancashire, BB7 4NH **Tel** *01200 441202*

Built over the ruins of an old abbey, this restaurant offers a scenic, riverbank setting. One of the specialities is braised neck of lamb, slow cooked with layers of buttered potatoes, onions and black pudding – a great interpretation of the traditional Lancashire hot-pot. The select wine and champagne list is supported by over 50 malt whiskies.

SAWREY Ees Wyke Country House
Ees Wyke Country House, nr Sawrey, Cumbria, LA22 0JZ **Tel** *015394 36393*

Formerly the holiday home of Beatrix Potter and close to Hill Top, this charming restaurant is set in one of the most beautiful parts of the Lake District. The five-course set dinner is served in a small and intimate dining room. The menu changes daily and only local produce is used. Eight rooms are available for accommodation.

SILVERDALE Wolf House Gallery
Lindeth Rd, Silverdale, Lancashire, LA5 0TX **Tel** *01524 701405*

Set within a discerning arts and crafts gallery, in lovely limestone countryside overlooking Morecambe Bay, this friendly café, which is open during the day, has home-made soups, tasty snacks and a tempting range of home baking. On Friday and Saturday evenings, it offers an unusual venue for fine dining, but bring your own wine.

Key to Price Guide *see p608*   **Key to Symbols** *see back cover flap*

TROUTBECK Queens Head   ⚤ ♿ 🅿   £££

Queen's Head, Troutbeck, Windermere, Cumbria, LA23 1PW **Tel** *01539 432174*

Flag floors, oak beams and an Elizabethan four-poster bar are some of the timeless features of this 17th-century inn. The atmosphere is homely, and the food traditional. Try the roast loin of venison with redcurrant and red wine *jus*. While there is a good choice of wines, it is a great place to taste local ales such as Coniston Bluebird and Jennings.

ULLSWATER Sharrow Bay Country House Hotel   ♿ 🅿   ££££

Lake Ullswater, Penrith, Cumbria, CA10 2LZ **Tel** *01768 486301*

Traditional country house, superbly located in its vast grounds beside idyllic Ullswater. Sample Michelin-starred cuisine from a six-course menu that has evolved over time, but where time-honoured favourites such as Stilton, onion and spinach soufflé or fillet of salmon with lemon and martini sauce make regular appearances.

ULVERSTON The Bay Horse Hotel   ⚤ ♿ 🅿   ££

The Bay Horse Hotel, Canal Foot, Ulverston, Cumbria, LA12 9EL **Tel** *01229 583972*

An 18th-century inn, once serving coaches crossing the Morecambe Bay sands. This comfortable, family-run hotel and restaurant on the banks of Leven enjoys outstanding views of both the Cumbrian and Lancashire fells. The menu is equally superb and draws on fresh local ingredients such as shrimps, wild salmon and salt marsh lamb.

WATERMILLOCK Macdonald Leeming House   ♿ 🅿   ££££

Leeming House, Watermillock, Ullswater, nr Penrith, Cumbria, CA11 0JJ **Tel** *0844 8799142*

Beautifully positioned above the shores of Ullswater, this splendid early 19th-century country house, set within extensive grounds, retains the charm of its past. The elegance of its setting is matched by the simple perfection of its award-winning Modern British cuisine. Come for an informal lunch in the conservatory or dinner in the Regency Restaurant.

WATERMILLOCK The Rampsbeck Country House Hotel   ♿ 🅿   ££££

Watermillock, Ullswater, Cumbria, CA11 0LP **Tel** *01768 486442*

Fantastic views and fine dining are some of the highlights of this 18th-century country house, located on the shores of Ullswater, in one of the most picturesque corners of the Lake District. The AA Rosette-winning restaurant serves imaginative dishes, using regional delicacies such as wild salmon, rabbit, Cumbrian ham and local lamb.

WHITEWELL Inn at Whitewell   ⚤ 🅿   £££

Whitewell, Forest of Bowland, Clitheroe, Lancashire, BB7 3AT **Tel** *01200 448222*

Dating back to the 15th century, this remote inn originally provided a welcome rest to travellers passing through the wilds of the Trough of Bowland, on their way to Lancaster. The stunning location is matched by the cooking of chef Jamie Cadman, whose contemporary style of British cooking incorporates many seasonal local specialities.

WINDERMERE Miller Howe   ⚤ 🎵 ♿ 🍴 🅿   ££££

Rayrigg Rd, Windermere, Cumbria, LA23 1EY **Tel** *01539 442536*

A delightful restaurant that serves fine gourmet food in striking surroundings. Try the chef's set evening menu, which includes recommendations from the extensive wine list, or replace any course with the à la carte alternatives. Also offers a range of imaginative vegetarian options.

WINDERMERE Holbeck Ghyll Country House Hotel   ⚤ ♿ 🅿   £££££

Holbeck Lane, Windermere, Cumbria, LA23 1LU **Tel** *01539 432375*

Set in a 19th-century hunting lodge, this intimate, Michelin-star restaurant (voted Cumbrian Restaurant of the Year) has good views across the lake. Serves English cuisine which reflects just a hint of France. The set dinner offers a tempting range of choices at each course, such as scallops or langoustine followed by beef, pigeon or venison, with a port-based sauce.

WINSTER Low Sizergh Barn   ⚤   ££

Alison Park, Low Sizergh Farm, Sizergh, Kendal, Cumbria, LA8 8AE **Tel** *01539 560426*

Organic milk, cheese and eggs from the family-run farm are among the ingredients used in this unique tea room. Open throughout the day for snacks, lunch and tea. Part of a craft and farm produce shop, in a converted Westmorland slate barn, this eatery overlooks the milking parlour. Watch the cows being brought in for afternoon milking.

WRIGHTINGTON BAR The Mulberry Tree   ⚤ ♿ 🅿   £££

9 Wood Lane, Wrightington Bar, Standish, Wigan, Lancashire, WN6 9SE **Tel** *01257 451400*

The restaurant of this former local pub has an enviable reputation for imaginative cuisine. French influences add an unexpected twist to typically English dishes. Try the entrée of black pudding topped with a poached egg and hollandaise sauce, followed by roast loin of cod on a saffron and spring pea risotto. Look for reasonably-priced specials.

YORKSHIRE AND THE HUMBER REGION

ASENBY Crab and Lobster   ⚤ 🎵 ♿   £££

Crab Manor, Dishforth Rd, Asenby, Thirsk, North Yorkshire, YO7 3QL **Tel** *01845 577286*

Step back into time at this charming seafood eatery, decorated with antiques and artifacts. The chef's signature dish is lobster Thermidor, but the fish-and-chips is equally good. Lamb and chicken dishes are also featured on the menu. Located in the quiet countryside of the Vale of York and not far from Ripon. Jazz music on Sunday lunchtimes.

BOLTON ABBEY Devonshire Arms Brasserie 🏃♿🅿 ⓔⓔⓔ

*The Devonshire Arms Country House Hotel, Bolton Abbey, Skipton, North Yorkshire, BD23 6AJ **Tel** 01756 718111*

Fringing the Yorkshire Dales and close to Bolton Priory, this characterful coaching inn has been in the family of the Duke and Duchess of Devonshire since 1753. The setting here is informal and relaxed, and the cuisine is a blend of modern British and French. Most of the dishes are available as either starters or main courses.

BOROUGHBRIDGE thediningroom 🏃🅿 ⓔⓔⓔ

*20 St James Square, Boroughbridge, North Yorkshire, YO51 9AR **Tel** 01423 326426*

Overlooking the Georgian square of a small market town, this cosy and friendly eating place is highly popular with the locals. Fish features prominently on the menu, which offers dishes best described as modern English. Everything is home-made and locally sourced where possible, and there is a good selection of wines and champagne.

BURNSALL The Devonshire Fell Hotel and Bistro 🏃♿🅿 ⓔⓔⓔⓔ

*Burnsall, Skipton, North Yorkshire, BD23 6BT **Tel** 01756 729000*

Originally a club for 19th-century gentlemen mill owners, this hotel and restaurant is situated on a hillside, and offers spectacular views over Wharfedale. Recently refurbished, the hotel's interior is striking as well. A bright and colourful bar leads to an inviting dining room. The menu is simple, but innovative, with seafood, poultry and game.

EAST WITTON The Blue Lion 🏃♿🅿 ⓔⓔⓔ

*E Witton, nr Leyburn, North Yorkshire, DL8 4SN **Tel** 01969 624273*

Former coaching inn full of character, on the edge of the Yorkshire Dales and not far from Jervaulx Abbey. The home-prepared food, available both in the bar and restaurant, ranges from traditional hearty dishes, such as steak and kidney pudding, to more exotic creations reflecting Asian influences. Extensive wine list and hand-drawn beers.

ELLAND La Cachette 🅿 ⓔⓔⓔ

*31 Huddersfield Rd, Elland, West Yorkshire, HX5 9AW **Tel** 01422 378833*

A busy and highly popular brasserie-style restaurant serving modern British food in a Mediterranean ambience. Fish features prominently on the menu, and there is a good choice of daily specials as well. The light, two-course lunch is of great value and the three-course dinner includes a half bottle of wine. The à la carte menu is extensive.

FERRENSBY The General Tarleton Inn 🏃♿🅿 ⓔⓔⓔ

*Boroughbridge Rd, Ferrensby, nr Knaresborough, North Yorkshire, HG5 0PZ **Tel** 01423 340284*

Named after a British general in the American War of Independence, this former, 18th-century coaching inn is renowned for its excellent fish dishes such as royal scallops or lung fish wrapped in Parma ham. Although the wine list is extensive, real ale fans can opt for a pint of Black Sheep or Timothy Taylor's, two of the best beers in the area.

HALIFAX Design House 🏃♿🅿 ⓔⓔⓔ

*Dean Clough (Gate 5), Halifax, West Yorkshire, HX3 5AX **Tel** 01422 383242*

A stylishly modern restaurant set within a former mill, which has found a new lease of life as the Dean Clough Arts and Business Complex. There is a distinct Mediterranean feel to the place. Tapas and lighter meals are popular during the day. The three-course set menu is of excellent value, while in the evening, there is full à la carte.

HAROME The Star Inn 🏃♿🅿 ⓔⓔⓔⓔ

*Harome, nr Helmsley, North Yorkshire, YO62 5JE **Tel** 01439 770397*

This attractive, 14th-century thatched inn exudes rustic charm, with original cow byres and a dormitory formerly used by travelling monks. The intimate, award-winning restaurant serves traditional British fare, and is justifiably popular. Advance reservations are recommended. The same menu is served in the bar.

HARROGATE Drum and Monkey 🏃🅿 ⓔⓔⓔ

*5 Montpellier Gardens, Harrogate, North Yorkshire, HG1 2TF **Tel** 01423 502650*

Elegant, but unpretentious, the old world ambience of this superb fish and seafood restaurant reflects the traditional character of the famous spa town of Harrogate. Dine in either the bar or the restaurant above. Dishes such as queen scallops with cheese and garlic butter, fisherman's pie and the shellfish platter are popular choices.

HAWORTH Weaver's 🏃🅿 ⓔⓔⓔ

*15–17 W Lane, Haworth, West Yorkshire, BD22 8DU **Tel** 01535 643822*

This long-established restaurant is set within three 17th-century weaver's cottages that once incorporated a café frequented by the Brontës. Flagged floors, bric-à-brac, low lighting and intimate alcoves in the dining room add to the atmosphere. Northern regional cooking is the hallmark, a popular choice being the Whitby fisherman's pie.

HETTON Angel Inn 🏃♿🅿 ⓔⓔⓔⓔ

*Hetton, Skipton, North Yorkshire, BD23 6LT **Tel** 01756 730263*

About 500 years old, this traditional inn once served cattle drovers. Wooden beams, nooks and crannies and log fires re-create the atmosphere of a bygone era. Dine in either the elegant restaurant or the more informal bar-brasserie. The separate menus offer a range of interesting dishes, including a choice of vegetarian and gluten-free options.

HUSTHWAITE The Balmoral 🏃♿🅿 ⓔⓔⓔ

*Low St, Husthwaite, North Yorkshire, YO61 4QA **Tel** 01347 868007*

This former village pub has been transformed into a restaurant offering traditional British fare. Features an outside terrace, perfect for alfresco dining on sunny days or balmy evenings. There is an exciting à la carte menu or, for more informal meals, choose from the speciality sandwiches. There is also an early bird menu.

ILKLEY Box Tree

35–37 Church St, Ilkley, West Yorkshire, LS29 9DR **Tel** *01943 608484*

Enjoy fine dining in the luxurious setting of one of Ilkley's oldest buildings. Awarded a Michelin star, the cuisine is modern French and draws upon the best of local and regional produce. The menu changes constantly, but dishes such as the hand-dived scallops served with white truffle oil are highly recommended.

LEEDS Chino Latino

Boar Lane, Leeds, West Yorkshire, LS1 6EA **Tel** *0113 380 4080*

Located in the city centre, Chino Latino offers an innovative fusion of Far East cuisine combining the delicate flavours of Chinese, Thai, South East Asian and modern Japanese food. Before dining, try a cocktail in the Latino bar. Relaxed atmosphere and good wine list.

LEEDS Anthony's Restaurant

19 Boar Lane, Leeds, West Yorkshire, LS1 6EA **Tel** *0113 245 5922*

Close to the station, passers-by would be surprised to find a restaurant of such gastronomic ambition among the everyday shops and bars. Complex constructions and compelling flavour juxtapositions are what to expect: roast duck with apple or seared tuna with broccoli puree and roast rhubarb, for instance.

OSMOTHERLEY Golden Lion

6 W End, Osmotherley, North Yorkshire, DL6 3AA **Tel** *01609 883526*

Traditional country pub in a picturesque village of 17th-century stone cottages. Serves as a starting point for the Lyke Wake Walk, and is close to Mount Grace Priory. Very popular with hill walkers, the pub offers well cooked, wholesome food using fresh local produce. The steak and kidney pie and tasty casseroles are firm favourites.

RAMSGILL IN NIDDERDALE The Yorke Arms

Ramsgill-in-Nidderdale, Pateley Bridge, nr Harrogate, North Yorkshire, HG3 5RL **Tel** *01423 755243*

Acclaimed chef Frances Atkins is one of only four female chefs in the country to gain the coveted Michelin star. Her creative dishes in the modern British style are superb, using seasonal meats, fish and game in unusual combinations. Discreet service in the relaxing ambience of this 17th-century shooting lodge makes dining here a real pleasure.

RIDGEWAY The Old Vicarage

Ridgeway Moor, Ridgeway Village, Sheffield, South Yorkshire, S12 3XW **Tel** *01142 475814*

Michelin-starred restaurant set within a Victorian vicarage. Welcoming winter log fires and an attractive garden terrace for apéritifs on balmy evenings are some of the attractions here. Produce from the kitchen garden and seasonal delicacies, often combined with unexpected ingredients, are at the heart of the inventive dishes on offer.

RIPLEY The Boar's Head Hotel

Ripley, Harrogate, North Yorkshire, HG3 3AY **Tel** *01423 771888*

A former coaching inn beside the castle, in the heart of a charming estate village. The menus are nothing short of inspirational, whether you dine in the elegant restaurant or the more casual and informal setting of the bistro. Seasonal fish, meat and game feature prominently on the menu.

SHEFFIELD Baldwins Omega

Brincliffe Hill, Psalter Lane, Sheffield, S11 9DF **Tel** *0114 255 1818*

This restaurant, family owned for the past 25 years, offers simple lunches through to a real banqueting experience. A reputation for fine cuisine has been built on excellent food combined with impeccable service. Menus offer both traditional and modern English styles.

SHEFFIELD Greenhead House

84 Burncross Rd, Chapeltown, Sheffield, South Yorkshire, S35 1SF **Tel** *0114 246 9004*

Set within a 17th-century house to the north of Sheffield. Features a delightful walled garden, a comfortable lounge warmed by open fires and an intimate dining room that creates a distinctively homely feel. The husband and wife team offer carefully prepared dishes in an all-inclusive meal, supported by a comprehensive selection of wines.

SOWERBY BRIDGE The Millbank

Mill Bank Rd, Mill Bank, Sowerby Bridge, West Yorkshire, HX6 3DY **Tel** *01422 825588*

This country pub lies in a small Pennine village, not far from the bustling towns of Halifax and Hebden Bridge. Bare floors and chunky furniture create a contemporary feel, while the garden offers a splendid view along the valley. Serves traditional food with a modern twist. An unusual feature of the bar is its gin list.

STOKESLEY Chapter's

27 High St, Stokesley, Middlesborough, North Yorkshire, TS9 5AD **Tel** *01642 711888*

Set in a recently refurbished and characterful Grade II listed building, this stylish eatery overlooks Stokesley's market square, below the northern escarpment of the Cleveland Hills. Dine in the gourmet restaurant or the more casual brasserie bar. Serves a variety of seafood, game and poultry dishes.

SUTTON ON THE FOREST The Rose and Crown Inn

Main St, Sutton-on-the-Forest, North Yorkshire, YO61 1DP **Tel** *01347 811333*

Informal dining in this village inn restaurant, which specializes in fish dishes presented in a classic brasserie style. Surrounded by pleasant gardens and set in the rural heart of Yorkshire, it is well placed between the attractive centres of Helmsley and York, and surrounded by a wealth of stately homes and abbeys.

WATH-IN-NIDDERDALE The Sportsman's Arms 🛱 🛦 🖵 ⓔⓔⓔ

Wath-in-Nidderdale, Pateley Bridge, Harrogate, North Yorkshire, HG3 5PP **Tel** *01423 711306*

Set within an old farmhouse and converted barn, this characterful inn emanates the charm of a former age. The food, served in a comfortable room, is cooked with a French influence, and includes fresh, seasonal fish and seafood brought from Whitby. Steaks, lamb, duck and guinea fowl also appear on the menu.

WHITBY Magpie Café 🛱 🛦 🖵 ⓔⓔ

14 Pier Rd, Whitby, North Yorkshire, YO21 3PU **Tel** *01947 602058*

Looking out across the historic port towards St Mary's Church and the abbey, this distinctive black-and-white, former merchant's house became a café in the 1930s. Specialities revolve around seafood and fish-and-chips, of which there are some eight different varieties. However, there is also a wide selection of other dishes too.

YORK Melton's Too 🛱 🛦 ⓔⓔⓔ

25 Walmgate, York, North Yorkshire, YO1 9TX **Tel** *01904 629222*

Located in a former saddler's, this open-plan bistro retains many original features, but has a distinctively modern feel. While losing nothing of the original Melton's dedication to good cooking, this place has a more informal appeal; an ideal venue whether you want just a light bite or a full dinner. The bar has a good range of speciality beers.

YORK The Blue Bicycle Restaurant 🛱 🎜 🖵 ⓔⓔⓔ

34 Fossgate, York, North Yorkshire, YO1 9TA **Tel** *01904 673990*

Seafood and modern European dishes are the specialities at this atmospheric restaurant. Situated beside River Foss, in a building that housed a 19th-century brothel, it still retains some of the original booths in the cellar. A guitarist provides an added attraction on Saturday evenings.

NORTHUMBRIA

AYCLIFFE The County 🛱 🖵 ⓔⓔⓔ

13 The Green, Aycliffe, Darlington, County Durham, DL5 6LX **Tel** *01325 312273*

Overlooking Aycliffe village green, the County is a historic building with a contemporary interior. The relaxed setting extends to the menu, you can combine dishes to get exactly what you want. The food is simply cooked and focuses on traditional and modern British cuisine. The wines are from the New World and there's a good range of real ales.

CARTERWAY HEADS The Manor House Inn 🛱 🛦 🖵 ⓔⓔ

Carterway Heads, Shotley Bridge, Northumberland, DH8 9LX **Tel** *01207 255268*

Located in isolation, this 18th-century inn has stunning views across the open moors. Dine in a quiet, relaxed atmosphere, either in the restaurant or more informally at the bar, which is popular with walkers and cyclists. The home-made food is good and a small shop sells some of the chutneys, jams and ready meals on the menu.

CORBRIDGE The Angel of Corbridge 🛱 🛦 ⓔⓔⓔ

1 Main St, Corbridge, Northumberland, NE45 5LA **Tel** *01434 632119*

Known for its discerning shops, Corbridge is an attractive stop-over. The Angel, a former coaching inn and one of the oldest buildings in town, prides itself on good food and excellent service. Traditional dishes, often with an unusual tweak, appear on the constantly changing menu and are served in both the bar and dining room.

DURHAM Bistro 21 🛱 🛦 ⓔⓔⓔ

Aykley Heads House, Aykley Heads, Durham, County Durham, DH1 5TS **Tel** *0191 384 4354*

Set within an early 18th-century building, originally a farmhouse, this popular bistro retains a distinct bucolic feel and, in summer, tables appear in the courtyard for al fresco dining. The cuisine is modern British with overtones of the Mediterranean and there's an ever-changing list of special dishes exploiting seasonal fresh produce.

GATESHEAD Eslington Villa Hotel 🛱 🛦 🖵 ⓔⓔⓔ

8 Station Rd, Low Fell, Gateshead, Tyne and Wear, NE9 6DR **Tel** *0191 487 6017*

This stunning 19th-century house combines the charm of an earlier age with modern creativity and offers dining in the comfortable restaurant or the less formal setting of the conservatory. The award-winning kitchen team are passionate about food and conceive eclectic menus featuring the best in contemporary and original cuisine.

GATESHEAD Fresh Element 🛱 🛦 🖵 ⓔⓔⓔ

BALTIC Centre for Contemporary Arts, South Shore Road, Gateshead, Tyne and Wear, NE8 3BA **Tel** *0191 478 1810*

Innovative development has transformed the quayside warehouses of the former Baltic Flour Mill into a vibrant centre for contemporary art. Above it all is McCoys Rooftop Restaurant, offering guests a spectacular view across the city skyline. The cuisine is equally impressive and modern in style, served in the best traditions of fine dining.

GREAT WHITTINGTON Queens Head Inn 🛱 🛦 🖵 ⓔⓔⓔ

Great Whittington, Corbridge, Tynedale, Newcastle upon Tyne, Tyne and Wear, NE19 2HP **Tel** *01434 672267*

A welcoming early 17th-century village coaching inn not far from Hadrian's Wall. The very comfortable restaurant serves a bistro-style menu of freshly prepared tempting dishes featuring local meat, game and fish from the coast. There's a well-devised wine list and extensive range of malt whiskies as well as several fine ales at the bar.

HAYDON BRIDGE General Havelock Inn

9 Ratcliffe Rd, Haydon Bridge, Hexham, Northumberland, NE47 6ER **Tel** *01434 684376*

Named after a famous general who helped put down the Indian Mutiny, this former roadside inn enjoys a delightful setting beside the river. Ingredients are sourced locally as much as possible, the dishes reflecting whatever is in season. One of the chef's signature dishes is Cullen Skink, a rich broth based around smoked haddock.

HEXHAM Valley Connection 301

Market Place, Hexham, Northumberland, NE46 3NX **Tel** *01434 601234*

This Bangladeshi restaurant enjoys a pretty location off the main street beside Hexham Abbey. Unique dishes include Mr Daraz's very own *bhuna gosht* (stir-fired lamb) and *bongo po curry*, created around king prawns from the Bay of Bengal. The winner is *shat kora*, flavoured with a variety of lemon found in the valley of Sylhet in Bangladesh.

HUTTON MAGNA The Oak Tree Inn

Hutton Magna, Durham, County Durham, DL11 7HH **Tel** *01833 627371*

Unassuming Oak Tree Inn is local favourite and a real gem. The chef at this restaurant hails from the Savoy, bringing imaginative fine cuisine to the informality of an 18th-century village pub. A warm salad of crispy pork belly with black pudding precedes royal sea bream with wild mushroom and asparagus noodles. Booking is essential.

MATFEN Matfen Hall Country House Hotel

Matfen, Northumberland, NE20 0RH **Tel** *01661 886500*

This beautifully restored 19th-century country mansion, set within its own extensive grounds, offers a dining experience to remember. Both the library and smaller print room provide a truly atmospheric candlelit setting for an intimate meal. The food is superb and the service is discreet, but attentive.

NEWCASTLE Paradiso

1 Market Lane, Newcastle upon Tyne, Tyne and Wear, NE1 6QQ **Tel** *0191 221 1240*

This stylish eatery is one of Newcastle's most popular restaurants. It combines old and new, its contemporary design blending well with the exposed brickwork of the traditional building. Diners can enjoy modern Italian cuisine with unusual influences from Africa, Asia and beyond. Sandwiches and snacks are served throughout the day. Closed Sun.

NEWCASTLE Blackfriars Restaurant

Friars St, Newcastle upon Tyne, Tyne and Wear, NE1 4XN **Tel** *0191 261 5945*

Housed within a medieval Dominican monks' refectory, this restaurant is perhaps the oldest dining room still in use in the country. The atmospheric courtyard lends itself to al fresco dining in summer. The style of cooking is modern British using locally sourced and organic produce. AA Rosette awarded.

NEWCASTLE Fisherman's Lodge

Jesmond Dene, Jesmond, Newcastle upon Tyne, Tyne and Wear, NE7 7BQ **Tel** *0191 281 3281*

Close to the city centre, but lying in the secluded wooded valley of Jesmond Dene, Fisherman's Lodge has earned an outstanding reputation for its fine dining. Seafood dishes are the speciality, but local meat and game also feature prominently on the menu. Exotic deserts and a carefully selected cheese board round off the meal. Closed Sundays and Mondays.

PONTELAND Café Lowrey

33–35 The Broadway, Darras Hall Estate, Tyne and Wear, NE20 9PW **Tel** *01661 820357*

Recently renamed when the chef took over ownership, Café Lowrey offers bistro-style dining with a distinct French influence to the food. The service is friendly and the atmosphere relaxed, though there's generally a lively buzz to the place at the weekend. However, go mid-week when there's usually a quiet corner to be had.

REDWORTH Barcelo Redworth Hall Hotel

Redworth, Bishop Auckland, Darlington, County Durham, DL5 6NL **Tel** *01388 770600*

Built in 1693 as a private house, Redworth Hall retains many of its original features and stands in 25 acres of beautifully kept grounds. The elegant 1744 dining room, named after the year in which it was added, offers fine dining in luxurious surroundings. For a less formal meal, opt for the conservatory restaurant.

ROMALDKIRK The Rose and Crown Inn

Romaldkirk, Barnard Castle, County Durham, DL12 9EB **Tel** *01833 650213*

This traditional stone-built coaching inn dates from the 18th century and stands on the green beside the church in the heart of a North Yorkshire village. Dine in style in the oak-panelled restaurant at tables bedecked in crisp white linen or choose the more rustic setting of the brasserie, perhaps selecting only one or two courses as you please.

TYNEMOUTH Sidney's Restaurant

3–5 Percy Park Rd, Tynemouth, Tyne and Wear, NE30 4LZ **Tel** *0191 257 8500*

A vibrant modern decor and constantly changing artwork set the scene for this bustling place. The kitchen team use the best fresh produce, meticulously creating an interesting variety of modern dishes, often European, but with underlying themes from across the globe. A variety of creative fish and vegetarian options give balance to the menu.

YARM Chadwick's

104B Yarm High St, Yarm, Stockton-on-Tees, County Durham, TS15 9AU **Tel** *01642 788558*

The attractive town of Yarm, surrounded by the snaking River Tees, is home to this bustling restaurant on the high street. The distinctly continental lunch offers lighter meals and snacks including pizzas and pasta. The evening menu is more formal, with a good range of specials and some interesting creations. Great service by the enthusiastic staff.

NORTH WALES

ABERDOVEY Penhelig Arms
Aberdyfi, Gwynedd, LL35 0LT **Tel** *01654 767215*

This small, friendly hotel has a reputable restaurant that enjoys panoramic views of the Dovey estuary. On offer is a good range of locally sourced fish and meat. Indulge in a glass of champagne and fresh dressed crab, or try the reasonably priced fixed menu.

ABERSOCH Porth Tocyn Country Hotel
Abersoch, Gwynedd, LL53 7BU **Tel** *01758 713303*

Panoramic hotel restaurant Porth Tocyn has appeared in good food guides for over 50 years. There's a choice between a three- and two-course evening menu. Ask for a table at the "picture window" for the best views over the peninsula. Tables in the garden for informal lunchtime dining.

BARMOUTH The Bistro
Church St, Barmouth, Gwynedd, LL42 1EW **Tel** *01341 281009*

Small restaurant recommended by *Les Routiers,* the Bistro uses locally-produced ingredients to create its award-winning range of seasonal dishes. The menu lays stress on the Welsh lamb and beef, but there's also a good choice of fish and excellent vegetarian choices. Booking is advised.

BEAUMARIS Ye Olde Bull's Head Inn
Castle St, Beaumaris, Isle of Anglesey, LL58 8AP **Tel** *01248 810329*

Locally known as "the Bull", this restaurant-with-rooms is based in the centre of town. An ancient coaching inn, built in 1472, the building provides an elegant setting for the main restaurant in its oldest part. There's also a less formal brasserie and a popular bar.

CAERNARFON The Prince's Brasserie
The Prince of Wales Hotel, Bangor St, Caernarfon, Gwynedd, LL55 1AR **Tel** *01286 673367*

Restaurant in Caernarfon's Prince of Wales Hotel, The Prince's Brasserie provides a good range of home-cooked meals. The steaks are renowned, and equally good are the vegetable dishes. You can get anything from home-made paté (with peach and pineapple chutney) to liver and bacon casserole.

CAPEL COCH Tre-Ysgawen Hall
Capel Coch, Llangefni, Isle of Anglesey, LL77 7UR **Tel** *01248 750750*

Hotel and spa with seasonal menu and excellent accompanying wine list, Tre-Ysgawen Hall has a delicious evening menu. The chef provides vegetarian and low-calorie fare on request. Residents have use of a gym and a golf course, available to help burn off the calories. There's also an atmospheric bar.

COLWYN BAY Stars Café Bar & Restaurant
124 Abergele Road, Colwyn Bay, Conwy, LL29 7PS **Tel** *01492 531555*

A café-bar-style restaurant in the heart of Colwyn Bay, Stars Café serves modern European fare. The locally-sourced produce is put to effective use, and breakfast, light lunch and full evening meals are served. A range of desserts are available. Good for families.

DOLGARROG The Lord Newborough
Dolgarrog, Conwy, LL32 8JX **Tel** *01492 660549*

Recently renovated and under a new ownership, the Lord Newborough prides itself on its simple, but tasty cuisine and friendly dining atmosphere. Using the best of Snowdonia's ingredients, the menu features Welsh lamb shank, Conwy Valley steak pie, Welsh potato bake (with leeks) and a delicious cheese board.

DOLGELLAU Bwyty Dylanwad Da
2 Ffos-y-felin, Dolgellau, Gwynedd, LL40 1BS **Tel** *01341 422870*

Small friendly café-restaurant with a long and impressive reputation, Bwyty Dylanwad Da also offers one of the best cappuccinos in town. Menu features traditional dishes such as faggot with spiced apple sauce, Welsh beef steak and Welsh honey and almond ice cream.

EWLOE The Borders Restaurant
St David's Park Hotel, Ewloe, nr Chester, Flintshire, CH5 3YB **Tel** *01244 520800*

This award-winning restaurant is in a four-star hotel on the Welsh border. It offers a delicious seasonal menu, an informal carvery perfect for family dining, and a tasty range of bar snacks. The classy surroundings create an ideal ambience to enjoy the superb food accompanied by an exceptional choice of wines.

HARLECH Castle Cottage
Y Llech, Harlech, Gwynedd, LL46 2YL **Tel** *01766 780479*

The award-winning restaurant (with rooms) at the Castle Cottage is a popular destination for locals and visitors alike. The seasonal menu features locally caught lobster, sea bass and black bream, and there is also venison from the Brecon Beacons National Park. Won the 2008/9 True Taste award for Best Restaurant in Wales.

Key to Price Guide *see p608* **Key to Symbols** *see back cover flap*

LLANBEDROG Glyn-Y-Weddw Arms   ⓔⓔ

*Lon Pin, Llanbedrog, Pwllheli, LL53 7TH **Tel** 01758 740212*

This low-key village pub and restaurant serves good, hearty food using fresh local produce. Daily specials and fixed-price menus include vegetarian options. Draught ales are also available and there is a lovely beer garden. A carvery is held on Sundays and there is an international buffet every Saturday.

LLANBERIS The Gwynedd Hotel & Restaurant   ⓔⓔⓔ

*Llanberis, Snowdonia, Gwynedd, LL55 4SU **Tel** 01286 870203*

Fabulously situated at the foot of Mount Snowdon, this restaurant prides itself on the varied menu of local and seasonal cuisine. The owners, Mark and Dita Bartlett, pay meticulous attention to every detail. Dinner and lunch come complete with sightseeing information.

LLANDRILLO Tyddyn Llan   ⓔⓔⓔⓔ

*Llandrillo, nr Corwen, Denbighshire, LL21 0ST **Tel** 01490 440264*

The rural location of this restaurant-with-rooms makes it the perfect stopping-off point after a hearty walk in the countryside. Set in a small elegant Georgian house, it is famed for the award-wining cuisine by owner Brian Webb. The imaginative menu, featuring local lamb and beef, justifies its reputation as one of Wales's finest restaurants.

LLANGOLLEN Greenbank Hotel and Restaurant   ⓔⓔ

*Victoria Square, Llangollen, Denbighshire LL20 8EU **Tel** 01978 861835*

This relaxed and friendly 18th-century water mill is in a beautiful location overlooking the River Dee. In the summer months, diners can sit out on the jetty and enjoy the stunning views of the river. The extensive menu offers a range of traditional food, including Welsh black beef and Yorkshire pudding.

LLANGOLLEN The Corn Mill   ⓔⓔ

*Dee Lane, Llangollen, Denbighshire, LL20 8NN **Tel** 01978 869555*

Informal restaurant in a heritage building, Green Bank is a preferred family destination. Children can enjoy fish fingers with baked beans, while their parents dine on venison sausage with parsnip, carrot and potato mash or pan-fried steak on black pudding, paté and Brie.

NORTHOP Stables Bar Restaurant   ⓔⓔⓔ

*Soughton Hall, Northop, Flintshire, CH7 6AB **Tel** 01352 840577*

Part of the luxurious Soughton Hall Hotel, Stables Bar Restaurant offers a truly atmospheric setting with open fires, cobbled floors and timber-roofs. The menu features modern British cuisine. Evening dinner is served in the hayloft and the accompanying wine is chosen from the extensive restaurant cellars.

PENMAENPOOL Penmaenuchaf Hall   ⓔⓔⓔⓔ

*Penmaenpool, Dolgellau, Gwynedd, LL40 1YB **Tel** 01341 422129*

The reputation of Penmaenuchaf Hall rests on its award-winning cuisine. Modern British cooking, thoughtfully kept simple and light, is served in the elegant dining room with fine linen, silver cutlery and crystal wine glasses. Welsh beef and lamb make a good showing. A Celtic cheese board is also available.

PORTMEIRION Hotel Portmeirion   ⓔⓔⓔⓔ

*Off A487, Portmeirion, Gwynedd, LL48 6ET **Tel** 01766 770228*

Designed by Clough Williams-Ellis in 1931, the formal hotel dining room has fabulous views overlooking the estuary. The modern Welsh menu uses the best of local Welsh produce. Castell Deudraeth Bar & Grill, another restaurant on the premises, specializes in fresh seafood, while the Town Hall Restaurant serves well-cooked meals and snacks.

PWLLHELI Plas Bodegroes   ⓔⓔⓔⓔ

*Nefyn Rd, Pwllheli, Gwynedd, LL53 5TH **Tel** 01758 612363*

One of Wales's most well-known restaurants, Michelin-starred Plas Bodegroes may be pricey, but it's more than worth the expense. Locally reared meat, fish and freshly caught game make for a great menu, but the desserts are the main draw. Try the heart-shaped cinnamon biscuit of rhubarb and apple with elderflower custard.

RHOS-ON-SEA Forte's Restaurant   ⓔ

*Penrhyn Avenue, Rhos-on-Sea, Conwy, LL28 4NH **Tel** 01492 544662*

With contemporary decor, Forte's is a perfect lunch venue for families exploring Rhos-on-Sea. It doubles as an ice cream parlour with a delicious range of sundaes, all made with the house ice cream. The restaurant closes at 5:30pm, except during July and August when it remains open in the evening. Breathtaking views of the harbour.

RHYDLYDAN Y Giler Arms   ⓔⓔ

*Rhydlydan, nr Betws-y-Coed, Conwy, LL24 0LL **Tel** 01690 770612*

Friendly country pub and hotel with its own fishing lake, the Giler Arms serves a flavourful seasonal menu in its atmospheric bar-restaurant. There's a good range of local ales, including Batham's traditional draught beers. Enjoys stunning views of the lake.

TALSARNAU Maes-y-Neuadd   ⓔⓔⓔ

*Talsarnau, Gwynedd, LL47 6YA **Tel** 01766 780200*

Housed in a scenic country house hotel, the restaurant at Maes-y-Neuadd serves an innovative four-course menu. Fresh meats and cheese come from local farms, fish from Cardigan Bay, and fresh vegetables and strawberries from the hotel garden. The courses in the set menus are carefully crafted to maintain harmony.

TAL-Y-BONT Ysgethin Inn ★ 🚹 🏄 ££

Tal-y-bont, nr Barmouth, Gwynedd, LL43 2AN **Tel** *01341 247578*

Informal family pub in a converted mill house on the banks of the River Ysgethin, serving a mix of simple bar snacks, classic roasts and house specials, such as Ysgethin steak pie. There's an extensive children's menu. Riverside patio and children's adventure playground. The new Black Rock grill restaurant cooks on volcanic stone.

TREMEIRCHION Starters Restaurant 🚹 🏄 ££

Ffynnon Beuno, Tremeirchion, St Asaph, Denbighshire, LL17 0UE **Tel** *01745 710475*

Cosy restaurant in Ffynnon Beuno Country House Hotel, Starters overlooks a sprawling open garden, including a 6th-century enclosed pool and a prehistoric cave thought to have been inhabited more than 30,000 years ago. It is so called because there are only starters and sweets served here.

SOUTH AND MID-WALES

BRECON Felin Fach Griffin 🚹 🏄 🛏 £££

Felin Fach, Brecon, Powys, LD3 0UB **Tel** *01874 620111*

Award-winning pub with rooms midway between Brecon and Hay-on-Wye, the Felin Fach Griffin has been acclaimed as exceptional by critics. A delicious lunch and supper menu of traditional Welsh cuisine is on offer. Starters include squab pigeon, while mains range from fresh salted cod to local Welsh rib-eye. Great local cheese board.

BRIDGEND Elliot Restaurant 🚹 🏄 🛏 £££

Coed-y-Mwstwr Hotel, Coychurch, Bridgend, CF35 6AF **Tel** *01656 860621*

In a country-house hotel, Coed-y-Mwstwr ("whispering trees"), Elliot Restaurant provides fabulous views over the picturesque Vale of Glamorgan. Daily table d'hôte menu includes duck breast with wilted spinach and cherry port sauce, or rabbit leg stuffed with garlic and spinach pancetta. There's also a family Sunday lunch menu.

BUILTH WELLS The Drawing Room 🏄 🛏 £££

Twixt Cwmbach and Newbridge-on-Wye, Builth Wells, Powys, LD2 3RT **Tel** *01982 552493*

Five-star restaurant-with-rooms in the heart of Wales, the Drawing Room occupies an elegant Georgian country residence. Its location in the plush Wye Valley provides plenty of delicious seasonal ingredients, including prime Welsh black beef and lamb from local farms.

BUILTH WELLS Tudor Restaurant 🚹 🏄 🛏 £££

Caer Beris Manor Hotel and Restaurant, Builth Wells, Powys, LD2 3NP **Tel** *01982 552601*

Popular restaurant in picturesque Caer Beris Manor Hotel, the Tudor uses the finest local produce to create its comprehensive à la carte menu. Dishes are seasonal, but Welsh lamb and Welsh black beef always make a good showing. The impressive wine list features over 150 bottles.

CARDIFF The Armless Dragon 🚹 🏄 🛏 ££

97 Wyeverne Road, Cathays, Cardiff, CF24 4BG **Tel** *029 2038 2357*

At the Armless Dragon, one of Cardiff's most popular dining venues, contemporary Welsh cuisine is served in a smart, but laid-back setting. The menu is arranged by theme, using local produce from Wales, such as chicken from Monmouthshire, ham from Carmarthen, spider crab from Pembrokeshire and lamb from Brecon.

CARDIFF The Greendown Inn 🚹 🏄 ££

Drope Rd, St Georges-Super-Ely, Cardiff, Vale of Glamorgan, CF5 6EP **Tel** *01446 760310*

Friendly inn in a pleasant country setting, the Greendown Inn is just a short drive from the bustling city of Cardiff. The menu showcases simple but well-prepared dishes, and the home-made beef pie is a continual favourite. Well priced for the decent quality of the cuisine.

CARDIFF Benedicto's 🚹 🛏 £££

4 Windsor Place, Cardiff, CF10 3BX **Tel** *029 2037 1130*

Well-reputed restaurant with an elegant dining room, Benedicto's is best known for its tasty menu of "treasures from the sea". Choose from mixed fish *brodetto* (a selection of fish with saffron and light tomato sauce), *pauppiettes* of sole (stuffed with crab, flavoured with ginger set on a prawn sauce) or fresh lobster.

CARDIFF New House Country Hotel 🚹 🏄 🛏 ££££

Thornhill, Cardiff, CF14 9UA **Tel** *029 2052 0280*

The panoramic restaurant at this country-house hotel on the outskirts of Cardiff, is known to blend international flavours with the best local produce from the Vale of Glamorgan. Traditional Sunday lunch menu offers discounts for children. Ask for a table on the patio if you don't want to feel that you are dining at a hotel.

CRICKHOWELL Nantyffin Cider Mill 🚹 🏄 🛏 ££

Brecon Road, Crickhowell, Powys, NP8 1SG **Tel** *01873 810775*

Pretty country restaurant in a converted mill at the base of the Black Mountains, the Nantyffin remains popular with locals and tourists alike. Dining is split between the bar and the high-beamed, stone-walled restaurant. Dishes are a mix of the local (Glanusk pheasant) and the international (feta, artichoke and olive tart).

Key to Price Guide *see p608* **Key to Symbols** *see back cover flap*

FISHGUARD Diners' Circle

Tregynon, Gwaun Valley, nr Fishguard, Pembrokeshire, SA659TU **Tel** *01239 820531*

A 14th-century farmhouse restaurant, Diner's Circle has been steadily building itself a reputation since it first opened 25 years ago. All food is made on the premises by the owner, with an emphasis on beef and lamb reared on the nearby land. Only members can book to eat here, but one-night membership is available and well worth it.

HAY-ON-WYE Old Black Lion

Lion St, Hay-on-Wye, Via Hereford, HR3 5AD **Tel** *01497 820841*

Colourful restaurant in a 17th-century inn, the Old Black Lion is consistently rated one of the UK's top 100 inns. Dating back to the 1300s, the dining room comes complete with exposed timber beams. Menus feature British produce, including seafood from Cornwall and seasonal vegetables and herbs from the hotel's gardens.

HAY-ON-WYE Three Cocks Hotel & Restaurant

Three Cocks, nr Hay-on-Wye, Brecon, Powys, LD3 0SL **Tel** *01497 847215*

Listed hotel-restaurant on the main Hereford to Brecon road, the Three Cocks serves tasty home-made dishes using the best of local cuisine. The dining room is quiet, but inviting, with stone fireplaces, comfortable chairs and great views over the hotel garden. Booking recommended.

LLANWRTYD WELLS Carlton Riverside

Llanwrtyd Wells, Powys, LD5 4RA **Tel** *01591 610248*

Restaurant-with-rooms, the Carlton Riverside extends a warm welcome and an award-winning menu that uses the best locally sourced ingredients. All-inclusive gourmet breakfasts are on offer and the fantastic desserts include home-made sorbets, lime posset and Welsh cheeses. The restaurant has three AA rosettes.

LLANWRTYD WELLS The Lasswade Country House Hotel & Restaurant

Station Rd, Llanwrtyd Wells, Powys, LD5 4RW **Tel** *01591 610515*

The Lasswade, an Edwardian country-house hotel, is renowned for its fresh and locally sourced, mostly organic, produce. This AA Rosette restaurant won the "True Taste of Wales" and "Sustain Food Challenge" awards and has been in the Good Food Guide since 2004. The Welsh black beef is a speciality. Booking is recommended.

MONMOUTH The Stone Mill

Rockfield, Monmouth, NP25 5SW **Tel** *01600 716273*

On the outskirts of the Forest of Dean, picturesque Stone Mill occupies a converted 16th-century barn with oak beams and vaulted ceiling offset by modern furnishings. The menu features the best of Welsh cuisine, including locally sourced Longhorn beef, pork from Monmouth, chicken from Chepstow and fish from Brixham.

MONMOUTH Prego Bistro

7 Church St, Monmouth, Monmouthshire, NP25 3BX **Tel** *01600 712600*

Informal restaurant-with-rooms on Monmouth's main shopping street. Consultant chef Franco Taruschio delights with a mix of Mediterranean food with a predominantly Italian influence. The lunch menu is perfect for a break from shopping.

PEMBROKE George Wheeler Restaurant

Old Kings Arms Hotel, Main St, Pembroke, Pembrokeshire, SA71 4JS **Tel** *01646 683611*

Award-winning restaurant in Pembrokeshire's oldest hotel, George Wheeler showcases the best of Wales's local produce, especially fish, sourced daily from Milford Haven. Traditional dishes, such as hot Welsh cockles with laver bread and bacon, sit neatly alongside more modern fare, such as the ever-popular king prawns with garlic butter.

SKENFRITH The Bell at Skenfrith

Skenfrith, Monmouthshire, NP7 8UH **Tel** *01600 750235*

Renovated 17th-century coaching inn with guestrooms, the Bell is well worth the short drive out of Monmouth. The restaurant menu here ties in with the farmer's market at nearby Abergavenny. Welsh beef, lamb and wild mushrooms popularly feature on the menu.

SOLVA The Old Pharmacy

5 Main St, Solva, Pembrokeshire, SA62 6UU **Tel** *01437 720005*

Formerly a chemist shop, this quaint little restaurant in the harbour village of Lower Solva specializes in local fish and seafood. The menu's star attraction is the bouillabaisse with freshly baked olive oil bread. The Solva lobster and crab, and Welsh organic beef and lamb are good too. There's a charming riverside patio. Children's menu available.

ST DAVIDS Morgan's Restaurant

20 Nun St, St Davids, Pembrokeshire, SA62 6NT **Tel** *01437 720508*

Since it re-opened in April 2004, Morgan's Brasserie has gone from strength to strength. The menu is well priced with some innovative combinations, including monkfish medallions with mushrooms and laver bread sauce, and rack of lamb with Welsh honey and stem ginger. Save some room for the home-made desserts.

ST DAVIDS Warpool Court Hotel

St Davids, Pembrokeshire, SA62 6BN **Tel** *01437 720300*

Hotel-restaurant with enviable views over St Davids peninsula, the Warpool Court boasts a delicious daily changing menu of modern British fare. Roast venison saddle comes with venison faggot and cassis *jus*, while the roast corn-fed chicken breast is laid on a bed of Parmesan, chorizo and spinach risotto.

SWANSEA Labaire's
93 Newton Rd, Mumbles, Swansea, SA3 4BN **Tel** *01792 366006*

Elegant restaurant with a welcoming ambience, Labaire's serves quality cuisine with a reasonable price tag. The eclectic menus offer everything from fillet of fresh local sea bass to rack of spring Welsh lamb. Booking recommended. Traditional roasts, served on Sundays, include Yorkshire puddings.

SWANSEA Patrick's with Rooms
638 Mumbles Rd, Mumbles, Swansea, SA3 4EA **Tel** *01792 360199*

Fantastic restaurant-with-rooms overlooking the Mumbles, Patrick's caters for everyone: it also has a menu in Braille. The food is delicious with an accompanying wine list. Many of the ingredients used are sourced from the nearby countryside and sea, such as the tasty Gower mussels with leek and laver bread and St lystydd cheese gratin.

SWANSEA Morgans Restaurant
Somerset Place, Swansea, West Glamorgan, SA1 1RR **Tel** *01792 484848*

Morgans is Swansea's only five-star hotel and it has a fantastic menu to match. The main restaurant serves an elegant range of European dishes with an emphasis on locally-grown produce. The menu is constantly changing and there are also special lunch and two-course dinner menus. You can also visit the less expensive Café Bar.

TALYBONT-ON-USK Usk Inn
Talybont-on-Usk, Brecon, Powys, LD3 7JE **Tel** *01874 676251*

Fabulous country pub with rooms in the heart of the Brecon Beacons National Park, Usk Inn sources its ingredients daily from all over Wales: fresh milk and cheese from Brecon, vegetables from Merthyr, meat from Bwlch. The menu caters for everything from bar snacks to three-course table d'hôte.

USK Three Salmons Hotel
Bridge St, Usk, Monmouthshire, NP15 1RY **Tel** *01291 672133*

Restaurant in a beautifully timbered 17th-century coaching inn, Three Salmons Hotel, in the market town of Usk, serves a carefully crafted menu of fresh, local fare with an Italian twist. The carpaccio of beef and baked salmon with pistachio and Parmesan crust, gives a flavour of what is on offer; however, the menu changes regularly.

WHITEBROOK Crown at Whitebrook
Whitebrook, nr Monmouth, Monmouthshire, NP25 4TX **Tel** *01600 860254*

Elegant restaurant in a charming hotel just outside of Monmouth, Crown at Whitebrook dates back to 1670. Head chef James Sommerin uses local ingredients but classic French training to create a mouthwatering menu, which mixes game with local beef, lamb and fish.

WOLFSCASTLE Wolfscastle Country Hotel
Wolfscastle, Haverfordwest, Pembrokeshire, SA62 5LZ **Tel** *01437 741225*

One of Wales's grandest country-house hotel-restaurants, the Wolfscastle occupies a panoramic old riverside vicarage near to Haverfordwest and Fishguard. The menu is, unsurprisingly, big on fish with salmon, monkfish and halibut making a good showing next to Welsh beef, lamb and duck. Gourmet breaks available.

THE LOWLANDS

ANSTRUTHER The Cellar
24 E Green, Anstruther, Fife, KY10 3AA **Tel** *01333 310378*

Housed in one of Fife's oldest buildings, this cosy restaurant was voted UK Seafood Restaurant of the Year 2008. Chef Peter Jukes serves excellent seafood cuisine, with fish, crabs, lobsters and scallops playing a prominent role. Uses fresh local produce. Ideal for those looking for an intimate, romantic meal.

AYR Fouters Bistro
2A Academy St, Ayr, Ayrshire, KA7 1HS **Tel** *01292 261391*

A popular, lively bistro in a vaulted basement, located in the town centre, just off the main street. The ambience is warm and welcoming, and the menu offers modern Scottish cuisine with world influences; all produce is locally sourced. The dishes are skilfully prepared and served in an accomplished, yet informal style.

CUPAR Ostlers Close
25 Bonnygate, Cupar, Fife, KY15 4BU **Tel** *01334 655574*

A cosy, comfortable restaurant serving modern Scottish cuisine. The menu features a variety of seafood, as well as poultry and seasonal game. Uses fresh local produce. The wild mushrooms are highly recommended. Open for dinner from Tuesday to Saturday; lunch is offered only on Saturday.

DIRLETON The Open Arms
Main St, Dirleton, East Lothian, EH39 5EG **Tel** *01620 850241*

Situated on the edge of the village green, overlooking the 13th-century Dirleton Castle, this popular, family-owned country hotel has a well deserved reputation for good food. Guests can choose between the elegant, formal restaurant or the bright, informal brasserie. The convivial surroundings add to the charm.

EDINBURGH Susie's Diner

51–53 W Nicolson St, Edinburgh, EH8 9DB **Tel** *0131 667 8729*

A well-established vegetarian café, centrally located near Edinburgh University. The food at this self-service diner has a Mexican and Middle Eastern theme, with an extensive repertoire of dishes that include enchiladas, moussaka and large salads. Follows a "bring your own booze" policy. Relaxed and welcoming atmosphere.

EDINBURGH Daniel's Bistro

88 Commercial St, Leith, Edinburgh, EH3 6SF **Tel** *0131 553 5933*

Located in the city centre, this stylish restaurant serves modern French (Alsacian-style) fare, with a Scottish influence. The ambience is light and airy, and the cooking is of good value and excellent quality. An award-winning bistro with friendly service.

EDINBURGH Hendersons

94 Hanover St, Edinburgh, EH2 1DR **Tel** *0131 225 2131*

Established for more than 40 years, this vegetarian restaurant is an Edinburgh institution. The family-run eatery is open all day, and serves a wide variety of snacks and complete meals. Favourites include chunky vegetable soup, baked lasagne and spring rolls. Also offers gluten-free and dairy-free specialities.

EDINBURGH Indigo Yard

7 Charlotte Lane, Edinburgh, EH2 4QZ **Tel** *0131 220 5603*

Situated in the centre of the city's West End, this highly acclaimed café-restaurant is a popular meeting venue as well. Open all day for coffee, snacks, lunch and dinner, and offers a wide variety of dishes, designed to suit all tastes. The ambience is contemporary, the servings are generous and the service friendly and efficient.

EDINBURGH Room in Leith

1c Dock Place, Edinburgh, EH6 6LU **Tel** *0131 554 7427*

This Scottish bistro serving fish, seafood and a wide range of meats, is located on the water's edge and offers a cosy place to relax. Friendly, knowledgeable staff and contemporary dishes ensure a good experience all round. The café is extremely popular and usually packed with locals and visitors to the area.

EDINBURGH Le Café St Honore

34 N W Thistle St Lane, Edinburgh, EH2 1EA **Tel** *0131 226 2211*

Located close to the main shopping streets, but in a quiet lane, this traditional French restaurant with a typical Parisian-style interior, is a favourite of many. All produce is of the finest quality, the dishes are imaginative and skilfully cooked and the staff are friendly and helpful.

EDINBURGH The Vintners Rooms Restaurant and Bar

The Vaults, 87 Giles St, Leith, Edinburgh, EH6 6BZ **Tel** *0131 554 6767*

This unusual candlelit restaurant is housed in a wine warehouse, and is one of Leith's more established eateries. Offers imaginative, contemporary Scottish menus. Guests can opt for a light lunch in the wine bar or a complete meal in the restaurant – the standard of food, service and atmosphere is admirable in both.

EDINBURGH Atrium and Blue Bar Café

10 Cambridge St, Edinburgh, EH1 2ED **Tel** *0131 228 8882*

Two restaurants run by consummate professionals. The more formal Atrium is open for lunch and dinner, and offers a fine, contemporary dining experience, while the informal Blue Bar Café is open all day for snacks, coffee, drinks, lunch and dinner. The cuisine is modern British with a Mediterranean twist. Superb quality in both places.

EDINBURGH Restaurant Martin Wishart

54 The Shore, Edinburgh, EH6 6RA **Tel** *0131 553 3557*

Possibly the finest dining experience in all of Scotland. Chef Martin Wishart's creative and innovative cuisine is in great demand by lovers of fine food, and justifiably so. Serves modern French fare, using the best produce available. The service is excellent, the ambience welcoming and the experience truly memorable.

EDINBURGH The Balmoral

The Balmoral Hotel, 1 Princes St, Edinburgh, EH2 2EQ **Tel** *0131 557 6727*

This classy and up-market restaurant is located in The Balmoral Hotel, and has its own entrance on Princes Street. Acclaimed chef Jeff Bland is renowned for his skill, imagination and passion for fine Scottish cuisine. The service at this Michelin-starred and multiple award-winning dining venue is also exceptional.

ELIE Sangster's

51 High St, Elie, Fife, KY9 1BZ **Tel** *01333 331001*

Located in a popular, coastal East Neuk village, this small, fine restaurant is run by one of Scotland's most recognized and skilled chefs, Bruce Sangster. Specialities include twice baked cheese soufflé, slow cooked noisette of lamb and delicious desserts. Closed on Monday, as well as for dinner on Sunday and for lunch on Tuesday and Saturday.

GLASGOW Firebird

1321 Argyle St, nr Museum of Transport, Glasgow **Tel** *0141 334 0594*

A popular bar-restaurant hang-out for drinks and an informal evening meal. All produce is of the freshest and highest quality, and the pizzas are among the best in Glasgow. It can get quite noisy at the weekends; if you like it quieter, go during the week instead.

GLASGOW City Merchant
97–99 Candleriggs, Glasgow, G1 1NP Tel 0141 553 1577

A warm and welcoming, family-run restaurant located in Glasgow's Merchant City. This bustling venue serves excellent seafood cuisine with a Scottish influence and uses the best local produce. The ambience is informal and rustic. Can accommodate up to 120 guests. Offers good value for money.

GLASGOW The Fat Ladies at the Buttery
652 Argyle St, Glasgow, G3 8UF Tel 0141 221 8188

Although located in a less than salubrious part of the city centre, this is one place that is well worth seeking out. This attractive pub has been converted into an elegant dining room, but retains elements of its past. Largely a fish restaurant, it also serves hearty Scottish fare, made from fresh local produce. Also offers a wide selection of desserts and cheeses.

GLASGOW Gamba
225A W George St, Glasgow, G2 2ND Tel 0141 572 0899

Popular, seafood restaurant, recognized for its high quality, varied cuisine. The food is meticulously prepared, using fresh seasonal produce such as fish, lobsters and oysters, and beautifully presented. The interior of this city centre eatery is modern, stylish and comfortable, while the ambience is cosy.

GLASGOW Stravaigin
28 Gibson St, Hillhead, Glasgow, G212 8NX Tel 0141 334 2665

Well placed in the popular Gibson Street, in the Glasgow University neighbourhood. Features a popular café-bar and a highly successful restaurant. Serves award-winning pub fare: the best of Scottish produce flavoured with the world's sauces, herbs and spices.

GLASGOW Brian Maule at Chardon d'Or
176 W Regent St, Glasgow, G2 4RL Tel 0141 248 3801

One of the finest restaurants in the city. Highly acclaimed chef Brian Maule provides an innovative menu of French cuisine, using locally sourced Scottish ingredients. Serves a variety of fish, poultry and game. The stylish, yet unpretentious, ambience and the friendly and efficient staff complete the experience.

GLASGOW Ubiquitous Chip
12 Ashton Lane, Glasgow, G12 8SJ Tel 0141 334 5007

A Glasgow West-End institution, this prestigious restaurant serves traditional Scottish cuisine, made with fresh local ingredients, and has been a home of culinary excellence for over 30 years. Great atmosphere and a friendly staff make this a notable place.

GULLANE La Potinière
Main St, Gullane, East Lothian, EH31 2AA Tel 01620 843214

Superior restaurant situated in a pretty East Lothian village. The menu changes from season to season, and offers well-prepared food, using fresh local produce. Boasts a caring and hospitable staff, as well as a private parking facility. The restaurant is closed on Monday and Tuesday.

KIPPFORD The Anchor Hotel
Main St, Kippford, Dalbeattie, Kirkudbrightshire, DG5 4LN Tel 01556 620205

This seaside hotel and pub is situated on the waterfront in the pretty village of Kippford, with great views of the coastal activity. The friendly bar serves appetizing pub food, using seasonal, locally sourced produce. A popular spot to enjoy real ale and a filling meal. The hotel is comfortable and of good value.

LARGS Nardinis
The Esplanade, Largs, KA30 8NF, Ayrshire, Tel 01475 689313

A splendid Art Deco interior sets the scene of this seafront lounge café. This well-known Scottish institution is definitely worth a visit if in the area. Breakfasts, cakes and Italian and British dishes are served all day. A perfect place to relax, sit back and read the paper. Extremely popular with both locals and tourists.

LINLITHGOW Champany Inn
Champany, nr Linlithgow, West Lothian, EH49 7LU Tel 01506 834532

Located on the outskirts of Linlithgow, not far from Edinburgh, this charming restaurant has a well-earned reputation for offering some of the best steaks in Scotland. Diners can choose from strip loin, rib eye, fillet and porterhouse; all cooked to perfection. Must-try specialities include delicious Loch Gruinart oysters and succulent hot smoked salmon.

MOFFAT Well View Hotel
Ballplay Rd, Moffat, Dumfriesshire, DG10 9JH Tel 01683 220184

An intimate hotel situated in a quiet residential street, a few minutes walk from the main street. Modern French cooking with some Scottish elements, using the best local produce available, is served in the dining room of this family-run establishment. Presents a peaceful atmosphere and comfortable surroundings.

PORTPATRICK Knockinaam Lodge
Off A77, nr Portpatrick, Dumfries and Galloway, DG9 9AD Tel 01776 810471

This attractive country house has an idyllic location overlooking the sea, and even boasts its own small private beach. Comfort and pampering are top priority at this beautiful and stylish lodge. The dining room serves international cuisine, with modern Scottish influences. A welcoming ambience adds to the charm.

Key to Price Guide *see p608* **Key to Symbols** *see back cover flap*

ST ANDREWS The Peat Inn   £££
On B940, Cupar, nr St Andrews, Fife, KY15 5LH **Tel** *01334 840206*

Highly accomplished modern cooking, using regional produce and seasonal vegetables, has established this smart hotel-restaurant as one of the best in Britain. The innovative cuisine is prepared by renowned chef David Wilson, whose passion for good Scottish fare is evident in his creations. Lunch is particularly good value.

ST ANDREWS The Seafood Restaurant   ££££
Bruce Embankment, St Andrews, Fife, KY16 9AS **Tel** *01334 479475*

Located in an enviable seafront location, this superb restaurant offers a memorable dining experience, along with striking views of the coastline. The menu features a variety of seafood, which is carefully prepared and beautifully presented. The ambience at this stylish eatery is warm and cosy.

ST MONANS The Seafood Restaurant   ££££
16 W End, St Monans, Fife, KY10 2BX **Tel** *01333 730327*

An excellent place to enjoy the very best of local seafood. Set in a stunning water's edge location, this fine, modern restaurant is attractively and elegantly fitted out. Serves a wide range of fresh, seasonal fish and seafood, including prawns, crabs, scallops and more. The food is meticulously prepared, and the staff friendly and attentive.

SOUTH QUEENSFERRY Orocco Pier   £££
17 High St, S Queensferry, Edinburgh, EH30 9PP **Tel** *0131 331 1298*

Situated on the main street in South Queensferry, a short distance from Edinburgh city centre. Open all day for light snacks, coffees and meals, this elegant restaurant is a great place to enjoy the splendid views of the Forth estuary and its bridges. Fish and seafood play a prominent role in the menu.

TROON Highgrove House Hotel   ££
Old Loans Rd, Troon, Ayrshire, KA7 7HL **Tel** *01292 312511*

Perched high on Dundonald Hill, this hotel-restaurant occupies a retired sea captain's house, and enjoys magnificent views over the Firth of Clyde and the Mull of Kintyre. The atmosphere is comfortable and welcoming. Serves informal meals from a varied menu, featuring some old favourites and newer innovations.

THE HIGHLANDS AND ISLANDS

ABERDEEN The Udny Arms   ££
Main St, Newburgh, Nr Aberdeen, Aberdeenshire, AB41 6BL **Tel** *01358 789444*

This family-run, village hotel has a bistro and pub that is cosy, full of character, and serves up honest, wholesome food. The locals rate this place very highly, not least because it is great value for money. The staff are friendly and efficient which makes for a pleasant dining experience.

ABERDEEN Priory   ££££
Mary Culter House Hotel, South Deeside Rd, Aberdeen, Aberdeenshire, AB12 5GB **Tel** *01224 732124*

Located on the banks of the River Dee, the Priory restaurant provides a lovely setting for a romantic candle-lit dinner, with its stone walls, open fire and intimate atmosphere. The menu is modern European with a Scottish twist, and every dish on it is prepared using excellent local produce. Closed Sun.

ABERDEEN The Silver Darling   ££££
Pocra Quay, Footdee, N Pier, Aberdeen, Aberdeenshire, AB11 5DQ **Tel** *01224 576229*

A superb seafood bistro restaurant located on the north side of Aberdeen harbour. This well-established venue is one of the best places to enjoy the daily catch, which has been carefully cooked and presented. Try and sit by the window if you can to make the most of the splendid coastline views. Closed Sun.

ALEXANDRIA Lomond's Restaurant at Cameron House Hotel   ££££
Off A82, Loch Lomond, Alexandria, West Dunbartonshire, G83 8QZ **Tel** *01389 755565*

A formal dining room at a luxurious country house, situated on the tranquil shores of Loch Lomond and set amid beautiful grounds. This elegant and stylish restaurant has won several awards, and offers exquisitely prepared meals in comfortable surroundings. The staff are well trained and friendly. An experience of a lifetime.

AUCHMITHIE But 'n' Ben   ££
Off A92, 1 Auchmithie, nr Arbroath, Angus, DD11 5SQ **Tel** *01241 877223*

Housed in twin cottages in a working fishing village. The restaurant is open for lunch, dinner and the traditional high tea. Menus naturally feature the day's catch and offer superb value for money. This small eatery is somewhat of a local institution and worth taking the trouble to find. Welcoming ambience.

AUCHTERARDER Andrew Fairlie @ Gleneagles   £££££
Gleneagles Hotel, Auchterarder, Perthshire, PH3 1NF **Tel** *01764 694267*

One of the finest dining experiences in Scotland. This elegant restaurant is set within the luxurious Gleneagles Hotel. The highly acclaimed chef presents imaginative French cuisine with a Scottish flavour. The must-try specialities include smoked lobster, roast Anjou squab with black truffle gnocchi and delicious hot chocolate biscuit dessert.

BALLATER Darroch Learg

Braemar Rd, Ballater, Royal Deeside, AB35 AUX **Tel** *013397 55443*

A great restaurant, with a well-deserved reputation for excellence, set within a Victorian shooting lodge. The modern British cuisine is particularly outstanding, as the best local produce is used to create imaginative and flavoursome dishes. The setting of this award-winning venue is relaxed, and the adjacent conservatory adds to the charm.

BLAIRGOWRIE The Loft Restaurant

Golf Course Rd, Blair Atholl by Pitlochry, Perthshire, PH18 5TE **Tel** *01796 481377*

An elegant venue with old-worldly beams and stone walls where guests can choose to dine in the more formal restaurant or enjoy a casual meal at the bistro. Both places offer skilfully prepared food using fresh local ingredients and a varying menu of seafood, poultry and game.

CAIRNDOW Loch Fyne Oyster Bar

Clachan, Cairndow, Argyll, PA26 8BL **Tel** *01499 600236*

Highly renowned restaurant offering an impressive array of fish and seafood. The menu features an excellent selection of both hot and cold meals, including delicious oysters, mussels, two veggie options and a lobster platter. Also offers steaks, lamb, and chicken dishes, as well as vegetarian choices.

CARNOUSTIE Ganges

11 Park Ave, Carnoustie, Angus, DD7 7JA **Tel** *01241 853336*

Located in a former Masonic hall just off Carnoustie's high street, this relatively new Indian restaurant has already earned a reputation for its tasty food and affordable prices. All the classic Indian dishes can be found here, cooked to an excellent standard. Closed Mon.

COLBOST BY DUNVEGAN Three Chimneys

Colbost, Dunvegan, Isle of Skye, Inverness-shire, IV55 8ZT **Tel** *01470 511258*

Situated a short distance from Dunvegan, on the western shores of the loch. Once a stone-built crofter's cottage, this award-winning restaurant offers seafood and game, lovingly prepared with fresh local produce. The ambience is peaceful and relaxed, and the service friendly. One of the "not to miss" places in Scotland.

DRYMEN The Pottery

The Square, Drymen, Argyll, G63 OBJ **Tel** *01360 660458*

Delightful restaurant and coffee shop, located in the square of the pretty little village of Drymen. Offers good, home-cooked food all day and delicious afternoon teas and lunches – all prepared fresh. Boasts a charming terrace. A popular stopping point for locals as well as tourists exploring the area.

DUFFTOWN A Taste of Speyside

10 Balvenie St, Dufftown, Moray, AB55 4AB **Tel** *01340 820860*

Set amid the mountains and glens of the Spey Valley, this restaurant has been offering an enjoyable culinary experience to customers for many years. The food here is wholesome and simply prepared, showing a strong commitment to quality local produce such as fish, poultry and game.

DUNKELD Kinnaird Estate

Kinnaird Estate, off B898, nr Dunkeld, Perthshire, PH8 0LB **Tel** *01796 482440*

This stylish restaurant, located in an estate hotel, produces food of great originality. Lunch is more affordable and worth trying. The property is beautifully maintained, with a range of accommodation available. The surroundings are elegant and welcoming, and the staff professional and friendly. An excellent experience.

FORT WILLIAM Crannog Seafood Restaurant

The Waterfront, Fort William, Perthshire, PH33 7PT **Tel** *01397 705589*

Nothing can detract from the simple pleasure of eating exquisitely fresh seafood while overlooking a panoramic loch view. The helpings at this restaurant are generous, the atmosphere is warm and relaxing and the service quite efficient.

INVERNESS Culloden House

Culloden, Inverness, Inverness-shire, IV2 7BZ **Tel** *01463 790461*

A historic building with loads of character, set in lovely grounds, close to the Culloden Visitor Centre. Offers Scottish country house-style food, with sauces, jellies, sorbets and mousses interspersing a wide variety of hearty and appetizing meat, game and fish dishes. Accommodation is also available.

KILBERRY Kilberry Inn

Kilberry, by Tarbert, Loch Fyne, Argyll, PA29 6YD **Tel** *01880 770223*

This former post office is now run as a pub in a quiet coastal village. Serves modern Scottish cuisine, with a constantly changing menu. However, a good selection of old favourites is also featured so not to disappoint the regular customers. Has a warm and cosy atmosphere.

KILLIECRANKIE Killiecrankie Hotel

Off A9, nr Pitlochry, Perthshire, PH16 5LG **Tel** *01796 473220*

Attractive, well-appointed hotel, which has the feel of a village inn. The food served here is healthy and wholesome, with some unusual, yet innovative twists. The excellent bar meals supplement the fine, dinnertime fare, both of which are served in cosy and inviting surroundings. The staff are friendly and hospitable.

Key to Price Guide *see p608* **Key to Symbols** *see back cover flap*

KINCRAIG The Boathouse Restaurant
🏃 ♿ £££

Loch Insh, Kincraig, Inverness-shire, PH21 1NU **Tel** *01540 651272*

Charming log-cabin restaurant overlooking Loch Insh. Features a traditional Scottish menu with local fish, haggis and steak, and serves tea, coffee, snacks and home-baked dishes throughout the day. Offers a special menu for children, and encourages outdoor meals on the balcony in summer. Also has a gift shop and a bar.

KIRRIEMUIR Lochside Lodge
♿ 🍷 £££

Bridgend of Lintrathen, by Kirriemuir, Angus, DD8 5JJ **Tel** *01575 560340*

Situated deep in the countryside, this tastefully converted restaurant was once a farm steading. Located near the loch, this cosy lodge is a welcoming place to enjoy some of the best cooking in the area. The menu features well balanced and simply prepared meals, and the use of local produce is imaginative and highly successful.

KYLESKU The Kylesku Hotel
🏃 🍷 £££

On A894 by Lairg, Sutherland, IV27 4HW **Tel** *01971 502231*

Lochs and mountains provide a magnificent backdrop to this hotel, which is located on the quayside. The bar and restaurant menus are extensive, and feature an array of local dishes. However, the speciality here is the freshly caught fish. The tranquil surroundings create an excellent setting in which to unwind and relax.

OBAN Wide Mouthed Frog
🏃 ♿ ££

Dunstaffnage Bay, by Oban, Argyll, PA37 1PX **Tel** *01631 567005*

Situated between the villages of Connel and Oban, this restaurant is a popular meeting place, particularly with the sailing fraternity. Good food and convivial surroundings make this a deservedly bustling venue. The menus feature local produce and the food is well cooked and presented. Accommodation also available.

OBAN The Knipoch Hotel
🏃 ♿ 🍷 £££

On A816, nr Oban, Argyll, PA34 4QT **Tel** *01852 316251*

Situated on the outskirts of Oban, this traditional country hotel has been a popular stopping place for many years. The bar meals here are excellent, while the dinners range from three to five courses. In addition, the huge array of vegetables and flamboyant puddings are as eyecatching as they are tasty.

OBAN Ee'usk
🏃 ♿ ££££

N Pier, Oban, Argyll, PA34 5QD **Tel** *01631 565666*

A recent addition to the eating scene in Oban, this stylish restaurant is located in a great waterside setting, and has something for everyone. Serves mouthwatering seafood, using fresh catches of the day. A must-visit for those who enjoy fish. A favoured choice of many, this eatery also offers great views of the coastline.

PERTH 63 Tay Street
🍷 ££££

63 Tay St, Perth, Perthshire, PH2 8NN **Tel** *01738 441451*

Run by a husband and wife team, this central Perth restaurant has been justifiably recognized for the quality and modern Scottish cuisine it offers. The cooking is superb, and the service friendly and professional. The menus feature the best regional produce available, which is used to create imaginative, flavoursome and thoroughly enjoyable dishes.

PERTH Let's Eat
🏃 ♿ 🍷 ££££

77–79 Kinnoull St, Perth, Perthshire, PH1 5EZ **Tel** *01738 643377*

Local ingredients and skilled and passionate owners play a prominent role in this restaurant's success. Offers relaxing and comfortable surroundings, innovative menus and skilled cooking. Fish, game, beef and lamb are the mainstay of the delicious meals, and are usually accompanied by fresh vegetables and creative sauces.

PLOCKTON Plockton Shores Restaurant
🏃 🍷 ££

Harbour St, Plockton, Ross-shire, IV52 8YX **Tel** *01599 544263*

Nestled on the shores of Loch Carron, this restaurant specializing in fish and shellfish. Diners can take in the spectacular views from across the bay while enjoying dishes such as Cullen skink (smoked haddock in a potato and parsley soup) or seared fillets of Mallaig sea bass served with aubergines and oven-roasted tomatoes.

PORT APPIN The Airds Hotel
🏃 🍷 £££££

Port Appin, Argyll, PA38 4DF **Tel** *01631 730236*

This hotel-restaurant is set on a fine waterfront location in Appin, and has a cheerful and comfortable interior. Offers a well balanced menu, with a variety of seafood, poultry and game, and uses fresh local produce to prepare appetizing dishes. The service is excellent, and the ambience warm and inviting.

ST MARGARET'S HOPE The Creel
🏃 🍷 £££

Front Rd, St Margaret's Hope, Orkney, KW17 2SL **Tel** *01856 831311*

A front-runner for one of the best places to eat in Orkney. The dishes are emphatically Orcadian in style, with a commitment to the wonderful, locally sourced seafood – which features frequently on the menu – as well as beef and seaweed fed lamb. The service is friendly and helpful. Also offers accommodation.

ULLAPOOL The Ceilidh Place
🏃 🎵 🍷 ££

14 W Argyle St, Ullapool, Sutherland, IV26 2TY **Tel** *01854 612103*

An interesting building, with a great atmosphere. Situated in an award-winning hotel with its own bookshop, rooms and bar, this restaurant serves superbly skilled and imaginative dishes, which are unashamedly local and of the highest quality. Meals incorporate fish, meat, poultry, vegetables and fruits – all prepared simply, yet excellently.

British Pubs

No tour of Britain could be complete without some exploration of its public houses. These are a great social institution, descendants of centuries of hostelries, ale houses and stagecoach halts. Some have colourful histories or fascinating contents, and occupy a central role in the community, staging quiz games and folk dancing. Many of those listed below are lovely buildings, or have attractive settings. Most serve a variety of beers, spirits and wine by the glass.

A "free house" is independent and will stock several leading regional beers, but most pubs are "tied" – this means that they are owned by a brewery and only stock that brewery's selection.

Many pubs offer additional attractions such as live music and beer gardens with picnic tables. Traditional pub food is often served at lunchtime, and increasingly, in the evenings as well. Traditional pub games take many forms, including cribbage, shove ha'penny, skittles, dominoes and darts.

LONDON

Bloomsbury: *Lamb*
94 Lamb's Conduit St, WC1.
Tel 020 7405 0713. **Map** 3 C5
Unspoilt Victorian pub with lovely cut-glass "snob screens" and theatrical photographs. Small courtyard at the rear. 🍴 🔊

City: *Black Friar*
174 Queen Victoria St, EC4.
Tel 020 7236 5474. **Map** 12 F2
Eccentric inside and out, with intriguing Art Nouveau decor. Attentive service. 🍴 🚶

City: *Ye Olde Cheshire Cheese*
145 Fleet St EC4.
Tel 020 7353 6170. **Map** 12 E1
Authentic 17th-century inn that evokes shades of Dickens's London. Its stark glory is best enjoyed in front of the open fires. 🍴 🚶

Hammersmith: *Dove*
19 Upper Mall, W6.
Tel 020 8748 9474.
One of west London's most attractive riverside pubs – you can watch rowing crews from the terrace. 🍴 🔊

Hampstead: *Spaniards Inn*
Spaniards Lane, NW3.
Tel 020 8731 8406.
Famous Hampstead landmark dating from the 18th century, once part of a tollgate. 🍴 🔊 🚶

Kensington: *Windsor Castle*
114 Campden Hill Rd, W8.
Tel 020 7243 8797. **Map** 7 C4
A civilized Georgian inn with oak furnishings and open fires.
The walled garden attracts well-heeled crowds in summer. Hearty English food. 🍴 🔊

Southwark: *George Inn*
77 Borough High St, SE1.
Tel 020 7407 2056. **Map** 13 B4
Quaint coaching inn with unique galleried courtyard. Rooms ramble upstairs and downstairs, and the overspill sits outside. Morris dancers may be seen performing here at times (see p120). 🍴 🔊 🚶

THE DOWNS AND CHANNEL COAST

Alciston: *Rose Cottage Inn*
Alciston nr Polegate.
Tel 01323 8703774.
In a creeper-covered cottage, this rural Sussex pub is decorated in classic rustic style, with beamed ceilings and open fireplaces. The local ales and busy kitchen add to its warmth. 🍴 🔊

Brighton: *Market Inn*
Market St, BN1 1HH.
Tel 01273 329483.
Once home to the Prince of Wales's chimney sweep, this is now something of a Brighton institution, spilling out onto The Lanes in the summer months. 🍴

Ditchling: *The Bull Hotel*
2 High St, BN6 8SY.
Tel 01273 843147.
Housed in a 14th-century building, the main bar is large, rambling and pleasantly traditional with characterful old wooden floorboards, beams and furniture, and a blazing fire. 🍴 🎵 🔊 🚶

Faversham: *White Horse Inn*
The Street, Boughton.
Tel 01227 751343.
Chaucer gave this place a passing mention in *The Canterbury Tales*. Among hop gardens and orchards, this genial country pub resounds with echoes from the past. Thirteen en suite bedrooms. 🍴 🎵 🔊 🚶 🚻

Goodwood: *Star and Garter*
East Dean, nr Goodwood.
Tel 01243 811318.
This lovely 18th-century inn is nestled at the foot of the South Downs. Local ales and cider are served straight from barrels. A good selection of wines. Excellent seafood dishes in summer and game dishes in winter. 🍴 🔊 🚶

Isle of Wight:
The Wight Mouse Inn
Newport Rd, Chale.
Tel 01983 730431.
This pub draws in the locals with its range of real ales. Jazz music on Thursdays. 🍴 🎵 🔊 🚶

Lewes: *Six Bells Inn*
Chiddingly, nr Lewes.
Tel 01825 872227.
Once a stopover for stagecoaches, this cosy drop-in now does a fine job of reviving weary ramblers and thirsty locals. Supposedly haunted by a grey cat and one Sara French, hanged in 1852 after serving her husband a pie seasoned with arsenic. 🍴 🎵 🔊 🚶 🚻

Romsey: *The Star Inn*
East Tytherley, nr Romsey.
Tel 01794 340225.
Popular watering hole on the edge of the New Forest, overlooking the village cricket pitch. The rivers Test and Dunn are nearby. Overnight accommodation available. 🍴 🔊 🚶

Rye: *The Mermaid*
Mermaid St. *Tel* 01797 223065.
Dating from 1136, this is one of the country's oldest inns. Constructed from old ship timbers, The Mermaid is an evocative slice of England's nautical history. Sit by the open fire and spot the celebrities having a quiet drink. 🍴 🔊 🚶

Walliswood: *The Scarlett Arms*
Walliswood Green Rd.
Tel 01306 627243.
Handsome inn with flagstone bar, wooden benches and a grand inglenook fireplace. The staff make the experience all the more congenial. Occasional live music. 🍴 🎵 🔊 🚶 🎶

EAST ANGLIA

Cambridge: *The Boathouse*
14 Chesterton Rd. **Tel** 01223 460905.
This riverside pub boasts a natty nautical theme and exceedingly comfortable armchairs. The beer garden is always warm and toasty, courtesy of heaters, allowing you to watch the river flow all year around. 🍴 🎵 🛏 🎿 🚬 🖋

Itteringham:
The Walpole Arms
The Common. **Tel** 01263 587258.
Oak-beamed inn that has been serving locally brewed ales since the 1700s. The restaurant is also highly regarded. 🍴 🛏 🎿 🚬

Kings Lynn: *The Lord Nelson*
Walsingham Rd, Burnham Thorpe.
Tel 01328 738241.
This watering hole was once one of Lord Nelson's favourite haunts. Kick back on any of the old high-backed benches, and wait for the attentive staff to take your order. Private functions are held in the handsome, flagstoned Victory Bar. Quiz all Sunday. 🍴 🎵 🛏 🎿 🖋

Norfolk: *Red Lion*
Wells Rd, Stiffkey. **Tel** 01328 830552.
The oldest parts of the simple bars have a few beams, aged flooring tiles or bare boards, and big open fires. A back gravel terrace has seats and tables for enjoying the bar food on a sunny day, and some pleasant walks are nearby. Real ale and 30 malt whiskies are available.
🍴 🎵 🛏 🎿 🚬

Norwich: *The Fat Cat*
49 W End St. **Tel** 01603 624364.
Rightly famed for its extensive real ale selection, The Fat Cat is full of attractions, starting with the well-stocked bar and the lively local clientele. 🍴 🚬

Ringstead: *The Gin Trap Inn*
6 High St. **Tel** 01485 525264.
Close to the Norfolk coastline and just on the edge of the Ringstead Downs nature reserve, this classic country pub features hand-pumped real ales and cosy log fires. The restaurant has a devoted following. Overnight accommodation available.
Quiz all Sunday.
🍴 🛏 🚬

Southwold: *The Crown Hotel*
High St. **Tel** 01502 722186.
The pub remains the star of this newly converted hotel, though the chic restaurant is becoming a firm local favourite. Excellent selection of wines at the bar. 🍴 🎿 🚬

Stowmarket:
The Buxhall Crown
Mill Rd, Buxhall. **Tel** 01449 736521.
Local real ales take pride of place in this old village pub that also does a roaring trade in home-cooked food with locally sourced ingredients. Good list of wine by the glass. 🍴

Suffolk:
The Six Bells at Bardwell
Bardwell, Bury St Edmunds.
Tel 01359 250820.
This village green charmer, dating from the 1500s, offers superb food and peaceful accommodation.
🍴 🛏 🎿 🚬

Walden: *Queen's Head Inn*
High St, Littlebury, Saffron Walden.
Tel 01799 522251.
Attractive coaching inn with a relaxed, family ambience. Stocks a decent selection of ales and has a heady wine list. There are six en suite rooms. 🍴 🎵 🛏 🎿 🖋

THAMES VALLEY

Aylesbury: *The King's Head*
Kings Head Passage, Market Sq, Buckinghamshire. **Tel** 01296 718812.
A small oasis in the heart of a pretty market town, this airy pub has award-winning food and ales and a courtyard for whiling away long summer afternoons. 🍴 🛏

Bedford: *The Park*
98 Kimbolton Rd, Bedfordshire.
Tel 01234 409305.
This warm and friendly pub has traditional features such as oak beams and old fireplaces. Good, wholesome food on offer. 🍴 🎵 🛏 🎿 🚬

Bicester: *The Hundred Acres*
Hart Place, Oxfordshire.
Tel 01869 329981.
A homely pub serving food and open late on weekends. Welcomes children until 8pm.
🍴 🛏 🎿 🚬

Chipping Norton:
The Falkland Arms
Great Tew, Chipping Norton, Oxfordshire. **Tel** 01608 683653.
Award-winning cask ales and a wonderful atmosphere. You can try beer tasters before you buy at this traditional gem of a place.
🍴 🎵 🛏 🖋

Faringdon: *The Trout*
Tadpole Bridge, Buckland Marsh, nr Faringdon. **Tel** 01367 870382.
Always busy and bustling, this 17th-century pub boasts a river-front garden where customers can savour local dishes.
🍴 🛏 🎿 🚬

Great Hormead:
The Three Tuns
High Street, Hertfordshire.
Tel 01763 289409.
A traditional thatched and beamed village pub with a cosy open fire in winter and a patio in summer. Hearty and reasonably priced food. 🍴 🛏 🎿 🚬 🖋

Luton: *The Bricklayers Arms*
High Town Rd, Bedfordshire.
Tel 01582 611017.
A friendly pub with ice-cold beers and plenty of quiz machines. Order whatever's on the left-hand pump, since its contents are changed constantly. 🖋

Newbury: *The Monument*
Northbrook St, Berkshire.
Tel 01635 41964.
The busiest pub around, there are different events every night of the week and a wide range of pub games. There is also a beer garden. 🍴 🎵 🛏 🖋

Oxford: *The White Horse*
52 Broad St. **Tel** 01865 728318.
This cosy pub has loads of character, with pictures of old sports stars on the walls and a great range of beers. 🍴

Watton-at-Stone: *The Bull*
113 High St, Herts. **Tel** 01920 831032.
Sit around the open-hearth fire at this 14th-century inn, or in the picturesque garden. 🍴 🛏 🎿

WESSEX

Abbotsbury: *Ilchester Arms*
Market St, Dorset. **Tel** 01305 871243.
A prominent landmark in this quaint village, the 18th-century stone Grade II listed inn features a deluxe conservatory. 🍴 🎵 🛏 🎿 🚬 🖋

Bath: *The Bell*
103 Walcot St, Bath, Avon.
Tel 01225 460426.
Splendid little pub, with billiards, live music and organic food. Soak in the friendly atmosphere while tucking into tasty sandwiches and cold plates. 🎵 🛏 🖋

Bridport: *Shave Cross Inn*
Shave Cross, Marshwood Vale, Dorset. **Tel** 01308 868358.
Award-winning inn with fine ales as well as English, Caribbean and international food. Five rooms.
🍴 🎵 🛏 🎿 🚬 🖋

Pensford: *Carpenter's Arms*
Stanton Wick, nr Pensford, Somerset.
Tel 01761 490202.
Overlooking the lovely Chew
Valley, this welcoming pub is set
among a row of small miners'
houses. It has an excellent menu
and a comprehensive wine list.

Salisbury: *Haunch of Venison*
1 Minster St, Salisbury, Wiltshire.
Tel 01722 411313.
The severed, mummified hand of
an 18th-century card player is on
display (along with more pleasant
antiques) at this 650-year-old pub.
The restaurant is a must-visit for a
good meal. Keep an eye out for
the resident ghost.

Salisbury: *The New Inn*
41/47 New St, Wiltshire.
Tel 01722 326662.
The low-beamed ceilings and
intimate interior lighting here
are offset by fine views of the
cathedral spire opposite. The
menu is broad and vegetarian-
friendly.

DEVON AND CORNWALL

Dawlish: *The Mount Pleasant*
Mount Pleasant Rd, Dawlish Warren,
Devon. *Tel 01626 863151.*
This pub is renowned for its views
over Exmouth from the dining
area. Drinkers visit once and
become loyal customers for years.
The warm ambience makes a
winning combination with super
value for money.

Exeter: *The Bridge Inn*
Bridge Hill, Topsham, Devon.
Tel 01392 873862.
With its pink exterior, you can't
miss this riverside pub, which has
been run by the same family for
111 years. Its several separate
rooms with fireplaces are truly
snug in winter, while the garden
is gorgeous on sunny days.
A pub with no bar, they serve
drinks and bar snacks through a
hatch in the corridor.

Falmouth: *Pandora Inn*
Restronguet Creek, Mylor Bridge,
nr Falmouth, Cornwall.
Tel 01326 372678.
Medieval pub with a thatched
roof by the waterside. Full of cosy
corners, low wooden ceilings, panelled walls and a variety of maritime
memorabilia.

Knowstone: *Masons Arms*
Inn Devon. *Tel 01398 341231.*
An atmospheric Grade II listed
cottage that is full of character.

The decor includes farm tools
and a bread-oven fireplace.
Delicious restaurant food and
friendly hosts.

Lynton: *Fox and Goose*
Parracombe, Barnstaple.
Tel 01598 763239.
A friendly and welcoming pub/
B&B with very good food and
beer. The log fire, plank ceiling
and assorted mounted antlers and
horns give a proper Exmoor feel
to the place. Serves real ale and
local cider.

Newton Abbot: *Two Mile Oak*
Totnes Rd, Abbotskerswell.
Tel 01803 812411.
An old coaching inn with a beamed
lounge and an alcove just for two.
A mix of wooden tables and chairs,
and a fine winter log fire.

Penzance: *The Pirate Inn*
Alverton Rd, Alverton, Cornwall.
Tel 01736 366094.
Recommended by the local youth
hostel, this is a friendly stop for a
beer and sandwich. Visitors often
invest in the souvenir T-shirts sold
here.

Porthleven: *Harbour Inn*
Commercial Rd, Cornwall.
Tel 01326 573876.
Watch the sun go down and sip
a top-quality pint as you sit by
Porthleven's harbour. Recently
refurbished, this pub retains its
original character, the modern
sofas and coffee tables notwith-
standing.

Saltash: *The Cecil Arms*
St Stephens, Cornwall.
Tel 01752 843408.
A pub with its own dedicated community, it serves wonderful ales and
food. The bartenders are exceedingly friendly. Children welcome
until 8.30pm.

Tiverton: *The White Ball Inn*
Bridge St, Devon. *Tel 01884 251525.*
Although the decor is slightly
generic, there is an unusual visible
well with a glass top. Vertigo
sufferers should not look down.

THE HEART OF ENGLAND

Alderminster: *The Bell*
Warwickshire. *Tel 01789 450414.*
Smart 18th-century coach inn
just 6.4 km (4 miles) out of
Stratford-upon-Avon, The Bell
also boasts a high-class restaurant.
Great views over Stour Valley
from the garden and conservatory.

Armscote: *Fox & Goose*
Warwickshire. *Tel 01608 682293.*
This atmospheric bar-restaurant
(and B&B) is perfect for a light
supper or relaxing drink. Sit in the
vast lawns during summer. The
bar has an open fire in winter.

Ashleworth: *Queen's Arms*
The Village, Gloucestershire.
Tel 01452 700395.
Sixteenth-century inn with a
noticeable Victorian makeover,
this pub features wood-beamed
ceilings and antique furnishings.
The fantastic kitchen serves traditional pub food as well as more
international flavours.

Bickley Moss:
Cholmondeley Arms
Malpas, Cheshire. *Tel 01829 720300.*
The menu in this family-friendly
pub includes the very best of
traditional local cuisine. Children
will adore the desserts – baked
syrup sponge, black cherry
Pavlova, bakewell tart, ice creams
and sorbets. Accommodation is
also available.

Bretforton: *Fleece Inn*
Near Evesham. *Tel 01386 831173.*
This real ale pub with its half-
timbered façade is a National
Trust property. Beautifully located
in the Vale of Evesham. Rooms
available. Parking in village square.

Farnborough:
Inn at Farnborough
Near Banbury. *Tel 01295 690615.*
Classy inn in a Grade II listed
free house from the 1700s, this
inn serves delicious local cuisine,
including sumptuous organic
steak burgers. Large garden and
conservatory.

Shrewsbury: *Armoury*
Welsh Bridge, Victoria Quay.
Tel 01743 340525.
This converted 18th-century
warehouse, with views over the
river, is a popular open-plan
venue. Go early if you want
to enjoy a leisurely sit-down
meal. Children are welcome
till 7pm.

Welford-on-Avon:
The Bell Inn
Nr Stratford-upon-Avon,
Warwickshire. *Tel 01789 750353.*
This lovely 17th-century country
pub serves wonderful real ale and
traditional bar food. The Bell Inn
lies just a short distance southwest
of Stratford-upon-Avon. Recently
renovated, there is a delightful
seating area in the garden.

Wenlock Edge:
Wenlock Edge Inn
Hilltop, nr Much Wenlock, Shropshire.
Tel 01746 785678.
This award-winning pub, under new ownership, is popular with walkers – there is a comprehensive selection of maps and guidebooks on stand-by. A fairly homely affair, Wenlock Edge Inn serves good bar food and ales. Three rooms on a bed and breakfast basis.
⊪ 🖾 ⚐

EAST MIDLANDS

Alderwasley: *The Bear Inn*
Belper, Derbyshire. *Tel* 01629 822585.
Friendly country pub with real olde-worlde charm, The Bear Inn serves a good range of real ales and delicious cuisine. Popular with locals and visitors alike. Ten rooms are also available. ⊪ 🖾

Birchover: *Druid Inn*
Main St, nr Matlock Derbyshire.
Tel 01629 650302.
In the lovely village of Birchover, the old but recently revamped Druid Inn has an excellent local menu. Legend has it that the nearby Row Tor rocks were once a place of Druid rituals.
⊪ 🎵 🖾 ⚐ ✏

Grimsthorpe: *Black Horse*
Grimsthorpe Bourne, Lincolnshire.
Tel 01788 591093.
Nestled just below Grimsthorpe Castle, this early 18th-century inn has been renovated into a high-class pub-eaterie. Lovers of the outdoors will enjoy the rambling grounds and lakeside nature trail. Return to enjoy the cosy atmosphere of the bar and spend the night in one of the six charmingly old-fashioned rooms. ⊪ 🖾 ⚐

Hathersage:
Plough Inn
Leadmill Bridge, Hope Valley, Derbyshire. *Tel* 01433 650319.
Enjoying an idyllic location on the banks of River Derwent, the 16th-century Plough Inn is set on nine acres of private parklands and offers the perfect summer stop off. Fabulous food, great views and six en suite rooms. ⊪ 🖾 ⚐

Lyddington:
Old White Hart
51 Main St, Rutland.
Tel 01572 821 703.
Charming country inn with an award-winning à la carte menu. The Old White Hart has lovingly retained the oak-beamed ceilings, exposed brick walls and open fires of the renovated 17th-century stone building. ⊪ 🖾 ⚐ ✏

Mumby: *Red Lion*
Hogsthorpe Rd, Lincolnshire.
Tel 01507 490391.
Run by the local Bateman's Brewery, this pub is an excellent choice to sample the flavours of Lincolnshire. On the menu are traditional dishes prepared with locally sourced ingredients.
⊪ 🖾 ⚐ ♿

Nottingham: *Cock and Hoop*
25 High Pavement, Nottingham.
Tel 0115 852 3231.
This traditional Victorian Ale House offers a friendly, civilised retreat where punters can enjoy superb real ale and excellent wines. The restaurant serves excellent British home cooking. Small dogs welcome. ⊪ ⚐

Stamford:
The George of Stamford
71 St Martins, Lincolnshire.
Tel 01780 750750.
One of England's most famous coaching inns, the George's bar, restaurant and rooms are all rich in history. Other than the award-winning restaurant menu, there are also more informal pub food choices served in the ivy-covered courtyard and in the York Bar.
⊪ 🎵 🖾 ⚐ ♿

LANCASHIRE AND THE LAKES

Ambleside: *The Britannia Inn*
Elterwater, Cumbria.
Tel 015394 37210.
This traditional inn began life as a farmhouse and cobbler's. Standing on the village green and surrounded by stunning scenery, it is a delightful place to unwind in after a day's walk. There are also nine en suite rooms. ⊪ 🖾 ⚐

Clitheroe: *The Shireburn Arms*
Hurst Green, Lancashire.
Tel 01254 826518.
Located in a picturesque village, this characterful 17th-century inn was one of author JRR Tolkein's favourite haunts. The Shireburn Arms takes its name from the family who built Stonyhurst College and nearby almshouses. ⊪ 🖾 ⚐

Downham: *Assheton Arms*
Downham, Lancashire.
Tel 01200 441227.
Previously known as The George and Dragon, this pub was renamed following the elevation of the local squire, Ralph Assheton, to Lord Clitheroe. Facing the old church in a pretty village of stone cottages, it has even been featured in films and television series. Specialities on the menu include seafood and stone-cooked steaks. ⊪ ⚐

Hawkshead:
Queen's Head Hotel
Main St, Cumbria. *Tel* 01539 436271.
Situated at the heart of one of the prettiest Lake District villages. The superb food ranges from simple sandwiches at the bar to full meals at the restaurant. William Wordsworth was schooled in this village. ⊪ 🖾 ⚐

Hawkshead: *Tower Bank Arms*
Near Sawrey, Hawkshead, Cumbria.
Tel 01539 436334.
Standing in a picturesque village, this 17th-century inn is very close to Hill Top, where the legendary children's book author Beatrix Potter once lived. It even features in one of her well-known stories, *The Tale of Jemima Puddle-Duck*. Three letting rooms. ⊪ 🖾 ⚐

Liverpool: *Ship and Mitre*
133 Dale St, Merseyside.
Tel 0151 236 0859.
Close to the city centre, this traditional pub has a reputation for serving a wide range of real ales. Hot food served daily. ⊪

Lonsdale: *Snooty Fox Tavern*
Main St, Kirkby Lonsdale, Cumbria.
Tel 01524 271308.
A listed Jacobean coaching inn in the centre of the town, the Snooty Fox lies in the picturesque Lune Valley. Its rambling bars and cobbled courtyard exude a quaint charm. ⊪ 🎵 🖾 ⚐ ♿ ✏

Manchester: *Lass o' Gowrie*
36 Charles St, Chorlton-cum-Medlock. *Tel* 0161 273 6932.
Famous for its cask ales, this lively pub is popular with students. The menu offers a range of freshly cooked food. Entertainment comes in the form of live music and comedy nights. ⊪ 🎵 ⚐ ✏

YORKSHIRE AND HAMBERSIDE

Askrigg: *Kings Arms*
Market Place, N Yorks.
Tel 01969 650817.
Fans of James Herriot's *All Creatures Great and Small* will recognize this as "The Drover's Arms". There is a broad menu of appetizing food and five real ales on tap in the bar. ⊪ 🖾 ⚐ ✏

Byland Abbey: *Abbey Inn*
Byland Abbey, N Yorks.
Tel 01347 868204.
This charming inn, opposite the evocative ruins of a 12th-century abbey, serves excellent snacks for bar lunches. It also has three rooms. 🖾 ⚐

Driffield: *Wellington Inn*
19 The Green, Lund, Driffield, E Yorks.
Tel 01377 217294.
Just north of the minster town of Beverley, this attractive pub overlooks a charming village green. Its fine food and friendly service have won it an enviable reputation. 🍴 🛏 🚶 ♿ ↗

Flamborough: *The Seabirds*
Tower St, Flamborough, E Yorks.
Tel 01262 850242.
Near the bird sanctuary *(see pp400–401)* on the chalk cliffs of Flamborough Head, this pub is popular with both locals and walkers. The specialities on the menu revolve around fish, but a range of other dishes is on offer too. 🍴 🛏 🚶

Lancaster:
The Game Cock Inn
The Green Austwick, via Lancaster, N Yorks. *Tel* 01524 251226.
Close to the Yorkshire "Three Peaks", this 17th-century coaching inn is the focal point of the tiny village. The award-winning food is home-cooked by a French chef, and the menus offer a range of options – everything from a simple snack to an elaborate dinner.
🍴 🛏 🚶

Leyburn: *The Blue Lion*
E Witton, Leyburn, N Yorks.
Tel 01969 624273.
An 18th-century coaching and drover's inn within a charming Wensleydale village, it retains many original features. Open fires warm the rooms in winter. The food is traditional, but often with an unusual twist.
🍴 🛏 🚶 ♿

Skipton: *The Red Lion Hotel*
By the Bridge, Burnsall, N Yorks.
Tel 01756 720204.
Before the bridge was built across the Wharfe at Burnsall, this 16th-century inn used to operate a ferry across the river. Today, it has a reputation for fine food and its generous range of real ales and wine. Dogs welcome. 🍴 🛏 🚶 ♿

NORTHUMBRIA

Barnard: *The Morritt Arms Hotel*
Greta Bridge, Barnard Castle, Co Durham. *Tel* 01833 627232.
Located between Carlisle and London, this 17th-century stone farmhouse eventually became a coaching inn. Dickens stayed here while writing *Nicholas Nickleby*. A mural by local artist John Gilroy depicts Dingley Dell from *The Pickwick Papers*. Twenty-one rooms are available. 🍴 🛏 🚶 ♿

Key to Symbols *see back cover flap*

Consett: *Lord Crewe Arms*
Blanchland, nr Consett, Co Durham.
Tel 01434 675251.
Built in 1160 as the abbot's house, this delightful hotel faces an unusual, enclosed cobbled square at the heart of a very pretty village. Dine in the formal restaurant or opt for the more casual style and menu at the bar. Dog friendly. Accommodation available. 🍴 🛏 🚶

Cornhill on Tweed: *Black Bull*
Etal Village, Northumb.
Tel 01890 820200.
Close to the Norman castle in this attractive estate village, the award-winning Black Bull is famous as the only thatched pub in Northumberland. Ingredients for the home-cooked food are sourced locally wherever possible and the menu always includes tasty vegetarian options. 🍴 🛏 🚶 ♿ ↗

Craster: *Jolly Fisherman*
Off B1339 nr Alnwick, Northumb.
Tel 01665 576461.
Unassuming local pub with lovely sea views. Home-made crab soup and seafood are specialities.
🍴 🛏 🚶 ♿ ↗

Hedley on the Hill:
The Feathers Inn
Northumb. *Tel* 01661 843607.
This family-run pub is popular with foodies, and serves traditional British fare. There is always a good selection of vegetarian dishes too and at least four guest ales on tap at the bar. 🍴 🛏 🚶 ↗

Hexham: *Dipton Mill Inn*
Dipton Mill Rd, Northumb.
Tel 01434 606577.
Originally an 18th-century mill, this family-run pub lies beside Dipton Burn in a wooded valley. The characterful bar stocks a range of locally brewed beers and serves home-made food. 🍴 🛏 🚶 ♿ ↗

Kielder Water:
The Pheasant Inn
Stannersburn, Falstone, Northumb.
Tel 01434 240382.
This 17th-century farmhouse has functioned as a pub for the last 250 years. Popular with visitors to Kielder Water and the surrounding forest. Meals are served at the bar, with the dining room opening for Sunday lunch and evening dinner.
🍴 🛏 🚶 ♿ ↗

Newton: *Cook and Barker Inn*
Newton on the Moor, Northumberland.
Tel 01665 575234.
Once a forge, the inn got its name from its first proprietors, a Captain Cook who married a Miss Barker. Dine à la carte in the restaurant, where the original fireplace and well remain. Hearty pub meals are available at the bar. Accommodation available. 🍴 🛏 🚶 ♿

Seahouses: *The Olde Ship Hotel*
Northumb. *Tel* 01665 720200.
Situated above the tiny fishing harbour with a view across Farne Islands. Interesting nautical memorabilia decorate the bars. Pleasant beer garden. Accommodation is also available. 🍴 🛏 🚶 ♿

NORTH WALES

Capel Curig: *Bryn Tyrch Hotel*
Conwy. *Tel* 01690 720223.
Pretty country inn in the heart of Snowdonia National Park, this is a popular stop-off point for walkers and climbers. Traditional Welsh cuisine. Great views of Mt Snowdon from the bar. 🍴 🛏 🚶 ♿ ↗

Denbigh: *Hope & Anchor*
94 Vale St, Denbighshire.
Tel 01745 815115.
Small, traditional village pub with a bustling beer garden. Darts competitions and weekly quizzes are also hosted, and there is music on Fridays and Saturdays. Rooms on a B&B basis. 🍴 🎵 🛏 🚶 ↗

Ganllwyd: *Tyn-y-groes*
Dolgellau, Gwynedd.
Tel 01341 440275.
Picturesque 16th-century inn in the heart of the Snowdonia National Park, Tyn-y-groes hotel and pub offers a friendly base for walking, mountain biking and fishing in the park. 🍴 🛏 🚶 ♿ ↗

Glanwydden: *Queen's Head*
Llandudno. *Tel* 01492 546570.
This bustling village pub has a reputed bar menu. Tables at the Queen's Head fill quickly so it is wise to arrive early. Great range of real ales. 🍴 🛏 🚶

Maentwrog: *Grapes Hotel*
Blaenau Ffestiniog, Gwynedd.
Tel 01766 590365.
Said to be haunted, this Grade II listed coaching inn serves fine ales and home-made cuisine in a stunning setting. Pitch pine pews, exposed stone walls and a roaring fire in winter all add to the effect.
🍴 🎵 🛏 🚶 ♿

Mold: *Glasfryn*
Raikes Lane, Sychdyn, Mold.
Tel 01352 750500.
Pretty village pub known for its theatre-going clientele (Theatre Clwyd is just next door), Glasfryn is a converted farmhouse pub with a warm welcome. Award-winning menu and wine list. 🍴 🛏 🚶

Nant Gwynant: *Pen-y-Gwryd*
Gwynedd. *Tel* 01286 870211.
Hotel with a bustling pub in
the shadow of Mt Snowdon. It is
here that the 1953 Everest team
holed up here while training for
the ultimate ascent. Popular with
walkers for its prime location, it
also serves great food and drink.
⊞ ♨ ♣ &

Overton Bridge:
Cross Foxes Inn
Erbistock, Wrexham, Clwyd.
Tel 01978 780380.
Fabulous food in a fabulous
setting, Cross Foxes Inn, on the
banks of the River Dee, is a very
welcoming 18th-century coaching
inn with a distinctive dining room.
Good choice of real ales.
⊞ ♨ ♣ &

SOUTH AND MID-WALES

Aberaeron: *Harbourmaster*
Pen Cei, Ceredigion.
Tel 01545 570755.
Fabulous hotel-pub overlooking
the town's picturesque harbour.
This blue-washed building serves
tasty seafood such as Cardigan
Bay crab and lobster, Aberaeron
mackerel and several other such
freshly caught delicacies in its
restaurant. ⊞ ♣ &

Aberystwyth: *Halfway Inn*
Devils Bridge Rd, Pisgah.
Tel 01970 880631.
Halfway between Aberystwyth and
Devil's Bridge (hence the name),
this large inn has steadily built a
strong reputation for its fine food
and fabulous real ale. Designated
restaurant area away from the bar.
⊞ ♨ ♣ ✈

East Aberthaw: *Blue Anchor*
Barry, S Glamorgan.
Tel 01446 750329.
This recently refurbished, thatched
pub in the seaside town of Barry is
just 16 km (10 miles) from Cardiff,
Blue Anchor has a friendly little bar
as well as an elegant restaurant
serving superior cuisine. Estuary
walks nearby. ⊞ ♨ ♣ &

Hay-on-Wye: *The Pandy Inn*
Dorstone, Herefordshire.
Tel 01981 550273.
A picturesque pub with rooms
just over the border in Herefordshire, The Pandy Inn boasts a long
and illustrious history. Supposedly
the oldest pub in the county, it
played host to Oliver Cromwell
during the 17th-century Civil
War. The restaurant seats 50
and serves wholesome, filling
and tasty food. Dogs welcome.
⊞ ♬ ♨ ♣

Pembroke Ferry: *Ferry Inn*
Pembroke Dock.
Tel 01646 682947.
This early 17th-century inn
serves delicious seafood in a
prime location overlooking
the harbour. Ferry Inn has an
extensive waterfront terrace,
which is a perfect setting for
languid summer dining. Check
out the specials board for
locally caught fish.
⊞ ♬ ♨ ♣ &

Penallt: *Boat Inn*
Lone Lane. *Tel* 01600 712615.
With a stunning location on the
banks of River Wye, the beer
garden of Boat Inn is a great
place to relax with a chilled
drink on a warm summer's day.
Bar food is available. Access is
via a footbridge. ⊞ ♬ ♨ ♣

Pontyclun:
High Corner House
The Square, Llanharan.
Tel 01443 238056.
An old inn dating from the early
1700s with three luxury rooms,
High Corner House serves
traditional, hearty pub food in
its jazzed-up restaurant. It is
conveniently located between
Cardiff and the Swansea coast.
⊞ ♬ ♣ &

Tintern:
The Rose & Crown Inn
Monmouth Rd, Monmouthshire.
Tel 01291 689254.
On the banks of the River Wye, in
a designated Area of Outstanding
Natural Beauty, the Rose & Crown
dates back to at least 1835. There
is live music on Friday nights, and
B&B accommodation is available.
Families, walkers and dogs
welcome. ⊞ ♬ ♣

Usk: *Nag's Head*
Twyn Sq. *Tel* 01291 672820.
Atmospheric village pub with
an extensive menu that is very
reasonably priced for the size
of the portions. The warmly
welcoming establishment places
an emphasis on the home-made
food, but there is also a bustling
bar area. ⊞ ♨ ♣ &

THE LOWLANDS

Edinburgh:
Café Royal Circle Bar
West Register St. *Tel* 0131 556 1884.
Refurbished in Victorian style,
this pub features tiled portraits
of Scottish worthies and ornate
chandeliers. Sink back into one
of the comfortable leather
chairs for a drink before making
your way to the oyster bar and
restaurant. ⊞

Elie: *Ship Inn*
The Harbour, Fife. *Tel* 01333 330 246.
Quayside pub with nautical decor
and attractive views. Summer
barbecues. ⊞ ♬ ♨ ♣ ✈

Glasgow: *Horseshoe*
17–19 Drury St. *Tel* 0141 229 5711.
Busy Victorian pub with a long
bar and plenty of period features.
Good value bar snacks. Karaoke
in the evenings. ⊞ ♬ ♣

Isle of Whithorn: *Steam Packet*
Isle of Whithorn, Dumfries &
Galloway. *Tel* 01988 500 334.
Superb setting on a lovely harbour.
Pleasant eating areas and a good
selection of real ales. Boat trips
from the harbour. ⊞ ♨ ♣

THE HIGHLANDS AND ISLANDS

Applecross: *Applecross Inn*
Shore St, Wester Ross, Highland.
Tel 01520 744262.
Spectacularly located beyond
Britain's highest mountain pass,
this pub overlooks the Isle of Skye.
Local seafood is served, and there
is music once a week in season.
⊞ ♬ ♨ ♣ &

Dundee: *Fishermans Tavern*
10–16 Fort St, Broughty Ferry, Tayside.
Tel 01382 775941.
Choose between award-winning
real ales and the extensive
selection of malts, or savour a
little of both. Good seafront and
views of the Tay Rail Bridge.
Rooms available. ⊞ ♣ ♬

Isle of Skye: *Tigh Osda Eilean*
Iarmain. Off A851, Isle Ornsay, Isle
of Skye. *Tel* 01471 833332.
Welcoming hotel bar. Lots of malts
and good bar food. Gorgeous
setting. ⊞ ♬ ♨ ♣ &

Loch Lomond: *Oak Tree Inn*
Balmaha, (E side). *Tel* 01360 870357.
Traditional stone inn with a well-
stocked bar, restaurant and B&B.
Sit by the roaring fires in winter
and snack on the tasty bar food
that is served all day. ⊞ ♬ ♨ ♣

Portsoy: *The Shore Inn*
The Old Harbour, Banffshire.
Tel 01261 842831.
A 300-year-old seafaring inn
nestled in a picturesque harbour.
Traditional cask ale and a real
open fire. ⊞ ♬ ♣ ✈

Ullapool: *Ferry Boat*
Shore St, Highland. *Tel* 01854 612366.
Good whiskies, bar lunches and
fine views over the harbour. Coal
fires and big windows overlooking
the loch. ⊞ ♬ ♣

SHOPPING IN BRITAIN

Vivienne Westwood's designer label

While the West End of London (see pp148–51) is undeniably the most exciting place to shop in Britain, many of the regional towns and cities offer nearly as wide a range of goods. Moreover, regional shopping can be less stressful, less expensive, and remarkably varied, with craft studios, farm shops, street markets and factory outlets adding to the enjoyment of bargain-hunting. Britain is famous for its country clothing: wool, waxed cotton and tweed are all popular, along with classic prints such as Liberty or Laura Ashley and tartan. Other particularly British goods include antiques, floral soaps and scents, porcelain, glass and local crafts.

Antiques stall at Bermondsey Market

SHOPPING HOURS

In general, shops in Britain open during the week from 9am or 10am, and close after 5pm or 6pm. Hours on Saturdays may be shorter. Many town centre shops open on Sundays. Some stores open late for one evening a week – Thursday in London's West End – while village shops may close at lunch-time, or for one afternoon each week. Market days vary from town to town.

HOW TO PAY

Most large shops all over the UK accept well-known credit cards such as Access and VISA. Charge cards such as American Express or Diners Club are acceptable in some places, but markets and some small shops do not take credit cards. Traveller's cheques can be used in larger stores, though exchange rates for non-sterling cheques may be poor. Take your passport with you for identification. Few places accept cheques drawn on foreign banks. Cash is still the most popular way to pay for small purchases.

RIGHTS AND REFUNDS

If something you buy is defective, you are entitled to a refund, provided you have kept your receipt as proof of purchase and return the goods in the same condition as when you bought them, preferably in the same packaging. This may not always apply to sale goods clearly marked as seconds, imperfect, or shop-soiled. Inspect these carefully before you buy. You do not have to accept a credit note in place of a cash refund.

ANNUAL SALES

Sales take place during January, and in June and July, when nearly every shop cuts prices to get rid of old stock. But you may find special offers at any time of the year. Some

Sign for the Lanes, Brighton (see p175)

shops begin winter sales just before Christmas. Department stores and fashion houses have some excellent bargains for keen shoppers; one of the most prestigious sales is at Harrods (see p97), where queues form long before opening time.

VAT AND TAX-FREE SHOPPING

Value added tax (VAT) is charged on most goods and services sold in Britain – exceptions are food, books and children's clothes. It is usually included in the advertised price. Visitors from outside the European Union who stay less than three months may claim this tax back. Take your passport with you when you go shopping. You must complete a form in the shop when you buy goods and give a copy to the customs authorities when you leave the country. You may have to show your goods as proof of purchase. If you arrange to have goods shipped from the store, VAT should be deducted before you pay.

OUT-OF-TOWN SHOPPING CENTRES

These large complexes, built in the style of North American malls, are rapidly increasing around Britain. The advantages of car access and cheap parking are undeniable, and most centres are accessible by public transport too. The centres usually feature popular high street stores, with facilities such as cafés, crèches, restaurants and cinemas.

A traditional shop front in Stonegate, York (see p404)

DEPARTMENT STORES

A few big department stores, such as Harrods, are only found in London, but others have provincial branches. John Lewis, for example, has shops in 22 locations. It sells a huge range of fabrics, clothing and household items, combining quality service with good value. Marks & Spencer, with branches in most major towns and cities in Britain, is famed for its good-value clothing and pre-prepared food. Debenhams and British Home Stores (BhS) are other well-known general stores with inexpensive clothing and home furnishings. Habitat is a reputable supplier of modern furniture. The sizes of all these stores, and the range of stock they carry, differs from region to region.

CLOTHES SHOPS

Once again, London has the widest range, from *haute couture* to cheap and cheerful items ready-made. Shopping for clothing in the regions, however, can often be less tiring. Many towns popular with tourists – Oxford, Bath and York for instance – have independently owned clothes shops where you are likely to receive a more personal service. Or you could try one of the chain stores in any high street such as Principles or Next for smart, reasonably

priced clothes, and Top Shop, Oasis and Miss Selfridge for younger and cheaper fashions.

SUPERMARKETS AND FOODSHOPS

Supermarkets are a good way to shop for food. The range and quality of items is usually excellent. Several large chains compete for market share and as a result prices are generally lower than in smaller shops. Sainsbury, Tesco, Asda, Safeway and Waitrose are some of the national names. The smaller town-centre shops such as bakeries, greengrocers or farm shops, may give you a more interesting choice of regional produce, and a more personal service.

Local Teesdale cheeses

SOUVENIR, GIFT AND MUSEUM SHOPS

Buying presents is a must for most travellers. Most reputable, large stores can arrange freight of high-value

The Mustard Shop (see p201), Norwich

items. If you want to buy things you can carry back in your suitcase, the choice is wide. You can buy attractive, well-made, portable craft items all over the country, especially in areas tourists are likely to visit. For slightly more unusual presents, have a look in museum shops and the gifts available in National Trust (see p29) and English Heritage (see p671) properties.

SECONDHAND AND ANTIQUE SHOPS

Britain's long history means there are many interesting artifacts to be found. A visit to any of Britain's stately homes will reveal a passion for antiques. Most towns have an antique or bric-a-brac (miscellaneous second-hand items) shop or two. Look for auctions – tourist information centres (see pp668–9) can help you to locate them. You may like to visit a jumble or car boot sale in the hope of picking up a bargain.

Book stall, Hay-on-Wye, Wales (see p461)

MARKETS

Large towns and cities usually have a central covered market which operates most weekdays, selling everything from fresh produce to pots and pans. The information under each town entry in this guide lists market days. Many towns hold weekly markets in the main square, while Farmers' Markets have become increasingly popular and are a good place to source fresh, organic produce from British farms.

ENTERTAINMENT IN BRITAIN

London is without a doubt the entertainment capital of Britain *(see pp152–5)*, with a whole wealth of shows, films and concerts to choose from, but many regional theatres, opera houses and concert halls also have varied programmes. Edinburgh, Manchester, Leeds,

Punch and Judy show

Birmingham, and Bristol in particular have a lot to offer and there are a number of summer arts festivals around the country such as those at Bath and Aldeburgh *(see pp62–3)*. Ticket prices vary but are usually cheaper outside the capital and when booked in advance.

SOURCES OF INFORMATION

In London, check the listings magazines, such as *Time Out*, or the *Evening Standard*, London's evening newspaper. All of the high-brow newspapers *(see p679)* provide comprehensive arts reviews and listings of the cultural events and shows throughout the country. Local newspapers, libraries, or tourist offices *(see p669)* can supply details of regional events. Specialist magazines such as *NME* give up-to-date news of the pop music scene and are available from any newsagent.

THEATRES

Britain has an enduring theatrical tradition dating back to Shakespeare *(see pp324–5)* and beyond. All over the country, amateurs and professionals tread the boards in auditoriums, pubs, clubs and village halls. Production and performance standards are generally high, and British actors have an

international reputation. London is the place to enjoy theatre at its most varied and glamorous *(see p152)*. The West End alone has more than 50 theatres *(see p153)* ranging from elaborate Edwardian, to Modernist-style buildings such as the National Theatre on the South Bank.

In Stratford-upon-Avon, the Royal Shakespeare Company presents a year-round programme of Shakespeare, as well as avant-garde and experimental plays. Bristol also has a long dramatic tradition, the Theatre Royal *(see p256)* is the oldest working theatre in Britain. Some of the best productions outside the capital can be found at the West Yorkshire Playhouse in Leeds, the Royal Exchange in Manchester *(see p372)* and the Traverse in Edinburgh. Open-air theatre ranges from the free street entertainment found in many

city centres, to student performances on the grounds of university colleges, or a production at Cornwall's clifftop amphitheatre, the Minack Theatre *(see p276)*. Every fourth year, York also stages a series of open-air medieval mystery plays called the York Cycle. Perhaps the liveliest theatrical tradition in Britain is the Edinburgh Festival *(see p509)*. Ticket availability varies from show to show. For a midweek matinee, you may be able to buy a ticket at the door, but for the more popular West End shows tickets may have to be booked weeks or months in advance. You can book through agencies and some travel agents, and most hotels will organize tickets for you. Booking fees are often charged. Beware of tickets offered by touts *(see p67)* – these may be counterfeit. There are no age restrictions in Britain's theatres.

Street entertainer

MUSIC

A diverse musical repertoire can be found in a variety of venues. Church choral music is a national tradition and many churches and cathedrals host concerts. London, Manchester, Birmingham, Liverpool, Bristol and Bournemouth all have their own excellent orchestras.

Rock, jazz, folk and country-and-western concerts are staged periodically in pubs, clubs and sometimes outdoors. Wales has a strong musical tradition which is evident in many of its pubs; northern England is known for its booming brass and silver bands; and Scotland has its famous bag-pipers *(see p480)*.

The Buxton Opera House, the Midlands

The multiplex Warner West End cinema, Leicester Square, London

CINEMAS

The latest films can be seen in any large town. Check the local papers or the tourist office to find out what is on.

Cinemas are having a revival, with luxurious multi-screen cinemas taking over from the local, single-screen cinemas. In larger cities a more diverse range of films is often on offer including foreign-language productions. These tend to be shown at arts or repertory cinemas. Mainstream English-speaking films are usually shown by the big chains. Age limits apply to certain films. Young children are allowed to see any feature film which is graded with a U (universal) or PG (parental guidance) certificate. Cinema prices vary widely; some are cheaper at off-peak times, such as Mondays or afternoons. For new releases it is advisable to book in advance.

CLUBS

Most cities have some sort of club scene, though London has the most famous venues (see p155). These may feature live music, discos, or DJ or dance performances. Some insist on dress codes or

members only, and most have doormen, or "bouncers". Apart from the major cities, Brighton and Bristol have lively clubs.

DANCE

This covers a multitude of activities: everything from classical ballet and acid-house parties to traditional English Morris dancing or the Scottish Highland fling, which you may come upon in pubs and villages around the country.

Dance halls are rarer than they were, but ballroom dancing is alive and well. Other dance events you may find are ceilidhs (pronounced kay-lee), which is Celtic dancing and music; May Balls often held at universities (invitation only); dinner or tea dances and square dancing.

Birmingham is home to the Birmingham Royal Ballet and is the best place to see performances outside London. Avant-garde contemporary dance is also performed.

GAY

Most large communities will have some gay meeting places, mostly bars and clubs. You can find out about them from publications such as the free *Pink Paper* or *Gay Times* on sale in some newsagents, and in gay bars and clubs. London's gay life is centred around Soho *(see p80)* with its many European-style cafés and bars. Outside London, the most active gay scenes

Three revellers, Gay Pride Festival

are in Manchester and Brighton. Gay Pride is the largest free outdoor festival in Europe.

CHILDREN

London offers children a positive goldmine of fun, excitement and adventure, though it can be expensive. From the traditional sights to something more unusual such as a discovery centre, London

has a wide range of activities, many interactive, to interest children of all ages. The weekly magazine *Time Out* has details of children's events.

Outside London, activities for children range from nature trails to fun fairs. Your local tourist office or the local library will have information on things to do with children.

Pirate Ship, Chessington World of Adventures, Surrey

THEME PARKS

Theme parks in Britain are enjoyed by children of all ages. Alton Towers has conventional rides plus a motor museum. Chessington World of Adventures is a huge complex south of London. Based on a zoo, it includes nine themed areas, such as Calamity Canyon and Circus World. Legoland, the latest park, opened in March 1996. Thorpe Park is a large watery theme park full of model buildings and a peaceful pet farm.

Alton Towers
Alton, Staffordshire.
Tel 0870 20 40 60.
www.altontowers.com

Chessington World of Adventures
Leatherhead Rd, Chessington, Surrey.
Tel 0870 9990045.
www.chessington.co.uk

Legoland
Winkfield Rd, Windsor, Berkshire.
Tel 0871 222 2001.
www.lego.co.uk

Thorpe Park
Staines Rd, Chertsey, Surrey.
Tel 08704 444466.
www.thorpepark.com

SPECIALIST HOLIDAYS AND OUTDOOR ACTIVITIES

Britain offers a wide variety of special interest holidays and courses, where you can learn a new sport or skill, practise an activity you enjoy, or simply have fun and meet people. If you prefer less structured activities, there are numerous options to choose from, such

Cycling on the Gower Peninsular, Wales

as walking in Britain's national parks, pony trekking in Wales, surfing in Cornwall or skiing in Scotland. There are also several spectator sports for those who like to watch rather than participate, including Premier League football, test match cricket and historic horse races.

Arvon Foundation writing week at Totleigh Barton in Devon

SPECIAL INTEREST HOLIDAYS

There are a number of special interest holidays and residential courses available in Great Britain. One advantage of this type of vacation is that you can attend a course alone, and yet have plenty of congenial company – most people are delighted to meet others who share their interests. Whatever your passion, you are likely to come across a holiday package that suits your needs.

Centres such as **Wye Valley Art Centre** in Gloucestershire and **West Dean College**, West Sussex, offer engaging, residential courses in arts and crafts. These can range from familiar activities such as drawing and painting to more esoteric subjects such as mosaic art and glass engraving. Those interested in writing can enroll at the **Arvon Foundation**, which organizes week-long courses in fiction, poetry, songwriting and TV drama at four rural retreats in Devon,

Shropshire, West Yorkshire and Invernesshire. The **Ashburton Cookery School** in Devon and **Cookery at the Grange** in Somerset offer fun cookery courses with lots of hands-on involvement. Non-carnivores might try the Vegetarian Society's **Cordon Vert School** in Cheshire, which has innovative cookery courses catering to chefs at all levels – from complete beginners to talented amateurs.

Companies such as **Hidden Britain Tours**, **Inscape Tours** and the **Back-Roads Touring Company** provide themed holidays. History lovers can opt for a tour of King Arthur's Country or Shakespeare's England. Other tours designed for motor enthusiasts, garden lovers or fans of rock and roll are also available.

The prices of such holidays include expert guidance, transport, entry fees to attractions and accommodation, which could be anything from a farmhouse to a medieval castle.

WALKING

Walking is a popular activity in Britain and a network of long-distance footpaths and shorter routes criss-crosses the country (*see pp36–7*). It is also an excellent way to experience the spectacular variety of the British landscape, either by yourself or with a group. An advantage is that most routes are away from major tourist sites and often pass through picturesque villages that are off the beaten track.

The **Ramblers' Association** is Britain's main walking body, and its website provides useful information on most routes and walking areas. It also publishes a range of books, including *Walk Britain*, which lists many good walks as well as suitable hotels, bed and breakfasts and hostels along the way.

There is no shortage of companies providing guided and self-guided holidays for walkers. The cost of these holiday packages should cover

Walking on Holyhead Mountain near South Stack Anglesey, Wales

accommodation, transport and detailed route guides. **Ramblers' Countrywide Holidays** offers guided group walks through some of the country's most splendid landscapes. **Sherpa Expeditions** has a variety of self-led walks. Pick a challenging 15-day coast-to-coast walk, or a more leisurely ramble along South Downs Way. Individual companies will advise you on the level of fitness required and the type of clothing and footwear that will be needed.

If you are planning to walk on your own, especially in remote areas, remember that it is essential to not only be well equipped, but to also leave details of your route with someone.

Mountain biking in Yorkshire

CYCLING

The country's tranquil lanes, bridleways and designated tracks are perfect for cyclists who want to explore the back roads of Britain. Depending on your level of fitness, you may opt for demanding routes through mountainous areas such as the magnificent West Highland Way in Scotland *(see p494)*. Those who would like to take it easy can enjoy a relaxed tour along Devon's lanes and take the opportunity to stop off for a sinfully rich cream tea.

Country Lanes offers a good variety of guided holidays in small groups around the west of England. The price includes an experienced leader, high quality bicycle equipment, accommodation, meals and

entry to attractions along the way. **Compass Holidays** and **Wheely Wonderful Cycling** concentrate on self-led tours, with routes throughout the country. They also provide bicycles, accommodation, detailed route maps, (including details of pubs, cafés and places of interest along the way) and appropriate luggage transport. Such self-guided bicycling holidays are ideal for families or groups of friends.

If you wish to organize your own cycling holiday, you may contact the **Cyclists' Touring Club**, which is Britain's main recreational cycling body, and **Sustrans**, the organization that formed the National Cycle Network. Both can provide a wealth of information about cycling in the country, including advice on matters such as bringing a bike into Britain, taking your bike on the train and the rules of the road. *Cycling in the UK*, the official guide book for the National Cycle Network, has route details and maps for many of the best rides, and also offers tips on how to hire a bike and what to do along the way.

HORSE RIDING AND PONY TREKKING

There are good riding centres in most parts of Britain, but certain areas are especially suitable for this invigorating activity. The best of these locations include the New Forest *(see p168)*, the South Downs *(see p181)*, the Yorkshire Dales National Park *(see pp384–6)* and the Brecon Beacons on the border between Wales and England *(see pp468–9)*.

Pony trekking holidays are also becoming very popular, and generally include basic training, a guide, meals and accommodation. These vacations are perfect for novice riders and children since the ponies are very well-trained and rarely proceed above a canter. The **British Horse Society** has all the information on where to ride as well as a list of approved riding schools that offer training. You can also consult the **Equine Tourism** website for information on riding centres

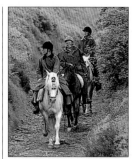

Horse riding on a country bridleway *(see p37)*

and horse-riding holidays. National park information offices can also provide details of the many equestrian centres that organize riding holidays in or around national parks.

GOLF

Over a quarter of Britain's 2000-odd golf clubs are in Scotland, which is unsurprising given that the ancient game was invented here. The first formal club was established in Edinburgh in 1744.

Today, the best known clubs are Carnoustie and St Andrews in Scotland, Royal St George's in England and Celtic Manor in Wales. These high-profile clubs only admit players above a certain handicap. Most other clubs, however, are more relaxed and welcome visitors.

Green fees vary greatly, as do the facilities offered by various clubs. Some clubs may ask to see a valid handicap certificate before they allow a player on the course. Failing that, a letter of introduction from a home club may be sufficient.

Specialist operators such as **Golf Vacations UK** and **Great Golf Holidays** can smooth the way to the first hole considerably by booking golf packages. They will organize travel and accommodation, reserve tee times and pay the green fees. They will also help you get temporary membership of a club if required.

If you wish to go it alone, the **Golf Club of Great Britain** can provide information on where to play. They also have an affiliated website for nonresidents of the UK.

SURFING

The best areas for surfing are in the West Country and South Wales. Tuition is available at many resorts, and equipment can be hired.

The Cornwall-based **British Surfing Association** runs its own surf school with professional coaching catering to a range of abilities, from novices to advanced competition surfers. Other companies that offer good surfing courses include **Surf South West** in Devon and the **Welsh Surfing Federation Surf School** in South Wales.

Sailing in Cardigan Bay, Welsh coast

BOATING AND SAILING

The British are extremely enthusiastic about boating and sailing. The network of rivers, lakes and canals ensures an abundance of boating sites. Many excellent choices are available – the Isle of Wight and the south coast are full of pleasure crafts. Several inland areas such as the Lake District (see pp354–69) are among the most widely favoured. Canal cruising is also very popular (see p689) and the Norfolk Broads (see p198) provide one of the best inland boating experiences. Check with the **Broads Authority** for details.

Many sailing courses are available. The **Royal Yachting Association** can provide lists of approved courses and training centres around Britain. One of the most trusted is Dorset's **Weymouth & Portland National Sailing Academy**, which has a range of courses to suit all ages and levels of ability. The **Falmouth School**

of Sailing in Cornwall is a privately owned sailing and powerboat school, which conducts lessons in the enclosed, safe waters of the Fal Estuary. Courses include basic "taster sessions", one-to-one tuition for adults and children, as well as group lessons.

SKIING

Facilities for skiing are limited in the UK, especially since the weather is rather unreliable. However, skiing enthusiasts can head for Scotland, which has a range of challenging slopes. **Ski Scotland**, the official ski site of the Scottish Tourist Board, has information about ski packages, accommodation, up-to-date weather conditions and details of the main ski areas, including the Cairngorms and the Nevis Range. **Snowsport Scotland**, the governing body for all Scottish snowsports, provides information on other snow-based activities such as Nordic skiing and snowboarding.

FISHING

Fishing, both on the sea and in rivers, is one of Britain's most popular participation sports. Regulations, however, are strict and can be rather complicated. It is advisable to check for details about rod licences, close seasons and other restrictions at tourist offices, tackle shops or with the **National Federation of Anglers** in Nottingham.

The best game fishing (trout and salmon) is in the West Country, the Northeast, Wales and Scotland. Also, there are several websites with links to specialist operators who arrange fishing holidays.

Solitary sea fisherman, England's southeast coast

SPECTATOR SPORTS

Football (soccer) is a passion for a large section of the population. The English Premier League is run by the **Football Association** and is home to some of the world's top clubs, including **Manchester United** (see p375), **Arsenal FC** and **Chelsea FC**. The domestic football season runs from August to May. Tickets for Premier League games can be expensive and difficult to obtain, but it is worth attempting to get hold of returned or unsold tickets directly from the clubs.

The main tennis event of the year is Wimbledon, which is held at the **All England Lawn Tennis Club (AELTC)** in London. This two-week event takes place in the last week of June and the first week of July. The tournament sparks off a period of tennis fever in England, especially when British players such as Tim Henman progress in the competition. Most tickets for Centre Court are allocated by a public ballot. Check the official website of the AELTC for details on how to procure tickets. Around 6,000 tickets are available on the day of play (payment by cash only), except for the final four days of the tournament.

Rugby Football is administered by the **Rugby Football Union** and also has a good following. Games are played in cities such as Edinburgh, London and Cardiff.

Cricket, the English national game, is played from April to September. Tickets for country matches are relatively cheap. International test matches are played on historic grounds such as **Surrey County Cricket Club's** ground at the Oval in London, and the **Yorkshire County Cricket Club** situated at Headingley in Leeds.

Both steeplechasing and flat-racing are very popular, and betting is big business. The Grand National is the best known steeplechase and runs at **Aintree Racecourse** in early April. The main meeting is **Royal Ascot**, which takes place in Berkshire towards the end of June.

DIRECTORY

SPECIAL INTEREST HOLIDAYS

Arvon Foundation
42A Buckingham Palace Rd, London SW1. *Tel 020 7931 7611*. **www.** arvonfoundation.org

Ashburton Cookery School
Hare's Lane Cottage, 76 E St, Ashburton TQ13. *Tel 01364 652784*. **www.**ashburtoncookery school.co.uk

Back-Roads Touring Company
14A New Broadway, London W5. *Tel 020 8566 5312*.

Cookery at the Grange
The Grange, Whatley, Frome, Somerset BA11. *Tel 01373 836579*.

Cordon Vert School
The Vegetarian Society, Parkdale, Dunham Rd, Altrincham, Cheshire WA14. *Tel 0161 9252014*.

Hidden Britain Tours
28 Chequers Rd, Basingstoke, Hampshire RG2 7PU. *Tel 01256 814222*.

Inscape Tours
35 Whitehall, London SW1A 2BX. *Tel 020 7839 3988*.

West Dean College
West Dean, Chichester, W Sussex PO18. *Tel 01243 811301*.

Wye Valley Art Centre
The Coach Hse, Mork, St Briavel's, Lydney, Gloucestershire GL15. *Tel 01594 530214*.

WALKING

Ramblers' Association
2nd Floor, Camelford Hse, 87–90 Albert Embankment, London SE1. *Tel 020 7339 8500*. **www**.ramblers.org.uk

Ramblers' Countrywide Holidays
Box 43, Welwyn Garden City AL8. *Tel 01707 386800*.

Sherpa Expeditions
131A Heston Rd, Hounslow TW5. *Tel 020 8577 2717*.

CYCLING

Compass Holidays
Cheltenham Spa Railway Station, Queens Rd, Cheltenham, Gloucestershire GL51. *Tel 01242 250642*.

Country Lanes
Brokenhurst New Forest. *Tel 01590 622627*.

Cyclists' Touring Club
69 Meadrow, Godalming, Surrey GU7. *Tel 0870 8730060*.

Sustrans
National Cycle Network Centre, 2 Cathedral Sq, College Green, Bristol BS1. *Tel 0845 1130065*.

Wheely Wonderful Cycling
Petchfield Farm, Elton, Ludlow, Shropshire SY8. *Tel 01568 770755*.

HORSE RIDING AND PONY TREKKING

British Horse Society
Stoneleigh Deer Park, Kenilworth, Warwickshire CV8. *Tel 0844 848 1666*. **www**.bhs.org.uk

Equine Tourism
www.equinetourism.co.uk

GOLF

Golf Club of Great Britain
3 Sage Yard, Douglas Rd, Surbiton, Surrey KT6. *Tel 020 8390 3113*. **www**.golfclubgb.co.uk

Golf Vacations UK
Tel 01228 527136. **www**.golfvacationsuk.com

Great Golf Holidays
2nd Floor, Central Hse, 4–6 Crantock St, Newquay, Cornwall TR7. *Tel 01637 879991*.

SURFING

British Surfing Association
The International Surfing Centre, Fistral Beach, Newquay, Cornwall TR7. *Tel 01637 876474*.

Surf South West
PO Box 39, Croyde, N Devon EX33. *Tel 01271 890400*.

Welsh Surfing Federation Surf School
The Barn, The Croft, Llangennith, Swansea SA3. *Tel 01792 386426*.

BOATING AND SAILING

Broads Authority
18 Colegate, Norwich, Norfolk NR3. *Tel 01603 610734*.

Falmouth School of Sailing
Grove Place, Falmouth, Cornwall TR11. *Tel 01326 211311*.

Royal Yachting Association
RYA Hse, Ensign Way, Hamble, Southampton, Hampshire SO31. *Tel 0845 345 0400*.

Weymouth & Portland National Sailing Academy
Osprey Quay, Portland, Dorset DT5. *Tel 01305 866000*.

SKIING

Ski Scotland
www.ski.visitscotland.com

Snowsport Scotland
Hillend, Biggar Rd, Midlothian EH10. *Tel 0131 445 4151*.

FISHING

Fishing Net
www.fishingnet.com

Fishing UK
www.fishing.co.uk

National Federation of Anglers
National Water Sports Centre, Adbolton Lane, Holme Pierrepont, Nottingham NG12. *Tel 0115 981 3535*.

SPECTATOR SPORTS

Aintree Racecourse
Ormskirk Rd, Aintree, Liverpool L9. *Tel 0151 523 2600*.

All England Lawn Tennis Club (AELTC)
Church Rd, Wimbledon, London SW19. *Tel 020 8946 2244*. **www**.wimbledon.org

Arsenal FC
Arsenal Stadium, Avenell Rd, Highbury, London N5. *Tel 020 7704 4040*.

Chelsea FC
Stamford Bridge, Fulham Rd, London SW6. *Tel 0871 984 1955*.

Football Association
16 Lancaster Gate, London W2. *Tel 020 7745 4545*.

Manchester United
Sir Matt Busby Way, Old Trafford, Manchester M16. *Tel 0161 868 8000*.

Royal Ascot
Ascot Racecourse, Ascot, Berkshire SL5. *Tel 0870 7271234*.

Rugby Football Union
Rugby Rd, Twickenham, Middlesex TW1. *Tel 020 8831 6527*.

Surrey County Cricket Club
The Brit Oval, Kennington, London SE11. *Tel 020 7820 5700*.

Yorkshire County Cricket Club
Headingley Cricket Ground, Leeds LS6. *Tel 0871 222 0994*.

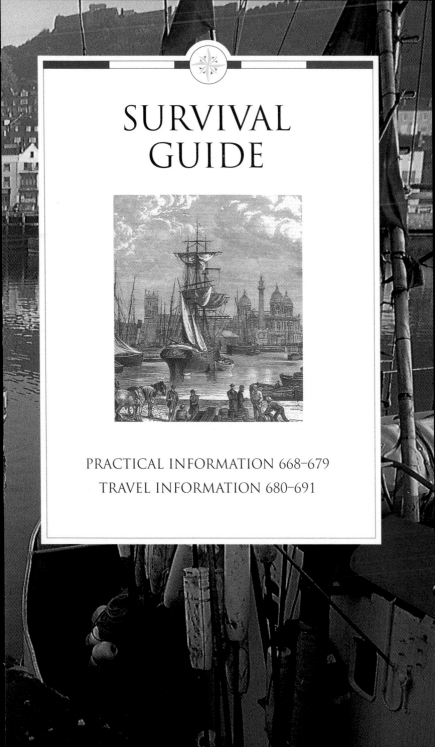

SURVIVAL
GUIDE

PRACTICAL INFORMATION

Every year, millions of people from all over the world seek out what the British often take for granted: the country's ancient history, colourful pageantry, spectacularly varied countryside and wonderful coastline. The range of facilities on offer to visitors in Britain has improved considerably over the past few years. Be aware that prices vary within Britain, and regional differences can be very noticeable. London, not surprisingly, is the most expensive city, and the knock-on effect extends to most of southern England, Britain's most affluent region. Food, accommodation, entertainment, transport and consumer items in shops are generally cheaper in other parts of the country. It is always advisable to plan your trip before you travel and to enjoy Britain fully, it is important to be aware of the basics of British life: when to visit, what to take, how to get around, where to find information and what to do if things go wrong.

A mounted sentry, London

Weymouth Beach, Dorset, on a busy public holiday weekend

WHEN TO GO

Britain's temperate climate does not produce many temperature extremes (see p68). However, weather patterns shift constantly, and the climate can vary widely in places only a short distance apart. Since it is impossible to predict rain or shine reliably in any season, be sure to pack a mix of warm and cool clothes and an umbrella, irrespective of when you plan to visit. Always get an up-to-date weather forecast before you set off on foot to remote mountain areas or moorland. Walkers can be surprised by the weather, and the Mountain Rescue services are often called out due to unexpectedly severe conditions. Weather reports can be found on television and radio,

A sign for the Mountain Rescue

as well as in newspapers. They can also be provided by phone services (see p678).

Britain's towns and cities are all-year destinations, but many attractions are open only between Easter and October. The main family holiday months, July and August, and public holidays (see p65) are always busy, and some hotels are full around Christmas. Spring and autumn offer a good compromise between reasonably good weather and a relative lack of crowds.

VISAS AND PASSPORTS

A valid passport is required to enter Britain. Visitors from the European Union (EU), the United States, Canada, New Zealand and Australia do not need visas to enter the country. Visit www.ukvisas.gov.uk to check your visa status. Visas can be arranged online at www.fco.gov.uk. When you arrive at any British air- or seaport, you will find separate queues at immigration control – one set for EU nationals, and another for everyone else. Residents of the EU are allowed to work in Britain with no permit, while Commonwealth citizens under the age of 27 may work part time for up to two years. North American students can get a Blue Card through their university. This enables them to work for up to six months, but it must be obtained before arrival in Britain. BUNAC (see p672) is a student club that organizes exchange schemes for students to work abroad.

CUSTOMS INFORMATION

Britain is part of the European Union, so anyone who arrives here from a member country can pass through a blue channel. However, random checks are still being made to detect entry of prohibited goods, particularly drugs, indecent material and weapons. Never, under any circumstances, carry luggage or parcels through customs for someone else. For most EU members there is no limit to the amount of excise goods (such as tobacco or alcohol) that can be brought into Britain, provided these are for your own use. This legislation does not apply to some new member states; check if you are unsure.

Travellers entering from outside the EU have to pass through customs channels. Go through the green channel if you have nothing to declare over the customs allowances, and use the red channel if you have goods to declare. If you are unsure of importation restrictions, go through the red channel. On departure, non-EU residents can apply for a VAT refund on goods bought in Britain (see p658).

Britain is free of rabies, and no live animals may be imported without a permit. Any animals found will be impounded and may be destroyed.

◁ Fishing boats in Scarborough port, North Yorkshire

TOURIST INFORMATION

Tourist information is available in many towns and public places, including airports and main rail and coach stations, and some places of historical interest. Look out for the tourist information symbol, which can indicate anything from a large and busy central tourist bureau to a simple kiosk or even simply an information board in a parking area.

Tourist offices will be able to help you on almost anything in their area, including places of interest and guided walks. Both the regional and national tourist boards produce comprehensive lists of local attractions and registered accommodation options. A range of leaflets is generally available for free at tourist offices, but a charge may be made for more detailed maps and booklets. For route planning, consider the excellent large-format motoring atlases produced by both the RAC and the AA (see p685). For rural exploration, Ordnance Survey maps are ideal (www.ordnancesurvey.co.uk).

It's wise to book accommodation well in advance of your visit. **VisitBritain** is a good resource for this. Out of season, you should have few problems booking transport, restaurants or even theatre performances at short notice, but in the high season, if you have set your heart on a luxury hotel, popular West End show or specific tour, you should try to book in advance. Contact VisitBritain in your country, or see a travel agent for advice and general information.

The most common English tourist information sign

OPENING HOURS

Outside of London and other main cities, many businesses and shops still close on Sundays, even though trading is legal. During the week, opening hours are generally from 9 or 10am until 5 or 5:30pm. Shop hours may include a late opening one evening a week, usually Thursday. In big city centres, particularly London, shops are generally open longer – often until 7pm and seven days a week.

Museums in London tend to operate late opening hours one day a week, while those outside the capital may be less flexible, sometimes closing in the morning or for one day a week, often on Mondays.

On public holidays, also known as bank holidays in Britain, banks, offices and some shops, restaurants and attractions often close, and transport networks run a limited service.

DIRECTORY

CUSTOMS AND IMMIGRATION

HM Customs & Excise
Dorset House,
27–45 Stamford St,
London SE1 9PY.
Tel 020 7865 3000
or 0845 010 9000
(advice line).

Home Office
Border & Immigration
Agency, Lunar House,
40 Wellesley Rd,
Croydon, Surrey.
Tel 0870 606 7766.
www.ind.homeoffice.
gov.uk

For information on import or export restrictions, visit
www.hmrc.gov.uk

EMBASSIES AND CONSULATES

Australian High Commission
Australia House,
Strand, London WC2.
Tel 020 7379 4334.
www.uk.embassy.gov.au

Canadian High Commission
Canada House, Trafalgar
Square, London SW1.
Tel 020 7258 6600.
www.canada.gc.ca

New Zealand High Commission
New Zealand House,
80 Haymarket,
London SW1.
Tel 020 7930 8422.
www.nzembassy.com

United States Embassy
24 Grosvenor Sq,
London W1.
Tel 020 7499 9000.
www.usembassy.org.uk

INTERNATIONAL TOURIST INFORMATION

VisitBritain Australia
Tel 02 9021 4400
or 1300 85 8589.
www.visitbritain.com

VisitBritain Canada
Tel 1 888 847 4885
or 1 905 405 1720.
www.visitbritain.com

VisitBritain Ireland
www.enjoyengland.ie

VisitBritain USA
Tel 1 800 462 2748
or 1 212 986 2266.
www.visitbritain.com

REGIONAL TOURIST BOARDS

Britain
Thames Tower, Blacks Rd,
London W6 9EL.
Tel 020 8846 9000.
www.visitbritain.com

Cumbria
Tel 01539 822222.
www.golakes.co.uk

East of England
Tel 01284 727470.
www.visiteastof
england.com

East Midlands
Tel 01159 888365.
www.discover
eastmidlands.com

London
Tel 0871 222 3318.
www.visitlondon.com

Northumbria
Tel 01271 336182.
www.visitnortheast
england.com

Northwest
Tel 01942 821222.
www.visitnorthwest.com

Scotland
Tel 0131 472 2222.
www.visitscotland.com

Southeast
Tel 023 8062 5400.
www.visitsoutheast
england.com

South West
Tel 0870 442 0880.
www.visitsouthwest.
co.uk

Wales
Tel 0870 830 0306.
www.visitwales.co.uk

Yorkshire and the Humber Region
Tel 01904 707961.
www.yorkshire.com

A Cotswolds church, one of hundreds of parish churches open to the public

required when purchasing a ticket. Visitors from overseas may buy a Great British Heritage Pass, which gives access to more than 600 sights including Stonehenge *(see pp262–3)* and Warwick Castle *(see pp322–3)*. The pass is also available as a Family Pass. Families of two adults and up to three children, aged 5–15, can benefit. The pass can be bought from VisitBritain offices abroad. In the UK, it is sold at the Britain Visitor Centre in Lower Regent Street in London, as well as at some ports of entry and tourist information centres across Britain *(see p669)*.

PUBLIC CONVENIENCES

Although some old-style supervised public toilets still exist, these have been largely replaced by the modern, free-standing, coin-operated "superloos". Main railway stations usually have toilet facilities for which there is a small charge. Young children should never use these toilets on their own.

TIPPING, ETIQUETTE AND SMOKING

In Britain it is the norm to tip taxi drivers and waiting staff in restaurants. Between 10 and 15 per cent is standard. Many restaurants automatically add a service charge to the bill, so do check before leaving a tip. It is not customary to leave a tip when buying a drink in a pub or bar.

Smoking is now forbidden in all of Britain's public indoor spaces, including pubs, restaurants, nightclubs, transport systems, taxis, theatres and cinemas. For advice on smoking-related issues, contact **ASH** (Action on Smoking and Health). It is illegal to buy cigarettes if you are under the age of 18.

Age restrictions also apply in pubs and bars, where you must be over 18 to be served. Some bars are for over-21s only, and patrons may be asked for identification before being served.

ADMISSION PRICES

Admission fees for museums and sights vary widely, from a nominal 50p to in excess of £10 for the more popular attractions. Many of the major national museums are free, although donations are encouraged. The same is true of a few local authority museums and art galleries. Some sights are in private hands, run either as a commercial venture or on a charitable basis. Stately homes open to the public may still belong to the gentry who have lived there for centuries; a charge is usually made to offset the enormous costs of upkeep. Many of these houses, such as Woburn Abbey *(see p230)*, have added safari parks or garden centres to attract larger numbers of visitors.

Great British Heritage Pass

Britain's thousands of small parish churches are among the country's greatest architectural treasures. None of these churches charges an entrance fee, although you may find that some are locked because of vandalism. Increasingly, many of the great cathedrals expect a donation from visitors.

Reductions are often available for groups, senior citizens, children and students. Proof of eligibility will be

TRAVELLERS WITH SPECIAL NEEDS

The facilities on offer for disabled visitors to Britain are steadily improving. Recently designed or newly renovated buildings and public spaces now offer lifts and ramps for wheelchair access (this information is given in the headings for each entry in this guide); specially designed toilets; grab rails; and, for the hearing-impaired, earphones. Buses are also becoming increasingly accessible, and, if given advance notice, train, ferry or bus staff will help any disabled passengers. Ask a travel agent about the Disabled Persons Railcard, which entitles you to discounted rail fares.

Many banks, theatres and museums now provide aids for the visually or hearing-impaired. Specialist tour operators, such as **Tourism for All**, cater for physically handicapped visitors.

If renting a car, Hertz *(see p685)* offers hand-controlled vehicles for hire at no extra cost. In order to use any of the disabled parking spaces, you need to display a special badge in your car.

For more general information on facilities for disabled travellers, contact **RADAR**.

This association also publishes two books that carry a wealth of information for disabled holiday-makers: *Holidays in Britain and Ireland* and *There and Back*. The latter is a comprehensive guide to non-local travel. It pays particular attention to the links between the different methods of transport, whether by air, rail, road or sea.

TRAVELLING WITH CHILDREN

The Natural History Museum, a great day out for the whole family

Britain offers a wealth of activities and fun days out for those travelling with children. The VisitBritain website *(see p669)* is a great resource for offering ideas, tips and useful information for the family.

Peak holiday times – Easter, July and August – and half-term school holidays have most to offer in terms of entertainment for children. There is always something child-friendly going on at Christmas, too, like panto-mimes and winter skating rinks. It is worth checking the websites of individual muse-ums and art galleries, because these often host child-centred events at key times of year. A couple of useful websites for information on things to do with children are www. kidslovelondon.com and www.whatson4kids.com.

Discounts for children or family tickets are available for travel, theatre shows and other forms of entertainment.

Choose a hotel that welcomes children, or opt for self-catering quarters with hard-wearing furnishings and lots of room in which to run around. Many hotels now provide baby-sitting or baby-listening services, and may offer reductions or even free accommodation for very young children *(see pp552–99)*.

Restaurants are also becom-ing more welcoming of tiny patrons, and many provide high chairs and special menus *(see pp600–51)*. Italian eateries are often the most friendly and informal, but even the traditional British pub, once resolutely child-free, has relented, with beer gardens and family rooms. Under-18s are not permitted near the bars, nor are they

allowed to buy or consume alcohol. The over-16s however, are permitted to consume wine, beer or cider with a table meal provided the alcohol is bought by an adult.

Baby-changing facilities are often provided at larger shops, department stores and shopping centres, as well as at most large museums and art galleries. For those who don't want to travel with all the paraphernalia necessary for their offspring (baby food, nappies, sunscreen), **Tinytots-away** provides a great serv-ice. This web-based company will deliver everything you need for your trip directly to your accommodation.

DIRECTORY

HELPLINE

Action on Smoking and Health (ASH)
Tel 020 7739 5902.
www.ash.org.uk

TRAVELLERS WITH SPECIAL NEEDS

RADAR
Tel 020 7250 3222.
www.radar.org.uk

Tourism for All
Tel 08451 249971.
www.tourismforall.org.uk

TRAVELLING WITH CHILDREN

Tinytotsaway
Tel 01275 424421
www.tinytotsaway.com

The privately owned, admission-charging Hever Castle *(see p189)*

International Student Identity Card

STUDENT TRAVELLERS

Full-time students in posses-
sion of a valid International
Student Identity Card (ISIC)
are often entitled to discounts
on things such as travel,
entrance fees and sports
facilities. North American students can also get medical
cover, although it may be
very basic *(see p675)*. ISICs
can be purchased from **STA
Travel**, the **National Union of
Students** or online. Proof of
student status is required.

A **Hostelling International**
card enables you to stay in
Britain's youth hostels. Outside
of term time, inexpensive
accommodation is also available at many of the university
halls of residence, such as the
University of London. This is
a good way of staying in city
centres on a tight budget.
Those who are exploring
the wilder regions of Britain
can find affordable sleeping
quarters in camping barns
(dormitory-style bunkhouses).
Though spartan, they cost very
little. The YHA website (www.
yha.org.uk) has a full list of
camping barns across Britain.

US and Canadian students
interested in working in Britain should contact **BUNAC**.

ENGLISH HERITAGE AND THE NATIONAL TRUST

Many of Britain's historic
buildings, parks and gardens,
not to mention vast tracts of
countryside and coastline,
are cared for by associations
such as **English Heritage**
(EH), the **National Trust**
(NT) or the **National Trust
for Scotland** (NTS). Entrance
fees for these sights are often
quite steep, so if you wish to
visit several of them during
your stay, it may be worth
taking out an annual mem-
bership, which allows free
access to any of these
properties for a calendar
year. Be aware that many
may be closed in winter.

Many of the National Trust's
properties are "listed", meaning that they are recognized
as having special architectural
or historical interest and are
therefore protected from alterations and demolition. This
guide identifies EH, NT and
NTS properties at the beginning of each entry.

E N G L I S H   H E R I T A G E

**The sign and symbol
of English Heritage**

ELECTRICITY

The voltage in Britain is
220/240 AC, 50 Hz. Electrical
plugs have three rectangular
pins and take fuses of 3, 5
and 13 amps. Visitors from

abroad will need an adaptor
for appliances that have been
brought from home, such
as portable computers, hairdryers and phone chargers.
Most hotels will have two-
pronged European-style
sockets for shavers only.

**Clock at the Royal Observatory,
Greenwich *(see p125)***

TIME

During the winter months,
Britain is on Greenwich
Mean Time (GMT), which is
five hours ahead of Eastern
Standard Time and 10 hours
behind Sydney. From about
the middle of March until
October, the clocks go for-
ward one hour to British
Summer Time (BST).

To check the correct time,
contact the Speaking Clock
service by dialling 123.

CONVERSION CHART

Britain is officially metric,
in line with the rest of
Europe. However, imperial
measures are still in use,
especially for road distances, which are measured in
miles. Imperial pints and
gallons are 20 per cent
larger than US measures.

Imperial to metric
1 inch = 2.5 centimetres
1 foot = 30 centimetres
1 mile = 1.6 kilometres
1 ounce = 28 grams
1 pound = 454 grams
1 pint = 0.6 litres
1 gallon = 4.6 litres

Metric to imperial
1 millimetre = 0.04 inch
1 centimetre = 0.4 inch
1 metre = 3 feet 3 inches
1 kilometre = 0.6 mile
1 gram = 0.04 ounce
1 kilogram = 2.2 pounds

Lorna Doone Cottage and National Trust Information Centre, Somerset

RESPONSIBLE TRAVEL

Like many European countries, Britain is aware of the need to be greener and is making a concerted effort to reduce emissions and waste. While most rubbish is still sent to landfill sites, there are recycling campaigns in every town and city, and the amounts of household waste are gradually diminishing.

Many holiday properties across the country publish their green policies, showing how they minimize energy use. Some lodgings even offer discounts to guests arriving by public transport or on foot, particularly in heavily congested areas such as national parks. These themselves vary in the environmental schemes they operate, but all are committed to encouraging green tourism.

The **Green Tourism Business Scheme** is a national scheme that has vetted 1,500 places to stay in England, Scotland and Wales, from small B&Bs to

Colourful stalls at a farmers' market

luxury five-star hotels, as well as about 500 visitor attractions. The scheme requires owners to provide details on more than 145 criteria, ranging from energy and waste control to use of local produce and transport. A qualified environmental auditor visits each property and allocates an award based on the standards met. There are also more than 20 regional accommodation certification schemes across Britain, including **Green Leaf** (New Forest) and **Green Island** (Isle of Wight).

Another green accommodation solution is the great outdoors. Campsites are located across Britain, and pitches are available from as little as £4.50 per night. Note, however, that sites are often fairly far from the main towns and may not be served by public transport.

Organic and fair-trade products can be bought at most supermarkets. Many towns and cities hold a weekly food market, and farmers' markets are also on the increase. These stock locally sourced produce, and shopping here is a great way to give back to the local economy. Visit www.farmersmarkets.net. to find your nearest farmers' market. When in rural areas, look out for farm shops that stock fresh products from local farms. "Slow Food" fairs are held occasionally across the country. These tend to last several days and are a great opportunity for small vendors to set up stalls and for visitors to sample food from sustainable sources.

DIRECTORY

STUDENT TRAVELLERS

BUNAC
16 Bowling Green Lane, London EC1R 0QH.
Tel 020 7251 3472.
www.bunac.org

Hostelling International
Tel 01707 324170.
www.hihostels.com

National Union of Students
Tel 0871 221 8221.
www.nus.org.uk

STA Travel
Priory House,
6 Wrights Lane,
London W8 6TA.
Tel 0871 230 8558.
www.statravel.co.uk

University of London
Malet St,
London WC1.
Tel 020 7862 8000.
www.housing.lon.ac.uk

HERITAGE ORGANIZATIONS

English Heritage
Tel 0870 333 1181.
www.english-heritage.org.uk

National Trust
Tel 0844 800 1895.
www.nationaltrust.org.uk

National Trust for Scotland
28 Charlotte Sq,
Edinburgh EH2 4ET.
Tel 0844 493 2100.
www.nts.org.uk

RELIGIOUS ORGANIZATIONS

Baptist
London Baptist Assn,
235 Shaftesbury Ave,
London WC2. *Tel* 020 7692 5592. **www**.londonbaptist.org.uk

Buddhist
Buddhist Society,
58 Eccleston Sq, London SW1. *Tel* 020 7834 5858.
www.thebuddhist society.org

Church of England
Great Smith St, London SW1. *Tel* 020 7898 1000.
www.cofe.anglican.org

Evangelical Alliance
Whitefield House,
186 Kennington Park Rd, London SE11.
Tel 020 7207 2100.
www.eauk.org

Jewish
Liberal Jewish Synagogue,
28 St John's Wood Rd, London NW8. *Tel* 020 7286 5181. **www**.ljs.org

Muslim
Islamic Cultural Centre,
146 Park Rd, London NW8. *Tel* 020 7725 2213. **www**.iccuk.org

Quakers
Friends House, 173–177 Euston Rd, London NW1.
Tel 020 7663 1000.
www.quaker.org.uk

Roman Catholic
Westminster Cathedral,
Victoria St, London SW1.

Tel 020 7798 9055.
www.westminster cathedral.org.uk

United Synagogue (Orthodox)
Adler House,
735 High Rd, North Finchley, London N12.
Tel 020 8343 8989.
www.theus.org.uk

RESPONSIBLE TRAVEL

Green Business
www.green-business.co.uk

Green Island Tourism
www.greenislandtourism.org

Green Leaf Tourist Scheme
www.thegreenforest.org

Green Tourism Business Scheme
www.green-business.co.uk

Tourism Concern
www.tourismconcern.org.uk

Personal Security and Health

Britain is a densely populated country that, like any other, has its share of social problems. However, it is very unlikely that you will come across any violence. If you do encounter difficulties, do not hesitate to contact the police for help. Britain's National Health Service can be relied upon for both emergency and routine treatment. Note that you may have to pay if your country has no reciprocal arrangement with Britain.

Police car

Ambulance

Fire engine

POLICE

The sight of a traditional bobby walking the streets is now less common than that of the police patrol car, but the old-fashioned police constable does still exist, particularly in rural areas and crowded city centres.

Unlike in many other countries, the police force in Britain does not carry guns, although 10 per cent of the London Metropolitan police are armed.

If you are lost, ask a policeman or woman – they are courteous, approachable and helpful. Traffic wardens may also be able to help you with directions. If you have been the victim of a robbery or an assault, contact the police by dialling 999. All Britain's major cities have community police support officers who patrol the city streets working alongside the police. They are able to deal with anti-social behaviour, can offer advice on crime prevention and can also help you with directions and information.

LOST AND STOLEN PROPERTY

If you lose anything or have anything stolen, report it at the nearest police station as soon as you are able. A written report from the local police is required to make a claim on your insurance for any theft. All of the main bus and rail stations have lost-property offices.

CRIME

Britain is not a dangerous place for visitors, and it is most unlikely that your stay will be blighted by crime. Due to terrorist threats, there are occasional security alerts, especially on the Underground, but these are mainly false alarms often due to people accidentally leaving a bag or parcel unattended. Always co-operate with the authorities if your bag has to be searched or if you are asked to evacuate a building.

WHAT TO BE AWARE OF

Make sure that your possessions are adequately insured before you arrive in Britain, and never leave them unattended in public places. Keep your valuables concealed (particularly mobile phones), especially in crowded places. Pickpockets love markets, busy shops and all modes of transport during rush hour. Keep handbags on your lap, never on the floor or on the back of your chair. It is advisable not to carry too much cash or jewellery with you. Take what you need for the day, and leave the rest in your hotel safe instead. It is also advisable not to leave any valuables on display in your hotel room.

At night, try to avoid deserted and poorly lit places such as back streets and car parks.

Begging is an increasingly common sight in many British cities, and foreign visitors are frequent targets for hard-luck stories. Requests for money are usually polite, but any abuse should be reported to the police immediately.

Female police constable

Traffic police officer

Male police constable

WOMEN TRAVELLERS

It is not unusual in Britain for women to travel unaccompanied or to visit a bar or restaurant with a group of female friends. However, caution is advisable in deserted places, especially after dark. Always summon a licensed taxi *(see pp690–91)* and do not walk through a quiet area at night, especially if you are not familiar with the district. Try to avoid using train carriages where there is just one other passenger or a group of young men.

It is illegal to carry any offensive weapons such as knives, guns and even tear gas around with you, even for self-defence. However, personal alarms are allowed.

IN AN EMERGENCY

The police, fire and ambulance services are on call 24 hours a day and can be reached by dialling 999. Along the coastal areas, this number will also put you in touch with Britain's voluntary coastguard rescue service, the Royal National Lifeboat Institute. Calls are free from any public or private phone, but they should be made only in real emergencies.

PHARMACIES

You can buy a wide range of over-the-counter drugs in Britain. **Boots** (www.boots.com) is the best-known chemist, with branches in most towns. Many medicines, however, are available only with a doctor's prescription. If you are likely to need medication, either bring your own or get your doctor to write out the generic (as opposed to the brand) name of the drug. If you are entitled to an NHS prescription, you will be charged a standard rate; if not, you will be charged the full cost of the drug. Do ask for a receipt for any insurance claim.

Some pharmacies are open until midnight; contact your local hospital for a list. You can call the NHS Direct 24-hour helpline (0845 4647) or go to a hospital casualty department any time. In an emergency, dial 999 for an ambulance.

Pharmacy sign

HEALTH INSURANCE

It is sensible to take out travel insurance to cover cancellation or curtailment of your holiday, theft or loss of money and possessions, and the cost of any medical treatment, which may include emergency hospital care, repatriation and specialists' fees. This is particularly important for visitors from outside the European Union. Emergency medical treatment in a British NHS casualty ward is free, but any kind of additional medical care could prove very expensive.

Those with a European Health Insurance Card (EHIC) are entitled to free treatment under the NHS. This applies to visitors from EU and European Economic Area (EEA) countries, as well as some Commonwealth countries, such as Australia and New Zealand. Be aware, though, that certain benefits covered by medical insurance will not be included. North American and Canadian health plans or student identity cards *(see p672)* may give you some protection against costs, but do always check the small print.

Royal National Lifeboat Institute logo

If you need to see a dentist while staying in Britain, be aware that you will have to pay. The cost varies, depending on your entitlement to NHS treatment and whether you can find an NHS dentist to treat you (many dental practices no longer take on NHS patients). Emergency dental treatment is available in some hospitals, but if you prefer to be seen by a private dentist, try looking in the *Yellow Pages (see p678)* .

DIRECTORY

EMERGENCY NUMBERS

Police, Fire and Ambulance services
Tel 999.

Accident and Emergency Departments
For your nearest unit, check the phone directory or contact the police.

Emergency Dental Care
Tel 020 7188 7188 *(Guy's Hospital, London) or* 020 7837 3646 *(children only, 24 hours).*

HELPLINES

Alcoholics Anonymous
Tel 0845 769 7555. www.alcoholics-anonymous.org.uk

British Deaf Association
www.signcommunity.org.uk

British Pregnancy Advisory Service
Tel 08457 30 40 30.
www.bpas.org

Childline
Tel 0800 1111 *(24-hour free phoneline for children in need of help).*
www.childline.org.uk

Dial UK
Tel 01302 310123
(helpline for the disabled).
www.dialuk.org.uk

Disabled Living Foundation
Tel 0845 130 9177.
www.dlf.org.uk

Frank
Tel 0800 77 66 00 *(24-hour substance-abuse helpline).*
www.talktofrank.com

NHS Direct
Tel 0845 4647.
www.nhsdirect.nhs.uk

Rape Crisis Centre
Regional numbers found at
www.rapecrisis.co.uk

Royal National Institute of Blind People
Tel 08457 66 99 99.
www.rnib.org.uk

Samaritans
Tel 08457 90 90 90 *(24 hours).*
www.samaritans.org

Victim Support
Tel 0845 30 30 900.
www.victimsupport.org

Banking and Local Currency

The high-street banks usually offer the best rates of currency exchange, though commission fees may vary. However, if you do find yourself having to use one of the many privately owned bureaux de change that are found at nearly every major airport, train station and tourist area, take care to check the commission and minimum charges before completing any transaction.

A branch of Lloyds TSB

BUREAUX DE CHANGE

Private bureaux de change may be more conveniently located and have more flexible opening hours than banks. However, rates of exchange vary and commission charges can be high, so it is always worth shopping around. **Exchange International**, **Travelex**, **American Express** and **Chequepoint** all have branches throughout Britain and usually offer good exchange facilities. Marks & Spencer (www.marksand spencer.com) has bureaux de change in more than 110 of its stores across the UK. They charge no commission on foreign-currency travellers' cheques and only 1 per cent on sterling travellers' cheques.

BANKS

Every large town and city in Britain has a branch of at least one of these five high-street banks: Barclays, Lloyds TSB, HSBC, NatWest and Royal Bank of Scotland.

Banking hours vary but the majority are open 9am to 5:30pm Monday to Friday. Most main branches open on Saturday mornings, too. All banks close on public holidays (*see p65*).

If you run out of funds, it is possible to have money wired from your country to your nearest British bank. Branches of Travelex and American Express will also do this for you. North American visitors can get cash dispatched through **Western Union** to a bank or post office. Remember to take along your passport as proof of identity.

CASH DISPENSERS

Most banks have a cash dispenser, or ATM, from which you can obtain money with a credit card and your personal identification number (PIN). Cash machines can also be found in some supermarkets, post offices, petrol stations, train stations and London Underground stations. Some of the most modern ATMs have on-screen instructions in several languages. Some make a charge for cash withdrawals (typically £1.50 per transaction). American Express cards may be used at all cash-dispensing machines, but there is a 2 per cent handling charge for each transaction.

There have been some incidences of card crime at ATMs; be vigilant and cover the keypad with your hand when entering your PIN.

CREDIT CARDS

Credit cards are widely used throughout Britain. Indeed, a credit card is necessary in order to rent a car and for some hotel bookings. However, many small shops, guesthouses, markets and cafés may not accept them, so always check in advance of your purchase. Cards that are accepted are usually displayed on the windows of the establishment. Britain uses the "chip and PIN" system instead of a signature on a credit slip. You will need a four-digit PIN, so ask your bank for one before you leave.

A credit card allows you to obtain cash advances up to your credit limit at any bank and cash dispenser displaying the appropriate card sign. You will be charged the credit card company's interest rate for obtaining cash, and this will appear on your statement with the amount advanced. You will probably also incur a currency-exchange fee.

BRITISH BANKS

These high-street banks have branches in most of Britain's towns and cities. Many will also offer currency-exchange facilities, but proof of identity may be required.

The Royal Bank of Scotland
Royal Bank of Scotland logo

National Westminster logo

HSBC
HSBC logo

BARCLAYS
Barclays Bank logo

Lloyds TSB logo

American Express
Tel 020 7834 5555.
www.americanexpress.co.uk

Chequepoint
Tel 020 7225 4600.
www.chequepoint.com

Exchange International
Tel 020 7630 1107.

Travelex
www.travelex.co.uk

Western Union
Tel 0800 833 833.
www.westernunion.co.uk

CURRENCY

Britain's currency is the pound sterling (£), which is divided into 100 pence (p). There are no exchange controls in Britain, so you may bring in and take out as much cash as you like. Scotland has

A Scottish one pound (£1) bank note

its own notes. Although these are legal tender throughout Britain, they are not always accepted in England and Wales. Travellers' cheques are the safest alternative to carrying large amounts of cash. Always keep the receipts from your

travellers' cheques separate from the cheques themselves. This simple precaution makes it easier to obtain a refund if your cheques are lost or stolen. Some high-street banks issue travellers' cheques free of commission to their account holders, but the normal rate is about 1 per cent. When changing money, ask for some smaller notes, since these are easier to use.

Bank Notes
English notes are produced in denominations of £5, £10, £20 and £50. Some shops may refuse the larger notes, so always get small denominations.

£50 note

£20 note

£10 note

£5 note

Coinage
Coins currently in use are £2, £1, 50p, 20p, 10p, 5p, 2p and 1p.

2 pounds (£2)

1 pound (£1)

50 pence (50p)

20 pence (20p)

10 pence (10p)

5 pence (5p)

2 pence (2p)

1 penny (1p)

Communications and Media

With constantly improving telecommunication systems and email, staying in touch and making plans while travelling has never been easier. The telephone system in Britain is efficient and inexpensive. Charges depend on when, where and for how long you talk. The cheapest time to call is between 6pm and 8am Monday to Friday and throughout the weekend. Local calls made on public payphones, however, are charged at a fixed rate per minute.

Modern BT phone box

PUBLIC TELEPHONES

You can use a payphone with coins or a card. All payphones accept 10p, 20p, 50p and £1 pieces; the newer ones also accept £2 coins. The minimum cost of a call is 40p. Phone cards are more convenient than coins and can be bought from newsagents and post offices. If you use a credit card, note that it carries a minimum charge and that your calls will be charged at a higher rate.

MOBILE PHONES

Mobile phones are widespread in Britain, and every high street has at least one mobile-phone shop, the most common being **Vodafone**, **Carphone Warehouse**, **Orange** and **Phones4U**. The UK network uses the 900 or 1800 GSM system, so visitors from the United States (where the system is 800 or 1900 MHz band) will need to acquire a tri- or quad-band set. Contact your service provider for details. You may need to inform your network operator in advance of your trip, so that the "roaming" facility can be enabled. When abroad,

you will be charged for the calls you receive, as well as for the calls you make; in addition, you have to pay a substantial premium for the international leg of the call.

It is easier and cheaper to purchase a SIM card locally and top it up with credit. This will allow you to use the local mobile-phone networks, though you can only do this if your handset is not "locked" to a specific network. Alternatively, you could buy a brand-new phone and top up with a pay-as-you-go card. Make sure the phone you buy can accept international calls. Check that your insurance policy covers you in case your phone gets stolen, and keep your network operator's helpline number handy for emergencies.

ACCESSING THE INTERNET

Most cities and towns now have some form of public access to computers and the Internet, including specially adapted payphones in the street. Many hotels include Internet facilities as part of their service, and free Internet access is often available at libraries, though you may have to book a time slot. Many cafés now offer free WiFi (wireless) Internet access, so you can use your laptop computer.

Internet cafés usually charge for computer use by the minute. Internet access is generally very cheap, but it is most reasonable during off-peak times. However, charges can build up quickly,

especially when including the cost of printing.

VoIP (Voice over Internet Protocol) is a way of communicating telephonically via your computer. Most Internet cafés will have at least one such system installed. In order to use it, you will need a Skype account (free to set up), a set of headphones and a microphone (usually provided by the café). It is free to call other Skype accounts. Calling land lines and mobiles is very cheap, but you need to buy Skype credits using credit/debit cards or PayPal.

DIRECTORY

The following services exist to help you find or reach a specific phone number. You will be charged more for enquiries if calling from a mobile phone.

BT Directory Enquiries
Tel 118 500 (charge applies).

International Directory Enquiries
Tel 118 505 (charge applies).

International Operator
Tel 155 (freephone).

Operator Assistance
Tel 100.

Overseas Calls
Tel 00 followed by country code: Australia (61), Canada (1), Ireland (353), New Zealand (64), South Africa (27), United States (1).

Yellow Pages
Tel 118 247 (charge applies).
www.yell.com
Provides numbers for shops or services in any area, as well as maps and driving directions.

DIRECTORY

Carphone Warehouse
www.carphonewarehouse.co.uk

Orange
www.orange.co.uk

Phones4U
www.phones4u.co.uk

Vodafone
www.vodafone.co.uk

Round-the-clock Internet access at the Europe-wide chain easyInternetcafe

POSTAL SERVICES

Stamps can be bought at many outlets, including supermarkets and petrol stations. When writing to a British address, always include the postcode, which can be obtained from **Royal Mail**. Within the UK, letters and postcards can be sent either first or second class; second-class mail is cheaper and takes a day or two longer. The price of postage depends on the size and weight of your letter. For more details, visit the Royal Mail website or take your letter/parcel to any post office, where they will weigh it and give you the price of postage.

Large urban post office branches have a *poste restante* service where letters can be collected. Correspondence should be sent to the recipient at *Poste Restante*, followed by the address of the relevant post office branch. To collect your post, you will have to show your passport or other form of identification. Post is kept for one month. London's main post office is in William IV Street, WC2. The American Express office on Haymarket also has a *poste restante* service for customers.

Main post office branches offer all the mail services available. In more isolated areas, there are often small branches in newsagents, grocery stores and general information centres. In many villages, the post office is also the only shop.

Post offices are usually open from 9am to 5:30pm Monday to Friday, and until 12:30pm on Saturday.

Royal Mail
Tel 08457 740 740.
www.royalmail.com

POST BOXES

Post boxes can be found throughout cities, towns and villages in Britain. They may be either free-standing pillar boxes or wall safes, but they are always painted bright red. Collections are usually made several times a day during weekdays (less often on Saturdays and Sundays). The last collection time of the day is marked on the box.

MAILING ABROAD

Pillar box

Air letters go by Royal Mail's airmail service anywhere in the world; the cost depends on the destination. On average, it takes three days for them to reach cities in Europe, and four to six days for other destinations. Royal Mail also offers an express airmail service called **Airsure**, available from all post office branches. Mail goes on the first available flight to the country of destination.

Parcelforce Worldwide offers courier-style services to most destinations and is comparable in price to **DHL**, **Crossflight**, **Expressair** or **UPS**.

Airsure (Royal Mail)
Tel 08457 740 740.
www.royalmail.com

Crossflight
Tel 08702 241 122.
www.crossflight.co.uk

DHL
Tel 08701 100 300.
www.dhl.co.uk

Expressair
Tel 08450 77 55 33.
www.expressair.co.uk

Parcelforce Worldwide
Tel 08708 50 11 50.
www.parcelforce.com

UPS
Tel 08457 877 877.
www.ups.com

NEWSPAPERS AND MAGAZINES

British national newspapers fall into two categories: quality papers, such as *The Times*, *The Daily Telegraph* and *The Guardian*; and those heavy on gossip, such as *The Sun* or the *Daily Mirror*. The weekend newspapers, more expensive than dailies, are packed with supplements of all kinds, including sections on the arts, entertainment, travel, listings and reviews. Free newspapers, with an emphasis on news and celebrity gossip, are given away, morning and evening, at main railway stations in major cities such as London and Manchester.

Specialist periodicals on just about every topic are available from newsagents. For a more in-depth analysis of current events, buy *The Economist*, *New Statesman* or *The Spectator*, while *Private Eye* cocks a satirical snook at public figures. A few foreign magazines and newspapers are available in large towns, often at main train stations, but mostly in London. One of the most popular is the *International Herald Tribune*, which is available on the day of issue.

Some of Britain's national newspapers

TELEVISION AND RADIO

The state-run BBC (British Broadcasting Corporation) operates eight channels and has a reputation for making some of the world's best television. These channels have no advertising breaks. Its commercial rivals include ITV, Channel 4 and Five. ITV is liked for its soap operas and game shows; Channel 4 caters for trendy and minority tastes (art films, documentaries, offbeat chat shows); and Five relies on US imports and TV movies.

The BBC also has a number of radio stations, ranging from pop music (Radio 1) to the middle-brow Radio 4. There are many local commercial radio stations.

Full TV and radio schedules appear in newspapers and listings magazines, as well as online and in the *Radio Times*, a weekly publication.

TRAVEL INFORMATION

Britain is an international gateway for both air and sea traffic, which translates into a variety of options in terms of travel. Visitors enjoy a large selection of air carriers linking Britain to the rest of Europe, North America and Australasia. Coach travel is a cheap, if rather slow, form of transport from Europe, while travelling by train has been transformed thanks to the Channel Tunnel. It takes less than two and a half hours from Paris to London on Eurostar. Travelling within Britain is also easy. There is an extensive network of roads to all parts of the country, and hiring a car can be a convenient way of travelling around. The railway network is efficient and far-reaching, especially around London. Travelling by coach is the cheapest option. The coach network reaches most areas but can be slow. If time is short, air travel is possible if expensive.

BRITISH AIRWAYS
British Airways logo

Eurostar trains at St Pancras International Station, London

TRAVELLING AROUND BRITAIN

Choosing the best form of transport depends on where and when you want to go, although the quickest and most convenient methods are generally also the most expensive. The **Transport Direct** website offers a number of alternative ways of getting to your chosen destination.

Distances between any two points within mainland Britain are relatively small, so air travel usually makes sense only between the extremes, such as London to Edinburgh.

Train travel is the best option if you want to visit Britain's major cities, though fares, especially at peak times, can be expensive. If you plan to do much travelling within Britain, invest in a rail pass (see p686). You can buy one before you arrive in the UK since several schemes cater for overseas visitors. **BritRail** has several options on offer, from a few days' to two weeks' worth of rail travel.

Coaches (see p688) cover a wide number of UK destinations and are cheaper than trains, but they take longer and may be less comfortable.

For a touring holiday, hiring a car (see p685) is easier than relying on public transport. Car rental can be arranged at major airports, large train stations and city centre outlets. Small local firms often undercut the large operators in price but may not be as reliable or convenient. To get the best deals, book from abroad.

For detailed exploration of smaller areas, such as Britain's national parks, you may prefer more leisurely forms of transport such as bike, narrowboat or horse. Sometimes there are picturesque local options, like the rowing-boat ferry between Southwold and Walberswick on the Blyth Estuary (see p202). Larger car ferries travel to Britain's islands.

Taxis (see p690) are available at all main coach and train stations; without a car you will avoid the stress of driving in congested city centres.

GREEN TRAVEL

With congestion charges in London and limited parking throughout the urban areas, driving in British cities is not recommended. Instead, make use of the country's extensive public transport network.

Covering a lot of ground without a car is possible, although this does take careful planning to ensure you catch all of your connections. Most areas are served by trains and/or buses, and services tend to be fairly regular. Travelling around the countryside without private transport, however, can be difficult, because bus services can be infrequent (particularly on Sundays). It may be sensible to hire a car.

Trains in Britain can be over-crowded at peak times, and they are often expensive, although booking tickets in advance can bring the cost down. The GroupSave ticket scheme allows discounted rail travel for groups of three or four, and various other discounts are available with a travel card.

The National Trust (see p672) offers some incentives, including discounted entry, to those who use public transport when visiting some of their sites.

The National Cycle Network provides more than 20,000 km (12,430 miles) of cycle paths across Britain. A bike can be taken on most off-peak trains, but you may have to book a spot for it. Check before you travel.

For more information on environmentally friendly travel options, contact **Sustrans**.

Arriving by Sea, Rail and Coach

Irrespective of how you are travelling from Europe, you will have to cross the English Channel or the North Sea. Ferry services operate from a huge number of ports on the European mainland and have good link-ups with international coaches, with services from most European cities to Britain. The Channel Tunnel means there is a non-stop rail link between Europe and Britain. Prices between the ferries and the tunnel services remain competitive, and both options are good green alternatives to flying.

FERRY SERVICES FROM EUROPE

A complex network of car and passenger ferry services links over a dozen British ports to many ports in northern and southern Europe.

Ferries can be convenient and economical for those travelling by car or on foot. Fares vary greatly according to the season, time of travel and duration of stay. Early booking means big savings – a Dover–Calais return crossing can cost as little as £22. The shortest crossings are not always the cheapest, since you often pay a premium for the speed of the journey.

CROSSING TIMES

Crossing times vary from just over an hour on the shortest routes to a full 24 hours on services from Spain and Scandinavia. If you take an overnight sailing, it is often worth paying extra for sleeping quarters to avoid feeling exhausted when you arrive.

Speed Ferries runs fast Seacat (catamaran) services between Dover and Boul-

ogne, in France, taking just under an hour. Catamarans can carry vehicles and lack the dip and sway of a conventional ship, so may be less painful for those who tend to get seasick.

SEAPORT BUREAUCRACY

Visitors from outside the EU should allow plenty of time for immigration control and customs clearance at British seaports *(see p668).*

CHANNEL TUNNEL

Thanks to the Channel Tunnel, there is access to Britain via **Eurostar** and **Eurotunnel** from the French and Belgian high-speed rail networks. In France and Belgium, trains reach speeds of up to 186 mph (300kmph). The cost is comparable to flying but the train is much more convenient and much less environmentally damaging. Typically, a ticket from London to Paris costs about £99 but can be as low as £59.

Eurotunnel logo

Passengers on buses and cars get on to a freight train run by Eurotunnel

that takes 35 minutes to travel between Calais and Folkestone. For those travelling by rail there are about 40 scheduled passenger-only Eurostar services, operated by the French, Belgians and British. They run direct services from Brussels, Paris, Lille and Calais to Ashford, Ebbsfleet and St Pancras in London. There are two passenger tunnels and one service tunnel, both lying 25–45 m (82–147 ft) below the sea bed.

INTERNATIONAL COACH TRAVEL

Although coach (bus) travel is considerably cheaper than other forms of travel, it is not the most comfortable. If you have a lot of spare time and want to stop off en route, however, it can be convenient. Once you have paid for your ticket, you will not have to pay extra for the ferry or the Channel Tunnel.

DIRECTORY

FERRIES, RAIL AND COACH TRAVEL

BritRail
www.acprailnet.com

Brittany Ferries
Tel 08709 076 103.
www.brittanyferries.co.uk

European Rail Travel
Tel 08448 484 064.
www.raileurope.co.uk

Eurostar
Tel 08705 186 186.
www.eurostar.com

Eurotunnel/Le Shuttle
Tel 08705 35 35 35.
www.eurotunnel.com

National Express
www.nationalexpress.com
(coaches)

Norfolk Line
www.norfolkline.com *(ferries)*

P&O Ferries
www.poferries.com

Speed Ferries
www.speed.ferries.org

Transport Direct
www.transportdirect.info

GREEN TRAVEL

Sustrans
www.sustrans.org.uk

Ferry arriving at Dover

Arriving by Air

Britain has about 130 licensed airports, only a handful of which deal with long-haul traffic. The largest one, London's Heathrow, is the world's busiest international airport and one of Europe's main routing points for international air travel. Heathrow is served by most of the world's leading airlines, with direct flights from nearly all the major cities. Other international airports include Gatwick, Stansted, Manchester, Glasgow, Newcastle, Birmingham and Edinburgh. Smaller airports, such as London City, Bristol, Norwich and Cardiff, have daily flights to European destinations. Strict anti-terrorist measures are currently in force at all airports.

A British Airways 747 jet at Heathrow Airport

BRITISH AIRPORTS

Most of Britain's largest and best-known airports are run by the British Airports Authority (BAA); the rest are either owned by a local authority or in private hands. BAA airports offer up-to-date facilities, including 24-hour banking, shops, cafés, hotels and restaurants. Security is strict at all British airports, and it is important never to leave your luggage unattended.

For visitors to London, Heathrow, Gatwick or Stansted are equally convenient. If you plan to visit northern England, there are now many flights going to Birmingham, Newcastle and Manchester, while for Scotland you can fly to Glasgow or Edinburgh.

Heathrow has five terminals and other airports have two. Before you fly, check with the airport from which terminal your flight leaves.

During severe weather conditions in the winter months, your flight may be diverted to another airport. If this happens, the airline will organize transportation back to your original destination.

British Airways has flights to most of the world's important destinations. Other British international airlines include

Virgin Atlantic, with routes to the USA and the Far East, and **British Midland**, which flies to Western Europe.

American airlines offering scheduled services to Britain include **Delta**, **US Air** and **American Airlines**. From Canada, the main carrier is **Air Canada**. From Australasia, the national carriers **Qantas** and **Air New Zealand** vie with several Far Eastern rivals.

Britain imposes an airport tax on all departing passengers. This is currently £10 for domestic and EU routes, and £20 for non-EU and long-haul flights. It is included in the price of the ticket.

TRANSPORT FROM THE AIRPORT

Britain's international airports lie some way from the city centres, but transport to and from them is efficient. The most convenient form of door-to-door travel is a taxi, but it is also the most expensive. In addition, taxis can be slow if there is road congestion. This is also a problem with buses or coaches, although they are a lot cheaper.

Heathrow and Newcastle airports are linked to the city centres by the Underground *(see p691)*, which is efficient, quick and cheap. Visitors to London arriving at Heathrow can also take the Heathrow Express, the fast train to Paddington Station

AIRPORT	INFORMATION	DISTANCE TO CITY CENTRE	TAXI FARE TO CITY CENTRE	PUBLIC TRANSPORT TO CITY CENTRE
Heathrow	08700 000 123	23 km (14 miles)	£40–£45	Rail: 15 mins Tube: 45 mins
Gatwick	08700 002 468	45 km (28 miles)	£75	Rail: 30 mins Bus: 70 mins
Stansted	08700 000 303	60 km (37 miles)	£80	Rail: 45 mins Bus: 75 mins
Manchester	0161 489 3000	16 km (10 miles)	£15–£16	Rail: 15 mins Bus: 30 mins
Birmingham	08707 33 55 11	13 km (8 miles)	£12–£15	Bus: 30 mins
Newcastle	08718 821 131	8 km (5 miles)	£10–£12	Metro: 20 mins Bus: 20 mins
Glasgow	08700 400 008	13 km (8 miles)	£12–£15	Bus: 20 mins
Edinburgh	08700 400 007	13 km (8 miles)	£17–£18	Bus: 25 mins

Terminal 5 at Heathrow Airport

(www.heathrowexpress.com
or 0845 600 1515). Trains run
every 15 minutes from 5am
until around midnight, taking
15 minutes from Terminals 1,
2 and 3, and 21 minutes
from Terminal 5. Terminal 4
requires a change of train and
takes a total of 23 minutes.
Those arriving at Gatwick can
take the Gatwick Express to
London Victoria (www.gatwick
express.com or 08705 30 15
30). Trains run every 15 minutes and
take 30
minutes.

Stansted
and Man-
chester also
have regu-
lar express
trains that are not
too expensive and
are a reliable method for travelling into the heart of the city.

National Express coaches
(see p688) provide direct connections from major airports
(London's Heathrow, Gatwick
and Stansted, Luton, Birmingham, Liverpool, Manchester,
Coventry, East Midlands and
Bristol) to many British destinations. They also have a regular service between Gatwick
and Heathrow.

CHOOSING A TICKET

Finding the right flight at the
right price can be difficult.
Promotional fares do come
up, and it is always worth
checking with the airlines.
Cheap deals are often available from package operators

Heathrow **express** ⊗

Gatwick **express**

**Signs for express railway
services to London**

and are advertised in newspapers and travel magazines.
Even if you enjoy independent travel, it may be worth
considering a package, since
sometimes car rental or rail
travel is included, and this
can be cheaper than arrang-
ing it yourself once in Britain.

Fares are usually seasonal,
the most expensive falling
between June and September.
The best deals can be had
from November to April,
excluding
Christmas
– if you
want to
travel then,
be sure to
book well
in advance.
APEX (Advance
Purchase Excur-
sion) fares are often the best
value, though they must be
booked up to a month ahead
and are subject to restrictions.
Charter flights offer even
cheaper seats but are not
usually flexible.

Budget airlines such as
easyJet and **Ryanair** offer
exceptionally cheap flights if
booked long enough in
advance. Always buy discount
fares from a reputable operator, and do not part with any
cash until you have seen your
ticket and ensured your seat
has been confirmed.

Students, the under-26s,
senior citizens and frequent
travellers may obtain a discount through student travel
agencies. Children also travel
at cheaper rates.

TRAVELLING WITHIN BRITAIN BY AIR

Internal air travel in Britain
only makes sense over
long distances, where it
can save a great deal
of time – for example,
London to Scotland, or
to one of the many off-
shore islands. Fares can be
expensive, but if you book
well ahead, they can be up
to three times cheaper than
if you just turn up at the
airport. The British Airways
shuttle flights that operate
between London and cities
such as Glasgow, Edin-
burgh and Manchester are
very popular with business
travellers. At peak times of
the day, flights leave every
hour, while at other times
there is usually a flight
every two hours. Even on
domestic flights, security
is strict. Never leave your
bags unattended.

DIRECTORY

AIR TRAVEL

Air Canada
Tel 0871 220 111.

Air New Zealand
Tel 0800 028 4149.

American Airlines
Tel 020 7365 0777.

British Airports Authority
Tel 020 8745 9800.
www.baa.com

British Airways
Tel 0870 850 9850.

British Midland
Tel 0870 607 0555.

Continental Airlines
Tel 0800 776 464.

Delta Airlines
Tel 0845 600 0950.

EasyJet
www.easyjet.com

Qantas
Tel 08457 747 767.

Ryanair
www.ryanair.com

US Airways
Tel 08456 003 300.
www.usairways.com

Virgin Atlantic
Tel 08705 747 747.

Travelling Around by Car

The most startling difference for most foreign motorists is that in Britain you drive on the left, with corresponding adjustments at roundabouts and junctions. Distances are measured in miles. Once you adapt, rural Britain is an enjoyable place to drive, though traffic density in towns and at busy holiday times can cause long delays – public holiday weekends near the south coast can be particularly horrendous. An extensive network of toll-free motorways and trunk roads has now cut travelling time to most parts of the country.

The A30 dual carriageway going through Cornwall

WHAT YOU NEED

To drive in Britain you need a current driving licence with an international driving permit, if required. You must also carry proof of ownership or a rental agreement in your vehicle, plus any insurance documents.

ROADS IN BRITAIN

Rush hour can last from 8 to 9:30am and from 5 to 7pm on weekdays in the cities; at these times, traffic can grind to a halt.

A good touring map is vital for driving in the country. The AA or RAC motoring atlases are fairly straightforward to use. For exploration of more rural areas, the Ordnance Survey series is the best. Motorways are marked with an "M" followed by their identifying number. "A" roads, sometimes

dual carriageways (that is, with two lanes in each direction), are main routes, while "B" roads are secondary roads. The latter are often less congested and more enjoyable. Rural areas are criss-crossed by a web of tiny lanes.

ROAD SIGNS

Signs are mostly standardized in line with Europe. Directional signs are colour-coded: blue for motorways, green for major routes and white for minor routes. Brown signs indicate places of interest. Advisory or warning signs are usually triangles in red and white, with easy-to-understand pictograms. Watch for electronic notices on motorways that warn of roadworks, accidents or patches of fog.

Level crossings, found at railway lines, often have auto-

matic barriers. If the lights are flashing red, it means a train is coming and you must stop.

The UK Highway Code Manual, available online at the Department of Transport website, is an up-to-date guide to all the current British driving regulations and traffic signs.

RULES OF THE ROAD

Speed limits are 30–40 mph (50–65 km/h) in built-up areas and 70 mph (110 km/h) on motorways or dual carriageways. Look out for speed signs on other roads. It is compulsory to wear seatbelts in Britain. Drink-driving penalties are severe; see the UK Highway Code Manual for legal limits. It is illegal to use a mobile phone while driving.

PARKING

Parking meters operate during working hours (usually 8am–6:30pm Mon–Sat). Be sure to keep a supply of coins for them. Some cities have "park and ride" schemes, where you can take a bus from an out-of-city car park into the centre. Other towns have parking schemes where you buy a card at the tourist office or newsagents, fill in your parking times and display it on your dashboard. Avoid double yellow lines at all times; single lines sometimes mean you can park in the evenings and at weekends, but check carefully. Traffic wardens will not hesitate to ticket, clamp or tow away your car. If in doubt, find a car park. Outside urban

DISTANCE CHART

LONDON

492 792	ABERDEEN						**10**	**Distance in miles**			
111 179	**411** 658	BIRMINGHAM					10	Distance in kilometres			
114 182	**490** 784	**88** 101	BRISTOL								
150 240	**493** 789	**102** 163	**44** 70	CARDIFF							
74 118	**563** 901	**185** 296	**189** 302	**228** 365	DOVER						
372 600	**121** 194	**290** 464	**369** 590	**373** 597	**442** 707	EDINBURGH					
170 272	**565** 904	**164** 262	**75** 120	**120** 192	**244** 342	**444** 710	EXETER				
198 317	**792** 492	**90** 144	**161** 258	**165** 264	**270** 432	**214** 342	**237** 380	LIVERPOOL			
184 294	**333** 533	**81** 130	**162** 258	**173** 277	**257** 411	**213** 341	**238** 381	**34** 54	MANCHESTER		
274 438	**228** 365	**204** 326	**288** 461	**301** 482	**343** 549	**107** 171	**364** 582	**155** 248	**131** 210	NEWCASTLE	
56 90	**473** 757	**63** 101	**70** 112	**104** 166	**129** 206	**353** 565	**141** 226	**153** 245	**144** 230	**254** 406	OXFORD
194 310	**307** 491	**129** 206	**217** 347	**231** 397	**264** 422	**186** 297	**292** 467	**97** 155	**65** 104	**82** 131	**174** 278	YORK

areas and popular tourist zones, parking is much easier. Look out for signs with a blue "P", indicating parking spaces. Never leave any valuables or luggage in your car: thefts are common, especially in cities.

PETROL

Large supermarkets often have the best deals; look out for branches of Asda, Tesco or Sainsbury's with petrol stations. Motorway service areas are generally more expensive. Petrol is sold in three grades: diesel, LRP (lead replacement petrol) and unleaded. Most modern cars in Britain use unleaded petrol, and any vehicle you hire will probably do too. Unleaded and diesel are cheaper than LRP. Most petrol stations in Britain are self-service, but the instructions at pumps are easy to follow.

Sign for a car park

BREAKDOWN SERVICES

Britain's major motoring organizations are the **AA** (Automobile Association) and the **RAC** (Royal Automobile Club). They provide a comprehensive 24-hour breakdown service for members, as well as many other motoring services. Both offer reciprocal assistance for members of overseas motoring organizations – before arrival, check with your own group to see if you are covered. You can contact the AA or RAC from the roadside SOS phones found on motorways. **Green Flag** is the other major rescue service in Britain.

Most car-hire agencies have their own cover, and their

charges include membership of the AA, the RAC or Green Flag. Be sure to ask the rental company for the service's emergency number.

If you are not a member of an affiliated organization, you can still call out a rescue service, although it will be expensive. Always follow the advice given on your insurance policy or rental agreement. If you have an accident that involves injury or another vehicle, call the police as soon as possible (*see p675*).

The Environmental Transport Association gives advice on reducing the impact of carbon emissions, as well as offering a number of ethical breakdown services.

CAR HIRE

Hiring a car in Britain can be expensive. Details of car-hire companies at Britain's airports are on the VisitBritain website (*see p669*). One of the most competitive national companies is **Autos Abroad**, but small local firms may undercut even these rates. Other reputable car-hire companies include **Avis**, **Hertz**, **Europcar** and **Budget**. It is illegal to drive without third-party insurance, and it is advisable to take out fully comprehensive insurance. Many companies prefer you to leave a credit card number; if not, you may have to part with a substantial cash deposit. You need your driving licence and a passport when you hire. Most companies will not hire cars to novice drivers, and may have age limits (normally 21–74). Automatic cars are also usually available for hire. If you are touring Britain for three weeks or more, you may find a leasing arrangement cheaper than hiring. Remember to add VAT and insurance costs when you check hire rates.

A small petrol station in Goathland, North Yorkshire

HITCHHIKING

It is not advisable to hitchhike in Britain, and there is a risk in hitchhiking alone, especially for a woman. If you must, stand near a busy exit road junction. In rural or walking areas like the Lake District, tired hikers may well be offered a lift. It is illegal to hitch on motorways or their approach roads.

Lift-sharing is now a common practice. The small-ads magazine *Loot* (sold in London, Manchester and Bristol, and also available online) has a large section for lift-seekers.

Travelling Around by Rail

Britain has a privatized rail network that covers the whole of the country, serving more than 2,500 stations. Divided into regional sections, the system is generally efficient and reliable. Parts of the network are occasionally closed for repairs, mostly at weekends, so check with your local station or online before travelling. Journeys across the country may involve a number of changes, since most lines radiate from London, which has seven major terminals. There is also a rail link with continental Europe on Eurostar, from King's Cross St Pancras station in London and Ebbsfleet and Ashford in Kent *(see p680)*.

The concourse at Liverpool Street Station, London

TICKETS

Large travel agents and all railway stations sell train tickets. First-class tickets cost about one-third more than standard fares, and buying a return fare is generally cheaper than buying two singles.

Allow plenty of time to buy your ticket, and always ask about any special offers or reduced fares. There are four types of discounted fares for adults. Apex tickets are available in limited numbers on some long-distance routes, but they have to be booked at least one week in advance. SuperApex fares, also available in limited numbers on a few mainline services, have to be purchased 14 days in advance. Savers can be used at weekends and on most weekday trains outside rush

hours, while Supersavers cannot be used on Fridays or on any peak-hour services to, from or through London.

Inspectors can levy on-the-spot fines if you do not have a valid ticket, so it is wise to buy a ticket before boarding the train. Ticket offices in rural areas may close at weekends, but small branch lines have a conductor on board who sells tickets. Many stations have automatic ticket machines.

RAIL PASSES

If you plan to do much train travelling around Britain, buy a rail pass. This can be purchased from many agents abroad, such as **Rail Europe**

or **Cie Tours International**. National Rail's All Line Rail Rover gives adults unlimited travel throughout England, Scotland and Wales for seven or 14 days. A Family Rail Card can be used for up to four adults and four children, while a Young Person's Rail Card allows 16- to 25-year-olds or full-time students attending a UK educational establishment to benefit from a series of discounts. The Senior Rail Card entitles those over the age of 60 to a discount of one-third on most fares. There are special passes for London transport, too, and a pass that covers London, Oxford, Canterbury and Brighton. Children aged five to 15 pay half fare; those under the age of five travel free. Disabled travellers qualify for many discounts.

Keep a passport-sized photograph handy for buying passes. If you have a pass, make sure you always show it when you buy a ticket.

GENERAL TIPS

Britain's fastest and most comfortable trains are those on the mainline routes. These are very popular services and get booked up quickly. It is always advisable to reserve your seat in advance, especially if you want to travel at peak times, such as Friday evenings. Mainline trains have dining cars and air-conditioning, and they are fast – travelling to Edinburgh from London, for example, takes just over four hours.

Porters are rare on British stations, although trolleys are often available for passengers to help themselves. If you are disabled and need help, call the Mobility Helpline to book assistance at least 24 hours

Mainline train at platform

Reconditioned steam trains on the tracks in North Yorkshire

ahead of your journey. A yellow line above a train window indicates a first-class compartment. Note that even if the train is full, you cannot sit in the first-class area without paying the full fare.

Trains sometimes split en route, each section proceeding to different destinations, so always check which section you should be on. Trains stop for only a minute at each station, so gather your belongings in advance and be ready to get on and off.

Some stations are a little way from town centres, but they are usually well signposted and mostly on a bus route. Trains on Sundays and public holidays can be slower and less frequent than normal.

SCENIC TRAIN RIDES

After motor transport made many rural railways redundant in the mid-20th century, some picturesque sections of track, as well as many old steam engines, were rescued and restored to working order by enthusiasts. These services are often privately run; the local tourist office, railway station ticket office or travel agents will provide you with more information. This is one of the best ways to enjoy Britain's spectacular scenery. Most of the lines are short – around 20 miles (32 km) – but cover some of the prettiest parts of the country. Lines include the Ffestiniog Railway *(see pp452–3)* in North Wales; the North York Moors Railway *(see p394)*; the Strathspey Steam Railway in the Cairngorm Mountains of the Scottish Highlands *(see p544)* and the La'l Ratty Railway in Cumbria *(see p364)*.

NATIONAL RAIL NETWORK

KEY

— Principal routes
— Other routes
● Principal stations
○ Other stations
▢ London area

Thurso
Wick
Kyle of Lochalsh
Inverness
Fort William
Oban
Perth
Dundee
Stirling
Aberdeen
Edinburgh
Glasgow
Paddington
Liverpool Street
St Pancras
King's Cross
Euston
Charing Cross
Victoria
Waterloo
Fenchurch St
Stranraer
Carlisle
Newcastle
Durham
Middlesborough
Windermere
Barrow
Scarborough
Blackpool
Preston
Leeds
York
Hull
Holyhead
Liverpool
Manchester
Cleethorps
Sheffield
Lincoln
Stoke
Derby
Nottingham
Wolverhampton
Leicester
Norwich
Great Yarmouth
Aberystwyth
Birmingham
Peterborough
Coventry
Cambridge
Ipswich
Harwich
Fishguard
The Welsh Valleys
Gloucester
Luton
Heathrow
LONDON
Southend
Pembroke Dock
Swansea
Cardiff
Bristol
Reading
Gatwick
Ramsgate
Canterbury
Dover
Barnstaple
Bath
Ashford
Taunton
Southampton
Brighton
Hastings
Exeter
Portsmouth
Eastbourne
Newquay
Torquay
Weymouth
Plymouth
Penzance
Falmouth

DIRECTORY

UK RAIL NUMBERS

Mobility Helpline
Tel 08457 44 33 66.

Great North Eastern Railways
Tel 08457 225 225 (bookings).

Great Western Trains
Tel 08457 000 125 (bookings).

Lost Property
*Tel 020 7387 8699 (Euston)
or contact the relevant train
company.*

Midland Mainline
Tel 08457 22 11 25 (bookings).

National Rail Enquiries Timetables
Tel 08457 48 49 50.
www.nationalrail.co.uk

Rail Europe
Tel 08448 484 064 (London).
www.raileurope.co.uk

Virgin Trains
Tel 08457 222 333 (bookings).

OVERSEAS RAIL NUMBERS

CIE Tours International
*Tel (201) 292 3438 or
(212) 319 0561 (United States);
(800) 243 8687 (Canada).*

Rail Europe
*Tel (914) 682 2999 (United
States); (800) 848 7245 (Canada).*

Travelling around by Coach

In Britain, the word "coach" refers to a long-distance express bus and one used for sightseeing excursions. What the British refer to as "buses" covers those vehicles that operate on regular routes with scheduled stops around or between villages, towns and cities. Many coach services duplicate rail routes but are generally cheaper. Journey times, however, are longer and much less predictable on crowded roads. Modern coaches are comfortable, sometimes with refreshments and toilets on board. Some city-to-city routes, especially at weekends, are so popular that it is a good idea to buy a reserved journey ticket, which guarantees you a seat. For ideas on visits to make, consult the VisitBritain website.

A coach tour on the Royal Mile, Edinburgh

NATIONAL COACH NETWORK

There are many regional coach companies, but the largest British coach operator is **National Express**, with a nationwide network of more than 1,200 destinations *(see pp16–19)*. Always book ahead for the more popular routes. The company offers a number of discounts, such as their £5 Funfares (50p booking fee), which are available online, to over 50 destinations. **Megabus** offers tickets for destinations all over Britain from as little as £1 (50p booking fee). As you would expect, you will need to book early, and the less popular destinations and travel times have the best deals.

The **Oxford Tube** and **Oxford Express** run frequent, wheelchair-friendly services between Oxford and London, while **Scottish Citylink** is a major operator running regular services between London, the north and Scotland. Some

services run from Heathrow, Gatwick and Stansted airports. Allow plenty of time to buy your ticket before boarding.

Discounts are available for full-time students and anyone under 25. The over-50s can also qualify for a discount coach card, saving up to 30 per cent on many fares.

COACH TOURS

A range of coach tours, covering all interests, age groups and destinations, is available. Some include a tour guide. They may last anything from a couple of hours to two weeks or more, touring coast or countryside and visiting places of interest. Some are highly structured, organizing every break en route; others leave you to sightsee or shop at your own pace. You can opt for a prearranged route, or commission your own itinerary for a group. Visit the **Enjoy England** website for inspiration.

Any large town will have a selection of coach companies. Check the local Yellow Pages *(see p678)* or ask at your hotel or local tourist office. You can also book coach trips direct from overseas through a specialist travel agent.

Seaside resorts and tourist sites are destinations for many day trips, especially in high season. In some of the more popular rural areas, such as the Lake District, special small coaches operate for ease of movement. You can book these in advance, or just turn up before the coach leaves, although the tour is likely to be fully booked, especially in high season. The local tourist information point or travel agent will be able to tell you where these trips leave from, the cost and may even sell you tickets. It is customary to tip the guide after your tour.

REGIONAL BUSES

Regional bus services are run by a number of companies, some private and some operated by local authorities. Services to remote areas tend to be sporadic and expensive, with some buses running just once a week and many isolated villages having no service at all. Only a few rural buses are equipped for wheelchairs.

As a rule, the further you get from a city, the fewer the buses and the more expensive the fare. On the plus side, local buses can be a pleasant and often sociable

A National Express coach

way of travelling around Britain's lovely countryside.

Most buses run with just one operator – the driver. All drivers prefer you to have the correct fare, so always keep a selection of coins handy. Some routes do not operate on Sundays and public holidays; those that do are much reduced. Always check your routes, schedules and fares at the local tourist office or bus station before you depart on a bus to avoid being stranded somewhere with no return transport.

DIRECTORY

British Travel Associates
*Tel 800 327 6097
(in North America).*

Enjoy England
www.enjoyengland.com

VisitBritain
www.visitbritain.com

COACH TRAVEL

Megabus
Tel 08705 50 50 50.
www.megabus.com

National Express
Tel 08717 81 81 81.
www.nationalexpress.com

Oxford Espress
Tel 01865 785400.
www.oxfordbus.co.uk

Oxford Tube
Tel 01865 772250.
www.stagecoachbus.com/
oxfordshire

Scottish Citylink
Tel 08705 50 50 50.
www.citylink.co.uk

Victoria Coach Station
Tel 020 7730 3466.
www.tfl.gov.uk/vcs

FERRY & WATERWAY TRAVEL

British Waterways
*Tel 01923 201120
(head office).*
www.britishwaterways.co.uk

Caledonian MacBrayne
Tel 01475 650100.
www.calmac.co.uk

Waterscape
www.waterscape.com

Travelling Britain's Coasts and Waterways

Britain has thousands of miles of inland waterways and hundreds of islands scattered along its beautiful coastline. Cruising along a canal in the Midlands countryside or travelling on one of the small local ferries to a remote Scottish island are both wonderful experiences. Canal boats can be hired, and scores of ferries run between Britain's offshore islands. For information on Britain's canals, rivers and lakes and to book accommodation, a boat or a hotel boat, visit the Waterscape website.

A barge on the Welsh Backs, Bristol

CANALS

As industrial production grew in the 18th century, it became vital to find a cheap and effective way of transporting heavy loads. Canals fulfilled this need, and a huge network was built, linking most industrial areas in the north and sea ports.

The arrival of the railways and their immediate success for freight made most canals redundant, but there are still some 3,200 km (2,000 miles) left, most in the old industrial heartland of the Midlands.

Today these canals lure travellers who are content to cruise on old-fashioned, slow narrowboats, taking their time to enjoy the views and the canalside inns, originally built to satisfy the bargees' thirsts and to supply stabling for the barge horses. These canal holidays can be very relaxing if you have the time.

If you wish to hire a narrowboat, you can book with a specialist travel firm or contact **British Waterways**.

LOCAL FERRIES

Britain's local ferries can offer anything from a ten-minute river journey to a seven-hour sea cruise.

Many of Scotland's ferries are operated by **Caledonian MacBrayne**. They sail to lots of different destinations, such as the Isle of Skye to the Kyle of Lochalsh, or the five-hour journey from Oban to Lochboisdale in the Western Isles. They offer a variety of different ticket types, from unlimited rover tickets for a specific period of time, to island-hop passes or all-inclusive coach tour and ferry tickets. Not all the island ferries take cars.

River ferries make an interesting alternative to the more usual forms of transport. The ferry across the Mersey, between the cities of Liverpool and Birkenhead, is still

A car ferry travelling from Oban to Lochboisdale

used by many commuters. London's river trips, such as the one that runs from Westminster to Tower Bridge, offer a different perspective on the city and make a change from tubes, buses and cars. Local tourist information centres can give you information about ferries in their area.

Travelling within Cities

Urban public transport in Britain is efficient and can be fun – children love London's double-decker buses. Fares are good value, especially compared to the expense of parking a car. Most of the larger cities have good bus services. London, Newcastle and Glasgow also have an underground system, while Blackpool, Manchester and Nottingham have trams. Taxis are available at every train station and at ranks near hotels and city centres. The best way to see many cities is on foot, but whatever transport you opt for, try to avoid the rush hours, from 8am to 9:30am and 5pm to 6:30pm.

Double-decker buses on the Strand, in London

LOCAL BUSES

Buses come in all shapes and sizes, with automatic doors and comfortable interiors. They include driver-operated double-deckers, the single-decker "bendy" bus and even smaller single-deckers that are able to weave in and out of traffic more easily. The old "big red bus" with a conductor still exists in London, but only as Heritage route numbers 9 and 15 (through the West End and the City respectively).

On most buses you pay the driver as you enter. They will not always accept notes, so keep a few pound coins handy. Credit cards and cheques are not accepted. The fare depends on the distance you travel. If you are exploring a city by bus, a daily pass is a good idea. Many of the larger cities have daily or weekly passes that can be used on all public transport in that city; these can often be bought from newsagents. Check with the tourist office for schedules and fares.

Night services are available only in major cities, from about 11pm until early morning.

Day passes are valid on these until 4:30am. In London, night buses are prefixed with the letter "N", and most of them pass through Trafalgar Square. Be on your guard when travelling alone late at night, when there may be few other passengers on board.

At some stops, called request stops, the driver will not halt unless you signal that you want to get on or off. If you want to board, raise your arm as the bus approaches; if you want to get off, ring the bell once before your stop. Destinations are shown on the front of buses. If you are not sure which stop you need, ask the driver or conductor to alert you and stay on the lower deck. Always keep your ticket until the end of the journey in case an inspector gets on board. They can impose an on-the-spot fine if you are without a valid ticket.

Cities have bus lanes, intended to bypass car traffic jams during the rush hours. These can be effective, but your journey could still take a long time. Schedules are hard to keep to, so regard timetables as advisory.

DRIVING IN CITIES

Driving in city centres is increasingly discouraged. In 2003 London introduced a congestion charge – if you drive or park within the congestion zone from Monday to Friday (7am to 6:30pm), you will be charged an £8 fee to pay before 10pm that day at a newsagent, petrol station or post office. Not paying the charge will lead to a large fine. See **Transport for London**'s website for more information. Other cities are considering similar steps to keep drivers out of the centres. Parking in city centres is also strictly controlled to prevent congestion *(see p684)*.

TAXIS

In large towns, taxis can be found at taxi ranks and train stations. Some operate by radio, so you have to phone. The local Yellow Pages *(see p678)*, pubs, restaurants and hotels will all have a list of taxi numbers. Prices are usually regulated. Always ask the price before you start your journey if there is no taxi meter. If you are not sure of the correct fare, ask the local tourist information point.

The famous London black cabs are almost as much of an institution as the big red buses. These are the safest cabs to use in London since all the drivers are licensed and have undergone strict tests. All licensed cabs must display a "For hire" sign, which is lit up whenever they are free. The newer cab designs are equipped to carry wheelchairs. If a cab stops for you in London, it must by law take you anywhere within a radius of 6 miles (10 km) so long as it is within the Metropolitan Police District. This includes most of London and Heathrow Airport. All licensed cabs have meters that start ticking

One of London's black cabs

as soon as the driver accepts your custom. The fare will increase minute by minute or for each 311 m (1,020 ft) travelled. Most drivers expect a tip of between 10 and 15 per cent of the fare. If you have a complaint, note the serial number found in the back of the cab.

Do not use unlicensed minicabs – they may be mechanically unsound or even uninsured. Never accept an unbooked minicab ride in the street.

GUIDED BUS TOURS

Most major tourist cities offer sightseeing bus tours. Weather permitting, a good way to see the cities is from a traditional open-topped double-decker bus. Private tours can be arranged with many companies. Contact the local tourist information centre for more details.

TRAMS

Trams are making a comeback throughout Britain in clean, energy-efficient and more modern guises. One of the best tram schemes in Britain is Manchester's Metrolink. The oldest tramway is in Blackpool, which opened in 1885.

LONDON UNDERGROUND

The Underground network in London, known as the Tube, has more than 270 sta-

A tram along Blackpool's famous promenade

CYCLING

Cycling is one of the greenest ways of getting around town. Even modest towns have somewhere you can hire bikes. Cyclists may not use motorways or their approach roads, nor can they ride on pavements, footpaths or pedestrianized zones. Many city roads have cycle lanes and their own traffic lights. You can take a bike on most trains; see the **National Rail** website for more information. Never leave your bike unlocked, and always wear a helmet.

Cycling under the Bridge of Sighs, Oxford

tions, each of which is marked with the London Underground logo. The only other cities with an underground system are Newcastle and Glasgow. Newcastle's system is limited to the city centre, while Glasgow's skirts around the centre. Both are clean and efficient, running the same hours as London's.

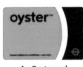

A London Underground sign outside a station

London tube trains run every day, except Christmas Day, from about 5:30am until just after midnight. Fewer trains run on Sundays and bank holidays. Note that the tube can get very crowded during rush hour.

The 11 tube lines are colour-coded and maps called Journey Planners are posted at every tube station, while maps of the central section are displayed in each train.

Most tube journeys between central destinations in London can be completed with only one or two changes of line. Smoking is not permitted on the Underground.

Tickets are purchased at the station, but many travellers use an Oystercard, an electronic card that can be topped up for use on buses and the tube. Using an Oystercard is, by far, the cheapest way of travelling

An Oystercard

on London Transport's tubes and buses. For information on how to get one, see the Transport for London website. Oystercards can be purchased from abroad. There are similar electronic card schemes in other major British cities, such as Oxford.

WALKING IN CITIES

Once you get used to traffic on the left, Britain's cities can be safely and enjoyably explored on foot. Instructions written on the road will tell you from which direction you can expect the traffic to come.

There are two types of pedestrian crossing: striped zebra crossings and push-button crossings at traffic lights. At a zebra crossing, traffic should stop for you, but at push-button crossings, cars will not stop until the lights change in your favour. More and more cities and towns are creating traffic-free zones in the city centre for pedestrians.

DIRECTORY

National Rail
Tel 08457 48 49 50
(enquiries).
www.nationalrail.co.uk

Transport for London
Tel 020 7222 1234 *(head office).*
www.tfl.com

General Index

Acknowledgments

Dorling Kindersley would like to thank the following people whose contributions and assistance have made the preparation of this book possible.

MAIN CONTRIBUTOR

Michael Leapman was born in London in 1938 and has been a professional journalist since he was 20. He has worked for most British national newspapers and now writes about travel and other subjects for several publications, among them *The Independent, Independent on Sunday, The Economist* and *Country Life*. He has written 11 books, including the award-winning *Companion Guide to New York* (1983, revised 1995) and *Eyewitness Travel Guide to London*. In 1989 he edited the widely praised *Book of London*.

ADDITIONAL CONTRIBUTORS

Paul Cleves, James Henderson, Lucy Juckes, John Lax, Marcus Ramshaw.

ADDITIONAL ILLUSTRATIONS

Christian Hook, Gilly Newman, Paul Weston.

DESIGN AND EDITORIAL

MANAGING EDITOR Georgina Matthews
SENIOR ART EDITOR Sally Ann Hibbard
DEPUTY EDITORIAL DIRECTOR Douglas Amrine
DEPUTY ART DIRECTOR Gaye Allen
PRODUCTION David Proffit
PICTURE RESEARCH Ellen Root, Rhiannon Furbear
DTP DESIGNER Ingrid Vienings
MAP CO-ORDINATORS Michael Ellis, David Pugh
RESEARCHER Pippa Leahy
Eliza Armstrong, Sam Atkinson, Moerida Belton, Lydia Baillie, Josie Barnard, Sonal Bhatt, Hilary Bird, Louise Boulton, Julie Bowles, Roger Bullen, Robert Butt, Chloe Carleton, Deborah Clapson, Elspeth Collier, Gary Cross, Cooling Brown Partnership, Guy Dimond, Nicola Erdpresser, Mariana Evmolpidou, Danny Farnham, Joy Fitzsimmons, Fay Franklin, Ed Freeman, Janice Fuscoe, Richard Hammond, Charlie Hawkings, Martin Hendry, Andrew Heritage, Annette Jacobs, Gail Jones, Steve Knowlden, Nic Kynaston, Esther Labi, Kathryn Lane, Pippa Leahy, Caroline Mead, James Mills Hicks, Rebecca Milner, Kate Molan, Elaine Monaghan, Mary Ormandy, Catherine Palmi, Marianne Petrou, Chez Picthall, Clare Pierotti, Andrea Powell, Mani Ramaswamy, Mark Rawley, Jake Reimann, Carolyn Ryden, David Roberts, Sands Publishing Solutions, Mary Scott, Meredith Smith, Alison Stace, Hugh Thompson, Simon Tuite, Conrad Van Dyk, Mary Villabona, Alice Wright.

ADDITIONAL PHOTOGRAPHY

Max Alexander, Peter Anderson, Apex Photo Agency: Stephen Bere, Deni Bown, June Buck, Simon Burt, Lucy Claxton, Michael Dent, Philip Dowell, Tim Draper, Mike Dunning, Chris Dyer, Andrew Einsiedel, Philip Enticknap, Jane Ewart, DK Studio/Steve Gorton, Frank Greenaway, Alison Harris, Stephen Hayward, John Heseltine, Ed Ironside, Dave King, Neil Mersh, Robert O'Dea, Ian O'Leary, Stephen Oliver, Vincent Oliver, Roger Phillips, Kim Sayer, Karl Shone, Chris Stevens, Jim Stevenson, Clive Streeter, Harry Taylor, Conrad Van Dyk, David Ward, Mathew Ward, Alan Williams, Stephen Wooster, Nick Wright, Colin Yeates.

PHOTOGRAPHIC AND ARTWORK REFERENCE

Christopher Woodward of the Building of Bath Museum, Franz Karl Freiherr von Linden, Gendall Designs, NRSC Air Photo Group, The Oxford Mail and Times, and Mark and Jane Rees.

PHOTOGRAPHY PERMISSIONS

DORLING KINDERSLEY would like to thank the following for their assistance and kind permission to photograph at their establishments: Banqueting House (Crown copyright by kind permission of Historic Royal Palaces); Cabinet War Rooms; Paul Highnam at English Heritage; Dean and Chapter Exeter Cathedral; Gatwick Airport Ltd; Heathrow Airport Ltd; Thomas Woods at Historic Scotland; Provost and Scholars Kings College; Cambridge; London Transport Museum; Madame Tussaud's; National Museums and Galleries of Wales (Museum of Welsh Life); Diana Lanham and Gayle Mault at the National Trust; Peter Reekie and Isla Roberts at the National Trust for Scotland; Provost Skene House; Saint Bartholmew the Great; Saint James's Church; London St Paul's Cathedral; Masters and Wardens of the Worshipful Company of Skinners; Provost and Chapter of Southwark Cathedral; HM Tower of London; Dean and Chapter of Westminster; Dean and Chapter of Worcetser Cathedral and all the other churches, museums, hotels, restaurants, shops, galleries and sights too numerous to thank individually.

PICTURE CREDITS

t = top; tl = top left; tlc = top left centre; tc = top centre; tr = top right; cla = centre left above; ca = centre above; cra = centre right above; cl = centre left; c = centre; cr = centre right; clb = centre left below; cb = centre below; crb = centre right below; bl = bottom left; b = bottom; bc = bottom centre; bcl = bottom centre left; br = bottom right; d = detail.

Works of art have been reproduced with the permission of the following copyright holders: © ADAGP, Paris and DACS, London 2006: 171t; © Alan Bowness, Hepworth Estate 277bl; © Fondazione Lucio Fontana 121tr; © The Estate of Patrick Heron/DACS, London 2006: 240cb; © D Hockney: 91tr, 411t; © Estate of Stanley Spencer/DACS, London 2006 235t; © Cy Twombly 121clb; © Angela Verren-Taunt/DACS, London 2006: 277br.

The work of Henry Moore, *Large Two Forms*, 1966, illustrated on page 413b and *Recumbent Figure* 1938 illustrated on page 91c has been reproduced by permission of the Henry Moore Foundation.

The publisher would like to thank the following individuals, companies and picture libraries for permission to reproduce their photographs:

ABBOT HALL ART GALLERY AND MUSEUM, Kendal: 370b(d); ABERDEEN ART GALLERIES 540t; ABERDEEN AND GRAMPIAN TOURIST BOARD 479ca; ACTION PLUS: 67t; 480t; 434c; David Davies 67cr; Peter Tarry 66cla, 67bl; AIRPORT EXPRESS ALLIANCE: 683c; Printed by kind permission of MOHAMED AL FAYED: 97t; ALAMY IMAGES: Peter Adams Photography 11tr; Gina Calvi 373tl; Bertrand Collet 488cl; Nick Higham 375b; gkphotography 607 tl; Bjanka Kadic 671tr; B. O'Kane 683tl; Angus Palmer 217b; Edward Parker 11br; The Photolibrary Wales 607c, 662tc, 662b; Seb Rogers 663cl; Neil Setchfield 606cl; Andrew Wiard 61crb; AMERICAN MUSEUM, Bath: 261tl; ANCIENT ART AND ARCHITECTURE COLLECTION: 42cb, 44ca, 44clb, 45ca, 45clb, 46bl, 46br, 48crb, 51ca, 232tl, 235br, 439t; THE ARCHIVE & BUSINESS RECORDS CENTRE, University of Glasgow: 483t; T & R ANNAN AND SONS: 516b(d); ASHMOLEAN MUSEUM, OXFORD: 47t. BARNABY'S PICTURE LIBRARY: 60ca; BEAMISH OPEN AIR MUSEUM: 424c, 415b, 425ca, 425cb, 425b; BLACKFRIARS CAFE BAR, NEWCASTLE: Andy Hook 602c; BRIDGEMAN ART LIBRARY, LONDON AND NEW YORK: Agnew and Sons, London 323t; Museum of Antiquities, Newcastle upon Tyne 44tl; Apsley House, The Wellington Museum, London 30tl; Bibliotheque Nationale, Paris *Neville Book of Hours* 322t(d); Birmingham City Museums and Gallery 319t; Bonham's, London, *Portrait of Lord Nelson with Santa Cruz Beyond*, Lemeul Francis Abbot 54cb(d); Bradford Art Galleries and Museums 49clb; City of Bristol Museums and Art Galleries 256c; British Library, London, *Pictures and Arms of English Kings and Knights* 4t(d), 39t(d), *The Kings of England from Brutus to Henry* 26bl(d), *Stowe manuscript* 40tl(d), *Liber Legum Antiquorum Regum* 46t(d), *Calendar Anglo-Saxon Miscellany* 46–7t(d), 46–7c(d), 46–7b(d), *Decrees of Kings of Anglo-Saxon and Norman England* 47clb, 49bl(d), *Portrait of Chaucer*, Thomas Occleve 49br(d), *Portrait of Shakespeare*, Droeshurt 51bl(d), *Historia Anglorum* 40bl(d), 236tl(d), *Chronicle of Peter of Langtoft* 285bl(d), *Lives and Miracles of St Cuthbert* 419tl(d), 419cl(d), 419cr(d), *Lindisfarne Gospels* 419br(d), *Commendatio Lamentabilis intransitu Edward IV* 436b(d),

Histoire du Roy d'Angleterre Richard II 438t(d), 537b; Christies, London 445t; Claydon House, Bucks, *Florence Nightingale*, Sir William Blake Richmond 162t; Department of Environment, London 48tr; City of Edinburgh Museums and Galleries, *Chief of Scottish Clan*, Eugene Deveria 484bl(d); Fitzwilliam Museum, University of Cambridge, *George IV as Prince Regent*, Richard Cosway 179cb, 212bl, *Flemish Book of Hours* 350tl(d); Giraudon/Musee de la Tapisserie, with special authorization of the city of Bayeux 47b,181b; Guildhall Library, Corporation of London, *The Great Fire*, Marcus Willemsznik 53bl(d); *Bubbler's Melody* 54br(d), *Triumph of Steam and Electricity*, The Illustrated London News 57t(d), *Great Exhibition, The transept from Dickenson's Comprehensive Pictures* 56–7, *A Balloon View of London as seen from Hampstead* 105c(d); Harrogate Museum and Art Gallery, North Yorkshire 388t; Holburne Museum and Crafts Study Centre, Bath 53t; Imperial War Museum, *London Field Marshall Montgomery*, J Worsley 31cbr(d); Kedleston Hall, Derbyshire 28br; King Street Galleries, London, *Bonnie Prince Charlie*, G Dupré 482tl; Lambeth Palace Library, London, *St Alban's Chronicle* 49t; Lever Brothers Ltd, Cheshire 349cra; Lincolnshire County Council, Usher Gallery, Lincoln, *Portrait of Mrs Fitzherbert after Richard Cosway* 179b; London Library, *The Barge Tower from Ackermann's World in miniature*, F Scoberl 55t; Manchester Art Gallery, UK, *Etruscan Vase Painters* 1871, Sir Lawrence Alma-Tadema 374b; Manchester City Art Galleries 373b; David Messum Gallery, London 447b; National Army Museum, London, *Bunker's Hill*, R Simkin 54ca; National Gallery, London, *Mrs Siddons the Actress*, Thomas Gainsborough 54t(d), 163ca; National Museet, Copenhagen 46ca; Phillips, the International Fine Art Auctioneers, *James I*, John the Elder Decritz 52b(d); Private collections: 8–9, 30ca(d), 604tl, 48–9, 55cla, 55bl, 56clb, Vanity Fair 57br, 163t, *Ellesmere Manuscript* 188b(d), *Armada: map of the Spanish and British Fleets*, Robert Adam 298t, 396t, 422b; Royal Geographical Society, London 163cb(d); Royal Holloway & Bedford New College, the *Princes Edward and Richard in the Tower*, Sir John Everett Millais 121b; Smith Art Gallery and Museum, Stirling 496b; Tate Gallery, London: 56crb, 237t; Thyssen-Bornemisza Collection, Lugo Casta, *King Henry VIII*, Hans Holbein the Younger 50b(d); Victoria and Albert Museum, London 28t(d), 56b, 97c, 204t, 351cr, 393b, *Miniature of Mary Queen of Scots*, by a follower of Francois Clouet 511br, 537t(d); Walker Art Gallery, Liverpool 378c; Westminster Abbey, London, *Henry VII Tomb effigy*, Pietro Torrigiano 30br(d), 40bc(d); The Trustees of the Weston Park Foundation, *Portrait of Richard III*, Italian School 49cla(d); Christopher Wood Gallery, London, *High Life Below Stairs*, Charles Hunt 29c(d); Courtesy of BRITISH AIRWAYS: 680t; BFI LONDON IMAX CINEMA WATERLOO: Richard Holttum 153c; BRITISH LIBRARY BOARD: *Cotton Faustina BVII folio 85* 49cb, 109cl; © THE BRITISH MUSEUM: 42cr, 43cb, 73tl, 85c, 103, 106–7 all except 107t and 107bl; © THE BRONTE SOCIETY: 412 all; BT PAYPHONES: 678tl; BURTON CONSTABLE FOUNDATION: Dr David Connell 350t. CADOGEN MANAGEMENT: 84b; CADW – Welsh Historic Monuments (Crown Copyright): 474t; CAMERA PRESS: Cecil Beaton 92bl; CARDIFF CITY COUNCIL: 472tr, 473t, 473c; FKB CARLSON: 605bcl; CASTLE HOWARD ESTATE LTD: 399tl; COLIN DE CHAIRE: 197c; TRUSTEES OF THE CHATSWORTH SETTLEMENT: 334b, 335b; MUSEUM OF CHILDHOOD, Edinburgh: 510b; BRUCE COLEMAN LTD: 35br; Stephen Bond 294b; Jane Burton 35cra; Mark N. Boulton 35cl; Patrick Clement 34clb; Peter Evans 544tl; Paul van Gaalen 250tl; Sir Jeremy Grayson 35bl; Harald Lange 34bc; Gordon Langsbury 545t; George McCarthy 34t, 35bl, 242b, 285br; Paul Meitz 528clb; Dr. Eckart Pott 34bl, 528t; Hans Reinhard 34cb, 35tc, 294t, 494tl; Dr Frieder Sauer 534t; N Schwiatz 35clb; Kim Taylor 35tl, 528cra; Konrad Wothe 528ca; COLLECTIONS: Liz Stares 30tr, Yuri Lewinski 373tl; CORBIS: Bruce Burkhardt 295c; Ashley Cooper 12tr; Eurasia Press/Steven Vidler 437br; Tim Graham 3br, 95bl; John Heseltine 111br; Angelo Hornak 117tc; Sygma/Sandro Vannini 11bl; JOE CORNISH: 403b; DOUG CORRANCE: 485b; JOHN CROOK: 171b; DESIGN MUSEUM: Amelia Webb 117bl; EASYEVERYTHING: James Hamilton 678br; 1805 CLUB: 31t; 1853 Gallery, Bradford 411t; EMPICS LTD: Nigel French 66bl; Tony Marshall 66tl, 66c; ENGLISH HERITAGE: 126b, 208c, 208b, 209b, 248–9b, 263b, 350br, 351b, 394t, 419tr, 419c; Avebury

Museum 42ca; Devizes Museum 42br, drawing by Frank Gardiner 423br; Salisbury Museum 42t, 42bl; Skyscan Balloon Photography 43t, 262b, 394t; 423bl; ENGLISH LIFE PUBLICATIONS LTD, Derby: 342tl, 342tr, 343t, 343b; ET ARCHIVE: 41tc, 41cr, 52cb, 53clb, 58crb, 162b; Bodleian Library, Oxford 48crb; British Library, London 48tl, 48ca; Devizes Museum 42cl, 43b, 262c; Garrick Club 436tl(d); Imperial War Museum, London 58clb(d), 59br; Labour Party Archives 60bc; London Museum 43cla; Magdalene College 50ca; National Maritime Museum, London 39b; Stoke Museum Staffordshire Polytechnic 41bc, 52tl; Victoria & Albert Museum, London 50t(d); MARY EVANS PICTURE LIBRARY: 9 inset, 604tr, 40br, 41tl, 41cl, 41bl, 41br, 44bl, 44br, 46cb, 47cla, 51t, 51cb, 51br, 53crb, 54bl, 55br, 56tl, 58ca, 59ca, 59clb, 59crb, 79cb, 104t,105t, 157 inset, 162cb, 163b, 187c, 189c, 195b, 206c, 222bl, 228tl, 231c, 231bl, 231br, 234bl, 239 inset, 278t, 295 inset, 336b, 349t, 349cla, 420t, 447tl, 482b, 499b, 512bl, 514b, 515t, 535b, 667 inset. CHRIS FAIRCLOUGH: 295b, 352b, 688b; FALKIRK WHEEL: 507b; PAUL FELIX: 234c; FFOTOGRAFF © Charles Aithie: 435t; FISHBOURNE ROMAN VILLA: 45t; LOUIS FLOOD: 484br; FOREIGN AND BRITISH BIBLE SOCIETY: Cambridge University Library 435c; FOTOMAS INDEX: 105cra. GARDEN PICTURE LIBRARY: J S Sira 27crt; John Glover 27tb; Steven Wooster 26–27t; GETTY IMAGES: 61cr, Travel Ink 673tc; Matthew Stockman 66crb; GLASGOW MUSEUMS: Burrell Collection 521ca, 520–1 all except 520tl; Art Gallery & Museum, Kelvingrove 519t, 531b, 543b(d); Saint Mungo Museum of Religious Life and Art 517tl; Museum of Transport 518cr; JOHN GLOVER: 62cr, 160cb, 205b; THE GORE HOTEL, London: 554c.

SONIA HALLIDAY AND LAURA LUSHINGTON ARCHIVE: 409t; ROBERT HARDING PICTURE LIBRARY: 182t, 548t, 60cra; Jan Baldwin 287b; M H Black 288t; Teresa Black 674crb; L Bond 337b; Michael Botham 36br; C Bowman 661c; Nelly Boyd 374tl; Lesley Burridge 304tr; Martyn F Chillman 305bc; Philip Craven 103t, 200b, 324b; Nigel Francis 219b; Robert Francis 66–7; Paul Freestone 226b; Sylvain Gradadom 295tl; Brian Harrison 529b; Van der Hars 538t; Michael Jenner 45b, 529c; Norma Joseph 65b; Christopher Nicholson 253t; B O'Connor 37ca; Jenny Pate 161bc; Rainbird Collection 417cb; Roy Rainsford 37b, 168t, 298b, 338cr, 368t, 386t, 475b; Walter Rawling 25t; Hugh Routledge 2–3; Peter Scholey 299t; Michael Short 305br; James Strachen 384b; Julia K Thorne 486bl; Adina Tovy 61tl, 486br; Andy Williams 179t, 234br, 346c, 432t, 524; Adam Woolfitt 24t, 24c, 44tr, 45crb, 260b, 272, 287ca, 305bl, 439bl, 468tl, 544tr; HAREWOOD HOUSE: 410c; PAUL HARRIS: 36t, 62cl, 301bl(d), 338b, 367b, 666–7, 663tr; HARROGATE INTERNATIONAL CENTRE: 389b; HAYWARD GALLERY: Richard Haughton 273tl; Crown copyright is reproduced with the permission of the Controller of HMSO: 73br, 118bl, 118br, 119tl; CATHEDRAL CHURCH OF THE BLESSED VIRGIN MARY AND ST ETHELBERT IN HEREFORD: 316b; HERTFORDSHIRE COUNTY COUNCIL: Bob Norris 58–9; JOHN HESELTINE: 76t, 102, 107t, 108, 250tr, 250c, 469tl; HISTORIC ROYAL PALACES (Crown Copyright): 4crb, 118cla, 173, 235 all; HISTORIC SCOTLAND (Crown Copyright): 497c, 506tr, 506c, 5-7bl; PETER HOUNSLES: 348bl; NEIL HOLMES: 258b(d), 260c, 286t, 371b, 429tl, 429tr, 451b; ANGELO HORNAK LIBRARY: 406bl, 406bl, 406br, 409br; Reproduced by permission of the CLERK OF RECORDS, HOUSE OF LORDS: 483c; DAVID MARTIN HUGHES: 156–7, 164; HULTON-DEUTSCH COLLECTION: 26c, 26tr, 31cl, 31cr, 53cla, 54c, 56c, 57cb, 58tl 58tr, 58b, 59t, 60bl, 162ca, 169c, 233b, 300t, 348c, 349crb, 350bl, 377b, 397b, 398br, 437t, 495b, 522tl, 536b; HUNTERIAN ART GALLERY: 519b; HUTCHISON LIBRARY: Catherine Blacky 604cb; Bernard Gerad 481t; HUTTON IN THE FOREST: Lady Inglewood 358t. THE IMAGE BANK, London: Derek Berwin 552t; David Gould 357b; Romilly Lockyer 604bl; Colin Molyneux 469bl; Trevor Wood 286b; Simon Wilkinson 180b; Terry Williams 112tc; IMAGES COLOUR LIBRARY: 34cla, 43c, 221b, 234t, 249t, 250bl, 251b, 336t, 338cl, 339t, 352c, 686cl; Horizon/Robert Estall 438c; Landscape Only 37cb, 248, 365, 439br; IMPERIAL WAR MUSEUM NORTH: 395t; IRONBRIDGE MUSEUM: 317b. JARROLD PUBLISHERS: 212br, 229t(d), 304bl; MICHAEL JENNER: 304tl, 340b, 528b; JORVIK VIKING CENTRE, York: 405t. FRANK LANE PICTURE AGENCY: 400b(d); W Broadhurst 254b; Michael Callan 242crb; ANDREW LAWSON: 27c, 27cb, 244br, 245tl, 245tr, 245br; LANGAN'S BRASSERIE: 603t; LEEDS CASTLE ENTERPRISES: 165b; LEIGHTON HOUSE, Royal Borough of Kensington: 122br; THE LEISURE PASS GROUP: 670cr; published by kind permission DEAN AND CHAPTER OF LINCOLN 340t, 341cb, 341bl; LINCOLNSHIRE COUNTY COUNCIL: USHER GALLERY, Lincoln: c 1820 by William

Ilbery 341bl; Llangollen International Musical Eisteddfod 450c; London Ambulance Service: 674cra; London Aquarium: 3c; London Film Festival: 62t; London Transport Museum: 84t; Longleat House: 266t; The Lowry Collection, Salford: *Coming From the Mill*, 1930, L.S. Lowry 371tr. Madame Tussauds: 104b; Magna: 353b; Maldom Millennium Trust: 209t; Mansell Collection, London: 31clb, 40tr, 52ca, 55cb, 261tr, 323bl, 349clb, 402b; Nick Meers: 22t, 238–9; Metropolitan Police Service: 675t; Archie Miles: 240ca; Simon Miles: 352tr; Minack Theatre: Murray King 276b; Mirror Syndication International: 74b, 87b, 112; BTA/Juilian Nieman 604ca; Museum Of London: 44crb, 113t; National Express Ltd: 688bl; National Fishing Heritage Centre, Grimsby: 403t; National Gallery, London: 73tr, 82–3 all; National Gallery Of Scotland: *The Reverend Walker Skating on Duddingston Loch*, Sir Henry Raeburn 504c(d); National Library Of Wales: 436tr, 439c(d), 467b; National Museum Of Film And Television, Bradford: 411c; Board of Trustees of the National Museums and Galleries on Merseyside: Liverpool Museum 379t; Maritime Museum 377t; Walker Art Gallery 346b, 378tl, 378tr, 378b, 379c; National Museums Of Scotland: 505t, 511bl; National Museum of Wales: 436c; By courtesy of the National Portrait Gallery, London: *First Earl of Essex*, Hans Peter Holbein 351t(d); National Tramway Museum, Crich: 339c; National Trust Photographic Library: *Bess of Hardwick (Elizabeth, Countess of Shrewsbury)*, Anon 334tl(d); Mathew Antrobus 302br, 390cl, 391bl; Oliver Benn 29br, 278c, 293bl, 390b; John Bethell 279c, 279bl, 279br, 303t; Nick Carter 255b; Joe Cornish 456; Prudence Cumming 267c; Martin Dohrn 50crb; Andreas Von Einsiedel 29bl, 302cb, 303ca; Roy Fox 271t; Geoffrey Frosh 289t; Jerry Harpur 244t, 244bl; Derek Harris 244clb, 267t; Nadia MacKenzie 28cl; Nick Meers 266b, 267b, 320b, 672bl; Rob Motheson 292t; Cressida Pemberton Piggot 554t; Ian Shaw 460t; Richard Surman 303br, 362b; Rupert Truman 303br, 379; Andy Tryner 302bl; Charlie Waite 391t; Jeremy Whitaker 303bl, 393t, 460b; Mike Williams 302ca, 391c; George Wright 244crb, 292c; National Trust For Scotland: 478b, 500b, 501c, 508b, 522tr, 523tl, 523tr, 523br; Glyn Satterley 523tr; Lindesey Robertson 523bl; National Waterways Museum at Gloucester: 301bc, 301br; NHPA: Martin Garwood 395ca; Daniel Heuclin 282la; Nature Photographers: Andrew Cleave 242cla; E A James 35cla, 360t; Hugh Miles 421t; Owen Newman 35ca; William Paton 528crb; Paul Sterry 34crb, 34br, 35cb, 35crb, 234c, 255t, 387t, 528cla; Roger Tidman 197b; Network Photographers: Laurie Sparham 480b; New Shakespeare Theatre Co: 153t; Norfolk Museums Service: Norwich Castle Museum 201b; Oxford Scientific Films: Okapia 282lb; 'PA' News Photo Library: John Stillwell 61cr. Palace Theatre Archive: 152c; Photos Horticultural: 161tlc, 161cra, 161cb, 161crb, 244ca, 245c; Pictures: 680t; Planet Earth Pictures: David Phillips 27crca; Popperfoto: 31br, 59bl, 60cb, 60br, 61bc, 86tl, 160tr, 203t, 284cl, 444b; AFP/ Eric Feferber 61br; SG Forester 67br; Port Merion Ltd: 454cr, 454tl; Press Association: Martin Keene 62b; Public Record Office (Crown Copyright): 48b. Rob Reichenfeld: 174t, 175c, 175b, 300b, 658b, 663t; RBS Group: 676bl, 676cb; Reuters: Ho New 61b; Rex Features Ltd: 31ca, 41tr, 60tl, 61lb, 236c, 237br; Barry Beattie 259cl; Peter Brooke 31bc, 678br; Nils Jorgensen 30c, 661t; Eileen Kleinman 661br; Hazel Murray 61tl; Tess, Renn-Burrill Productions 269b; Brian Rasic 63t; Nick Rogers 61tr; Tim Rooke 64cr, 66tr; Sipa/Chesnot 31bl; Today 25c; Richard Young 60tl; Rex Features: Jonathon Player 294cla; The Ritz, London: 81t; Royal Academy Of Arts, London: 84ca; Royal Collection © 1995 Her Majesty Queen Elizabeth II: *The Family of Henry VIII*, Anon 38(d), 85c, 86tr, 86bl, 87t, 236tr, 237tl(d), 237tr, 237bl, *George IV, in full*

Highland dress, Sir David Wilkie 485t; David Cripps 87c; John Freeman 88br; Royal College Of Music, London: 96c; Royal Pavilion, Art Gallery And Museums, Brighton: 178c, 178bl, 178br, 179cl, 179cr; Royal Botanic Gardens, Kew:74ca; Royal Shakespeare Theatre Company: Donald Cooper 327c(d). St. Alban's Museums: Verulamium Museum 232b; St. Pauls Cathedral: Sampson Lloyd 114tr, 114cl, 114clb; Sartaj Balti House: Clare Carnegie 411b; Scottish National Gallery Of Modern Art: Roy Lichtenstein In the Car 507c; Scottish National Portrait Gallery: on loan from the collection of the Earl of Roseberry, *Execution of Charles I*, Unknown Artist 52–3; Sidmouth Folk Festival: Derek Brooks 289b; Skyscan Balloon Photo-graphy: 262t; John Snocken: 27c, 27ra; Southbank Press Office: 154t; Sporting Pictures: 66cra, 66bc, 66br, 67cl, 358b; STA Travel Group: 672tl; Still Moving Pictures: Doug Corrance 548b; Wade Cooper 483b; Derek Laird 482c; Robert Lees 65t; STB 544br, 545c, Paisley Museum 515b, Paul Tomkins 529tr; SJ Whitehorn 495t; David Tarn: 389tl; Tony Stone Images: 604–5, 550–1; Rex A.Butcher 81c; Richard Elliott 64b; Rob Talbot 353ca; David Woodfall 440; © Tate Britain: 73bl, 91all, ; © Tate Modern: 121tr, 121clb, 121br; *Soft Drain Pipe – Blue (Cool) Version*, 1967 © Claes Oldenburg 121cr; © Tate St. Ives: 277cr, 277clb, 277br; Rob Talbot: 353cb; Transport for London: 378cl, 691cb; Troika Photos Limited: Michael Walter 680cl; Tuille House Museum, Carlisle: 358c; Urbis: 372c; courtesy of the Board of Trustees of the Victoria And Albert Musuem, London: 72b, 98–99. Charlie Waite: 549t; © Wales Tourist Board: 433c, 434b, 438–9, 468br, 469tr, 469br; Roger Vitos 468tl, 468bl; The Wallace Collection, London: 104cb; David Ward: 525b, 543t; Frederick Warne & Co: 367t(d); © Warwick Castle: 323cra; Roger Vitos 468tl, 468bl; Courtesy of the Trustees of The Wedgwood Museum, Barlaston, Staffordshire, England: 311b; West Midlands Police: 674bl, 674br, 674tr; Dean and Chapter of Westminster: 93bl; Tony Middleton 92bc; Jeremy Whitaker: 228tr, 228c, 229b; Whitbread Plc: 604bl; Whitworth Art Gallery, University of Manchester: courtesy of Granada Television Arts Foundation 374c; Christopher Wilson: 404bl; Wilton House Trust: 265b; Winchester Cathedral: 171t; Woburn Abbey – by kind permission of the Marquess of Tavistock and Trustees of the Bedford Estate: 50–1, 230t; Timothy Woodcock Photolibrary: 5b; Photo © Woodman-sterne, Watford, UK: Jeremy Marks 114t, 115t. York Castle Museum: 405cb; York City Art Gallery: 407bl; Dean & Chapter York Minster: 409cla, 409ca, 409cl; Peter Gibson 409cra, 409cr, 409cl; Jim Korshaw 406tr; Reproduced couresty of the Yorkshire Museum: 408c; Yorkshire Sculpture Park: Jerry Hardman Jones 413t. ZEFA: 64t, 154b, 263t, 269t, 486c, 659t, 682c, 684tr; Bob Croxford 63cr; Weir 19t.

Front Endpaper: All special photography except Robert Harding Picture Library/Andy Williams tl, Adam Woolfitt bl; David Martin Hughes brl; National Trust Photographic Library/Joe Cornish clc; Tony Stone Images/David Woodfall cl. Back Endpaper: All special photography except John Heseltine tl, br.

Jacket
Front – Dorling Kindersley: Kim Sayer clb; Frame Muller Photography: Ephraim Muller main. Back – Nick Board: cla; Robert Harding Picture Library: Hugh Routledge bl; William Lee: tl; SuperStock: Digital Vision/Alan Baxter clb. Spine – Dorling Kindersley: Stephen Oliver b; Frame Muller Photography: Ephraim Muller t.

All other images © Dorling Kindersley. For further information see www.DKimages.com

SPECIAL EDITIONS OF DK TRAVEL GUIDES

Central London

**REGENT'S PARK
AND BLOOMSBURY**
See pp102–107
Street Finder maps 1, 2, 3

REGENT'S PARK

GLOUCESTER PLACE

MARYLEBONE ROAD

EUSTON ROAD

GOWER ST

TOTTENHAM COURT

HARLEY STREET

PORTLAND PLACE

CLEVELAND STREET

GREAT PORTLAND STREET

MORTIMER STREET

BAKER STREET

WIGMORE STREET

OXFORD STREET

OXFORD STREET

BROOK STREET

REGENT STREET

WARDOUR STREET

SO

SHA

MARBLE ARCH

BAYSWATER ROAD

PARK LANE

MOUNT ST

CONDUIT ST

BERKELEY ST

PICCADILLY

ST JAMES'S ST

PALL MALL

KENSINGTON

HYDE PARK

THE M

KENSINGTON PALACE GDNS

Round Pond

GARDENS

SERPENTINE ROAD

Serpentine

ROTTEN ROW

GREEN PARK

ST JAME
PAR

KENSINGTON ROAD

KNIGHTSBRIDGE

KNIGHTSBRIDGE

HYDE PARK CORNER

BUCKINGHAM PALACE GARDENS

Buckingham Palace

BUCKINGHAM GATE

EXHIBITION ROAD

Victoria and Albert Museum

BROMPTON ROAD

GROSVENOR PLACE

LOWER GROSVENOR PLACE

VICTORIA ST

VAUXHALL BRIDG

ROCHESTER ROW

**SOUTH KENSINGTON
AND HYDE PARK**
See pp94–101
Street Finder maps 8, 9, 16, 17

**WEST END AND
WESTMINSTER**
See pp76–93
Street Finder maps 10, 11, 18, 19